Rethinking *the* Color Line

Rethinking *the* Color Line

Readings in Race and Ethnicity

FOURTH EDITION

CHARLES A. GALLAGHER
La Salle University

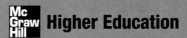
Higher Education

Boston   Burr Ridge, IL   Dubuque, IA   New York   San Francisco   St. Louis
Bangkok   Bogotá   Caracas   Kuala Lumpur   Lisbon   London   Madrid   Mexico City
Milan   Montreal   New Delhi   Santiago   Seoul   Singapore   Sydney   Taipei   Toronto

McGraw Hill **Higher Education**

Published by McGraw-Hill, an imprint of The McGraw-Hill Companies, Inc., 1221 Avenue of the Americas, New York, NY 10020. Copyright © 2009, 2007, 2003, 1999. All rights reserved. No part of this publication may be reproduced or distributed in any form or by any means, or stored in a database or retrieval system, without the prior written consent of The McGraw-Hill Companies, Inc., including, but not limited to, in any network or other electronic storage or transmission, or broadcast for distance learning.

This book is printed on acid-free paper.

1 2 3 4 5 6 7 8 9 0 DOC/DOC 0 9 8

ISBN 978-0-07-340427-1
MHID 0-07-340427-6

Editor in Chief: *Michael Ryan*
Publisher: *Frank Mortimer*
Sponsoring Editor: *Gina Boedeker*
Executive Marketing Manager: *Leslie Oberhuber*
Developmental Editor: *Larry Goldberg*
Production Editor: *Karol Jurado*
Production Service: *Anne Draus, Scratchgravel Publishing Services*
Manuscript Editor: *Margaret C. Tropp*
Text Designer: *Kay Lieberherr*
Design Manager: *Ashley Bedell*
Cover Designer: *Stacy Anthony*
Production Supervisor: *Louis Swaim*
Composition: *10/12 Palatino by Laserwords Private Limited*
Printing: *45# New Era Matte Plus, R. R. Donnelley & Sons/Crawfordsville, IN*

Library of Congress Cataloging-in-Publication Data
Rethinking the color line : readings in race and ethnicity / [edited by] Charles A. Gallagher. — 4th ed.
   p. cm.
  Includes bibliographical references and index.
  ISBN-13: 978-0-07-340427-1 (alk. paper)
  ISBN-10: 0-07-340427-6 (alk. paper)
 1. United States—Race relations. 2. United States—Ethnic relations. 3. Minorities—Civil rights—United States.
I. Gallagher, Charles A. (Charles Andrew), 1962–
  E184.A1R4485 2009
  305.800973—dc22

                                                                    2008031078

This book is dedicated to Tom and Marie Gallagher. One could not ask for better parents.

About the Author and Rethinking the Color Line

An old saying suggests that if you "scratch" at any creative endeavor you will uncover personal biography. The genealogy of *Rethinking the Color Line* reflects this adage. As a boy I grew up in Overbrook Park, an all-white, working- and lower-middle-class neighborhood in Philadelphia. My world was a mix of first- and second-generation immigrants from Poland, Russia, Ireland, and Italy. Race was something I experienced when we left our completely self-contained, row house community and went "downtown." Race was typically presented to me in terms of geography: blacks lived in North and West Philly, Asians clustered in Chinatown, and Latinos resided off of N. Broad Street. The "race as geography" analogy was cemented as I got older and was taken on class trips to museums of art and natural history. The dioramas in the museums had each of the "major races of mankind" frozen in a variety of daily, primitive routines: some were engaged in tepee making, others were spearing fish or seals, farmers tended rice paddies, peasants worked the land. Typically there was a map that explained that black people were from this continent, brown people from there, and so on until all the racial groups had been repatriated back to their "original" homeland.

I saw parallels to the representations of race I experienced as a boy and the textbooks available to me as a student teacher almost twenty years ago. Race and ethnicity readers and textbooks typically presented each group's history as discrete events that took place in a social vacuum, rather than weaving a narrative that reflects the constant interaction within and between racial and ethnic groups. Race relations plays out in housing, the economy, criminal justice, schooling, love, culture, and politics. This perspective shows the social relations that link all racial and ethnic groups together, rather than an approach in which week four is dedicated to African Americans and week seven to American Indians. What I have attempted to do in this book is take the study of race out of the museum and into the spaces we live in and share across the color line.

Contents

Preface

When it comes to race and ethnic relations in the United States, we are two nations: the nation we imagine ourselves to be as depicted in the media and the nation we actually inhabit. Reflect for a moment about how race is depicted in popular culture. Turn on the television and you enter a fantasyland where whites, blacks, Latinos, and Asians gather together to shop, eat, work, and interact in spaces where race is meaningless. In this racial utopia, a car packed with young adults from *every* racial group drives through a Checker's fast-food take-out window as the hip-hop voice-over tells us "Ya gotta eat." Car commercials as well as advertisements for antacids, snack foods, soda, and fast-food restaurants routinely show an America that is integrated, assimilated, and color-blind. In this carefully manufactured racial utopia, television commercials depict actors of different races interacting in race-neutral environments like Chili's or Applebee's. In Hollywood's version of U.S. race relations, one of your best friends is always from a different race. In this racial nirvana, handsome, middle-class men of varying races relax in upper-middle-class living rooms backslapping and bonding over football, Coor's beer, and Domino's pizza. America's racial "presentation of self" in the media is overwhelmingly depicted as an environment that is integrated, multiracial, and for the most part color-blind. The media now present America as a kind of United Nations reunion party where everyone has equal social standing and equal opportunity, and everyone is middle class.

These representations of a color-blind America seriously misrepresent the extent to which race continues to shape the life chances of racial minorities in the United States. Consider, for example, racial diversity in corporate America. Significant movement into the upper ranks of top management would indicate that racial barriers have fallen. Progress has been made in the upper ranks of corporate America, but the proportion of racial minorities now in these positions is minuscule. "The Glass Ceiling Report" produced by the U.S. Department of Labor found

that "97% of the senior managers of Fortune 1000 industrial and Fortune 500 are white; 95 to 97% are male." Racial minorities make up about 30% of the U.S. population. All things being equal, we should expect to see about 30% of the top jobs going to racial minorities. What we see, however, is that only 3% not 30% of senior managers at Fortune 1000 and Fortune 500 companies are members of racial minorities. What does this figure say about the notion that we are now a color-blind nation?

The United States Senate provides a rather good test of the fit between how groups are presented in television dramas like CSI or in films at the multiplex and the political power these groups have achieved. Since there are 100 members in the U.S. Senate and racial minorities in the United States account for about 30% of the population, all things being equal, the Senate should have about 30 members from racial minorities. When we look at the membership of the 110th Congress, however, we find only 6 racial minority members, which means that 94 senators are white. Since whites constitute about 70% of the population, proportional representation suggests that they should hold 70 Senate seats not 94. There are currently no American Indians in the U.S. Senate. Women too are underrepresented in the Senate. Although women comprise about 52% of the adult population (which means we should see 52 women in the Senate), there are only 16 female U.S. senators.

It is difficult to think about life in America without directly confronting issues of race and ethnicity. Reflect for a moment on how recent events and trends both dominate and alter American social and cultural life: White racists tie a black Texan to the back of a pickup truck and drag him to his death, while white rapper Eminem wins three Grammy awards; challenges to the University of Michigan's affirmative action program move up to the Supreme Court, creating a national dialogue on the extent to which the racial "playing field" is level; after 9/11 politicians called for tougher immigration laws, while U.S. farmers and agribusiness discuss institution of a new *bracero* farm labor program that would ease restrictions on seasonal immigrant farmworkers; Oprah Winfrey has a net worth of more than a billion dollars, while almost of a quarter of the total black population lives below the poverty line; racial profiling brings about a new term, DWB (driving while black), while Colin Powell, Denzel Washington, and Tiger Woods are consistently voted among America's most celebrated and respected people; white suburban teenagers continue to be the largest consumers of rap and hip-hop, yet racially motivated hate crimes continue to happen on campuses throughout the country; Latinos now outnumber the black population, yet each group is significantly under-represented in Congress and in corporate America. The readings in *Rethinking the Color Line* will allow students to examine the contradictions of race and ethnicity and pre-pare them to live in an increasingly racially and ethnically diverse society.

Although the media have seized on a U.S. Census Bureau figure predicting that by the year 2060 whites will be outnumbered by Asians, blacks, Hispanics, and American Indians, this rather simplistic demographic forecast misses the conflicts, contradictions, and cultural convergences that currently define race and ethnic relations in the United States. *Rethinking the Color Line* is designed to help make sense of how race and ethnicity influence aspects of social life in ways that are often made invisible by culture, poli-tics, and economics. This theoretically informed, empirically grounded reader uses a social constructionist perspective to frame and define the concepts of race and ethnicity in the United States. The selections should stimulate conversation in the classroom and allow students to think through solu-tions to what often seem intractable problems. As a peda-gogical strategy, this text raises a number of questions in the part introductions that guide students through the readings by providing an overview of how each reading is conceptu-ally linked to the others. Each chapter starts with "Questions to Consider," asking students to focus their attention on spe-cific themes, issues, or questions raised in the reading. It is important to me that my students be exposed to the classic paradigms in the study of race and ethnic relations in the United States. However, just as important is my desire that students be exposed to and explore new theories and para-digms that are challenging, supplanting and redefining the classic race and ethnicity "canon," which itself changes over time. The biologically based, pseudoscientific assumptions that defined and guided race and ethnicity scholarship for

much of this and the previous century have been debunked, discredited, and discarded. What has emerged in the last 30 years are competing narratives of what race and ethnic iden-tity mean and the social pressures that shape those mean-ings. Postcolonial, postmodern, postethnic, class-based, and primordialist perspectives all claim to elucidate how race and ethnicity have been, and continue to be, thoroughly rethought.

The readings in the first part of this text provide stu-dents with the theoretical framework and analytical tools they will use throughout the book. Students come to understand what is meant by race and ethnicity as social constructions. The news, situation comedies, MTV, and racial topography of neighborhoods all become subjects for sociological scrutiny. *Rethinking the Color Line* allows students to learn how race and ethnicity influence life in ways that many students routinely take for granted. It has been my experience that a majority of students who read these articles internalize a version of the "sociological imagination" that forever changes how they understand race and ethnic relations. Raising consciousness about how each of us influences and in turn is influenced by race and ethnic relations is an explicit goal of this book.

Over the last decade I have had the luxury of test-ing a large number of varied readings on hundreds of students in dozens of race and ethnic relations classes at large public universities as well as small, elite liberal arts colleges. The readings in this book represent the final out-come of classroom "hits and misses." I have used classroom experiences, the results of examinations, and how easily students were able to integrate the readings into research papers to gauge (1) the extent to which the reading con-tributed to students' understanding of a particular theory or concept, (2) if the reading was intellectually engaging, and (3) if it lent itself to active learning in the classroom. If a reading could pass these hurdles in at least three of my classes, then it made it into this book. Teaching at both public universities and private colleges also provided me with the opportunity to observe how students from dif-ferent regions, class backgrounds, and racial and ethnic identities reacted to the assigned readings. The articles speak to, challenge, and find common ground among stu-dents from racially, ethnically, culturally, and economically diverse backgrounds. *Rethinking the Color Line* is a response to my students' calls for a book that was user-friendly but did not sacrifice intellectual or theoretical rigor.

This book has been designed to be relevant for students on an individual level while also helping them understand that race and ethnic relations are embedded in the institutions that structure their lives. The readings require students to constantly negotiate the tensions between individual agency and the often determined constraints of social structure. The common thread that links these readings is the ongoing debate about the relationship between agency and structure. It is this conceptual framework that will allow students to think about race and ethnicity in fluid rather than static terms.

Changes in the Fourth Edition

One obvious change to the fourth edition of *Rethinking the Color Line* is that the book is more colorful. The book now features a two-color design that better highlights key features like "Seeing the Big Picture" and "Questions to Consider." Another new feature that provides greater accessibility to the articles is that vocabulary words have been **boldfaced** throughout the text and defined at the bottom of the page. Five new "Seeing the Big Picture" features have been added to better link the subsections to questions raised in the readings. The nine new articles explore topics that are currently redefining race relations in the United States. F. James Davis (Reading 9) examines the multiple racial locations one can occupy because the idea of race itself is so contingent and fluid. Lawrence Bobo (Reading 20), expands upon the idea that laissez-faire racism has in large part supplanted blatant kinds of racism, creating an even greater obstacle to achieving racial equality. Michael Emerson (Reading 24) addresses a fact that most Americans would like to ignore: our houses of worship are hypersegregated. Why is this the case, and what does it say about U.S. race relations? Kenneth Bolton and Joe Feagin (Reading 27) detail the extent to which black police officers are subject to racism from other officers. John Logan (Reading 41) details the experiences of blacks from Africa and the Caribbean and the treatment these groups receive relative to other blacks and Latinos. Kimberly McClain DaCosta's very forward thinking chapter (Reading 47) attempts to explain the implications of multiracial families in terms of how individuals define themselves racially. Finally, Meizhu Lui and associates (Reading 48) attempt to outline ways to minimize race-based inequality.

Appendix

The appendix, "Race by the Numbers: America's Racial Report Card," is meant to capture almost every quality-of-life measure (income, education, health, etc.) by race and ethnicity. The appendix is linked to each reading in the "Seeing the Big Picture" questions at the end of each chapter. It was designed for faculty and students to have a ready comparative reference of racial and ethnic social statistics relevant for classroom discussions and research assignments.

Supplements

Visit our Online Learning Center Web site at www.mhhe.com/Gallagher4 for robust student and instructor resources.

For students: Student resources include multiple-choice quizzes for each reading, Web links, and other study tools.

For instructors: The password-protected instructor portion of the Web site includes the instructor's manual, a comprehensive test bank, and other instructor resources.

Acknowledgments

Many thanks go to the following reviewers who provided suggestions about the form and content of *Rethinking the Color Line:* Kholoud Al-Qubbaj, Southern Utah University; Patrick C. Archer, Iowa State University; Rod Golden, Mesa Community College; Kevin Lamarr James, University of Illinois at Chicago; Demetrius Semien, University of North Carolina at Chapel Hill; Victor Thompson, San Jose State University; Will Tyson, University of South Florida; and Kathy Westman, Waubonsee Community College.

I welcome any comments, suggestions, or criticism concerning this reader. Please feel free to contact me about which readings work, which do not, or readings I might include in future editions. Please send any comments directly to me. I look forward to your feedback.

CHARLES A. GALLAGHER
Department of Sociology
Social Work and Criminal Justice
La Salle University
1900 W. Olney Ave.
Philadelphia, PA 19141

THE SOCIOLOGICAL PROMISE IMPLICIT IN THE TITLE *RETHINKING THE COLOR LINE* IS THAT WE WILL EXPLORE THE CONTEMPORARY MEANINGS OF RACE AND ETHNICITY AND EXAMINE HOW SOCIAL, POLITICAL, ECONOMIC, AND CULTURAL FORCES SHAPE THOSE MEANINGS. This may seem like a straightforward task. It is not. Race and ethnicity are slippery concepts because they are always in a state of flux. Imagine for a moment the shape of the United States as analogous to a definition of race or ethnicity. It may appear that an outline or sketch of the U.S. border, like a definition of race or ethnicity, can be neatly described or mapped out; that is, just as we can imagine the borders of the United States, we can, with reasonable certainty, identify someone as black, white, Asian, or American Indian. We place people in these racial categories because we have been trained to focus on a combination of traits like skin color, hair texture, and eye shape. After we have placed individuals in racial categories, we typically use cultural markers, such as their ethnic background or ancestry, to further sort them. For instance, if a white person walks into a room, we *see* that individual's race. What happens when he or she starts talking and we pick up on an Irish brogue or a New York City accent or a southern dialect? What happens when the brown woman in front of us in the supermarket talks to the cashier and we recognize her accent as Jamaican or English? We tend to sort first by color and then by cultural background.

Since the founding of the United States more than two hundred years ago, the lines that have defined the nation's borders have been redrawn dozens of times. Just as there was no United States of America prior to 1776, the idea of race as it is currently understood did not exist until the Europeans colonized the Americas, Africa, and parts of Asia. The mental map we conjure up of the United States today is only about forty years old. The map was last redrawn in 1959 when Hawaii was admitted into the Union as the fiftieth state. Previously, the map had been

RETHINKING THE COLOR LINE ~ *Understanding How Boundaries Shift*

redrawn after the Louisiana Purchase of 1803 and again after the Missouri Compromise of 1820, as well as after the admittance of every new state to the Union. And we will have to redraw our mental map yet again if the Commonwealth of Puerto Rico votes to enter the Union as the fifty-first state.

The problem with definitions of race and ethnicity, as with the shape of the United States, is that the borders or contours that give form and meaning to these concepts change over time. A person defined as white in the year 2010 might have been defined as black or Irish or Italian at various times in American history. For example, around the turn of the twentieth century, Irish and Italian immigrants were *not* viewed as white when they first arrived in the United States. At that time, members of those groups did not easily fit into the existing racial hierarchy; they were in a racial limbo—not white, not black, not Asian. Their ethnic background—that is, the language, culture, and religious beliefs that distinguished these Irish and Italian immigrants from the dominant group—was used in various ways to define them as a racial group. Within a generation or two, these so-called Irish and Italian racial groups assimilated and were absorbed into the category we now know as white. The journey from being considered not white or racially ambiguous to white was rather swift. It may seem odd, and may even shock our racial sensibilities, to think of Supreme Court Justice Antonin Scalia's or Senator Ted Kennedy's parents or

1

grandparents as possibly being defined as nonwhite Italians or nonwhite Irish at different times in American history. But is a nonwhite Italian or nonwhite Irish any less curious an idea than a black-Irish American or an Asian-Italian American? If one's ethnic identity is subsumed or taken over by a racial identity, the question we need to ask as sociologists is, why?

Just as the shape of the United States has changed over time, so have the definitions of race and ethnicity. Do you think your view of race and ethnicity is different from that of your parents or grandparents? How you understand race and ethnicity reflects a definition specific to this moment in time, one that, in all likelihood, will look quite different in three or four decades. *Rethinking the Color Line* will provide you with a theoretical framework for understanding how and why definitions of race and ethnicity change over time, what sociological forces bring about these changes, and what these categories might look like in the future.

What these examples suggest, and what many of the readings in *Rethinking the Color Line* consciously explore, is how race and ethnicity are socially constructed. When we say that something is "socially constructed," we mean that *the characteristics deemed relevant to that definition are based on societal and cultural values.* Race and ethnicity are social constructions because their meanings are derived by focusing on arbitrary characteristics that a given society deems important. Race and ethnicity are social products based on cultural values, not scientific facts.

Think for a moment about gravity. If you push this book off your desk, do you expect it to fall to the ground? Obviously, you do. If you lived in Brazil or South Africa or Puerto Rico, would you expect the same thing to happen to your book? Of course you would, because you know that gravity is a universal constant. However, someone defined as black in the United States could be defined as white in Brazil, Trigueno (intermediate) in Puerto Rico, and "coloured" in South Africa. Gravity is the same everywhere, but racial classifications vary across place and time because definitions of race and ethnicity are based on the physical traits a society chooses to value or devalue. Because each society's values are based on a different set of historical experiences, cultural circumstances, and political definitions, ideas about race and ethnicity can vary quite a bit, not only between countries

but within them as well. For example, historically, it was not uncommon for someone to have been socially and legally defined as black in the southern part of the United States but to "pass" for white after migrating north. The beliefs and definitions that undergird the idea of race are very unstable and, as we will see in the readings, quite susceptible to political manipulation.

Racial and ethnic identity is culturally meaningful only because we define and understand it in that way. In other words, race exists because we say race exists. And because the characteristics that make up the idea of race and ethnicity reflect a social process, it is possible to imagine these concepts in a different way. Instead of looking at skin color, facial features, or hair texture as a way to sort individuals, we could create a racial category based on the size of people's feet. People with shoe sizes between 4 and 7 would be labeled the Petite Race, those with sizes 8–11 would be designated the Bigger Race, and the 12–15 shoe size crowd would be categorized as the Monster Foot Race. Those with feet smaller or larger than the existing categories would be the "Other" Race. Likewise, we could use eye color, height, glove size, or nose length to create racial categories. Because the physical markers we use to define race are arbitrary and have no basis in genetics, biology, anthropology, or sociology, using shoe size as the criterion to fashion a new definition of race would be just as valid as the system currently in place. Similarly, we could redefine ethnicity by changing the focus from language, culture, religion, or nationality as a method of sorting people and instead create categories of people based on the amount of meat they eat or the way they style their hair.

What complicates our ability to accurately and easily map these definitions of race and ethnicity is that the definitions are constantly changing. Are the 30 million Latinos in the United States an ethnic group because they are defined by the U.S. Census Bureau as such, or are Latinos a racial group? If the current census categories of white, black, Asian, and American Indian do not adequately reflect what Latinos experience or how Latinos are viewed by non-Latinos, should a "brown" category be added to the census? Would a newly created "brown" category link Puerto Ricans in New York City with Cuban Americans in Miami and Mexican Americans in San Diego? Why or why not? How should we define the race of a child whose father is Mexican-African American and whose mother is Japanese-Irish American? What is this child's ethnicity? For that matter, how and in what ways are race and ethnicity related?

In 1903, sociologist W. E. B. Du Bois wrote "the problem of the twentieth century is the problem of the color-line." It appears that a key problem of the twenty-first century, while different in degree and context from the one Du Bois chronicled, will still be the color line. A topic or issue may not initially seem to be linked to race or ethnicity, but on closer sociological scrutiny, patterns often emerge that make it clear that race and ethnicity matter quite a bit. How do you see race and ethnicity being connected to who gets a good education or adequate health care, who is likely to be poor, where toxic waste sites are built, who gets hired or promoted, or which racial or ethnic groups are more likely to have members sentenced to death and executed? Race and ethnicity are intertwined in every aspect of our lives.

Rethinking the Color Line will provide you with the tools necessary to navigate the complicated and often contradictory meanings of race and ethnicity in the United States. The readings will take you on a sociological journey and explore how you, your classmates, your family, and your friends fit into the racial and ethnic mosaic of the United States. If you focus carefully on the readings, the "Questions to Consider" chapter introductions, and the "Seeing the Big Picture" discussion at the end of most chapters, your perspective on race and ethnic relations in the United States will be changed forever. ✳

WHO TAUGHT YOU HOW TO "BE" BLACK or American Indian or white or Asian? Did you learn to "do" your race by watching sitcoms on television or by watching your peers in the schoolyard? Was it your parents or an older sibling or cousin who taught you how to act both your age and your race? In what social situations do you think about your racial identity? Is it only when you interact with an individual from a different racial background? Do you think about your race, about other racial groups, or about race relations when you watch football games or MTV or the nightly news? Do you think about your race while you are in your neighborhood or only when you drive through an area with a different racial population? Were you ever in a social setting in which you were the only person of your color? How did that make you feel?

How did you learn to "be" Korean or Jamaican or German? In what situations do you think about your ancestry? Is it during the holidays or when you spend time with your family? Or has your family been in the United States for so many generations that the family tree linking you to the homeland is unimportant, nonexistent, or untraceable? Does that mean you have a racial identity but not an ethnic identity? Or does "American" best mirror your social identity?

The readings in Part I answer these questions by exposing you to the social theories used to define and understand the dynamics of race and ethnicity. The first five readings, in **Race and Ethnicity: Sociohistoric Constructions,** examine how the natural variation in human skin color has been used as a way to sort people into groups, create a racial hierarchy, and justify exploitation based on skin color. Marvin Harris explains why gradations of color, from black to white, are "beautiful" sociocultural responses to the environment. Howard Zinn charts the evolution of the idea of race in early U.S. history and how the idea of racial categories was synonymous with who would be free and who would be enslaved. Michael Omi and Howard Winant explain the emergence of racial categories as a "sociohistoric" process they call

SORTING BY COLOR ~
Why We Attach Meaning to Race

racial formation; that is, the way we define ourselves racially reflects a political and social process that was hundreds of years in the making. Joe Feagin and Clairece Booher Feagin provide an overview of the theories central to ethnic and racial studies, theories that will reemerge throughout the book. Eduardo Bonilla-Silva suggests that race, like class or gender, takes on a "life of its own," creating hierarchical social relations that are exploitive and coercive. As you will see throughout the text, many of the articles in this reader draw on one or more of these theories to explain a particular aspect of racial inequality and race and ethnic relations.

The next three readings, in **Race and Ethnicity: Contemporary Socioeconomic Trends,** draw on theories outlined in the first section while emphasizing socioeconomic disparities between racial and ethnic groups. Rebecca Blank provides descriptive statistics on the social and economic well-being of non-Hispanic whites, non-Hispanic blacks, Hispanics, Asian and Pacific Islanders, and American Indians and Alaska natives. Very real differences exist between groups in terms of income, rates of poverty and incarceration, access to computers, and health status. How might you explain these between-group differences in quality-of-life markers? David Williams and Chiquita Collins present a rather disturbing overview of racial disparities in health. Not only are racial minorities worse off compared to whites on almost every health measure, but it is likely this gap will continue to grow as the United States limits access to public health care for the poor. Using national data on wealth, Thomas Shapiro examines the racial dynamics of how

5

transformative assets, the financial assistance one gets from families, shapes life chances.

In **Race as Chameleon: How the Idea of Race Changes over Time and Place,** F. James Davis uses the "one-drop rule" to map the ever changing definition of race by focusing on the various "status and identity positions" that emerged as groups mixed across the color line. What is important to note is that the definitions forced on mixed race groups reflected power relations and the desire to fashion various social buffers that maintained white supremacy.

Both David Wilkins and Yen Le Espiritu demonstrate how, why, and in what situations racial and ethnic identities are used to organize politically. It is often the case that those in power thrust a racial identity upon a group even though there may be enormous cultural diversity within that group. Chinese, Japanese, and Koreans "became" Asian through the racialization process.

Throughout this book I will be arguing that the idea of race is not static. Jennifer Lee and Frank Bean suggest that we are yet again at a crossroads in the construction of how we think about racial categories as the number of individuals who define themselves as "multiracial" grows. As

these readings demonstrate, the creation of racial categories is as much a historical process as it is a political one.

The next three readings, in **Color-Blind America: Fact, Fantasy, or Our Future,** focus on how different social conditions can exacerbate racial and ethnic relations and what might be done at both the macro and micro levels to ameliorate racial inequality. Professor Charles A. Gallagher notes that current trends in popular culture have blurred the color line by linking the consumption of products across racial groups to racial harmony. Gallagher asks, if groups from various races now share and consume the same products (hip-hop, McDonalds, reality TV), has racial equality been achieved? Lani Guinier and Gerald Torres make the case that descriptions of the United States as a color-blind nation are quite premature, and Herbert Gans argues that a "beige-ing" of America is taking place that will incorporate some parts of the Latino and Asian populations but not blacks. The color line will shift, Gans argues, but not necessarily in a way that is inclusive. Each of these readings points to the various social, economic, and cultural barriers to racial equality and the rather lofty goal of becoming a truly color-blind nation. ✳

1   How Our Skins Got Their Color

Marvin Harris

The late MARVIN HARRIS spent a portion of his life teaching in the anthropology department at Columbia University, where he served as department chair. He has published sixteen books, including *Cannibals and Kings; Culture, People, and Nature;* and *Our Kind.*

Questions to Consider   Cultural anthropologist Marvin Harris links the variations in skin color one can observe in traveling around the world to the human body's ability to adapt physically to changes in exposure to solar radiation. How do you explain his assertion that "white was beautiful because white was healthy" and "black was beautiful because black was healthy"?

MOST HUMAN BEINGS ARE NEITHER VERY fair nor very dark, but brown. The extremely fair skin of northern Europeans and their descendants, and the very black skins of central Africans and their descendants, are probably special adaptations. Brown-skinned ancestors may have been shared by modern-day blacks and whites as recently as 10,000 years ago. Human skin owes its color to the presence of particles known as **melanin.** The primary function of melanin is to protect the upper levels of the skin from being damaged by the sun's ultraviolet rays. This radiation poses a critical problem for our kind because we lack the dense coat of hair that acts as a sunscreen for most mammals. . . . Hairlessness exposes us to two kinds of radiation hazards: ordinary sunburn, with its blisters, rashes, and risk of infection; and skin cancers, including malignant melanoma, one of the deadliest diseases known. Melanin is the body's first line of defense against these afflictions. The more melanin particles, the darker the skin, and the lower the risk of sunburn and all forms of skin cancer. This explains why the highest rates for skin cancer are found in sun-drenched lands such as Australia, where light-skinned people of European descent spend a good part of their lives outdoors wearing scanty attire.

melanin The pigment that gives the skin its color. Melanin protects the skin from the ultraviolet rays associated with various skin cancers. Populations living near the equator have darker skin to protect them from the harsh effects of the sun.

Very dark-skinned people such as heavily pigmented Africans of Zaire seldom get skin cancer, but when they do, they get it on depigmented parts of their bodies—palms and lips.

If exposure to solar radiation had nothing but harmful effects, natural selection would have favored inky black as the color for all human populations. But the sun's rays do not present an unmitigated threat. As it falls on the skin, sunshine converts a fatty substance in the epidermis into vitamin D. The blood carries vitamin D from the skin to the intestines (technically making it a hormone rather than a vitamin), where it plays a vital role in the absorption of calcium. In turn, calcium is vital for strong bones. Without it, people fall victim to the crippling diseases rickets and osteomalacia. In women, calcium deficiencies can result in a deformed birth canal, which makes childbirth lethal for both mother and fetus.

Vitamin D can be obtained from a few foods, primarily the oils and livers of marine fish. But inland populations must rely on the sun's rays and their own skins for the supply of this crucial substance. The particular color of a human population's skin, therefore, represents in large degree a trade-off between the hazards of too much versus too little solar radiation:acute sunburn and skin cancer on the one hand, and rickets and osteomalacia on the other. It is this trade-off that largely accounts for the preponderance of brown people in the world and for the general tendency for skin color to be darkest among **equatorial populations** and lightest among populations dwelling at higher latitudes.

At middle latitudes, the skin follows a strategy of changing colors with the seasons. Around the Mediterranean basin, for example, exposure to the summer sun brings high risk of cancer but low risk for rickets; the body produces more melanin and people grow darker (i.e., they get suntans). Winter reduces the risk of sunburn and cancer; the body produces less melanin, and the tan wears off.

The correlation between skin color and latitude is not perfect because other factors—such as the availability of foods containing vitamin D and calcium, regional cloud cover during the winter, amount of clothing worn, and cultural preferences—may work for or against the predicted relationship. Arctic-dwelling Eskimo, for example, are not as light-skinned as expected, but their habitat and economy afford them a diet that is exceptionally rich in both vitamin D and calcium.

Northern Europeans, obliged to wear heavy garments for protection against the long, cold, cloudy winters, were always at risk for rickets and osteomalacia from too little vitamin D and calcium. This risk increased sometime after 6000 B.C., when pioneer cattle herders who did not exploit marine resources began to appear in northern Europe. The risk would have been especially great for the brown-skinned Mediterranean peoples who migrated northward along with the crops and farm animals. Samples of Caucasian skin (infant penile foreskin obtained at the time of circumcision) exposed to sunlight on cloudless days in Boston (42°N) from November through February produced no vitamin D. In Edmonton (52°N) this period extended from October to March. But further south (34°N) sunlight was effective in producing vitamin D in the middle of the winter. Almost all of Europe lies north of 42°N. Fair-skinned, nontanning individuals who could utilize the weakest and briefest doses of sunlight to synthesize vitamin D were strongly favored by **natural selection.** During the frigid winters, only a small circle of a child's face could be left to peek out at the sun through the heavy clothing, thereby favoring the survival of individuals with translucent patches of pink on their cheeks characteristic of many northern Europeans. (People who could get calcium by drinking cow's milk would also be favored by natural selection.)

If light-skinned individuals on the average had only 2 percent more children survive per generation, the changeover in their skin color could have begun 5,000 years ago and reached present levels well before the beginning of the Christian era. But natural selection need not have acted alone. **Cultural selection** may also have played a role. It seems likely that whenever people consciously or unconsciously had to decide which infants to nourish and which to neglect, the advantage would go to those with lighter skin, experience having shown that such individuals tended to grow up to be taller, stronger, and healthier than their darker siblings. White was beautiful because white was healthy.

To account for the evolution of black skin in equatorial latitudes, one has merely to reverse the combined effects of natural and cultural selection. With the sun directly overhead most of the year, and clothing a hindrance to work and survival, vitamin D was never in short supply (and calcium was easily obtained from vegetables). Rickets and osteomalacia were rare. Skin cancer was the main problem, and what nature started, culture amplified. Darker infants were favored by parents because experience showed that they grew up to be freer of disfiguring and lethal malignancies. Black was beautiful because black was healthy.

equatorial populations Populations living near the equator.

natural selection In his 1859 book *The Origin of Species,* Charles Darwin describes the process by which nature "selects" the best-adapted varieties of animals for survival.

cultural selection The idea that, in ways that mirror natural selection, society "selects" those cultural traits that will enhance the survival of a particular civilization.

2 Drawing the Color Line
Howard Zinn

HOWARD ZINN professor, activist, and author, has dedicated his life to the notion that the knowledge of history is important to people's everyday lives and can be a powerful force for social change.

Questions to Consider   In this article Howard Zinn chronicles the beginning of slavery in North America. How did law, custom, and culture reconcile the emergence of chattel slavery with Christian precepts, which reject the idea that one human can own or forcibly control another human being? What arguments were used to justify slavery? List which groups profited from the slave trade.

A BLACK AMERICAN WRITER, J. SAUNDERS Redding, describes the arrival of a ship in North America in the year 1619:

> Sails furled, flag drooping at her rounded stern, she rode the tide in from the sea. She was a strange ship, indeed, by all accounts, a frightening ship, a ship of mystery. Whether she was trader, privateer, or man-of-war no one knows. Through her bulwarks black-mouthed cannon yawned. The flag she flew was Dutch; her crew a motley. Her port of call, an English settlement, Jamestown, in the colony of Virginia. She came, she traded, and shortly afterwards was gone. Probably no ship in modern history has carried a more portentous freight. Her cargo? Twenty slaves.

There is not a country in world history in which racism has been more important, for so long a time, as the United States. And the problem of "the color line," as W. E. B. Du Bois put it, is still with us. So it is more than a purely historical question to ask: How does it start?—and an even more urgent question: How might it end? Or, to put it differently: Is it possible for whites and blacks to live together without hatred?

If history can help answer these questions, then the beginnings of slavery in North America—a continent where we can trace the coming of the first whites and the first blacks—might supply at least a few clues.

Some historians think those first blacks in Virginia were considered as servants, like the white **indentured servants** brought from Europe. But the strong probability is

indentured servant Historically, a laborer under contract to an employer for some period of time, usually seven years, in exchange for travel, food, and accommodations. Servants often became indebted to their employer and were often subject to violence.

that, even if they were listed as "servants" (a more familiar category to the English), they were viewed as being different from white servants, were treated differently, and in fact were slaves. In any case, slavery developed quickly into a regular institution, into the normal labor relation of blacks to whites in the New World. With it developed that special racial feeling—whether hatred, or contempt, or pity, or patronization—that accompanied the inferior position of blacks in America for the next 350 years—that combination of inferior status and derogatory thought we call racism.

Everything in the experience of the first white settlers acted as a pressure for the enslavement of blacks.

The Virginians of 1619 were desperate for labor, to grow enough food to stay alive. Among them were survivors from the winter of 1609–1610, the "starving time," when, crazed for want of food, they roamed the woods for nuts and berries, dug up graves to eat the corpses, and died in batches until five hundred colonists were reduced to sixty.

In the *Journals* of the House of Burgesses of Virginia is a document of 1619 which tells of the first twelve years of the Jamestown colony. The first settlement had a hundred persons, who had one small ladle of barley per meal. When more people arrived, there was even less food. Many of the people lived in cavelike holes dug into the ground, and in the winter of 1609–1610, they were driven thru insufferable hunger to eat those things which nature most abhorred, the flesh and excrements of man as well of our own nation as of an Indian, digged by some out of his grave after he had lain buried three days and wholly devoured him; others, envying the better state of body of any whom hunger has not yet so much wasted as their own, lay wait and threatened to kill and eat them; one among them slew his wife as she slept in his bosom, cut her in pieces, salted her and fed upon her till he had clean devoured all parts saving her head.

A petition by thirty colonists to the House of Burgesses, complaining against the twelve-year governorship of Sir Thomas Smith, said:

In those 12 years of Sir Thomas Smith, his government, we aver that the colony for the most part remained in great want and misery under most severe and cruel laws . . . . The allowance in those times for a man was only eight ounces of meale and half a pint of peas for a day . . . mouldy, rotten, full of cobwebs and maggots, loathsome to man and not fit for beasts, which forced many to flee for relief to the savage enemy, who being taken again were put to sundry deaths as by hanging, shooting and breaking upon the wheel . . . of whom one for stealing two or three pints of oatmeal had a bodkin thrust through his tongue and was tied with a chain to a tree until he starved.

The Virginians needed labor, to grow corn for subsistence, to grow tobacco for export. They had just figured out how to grow tobacco, and in 1617 they sent off the first cargo to England. Finding that, like all pleasurable drugs tainted with moral disapproval, it brought a high price, the planters, despite their high religious talk, were not going to ask questions about something so profitable.

They couldn't force Indians to work for them, as Columbus had done. They were outnumbered, and while, with superior firearms, they could massacre Indians, they would face massacre in return. They could not capture them and keep them enslaved; the Indians were tough, resourceful, defiant, and at home in these woods, as the transplanted Englishmen were not.

White servants had not yet been brought over in sufficient quantity. Besides, they did not come out of slavery, and did not have to do more than contract their labor for a few years to get their passage and a start in the New World. As for the free white settlers, many of them were skilled craftsmen, or even men of leisure back in England, who were so little inclined to work the land that John

Smith, in those early years, had to declare a kind of martial law, organize them into work gangs, and force them into the fields for survival.

There may have been a kind of frustrated rage at their own ineptitude, at the Indian superiority at taking care of themselves, that made the Virginians especially ready to become the masters of slaves. Edmund Morgan imagines their mood as he writes in his book *American Slavery, American Freedom:*

If you were a colonist, you knew that your technology was superior to the Indians'. You knew that you were civilized, and they were savages. . . . But your superior technology had proved insufficient to extract anything. The Indians, keeping to themselves, laughed at your superior methods and lived from the land more abundantly and with less labor than you did. . . . And when your own people started deserting in order to live with them, it was too much. . . . So you killed the Indians, tortured them, burned their villages, burned their cornfields. It proved your superiority, in spite of your failures. And you gave similar treatment to any of your own people who succumbed to their savage ways of life. But you still did not grow much corn.

Black slaves were the answer. And it was natural to consider imported blacks as slaves, even if the institution of slavery would not be regularized and legalized for several decades. Because, by 1619, a million blacks had already been brought from Africa to South America and the Caribbean, to the Portuguese and Spanish colonies, to work as slaves. Fifty years before Columbus, the Portuguese took ten African blacks to Lisbon—this was the start of a regular trade in slaves. African blacks had been stamped as slave labor for a hundred years. So it would have been strange if those twenty blacks, forcibly transported to Jamestown, and sold as objects to settlers anxious for a steadfast source of labor, were considered as anything but slaves.

Their helplessness made enslavement easier. The Indians were on their own land. The whites were in their own European culture. The blacks had been torn from their land and culture, forced into a situation where the heritage of language, dress, custom, family relations, was bit by bit obliterated except for the remnants that blacks could hold on to by sheer, extraordinary persistence.

Was their culture inferior—and so subject to easy destruction? Inferior in military capability, yes—vulnerable to whites with guns and ships. But in no other way—except that cultures that are different are often taken as inferior, especially when such a judgment is practical and profitable. Even militarily, while the Westerners could secure forts on the African coast, they were unable to subdue the interior and had to come to terms with its chiefs.

The African civilization was as advanced in its own way as that of Europe. In certain ways, it was more admirable; but it also included cruelties, hierarchical privilege, and the readiness to sacrifice human lives for religion or profit. It was a civilization of 100 million people, using iron implements and skilled in farming. It had large urban centers and remarkable achievements in weaving, ceramics, sculpture.

European travelers in the sixteenth century were impressed with the African kingdoms of Timbuktu and Mali, already stable and organized at a time when European states were just beginning to develop into the modern nation. In 1563, Ramusio, secretary to the rulers in Venice, wrote to the Italian merchants: "Let them go and do business with the King of Timbuktu and Mali and there is no doubt that they will be well-received there with their ships and their goods and treated well, and granted the favours that they ask."

A Dutch report, around 1602, on the West African kingdom of Benin, said: "The Towne seemeth to be very great, when you enter it. You go into a great broad street, not paved, which seemeth to be seven or eight times broader than the Warmoes Street in Amsterdam . . . . The Houses in this Towne stand in good order, one close and even with the other, as the Houses in Holland stand."

The inhabitants of the Guinea Coast were described by one traveler around 1680 as "very civil and good-natured people, easy to be dealt with, condescending to what Europeans require of them in a civil way, and very ready to return double the presents we make them."

Africa had a kind of **feudalism,** like Europe based on agriculture, and with hierarchies of lords and vassals. But African feudalism did not come, as did Europe's, out of the slave societies of Greece and Rome, which had destroyed ancient tribal life. In Africa, tribal life was still powerful, and some of its better features—a communal spirit, more kindness in law and punishment—still existed. And because the lords did not have the weapons that European lords had, they could not command obedience as easily.

feudalism A medieval European political system in which land was leased through the king to barons and knights who engaged serfs to work the land in return for military protection. The system was based on military, social, and economic obligations and enforced through law, custom, and religion.

In his book *The African Slave Trade,* Basil Davidson contrasts law in the Congo in the early sixteenth century with law in Portugal and England. In those European countries, where the idea of private property was becoming powerful, theft was punished brutally. In England, even as late as 1740, a child could be hanged for stealing a rag of cotton. But in the Congo, communal life persisted, the idea of private property was a strange one, and thefts were punished with fines or various degrees of servitude. A Congolese leader, told of the Portuguese legal codes, asked a Portuguese once, teasingly: "What is the penalty in Portugal for anyone who puts his feet on the ground?"

Slavery existed in the African states, and it was sometimes used by Europeans to justify their own slave trade. But, as Davidson points out, the "slaves" of Africa were more like the serfs of Europe—in other words, like most of the population of Europe. It was a harsh servitude, but they had rights which slaves brought to America did not have, and they were "altogether different from the human cattle of the slave ships and the American plantations." In the Ashanti Kingdom of West Africa, one observer noted that "a slave might marry; own property; himself own a slave; swear an oath; be a competent witness and ultimately become heir to his master. . . . An Ashanti slave, nine cases out of ten, possibly became an adopted member of the family, and in time his descendants so merged and intermarried with the owner's kinsmen that only a few would know their origin."

One slave trader, John Newton (who later became an antislavery leader), wrote about the people of what is now Sierra Leone:

> The state of slavery, among these wild barbarous people, as we esteem them, is much milder than in our colonies. For as, on the one hand, they have no land in high cultivation, like our West India plantations, and therefore no call for that excessive, unintermitted labour, which exhausts our slaves: so, on the other hand, no man is permitted to draw blood even from a slave.

African slavery is hardly to be praised. But it was far different from plantation or mining slavery in the Americas, which was lifelong, morally crippling, destructive of family ties, without hope of any future. African slavery lacked two elements that made American slavery the most cruel form of slavery in history: the frenzy for limitless profit that comes from capitalistic agriculture; the reduction of the slave to less than human status by the use of racial hatred, with that relentless clarity based on color, where white was master, black was slave.

In fact, it was because they came from a settled culture, of tribal customs and family ties, of communal life and traditional ritual, that African blacks found themselves especially helpless when removed from this. They were captured in the interior (frequently by blacks caught up in the slave trade themselves), sold on the coast, then shoved into pens with blacks of other tribes, often speaking different languages.

The conditions of capture and sale were crushing affirmations to the black African of his helplessness in the face of superior force. The marches to the coast, sometimes for 1,000 miles, with people shackled around the neck, under whip and gun, were death marches, in which two of every five blacks died. On the coast, they were kept in cages until they were picked and sold. One John Barbot, at the end of the seventeenth century, described these cages on the Gold Coast:

> As the slaves come down to Fida from the inland country, they are put into a booth or prison . . . near the beach, and when the Europeans are to receive them, they are brought out onto a large plain, where the ship's surgeons examine every part of everyone of them, to the smallest member, men and women being stark naked. . . . Such as are allowed good and sound are set on one side . . . marked on the breast with a red-hot iron, imprinting the mark of the French, English, or Dutch companies. . . . The branded slaves after this are returned to their former booths where they await shipment, sometimes 10–15 days.

Then they were packed aboard the slave ships, in spaces not much bigger than coffins, chained together in the dark, wet slime of the ship's bottom, choking in the stench of their own excrement. Documents of the time describe the conditions:

> The height, sometimes, between decks, was only eighteen inches; so that the unfortunate human beings could not turn around, or even on their sides, the elevation being less than the breadth of their shoulders; and here they are usually chained to the decks by the neck and legs. In such a place the sense of misery and suffocation is so great, that the Negroes . . . are driven to frenzy.

On one occasion, hearing a great noise from below decks where the blacks were chained together, the sailors opened the hatches and found the slaves in different stages of suffocation, many dead, some having killed others in desperate attempts to breathe. Slaves often jumped overboard to drown rather than continue their suffering.

To one observer a slave-deck was "so covered with blood and mucus that it resembled a slaughter house."

Under these conditions, perhaps one of every three blacks transported overseas died, but the huge profits (often double the investment on one trip) made it worthwhile for the slave trader, and so the blacks were packed into the holds like fish.

First the Dutch, then the English, dominated the slave trade. (By 1795 Liverpool had more than a hundred ships carrying slaves and accounted for half of all the European slave trade.) Some Americans in New England entered the business, and in 1637 the first American slave ship, the *Desire,* sailed from Marblehead. Its holds were partitioned into racks, 2 feet by 6 feet, with leg irons and bars.

By 1800, 10 to 15 million blacks had been transported as slaves to the Americas, representing perhaps one-third of those originally seized in Africa. It is roughly estimated that Africa lost 50 million human beings to death and slavery in those centuries we call the beginnings of modern Western civilization, at the hands of slave traders and plantation owners in Western Europe and America, the countries deemed the most advanced in the world.

In the year 1610, a Catholic priest in the Americas named Father Sandoval wrote back to a church functionary in Europe to ask if the capture, transport, and enslavement of African blacks was legal by church doctrine. A letter dated March 12, 1610, from Brother Luis Brandaon to Father Sandoval gives the answer:

> Your Reverence writes me that you would like to know whether the Negroes who are sent to your parts have been legally captured. To this I reply that I think your Reverence should have no scruples on this point, because this is a matter which has been questioned by the Board of Conscience in Lisbon, and all its members are learned and conscientious men. Nor did the bishops who were in Sao Thome, Cape Verde, and here in Loando—all learned and virtuous men—find fault with it. We have been here ourselves for forty years and there have been among us very learned Fathers . . . never did they consider the trade as illicit. Therefore we and the Fathers of Brazil buy these slaves for our service without any scruple.

With all of this—the desperation of the Jamestown settlers for labor, the impossibility of using Indians and the difficulty of using whites, the availability of blacks offered in greater and greater numbers by profit-seeking dealers in human flesh, and with such blacks possible to control because they had just gone through an ordeal which if it did not kill them must have left them in a state of psychic and physical helplessness—is it any wonder that such blacks were ripe for enslavement?

And under these conditions, even if some blacks might have been considered servants, would blacks be treated the same as white servants?

The evidence, from the court records of colonial Virginia, shows that in 1630 a white man named Hugh Davis was ordered "to be soundly whipt . . . for abusing himself . . . by defiling his body in lying with a Negro." Ten years later, six servants and "a negro of Mr. Reynolds" started to run away. While the whites received lighter sentences, "Emanuel the Negro to receive thirty stripes and to be burnt in the cheek with the letter R, and to work in shackle one year or more as his master shall see cause."

Although slavery was not yet regularized or legalized in those first years, the lists of servants show blacks listed separately. A law passed in 1639 decreed that "all persons except Negroes" were to get arms and ammunition—probably to fight off Indians. When in 1640 three servants tried to run away, the two whites were punished with a lengthening of their service. But, as the court put it, "the third being a negro named John Punch shall serve his master or his assigns for the time of his natural life." Also in 1640, we have the case of a Negro woman servant who begot a child by Robert Sweat, a white man. The court ruled "that the said negro woman shall be whipt at the whipping post and the said Sweat shall tomorrow in the forenoon do public penance for his offense at James citychurch."

This unequal treatment, this developing combination of contempt and oppression, feeling and action, which we call "racism"—was this the result of a "natural" antipathy of white against black? The question is important, not just as a matter of historical accuracy, but because any emphasis on "natural" racism lightens the responsibility of the social system. If racism can't be shown to be natural, then it is the result of certain conditions, and we are impelled to eliminate those conditions.

We have no way of testing the behavior of whites and blacks toward one another under favorable conditions—with no history of subordination, no money incentive for exploitation and enslavement, no desperation for survival requiring forced labor. All the conditions for black and white in seventeenth-century America were the opposite of that, all powerfully directed toward antagonism and mistreatment. Under such conditions even the slightest

display of humanity between the races might be considered evidence of a basic human drive toward community.

Sometimes it is noted that, even before 1600, when the slave trade had just begun, before Africans were stamped by it—literally and symbolically—the color black was distasteful. In England, before 1600, it meant, according to the *Oxford English Dictionary:* "Deeply stained with dirt; soiled, dirty, foul. Having dark or deadly purposes, malignant; pertaining to or involving death, deadly; baneful, disastrous, sinister. Foul, iniquitous, atrocious, horribly wicked. Indicating disgrace, censure, liability to punishment, etc." And Elizabethan poetry often used the color white in connection with beauty.

It may be that, in the absence of any other overriding factor, darkness and blackness, associated with night and unknown, would take on those meanings. But the presence of another human being is a powerful fact, and the conditions of that presence are crucial in determining whether an initial prejudice, against a mere color, divorced from humankind, is turned into brutality and hatred.

In spite of such preconceptions about blackness, in spite of special subordination of blacks in the Americas in the seventeenth century, there is evidence that where whites and blacks found themselves with common problems, common work, common enemy in their master, they behaved toward one another as equals. As one scholar of slavery, Kenneth Stampp, has put it, Negro and white servants of the seventeenth century were "remarkably unconcerned about the visible physical differences."

Black and white worked together, fraternized together. The very fact that laws had to be passed after a while to forbid such relations indicates the strength of that tendency. In 1661 a law was passed in Virginia that "in case any English servant shall run away in company of any Negroes" he would have to give special service for extra years to the master of the runaway Negro. In 1691, Virginia provided for the banishment of any "white man or woman being free who shall intermarry with a negro, mulatoo, or Indian man or woman bond or free."

There is an enormous difference between a feeling of racial strangeness, perhaps fear, and the mass enslavement of millions of black people that took place in the Americas. The transition from one to the other cannot be explained easily by "natural" tendencies. It is not hard to understand as the outcome of historical conditions.

Slavery grew as the plantation system grew. The reason is easily traceable to something other than natural racial repugnance: the number of arriving whites, whether free or indentured servants (under four to seven years contract), was not enough to meet the need of the plantations. By 1700, in Virginia, there were 6,000 slaves, one-twelfth of the population. By 1763, there were 170,000 slaves, about half the population.

Blacks were easier to enslave than whites or Indians. But they were still not easy to enslave. From the beginning, the imported black men and women resisted their enslavement. Ultimately their resistance was controlled, and slavery was established for 3 million blacks in the South. Still, under the most difficult conditions, under pain of mutilation and death, throughout their two hundred years of enslavement in North America, these Afro-Americans continued to rebel. Only occasionally was there an organized insurrection. More often they showed their refusal to submit by running away. Even more often, they engaged in sabotage, slowdowns, and subtle forms of resistance which asserted, if only to themselves and their brothers and sisters, their dignity as human beings.

The refusal began in Africa. One slave trader reported that Negroes were "so wilful and loth to leave their own country, that they have often leap'd out of the canoes, boat and ship into the sea, and kept under water till they were drowned."

When the very first black slaves were brought into Hispaniola in 1503, the Spanish governor of Hispaniola complained to the Spanish court that fugitive Negro slaves were teaching disobedience to the Indians. In the 1520s and 1530s, there were slave revolts in Hispaniola, Puerto Rico, Santa Marta, and what is now Panama. Shortly after those rebellions, the Spanish established a special police for chasing fugitive slaves.

A Virginia statute of 1669 referred to "the obstinacy of many of them," and in 1680 the Assembly took note of slave meetings "under the pretense of feasts and brawls" which they considered of "dangerous consequence." In 1687, in the colony's Northern Neck, a plot was discovered in which slaves planned to kill all the whites in the area and escape during a mass funeral.

Gerald Mullin, who studied slave resistance in eighteenth-century Virginia in his work *Flight and Rebellion,* reports:

> The available sources on slavery in 18th-century Virginia—plantation and county records, the newspaper advertisements for runaways—describe rebellious

slaves and few others. The slaves described were lazy and thieving; they feigned illnesses, destroyed crops, stores, tools, and sometimes attacked or killed overseers. They operated blackmarkets in stolen goods. Runaways were defined as various types, they were truants (who usually returned voluntarily), "outlaws" . . . and slaves who were actually fugitives: men who visited relatives, went to town to pass as free, or tried to escape slavery completely, either by boarding ships and leaving the colony, or banding together in cooperative efforts to establish villages or hide-outs in the frontier. The commitment of another type of rebellious slave was total; these men became killers, arsonists, and insurrectionists.

Slaves recently from Africa, still holding on to the heritage of their communal society, would run away in groups and try to establish villages of runaways out in the wilderness, on the frontier. Slaves born in America, on the other hand, were more likely to run off alone, and, with the skills they had learned on the plantation, try to pass as free men.

In the colonial papers of England, a 1729 report from the lieutenant governor of Virginia to the British Board of Trade tells how "a number of Negroes, about fifteen . . . formed a design to withdraw from their Master and to fix themselves in the fastnesses of the neighboring Mountains. They had found means to get into their possession some Arms and Ammunition, and they took along with them some Provisions, their Cloths, bedding and working Tools . . . . Tho' this attempt has happily been defeated, it ought nevertheless to awaken us into some effectual measures."

Slavery was immensely profitable to some masters. James Madison told a British visitor shortly after the American Revolution that he could make $257 on every Negro in a year, and spend only $12 or $13 on his keep. Another viewpoint was of slaveowner Landon Carter, writing about fifty years earlier, complaining that his slaves so neglected their work and were so uncooperative ("either cannot or will not work") that he began to wonder if keeping them was worthwhile.

Some historians have painted a picture—based on the infrequency of organized rebellions and the ability of the South to maintain slavery for two hundred years—of a slave population made submissive by their condition; with their African heritage destroyed, they were, as Stanley Elkins said, made into "Sambos," "a society of helpless dependents." Or as another historian, Ulrich Phillips, said, "by racial quality submissive." But looking at the totality of slave behavior, at the resistance of everyday life, from quiet noncooperation in work to running away, the picture becomes different.

In 1710, warning the Virginia Assembly, Governor Alexander Spotswood said:

> freedom wears a cap which can without a tongue, call together all those who long to shake off the fetters of slavery and as such an Insurrection would surely be attended with most dreadful consequences so I think we cannot be too early in providing against it, both by putting our selves in a better posture of defence and by making a law to prevent the consultations of those Negroes.

Indeed, considering the harshness of punishment for running away, that so many blacks did run away must be a sign of a powerful rebelliousness. All through the 1700s, the Virginia slave code read:

> Whereas many times slaves run away and lie hid and lurking in swamps, woods, and other obscure places, killing hogs, and commiting other injuries to the inhabitants . . . if the slave does not immediately return, anyone what soever may kill or destroy such slaves by such ways and means as he . . . shall think fit . . . . If the slave is apprehended . . . it shall . . . be lawful for the county court, to order such punishment for the said slave, either by dismembering, or in any other way . . . as they in their discretion shall think fit, for the reclaiming any such incorrigible slave, and terrifying others from the like practices.

Mullin found newspaper advertisements between 1736 and 1801 for 1,138 men runaways, and 141 women. One consistent reason for running away was to find members of one's family—showing that despite the attempts of the slave system to destroy family ties by not allowing marriages and by separating families, slaves would face death and mutilation to get together.

In Maryland, where slaves were about one-third of the population in 1750, slavery had been written into law since the 1660s, and statutes for controlling rebellious slaves were passed. There were cases where slave women killed their masters, sometimes by poisoning them, sometimes by burning tobacco houses and homes. Punishments ranged from whipping and branding to execution, but the trouble continued. In 1742, seven slaves were put to death for murdering their master.

Fear of slave revolt seems to have been a permanent fact of plantation life. William Byrd, a wealthy Virginia slave owner, wrote in 1736:

> We have already at least 10,000 men of these descendants of Ham, fit to bear arms, and these numbers increase every day, as well by birth as by importation. And in case there should arise a man of desperate fortune, he might with more advantage than Cataline kindle a servile war . . . and tinge our rivers wide as they are with blood.

It was an intricate and powerful system of control that the slaveowners developed to maintain their labor supply and their way of life, a system both subtle and crude, involving every device that social orders employ for keeping power and wealth where it is. As Kenneth Stampp puts it:

> A wise master did not take seriously the belief that Negroes were natural-born slaves. He knew better. He knew that Negroes freshly imported from Africa had to be broken into bondage; that each succeeding generation had to be carefully trained. This was no easy task, for the bondsman rarely submitted willingly. Moreover, he rarely submitted completely. In most cases there was no end to the need for control—at least not until old age reduced the slave to a condition of helplessness.

The system was psychological and physical at the same time. The slaves were taught discipline, were impressed again and again with the idea of their own inferiority to "know their place," to see blackness as a sign of subordination, to be awed by the power of the master, to merge their interest with the master's, destroying their own individual needs. To accomplish this there was the discipline of hard labor, the breakup of the slave family, the lulling effects of religion (which sometimes led to "great mischief," as one slaveholder reported), the creation of disunity among slaves by separating them into field slaves and more privileged house slaves, and finally the power of law and the immediate power of the overseer to invoke whipping, burning, mutilation, and death. Dismemberment was provided for in the Virginia Code of 1705. Maryland passed a law in 1723 providing for cutting off the ears of blacks who struck whites, and that for certain serious crimes, slaves should be hanged and the body quartered and exposed.

Still, rebellions took place—not many, but enough to create constant fear among white planters. The first large-scale revolt in the North American colonies took place in New York in 1712. In New York, slaves were 10 percent of the population, the highest proportion in the northern states, where economic conditions usually did not require large numbers of field slaves. About twenty-five blacks and two Indians set fire to a building, then killed nine whites who came on the scene. They were captured by soldiers, put on trial, and twenty-one were executed.

The governor's report to England said: "Some were burnt, others were hanged, one broke on the wheel, and one hung alive in chains in the town." One had been burned over a slow fire for eight to ten hours—all this to serve notice to other slaves.

A letter to London from South Carolina in 1720 reports:

> I am now to acquaint you that very lately we have had a very wicked and barbarous plot of the designe of the negroes rising with a designe to destroy all the white people in the country and then to take Charles Town in full body but it pleased God it was discovered and many of them taken prisoners and some burnt and some hang'd and some banish'd.

Around this time there were a number of fires in Boston and New Haven, suspected to be the work of Negro slaves. As a result, one Negro was executed in Boston, and the Boston Council ruled that any slaves who on their own gathered in groups of two or more were to be punished by whipping.

At Stono, South Carolina, in 1739, about twenty slaves rebelled, killed two warehouse guards, stole guns and gunpowder, and headed south, killing people in their way, and burning buildings. They were joined by others, until there were perhaps eighty slaves in all and, according to one account of the time, "they called out Liberty, marched on with Colours displayed, and two Drums beating." The militia found and attacked them. In the ensuing battle perhaps fifty slaves and twenty-five whites were killed before the uprising was crushed.

Herbert Aptheker, who did detailed research on slave resistance in North America for his book *American Negro Slave Revolts,* found about 250 instances where a minimum of ten slaves joined in a revolt or conspiracy.

From time to time, whites were involved in the slave resistance. As early as 1663, indentured white servants and black slaves in Gloucester County, Virginia, formed a conspiracy to rebel and gain their freedom. The plot was betrayed, and ended with executions. Mullin reports that the newspaper notices of runaways in Virginia often warned "ill-disposed" whites about harboring fugitives. Sometimes slaves and free men ran off together, or cooperated in crimes together. Sometimes, black male slaves ran off and joined white women. From time to time, white ship captains and watermen dealt with runaways, perhaps making the slave a part of the crew.

In New York in 1741, there were ten thousand whites in the city and two thousand black slaves. It had been a hard winter and the poor—slave and free—had suffered greatly. When mysterious fires broke out, blacks and whites were accused of conspiring together. Mass hysteria developed against the accused. After a trial full of lurid accusations by informers, and forced confessions, two white men and two white women were executed, eighteen slaves were hanged, and thirteen slaves were burned alive.

Only one fear was greater than the fear of black rebellion in the new American colonies. That was the fear that discontented whites would join black slaves to overthrow the existing order. In the early years of slavery, especially, before racism as a way of thinking was firmly ingrained, while white indentured servants were often treated as badly as black slaves, there was a possibility of cooperation. As Edmund Morgan sees it:

> There are hints that the two despised groups initially saw each other as sharing the same predicament. It was common, for example, for servants and slaves to run away together, steal hogs together, get drunk together. It was not uncommon for them to make love together. In Bacon's Rebellion, one of the last groups to surrender was a mixed band of eighty negroes and twenty English servants.

As Morgan says, masters, "initially at least, perceived slaves in much the same way they had always perceived servants . . . shiftless, irresponsible, unfaithful, ungrateful, dishonest." And "if freemen with disappointed hopes should make common cause with slaves of desperate hope, the results might be worse than anything Bacon had done."

And so, measures were taken. About the same time that slave codes, involving discipline and punishment, were passed by the Virginia Assembly,

> Virginia's. ruling class, having proclaimed that all white men were superior to black, went on to offer their social (but white) inferiors a number of benefits previously denied them. In 1705 a law was passed requiring masters to provide white servants whose indenture time was up with ten bushels of corn, thirty shillings, and a gun, while women servants were to get 15 bushels of corn and forty shillings. Also, the newly freed servants were to get 50 acres of land.

Morgan concludes: "Once the small planter felt less exploited by taxation and began to prosper a little, he became less turbulent, less dangerous, more respectable. He could begin to see his big neighbor not as an extortionist but as a powerful protector of their common interests."

We see now a complex web of historical threads to ensnare blacks for slavery in America: the desperation of starving settlers, the special helplessness of the displaced African, the powerful incentive of profit for slave trader and planter, the temptation of superior status for poor whites, the elaborate controls against escape and rebellion, the legal and social punishment of black and white collaboration.

The point is that the elements of this web are historical, not "natural." This does not mean that they are easily disentangled, dismantled. It means only that there is a possibility for something else, under historical conditions not yet realized. And one of these conditions would be the elimination of that class exploitation which has made poor whites desperate for small gifts of status, and has prevented that unity of black and white necessary for joint rebellion and reconstruction.

Around 1700, the Virginia House of Burgesses declared:

> The Christian Servants in this country for the most part consists of the Worser Sort of the people of Europe. And since . . . such numbers of Irish and other Nations have been brought in of which a great many have been soldiers in the late warrs that according to our present Circumstances we can hardly governe them and if they were fitted with Armes and had the Opertunity of meeting together by Musters we have just reason to fears they may rise upon us.

It was a kind of **class consciousness,** a class fear. There were things happening in early Virginia, and in the other colonies, to warrant it.

class consciousness Karl Marx argued that the working classes were not conscious of the ways in which the ruling class oppressed them. Class consciousness refers to the ability of the laboring class (the proletariat) to challenge the reasons given to them by economic elites as to why they were impoverished.

3　Racial Formations
Michael Omi • Howard Winant

MICHAEL OMI is a professor in the Department of Ethnic Studies at the University of California, Berkeley, and the co-author of *Racial Formation in the United States from the 1960s to the 1980s* (1986). He has also written about racial theory and politics, right-wing political movements, Asian Americans and race relations, and race and popular culture. In 1990, he was the recipient of Berkeley's Distinguished Teaching Award.

HOWARD WINANT is a professor of sociology at the University of California, Santa Barbara. He is the author of numerous books and articles, including *Racial Formation in the United States from the 1960s to the 1990s* (1994) (with Michael Omi), *Racial Conditions: Politics, Theory, Comparisons* (1994), and *Stalemate: Political Economic Origins of Supply-Side Policy* (1988).

Questions to Consider If race is not "real" in a scientific sense, why can I look around the classroom or campus and see that someone is black or Asian or white? What is the difference between something being "real" (like the book in front of you) and something being a "social construction" (like race or gender)? Use Omi and Winant's theory of racial formation to explain how and why we "see" race as we do.

IN 1982–83, SUSIE GUILLORY PHIPPS unsuccessfully sued the Louisiana Bureau of Vital Records to change her racial classification from black to white. The descendant of an eighteenth-century white planter and a black slave, Phipps was designated "black" in her birth certificate in accordance with a 1970 state law which declared anyone with at least one-thirty-second "Negro blood" to be black. The legal battle raised intriguing questions about the concept of **race,** its meaning in contemporary society, and its use (and abuse) in public policy. Assistant Attorney General Ron Davis defended the law by pointing out that some type of racial classification was necessary to comply with federal record-keeping requirements and to facilitate programs for the prevention of genetic diseases. Phipps's attorney, Brian Begue, argued that the assignment of racial categories on birth certificates was unconstitutional and that the one-thirty-second designation was inaccurate. He called on a retired Tulane University professor who cited research indicating that most whites have one-twentieth "Negro" ancestry. In the end, Phipps lost. The court upheld a state law which quantified racial identity, and in so doing affirmed the legality of assigning individuals to specific racial groupings.[1]

The Phipps case illustrates the continuing dilemma of defining race and establishing its meaning in institutional life. Today, to assert that variations in human physiognomy are racially based is to enter a constant and intense debate. *Scientific* interpretations of race have not been alone in sparking heated controversy; *religious* perspectives have done so as well.[2] Most centrally, of course, race has been a matter of *political* contention. This has been particularly true in the United States, where the concept of race has varied enormously over time without ever leaving the center stage of US history.

What Is Race?

Race consciousness, and its articulation in theories of race, is largely a modern phenomenon. When European explorers in the New World "discovered" people who looked different than themselves, these "natives" challenged then existing conceptions of the origins of the human species, and raised disturbing questions as to whether *all* could be considered in the same "family of man."[3] Religious debates flared over the attempt to reconcile the Bible with the existence of "racially distinct" people. Arguments took place over creation itself, as theories of polygenesis questioned whether God had made only one species of humanity ("monogenesis"). Europeans wondered if the natives of the New World were indeed human beings with redeemable

souls. At stake were not only the prospects for conversion, but the types of treatment to be accorded them. The expropriation of property, the denial of political rights, the introduction of slavery and other forms of coercive labor, as well as outright extermination, all presupposed a worldview which distinguished Europeans—children of God, human beings, etc.—from "others." Such a worldview was needed to explain why some should be "free" and others enslaved, why some had rights to land and property while others did not. Race, and the interpretation of racial differences, was a central factor in that worldview.

In the colonial epoch science was no less a field of controversy than religion in attempts to comprehend the concept of race and its meaning. Spurred on by the classificatory scheme of living organisms devised by Linnaeus in *Systema Naturae,* many scholars in the eighteenth and nineteenth centuries dedicated themselves to the identification and ranking of variations in humankind. Race was thought of as a *biological* concept, yet its precise definition was the subject of debates which, as we have noted, continue to rage today. Despite efforts ranging from Dr. Samuel Morton's studies of cranial capacity[4] to contemporary attempts to base racial classification on shared gene pools,[5] the concept of race has defied biological definition . . . .

Attempts to discern the *scientific meaning* of race continue to the present day. Although most physical anthropologists and biologists have abandoned the quest for a scientific basis to determine racial categories, controversies have recently flared in the area of genetics and educational psychology. For instance, an essay by Arthur Jensen argued that hereditary factors shape intelligence not only revived the "nature or nurture" controversy, but raised highly volatile questions about racial equality itself.[6] Clearly the attempt to establish a *biological* basis of race has not been swept into the dustbin of history, but is being resurrected in various scientific arenas. All such attempts seek to remove the concept of race from fundamental social, political, or economic determination. They suggest instead that the truth of race lies in the terrain of innate characteristics, of which skin color and other physical attributes provide only the most obvious, and in some respects most superficial, indicators.

Race as a Social Concept

The social sciences have come to reject biologistic notions of race in favor of an approach which regards race as a *social* concept. Beginning in the eighteenth century, this trend has

race Sociologists view race as a social concept because the idea of race has changed over time, the categories of race are not discrete (they blend into one another), and the definition of race changes from country to country. We tend to think about race in terms of skin color, but the reason we place human beings into skin color categories is as arbitrary as grouping individuals by height, blood type, weight, eye color, or finger length.

been slow and uneven, but its direction clear. In the nine-teenth century Max Weber discounted biological explanations for racial conflict and instead highlighted the social and political factors which engendered such conflict.[7] The work of pioneering cultural anthropologist Franz Boas was crucial in refuting the scientific racism of the early twentieth century by rejecting the connection between race and culture, and the assumption of a continuum of "higher" and "lower" cultural groups. Within the contemporary social science literature, race is assumed to be a variable which is shaped by broader societal forces.

Race is indeed a pre-eminently *sociohistorical* concept. Racial categories and the meaning of race are given concrete expression by the specific social relations and historical context in which they are embedded. Racial meanings have varied tremendously over time and between different societies.

In the United States, the black/white color line has historically been rigidly defined and enforced. White is seen as a "pure" category. Any racial intermixture makes one "nonwhite." In the movie *Raintree County,* Elizabeth Taylor describes the worst of fates to befall whites as "havin' a little Negra blood in ya'—just one little teeny drop and a person's all Negra."[8] This thinking flows from what Marvin Harris has characterized as the principle of *hypo-descent:*

> By what ingenious computation is the genetic tracery of a million years of evolution unraveled and each man [sic] assigned his proper social box? In the United States, the mechanism employed is the rule of hypo-descent. This descent rule requires Americans to believe that anyone who is known to have had a Negro ancestor is a Negro. We admit nothing in between . . . . "Hypo-descent" means affiliation with the subordinate rather than the superordinate group in order to avoid the ambiguity of intermediate identity . . . . The rule of hypo-descent is, therefore, an invention, which we in the United States have made in order to keep biological facts from intruding into our collective racist fantasies.[9]

The Susie Guillory Phipps case merely represents the contemporary expression of this racial logic.

By contrast, a striking feature of race relations in the lowland areas of Latin America since the abolition of slavery has been the relative absence of sharply defined racial groupings. No such rigid descent rule characterizes racial identity in many Latin American societies. Brazil, for example, has historically had less rigid conceptions of race, and thus a variety of "intermediate" racial categories exist. Indeed, as Harris notes, "One of the most striking consequences of the Brazilian system of racial identification is that parents and children and even brothers and sisters are frequently accepted as representatives of quite opposite racial types."[10] Such a possibility is incomprehensible within the logic of racial categories in the US.

To suggest another example: the notion of "passing" takes on new meaning if we compare various American cultures' means of assigning racial identity. In the United States, individuals who are actually "black" by the logic of hypo-descent have attempted to skirt the discriminatory barriers imposed by law and custom by attempting to "pass" for white.[11] Ironically, these same individuals would not be able to pass for "black" in many Latin American societies.

Consideration of the term "black" illustrates the diversity of racial meanings which can be found among different societies and historically within a given society. In contemporary British politics the term "black" is used to refer to all nonwhites. Interestingly this designation has not arisen through the racist discourse of groups such as the National Front. Rather, in political and cultural movements, Asian as well as Afro-Caribbean youth are adopting the term as an expression of self-identity.[12] The wide-ranging meanings of "black" illustrate the manner in which racial categories are shaped politically.[13]

The meaning of race is defined and contested throughout society, in both collective action and personal practice. In the process, racial categories themselves are formed, transformed, destroyed and reformed. We use the term **racial formation** to refer to the process by which social, economic and political forces determine the content and importance of racial categories, and by which they are in turn shaped by racial meanings. Crucial to this formulation is the treatment of race as a *central axis* of social relations which cannot be subsumed under or reduced to some broader category or conception.

Racial Ideology and Racial Identity

The seemingly obvious, "natural" and "common sense" qualities which the existing racial order exhibits themselves testify to the effectiveness of the racial formation process in constructing racial meanings and racial identities.

---

racial formation The process in which race operates as a central axis of social relations, which then determine social, economic, and political institutions and practices.

One of the first things we notice about people when we meet them (along with their sex) is their race. We utilize race to provide clues abut *who* a person is. This fact is made painfully obvious when we encounter someone whom we cannot conveniently racially categorize—someone who is, for example, racially "mixed" or of an ethnic/racial group with which we are not familiar. Such an encounter becomes a source of discomfort and momentarily a crisis of racial meaning. Without a racial identity, one is in danger of having no identity.

Our compass for navigating race relations depends on preconceived notions of what each specific racial group looks like. Comments such as, "Funny, you don't look black," betray an underlying image of what black should be. We also become disoriented when people do not act "black," "Latino," or indeed "white." The content of such stereotypes reveals a series of unsubstantiated beliefs about who these groups are and what "they" are like.[14]

In US society, then, a kind of "racial etiquette" exists, a set of interpretive codes and racial meanings which operate in the interactions of daily life. Rules shaped by our perception of race in a comprehensively racial society determine the "presentation of self,"[15] distinctions of status, and appropriate modes of conduct. "Etiquette" is not mere universal adherence to the dominant group's rules, but a more dynamic combination of these rules with the values and beliefs of subordinated groupings. This racial "subjection" is quintessentially ideological. Everybody learns some combination, some version, of the rules of racial classification, and of their own racial identity, often without obvious teaching or conscious inculcation. Race becomes "common sense"—a way of comprehending, explaining and acting in the world.

Racial beliefs operate as an "amateur biology," a way of explaining the variations in "human nature."[16] Differences in skin color and other obvious physical characteristics supposedly provide visible clues to differences lurking underneath. Temperament, sexuality, intelligence, athletic ability, aesthetic preferences and so on are presumed to be fixed and discernible from the palpable mark of race. Such diverse questions as our confidence and trust in others (for example, clerks or salespeople, media figures, neighbors), our sexual preferences and romantic images, our tastes in music, films, dance, or sports, and our very ways of talking, walking, eating and dreaming are ineluctably shaped by notions of race. Skin color "differences" are thought to explain perceived differences in intellectual, physical and artistic temperaments, and to justify distinct treatment of racially identified individuals and groups.

The continuing persistence of racial ideology suggests that these racial myths and stereotypes cannot be exposed as such in the popular imagination. They are, we think, too essential, too integral, to the maintenance of the US social order. Of course, particular meanings, stereotypes and myths can change, but the presence of a *system* of racial meanings and stereotypes, of racial ideology, seems to be a permanent feature of US culture.

Film and television, for example, have been notorious in disseminating images of racial minorities which establish for audiences what people from these groups look like, how they behave, and "who they are."[17] The power of the media lies not only in their ability to reflect the dominant racial ideology, but in their capacity to shape that ideology in the first place. D. W. Griffith's epic *Birth of a Nation,* a sympathetic treatment of the rise of the Ku Klux Klan during Reconstruction, helped to generate, consolidate and "nationalize" images of blacks which had been more disparate (more regionally specific, for example) prior to the film's appearance.[18] In US television, the necessity to define characters in the briefest and most condensed manner has led to the perpetuation of racial caricatures, as racial stereotypes serve as shorthand for scriptwriters, directors and actors, in commercials, etc. Television's tendency to address the "lowest common denominator" in order to render programs "familiar" to an enormous and diverse audience leads it regularly to assign and reassign racial characteristics to particular groups, both minority and majority.

These and innumerable other examples show that we tend to view race as something fixed and immutable—something rooted in "nature." Thus we mask the historical construction of racial categories, the shifting meaning of race, and the crucial role of politics and ideology in shaping race relations. Races do not emerge full-blown. They are the results of diverse historical practices and are continually subject to challenge over their definition and meaning.

Racialization: The Historical Development of Race

In the United States, the racial category of "black" evolved with the consolidation of racial slavery. By the end of the seventeenth century, Africans whose specific identity was Ibo, Yoruba, Fulani, etc., were rendered "black" by an ideology of exploitation based on racial logic—the establishment and maintenance of a "color line." This of course did not occur overnight. A period of indentured servitude which was not rooted in racial logic preceded the consolidation of racial slavery. With slavery, however, a racially based understanding of society was set in motion which resulted in the shaping of a specific *racial* identity not only for the slaves but for the European settlers as well. Winthrop Jordan has observed: "From the initially common term *Christian,* at mid-century there was a marked shift toward the terms *English* and *free.* After about 1680, taking the colonies as a whole, a new term of self-identification appeared—*white.*"[19]

We employ the term **racialization** to signify the extension of racial meaning to a previously racially unclassified relationship, social practice or group. Racialization is an ideological process, an historically specific one. Racial ideology is constructed from pre-existing conceptual (or, if one prefers, "dis-cursive") elements and emerges from the struggles of competing political projects and ideas seeking to articulate similar elements differently. An account of racialization processes that avoids the pitfalls of US ethnic history[20] remains to be written.

Particularly during the nineteenth century, the category of "white" was subject to challenges brought about by the influx of diverse groups who were not of the same Anglo-Saxon stock as the founding immigrants. In the nineteenth century, political and ideological struggles emerged over the classification of Southern Europeans, the Irish and Jews, among other "nonwhite" categories.[21] Nativism was only effectively curbed by the institutionalization of a racial order that drew the color line *around,* rather than *within,* Europe.

By stopping short of racializing immigrants from Europe after the Civil War, and by subsequently allowing their assimilation, the American racial order was reconsolidated in the wake of the tremendous challenge placed before it by the abolition of racial slavery.[22] With the end of Reconstruction in 1877, an effective program for limiting the emergent class struggles of the later nineteenth century was forged: the definition of the working class *in racial terms*—as "white." This was not accomplished by any legislative decree or capitalist maneuvering to divide the working class, but rather by white workers themselves. Many of them were recent immigrants, who organized

racialization The social process by which a racial identity is attached to a group and that group is placed in a race-based social hierarchy. Upon their arrival in America, for example, Europeans labeled the hundreds of indigenous tribal populations "Indians" and placed them in a single group in a racial hierarchy.

on racial lines as much as on traditionally defined class lines.[23] The Irish on the West Coast, for example, engaged in vicious anti-Chinese race-baiting and committed many pogrom-type assaults on Chinese in the course of consolidating the trade union movement in California.

Thus the very political organization of the working class was in important ways a racial project. The legacy of racial conflicts and arrangements shaped the definition of interests and in turn led to the consolidation of institutional patterns (e.g., segregated unions, dual labor markets, exclusionary legislation) which perpetuated the color line *within* the working class. Selig Perlman, whose study of the development of the labor movement is fairly sympathetic to this process, notes that:

> The political issue after 1877 was racial, not financial, and the weapon was not merely the ballot, but also "direct action"—violence. The anti-Chinese agitation in California, culminating as it did in the Exclusion Law passed by Congress in 1882, was doubtless the most important single factor in the history of American labor, for without it the entire country might have been overrun by Mongolian [sic] labor and *the labor movement might have become a conflict of races instead of one of classes.*[24]

More recent economic transformations in the US have also altered interpretations of racial identities and meanings. The automation of southern agriculture and the augmented labor demand of the postwar boom transformed blacks from a largely rural, impoverished labor force to a largely urban, working-class group by 1970.[25] When boom became bust and liberal welfare statism moved rightwards, the majority of blacks came to be seen, increasingly, as part of the "underclass," as state "dependents." Thus the particularly deleterious effects on blacks of global and national economic shifts (generally rising unemployment rates, changes in the employment structure away from reliance on labor intensive work, etc.) were explained once again in the late 1970s and 1980s (as they had been in the 1940s and mid-1960s) as the result of defective black cultural norms, of familial disorganization, etc.[26] In this way new racial attributions, new racial myths, are affixed to "blacks."[27] Similar changes in racial identity are presently affecting Asians and Latinos, as such economic forces as increasing Third World impoverishment and indebtedness fuel immigration and high interest rates, Japanese competition spurs resentments, and US jobs seem to fly away to Korea and Singapore.[28] . . .

Once we understand that race overflows the boundaries of skin color, super-exploitation, social stratification, discrimination and prejudice, cultural domination and cultural resistance, state policy (or of any other particular social relationship we list), once we recognize the racial dimension present to some degree in *every* identity, institution and social practice in the United States—once we have done this, it becomes possible to speak of *racial formation.* This recognition is hard-won; there is a continuous temptation to think of race as an *essence,* as something fixed, concrete and objective, as (for example) one of the categories just enumerated. And there is also an opposite temptation: to see it as a mere illusion, which an ideal social order would eliminate.

In our view it is crucial to break with these habits of thought. The effort must be made to understand race as *an unstable and "decentered" complex of social meanings constantly being transformed by political struggle.*

---

4 Theoretical Perspectives in Race and Ethnic Relations

Joe R. Feagin • Clairece Booher Feagin

JOE R. FEAGIN is the Ella C. McFadden Professor of sociology at Texas A&M. He is author of more than 100 books and articles on race relations.

CLAIRECE BOOHER FEAGIN is the author of *What Will School Be Like?* (1991) and co-author of *Stories for Parents* (1990) and *Discrimination American Style: Institutional Racism and Sexism* (1978).

Assimilation and Other Order Perspectives

In the United States much social theorizing has emphasized **assimilation,** the more or less orderly adaptation of a migrating group to the ways and institutions of an established group. Hirschman has noted that "the assimilation perspective, broadly defined, continues to be the primary theoretical framework for sociological research on racial and ethnic inequality." The reason for this dominance, he suggests, is the "lack of convincing alternatives."[1] The English word *assimilate* comes from the Latin *assimulare,* "to make similar."

Robert E. Park

Robert E. Park, a major sociological theorist, argued that European out-migration was a major catalyst for societal reorganization around the globe. In his view intergroup

assimilation To make "similar" to the dominant group; the process by which newly arrived ethnic and racial groups take on the language, mannerism, and customs of the dominant culture.

> **Questions to Consider**   Which theories outlined by Feagin and Feagin do you believe best explain contemporary race relations in the United States? Do you need to pull together theories in this reading to explain the experiences of different racial and ethnic groups in the United States? Can one theory explain or fully capture the dynamics of race and ethnic relations in the United States? Why or why not?

contacts regularly go through stages of a *race relations cycle.* Fundamental social forces such as out-migration lead to recurring cycles in intergroup history: "The race relations cycle which takes the form, to state it abstractly, of *contacts, competition, accommodation* and eventual *assimilation,* is apparently progressive and irreversible."[2] In the contact stage migration and exploration bring people together, which in turn leads to economic competition and thus to new social organization. Competition and conflict flow from the contacts between host peoples and the migrating groups. Accommodation, an unstable condition in the race relations cycle, often takes place rapidly. It involves a forced adjustment by a migrating group to a new social situation. . . . Nonetheless, Park and most scholars working in this tradition have argued that there is a long-term trend toward assimilation of racial and ethnic minorities in modern societies. "Assimilation is a process of interpenetration and fusion in which persons and groups acquire the memories, sentiments, and attitudes of other persons or groups, and, by sharing their experience and history, are incorporated with them in a common cultural life."[3] Even racially subordinate groups are expected to assimilate.[4]

Stages of Assimilation: Milton Gordon

Since Park's pioneering analysis in the 1920s, many U.S. theorists of racial and ethnic relations and numerous textbook writers have adopted an assimilationist perspective, although most have departed from Park's framework in a number of important ways. Milton Gordon, author of the influential *Assimilation in American Life,* distinguishes a variety of initial encounters between race and ethnic groups and an array of possible assimilation outcomes. While Gordon presents three competing images of assimilation—the melting pot, cultural pluralism, and Anglo-conformity—he focuses on Anglo-conformity as the descriptive reality. That is, immigrant groups in the United States, in Gordon's view, have typically tended to give up much of their heritage for the dominant, preexisting Anglo-Saxon core culture and society. The touchstone of adjustment is viewed thus: "If there is anything in American life which can be described as an overall American culture which serves as a reference point for immigrants and their children, it can best be described, it seems to us, as the middle-class cultural patterns of, largely, white Protestant, Anglo-Saxon origins, leaving aside for the moment the question of minor reciprocal influences on this culture exercised by the cultures of later entry into the United States."[5]

Gordon notes that Anglo-conformity has been substantially achieved for most immigrant groups in the United States, especially in regard to cultural assimilation. Most groups following the English have adapted to the Anglo core culture. Gordon distinguishes seven dimensions of adaptation:

1. *cultural assimilation:* change of cultural patterns to those of the core society;
2. *structural assimilation:* penetration of cliques and associations of the core society at the primary-group level;
3. *marital assimilation:* significant intermarriage;
4. *identification assimilation:* development of a sense of identity linked to the core society;
5. *attitude-receptional assimilation:* absence of prejudice and stereotyping;
6. *behavior-receptional assimilation:* absence of intentional discrimination;
7. *civic assimilation:* absence of value and power conflict.[6]

Whereas Park believed structural assimilation, including primary-group ties such as intergroup friendships, flowed from cultural assimilation, Gordon stresses that these are separate stages of assimilation and may take place at different rates.

Gordon conceptualizes structural assimilation as relating to primary-group cliques and relations. Significantly, he does not highlight as a separate type of structural assimilation the movement of a new immigrant group into the *secondary groups* of the host society—that is, into the employing organizations, such as corporations or public bureaucracies, and the critical educational and political institutions. The omission of secondary-structural assimilation is a major flaw in Gordon's theory. Looking at U.S. history, one would conclude that assimilating into the core society's secondary groups does *not necessarily* mean entering the dominant group's friendship cliques. In addition, the dimension Gordon calls *civic assimilation* is confusing since he includes in it "values," which are really part of cultural assimilation, and "power," which is a central aspect of structural assimilation at the secondary-group level.

Gordon's assimilation theory has influenced a generation of researchers. . . . In a recent examination of Gordon's seven dimensions of assimilation, J. Allen Williams and Suzanne Ortega drew on interviews with a midwestern sample to substantiate that cultural assimilation was not necessarily the first type of assimilation to occur. For example, the Mexican Americans in the sample were found to be less culturally assimilated than African Americans, yet were more assimilated structurally. Those of Swiss and Swedish backgrounds ranked about the same on the study's measure of cultural assimilation, but the Swedish Americans were less assimilated structurally. Williams and Ortega conclude that assimilation varies considerably from one group to another and that Gordon's seven types can be grouped into three more general categories of structural, cultural, and receptional assimilation.[7]

In a later book, *Human Nature, Class, and Ethnicity* (1978), Gordon has recognized that his assimilation theory neglects power issues and proposed bringing these into his model, but so far he has provided only a brief and inadequate analysis. Gordon mentions in passing the different resources available to competing racial groups and refers briefly to black-white conflict, but gives little attention to the impact of economic power, inequalities in material resources, or capitalistic economic history on U.S. racial and ethnic relations.[8]

Focused on the millions of white European immigrants and their adjustments, Gordon's model emphasizes *generational* changes within immigrant groups over time. Substantial acculturation to the Anglo-Protestant core culture has often been completed by the second or third generation for many European immigrant groups. The partially acculturated first generation formed protective communities and associations, but the children of those immigrants were considerably more exposed to Anglo-conformity pressures in the mass media and in schools.[9] Gordon also suggests that substantial assimilation along certain other dimensions, such as the civic, behavior-receptional, and attitude-receptional ones, has occurred for numerous European groups. Most white groups have also made considerable progress toward equality at the secondary-structural levels of employment and politics, although the dimensions of this assimilation are neither named nor discussed in any detail by Gordon.

For many white groups, particularly non-Protestant ones, structural assimilation at the primary-group level is underway, yet far from complete. Gordon suggests that substantially complete cultural assimilation (for example, adoption of the English language) along with structural (primary-group) pluralism form a characteristic pattern of adaptation for many white ethnic groups. Even these relatively acculturated groups tend to limit their informal friendships and marriage ties either to their immediate ethnic groups or to *similar* groups that are part of their general religious community. Following Will Herberg, who argued that there are three great community "melting pots" in the United States—Jews, Protestants, and Catholics—Gordon suggests that primary-group ties beyond one's own group are often developed with one's broad socioreligious community, whether that be Protestant, Catholic, or Jewish.[10]

In his influential books and articles Gordon recognizes that structural assimilation has been retarded by racial prejudice and discrimination, but he seems to suggest that non-European Americans, including African Americans, will eventually be absorbed into the core culture and society. He gives the most attention to the gradual assimilation of middle-class non-Europeans. In regard to blacks he argues, optimistically, that the United States has "moved decisively

down the road toward implementing the implications of the American credo of [equality and justice] for race relations"—as in employment and housing. This perceived tremendous progress for black Americans has created a policy dilemma for the government: should it adopt a traditional political liberalism that ignores race, or a "corporate liberalism" that recognizes group rights along racial lines? Gordon includes under corporate liberalism government programs of affirmative action, which he rejects.[11] . . .

Some assimilation-oriented analysts such as Gordon and Alba have argued that the once prominent ethnic identities, especially of European American groups, are fading over time. Alba suggests that there is still an ethnic identity of consequence for non-Latino whites, but declares that "a new ethnic group is forming—one based on a vague *ancestry* from anywhere on the European continent."[12] In other words, such distinct ethnic identities as English American and Irish American are gradually becoming only a vague identification as "European American," although Alba emphasizes this as a trend, not a fact. Interestingly, research on intermarriages between members of different white ethnic groups has revealed that large proportions of the children of such marriages see themselves as having multiple ethnic identities, while others choose one of their heritages, or simply "American," as their ethnic identity.[13]

Ethnogenesis and Ethnic Pluralism

Some theorists working in the assimilation tradition reject the argument that most European American groups have become substantially assimilated to a generic Anglo-Protestant or Euro-American identity and way of life. A few have explored models of adjustment that depart from Anglo-conformity in the direction of ethnic or cultural pluralism. Most analysts of pluralism accept some Anglo-conformity as inevitable, if not desirable. In *Beyond the Melting Pot,* Glazer and Moynihan agree that the original customs and home-country ways of European immigrants were mostly lost by the third generation. But this did not mean the decline of ethnicity. The European immigrant groups usually remained distinct in terms of name, identity, and, for the most part, primary-group ties.[14]

Andrew Greeley has developed the interesting concept of *ethnogenesis* and applied it to white immigrant groups, those set off by nationality and religion. Greeley is critical of the traditional assimilation perspective because it assumes "that the strain toward homogenization in a modern industrial society is so great as to be virtually irresistible."[15] Traditionally, the direction of this assimilation in the United States is assumed to be toward the Anglo-Protestant core culture. But from the ethnogenesis perspective, adaptation has meant more than this one-way conformity. The traditional assimilation model does not explain the persistence of ethnicity in the United States—the emphasis among immigrants on ethnicity as a way of becoming American and, in recent decades, the self-conscious attempts to create ethnic identity and manipulate ethnic symbols.[16]

. . . Greeley suggests that in many cases host and immigrant groups had a somewhat similar *cultural* inheritance. For example, some later European immigrant groups had a cultural background initially similar to that of earlier English settlers. As a result of interaction in schools and the influence of the media over several generations the number of cultural traits common to the host and immigrant groups often grew. Yet late in the adaptive process certain aspects of the heritage of the home country remained very important to the character of the immigrant-ethnic group. From this perspective, ethnic groups share traits with the host group *and* retain major nationality characteristics as well. A modern ethnic group is one part home-country heritage and one part common culture, mixed together in a distinctive way because of a unique history of development within the North American crucible.[17]

A number of research studies have documented the persistence of distinctive white ethnic groups such as Italian Americans and Jewish Americans in U.S. cities, not just in New York and Chicago but in San Francisco, New Orleans, and Tucson as well. Yancey and his associates have suggested that ethnicity is an "emergent phenomenon"—that its importance varies in cities and that its character and strength depend on the specific historical conditions in which it emerges and grows.[18]

Some Problems with Assimilation Theories

Most assimilation theorists take as their examples of ethnic adaptation white European groups migrating more or less voluntarily to the United States. But what of the adaptation and assimilation of non-European groups beyond the stage of initial contact? Some analysts of assimilation include non-white groups in their theories, despite the problems that arise from such an inclusion. Some analysts have argued that assimilation, cultural and structural, is the necessary, if long-term, answer to the racial problem in the United States. . . .

More optimistic analysts have emphasized progressive inclusion, which will eventually provide black Americans and other minority groups with full citizenship, in fact as well as principle. For that reason, they expect ethnic and racial conflict to disappear as various groups become fully assimilated into the core culture and society. Nathan Glazer, Milton Gordon, and Talcott Parsons have stressed the egalitarianism of U.S. institutions and what they view as the progressive emancipation of non-European groups. Gordon and others have underscored the gradual assimilation of middle-class black Americans over the last several decades. Full membership for black Americans seems inevitable, notes Parsons, for "the only tolerable solution to the enormous [racial] tensions lies in constituting a single societal community with full membership for all."[19] The importance of racial, as well as ethnic, stratification is expected to decline as powerful, universalistic societal forces wipe out the vestiges of earlier ethnocentric value systems. White immigrants have desired substantial assimilation, and most have been absorbed. The same is expected to happen eventually for non-European groups.

Assimilation theories have been criticized as having an "establishment" bias, as not distinguishing carefully enough between what *has* happened to a given group and what the establishment at some point felt *should have* happened. For example, a number of Asian American scholars and leaders have reacted vigorously to the application of the concept of assimilation to Asian Americans, arguing that the very concept originated in a period (1870–1925) of intense attacks by white Americans on Asian Americans. The term was thus tainted from the beginning by its association with the dominant European American group's ideology that the only "good groups" were those that assimilated (or could assimilate) in Anglo-conformity fashion.

Unlike Park, who paid substantial attention to the historical and world-economy context of migration, many of today's assimilation theorists do not analyze sufficiently the historical background and development of a particular racial or ethnic group within a national or world context. In addition, assimilation analysts such as Gordon tend to neglect the power imbalance and inequality in racial and ethnic relations, which are seen most clearly in the cases of non-European Americans. As Geschwender has noted, "they seem to have forgotten that exploitation is the driving force that gives meaning to the study of racial and ethnic relations."[20]

Biosocial Perspectives

Some U.S. theorists, including assimilationists, now accent a biosocial perspective on racial and ethnic relations. The idea of race and ethnicity being deeply rooted in the biological makeup of human beings is an old European and American notion that has received renewed attention from a few social scientists and biologists in the United States since the 1970s. In *Human Nature, Class, and Ethnicity,* for example, Gordon suggests that ethnic ties are rooted in the "biological organism of man." Ethnicity is a fundamental part of the physiological as well as the psychological self. Ethnicity "cannot be shed by social mobility, as for instance social class background can, since society insists on its inalienable ascription from cradle to grave." What Gordon seems to have in mind is not the old racist notion of the unchanging biological character and separateness of racial groups, but rather the rootedness of intergroup relation, including racial and ethnic relations, in the everyday realities of kinship and other socially constructed group boundaries. Gordon goes further, however, emphasizing that human beings tend to be "selfish, narcissistic and perpetually poised on the edge of aggression." And it is these selfish tendencies that lie behind racial and ethnic tensions.[21] Gordon is here adopting a Hobbesian (dog-eat-dog) view of human nature. . . .

Although decidedly different from the earlier biological theories, the modern biosocial analysis remains problematical. The exact linkages between the deep genetic underpinnings of human nature and concrete racial or ethnic behavior are not spelled out beyond some vague analysis of kin selection and selfish behavior. . . .

Another difficulty with the biosocial approach is that in the everyday world, racial and ethnic relations are *immediately social* rather than biological. As Edna Bonacich has pointed out, many racial and ethnic groups have mixed biological ancestry. Jewish Americans, for example, have a very mixed ancestry: as a group, they share no distinct biological characteristics. Biologically diverse Italian immigrants from different regions of Italy gained a sense of being Italian American (even Italian) in the United States. The bonds holding Jewish Americans together and Italian Americans together were not genetically based or biologically primordial, but rather the result of real *historical* experiences as these groups settled into the United States. Moreover, if ethnicity is primordial in a biological sense, it should always be a prominent force in human affairs.

Sometimes ethnicity leads to recurring conflict, as in the case of Jews and Gentiles in the United States; in other cases, as with Scottish and English Americans, it quietly disappears in the assimilation process. Sentiments based on common ancestry are important, but they are activated primarily in the concrete experiences and histories of specific migrating and host groups.[22]

Emphasizing Migration: Competition Theory

. . . The *human ecology* tradition in sociological thought draws on the ideas of Park and other ecologists and emphasizes the "struggle of human groups for survival" within their physical environments. This tradition, which highlights demographic trends such as the migration of groups and population concentration in cities, has been adopted by competition analysts researching racial and ethnic groups.[23]

Competition theorists such as Susan Olzak and Joane Nagel view ethnicity as a social phenomenon distinguished by boundaries of language, skin color, and culture. They consider the tradition of human ecology valuable because it emphasizes the stability of ethnic population boundaries over time, as well as the impact of shifts in these boundaries resulting from migration; ethnic group membership often coincides with the creation of a distinctive group niche in the labor force. Competition occurs when two or more ethnic groups attempt to secure the same resources, such as jobs or housing. Competition theorists have accented the ways in which ethnic group competition and the accompanying ethnic solidarity lead to collective action, mobilization, and protest.[24]

According to competition theorists, collective action is fostered by immigration across borders and by the expansion of once-segregated minorities into the same labor and housing markets to which other ethnic groups have access. A central argument of these theorists is that collective attacks on a subordinate ethnic group—immigrant and black workers, for instance—increase at the local city level when the group moves up and out of segregated jobs and challenges other groups and not, as one might expect, in cities where ethnic groups are locked into residential segregation and poverty. . . .

Competition theorists explicitly contrast their analyses with the power-conflict views we will discuss in the next section, perspectives that emphasize the role of capitalism, economic subordination, and institutionalized discrimination. Competition theorists write about urban ethnic worlds as though institutionalized racism and capitalism-generated exploitation of workers are not major forces in recurring ethnic and racial competition in cities. As we have seen, they emphasize migration and population concentration, as well as other demographic factors. . . .

Power-Conflict Theories

The last few decades have witnessed the development of power-conflict frameworks explaining U.S. racial and ethnic relations, perspectives that place much greater emphasis on economic stratification and power issues than one finds in assimilation and competition theories. Within this broad category of power-conflict theories are a number of subcategories, including the internal colonialism viewpoint, and a variety of class-based and neo-Marxist theories. . . .

Internal Colonialism

Analysts of internal colonialism prefer to see the racial stratification and the class stratification of U.S. capitalism as *separate but related* systems of oppression. Neither should be reduced in social science theories to the other. An emphasis on power and resource inequalities, particularly white-minority inequalities, is at the heart of the internal colonialism model.

The framework of internal colonialism is built in part upon the work of analysts of *external colonialism*—the worldwide imperialism of certain capitalist nations, including the United States and European nations.[25] For example, Balandier has noted that capitalist expansion has affected non-European peoples since the fifteenth century: "Until very recently the greater part of the world population, not belonging to the white race (if we exclude China and Japan), knew only a status of dependency on one or another of the European colonial powers."[26] External colonialism involves the running of a country's economy and politics by an outside colonial power. Many colonies eventually became independent of their colonizers, such as Britain or France, but continued to have their economies directed by the capitalists and corporations of the colonial powers. This system of continuing dependency has been called **neocolonialism.** Neocolonialism is common

neocolonialism When powerful countries control less powerful countries through political and economic means in order to extract profits and/or exert regional control. The term typically applies to the continued control of formal colonies by hand-picked local elites who do the bidding of the former occupier.

today where there are few white settlers in the colonized country. Colonies experiencing a large in-migration of white settlers often show a different pattern. In such cases external colonialism becomes *internal colonialism* when the control and exploitation of non-European groups in the colonized country passes from whites in the home country to white immigrant groups within the newly independent country.[27]

Non-European groups entering later, such as African slaves and Mexican farm workers in the United States, can also be viewed in terms of internal colonialism. Internal colonialism here emerged out of classical European colonialism and imperialism and took on a life of its own. The origin and initial stabilization of internal colonialism in North America predate the Revolutionary War. The systematic subordination of non-Europeans began with "genocidal attempts by colonizing settlers to uproot native populations and force them into other regions."[28] Native Americans were killed or driven off desirable lands. Slaves from Africa were a cheap source of labor for capital accumulation before and after the Revolution. Later, Asians and Pacific peoples were imported as contract workers or annexed in an expansionist period of U.S. development. Robert Blauner, a colonialism theorist, notes that agriculture in the South depended on black labor; in the Southwest, Mexican agricultural development was forcibly taken over by European settlers, and later agricultural development was based substantially on cheap Mexican labor coming into what was once northern Mexico.[29]

In exploiting the labor of non-European peoples, who were made slaves or were paid low wages, white agricultural and industrial capitalists reaped enormous profits. From the internal colonialism perspective, contemporary racial and ethnic inequality is grounded in the economic *interests* of whites in low-wage labor—the underpinning of capitalistic economic exploitation. Non-European groups were subordinated to European American desires for *labor* and *land.* Internal colonialism theorists have recognized the central role of *government* support of the exploitation of minorities. The colonial and U.S. governments played an important role in legitimating slavery in the sixteenth through the nineteenth centuries and in providing the government soldiers who subordinated Native Americans across the nation and Mexicans in the Southwest.

Most internal colonialism theorists are not concerned primarily with white immigrant groups, many of which entered the United States after non-European groups were subordinated. Instead, they wish to analyze the establishment of racial stratification and the control processes that maintain persisting white dominance and ideological racism. Stokely Carmichael and Charles Hamilton, who in their writings in the 1960s were among the first to use the term *internal colonialism,* accented institutional racism—discrimination by the white community against blacks as a group.[30] From this perspective African Americans are still a "colony" in the United States in regard to education, economics, and politics. . . .

A Neo-Marxist Emphasis on Class

Analysts of racial and ethnic relations have combined an internal colonialism perspective with an emphasis on class stratification that draws on the Marxist research pioneered by [black sociologists W. E. B.] Du Bois and [Oliver] Cox. Mario Barrera, for example, has suggested that the heart of current internal colonialism is an interactive structure of class *and* race stratification that divides our society. Class, in the economic-exploitation sense of that term, needs to be central to a colonialism perspective. Basic to the U.S. system of internal colonialism are four classes that have developed in U.S. capitalism:

1. *capitalists:* that small group of people who control capital investments and the means of production and who buy the labor of many others;

2. *managers:* that modest-sized group of people who work as administrators for the capitalists and have been granted control over the work of others;

3. *petit bourgeoisie:* that small group of merchants who control their own businesses and do most of their work themselves, buying little labor power from others;

4. *working class:* that huge group of blue-collar and white-collar workers who sell their labor to employers in return for wages and salaries.

The dominant class in the U.S. political-economic system is the capitalist class, which in the workplace subordinates working people, both nonwhite and white, to its profit and investment needs. And it is the capitalists who decide whether and where to create jobs. They are responsible for the flight of capital and jobs from many central cities to the suburbs and overseas.

Barrera argues that each of these classes contains important segments that are set off in terms of race and ethnicity. Figure 1 suggests how this works. Each of the major classes is crosscut by a line of racial segmentation that separates those suffering institutionalized discrimination, such as black Americans and Mexican Americans, from those who do not. Take the example of the working

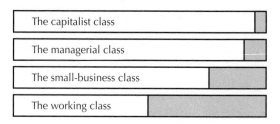

FIGURE 1   The Class and Race Structure of Internal Colonialism. Shaded area represents nonwhite segment.

class. Although black, Latino, and other minority workers share a similar *class* position with white workers, in that they are struggling against capitalist employers for better wages and working conditions, they are *also* in a subordinate position because of structural discrimination along racial lines within that working class. Barrera notes that the dimensions of this discrimination often include lower wages for many minority workers, as well as their concentration in lower-status occupations. Many Americans suffer from both class exploitation (as wage workers) and racial exploitation (as workers of color).

Ideology and Oppositional Culture

Internal colonialism theorists have studied the role of cultural stereotyping and ideology in limiting the opportunities of subordinate groups of color. A racist ideology dominates an internal colonialist society, intellectually dehumanizing the colonized. Stereotyping and prejudice, seen in many traditional assimilation theories as more or less temporary problems, are viewed by colonialism analysts as a way of rationalizing exploitation over a very long period, if not permanently. Discrimination is a question not of individual bigots but rather of a system of racial exploitation rationalized by prejudice.[31]

In his book on the English colonization of Ireland, Michael Hechter has developed a theory of internal colonialism that emphasizes how the subordinate group utilizes its own culture to *resist* subordination. Hechter argues that in a system of internal colonialism, cultural as well as racial markers are used to set off subordinate groups such as African Americans in the United States and the Irish in the United Kingdom. Resistance to the dominant group by the subordinate group often takes the form of cultural solidarity in opposition to the dominant culture. This solidarity can become the basis for protest movements by the subordinated group.[32]

Beginning in the 1960s, a number of power-conflict scholars and activists have further developed this idea of **oppositional culture** as a basis for understanding the resistance of non-European groups to the Euro-American core culture. Bonnie Mitchell and Joe Feagin have built on the idea of oppositional culture suggested in the work of Hechter and Blauner.[33] They note that in the centuries of contact before the creation of the United States, Mexico, and Canada, North America was populated by a diverse mixture of European, African, and Native American cultures. The U.S. nation created in the late 1700s encompassed African enslavement and the genocide of Native Americans. Faced with oppression, these and other victims of internal colonialism have long drawn on their own cultural resources, as well as their distinctive knowledge of Euro-American culture and society, to resist oppression in every way possible.

The cultures of those oppressed by European Americans have not only provided a source of individual, family, and community resistance to racial oppression and colonialism but have also infused, albeit often in unheralded ways, some significant elements into the evolving cultural mix that constitutes the core culture of the United States. The oppositional cultures of colonized groups such as African Americans, Latino Americans, and Native Americans have helped preserve several key elements of U.S. society, including its tradition of civil rights and social justice. Another key element, ironically enough given the usual white image of minority families, is the value of extended kinship relations. The tendency toward extended kin networks is both culturally encouraged and economically beneficial for oppressed minority groups. For example, research on black and Latino communities has found extensive kinship networks to be the basis of social and economic support in difficult times. Native American groups have also been known for their communalism and extended family networks.[34]

. . . This reality contrasts with the exaggerated stereotypes of endemic family pathology in these groups. Internal colonialism theories accent both the oppression of minority Americans and the oppositional cultures that enable minority groups not only to survive but also to resist oppression, passively and actively.

oppositional culture Subcultures that reject mainstream, typically middle-class, behavior. Street and biker gangs, gangsta rap, and cults are examples of oppositional culture.

Criticism of Internal Colonialism Theories

. . . Joan Moore has criticized the term *neocolonialism*. As we have noted, a neocolonial situation is one in which a Third World country (for example, an African country) has separated itself politically from a European colonial power but continues to be dependent on that country. The former colony needs "foreign experts." It has a class of indigenous leaders who help the former colonial power exploit the local population. It has a distinct territorial boundary. Moore suggests that this neocolonialism model does not apply very well to subordinate nonwhite groups in the United States, in that these groups are not generally confined to a specific bounded territory, nor do they contain the exploitative intermediary elite of Third World neocolonialism. This space-centered critique has been repeated by Omi and Winant, who argue that the social and spatial intermixing of white and nonwhite groups in the United States casts serious doubt on the internal colonialism argument about territorially bounded colonization.[35]

However, most internal colonialism researchers have recognized the differences between internal colonial and neocolonial oppression. These theorists note that the situations of minority groups in the United States are different from those of, for instance, Africans in a newly independent nation still dependent on a European country. In response to Moore's critique, internal colonialism analysts might argue that there are many aspects of colonialism evident in U.S. racial and ethnic relations; they might emphasize that non-European groups in the United States (1) are usually residentially segregated, (2) are typically "super-exploited" in employment and deficient in other material conditions when compared with white immigrants, (3) are culturally stigmatized, and (4) have had some of their leaders co-opted by whites. While these conditions in the United States are not defined as precisely as they are in the case of Third World neocolonialism, they are similar enough to allow the use of the idea of colonialism to assess racial and ethnic relations in the United States.

The Split Labor Market View: Another Class-Based Theory

Colonialism analysts such as Blauner are sometimes unclear about whether all classes of whites benefit from the colonization of nonwhites, or just the dominant class of capitalist employers. A power-conflict perspective that helps in assessing this question is the *split labor market* view, which treats class in the sense of position in the "means of production." This viewpoint has been defended by Edna Bonacich. She argues that in U.S. society the majority-group (white) workers do not share the interests of the dominant political and economic class, the capitalists. Yet both the dominant employer class and the white part of the working class discriminate against the nonwhite part of the working class.[36]

. . . Bonacich emphasizes that discrimination against minority workers by ordinary white workers seeking to protect their own privileges, however limited these may be, is important. Capitalists bring in nonwhite laborers to decrease labor costs, but white workers resist because they fear job displacement or lower wages. For example, over the last century white workers' unions have restricted the access of black workers to many job ladders, thus splitting the labor market and reducing black incomes. . . . White workers gain and lose from this structural racism. They gain in the short run, because there is less competition for privileged job categories from the nonwhites they have excluded. But they lose in the long run because employers can use this cordoned-off sector of nonwhites to undercut them.[37]

"Middleman" Minorities and Ethnic Enclaves

Drawing on insights of earlier scholars, Bonacich has explored the in-between position, in terms of power and resources, that certain racial and ethnic groups have occupied in stratified societies. These groups find their economic niche serving elites and workers as small-business people positioned between producers and consumers. Some ethnic and racial groups become small-scale traders and merchants doing jobs that dominant groups are not eager to do. For example, many first-generation Jewish and Japanese Americans, excluded from mainstream employment by white Protestants, became small-scale merchants, tailors, restaurant operators, or gardeners. These groups have held "a distinctive class position that is of special use to the ruling class." They "act as a go-between to this society's more subordinate groups."[38]

Bonacich and Modell have found that Japanese Americans fit the middleman minority model. Before World War II Japanese Americans resided in highly organized communities. Their local economies were based on self-employment, including gardening and truck farming, and on other non-industrial family businesses. The group solidarity of the first generation of Japanese Americans helped them establish successful small businesses. However, they faced hostility

from the surrounding society, and in fact were driven into the businesses they developed because they were denied other employment opportunities. By the second generation there was some breakdown in the middleman position of Japanese Americans, for many of that generation moved into professional occupations outside the niche economy.[39]

Some middleman minorities, such as Jewish and Korean American merchants in central cities, have become targets of hostility from less well off groups, such as poor African Americans. In addition, strong ethnic bonds can make the middleman group an effective competitor, and even Anglo-Protestant capitalists may become hostile toward an immigrant middleman minority that competes too effectively. Thus Jewish Americans have been viewed negatively by better-off Anglo-Protestant merchants, who have the power to discriminate against them, as well as by poor black renters and customers with whom Jews deal as middleman landlords and merchants. . . .

A somewhat similar perspective, *enclave theory,* examines secondary-structural incorporation into the economy, especially the ways in which certain non-European immigrant groups have created social and economic enclaves in cities. Both the middleman and the enclave perspectives give more emphasis to economic inequality and discrimination than assimilation perspectives, and they stress the incorporation of certain groups, such as Asians and Cubans, into the United States through the means of small businesses and specialized ethnic economies. The major differences between the two viewpoints seem to stem from the examples emphasized. Groups accented by enclave theorists, such as Cuban Americans, have created ethnic enclaves that are more than merchant or trading economies—they often include manufacturing enterprises, for example. In addition, ethnic enclaves usually compete with established Anglo-Protestant business elites. In contrast, the middleman minorities and those described as enclave minorities develop trading economies and are likely to fill an economic niche that *complements* that of established white elites. However, the aforementioned research of Bonacich on Jewish Americans suggests that there is little difference between the real-world experiences of those described as middleman minorities. . . .

Women and Gendered Racism: New Perspectives

Most theories of racial and ethnic relations have neglected gender stratification, the hierarchy in which men as a group dominate women as a group in terms of power and resources. In recent years a number of scholars have researched the situations of women within racial and ethnic groups in the United States. Their analyses assess the ways in which male supremacy, or a patriarchal system, interacts with and operates within a system of racial and ethnic stratification. Discussing racial and ethnic cultures around the globe, Adrienne Rich has defined a *patriarchal system* as "a familial-social, ideological, political system in which men—by force, direct pressure, or through ritual, tradition, law and language, customs, etiquette, education, and the division of labor—determine what part women shall or shall not play, and in which the female is everywhere subsumed under the male."[40]

Asking whether racism or patriarchy has been the primary source of oppression, social psychologist Philomena Essed examined black women in the United States and the Netherlands.[41] She found racism and sexism interacting regularly. The oppression of black women can be seen as *gendered racism*. For example, under slavery African American women were exploited not only for labor but also as sex objects for white men. And after slavery they were excluded from most job categories available to white men and white women; major employment changes came only with the civil rights movement of the 1960s. Today racism has many gendered forms. In the U.S. mass media the white female is the standard for female beauty. Minority women are often stereotyped as matriarchs in female-headed families and are found disproportionately in lower-status "female jobs," such as typists. Some women of color are closely bound in their social relations with those who oppress them in such areas as domestic employment ("maids") and other low-paid service work.[42]

In her book *Black Feminist Thought* Patricia Hill Collins argues that a black feminist theoretical framework can help highlight and analyze the negative stereotypes of black women in white society—the stereotypes of the docile mammy, the domineering matriarch, the promiscuous whore, and the irresponsible welfare mother. These severely negative images persist among many whites because they undergird white discrimination against black women in the United States.[43]

Scholars assessing the situations of other women of color, including Native American, Asian, and Latino women, have similarly emphasized the cumulative and interactive character of racial and gender oppression and the necessity of liberating these women from white stereotypes and discrimination. For example, Denise Segura has examined labor-force data on Mexican American women and developed the concept of "triple oppression," the mutually reinforcing and interactive set of race, class, and gender forces whose cumulative effects "place women of color in a subordinate social and economic position relative to men of color and the majority white population."[44]

Class, the State, and Racial Formation

Looking at the important role of governments in creating racial and ethnic designations and institutionalizing discrimination, Michael Omi and Howard Winant have developed a theory of *racial formation*. Racial tensions and oppression, in their view, cannot be explained solely in terms of class or nationalism. Racial and ethnic relations are substantially defined by the actions of governments, ranging from the passing of legislation, such as restrictive immigration laws, to the imprisonment of groups defined as a threat (for example, Japanese Americans in World War II). Although the internal colonialism viewpoint gives some emphasis to the state's role in the exploitation of non-white minorities, it has not developed this argument sufficiently.

Omi and Winant note that the U.S. government has shaped the politics of race: the U.S. Constitution and a lengthy series of laws openly defined racial groups and interracial relationships (for example, slavery) in racist terms. The U.S. Constitution counted each African American slave as three-fifths of a person, and the Naturalization Law of 1790 explicitly declared that only *white* immigrants could qualify for naturalization. Many non-Europeans, including Africans and Asians, were prevented from becoming citizens. Japanese and other Asian immigrants, for example, were until the 1950s banned by law from becoming citizens. In 1854 the California Supreme Court ruled that Chinese immigrants should be classified as "Indians"(!), therefore denying them the political rights available to white Americans.[45]

For centuries, the U.S. government officially favored northern European immigrant groups over non-European and southern European groups such as Italians. For example, the Immigration Act of 1924 was used to exclude Asian immigrants and most immigrants from southern and eastern Europe, whom political leaders in Congress saw as racially inferior and as a threat to their control of the society. North European Americans working through the government thereby shaped the subsequent racial and ethnic mix that is the United States.

Another idea accented by Omi and Winant is that of *social rearticulation,* the recurring historical process of rupturing and reconstructing the understandings of race in this country. The social protest movements of various racial and ethnic groups periodically challenge the governments' definition of racial realities, as well as individual definitions of those realities. The 1960s civil rights movement, for instance, rearticulated traditional cultural and political ideas about race in the United States, and in the process changed the U.S. government and broadened the involvement of minority Americans in the politics of that government. New social movements regularly emerge, sometimes bringing new identities and political norms.[46]

Resistance to the Dominant Group

Recent research has highlighted the many ways in which powerless groups fight back against the powerful. One power-conflict theorist who has made an important contribution to our understanding of how the oppressed react to oppression is James Scott. Influenced by the work of scholars such as John Gaventa on the many "faces of power" Scott has shown that at the heart of much interaction between the powerless and the powerful is intentional deception.[47] For example, the African American slaves were not free to speak their minds to their white masters, but they did create a crucial discourse among themselves that was critical of their white oppressors. Scott cites a proverb of African slaves on the Caribbean island of Jamaica: "Play fool, to catch wise." Looking closely at the lives of slaves and the poor everywhere, Scott has developed the idea of a backstage discourse by the oppressed that includes views that cannot be discussed in public for fear of retaliation. In addition to secret ideological resistance on the part of slaves and other poor people, a variety of other resistance tactics are used, including foot-dragging, pilfering, dissimulation, and flight. Scott cites Afro-Christianity as an example of how African American slaves resisted the "ideological hegemony" (attempts to brainwash) of white slavemasters. In public

religious services African American slaves controlled their gestures and facial expressions and pretended to accept Christian preaching about meekness and obedience. Backstage, where no whites were present, Afro-Christianity emphasized "themes of deliverance and redemption, Moses and the Promised Land, the Egyptian captivity, and emancipation."[48] For slaves the Promised Land meant the North and freedom, and the afterlife was often viewed as a place where the slaves' enemies would be severely punished.

Historian Sterling Stuckey has noted that slave spirituals, although obviously affected by Christianity, "take on an altogether new coloration when one looks at slave religion on the plantations where most slaves were found and where African religion, contrary to the accepted scholarly wisdom, was practiced." The religion of African Americans mixed African and European elements from the beginning. Yet at its core the expressive, often protest-inclined African values prevailed over the European values.[49] Stuckey has shown that African culture and religion were major sources of the slaves' inclination to rebellion. The work of Scott and Stuckey can be linked to the analyses of Hechter and Mitchell and Feagin that we cited previously, for they too have accented the role of an oppositional culture in providing the foundation of resistance to racial oppression.

We can conclude this discussion of the most important critical power-conflict theories by underscoring certain recurring themes:

1. a central concern for racial and ethnic inequalities in economic position, power, and resources;
2. an emphasis on the links of racial inequalities to the economic institutions of capitalism and to the subordination of women under patriarchal systems;
3. an emphasis on the role of the government in legalizing exploitation and segregation and in defining racial and ethnic relations;
4. an emphasis on resistance to domination and oppression by those oppressed.

5 Racialized Social System Approach to Racism

Eduardo Bonilla-Silva

EDUARDO BONILLA-SILVA is professor of sociology at Duke University. He is best known for his 1997 piece in the *American Sociological Review* entitled "Rethinking Racism: Toward a Structural Interpretation." He is the author of three books: *White Supremacy and Racism in the Post–Civil Rights Era* (2001), *Racism Without Racists: Color Blind Racism and the Persistence of Racial Inequality in the USA* (2003), and *Whiteout: The Continuing Significance of Racism* (with Ashley Doane, 2003).

Questions to Consider   Eduardo Bonilla-Silva argues that "after a society becomes racialized, racialization develops a life of its own." What does this mean? How does society become "racialized," and how is it possible that the idea of race can develop a "life" of its own? How, according to the author, is the United States characterized by racialized social systems?

IN ORDER TO CAPTURE THE SOCIETY-WIDE, organized, and institutional character of racism I build my alternative theory around the notion of **racialized social systems.**[1] This term refers to societies in which economic, political, social, and ideological levels are partially structured by the placement of actors in racial categories or races. Races typically are identified by their phenotype, but (as we see later) the selection of some human traits to designate a racial group is always socially rather than biologically based.

These systems are structured partially by race because modern social systems incorporate two or more forms of hierarchical patterns. Although processes of racialization are always embedded in other forms of hierarchy, they acquire autonomy and have independent social effects. This implies that the phenomenon that has been conceived as a free-floating ideology in fact has its own structural foundation.

In all racialized social systems the placement of actors in racial categories involves some form of hierarchy[2] that produces definite social relations among the races. The race placed in the superior position tends to receive greater economic remuneration and access to better occupations and prospects in the labor market, occupies a

racialized social systems The idea that society is organized along racial lines and that economic, political, social, and even psychological rewards differ according to one's placement in a racial hierarchy. Once established, the system of racial hierarchy takes on a life of its own.

primary position in the political system, is granted higher social estimation (e.g., is viewed as "smarter" or "better looking"), often has the license to draw physical (segregation) as well as social (racial etiquette) boundaries between itself and other races, and receives what W. E. B. Du Bois called a "psychological wage."[3] The totality of these racialized social relations and practices constitutes the racial structure of a society.

Although all racialized social systems are hierarchical, the particular character of the hierarchy, and, thus, of the racial structure, is variable. For example, the domination of blacks in the United States was achieved through dictatorial means during slavery, but in the post–civil rights period this domination has been *hegemonic,* that is in the Gramscian sense of the term, achieved through consent rather than coercion.[4] Similarly, the form of securing domination and white privilege is variable too. For instance, the racial practices and mechanisms that kept blacks subordinated changed from overt and eminently racist in the Jim Crow era to covert and indirectly racist in the contemporary period. The unchanging element of these systems is racial inequality—that the subordinated races' life chances are significantly lower than those of the dominant race. This is the feature that ultimately distinguishes this form of hierarchical social organization. Generally, the higher the level of racial inequality, the more racialized the social system, and vice versa.

Because the races receive different social rewards at all levels, they develop different interests, which can be detected in their struggles to either transform or maintain a particular racial order. These interests are collective rather than individual, are based on relations among races rather than on particular group needs, and are practical; that is, they are related to concrete struggles. Although one race's general interest may ultimately lie in the complete elimination of a society's racial structure, its array of alternatives may not include that possibility. For instance, the historical struggle against chattel slavery led not to the development of race-free societies but to the establishment of social systems with a different kind of racialization. Race-free societies were not among the available alternatives because the nonslave populations had the capacity to preserve some type of racial privilege. The historical "exceptions" occurred in racialized societies in which the nonslaves' power was almost completely superseded by that of the slave population.[5]

A simple criticism of the argument I have advanced so far is that it ignores the internal divisions of the races along class and gender lines. Such criticism, however, does not deal squarely with the issue at hand. The fact that not all members of the dominant race receive the same level of rewards and (conversely) that not all members of the subordinate race or races are at the bottom of the social order does not negate the fact that races, as social groups, are in either a superordinate or a subordinate position in a social system. Historically the racialization of social systems did not imply the exclusion of other forms of oppression. In fact, racialization occurred in social formations also structured by class and gender. Hence, in these societies, the racialization of subjects is fragmented along class and gender lines. The important question— Which interests move actors to struggle?—is historically contingent and cannot be ascertained a priori.[6] Depending on the character of racialization in a social order, class interests may take precedence over racial interests as in contemporary Brazil, Cuba, and Puerto Rico. In other situations, racial interests may take precedence over class interests as in the case of blacks throughout most of U.S. history.

In general, the systemic salience of class in relation to race increases when the economic, political, and social inequality among the races decreases substantially. Yet this broad argument generates at least one warning: The narrowing of within-class differences among racial actors usually causes *more* rather than *less* racial conflict, at least in the short run, as the competition for resources increases.[7] More significantly, even when class-based conflict becomes more salient in a social order, this cannot be interpreted as prima facie evidence that race has subsided as a social factor. For instance, because of the way in which Latin American racial formations rearticulated race and racial discourse in the nineteenth-century post-emancipation era,[8] these societies silenced from above the political space for public racial contestation. Yet more than 100 years after these societies developed the myth of racial democracy, they have more rather than less racial inequality than countries such as the United States.[9]

Because racial actors are also classed and gendered (that is, they belong to class and gender groups), analysts must control for class and gender to ascertain the material advantages enjoyed by a dominant race. In a racialized society such as the United States, the independent effects of race are assessed by analysts who (1) compare data between whites and nonwhites in the *same* class and gender positions, (2) evaluate the proportion as well as the general character of the races' participation in some domain of life, and (3) examine racial data at all levels— social, political, economic, and ideological—to ascertain the general position of racial groups in a social system.

The first of these procedures has become standard practice in sociology. No serious sociologist would present racial statistics without controlling for gender and class (or at least the class of persons' socioeconomic status). By doing this, analysts assume they can measure the unadulterated effects of "discrimination" manifested in unexplained "residuals." Despite its usefulness, however, this technique provides only a partial account of the "race effect" because (1) a significant amount of racial data cannot be retrieved through surveys and (2) the technique of "controlling for" a variable neglects the obvious—why a group is over- or underrepresented in certain categories of the control variables in the first place.[10] Moreover, these analysts presume that it is possible to analyze the amount of discrimination in one domain (e.g., income, occupational status) "without analyzing the extent to which discrimination also affects the factors they hold constant."[11] Hence to evaluate "race effects" in any domain, analysts must attempt to make sense of their findings in relation to a race's standing in other domains.

But what is the nature of races or, more properly, of racialized social groups? Omi and Winant state that races are the outcome of the racialization process, which they define as "the extension of racial meaning to a previously racially unclassified relationship, social practice, or group."[12] Historically the classification of a people in racial terms has been a highly political act associated with practices such as conquest and colonization, enslavement, peonage, indentured servitude, and, more recently, colonial and neocolonial labor immigration. Categories such as "Indians" and "Negroes" were invented in the sixteenth and seventeenth centuries to justify the conquest and exploitation of various peoples.[13] The invention of such categories entails a dialectical process of construction; that is, the creation of the category "Other" involves the creation of a category "Same." If "Indians" are depicted as "savages," Europeans are characterized as "civilized"; if "blacks" are defined as natural candidates for slavery, "whites" are defined as free subjects.[14] Yet although the racialization of peoples was socially invented and did not override previous forms of social distinction based on class or gender, it did not lead to imaginary relations but generated new forms of human association with definite status differences. After the process of attaching meaning to a "people" is instituted, race becomes a real category of group association and identity.[15]

Because racial classifications partially organize and limit actors' life chances, racial practices of opposition emerge. Regardless of the form of racial interaction (overt, covert, or inert), races can be recognized in the realm of racial relations and positions. Viewed in this light, races are the effect of racial practices of opposition ("we" versus "them") at the economic, political, social, and ideological levels.[16]

Races, as most social scientists acknowledge, are not biologically but socially determined categories of identity and group association. In this regard, they are analogous to class and gender.[17] Actors in racial positions do not occupy those positions because they are of X or Y race, but because X or Y has been socially defined as a race. Actors' **phenotypic** (i.e., biologically inherited) characteristics, such as skin tone and hair color and texture, are usually,

phenotype A biological term that refers to how we look (skin color, facial features, hair texture, etc.).

although not always, used to denote racial distinctions.[18] For example, Jews in many European nations and the Irish in England have been treated as racial groups.[19] Also, Indians in the United States have been viewed as one race despite the tremendous phenotypic and cultural variation among nations. Because races are socially constructed, both the meaning and the position assigned to races in the racial structure are always contested. Who is to be black or white or Indian reflects and affects the social, political, ideological, and economic struggles among the races. The global effects of these struggles can change the meaning of the racial categories as well as the position of a racialized group in a social formation.

This latter point is illustrated clearly by the historical struggles of several "white ethnic" groups in the United States in their efforts to become accepted as legitimate whites or "Americans."[20] Neither light-skinned nor, for that matter, dark-skinned immigrants necessarily came to this country as members of X or Y race. Light-skinned Europeans, after brief periods of "not-yet white," became "white" but did not lose their "ethnic" character.[21] Their struggle for inclusion had specific implications: racial inclusion as members of the white community allowed Americanization and class mobility. On the other hand, among dark-skinned immigrants from Africa, Latin America, and the Caribbean, the struggle was to avoid classification as "black." These immigrants challenged the reclassification of their identity for a single reason: In the United States "black" signified a subordinate status in society. Hence many of these groups struggled to keep their own ethnic or cultural identity, as denoted in expressions such as "I am not black; I am Jamaican," or "I am not black; I am Senegalese."[22] Yet eventually many of these groups resolved this contradictory situation by accepting the duality of their situation: In the United States, they were classified socially as black yet they retained and nourished their own cultural or ethnic heritage—a heritage deeply influenced by African traditions.

Although the content of racial categories changes over time through manifold processes and struggles, race is not a secondary category of group association. The meaning of black and white, the "racial formation," changes within the larger racial structure. This does not mean that the racial structure is immutable and completely independent of the action of racialized actors. It means only that the social relations among the races become institutionalized (form a structure as well as a culture) and affect social life whether or not individual members of the races want it to. In Frederick Barth's words, "Ethnic identity implies a series of constraints on the kinds of roles an individual is allowed to play [and] is similar to sex and rank, in that it constrains the incumbent in all his activities."[23] For instance, free blacks during the slavery period struggled to change the meaning of "blackness," specifically to dissociate it from slavery. Yet they could not escape the larger racial structure that restricted their life chances and their freedom.[24]

The placement of a group of people in a racial category stemmed initially[25] from the interests of powerful actors in the social system (e.g., the capitalist class, the planter class, and colonizers). After racial categories were employed to organize social relations in societies, however, race became an independent element of the operation of the social system.

What are the dynamics of racial issues in racialized systems? Most important, after a social formation is racialized, its "normal" dynamics always include a racial component. Societal struggles based on class or gender contain a racial component because both of these social categories are also racialized; that is, both class and gender are constructed along racial lines. In 1922, for example, white South African workers in the middle of a strike inspired by the Russian revolution rallied under the slogan "Workers of the world unite for a white South Africa." One of the state's "concessions" to this "class" struggle was the passage of the Apprenticeship Act of 1922, "which prevented Black workers acquiring apprenticeships."[26] In another example, the struggle of women in the United States to attain their civil and human rights has always been plagued by deep racial tensions.[27]

Nonetheless, some of the strife that exists in a racialized social formation has a distinct racial character; I call such strife *racial contestation*—the struggle of racial groups for systemic changes regarding their position at one or more levels. Such a struggle may be social (Who can be here? Who belongs here?), political (Who can vote? How much power should they have? Should they be citizens?), economic (Who should work, and what should they do? They are taking our jobs!), or ideological (Black is beautiful!).

Although much of this contestation is expressed at the individual level and is disjointed, sometimes it becomes collective and general and can effect meaningful systemic changes in a society's racial organization. The form of

contestation may be relatively passive and subtle (e.g., in situations of fundamental overt racial domination such as slavery and apartheid) or more active and overt (e.g., in quasi-democratic situations such as the contemporary United States). As a rule, however, fundamental changes in racialized social systems are accompanied by struggles that reach the point of overt protest.[28] This does not mean that a violent racially based revolution is the only way of accomplishing effective changes in the relative position of racial groups. It is simply an extension of the argument that social systems and their supporters must be "shaken" if fundamental transformations are to take place.[29] On this structural foundation rests the phenomenon labeled racism by social scientists.

I reserve the term *racial ideology* for the segment of the ideological structure of a social system that crystallizes racial notions and stereotypes. Racial ideology provides the rationalization for social, political, and economic interactions among the races. Depending on the particular character of a racialized social system and on the struggles of the subordinated races, racial ideology may be developed highly (as in apartheid) or loosely (as in slavery) and its content expressed in overt or covert terms.

Although racial ideology originates in race relations, it acquires relative autonomy in the social system and performs practical functions.[30] In Paul Gilroy's words, racial ideology "mediates the world of agents and the structures which are created by their social praxis."[31] Racism crystallizes the changing "dogma" on which actors in the social system operate and becomes "common sense"; it provides the rules for perceiving and dealing with the Other in a racialized society. In the United States, for instance, because racial notions about what blacks and whites are or ought to be pervade their encounters, whites still have difficulty in dealing with black bankers, lawyers, professors, and doctors.[32] Thus, although racist ideology is ultimately false, it fulfills a practical role in racialized societies.

At this point it is possible to sketch the framework of the racialized social system. First, racialized social systems are societies that allocate differential economic, political, social, and even psychological rewards to groups along racial lines, lines that are socially constructed. After a society becomes racialized, a set of social relations and practices based on racial distinctions develops at all societal levels. I designate the aggregate of those relations and practices as the racial structure of a society. Second, races historically are constituted according to the process of racialization; they become the effect of relations of opposition among racialized groups at all levels of a social formation. Third, on the basis of this structure, a racial ideology develops. This ideology is not simply a "superstructural" phenomenon (a mere reflection of the racialized system) but becomes the organizational map that guides actions of racial actors in society. It becomes as real as the racial relations it organizes. Fourth, most struggles in a racialized social system contain a racial component, but sometimes they acquire or exhibit a distinct racial character. Racial contestation is the logical outcome of a society with a racial hierarchy. A social formation that includes some form of racial contestation. Finally, the process of racial contestation reveals the different objective interests of the races in a racialized social system.

Conclusion

My central argument in this chapter is that the common-sense understanding of racism, which is not much different than the definition developed by mainstream social scientists or even by many critical analysts, does not provide an adequate theoretical foundation for understanding racial phenomena. With notable exceptions,[33] analysts in academia are still entangled in ungrounded ideological interpretations of racism. Lacking a structural view, they tend to reduce racial phenomena to a derivation of the class structure (as Marxist interpreters do) or the result of an irrational ideology (as mainstream social scientists do).

In the racialized social system framework, I suggest, as do Omi and Winant, that racism should be studied from the viewpoint of racialization. I contend that after a society becomes racialized, racialization develops a life of its own.[34] Although racism interacts with class and gender structurations in society, it becomes an organizing principle of social relations in itself. Race, as most analysts suggest, is a social construct, but that construct, like class and gender, has independent effects in social life. After racial stratification is established, race becomes an independent criterion for vertical hierarchy in society. Therefore different races experience positions of subordination and superordination in society and develop different interests. This framework has the following advantages over traditional views of racism:

Racial phenomena are regarded as the "normal" outcome of the racial structure of a society. Thus we can account for all racial manifestations. Instead of explaining racial phenomena as deriving from other structures or from racism (conceived of as a free-floating ideology), we can trace cultural, political, economic, social, and even psychological racial phenomena to the racial organization of that society.

The changing nature of what analysts label "racism" is explained as the normal outcome of racial contestation in a racialized social system. In this framework, changes in racism are explained rather than described. Changes are due to specific struggles at different levels among the races, resulting from differences in interests. Such changes may transform the nature of racialization and the global character of racial relations in the system (the racial structure). Therefore, change is viewed as a normal component of the racialized system.

The racialized social system framework allows analysts to explain overt as well as covert racial behavior. The covert or overt nature of racial contacts depends on how the process of racialization is manifested; this in turns depends on how race originally was articulated in a social formation and on the process of racial contestation. This point implies that rather than conceiving of racism as a universal and uniformly orchestrated phenomenon, analysts should study "historically-specific racisms."[35] This insight is not new: Robert Park, Oliver Cox, Pierre van den Bergue, and Marvin Harris described varieties of "situations of race relations" with distinct forms of racial interaction.

Racially motivated behavior, whether or not the actors are conscious of it, is regarded as "rational"—that is, based on the given race's individual interests.[36] This framework accounts for Archie Bunker–type racial behavior as well as for more "sophisticated" varieties of racial conduct. Racial phenomena are viewed as systemic; therefore all actors in the system participate in racial affairs. Some members of the dominant racial group tend to exhibit less virulence toward members of the subordinated races because they have greater control over the form and outcome of their racial interactions. When they cannot control that interaction—as in the case of revolts or blacks moving into "their" neighborhood—they behave much like other members of the dominant race.

The reproduction of racial phenomena in contemporary societies is explained in this framework not by reference to a long-distant past but in relation to its contemporary structure. Because racism is viewed as systemic (possessing a racial structure) and as organized around the races' different interests, racial aspects of social systems today are viewed as fundamentally related to hierarchical relations among the races in those systems. Elimination of the racialized character of a social system entails the end of racialization, and hence of races altogether. This argument clashes with social scientists' most popular policy prescription for "curing" racism, namely education. This "solution" is the logical outcome of defining racism as a belief. Most analysts regard racism as a matter of individuals subscribing to an irrational view, thus the cure is educating them to realize that racism is wrong. Education is also the choice pill prescribed by Marxists for healing workers from racism. The alternative theory offered here implies that because the phenomenon has structural consequences for the races, the only way to cure society of racism is by eliminating its systemic roots. Whether this can be accomplished democratically or only through revolutionary means is an open question, and one that depends on the particular racial structure of the society in question.

A racialization framework accounts for the ways in which racial and ethnic **stereotypes** *emerge, are transformed, and disappear.* Racial stereotypes are crystallized at the ideological level of a social system. These images ultimately indicate—although in distorted ways—and justify the stereotyped group's position in a society. Stereotypes may originate out of (1) material realities or conditions endured by the group, (2) genuine ignorance about the group, or (3) rigid, distorted views on the group's physical, cultural, or moral nature. Once they emerge, however, stereotypes must relate—although not necessarily fit perfectly—to the group's true social position in the racialized system if they are to perform their ideological function. Stereotypes that do not tend to reflect a group's situation do not work and are bound to disappear. For example, notions of the Irish as stupid or of Jews as athletically talented have

all but vanished since the 1940s, as the Irish moved up the educational ladder and Jews gained access to multiple routes of social mobility. Generally, then, stereotypes are reproduced because they reflect a group's distinct position and status in society. As a corollary, racial or ethnic notions about a group disappear only when the group's status mirrors that of the dominant racial or ethnic group in the society.

The framework of the racialized social system is not a universal theory explaining racial phenomena in societies. It is intended to trigger a serious discussion of how race shapes social systems. Moreover, the important question of how race interacts and intersects with class and gender has not yet been addressed satisfactorily. Provisionally I maintain that a nonfunctionalist reading of the concept of social system may give us clues for comprehending societies *structured in dominance,* to use Stuart Hall's term. If societies are viewed as systems that articulate different structures (organizing principles on which sets of social relations are systematically patterned), it is possible to claim that race—as well as gender—has both individual and combined (interactive) effects in society.

To test the usefulness of the racialized social system framework as a theoretical basis for research, we must perform comparative work on racialization in various societies. One of the main objectives of this comparative work should be to determine the specific mechanisms, practices, and social relations that produce and reproduce racial inequality at all levels—that is, uncover the society's racial structure. Unlike analysts who believe that "racism" has withered away, I argue that the persistent inequality experienced by blacks and other racial minorities in the United States today is due to the *continued* albeit *changed* existence of a racial structure. In contrast to race relations in the Jim Crow period, however, racial practices that reproduce racial inequality in contemporary America are (1) increasingly covert, (2) embedded in normal operations of institutions, (3) void of direct racial terminology, and (4) invisible to most whites.

stereotype A simplfied picture we paint of an entire group of people. The tendency is to generalize about everyone in that group based on ignornance, limited information, or prejudice. Examples of racial stereotypes: all Asians are good at math, white people can't jump, and all black people have rhythm.

Seeing the Big Picture **The Social Construction of Race, 1790–2000**
The Appendix provides the official racial definitions used by the U.S. Census. Figure 1 shows how racial and ethnic categories changed from 1790 to 2000. How do these changing definitions reflect the idea that race is a "social construction"?

6 An Overview of Trends in Social and Economic Well-Being, by Race

Rebecca M. Blank

REBECCA M. BLANK is dean of the Gerald R. Ford School of Public Policy, Henry Carter Adams Collegiate Professor of Public Policy, and professor of economics at the University of Michigan. Prior to going to Michigan, she served as a member of the President's Council of Economic Advisers from 1997 to 1999. Blank's research has focused on the interactions among the macroeconomy, government antipoverty programs, and the behavior and well-being of low-income families. She is the author of *It Takes a Nation: A New Agenda for Fighting Poverty* (1997), *Finding Jobs: Work and Welfare Reform* (2000), *and The New World of Welfare* (2001).

Questions to Consider   In this reading, Rebecca Blank discusses seven indicators of "well-being" for various racial and ethnic groups in the United States. As you read this chapter take note of which racial groups appear to be socially disadvantaged relative to one another. How do you explain group-level disparities in these quality-of-life indicators? Do you agree with the three explanations she provides at the end of this chapter as to why these quality-of-life disparities exist?

Introduction

In general, there are many signs of improvement across all racial and ethnic groups in a wide variety of measures of measures of well-being, such as educational achievement, health status, and housing quality. In some cases, disparities between different racial groups have narrowed, as all groups have experienced improvements. But in too many cases, overall improvement in well-being among all groups has brought about no lessening of racial or ethnic disparities. In a few key measures, disparities have actually widened. The primary conclusion of this paper is that race and ethnicity continue to be salient predictors of well-being in American society. To understand what is happening in America today and what will be happening in America tomorrow, one must understand the role of race.

Indicators of Well-Being

This chapter discusses trends in seven areas:

1. population/demographic change,
2. education,
3. labor markets,
4. economic status,
5. health status,
6. crime and criminal justice, and
7. housing and neighborhoods.

Wherever possible, trends over time are presented for key variables, focusing on five major population groups: non-Hispanic Whites, non-Hispanic Blacks, Hispanics, Asian and Pacific Islanders, and American Indians and Alaska Natives. These data are taken almost entirely from U.S. government sources. In many cases, however, data for all groups are not available, or not available for the entire time period. Data available for as many groups as possible are presented in the 10 figures. The term "minority" is used to refer to a group that composes a minority of the total population. Although these five groups are currently minorities in the population, current trends project they will, together, constitute more than half the U.S. population by 2050.

This brief introduction does not attempt to provide anything like a comprehensive discussion of the available data. Provided here is an overview of some of the more interesting trends, particularly focusing on issues that introduce key topics that will be addressed in this book. One particular limitation of these data is that they present averages across very large aggregate categories of racial and ethnic classification. This hides much of the rather important information about subgroups. For instance, although data for Dominican and Cuban Americans might show very different trends, they are both combined within the Hispanic category. Similarly, Japanese and Laotian Americans are grouped together in the Asian and Pacific Islander category; Italian and Norwegian Americans are grouped together as non-Hispanic Whites.

An Increasingly Diverse Population

The U.S. population is becoming increasingly diverse. Hispanics, non-Hispanic Blacks, Asian and Pacific Islanders, and American Indians and Alaska Natives currently constitute 27 percent of the population. By 2005, Hispanics will be the largest of these groups in the United States, surpassing non-Hispanic Blacks. These changes will present this nation with a variety of social and economic opportunities and challenges.

Recent high levels of immigration are also increasing diversity within these groups. At present, 38 percent of Hispanics are foreign-born; 61 percent of Asian and Pacific Islanders are foreign-born. This raises questions of assimilation and generational change. Will the second generation among these groups show a narrowing of the disparities that distinguish their foreign-born parents from the U.S.-born population?

Where people live and who they live next to is important in determining how individuals experience racial and ethnic diversity. The population in the West is the most diverse, with more than one-third of the population composed of racial and ethnic minorities. The West is also the region where a higher percentage of Hispanics, Asian and Pacific Islanders, and American Indians and Alaska Natives reside. The South is the second most diverse region and has the largest percentage of non-Hispanic Blacks. The Midwest is the region with the least population diversity; 85 percent of its population is non-Hispanic Whites.

The household structure of these different groups varies greatly. Household structure, based on data for 1970 and 1996, correlates with a variety of other variables, particularly variables relating to economic well-being. More adults in a family means more potential earnings as well as more available adults to care for children. Single-parent households are among the poorest groups in the country. Individuals who live alone are also often more economically vulnerable than are persons who live with other family members.

All groups show significant increases in the number of people living alone or in single-parent families between 1970 and 1996, but the percentage living in single-parent families is much larger among Blacks, Hispanics, and American Indians and Alaska Natives. In fact, the biggest recent percentage of all families are in single-father families, rather than single-mother families, although single-father families continue to be a small percentage of all families. The reasons for these trends—and why some groups have much larger percentages of single-parent families in particular—are much debated.

Household structure is closely related to age distribution as well. Minority populations have a significantly larger percentage of children under the age of 17 than do non-Hispanic Whites, whereas Whites have a much larger percentage of elderly persons. The result is that the school-aged population—persons aged 5 to 17—is more racially and ethnically diverse than the population as a whole, so that today's schools reflect tomorrow's more diverse adult population—and also mirror some of the conflicts and the benefits that accompany growing diversity.

Educational Attainment

In a society growing increasingly complex, educational skills are key to future life opportunities. Disparities in education are fundamental because they can determine lifetime earning opportunities and influence an individual's ability to participate in civic activities as well.

The labor market of the twenty-first century will rely increasingly on computers; thus, obtaining computer skills is fundamental. Figure 1 shows how children's access to computers has changed over time, both in their schools and in their homes. Clearly, more and more children have access to computers, particularly in their schools; but there is an ongoing gap in computer use between White children versus Black and Hispanic children. Between

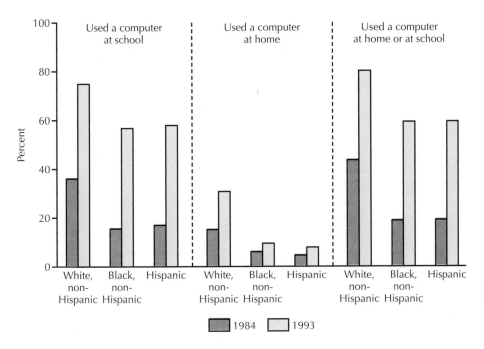

FIGURE 1   **Computer Use by Children in First Through Sixth Grades.**
Source: Council of Economic Advisers (1998).

1984 and 1993, the years for which these data are available, this gap increased for computer use at home, leaving children in minority groups further behind.

Other more conventional measures of achievement in elementary and secondary schooling have generally shown narrowing gaps across racial groups. Mathematics proficiency scores, as measured among children of different ages by the National Assessment of Educational Progress, have shown ongoing gains, particularly by Black children. High school completion continues to inch up among both Whites and Blacks, with substantially greater progress among Blacks; so that the White-Black high school dropout rates are slowly converging over time. Among Hispanics, high school completion has been stagnant at approximately 60 percent since the early 1980s. Hence, the gap between Hispanics and other groups in terms of educational achievement is widening.

Figure 2 shows trends in attainment of college degrees, through 1997, among Whites, Blacks, and Hispanics. Economic returns to a college education have increased dramatically in recent years, and college degrees continue to be an important credential for entry into many white-collar jobs. Although college completion has increased steeply among Whites, it has increased only modestly among Blacks, leading to a widening gap since the early 1990s. Among Hispanics, college completion rates are not much higher now than they were in the mid-1980s.

The more stagnant educational trends among Hispanics reflect, in part, the growing immigrant percentage of that population. Immigrants are less likely to hold high school or college degrees. U.S.-born Hispanics are making progress in increasing both their high school and college completion levels, but this progress is being diluted by the growing pool of less-educated immigrants. This re-emphasizes the question of how second-generation Hispanic children will fare. If they follow the trends of other U.S.-born populations, Hispanic educational attainment will start to increase over time.

Labor-Market Involvement

Involvement in the labor force means integration with the mainstream U.S. economy. Earnings are the primary source of income for most persons. Although job-holding may create some stress, it also produces economic rewards. Access to jobs is key for economic progress.

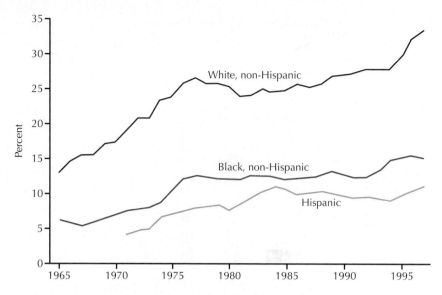

FIGURE 2   Persons Aged 25 to 29 with a Four-Year College Degree or Higher. Prior to 1971, data for Whites include Hispanic Whites, and data for Blacks include Hispanic Blacks. Data for non-Hispanic Blacks and Hispanics are three-year centered averages. Prior to 1991, data are for persons having completed four or more years of college. *Source:* Council of Economic Advisers (1998).

Figure 3 plots the labor-force participation rates from the 1950s to 1997 for Whites, Blacks, and Hispanics, by gender. The chart shows rapidly increasing convergence in labor-force participation rates, as men's rates have slowly decreased while women's rates have increased steadily. White women, who used to be much less likely to work than Black women, are now just as likely to be in the labor force. In fact, both White women's and Black women's labor-force participation rates are rapidly converging with those of Black men, who have experienced steady decreases in work involvement.

Hispanic women also have shown increases in labor-force participation, but remain much less likely to work than other women. A major question for the Hispanic population is whether adult women will show rapid increases in labor-force participation, to the level of women from other groups. Such changes in women's labor-market involvement not only mean changes in the economic base of families—and probably in the economic security and decision-making power of husbands versus wives—but may also mean substantial changes in family functioning and in child-rearing practices.

Along with labor-force participation, unemployment is another measure of access (or lack of access) to jobs. After two decades of higher unemployment rates, unemployment in the late 1990s was at 25-to-30-year lows among all groups. The differentials between groups, however, remained quite large. For instance, unemployment rates among Blacks have consistently been at least twice as high as those of Whites.

The labor-market issue that has received the most attention in recent years is wage opportunities. Figure 4 plots median weekly earnings among male and female full-time workers from 1965 through the first two quarters of 1998. Among all groups, men's wages decreased steadily from 1980 until 1995, when there was evidence of an upturn. The pay gap between White and Black men changed little, however, with no sign of relative progress in wages for Black men. Hispanic men have actually seen decreases in both absolute and relative wages, compared with White and Black men. Again, this pattern is at least partially the result of the growing percentage of less-educated immigrants in the Hispanic population.

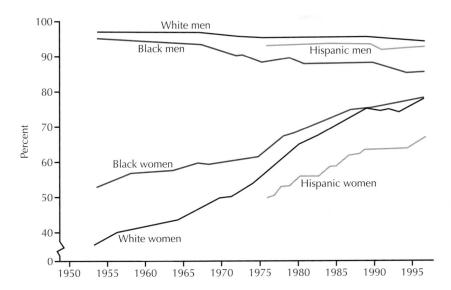

FIGURE 3 **Labor Force Participation Rates of Persons Aged 25 to 54.**
Prior to 1972, data for Blacks include all non-Whites. *Source:* Council of
Economic Advisers (1998).

In contrast, women have not experienced wage decreases. In fact, White women's wages have grown slowly since the 1980s, so that they now earn more than both Hispanic and Black men. Black women's wages have been largely stagnant, although they show a recent upturn; and Hispanic women's wages have decreased slightly. Thus, the wage gap between White women and both Black and Hispanic women has increased.

Economic Status

Continued and even growing gaps in earnings imply that the economic situation is not improving for minority populations relative to the White population. Other measures of family economic well-being reinforce this conclusion. Figure 5 shows median family income for Asian and Pacific Islanders, non-Hispanic Whites, Hispanics, and Blacks through 1996. Family income is probably the most widely used measure of overall economic well-being. Among non-Hispanic Whites, family income has been rising steadily. Essentially, the growth in female labor-force participation and increases in White women's wages have resulted in more family income, even though men's earnings have deteriorated somewhat. Asian families earn even more than Whites. Black family income has been relatively

stagnant since the 1970s, although there were signs of increase after 1993. Hispanic family income decreased in the 1990s.

This means that income differentials have widened between Whites and Asian and Pacific Islanders on the upper end of the income brackets and Blacks and Hispanics on the lower end. American Indians and Alaska Natives, for whom we only have data from the 1990 Census, show lower income than Blacks in that year.

These median family income numbers hide very different experiences at different points in the income distribution. Households headed by less skilled workers—particularly those headed by single parents—have generally experienced income decreases over the past several decades. Households headed by a person with a college degree have generally experienced income increases.

One might be particularly concerned with the number of families at very low income levels. Figure 6 shows poverty rates among individuals by racial group, indicating the percentage of the population in each group living in families with incomes below the official U.S. poverty line, which was less than $8,000 per year in the late 1990s. In general, poverty rates have been relatively flat since the early 1970s. About 10 percent of the White population has been poor over this period. Asian and Pacific Islanders show

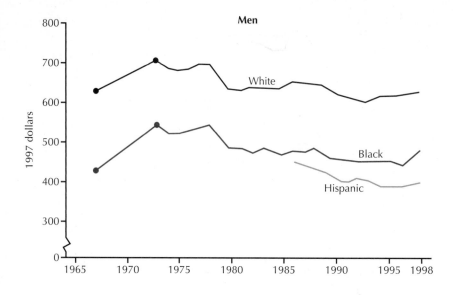

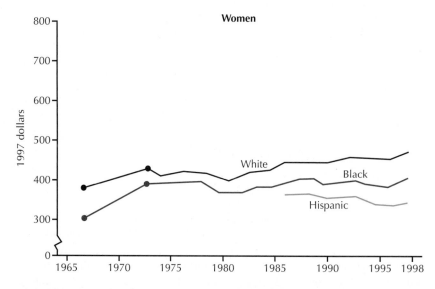

FIGURE 4   **Median Weekly Earnings of Male and Female Full-Time Workers.** Straight line between dots indicates data are not available for intervening years. Prior to 1979, data for Blacks include all non-Whites. Data for 1998 are from the first two quarters. *Source:* Council of Economic Advisers (1998).

a slightly higher poverty rate, underscoring the diversity within the Asian and Pacific Islander populations—they have both higher median incomes than Whites as well as higher poverty rates, reflecting the fact that at least some Asian groups are experiencing economic difficulties.

Black poverty has also been relatively constant, but at nearly 30 percent—three times the White poverty rate. Hispanic poverty rates are now higher than Black poverty rates. Poverty rates among subgroups, such as children or the elderly, show similar differentials between racial and ethnic groups.

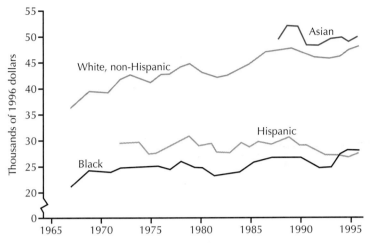

FIGURE 5   Median Family Income. Prior to 1972, data for Whites include Hispanic Whites. *Source:* Council of Economic Advisers (1998).

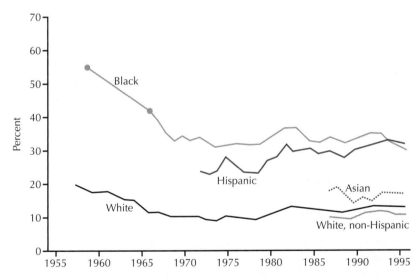

FIGURE 6   Poverty Rates for Individuals. Straight line between dots indicates data not available for intervening years. *Source:* Council of Economic Advisers (1998).

Health Status

Economic well-being is often closely linked to other aspects of well-being, such as health status. Interestingly, health differences do not necessarily show the same patterns as economic differences. Infant-mortality rates provide a primary indicator of both health status and access to

health care in a population. Figure 7 plots infant-mortality rates by race from the early 1980s through 1995. Infant mortality has been steadily decreasing among all groups, indicating major health improvements within all populations. The disparities between groups, however, have remained largely constant. Black infant-mortality rates are about two-and-a-half times White rates. American Indian

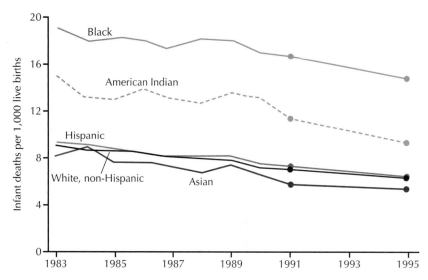

FIGURE 7   Infant Mortality Rates. Straight line between dots indicates data not available for intervening years. *Source:* Council of Economic Advisers (1998).

and Alaska Native rates have fallen a bit faster than other groups, but remain well above White rates.

Figure 7 also shows a pattern visible in much health data—namely, although Hispanics show substantial educational and economic differentials, they show far fewer health differentials. Hispanic infant-mortality rates are almost identical to White and Asian and Pacific Islander infant mortality rates.

Clearly, smoking is a health issue that emerges in adolescence. Smoking is correlated with a shorter life expectancy and greater health risks. In general, smoking rates have fallen for both young women and men over the past 30 years; and this is one of the few indicators where Blacks and Hispanics do better than Whites. Black smoking rates have fallen faster than White rates, so that young Blacks, who used to be more likely to smoke than Whites, are now less likely to smoke.

In contrast, Figure 8 shows death rates among 15- to 34-year-olds in the mid-1990s. There are very large differences in death rates by cause among different racial groups. American Indians and Alaska Natives are far more likely to die as a result of unintentional injuries—typically automobile accidents—and suicide. Blacks are far more likely to die as a result of homicide and HIV infection. These differences emphasize that living conditions and health-risk factors are quite different among different populations.

Crime and Criminal Justice

There is no single aggregate measure of the likelihood of being a victim of crime. Figure 9 plots homicide rates, which constitute a small percentage of all crimes but are among the best measured crime statistics (few homicides go unnoticed or unreported). Figure 9 shows that Blacks are far more likely to be homicide victims than is any other group. The homicide victimization rate of Blacks is more than twice that of Hispanics and six times that of non-Hispanic Whites and Asian and Pacific Islanders. American Indian and Alaska Native homicide rates are about twice those of Whites and Asian and Pacific Islanders, and slightly below those of Hispanics. Although public discussion often focuses on the higher likelihood that Blacks will be arrested for crimes, there is little discussion of the fact that Blacks are also much more likely to be victims. There are large disparities by race in the likelihood of being a victim of a crime, as well as in the likelihood of being arrested and incarcerated by the criminal justice system. Although other crime statistics, such as property crimes, show smaller racial disparities, they also show higher victimization among minority groups.

Data on experience within the criminal justice system are largely tabulated only for Whites and Blacks, and hence provide less comprehensive measures across racial groups. Blacks are far more likely to be arrested and incarcerated than are Whites. Some of these differences reflect

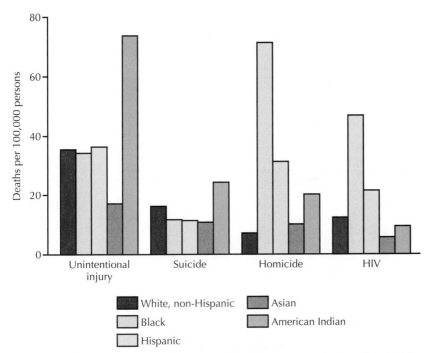

FIGURE 8 **Death Rates by Cause, for Persons Aged 15 to 34, 1996 to 1995.** Data for 1994 and 1995 are averaged to provide more reliable estimates. HIV data for American Indians are for 1993–1995. *Source:* Council of Economic Advisers (1998).

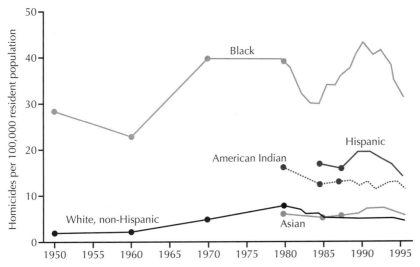

FIGURE 9 **Victims of Homicide.** Straight line between dots indicates data not available for intervening years. Data include deaths from "legal intervention" (use of police force). Prior to 1985, data for Whites include Hispanic Whites. Prior to 1970, data include nonresidents. *Source:* Council of Economic Advisers (1998).

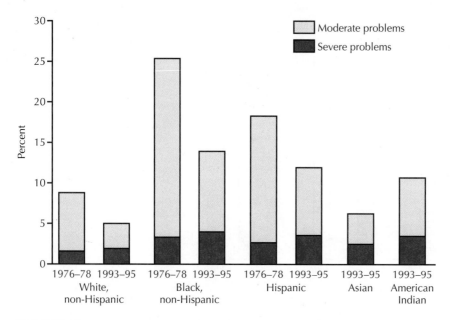

FIGURE 10   Housing Units with Physical Problems. Data for 1976 and 1978, or 1993 and 1995, are averaged to provide more reliable estimates. Data for Asians exclude Hispanic Asians, and data for American Indians exclude Hispanic American Indians. *Source:* Council of Economic Advisers (1998).

differences in the crimes for which Blacks are disproportionately arrested, and some may reflect discriminatory behavior on the part of the police and other persons within the criminal justice system. In 1995, more than 9 percent of the Black population was under correctional supervision, either on probation or parole, or in jail or prison, compared to 2 percent of the White population. Among young Black men 20 to 29 years old, more than 25 percent are under correctional supervision. Because arrests and prison stays often fracture families and reduce future labor-market opportunities, these high rates of involvement with the criminal justice system are correlated with the reduced economic opportunities of Black families.

Housing and Neighborhoods

Where people live, and the housing they live in, is correlated with their health and economic status. Increasing concern among social scientists about "neighborhood effects"—the influence of peers and of neighborhood characteristics on individual health and behavior—has raised interest in housing and neighborhood issues. Figure 10 shows the percentage of populations living in housing units with physical problems, such as substandard plumbing or heating as well as electrical and other serious upkeep problems. All groups for which we have data, from the mid-1970s to the mid-1990s, show substantial improvement in housing quality; but, as in other areas, large disparities remain across groups. Non-Hispanic Blacks, Hispanics, and American Indians and Alaska Natives are far more likely to live in substandard housing than are Whites or Asian and Pacific Islanders. Other measures of housing adequacy, such as crowding, show similar trends, with overall improvement among all groups, but continuing large disparities between groups.

Information about neighborhoods raises again the question of where people live and who they live next to. The diversity of a person's neighborhood can affect his or her overall sense of national diversity and knowledge of members of other races or ethnicities.

Whites are by far the most segregated population, even more than their larger population percentage would justify. The average White person lives in a neighborhood that is more than 80 percent White. Blacks are the next most segregated, living in neighborhoods that are, on average, about 60 percent Black and 30 percent White.

Hispanics live in neighborhoods that have close to equal amounts (about 40 percent each) of Whites and Hispanics. Asian and Pacific Islanders live in the most diverse neighborhoods, composed of a mix of Whites, Blacks, Hispanics, and other Asian and Pacific Islanders. This suggests that these two population groups are experiencing and living in the midst of diversity in this country to a much greater degree than Whites or Blacks.

What Do These Disparities Mean?

This very quick and quite limited review of some of the key indicators of economic and social well-being underscores the ongoing importance of disparities by race and by Hispanic origin in U.S. society. Of course, there are multiple reasons behind these disparities. Many of the other chapters in this book summarize what the research literature indicates about the causes and effects of racial disparities in key areas of society. Three overarching conclusions, based on the data, are presented here.

First, race and Hispanic origin continue to be defining characteristics for many Americans. They are correlated with educational and economic opportunities, with health status, and with where people live and who they live next to. The magnitude of these differences, especially for Blacks and Hispanics, is extremely significant on average, suggesting that these disparities are widely experienced. Relative to the White and Asian populations, the Black population on average has only two-fifths as many college graduates, three-fourths as much earnings, and only slightly more than one-half as much income. The Hispanic population fares even worse. Although we do not have as much comparable information for American Indians and Alaska Natives, their data tend to be closer to those of Blacks and Hispanics than to those of Whites. Whatever their causes, these are substantial differentials; they shape our life opportunities and they shape our opinions about behavior toward each other. To repeat the point I started with at the beginning of this chapter, race continues to be a salient predictor of well-being in America.

Second, the growing presence of Hispanic and Asian and Pacific Islander populations is fundamentally changing the face of America. The displacement of Blacks as the largest minority group in the population in the early 2000s may cause some political and social tension. High numbers of immigrants within the Hispanic and Asian and Pacific Islander groups make questions of assimilation and second-generation progress particularly important in the years ahead. If second-generation Hispanic women behave more like other U.S.-born women, there will be many more Hispanic families with wives in the labor market two decades from now. If second-generation Hispanics acquire education at the rate of other U.S.-born populations, the education levels within the Hispanic community will rise substantially.

Third, Whites may be less aware of the changes and the challenges of growing population diversity than any other group. In part, there is often a "blindness" among the majority to the situation of other groups, because their own situation is typically taken as the norm. This "blindness" is reinforced by locational patterns and neighborhood choice. Whites are much more likely to live in the Midwest than other groups, the least diverse part of the nation; and they tend to live in the most segregated neighborhoods in the other regions. In contrast, Asian and Pacific Islanders—who do as well as Whites on many measures of well-being—live in much more diverse neighborhoods and are almost surely more aware of issues relating to diversity and difference, even when these issues do not translate into personal economic differentials. In short, the growing population of Hispanics and Asian and Pacific Islanders, as well as many Blacks, may be better prepared to address the challenges, and to take advantage of the benefits, of an increasingly diverse population than are Whites.

Seeing the Big Picture   **The Role of Race in Social Mobility**
Think for a moment about three important indicators of "living the good life" (for example, good health, high income, and a college degree). Now look up those indicators in the Appendix and determine whether those indicators vary by race and ethnicity. How do you explain group-level differences in these quality-of-life indicators?

The Color of Health in the United States

David R. Williams • Chiquita A. Collins

DAVID R. WILLIAMS is the Harold W. Cruse Collegiate Professor of Sociology at the University of Michigan. His major areas of research and interest include medical sociology, social psychology, race and SES differences in health, racism and health, and religion and mental health.

CHIQUITA A. COLLINS is an assistant professor in the department of sociology and research associate with the Population Research Center at the University of Texas at Austin.

Questions to Consider   We tend to think about health in individual terms: a parent's battle with cancer, a brother struggling with diabetes, or a sister coping with acute asthma. But upon closer inspection, what appears to be an individual malady or a family tragedy is linked to racial inequality. Medical researchers found that the odds of babies dying in Central Harlem before their first birthday was 1 in 50 while just one zip code away on the Upper East Side the death odds were only 1 in 600. Put another way, babies in Central Harlem are 12 times more likely to die before they reach their first birthday than are babies on the Upper East Side of New York City. In this reading Williams and Collins explain how race, poverty, and health outcomes are linked. How likely is it, given increased levels of socioeconomic inequality and health care cuts by both federal and state governments, that the United States can follow the policy recommendations suggested by the authors?

T HE UNITED STATES IS RELATIVELY UNUSUAL among industrialized countries in that it reports the health status of its population based on race.[1] Most other countries focus on social class differences. For most of this century, the contrast between whites and nonwhites (a category that consisted almost exclusively of blacks) was the basis of differentiation. Since the late 1970s there has been a growing emphasis on collecting more data on the racial and ethnic minority populations that constitute an increasing proportion of the American population. Recent reviews reveal that race and ethnicity remain potent predictors of variations in health status.[2–5]

The most recent report card on the health of the U.S. population presents infant and adult mortality rates by race.[6] Infant **mortality rates** are reported for major subgroups of the Asian and Pacific Islander American (APIA) and the Hispanic population, but subgroup differences were not available for adult mortality. The infant mortality rate for blacks is twice that of whites, and American Indians also have elevated infant mortality rates compared to the white population. The APIA population and its four major subgroups have rates that are lower than those of whites, while

the rate for Hispanics is equivalent to that of whites. However, variation occurs within the Hispanic category: Puerto Ricans have higher infant mortality rates than do the other Hispanic groups and the white population. The report also revealed that the age-adjusted death rate for the entire black population is dramatically higher than that of whites, but all of the other racial/ethnic populations have death rates lower than the white population, with the APIA population having the lowest death rates.

These overall data mask important patterns of variation for subgroups of these populations and for specific health

mortality rates The number of deaths per 1000 within a given population, typically measured over one year. One could look at infant mortality (baby deaths) or maternal mortality (deaths resulting from childbirth) in a given population.

conditions, a point readily evident in recent overviews of the health of the Hispanic population.[7,8] While Latinos have lower death rates for the two leading causes of death (heart disease and cancer) than do non-Hispanics, they also have higher mortality rates than do non-Hispanic whites for tuberculosis, septicemia, chronic liver disease and cirrhosis, diabetes, and homicide. Death rates of Hispanics also exceed those of whites in the fifteen to forty-four age group.[9] Moreover, Hispanics have elevated rates of infectious diseases such as measles, rubella, tetanus, tuberculosis, syphilis, and AIDS. The prevalence of obesity and glucose intolerance are also particularly high, especially among Mexican Americans. Similar to the findings for infant mortality, adult mortality rates for Puerto Ricans are higher than the rates of other Hispanic groups. However, even among Puerto Ricans, the mortality rate is lower than for white non-Hispanics and considerably lower than for African Americans.

Specific subgroups of the APIA population have elevated rates of morbidity and mortality across a number of health indicators. The Native Hawaiian population has the highest cancer rates of any APIA population in the United States[10] and the highest death rates due to heart disease of any racial group in the United States.[11] Rates of stomach cancer are high among Japanese Americans, and Chinese Americans have an incidence of liver cancer that is four times higher than that of the white population.[10] Very high rates of obesity are evident for Native Hawaiians and Samoans, and these populations, along with Asian Indians, Japanese Americans, and Korean Americans, have prevalence rates of diabetes that are more similar to those of the black population than those of the white population.[12] Death rates for Native Americans are high for the under-forty-five age group, and suicide rates for American Indian youth are two to four times higher than those of any other racial group.[9] Native American youth also have higher levels of alcohol and other drug use than does any other racial group.[13]

Worsening Health Status

As part of the increasing income inequality in the United States, the gains in economic status of blacks relative to that of whites have stagnated in recent years.[14] Moreover, on several economic indicators there has been an absolute decline in the economic status of African Americans. For example, unlike the pattern for white families, the pattern for low-income black and Hispanic families shows an absolute decline in family income since 1973, and weekly wage and salary income declined for all black and Hispanic males below the 90th percentile of income between 1979 and 1987. Similarly, the percentage of black children living in poverty increased from 41 percent to 44 percent between 1979 and 1988.[15] Similar to the findings noted earlier for **socioeconomic status (SES),** this decline in black economic well-being and increase in black-white inequality is associated with worsening black health across a number of health status indicators.

The gap in life expectancy between blacks and whites widened between 1980 and 1991 from 6.9 years to 8.3 years for males and from 5.6 years to 5.8 years for females.[16] Moreover, for every year between 1985 and 1989, the life expectancy for both African American men and women declined from the 1984 level, although an upturn has been reported in the most recent data.[6] A slower rate of decline among blacks than whites for heart disease is the chief contributor to the widening racial gap in life expectancy, while HIV infection, homicide, diabetes, and pneumonia are major causes of decreasing life expectancy for blacks.[17]

The age-adjusted death ratios for blacks and whites were greater in 1991 than in 1980, and the annual number of excess deaths for the African American population, compared to the white population, increased from 60,000 in 1980 to 66,000 in 1991.[16] During this period, the overall age-adjusted death rate decreased more rapidly for white males and females than for their black counterparts. Under the age of seventy, three causes of death—cardiovascular disease, cancer, and problems resulting in infant mortality—account for 50 percent of the excess deaths for black males and 63 percent of the excess deaths for black females. Homicide accounts for 19 percent of the excess deaths for black males and 6 percent for black females. An analysis of death rates between 1900 and the present reveals that black-white health inequality among men is currently at an all-time high for this century.[18] In some depressed urban environments there has been no improvement in the health status of the black population over time. For example, Freeman[19] shows that in contrast to a steady decline in national mortality rates for both blacks and whites between 1960 and 1980, there

socioeconomic status (SES) A measure of an individual's or family's relative economic and social ranking, which may include income, education, social standing, and occupation.

was no change in mortality for African Americans in Harlem over this twenty-year period. However, the potential contribution of selection processes via migration to this pattern was not assessed.

The gap in infant mortality rates for white and black babies widened for each sex between 1980 and 1991.[16] Rates of both preterm delivery[20] and low birth-weight[16] have remained stable for white women but have been increasing among African Americans. A widening differential between African Americans and whites is also evident for rates of sexually transmitted diseases.[21] Between 1986 and 1989, cases of gonorrhea and syphilis decreased by 50 percent and 11 percent, respectively, for whites. In contrast, gonorrhea declined by only 13 percent for blacks while syphilis increased by 100 percent. The increase in syphilis is thought to be associated with increases in the use of crack cocaine and related increases in prostitution.

Major Historical Events

This recent evidence of deterioration in the health of the African American population emphasizes the importance of considering the larger historical context in understanding the health status of population groups. Mullings has suggested that the civil rights movement, for example, has had important positive effects on black health.[22] By reducing occupational and educational segregation, it improved the SES position of at least a segment of the black population and also influenced public policy to make health care accessible to larger numbers of people. Consistent with this hypothesis, one study found that between 1968 and 1978, blacks experienced a larger decline in mortality rates (both on a percentage and absolute basis) than whites.[23]

More recently, the presidential campaign of Jesse Jackson may have had a positive short-term impact on the health of the African American population. Using four-wave data from the National Study of Black Americans that span the period 1979–80 to 1992, Jackson et al. found that during the third wave of data collection (1988), the reported levels of physical and mental well-being were at their highest.[24] In addition, the proportions of respondents reporting that they had experienced racial discrimination and that they perceived whites as wanting to keep blacks down were at their lowest levels. Contemporaneously, Jesse

Jackson, a black male, was making the most successful run for the presidency of the United States that had ever been made by an African American in the history of the United States. These researchers suggest that this political event may have had spillover effects for black adults' perceptions of America's racial climate and their health status.

The massive internal migration of blacks in the United States earlier this century has been an important influence on the African American population. Although the initial economic and longer-term political gains linked to migration may have had positive health consequences, the black migration may have also had profound adverse effects on health.[25] First, the black migration disproportionately distributed the African American population to urban residential areas where living conditions are hostile to life and health. Unlike the white urban poor who are dispersed throughout the city, with many residing in relatively safe and comfortable neighborhoods, the black poor are concentrated in depressed central-city neighborhoods[26] where the stress of poor urban environments can lead to illness.[27,28] A recent study in Harlem, one of the poorest areas of New York City, documented that black males between the ages of twenty-five and forty-four in Harlem are six times more likely to die than are their white counterparts in the United States.[29] Moreover, the life expectancy of blacks in Harlem is lower than that of persons in Bangladesh, one of the poorest countries in the world.

Wilson suggests that the concentration of black poverty in the inner city is due to the out-migration of middle-class blacks to other areas.[26] In contrast, Massey and Gross found that three complementary mechanisms were responsible:[30] the wholesale abandonment of black and racially mixed areas by middle-class whites, the selective migration of poor people into black neighborhoods, and the net movement into poverty of blacks living in segregated areas. Living conditions in inner-city areas are also deteriorating over time. The economic status of central-city African Americans has declined relative to other urban blacks. In 1940, central-city blacks earned 10 percent more than did other black urban dwellers, but by 1980 they were receiving 10 percent less.[14] There is also growing concern about the health consequences of stress in residential environments, such as the high level of community violence in many depressed urban environments.[31]

The internal migration of the African American population also affected health by changing health behaviors in ways that lead to high risks of disease and death. With the great migration and urbanization of black Americans came a dramatic rise in their use of alcohol and tobacco, and a reversal in the racial distribution of alcohol and tobacco use.[32] During the first half of the twentieth century, the prevalence of cigarette smoking and alcohol abuse was higher for whites than for blacks. The great migration shifted a considerable portion of the black population from the relatively "dry" rural South, where social life revolved around churches and family associations, to the "wet" areas of the urban North, where taverns and associated alcohol use were an integral part of social life.[33] Moreover, by producing feelings of alienation, powerlessness, and helplessness, life in urban settings created the need for individuals to mask these feelings or obtain temporary relief from them by consuming tobacco and alcohol. African Americans have been special targets of the advertising of both the tobacco and the alcohol industries,[34,35] targeting that dates back to the 1950s.[36]

A recent provocative theory designed to account for the high rates of hypertension among African Americans also gives a central role to historical factors.[37] According to the "slavery hypothesis," the historic conditions of slavery, especially those linked to capture in Africa and the transatlantic slave voyage, resulted in the preferential survival of those Africans who had a genetic propensity to conserve sodium and water. Contemporary African Americans have inherited this trait, which is responsible for the elevated rates of high blood pressure. Despite its deceptive simplicity and intuitive appeal, like earlier biological explanations, this hypothesis locates racial disparities in health inside the individual and pays scant attention to current living conditions. Serious questions have been raised regarding the plausibility of a historic genetic "bottleneck" being a key determinant of current genetic characteristics,[38] and about the validity of the historic data that have been invoked to support this theory.[39] Moreover, there is abundant evidence that the current social circumstances of African Americans play a major role in accounting for their elevated rates of high blood pressure.[40]

Race and SES

Socioeconomic differences between racial groups are largely responsible for the observed patterns of racial disparities in health status. Race is strongly correlated with SES and is sometimes used as an indicator of SES. For example, while 11 percent of the white population is poor, poverty rates for the African American and Hispanic population are 33 percent and 29 percent, respectively. Not surprisingly, differentials in health status associated with race are smaller than those associated with SES. For example, in 1986, persons with an annual household income of $10,000 or less were 4.6 times more likely to be in poor health than those with income over $35,000, while blacks were 1.9 times more likely to be in poor health than whites.[1] Thus, race differentials were less than half of the SES differentials.

Researchers frequently find that adjusting racial disparities in health for SES substantially reduces these differences. In some cases the race disparity disappears altogether when adjusted for SES.[41,42] Two recent studies provide striking evidence of the contribution of SES to observed racial differences in violence and illegal drug use. Greenberg and Schneider[43] showed that rates of violent deaths in New Jersey were associated not with race per se, but with residence in urban areas with a high concentration of undesirable environmental characteristics such as waste incinerators, landfills, and deserted factories. Violent deaths from homicide, poisoning/drug use, falls, fires, and suicide in these marginal areas were ten times higher for males and six times higher for females than for their counterparts in the rest of New Jersey. Moreover, deaths in these marginal areas were high for whites and Hispanics as well as blacks, females as well as males, and middle-aged and elderly populations as well as youthful populations. Lillie-Blanton et al.[44] also found that a twofold higher prevalence of crack cocaine use for blacks and Hispanics compared to whites was reduced to nonsignificance when adjusted for census indicators of social environmental risk factors. Thus, failure to adjust racial differences for SES can reinforce racial prejudices and perpetuate racist stereotypes, diverting both public opinion and research dollars from the underlying social factors that are responsible for the pattern of risk distribution.

More frequently, it is found that adjustment for SES substantially reduces but does not eliminate racial disparities in health.[18,45,46] That is, within each level of SES, blacks generally have worse health status than whites. One recent study found higher infant mortality rates among college-educated black women than among their similarly situated white peers.[47] Moreover, some studies find that the black-white mortality ratio actually increases with rising SES. This is clearly the case for infant mortality, where the black-white gap is narrowest among women who have not completed high school, and highest among women with a college education.[48]

Kessler and Neighbors emphasize the importance of systematically testing for interactions between race and socioeconomic status.[49] They reanalyzed data from eight epidemiologic surveys and demonstrated that although controlling for SES reduced to nonsignificance the association between race and psychological distress, low-SES blacks had higher rates of distress than did low-SES whites. However, the findings have not been uniform. Analyses of data from the large ECA study found that low-SES white males had higher rates of psychiatric disorders than did their black peers.[50] Among women, low-SES black females had higher levels of substance abuse disorders than did their white peers. These findings suggest the importance of distinguishing distress from disorder, as well as the need to understand the interactions among race, gender, and class.

One reason for the persistence of racial differences despite adjustment for SES is that the commonly used SES indicators do not fully capture the economic status difference between households of different races. For example, racial differences in wealth are much larger than those for income. There are large racial differences in the inheritance of wealth and intergenerational transfers of wealth. Table 1 shows that while white households have a median net worth of $44,408, the net worth was $4,604 for black households and $5,345 for Hispanic households.[51] Compared to white households, black households had a significantly greater percentage of their net worth in durable goods such as housing and motor vehicles, and a significantly lower percentage of their net worth in financial assets. Moreover, at every income level, the net worth of black and Hispanic households is dramatically less than that of white households. Thus, in studies of racial comparisons, measures of assets are necessary for the identification of the economic status of the household.

In some cases where blacks are more exposed to particular risk factors, these risk factors appear to have weaker effects for the black population. In a national study in which black children constituted 75 percent of those in the category of lowest long-term income, persistent poverty was unrelated to either stunting or wasting for blacks, unlike the strong pattern evident for non-Hispanic whites and Hispanics.[52] Similarly, although black infants have twice the low birthweight risk of whites, low birthweight is more strongly linked to infant mortality in the neonatal period for blacks than for whites.[53]

TABLE 1   Median Net Worth in 1991 by Monthly Household Income Quintiles for Whites, Blacks, and Hispanics

Household Income	White	Black	Hispanic
All	$ 44,408	$ 4,604	$ 5,345
Lowest quintile	$ 10,257	$ 1	$ 645
Second quintile	$ 25,602	$ 3,299	$ 3,182
Third quintile	$ 33,503	$ 7,987	$ 7,150
Fourth quintile	$ 52,767	$20,547	$19,413
Highest quintile	$129,394	$54,449	$67,435

Source: Eller, T. J. (1994). *Household wealth and asset ownership, 1991* (U.S. Bureau of the Census, Current Population Reports, P70–34). Washington DC: U.S. Government Printing Office.

TABLE 2   Median Earnings in 1990 by Education (Years of School Completed) for White, Black, and Hispanic, Male and Female Full-Time Workers

	Males		
Education Level	*White*	*Black*	*Hispanic*
8 years or less	16,906	16,961	13,913
9–11 years	21,048	16,778	17,868
12 years	26,526	20,271	20,932
Some college	31,336	25,863	26,380
College degree	28,263	30,532	33,074
Graduate	47,787	36,851	42,315
	Females		
Education Level	*White*	*Black*	*Hispanic*
8 years or less	11,826	11,364	11,231
9–11 years	14,010	13,643	12,586
12 years	17,552	16,531	16,298
Some college	21,547	19,922	20,881
College degree	26,822	26,881	22,555
Graduate	31,991	31,119	30,133

Source: U.S. Bureau of the Census. (1991). *Money income of households, families, and persons in the United States* (Current Population Reports, P-60, No. 174). Washington, DC: U.S. Government Printing Office.

Racism

Another reason for the failure of SES indicators to completely account for racial differences in health is the failure of most studies to consider the effects of **racism** on health. A growing body of theoretical and empirical work suggest that racism is a central determinant of health status of oppressed racial and ethnic populations.[18,48,54–56] Racism is viewed as incorporating ideologies of superiority, negative attitudes and beliefs toward racial and ethnic outgroups, and differential treatment of members of those groups by both individuals and societal institutions. Racism can affect health in at least three ways.[18,54]

racism The assigning of attitudes, behaviors, and abilities to individuals or groups based on skin color; includes the institutional arrangements that privilege one group over another and the ideological apparatus that perpetuates and makes those arrangements possible.

First, it can transform social status so that SES indicators are not equivalent across race. There are large differences related to race in the quality of elementary and high school education, so that blacks bring fewer basic skills to the labor market than whites do.[57] In addition, as Table 2 indicates, whites receive higher income returns from education than blacks and Hispanics.[58]

These racial differences are larger among males than among females, and the black-white income gap for males does not become narrower with increasing years of education. In addition, although Hispanic males do better than their black peers at the higher levels of education, the same is not true for Hispanic females. These data indicate that simply equalizing levels of education would still leave a large racial gap in earned income.

Dressler also indicates that the pattern of income production varies for black and white households.[59] Black households are more likely than white ones to rely on several wage earners to contribute to total household income. Middle-class blacks are also more likely than their white peers to be recent and tenuous in that class status.[60] College-educated blacks, for example, are almost four times more likely than their white peers to experience unemployment.[61] Researchers have also emphasized that the purchasing power of a given level of income varies by race,[55,62] with blacks paying higher prices than whites for a broad range of goods and services in society, including food and housing. African Americans also have higher rates of unemployment and underemployment than do whites. Moreover, employed blacks are more likely than their white peers to be exposed to occupational hazards and carcinogens, even after adjusting for job experience and education.[63]

Second, racism can restrict access to the quantity and quality of health-related desirable services such as public education, health care, housing, and recreational facilities. Recent studies have found a positive association between residential segregation and mortality rates for both adults[64] and infants.[65,66] The relationship between segregation and infant mortality exists for blacks but not for whites. A recent review of racial differences in medical care found that even after adjusting for severity of illness, SES, and/or insurance status, blacks were less likely to receive a wide range of medical services than were whites.[67]

Third, the experience of racial discrimination and other forms of racism may induce psychological distress than may adversely affect physical and mental health status as well as the likelihood of engaging in violence and addiction. Recent reviews reveal that a small but growing body of evidence indicates that the experience of racial discrimination is adversely related to a broad range of health outcomes.[48,54] In addition, the internalization of racist ideology is also adversely associated with morbidity.[54]

In color-conscious American society, skin color may be an important determinant of the degree of exposure to racial discrimination, access to valued resources, and the intensity of the effort necessary to obtain those resources.[59] Dressler[59] has employed darker skin color as an objective indicator of low social status within the black population and found that status inconsistency based on the relation of skin color to lifestyle (ownership of material goods and engaging in status-enhancing behaviors) is associated with elevated rates of hypertension. Independent of education level, persons with darker skin color and higher lifestyle had the highest levels of blood pressure. Klag et al. also found an interaction between skin color and SES in a sample of blacks.[68] Darker skin color was associated with elevated rates of hypertension for low- but not high-SES blacks. Consistent with the notion that darker-skinned African Americans may experience higher levels of discrimination, analyses of data from the National Study of Black Americans found that skin color was a stronger predictor of occupational status and income of blacks than was parental SES.[69]

Racial and socioeconomic inequality in health is arguably the single most important public health issue in the United States. The evidence reviewed indicates that SES inequalities in health are widening, and the health status of at least some racial groups has worsened over time. The ranking of the United States relative to other industrialized countries in terms of health has been declining over time, while America continues to spend more on medical care per capita than any other country in the world. The evidence reviewed suggests that a serious and sustained investment in reducing societal inequalities can enhance the quantity and quality of life of all Americans and create the necessary liberty for the pursuit of health and happiness.

Seeing the Big Picture   **How Race Can Be Hazardous to Your Health**

Look at Section III in the Appendix on race and health. What trends do you observe? Why do certain diseases affect one group more than others? Are you able to discern the role of race and class in these health disparities?

Transformative Assets, the Racial Wealth Gap, and the American Dream

Thomas M. Shapiro

THOMAS M. SHAPIRO is the Pokross Professor of Sociology at Brandeis University. Shapiro and Melvin L. Oliver have been awarded the C. Wright Mills Award and the American Sociological Association's Distinguished Scholarly Publication Award for *Black Wealth/White Wealth.* Shapiro's books include *Population Control Politics: Women, Sterilization, and Reproductive Choice* and *Great Divides: Readings in Social Inequality in the United States.*

Questions to Consider There is a saying that the color of America is green (money!). But using income as a way to measure the relative success of racial groups does not, according to Professor Tom Shapiro, paint an accurate portrait of social inequality or who is likely to achieve the American Dream. What are "transformative assets," who is likely to have them, and how are these intergenerational perks a form of unearned privilege? Are these intergenerational transfers of wealth throughout the life course "fair"? Are they racist? Do these transfers of wealth undermine the deeply held belief that individuals should pull themselves up by their own bootstraps?

Race and Wealth

Racial inequality remains a festering public and private issue in American society. After dismantling the most oppressive racist policies and practices of its past, many have come to believe that the United States has moved beyond race and that our most pressing racial concerns should center now on race-neutrality and color blindness. Proclaiming the successes of the civil rights agenda and the dawning of a postracial age in America, books by Shelby Steele, Abigail and Stephan Thernstrom, and others influenced not only the academic debates but elite, media, and popular opinion as well.[1] Indeed, a review of the record shows impressive gains since the mid-1960s, most particularly in the areas of law, education, jobs, and earnings. During the 2004 Presidential election, for instance, and into the second term of the Bush Administration, politicians and the media treat racial inequality as a non-issue, or as if it no longer existed. Even though progress is real, this new political sensibility about racial progress and equality incorporates illusions that mask an enduring and robust racial hierarchy and continue to hinder efforts to achieve our ideals of democracy and justice.

In fact, we can consider seriously the declining economic significance of race because the measures we have traditionally used to gauge racial inequality focus almost exclusively on salaries and jobs. The black-white earning gap narrowed considerably throughout the 1960s and 1970s.

The earnings gap has remained relatively stable since then, with inequality rising again in the 1980s and closing once more during tight labor markets in the 1990s. The average black family earned 55 cents for every dollar earned by the average white family in 1989; by 2000, it reached an all-time high of 64 cents on the dollar. For black men working full-time, the gains are more impressive, as their wages reached 67 percent of those of fully employed white men, up from 62 percent in 1980 and only 50 percent in 1960. How much the racial wage gap has closed, why it has closed, and what it means are the subjects of academic and political debate. One study, for example, argues that the racial wage gap is really 23 percent higher than the official figures because incarceration rates hide low wages and joblessness among blacks. In any case, it takes more African American family members to work to earn the same money as white families.

For example, middle-income black families worked the equivalent of 12 more weeks than white families to earn the same family income in 2000.[2]

The tremendous growth of the black middle class often is cited as the triumphant sign of progress toward racial equality. The raw numbers appear to justify celebration: In 1960, a little more than three-quarters of a million black men and women worked in middle class occupations. By 1980, the number increased to nearly three and a half million and nearly seven million African Americans worked in middle class jobs in 1995. This impressive growth in achieving middle class status, however, does not tell the whole story, as one can point out that stagnating economic conditions and blacks' lower middle class occupational profile have stalled the march into the great American middle class since the mid-1970s.

The case I want to make is that the real story of the meaning of race in modern America, however, must include a serious consideration of how one generation passes advantage and disadvantage to the next—how individuals' starting points are determined. While ending the old ways of outright exclusion and violence, our nation continues to reproduce racial inequality, racial hierarchy, and social injustice that is very real and formidable for those who experience [it]. This contribution will explore the bedrock of racial inequality in modern America.

The racial wealth gap—which has more to do with race than with merit or accomplishments—translates into different worlds, opportunities, and rewards for black and white families. My argument is grounded in three big ideas. First, I argue that family inheritance and continuing discrimination in really vital areas like homeownership are reversing gains earned in schools and on the job and making racial inequality worse. In addition to money passed at death, family inheritance includes paying for college education, substantial down payment assistance in buying a first home, and other continuing parental financial assistance. Consequently, it is virtually impossible for people of color to earn their way to equal wealth through wages. No matter how much blacks earn, they cannot pass their occupational status along to their children; they cannot outearn the wealth gap. Many believe that African Americans do not do as well as whites, other minorities, or immigrants because they spend too much money rather than save and invest in the future of their

families. They are unable to defer gratification, do not sacrifice for the future, and consume excessively. The facts speak otherwise. Second, these inheritances amount to **transformative assets**. This involves the capacity of unearned, inherited wealth to lift a family economically and socially beyond where their own achievements, jobs, and earnings would place them. Since the vast majority of African Americans were first excluded and later precluded from the kind of occupations, investments, and government policies and programs that lead to wealth generation, transformative assets typically apply to whites from financial advantaged families and not blacks. These head-start assets set up different starting lines, establish different rules for success, fix different rewards for accomplishments, and ultimately perpetuate racial inequality. Third, the way families use head-start assets to transform their own lives—within current structures that reward them for doing so—has racial and class consequences for the homes they buy, the communities they live in, and the quality of schools their children attend. The same set of processes typically advantages whites while disadvantaging African Americans.

These big ideas help us understand one of the most important issues facing America as we start the twenty-first century. African American were frozen out of the mainstream of American life over the first half of the last century, but since 1954 the civil rights movement has won many battles against racial injustice, and America has reached a broad national consensus in favor of a more tolerant, more inclusive society. Yet we live with a great paradox: Why is racial inequality increasing in this new era?

The Racial Wealth Gap

The typical black household makes 59 cents earned by the typical white household. This income comparison is the most widely used indicator of current racial and ethnic material inequality.[3] However, changing the lens of analysis to wealth dramatically shifts the perspective. For example,

transformative assets Assets that individuals receive, typically from parents and grandparents, that socially and economically "transform" their lives. For example, getting a down payment for a house in a neighborhood you could not afford on your own, having your parents pay for your college education so you start life without college debt, or receiving an inheritance.

the 1999 net worth (all assets minus all liabilities) of typical white families is $81,000 compared to $8,000 for black families. This baseline racial wealth gap, then, shows the black families possess only 10 cents for every dollar of wealth held by white families. The socioeconomic yardstick is no longer how to get from 59 cents on the dollar to parity but how to think about going from 10 cents on the dollar to a figure approaching parity. In dollars, the baseline racial wealth gap is robust: The typical white family's wealth is almost $74,000 more than the typical black family's. Even though both white and black families increased their net worth between 1988 and 1999, the black-white gap actually grew by $16,000 (in 1999 dollars). During this period, typical white and black families improved financially but inequality grew. The figures for net financial assets (excluding home equity and vehicles) do not paint a better picture. Later we will examine the impact of the recession and jobless recovery that started in the late 1990s.

The classic argument is that racial inequality in significant areas like family wealth represents huge disparities in education, jobs, and income. Once these disparities are alleviated, our traditional understanding and theory lead to an expectation that racial inequality will be diminished to a great extent.[4] Confounding this traditional understanding, and demonstrating the need for new thinking about civil rights in the twenty-first century, examining middle class families demonstrates that even black and white families with equal accomplishments are separated by a dramatic wealth gap. Defining middle class by income, we see a reduction in the baseline racial wealth gap to $44,500 for whites and $17,000 for blacks. Clearly, income is important to wealth accumulation. At the same time, however, middle class black families with similar incomes to white own only 26 cents of wealth for every dollar owned by whites. Defining middle class by occupation changes the ratio to 22 cents on the dollar. And, using a college education as a hallmark of middle class status moves the wealth ratio to 27 cents on the dollar. One needs to be asking how it is that blacks with equal accomplishments in income, jobs, and degrees possess only about a quarter of the wealth of their white counterparts.

The black middle class that emerged between the mid-1960s and early 1980s is a success story written in the accomplishments of education, occupation, and earnings. An asset perspective, however, shows that the white middle class stands for the most part on the two legs of good earning and substantial financial assets while the black middle class stands for the most part on the earning leg alone. Middle class status is thus more precarious for blacks than it is for whites; blacks are more susceptible to falling from middle class grace, less capable of cushioning hard times, and less able to retool careers or change directions. And, of course, they are far less able to pass along their hard-earned successes to their children.

We can examine the relationship between family wealth and what we think predicts wealth, such as education, income, age, marital status, family size, region, and job. To make our findings more graphic, we can estimate the cost of being African American, that is, the wealth difference between typical white and black families with equal accomplishments on all the factors that we think lead to wealth accumulation. The cost of being black amounts to $136,174. This is a measure of the accumulative disadvantage of being African-American. Flipping the perspective, the accumulative advantage or the legacy of whiteness for the typical white family also is $136,174.[5]

Is the Racial Wealth Gap Narrowing or Growing?

Among the crucial issues facing families today is how the recent recession and jobless recovery have affected family economic security. My recent research argues that a widening wealth gap between minorities and whites is reversing gains earned in schools and on jobs and making inequality worse. A 2004 report from the Pew Hispanic Center provides new data on family wealth and offers a sobering assessment of the precarious and fragile status of middle class families, including whites, but most particularly Hispanics and African-Americans.[6]

In the years prior to the 2001 recession, white, Hispanic, and African-American families were generating wealth through savings, investment, and homeownership. More families were acquiring assets and family portfolios were growing. In this context of wealth accumulation, however, the wealth gap between minority and white families was widening. The recession and recovery brought wealth growth to an abrupt halt for millions of American families. During the recession and jobless recovery, Hispanic and African-American families lost over one-quarter of their wealth while the wealth of white families grew slowly. In 2002, a typical Hispanic family owned 11 cents of wealth for every dollar owned by a typical white family, and African-American families owned only 7 cents.

Net wealth losses illustrate how Hispanic and African-American families, and low-to-middle income families in general, have shouldered the burden of tightening economic times in the Bush administration. And the wealth data show that the current combination of recession and recovery has tightened the financial vice on millions of American families. Over one in four Hispanic and African-American families are asset-poor, having no liquid financial assets, compared to 6 percent of whites. Families with small or moderate amounts of wealth drew down their meager stockpile of savings to use as private safety nets. In addition to making tough choices like giving up health insurance or spacing out medical appointments and refilling prescriptions, this is the real story of how families are adapting to the recession, jobless recovery, stagnating wages, outsourcing, and dwindling federal commitment to important safety nets like unemployment benefits and the minimum wage, which are not keeping pace with inflation.

For example, interest-earning assets like savings bonds, IRA and Keogh accounts, 401(k) and thrift accounts, stocks and mutual funds, and business capital declined precipitously in Hispanic families with assets. In African-American families, stock and mutual fund investments plummeted by nearly two-thirds. Surely, this reflects investment losses, but it also represents families tapping accounts to cover insecurities about employment and losses of job-related income. These families are adapting by eating the acorns they were storing for their future economic mobility and security. These setbacks will not be made up easily or in a short time span.

While the income, educational achievement, and job gaps among Hispanics, African-Americans and whites remain steady or show some slight narrowing, the wealth gap increases. I made this argument in my recent book, *The Hidden Cost of Being African American*. The report and current data from the Pew Hispanic Center further corroborate how a growing wealth gap reverses gains in schools, on jobs, and in paychecks. An added compounding change is that the financial portfolios of Hispanics and African-Americans have been shrinking in the current economy.

More than any other economic attribute, wealth represents the sedimentation of historical inequalities in the American experience, in a sense the accumulation of advantages and disadvantages for different racial, class, and ethnic groups. In this way, it allows us a window to explore how our past influences realities today.

This is not simply a story about counting money, because families think about using wealth first as a private safety net, and then as a vehicle to launch mobility into middle class status, homeownership, business development, or a more secure retirement. The recent recession and recovery—along with public policies— are a real step backward for the self-reliance and independence of Hispanics, African-Americans, and other low-to-middle income families. They are a double blow against equality and family well-being in America. Missing from the current national political scene is a serious conversation about the economic status of America's families and the role of government in enabling families to build a wealth pillar for their mobility, stability, and well-being. Finally, family wealth is not a story about counting dollars to determine who has played the game best. Far more importantly, family wealth is crucial to opportunities and success in a way that allows families to launch their own social mobility in a self-reliant and independent manner. Closing the racial wealth gap needs to be at the forefront of the civil rights agenda moving into the twenty-first century.

Seeing the Big Picture   The Color of Money

Section VI in the Appendix lists households making more than $250,000 and those in poverty, which the government defines as $19,484 for a family of four (2004). Using these two income categories as your reference points, explain how race is linked to transformative assets and upward mobility.

RACE AS CHAMELEON~
How the Idea of Race Changes
over Time and Place COLOR SORTING BY C

Defining Race: Comparative Perspectives

9

F. James Davis

F. JAMES DAVIS is professor emeritus of sociology at Illinois State University. Dr. Davis conducted research for the Air Force at the University of Washington during the years 1951–1952. He is the author of the classic work *Who Is Black? One Nation's Definition,* as well as *Society and the Law, Social Problems,* and *Minority-Dominant Relations.*

A BLACK PERSON IN THE UNITED STATES HAS long been defined as a person with any known African black ancestry, no matter how little or how distant. The aphorism for this so-called one-drop rule is that "one drop of black blood makes you black." So deeply rooted in the American psyche is this rule that a person can have predominantly white ancestry and even look white, yet unquestionably be defined as black. Such people as Halle Berry, Lena Horne, Julian Bond, or Muhammad Ali come to mind. Is it any wonder that foreign visitors and television viewers have trouble understanding why we define such people as black? No other nation defines blacks in this way, and our one-drop rule does not apply to any minority other than African Americans.

Walter White, president of the National Association for the Advancement of Colored People (NAACP) from 1931 to 1955, had blue eyes, blond hair, and fair skin, and his ancestry was no more than one sixty-fourth African black (Ottley 1943). He had been raised in Georgia in the black community and had been subjected to white discrimination and violence (White 1948). He passed as white in order to investigate lynchings in the Jim Crow South. White's second marriage, to a brunette white woman, provoked outrage from the black press for his betrayal. He had married outside the black community, across the ethnic barrier. When the White family made an international goodwill tour and were

Questions to Consider For most of U.S. history the "one-drop" rule defined someone as black if he or she had a single "drop" of black blood—that is, any African ancestry. This "rule" was designed to maintain white supremacy by keeping the color line rigid and guaranteed there would be a constant source of slaves even after the importation of enslaved Africans was banned in 1808 (slavery wouldn't end until 1865). Professor F. James Davis makes the point that for many in the United States the law of hypodescent placed individuals within the black community even if they did not phenotypically "look" black. What Professor Davis brings to light is that there are many other identities (he outlines six) that mixed-raced individuals occupy. Are these categories still relevant today?

publicized as an interracial couple, White was often asked how he happened to marry a black woman (Cannon 1956).

A former law professor, now a university president, grew up in a white, middle-class neighborhood in Virginia and had always thought he was white until he was ten years old. He certainly looks white. His father, after a financial collapse and a broken marriage, took him and his younger brother to live in his home community in Muncie, Indiana, in the 1950s. While en route there by bus, their father told the boys that he had passed as white and they would be living in a black neighborhood. There the boys were discriminated against and harassed by both whites and blacks. Against all odds, this older brother's abilities, both in the classroom and in athletics, enabled him to achieve outstanding success. When asked why he does not pass as white, he answers that he has been taught through bitter experience that in the United States he is black (G. H. Williams 1995).

Although there are average differences in visible physical traits in human populations, there are no pure races. When I use the term "unmixed African black," I mean someone whose entire ancestry derives from populations in sub-Saharan Africa. Originally the term "mulatto" meant half African black and half white, but it came to mean any degree of mixture. Often people now say that a child of an African American and a white is "half and half," which correctly describes the child's racial background. However, one such child may have a parent whose ancestry is three-fourths African, whereas another's is one-fourth. The ancestry of the first child would be three-eighths black, the second one-eighth. Regardless of the ancestral fractions and physical appearances, both children are black under the American one-drop rule. Due to strong social conditioning, most light-hued African Americans identify themselves as black, but as we shall see, some do not.

Because of the one-drop rule, mixed offspring with any African ancestry are assigned to the black community. The result of over 350 years of **miscegenation** in the United States is a "new people," derived predominantly from African black populations but with a large infusion of genes from European whites and a substantial amount from Native Americans (Reed 1969; Williamson 1980). Estimates of the number of African Americans who have some white ancestry range from three-fourths to above 90 percent, and as many as one-fourth have Native American ancestry. The color spectrum in the black community ranges from ebony to lighter than most whites, and other visible physical traits show a similar range of variation.

The one-drop rule is unique in the world because it has resulted from our particular experiences with slavery and racial segregation in the United States. The social statuses and identities of racially mixed people are determined by group power dynamics, just as those of their parent groups are. The varying social structures and histories of societies around the globe have produced sharply contrasting status positions and terms of identity for mixed-race people.

miscegenation The social and intimate "mixing" of different racial groups and the children resulting from such unions.

Seven different status positions are identified here to help readers gain perspective on current issues of racial identity in the United States. First, we need to examine further the development and effects of the one-drop rule.

The Hypodescent Status

Anthropologists call our one-drop rule a hypodescent rule because mixed black/white children are assigned the status position of the lower status parent group—that of blacks. Evidently this first occurred in the mid-1600s in the Chesapeake area of Maryland and Virginia, where miscegenation between white indentured servants and slaves from Africa became widespread. The mixed persons generally were assigned the status of slaves and the same racial identity as African blacks (Williamson 1980). By the early 1700s, the one-drop rule had become the social definition of a black person in the upper South, and from there it spread southward.

Also in the 1600s, a competitor to the one-drop rule emerged. In Louisiana and South Carolina, free mulattoes came to have an in-between, buffer status. These free mulattoes were allied with whites and not considered to be blacks (Williamson 1980). Until the 1840s in South Carolina, mulattoes could become white by behavior and reputation and could marry into white families (Catterall 1926–1937). Louisiana also rejected the one-drop rule, accepting miscegenation and the intermediate status of mulattoes until 1808, when the Louisiana Civil Code prohibited "free people of color" from marrying either whites or blacks (Domínguez 1986).

In a number of states before the Civil War, there were court cases in which persons who had as much African ancestry as one-fourth were declared to be white. The United States had not yet lined up solidly behind the one-drop rule. Finally in the 1850s, in order to preserve slavery, the South came together in firm support of the one-drop rule (Williamson 1980). Although the competing rule was put down, for several decades there were statutes and court decisions that limited the definition of a black person to at least one-fourth, one-eighth, or some other fraction of ancestry.

The Civil War and Reconstruction accelerated the alienation of mulattoes from whites, who made it clear that mulattoes of all shades would be defined as blacks. The one-drop rule gained support in the North as well as the South and was further strengthened at the turn of the twentieth century by the passage of Jim Crow laws in the southern states. These segregation laws were reinforced by extralegal threats and terrorism. Light blacks were as likely as darker ones to pay the ultimate price for alleged violations of the master-servant etiquette for "getting out of their place" (Vander Zanden 1972). The lynching of blacks peaked from 1885 to 1909, and the peak of passing also occurred during this period, although most of those who could pass permanently did not do so (Burma 1946; Eckard 1947). By World War I, the one-drop rule was backed uniformly by US whites.

The one-drop rule was crucial to maintaining Jim Crow segregation, in which widespread miscegenation, not racial "purity," prevailed. The racial double standard of sexual relations gave white men access to black women but protected white women from black men. The entire system of white domination would be threatened by a mixed child living in a white home. Mixed children fathered by white males, defined as black by the one-drop rule, stayed with the mother in the black community (Blaustein and Ferguson 1957; Myrdal, Sterner, and Rose 1944; Rose 1956). US senator Theodore Bilbo of Mississippi trumpeted in a 1947 book that protecting white women from black men was preventing "**mongrelization**," keeping the white race pure (Bilbo 1947).

By 1925, the African American community had fully accepted the one-drop rule and was giving it strong support. The black community had developed a vested interest in a rule used for centuries to preserve slavery and legalized segregation. The rule had forced all shades of mixed persons into the black community, where, over time, white oppression and other common experiences created a common culture and a sense of ethnic unity and pride. Lighter mulattoes, discriminated against and terrorized by whites, allied themselves more firmly than ever with blacks. Many leaders of the Harlem Renaissance of the 1920s, including Langston Hughes and A. Philip Randolph, were light mulattoes.

The civil rights movement of the 1950s and 1960s put an end to the Jim Crow laws and saw major civil rights legislation passed in Washington, D.C. At the same time, white backlash to the movement strengthened African American support for the one-drop rule. In the 1960s, lighter blacks often felt heavy pressure to affirm their blackness (Williamson 1980). In 1972, the National Association of Black Social Workers (NABSW) strongly endorsed the one-drop rule by passing a resolution against the adoption of black children by white parents (Day 1979). Rejecting the terms "biracial" and "racially mixed," the Association insisted that mixed children be taught to acknowledge their blackness and raised to survive as blacks (Ladner 1977). By the mid-1970s, "cross-racial" adoption had almost stopped, and by 1987, thirty-five

mongrelization Used as a pejorative, a blending of different populations as a result of widespread miscegenation.

or more states had a policy against it. Although the issue has been revived, the NABSW has not changed its position.

In general the one-drop rule has had the support of law. The rule was challenged often in court in the nineteenth century and earlier but not much in the twentieth. State laws defining who is black in terms of fractions of ancestry, or an explicit one-drop rule, have generally been rescinded in recent decades. However, the courts have not invalidated the one-drop rule. In 1983, the rule was upheld by a district court in Louisiana in a lawsuit brought by Susie Phipps (*Jane Doe v. Louisiana*), whose application for a passport was denied because she checked "white" as her race. She looks white, had always lived as white, and thought she was white (Trillin 1986). Lawyers for the state produced evidence that Mrs. Phipps was three thirty-seconds black, and by a 1970 statute, one thirty-second was enough. Before 1970, a "traceable amount" was enough in Louisiana. In 1986 the US Supreme Court refused to review this decision on the ground that no substantial federal question was involved (107 Sup.Ct.Reporter, interim ed. 638). Louisiana has abolished the one thirty-second criterion, but its courts have not ruled against the one-drop rule.

Despite the general support for the one-drop rule by both whites and blacks, there are long-standing examples of rejection of it in both communities (Daniel 1992). Some of the African American children adopted by whites and some children of mixed marriages are socialized to reject the black-only identity. Many Creoles of color in New Orleans and vicinity still reject both the black and the white identity (Domínguez 1986: 163–164). Many Hispanic Americans with some black ancestry resist the rule if they can and embrace a Latino identity. Although a majority of Puerto Rican immigrants have some African ancestry, few of them were identified as black when they were still on the island (Jorge 1979).

Native Americans with some African ancestry generally try to avoid the one-drop rule, usually by staying on a reservation (Bennett 1962). Those who leave the reservation are often treated as blacks. In Virginia, persons who are one-fourth or more Native American and less than one-sixteenth African black have been defined as Indians while on the reservation but as blacks when they leave (Berry 1965). States and tribes differ in their definitions of who is Indian. In the East and South, there are 200 or so small triracial communities that have long evaded the rule by remaining isolated (Berry 1963).

The most common response to deviations from the rule in both the black and the white communities is to condemn the deviations and affirm the rule. Deviant acts and rhetoric call attention to a violated rule and can strengthen the consensus that supports it (Durkheim 1960). For most African Americans of all hues, apparently, the rule gets such constant reinforcement that it provides a clear sense of black ethnic identity. After the US Census Bureau offered respondents the opportunity to designate their own race in 1960, the percentage who checked "black" did not decline significantly.

Problems engendered by the rule, some of them painfully distressing, are borne primarily by the black community. Public concern about these problems does not rise very high because the one-drop rule is so taken for granted by both blacks and whites. All the problems stem from defining as black a mixed population with a rainbow of physical characteristics. The ambiguity of the racial identity of very light blacks often leads to everyday strains and embarrassments, even to traumatic experiences and deep dilemmas of identity.

The rule has other costs, including conflicts in black families and communities over differences in color, hair, and other traits. Darker and "nappier" blacks often receive stinging criticism of their appearance, and the lightest ones are also often harassed and humiliated (Gwaltney 1980). As filmmaker Spike Lee has shown in *School Daze* and later in *Jungle Fever,* intense conflicts among blacks over color and hair accompany dating, sexual relations, and marriage. Color discrimination among blacks also occurs in the workplace, in the media, and elsewhere (Russell, Wilson, and Hall 1992). Is discrimination based on racial traits not a violation of civil rights laws?

Among still other problems are collective anxieties of whites about "invisible blackness" (Williamson 1980) and of blacks about persons who "deny their color." Many white parents of mixed children worry about the suppression of their white ancestry. There is profound anxiety about the rare resort to passing to gain opportunities. There are complex administrative and legal problems in implementing the one-drop rule. The rule causes gross misperceptions of the racial classification of very large populations in Asia, the Middle East, Latin America, and elsewhere. It poses problems of sampling and interpretation in medical and scientific research on racial differences (Davis 1991).

Elsewhere in the world, persons whose ancestry is part African black are perceived as mixed, not as just black. However, the status positions of mixed-race persons vary greatly from one society to another, reflecting different group power dynamics. We now examine six other status and identity positions.

The In-Between Status

Remember that the one-drop rule assigns to mixed-race persons the identical status position occupied by the lower status parent group. A second rule assigns persons of mixed heritage a status between that of the parent groups, as occupied by the mulattoes of South Carolina and Louisiana before 1850. Such groups are seen as marginal to both parent groups, but often there is a firmer tie with one than the other. Some middle groups develop a strong separate identity.

Many, if not most, in-between minorities, whether racial hybrid groups or not, meet special occupational needs the dominant community is unable or unwilling to meet. "Middleman minorities," as the economists call them, may or may not have had previous experience with such work. Often the work is onerous, highly stigmatized, or very risky, or it involves long hours. This in-between group serves as a buffer between the groups above and below it. Political and economic changes, especially when they eliminate the group's special occupations, can have drastic consequences for the middle minority. When crises come, the dominant group rarely protects the middle group from the animosity of lower-status groups (Blalock 1967). The vulnerability of the middle minority is especially great when it is occupied by a mixed-race group because of special problems with identity and group acceptance.

Under the apartheid system in the Republic of South Africa, there were two buffer groups between the dominant whites and the native blacks: the Asians and the Coloureds. This system of fourfold segregation was legalized in 1948 (Van den Berghe 1971) and lasted for half a century. During the prolonged crisis that preceded the downfall of the system and of white domination in 1994, the two buffer groups experienced much harassment and violence. Major adjustments in group statuses in recent years are complex and have been proceeding with much less conflict than was expected.

The definitions of the four "race groups" in South Africa remain essentially as they were under the apartheid system. Blacks are unmixed Africans. South African whites often explain who the Coloureds are by saying they are not black and not Asian. Coloureds are any "mixed-blood" persons, including children and descendants of black/Asian and white/Asian unions, not just those of black/white and black/Coloured unions. The bulk of the Coloureds are mulattoes, ranging from very dark to very light, and thus are very similar to most African Americans. Under apartheid, both legal and informal controls were designed to prevent or punish all white/nonwhite sexual contacts, not just those involving white women. There was no double standard. White men were punished as severely for white/nonwhite sexual contacts as black, Asian, and Coloured men were.

Under apartheid, passing as white was facilitated by the infinite gradations of racial traits among the Coloureds, with many mixed persons appearing white. However, far from being secret as in the United States, passing was open, legalized, and administered by a complex bureaucracy. Passing required official reclassification to a different "racial" category, usually from Coloured to white. Some individuals and couples were reclassified more than once, and different members of a family were sometimes classified differently (Watson 1970). Such reclassification could not occur under a one-drop rule.

Bottom of the Ladder

By a third rule, persons of mixed race are assigned a status lower than that of either parent group. Not accepted on equal terms by either of the parent race groups, such people are defined as a separate and lowly people, as outcasts. In East Africa, mulattoes among the Ganda peoples of Uganda are regarded with condescension and contempt by the Ganda and not accepted by the English or other whites. For a time there was discussion of a plan to remove all the mulattoes to an island in Lake Victoria where they could be completely isolated (Berry 1965). A similar position is occupied by the métis in Canada, the Anglo-Indians in India, Korean Americans in Korea, and Vietnamese Americans in Vietnam.

The métis population originated in the seventeenth century from unions in the Canadian wilderness between Indian women and French and Scottish trappers. At first, the children were called métis if they spoke French, or "half-breeds" if they spoke English, but eventually all racial hybrids were known as métis. They were regarded as neither white nor Indian. They felt superior to the Indians and would not marry them. They became valued

middlemen—buffalo hunters, interpreters, and transporters of supplies and furs by canoe or carts. They plummeted from middle to bottom-of-the-ladder status when white settlement and the coming of the railroads in the latter half of the nineteenth century ended the need for their special occupations.

After the métis rebelled against the Canadian government in 1879 and 1884, they dispersed throughout the Canadian West, despised by whites and Indians alike. Some managed to get accepted on Indian reservations, but most lived as outcasts in poor, isolated areas or moved to towns and cities to become an urban underclass. There may be as many as 750,000 métis now in Canada, more than the number of full Indians. They remain a broken, desperately poor people.

Similarly, the mixed Anglo-Indian population in India went from a relatively secure middle minority status under British colonial rule to a precarious and lowly position, especially after India became independent in 1947 (Gist and Dean 1973). Anthropologists classify South Asians as "Hindu Caucasoids," but the British consider all dark-skinned "native peoples" to be nonwhite, and race is what people believe it to be. There is no place for "mixed-blood" people in the Hindu caste tradition (Ballhatchet 1980). Many Anglo-Indians fled to Australia or England as Indian nationalism grew (Berry 1965), but around a quarter of a million remain in India. Caste has been legally abolished, but the traditions still have force, and the Eurasians remain a despised out-group.

Thousands of Korean American children were born to women in Korea during the Korean War, some fathered by white servicemen and some by African Americans, and many more have been born since. Mixed children face extreme difficulties in Korea, where there is a strong prejudice against marrying someone of a different racial or ethnic group. Citizenship there is paternal, so the mixed children have been defined not as Koreans but as Americans. Children of American males are not granted US citizenship if born out of wedlock outside the United States. The great majority of the children thus have had no country and have been denied the rights of Korean citizens. These children are seen as debased and polluted, and some Korean families have refused to accept them. Mixed children under fifteen years of age can be adopted if the mothers give them up and register them with the Korean government as orphans.

The 80,000 or so mixed children fathered in Vietnam by white and black American military personnel during the war there are called the "dust of life" and treated with contempt. They are virtual outcasts in their own society, where, as in Korea, the child's identity and citizenship rights derive from the father. The US approach to this contrasts sharply with that of the French, who took 25,000 mixed children with them when they left in 1954 and offered them French citizenship. In 1982, the United States began allowing the mixed children to emigrate, provided that Americans adopt the younger ones and sponsor the older ones. Although many of these mixed children in both Vietnam and Korea have been adopted in the United States in recent years, most of them and their descendants remain lowly outcasts (Valverde 1992).

Top of the Ladder

Sometimes racially mixed people have achieved a higher status than that of either parent group, as experienced by the mulattoes of Haiti, Liberia, and Namibia, and the mestizos of Mexico (Nicholls 1981; Stoddard 1973). The two examples discussed here required a successful political revolution. In the wealthy French colony on Saint Domingue (Hispaniola), later called Haiti, a slave named Toussaint L'Ouverture began a revolution in 1791 that ended slavery. Previously there had been some 30,000 whites exercising extremely harsh control over half a million black slaves, with about 24,000 free blacks and mulattoes occupying an in-between status. After the rebels achieved independence in 1804, the mulattoes emerged as the economically and politically dominant elites and retained their ascendancy for more than a century and a half. They maintained tight kinship ties among mulatto families, preventing intermarriage with both whites and African blacks. They looked down on both unmixed Africans and the small white population, although the Lebanese, Syrians, and other whites performed valuable middle minority commercial functions (Nicholls 1981). The mulattoes lost control to the Duvalier regime in 1957, later regained it, and lost it again, and the volatile struggle for political power goes on.

The Spanish ruled Mexico for three centuries. During the long colonial period, there was massive miscegenation between the Spanish and Indian populations and some that involved African blacks. At first the term "mestizo" meant half-Spanish and half-Indian, but it came to refer to the entire mixed population, regardless of the degree of mixture. Under Spanish rule, mestizos occupied a middle status position, with Indians on the bottom. The mestizos took pride in their Spanish ancestry and played down their Indian backgrounds (Stoddard 1973). Mestizos became the rulers when Spanish control was overthrown in 1821, and today they are by far the largest group in Mexico. Some Spanish and other whites have retained considerable wealth and influence, but political power remains chiefly in mestizo hands. The overwhelming size of the mestizo group would appear to be a major factor in its political dominance, yet in Haiti the mulatto elites retained control for a long time with relatively small numbers.

Highly Variable Status: Latin America

Under a fourth rule, mixed-race persons are assigned a status that may vary from quite low to very high, depending more on education and wealth than on color or other racial traits. In Brazil and lowland Latin America generally, the upper class is called white, but it also includes light mulattoes and mestizos. The middle class is a long ladder with many rungs and is composed mainly of mulattoes, although in some countries it also includes many mestizos. The lower class includes most of the unmixed blacks and Indians, along with a few whites and some mulattoes and mestizos.

Race influences class placement, but it is only one factor, and it may be overcome by wealth and education. A plethora of terms is used for the innumerable gradations of racial mixture, but the color designations depend more on the place on the class ladder than on actual racial traits. As people use educational and economic success to climb the class ladder, their racial designations often change. No secrecy is needed to "pass" to another racial identity (Wagley 1963).

Latin Americans can accept light mulattoes and mestizos as whites, referring to any visible traces of African traits in such euphemistic terms as "brunette" or "a little mulatto" (Solaun and Kronus 1973). In Brazil it is class rather than racial discrimination that is pervasive, sharp, and persistent, even involving class-segregated public facilities and a class-based master-servant etiquette (Harris 1964). The expression "money whitens" indicates that class can have more weight than physical traits in determining racial classification. Census estimates of the number of people in different racial categories can be very misleading when compared with the estimates in the United States or other nations.

In Puerto Rico, as in Latin America generally, miscegenation of whites, native Indians, and African blacks has produced the entire range of skin color and other racial features. A substantial proportion of the mixed population is considered white, including many who are quite dark. Individuals are allowed some choice and room to negotiate for a racial identity (Domínguez 1986). Around 10 percent of Puerto Rican migrants to the United States are unmixed blacks, and half or more of the remainder have some African ancestry. Therefore, some three-fifths of the migrants are perceived as black in the United States, whereas on the island most of them were known either as whites or by one of the many color designations other than black. It comes as a shock to the majority of the migrants to be defined as black in the United States. Some manage to become known as Hispanic whites by emphasizing their Spanish language and heritage, but others fail. Parents in the Puerto Rican immigrant community pressure their young to "whiten" the family in order to succeed, which puts them in conflict with the African American community.

On the Caribbean islands colonized by the Spanish and Portuguese, Iberian whites have readily married lighter mulattoes with visible African traits. Iberian colonists brought with them an ideal image of beauty known as Morena (meaning Moorish) and the acceptance of marriage with mulattoes. By contrast, whites on the Caribbean islands colonized by the English, French, and Dutch have accepted intermarriage only with those mulattoes who look white (Hoetink 1967). It is appearance that counts, however, not known African ancestry, so there is no one-drop rule. The Iberian approach seems to be the general rule in southern Europe and the Near and Middle East. The intermarriage rule on the English, French, and Dutch islands was brought from northern Europe. The one-drop rule is not inherent in British culture, then, or in northwestern Europe generally. It emerged on US soil.

Egalitarian Pluralism for the Racially Mixed: Hawai'i

As in Latin America, the status of mixed-race people in Hawai'i can range from quite low to very high, depending on educational and economic achievement. However, color and other racial traits do not affect the class placement in Hawai'i as they do to some extent in Latin America. There is no preoccupation with race in Hawai'i and no color ladder

with a preferred hue at the top. Hawai'i has a long tradition of treating the racially mixed in an egalitarian manner that contrasts sharply with the hypodescent status on the US mainland. Despite the eventual wresting of political and economic power from the original Hawaiians by US economic interests in the 1890s, the competitive struggles and occasional conflicts have essentially been those of class and ethnicity, not race.

The Polynesian settlers in the Hawaiian Islands some 1,500 years ago were probably a racial blend of Mongoloid peoples from Southeast Asia and Caucasoid stocks from Indonesia and South Asia (Howard 1980). Further miscegenation with many different peoples began when the first **haoles** (non-Polynesians) came. Captain Cook found in 1778 that Hawaiian hospitality included openness to sexual relations and marriage with outsiders. The haoles never stopped coming, first for a way station for the fur trade; next for sandalwood; then for whales; then for sugarcane, pineapples, and other agricultural products; and finally as tourists. Many white traders and planters took Hawaiian wives, and eventually some of the children of Congregational missionaries from New England took native Hawaiian wives.

The demand for sugarcane workers escalated in the 1850s, and large numbers were brought from China and later from Portugal, other European countries, and Japan. By 1900 the Japanese were the largest ethnic group in Hawai'i. Migrants then came from Puerto Rico, Korea, and the Philippines. Still later, more came from South and East Asia, other Pacific Islands, Mexico, the Middle East, Europe, the United States, and elsewhere. Miscegenation never stopped. By 1930 there were more part-Hawaiians than unmixed ones, and by 1960 nine times as many. By the 1970s, Hawaiians and part-Hawaiians (one-eighth or more) were not quite one-fifth of the population, behind whites and Japanese (Howard 1980: 449–451). Native chiefs had made overly generous trade concessions and had lost much of their land. Revival of traditional culture began in the 1970s, along with charges of past and present discrimination against Hawaiians and part-Hawaiians by wealthy whites and other haole groups. This has been an ethnic and class protest, not a racial one. Clearly the native Hawaiians have been badly exploited, but the basis for it has been greed, not racism. The rhetoric of racist ideology is absent.

haoles The Hawaiian word for whites.

There has been no systematic racial segregation and discrimination, either de jure or de facto, and the various peoples in Hawai'i generally are scornful of anyone who exhibits racial prejudice. Many of the Pacific Island peoples are relatively dark-skinned, and the class status of the mixed people in Hawai'i seems to be unaffected by color or other racial traits. Ethnic and racial intermarriages are common, and many people can identify ancestry in several groups. It is considered bad manners to express disapproval of miscegenation. The tolerant, egalitarian balance of pluralism and assimilation extends to racially mixed persons, whose status is no lower or higher than that of the parent groups involved. The first racial hybrids in Hawai'i were highly respected, and this model has had a lasting impact (Adams 1969; Berry 1965).

Assimilating Minority Status

The seventh rule accounts for the status of persons in the United States who are partly descended from racial minorities other than African American. The children of the first generation of miscegenation may experience ambiguity or be identified as members of the minority group. However, when the proportion of minority ancestry becomes one-fourth or less in the next generation of mixture, the children are accepted unambiguously as assimilating Americans. There is no need for them to "pass" in order to hide the minority background. In fact, they can be proud of having ancestry that is part Native American, Mexican, Chinese, Japanese, Filipino, Vietnamese, or other Asian, and they find little opposition to intermarriage with whites. There is no one-drop rule to deter their further miscegenation and full assimilation into the dominant Anglo-American community.

For many decades, Chinese immigrants in the United States were despised and did not have the benefit of the status of an assimilating minority. Neither did the earlier Japanese Americans, especially during the days of their relocation to prison camps as enemy aliens during World War II. The operating rule was that everyone with one-eighth or more Japanese ancestry was to be removed to the camps. Since the Japanese had been immigrating to the United States only since 1885, this one-eighth criterion was a sure way to intern everyone with any known Japanese ancestry (Williams 1996). During the war years, then, what was in effect a one-drop rule was used for Japanese Americans.

The foregoing comparative discussion dramatizes the uniqueness of America's one-drop rule. It also shows that the status occupied by mixed-race people in a society can change in response to major shifts in racial group power relations. Experiences in other societies can provide valuable perspective on current issues about racial identity and the one-drop rule. They also suggest the need for caution in extrapolating to other societies the findings on the dynamics of the personal identity of mixed-race people in the United States.

The Multiracial Identity Movement

In recent years, new challenges to the one-drop rule have emerged. In the 1980s and 1990s, a movement to allow mixed-race persons to adopt a biracial or multiracial identity rapidly gained momentum. Campus groups were organized at many colleges and universities. A national organization called the Association of Multiethnic Americans (AMEA) was created to coordinate groups in thirty or more cities (Grosz 1989). The emphasis, rather than a frontal attack on the one-drop rule, has been on the freedom to acknowledge all of one's ancestries, including black (Nakashima 1992). The movement includes all racial blends, not just those with African black ancestry.

Mixed-race people with no black ancestry, although not subject to a one-drop rule, have been well aware that the rule for blacks has been responsible for the "check only one" instruction. Until the 2000 census, this rendered persons with Native American, Mexican, Asian, or Pacific Islander forebears unable to acknowledge two or more ancestries. Mexican Americans, the majority of whom are mestizos, had to check "black," "white," or "other." In 1990, 48 percent of them checked "other," and 97 percent of all Americans who checked "other" were Hispanics, who may be of any race or blend.

The marked increase in interracial marriages, although still a small proportion of all marriages, is one argument for recognizing the multiracial identity. The trend that began in the 1960s has accelerated, especially since the *Loving* case, in which the US Supreme Court in 1967 held the Virginia statute prohibiting interracial marriage to be unconstitutional. From 1970 to 1991, mixed-race marriages in the United States tripled. During this same period, births for one black and one white parent increased more than fivefold, and increases almost this large occurred in marriages involving one white and one Asian-American parent (Page 1996).

The vast majority of black/white sexual unions over 350 years have not had the benefit of marriage and have involved white males and black females. By contrast, a large majority of black/white marriages in recent decades have been between a black man and a white woman. One estimate is that at least 30 percent of these couples want to identify their children as biracial or multiracial. Many of these wives do not want their children to have to deny their mother's ancestry.

The multiracial identity movement has faced determined opposition. Many blacks fear that persons who want to affirm their European, Native American, or Asian ancestry want to deny their African roots (Bates 1993). There is also fear that the movement will divide the black community, reduce its numbers, weaken black political power, and undermine civil rights remedies (Daniel 1992). Some fear that whites want to create a buffer class with a status above that of blacks or a system of "colorism" like the one in lowland Latin America.

Despite the opposition, the movement has had some successes. PROJECT RACE (Reclassify All Children Equally) has persuaded a number of states to require the multiracial option on some official forms, and school districts in several states have added the option (Graham 1995). In 1993, both PROJECT RACE and the AMEA testified in favor of the multiracial option before the Subcommittee on Census, Statistics, and Postal Personnel of the US House of Representatives. These organizations later gave similar testimony to the US Office of Management and Budget (OMB), which defines racial categories for all levels of government in the country, including the public schools (Fernandez 1995).

The policy debate centered mainly on the possible use of the multiracial category on the Census Bureau forms for 2000, an option strongly opposed by the NAACP and other black leaders (Daniel 2000b). The OMB decided to reject the multiracial category but to change the traditional instruction, "check only one," to "check one or more." This compromise was approved by the NAACP, the Urban League, the Congressional Black Caucus, and other black groups (Daniel 2000b). Although it was only a partial victory for the multiracial identity movement, the federal government had finally acknowledged the reality of multiple racial ancestries. To counter the fears of civil rights leaders, the OMB instruction was that persons who check "white" and any minority race are to be counted as members of that minority for the purpose of enforcing civil rights laws. Also, the term "multiracial" was not to be used in interpreting the responses. The plan received unanimous support from thirty federal agencies and was adopted for the collection of all governmental data on race, not just census data (Lew 2000).

The percentage of Americans who checked more than one race in the 2000 census was 2.3. That percentage varies according to age group, however. Among African Americans over the age of fifty, 2.3 percent checked more than one race. However, for blacks eighteen years of age or younger, the percentage was 8.3. This age difference is probably due in part to the increase in the number of young interracial parents, in part to the multiracial identity movement, but also to the public rejection of the one-drop rule by a number of black celebrities. These rejections have been a prominent part of the increased publicity about mixed-race experiences in the past two decades. Issues of identity have been featured in books, articles, films, and newscasts and on talk shows.

One of the most dramatic news stories of the 1990s was the DNA testing that showed the high likelihood that Thomas Jefferson was the father of the last son of his slave Sally Hemmings (Foster 1998). Alex Haley's 1976 book *Roots* and the television series based on it had demonstrated how fully both African Americans and whites accept the one-drop rule. It seemed perfectly natural for Haley to pursue his African roots. In his 1993 book *Queen,* however, Haley focused on his white-appearing grandmother, played by Halle Berry in the television series. In 1990, when Renee Tenison was hailed as the first black woman to be Playboy's "Playmate of the Year," she protested that it was unfair for her to have to deny her white mother (Russell, Wilson, and Hall 1992). When Chelsi Smith was portrayed as the first black winner of the Miss USA pageant in 1995, she insisted that she is both black and white. (The first black winner was actually Carole Gist, in 1990.) It seems unlikely that such celebrities would so publicly reject the one-drop rule without the encouragement of the multiracial identity movement and the heightened awareness in the media.

Shirley Haizlip and her book *The Sweeter the Juice* (1994) were featured on the Oprah Show in 1994. The family members on the show all looked white, but some had passed while others had not. The author appeared on the show to explain how this can happen. In subsequent years, there have been other Oprah shows featuring similar experiences with the color line.

When Tiger Woods won the Masters Championship in 1997 and sports reporters asked how it felt to be the first black winner, he replied that he is not only black. He pointed out that his mother is from Thailand. Evidently he is one-fourth Thai, one-fourth Chinese, one-fourth black, one-eighth Native American, and one-eighth white. In the fall of 2003 in South Africa, US television reporters repeatedly referred to both Tiger and Vijay Singh as blacks. Tiger says he checks "Asian" on forms calling for race, and Singh is from India, not Africa. In South Africa, Tiger would be defined as Coloured, Singh as Asian, and neither one as black.

Whither the One-Drop Rule?

Do the successes of the multiracial identity movement, along with the increased media attention, foreshadow the end of the one-drop rule? Or will they join the several patterned deviations that point to the rule and reinforce it? Some states that have passed statutes to legitimate a multiracial category are finding them difficult to implement. It remains to be seen how much the states will follow the OMB's instruction to "check one or more" in collecting governmental data. Evidently it will take a lot to convince most African Americans that they have more to gain than to lose by backing away from the one-drop rule, especially in the face of continuing prejudice and discrimination.

Exceptions can become so blatant, however, that a rule becomes conspicuously obsolete. Significant further changes might be a long time coming, yet the fall of the apartheid system in South Africa in 1994 shows that momentum sometimes builds to a point at which major change can occur very fast. Increasing global awareness puts a spotlight on the US one-drop rule and its uniqueness in the world. Since national origins immigration quotas were abolished in the 1960s, the United States has increasingly become a multiracial, multiethnic society. How rapidly might the view grow that persons with partly black ancestry have a human right to have both or all of their racial backgrounds recognized?

If and when the one-drop rule loses its hold, what then? Of the six other status positions for mixed-race people discussed here, which one might incur the least opposition from most whites and most blacks? Is there one that would be accompanied by problems that are less serious than those resulting from the one-drop rule? Some of the six

alternatives could not possibly fit conditions in the United States, especially the bottom-of-the-ladder and the top-of-the-ladder statuses. The idea of a return to the in-between, buffer status would arouse intense hostility in the black community. Light mulatto leaders are highly valued and are held tightly in the embrace of black pride. African Americans also disdain the "colorism" of the Latin American pattern, and most whites would abhor very frequent intermarriage between whites and persons with visibly African traits.

The northern European status for mixed-race people would appear to be the closest alternative to the US hypo-descent position. To some whites, marriage with persons with known black ancestry but who look white might seem but a limited and beneficial exception to the one-drop rule. After all, "white blacks" carry very few genes from African ancestors, and many common beliefs about miscegenation are false and racist. Other whites, however, would be dominated by irrational fears of massive miscegenation, widespread passing, and "invisible blackness." As for the black community, few would likely consider it a good thing that those wishing to be assimilated could do so without having to pass secretly and abandon their black families and community. It would require the belief that very few persons would be lost to the white community and that black unity would not be impaired. This leap of faith seems highly unlikely so long as fully equal treatment of blacks is still an elusive goal.

Opposition to the assimilating minority status for the racially mixed would no doubt be very strong. That alternative would require acceptance of widespread intermarriage between whites and persons with one-fourth or less African ancestry. This process has helped visible minorities other than blacks to climb the class ladder and achieve equal treatment. To many, if not most, whites, it would probably seem to be an extreme departure from the one-drop rule, which has been designed to prevent total assimilation of persons with invisible as well as visible black ancestry.

Most blacks want equal treatment and economic and political integration, not total assimilation. Some barriers to opportunities have been lowered, but there is still considerable opposition by both whites and blacks to more informal contacts. Churches are as segregated as ever, urban housing segregation has been increasing, and pressures for black unity have limited social contacts between blacks and whites. Neither the black nor the white community exhibits any enthusiasm for complete assimilation.

Unlikely as it may now seem, the mainland United States might someday move toward the Hawaiian approach as most feasible. Mainlanders who move to Hawai'i have seemed able to accept the island pattern, different though it is, within a few months (Adams 1969). The implicit rule for mixed-race status in Hawai'i is consistent with egalitarian pluralism, an outcome that African Americans and Hispanics generally prefer to full assimilation (Davis 1995). Although that may not be the road taken sooner or even later, we have seen that the status of racially mixed people can be changed by shifts in group power relations. Deeply rooted as it has been, then, the one-drop rule may not be perpetuated forever.

Seeing the Big Picture

What Was *Your* Race in 1890?

Look at Figure 1 in the Introduction of the Appendix. What parallels do you see between the six "status and identity" positions described by F. James Davis and the changing categories used by the U.S. Census? What do you make of the census categories in 1790 and 2000? Why are they so different?

---

10 A Tour of Indian Peoples and Indian Lands
David E. Wilkins

DAVID E. WILKINS is an associate professor of American Indian studies, political science, and law at the University of Minnesota, Twin Cities Campus. He has authored several books and a number of articles dealing with the political/legal relationship between indigenous nations and the United States and state governments. His most recent book is *American Indian Politics and the American Political System* (2002).

One of the greatest obstacles faced by the Indian today in his desire for self-determination . . . is the American public's ignorance of the historical relationship of the United States with Indian tribes and the lack of general awareness of the status of the American Indian in our society today.
— AMERICAN INDIAN POLICY REVIEW COMMISSION, 1977[1]

Questions to Consider Why has it been so difficult to find a political and cultural definition of who is an American Indian, what constitutes a tribe, and what criteria need to be met to claim tribal membership? How are race, culture, identity, and politics linked in Wilkins's discussion of American Indians?

THIS CHAPTER PROVIDES DESCRIPTIONS, definitions, and analysis of the most important concepts necessary for a solid foundation for the study of Indian politics. I will attempt to clarify how indigenous peoples, variously grouped, are defined, and discuss why such definitions are necessary. I will then analyze how the term Indian is defined and discuss what constitutes a reservation or Indian Country. Finally, I will conclude the chapter with a description of the basic demographic facts and socioeconomic data that applies throughout Indian lands.

What Is an Indian Tribe?

American Indians, tribal nations, Indian **tribes,** indigenous nations, Fourth World peoples, Native American peoples, aboriginal peoples, First Nations, and native peoples—these are just a sample of current terms that are used to refer to indigenous peoples in the continental United States in a collective sense. Alaska Natives, including Aleuts, Inuit, and Indians, and Native Hawaiians are the indigenous people of those respective territories. While I will provide some descriptive details about Alaska Natives, I will have less to say about Native Hawaiians because their legal status is unique among aboriginal peoples of the United States.[2]

This was brought to light in the Supreme Court's 2000 ruling in *Rice v. Cayetano.*[3] In that case, the Court struck down restrictions that had allowed only persons with Native Hawaiian blood to vote for the trustees of the Office of Hawaiian Affairs, a state agency created to better the lives of Hawaii's aboriginal people. While *Cayetano* did not specifically address the political relationship of the Native Hawaiians to the federal government, it called into question the status of the more than 150 federal statutes that recognize that Hawaii's native peoples do, in fact, have a unique legal status.

The departments of the Interior and Justice issued a preliminary report of August 23, 2000, that recommended that Congress "enact further legislation to clarify Native Hawaiians' political status and to create a framework for recognizing a government-to-government relationship with a representative Native Hawaiian governing body."[4] If Congress acts to create such a framework, and a bill was introduced on July 20, 2000 (S. 2898), by Senator Daniel K. Akaka (D-HI), then Hawaii's Natives would have a political relationship with the federal government similar to that of federally recognized tribes. The sovereignty movement in Hawaii is very complex, however, and some segments of the population desire more than mere federal recognition of their status because of their nation's preexisting sovereign status.[5]

Indigenous communities expect to be referred to by their own names—Navajo or Diné, Ojibwe or Anishinabe, Sioux or Lakota, Suquamish, or Tohono O'odham—since they constitute separate political, legal, and cultural entities. In fact, before Europeans arrived in the Americas, it is highly doubtful whether any tribes held a "conception of that racial character which today we categorize as 'Indian.' People recognized their neighbors as co-owners of the lands given to them by the Great Spirit and saw themselves sharing a basic status within creation as a life form."[6] However, when discussing Indian people generically, *American Indian tribes* and *Native Americans* remain the most widely used terms despite the inherent problems with both. For instance, America's indigenous people are not *from* India, and the term *Native American* was "used during the nativist (anti-immigration, anti-foreign) movement (1860s–1925) and the anti-black, anti-Catholic, and anti-Jewish Ku Klux Klan resurgence during the early 1900s."[7]

There is no universally agreed upon definition of what constitutes an Indian tribe, in part because each tribal community defines itself differently and because the U.S. government in its relations with tribes has operated from conflicting sets of cultural and political premises across time. Although no universal definition exists, many statutes give definitions for purposes of particular laws, federal agencies like the Bureau of Indian Affairs generate their own definitions, numerous courts have crafted definitions, and the term *tribe* is found—though not defined—in the Constitution's commerce clause.

For example, the Indian Self-Determination Act of 1975 (as amended) defines an Indian tribe as "any Indian tribe, band, nation, or other organized group or community . . . which is recognized as eligible for the special programs and services provided by the United States to Indians because of their status as Indians." By contrast, the Supreme Court in *Montoya v. United States* (1901) even more ambiguously said that "by a 'tribe' we understand a body of Indians of the same or a similar race united in a community under one leadership or government, and inhabiting a particular though sometimes ill-defined territory."[8]

Broadly, the term *tribe* can be defined from two perspectives—**ethnological** and *political-legal.*[9] From

---

tribe A social unit organized around ancestry, ethnicity, race, or a common culture.

ethnology The branch of anthropology that compares human cultures; includes the study of the origin and history of racial groupings.

an ethnological perspective, a tribe may be defined as a group of indigenous people connected by biology or blood; kinship, cultural, and spiritual values; language; political authority; and a territorial land base. But for our purposes, it is the political-legal definition (since there is no single definitive legal definition) of tribe, especially by the federal government, which is crucial since whether or not a tribal group is *recognized* as a tribe by the federal government has important political, cultural, and economic consequences, as we shall see shortly.

Federally Recognized Tribal and Alaska Native Entities

The extension of federal recognition by the United States to a tribal nation is the formal diplomatic acknowledgment by the federal government of a tribe's legal status as a sovereign. This is comparable to when the United States extended "recognition" to the former republics of the Soviet Union after that state's political disintegration. It is the beginning point of a government-to-government relationship between an indigenous people and the U.S. government.[10] The reality is that an American Indian tribe is not a legally recognized entity in the eyes of the federal government unless some explicit action by an arm of the government (i.e., congressional statute, administrative ruling by the BIA, presidential executive order, or a judicial opinion) decides that it exists in a formal manner.

Federal recognition has historically had two distinctive meanings. Before the 1870s, "recognize" or "recognition" was used in the cognitive sense. In other words, federal officials simply acknowledged that a tribe existed, usually by negotiating treaties with them or enacting specific laws to fulfill specific treaty pledges.[11] During the 1870s, however, "recognition," or more accurately, "acknowledgment," began to be used in a formal jurisdictional sense. It is this later usage that the federal government most often employs to describe its relationship to tribes. In short, federal acknowledgment is a formal act that establishes a political relationship between a tribe and the United States. It affirms a tribe's sovereign status. Simultaneously, it outlines the federal government's responsibilities to the tribe.

More specifically, federal acknowledgment means that a tribe is not only entitled to the immunities and privileges available to other tribes, but is also subject to the same federal powers, limitations, and other obligations

of recognized tribes. What this means, particularly the "limitations" term, is that "acknowledgment shall subject the Indian tribe to the same authority of Congress and the United States to which other federally acknowledged tribes are subjected."[12] In other words, tribes are informed that they are now subject to federal plenary power and may, ironically, benefit from the virtually unlimited and still largely unreviewable authority of the federal government. For example, recognized tribes have exemptions from most state tax laws, enjoy sovereign immunity, and are not subject to the same constitutional constraints as are the federal and state governments.

Until 1978, federal recognition or acknowledgment was usually bestowed by congressional act or presidential action. But in 1978 the BIA, the Department of the Interior agency primarily responsible for carrying out the federal government's treaty and trust obligations to tribal nations, published regulations which contained specific criteria that unacknowledged or nonrecognized tribal groups had to meet in order to be formally recognized by the United States. The set of guidelines was based mainly on confirmation by individuals and groups outside the petitioning tribe that members of the group were Indians. The mandatory criteria were the following: the identification of the petitioners "from historical times until the present on a substantially continuous basis, as 'American Indian' or 'Aboriginal' by the federal government, state or local governments, scholars, or other Indian tribes; the habitation of the tribe on land identified as Indian; a functioning government that had authority over its members; a constitution; a roll of members based on criteria acceptable to the secretary of the interior; not being a terminated tribe, and members not belonging to other tribes.[13]

These criteria largely were designed to fit the **"aboriginal"** or "mythic" image of the western and already recognized tribes. They were problematic for many eastern tribes who sought recognition, since they paid little heed to the massive historical, cultural, economic, and legal barriers those tribes had to endure merely to survive as tribes into the late twentieth century, lacking any semblance of federal support or protection.

aboriginal Usually refers to the first people to inhabit a particular region; often used as shorthand for native groups who were geographically displaced, mistreated, or slaughtered by settlers, as in the case of the indigenous population of Australia.

Since the late 1970s there has been tension between those who support BIA or administrative recognition versus those who believe that only the Congress has authority to recognize tribes. The debate over administrative versus legislative recognition rages on, with some advocates from each camp asserting their exclusive right to extend or withhold recognition. This raises an important question: Is there a qualitative difference between the two types of recognition? There are two important differences. First, tribes that opt for administrative variety must meet the formalized set of criteria mentioned earlier. Tribes that pursue congressional recognition, provided they can muster enough proof that they are a legitimate group composed of people of Indian ancestry, have only to make a compelling case to the congressional representative(s) of the state they reside in. The congressional sponsor(s) then make(s) the case for the tribe via legislation.

The second major difference involves the administrative law component known as "subordinate delegation." The major grant of authority the Congress has delegated to the secretary of the interior is located in title 25—*Indians*—of the *U.S. Code*. Section 1 states that the head of Indian affairs, formerly the commissioner of Indian Affairs, today the assistant secretary of Indian Affairs, is "appointed by the President, by and with the advice and consent of the Senate."[14] In section 2, the head is authorized to "have the management of all Indian affairs and of all matters arising out of Indian relations."[15] As William Quinn states, this law "would arguably not authorize the Secretary or Commissioner to establish a perpetual government-to-government relationship via federal acknowledgment with an Indian group not already under the Department's aegis."[16] Nevertheless, Quinn asserts that the secretary of the interior, with the U.S. Supreme Court's approval, has historically exercised the authority to "recognize" tribes "when a vacuum of responsibility existed over decades, resulting in a gradual and unchallenged accretion of this authority."[17]

The problem, however, is not that the secretary is usurping unused congressional authority; instead, it is the manner and degree to which secretarial discretion and interpretation of federal laws have been discharged by BIA officials. As Felix Cohen said more than forty years ago, "Indians for some decades have had neither armies nor lawyers to oppose increasingly broad interpretations of the power of the Commissioner of Indian Affairs, and so little by little 'the management of all Indian affairs' has come to

be read as 'the management of all the affairs of Indians.'"[18] This statement has relevance today, notwithstanding the federal government's policy of Indian self-determination and the more recent policy of tribal self-governance.

The Congress's track record is problematic as well. Generally speaking, however, tribes with explicit congressional acknowledgment have found their status less subject to the whims of BIA officials, though even that is no guarantee of smooth affairs, because BIA oversees and administers most of the government's political relationship with tribes.

A prime example involves the Pascua Yaqui tribe of southern Arizona. The Yaqui were legislatively recognized in 1978. However, in the late 1980s, when they solicited the approval of the BIA on some changes in their constitution, they were informed by bureau officials that they were limited in what governmental powers they could exercise because they were not a "historic tribe," but were instead merely a "created adult Indian community":

> A historic tribe has existed since time immemorial. Its powers derive from its unextinguished, inherent sovereignty. Such a tribe has the full range of governmental powers except where it has been removed by Federal law in favor of either the United States or the state in which the tribe is located. By contrast, a community of adult Indians is composed simply of Indian people who reside together on trust land. A community of adult Indians may have a certain status which entitles it to certain privileges and immunities. . . . However, that status is derived as a necessary scheme to benefit Indians, not from some historical inherent sovereignty.[19]

The bureau's attempt to create two categories of recognized tribes, a novel and disturbing approach to determining tribal identity, was halted by Congress, which declared that no department or agency of the government could develop regulations that negated or diminished the privileges and immunities of any federally recognized tribes.[20] The Congress has, moreover, in recent years tried to reassert its constitutional authority in the field by introducing legislation that would transfer administrative and congressional consideration of applications for federal recognition to an independent commission.[21]

Congress's actions, along with the increasing politicization of the administrative recognition process because of Indian gaming operations and state concerns, compelled Kevin Gover, the assistant secretary of Indian Affairs (head of the BIA), in May 2000 to testify before Congress that his agency was no longer able to do the job of recognizing tribes. Gover admitted that he had been unable to streamline the recognition process, which in some cases had taken years to resolve, but he placed larger blame on the fact that Indian gaming revenues had enabled some groups to wage protracted legal battles that often involved nonrecognized tribes, non-Indian citizens and towns, and recognized tribes.[22]

As of 2001, the Department of the Interior officially recognizes 561 indigenous entities—332 are Indian nations, tribes, bands, organized communities, or Pueblos in the lower forty-eight states; 229 are Alaska Native villages or corporations—on a list annually prepared by the BIA. These constitute the indigenous people eligible for special programs and services provided by the United States to indigenous communities because of their status as Indians or Alaska Natives.

The situation of Alaska Native villages and corporations is complicated not only by distinctive ethnological differences but also by their unique political and legal status. Although Alaska Natives are eligible to receive services from the BIA, their political sovereignty as self-governing bodies has been questioned and at times constrained by the federal government. A recent Supreme Court case, *Alaska v. Native Village of Venetie Tribal Government* (1998),[23] cast some doubts on the sovereign status of Alaskan villages. *Venetie* dealt with the jurisdictional status of Alaska Native villages and whether or not lands owned in fee simple by these communities—a type of ownership defined by the Alaska Native Claims Settlement Act of 1971—constituted "Indian Country."

In a major victory for Alaskan state authorities and a blow to the sovereignty of the village of Venetie, an Athabaskan community of some 350 people, Justice Clarence Thomas for a unanimous court held that Venetie's 1.8 million acres of fee-simple lands did not qualify as "Indian Country" because they had not been set aside by the federal government for tribal use and were not "under federal supervision." Thus, the tribal government lacked the inherent authority to impose a 5 percent business tax on a contractor building a state-funded school in the village. In denying Venetie, and by extension every other Alaskan village, the power to tax, this ruling called into question what the actual political status of these villages was.

In addition, the indigenous people of Hawaii, who prefer to be called Hawaiians, Hawaiian Natives, or Native Hawaiians, although they are treated as Native Americans for some legal purposes, are not on the Department of the Interior's list of federally recognized tribal entities and have a unique status under federal law.[24]

But there are other indigenous people in the United States who are *not federally recognized,* who had their recognized status *terminated* by the federal government, or who have *state recognition* only. I will discuss these three categories briefly.

Nonrecognized or Unacknowledged Groups

These are groups exhibiting a tremendous degree of racial, ethnic, and cultural diversity. In some cases, they are descendants of tribes who never fought the United States, had no resources desired by the federal government, or lived in geographic isolation and were simply ignored, and hence may never have participated in a treaty or benefited from the trust relationship which forms the basis of most contemporary recognized tribes' status. Despite these circumstances, some of these groups retain their aboriginal language, hold some lands in common, and in some cases have retained some degree of traditional structures of governance. These groups feel entitled to recognition status and have petitioned the United States to be so recognized.[25]

In other cases, groups have questionable genealogical connections to legitimate historical tribes but, for varying reasons, have chosen to self-identify as particular tribes and desire to be recognized by the federal government.[26] As of 2000, the BIA had received a total of 237 letters of intent and petitions for federal recognition. The acknowledgment process, established in 1978 and administered by the Branch of Acknowledgment and Research (BAR) in the BIA, proved to be an extremely slow, expensive, and politicized process that required excessive historical documentation and was greatly influenced by already recognized tribes who were reluctant to let other groups, regardless of their historical legitimacy, gain politically recognized status.[27] Because of these and other problems, the bureau surrendered its power to administratively recognize tribal groups in the fall of 2000. Between 1978 and 2000, the BIA officially recognized only fifteen tribes (e.g., Grand Traverse Band of Ottawa & Chippewa and Jamestown S'Klallam) and denied the petitions of fifteen groups (e.g., Lower Muscogee Creek Tribe east of Mississippi, Kaweah Indian Nation, Southeastern Cherokee Confederacy).[28]

Terminated Tribes

From 1953 to the mid-1960s, the federal government's Indian policy was called "termination" because the United States wanted to sever the trust relationship and end federal benefits and support services to as many tribes, bands, and California rancherias as was feasible in an effort to expedite Indian assimilation and to lift discriminatory practices and policies that negatively affected indigenous peoples.[29] This policy was exemplified by House Concurrent Resolution No. 108, passed in 1953. This measure declared that,

> Whereas it is the policy of Congress, as rapidly as possible, to make the Indians within the territorial limits of the United States subject to the same laws and entitled to the same privileges and responsibilities as are applicable to other citizens of the United States, to end their status as wards of the United States, and to grant them all the rights and prerogatives pertaining to American citizenship; and Whereas the Indians within the territorial limits of the United States should assume their full responsibilities as American citizens: Now, therefore, be it resolved . . . that it is declared to be the sense of Congress that, at the earliest possible time, all of the Indian tribes and the individual members thereof located within the States of California, Florida, New York . . . should be freed from Federal supervision and control and from all disabilities and limitations specially applicable to Indians.[30]

Over one hundred tribes, bands, and California rancherias—totaling a little more than eleven thousand Indians—were "terminated" and lost their status as "recognized" and sovereign Indian communities. Termination thus subjected the tribes and their members to state law, their trust assets were usually individualized and either sold or held by the banks, and they were no longer eligible for the other benefits and exemptions recognized tribes enjoy.

The terminated tribes, other tribes faced with termination, and Indian and non-Indian interest groups began to lobby Congress to end this disastrous policy, because of the economic and political hardships it was causing. By the mid-1960s, the policy was stifled. Gradually, terminated tribes began to push for "restoration" of their recognized status. The first tribe terminated, the Menominee of Wisconsin (terminated in 1954), was also the first tribe to be legislatively "restored," in 1973.

Although discredited as policy by the mid-1960s, and rejected by presidents Nixon and Reagan in their Indian policy statements, termination was not officially rejected by Congress until 1988 in a largely symbolic gesture that declared that "the Congress hereby repudiates and rejects HCR 108 of the 83rd Congress and any policy of unilateral termination of federal relations with any Indian nation."[31]

State-Recognized Tribes

Some Indian tribes have been recognized by their host states since the colonial era (e.g., Pamunkey Tribe of Virginia), although others have been recognized by state decrees (governor's action or state statute) in contemporary times. There are currently over fifty state-recognized tribes in Alabama, Connecticut, Georgia, Louisiana, Massachusetts, Michigan, Montana, New Jersey, North Carolina, New York, Oklahoma, Virginia, Washington, and West Virginia. See Table 1 for a list of these tribes. Depending on the policy established by the individual state, state recognition may or may not depend on prior federal recognition. Importantly, state recognition is not a prerequisite for federal recognition, although a long-standing relationship with a state is one factor in the federal recognition criteria that the BIA weighs in its determination of whether a group has historical longevity in a particular place.

For example, the Lumbee Tribe of North Carolina was legislatively recognized by the state in 1953.[32] Confident, the Lumbee leadership two years later asked Representative Frank Carlyle (D-NC) to introduce a bill before Congress that would extend federal recognition to the Lumbee. On June 7, 1956, the Congress passed an act which provided a measure of recognition to the Lumbee Nation,[33] without giving them the full range of benefits and services other federally recognized tribes received because federal policy at the time was focused on terminating the unique trust relationship between tribes and the United States. To date, the Lumbee Tribe is still not considered a federally recognized tribe by the BIA or the Indian Health Service, though they qualify for and receive other federal services as a recognized tribe.[34]

Who Is an American Indian?

Having established the complexity of determining what an Indian tribe is from a legal-political perspective, we now turn to a brief but necessary examination of the equally if not more cumbersome question of "Who is an Indian?" This is important, as McClain and Stewart note, because "the question of who is an Indian is central to any discussion of

TABLE 1   State Recognized Tribes

Alabama	Nansemond Indian Tribe
Echota Cherokee	Pamunkey Indian Tribe
Northeast Alabama Cherokee	United Rappahannock Tribe
MaChis Lower Creek	Upper Mattaponi Indian Tribe
Southeast Alabama Cherokee	**West Virginia**
Star Muscogee Creek	Appalachian American Indians of West Virginia
Mowa Band of Choctaw	**Connecticut**
Georgia	Golden Hill Paugussett
Georgia Eastern Cherokee	Paucatuck Eastern Pequot
Cherokee of Georgia	Schagticoke
Lower Muskogee Creek	**Louisiana**
Tama Tribal Town	Choctaw-Apache of Ebarb
New Jersey	Caddo Tribe
Nanticoke Lenni-Lanape	Clifton Choctaw
Powhatan Renape	Four Winds Cherokee
Ramapough Mountain	United Houma Nation
Michigan	**New York**
Burt Lake Band of Ottawa & Chippewa Indians	Shinnecock
Gun Lake Band of Grand River Ottawa Indians	Poospatuk
Grand River Band of Ottawa Indians	**Montana**
Swan Creek Black River Confederated Tribes	Little Shell Tribe of Chippewa
North Carolina	**Oklahoma**
Coharie Intra-Tribal Council	Delaware Tribe of East Oklahoma
Haliwa-Saponi Tribe	Loyal Shawnee Tribe
Lumbee	Yuchi Tribe
Meherrin Tribe	**Washington**
Person County Indians	Chinook Indian Tribe
Waccamaw-Siouan Tribe	Duwamish Tribe
Virginia	Kikiallus Indian Nation
Chickahominy Indian Tribe	Marietta Band of Nooksack Indians
Eastern Chickahominy Indian Tribe	Steilacoom Indian Tribe
Mattaponi Indian Tribe	Snohomish Tribe of Indians
Monacan Indian Tribe	

Source: http://www.thespike.com/tablest.htm.

American Indian politics."[35] The political relationship that exists between tribes and the federal government, bloated with issues of disparate power, **cultural biases,** and race and ethnicity, makes this so. Of course, like the concept of "Indian tribe," before Columbus arrived in 1492 there were no peoples in the Americas known as "Indians" or "Native Americans." Each indigenous community had its

cultural bias The assumption that one's own cultural practices or beliefs are better and as such should be the norm by which other cultures are measured.

own name relating to the character of its people and the lands they inhabited.

With the political status of Indian nations defined, the question of deciding just "who is an Indian" would not appear to be a difficult one to answer. The decision rests with the tribal nations who retain, as one of their inherent sovereign powers, the power to decide who belongs in their nation. Unless this right has been expressly ceded in a treaty, it remains probably the most essential component of self-government. If tribes were to lose the right to decide who their citizens/members were, then it would logically follow that any government could dictate or influence what the tribe's membership should entail.

Since the identification of individuals as Indians depends upon or coincides with their association in a unique body politic and distinctive cultural and linguistic systems, historically, at least, "allegiance rather than ancestry per se [was] the deciding factor" in determining who was an Indian.[36] In other words, historically, to be considered an Indian one had to meet certain basic tribally defined criteria, including the social, cultural, linguistic, territorial, sociopsychological, and ceremonial. These criteria, of course, varied from tribal nation to tribal nation. However, as the federal government's power waxed by the late nineteenth century, with the corresponding waning of tribal power, indigenous cultural-social-territorial–based definitions of tribal identity were sometimes ignored and replaced by purely legal and frequently race-based definitions often arbitrarily articulated in congressional laws, administrative regulations, or court cases.

Congress, in particular, began to employ and still uses ethnological data, including varying fractions of blood quantum. In fact, blood quantum remains one of the most important criteria used by the federal government and tribal governments to determine Indian status, despite the fact that its continued use "poses enormous conceptual and practical problems" since blood is not the carrier of genetic material and cultural traits as was thought in the nineteenth century.[37]

When blood quantum was first used in the Indian context in the early part of the twentieth century as a mechanism to reduce federal expenditures for Indian education, it "was meant to measure the amount of Indian blood possessed by an individual. Because racial blood types could not be observed directly, Indian blood quantum was inferred from the racial backgrounds of parents. If both parents were reputed to have 'unadulterated' Indian blood, then the blood quantum of their children was fixed at 100 percent. For children of racially mixed parents, their Indian blood quantum might be some fractional amount such as ¾, ½, or ⅛."[38]

The federal government's principal function in formulating definitions of "Indian," since like the concept "tribe" there is no single constitutional or universally accepted definition, is to "establish a test whereby it may be determined whether a given individual is to be excluded from the scope of legislation dealing with Indians."[39] The most widely accepted "legal" definition of "Indian" is from Felix Cohen, who wrote in 1943 that:

> The term "Indian" may be used in an ethnological or in a legal sense. Ethnologically, the Indian race may be distinguished from the Caucasian, Negro, Mongolian, and other races. If a person is three-fourths Caucasian and one-fourth Indian, it is absurd, from the ethnological standpoint, to assign him to the Indian race. Yet legally such a person may be an Indian. From a legal standpoint, then, the biological question of race is generally pertinent, but not conclusive. Legal status depends not only upon biological, but also upon social factors, such as the relation of the individual concerned to a white or Indian community. . . . Recognizing the possible diversity of definitions of "Indianhood," we may nevertheless find some practical value in a definition of "Indian" as a person meeting two qualifications: (a) That some of his ancestors lived in America before its discovery by the white race, and (b) That the individual is considered an "Indian" by the community in which he lives.[40]

Because of the Constitution's silence on the issue of who is an Indian, Congress, the BIA, and the federal courts have had great latitude in developing specific meanings for specific situations which only sometimes reflect the definitions of particular tribes. But because of the plenary power doctrine and the trust doctrine, these federal actors, but especially the Congress, have vested themselves with the right to define "who an Indian is" for purposes relating to legislation and have sometimes established base rolls which actually identify who a tribe's members are. This was done in the case of the so-called Five Civilized Tribes of present-day Oklahoma. Congress, in 1893, enacted a law that all but secured to the federal government the right to determine membership of these tribes.[41]

Over thirty "legal" definitions have been promulgated by various agencies, departments, and congressional committees and subcommittees that explain who is and is not an Indian eligible for federal services.[42] These definitions can be grouped into six categories. First, and most common, are those definitions that require a specific blood quantum, with one-fourth being the most widely accepted fraction. Second, there is a set of definitions clustered under the requirement that the individual be a member of a federally recognized indigenous community.

A third category includes definitions that mandate residence "on or near" a federal Indian reservation. A fourth class includes definitions grouped under descendancy. These entail definitions that extend eligibility not only to tribal members but also to their descendants up to a specified degree. For example, the definition of Indian found in a 1998 bill, Indian Trust-Estate Planning and Land Title Management Improvement Act, declares that "the term 'Indian' means any individual who is a member, or a descendant of a member, of a North American tribe, band, pueblo, or other organized group of natives who are indigenous to the continental U.S., or who otherwise has a special relationship with the U.S. through a treaty, agreement, or other form of recognition." The bill's sponsors described an "Alaska Native" as "an individual who is an Alaskan Indian, Eskimo, Aleut, or any combination thereof, who are indigenous to Alaska."

Under the fifth grouping are several definitions that rely on self-identification. The U.S. Census Bureau, for example, allows individuals to simply declare that they are Indian. Finally, the sixth class is a miscellaneous category that includes definitions which do not easily fit in the other categories.[43]

Defining "Indian" and "tribe" are not simple tasks in part because of the political and economic resources involved and because of the number and power of the respective actors: tribal governments, individual Indians, Congress, the president, the Department of the Interior, the BIA, federal courts and, increasingly, state governments and the various agencies and individuals who constitute those sovereigns. But who does the defining and how these emotionally laden terms are defined are crucial in expanding our understanding of the politics of individual tribes, intertribal relations, and intergovernmental relations.

For example, in terms of identity, high outmarriage rates, steadily decreasing federal dollars, and an intensified tribal-state relationship have prompted questions about "whether the rules defining Indianness and tribal membership should be relaxed or tightened—that is, made more inclusionary or more exclusionary."[44] For instance, some tribes are eliminating **blood quantum** and adopting descent criteria, while others are pursuing an "ethnic purification strategy" by adopting a stricter set of blood

blood quantum The idea of counting the percentage of racial heritage, which comes from racist laws that were used to place American Indians on reservations. The laws asked the question, in terms of a percentage, how black, or Indian, or white you were.

quantum rules concerning tribal enrollment. These decisions impact tribes and their political relationship with the federal government.

While tribes retain the right to establish their own membership criteria, the BIA in August 2000 published proposed regulations on the documentation requirements and standards necessary for Indians to receive a "certificate of degree of Indian blood" (CDIB), which is the federal government's way of determining whether individuals possess sufficient Indian blood to be eligible for certain federal programs and services provided exclusively to American Indians or Alaska Natives.[45]

But a number of Indian leaders, like W. Ron Allen, chairman of the Jamestown S'Klallam Tribe of Washington, charged that the federal government should not be in the business of determining who is Indian. The proposed regulations, he argued, by requiring applicants to show a relationship to an enrolled member of a federally recognized tribe, would potentially exclude members of descendants of terminated tribes, state-recognized tribes, and nonrecognized tribes.

Since the BIA's standard blood quantum is one-fourth, and with the high rates of out-marriage, Russell Thornton, an anthropologist, suggests that sometime in this century the proportion of the Indian population with less than one-fourth blood quantum will rise to 60 percent. If this trend is correct, from the federal government's standpoint "decreasing blood quanta of the total Native American population may be perceived as meaning that the numbers of Native Americans to whom it is obligated have declined."[46] This will not mean the extinction of Indian tribes, but it will mean a new form of federal termination of Indians who are eligible for federal aid and services.

Questions around whether a tribe is federally recognized, state-recognized, nonrecognized, or terminated have direct bearing on the internal and external political dynamics of tribes, and directly affect intergovernmental relations, since only recognized tribes may engage in gaming operations that are not directly subject to state law, may exercise criminal jurisdiction over their members and a measure of civil jurisdiction over nonmembers, and are exempt from a variety of state and federal taxes.

What Are Indian Lands?

The first and most obvious difference between Indian peoples and all other groups in the United States is that

Indians were here before anyone else. All the land in the continental United States, Alaska, and Hawaii was inhabited and revered by the over six hundred distinctive indigenous peoples who dwelt here. Gradually, however, from 1492 forward, various foreign nations—Russia, Holland, Spain, Great Britain, France, Sweden, and later the United States—competed for an economic foothold in North America. For the three most dominant European states, France, Spain, and Great Britain (and later the United States, as Britain's successor), this usually included efforts to secure title to indigenous lands through formal treaties, which were sometimes coercive and occasionally fraudulent, while some were fairly negotiated.[47]

When the United States declared independence in 1776, it wisely opted to continue the policy of negotiating treaties with tribes, which it continued to do until 1871, when Congress unilaterally declared that "hereafter no Indian nation or tribe within the territory of the United States shall be acknowledged or recognized as an independent nation, tribe, or power with whom the United States may contract by treaty."[48] However, this stance proved unworkable and within a short period the United States was again negotiating *agreements* with tribal nations that were often referred to and accorded the legal status of treaties. The negotiation of agreements continued until 1912.

Many of these documents were primarily viewed as land cession arrangements by the federal government, in which the United States purchased varying amounts of tribal lands in exchange for monies, goods, and services. In addition, tribes "reserved" their remaining lands, or agreed to relocate to new lands, which were usually designated as reservations. These reserved lands were to be held "in trust" by the United States on behalf of the tribe(s), who were deemed the beneficiaries. As the tribes' "trustee," the federal government theoretically exercised the responsibility to assist the tribes in the protection of their lands, resources, and cultural heritage and pledged that it would hold itself to the highest standards of good faith and honesty in all its dealings with the tribes.

For example, article 1 of a treaty the Kickapoo signed on October 24, 1832, contained a cession of land:

> The Kickapoo tribe of Indians, in consideration of the stipulations hereinafter made, do hereby cede to the United States, the lands assigned to them by the treaty of Edwardsville, and concluded at St. Louis . . . and all other claims to lands within the State of Missouri.[49]

The second article, however, described the lands the tribe had secured for their land cessions:

> The United States will provide for the Kickapoo tribe, a country to reside in, southwest of the Missouri river, as their permanent place of residence as long as they remain a tribe . . . [and] it is hereby agreed that the country within the following boundaries shall be assigned, conveyed, and forever secured . . . to the said Kickapoo tribe.[50]

In this case the Kickapoo agreed to relocate to a little over 700,000 acres of new lands in Kansas that were to serve as their permanent "reservation."

In short, a reservation is an area of land—whether aboriginal or new—that has been reserved for an Indian tribe, band, village, or nation. Generally, the United States holds, in trust for the tribe, legal title to the reserved territory. The tribe in these instances holds a beneficial title to the lands, or, in other words, an exclusive right of occupancy. Of course, reservations were not all created by treaty. Congress established a number of reservations by statute.

The president, through the use of executive order power, established many other reservations. For instance, the state of Arizona has twenty-one reservations—twenty of which were created by presidents. The core foundation of the Navajo Reservation (the largest in the country), was treaty-established in 1868, though the many additions to it were mostly by executive orders. In 1919, Congress forbade the president from establishing any more reservations via executive order. Finally, the secretary of the interior is empowered under the 1934 Indian Reorganization Act to establish, expand, or restore reservations.

As of 1998, there were 314 reservations and other restricted and trust lands in the United States. These reserved lands are located in thirty-one states, mostly in the West. There are also twelve state-established reservations in Connecticut, Massachusetts, Michigan, New York, New Jersey, South Carolina, Georgia, and Virginia. Despite the large number of federally recognized Alaska Native groups, there is only one reservation, the Annette Island Indian Reserve.[51]

At present, the indigenous land base in the United States, including Alaska, is approximately 100 million acres—fifty-six million in the continental United States, forty-four million in Alaska. This represents approximately 4 percent of all lands in the United States. Map 1 graphically shows the rapid and enormous loss of aboriginal

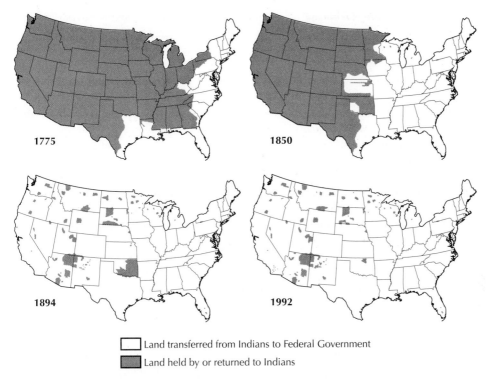

1775

1850

1894

1992

☐ Land transferred from Indians to Federal Government

■ Land held by or returned to Indians

MAP 1 **American Indian Land Losses.** *Source: Encyclopedia of North American Indians,* edited by Frederick E. Hoxie. Copyright © 1996 by Houghton Mifflin Company. All rights reserved.

territory to the United States from the birth of the American republic to the present day.

The roughly one hundred million acres constitutes territory over which tribal governments and Alaska Native villages and corporations exercise varying amounts of governmental jurisdiction, and where state laws are generally inapplicable, with exceptions.

In 1999, 1,397,931 Indians were identified in a BIA report out of the total U.S. Indian population in 2000 of 2,475,956 (individuals self-identifying as single race American Indian or Alaska Native).

What Is Indian Country?

For an indigenous government to be able to exercise criminal or civil jurisdiction over their territory, their own members, and, in some limited cases, non-Indians, the land in question must be designated as *Indian Country*. In the colonial era, Indian Country encompassed all the lands beyond the frontier lands "populated by tribes and bands

of Indians who rejected contact with 'civilized' populations."[52] Today, however, the concept "has been elevated by federal law above other ideas because it transcends mere geographical limitations and represents that sphere of influence in which Indian traditions and federal laws passed specifically to deal with the political relationship of the United States to American Indians have primacy."[53]

Indian Country: Beyond the Reservation

Broadly, the term "Indian Country" means land within which Indian laws and customs and federal laws relating to Indians are generally applicable. But it is also defined as all the land under the supervision and protection of the federal government that has been set aside primarily for the use of Indians. Federal law defines it, first, as all land within the boundaries of an Indian reservation, whether owned by Indians or non-Indians. Second, it includes all "dependent Indian communities" in the United States.

These are lands—pueblos of New Mexico, Oklahoma Indian tribal lands, and California rancherias—previously recognized by European nations and now by the successor government, the United States, as belonging to the tribes or as set aside by the federal government for use and benefit of the Indians.

Pueblo lands, because they were previously recognized as belonging to the pueblos under Spanish, Mexican, and later U.S. law, are not, strictly speaking, reservations, but are considered Indian lands and are held in trust by the federal government because they are held in communal ownership with fee-simple title residing in each pueblo. Some Pueblo Indian lands are held in equitable ownership by various pueblos, with the United States holding legal title. These lands include reservations created by congressional statute and executive order reservations established by the president.

Oklahoma's numerous Indian tribes also have a distinctive history, though their lands also constitute Indian Country. It is important to note that the tribes in the eastern part of the state, what was called "Indian Territory," home of the Five Civilized Tribes, have a somewhat different history from tribes in the western part of the state, or what was called "Oklahoma Territory," home of the Cheyenne, Arapaho, Kiowa, Comanche, etc. Although the BIA and the Bureau of the Census have asserted that there are no Indian reservations in Oklahoma, except for the Osage, John Moore argues that the reservation status of Oklahoma tribes persists, notwithstanding allotment and other policies designed to terminate Indian communal land holdings.[54]

Some California tribes, because of heavy Spanish influence dating from 1769, live on rancherias, a Spanish term meaning "small reservation" and originally applied to Indians who had not been settled in Christian mission communities. The history of death and dispossession visited upon California's indigenous population may well be the worst of any aboriginal peoples in the United States. From a population of well over 300,000 at the time of contact, California Indians experienced a staggering rate of decline from diseases, outright **genocide,** and displacement.[55] That they have retained any lands at all is a remarkable testimony to their fortitude.

Finally, the Indian Country designation includes all individual Indian allotments (I will discuss the allotment

genocide The systematic wholesale killing of individuals because of their race, religion, ethnicity, or political affiliation. The idea behind genocide is the total eradication of a group, motivated by hatred.

policy shortly) that are still held in trust or restricted status by the federal government—whether inside or outside an Indian reservation.[56]

For political and legal purposes, the designation of Indian Country is crucial because the reach of a tribal nation's jurisdiction is generally restricted to lands so designated. And it is Indian Country where most jurisdictional disputes arise between tribes and their members, tribes and non-Indians, and tribes and the local, county, state, or federal governments.

For example, this was the central question in the recent U.S. Supreme Court case involving indigenous people, *Alaska v. Native Village of Venetie Tribal Government* (1998). In this case, the court had to decide whether the village of Venetie constituted Indian Country. If so, then the tribal government had the right to impose a tax on a construction company; if not, then it lacked such taxing power. In a harmful ruling for Alaska Native sovereignty, the Supreme Court held that the village's fee-simple lands did not constitute Indian Country, thus depriving Alaska villages and corporations of the power to exercise a number of governmental powers that tribal nations in the lower forty-eight states exercise routinely. The Supreme Court, however, need not have relied so exclusively on the question of whether or not Venetia constituted "Indian Country" since the statutes articulating this concept clearly did not encompass Alaska at the time they were enacted.

Demography and Indian Country

According to a report, *Changing America,* prepared by the Council of Economic Advisers for President Clinton's Race Initiative in 1998, the population of the United States is increasingly diverse. In recent years the four major racial/ethnic minority groups—Latinos, Asian Americans, African Americans, and American Indians—have each grown faster than the population as a whole. Whereas in 1970 the combination of these four groups represented only 16 percent of the entire population, by 1998 this had increased to 27 percent.[57] The Bureau of the Census, the report noted, projects that by 2050, these groups will account for "almost half of the U.S. Population." Early data from the 2000 U.S. census, which shows a total population of 281,421,906, indicate the continuing transformation of race and ethnicity in America. While the categories of white (211,460,626), Hispanic or Latino (35,305,818), black or African American (34,658,190), American Indian

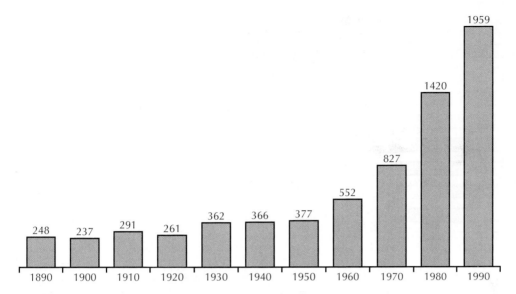

FIGURE 1   **American Indian Population, 1890–1990 (thousands).** *Source:* Larry Hajime Shinagawa and Michael Jang, *Atlas of American Diversity* (Walnut Creek, Calif.: AltaMira, 1998), 107–8. *Notes:* 1900, partially estimated; 1940 Eskimo and Aleut populations are based on 1939 counts.

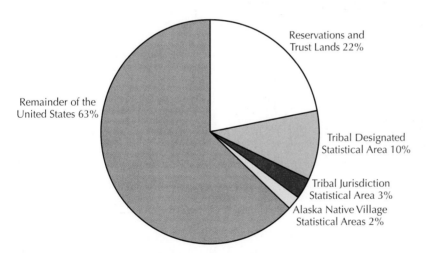

FIGURE 2   **American Indian Population by Type of Area, 1990 (percent).** *Source:* Larry Hajime Shinagawa and Michael Jang, *Atlas of American Diversity* (Walnut Creek, Calif.: AltaMira, 1998), 107–8.

or Alaska Native (2,475,956), Asian (10,242,998), and Native Hawaiian or other Pacific Islander (398,835) were familiar, for the first time in history individuals could choose self-identify as having more than one race. Some 6,826,228 people, 2.4 percent of the total population, claimed affiliation with two or more races.[58]

While this projected growth has potentially staggering political and economic implications, the fact is that the total indigenous population, despite the large number of indigenous nations—561 and counting—is comparatively quite small (see Figures 1–5). In 2000, there were a reported 2,475,956 self-identified Indians and Alaska

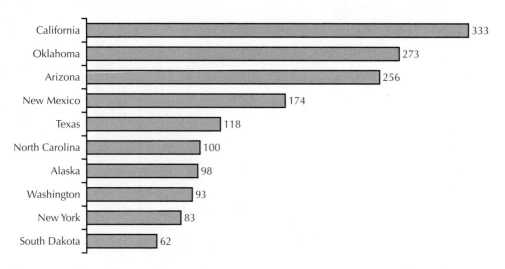

FIGURE 3   **States with the Ten Largest American Indian Populations, 2000 (thousands).** *Source:* www.census.gov/clo/www/redistricting.html.

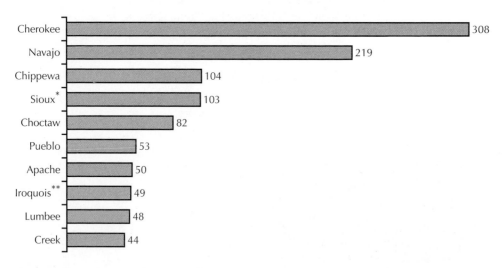

FIGURE 4   **Ten Largest American Indian Tribes, 1990 (thousands).** *Source:* Larry Hajime Shinagawa and Michael Jang, *Atlas of American Diversity* (Walnut Creek, Calif.: AltaMira, 1998), 107–8. [*]Any entry with the spelling "Siouan" was miscoded to Sioux in North Carolina. [**]Reporting and/or processing problems have affected the data for this tribe.

Natives, a 26 percent increase since 1990. This is a drastic decline from pre-European figures of over seven million, but it is far more than the nadir of perhaps only 250,000 around 1900.[59] The 2000 figure represents only 0.9 percent of the total U.S. population of 281,421,906.

Although the overall population of self-identified American Indians and Alaska Natives is still quite small, because of the new category allowing individuals to identify as belonging to more than one race (sixty-three racial options were possible), the 2000 census data are not

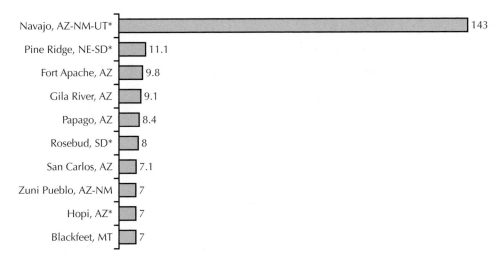

FIGURE 5   **Reservations with the Largest Numbers of American Indians, 1990 (thousands).** *Source:* Larry Hajime Shinagawa and Michael Jang, *Atlas of American Diversity* (Walnut Creek, Calif.: AltaMira, 1998), 107–8. *Includes trust lands.

directly comparable with data from the 1990 census or previous censuses. Thus, while approximately 2.5 million individuals identified themselves as American Indian and Alaska Native alone, an additional 1.6 million people reported themselves as being indigenous and belonging to "at least one other race." Within this group, the most common combinations were "American Indian and Alaska Native *and* White" (66 percent of the population reported this); "American Indian and Alaska Native *and* Black or African American" (11 percent of the population); and "American Indian and Alaska Native *and* White *and* Black or African American" (7 percent). In sum, approximately 4.1 million people reported themselves as being American Indian and Alaska Native "alone or in combination with one or more other races."[60] The wide diversity within this population will be discussed in greater detail in forthcoming Census reports not yet available.

Suffice it to say, the amount of racial mixing acknowledged in the American Indian context is extreme when compared to that of other racial/ethnic groups. As Russell Thornton, a Cherokee anthropologist, noted in his analysis of the 2000 census data, American Indians have a racial mixture of 37 percent, which "far exceeds percentages for other groups." Thornton noted that only about 5 percent of African Americans reported mixed ancestry.[61]

In Alaska, there is only one small reservation, Annette Island Reserve, though for census purposes lands are designated as "Alaska Native Village Statistical areas" that are inhabited and recognized as indigenous areas. Approximately 47,244 Alaska Natives live on these lands. In sum, more than 60 percent, over one million, of all Indian people do not live on Indian reservations.[62] A majority of indigenous peoples, in fact some 56.2 percent, live in metropolitan or suburban areas. And roughly half of all urban Indians can be found in as few as sixteen cities, largely as a result of the 1950s and 1960s termination, relocation, and educational programs of the federal government.

In the early days of relocation, the BIA generally helped send Indians to Chicago, Los Angeles, Denver, or Salt Lake City. By 1990, Indians had migrated to a number of other metropolitan areas. Cities with the largest Indian populations in 1990 were Tulsa, Oklahoma (48,348); Oklahoma City, Oklahoma (46,111); Los Angeles–Long Beach, California (43,689); Phoenix, Arizona (38,309); and Seattle-Tacoma, Washington (32,980).[63] The vast majority of Indians still live in the western half of the United States.

The states with the ten largest indigenous populations are shown in Figure 3. The District of Columbia had the fewest Indians, 1,466.

There is also great variation in the population of individual tribes (see Figure 5). The largest tribe is the Cherokee Nation of Oklahoma, with 369,035 members. The smallest tribes have fewer than one hundred members. The indigenous population is also a young population, with more than 35 percent younger than age seventeen. In fact, the median age for reservation Indians is more than ten years younger than that of the general U.S. population. The Indian population, like that of the Jews and the Japanese Americans in Hawaii, is also one that experiences an extremely high level of intergroup marriage (marriage between persons of different races). Although intergroup marriage couples accounted for only 4 percent of all married couples in the United States in 1990, American Indians had a 53 percent intergroup marriage rate. Potentially, this figure could have severe cultural and political implications for indigenous nations.[64]

As Snipp mused:

> The extraordinarily high level of racial intermarriage for American Indians provides a good reason to expect that growing numbers of American Indians and their descendants will choose non-Indians for spouses and to a greater or lesser degree become absorbed into the dominant culture. Some of these Indians will abandon their cultural heritage altogether, while others may make only minor accommodations as a result of having a non-Indian spouse. This raises a question that is extremely controversial within many quarters of the American Indian community: Are American Indians assimilating so quickly through racial intermarriage that they will eventually, in the not to distant future, marry themselves out of existence?[65]

Predicting the future is an impossible task and I will not hazard a guess as to whether this intermarriage rate will continue. Suffice it to say, this is viewed as a serious predicament by some tribes and raises some important questions. For instance, will Indians, like many intermarried Jews, be able to show a propensity for combining extensive intermarriage with a surge in ethnic and religious pride? For while the rate of Jewish intermarriage is higher today than at any other point, American Jewish culture and community life appear to be flourishing, including a resurgent interest in Yiddish.[66]

Other questions confront tribes as well. Will they continue to use blood quantum as their primary definitional criteria? Will the federal government claim that its legal and moral obligations to Indians dissipate if a tribal nation's blood quantum falls below a certain percentage? Will tribes be able to exercise jurisdiction over a multiracial citizenry? These are questions some tribes are beginning to address as we begin the new millennium.

Conclusion

The power to define—what is a tribe, who is an Indian, what constitutes Indian Country, which group gets recognized—along with the power to decide whether or not to act in a colonial capacity in relation to indigenous nations are important means by which the federal government has gained and retains a dominant position vis-à-vis tribal groups. While on one hand supporting the right of indigenous polities to exercise self-determination, the United States on the other still insists that it has the power and the right to trump important tribal governmental decisions regarding identity and has shown throughout its history that it will so act if it deems it necessary to further its own economic, political, and cultural interests.

The demographic data presented glaringly show that diversity and uncertainty are hallmarks of Indian Country, with more than half the indigenous population living off reservations and Indians outmarrying at increasing rates. What the impact of such movement and marriage rates will be on tribal national identity, federal Indian policy, and the government-to-government relationship is, however, impossible to predict.

Seeing the Big Picture   **From Riches to the "Res" (Reservation System)**
Map 1 in this reading shows land held by Indians in 1750 and 1992. Glance at the quality-of-life indicators in the Appendix. Do you believe that socioeconomic standing and the loss of Indian lands are connected? How?

11   Asian American Panethnicity: Contemporary National and Transnational Possibilities

Yen Le Espiritu

YEN LE ESPIRITU is professor of ethnic studies at the University of California, San Diego.

IN AN ARTICLE PUBLISHED IN *GIDRA,* AN activist Asian American news magazine, Naomi Iwasaki (1999, under "Asian American or Not") writes, "You know, the hardest thing about pan-Asian solidarity is the 'pan' part. It forces us all to step outside of our comfort zones, whether they be constructed by ethnicity, class, home city, identity, whatever." Iwasaki's statement calls attention to the social constructedness of panethnicity—panethnic identities are self-conscious products of political choice and actions, not of inherited phenotypes, bloodlines, or cultural traditions. . . . Employing a racial formation perspective (Omi and Winant 1986), I argue that the racialist constructions of Asians as homogeneous and interchangeable spawn important alliances and affiliations among ethnic and immigrant groups of Asian origin. Adopting the dominant group's categorization of them, Asian Americans have institutionalized pan-Asianism as their political instrument, thereby enlarging their own capacities to challenge and transform the existing structure of power. In other words, Asian Americans did not just adopt the pan-Asian concept but also transformed it to conform to their political, economic, and ideological needs.

Though powerful, pan-Asianism is not unproblematic: it can mask salient divisions, subsume nondominant groups, and create marginalities, all of which threatens the legitimacy and effectiveness of pan-Asianism and bolsters (however inadvertently) the racist discourses and practices that construct Asians as homogeneous. In the three decades since the emergence of the pan-Asian concept in the late 1960s, Asian American communities have changed in dramatic ways. No longer constrained by race-based exclusion laws, Asian immigrants began arriving in much larger numbers than before. Many of the post-1965 immigrants have little direct experience with the Asian American movement and little reason to think of themselves as Asian American rather than as immigrants, as low-wage workers, or as members of different national and ethnic groups (Espiritu et al. 2000, 131). Moreover, recent immigration has further diversified Asian Americans along cultural, generational, economic, and political lines—all of which have compounded the difficulties of forging pan-Asian identities and institutions.

This chapter reviews the history of Asian American panethnicity in the United States *then to now,* paying particular attention to the ways in which pan-Asian identities and institutions have been transformed by the post-1965 immigration and by changes in the global economy. The first section documents the social, political, and demographic factors that led to the emergence of pan-Asianism in the late 1960s and early 1970s. The second details how the post-1965 immigration has diversified the Asian American population and made it more difficult for groups to imagine shared origins and destinies. The third establishes that the construction of Asian American identities not only is a response to conditions in the United States but also is deeply bound to U.S. colonial and imperialist practices that propel the contemporary migration of Asians to the United States in the first place. The fourth discusses the political importance of cross-group affiliation, not only among Asians but also with other groups across class, ethnic, racial, and national lines. Of the four sections, the third conveys the chapter's central argument: pan-Asianism in the United States has been determined not exclusively by events and population changes in the United States but also by U.S. colonialism and imperialism in Asia. Much of the published work in the field of U.S. immigration studies has remained "America-centric," focusing on the immigrants' "modes of incorporation" and the process of their "becoming American." In contrast, this chapter takes a *critical transnational* approach to the study of Asian Americans, calling attention to the deep historical entanglements of immigration and imperialism.[1]

Coming Together: The Emergence of Pan-Asianism

Arriving in the United States, nineteenth-century immigrants from Asian countries did not think of themselves as "Asians." Coming from specific districts and provinces in different nations, Asian immigrant groups did not even think of themselves as Chinese, Japanese, Korean, and so forth, but rather as people from Toishan, Hoiping, or some other district in Guandong Province in China or from Hiroshima, Yamaguchi, or some other prefecture in Japan. Members of each group considered themselves culturally and politically distinct. Historical enmities between their countries of origin further separated the groups even before their arrival in the United States. However, non-Asians had little understanding or appreciation of these distinctions. For the most part, outsiders accorded to people from Asia certain common characteristics and traits that were essentially supranational. Indeed, the exclusion acts and quotas limiting Asian immigration to the United States relied on racialist constructions of Asians as homogeneous (Lowe 1991, 28).

The development of panethnicity among Asian Americans has a short history. It was not until the late 1960s, with the advent of the Asian American movement, that a pan-Asian consciousness and constituency were first formed. Before the 1960s, Asians in the United States frequently practiced ethnic disidentification: distancing one's group from another group so as not to be mistaken for a member of that group and to avoid suffering the blame for its presumed misdeeds (Hayano 1981, 161, 162; Daniels 1988, 113). For example, in the late nineteenth century, aware of Chinese exclusion, Japanese immigrant leaders did everything possible to distinguish themselves from the Chinese immigrants (Ichioka 1988, 250). In the end Japanese attempts at disidentification failed. With the passage of the 1924 Immigration Act, the Japanese joined the Chinese as a people deemed unworthy of becoming Americans. Less than two decades later, after the bombing of Pearl Harbor, it was the turn of the Chinese to disassociate themselves from the Japanese. Fearful that they would be targets of anti-Japanese

activities, many Chinese immigrants took to wearing buttons that proclaimed positively, "I'm Chinese." Some Chinese immigrants—and also Korean and Filipino migrants—even joined the white persecution with buttons that added, "I hate Japs worse than you do" (Daniels 1988, 205; Takaki 1989, 370–71). These two examples are instructive not only as evidence of ethnic disidentification but also as documentation of the pervasiveness of racial lumping. Precisely because of racial lumping, persons of Asian ancestry found it necessary to disassociate themselves from other Asian groups.

The development of a pan-Asian consciousness and constituency reflected broader societal developments and demographic changes as well as the group's political agenda. Before World War II, pan-Asian unity was not feasible because the predominantly foreign-born Asian population did not share a common language. During the postwar years, owing to immigration restrictions and the growing dominance of the second and even third generations, U.S.-born Asians outnumbered immigrants. By 1960 approximately two-thirds of the Asian population in California had been born in the United States (Ong 1989, 5–8). With English as the common language, persons from different Asian backgrounds were able to communicate with one another (Ling 1984, 73) and in so doing to create a common identity associated with the United States. Also, the breakdown of economic and residential barriers during the postwar period provided the first opportunity for an unprecedented number of Asian Americans to come into intimate, sustained contact with the larger society—and with one another. Formerly homogeneous, the Asian ethnic enclaves started to house mixed-Asian communities, as well as non-Asian groups. Multigroup suburban centers also emerged. Paul Wong (1972, 34) reported that since the early 1960s Asian Americans of diverse national origins had moved into the suburbs outside the major Asian communities such as Berkeley and San Mateo, California. Although a small proportion of the local population, these Asian Americans tended to congregate in pockets; consequently, in some residential blocks a majority of the residents were Asian Americans.

Although broader social struggles and internal demographic changes provided the impetus for the Asian American movement, it was the Asian Americans' politics—explicitly radical, confrontational, and

---

transnational The movement of individuals, families, culture, and ideas back and forth between one's country of origin and a new place of residence.

pan-Asian—that shaped the movement's content. Inspired by anticolonial revolutions in Asia and by black and Chicano revolutionary nationalism, college students of Asian ancestry sought to transcend inter-Asian ethnic divisions and to ally themselves with other "Third World" minorities (Blauner 1972, ch. 2; Omatsu 1994). Through pan-Asian organizations, publications, and Asian American studies programs, Asian American activists forged a pan-Asian consciousness by highlighting their shared resistance to Western imperialism and to U.S. racism. The pan-Asian concept enabled diverse Asian American groups to understand their "unequal circumstances and histories as being related" (Lowe 1991, 30). By the mid-1970s, "Asian American" had become a familiar term (Lott 1976, 30). Although first coined by college activists, the pan-Asian concept began to be used extensively by professional and community spokespersons to lobby for the health and welfare of Americans of Asian descent. Commenting on the "literally scores of pan-Asian organizations" in the mid-1970s, William Liu (1976, 6) asserted that "the idea of pan-Asian cooperation [was] viable and ripe for development."

The advent of state-sponsored affirmative action programs provided another material reason for Asian American subgroups to consolidate their efforts. Because the welfare state bureaucracy often treats all Asian Americans as a single administrative unit in distributing economic and political resources, it imposes a pan-Asian structure on persons and communities dependent on government support. As dealings with government bureaucracies increased, political organization along a pan-Asian line became necessary, not only because numbers confer power but also because the pan-Asian category is the institutionally relevant category in the political and legal system. Administratively treated as a homogeneous group, Asian Americans found it necessary—and even advantageous—to respond as a group. The pan-Asian strategy has led to some political victories. For example, Asian American legislators, community leaders, and organizations united to fight the Census Bureau's proposal to collapse all Asian racial codes into one summary category for the 1980 and 1990 censuses. Partly in response to the strength of their political lobbying, the Census Bureau finally conceded to the coalition's demand for a detailed enumeration of Asian subgroups.[2] Indeed, the emergence of the

pan-Asian entity may be one of the most significant political developments in Asian American affairs.

Changing Demographic and Economic Characteristics

The post-1965 immigration surge from Asia has transformed Asian America—and thus the feasibility of pan-Asian ethnicity—in dramatic ways. The share of immigrants to the United States from Asia as a proportion of total admission grew from a tiny 5 percent in the 1950s to 11 percent in the 1960s and 33 percent in the 1970s, and it has remained at 35 percent since 1980 (Zhou and Gatewood 2000, 9). In sheer numbers, the Asian American population grew from a total of 1.4 million in 1970 to 7.3 million in 1990, to 10.2 million in 2000.[3] According to Zhou and Gatewood (2000, 14), immigration accounted for more than two-thirds of this spectacular population growth. For the new national origins groups (Indians, Koreans, Vietnamese, Cambodians, Laotians, and the Hmong), population growth can be attributed almost entirely to immigration (Zhou and Gatewood 2000, 14). Projections from the Census Bureau suggest that the Asian American population will increase from 9 million in 1995 to 34 million in 2050, growing from 3 to 8 percent of the total U.S. population (Smith and Edmonston 1997). The dramatic growth in the absolute numbers of Asian Americans has been accompanied by increasing ethnic, generational, and socioeconomic diversity within Asian America, all of which has important implications for pan-Asian identities and practices. As Michael Omi (1993, 205) succinctly states, "The irony is that the term ["Asian American"] came into vogue at precisely the historical moment when new Asian groups were entering the U.S. who would render the term problematic."

Ethnic Diversification

Before the post-1965 immigration surge, the Asian American population was composed mainly of three ethnic groups: Japanese, Chinese, and Filipino. In 1970 Japanese Americans constituted the single largest group (41 percent of the Asian American population), followed by Chinese Americans (30 percent) and Filipino Americans (24 percent). Members of other national origins groups (mostly

Koreans) represented less than 5 percent of the Asian American population total (Zhou and Gatewood 2000, 13). Coming of age in the 1960s, U.S.-born Japanese and Chinese Americans formed the core force of the Asian American movement on West Coast college campuses and in the Northeast (Espiritu 1992). In contrast, in 2000 the U.S. census recorded twenty-four national origins groups, and no single group accounted for more than one-quarter of the Asian American population. Although Japan has sent very few immigrants to the United States, the Philippines, China and Taiwan, Korea, India, and Vietnam have been on the list of the top ten sending countries since 1980 (USINS 1997). Reflecting these changing immigration patterns, in 2000 the Japanese American share of the Asian American population fell to only 8 percent, and the five largest Asian American groups were Chinese and Taiwanese (24 percent), Filipino (18 percent), Asian Indian (17 percent), Korean (11 percent), and Vietnamese (11 percent) (Barnes and Bennett 2002).[4] The new Asian American demographics have complicated the delicate pan-Asian alignments created in the 1960s and 1970s among the then-largest Asian American groups: Japanese, Chinese, and, to a lesser extent, Filipino Americans.

Generational Diversification

Between the 1940s and 1960s, when immigration from Asia was restricted, U.S.-born Asian Americans dominated the Asian American population. By the 1970s the foreign-born reemerged as a large majority. In 2000, 7.2 million Asian Pacific Americans—approximately 70 percent of the total Asian American population—were foreign-born (U.S. Department of Commerce 2002). The foreign-born component dominated all Asian American groups except for Japanese Americans; over 60 percent of Filipinos and nearly 80 percent of Vietnamese and other Asians were foreign-born (Zhou and Gatewood 2000, 14). Because of legal exclusion in the past, it is only among the two oldest immigrant groups—the Japanese and Chinese Americans—that a sizable third or fourth generation exists. Among Asian American children under eighteen years of age, more than 90 percent are either foreign-born or children of foreign-born parents (Zhou and Greenwood 2000, 23). Paul Ong and Suzanne Hee (1993) have predicted that the foreign-born segment will still be a majority in the year 2020.

Class Diversification

Post-1965 immigration has also increased the economic diversity of Asian Americans. In contrast to the largely unskilled immigrant population of the pre–World War II period, the new arrivals include not only low-wage service-sector workers but also significant numbers of white-collar professionals. According to the 1990 U.S. census, more than 60 percent of immigrants (age twenty-five or older) from India and Taiwan reported having attained a college degree (three times the proportion of average Americans), but fewer than 5 percent of those from Cambodia and Laos made such a report. Among the employed workers, about 45 percent of immigrants from India and Taiwan held managerial or professional occupations, more than twice the proportion of average American workers, but fewer than 5 percent of those from Laos and only about 10 percent of those from Cambodia had held such a position. Further, immigrants from India, the Philippines, and Taiwan reported a median household income of about $45,000, compared to $30,000 for average American households; those from Cambodia and highland Laos reported a median household income below $20,000. Poverty rates for Asian immigrants ranged from a low of 7 percent for Filipinos, Indians, and Japanese to a high of more than 60 percent for Hmongs and 42 percent for Cambodians, compared to about 10 percent for average American families (Zhou 1999). Given the diversity of economic background, Asian Americans can be found throughout the income spectrum of the United States. In other words, today's Asian Americans join whites in the well-paid, educated, white-collar service sector of the workforce as well as Latino immigrants in lower-paying service and manufacturing jobs (Ong and Hee 1994). Responding to limited job opportunities for highly skilled immigrants, a large number of Asian immigrants have also turned to self-employment (Ong and Hee 1994).

Implications for Panethnicity in Contemporary Asian America

By most accounts, the expanding diversity of Asian Americans has brought into question the very definition of Asian America—and along with it, the feasibility and appropriateness of pan-Asian identities and practices. In a major public policy report on the state of Asian America, editor

Paul Ong (2000) suggests that the pan-Asian identity is "fragile," citing as evidence the group's ethnic and economic diversity as well as the growing population of bi- and multiracial Asian Americans who want to acknowledge their combined racial heritage.[5] Similarly, in the introduction to their substantial multidisciplinary reader on contemporary Asian America, editors Min Zhou and James Gatewood (2000, 27) caution that "differences in class background among the immigrant generation and divergent modes of incorporation of that generation can deter the formation of panethnicity." Comparing the experiences of affluent Chinese immigrants and Cambodian refugees, Aihwa Ong (1996, 751) concludes that the category "Asian American" "must confront the contradictions and instabilities within the imposed solidarity, brought about by the group's internal class, ethnic, and racial stratifications." In Asian American studies, many scholars have critically pointed to the field's privileging of East Asians (the "old" Asian Americans) over South and Southeast Asians (the "new" Asian Americans)—a clear indictment of the suppression of diverse histories, epistemologies, and voices within the pan-Asian framework. For example, in an edited volume on South Asians in Asian America aptly titled *A Part, Yet Apart,* Rajiv Shankar (1998, x) laments that South Asians "find themselves so unnoticed as an entity that they feel as if they are merely a crypto-group, often included but easily marginalized within the house of Asian America.". . .

Pan-Asian National and Transnational Possibilities

As we begin the twenty-first century, the Asian American community is at a crossroads: how is it to build pan-Asian solidarity amid increasing internal diversities and amid an increasingly racially polarized U.S. society? As I have argued here, Asian American panethnicity is a socially constructed identity that emerged in large part from the violence of racism and imperialism to contest and disrupt these structures of inequality and domination. But it is also a contested category, encompassing not only cultural differences but also social, political, and economic inequalities. In the past two decades underrepresented groups within the pan-Asian coalition have decried the dangers of an Asian American cultural and political agenda that erases differences or tokenizes and patronizes its less dominant members (Strobel 1996; Misir 1996; Nguyen 2002). But

pan-Asian possibilities also abound. Since panethnic identities are self-conscious products of political choice and actions, I provide here examples of instances where Asian Americans have made conscious choices to organize politically across difference.

The growing population of bi- and multiracial Asian Americans poses an immediate challenge to pan-Asianism. On the other hand, some existing evidence suggests that the growth in the population of multiracial Asians need not spell the end of pan-Asianism. For example, in their analyses of Asian American intermarriages from 1980 and 1990 census data, Larry Hajime Shinagawa and Gin Yong Pang (1996, 140–41) report a prominent countertrend toward pan-Asian interethnic marriages, regardless of gender, nativity, region, and generation: "For a span of ten years (1980 to 1990), nationally and for California, the number of Asian interethnic marriages approaches or now exceeds interracial marriages. Meanwhile, interethnic marriages for Asian Pacific men increased from 21.1 percent in 1980 to 64 percent in 1990, and for women from 10.8 percent to 45.5 percent." They attribute this rise to a combination of factors, including the large population increases and concentrations of Asian Americans, their growing similarities in socioeconomic attainment and middle-class orientation, and their growing racial consciousness in an increasingly racially stratified U.S. society.

But what of the multiracial children? According to the 2000 U.S. census, approximately 850,000 people reported that they were Asian and white, and 360,000 reported that they were two or more Asian groups (Barnes and Bennett 2000, table 4). While there exist no comprehensive data on the racial identification of multiracial Asians, the close contact with Asian American advocacy groups maintained by the Hapa Issues Forum (HIF)—a national multiracial Asian American organization—suggests that multiracial Asian and pan-Asian identities need not be mutually exclusive. From its inception, HIF has pursued a double political mission: pushing for recognition of multiracial Asians as well as for the civil rights agendas of existing Asian American groups. These two goals are most evident in the group's response to the controversy over the classification of multiracials in the 2000 census. Denouncing the government's past attempts to wedge mixed-race Americans into one rigid racial category, most mainstream multiracial groups favored adding a "multiracial" category to the 2000 census. However, most civil rights groups, including many pan-Asian groups, argued that such a category would dilute the numbers of people who identify with a particular race and cause their respective communities to lose hard-won gains in civil rights, education, and electoral arenas (Espiritu 2001, 31). Refusing this "splitting" of their multiple personal and political identities, HIF's board of directors rejected the "stand-alone multiracial" category and endorsed the "check more than one" format, contending that the latter option would allow them to identify as multiracial *and* "still be counted with their Asian American brethren and sisters" (King 2000, 202). In other words, the "check more than one" format would allow the data to be collected in a way that recognized the existence of multiracial Asians and still make it possible to use the data in "the five racial category format to track discrimination against Asian Americans" (King 2000, 202).

Asian American activists have also engaged in *proactive* efforts to draw together Asian Americans of different classes to organize against anti-Asian racism, defined not as random attacks against Asians but as a product of structural oppression and everyday encounters (Kurashige 2000, 15). The activities of the Asian Americans United, a panethnic community-based organization in Philadelphia, provide an example (Kurashige 2000). When large numbers of Southeast Asian immigrants began experiencing problems in Philadelphia with racist violence, educational inequality, and poor housing, a small group of educated East and South Asian American activists responded. Modeling themselves after the militant Yellow Seeds organization in the 1970s, group members insisted on anti-imperialist politics, a critique of racism as institutional and structural, and a focus on activist organizing and politics. They organized a successful rent strike and were part of a victorious legal campaign to institute bilingual education in the local schools. Most important, they sought to build relationships with working-class Southeast Asian communities by creating a youth leadership training program organized around a pan-Asian identity and radical politics. When a violent attack on Southeast Asian youths in that city by a group of white youths led to a fight that left one of the white attackers dead, city police and prosecutors portrayed the attackers as victims and laid the responsibility for the violence at the hands of the Southeast Asians. Although unable to secure full justice in the court cases that ensued, Asian Americans United seized on the incident as a means of educating its constituency about institutionalized racism. The group succeeded in mobilizing

parts of the Asian American community around these efforts, and its success enabled it to move from panethnic to interethnic affiliation through an alliance with a Puerto Rican youth group also plagued by hate crimes, police brutality, and prosecutorial racism (Espiritu et al. 2000, 132). This example suggests that class need not be a source of cleavage among Asian Americans, and that the concerns of working-class Asian Americans *can* unite people at the grassroots level with class-conscious members of the intellectual and professional strata (Kurashige 2000).

Given our globalizing world and the resultant demographic changes, the construction of an Asian American identity is no longer situated—if indeed it ever was—only within Asian America but also through relations and struggles with other communities of color. Today working-class immigrants of diverse backgrounds coexist with African American and U.S.-born Latinos in urban communities across the country. This "social geography of race" has produced new social subjects and new coalitions. For example, young Laotian women in northern California joined Chinese and Japanese Americans in panethnic struggles against anti-Asian racism and also against the "neighborhood race effects" of underfunded schools, polluted air and water, and low-wage jobs that they and their families share with their African American, Latino, Arab American, and poor white neighbors (Espiritu et al. 2000; Shah 2002). In the same way, recognizing their common histories of political fragmentation and disfranchisement, Japanese, Chinese, and Mexicans in the San Gabriel Valley of Los Angeles County formed political alliances to work together on the redistricting and reapportionment process in the Valley (Saito 1998, 10).

Finally, given the internationalization and feminization of the labor force in recent decades, some Asian women in the United States *and* in Asia have begun to conceive of themselves as similarly situated racial, gendered, and classed subjects. The dominance of women in contemporary immigration reflects the growth of female-intensive industries in the United States, particularly in services, health care, microelectronics, and apparel manufacturing. To escape the tightening labor market, employers in the United States have opted either to shift labor-intensive processes to less-developed countries or to import migrant labor, especially female, to fill low-wage, insecure assembly and service-sector jobs (Lim 1983; Hossfeld 1994). Women thus have become a rapidly growing segment of the world's migratory and international work-force (Sacks and Scheper-Hughes 1987).

For post-1965 immigrant women from Asia, their politically insecure status as "alien" and their limited English proficiency have interacted with geographical segregation, racist and sexist hiring practices, and institutional barriers to recertification by U.S. professional boards to narrow greatly their occupational choices. Consequently, many Asian immigrant women, instead of gaining access to a better, more modern, and more liberated life in the United States, have been confined to low-paying service jobs and factory assembly-line work, especially in the garment and microelectronics industries. The similarities in the labor conditions for Asian women here and in Asia, brought about by global capitalism, constitute the "situating grounds for a strategic transnational affiliation" (Kang 1997, 415). Moreover, examples abound of collaboration amongst capitalists *across* geopolitical boundaries. In the case of the garment industry, the small Asian immigrant garment factories in New York and Los Angeles are significant and fairly well integrated components in a globalized production process (Kang 1997). In other words, Asian women working in the garment and electronics factories in major cities in the United States are virtually part of the same labor force as those employed in export-processing zones in Asia or Latin America. Such simultaneous, transnational linkages in Asian women's working conditions—the similarities between exploitive labor conditions for Asian women in Asia and Asian American women in the United States—could disrupt the First World–Third World binary and call attention to their shared lives across geopolitical boundaries (Kang 1997, 429). Since this is the case, the focus on women's labor within the global economy provides *one* means for linking Third World women, immigrant women, and U.S. women of color. The racialized feminization of labor gives rise to a "common context of struggle" among Asian women within, outside, and across the borders of the United States and has resulted in the establishment of numerous cross-border and transnational women's organizations, such as Gabriela, the support committee for Maquiladora workers, and Asian Immigrant Women Advocates (Lowe 1996).

These cross-racial and cross-border alliances and the radical mobilization around gender issues underscore the centrality of "unlikely coalitions" in contemporary political organizing. As Angela Davis (1997, 322) points out,

we can accomplish important things in the struggle for social justice if we focus on the creation of "unpredictable or unlikely coalitions grounded in political projects." A complex world requires a complex set of alliances. These unlikely coalitions, including pan-Asian coalitions, along with the antiglobal organizations that are seeking to impose workplace and environmental restraints on multinational corporations and capital, could prove a potent force for social change at both the national and global levels.

Conclusion

Since the pan-Asian concept was forged in the late 1960s, the Asian American population has become much more variegated. The post-1965 immigration surge from Asia has fragmented Asian America more clearly than in the past along ethnic, generational, and class lines. This increasing diversity has brought into question the very feasibility and appropriateness of pan-Asian identities and practices, challenging Asian Americans to take seriously the social, political, and economic inequalities that exist within their communities. My main contention in this chapter is that we cannot examine Asian American panethnicity solely in terms of racial politics within the framework of the U.S. nation-state. While important, this framework narrowly focuses on identity politics within Asian America, not on the global politics and power that produced massive displacements and migrations of Asians in the first place. Calling for a critical transnational perspective on the study of panethnicity, I argue instead that different circumstances of exit—the product of different types of U.S. engagement in different Asian countries—have shaped the size and timing of migration and the socioeconomic profile of different Asian groups and thus have profoundly affected their group formation and differentiation in the United States. This approach expands the discussion on pan-Asian ethnicity by viewing it as an integral part not only of Asian American studies or American studies but also of international and transnational studies. In all, the examples cited in this chapter confirm the plural and ambivalent nature of panethnicity: it is a highly contested terrain on which Asian Americans merge and clash over terms of inclusion but also an effective site from which to forge crucial alliances with other groups both within and across the borders of the United States in their ongoing efforts to effect larger social transformation.

Seeing the Big Picture **Panethnic Fortunes: Riches *and* Rags**

Look at Asians relative to other groups in Sections VI (Income, Wealth, and Poverty), VII (Employment), and VIII (Occupations) in the Appendix. Might panethnic identity formation as a political strategy explain the relative success of Asians? How?

12 Beyond Black and White: Remaking Race in America

Jennifer Lee • Frank D. Bean

Jennifer Lee is an associate professor in the department of sociology at the University of California, Irvine, and received her B.A. and Ph.D. degrees from Columbia University. She is author of *Civility in the City: Blacks, Jews, and Koreans in Urban America* (2002) and co-editor (with Min Zhou) of *Asian American Youth: Culture, Identity, and Ethnicity* (2004).

Frank D. Bean is a professor of sociology at the University of California, Irvine, and the co-director of the Center for Research on Immigration, Population and Public Policy. He is former director of the Center for U.S./Mexico Border and Migration Research at the University of Texas, Austin. His current research examines four areas: the intersection of race/ethnicity in the United States, immigration and U.S. welfare patterns, migration within and from Mexico, and the effects of immigration on labor markets. He is the author of *America's Newcomers and the Dynamics of Diversity* (2003).

S TARTING WITH THE 2000 CENSUS, AMERICANS could officially label themselves and their children as members of more than one race. Nearly 7 million Americans, 2.4 percent of the nation's population, were recorded as being multiracial. This option and these numbers signal a profound loosening of the rigid racial and ethnic boundaries that have so long divided the country. The immigration patterns behind these changes also

Questions to Consider   Much has been made of recent U.S. Census reports that Latinos are now the largest racial minority in the United States. Equally important but not as widely addressed in the media has been the relative explosion of individuals who self-identify as "multiracial." Tiger Woods (Cablinasian: Caucasian-Black-Indian-Asian), Vin Diesel (white Italian-American and African American) and Halle Berry (white mother and African American father) each have made a point to publicly celebrate and affirm their hybrid ethnic and racial identities. What do Lee and Bean say these trends mean for the future of the color line as the children of mixed-race unions age out and have their own children? Will racial categories as we know them blur into one another or are we likely to see new categories emerge that serve to maintain racial hierarchy and inequality?

point to potentially important realignments in America's color lines.

How might a black father and a white mother fill out official government documents, like U. S. Census forms, requiring them to designate the race of their child? Before 2000, such an intermarried couple had no alternative but to list their child as either black or white. Similarly, a child born to a white father and an Asian mother had to be listed as either Asian or white, but not Asian and white. Not any more. Americans can now officially identify themselves and their children as black and white, or white and Asian. Indeed, respondents can now choose a combination of up to six different categories of races, including "Other." The 2000 Census reported one in every forty Americans was registered as belonging to two or more racial groups. Many sociologists think this ratio could soar to one in five Americans by the year 2050.

Why does this checking of additional boxes matter? For one thing, how people report themselves racially provides information needed to implement and enforce important legislation, such as the **Voting Rights Act.** The Department of Justice uses the statistics to identify places where substantial minority populations exist and may be subject to disenfranchisement. For another, the counts document social and economic disparities among racial groups in America. Countries like France that do not collect data on race cannot verify the existence and effects of racial discrimination even when other evidence suggests such discrimination is a major problem. These data also signal the official recognition and hence the influence of groups that define themselves on the basis of common national origin, skin color or ancestry. Americans of Pacific Islander origin, for example, recently asked to be separately classified. On the other hand, critics worry that official data on race perpetuate rather than eliminate racial identities and divisions. A ballot initiative being circulated in California, for example, would largely ban the state's collection of racial information.

But the new opportunity to mark more than one race is also important because it indicates that people can now officially recognize the mixing of racial backgrounds in American society. If the United States was once thought of as a black-and-white society, this is certainly no longer so. Continued immigration from Latin America and Asia, the rise in intermarriage over the past 30 years, and the formal

Voting Rights Act Civil rights legislation signed into law by President Lyndon Johnson in 1965, making obstacles to voting (poll taxes and literacy tests) illegal. These measures had been used in the South to disenfranchise blacks.

recognition of the multiracial population are moving America far beyond black and white. Yet while America's increasing diversity implies that racial divisions may be weakening, it does not mean that race has become irrelevant. Instead, new kinds of color lines may be emerging. For now, however, the rearrangement seems to leave African Americans facing a new black-nonblack, instead of the old black-white, racial divide.

Why There Are More Multiracial Americans

The growth of the multiracial population is a result both of increasing intermarriage between whites and nonwhites and of people's increasing willingness to report their multiracial backgrounds. The number of racial intermarriages in the United States grew from 150,000 in 1960 to 1.6 million in 1990—a tenfold increase over three decades. It is still the exception rather than the rule for whites and blacks in this country, however. Just 6 percent of whites and 10 percent of blacks marry someone of a different race. By contrast, more than one-quarter of all native-born Asians and Latinos marry someone of a different race. (For this discussion, we will speak of Latinos as if they were a "race," although government forms count Hispanic background separately, so that people who say they are Latino can report themselves as belonging to any racial group, such as white, black, or Asian.) Even more striking is that two of every five young Latinos and two of every three young Asians born in the United States marry someone of a different race, and the majority marry whites. Asians and Latinos—many of whom are either immigrants or the children of immigrants—are three times as likely to marry whites as blocks are to marry whites.

Coinciding with the rise in intermarriage has been the growth of a new immigrant stream from Latin America and Asia. Today, immigrants and their children total more than 60 million people, approximately 22 percent of the U.S. population. The increase in immigration from non-European countries over the past 35 years has converted the United States from a largely white and black society into one that is comprised of numerous racial and ethnic groups. This, plus increasing intermarriage, and the increasing willingness of Americans to call themselves multiracial has changed the way race is measured in America.

Constructing Race

Social scientists generally agree that race is not a biological category, but a social and cultural construction, meaning that racial distinctions have not existed since time immemorial, are not rooted in biology and are not fixed. Rather, they have changed and been reinterpreted throughout our nation's history. For instance, when the Irish, Italians, and Jews first arrived in the United States in the 19th century, Anglo Americans considered them racially distinct and inferior. They were not considered white. However, they successfully achieved "whiteness" by deliberately and forcefully distinguishing themselves from African Americans. Today, few would contest the claim that the Irish, Italians and Jews are white.

Race and racial boundaries have changed for other groups as well. For example, Asian ethnic groups like the Chinese in Mississippi have changed their racial status from almost black to almost white. Sociologist James Loewen details how the Chinese there achieved near-white status by becoming as economically successful as whites, copying their cultural and social practices, and distancing themselves from African Americans and Chinese Mississippians who married African Americans.

As historian Gary Gerstle explains, whiteness as a category "has survived by stretching its boundaries to include Americans—the Irish, eastern and southern Europeans—who had been deemed nonwhite. Contemporary evidence suggests that the boundaries are again being stretched as Latinos and Asians pursue whiteness much as the Irish, Italians, and Poles did before them." Given the change in racial boundaries over time, it is likely that the boundaries may continue to stretch to include newer groups. For instance, some sociologists argue that Asians are the next in line to become white. Whether or not they do, we should understand that race is a cultural product that has changed over time, rather than a fixed, primordial category rooted in biology.

The Origin of "Mark One or More Races"

Since its inception in 1790, the decennial U.S. Census has determined taxation, the numbers of representatives from each state, and the boundaries of Congressional districts. And it has always counted the U.S. population by race. The way that race is measured and even the racial categories themselves, however, have changed considerably. For example, in 1850, the Census added the category "mulatto," and in 1890, it added the categories "quadroon" and "octoroon" in an effort to more precisely measure the representation of black mixtures in the population. ("Mulatto" refers to people of mixed black and white "blood," "quadroon" to people with one-fourth black blood, and "octoroon" to those with one-eighth black blood.) However, "quadroon" and "octoroon" were promptly removed in 1900 because they caused countless statistical inaccuracies. The Census Board determined that the "mulatto" category provided clearer data on the U.S. population with mixed blood, but eventually dropped this category in 1930. By that time, the law of the country, with the census following suit, had adopted the "one-drop rule" of hypodescent (by which all persons with any trace of black ancestry were labeled racially black) as an appropriate criterion by which to attempt to measure race. Importantly, census enumerators classified the people they interviewed by race.

In the 1960s, racial categories came under scrutiny once again, and the Civil Rights Movement prompted one of the most significant changes in the political context and purpose of racial categorization. The argument spread that Americans should be able to mark their own race to identify themselves and their children rather than leaving this to enumerators. Some politicians and experts asserted that the racial categories should more accurately reflect America's diversity and lobbied for new categories, distinguishing among categories of whites, and substituting the term "ethnic" in place of "race." Changes in the 1970 Census reflected some of these currents, with self-identification replacing enumerator identification in order to satisfy public sentiments. By the mid-1970s, groups wanting to be recognized as racial minorities organized advisory committees to seek official statistical representation so that they could participate in federal programs designed to assist racial "minorities." These advisory committees lobbied for the adoption of five racial categories—white, black, Asian, Native American, and other—by the Census and all federal agencies. In 1980, the Census categories changed yet again, this time including the category of Hispanic origin separately from race, and modifying one of the racial categories to Asian–Pacific Islander.

During the early 1990s, new advocacy groups arose with a different agenda. These groups criticized the government standards for not accurately reflecting the diversity in the country brought about by increases in immigration and interracial marriage. In particular, advocates from groups such as the Association for Multi-Ethnic Americans (AMEA) and Project RACE (Reclassify All Children Equally) lobbied the Census Bureau to adopt a "multiracial" category. Advocates argued that it was an affront to force them or their children into a single racial category. Furthermore, they argued that forced mono-racial identification was inaccurate because it denies the existence of interracial marriages, and is ultimately discriminatory. A year later in 1994, the Office of Management and Budget (OMB), which managed this issue, acknowledged that the racial categories were of decreasing value and considered an alternate strategy: allowing respondents to identify with as many races as they wished. While the spokespeople for the multiracial movement were not entirely satisfied with this option, they conceded that it was an improvement over forced mono-racial identification.

Not everyone favored adding a multiracial category or allowing Americans to mark more than one race. Civil rights groups—and in particular, black civil rights groups such as the NAACP—strongly objected. They feared that those who would otherwise be counted as black or Hispanic would now choose to identify as multiracial, and, depending on how such persons were counted, diminish their official counts. This, in turn, could undermine enforcement of the Voting Rights Act and potentially reduce the size and effectiveness of government programs aimed at helping minorities.

On October 30, 1997 the Census Bureau announced its final decision that all persons would have the option to identify with two or more races, starting with the 2000 Census and extending to all federal data systems by the year 2003. The racial options on the 2000 Census included "White," "Black," "Asian," "Native Hawaiian or Other Pacific Islander," "American Indian and Alaska Native," and "Other." While "Latino" or "Hispanic" was not a racial category on the 2000 Census, OMB mandated two distinct questions: one on race and a second asking whether a person is "Spanish/Hispanic/Latino." Because those who classify themselves as "Spanish/Hispanic/Latino" can be of any race, the Census asks both questions in order to identify the Latino population in the United States.

The Census Bureau's decision to allow Americans to "mark one or more races" is a landmark change in the way the U.S. government collects data on race. Perhaps even more importantly, it gives official status and recognition to individuals who see themselves or their children as having mixed racial heritage—an acknowledgement that speaks volumes about how far the country has come since the days when the "one-drop rule" enjoyed legal legitimacy. Moreover, such changes may mean that old racial divides are beginning to fade. Multiracial reporting, however, has not been equally distributed across all racial and ethnic groups. Rather, those who choose to mark two or more races are distinctive.

Who Are the Multiracials?

Interracial marriage was illegal in 16 states as recently as 1967, but today, about 13 percent of American marriages involve persons of different races. If we go back even further to 1880, the rates of intermarriage among Asians and Latinos in this country were close to zero, but now, more than a quarter of all native-born Asians and Latinos marry someone of a different racial background, mostly whites. As we noted, in 2000, 6.8 million people, or 2.4 percent of the population, were reported as multiracial. While these figures may not appear large, a recent National Academy of Science study estimated that the multiracial population could rise to 21 percent by the year 2050 because of rising intermarriage, when as many as 35 percent of Asians and 45 percent of Hispanics could claim a multiracial background. Of the multiracial population in 2000, 93 percent reported two races, 6 percent reported three races, and 1 percent reported four or more races.

As Table 1 illustrates, the groups with high percentages of multiracial persons include "Native Hawaiian or Other Pacific Islander," "American Indian and Alaska Native," "Other," and "Asian." The categories with the lowest proportion of persons who claim a multiracial background are "White" and "Black."

The proportion of blacks who identify as multiracial is quite small, accounting for just 4.2 percent of the total black population. These figures stand in sharp contrast to those among American Indian/Alaska Natives and Native Hawaiian or other Pacific Islanders who have the highest percentage of multiracials as a proportion of their populations at 36.4 and 44.8 percent, respectively. The particular combinations are of interest. Among those identified as black, Asian, or Latino, 2 percent, 7 percent, and

TABLE 1   Multiracial Identification by Race: People Recorded as One Race Who Are Also Recorded as One or More Other Races

	Racial Identification (millions)	Multiracial Identification (millions)	Percent Multiracial
White	216.5	5.1	2.3%
Black	36.2	1.5	4.2
Asian	11.7	1.4	12.4
Other	18.4	3.0	16.4
American Indian and Alaska Native	3.9	1.4	36.4
Native Hawaiian or other Pacific Islander	0.7	0.3	44.8

Source: U.S. Census 2000.

5 percent, respectively, also claim a White identity. Among Asians, the Asian-white multiracial combination is about three and a half times more likely to occur, and among Latinos, the Latino-white combination is more than two and a half times more likely to occur, as the black-white combination occurs among blacks. Why this is so is particularly perplexing when we consider that the Census Bureau has estimated that at least three-quarters of black Americans have some white ancestry and thus could claim a multiracial identity on this basis alone.

The tendency of black Americans not to report multiracial identifications undoubtedly owes in part to the legacy of slavery, lasting discrimination, and both the legal and de facto invocation of the "one-drop rule." For no other racial or ethnic group in the United States does the one-drop rule limit identity choices and options. Recent sociological studies find that about 50 percent of American Indian-white and Asian-white intermarried couples report a white racial identity for their children. In a study of multiracial Hispanic students, we found that 44 percent chose a Hispanic identity. Without the imposition of the "one-drop rule" that historically imposed a black racial identity on multiracial black Americans, multiracial Asians, Latinos, and American Indians appear to have much more leeway to choose among different racial options.

In addition, because a significant proportion of Latinos and Asians in the United States are either immigrants

or the children of immigrants, their understanding of race, racial boundaries, and the black-white color divide is shaped by a different set of circumstances than those of African Americans. Most importantly, Latinos' and Asians' experiences are not rooted in the same legacy of slavery with its systematic and persistent patterns of legal and institutional discrimination and inequality through which the tenacious black-white divide was formed and cemented. For these reasons, racial and ethnic boundaries appear more fluid for the newest immigrants than for native-born blacks, providing multiracial Asians and Latinos more racial options than their black counterparts.

Remaking Race and Redrawing the Color Line

What do current trends and patterns in immigration, intermarriage, and multiracial identification tell us about the remaking of race in America? It appears that increases in intermarriage and the growth of the multiracial population reflect a blending of races and the shifting of color lines. Because interracial marriage and multiracial identification indicate a reduction in social distance and racial prejudice, these phenomena provide evidence of loosening racial boundaries. At first glance, these patterns offer an optimistic portrait of the weakening of color lines. For instance, interracial marriage was illegal in 16 states as recently as 1967, but today, about 13 percent of American marriages involve persons of different races. If we go back even further to 1880, the rates of intermarriage among Asians and Latinos in this country were close to zero, but now, more than a quarter of all native-born Asians and Latinos marry someone of a different racial background, mostly whites.

Yet, upon closer examination, we find that patterns of intermarriage and multiracial identification are not similar across all groups. Not only are Latinos and Asians more likely to intermarry than blacks, they are also more likely to report a multiracial identification. These different rates suggest that while racial boundaries may be fading, they are not disappearing at the same pace for all groups.

What is crucial here is how we interpret the intermarriage and multiracial identification rates for Latinos and Asians. If we consider Latinos and Asians as discriminated-against racial minorities, closer to blacks than whites in their social disadvantages, then their high levels of multiracial identification suggest that racial border lines might be fading for all nonwhite groups. Latinos and Asians look more, however, like immigrant groups whose disadvantages derive from their not having had time to join the economic mainstream, but who soon will. Their high levels of intermarriage and multiracial reporting therefore signal an experience and trajectory different from that of blacks. Their situations do not necessarily indicate that similar assimilation can be expected among blacks.

Based on the patterns of intermarriage and multiracial identification noted above, the color line appears less rigid for Latinos and Asians than blacks. Asians and Latinos have high rates of intermarriage and multiracial reporting because they were not and are not treated as blacks have been. While the color line may also be shifting for blacks, this shift is occurring more slowly, leaving Asians and Latinos socially nearer to whites. Much of America's racial history has revolved around who was white and who was not; the next phase may revolve instead around who is black and who is not.

The emergence of a black-nonblack divide in a context where diversity is increasing and other racial and ethnic boundaries are diminishing represents a good news–bad news outcome for America. That a white-nonwhite color line does not seem to be enduring is the good news. But that newer nonwhite immigrant groups appear to be jumping ahead of African Americans in a hierarchy still divided by race is the bad news. Based on immigration, intermarriage, and multiracial identification, it appears that Latinos and Asians are closer to whites than to blacks, and consequently may be participants in a new color line that continues to disadvantage blacks.

As a final matter, one might ask: What does all of this imply for the future of measuring race in the census? Critics of racial labels argue that if racial and ethnic boundaries are loosening, we should abandon the use of racial categories in the census altogether and learn to get along without them in our policy making. They argue that if racial labels could be eliminated, racial discrimination itself would be eradicated. However, in the United States today, because the practice of discrimination based on physical characteristics such as skin color continues to persist, at least for African Americans, eradicating racial labels would simply put us in a position where we know less about the disadvantages experienced by blacks and can do less about it.

Seeing the Big Picture   Check All That Apply (Finally!): The Institutionalization of Mixed Race Identity

Section X in the Appendix lists the percentage of Americans who identify with more than one race. How might you interpret the fact that Latino and American Indians are more likely than whites or blacks to claim more than one race?

COLOR-BLIND AMERICA ~
Fact, Fantasy, or Our Future?

SORTING BY COLOR SORTING BY COLOR
SORTING BY COLOR SORTING BY COLOR SO
BY COLOR SORTING BY COLOR SORTING
BY COLOR SORTING BY COLOR SORTING BY

13 Color-Blind Privilege: The Social and Political Functions of Erasing the Color Line in Post-Race America

Charles A. Gallagher

CHARLES A. GALLAGHER is professor and chair of the Department of Sociology, Social Work and Criminal Justice at La Salle University in Philadelphia. His research focuses on racial and social inequality, immigration, urban sociology, and the ways in which the media, the state, and popular culture construct, shape, and disseminate ideas of race. He has published articles on the sociological functions of color-blind political narratives, how racial categories expand and contract within the context of interracial marriages, race theory, racial innumeracy, and how one's ethnic history shapes perceptions of privilege. Professor Gallagher can be reached at gallagher@lasalle.edu.

Questions to Consider The dominant view in the United States is that we are now a color-blind nation. Rap and hip-hop are thoroughly mainstream commodities available for sale in every mall across the country. Celebrities, CEOs, high-level politicians, and opinion makers are drawn from every racial and ethnic group. Race, the mainstream media would have us believe, no longer matters. Charles A. Gallagher argues that the story of color blindness promoted in the mass media disguises a more troubling reality: continued racial inequality. How does presenting the United States as a color-blind nation serve various political, ideological, and social functions?

Introduction

An adolescent white male at a bar mitzvah wears a FUBU[1] shirt while his white friend preens his tightly set, perfectly braided corn rows. A black model dressed in yachting attire peddles a New England yuppie boating look in Nautica advertisements. It is quite unremarkable to observe whites, Asians, or African Americans with dyed purple, blond, or red hair. White, black, and Asian students decorate their bodies with tattoos of Chinese characters and symbols. In cities and suburbs, young adults across the color line wear hip-hop clothing and listen to white rapper Eminem and black rapper Jay-Z. A north Georgia branch of the NAACP installs a white biology professor as its president. The music of Jimi Hendrix is used to sell Apple Computers. Du-Rag kits, complete with bandana headscarf and elastic headband, are on sale for $2.95 at hip-hop clothing stores and family-centered theme parks like Six Flags. Salsa has replaced ketchup as the best-selling condiment in the United States.

Companies as diverse as Polo, McDonald's, Tommy Hilfiger, Walt Disney World, MasterCard, Skechers sneakers, IBM, Giorgio Armani, and Neosporin antibiotic ointment have each crafted advertisements that show a balanced, multiracial cast of characters interacting and consuming their products in a post-race, color-blind world.[2]

Americans are constantly bombarded by depictions of race relations in the media which suggest that discriminatory racial barriers have been dismantled. Social and cultural indicators suggest that America is on the verge, or has already become, a truly color-blind nation. National polling data indicate that a majority of whites now believe discrimination against racial minorities no longer exists. A majority of whites believe that blacks have as good a chance as whites in procuring housing and employment or achieving middle-class status while a 1995 survey of white adults found that a majority of whites (58%) believed that African Americans were better off finding jobs than whites.[3] Much of white America now sees a level playing field, while a majority of black Americans see a field which is still quite uneven. Best-selling books like *The End of Racism*[4] and *Color-Blind: Seeing Beyond Race in a Race-Obsessed World* suggest the United States is not very far from making **color blindness** a social and political reality.[5] The color-blind or race neutral perspective holds that in an environment where institutional racism and discrimination have been replaced by equal opportunity, one's qualifications, not one's color or ethnicity, should be the mechanism by which upward mobility is achieved. Whites and blacks differ significantly, however, on their support for affirmative action, the perceived fairness of the criminal justice system, the ability to acquire the "American Dream," and the extent to which whites have benefited from past discrimination.[6]

This article examines the social and political functions color blindness serves for whites in the United States. Drawing on information compiled from interviews and focus groups with whites around the country, I argue that color blindness maintains white privilege by negating racial inequality. Embracing a post-race, color-blind perspective provides whites with a degree of psychological comfort by allowing them to imagine that being white or black or brown has no bearing on an individual's or a group's relative place in the socioeconomic hierarchy. My research included interviews with seventeen focus groups and thirty individual whites around the country. While my sample is not representative of the total white population, I used personal contacts and snowball sampling to purposively locate respondents raised in urban, suburban, and rural environments. Twelve of the seventeen focus groups were conducted in a university setting, one in a liberal arts college in the Rocky Mountains and the other at a large urban university in the Northeast. Respondents in

these focus groups were selected randomly from the student population. The occupational range for my individual interviews was quite eclectic and included a butcher, construction worker, hair stylist, partner in a prestigious corporate law firm, executive secretary, high school principal, bank president from a small town, retail workers, country lawyer, and custodial workers. Twelve of the thirty individual interviews were with respondents who were raised in rural and/or agrarian settings. The remaining respondents lived in suburbs of large cities or in urban areas.

What linked this rather disparate group of white individuals together was their belief that race-based privilege had ended. As a majority of my respondents saw it, color blindness was now the norm in the United States. The illusion of racial equality implicit in the myth of color blindness was, for many whites, a form of comfort. This aspect of pleasure took the form of political empowerment ("what about whites' rights") and moral gratification from being liberated from "oppressor" charges ("we are not responsible for the past"). The rosy picture that color blindness presumes about race relations and the satisfying sense that one is part of a period in American history that is morally superior to the racist days of the past is, quite simply, a less stressful and more pleasurable social place for whites to inhabit.

The Norm of Color Blindness

The perception among a majority of white Americans that the socioeconomic playing field is now level, along with whites' belief that they have purged themselves of overt racist attitudes and behaviors, has made color blindness the dominant lens through which whites understand contemporary race relations. Color blindness allows whites to believe that segregation and discrimination are no longer an issue because it is now illegal for individuals to be denied access to housing, public accommodations, or jobs because of their race. Indeed, lawsuits alleging institutional racism against companies like Texaco, Denny's, Coca-Cola, and Cracker Barrel validate what many whites know at a visceral level is true; firms which deviate from the color-blind norms embedded in **classic liberalism** will be punished. As a political ideology, the commodification and mass marketing of products that signify color

---

color blindness This term can be understood in two ways: the idea that we *should* live in a society where people are treated equally regardless of their skin color, or the belief that we *are now* a color-blind society where race no longer shapes life chances.

classic liberalism A school of thought stressing individual freedom and limited government.

but are intended for consumption across the color line further legitimate color blindness. Almost every household in the United States has a television that, according to the U.S. Census, is on for seven hours every day.[7] Individuals from any racial background can wear hip-hop clothing, listen to rap music (both purchased at Wal-Mart) and root for their favorite, majority black, professional sports team. Within the context of racial symbols that are bought and sold in the market, color blindness means that one's race has no bearing on who can purchase an SUV, live in an exclusive neighborhood, attend private schools, or own a Rolex.

The passive interaction whites have with people of color through the media creates the impression that little, if any, socioeconomic difference exists between the races. Research has found that whites who are exposed to images of upper-middle-class African Americans, like the Huxtable family in *The Cosby Show,* believe that blacks have the same socioeconomic opportunities as whites.[8] Highly visible and successful racial minorities like Secretary of State Colin Powell and National Security Advisor Condoleezza Rice are further proof to white America that the nation's efforts to enforce and promote racial equality have been accomplished. Reflecting on the extent to which discrimination is an obstacle to socioeconomic advancement and the perception of seeing African Americans in leadership roles, Tom explained:

> If you look at some prominent black people in society today, and I don't really see [racial discrimination], I don't understand how they can keep bringing this problem onto themselves. If they did what society would want them to, I don't see that society is making problems for them. I don't see it.

The achievement ideology implicit in the color-blind perspective is also given legitimacy and stripped of any racist implications by black neoconservatives like anti–affirmative action advocate Ward Connerly, Shelby Steele, and Clarence Thomas, and Asian American Secretary of Labor Elaine Chou.[9] Each espouses a color-blind, race neutral doctrine that treats race-based government programs as a violation of the sacrosanct belief that American society only recognizes the rights of individuals. These individuals also serve as an important public example that in a post-race, color-blind society climbing the occupational ladder is now a matter of individual choice.

The new color-blind ideology does not, however, ignore race; it acknowledges race while ignoring racial hierarchy by taking racially coded styles and products and

reducing these symbols to commodities or experiences which whites and racial minorities can purchase and share. It is through such acts of shared consumption that race becomes nothing more than an innocuous cultural signifier. Large corporations have made American culture more homogenous through the ubiquity of fast food, television, and shopping malls but this trend has also created the illusion that we are all the same through consumption. Most adults eat at national fast-food chains like McDonald's, shop at mall anchor stores like Sears and J. C. Penney's, and watch major league sports, situation comedies, or television dramas. Defining race only as cultural symbols that are for sale allows whites to experience and view race as nothing more than a benign cultural marker that has been stripped of all forms of institutional, discriminatory or coercive power. The post-race, color-blind perspective allows whites to imagine that depictions of racial minorities working in high status jobs and consuming the same products, or at least appearing in commercials for products whites desire or consume, is the same as living in a society where color is no longer used to allocate resources or shape group outcomes. By constructing a picture of society where racial harmony is the norm, the color-blind perspective functions to make white privilege invisible while removing from public discussion the need to maintain any social programs that are race-based.

How then is color blindness linked to privilege? Starting with the deeply held belief that America is now a meritocracy, whites are able to imagine that the socioeconomic success they enjoy relative to racial minorities is a function of individual hard work, determination, thrift, and investments in education. The color-blind perspective removes from personal thought and public discussion any taint or suggestion of white supremacy or white guilt while legitimating the existing social, political, and economic arrangements that whites are privileged to receive. This perspective insinuates that class and culture, and not institutional racism, are responsible for social inequality. Color blindness allows whites to define themselves as politically progressive and racially tolerant as they proclaim their adherence to a belief system that does not see or judge individuals by the "color of their skin." This perspective ignores, as Ruth Frankenberg puts it, how whiteness is a "location of structural advantage societies structured in racial dominance."[10] Frankenberg uses the term "color and power evasiveness" rather than color blindness to convey how the ability to ignore race by members of the dominant group reflects a position of power and privilege. Color blindness hides white privilege behind a mask of assumed meritocracy while rendering invisible the institutional arrangements that perpetuate racial inequality. The veneer of equality implied in color blindness allows whites to present their place in the racialized social structure as one that was earned.

Given the pervasiveness of color blindness, it was not surprising that respondents in this study believed that using race to promote group interests was a form of racism. Joe, a student in his early twenties from a working-class background, was quite adamant that the opportunity structure in the United States did not favor one racial group over another.

> I mean, I think that the black person of our age has as much opportunity as me, maybe he didn't have the same guidance and that might hurt him. But I mean, he's got the same opportunities that I do to go to school, maybe even more, to get more money. I can't get any aid. . . . I think that blacks have the same opportunities as whites nowadays and I think it's old hat.

Not only does Joe believe that young blacks and whites have similar educational experiences and opportunity but it is his contention that blacks are more likely or able to receive money for higher education. The idea that race matters in any way, according to Joe, is anachronistic; it is "old hat" in a color-blind society to blame one's shortcomings on something as irrelevant as race.

Believing and acting as if America is now color blind allows whites to imagine a society where institutional racism no longer exists and racial barriers to upward mobility have been removed. The use of group identity to challenge the existing racial order by making demands for the amelioration of racial inequities is viewed as racist because such claims violate the belief that we are a nation that recognizes the rights of individuals, not rights demanded by groups. Sam, an upper-middle-class respondent in his twenties, draws on a pre– and post–civil rights framework to explain racial opportunity among his peers:

> I guess I can understand my parents' generation. My parents are older, my dad is almost sixty and my mother is in her mid-fifties, ok? But the kids I'm going to school with, the minorities I'm going to school with, I don't think they should use racism as an excuse for not getting a job. Maybe their parents, sure, I mean they were discriminated against. But these kids have *every* opportunity that I do to do well.

In one generation, as Sam sees it, the color line has been erased. Like Sam's view that there are opportunities for all, there is, according to Tara, a reason to celebrate the current state of race relations.

> I mean, like you are not the only people that have been persecuted—I mean, yeah, you have been, but so has every group. I mean, if there's any time to be black in America, it's now.

Seeing society as race neutral serves to decouple past historical practices and social conditions from present-day racial inequality. A number of respondents viewed society this way and pointed out that job discrimination had ended. Michelle was quite direct in her perception that the labor market is now free of discrimination, stating that "don't think people hire and fire because someone is black and white now." Ken also believed that discrimination in hiring did not occur since racial minorities now have legal recourse if discrimination occurs.

> I think that pretty much we got past that point as far as jobs. I think people realize that you really can't discriminate that way because you will end up losing . . . because you will have a lawsuit against you.

Critical race theorist David Theo Goldberg sees this narrative as part of the "continued insistence on implementing an ideal of color-blindness [that] either denies historical reality and its abiding contemporary legacies, or serves to cut off any claims to contemporary entitlements."[11] It also means that whites can picture themselves as victims of reverse discrimination and racism, as Anne, a woman in a focus group explained:

> Why is it so important to forget about, you know, white people's rights? I mean, not that, not being racist or anything, but why is it such a big deal that they have to have it their way or no way when it should be a compromise between the two, and the whites should be able to voice their opinions as much as the blacks do.

There is the belief that whites have been silenced by race politics and as Jodie explains, "The tables have turned where they're getting more rights than we have. Like it never balanced out."

The logic inherent in the color-blind approach is circular; since race no longer shapes life opportunities in a color-blind world, there is no need to take race into account when discussing differences in outcomes between racial groups. This approach erases America's racial hierarchy by implying that social, economic, and political power and mobility are equally shared among all racial groups. Ignoring the extent or ways in which race shapes life opportunities validates whites' social location in the existing racial hierarchy while legitimating the political and economic arrangements that perpetuate and reproduce racial inequality and privilege.

Color Is Now a Matter of Choice

Leslie Carr suggests "the roots of color-blind ideology are found in classic liberal doctrines of freedom—the freedom of the individual created by the free capitalist marketplace."[12] Within the context of a free-market model, color blindness has come to mean that ignoring or attending to one's racial identity is a matter of individual choice, much like the ways in which whites can choose whether or not to emphasize part of their ethnic background. Many whites, for example, claim to be Irish on St. Patty's Day. Some Italian Americans feel purchasing a meal at the Olive Garden Restaurant is an ethnic dining experience that reconnects them to their immigrant past or fictive ethnic family tree. Some whites don kilts at Highlander Fairs or dress as medieval artisans or knights at Renaissance Festivals. These individuals experience their ethnicity as an option. There is no social cost to "being ethnic" for a day, nor does this voluntary behavior circumscribe opportunities in life. The color-blind narrative holds that affirming racial identity is, like whites who have the luxury of an **optional ethnicity,** an individual, voluntary decision.[13] If pride in one's ethnicity and by extension one's color is a matter of choice, then race no longer matters as an independent force which organizes social life, allocates resources, or creates obstacles to upward mobility.[14] In **post-race,** color-blind America, one can now consume images and products for, from, and about any racial or ethnic group. Racial styles, like clothing fashion, food choices, or musical preferences are like interchangeable, mix-and-match commodities for sale at the mall.

The color-blind narrative allows racial identity to be acknowledged in individual and superficial ways but using

optional ethnicity A form of ethnicity that one can pick and choose. There is little or no social cost to engaging in optional ethnicity, as in someone is being "Irish" on St. Patrick's Day even though this person does not think about being Irish during the rest of the year.

post-race The notion that race is no longer relevant in politics, culture, or economics. The post-race perspective posits that racism no longer shapes individuals' life chances.

race to assert group demands violates the cherished notion that as a nation we recognize the rights of individuals rather than group rights. Within the color-blind perspective, it is understood that one does not choose one's race, but one should be conscious, or at least cautious, not to make race more than background cultural information. In a post-race, color-blind world, race can be seen, but pointing out race-based inequities should not be heard. The idea of identity, race, and the fluidity of individual choices was part of Jeff's explanation of race relations:

> It just seems like a gap's been bridged, where people don't have like separate things. You know, like in past generations there were things that each group had to itself, but now it's like there are plenty of things you can find in, like, black people that white people do. You know, there's music; rap music is no longer, . . . it's not a black thing anymore. . . . When it first came out, it was black music, but now it's just music. It's another choice, just like country music can be considered like white hick music or whatever. You know, it's just a choice.

Tom makes the point that race categories exist, but assimilation allows any individual to become an American, if they so choose:

> Blacks don't seem, poor blacks seem like they're more immigrant than we are.
> Interviewer: In what way?
> Because they try to keep pushing the differences. You know, like I said, the Asians just meld in a little bit better than the blacks. . . . Why do they have to be caught up in being African American? They've been in America all their lives. They were born here. They're not African Americans. That's just separate.

There was the perception that Asians did not embrace identity politics or use their racial identity to promote group rights. As Mike, a young white man in a focus group told me:

> It's just becoming like really, really popular for black students to be black and proud and racist. But with Asians, it's not that way. I mean there is a magazine *Ebony* for strictly black people— I've never really read it. I mean there is no magazine for just Asian people. There's nothing saying, like, "Asian power."

Comedian Chris Rock points to how erasing the color line and color blindness are linked when he asked rhetorically "What does it say about America when the greatest golfer in the world [Tiger Woods] is black and the greatest rapper [Eminem] is white." Rock's message is clear: No role or occupation (at least in sports and music) is now determined by skin color. By allowing anyone to claim ownership of racial styles, color-blind narratives negate the ways in which race continues to circumscribe opportunities in life. The color-blind approach requires that these preferences, while racially bracketed, be available to all for purchase or consumption. At its core, the color-blind philosophy holds that racial minorities can succeed if they rid themselves of any notion that their race entitles them to special treatment. Racial identity can still be expressed or acknowledged, but one's race should mean nothing more than a tendency towards individualistic expressions, like music, foods, or clothes.

Within the color-blind perspective, it is not race per se which determines upward mobility, but how much an individual *chooses* to pay attention to race that determines one's fate. According to this perspective, race is only as important as you allow it to be, as Kevin, a 33-year-old white male custodial worker in Colorado told me:

> I never really look at anyone as a color, you know. Your skin's a color, but that doesn't mean, . . . I don't know, I never look at someone being black or Chinese. Yeah, you're Chinese because of the way your eyes are slanted, but you talk just like me. You're just like me. I don't look at you any different than you being me. You know, that's how I've always looked at it. You know.

Implicit in this expression of color blindness is that color does not matter as long as blacks and Chinese assimilate to the point where they are "just like" Kevin. As a member of the dominant group, Kevin has the privilege of defining color blindness as the expectation that racial minorities will mirror his own cultural and social experiences while denying how racism shapes the experiences of racial minorities.[15]

When racial identity shifts from being an individual expression to one that is used to organize politically or make group-based grievances, whites view it as racist. Mary believes that race is used to force whites to think about color and inequality:

> I think that they are making it worse for themselves. I think that anybody can see in this country—I think it's you [blacks]. It doesn't matter what color you are. I mean, sure there are black things but why put it on a T-shirt? Why not just have a plain black T-shirt? Why would you have to make such a big statement that pushes people away, that threatens people. I would never want to threaten anybody.

As Mary's comments make clear, embracing racial symbols that serve to socially isolate and challenge the racial status quo is a "threat." Implicit in this exchange is that it is not very pleasurable for Mary to interact with those who would use race to promote a political agenda.

The respondents below were bothered by what they saw as a double standard concerning beauty pageants; blacks could have their own pageant but whites could not. Their anger is, at least based in part, on an understanding that the norm of color blindness has been violated. Jodie lamented that:

> You know, it's amazing. Like, even, like even, like the Miss America pageants. There's a black Miss America pageant. But there's also black contestants in the Miss America pageant and then there's a separate pageant for blacks only. And if we had a separate pageant for whites only I just think that things would be . . . more hell would be raised.

Michelle was also bothered by her perception that the idea of race was taken too seriously by blacks:

> You know, it just seems, even for silly things, even the fact that you have to have black women in the Miss America pageant but then they have their own Miss Black America pageant. You know, like that type of thing, and it's like, come on. . . .

John, a 22-year-old male from New Jersey, also felt that whites were held to a different set of social expectations than blacks:

> I watch Miss America and we've had what, a black Miss America three out of the last five years, yet they do have a black Miss America (contest). They don't have white contestants, they only have black contestants. Now, I'm not saying that a black person can't enter the white contest, but it's just kind of ironic that here a black woman enters a predominately white contest and, you know, usually a Miss America's supposed to be representative of the whole population, yet only 12% of the population is black. . . . It just kind of seems strange that if a white person tried to enter a black contest, forget it, you'd have mayhem.

Viewed within the color-blind perspective, the Miss Black America pageant is a form of institutional racism because it denies all racial groups full access to participation. The Miss Black America pageant is, as suggested above, racist for excluding whites because of the color of their skin. The long history of racial minorities being excluded from white organizations and institutions as the reason behind why black, Latino, and Asian organizations were formed in the first place is now only viewed as irrelevant.

Like the anger expressed over what was perceived as a racial double standard concerning the Miss America pageant, Malcolm X also came to represent challenges to the color-blind perspective, which were viewed as illegitimate because they advocate group solutions to race-based inequities. As one respondent told me about Malcolm X:

> He got into Buddha [sic] and changed his violence. When he was younger, I think that's when he was violent but in the years before he was killed I think he definitely went towards peace, like Martin Luther King. I don't know why they can't wear Martin Luther King hats [instead of Malcolm X hats].

Color blindness has emerged as America's newest racial mythology because it provides a level-playing-field narrative that allows whites to inhabit a psychological space that is free of racial tension. This new era of color blindness is a respite from the racial identity movements which often result in white guilt, defensiveness, or the avoidance of racially charged issues. Color blindness provides whites with the belief that they live in an era that is free of racism. Convinced that these racist attitudes and practices are over, whites today are able to define themselves as racially progressive and tolerant. Within this universe where racial differences are almost meaningless, whites are able to claim that their privileged social position relative to racial minorities reflects individual achievement rather than the fruits of white supremacy. The constant barrage of color-blind messages and messengers reinforces and confirms that the egalitarian and meritocractic norms that undergird American culture are intact. Embracing color blindness allows whites to be blind to or ignore the fact that racial and ethnic minorities lag behind whites on almost every measure of quality of life. Color-blind pleasure means whites are able to think about contemporary race relations as a clean slate where the crimes of slavery, Jim Crow, institutional racism, and white privilege have been ended and the racist sins of their grandparents have been erased.

Our Survey Says— "Color-Blind Nation"

National survey data suggest that a majority of whites view race relations through the lens of color blindness. A 1997 Gallup poll found that a majority of whites believe that blacks have "as good a chance as whites" in their community in procuring employment (79%).[16] A Kaiser Family Poll (1997) found that a majority of whites believe that blacks are doing at least as well or better than whites in income and educational attainment. The poll found that "almost two-thirds (64%) of whites do NOT believe that whites have benefited from past and present discrimination against African Americans."[17] In their study on racial attitudes, Schuman and associates found that when white Americans are asked to account for black disadvantage, the most popular explanation is that of black people's lack of motivation or willpower to get ahead.[18] These surveys suggest a majority of whites view the opportunity structure as being open to all, regardless of color. Not only do whites see parity compared to blacks in access to housing, employment, education, and achieving a middle-class life style, but where differences do exist, whites attribute racial inequities to the individual shortcomings of blacks.

Reflecting on affirmative action, Monica articulates an all-is-now-equal argument as to why color should no longer matter in hiring decisions or school admissions:

> I think all the backgrounds have come a long way to where they don't need it any more. Basically everyone has equal opportunity to get a certain job, to get into a certain school, and now it should be based on your performance and not for what you are.

Drawing on an ideology of egalitarianism and meritocracy, Monica believes, as most white Americans do, that color is no longer a factor in obtaining employment or a quality education. Given the premise that racial equality has now been achieved, Monica is able to argue that achievement and not skin color should shape the allocation of resources. In other words, since the playing field is now level, any group claims to address real or imagined inequities are illegitimate. Joan voiced the anger that whites should in some way be held accountable for past or present racial inequities.

> That's what bothers me. They say "we" have been oppressed. They have not. The students here at the university right now have not been oppressed. They did not experience the Watts riot, they didn't experience physically being hosed down by police. Granted, the white population was responsible for that, but we are not. We are not responsible. Therefore, we should not be put out because of that. We didn't do it. We're not doing it now, therefore they have no right to say, well, we've been oppressed.

Neither Joan, nor the white race, should be "put out" for past racist practices. The color-blind perspective is a historical rendering of the actions of the near and distant past as events which are disconnected from contemporary racial inequality.

James expresses a number of the trends found in the surveys cited earlier. After stating that "hey, everybody's got the same opportunity" when asked about what his views were on the idea of white privilege, James countered that:

> They say that I have white privileges. Uh, and if they say it's like because where I live, I live in a big house or something like that, they're wrong, because that's not a privilege. That's something my parents worked for. And if they don't live in a big fancy houses that's something that their parents didn't work for. And if they want to change that . . . I've got black people living across from me. Uh, they're no different than me. They're different from the black people down here because they worked for what they wanted. These people [blacks in a poor segregated part of the city], they don't have to live here. There's no one holding them back. They can get into school as well as everybody else can. I was lucky my parents could pay for school and I didn't need financial aid. . . . You know, the opportunity is there. You've just got to take hold of it.

James suggests that when class background is taken into account whites and blacks are the same. The blacks who are unable to leave poor, segregated neighborhoods reflect individual shortcomings on the part of blacks, not structural obstacles. Rob implies that it is hard work and individual merit, not one's skin color that matters. Examining his own mobility, Rob remarks, "I don't know if their situation is any different than mine. I mean, I can only gauge on the fact that I've been busting my ass for the last ten years to get to where I want to be."

How Color-Blind a Nation?

The beliefs voiced by whites in national survey data and my own interviews raise an empirical question; to what extent are we now a color-blind nation? If educational opportunity, occupational advancement, health, upward mobility, and equal treatment in the public sphere can be used as indicators of how color-blind we are as a nation, then we have failed. U.S. census figures present a picture of America that is far from color-blind. In 1999, over 73% of white households owned their own homes compared to 46% for blacks, 45% for Hispanics, 53% for Asians, and 56% for American Indians.[19] In 1993, whites had about ten times more in assets than blacks or Latinos.[20] Median family income in 1998 was $42,439 for whites, $25,351

for blacks, $27,330 for Latinos, and $46,637 for Asians. In 1997, almost 25% of whites over the age of 25 had four years of college or more compared to less than 14% for blacks and Latinos. In 1997, 8.6% of whites compared to 26.5% blacks, 27% of Latinos, and 14% of Asians lived at or below the poverty line.[21] A national study found that even after controlling for individual credit history, blacks in 33 states were charged more for car loans than whites.[22] Health statistics tell a similar tale. Whites have lower rates of diabetes, tuberculosis, pregnancy-related mortality, and sudden infant death syndrome (SIDS), and are more likely to have prenatal care in the first trimester than blacks, Latinos, or Asians. In 1997, 15% of whites did not have public or private health care coverage compared to 21.5% for blacks, 34% for Latinos, and 20.7% for Asians.[23]

In 1998, blacks and Latinos were also underrepresented as lawyers, physicians, professors, dentists, engineers, and registered nurses. A Glass Ceiling study commissioned by the federal government found that when one reaches the level of vice president and above at *Fortune* 1000 industrial companies and *Fortune* 500 service industries, 96.6% of the executives are white males. Nationally, white men comprise 90% of the newspaper editors and 77% of television news directors.[24] In 1999, the Department of Justice found that blacks and Latinos were twice as likely as whites to be subject to force when they encounter a police officer, were more likely to be subjected to car searches during a traffic stop, and were more likely to be ticketed than whites. Although blacks and whites are just as likely to use drugs, almost two-thirds of those convicted on drug charges are black.[25] Congress does not represent the racial and ethnic diversity of this country. In 2000, blacks were 13% of the population, Asians and Pacific Islanders 4%, and Latinos 12%. Yet the House of Representatives was only 9% black, 4% Latino, and 0.9% Asian. The U.S. Senate is 97% white and only 2% Asian and 1% American Indian, and therefore has no black or Latino members.[26] In early 2003, there were no black or Latino governors. According to another report, if you were black and living in Florida, you were four times as likely as whites to have your ballot invalidated in the 2000 presidential election.[27] We are not now, nor have we ever been, a color-blind nation.

The Cost of Racialized Pleasures

Being able to ignore or being oblivious to the ways in which almost all whites are privileged in a society cleaved on race has a number of implications. Whites derive pleasure in being told that the current system for allocating resources is fair and equitable. Creating and internalizing a color-blind view of race relations reflects how the dominant group is able to use the mass media, immigration stories of upward mobility, rags-to-riches narratives, and achievement ideology to make white privilege invisible. Frankenberg argues that whiteness can be "displaced," as is the case with whiteness hiding behind the veil of color blindness. It can also be made "normative" rather than specifically "racial," as is the case when being white is defined by white respondents as being no different than being black or Asian.[28] Lawrence Bobo and associates have advanced a theory of laissez-faire racism that draws on the color-blind perspective. As whites embrace the equality of opportunity narrative they suggest that

> laissez-faire racism encompasses an ideology that blames blacks themselves for their poorer relative economic standing, seeing it as a function of perceived cultural inferiority. The analysis of the bases of laissez-faire racism underscores two central components: contemporary stereotypes of blacks held by whites, and the denial of societal (structural) responsibility for the conditions in black communities.[29]

As many of my respondents make clear, if the opportunity structure is open ("It doesn't matter what color you are"), there must be something inherently wrong with racial minorities or their culture that explains group-level differences.

Leslie Carr argues "that color blindness is not the opposite of racism; it is another form of racism."[30] I would add that the form color blindness takes as the nation's hegemonic political discourse is a variant of laissez-faire racism. Historian David Roediger contends that in order for the Irish to have been absorbed into the white race in the mid-nineteenth century "the imperative to define themselves as whites came from the particular public and psychological wages whiteness offered" these new immigrants.[31] There is still a "wage" to whiteness, that element of ascribed status whites automatically receive because of their membership in the dominant group. But within the framework of color blindness the imperative has switched from whites overtly defining themselves or their interests as white, to one where they claim that color is irrelevant; being white is the same as being black, yellow, brown, or red. Some time ago, Ralph Ellison asked this important question about race relations that continues to go unanswered:

> What, by the way, is one to make of a white youngster who, with a transistor radio glued to his ear, screaming a Stevie Wonder tune, shouts racial epithets at black youngsters trying to swim at a public beach. . . . ?[32]

My interviews with whites around the country suggest that in this post-race era of color-blind ideology Ellison's keen observations about race relations need modification. The question now is what are we to make of a young white man from the suburbs who listens to hip-hop, wears baggy hip-hop pants, a baseball cap turned sideways, unlaced sneakers, and an oversized shirt emblazoned with a famous NBA player who, far from shouting racial epithets, lists a number of racial minorities as his heroes? It is now possible to define oneself as not being racist because of the clothes you wear, the celebrities you like, or the music you listen to while believing that blacks or Latinos are disproportionately poor or overrepresented in low-pay, dead-end jobs because they are part of a debased, culturally deficient group. Having a narrative that smooths over the cognitive dissonance and ofttimes schizophrenic dance that whites must do when they navigate race relations is likely an invaluable source of pleasure.

14   The Ideology of Colorblindness

Lani Guinier • Gerald Torres

LANI GUINIER is the Bennett Boskey Professor of Law at Harvard University. She was nominated by President Clinton to be the first black woman to head the civil rights division of the Department of Justice. She has authored ninety-seven publications, many examining the intersection of race, gender, and the law.

GERALD TORRES is the H.O. Head Centennial Professor of Real Property Law at the University of Texas. He was previously professor of law and associate dean at the University of Minnesota Law School and also served in the U.S. Department of Justice, first as deputy assistant attorney general for Environment and Natural Resources and then as counsel to Attorney General Janet Reno. His publications include *Environmental Justice: The Legal Meaning of a Social Movement* (1996), *Understanding Environmental Racism* (1992), *and Critical Race Theory: The Decline of the Universalist Ideal and the Hope of Plural Justice* (1991).

Questions to Consider
Dr. Martin Luther King Jr.'s plea that one day his children would be judged "not by the color of their skin, but by the content of their character" is perhaps the single most quoted statement about the goals of the modern civil rights movement. There is, however, a huge gap between the expressed societal goals of what we "ought to be" and what we are. Guinier and Torres suggest that the very idea of color blindness has become a way to turn a blind eye toward glaring racial inequality. What purpose is served by turning MLK's statement on color blindness on its head? How and in what ways has the idea of color blindness been appropriated by individuals or groups who believe race no longer matters in shaping individual or group socioeconomic outcomes?

THE DISCOURSE OF COLORBLINDNESS focuses on managing the appearance of formal equality without worrying overmuch about the consequences of real-world inequality. Proponents of a colorblind ethos define freedom and equality exclusively in terms of the autonomous—some would say atomized—individual. This individual has no historical antecedents, no important social relationships, and no political commitments. By structuring the primary concerns around the idea of freedom for an everyman or everywoman, proponents of colorblind analysis locate that atomized individual in an abstract universe of rights and preferences rather than within an obdurate social structure that may limit or even predetermine a person's choices. In relationship to the state and to the market, the paramount virtue of the colorblind universe resides in treating each abstract individual the same as every other. By subjecting rules to this metric of simple sameness, people are legitimized through the appearance of abstract fairness.

Three rules seem to govern this colorblind universe. First, race is all about skin color. It is not a marker for social status, history, or power but is simply a false construction of phenotype that relies improperly on ascriptive physical identifiers of "blood" or ancestry. This is what some commentators call "formal race." Others refer to it as "biological race." Formal or biological race treats all race as pigmentation and grants all racial classifications symmetrical status. When race is only pigmentation, all racial classifications are equally bad, despite hierarchies of privilege or disadvantage that accompany the racial assignation.

Thus, the second rule of colorblindness is that recognizing race is the equivalent of holding onto unscientific notions of racial biology. If race is essentially "made up," with no scientific basis, then critics of race argue that treating people differently based on these made-up categories is unacceptable. Even if members of different "races" are treated "the same," each person so identified is denied his or her essential individual humanity. Moreover, when one notices race, one is implicitly manifesting racial enmity or racial preference. Since racial classification enabled a Jim Crow legal system to perpetuate false assumptions about biological inferiority, noticing race is in essence a throwback to racism.

The third rule is that racism is a personal problem. Unlike capitalism or socialism which are economic systems, or democracy which is a political arrangement, racism, racial hierarchy, or any institutionalized racial discrimination is not an economic or historic system, political arrangement, or social structure. Under the third rule of colorblindness, racism lacks any necessary nexus to power or privilege, and any observed connection is incidental, merely a result of the actions of people with a bad heart. Racism is a psychological disease of individuals, not a social plague. Racism is not produced by environmental toxins, nor is it reinforced by cultural forms or institutional practice. It is simply an irrational defect of the individual mind. It afflicts the aberrant soul who is vulnerable to prejudice or even self-hatred. The challenge for the judiciary, therefore, is to discern and eliminate to the greatest extent possible any public identification of race, since the identification is per se stigmatizing.

For those who believe we are already close to a colorblind society, formal fairness outweighs other concerns. They prefer rules like colorblindness even when such rules hide or reinforce relationships of privilege and subordination. The dangers of continuing to notice race are so profound that they justify doing nothing about the historic and present effects of the nexus between race and political and economic power. Not only is it wrong for the government to notice race, it is wrong for the political system to permit racially affected groups to mobilize in either their own self-interest or the larger public good.

• • •

In response to the claims of those who take a colorblind approach, we argue, as a practical matter, that it is impossible to be colorblind in a world as color-conscious as ours. Moreover, efforts to be colorblind are undesirable because they inhibit racialized minorities from struggling against their marginalized status. The rule of colorblindness disguises (sometimes deliberately) or normalizes (sometimes unwittingly) relationships of privilege and subordination. It gives those who have enjoyed little power in our society no mechanisms for understanding and challenging the systemic nature of their oppression. It affirms the existing imbalance in power relations; all that must change is for the privileged within the society to learn to tolerate on an individual basis those who were previously raced black or brown. Racial difference is relegated to celebratory holidays that capture the nostalgia of a time when we once thought we were different, but whose celebration reaffirms how essentially "the same" we truly are. This approach does not involve any fundamental rethinking of how race has socially and politically constructed privilege. The way race has been used both to distribute resources and to camouflage the unfairness in that distribution remains invisible. And the political space, where groups come together to give voice to their collective experience and mobilize to engage in fundamental social change, vanishes.

• • •

Racial Inequality Is Not a Problem of Individuals

Most people who oppose racism today believe that it is a psychological condition which distorts a person's thinking about people of a different "racial" phenotype. They believe in the changing-people's-thinking approach to racism. This approach, we argue, poses several dangers.

First, it reaffirms an essentialist view of race as merely a biological holdover from a less enlightened time that lacks any present political or social meaning. It suggests that racism is simply an inappropriate way that some individuals categorize groups of people who are in fact phenotypically different but whose physical differences amount to nothing important. This approach does not leave any space for other kinds of differences that people of color do in fact experience. These experiences are written off as some aberrational individual commitment to racialism that is obsessive and negative.

Second, the changing-people's-thinking approach not only locates the problem in the individual but it locates the remedy there as well. All that is necessary to overcome racism is for an individual to become better informed about different racial groups.

Third, in the changing-people's-thinking approach, either not speaking of race at all or speaking of it as a uniformly bad thing trumps all other options. This so-called neutral stance becomes almost inevitable after one has defined racism solely as an individual problem and an aberrant one at that. Racism is chased into the closet, and we are surprised when someone openly expresses intolerant views. Conservatives and progressives alike get caught in this trap and end up as speaking police, monitoring what people may say but feeling no compulsion to do anything about the racial hierarchy that shelters the root sources of bigotry. What surprises us about open bigotry is that it is public, not that it exists.

If we do not shift the locus of conversation to make visible the effects of such deeply held but unspoken attitudes, they will tend to normalize inequality. We will all then be tempted to explain the terrible condition of people of color as resulting from the behavior of the victims themselves. Having cleansed the social discourse of any mention of race and having policed expressions of bigotry, we will come to view any remaining racial dimension to observed injustices and inequities as a function of the way "those people" of color conceive of and structure their social life.

Colorblindness Masks Entrenched Racial Inequality

The colorblindness doctrine assumes that race is an individual attribute that should be of no consequence. For that reason, those advocating colorblindness as both means and end fail to recognize patterns of racial inequality and perceive no need to look more closely at data associated with these collective accidents of birth. They fail to see that an economy which is largely unaccountable to democratic institutions and principles of justice merely compounds inequality through the generations.

Stripped of concrete features like race, a black family earning $50,000 a year, for example, seems financially identical to a white family with the same income. Yet, this assumption of sameness does not take into account the effects of structural inequality compounded over time. Data on the generational effects of inequality show that blacks earning $50,000 or more have a **median** net worth that is barely one-half the median net worth of their white counterparts.

median If you were to line up a list of numbers from the smallest to the largest, the median would be the place where half of the numbers were above and half were below the number in the middle.

Most Americans have difficulty accumulating wealth. Income, understood principally as wages and salaries, does not easily convert into wealth because immediate necessities deplete available resources. Although income is distributed in a highly unequal manner in the United States (the top 20 percent of earners receives 43 percent of all income, while the poorest 20 percent of the population receives 4 percent of the total income), the distribution of wealth is even more unequal, and that inequality grows with each succeeding generation. In 1900, 39 percent of the wealthiest men in America emerged from wealthy families; by 1950, 68 percent of the wealthiest were born into wealth. By 1970, this figure climbed to 82 percent. That same year, only 4 percent of the richest men came from modest origins.

Income has been used as a surrogate for wealth at least in part due to the existence of little reliable data on wealth accumulation. But income alone offers an incomplete, skewed assessment of the inequality in life chances among different individuals and groups. The reality for most families is that while income may supply basic necessities, wealth is a critical resource for improving life chances, securing prestige, passing status along to the next generation, and influencing the political process. Wealth also provides financial stability during times in which needs overwhelm income.

Even at a time when the economy is good and when the unemployment rate for people of color is at an all-time low, blacks will not be able to sustain their economic gains until they can convert income into asset accumulation. Yet as the sociologist Dalton Conley points out: "At the lower end of the income spectrum (less than $15,000 per year), the median African American family has no assets, while the equivalent white family holds $10,000 worth of equity. At upper income levels (greater than $75,000 per year), white families have a median net worth of $308,000, almost three times the figure for upper-income African American families ($114,600)." The median net worth of whites is twelve times that of blacks. Similarly, the average white household controls $6,999 in net financial assets while the average black household retains no net financial assets whatsoever.

Owning a home is the primary method of equity accumulation for most families in the United States. Not surprisingly, disparities in home-ownership rates contribute to the black-white wealth disparity. As of 1997, only 44 percent of blacks owned their homes, in contrast with 71 percent of whites. Not only are blacks less likely to own homes, but when they do own homes, their asset is less likely to accumulate value than that of white homeowners. The value of housing in black neighborhoods increases at a lower rate compared with similar units in predominantly white neighborhoods. Black households are less likely than white households to have their wealth invested in financial assets, rental property, and businesses or farms that are likely to produce income. Black assets more often are tied up in a home and consumables, such as a car or household goods. As a result, black families are less able to expand their income than white families, and thus the disparity in wealth perpetuates itself.

What these comparisons of income and wealth illustrate is not just the effects of historical discrimination in particular cases but the effects of an entire complex of social relations, reflected in poorer housing markets, less adequate schools, reduced access to banks and other sources of capital, hostile relations with police authority, and increased crime. The cumulative impact of these disparities requires an explanation that does not merely excuse the current distribution of assets.

Efforts to pass these effects off to class are unavailing. When trying to explain the wealth gap between blacks and whites, Melvin Oliver and Thomas Shapiro used a large number of controls in their work—income, age, sex, marriage, children, number of working people within the household, education, occupation, work history, and region. With these controls, Oliver and Shapiro confirmed that nonracial factors standing alone cannot explain the black-white wealth gap.

The status of both the black poor and the black middle class is much more precarious and unstable than that of their white peers. Between 1980 and 1996 the absolute incomes of the poorest blacks declined dramatically, as compared with a small decline in the income of the poorest white families. Even as poverty in the black community declined overall, those who remained poor became poorer still. The percentage of black men between ages 25 and 34 who earn less than the poverty line for a family of four jumped from about 20 percent in 1969 to just over 50 percent in 1991.

Even among blacks and whites who both start at low socioeconomic positions as measured by parental occupation, whites who make it into the middle class accumulate more wealth than blacks who have traveled the same path. Blacks' middle-class status entirely depends on income,

whereas the status of the white middle class rests on the stability and security of assets. The writer DeNeen L. Brown illustrates this marginality and fragility when she explains what it means to be first-generation black middle-class: "To me that term doesn't mean anything other than someone who is one step out of poverty and two paychecks from being broke. I have income but not true wealth."

The average net worth of middle-class whites is nearly four times that of comparably situated blacks, and their average net financial assets are nearly 55 times greater than that of their black counterparts. This is true even within the context of real economic success. As Oliver and Shapiro note: "No matter how high up the mobility ladder blacks climb, their asset accumulation remains capped at inconsequential levels, especially when compared to that of equally mobile whites." As a result, each generation passes on a form of "asset poverty" regardless of the level of mobility or occupational attainment achieved. Social mobility does not fully counteract the effects of the intergenerational transmission of wealth.

Access to higher education has always been an indicator of both social mobility and the capacity of families to transfer wealth across generations. What we find when we compare the opportunities of white and black people is a continuing gap in access to higher education between these two groups. Because of the dramatic changes occurring in our economy, what this differential means is that the distribution of access to our knowledge-based economy will be color-coded.

Most people believe (and the data confirm) that education positively affects wealth accumulation: high educational achievement typically leads to better-paying jobs, which in turn result in greater wealth accumulation. What is less clear is the effect that wealth has upon education. While ample research has explored the effect of family and neighborhood income upon student performance and attainment, few studies have focused on wealth. The studies that do exist provide some insight into this relationship. Conley found that financial contributions of parents to their children's educational expenses have strong effects upon children's educational expectations. Yet African-American young adults receive less financial help from their parents and return more money to their parents' households than their white counterparts during the period immediately following high school. These data suggest that African-American young adults are substituting work for schooling.

Conley found that the most significant wealth-based predictor of educational performance is parents' liquid assets. (The most significant *overall* predictor, according to Conley, is parental educational level—another instance of the compounding of wealth over generations.) From this he infers that family-based educational financing is "probably more important than the differences in school districts associated with housing values." Conley states that wealth-based resource disparities at the district level (created by reliance on local property taxes, which fund the schools) account for approximately 10 percent of the gap in black and white standardized test scores. Furthermore, a decline in our social commitment to providing access to higher education for people of color is widening the gap. The declining support for public education compounds the problems in higher education. Black and other non-white communities feel the impact of this decreased support first and most powerfully, but it will affect all poor communities, regardless of color, in the long run. Everyone who depends on public education for upward mobility will suffer. Recent dramatic changes in the economy promise to magnify this disadvantage.

When Conley incorporated wealth factors into traditional educational analyses, a number of important elements in the cultural-deficit model for explaining educational disparities disappear. These include the pathologies supposedly created by female heads of households, receipt of welfare payments, parental age, parental occupational prestige, and parental income level. As the economist Marcellus Andrews puts it: "Working-class black people are muddling through an economy that no longer offers the prospect of middle-class life to hard working but modestly educated adults." There is a simple way to look at the confluence of these facts. Black people as a group not only have lower incomes than whites but also reduced access to the major avenue of wealth creation and transfer in the middle and working classes, namely high-quality higher education. Race in this society tracks wealth, wealth tracks education, and education tracks access to power.

Race provides an analytic tool for understanding significant dynamics of American economic life, such as the largely unremarked upon absence of any automatic escalator from one class to the next, despite the Horatio Alger myth. The linkages between race and black poverty tell us more about race than they do about individual black people. Moreover, the linkage between race and poverty tells us as much about white people as it does about black people. It tells us that the most potent determinant of economic success lies in the accumulated assets that are passed on from one generation to the next. Racial disparities cannot be explained by reference to any simple binary in which blacks are poor and whites are not. Instead, the mechanisms making it so hard for black people to accumulate assets in a way that changes their life chances are the same mechanisms that keep poor whites poor. These mechanisms are compounded by race, but they are not totally explained by race. Race is instructive in identifying the workings of class, but it cannot be swallowed up into class.

Hugh Price, President of the National Urban League, challenged us in his 1999 State of Black America address to look at race as "endogenous," that is, "something that is defined within a political-economic system and not at all natural or immutable." Race cannot be defined outside the economic or political system; "it is defined by the economic system, to grant or deny access to wealth accumulation." For the individual who is raced black, Price is pointing out links in a chain that may provide an important context for what otherwise might be interpreted as individual deficits, behavioral flaws, or cultural pathology.

Seeing the Big Picture

Color-Blind or Blind to Color?

Briefly glance through the Appendix. Based on your observations of statistics on race in this section, can you make an argument that the United States is now color-blind? How might you reconcile the ideal of color blindness with the trends in the data?

The Possibility of a New Racial Hierarchy in the Twenty-First-Century United States

Herbert J. Gans

HERBERT J. GANS is the Robert Lynd Professor of Sociology at Columbia University. He received his Ph.D. from the University of Pennsylvania. He has worked as a research planner for public and private agencies, and prior to coming to Columbia taught at the University of Pennsylvania, MIT, and Teachers College of Columbia University. He is the author of nine books and more than 160 articles. His first book was *The Urban Villagers* (1962). Recent works include *War Against the Poor* (1995), *Making Sense of America* (1999), and *Democracy and the News* (2003).

Questions to Consider   In a timely and provocative article, Herbert Gans suggests that racial categories, as currently understood, are undergoing fundamental changes. He argues that the current racial hierarchy will collapse into two categories: black and nonblack. How will this happen? Which racial and ethnic groups will be placed in each of these two categories, and why?

OVER THE LAST DECADE, A NUMBER OF social scientists writing on race and ethnicity have suggested that the country may be moving toward a new racial structure (Alba 1990; Sanjek 1994; Gitlin 1995). If current trends persist, today's multiracial hierarchy could be replaced by what I think of as a dual or bimodal one consisting of "nonblack" and "black" population categories, with a third, "residual," category for the groups that do not, or do not yet, fit into the basic dualism.[1]

More important, this hierarchy may be based not just on color or other visible bodily features, but also on a distinction between undeserving and deserving, or stigmatized and respectable, races.[2] The hierarchy is new only insofar as the old white-nonwhite dichotomy may be replaced by a nonblack-black one, but it is hardly new for blacks, who are likely to remain at the bottom once again. I fear this hierarchy could develop even if more blacks achieve educational mobility, obtain professional and managerial jobs, and gain access to middle-class incomes, wealth, and other "perks." Still, the hierarchy could also end, particularly if the black distribution of income and wealth resembles that of the then-dominant races, and if interracial marriage eliminates many of the visible bodily features by which Americans now define race.

Since no one can even guess much less model the many causal factors that will influence the future, the observations that follow are not intended to be read as a prediction but as an exercise in speculative analysis. The weakness of such an analysis is its empirical reliance on the extrapolation of too many current trends and the assumed persistence of too many current phenomena. The analysis becomes a justifiable exercise, however, because it aims only to speculate about what future "scenarios" are possible, and what variables might shape these.

Obviously, the observations about such a hierarchy are not meant to suggest that it is desirable. Indeed, I wrote the paper with the hope that if such a future threatens to become real, it can be prevented.

The remainder of this paper elaborates the basic scenario, adds a set of qualifications, and considers the variables and alternative scenarios now most likely to be significant for the future. The paper concludes with observations about the contemporary construction of race in the United States raised by my analysis about a possible future.

The Dual Racial Hierarchy

Before what is now described, somewhat incorrectly, as the post-1965 immigration, the United States was structured as a predominantly Caucasian, or white, society, with a limited number of numerically and otherwise inferior races, who were typically called Negroes, Orientals, and American Indians—or blacks, yellows, and reds to go with the pinkish-skinned people called whites. There was also a smattering of groups involving a huge number of people who were still described by their national or geographic origins rather than language, including Filipinos, Mexicans and Puerto Ricans, Cubans, etc.[3]

After 1965, when many other Central and Latin American countries began to send migrants, the Spanish-speaking groups were all recategorized by language and called Hispanics. Newcomers from Southeast Asia were classified by continental origin and called Asians, which meant that the later Indian, Pakistani, and Sri Lankan newcomers had to be distinguished regionally, and called South Asians.

At the end of the twentieth century, the country continues to be dominated by whites. Nevertheless, both the immigrants who started to arrive after the end of World War II and the political, cultural, and racial changes that took place in the wake of their arrival have further invalidated many old racial divisions and labels. They have also set into motion what may turn out to be significant transformations in at least part of the basic racial hierarchy.

These transformations are still in an early phase but one of the first has been the elevation of a significant, and mostly affluent, part of the Asian and Asian-American population into a **"model minority"** that also bids to eradicate many of the boundaries between it and whites. Upward socioeconomic mobility and increasing intermarriage with whites may even end up in eliminating the boundary that now constructs them as a separate race. Thus, one possible future trend may lead to all but poor Asians and Asian-Americans being perceived and even treated so much like whites that currently visible bodily differences will no longer be judged negatively or even noticed, except when and where Asians or Asian-Americans threaten white interests (e.g., Newman 1993). The same treatment as quasi whites may spread to other successfully mobile and intermarrying immigrants and their descendants, for example Filipinos and white Hispanics.[4]

What these minorities have in common now with Asians, and might have in common even more in the future, is that they are all nonblack, although not as many are currently as affluent as Asians. Nonetheless, by the middle of the twenty-first century, as whites could perhaps become, or will worry about becoming, a numerical minority in the country, they might cast about for political and cultural allies.[5] Their search for allies, which may not even be conscious or deliberate, could hasten the emergence of a new,

nonblack racial category, whatever it is named, in which skin color, or in the case of "Hispanics," racially constructed ethnic differences, will be ignored, even if whites would probably remain the dominant subcategory.

The lower part of the emerging dual hierarchy will likely consist of people classified as blacks, including African-Americans, as well as Caribbean and other blacks, dark skinned or black Hispanics, Native Americans, and anyone else who is dark skinned enough and/or possessed of visible bodily features and behavior patterns, actual or imagined, that remind nonblacks of blacks. Many of these people will also be poor, and if whites and other nonblacks continue to blame America's troubles on a low-status scapegoat, the new black category will be characterized as an undeserving race.

In effect, class will presumably play nearly as much of a role in the boundary changes as race, but with some important exceptions. For example, if a significant number of very poor whites remain as the twenty-first-century equivalent of today's "white trash," they will probably be viewed as less undeserving than equally poor blacks simply because they are whites.[6]

Furthermore, the limits of class are indicated, at least for today, by the continued stigmatization of affluent and otherwise high-status blacks, who suffer some of the same indignities as poor blacks (Feagin and Sykes 1994).[7] So, of course, do moderate and middle-income members of the working class, who constitute the majority of blacks in America even if whites do not know it. The high visibility of "black" or Negroid physical features renders class position invisible to whites, so that even affluent blacks are suspected of criminal or pathological behavior that is actually found only among a minority of very poor blacks.

Despite continuing white hatreds and fears of blacks that continue almost 150 years after the Civil War, racial classification systems involving others have been more flexible. When the first Irish immigrants came to New York, they were so poor that they were perceived by Anglo-Saxon whites as the black Irish and often treated like blacks. Even so, it did not take the Irish long to separate themselves from blacks, and more important, to be so separated by the city's Anglo-Saxons. A generation later, the Irish were whites (Roediger 1991; Ignatiev 1995).

Perhaps their new whiteness was reinforced by the arrival of the next set of newcomers: people from Eastern and Southern Europe who were often described as members of "swarthy races." Even though the word *race* was used the way we today use *ethnicity*, the newcomers were clearly not white in the Anglo-Saxon sense, and Southern Italians were

---

model minority A minority ethnic or racial group that has been socioeconomicly successful relative to other racial minorities. The media typically frame this group as a "model" that other racial and ethnic groups should emulate.

sometimes called "guineas" because of their dark skin. Nonetheless, over time, they too became white, thanks in part to their acculturation, their integration into the mainstream economy, and after World War II, their entry into the middle class. Perhaps the disappearance of their swarthiness was also reinforced by the arrival in the cities of a new wave of Southern blacks during and after World War II.

A less typical racial transformation occurred about that time in Mississippi, where whites began to treat the Chinese merchants who provided stores for poor blacks as near whites. As Loewen (1988) tells the story, increased affluence and acculturation were again relevant factors. Although whites neither socialized nor intermarried with the Chinese, they accorded them greater social deference and political respect than when they had first arrived. They turned the Chinese into what I previously called a residual category, and in the process created an early version of the nonblack-black duality that may appear in the United States in the next century.

As the Mississippi example suggests, changes in racial classification schemes need not require racial or class equality, for as long as scarce resources or positions remain, justifications for discrimination also remain and physical features that are invisible in some social settings can still become visible in others. **Glass ceilings** supply the best example, because they seem to change more slowly than some other hierarchical boundaries. Even ceilings for Jews, non-Irish Catholics, and others long classified as whites are still lower than those for **WASPs** in the upper reaches of the class and prestige structures.

I should note that the racial hierarchy I have sketched here, together with the qualifications that follow, are described both from the perspective of the (overtly) detached social scientist, and also from the perspective of the populations that end up as dominant in the structure. A longer paper would analyze how very differently the people who are fitted into the lower or residual parts of the hierarchy see it.[8]

Qualifications to the Dual Hierarchy

Even if the country would someday replace its current set of racial classifications, the result would not be a simple dual structure, and this model needs to be qualified in at least three ways.

Residuals

The first qualification is the near certainty of a residual or middle category that includes groups placed in a waiting position by the dominant population until it becomes clear whether they will be allowed to become nonblack, face the seemingly permanent inferiority that goes with being black, or become long-term residuals.

If such a structure were to develop in the near future, those likely to be placed in a residual category would include the less affluent members of today's Asian, Hispanic and Filipino, Central and South American Indian, and mixed Indian-Latino populations. The future of the dark-skinned members of the South Asian newcomers is harder to predict. Indeed, their treatment will become an important test of how whites deal with the race-class nexus when the people involved are very dark skinned but are not Negroid—and when their class position is so high that in 1990 it outranked that of all other immigrants (Rumbaut 1997, table 1.4).[9]

Who is classified as residual will, like all other categorizations, be shaped by both class and race. To borrow Milton Gordon's (1964) useful but too rarely used notion of "ethclass," what may be developing are "race-classes," with lower-class members of otherwise racially acceptable groups and higher-class members of racially inferior ones being placed in the residual category.

It is also possible for two or more residual categories to emerge, one for nonwhite and Hispanic populations of lower- and working-class position, and another for nonwhites and Hispanics of higher-class position, with the latter more likely to be eligible eventually to join whites in the nonblack portion of a dual hierarchy. Yet other variations are conceivable, however, for white America has not yet given any clues about how it will treat middle-class Latinos of various skin colors and other bodily features. Perhaps today's ad hoc solution, to treat nonblack Hispanics as a quasi-racial ethnic group that is neither white nor black, may survive for another generation or more, particularly if enough Hispanics remain poor or are falsely accused of rejecting linguistic Americanization.

Being placed in a residual classification means more than location in a middle analytic category; it is also a socially enforced, even if covert, category, and it will be accompanied by all the social, political, and emotional uncertainties that go with being placed in a holding

---

glass ceiling A situation in which the advancement of a qualified person within the hierarchy of an organization is curtailed at a particular point due to sexist or racist discrimination. One is able to "see" the corporate path to the top but hits an imaginary "glass ceiling" where advancement stops.
WASP White Anglo-Saxon Protestant.

pattern and all the pains these create (Marris 1996). True, residuals may not know they are waiting, but then the second-generation white ethnic "marginal men" identified by Stonequist (1937) did not know they were waiting for eventual acculturation and assimilation.

Multiracials

A second qualification to the dual model is created by the emergence of biracials or multiracials that result from the rising intermarriage rates among Asian, Hispanic, and black and white immigrants as well as black and white native-born Americans.[10] Interracial marriages increased from 1 percent of all marriages in 1960 to 3 percent in 1990 (Harrison and Bennett 1995, 165).[11] They are expected to increase much faster in the future, particularly Asian-white ones, since even now, about a third of all Asian marriages, and more than half of all Japanese ones, are intermarriages.[12] If Hispanic-white marriages were also counted, they would exceed all the rest in current number and expected growth, but these are usually treated as ethnic rather than racial intermarriages.

Another set of recruits for a residual position includes the light-skinned blacks, once called mulattos, who today dominate the African-American upper class, some of whom may be sufficiently elite and light skinned to be viewed as nonblack. Even now, the most prominent among the light-skinned black-white biracials, including business and civic leaders, celebrities and entertainers, are already treated as honorary whites, although many refuse this option and take special pride in their blackness and become "race leaders."[13]

Meanwhile, "multiracial" is in the process of slowly becoming a public racial category, and someday it could become an official one codified by the U.S. Census.[14] At this writing, however, many people of mixed race are not ready to define themselves publicly as such, and those who can choose which racial origin to use are sometimes flexible on instrumental grounds, or may choose different racial origins on different occasions.[15] How people of various racial mixtures construct themselves in the longer run is impossible to tell, since issues of their identification and treatment by others, their own identity, and the social, occupational, financial, and political benefits and costs involved cannot be predicted either.

As far as the country's long-term future racial structure is concerned, however, what matters most is how whites will eventually view and treat multiracial people. This will be affected by the variations in class and visible physical features among multiracial people—for example,

how closely they resemble whites or other deserving races. Another question is the future of the traditional identification of race with "blood," which counts all nonwhites in halves, quarters, or even eighths, depending on how many and which ancestors intermarried with whom.[16] If the late-twentieth-century belief in the power of genes continues, blood might simply be replaced by genes someday.

Mixed race is a particularly complex category, for several reasons. In any racial intermarriage with more than one offspring, each sibling is likely to look somewhat different racially from the others, ranging from darker to lighter or more and less nonwhite. Thus, one black-white sibling could be viewed as black and another as nonblack—even before they decide how they view themselves. What happens in subsequent generations is virtually unimaginable, since even if mixed-race individuals marry others of the same mixture, their children will not resemble their grandparents and some may barely resemble their parents. Eventually, a rising number will be treated as, and will think of themselves as, white or nonblack, but this is possible only when people of multiracial origin can no longer bear children who resemble a black ancestor.

Empirical evidence about the effects of racial intermarriage from countries where it has taken place for a long time is unfortunately not very relevant. The closest case, the Caribbean islands, are for the most part, tiny. They are also former plantation societies, with a small number of white and light-skinned elites, and a large number of nonwhites—and a differential conception of white and nonwhite from island to island.[17] Caribbean nonwhites appear to intermarry fairly freely but skin color does count and the darkest-skinned peoples are invariably lowest in socioeconomic class and status (Mintz 1989; Rodriguez 1989).

The only large country, Brazil, also began as a plantation society, and it differs from the United States particularly in that the Brazilian state eschewed racial legislation. As a result, Brazil never passed Jim Crow laws, but as of this writing (January 1998) it has not passed civil rights legislation either. Racial stratification, as well as discrimination and segregation, has persisted nonetheless, but it has been maintained through the class system. Drastic class inequalities, including a high rate of illiteracy among the poor, have enabled whites to virtually monopolize the higher class and status positions.

The absence of state involvement has given Brazil an undeserved reputation as a society that encourages intermarriage but ignores racial differences, a reputation the state has publicized as "racial democracy." The reality is not very different from that of the United States, however, for while there has been more intermarriage, it appears to have taken place mainly among blacks and black-white biracials, who together make up about half the country's population. Moreover, biracials gain little socioeconomic advantage from their lighter skins, even as the darkest-skinned blacks are kept at the bottom, forced into slums and prisons as in the United States.[18]

In effect, the Brazilian experience would suggest an empirical precedent for my hypothesis that blacks will remain a separate, and discriminated-against, population in the United States of the future. Indeed, in just about every society in which blacks first arrived as slaves, they are still at the bottom, and the political, socioeconomic, and cultural mechanisms to keep them there remain in place. Although blacks obtain higher incomes and prestige than Asians or white Hispanics in a number of American communities, the descendants of nonblack immigrants are, with some notable exceptions, still able to overtake most blacks in the long run.

Since parts of the United States were also a plantation society in which the slaves were black, the leftovers of the racial stratification pattern will likely continue here as well. Thus, children of black-white intermarriages who turn out to be dark skinned are classified as blacks, even if the United States is on the whole kinder to light-skinned biracials than Brazil.

The future of Asian-white biracials remains more unpredictable, in part because no empirical data exist that can be used to shore up guesses about them. The same observation applies to the endless number of other multiracial combinations that will be created when the children of multiracial parents intermarry with yet other multiracials. There will be few limits to new variations in bodily features, though which will be visible or noticed, and which of the latter will be stigmatized or celebrated as exotic cannot be guessed now.[19] Most likely, however, the larger the number of multiracials and of multiracial variations, the more difficult it will be for nonblacks to define and enforce racial boundaries, or to figure out which of the many darker-skinned varieties of multiracials had black ancestors. In that case, an eventual end to racial discrimination is possible.

If future racial self-identification patterns will also resemble today's ethnic ones, the racial equivalent of today's voluntary white ethnicity and its associated lack of ethnic loyalty may mean that many future triracial, quadriracial, and other multiracial people may eventually know little, and care even less, about the various racial mixtures they have inherited. It is even conceivable that this change

will extend to black multiracials, and should race become voluntary for them as well, the possibility of an end to racial discrimination will be increased. Unfortunately, at the moment such extrapolations are far closer to utopian thinking than to sociological speculation.

Regional Variations

A third qualification to the dual model is that the portrait I have drawn is national, but given the regional variations in old racial groups and new immigrant populations, it fits no single U.S. region. Moreover, some parts of the country are now still so devoid of new immigrants, with the exception of the handful who come to establish "ethnic" restaurants, that the present racial hierarchies, categories, and attitudes, many of them based on stereotypes imported from elsewhere, could survive unchanged for quite a while in such areas. Furthermore, some areas that have experienced heavy immigration from Asia and Latin America are currently seeing an outmigration of whites, especially lower-income ones (Frey 1996). Thus, even current patterns in the racial makeup of U.S. regions could change fairly quickly.

In addition, regional differences remain in the demography of the lowest strata. The racial hierarchy of the Deep South will probably continue to bear many direct marks of slavery, although the de facto black experience elsewhere in the country has so far not been totally different. Moreover, in some regions, Latin American and other poor nonblack immigrants have already been able to jump over the poor black population economically and socially, partly because whites, including institutions such as banks, are less hostile—or less necessary—to them than they are to blacks.

In the Southwest, Mexicans and other Hispanics remain at the socioeconomic bottom, although in California, they may be joined by the Hmong, Laotians, and other very poor Asians. And Native Americans still occupy the lowest socioeconomic stratum in the handful of mostly rural parts of the country where they now live, although tribes with gambling casinos may be able to effect some changes in that pattern.

Even though some of the new immigrants can by now be found just about everywhere in America, the Los Angeles and New York City areas not only remain the major immigrant arrival centers but also contain the most diverse populations. As a result, a number of the issues discussed in this paper will be played out there, even as they are barely noticeable in the many smaller American cities that may have attracted only a handful of the newcomers. Since these two cities are also the country's prime creators of popular culture, however, their distinctive racial and ethnic characteristics will probably be diffused in subtle ways through the country as a whole.

Alternative Scenarios

Speculating about the future also requires some explicit consideration of the variables that could affect the guesses I have made here, which in turn could lead to alternative scenarios. Generally speaking these variables are macrosociological—major changes in the economy, demographic patterns including internal migration and immigration, as well as political realignments and racial divisions of labor, among others. These in turn can result in changes in racial and ethnic relations as well as in classification systems.

As noted earlier, dominant groups can alter racial categories and constructions. Model minorities are "chosen" by the dominant population precisely because they appear to share, and thereby to uphold, that population's behavior or values. If new behavior or values need to be upheld, new model minorities may be recruited. Scapegoats are populations that can be blamed for social problems, although the dominant populations choose, or even create, the social problems for which scapegoats will be blamed. Scapegoats, or targets for blame, generally come in two varieties: *higher* scapegoats, usually recruited from higher status minority groups that can be blamed for obtaining too much economic or cultural power; and *lower* ones, typically the undeserving poor, who can be accused of deviant behavior or values said to hold back economic growth, require public expenditures that could bankrupt governmental budgets, threaten familial and sexual norms, or impair the moral fabric of the rest of society. Blaming both types of scapegoats is a politically easy way of responding to a crisis, particularly one for which immediate and feasible solutions are lacking.

During the long Cold War, the Soviets and other foreign scapegoats could be blamed for American problems, but now, domestic scapegoats have again become the primary target. While illegal and even legal American immigrants are once again joining poor blacks as the country's principal lower scapegoats, only a few states have sufficient immigrants to serve as targets for blame, which may help to explain why conservative politicians, particularly Republicans, have more often demonized poor blacks.

The most likely candidates for change in current racial categories, other than of model minorities, are the people whites now call Hispanics, as well as descendants of some now

officially nonwhite populations in the new immigration. They will have to be allowed into the higher-status occupations in larger number if and when the supply of whites runs out, and in that case, today's forms of racial and ethnic discrimination against them, particularly those shaped by class considerations, would have to give way. In fact, by the middle of the twenty-first century, demographers and journalists may be amazed that fifty years earlier, whites expected to be swamped in 2050 by an aggregate of diverse peoples then all called Hispanics.

Two macrosocial factors are probably most important in thinking about alternative scenarios. One is the set of geopolitical and economic demographics that can be produced by cross-national population movements, including the one that has fueled the immigration from Central and Latin America, as well as Russia, Asia, and now Africa, during the last half century. These movements were controlled at least in part by U.S. government legislation, but world catastrophes could take place that could force even the United States to open its borders to much larger numbers of people who might alter the racial distribution significantly.

National demographics can also be changed by domestic political considerations, however, which could lead to a new search for white—and non-Hispanic—immigrants. The United States found its late-nineteenth-century industrial workforce in white Europe rather than among the newly freed slaves in the South. Likewise, Australia has recently looked for European immigrants to discourage the arrival of further Asians.

The second major factor is the state of the domestic economy. If late-twentieth-century trends in the world economy and on Wall Street continue in their present forms, the further disappearance of American firms, jobs, and high wages, as well as related changes in the country's economy, would persist too.

Suppose, for example, that unemployment, or the decline of real income, or both, worsened in the first quarter of the twenty-first century, and Americans in large numbers conclude that the country's economy can never again supply full-time jobs paying a living wage for everyone. While the descendants of the poorer immigrants would be the first to experience what I once called "second generation decline" (Gans 1992), other immigrants can also be dispatched into persistent poverty when not enough jobs are available, with the appropriate racial stereotypes invented or reinvented to justify their downward mobility. Even some middle-class descendants of Asian, Russian, and other newcomers could be transformed into lower scapegoats. Then, the dual racial hierarchy I have described would look very different or might not come to pass at all.

Should economic crises result in political crises as well, or raise religious and culture "wars" to more feverish pitches, the current movement toward a dual racial structure could also end quickly. Then, a modern version of the nineteenth-century American monoracial pattern might reappear, with the children of white newcomers joining older white ethnics and WASPs as the only acceptable race. Some members of the newly scapegoated races would probably react in turn, inaugurating political protest, intensifying identity politics and slowing down on intermarriage and other forms of acculturation and assimilation. Some descendants of today's newcomers might return to the old country.

What if a very different economic scenario were assumed, involving a return of old-style economic growth accompanied by a stronger U.S. position in the global economy, a shortage of domestic workers, and an upward trend in real income? In that case, the trend toward a dual structure might be hastened, and the erosion of perceived racial differences speeded up as well.

At that point, the now still visible bodily differences of Asian-Americans and their descendants might no longer be noticed, and these groups would repeat the post–World War II pattern by which Southern and Eastern European "races" were redefined as "ethnic groups." The reclassification of Hispanics, including the treatment of third-generation Central and Latin Americans, would probably move in the same direction.

The fate of blacks is more difficult to imagine. If the economy created a seller's market for people with job skills at all levels from blue collar to professional and managerial, all poverty would decline sharply, including that of blacks. Moreover, blacks would be able to enter the upper middle and middle classes in such numbers as to disturb white America's long association of poverty with blackness. Indeed, in an economy with enough decent jobs for all, private and public affirmative action policies to assure the spread of blacks at all levels of the occupational and socioeconomic structure would be likely as well.

Under such conditions, those aspects of white racism due to fear of and anger at black poverty would begin to decline, and if the federal government was committed to fight racial discrimination and segregation, so would the construction of blacks as an undeserving race. Black-white intermarriage rates might also rise more quickly.

If the prosperity were long term, and it as well as other events in the society and the world reduced the

country's resort to domestic scapegoats, a dual racial hierarchy might be replaced by the beginnings of a multiracial structure in which the boundaries of all races would become fuzzier and weaker. Since now-stigmatized visible bodily differences would then lose their negative connotations, they might not only be ignored but even come to be celebrated as positive contributions to American diversity, just as current ethnic differences among Europeans provide the country with nonthreatening cultural diversities.

Prosperity alone does not necessarily solve a society's other problems, however, and political, cultural, and religious conflicts could remain, encouraging dominant groups to choose and stigmatize an undeserving race, even if it is not a poor one. Anti-Semitic activities, for example, have occurred in prosperous times and societies, and in nations with minuscule Jewish populations.

Likewise, more economic prosperity and other positive economic tendencies alone do not necessarily produce more acculturation and assimilation of immigrants. Even the acculturation of large numbers of immigrants and their descendants does not automatically preclude identity politics, for today's college and university campuses are rife with rapidly acculturating newcomers who nevertheless feel strongly enough about their racial identity to become active in identity politics.

It is even possible that in a multiracial America, some latter-day descendants of WASPs and white ethnics will resort to identity politics as an attempt to retain or restore their political and cultural dominance.[20] And if a global economy also produced pressures toward global cultural and political homogeneities, nation-states or their successors might develop now unimagined forms of national identity politics or cultural revivals to maintain some kind of national distinctiveness. Immigrants and their descendants might be victimized by such developments more than blacks, however.

Three Tendencies in the Contemporary Construction of Race

Biological Constructions

The first tendency is the continuing construction of race from biological as well as social building blocks. Most scientific experts agree that there are no biologically definable races, and that race is therefore not a useful biological concept. The lay public, however, which is not ready to accept expert opinion, sees differences in visible bodily features, mostly facial, between people and treats them as racial differences caused by differences in "blood." People also racialize differences in personality traits such as "soul"—and national character in the case of immigrants.

The visible bodily differences are not imaginary, for people do differ by skin color, and the shapes or other characteristics of various body parts, including heads, eyelids, noses, hair, and others. To cite just a few examples, even in third-generation white ethnic America, one can find Irish and Welsh (or "Celtic") faces, southern Italian and Sicilian ones, and Slavic as well as Scandinavian ones.

What people notice are not scientifically defined races or subraces, but the descendants of once-isolated peoples who had been inbreeding for centuries.[21] Since most have now stopped doing so as a result of rural to urban and other migrations, their distinctiveness is disappearing with each new generation, but it has by no means disappeared.

Some of the variations in personality and social characteristics that laypeople correlate with race or "blood" can undoubtedly be traced in part to the societies and economies, as well as the racial hierarchies, in which these once-isolated peoples lived. The occupational and other social roles that immigrants play in their new societies also play a part, one reason why immigrant shopkeepers in "middlemen" roles are often seen as "clannish" by the populations they serve, for example.

Some visible bodily features that distinguish people are noticed and judged; some are noticed but not judged one way or another; and yet others are not even noticed, seeming to be virtually invisible. Although how features are judged can be traced in part to the popular Darwinisms of the last two centuries, in general, the bodily features of the most prestigious peoples are usually adopted as ideals of physical perfection, while features found among the lower social classes are judged pejoratively.[22]

Variations in skin color, as well as in head shapes, noses, eyes, lips, and hair, have been noticed in many societies, but differences in some bodily parts have been ignored, for example, the size of fingers and the shapes of ears and earlobes.[23] Yet other bodily features are not noticed because they are hidden by clothes; while a few are not noticed because people wear clothes to hide them. These often spur fantasies, for example about black penis size and other imagined racial differences in reproductive and other organs.[24]

A major ingredient of the social construction of race is the determination of which visible bodily features are noticed and used to delineate race and which remain unnoticed. In the process shaping that construction, various social constructors, including laypersons, experts, and, when relevant, commercial and political decision makers, take part. Unless explicit ideological, commercial, or political reasons are involved, the constructors may not be aware of the process in which they are involved, or the causes that shape the final determination. Usually, whites are the major constructors, but increasingly, representatives of the racial minorities to be constructed participate when they can politicize the process, or can frighten manufacturers or advertisers of national consumer goods.[25]

Strictly speaking, a biological construction should make racial characteristics and classifications relatively fixed, but lay biological construction is almost as flexible as social construction. The reason for the lack of fixity is not hard to find, for the choice of which visible bodily features are to be noticed has almost nothing to do with race and everything to do with stratification.

As the Brazilian and United States experiences indicate, the race of the lowest class became the lowest race because slaves were almost by definition the lowest class and race. That captured blacks were the only population economically and otherwise powerless to prevent their becoming enslaved in recent centuries led whites to use their distinguishable skin color and facial features to translate their class inferiority into a racial one (Fields 1990). Similarly, the stigmatization of "yellow" skin resulted from the serflike status of Chinese "coolies" on railroad construction gangs; the stigmatization of "swarthiness" followed from the low status of the Southern and Eastern European newcomers; and a century later, white Hispanic immigrants are sometimes called a race because of their low class position.[26] That the ancestors of now-respected Americans were once damned for their swarthy skins has been quietly forgotten, both among their descendants and among the peoples who "invented" the original stigma.

Ethnicity as Racial

The second, and related, tendency is the continuing lay practice of identifying ethnic and national differences as racial, particularly in private self-naming. Census analysts have discovered that in the 1990 census, respondents to open-ended questions claimed membership in nearly three hundred races or ethnic groups, including seventy Hispanic categories (Morganthau 1995, 64). In many instances, they equated their race with their nationality—or with their tribes in the case of Native Americans.[27] As Eleanor Gerber and Manuel de la Puente pointed out in reporting on a study of test questions for the 2000 census: "Most respondents recognized the term 'ethnic group' but . . . would indicate it was 'the same thing' as race . . . [and] often coined the term 'ethnic race' during our discussions" (Gerber and de la Puente 1996, 21).

The two Bureau of Census researchers suggest lack of education as the causal factor in this conflation, indicating that only the college educated could distinguish ethnic group from race. However, as long as Americans notice visible bodily differences among people of the same official race, they will hold on to *private* constructions of race that differ from the official definitions.[28] Even among the third- and fourth-generation white multiethnics whose "ethnic options" Mary Waters (1990) studied, some chose their ethnicities on the basis of racial conceptions of national origin.[29] In effect, ethnicity continues to be a matter of "blood."[30]

Racial Tolerance

The third and perhaps most important tendency is the apparently increasing white tolerance for racial differences, except with respect to blacks. At the same time, whites seem to use race less often as an indicator of class, except when they are considering poor blacks. This trend may become more widespread as racial intermarriage among people of similar class increases further. Today, class homogamy is apparently outranking racial homogamy among college-educated young people (Kalmijn 1991).

If this pattern spreads to other Americans of the same age and if it becomes permanent, and if whites were willing and able to see that their hatreds and fears of blacks and other very poor nonwhites are so often reactions to their extreme and persistent poverty rather than their race, class could become more important and more overt as a boundary and a principle of stratification in the future. If Americans could also realize that class is more than a matter of "lifestyle" differences among near equals, class stratification might someday become a matter of general public discussion. In that case, the myth of a classless America might eventually be laid to rest.[31]

Even a more modest increase in awareness of class would be desirable, because class is after all an achieved status, while race is not, even in its reasonably flexible lay construction. However, the shift from race to class would also require Americans to develop a more fundamental understanding of the United States and to invent a new conception of the American dream and its underlying myth to replace that of the classless society. So far, there is no indication of this happening.

In fact, it would probably not happen until events in the political economy make it possible to achieve a drastic reduction of joblessness and poverty, so that the correlation of poverty with blackness is significantly lowered. If and when blacks become roughly equal economically to nonblacks, blacks can no longer be treated as an undeserving race.

If poverty and inequality are not lessened, however, and if more poor blacks are condemned to work for nothing but their welfare benefits, they could be treated as an ever more undeserving race, and other populations who cannot enter, or stay in, the middle class, including poor Hispanics and Asians, might join them. In that case, the racial hierarchy of the next century's United States would look very different from the one I have sketched here.

Conclusion

A society's reconstruction of racial categories appears to require at least the following conditions: (1) an influx of immigrants who do not fit the existing racial categories and their associated class backgrounds; (2) a healthy economy with sufficient opportunity for upward mobility even for poorer immigrants; (3) a lack of demand for new lower (and higher) racial scapegoats; and (4) an at least temporary demand for model minorities.

If these conditions are met, existing racial definitions and categories will be altered, sometimes even quickly if there is a proliferation of interracial marriages. However, in a society with a history of slavery, one possible effect is a dual racial hierarchy, in which one part consists mostly of ex-slaves. However, since even the effects of slavery should eventually be eliminated, at least in theory, the United States could become a predominantly interracial or multiracial society someday.

Even then, the more prestigious racial mixtures are apt to remain somewhat whiter for a while than the rest, and the less prestigious ones darker. But if the country's racial mixing ever became so thorough that skin color and other currently used bodily features were sufficiently unrecognizable or no longer of sufficient interest to be noticed, race would no longer be associated with social ranking. If Americans then still needed to rank each other, new criteria would have to be found.

PREJUDICE, DISCRIMINATION, AND RACISM

I MAGINE YOU ARE A 57-YEAR-OLD WHITE VICE president with Friendly Bank. You earn a considerable amount of money, have large mortgage and car payments, and support four kids, two of whom are in college. You are the primary breadwinner in your family. At lunch, your boss asks you about the new manager you will be hiring. He hints to you in a subtle way, a way you could never prove in court, that he has had bad experiences working with Asian Americans and would be extremely upset if one was hired. You are not racist toward Asians. In fact, one of your best friends is an Asian American. You do, however, need this job, your family needs to eat, two of your children are in college, and you are at an age at which moving from one job to another would be very difficult and extremely costly. Of the three hundred people who apply for this position, several Asian American candidates appear to be highly qualified, and one unquestionably would make an excellent bank manager. Would you turn a blind eye to the resumes of the Asian Americans, or would you hire the most qualified person, even if that meant hiring an Asian American and being marginalized or conveniently downsized by your boss?

How do feelings of antipathy toward or dislike of a group of people because of their skin color, ethnicity, or religion culminate in actions against members of that group? As the preceding example indicates, individuals may act in discriminatory ways and not be prejudiced or racist. Conversely, someone may be prejudiced and racist toward a group and not discriminate. The Asian or black shoe salesperson who does not like whites may still sell a white customer a pair of shoes in order to earn a commission.

Prejudice and **discrimination** are linked in complicated ways. Since World War II, whites' views on integration, interracial marriage, voting for nonwhite politicians,

prejudice To "prejudge"; having preconceived notions, attitudes, or negative beliefs about a group.
discrimination The denial of goods or services to an individual or group for arbitrary reasons, such as a person's race, religion, or nationality.

and sharing social space with blacks and Asians suggest that whites are gradually embracing the idea of a color-blind society. However, things, particularly attitudes through surveys, are not always as they seem. Such survey findings are encouraging only if you believe that respondents' answers are an accurate reflection of what they really think or feel. Perhaps these trends reflect pressure to conform to what respondents believe is a socially desirable attitude. Typically, individuals want to present themselves to others in a positive way. This pressure to conform may lead respondents to conveniently forget or tightly monitor racist or prejudiced beliefs. Are answers to questions about racial attitudes merely a reflection of what takes place in the abstract, unnatural interview setting, or are these responses a valid and reliable window into Americans' racial attitudes? Frankly, social scientists are not always sure. To further complicate matters, it's not clear what connection, if any, exists between attitudes and action or between prejudice and discrimination. Demonstrating a strong, consistent causal link between attitudes and actions has proved elusive in the social sciences. The proposition that actions flow from attitudes may seem straightforward, but as we will see in the readings, it is not. It seems logical that individuals would behave in a manner consistent with their attitudes, opinions, or beliefs about a particular topic. If, for example, you define yourself as not being racist, you would not engage in racial discrimination. But as the example about the vice president of Friendly Bank suggests, various social and economic pressures mediate what we would like to do, what we should do, and what we actually do.

Prejudice and discrimination take many forms. The first five readings, in **Understanding Racism,** examine those forms and the way certain social and structural conditions can create an environment in which prejudice and discrimination are likely to emerge. In an insightful and classic piece of sociology, Herbert Blumer explains race prejudice (racism) as a reflection of how individuals place themselves in a racial hierarchy relative to other racial groups they encounter; that is, individuals attempt to maintain privilege and status by reserving the "prerogatives" of their racial group, even if they are not consciously aware of it. Robert Merton provides examples of the social context in which a nonprejudiced individual like our vice president at Friendly Bank might act in a discriminatory fashion. Like Blumer, Merton outlines how prejudice and discrimination are often rooted in efforts to maintain privileges or advantages that accrue to individuals because of their skin color. Susan Akram and Kevin Johnson discuss how Arab Americans and Muslims in the United States have been subject to discriminatory treatment, harassment, and increased surveillance by the government since the 9/11 terrorist attacks. The assumption among some, these authors point out, is that every Arab American is a potential terrorist until proven otherwise. George Lipsitz chronicles how racism by the federal government in housing, bank lending, and huge subsidies to spur suburbanization (and white flight from the cities) after World War II should be understood as institutional practices that resulted in sub-stantial long-term, intergenerational "investments" in the white population. Lawrence Bobo argues that the old-style Jim Crow racism of the past has been replaced by laissez-faire racism. This theory suggests that since the government and institutions can no longer legally engage in overt discrimination, individuals can no longer claim that racism affects upward mobility.

The five articles in **How Space Gets Raced** reveal a nation highly segregated by race and ethnicity. Douglas Massey argues that residential segregation results in a loss of occupational and educational mobility for racial minorities and cuts off communities from "mainstream" America. Elijah Anderson explains how many poor, young African Americans use fear and intimidation as a way to gain respect among their peers. Robert Bullard details how poor and nonwhite neighborhoods are disproportionately exposed to toxic waste, perhaps the most obvious way in which social space gets raced to the detriment of a racial minority.

The Reverend Martin Luther King commented, "The church is the most segregated institution in America . . . and Sunday service is the most segregated hour in the nation." Michael Emerson asks why this is the case and, perhaps more important, what are the social characteristics of racially integrated congregations. Finally, Shannon Zenk and associates expose the extent to which space gets raced in their study of which neighborhoods have access to large supermarkets and which ones must rely on the corner store or bodega for their groceries. ✳

16 Race Prejudice as a Sense of Group Position

Herbert Blumer

The late HERBERT BLUMER spent most of his professional career at the University of Chicago and the University of California, Berkeley. Blumer established symbolic interactionism as a major sociological perspective in American sociology.

> **Questions to Consider**
>
> Herbert Blumer writes, "to characterize another racial group is, by opposition, to define one's own group." How does a "sense of group position" shape how we see other racial and ethnic groups? Have you ever defined your racial group membership in such a way as to heighten your group's status at the expense of another? What was the context?

IN THIS PAPER I AM PROPOSING AN APPROACH to the study of race prejudice different from that which dominates contemporary scholarly thought on this topic. My thesis is that race prejudice exists basically in a sense of group position rather than in a set of feelings which members of one racial group have toward the members of another racial group. This different way of viewing race prejudice shifts study and analysis from a preoccupation with feelings as lodged in individuals to a concern with the relationship of racial groups. It also shifts scholarly treatment away from individual lines of experience and focuses interest on the collective process by which a racial group comes to define and redefine another racial group. Such shifts, I believe, will yield a more realistic and penetrating understanding of race prejudice.

There can be little question that the rather vast literature on race prejudice is dominated by the idea that such prejudice exists fundamentally as a feeling or set of feelings lodged in the individual. It is usually depicted as consisting of feelings such as antipathy, hostility, hatred, intolerance, and aggressiveness. Accordingly, the task of scientific inquiry becomes two-fold. On one hand, there is a need to identify the feelings which make up race prejudice—to see how they fit together and how they are supported by other psychological elements, such as mythical beliefs. On the other hand, there is need of showing how the feeling complex has come into being. Thus, some scholars trace the complex feelings back chiefly to innate dispositions; some trace it to personality composition, such as authoritarian personality; and others regard the feelings of prejudice as being formed through social experience. However different may be the contentions regarding the makeup of racial prejudice and the way in which it may come into existence, these contentions are alike in locating prejudice in the realm of individual feeling. This is clearly true of the work of psychologists, psychiatrists, and social psychologists, and tends to be predominantly the case in the work of sociologists.

Unfortunately, this customary way of viewing race prejudice overlooks and obscures the fact that race prejudice is fundamentally a matter of relationship between racial groups. A little reflective thought should make this very clear. Race prejudice presupposes, necessarily, that racially prejudiced individuals think of themselves as belonging to a given racial group. It means, also, that they assign to other racial groups those against whom they are prejudiced. Thus, logically and actually, a scheme of racial identification is necessary as a framework for racial prejudice. Moreover, such identification involves the formation of an image or a conception of one's own racial group and of another racial group, inevitably in terms of the relationship of such groups. To fail to see that racial prejudice is a matter (a) of the racial identification made of oneself and of others, and (b) of the way in which the identified groups are conceived in relation to each other, is to miss what is logically and actually basic. One should keep clearly in mind that people necessarily come to identify themselves as belonging to a racial group; such identification is not spontaneous or inevitable but a result of experience. Further, one must realize that the kind of picture which a racial group forms of itself and the kind of picture which it may form of others are similarly products of experience. Hence, such pictures are variable, just as the lines of experience which produce them are variable.

The body of feelings which scholars, today, are so inclined to regard as constituting the substance of race prejudice is actually a resultant of the way in which given racial groups conceive of themselves and of others. A basic understanding of race prejudice must be sought in the process by which racial groups form images of themselves and of others. This process, as I hope to show, is fundamentally *a collective process*. It operates chiefly through the public media in which individuals who are accepted as the spokesmen of a racial group characterize publicly another racial group. To characterize another racial group is, by opposition, to define one's own group. This is equivalent to placing the two groups in relation to each other, or defining their positions *vis-à-vis* each other. It is the *sense of social position* emerging from this collective process of characterization which provides the basis of race prejudice. The following discussion will consider important facets of this matter.

I would like to begin by discussing several of the important feelings that enter into race prejudice. This discussion will reveal how fundamentally racial feelings point to and depend on a positional arrangement of the racial groups. In this discussion I will confine myself to such feelings in the case of a dominant racial group.

There are four basic types of feeling that seem to be always present in race prejudice in the dominant group. They are (1) a feeling of superiority, (2) a feeling that the subordinate race is intrinsically different and alien, (3) a feeling of proprietary claim to certain areas of privilege and advantage, and (4) a fear and suspicion that the subordinate race harbors designs on the prerogatives of the dominant race. A few words about each of these four feelings will suffice.

In race prejudice there is a self-assured feeling on the part of the dominant racial group of being naturally superior or better. This is commonly shown in a disparagement of the qualities of the subordinate racial group. Condemnatory or debasing traits, such as laziness, dishonesty, greediness, unreliability, stupidity, deceit and immorality, are usually imputed to it. The second feeling, that the subordinate race is an alien and fundamentally different stock, is likewise always present. "They are not of our kind" is a common way in which this is likely to be expressed. It is this feeling that reflects, justifies, and promotes the social exclusion of the subordinate racial group. The combination of these two feelings of superiority and of distinctiveness can easily give rise to feelings of aversion and even antipathy. But in themselves they do not form prejudice. We have to introduce the third and fourth types of feeling.

The third feeling, the sense of proprietary claim, is of crucial importance. It is the feeling on the part of the dominant group of being entitled to either exclusive or prior rights in many important areas of life. The range of such exclusive or prior claims may be wide, covering the ownership of property such as choice lands and sites; the right to certain jobs, occupations or professions; the claim to certain kinds of industry or lines of business; the claim to certain positions of control and decision-making as in government and law; the right to exclusive membership in given institutions such as schools, churches and recreational institutions; the claim to certain positions of social prestige and to the display of the symbols and accoutrements of these positions; and the claim to certain areas of intimacy and privacy. The feeling of such proprietary claims is exceedingly strong in race prejudice. Again, however, this feeling even in combination with the feeling of superiority and the feeling of distinctiveness does not explain race prejudice. These three feelings are present frequently in societies showing no prejudice, as in certain forms of feudalism, in caste relations, in societies of chiefs and commoners, and under many settled relations of conquerors and conquered. Where claims are solidified into a structure which is accepted or respected by all, there seems to be no group prejudice.

The remaining feeling essential to race prejudice is a fear or apprehension that the subordinate racial group is threatening, or will threaten, the position of the dominant group. Thus, acts or suspected acts that are interpreted as an attack on the natural superiority of the dominant group, or an intrusion into their sphere of group exclusiveness, or an encroachment on their area of proprietary claim are crucial in arousing and fashioning race prejudice. These acts mean "getting out of place."

It should be clear that these four basic feelings of race prejudice definitely refer to a positional arrangement of the racial groups. The feeling of superiority places the subordinate people *below;* the feeling of alienation places them *beyond;* the feeling of proprietary claim excludes them from the prerogatives of position; and the fear of encroachment is an emotional recoil from the endangering of group position. As these features suggest, the positional relation of the two racial groups is crucial in race prejudice. The dominant group is not concerned with the subordinate group as such but it is deeply concerned with its position *vis-à-vis* the subordinate group. This is epitomized in the key and universal expression that a given race is all right in "its place." The sense of group position is the very heart of the relation of the dominant to the subordinate group. It supplies the dominant group with its framework of perception, its standard of judgment, its patterns of sensitivity, and its emotional proclivities.

It is important to recognize that this sense of group position transcends the feelings of the individual members of the dominant group, giving such members a common orientation that is not otherwise to be found in separate feelings and views. There is likely to be considerable difference between the ways in which the individual members of the dominant group think and feel about the subordinate group. Some may feel bitter and hostile, with strong antipathies, with an exalted sense of superiority and with a lot of spite; others may have charitable and protective feelings, marked by a sense of piety and tinctured by benevolence; others may be condescending and reflect mild contempt; and others may be disposed to politeness and considerateness with no feelings of truculence. These are only a few of many different patterns of feeling to be found among members of the dominant racial group. What gives a common dimension to them is a sense of the social position of their group. Whether the members be humane, or callous, cultured or unlettered, liberal or reactionary, powerful or impotent, arrogant or humble, rich or poor, honorable or dishonorable—all are led, by virtue of sharing the sense of group position, to similar individual positions.

The sense of group position is a general kind of orientation. It is a general feeling without being reducible to specific feelings like hatred, hostility or antipathy. It is also a general understanding without being composed of any set of specific beliefs. On the social psychological side it cannot be equated to a sense of social status as ordinarily conceived, for it refers not merely to vertical positioning but to many other lines of position independent of the vertical dimension. Sociologically it is not a mere reflection of the objective relations between racial groups. Rather, it stands for "what ought to be" rather than for "what is." It is a sense of where the two racial groups *belong.*

In its own way, the sense of group position is a norm and imperative—indeed a very powerful one. It guides, incites, cows, and coerces. It should be borne in mind that this sense of group position stands for and involves a fundamental kind of group affiliation for the members of the dominant racial group. To the extent they recognize or feel themselves as belonging to that group they will automatically come under the influence of the sense of position held by that group. Thus, even though given individual members may have personal views and feelings different from the sense of group position, they will have to conjure with the sense of group position held by their racial group. If the sense of position is strong, to act contrary to it is to risk a feeling of self-alienation and to face the possibility of ostracism. I am trying to suggest, accordingly, that the locus of race prejudice is not in the area of individual feeling but in the definition of the respective positions of the racial groups.

The source of race prejudice lies in a felt challenge to this sense of group position. The challenge, one must recognize, may come in many different ways. It may be in the form of an affront to feelings of group superiority; it may be in the form of attempts at familiarity or transgressing the boundary line of group exclusiveness; it may be in the form of encroachment at countless points of proprietary claim; it may be a challenge to power and privilege; it may take the form of economic competition. Race prejudice is a defensive reaction to such challenging of the sense of group position. It consists of the disturbed feelings, usually of marked hostility, that are thereby aroused. As such, race prejudice is a protective device. It functions, however short-sightedly, to preserve the integrity and the position of the dominant group.

It is crucially important to recognize that the sense of group position is not a mere summation of the feelings of position such as might be developed independently by separate individuals as they come to compare themselves with given individuals of the subordinate race. The sense of group position refers to the position of group to group, not to that of individual to individual. Thus, *vis-à-vis* the subordinate racial group the unlettered individual with low status in the dominant racial group has a sense of group position common to that of the elite of his group. By virtue of sharing this sense of position such an individual, despite his low status, feels that members of the subordinate group, however distinguished and accomplished, are somehow inferior, alien, and properly restricted in the area of claims. He forms his conception as a representative of the dominant group; he treats individual members of the subordinate group as representative of that group.

An analysis of how the sense of group position is formed should start with a clear recognition that it is an historical product. It is set originally by conditions of initial contact. Prestige, power, possession of skill, numbers, original self-conceptions, aims, designs and opportunities are a few of the factors that may fashion the original sense of group position. Subsequent experience in the relation of the two racial groups, especially in the area of claims, opportunities and advantages, may mould the sense of group position in many diverse ways. Further, the sense of group position may be intensified or weakened, brought to sharp focus or dulled. It may be deeply entrenched and tenaciously resist change for long periods of time. Or it may never take root. It may undergo quick growth and vigorous expansion, or it may dwindle away through slow-moving erosion. It may be firm or soft, acute or dull, continuous or intermittent. In short, viewed comparatively, the sense of group position is very variable.

However variable its particular career, the sense of group position is clearly formed by a running process in which the dominant racial group is led to define and redefine the subordinate racial group and the relations between them. There are two important aspects of this process of definition that I wish to single out for consideration.

First, the process of definition occurs obviously through complex interaction and communication between the members of the dominant group. Leaders, prestige bearers, officials, group agents, dominant individuals and ordinary laymen present to one another characterizations of the subordinate group and express their feelings and ideas on the relations. Through talk, tales, stories, gossip, anecdotes, messages, pronouncements, news accounts, orations, sermons, preachments and the like definitions are presented and feelings are expressed. In this usually vast and complex interaction separate views run against one another, influence one another, modify each other, incite one another and fuse together in new forms. Correspondingly, feelings which are expressed meet, stimulate each other, feed on each other, intensify each other and emerge in new patterns. Currents of view and currents of feeling come into being; sweeping along to positions of dominance and serving as polar points for the organization of thought and sentiment. If the interaction becomes increasingly circular and reinforcing, devoid of serious inner opposition, such currents grow, fuse and become strengthened. It is through such a process that a collective image of the subordinate group is formed and a sense of group position is set. The evidence of such a process is glaring when one reviews the history of any racial arrangement marked by prejudice.

Such a complex process of mutual interaction with its different lines and degrees of formation gives the lie to the many schemes which would lodge the cause of race prejudice in the makeup of the individual—whether in the form of innate disposition, constitutional makeup, personality structure, or direct personal experience with members of the other race. The collective image and feelings in race prejudice are forged out of a complicated social process in which the individual is himself shaped and organized. The scheme, so popular today, which would trace race prejudice to a so-called authoritarian personality shows a grievous misunderstanding of the simple essentials of the collective process that leads to a sense of group position.

The second important aspect of the process of group definition is that it is necessarily concerned with *an abstract image* of the subordinate racial group. The subordinate racial group is defined as if it were an entity or whole. This entity or whole—like the Negro race, or the Japanese, or the Jews—is necessarily an abstraction, never coming within the perception of any of the senses. While actual encounters are with individuals, the picture formed of the racial group is necessarily of a vast entity which spreads out far beyond such individuals and transcends experience with such individuals. The implications of the fact that the collective image is of an abstract group are of crucial significance. I would like to note four of these implications.

First, the building of the image of the abstract group takes place in the area of the remote and not of the near. It is not the experience with concrete individuals in daily association that gives rise to the definitions of the extended, abstract group. Such immediate experience is usually regulated and orderly. Even where such immediate experience is disrupted the new definitions which are formed are limited to the individuals involved. The collective image of the abstract group grows up not by generalizing from experiences gained in close, first-hand contacts but through the transcending characterizations that are made of the group as an entity. Thus, one must seek the central stream of definition in those areas where the dominant group as such is characterizing the subordinate group as such. This occurs in the "public arena" wherein the spokesmen appear as representatives and agents of the dominant group. The extended public arena is constituted by such things as legislative assemblies, public meetings, conventions, the press, and the printed word. What goes on in this public arena attracts the attention of large numbers of the dominant group and is felt as the voice and action of the group as such.

Second, the definitions that are forged in the public arena center, obviously, about matters that are felt to be of major importance. Thus, we are led to recognize the crucial role of the "big event" in developing a conception of the subordinate racial group. The happening that seems momentous, that touches deep sentiments, that seems to raise fundamental questions about relations, and that awakens strong feelings of identification with one's racial group is the kind of event that is central in the formation of the racial image. Here, again, we note the relative unimportance of the huge bulk of experiences coming from daily contact with individuals of the subordinate group. It is the events seemingly loaded with great collective significance that are the focal points of the public discussion. The definition of these events is chiefly responsible for the development of a racial image and of the sense of group position. When this public discussion takes the form of a denunciation of the subordinate racial group, signifying that it is unfit and a threat, the discussion becomes particularly potent in shaping the sense of social position.

Third, the major influence in public discussion is exercised by individuals and groups who have the public ear and who are felt to have standing, prestige, authority and power. Intellectual and social elites, public figures of prominence, and leaders of powerful organizations are likely to be the key figures in the formation of the sense of group position and in the characterization of the subordinate group. It is well to note this in view of the not infrequent tendency of students to regard race prejudice as growing out of the multiplicity of experiences and attitudes of the bulk of the people.

Fourth, we also need to perceive the appreciable opportunity that is given to strong interest groups in directing the lines of discussion and setting the interpretations that arise in such discussion. Their self-interests may dictate the kind of position they wish the dominant racial group to enjoy. It may be a position which enables them to retain certain advantages, or even more to gain still greater advantages. Hence, they may be vigorous in seeking to manufacture events to attract public attention and to set lines of issue in such a way as to predetermine interpretations favorable to their interests. The role of strongly organized groups seeking to further special interest is usually central in the formation of collective images of abstract groups. Historical records of major instances of race relations, as in our South, or in South Africa, or in Europe in the case of the Jew, or on the West Coast in the case of the Japanese, show the formidable part played by interest groups in defining the subordinate racial group.

I conclude this highly condensed paper with two further observations that may throw additional light on the relation of the sense of group position to race prejudice. Race prejudice becomes entrenched and tenacious to the extent the prevailing social order is rooted in the sense of social position. This has been true of the historic South in our country. In such a social order race prejudice tends to become chronic and impermeable to change. In other places the social order may be affected only to a limited extent by the sense of group position held by the dominant racial group. This I think has been true usually in the case of anti-Semitism in Europe and this country. Under these conditions the sense of group position tends to be weaker and more vulnerable. In turn, race prejudice has a much more variable and intermittent career, usually becoming pronounced only as a consequence of grave disorganizing events that allow for the formation of a scapegoat.

This leads me to my final observation which in a measure is an indirect summary. The sense of group position dissolves and race prejudice declines when the process of running definition does not keep abreast of major shifts in the social order. When events touching on relations are not treated as "big events" and hence do not set crucial issues in the arena of public discussion; or when the elite leaders or spokesmen do not define such big events vehemently or adversely; or where they define them in the direction of racial harmony; or when there is a paucity of strong interest groups seeking to build up a strong adverse image for special advantage—under such conditions the sense of group position recedes and race prejudice declines.

The clear implication of my discussion is that the proper and fruitful area in which race prejudice should be studied is the collective process through which a sense of group position is formed. To seek, instead, to understand it or to handle it in the arena of individual feeling and of individual experience seems to me to be clearly misdirected.

Seeing the Big Picture   **Racism: Group Position or Individual Belief?**

Blumer explains that four "feelings" make up race prejudice. Are you able to come up with an example of each of these four feelings for a specific racial or ethnic group? Are you convinced by his argument that racism is "a fundamental matter of relationship between racial groups" rather than individual-level feelings of animosity?

---

17   Discrimination and the American Creed
Robert K. Merton

The late ROBERT K. MERTON was an eminent sociological theorist and a well-known defender of sociology as a genuine science. His publications include *On the Shoulders of Giants: A Shandean Postscript* (1965) and *The Sociology of Science: Theoretical and Empirical Investigations* (1973).

Questions to Consider   Have you ever been in a situation in which social, economic, or peer pressure forced you to treat someone from a different racial group in an inappropriate way? Robert Merton suggests that individuals who are *not* prejudiced often act in bigoted and discriminatory ways. How and why does this happen? Is it possible to live our lives in the category Merton calls the "unprejudiced non-discriminator"?

THE PRIMARY FUNCTION OF THE SOCIOLOGIST is to search out the determinants and consequences of diverse forms of social behavior. To the extent that he succeeds in fulfilling this role, he clarifies the alternatives of organized social action in a given situation and of the probable outcome of each. To this extent, there is no sharp distinction between pure research and applied research. Rather, the difference is one between research with direct implications for particular problems of social action and research which is remote from these problems. Not infrequently, basic research which has succeeded only in clearing up previously confused concepts may have an immediate bearing upon the problems of men in society to a degree not approximated by applied research oriented exclusively to these problems. At least, this is the assumption underlying the present paper: clarification of apparently unclear and confused concepts in the sphere of race and ethnic relations is a step necessarily prior to the devising of effective programs for reducing intergroup conflict and for promoting equitable access to economic and social opportunities . . . .

The American Creed: As Cultural Ideal, Personal Belief and Practice

The American **creed** as set forth in the Declaration of Independence, the preamble of the Constitution and the Bill of Rights has often been misstated. This part of the cultural heritage does *not* include the patently false assertion that all men are created equal in capacity or endowment. It does *not* imply that an Einstein and a moron are equal in intellectual capacity or that Joe Louis and a small, frail Columbia professor (or a Mississippian Congressman) are equally endowed with brawny arms harboring muscles as strong as iron bands. It does *not* proclaim universal equality of innate intellectual or physical endowment.

Instead, the creed asserts the indefeasible principle of the human right to full equity—the right of equitable access to justice, freedom and opportunity, irrespective of race or religion or ethnic origin. It proclaims further the universalist doctrine of the dignity of the individual, irrespective of the groups of which he is a part. It is a creed announcing full moral equities for all, not an absurd myth affirming the equality of intellectual and physical capacity of all men everywhere. And it goes on to say that though men differ in innate endowment, they do so as individuals, not by virtue of their group memberships.

Viewed sociologically, the creed is a set of values and precepts embedded in American culture, to which Americans are expected to conform. It is a complex of affirmations, rooted in the historical past and ceremonially celebrated in the present, partly enacted in the laws of the land and partly not. Like all creeds, it is a profession of faith, a part of cultural tradition sanctified by the larger traditions of which it is a part.

It would be a mistaken sociological assertion, however, to suggest that the creed is a fixed and static cultural constant, unmodified in the course of time, just as it would be an error to imply that as an integral part of culture, it evenly blankets all subcultures of the national society. It is indeed dynamic, subject to change and in turn promoting change in other spheres of culture and society. It is, moreover, unevenly distributed throughout the society, being institutionalized as an integral part of local culture in some regions of the society and rejected in others.

creed In the context of this article, the belief system that a people share.

. . . Learned men and men in high public positions have repeatedly observed and deplored the disparity between ethos and behavior in the sphere of race and ethnic relations. In his magisterial volumes on the American Negro, for example, Gunnar Myrdal called this gulf between creed and conduct "an American dilemma," and centered his attention on the prospect of narrowing or closing the gap. The President's Committee on Civil Rights, in their report to the nation, and . . . President [Truman] himself, in a message to Congress, have called public attention to this "serious gap between our ideals and some of our practices."

But as valid as these observations may be, they tend so to simplify the relations between creed and conduct as to be seriously misleading both for social policy and for social science. All these high authorities notwithstanding, the problems of racial and ethnic inequities are not expressible as a discrepancy between high cultural principles and low social conduct. It is a relation not between two variables, official creed and private practice, but between three: first, the cultural creed honored in cultural tradition and partly enacted into law; second, the beliefs and attitudes of individuals regarding the principles of the creed; and third, the actual practices of individuals with reference to it.

Once we substitute these three variables of cultural ideal, belief and actual practice for the customary distinction between the two variables of cultural ideals and actual practices, the entire formulation of the problem becomes changed. We escape from the virtuous but ineffectual impasse of deploring the alleged hypocrisy of many Americans into the more difficult but potentially effectual realm of analyzing the problem in hand.

To describe the problem and to proceed to its analysis, it is necessary to consider the official creed, individuals' beliefs and attitudes concerning the creed, and their actual behavior. Once stated, the distinctions are readily applicable. Individuals may *recognize* the creed as part of a cultural tradition, *without having any private conviction of its moral validity or its binding quality.* Thus, so far as the beliefs of individuals are concerned, we can identify two types: those who genuinely believe in the creed and those who do not (although some of these may, on public or ceremonial occasions, profess adherence to its principles). Similarly, with respect to actual practices: conduct may or may not conform to the creed. But, and this is the salient consideration: *conduct may or may not conform with individuals' own beliefs concerning the moral claims of all men to equal opportunity.*

Stated in formal sociological terms, this asserts that attitudes and overt behavior vary independently. *Prejudicial attitudes need not coincide with discriminatory behavior.* The implications of this statement can be drawn out in terms of a logical syntax whereby the variables are diversely combined, as can be seen in the following typology.

By exploring the interrelations between prejudice and discrimination, we can identify four major types in terms of their attitudes toward the creed and their behavior with respect to it. Each type is found in every region and social class, though in varying numbers. By examining each type, we shall be better prepared to understand their interdependence and the appropriate types of action for curbing ethnic discrimination. The folklabels for each type are intended to aid in their prompt recognition.

Type I: The Unprejudiced Non-Discriminator or All-Weather Liberal

These are the racial and ethnic liberals who adhere to the creed in both belief and practice. They are neither prejudiced nor given to discrimination. Their orientation toward the creed is fixed and stable. Whatever the environing situation, they are likely to abide by their beliefs: hence, the *all-weather* liberal.

This is, of course, the strategic group which *can* act as the spearhead for the progressive extension of the creed into effective practice. They represent the solid foundation both for the measure of ethnic equities which now exist and for the future enlargement of these equities. Integrated with the creed in both belief and practice, they would seem most motivated to influence others toward the same democratic outlook. They represent a reservoir of culturally legitimatized goodwill which can be channeled into an active program for extending belief in the creed and conformity with it in practice.

Most important, as we shall see presently, the all-weather liberals comprise the group which can so reward others for conforming with the creed, as to transform deviants into conformists. They alone can provide the positive social environment for the other types who will no longer find it expedient or rewarding to retain their prejudices or discriminatory practices.

But though the ethnic liberal is a *potential* force for the successive extension of the American creed, he does not fully realize this potentiality in actual fact, for a variety of reasons. Among the limitations on effective action

are several fallacies to which the ethnic liberal seems peculiarly subject. First among these is the *fallacy of group soliloquies.* Ethnic liberals are busily engaged in talking to themselves. Repeatedly, the same groups of like-minded liberals seek each other out, hold periodic meetings in which they engage in mutual exhortation and thus lend social and psychological support to one another. But however much these unwittingly self-selected audiences may reinforce the creed among themselves, they do not thus appreciably diffuse the creed in belief or practice to groups which depart from it in one respect or the other.

More, these group soliloquies in which there is typically wholehearted agreement among fellow-liberals tend to promote another fallacy limiting effective action. This is the *fallacy of unanimity.* Continued association with like-minded individuals tends to produce the illusion that a large measure of consensus has been achieved in the community at large. The unanimity regarding essential cultural axioms which obtains in these small groups provokes an overestimation of the strength of the movement and of its effective inroads upon the larger population which does not necessarily share these creedal axioms. Many also mistake participation in the groups of like-minded individuals for effective action. Discussion accordingly takes the place of action. The reinforcement of the creed for oneself is mistaken for the extension of the creed among those outside the limited circle of ethnic liberals.

Arising from adherence to the creed is a third limitation upon effective action, the *fallacy of privatized solutions* to the problem. The ethnic liberal, precisely because he is at one with the American creed, may rest content with his own individual behavior and thus see no need to do anything about the problem at large. Since his own spiritual house is in order, he is not motivated by guilt or shame to work on a collective problem. The very freedom of the liberal from guilt thus prompts him to secede from any *collective* effort to set the national house in order. He essays a *private* solution to a *social* problem. He assumes that numerous individual adjustments will serve in place of a collective adjustment. His outlook, compounded of good moral philosophy but poor sociology, holds that each individual must put his own house in order and fails to recognize that privatized solutions cannot be effected for problems which are essentially social in nature. For clearly, if each person *were* motivated to abide by the American creed, the problem would not be likely to exist in the first place. It is only when a social environment is established by conformists to the creed that deviants can in due course be brought to modify their behavior in the direction of conformity. But this "environment" can be constituted only through collective effort and not through private adherence to a public creed. Thus we have the paradox that the clear conscience of many ethnic liberals may promote the very social situation which permits deviations from the creed to continue unchecked. Privatized liberalism invites social inaction. Accordingly, there appears the phenomenon of the inactive or passive liberal, himself at spiritual ease, neither prejudiced nor discriminatory, but in a measure tending to contribute to the persistence of prejudice and discrimination through his very inaction.

The fallacies of group soliloquy, unanimity and privatized solutions thus operate to make the potential strength of the ethnic liberals unrealized in practice.

It is only by first recognizing these limitations that the liberal can hope to overcome them. With some hesitancy, one may suggest initial policies for curbing the scope of the three fallacies. The fallacy of group soliloquies can be removed only by having ethnic liberals enter into organized groups not comprised merely by fellow-liberals. This exacts a heavy price on the liberal. It means that he faces initial opposition and resistance rather than prompt consensus. It entails giving up the gratifications of consistent group support.

The fallacy of unanimity can in turn be reduced by coming to see that American society often provides large rewards for those who express their ethnic prejudice in discrimination. Only if the balance of rewards, material and psychological, is modified will behavior be modified. Sheer exhortation and propaganda are not enough. Exhortation verges on a belief in magic if it is not supported by appropriate changes in the social environment to make conformity with the exhortation rewarding.

Finally, the fallacy of privatized solutions requires the militant liberal to motivate the passive liberal to collective effort, possibly by inducing in him a sense of guilt for his unwitting contribution to the problems of ethnic inequities through his own systematic inaction.

One may suggest a unifying theme for the ethnic liberal: goodwill is not enough to modify social reality. It is only when this goodwill is harnessed to social-psychological realism that it can be used to reach cultural objectives.

Type II: The Unprejudiced Discriminator or Fair-Weather Liberal

The fair-weather liberal is the man of expediency who, despite his own freedom from prejudice, supports discriminatory practices when it is the easier or more profitable course. His expediency may take the form of holding his silence and thus implicitly acquiescing in expresions of ethnic prejudice by others or in the practice of discrimination by others. This is the expediency of the timid: the liberal who hesitates to speak up against discrimination for fear he might lose status or be otherwise penalized by his prejudiced associates. Or his expediency may take the form of grasping at advantages in social and economic competition deriving solely from the ethnic status of competitors. This is the expediency of the self-assertive: the employer, himself not an anti-Semite or Negrophobe, who refuses to hire Jewish or Negro workers because "it might hurt business"; the trade union leader who expediently advocates racial discrimination in order not to lose the support of powerful Negrophobes in his union.

In varying degrees, the fair-weather liberal suffers from guilt and shame for departing from his own effective beliefs in the American creed. Each deviation through which he derives a limited reward from passively acquiescing in or actively supporting discrimination contributes cumulatively to this fund of guilt. He is, therefore, peculiarly vulnerable to the efforts of the all-weather liberal who would help him bring his conduct into accord with his beliefs, thus removing this source of guilt. He is the most amenable to cure, because basically he wants to be cured. His is a split conscience which motivates him to cooperate actively with those who will help remove the source of internal conflict. He thus represents the strategic group promising the largest returns for the least effort. Persistent re-affirmation of the creed will only intensify his conflict; but a long regimen in a favorable social climate can be expected to transform the fair-weather liberal into an all-weather liberal.

Type III: The Prejudiced Non-Discriminator or Fair-Weather Illiberal

The fair-weather illiberal is the reluctant conformist to the creed, the man of prejudice who does not believe in the creed but conforms to it in practice through fear of sanctions which might otherwise be visited upon him. You know him well: the prejudiced employer who discriminates against racial or ethnic groups until a Fair Employment Practice Commission, able and willing to enforce the law, puts the fear of punishment into him; the trade union leader, himself deeply prejudiced, who does away with Jim Crow in his union because the rank-and-file demands that it be done away with; the businessman who forgoes his own prejudices when he finds a profitable market among the very people he hates, fears or despises; the timid **bigot** who will not express his prejudices when he is in the presence of powerful men who vigorously and effectively affirm their belief in the American creed.

It should be clear that the fair-weather illiberal is the precise counterpart of the fair-weather liberal. Both are men of expediency, to be sure, but expediency dictates different courses of behavior in the two cases. The timid bigot conforms to the creed only when there is danger or loss in deviations, just as the timid liberal deviates from the creed when there is danger or loss in conforming. *Superficial similarity in behavior of the two in the same situation should not be permitted to cloak a basic difference in the meaning of this outwardly similar behavior,* a difference which is as important for social policy as it is for social science. Whereas the timid bigot is under strain when he conforms to the creed, the timid liberal is under strain when he deviates. For ethnic prejudice has deep roots in the character structure of the fair-weather bigot, and this will find overt expression unless there are powerful countervailing forces, institutional, legal and interpersonal. He does not accept the moral legitimacy of the creed; he conforms because he must, and will cease to conform when the pressure is removed. The fair-weather liberal, on the other hand, is effectively committed to the creed and does not require strong institutional pressure to conform; continuing interpersonal relations with all-weather liberals may be sufficient.

This is the one critical point at which the traditional formulation of the problem of ethnic discrimination as a departure from the creed can lead to serious errors of theory and practice. Overt behavioral deviation (or conformity) may signify importantly different situations, depending upon the underlying motivations. Knowing simply that ethnic discrimination is rife in a community does not, therefore, point to appropriate lines of social policy. It is necessary to know also the distribution of ethnic prejudices

bigot Someone deeply committed to his or her own prejudices, distortions, or biases regarding other people. Bigots are intolerant of difference.

and basic motivations for these prejudices as well. Communities with the same amount of overt discrimination may represent vastly different types of problems, dependent on whether the population is comprised by a large nucleus of fair-weather liberals ready to abandon their discriminatory practices under slight interpersonal pressure or a large nucleus of fair-weather illiberals who will abandon discrimination only if major changes in the local institutional setting can be effected. Any statement of the problem as a gulf between creedal ideals and prevailing practice is thus seen to be overly simplified in the precise sense of masking this decisive difference between the type of discrimination exhibited by the fair-weather liberal and by the fair-weather illiberal. That the gulf-between-ideal-and-practice does not adequately describe the nature of the ethnic problem will become more apparent as we turn to the fourth type in our inventory of prejudice and discrimination.

Type IV: The Prejudiced Discriminator or the All-Weather Illiberal

This type, too, is not unknown to you. He is the confirmed illiberal, the bigot pure and unashamed, the man of prejudice consistent in his departure from the American creed. In some measure, he is found everywhere in the land, though in varying numbers. He derives large social and psychological gains from his conviction that "any white man (including the village idiot) is 'better' than any nigger (including George Washington Carver)." He considers differential treatment of Negro and white not as "discrimination," in the sense of unfair treatment, but as "discriminating," in the sense of showing acute discernment. For him, it is as clear that one "ought" to accord a Negro and a white different treatment in a wide diversity of situations, as it is clear to the population at large that one "ought" to accord a child and an adult different treatment in many situations.

This illustrates anew my reason for questioning the applicability of the unusual formula of the American dilemma as a gap between lofty creed and low conduct. For the confirmed illiberal, ethnic discrimination does *not* represent a discrepancy between *his* ideals and *his* behavior. His ideals proclaim the right, even the duty, of discrimination. Accordingly, his behavior does not entail a sense of social deviation, with the resultant strains which this would involve. The ethnic illiberal is as much a conformist as the ethnic liberal. He is merely conforming to a different cultural and institutional pattern which is centered, not about the creed, but about a doctrine of essential inequality of status ascribed to those of diverse ethnic and racial origins. To overlook this is to overlook the well-known *fact* that our national culture is divided into a number of local subcultures which are not consistent among themselves in all respects. And again, to fail to take this fact of different subcultures into account is to open the door for all manner of errors of social policy in attempting to control the problems of racial and ethnic discrimination.

This view of the all-weather illiberal has one immediate implication with wide bearing upon social policies and sociological theory oriented toward the problem of discrimination. The extreme importance of the social surroundings of the confirmed illiberal at once becomes apparent. For as these surroundings vary, so, in some measure, does the problem of the consistent illiberal. The illiberal, living in those cultural regions where the American creed is widely repudiated and is no effective part of the subculture, has his private ethnic attitudes and practices supported by the local mores, the local institutions and the local power-structure. The illiberal in cultural areas dominated by a large measure of adherence to the American creed is in a social environment where he is isolated and receives small social support for his beliefs and practices. In both instances, the *individual* is an illiberal, to be sure, but he represents two significantly different *sociological types*. In the first instance, he is a *social conformist,* with strong moral and institutional reinforcement, whereas in the second, he is a *social deviant,* lacking strong social corroboration. In the one case, his discrimination involves him in further integration with his network of social relations; in the other, it threatens to cut him off from sustaining interpersonal ties. In the first cultural context, personal change in his ethnic behavior involves alienating himself from people significant to him; in the second context, this change of personal outlook may mean fuller incorporation in groups meaningful to him. In the first situation, modification of his ethnic views requires him to take the path of greatest resistance whereas in the second, it may mean the path of least resistance. From all this, we may surmise that any social policy aimed at changing the behavior and perhaps the attitudes of the all-weather illiberal will have to take into account the cultural and social structure of the area in which he lives . . . .

Implications of the Typology for Social Policy

. . . In approaching problems of policy, two things are plain. First, these should be considered from the standpoint of the militant ethnic liberal, for he alone is sufficiently motivated to engage in positive action for the reduction of ethnic discrimination. And second, the fair-weather liberal, the fair-weather illiberal and the all-weather illiberal represent types differing sufficiently to require diverse kinds of treatment.

Treatment of the Fair-Weather Liberal

The fair-weather liberal, it will be remembered, discriminates only when it appears expedient to do so, and experiences some measure of guilt for deviating from his own belief in the American creed. He suffers from this conflict between conscience and conduct. Accordingly, he is a relatively easy target for the all-weather liberal. He represents the strategic group promising the largest immediate returns for the least effort. Recognition of this type defines the first task for the militant liberal who would enter into a collective effort to make the creed a viable and effective set of social norms rather than a ceremonial myth . . . .

Since the fair-weather liberal discriminates only when it seems rewarding to do so, the crucial need is so to change social situations that there are few occasions in which discrimination proves rewarding and many in which it does not. This would suggest that ethnic liberals self-consciously and deliberately seek to draw into the social groups where they constitute a comfortable majority a number of the "expedient discriminators." This would serve to counteract the dangers of self-selection through which liberals come to associate primarily with like-minded individuals. It would, further, provide an interpersonal and social environment for the fair-weather liberal in which he would find substantial social and psychological gains from abiding by his own beliefs, gains which would more than offset the rewards attendant upon occasional discrimination. It appears that men do not long persist in behavior which lacks social corroboration.

We have much to learn about the role of numbers and proportions in determining the behavior of members of a group. But it seems that individuals generally act differently when they are numbered among a minority rather than the majority. This is not to say that minorities abdicate their practices in the face of a contrary-acting majority, but only that the same people are subjected to different strains and pressures according to whether they are included in the majority or the minority. And the fair-weather liberal who finds himself associated with militant ethnic liberals may be expected to forgo his occasional deviations into discrimination; he may move from category II into category I. . . .

Treatment of the Fair-Weather Illiberal

Because his *beliefs* correspond to those of the full-fledged liberal, the fair-weather liberal can rather readily be drawn into an interpersonal environment constituted by those of a comparable turn of mind. This would be more difficult for the fair-weather illiberal, whose beliefs are so fully at odds with those of ethnic liberals that he may, at first, only be alienated by association with them. If the initial tactic for the fair-weather liberal, therefore, is a change in interpersonal environment, the seemingly most appropriate tactic for the fair-weather illiberal is a change in the institutional and legal environment. It is, indeed, probably this type which liberals implicitly have in mind when they expect significant changes in behavior to result from the introduction of controls on ethnic discrimination into the legal machinery of our society.

For this type—and it is a major limitation for planning policies of control that we do not know his numbers or his distribution in the country—it would seem that the most effective tactic is the institution of legal controls administered with strict efficiency. This would presumably reduce the amount of *discrimination* practiced by the fair-weather illiberal, though it might *initially* enhance rather than reduce his *prejudices* . . . .

A second prevalent tactic for modifying the prejudice of the fair-weather illiberal is that of seeking to draw him into interethnic groups explicitly formed for the promotion of tolerance. This, too, seems largely ineffectual, since the deeply prejudiced individual will not enter into such groups of his own volition. As a consequence of this process of self-selection, these tolerance groups soon come to be comprised by the very ethnic liberals who initiated the enterprise.

This barrier of self-selection can be partially hurdled only if the ethnic illiberals are brought into continued association with militant liberals in groups devoted to significant common values, quite remote from objectives of ethnic equity as such. Thus, as our Columbia-Lavanburg researches have found, many fair-weather illiberals *will* live in interracial housing projects in order to enjoy the rewards of superior housing at a given rental. And some of the illiberals thus

brought into personal contact with various ethnic groups under the auspices of prestigeful militant liberals come to modify their prejudices. It is, apparently, only through interethnic collaboration, initially enforced by pressures of the situation, for immediate and significant objectives (other than tolerance) that the self-insulation of the fair-weather illiberal from rewarding interethnic contacts can be removed.

But however difficult it may presently be to affect the *prejudicial sentiments* of the fair-weather illiberal, his *discriminatory practices* can be lessened by the uniform, prompt and prestigeful use of legal and institutional sanctions. The critical problem is to ascertain the proportions of fair-weather and all-weather illiberals in a given local population in order to have some clue to the probable effectiveness or ineffectiveness of anti-discrimination legislation.

Treatment of the All-Weather Illiberal

It is, of course, the hitherto confirmed illiberal, persistently translating his prejudices into active discrimination, who represents the most difficult problem. But though he requires longer and more careful treatment, it is possible that he is not beyond change. In every instance, his social surroundings must be assiduously taken into account. It makes a peculiarly large difference whether he is in a cultural region of bigotry or in a predominantly "liberal" area, given over to verbal adherence to the American creed, at the very least. As this cultural climate varies, so must the prescription for his cure and the prognosis for a relatively quick or long delayed recovery.

In an unfavorable cultural climate—and this does not necessarily exclude the benign regions of the Far South—the immediate resort will probably have to be that of working through legal and administrative federal controls over extreme discrimination, with full recognition that, in all probability, these regulations will be systematically evaded for some time to come. In such cultural regions, we may expect nullification of the law as the common practice, perhaps as common as was the case in the nation at large with respect to the Eighteenth Amendment, often with the connivance of local officers of the law. The large gap between the new law and local mores will not *at once* produce significant change of prevailing practices; token punishments of violations will probably be more common than effective control. At best, one may assume that significant change will be fitful, and excruciatingly slow. But secular changes in the economy may in due course lend support to the new legal framework of control over discrimination. As the economic shoe pinches because the illiberals do not fully mobilize the resources of industrial manpower nor extend their local markets through equitable wage-payments, they may slowly abandon some discriminatory practices as they come to find that these do not always pay—even the discriminator. So far as discrimination is concerned, organized counteraction is possible and some small results may be expected. But it would seem that wishes father thoughts, when one expects basic changes in the immediate future in these regions of institutionalized discrimination.

The situation is somewhat different with regard to the scattered, rather than aggregated, ethnic illiberals found here and there throughout the country. Here the mores and a social organization oriented toward the American creed still have some measure of prestige and the resources of a majority of liberals can be mobilized to isolate the illiberal. In these surroundings, it is possible to move the all-weather illiberal toward Type III—he can be brought to conform with institutional regulations, even though he does not surrender his prejudices. And once he has entered upon this role of the dissident but conforming individual, the remedial program designed for the fair-weather illiberal would be in order.

---

18 Race and Civil Rights Pre–September 11, 2001: The Targeting of Arabs and Muslims

Susan M. Akram • Kevin R. Johnson

SUSAN M. AKRAM is an associate professor at the Boston University School of Law. She is the founding director of the Immigration Project at the public interest law firm Public Counsel in Los Angeles and of the Political Asylum/Immigration Representation Project in Boston, and the interim director of the Joint Voluntary Agency for resettlement of Iraqi refugees in refugee camps in Saudi Arabia after the Gulf War.

KEVIN R. JOHNSON is associate dean for academic affairs and Mabie-Apallas Public Interest Professor of Law and Chicana/o Studies at the University of California at Davis. He has published extensively on immigration law and policy, racial identity, and civil rights in national and international journals.

THE FEDERAL GOVERNMENT'S RESPONSE TO the tragedy of September 11, 2001, demonstrates the close relationship between immigration law and civil rights in the United States. Noncitizens historically have been vulnerable to civil rights deprivations, in no small part because the law permits, and arguably encourages, extreme governmental conduct with minimal protections for the rights of noncitizens. Unfortunately, the current backlash against Arabs and Muslims fits comfortably into a long history of US government efforts to stifle political dissent.[1] This backlash is especially troubling because of the possibility—exemplified by the internment of persons of Japanese ancestry during

Questions to Consider   Most Americans believe that what makes the United States a great country is our ability to learn from our mistakes. We identify a social injustice, correct it, and vow that such behavior will never happen again. We interned—a nice word for jailed—Japanese Americans throughout World War II, only to release them after the war and pay reparations to survivors decades later. When racial profiling (Driving While Black) emerged as a civil rights issue, the federal government set up a task force to end this practice. As a nation we tell ourselves that such discriminatory, immoral, and un-American actions against one of our own will never happen again. Akram and Johnson argue that like the objects of Japanese American internment in the 1940s and black profiling in the 1990s, Arab Americans and Muslims are America's "new" targets. How is the idea of racialization linked to nationality, stereotypes, and post–9/11 national security and the treatment of Arab and Muslim Americans?

World War II—that racial, religious, and other differences have fueled the animosity toward Arabs and Muslims.

It is in the context of a particular historical and legal environment that the post–September 11 targeting of Arabs and Muslims must be understood, as this context both explains Arab and Muslim fears in time of crisis and permits such targeting to be acceptable in the public eye. Such government, public, and private acts as the unjustified FBI investigations of Arab- or Muslim-owned businesses, or the closing of Muslim and Arab bank accounts, or the shutting down of Muslim charities, or FBI visits to mosques and Muslim/Arab academics, or "special registration" and other targeted monitoring of persons only of Arab origin or Muslim faith have become quite an accepted part of the "war on terrorism." Yet, should either the government or others target white Irish Catholics or Jews or another racial/ethnic minority in such a sustained manner, they would doubtless face significant and vociferous challenge for racial or religious profiling.

Commentators have observed how popular perceptions of racial and other minorities influence their treatment under the law.[2] As with other minority groups, this seems true for Arabs and Muslims. As Professor Natsu Saito summarizes,

> Arab Americans and Muslims have been "raced" as "terrorists": foreign, disloyal, and imminently threatening. Although Arabs trace their roots to the Middle East and claim many different religious backgrounds, and Muslims come from all over the world . . . , these distinctions are blurred and negative images about either Arabs or Muslims are often attributed to both. As Ibrahim Hooper of the Council on American-Islamic Relations notes, "The common stereotypes are that we're all Arabs, we're all violent and we're all conducting a holy war."[3]

The demonization of Arabs and Muslims in the United States, accompanied by harsh legal measures directed at them, began well before the tragedy of September 11, 2001.[4] It can be traced to popular stereotypes,[5] years of mythmaking by film and media,[6] racism during times of national crisis,[7] and a campaign to build political support for US foreign policy in the Middle East.[8] Since at least the 1970s, US laws and policies have been founded on the assumption that Arab and Muslim noncitizens are potential terrorists and have targeted this group for special treatment under the law.[9] The post–September 11 targeting of Muslims and Arabs is simply the latest chapter in this history.[10]

The Stereotyping of Arabs as Terrorists and Religious Fanatics

Similar to the animus toward other racial minorities, anti-Arab, anti-Muslim animus can be viewed as part of a dynamic process of "racialization."[11] Racialization, as used here, views "race" as "an unstable and 'decentered' complex of social meanings constantly being transformed by political struggle."[12] This understanding of race breaks with the traditional view that race is fixed by biology; it instead considers "racial formation" to explain how race operates in the United States.[13]

Defining race as a process in which racial difference is socially, not biologically, constructed assists in examining the treatment of Arabs and Muslims in the United States; their experiences show the severe damage that racialization can do and offer hope that the process can be reversed.[14] Recognizing that race is the product of social construction, the US Supreme Court held that different groups may be racialized and that Arabs can be discriminated against as members of a different "race" in violation of the civil rights laws.[15]

Through the process of racialization, Arabs and Muslims have been considered racially different from whites and other racial minorities. Professor Nabeel Abraham, a leading commentator on racism against Arabs and Muslims in the United States, identifies three distinct ways in which Arabs and Muslims have been racialized: (1) through political violence by extremist groups based on the Arab-Israeli conflict in the Middle East, (2) by xenophobic violence targeting Arabs and Muslims at the local level, and (3) through the hostility arising from international crises affecting the United States and its citizens.[16] The law and its enforcement also have contributed to hostility toward Arabs and Muslims in the United States.[17]

The Silencing of Arabs Through Politically Motivated Violence and Intimidation

Conflict in the Middle East provokes violence against Arabs and Muslims in the United States, as well as the lesser-known intimidation tactics followed by some mainstream activist organizations. A Rand Corporation study conducted for the US Department of Energy concludes that the Jewish Defense League (JDL) was, for more than a decade, one of the most active terrorist groups, as classified by the FBI, in the United States.[18] The study reviews the violence known to have been committed by the JDL, as well as incidents in which the JDL's involvement was suspected, all of which was described as part of a strategy "to eliminate perceived enemies of the Jewish people and Israel."[19] The violence included bombings of Arab foreign offices and planting bombs in American-Arab Anti-Discrimination Committee offices across the country.[20] According to the FBI, Jewish extremist organizations were responsible for twenty terrorist incidents in the 1980s.[21]

Despite the many incidents of anti-Arab violence at the hands of Jewish extremist groups, influential hate-crime studies fail to include these groups as perpetrators of these crimes.[22] According to Professor Abraham, "Jewish extremist groups constitute an undeniable source of anti-Arab hate violence not discussed in conventional accounts of racist violence in the United States."[23]

Even less publicized than the anti-Arab violence of extremist groups is the campaign by mainstream organizations, such as the Anti-Defamation League of B'nai B'rith (ADL), to intimidate and silence Arabs and Muslims. Established in the early 1900s as an organization with the mission of fighting anti-Semitism, the ADL gained a reputation as a leading antidiscrimination organization in the United States. Unfortunately, after the creation of Israel in 1948, the ADL added a new mission: to discredit or silence critics of Israel or defenders of Palestinian human rights.[24] The ADL has aggressively engaged in efforts to intimidate Arabs, Muslims, and others with similar views on the Middle East conflict, discouraging them from participating in political debate. In 1983, for example, the ADL released a handbook entitled *Pro-Arab Propaganda in America: Vehicles and Voices.*[25] It lists as "anti-Israel propagandists" some of the most prominent scholars on Middle East issues, including Columbia University's Edward Said and Harvard University's Walid Khalidi, as well as humanitarian organizations dealing with the Middle East or Palestine. Alfred Lilienthal, an influential commentator on Middle East issues, himself on the ADL's blacklist, claims, "Many ADL charges against critics of Israel are totally inaccurate, questionable, or based upon half-truths," and the ADL often characterizes groups or individuals who criticize Israel or Zionism as "extremists" intent on eradicating Israel or inciting antiSemitism in America.[26] The ADL handbook was widely distributed throughout the United States to, according to critics, challenge, harass, and silence groups and individuals on the list.

The ADL is not the only mainstream organization to distribute lists of Arab American individuals and groups and those working with them. The American Israel Public Affairs Committee (AIPAC) issued two similar lists.[27] Through a campaign, primarily on college campuses, organized against groups and individuals on these lists, AIPAC and the ADL have harassed and intimidated academics and activists for years.[28]

Aside from its campaign to discredit and silence academics on university campuses, the ADL has also sought to silence pro-Muslim and pro-Arab speakers from engaging in public debate concerning the Middle East. Most recently, the Florida ADL unsuccessfully lobbied the Florida Commission on Human Relations to exclude a Muslim representative from a panel at a civil rights conference.[29] Similarly, the American Jewish Committee sought to exclude Ghazi Khankan, executive director of the New York chapter of the Council on American-Islamic Relations (CAIR), from participating in a public forum on multicultural understanding because he was "anti-Israel."[30] The ADL demanded that CAIR's Northern California director be prevented from testifying about hate crimes before the California Select Committee on Hate Crimes.[31]

The full extent of the ADL's activities against Arabs did not come to light until January 1993, when the results of an FBI investigation of a veteran San Francisco Police Department officer and an ADL-paid undercover agent became public. Law enforcement authorities uncovered computerized files on thousands of Arab Americans and information on Arab organizations, as well as many other mainstream organizations.[32] These files reflected surveillance of organizations and leaders, including the NAACP, Greenpeace, the ACLU, the Asian Law Caucus, the National Lawyers Guild, the Rainbow Coalition, Jews for Jesus, and three current or past members of the US Congress.[33] The information included confidential law enforcement files and information from the Department of Motor Vehicles.[34] The FBI confirmed that the ADL provided information from the surveillance activities to the South African government.[35] The ADL's attorney admitted that the ADL had passed surveillance information to Israel.[36] At least one US citizen of Arab descent who had been the subject of surveillance was arrested in Israel when he visited the Israeli-occupied Palestinian territories.[37] When the spying became public, an array of civil rights lawsuits was filed.[38] As part of the settlement of a class action, the ADL was permanently enjoined from illegal spying on Arab American and other civil rights groups.[39]

Despite the settlement and the permanent injunction, the damage to the civil liberties of Arabs in the United States from the ADL's surveillance activities has been done. The discovery of espionage has contributed to the climate of fear for Arab and Muslim Americans. US intelligence agencies may have obtained information from the ADL that could potentially place politically active Arab groups and individuals under heightened government scrutiny.[40] Consequently, Arab Americans may perceive that the US government is in collusion with Israeli and anti-Arab organizations. Such perceptions have been reinforced by the revelation that information provided by the ADL triggered the FBI investigation and arrest of the "LA Eight," a group of noncitizens, for alleged technical violations of the Immigration and Nationality Act (INA).[41] Furthermore, "no . . . major American Jewish organization has condemned the ADL for its political excesses or its documented association with Israeli intelligence organizations."[42] Our research has not discovered any publication in which the ADL admitted culpability or disavowed these activities.

In sum, the ADL has engaged in surveillance of Arab and Muslim groups in an apparent effort to intimidate and silence those voices it deems "anti-Semitic."[43] As Professor Abraham summarizes: "The overall effect of the ADL's practices is to reinforce the image of Arabs as terrorists and security threats, thereby creating a climate of fear, suspicion, and hostility towards Arab-Americans and others who espouse critical views of Israel, possibly leading to death threats and bodily harm."[44]

The Impact of Anti-Arab Images in Popular Culture

Racism against Arabs is not all the work of political activists. Importantly, media and film, feeding on existing stereotypes in US society about Arabs and Muslims, have found a ready audience for dangerous and one-dimensional images. Such depictions contribute to the racialization of Arabs and Muslims. In addition, in a study on anti-Arab racism, Professor Abraham documents a range of racial epithets, intolerant speech, and violence directed at Arabs by private citizens and public officials.[45]

Jack Shaheen's review of US films offers convincing evidence of the vilification of Arabs and Muslims by the movie industry. Shaheen catalogs hundreds of Hollywood movies in which Arabs or Muslims are portrayed as terrorists or otherwise placed in a negative, often nonhuman, light. Muslims are shown as hostile invaders or "lecherous, oily sheikhs intent on using nuclear weapons."[46] A far-too-common scene shows a mosque with Arabs at prayer, then cuts away to show civilians being gunned down.

These movies show Westerners hurling such epithets at Arabs as "assholes," "bastards," "camel-dicks," "pigs," "devil-worshipers," "jackals," "rats," "rag-heads," "towelheads," "scum-buckets," "sons-of-dogs," "buzzards of the jungle," "sons-of-whores," "sons-of-unnamed goats," and "sons-of-she-camels."[47] Arab women are often portrayed as weak and mute, covered in black, or as scantily clad belly dancers.

The US Department of Defense has cooperated with Hollywood in making more than a dozen films showing US soldiers killing Arabs and Muslims. Audiences apparently embrace the demonization in these movies. As Shaheen notes,

> To my knowledge, no Hollywood WWI, WWII, or Korean War movie has ever shown America's fighting forces slaughtering children. Yet, near the conclusion of [the movie] Rules of Engagement, US marines open fire on the Yemenis, shooting 83 men, women, and children. During the scene, viewers rose to their feet, clapped and cheered. Boasts director Friedkin, "I've seen audiences stand up and applaud the film throughout the United States."[48]

One-sided film portrayals omit images of Arabs and Muslims as ordinary people with families and friends or as outstanding members of communities, scholars, writers, or scientists. Few US movies have depicted Arabs or Muslims in a favorable light and even fewer have included them in leading roles. Commentators rarely criticize the unbalanced depiction of Arabs and Muslims.[49] The stereotyping and demonization of Arabs and Muslims by American films may well have gone largely unnoticed because these characterizations are entirely consistent with widespread attitudes in US society.

Reinforcing the anti-Arab, anti-Muslim stereotypes in film, public officials have openly used intolerant speech toward Arabs and Muslims—speech that would be clearly unacceptable if directed at other minority groups.[50] For example, a mayoral candidate in Dearborn, Michigan, a suburb of Detroit, distributed a campaign brochure in which he claimed the city's Arab Americans "threaten our neighborhoods, the value of our property and a darned good way of life."[51] In 1981, the governor of Michigan proclaimed that Michigan's economic woes were due to the "damn Arabs."[52] Such statements by public officials fuel the perception that prejudice and animosity directed at Arabs and Muslims are socially acceptable.

Moreover, prominent politicians have returned financial contributions from Arab American and American Muslim groups, fearing the political risks of the acceptance of such monies. For example, in the 1984 presidential campaign, Walter Mondale returned five thousand dollars in contributions made by US citizens of Arab ancestry.[53] Philadelphia mayoral candidate Wilson Goode returned more than two thousand dollars in campaign contributions from Arab Americans.[54] In his first congressional race, Joe Kennedy returned one hundred dollars to James Abourezk, a former US senator who is Arab American.[55] New York senator Hillary Clinton returned fifty thousand dollars to Muslim organizations.[56] Although several of these politicians stated that they returned the funds because of the contributors' **anti-Semitic** remarks, the perception remains that Arabs and Muslims cannot participate in the body politic. For similar reasons, New York City mayor Rudolph Giuliani returned ten million dollars donated by a Saudi Arabian prince for the victims of the World Trade Center destruction due to a public outcry caused by the contributor's criticism of US foreign policy in the Middle East.[57]

Racism in Times of National Crisis

Hostility toward minorities often accompanies times of crisis in the United States. For Arabs and Muslims, this may be even more problematic. Perpetrators of hate crimes against Arabs and Muslims frequently fail to differentiate among persons based on religion or ethnic origin, from Pakistanis, Indians, Iranians, and Japanese to Muslims, Sikhs, and Christian Arabs.[58] The widespread perception in the United States is that Arabs and Muslims are identical and eager to wage a holy war against the United States. In fact, according to a 1993 report, only 12 percent of the Muslims in the United States are Arab,[59] and Arab Muslims at that time were even a minority in the Arab American community.[60] Although there are Muslim extremists, the majority of Muslims are "decent, law-abiding, productive citizens."[61]

Because of the lack of differentiation between different types of Arabs and Muslims, terrorist acts by small groups of Arabs and Muslims often have been followed by generalized hostility toward entire communities of Arabs and Muslims in the United States. For example, after Lebanese Shiite gunmen in 1985 hijacked TWA Flight 847 to Beirut, beat an American on the plane to death, and held the remaining passengers hostage for more than two weeks,[62] violent attacks against persons of Arab and Muslim origin occurred across the United States. Islamic centers and Arab American organizations were vandalized and threatened. A Houston mosque was firebombed. A bomb exploded in the American-Arab Anti-Discrimination Committee office in Boston, severely injuring two police officers.[63] Later that same year, after terrorists hijacked the *Achille Lauro* cruise liner and murdered a passenger, a wave of anti-Arab violence swept the country, including the bombing of an American-Arab Anti-Discrimination Committee office that killed its regional executive director.[64]

In 1986, in apparent response to the Reagan administration's "war on terrorism" directed at Libya, another episode of anti-Arab harassment and violence broke out. The same night as a US bombing raid on Libya, the American-Arab Anti-Discrimination Committee national office in Washington received threats. Shortly thereafter, the Detroit American-Arab Anti-Discrimination Committee office, the Dearborn Arab Community Center, and the Detroit Arab American newspaper received bomb threats.[65] Threats, beatings, and other violent attacks on Arabs were reported across the United States. At this time, someone broke into a Palestinian family's home, set off a smoke bomb inside the house, and painted slogans such as "Go Back to Libya" on the walls.[66]

The first Gulf War intensified anti-Arab hostility in the United States. The American-Arab Anti-Discrimination Committee reported four anti-Arab hate crimes for 1990 before the invasion of Kuwait in August of that year. Between the invasion and February 1991, the committee reported 175 incidents.[67] When US intervention commenced in January 1991, Arab and Muslim businesses and community organizations were bombed, vandalized, and subjected to harrassment.[68]

The US Government and the Role of Law

Institutional racism through the law and its enforcement has contributed to the racialization and targeting of Arabs and Muslims. The federal government's actions taken in the name of fighting terrorism have been followed by indiscriminate threats and violence against Arabs and

---

anti-Semitic Dislike, hatred, or mistreatment of Jews.

Muslims in the United States. This frightening pattern has repeated itself in the wake of September 11.[69]

The Nixon administration's "Operation Boulder" was an early effort of the US government to target Arabs in the United States for special investigation and discourage their political activism on Middle Eastern issues.[70] Ostensibly designed to confront the threat posed by terrorists who took hostages and murdered athletes at the 1972 Munich Olympics, the president's directives authorized the FBI to investigate people of "Arabic origin" to determine their potential relationship with "terrorist" activities related to the Arab-Israeli conflict.[71] The FBI admittedly wiretapped prominent Detroit lawyer Abdeen Jabara, then president of the Association of Arab-American University Graduates.[72]

Later in the 1970s, President Carter took numerous steps against Iranians and Iran in response to the crisis in which US citizens were held hostage in Tehran. In the 1980s, the Reagan administration's foreign policy also involved combating "terrorism." President Reagan in 1986 announced that the US government had evidence that Libyan leader Muammar Qaddafi was responsible for terrorist attacks, such as those at the Rome and Vienna airports, and was planning further attacks in the United States.[73] The US Navy later that year shot down two Libyan planes off the coast of Libya. President Reagan announced that "we have the evidence" that Qaddafi was sending hit teams to assassinate the US president.[74] Despite official responses from the Austrian, Italian, and Israeli governments that there was no evidence of Libyan involvement in the Rome and Vienna attacks or that any Libyan "hit squads" had been sent to the United States,[75] the United States bombed Libya. Violence against US residents of Arab or Middle Eastern origin and vandalism of their community centers, mosques, businesses, and homes followed the public announcements.

In the 1990s, after the US invasion of Kuwait, the US government's "war on terrorism" shifted focus to Iraq and its leader, Saddam Hussein. The Bush administration accused Iraqi forces of atrocities against Kuwaitis. The administration then launched a surveillance program directed at Arab Americans. The FBI interrogated Arab and Muslim leaders, activists, and antiwar demonstrators across the country.[76] The Department of Justice instituted fingerprinting of all residents and immigrants of Arab origin in the United States; the Federal Aviation

Administration commenced a system of airline profiling of persons from the Arab world.[77] Private harassment and violence against Arab and Muslim communities followed.

Foreign policy has played a large role in immigration measures directed at Arabs and Muslims in the United States. The Immigration and Naturalization Service (INS)[78] sought to deport noncitizens of Palestinian ancestry[79] at the same time that the federal government attempted to shut down Palestine Liberation Organization (PLO) offices in the United States and at the United Nations.[80] In the 1980s, President Reagan issued a secret National Security Decision Directive that authorized the creation of a network of agencies designed to prevent "terrorists" from entering or remaining in the United States. Under one proposal, intelligence agencies would provide the INS with "names, nationalities and other identifying data and evidence relating to *alien undesirables and suspected terrorists* believed to be in . . . the U.S."[81] The Alien Border Control Committee also considered an INS-created strategy outlined in a document entitled "Alien Terrorists and Undesirables: A Contingency Plan." The strategy called for mass arrests and detentions of noncitizens from Arab nations and Iran, and suggested using ideological exclusion grounds in the immigration laws to remove noncitizens from Arab countries and Iran already in the United States.[82]

Efforts to Stifle Political Dissent: The Case of the LA Eight

Critics long have pointed out that the United States has discriminated against Arabs and Muslims in applying the terrorist exclusion provisions of the INA, the comprehensive US immigration law.[83] Arabs, particularly Palestinians, are the primary groups subject to many of the terrorism provisions. During the first Gulf War crisis, for example, government officials fingerprinted and photographed all entrants to the US who held Iraqi or Kuwaiti passports without regard to evidence of past terrorist activities or sympathies.[84]

Related to the terrorist provisions in the immigration laws are those permitting exclusion of noncitizens based on political beliefs or associations, passed during the anticommunist fervor of the McCarthy era.[85] The courts generally upheld application of the ideological exclusions, which provoked sharp academic criticism. In 1977, Congress enacted the McGovern Amendment, which permitted the attorney general to waive the exclusion of any noncitizen affiliated with an organization proscribed by the United States.[86] In 1979, Congress created a single exception to the McGovern Amendment that denied the exclusion waiver for only one group: PLO officials or representatives.[87] In any event, through a variety of means, consular officers could continue to exclude a person based on ideology.

The federal government's efforts to remove the LA Eight illustrate the extremes to which it will resort in order to deport political dissidents from the country.[88] The case began before dawn on January 26, 1987, when officers of the FBI, INS, and Los Angeles Police Department descended on the home of Khader Hamide, a US lawful permanent resident, and his Kenyan-born wife, Julie Mungai. They were handcuffed, told they were being arrested for "terrorism," and taken into custody while police blocked the street and an FBI helicopter hovered overhead.[89] Six other individuals were arrested that morning.

The INS sought to remove the LA Eight from the United States based on political ideology. Both the director of the FBI and the regional counsel of the INS testified before Congress that the sole basis of the government's efforts to deport the LA Eight was their political affiliations. In the words of FBI director William Webster, "All of them were arrested because they are alleged to be members of a world-wide Communist organization which under the [INA] makes them eligible for deportation . . . *If these individuals had been United States citizens, there would not have been a basis for their arrest.*"[90] The evidence underlying the government's charges amounted to a claim that the LA Eight read or distributed literature linked to the Popular Front for the Liberation of Palestine (PFLP), which the district court found was engaged in a wide range of lawful activities from providing education, health care, social services, and day care to cultural and political activities.[91] The district court ruled that the ideological exclusion grounds violated the First Amendment.[92]

In 1990, while the LA Eight case was pending, Congress repealed the ideological exclusion grounds from the immigration laws. The INS then instituted new proceedings against the LA Eight based on charges of terrorism, as well as other grounds. The INA permits removal of noncitizens who have "engaged in terrorist activity," which is defined as having committed "in an individual capacity or as a member of an organization, an act of terrorist activity or an act which the actor knows, or reasonably should know, *affords*

material support to any individual, organization, or government in conducting a terrorist activity at any time.*"[93] This broad language authorizes the INS to deport or exclude an individual who has donated money to an organization for its legal, social, or charitable activities, if any part of that organization also has engaged in terrorism, as broadly defined.[94]

The thrust of the INS case was based on the LA Eight's affiliation with the PFLP. Because this provision previously had never been used by the INS to seek to deport a noncitizen from the United States, the LA Eight claimed that the federal government selectively enforced the immigration laws against them for exercising their First Amendment rights. In the end, the Supreme Court ruled that the 1996 amendments to the immigration laws barred judicial review of their claim.[95]

Following the court's decision, the case was remanded to the immigration court. In 2001, the court dismissed the primary removal charges on the grounds that they were not meant to apply retroactively. Nonetheless, the federal government continues its efforts to deport the LA Eight, even relying on secret evidence in seeking removal of two of the eight.[96]

The Secret Evidence Cases

The INS also has selectively targeted Arabs and Muslims through the use of secret evidence—evidence that it refuses to disclose to the noncitizen or his or her counsel—to charge, detain, and deny bond or release in removal proceedings. By 1999, twenty-five secret evidence cases were pending.[97]

In *Rafeedie v. INS*,[98] Fouad Rafeedie, a twenty-year lawful permanent resident of Palestinian origin, was arrested upon returning to the United States after a two-week trip to a conference in Syria sponsored by the Palestine Youth Organization. He was placed in summary exclusion proceedings based on ideological grounds. The INS claimed that disclosing its evidence against Rafeedie would be "prejudicial to the public interest, safety, or security of the United States."[99] The court of appeals rejected the INS position and required application of the ordinary due process analysis in deciding whether the federal government's national security interests outweighed Rafeedie's First Amendment rights. The court observed that the only way Rafeedie could have prevailed over the secret evidence proceeding would have been to "rebut the undisclosed evidence against him . . . It is difficult to imagine how even someone innocent of all wrong-doing could meet such a burden."[100]

Since repeal of the ideological exclusion provisions of the INA in 1990, the INS has relied on secret evidence to detain and deport Arabs and Muslims. Moreover, in response to the 1995 Oklahoma City bombing, Congress enacted antiterrorism legislation that has facilitated the targeting of Arab and Muslim noncitizens: the Antiterrorism and Effective Death Penalty Act (AEDPA)[101] and the Illegal Immigration Reform and Immigrant Responsibility Act (IIRIRA).[102] Both brought about radical changes to the immigration laws and effectively allowed for the possibility of ideological exclusion and removal through secret evidence proceedings.

Bolstered by the 1996 reforms curtailing the rights of noncitizens, the INS brought approximately two dozen deportation actions based on secret evidence, claiming that disclosing the evidence would compromise the security of the United States.[103] Although the INS denies that it selectively uses secret evidence against Arabs and Muslims, our research has not uncovered a single secret evidence case not involving an Arab or Muslim noncitizen.[104]

AEDPA established a special procedure for detaining and deporting "alien terrorists" that permits the use of secret evidence with certain procedural and constitutional safeguards designed to protect constitutional rights. The federal government, however, has not yet used the new procedure; instead, it has relied on preexisting regulations that it claims authorize the use of secret evidence in the immigration courts. By so doing, the government has avoided complying with AEDPA's safeguards, including requiring the production of an unclassified summary of the secret evidence to the noncitizen and having a federal court assess the constitutionality of the use of secret evidence. This strategy has allowed the US government to avoid charging the noncitizen under a substantive "terrorism" provision of the INA, which would require the government to prove such a charge.[105]

The cases of the "Iraqi Seven" arose out of the US government's resettlement of Iraqi Kurds after the Gulf War.[106] The Iraqi men, who had all worked for a CIA-funded Iraqi opposition group, were evacuated from Iraq by the United States. The INS commenced exclusion proceedings against them based on alleged visa violations. Fearing persecution if returned to Iraq, the seven sought asylum in the United States. Relying primarily on secret evidence, the immigration judge found them to be national security risks.

As a result of the litigation, the INS released five hundred pages of evidence used against the Iraqi Seven. James Woolsey, the former head of the CIA who directed the US government's efforts to organize the overthrow of Saddam Hussein, was one of the lawyers representing the Iraqis. Besides concluding that hundreds of pages had been erroneously classified, Woolsey found that the evidence was based on serious errors in Arabic-English translations; ethnic and religious stereotyping by the FBI; and reliance on unreliable information, including rumors and innuendo. He claimed that the US government made material misrepresentations to the immigration judge.[107] Despite the weakness of the government's case, the case was only concluded when five of the Iraqis entered into a settlement agreement, withdrawing their asylum claims in exchange for release from detention.

Mazen al-Najjar and Anwar Haddam experienced the longest detentions connected with secret evidence proceedings: Al-Najjar was detained for more than four years[108] and Haddam was jailed for four years,[109] both on allegations of association with terrorism. Al-Najjar, a stateless Palestinian, was editor of the journal of the World and Islam Studies Enterprise (WISE), a think tank based at the University of South Florida devoted to promoting discussion of Middle East issues. The INS arrested al-Najjar and placed him in removal proceedings as part of an FBI investigation against a former WISE administrator who became head of the Islamic Jihad. The arrest and detention was based on secret evidence.[110] Al-Najjar was held in custody for three years and seven months before his release in December 2000. He was then rearrested in November 2001, and remained in custody until his deportation in August 2002.[111] No terrorism charges were ever brought, but he was detained and his removal was sought on the basis of visa violations and on evidence the INS refused to disclose.[112]

Anwar Haddam was an elected member of the Algerian Parliament. A professor of physics at the University of Algiers, he ran for election as a member of the Islamic Salvation Front (FIS), a moderate Islamic party that swept the 1991 elections with 80 percent of the vote. The Algerian military staged a coup d'état, arrested the president of the FIS, and rounded up thousands of its members. Top FIS officials were killed or imprisoned, while thousands of FIS supporters were imprisoned, tortured, and executed. A civil war followed with tens of thousands of deaths. One of the few elected FIS officials who managed to escape Algeria, Haddam entered the United States on a valid nonimmigrant visa in 1992, and later filed an asylum claim. The INS took Haddam into custody and detained him based on secret evidence.[113]

In both the al-Najjar and Haddam cases, as the secret evidence was either unclassified or disclosed, it was demonstrated that the government's "terrorist" claims were based on unreliable evidence and apparently unfounded. Yet, the inability to challenge the secret evidence cost al-Najjar and Haddam years of their lives in custody.

Nasser Ahmed, a father of US-citizen children, was held in custody and denied bond for three-and-a-half years based on secret evidence.[114] Charged in April 1995 with overstaying his visa, he had been released on fifteen thousand dollars bond while he pursued a claim for political asylum. In 1996, while his own deportation proceedings were ongoing, Ahmed became the court-appointed translator for the attorneys representing Sheik Omar Abdel Rahman, later convicted in the 1993 World Trade Center bombing attempt. As Ahmed was going to immigration court for his asylum hearing, the INS arrested him and opposed his release on bond. On remand, the immigration court dismissed the evidence of the government's remaining contentions on the grounds that it was based on an informant who had personal reasons for seeking Ahmed's deportation.

As the secret evidence cases have slowly moved toward conclusion, the government's claims in all of the cases have evaporated. No case has included sufficient evidence of terrorism-related charges necessary to justify the years of detention. Besides the individual loss of liberty, the cases have chilled Arab and Muslim political speech.

Conclusion

Stereotypes about Arabs and Muslims have influenced immigration law and its enforcement, as well as the civil rights of Arab and Muslim noncitizens in the United States. This discussion is by no means comprehensive. Other examples of the US government's response to perceived fears of Arab and Muslim terrorism are plentiful. For example, in the 1990s, the much-publicized case of asylum-seeker Sheik Omar Abdel Rahman[115] by itself resulted in changes to the immigration laws that narrowed the rights of all asylum applicants.[116] An episode of the popular television show *60 Minutes*,[117] focusing on his alleged abuse of the asylum system, triggered a chain reaction that culminated in 1996 asylum reforms. These reforms included a summary exclusion procedure by which a noncitizen could be excluded from the country without a hearing on an asylum or other claim to relief.[118]

As shown above, demonization of Arabs and Muslims has had an impact on the evolution of the law and encouraged harsh governmental efforts to remove Arabs and Muslims from the United States. The same stereotypes have affected the civil rights of all persons of Arab and Muslim ancestry in the United States since September 11, 2001. Importantly, the aftermath of the security measures taken since then threatens to have enduring impacts on the civil rights of all immigrants, and on US citizens as well.

Seeing the Big Picture **America's New Public Enemy?**
The statistics on hate crimes in the Appendix (Section IV) show patterns that are analogous to the attacks on Arab Americans and Muslims in the United States as described by Akram and Johnson. How is the disproportionate number of hate crimes committed against racial minorities similar to what has happened to Arab Americans and Muslims since the 9/11 terrorist attacks?

19

The Possessive Investment in Whiteness: Racialized Social Democracy

George Lipsitz

GEORGE LIPSITZ researches racialization in U.S. society, including the racialization of space, urban culture, collective memory, and movements for social change. He is the author of *American Studies in a Moment of Danger* (2001) and *The Possessive Investment in Whiteness: How White People Profit from Identity Politics* (1998).

Questions to Consider   What does George Lipsitz mean by a "possessive investment in whiteness"? How is it possible that being a member of a particular racial group could confer social and economic privileges (or disadvantages) that are both institutional and intergenerational? How many specific programs does Lipsitz identify as being party to institutional racism?

SHORTLY AFTER WORLD WAR II, A FRENCH reporter asked expatriate Richard Wright his opinion about the "Negro problem" in the United States. The author replied "There isn't any Negro problem; there is only a white problem."[1] By inverting the reporter's question, Wright called attention to its hidden assumptions—that racial polarization comes from the existence of blacks rather than from the behavior of whites, that black people are a "problem" for whites rather than fellow citizens entitled to justice, and that unless otherwise specified "American" means whites.[2] But Wright's formulation also placed political mobilization by African Americans in context, attributing it "to the systemic practices of aversion, exploitation, denigration, and discrimination practiced by people who think of themselves as white."

Whiteness is everywhere in American culture, but it is very hard to see. As Richard Dyer argues, "white power secures its dominance by seeming not to be anything in particular."[3] As the unmarked category against which difference is constructed, whiteness never has to speak its name, never has to acknowledge its role as an organizing principle in social and cultural relations.[4]

To identify, analyze, and oppose the destructive consequences of whiteness, we need what Walter Benjamin called "presence of mind." Benjamin wrote that people visit fortune-tellers not so much out of a desire to know the future but rather out of a fear of not noticing some important aspect of the present. "Presence of mind," he argued, "is an abstract of the future, and precise awareness of the present moment more decisive than foreknowledge of the most distant events."[5] In our society at this time, precise awareness of the present moment requires an understanding of the existence and the destructive consequences of "white" identity.

In recent years, an important body of American studies scholarship has started to explore the role played by cultural practices in creating "whiteness" in the United States. More than the product of private prejudices, whiteness emerged as a relevant category in American life largely because of realities created by slavery and segregation, by immigration restriction and Indian policy, by conquest and colonialism. A fictive identity of "whiteness" appeared in law as an abstraction, and it became actualized in everyday life in many ways. American economic and political life gave different racial groups unequal access to citizenship and property, while cultural practices including Wild West shows, minstrel shows, racist images in advertising, and Hollywood films institutionalized racism by uniting ethnically diverse European-American audiences into an imagined community—one called into being through inscribed appeals to the solidarity of white supremacy.[6] Although cross-ethnic identification and pan-ethnic antiracism in culture, politics, and economics have often interrupted and resisted racialized white supremacist notions of American identity, from colonial days to the present, successful political coalitions serving dominant interests have often relied on exclusionary concepts of whiteness to fuse unity among otherwise antagonistic individuals and groups.[7]

In these accounts by American studies scholars, cultural practices have often played crucial roles in prefiguring, presenting, and preserving political coalitions based on identification with the fiction of "whiteness." Andrew Jackson's coalition of the "common man," Woodrow Wilson's "New Freedom," and Franklin D. Roosevelt's New Deal all echoed in politics the alliances announced on stage and screen by the nineteenth-century minstrel show, by D. W. Griffith's cinema, and by Al Jolson's ethnic and racial imagery.[8] This impressive body of scholarship helps us understand how people who left Europe as Calabrians or Bohemians became something called "whites" when they got to America and how that designation made all the difference in the world.

Yet, while cultural expressions have played an important role in the construction of white supremacist political alliances, the reverse is also true (i.e., political activity has also played a constitutive role in racializing U.S. culture). Race is a cultural construct, but one with sinister structural causes and consequences. Conscious and deliberate actions have institutionalized group identity in the United States, not just through the dissemination of cultural stories but also through systematic efforts from colonial times to the present to create a possessive investment in whiteness for European Americans. Studies of culture too far removed from studies of social structure leave us with inadequate explanations for understanding racism and inadequate remedies for combatting it.

From the start, European settlers in North America established structures encouraging possessive investment in whiteness. The colonial and early-national legal systems authorized attacks on Native Americans and encouraged the appropriation of their lands. They legitimated racialized chattel slavery, restricted naturalized citizenship to "white" immigrants, and provided pretexts for exploiting labor, seizing property, and denying the franchise to Asian Americans, Mexican Americans, Native Americans, and African Americans. Slavery and "Jim Crow" segregation institutionalized possessive identification with whiteness visibly and openly, but an elaborate interaction of largely *covert* public and private decisions during and after the days of slavery and segregation also produced a powerful legacy with enduring effects on the racialization of experience, opportunities, and rewards in the United States. Possessive investment in whiteness pervades public policy in the United States past and present—not just long ago during slavery and segregation but in the recent past and present as well—through the covert but no less systematic racism inscribed within U.S. social democracy.

Even though there has always been racism in American history, it has not always been the same racism. Political and cultural struggles over power shape the contours and dimensions of racism in any era. Mass mobilizations against racism during the Civil War and civil rights eras meaningfully curtailed the reach and scope of white supremacy, but in each case reactionary forces then engineered a renewal of racism, albeit in new forms, during successive decades. Racism changes over time, taking on different forms and serving different social purposes in different eras.

Contemporary racism is not just a residual consequence of slavery and **de jure segregation** but rather something that has been created anew in our own time by many factors including the putatively race-neutral liberal social democratic reforms of the past five decades. Despite hard-fought battles for change that secured important concessions during the 1960s in the form of civil rights legislation, the racialized nature of social democratic policies in the United States since the Great Depression has, in my judgment, actually increased the possessive investment in whiteness among European Americans over the past half-century.

The possessive investment in whiteness is not a simple matter of black and white; all racialized minority groups have suffered from it, albeit to different degrees and in different ways. Most of my argument here addresses relations between European Americans and African Americans because they contain many of the most vivid oppositions and contrasts, but the possessive investment in whiteness always emerges from a fused sensibility drawing on many sources at once—on antiblack racism to be sure, but also on the legacies of racialization left by federal, state, and local policies toward Native Americans, Asian Americans, Mexican Americans, and other groups designated by whites as "racially other."

During the New Deal, both the Wagner Act and the Social Security Act excluded farm workers and domestics from coverage, effectively denying those disproportionately minority sectors of the work force protections and benefits routinely channeled to whites. The Federal Housing Act of 1934 brought home ownership within reach of millions of citizens by placing the credit of the federal

---

de jure segregation Segregation that is imposed by law; versus de facto segregation, which exists "in fact" or practice but is not specified by law.

government behind private lending to home buyers, but overtly racist categories in the Federal Housing Administration's (FHA's) "confidential" city surveys and appraisers' manuals channeled almost all of the loan money toward whites and away from communities of color.[9] In the post–World War II era, trade unions negotiated contract provisions giving private medical insurance, pensions, and job security largely to the mostly white workers in unionized mass-production industries rather than fighting for full employment, universal medical care, and old age pensions for all or for an end to discriminatory hiring and promotion practices by employers.[10]

Each of these policies widened the gap between the resources available to whites and those available to aggrieved racial communities, but the most damaging long-term effects may well have come from the impact of the racial discrimination codified by the policies of the FHA. By channeling loans away from older inner-city neighborhoods and toward white home buyers moving into segregated suburbs, the FHA and private lenders after World War II aided and abetted the growth and development of increased segregation in U.S. residential neighborhoods. For example, FHA appraisers denied federally supported loans to prospective home buyers in the racially mixed Boyle Heights neighborhood of Los Angeles because it was a "'**melting pot**' area literally honeycombed with diverse and subversive racial elements."[11] Similarly, mostly white St. Louis County secured five times as many FHA mortgages as the more racially mixed city of St. Louis between 1943 and 1960. Home buyers in the county received six times as much loan money and enjoyed per capita mortgage spending 6.3 times greater than those in the city.[12]

In concert with FHA support for segregation in the suburbs, federal and state tax monies routinely provided water supplies and sewage facilities for racially exclusive suburban communities in the 1940s and 1950s. By the 1960s, these areas often incorporated themselves as independent municipalities in order to gain greater access to federal funds allocated for "urban aid."[13] At the same time that FHA loans and federal highway building projects subsidized the growth of segregated suburbs, urban renewal programs in cities throughout the country devastated minority neighborhoods.

During the 1950s and 1960s, federally assisted **urban renewal** projects destroyed 20 percent of the central city housing units occupied by blacks, as opposed to only 10 percent of those inhabited by whites.[14] Even after most major urban renewal programs had been completed in the 1970s, black central city residents continued to lose housing units at a rate equal to 80 percent of what had been lost in the 1960s. Yet white displacement declined back to the relatively low levels of the 1950s.[15] In addition, the refusal first to pass, then to enforce, fair housing laws, has enabled realtors, buyers, and sellers to profit from racist collusion against minorities without fear of legal retribution.

During the decades following World War II, urban renewal helped construct a new "white" identity in the suburbs by helping destroy ethnically specific European-American urban inner-city neighborhoods. Wrecking balls and bulldozers eliminated some of these sites, while others became transformed by an influx of minority residents desperately competing for a declining number of affordable housing units. As increasing numbers of racial minorities moved into cities, increasing numbers of European-American ethnics moved out. Consequently, ethnic differences among whites became a less important dividing line in American culture, while race became more important. The suburbs helped turn European Americans into "whites" who could live near each other and intermarry with relatively little difficulty. But this "white" unity rested on residential segregation and on shared access to housing and life chances largely unavailable to communities of color.[16]

During the 1950s and 1960s, local "pro-growth" coalitions led by liberal mayors often justified urban renewal as a program designed to build more housing for poor people, but it actually destroyed more housing than it created. Ninety percent of the low-income units removed for urban renewal were never replaced. Commercial, industrial, and municipal projects occupied more than 80 percent of the land cleared for these projects, with less than 20 percent allocated for replacement housing. In addition, the loss of taxable properties and tax abatements granted to new enterprises in urban renewal zones often meant serious tax increases for poor, working-class, and

melting pot The blending or "melting" of different racial, cultural, and ethnic groups into a new configuration.

urban renewal Also known as slum clearance, these policies attempted to renew blighted urban areas by redeveloping the land. Many have viewed these policies as a way to dislocate the urban poor and working classes, seize the land, and create development opportunity for the elites.

middle-class home owners and renters.[17] Although the percentage of black suburban dwellers also increased during this period, no significant desegregation of the suburbs took place. From 1960 to 1977, four million whites moved out of central cities, while the number of whites living in suburbs increased by twenty-two million.[18] During the same years, the inner-city black population grew by six million, but the number of blacks living in suburbs increased by only 500,000 people.[19] By 1993, 86 percent of suburban whites still lived in places with a black population below 1 percent. At the same time, cities with large numbers of minority residents found themselves cut off from loans by the FHA; in 1966, because of their growing black and Puerto Rican populations, Camden and Paterson, New Jersey, received no FHA-sponsored mortgages between them.[20]

Federally funded highways designed to connect suburban commuters with downtown places of employment destroyed already scarce housing in minority communities and often disrupted neighborhood life as well. Construction of the Harbor Freeway in Los Angeles, the Gulf Freeway in Houston, and the Mark Twain Freeway in St. Louis displaced thousands of residents and bisected previously connected neighborhoods, shopping districts, and political precincts. The process of urban renewal and highway construction set in motion a vicious cycle: population loss led to decreased political power, which made minority neighborhoods more likely to be victimized by further urban renewal and freeway construction, not to mention more susceptible to the placement of prisons, waste dumps, and other projects that further depopulated these areas.

In Houston, Texas—where blacks make up slightly more than one-quarter of the local population—more than 75 percent of municipal garbage incinerators and 100 percent of the city-owned garbage dumps are located in black neighborhoods.[21] A 1992 study by staff writers for the *National Law Journal* examined the Environmental Protection Agency's response to 1,177 toxic waste cases and found that polluters of sites near the greatest white population received penalties 500 percent higher than penalties imposed on polluters in minority areas—an average of $335,566 for white areas contrasted with $55,318 for minority areas. Income did not account for these differences—penalties for low-income areas on average actually exceeded those for areas with the highest median incomes by about 3 percent. The penalties for violating all federal environmental laws about

air, water, and waste pollution in minority communities were 46 percent lower than in white communities. In addition, **Superfund** remedies left minority communities with longer waiting times for being placed on the national priority list, cleanups that begin from 12 to 42 percent later than at white sites, and a 7 percent greater likelihood of "containment" (walling off a hazardous site) than cleanup, while white sites experienced treatment and cleanup 22 percent more often than containment.[22]

Urban renewal failed as a program for providing new housing for the poor, but it played an important role in transforming the U.S. urban economy away from factory production and toward producer services. Urban renewal projects subsidized the development of downtown office centers on land previously used for residences, and they frequently created buffer zones of empty blocks dividing poor neighborhoods from new shopping centers designed for affluent commuters. In order to help cities compete for corporate investment by making them appealing to high-level executives, federal urban aid favored construction of luxury housing units and cultural centers, such as symphony halls and art museums, over affordable housing for workers. Tax abatements granted to these producer-services centers further aggravated the fiscal crisis that cities faced, leading to tax increases on existing industries, businesses, and residences.

Workers from aggrieved racial minorities bore the brunt of this transformation. Because the 1964 Civil Rights Act came so late, minority workers who received jobs because of it found themselves more vulnerable to seniority-based layoffs when businesses automated or transferred operations overseas. Although the act initially made real progress in reducing employment discrimination, lessened the gaps between rich and poor and black and white, and helped bring minority poverty to its lowest level in history in 1973, that year's recession initiated a reversal of minority progress and a reassertion of white privilege.[23] In 1977, the U.S. Civil Rights Commission reported on the disproportionate impact of layoffs on minority workers. In cases where minority workers made up only 10 to 12 percent of the work force in their area, they accounted for from 60 to 70 percent of those laid off in 1974. The principle of seniority, a social democratic triumph, in this case worked

Superfund Aid to communities for cleanup and abatement of the effects of living near abandoned industrial waste sites.

to guarantee that minority workers would suffer most from technological changes because the legacy of past discrimination by their employers left them with less seniority than white workers.[24]

When housing prices doubled during the 1970s, white home owners who had been able to take advantage of discriminatory FHA financing policies received increased equity in their homes, while those excluded from the housing market by earlier policies found themselves facing higher costs of entry into the market in addition to the traditional obstacles presented by the discriminatory practices of sellers, realtors, and lenders. The contrast between European Americans and African Americans is instructive in this regard. Because whites have access to broader housing choices than blacks, whites pay 15 percent less than blacks for similar housing in the same neighborhood. White neighborhoods typically experience housing costs 25 percent less expensive than would be the case if the residents were black.[25]

A recent Federal Reserve Bank of Boston study showed that minority applicants had a 60 percent greater chance of being denied home loans than white applicants with the same credit-worthiness. Boston bankers made 2.9 times as many mortgage loans per one thousand housing units in neighborhoods inhabited by low-income whites than they did to neighborhoods populated by low-income blacks.[26] In addition, loan officers were far more likely to overlook flaws in the credit records of white applicants or to arrange creative financing for them than they were with black applicants.[27]

A Los Angeles study found that loan officers more frequently used dividend income and underlying assets criteria for judging black applicants than they did for whites.[28] In Houston, the NCNB Bank of Texas disqualified 13 percent of middle-income white loan applicants but disqualified 36 percent of middle-income black applicants.[29] Atlanta's home loan institutions gave five times as many home loans to whites as to blacks in the late 1980s. An analysis of sixteen Atlanta neighborhoods found that home buyers in white neighborhoods received conventional financing four times as often as those in black sections of the city.[30] Nationwide, financial institutions get more money in deposits from black neighborhoods than they invest in them in the form of home mortgage loans, making home lending a vehicle for the transfer of capital away from black savers and toward white investors.[31]

In many locations, high-income blacks were denied loans more often than low-income whites.[32]

Federal home loan policies have placed the power of the federal government behind private discrimination. Urban renewal and highway construction programs have enhanced the possessive investment in whiteness directly through government initiatives. In addition, decisions about the location of federal jobs have also systematically supported the subsidy for whiteness. Federal civilian employment dropped by 41,419 in central cities between 1966 and 1973, but total federal employment in metropolitan areas grew by 26,558.[33] While one might naturally expect the location of government buildings that serve the public to follow population trends, the federal government's policies in locating offices and records centers in suburbs helped aggravate the flight of jobs to suburban locations less accessible to inner-city residents. Since racial discrimination in the private sector forces minority workers to seek government positions disproportionate to their numbers, these moves exact particular hardships on them. In addition, minorities who follow their jobs to the suburbs generally encounter increased commuter costs because housing discrimination makes it harder and more expensive for them to relocate than for whites.

The racialized aspects of fifty years of these social democratic policies became greatly exacerbated by the anti-social democratic policies of neoconservatives in the Reagan and Bush administrations during the 1980s and 1990s. They clearly contributed to the reinforcement of possessive investments in whiteness through their regressive policies in respect to federal aid to education and their refusal to challenge segregated education, housing, and hiring, as well as their cynical cultivation of an antiblack, counter-subversive consensus through attacks on affirmative action and voting rights legislation. In the U.S. economy, where 86 percent of available jobs do not appear in classified advertisements and where personal connections provide the most important factor in securing employment, attacks on affirmative action guarantee that whites will be rewarded for their historical advantages in the labor market rather than for their individual abilities or efforts.[34]

Yet even seemingly race-neutral policies supported by both neoconservatives and social democrats in the 1980s and 1990s have also increased the absolute value of being white. In the 1980s, changes in federal tax laws decreased the value of wage income and increased the value of investment income—a move harmful to minorities who suffer from an even greater gap between their total wealth and that of whites than in the disparity between their income and white income. Failure to raise the minimum wage between 1981 and 1989 and the more than one-third decline in value of Aid for Families with Dependent Children payments hurt all poor people, but they exacted special costs on nonwhites facing even more constricted markets for employment, housing, and education than poor whites.[35]

Similarly, the "tax reforms" of the 1980s made the effective rate of taxation higher on investment in actual goods and services than it was on profits from speculative enterprises. This encouraged the flight of capital away from industrial production with its many employment opportunities and toward investments that can be turned over quickly to allow the greatest possible tax write-offs. Consequently, government policies actually discouraged investments that might produce high-paying jobs and encouraged investors to strip companies of their assets in order to make rapid short-term profits. These policies hurt almost all workers, but they exacted particularly high costs from minority workers who, because of employment discrimination in the retail and small business sectors, were overrepresented in blue-collar industrial jobs.

On the other hand, while neoconservative tax policies created incentives for employers to move their enterprises elsewhere, they created disincentives for home owners to move. Measures such as California's Proposition 13 granting tax relief to property owners badly misallocate housing resources because they make it financially unwise for the elderly to move out of large houses, further reducing the supply of housing available to young families. While one can well understand the necessity for protecting senior citizens on fixed incomes from tax increases that would make them lose their homes, the rewards and punishments provided by Proposition 13 are so extreme that they prevent the kinds of generational succession that have routinely opened up housing to young families in the past. This reduction works particular hardships on those who also face discrimination by sellers, realtors, and lending institutions.

Subsidies to the private sector by government agencies also tend to reward the results of past discrimination. Throughout the country, tax increment redevelopment programs give tax-free, low-interest loans to developers whose projects use public services, often without having to pay taxes to local school boards or county governments. Industrial development bonds resulted in a $7.4 billion tax loss in 1983, a loss that ordinary tax payers had to make up through increased payroll taxes. Compared to white Americans, people of color, who are more likely to be poor or working class, suffer disproportionately from these changes as tax payers, as workers, and as tenants. A study by the Citizens for Tax Justice found that wealthy Californians spend less than eleven cents in taxes for every dollar earned, while poor residents of the state paid fourteen cents out of every dollar in taxes. As groups overrepresented among the poor, minorities have been forced to shoulder this burden in order to subsidize the tax breaks given to the wealthy.[36] While holding property tax assessments for businesses and some home owners to about half of their market value, California's Proposition 13 deprived cities and counties of $13 billion a year in taxes. Businesses alone avoided $3.3 billion to $8.6 billion in taxes per year under this statute.[37]

Because they are ignorant of even the recent history of the possessive investment in whiteness—generated by slavery and segregation but augmented by social democratic reform—Americans produce largely cultural explanations for structural social problems. The increased possessive investment in whiteness generated by disinvestment in America's cities, factories, and schools since the 1970s disguises the general problems posed to our society by de-industrialization, economic restructuring, and **neoconservative** attacks on the welfare state as *racial* problems. It fuels a discourse that demonizes people of color for being victimized by these changes, while hiding the privileges of whiteness by attributing them to family values, fatherhood, and foresight—rather than to favoritism.

The demonization of black families in public discourse since the 1970s is particularly instructive in this regard. During the 1970s, the share of low-income households headed by blacks increased by one-third, while black family income fell from 60 percent of white family income in 1971 to 58 percent in 1980. Even when adjusting

neoconservatism A response to the liberalism of the 1960s, this political philosophy is an attempt to return to the conservatism of the 1950s. The movement is characterized by privatizing public goods, nation building through military intervention abroad, and minimum government regulation.

for unemployment and for African-American disadvantages in life-cycle employment (more injuries, more frequently interrupted work histories, confinement to jobs most susceptible to layoffs), the wages of full-time year-round black workers fell from 77 percent of white workers' income to 73 percent by 1986. In 1986, white workers with high school diplomas earned three thousand dollars per year more than African Americans with the same education.[38] Even when they had the same family structure as white workers, blacks found themselves more likely to be poor.

Among black workers between the ages of twenty and twenty-four, 46 percent held blue-collar jobs in 1976, but that percentage fell to only 20 percent by 1984. Earnings by young black families had reached 60 percent of the amount secured by white families in 1973, but by 1986 they fell back to 46 percent. Younger African-American families experienced a 50 percent drop in real earnings between 1973 and 1986, with the decline in black male wages particularly steep.[39]

Many recent popular and scholarly studies have explained clearly the causes for black economic decline over the past two decades.[40] Deindustrialization has decimated the industrial infrastructure that formerly provided high-wage jobs and chances for upward mobility to black workers. Neoconservative attacks on government spending for public housing, health, education, and transportation have deprived African Americans of needed services and opportunities for jobs in the public sector. A massive retreat from responsibility to enforce anti-discrimination laws at the highest levels of government has sanctioned pervasive overt and covert racial discrimination by bankers, realtors, and employers.

Yet public opinion polls conducted among white Americans display little recognition of these devastating changes. Seventy percent of whites in one poll said that African Americans "have the same opportunities to live a middle-class life as whites."[41] Nearly three-fourths of white respondents to a 1989 poll believed that opportunities for blacks had improved during the Reagan presidency.[42]

Optimism about the opportunities available to African Americans does not necessarily demonstrate ignorance of the dire conditions facing black communities, but, if not, it then indicates that many whites believe that blacks suffer deservedly, that they do not take advantage of the opportunities offered them. In the opinion polls, favorable assessments of

black chances for success often accompanied extremely negative judgments about the abilities, work habits, and character of black people. A National Opinion Research Report in 1990 disclosed that more than 50 percent of American whites viewed blacks as innately lazy and less intelligent and less patriotic than whites.[43] Furthermore, more than 60 percent of whites questioned in that survey said that they believed that blacks suffer from poor housing and employment opportunities because of their own lack of willpower. Some 56.3 percent of whites said that blacks preferred welfare to employment, while 44.6 percent contended that blacks tended toward laziness.[44] Even more important, research by Mary and Thomas Byrne Edsall indicates that many whites structure nearly all of their decisions about housing, education, and politics in response to their aversions to black people.[45]

The present political culture in this country gives broad sanction for viewing white supremacy and antiblack racism as forces from the past, as demons finally put to rest by the passage of the 1964 Civil Rights Act and the 1965 Voting Rights Act.[46] Jurists, journalists, and politicians have generally been more vocal in their opposition to "quotas" and to "reverse discrimination" mandating race-specific remedies for discrimination than to the thousands of well-documented incidents every year of routine, systematic, and unyielding discrimination against blacks.

It is my contention that the stark contrast between black experiences and white opinions during the past two decades cannot be attributed solely to ignorance or intolerance on the part of individuals but stems instead from the overdetermined inadequacy of the language of liberal individualism to describe collective experience.[47] As long as we define social life as the sum total of conscious and deliberate individual activities, then only *individual* manifestations of personal prejudice and hostility will be seen as racist. Systemic, collective, and coordinated behavior disappears from sight. Collective exercises of group power relentlessly channeling rewards, resources, and opportunities from one group to another will not appear to be "racist" from this perspective because they rarely announce their intention to discriminate against individuals. But they work to construct racial indentities by giving people of different races vastly different life chances.

The gap between white perceptions and minority experiences can have explosive consequences. Little more than a year after the 1992 Los Angeles rebellion, a six-teen-year-old high school junior shared her opinions with a reporter from the *Los Angeles Times*. "I don't think white people owe anything to black people," she explained. "We didn't sell them into slavery, it was our ancestors. What they did was wrong, but we've done our best to make up for it."[48] A seventeen-year-old senior echoed those comments, telling the reporter:

> I feel we spend more time in my history class talking about what whites owe blacks than just about anything else when the issue of slavery comes up. I often received dirty looks. This seems strange given that I wasn't even alive then. And the few members of my family from that time didn't have the luxury of owning much, let alone slaves. So why, I ask you, am I constantly made to feel guilty?[49]

More ominously, after pleading guilty to bombing two homes and one car, to vandalizing a synagogue, and attempting to start a race war by murdering Rodney King and bombing Los Angeles's First African Methodist Episcopal Church, twenty-year-old Christopher David Fisher explained that "sometimes whites were picked on because of the color of their skin. . . . Maybe we're blamed for slavery."[50] Fisher's actions were certainly extreme, but his justification of them drew knowingly and precisely on a broadly shared narrative about the victimization of innocent whites by irrational and ungrateful minorities.

The comments and questions raised about the legacy of slavery by these young whites illumine broader currents in our culture that have enormous implications for understanding the enduring significance of race in our country. These young people associate black grievances solely with slavery, and they express irritation at what they perceive as efforts to make them feel guilty or unduly privileged in the present because of things that happened in the distant past. Because their own ancestors may not have been slave owners or because "we've done our best to make up for it," they feel that it is unreasonable for anyone to view them as people who owe "anything" to blacks. On the contrary, Fisher felt that his discomfort with being "picked on" and "blamed" for slavery gave him good reason to bomb homes, deface synagogues, and plot to kill black people.

Unfortunately for our society, these young whites accurately reflect the logic of the language of liberal individualism and its ideological predispositions in discussions of race. They seem to have no knowledge of the disciplined, systemic, and collective *group* activity that has structured white identities in American history. They

are not alone in their ignorance; in a 1979 law journal article, future Supreme Court Justice Antonin Scalia argued that affirmative action "is based upon concepts of racial indebtedness and racial entitlement rather than individual worth and individual need" and is thus "racist."[51]

Yet liberal individualism is not completely color blind on this issue. As Cheryl I. Harris demonstrates, the legacy of liberal individualism has not prevented the Supreme Court from recognizing and protecting the group interests of *whites* in the Bakke, Croson, and Wygant cases.[52] In each case, the Court nullified affirmative action programs because they judged efforts to help blacks as harmful to whites: to white expectations of entitlement, expectations based on the possessive investment in whiteness they held as members of a group. In the Bakke case, for instance, neither Bakke nor the court contested the legitimacy of medical school admissions standards that reserved five seats in each class for children of wealthy donors to the university or that penalized Bakke for being older than most of the other applicants. The group rights of not-wealthy people or of people older than their classmates did not compel the Court or Bakke to make any claim of harm. But they did challenge and reject a policy designed to offset the effects of past and present discrimination when they could construe the medical school admission policies as detrimental to the interests of whites as a group—and as a consequence they applied the "strict scrutiny" standard to protect whites while denying that protection to people of color. In this case, as in so many others, the language of liberal individualism serves as a cover for coordinated collective group interests.

Group interests are not monolithic, and aggregate figures can obscure serious differences within racial groups. All whites do not benefit from the possessive investment in whiteness in precisely the same way; the experiences of members of minority groups are not interchangeable. But the possessive investment in whiteness always affects individual and group life chances and opportunities. Even in cases where minority groups secure political and economic power through collective mobilization, the terms and conditions of their collectivity and the logic of group solidarity are always influenced and intensified by the absolute value of whiteness in American politics, economics, and culture.[53]

In the 1960s, members of the Black Panther Party used to say that "if you're not part of the solution, you're part of the problem." But those of us who are "white" can only become part of the solution if we recognize the degree to which we are already part of the problem—not because of our race, but because of our possessive investment in it. Neither conservative **"free market"** policies nor liberal social democratic reforms can solve the "white problem" in America because both of them reinforce the possessive investment in whiteness. But an explicitly antiracist pan-ethnic movement that acknowledges the existence and power of whiteness might make some important changes. Pan-ethnic, antiracist coalitions have a long history in the United States—in the political activism of John Brown, Sojourner Truth, and the Magon brothers, among others—but we also have a rich cultural tradition of pan-ethnic antiracism connected to civil rights activism of the kind detailed so brilliantly in rhythm and blues musician Johnny Otis's recent book, *Upside Your Head! Rhythm and Blues on Central Avenue.*[54] These efforts by whites to fight racism, not out of sympathy for someone else but out of a sense of self-respect and simple justice, have never completely disappeared; they remain available as models for the present.[55]

Walter Benjamin's praise for "presence of mind" came from his understanding of how difficult it may be to see the present. But more important, he called for presence of mind as the means for implementing what he called "the only true telepathic miracle"—turning the forbidding future into the fulfilled present.[56] Failure to acknowledge our society's possessive investment in whiteness prevents us from facing the present openly and honestly. It hides from us the devastating costs of disinvestment in America's infrastructure over the past two decades and keeps us from facing our responsibilities to reinvest in human capital by channeling resources toward education, health, and housing—and away from subsidies for speculation and luxury. After two decades of disinvestment, the only further disinvestment we need is to disinvest in the ruinous pathology of whiteness that has always undermined our own best instincts and interests. In a society suffering so badly from an absence of mutuality, an absence of responsibility, and an absence of simple justice, presence of mind might be just what we need.

free market A system of exchange in which buyers and sellers come to agreement about pricing with no outside influences. The idea of a free market is that there is little or no government intervention in the private transactions of individuals.

Seeing the Big Picture — Race as an Investment

How do rates of homeownership (Section II in the Appendix) and occupations by race (Section VIII) point to historic investments that have privileged one group over another?

20 Laissez-Faire Racism, Racial Inequality, and the Role of the Social Sciences
Lawrence D. Bobo

LAWRENCE D. BOBO is the Norman Tishman and Charles M. Diker Professor of Sociology and of African and African American Studies at Harvard University.

Questions to Consider There is the tendency, particularly in the media, to frame racism as a practice and belief system of the past. We like to tell ourselves that the racism of yesterday, which was a core feature and organizing principle of the United States, has been laid to rest. In his discussion of laissez-faire racism, Professor Bobo suggests that racism hasn't gone away; it's merely morphed into a new discourse in which nonracial reasons or rationalizations (social class, culture, work ethic) are used to explain away continued institutional racism and discrimination. How is laissez-faire racism different from "old-fashioned" racism, and why is this new type of racism more problematic?

As PART OF RESEARCH ON THE INTERSECTION of poverty, crime, and race, I conducted two focus groups in a major eastern city in early September 2001, just prior to the tragic events of September 11. The dynamics of the two groups, one with nine white participants and another with nine black participants, drove home for me very powerfully just how deep but also just how sophisticated, elusive, and enduring a race problem the United States still confronts. An example from each group begins to make the point that the very nature of this problem and our vocabularies for discussing it have grown very slippery, very difficult to grasp, and therefore extremely difficult to name and to fight.

First let's consider the white focus group. In response to the moderator's early question, "What's the biggest problem facing your community?" a young working-class white male eagerly and immediately chimed in, "Section 8 housing." "It's a terrible system," he said. The racial implications hung heavy in the room until a middle-aged white bartender tried to leaven things a bit by saying:

> All right. If you have people of a very low economic group who have a low standard of living who cannot properly feed and clothe their children, whose speech patterns are not as good as ours [and] are [therefore] looked down upon as a low class. Where I live most of those people happen to be black. So it's generally perceived that blacks are inferior to whites for that reason.

The bartender went on to explain: "It's not that way at all. It's a class issue, which in many ways is economically driven. From my perspective, it's not a racial issue at all. I'm a bartender. I'll serve anybody if they're a class [act]." At this, the group erupted in laughter, but the young

working-class male was not finished. He asserted, a bit more vigorously:

> Why should somebody get to live in my neighborhood that hasn't earned that right? I'd like to live [in a more affluent area], but I can't afford to live there so I don't. . . . So why should somebody get put in there by the government that didn't earn that right?

And then the underlying hostility and stereotyping came out more directly when he said: "And most of the people on that program are trashy, and they don't know how to behave in a working neighborhood. It's not fair. I call it unfair housing laws."

Toward the end of the session, when discussing why the jails are so disproportionately filled with blacks and Hispanics, this young man said: "Blacks and Hispanics are more violent than white people. I think they are more likely to shoot somebody over a fender bender than a couple of white guys are. They have shorter fuses, and they are more emotional than white people."

In fairness, some members of the white group criticized antiblack prejudice. Some members of the group tried to point out misdeeds done by whites as well. But even the most liberal of the white participants never pushed the point, rarely moved beyond abstract observations or declarations against prejudice, and sometimes validated the racial stereotypes more overtly embraced by others. In an era when everyone supposedly knows what to say and what not to say and is artful about avoiding overt bigotry, this group discussion still quickly turned to racial topics and quickly elicited unabashed negative stereotyping and antiblack hostility.

When asked the same question about the "biggest problem facing your community," the black group almost in unison said, "Crime and drugs," and a few voices chimed in, "Racism." One middle-aged black woman reported: "I was thinking more so on the lines of myself because my house was burglarized three times. Twice while I was at work and one time when I returned from church, I caught the person in there."

The racial thread to her story became clearer when she later explained exactly what happened in terms of general police behavior in her community:

> The first two robberies that I had, the elderly couple that lived next door to me, they called the police. I was at work when the first two robberies occurred. They called the police two or three times. The police never even showed up. When I came in from work, I had to go . . . file a police report. My neighbors went with me, and they had called the police several times and they never came. Now, on that Sunday when I returned from church and caught him in my house, and the guy that I caught in my house lives around the corner, he has a case history, he has been in trouble since doomsday. When I told [the police] I had knocked him unconscious, oh yeah, they were there in a hurry. Guns drawn. And I didn't have a weapon except for the baseball bat, [and] I wound up face down on my living room floor, and they placed handcuffs on me.

The moderator, incredulous, asked: "Well, excuse me, but they locked you and him up?" "They locked me up and took him to the hospital."

Indeed, the situation was so dire, the woman explained, that had a black police officer who lived in the

neighborhood not shown up to help after the patrol car arrived with sirens blaring, she felt certain the two white police officers who arrived, guns drawn, would probably have shot her. As it was, she was arrested for assault, spent two days in jail, and now has a lawsuit pending against the city. Somehow I doubt that a single, middle-aged, churchgoing white woman in an all-white neighborhood who had called the police to report that she apprehended a burglar in her home would end up handcuffed, arrested, and in jail alongside the burglar. At least, I am not uncomfortable assuming that the police would not have entered a home in a white community with the same degree of apprehension, fear, preparedness for violence, and ultimate disregard for a law-abiding citizen as they did in this case. But it can happen in black communities in America today.

To say that the problem of race endures, however, is not to say that it remains fundamentally the same and essentially unchanged. I share the view articulated by historians such as Barbara Fields (1982) and Thomas Holt (2000) that race is both socially constructed and historically contingent. As such, it is not enough to declare that race matters or that racism endures. *The much more demanding challenge is to account for how and why such a social construction comes to be reconstituted, refreshed, and enacted anew in very different times and places.* How is it that we can find a working-class white man who is convinced that many blacks are "trashy people" controlled by emotions and clearly more susceptible to violence? How is it that a black woman defending herself and her home against a burglar ends up apprehended as if she were one of the "usual suspects"? Or cast more broadly, how do we have a milestone like the *Brown* decision and pass a Civil Rights Act, a Voting Rights Act, a Fair Housing Act, and numerous acts of enforcement and amendments to all of these, including the pursuit of affirmative action policies, and yet still continue to face a significant racial divide in America?

The answer I sketch here is but a partial one, focusing on three key observations. First, as I have argued elsewhere and elaborate in important ways here, I believe that we are witnessing the crystallization of a new racial ideology here in the United States. This ideology I refer to as laissez-faire racism. We once confronted a slave labor economy with its inchoate ideology of racism and then watched it evolve in response to war and other social, economic, and cultural trends into an explicit Jim Crow racism of the de jure segregation era. We have more recently seen the biological and openly segregationist thrust of twentieth-century Jim Crow racism change into the more cultural, free-market, and ostensibly color-blind thrust of laissez-faire racism in the new millennium. But make no mistake—the current social structure and attendant ideology reproduce, sustain, and rationalize enormous black-white inequality (Bobo and Kluegel 1997).

Second, race and racism remain powerful levers in American national politics. These levers can animate the electorate, constrain and shape political discourse and campaigns, and help direct the fate of major social policies. From the persistently contested efforts at affirmative action through a historic expansion of the penal system and the recent dismantling of "welfare as we know it," the racial divide has often decisively prefigured and channeled core features of our domestic politics (Bobo 2000).

Third, social science has played a peculiar role in the problem of race. And here I wish to identify an intellectual and scholarly failure to come to grips with the interrelated phenomena of white privilege and black agency. This failure may present itself differently depending on the ideological leanings of scholars. I critique one line of analysis on the left and one on the right. On the left, the problem typically presents as a failure of sociological imagination. It manifests itself in arguments that seek to reduce racialized social dynamics to some ontologically more fundamental nonracialized factor. On the right, the problem is typically the failure of explicit victim-blaming. It manifests itself in a rejection of social structural roots or causation of racialized social conditions. I want to suggest that both tactics—the left's search for some structural force more basic than race (such as class or skill levels or child-rearing practices) and the right's search for completely volitional factors (cultural or individual dispositions) as final causes of "race" differences—reflect a deep misunderstanding of the dynamics of race and racism. Race is not just a set of categories, and racism is not just a collection of individual-level anti–minority group attitudes. Race and racism are more fundamentally about sets of intertwined power relations, group interests and identities, and the ideas that justify and make sense out of (or challenge and delegitimate) the organized racial ordering of society (Dawson 2000). The latter analytic posture and theory of race in society is embodied in the theory of laissez-faire racism.

On Laissez-Faire Racism

. . . Laissez-faire racism involves persistent negative stereotyping of African Americans, a tendency to blame blacks themselves for the black-white gap in socioeconomic status, and resistance to meaningful policy efforts to ameliorate U.S. racist social conditions and institutions. It represents a critical new stage in American racism. As structures of racial oppression became less formal, as the power resources available to black communities grew and were effectively deployed, as other cultural trends paved the way for an assault on notions of biologically ranked "races," the stage was set for displacing Jim Crow racism and erecting something different in its place. . . .

The second point to emphasize here is that this is an argument about general patterns of group relations and ideology—not merely about variation in views among individuals from a single racial or ethnic category. As such, our primary concern is with the central tendency of attitudes and beliefs within and between racial groups and the social system as such, not within and between individuals. It is the collective dimensions of social experience that I most intend to convey with the notion of laissez-faire racism—not a singular attitude held to a greater or lesser degree by particular individuals. The intellectual case for such a perspective has been most forcefully articulated by the sociologist Mary R. Jackman (1994, 119). We should focus an analysis of attitudes and ideology on group-level comparisons, she writes, because doing so

> draws attention to the structural conditions that encase an intergroup relationship and it underscores the point that individual actors are not free agents but caught in an aggregate relationship. Unless we assume that the individual is socially atomized, her personal experiences constitute only one source of information that is evaluated against the backdrop of her manifold observations of the aggregated experiences (both historical and contemporaneous) of the group as a whole.

The focus is thus more on the larger and enduring patterns and tendencies that distinguish groups than on the individual sources of variation.

With this in mind, I want to focus on three pieces of data, the first of which concerns the persistence of negative stereotypes of African Americans. Figure 1 reports data from a national Web-based survey I recently conducted using eight of Paul Sniderman's stereotype questions (four

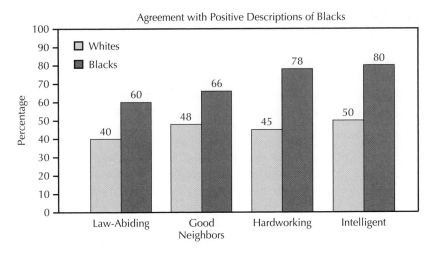

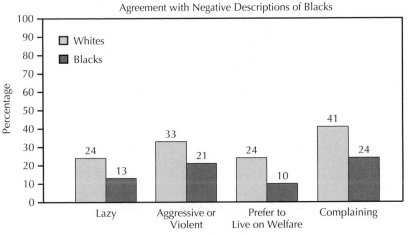

FIGURE 1 **Stereotype Items, by Race.** *Source:* Race, Crime, and Public Opinion Study (2001).

dealing with positive social traits and four dealing with negative social traits) (Sniderman and Piazza 1993). Several patterns stand out. It is easier for both blacks and whites to endorse the positive traits when expressing views about the characteristics of blacks than the negative traits. However, African Americans are always more favorable and less negative in their views than whites. Some of the differences are quite large. For instance, there is a thirty-percentage-point difference between white and black perceptions on the trait of intelligence and a thirty-three-percentage-point difference on the "hardworking" trait. . . .

Negative stereotypes of African Americans are common, though not uniform, and to a distressing degree they exist among both blacks and whites and presumably influence perceptions and behaviors for both groups. However, there is a sharp difference in central tendency within each group, in predictable directions. One cannot escape the conclusion that most whites have different and decidedly lesser views of the basic behavioral characteristics of blacks than do blacks themselves. And that generally these patterns indicate that African Americans remain a culturally dishonored and debased group in the American psyche. . . .

On the Peculiar Role of Social Science

Mainstream scholars on the left tend to treat race as a categorical designation that affects the outcomes that matter to us for reasons that have nothing to do with race as a sociological phenomenon. If African Americans have lower employment chances or earnings than whites, this is not a function of race but rather of purely "statistical discrimination" or other factors, such as different levels of education and skill, that somehow "explain" the extraneous influence of race. Since we do not believe in race as an inherent biological or primordial cultural factor that produces social outcomes, there must be other nonracial social conditions that account for any effect of race on outcomes that matter. The analog to this line of reasoning in examinations of political attitudes and public opinion is the treatment of African Americans as an out-group attitude object, an object toward which individual whites have been socialized to hold more or less negative attitudes.

To the credit of liberal social analysts, both approaches reject biological and inflexible cultural understandings of race and racial differences. Yet both approaches fail to come to grips with the condition of embedded white privilege and the import of constrained but quite real black agency. That is, there are sociologically meaningful "imagined communities," communities of identity as well as of typical residence, interaction, family connection, and larger interest defined as black and white that exist in relation to one another in the United States. And indeed, race has been used at various points and in various ways as one of the fundamental principles in organizing an array of conditions that define the relationship between those sociological units or imagined communities. Hence, its effects are not reducible to other, putatively more fundamental causes.

Let me be more specific by taking an example from the realm of racial attitudes and public opinion. The theory of symbolic racism contends that a new form of antiblack prejudice has arisen among whites reflecting a blend of early learned traditional values (for example, individualism and the Protestant work ethic) and early learned negative feelings and beliefs about blacks. This new attitude is an amalgamation. It consists of a resentment of demands made by blacks, a resentment of special favors received, especially from government, by blacks, and a denial of the contemporary relevance of discrimination. These views

constitute a coherent attitude, an attitude not bearing any functional relation to white advantage or privilege or to real-world black challenge and resistance to white privilege. Rather, the attitude is a learned ideation of centrally unreasoned, emotion-laden content. When political issues arise that make race and African Americans salient, this underlying psychological disposition becomes the basis of whites' political response. Hence, prejudice *intrudes* into politics.

What I want to suggest is that prejudice is *in and of* politics—not an ideational intrusion of the individual's emotionally expressive and irrational impulses upon the political sphere (Bobo and Tuan, forthcoming). As I have argued elsewhere, intergroup attitudes are not principally individual-level judgments of like and dislike (Bobo, Kluegel, and Smith 1997; Bobo and Smith 1998). Instead, following the inspiration of Herbert Blumer (1958), I argue that these attitudes centrally involve beliefs and feelings about the proper relation between groups. Racial attitudes capture aspects of the preferred group positions and those patterns of belief and affect that undergird, mobilize as needed, and make understandable the prevailing racial order.

These remarks have specific meaning with regard to the conceptualization and measurement of a notion like symbolic racism. Beliefs and feelings about whether blacks receive special treatment, favors, or an unfair advantage or have leaders and a political agenda that demand too much are not merely ventilations of atomistic feelings of resentment or hostility. These are highly political judgments about the status, rights, and resources that members of different *groups* are rightly entitled to enjoy or make claims on.

This difference in conceptualization is an important one and is directly linked to my concern with white privilege and black agency. From the vantage point of symbolic racism theory, there is no instrumental or rational objective whatsoever behind the intrusion of prejudice into politics. Whites are neither seeking the maintenance of privilege nor responding in any grounded fashion to real social, political, and economic demands arising from the black community and its leaders. Instead, the theory holds, a mixture of emotions, fears, anxieties, and resentments combines with important social values to occasion a hostile response when African Americans and their concerns are made politically salient (Kinder and Sanders 1996; Sears, van Laar, and Kosterman 1997).

Although not intended as such, this view trivializes African Americans' political activism and struggle that put issues like desegregation, antidiscrimination, affirmative action, and increasingly the matter of reparations on the national political agenda. Real political actors pursued deliberate strategies and waged hard-fought legal, electoral, and protest-oriented battles to advance the interests of black communities. These actions had powerful effects on the larger dynamics of politics and public opinion (Lee 2002). And however imperfect and imbued with exaggerated apprehensions they may have been, white Americans nonetheless perceived and responded to these very substantively political struggles (Bobo 1988). Hence, to classify white attitudes and beliefs about black demands, black leadership, and black responses to disadvantage as some sort of "pre-political," completely emotional ideation is to trivialize black America, to infantilize white America, and to skirt serious engagement with the many powerful "wages" that still accrue to whiteness.

Empirically and in terms of measurement, this argument raises serious doubts about how to understand the meaning of responses to the questions used to tap symbolic racism. For example, my own research suggests that when many whites say that blacks (or any other minority group) are "taking unfair advantage of privileges given to them by the government," these are not vague resentments (Bobo 1999). These sentiments are almost certainly not precisely calculated assessments of real risks and actual losses, but they are still expressly political judgments about the quality of life and about important resources, at once material and symbolic, that groups may get from the state.

In particular, whites who answer in the affirmative to this sort of survey question frequently speak of their tax dollars and their work effort going to support others, in the concrete language of a zero-sum resource transfer. A good illustration of the point comes from the cultural sociologist Michele Lamont's important new book, *The Dignity of Working Men: Morality and the Boundaries of Race, Class, and Immigration* (2000, 60–61). She writes of one of her subjects:

> Vincent is a workhorse. He considers himself "top gun" at his job and makes a very decent living. His comments on

blacks suggest that he associates them with laziness and welfare and with claims to receiving special treatment at work through programs such as affirmative action. He says: "Blacks have a tendency to . . . try to get off doing less, the least possible . . . to keep the job where whites will put in that extra oomph. I know this is a generality and it does not go for all, it goes for a portion. It's this whole unemployment and welfare gig. A lot of the blacks on welfare have no desire to get off it. Why should they? It's free money. I can't stand to see my hard-earned money [*said with emphasis*] going to pay for someone who wants to sit on his ass all day long and get free money."

As Lamont (2000, 62) concludes about a number of the white working-class men she interviewed: "They underscore a concrete link between the perceived dependency of blacks, their laziness, and the taxes taken from their own paychecks."

This is not an isolated finding of Lamont's in-depth interviews. For example, the sociologist Mary Waters (1999, 177) observed a very similar pattern among the white managers and employers she studied. She writes:

> Most white respondents were much more able to tap into their negative impressions of black people, especially "underclass" blacks whom they were highly critical of. These opinions were not just based on disinterested observation. There was a direct sense among many of the whites that they personally were being taken advantage of and threatened by the black population.

The language used is one of traits (laziness) and violations of values (hard work and self-reliance) coupled with moral condemnation, but the group comparison, sense of threat, and identity-engaging element is equally clear. Indeed, as the experimental social psychologist Eliot Smith (1993, 308–9) has persuasively argued, it is exactly this blend of important group identity and resource threat to the group that *should* be emotionally arousing: "These items and the definition all involve appraisals of an outgroup as violating ingroup norms or obtaining illegitimate advantages, leading to the emotion of anger." Conceptualizing such responses as the ventilation of resentment distorts the critical point that "the focus in the model advanced here is not the intrinsically negative qualities attributed to blacks themselves (which are the theoretical key in concepts of prejudice as a negative attitude) but *appraisals of the threats posed by blacks to the perceiver's own group*" (309, emphasis in original).

The substance of the theory and the interpretation of the measures of symbolic racism thus suffer from a failure of sociological imagination. The theory pushes out of analytical view the real and substantial linkage between the facts of white privilege and the facts of active black challenge to it. In their place, the theory gives us but the phantasms of racial resentments in the minds of individual whites. These phantasms somehow—but apparently unintentionally—enter politics, take note of black agitation and disruption, and then release in a spasm of reaction against race-targeted social policies. I would like to suggest that there is something decidedly wrong with the theory and conceptualization, even though the many sentiments identified in the concepts of symbolic racism and racial resentment are indeed at the heart of the contemporary political struggle over race (Krysan 2000).

On the right side of the political spectrum, the example I wish to draw attention to is the mounting speculation, most prominently offered by Stephan and Abigail Thernstrom (1997), that the pervasive patterns of racial segregation we observe in the United States are a function of "black self-segregation." In this case, African Americans are credited with agency, but that agency is said to be exercised in a manner that continues to disadvantage blacks. Only this time it is blacks themselves who, by choosing a self-handicapping preference, are responsible. The argument is a troubling one for anyone who believes that neighborhoods vary in school quality, safety, social services and amenities, and all that goes into the phrase "quality of life." It says that blacks are, perforce and of their own free will, placing racial solidarity above social mobility and a better quality of life.

The failure here is twofold. First, the Thernstroms' argument is contingent on the rejection of compelling empirical evidence of racial bias and discrimination in the housing market (for an authoritative review, see Charles 2003). It is clear that a powerful racial hierarchy continues to permeate thinking about communities, neighborhoods, and where to live. Using experimental data, Camille Z. Charles and I show that white Americans are systematically more open to residential contact with Asians and Latinos than with blacks—holding every other consideration constant (Zubrinsky and Bobo 1996). Several studies have now made it clear

that antiblack racial stereotypes are direct predictors of willingness to live in more integrated communities (Farley et al. 1994; Bobo and Zubrinsky 1996; Charles 2000).

These results are consistent with other demographic and behavioral data (Yinger 1998). Researchers at the State University of New York at Albany document the very small changes in high rates of black-white residential segregation between 1990 and 2000. Indeed, HUD auditing studies in 1989 found overall rates of discrimination in access to housing for African Americans that were only trivially different from those observed a decade earlier.

Second, the theory of black self-segregation treats black choice and action as if it exists in a vacuum. That is, it ignores altogether what are almost surely important feedback mechanisms that prompt many blacks to self-select into black neighborhoods out of the reasonable expectation that they would encounter hostility from some white neighbors. As formulated by the Thernstroms and others, the self-segregation hypothesis fails to address the immediately relevant question of whether African Americans would self-select into predominantly black communities in the absence of historic experience, current collective memory, and ongoing encounters with contemporary racism. The best available empirical evidence suggests that blacks as a group are the people who are the most likely to prefer integration and to comfortably accept living in minority group status in a neighborhood (Charles 2000).

Part of the message here concerning theoretical interpretation on the right and the left is that variables and data never speak for themselves. It is the questions we pose (and those we fail to ask) as well as our theories, concepts, and ideas that bring a narrative and meaning to marginal distributions, correlations, regression coefficients, and statistics of all kinds. If we suffer from failures of sociological imagination, if we conceive of race and racism in ways that disassociate them from white privilege, black agency, and the interrelations between the two phenomena, then we are bound to get things wrong however much we may have followed formal statistical criteria and other normative canons of science. Or, as the sociologist Tukufu Zuberi (2001, 144) puts it in his new book, *Thicker Than Blood: How Racial Statistics Lie:* "Most racial statistics lack a critical evaluation of racist structures that encourage pathological interpretations. These pathological interpretations have had a profound impact on our causal theories and statistical methods. Our theories of society, not our empirical evidence, guide how we interpret racial data."

Indeed, it is that perspective on racist structures, or what the political scientists Michael Dawson (2001) and Claire Jean Kim (2000) call the American racial order, that informs a very different reading of the import of white privilege and black agency.

Caveats

A series of interpretative caveats should be borne in mind here. First, although I have spoken extensively about black-white relations, I am mindful of the extent to which this is an increasingly partial view of American race relations. The rapid and continuing expansion of the Asian and Latino populations in the United States and the unique experiences and issues faced by members of these internally diverse communities will inevitably reshape the American social landscape. However, it is not at all clear that the continued diversification of the United States in any way fundamentally destabilizes the historic black-white divide. The urban sociologist Herbert Gans (1999) has written a provocative and I think more than suggestive essay arguing that we are evolving as a nation toward a new major racial dichotomy: the black versus the nonblack. Accordingly, we would still have racial hierarchy and some degree of heterogeneity, especially within the nonblack category (which include whites and those effectively earning the title of honorary whites, such as successful middle-class Asians). And much of the arsenal of analytical tools and perspectives that long helped to make sense of the black-white divide would have applicability in such a new context. Similarly, my colleague Mary Waters's (1999) powerful recent book, *Black Identities: West Indian Immigrant Dreams and American Realities,* makes clear just how salient the black-white divide remains even for an immigrant population that arrived committed to transcending race.

Second, wartime and the social upheaval occasioned by war can present a powerful opportunity for reshaping the landscape of race relations. Indeed, the political scientists Philip Klinkner and Rogers Smith (1999) craft a persuasive claim that war is a necessary but not sufficient precondition for improvements in the status of blacks. They argue that far-reaching qualitative changes in the status of African Americans have typically involved the convergence of three factors: a major wartime mobilization that ultimately required a large number of black troops; an enemy viewed as profoundly antidemocratic, thereby heightening the claims for fuller realization of democratic ideals at home; and significant internal political mobilization and contestation from below demanding reform.

Viewed in this light, the terrorist attacks on the United States of September 11, 2001, and the subsequent military actions in Afghanistan against the al Qaeda network and the ruling Taliban regime and the later war in Iraq raise again the possibility of this convergence of circumstances. That the early televised images of the devastation at the World Trade Center in New York were so thoroughly multiracial and multiethnic only heightens this potential. And that African Americans in the persons of Colin Powell and Condoleezza Rice occupy such high leadership posts adds to the salutary import of the moment. Certainly we are already witnessing journalistic accounts of a nation pulling together and uniting in ways that may heal otherwise deep racial divisions.

Yet at this moment there are no strong indications that these events will seriously shift the landscape of black-white relations. Not all wartime moments do, as Klinkner and Smith note with regard to the Spanish-American War, the Korean War, and the Vietnam War.

Third, I have scarcely touched upon the matter of class divisions within the African American community and the growth of the black middle class. Nor, for that matter, have I wrestled with the ways in which gender and sexuality also condition life along the color line. It must be stressed that class, gender, and sexuality all become dividing lines within the African American community (and outside it) in ways that shape agendas, the capacity for mobilization, and even ideas about who is a full member of the community (Cohen 1999; Dawson 1994, 2001). My objective has been to focus on those aspects of contemporary race relations that largely cut across these cleavages and thus are centrally experienced as "race," rather than examine the intersection of race with

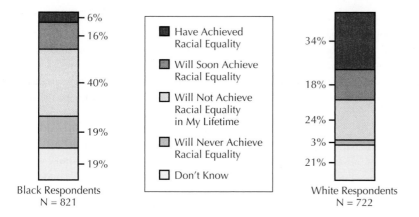

Do you think that blacks have achieved racial equality,
will soon achieve racial equality, will not achieve racial
equality in your lifetime, or will never achieve racial equality?

FIGURE 2   **Respondents Race and Beliefs About Racial Equality.**
Source: National African American Election Study (2000).

other statuses and identities. I do not mean to dismiss or disregard these other factors, but rather to stress that there remain social conditions we must understand and engage as a distinctive racial divide.

Conclusion

I opened with the words of a young, angry white male who saw "trashy" Section 8 blacks coming into his neighborhood with government subsidies and diminishing what he perceived as a standard of life that he had earned and that set him above and apart from them. And with the words of a middle-aged, churchgoing black woman who returned to her home one Sunday morning not only to do battle with a burglar but later with the racially biased police and criminal justice system. As these two cases attest, race remains a deep divide in America.

Of course, black and white Americans could scarcely be further apart in their own judgments about the severity of the racial divide. As part of an election study in 2000, Michael Dawson and I asked a large national sample of blacks and whites about the likelihood of achieving racial equality in America. Figure 2 shows the results. A full one-third of whites said that we had already achieved it, in

contrast to a mere 6 percent of African Americans. One in five blacks said that we never would achieve it, and another two out of five said that it would never happen in their lifetimes. Blacks see a deep and lingering social ill, and whites see a problem that is just about resolved. Without claiming to "know" the answer, I interpret responses of "have already achieved racial equality" and perhaps even of "will soon achieve racial equality" to constitute a deliberate evasion of responsibility more than a thoughtful assessment or response to social realities (Kluegel and Smith 1986; Kluegel and Bobo 2001). Too many friction points, inequalities, and signs of discrimination remain to take such views at face value.

Indeed, it is fair to still speak of white supremacy in America and of racism in America (Bonilla-Silva 2001; Feagin 2001). The persistence of white supremacy and the enduring potency of racism, I believe, trace to the adaptive capacity of racial ideologies. As Thomas Holt (2000, 27–28) has explained: "Race is ideological, but, being embedded in political economies that are quite historically specific, it cannot long survive changes in the material base from which it draws sustenance." The defeat of Jim Crow racism and the victories of the civil rights era did not eradicate black-white economic inequality, labor market discrimination, or gargantuan disparities in accumulated wealth; they did not end residential segregation by race and randomly disperse people in physical space; they did not reallocate political power; and they did not completely repudiate the racist stereotypes and other elements of American political culture and whites' sense of entitlement that feed and sustain racism.

These victories did, however, fundamentally restructure the terrain on which racism is now enacted, understood, and reproduced. This new regime of laissez-faire racism is more fluid and permeable than the Jim Crow regime. It works in ways that permit, on the one hand, the carefully delimited and controlled success of a Colin Powell, a Condoleezza Rice, or even an Oprah Winfrey, but that, on the other hand, do not eliminate the ghetto, black joblessness, and poverty and do not even wince at a despicable effort at black voter disenfranchisement. Indeed, it works in ways that allow a young working-class white man to seethe with anger at a social policy effort to extend a step up for poor blacks and in ways that allow a churchgoing black woman to endure the tragic burden of fighting a black burglar and the white police. These are all manifestations of our continued entrapment in the snare of racism.

I have no battle plan for defeating laissez-faire racism. What we can do as scholars is, first, to struggle to conceptualize, name, and understand as accurately as

possible what is happening and to make those ideas widely available. Let's tell the story of enduring inequality in its fullness and according to the highest standards that we can attain.

Second, we can push for changes and social policies that speak to what our analyses tell us are the central structural and cultural problems. In that regard, the push for a serious dialogue about race—for truth and reconciliation, for an apology, and most of all for reparations—is a major element of the next stage of the struggle (Dawson and Popoff 2004). Liberal and progressive voices must turn away from the demand that the black political agenda be entirely suppressed in favor of a race-neutral, purely universalistic or centrist political agenda (see Thompson 1998).

And third, I do not believe it is possible to accomplish a recognition of one's full humanity without demanding it as such. Careful political thinking and organizing is necessary, to be sure. Strategic coalitions reaching across lines of class, color, and ethnicity will be essential. Working through conventional legal and political channels will be necessary too. But I remain doubtful that hidden agendas and half-measures will do what it takes to finally crush the legacy of white supremacy in America, to dislodge laissez-faire racism, and to lead us to that mountaintop that Martin Luther King spoke of the night before he was assassinated.

21 Residential Segregation and Neighborhood Conditions in U.S. Metropolitan Areas

Douglas S. Massey

DOUGLAS S. MASSEY is the Henry G. Bryant Professor of Sociology and Public Affairs at Princeton University. His book *American Apartheid* (co-authored with Nancy A. Denton) won the 1995 Distinguished Scholarly Publication Award from the American Sociological Association.

> **Questions to Consider**
>
> Douglas Massey points out that almost all racial and ethnic groups are highly segregated in the United States. Racially integrated neighborhoods are an anomaly. Why is residential segregation the norm rather than the exception? Why are blacks subject to the most severe discrimination in the housing market?

SOCIAL SCIENTISTS HAVE LONG STUDIED patterns of racial and ethnic segregation because of the close connection between a group's spatial position in society and its socioeconomic well-being. Opportunities and resources are unevenly distributed in space; some neighborhoods have safer streets, higher home values, better services, more effective schools, and more supportive peer environments than others. As people and families improve their socioeconomic circumstances, they generally move to gain access to these benefits. In doing so, they seek to convert past socioeconomic achievements into improved residential circumstances, yielding tangible immediate benefits and enhancing future prospects for social mobility by providing greater access to residentially determined resources.

Throughout U.S. history, racial and ethnic groups arriving in the United States for the first time have settled in enclaves located close to an urban core, in areas of mixed land use, old housing, poor services, and low or decreasing socioeconomic status. As group members build up time in the city, however, and as their socioeconomic status rises, they have tended to move out of these enclaves into areas that offer more amenities and improved conditions—areas in which majority members are more prevalent—leading to their progressive spatial assimilation into society.

The twin processes of immigrant settlement, on the one hand, and spatial assimilation, on the other, combine to yield a diversity of segregation patterns across groups and times, depending on the particular histories of inmigration and socioeconomic mobility involved (Massey, 1985). Groups experiencing recent rapid inmigration and slow socioeconomic mobility tend to display relatively high levels of segregation, whereas those with rapid rates of economic mobility and slow rates of inmigration tend to be more integrated.

When avenues of spatial assimilation are systematically blocked by prejudice and discrimination, however, residential segregation increases and persists over time. New minorities arrive in the city and settle within enclaves, but their subsequent spatial mobility is stymied, and ethnic concentrations increase until the enclaves are filled, whereupon group members are forced into adjacent areas, thus expanding the boundaries of the enclave (Duncan and Duncan, 1957). In the United States, most immigrant groups experienced relatively few residential barriers, so levels of ethnic segregation historically were not very high. Using a standard segregation index (the **index of dissimilarity**), which varies from 0 to 100,

index of dissimilarity: An index or measure used to represent the level of residential segregation in region or city.

European ethnic groups rarely had indexes of more than 60 (Massey, 1985; Massey and Denton, 1992).

Blacks, in contrast, traditionally experienced severe prejudice and discrimination in urban housing markets. As they moved into urban areas from 1900 to 1960, therefore, their segregation indices rose to unprecedented heights, compared with earlier times and groups. By mid-century, segregation indices exceeded 60 virtually everywhere; and in the largest Black communities they often reached 80 or more (Massey and Denton, 1989b, 1993).

Such high indices of residential segregation imply a restriction of opportunity for Blacks compared with other groups. Discriminatory barriers in urban housing markets mean individual Black citizens are less able to capitalize on their hard-won attainments and achieve desirable residential locations. Compared with Whites of similar social status, Blacks tend to live in systematically disadvantaged neighborhoods, even within suburbs (Schneider and Logan, 1982: Massey et al., 1987; Massey and Fong, 1990; Massey and Denton, 1992).

In a very real way, barriers to spatial mobility are barriers to social mobility; and a racially segregated society cannot logically claim to be "color blind." The way a group is spatially incorporated into society is as important to its socioeconomic well-being as the manner in which it is incorporated into the labor force. It is important, therefore, that levels and trends in residential segregation be documented so that this variable can be incorporated fully into research and theorizing about the causes of urban poverty. To accomplish this, presented here is an overview and interpretation of historical trends in the residential segregation of Blacks, Hispanics, and Asians.

Long-Term Trends in Black Segregation

Massey and Hajnal (1995) examined historical trends in Black segregation at the state, county, municipal, and neighborhood levels.[1] Their interpretation focused on two

[1] Residential segregation was measured using the index of dissimilarity, and racial isolation was measured using the P* index (Massey and Denton, 1988). The index of dissimilarity is the relative number of Blacks who would have to change geographic units so that an even Black-White spatial distribution could be achieved. The P* index is the percentage of Blacks residing in the geographic unit of the average Black person.

specific time periods—pre–World War II; 1900 to 1940; and postwar, from 1950 to 1990. Table 1 presents their data on the geographic structure of Black segregation and racial isolation during the earlier period. Because of data limitations, segregation or isolation at the municipal level during this early period could not be measured.

As Table 1 shows, Blacks and Whites were distinctly segregated from one another across state boundaries early in the twentieth century. In 1900, for example, 64 percent of all Blacks would have had to move to a different state to achieve an even distribution across state lines, and most Blacks lived in a state that was 36 percent Black. These figures simply state the obvious, that in 1900, some 90 percent of Blacks lived in a handful of southern states, which contained only 25 percent of all Whites (U.S. Bureau of the Census, 1979).

The isolation index shows that in the South, most Blacks lived in rural counties that were approximately 45 percent Black, yielding a high degree of segregation and racial isolation at the county level as well. The dissimilarity index for 1900 reveals that nearly 70 percent of all Blacks would have had to shift their county of residence to achieve an even racial distribution across county lines.

At the beginning of this century, for Blacks, the typical residential setting was southern and rural; for Whites it was northern and urban. Under conditions of high state- and county-level segregation, race relations remained largely a regional problem centered in the South. Successive waves of Black migration out of the rural South into the urban North transformed the geographic structure of Black segregation during the twentieth century, however, ending the regional isolation and rural confinement of Blacks. From 1900 to 1940, the index of Black-White dissimilarity fell from 64 to 52 at the state level and from 69 to 59 at the county level. Black isolation likewise dropped from 36 to 24 within states, and from 45 to 32 within counties.

The movement of Blacks out of rural areas, however, was accompanied by their progressive segregation within cities. Although we lack indices of Black-White dissimilarity for 1900, research has demonstrated that blacks were not particularly segregated in northern cities during the nineteenth century. Ward-level dissimilarity for Blacks in 11 northern cities circa 1860 had average indices of approximately 46 (Massey and Denton, 1993).

By 1910, however, the eight cities listed in Table 1 had an average index of 56, and the level of Black-White

TABLE 1   Indices of Black-White Segregation Computed at Three Geographic Levels, 1900 to 1940

	Years				
	1900	*1910*	*1920*	*1930*	*1940*
Between states					
Dissimilarity	64	65	61	54	52
Isolation	36	34	30	25	24
Between counties					
Dissimilarity	69	70	66	60	59
Isolation	45	43	38	33	32
Between wards					
Dissimilarity					
Boston	—	64	65	78	79
Buffalo	—	63	72	81	82
Chicago	—	67	76	85	83
Cincinnati	—	47	57	73	77
Cleveland	—	61	70	85	86
Philadelphia	—	46	48	63	68
Pittsburgh	—	44	43	61	65
St. Louis	—	54	62	82	84
Average	—	56	62	76	78
Isolation					
Boston	06	11	15	19	—
Buffalo	04	06	10	24	—
Chicago	10	15	38	70	—
Cincinnati	10	13	27	45	—
Cleveland	08	08	24	51	—
Philadelphia	16	16	21	27	—
Pittsburgh	12	12	17	27	—
St. Louis	13	17	30	47	—
Average	10	13	23	39	—

Source: Massey and Hajnal (1995).

dissimilarity increased sharply during each decade after 1910, suggesting the progressive formation of black ghettos in cities throughout the nation. As Lieberson (1980) has shown, the growth of Black populations in urban areas triggered the imposition of higher levels of racial segregation within cities. Before the U.S. Supreme Court declared them unconstitutional in 1916, many U.S. cities actually passed apartheid laws establishing separate Black and White districts. Thereafter, however, segregation was achieved by less formal means (see Massey and Denton, 1993:26–42). Whatever the mechanism, the end result was a rapid increase in Black residential segregation, with the neighborhood segregation index rising from 56 to 78 between 1910 and 1940, a remarkable increase of 39 percent in just three decades.

The combination of growing urban Black populations and higher levels of segregation could only produce one possible outcome—higher levels of Black isolation. In 1900, the relatively small number of urban Blacks and the rather low level of Black-White segregation resulted in a low degree of racial isolation within neighborhoods. Among the eight cities shown in Table 1, the average isolation index was just 10; the typical urban Black resident lived in a ward that was 90 percent non-Black. Moreover, the index of isolation did not vary substantially from city to city. Urban Blacks early in the century were quite likely to know and interact socially with Whites (Massey and Denton, 1993:19–26). Indeed, on average they were more likely to share a neighborhood with a White person than with a Black person.

By 1930, however, the geographic structure of segregation had changed dramatically, shifting from state and county levels to the neighborhood level. The average isolation index was now 39 in neighborhoods, indicating that most Black residents in the cities under study lived in a ward that was almost 40 percent Black. In some cities, the degree of racial isolation reached truly extreme levels. The transformation was most dramatic in Chicago, where the isolation index went from 10 in 1900 to 70 in 1930, by which time, moreover, the dissimilarity index had reached 85. Similar conditions of intense Black segregation occurred in Cleveland, which by 1930 displayed a dissimilarity index of 85 and an isolation index of 51.

• • •

Despite the relative stability of segregation achieved by 1970 at the state, county, and neighborhood levels, a remarkable change was occurring at the city level. From 1950 onward, Blacks and Whites were becoming more and more segregated across *municipal* boundaries. After 1950, Blacks and Whites not only tended to live in different neighborhoods; increasingly they lived in different municipalities as well. After 1950, in other words, Blacks and Whites came to reside in wholly different towns and cities. From 1950 to 1980, the index of Black-White dissimilarity increased from 35 to 49 at the municipal level, a change of 40 percent in just 30 years, a shift that was remarkably similar to the rapid change observed in neighborhood-level segregation during the early period of ghetto formation. Black isolation went from an index of 19 to 35 at the municipal level, an increase of 84 percent. By the end of the 1970s, the average Black urban dweller lived in a municipality that was 35 percent Black; and one-half of all urban Blacks would have had to exchange places with Whites to achieve an even municipal distribution.

The emergence of significant municipal-level segregation in the United States reflects demographic trends that occurred in all parts of the urban hierarchy—in nonmetropolitan areas as well as central cities and suburbs. In 1950, there were no predominantly Black central cities in the United States. Among cities with more than 100,000 inhabitants, none had a Black percentage in excess of 50 percent. By 1990, however, 14 cities were at least 50 percent Black, including Atlanta, Baltimore, Detroit, Gary, Newark, New Orleans, and Washington; together they were home to 11 percent of all Blacks in the United States. In addition, another 11 cities were approaching Black majorities

by 1990, with percentages ranging from 40 percent to 50 percent, including Cleveland, St. Louis, and Oakland. Among cities with populations of 25,000 or more, only two municipalities in the entire United States were more than 50 percent Black in 1950, both in the South; but by 1990 the number had increased to 40. Some of these cities—such as Prichard, Alabama; Kinston, North Carolina; and Vicksburg, Mississippi—were located in nonmetropolitan areas of the South. Others—such as Maywood, Illinois; Highland Park, Michigan; and Inglewood, California—were suburbs of large central cities in the North and West.

Recent Trends in Black Segregation

Table 2 shows indicators of Black residential segregation for the 30 U.S. metropolitan areas with the largest Black populations. As in Table 1, these data are used to evaluate racial segregation from two vantage points. The first three columns show trends in the indices of spatial separation between Blacks and Whites using the index of dissimilarity, and the next three columns show trends in indices of Black residential isolation. The indices for 1970 and 1980, from Massey and Denton (1987), are metropolitan areas based on 1970 boundaries. Indices for 1990, from Harrison and Weinberg (1992), are based on 1990 geographic definitions. White and Black Hispanics were excluded, by both sets of researchers, from their subject sets of Whites and Blacks, and both sets of researchers computed indices using tracts as units of analysis.

Among the northern metropolitan areas shown, there is little evidence of any trend toward Black residential integration. Black segregation indices averaged about 85 in 1970, 80 in 1980, and 78 in 1990, a decline of only 8 percent in 20 years. Dissimilarity indices more than 60 are generally considered high, whereas those between 30 and 60 are considered moderate (Kantrowitz, 1973). At the rate of change observed between 1970 and 1990, the average level of Black-White segregation in northern areas would not reach the lower limits of the high range until the year 2043. At the slower rate of change prevailing from 1970 to 1980, it would take until 2067. As of 1990, no large northern Black community approached even a moderate level of residential segregation.

Indeed, in most metropolitan areas, racial segregation remained very high throughout the 20-year period. Dissimilarity indices were essentially constant in seven

TABLE 2 Trends in Black Segregation and Isolation in the 30 Metropolitan Areas with the Largest Black Populations, 1970 to 1990

Metropolitan	Dissimilarity Indices			Isolation Indices		
	1970[a]	1980[a]	1990[b]	1970[a]	1980[a]	1990[b]
Northern						
Boston, MA	81.2	77.6	68.2	56.7	55.1	51.2
Buffalo, NY	87.0	79.4	81.8	71.2	63.5	68.1
Chicago, IL	91.9	87.8	85.8	85.8	82.8	83.9
Cincinnati, OH	76.8	72.3	75.8	59.1	54.3	61.0
Cleveland, OH	90.8	87.5	85.1	81.9	90.4	80.8
Columbus, OH	81.8	71.4	67.3	63.5	57.5	52.5
Detroit, MI	88.4	86.7	87.6	75.9	77.3	82.3
Gary-Hammond-E. Chicago, IL	91.4	90.6	89.9	80.4	77.3	84.2
Indianapolis, IN	81.7	76.2	74.3	64.5	62.3	61.0
Kansas City, MO	87.4	78.9	72.6	74.2	69.0	61.6
Los Angeles-Long Beach, CA	91.0	81.1	73.1	70.3	60.4	69.3
Milwaukee, WI	90.5	83.9	82.8	73.9	69.5	72.4
New York, NY	81.0	82.0	82.2	58.8	62.7	81.9
Newark, NJ	81.4	81.6	82.5	67.0	69.2	78.6
Philadelphia, PA	79.5	78.8	77.2	68.2	69.6	72.2
Pittsburgh, PA	75.0	72.7	71.0	53.5	54.1	53.1
St. Louis, MO	84.7	81.3	77.0	76.5	72.9	69.5
San Francisco-Oakland, CA	80.1	71.7	66.8	56.0	51.1	56.1
Average	84.5	80.1	77.8	68.7	66.1	68.9
Southern						
Atlanta, GA	82.1	78.5	67.8	78.0	74.8	66.5
Baltimore, MD	81.9	74.7	71.4	77.2	72.3	70.6
Birmingham, AL	37.8	40.8	71.7	45.1	50.2	69.6
Dallas-Ft. Worth, TX	86.9	77.1	63.1	76.0	64.0	58.0
Greensboro-Winston Salem, NC	65.4	56.0	60.9	56.1	50.1	55.5
Houston, TX	78.1	69.5	66.8	66.4	59.3	63.6
Memphis, TN	75.9	71.6	69.3	78.0	75.9	75.0
Miami, FL	85.1	77.8	71.8	75.2	64.2	47.1
New Orleans, LA	73.1	68.3	68.8	71.3	68.8	71.9
Norfolk-Virginia Beach, VA	75.7	63.1	50.3	73.5	62.8	55.9
Tampa-St. Petersburg, FL	79.9	72.6	69.7	58.0	51.5	51.0
Washington, DC	81.1	70.1	66.1	77.2	68.0	66.7
Average	75.3	68.3	66.5	69.3	63.5	64.9

[a]Indices are from Massey and Denton (1987).
[b]Indices are from Harrison and Weinberg (1992).

metropolitan areas—Cincinnati, Detroit, Gary, New York, Newark, and Philadelphia; in seven others—Buffalo, Chicago, Cleveland, Indianapolis, Milwaukee, Pittsburgh, and St. Louis—small declines still left Blacks extremely segregated. All the latter metropolitan areas had dissimilarity indices exceeding 70 in 1990, and in four cases, the index was more than 80. No other ethnic or racial group in the history of the United States has ever, even briefly, experienced such high levels of residential segregation (Massey and Denton, 1993).

A few metropolitan areas experienced significant declines in the level of Black-White segregation between 1970 and 1990, although the pace of change slowed considerably during the 1980s, compared with the 1970s. In Columbus, Ohio, for example, Black-White dissimilarity fell by more than 10 index points from 1970 to 1980 (from 82 to 71), but then dropped by only 4 points through 1990. Likewise, San Francisco dropped from 80 to 72 during the 1970s, but went to just 68 by 1990.

The only areas that experienced a sustained decline in Black-White segregation across both decades were Los Angeles and Boston; but in each case, the overall index of segregation remained well within the high range. The drop in Los Angeles probably reflects the displacement of Blacks by the arrival of large numbers of Asian and, particularly, Hispanic immigrants (Massey and Denton, 1987). By 1990, for example, Watts, the core of the 1960s Black ghetto, had become predominantly Hispanic (Turner and Allen, 1991). The arrival of more than a million new immigrants in Los Angeles County between 1970 and 1980 put substantial pressure on the housing stock, and increased intergroup competition for residential units, especially at the low end of the market, leading to considerable neighborhood flux and residential mixing (Frey and Farley, 1996).

When large Black communities are subject to high levels of segregation, intense racial isolation is inevitable. In 1990, six metropolitan areas—Chicago, Cleveland, Detroit, Gary, New York, and Newark—had isolation indices of 80 or more, meaning that most Black people lived in neighborhoods that were more than 80 percent Black. Detailed analyses of neighborhoods show, however, that this overall average is misleading, because it represents a balance between a small minority of Blacks who reside in highly integrated neighborhoods and a large majority of Blacks who live in all-Black neighborhoods

(Denton and Massey, 1991). Moreover, in four of the six metropolitan areas, the level of Black isolation actually increased between 1970 and 1990.

In other northern areas, the prevailing pattern of change in racial isolation was one of stability, with shifts of less than 5 percent from 1970 to 1990. The average isolation index of 68.9 in 1990 was virtually identical to the index of 68.7 observed two decades earlier; in other words, 20 years after the Fair Housing Act, Blacks were still unlikely to come into residential contact with members of other groups. The large ghettos of the North have remained substantially intact and were largely unaffected by civil rights legislation of the 1960s.

Trends in Black segregation and isolation are somewhat different in the South, where segregation levels traditionally have been lower because of the distinctive history and character of southern cities. With social segregation enforced by Jim Crow legislation, Blacks and Whites before 1960 often lived in close physical proximity, with Black-inhabited alleys being interspersed between larger, White-occupied avenues (Demerath and Gilmore, 1954). During the postwar housing boom, moreover, rural Black settlements were often overtaken by expanding White suburbs, thereby creating the appearance of racial integration. For these and other reasons, Black-White segregation scores in the South traditionally have averaged about 10 points lower than in the North (Massey and Denton, 1993).

This regional differential is roughly maintained, as shown in Table 1, but southern areas display considerably greater diversity, despite the regional averages, than in the North. In some metropolitan areas, such as Baltimore, Houston, and Tampa, significant declines in segregation occurred during the 1970s, but declines slowed during the 1980s. In others, such as Dallas, Miami, and Norfolk, steady declines occurred throughout both decades. In Memphis and New Orleans, relatively small changes occurred, no matter which decade one considers. Two southern areas displayed increasing levels of Black-White segregation—Birmingham, where the increase was very sharp after 1970, and Greensboro, where an initial decline during the 1970s was reversed during the 1980s.

In general, then, Black-White segregation scores in the South appear to be converging on indices from 60 to 70, yielding an average of 67 and maintaining the traditional differential compared with the North. Metropolitan areas with segregation indices higher than the 60 to

70 range in 1970 experienced decreasing segregation, whereas those with indices less than 60 to 70 displayed increasing segregation; and those with indices within that range did not change much.

Only Norfolk differed from this pattern, with a significant and sustained decline in segregation during both decades, producing by 1990 a level of Black-White dissimilarity well within the moderate range. Many Norfolk residents are in the military, which has been more successfully integrated than other institutions in American life (Moskos and Butler, 1996). Frey and Farley (1994) demonstrated that areas dominated, economically, by military bases have significantly lower levels of Black-White segregation than others, controlling for a variety of other factors.

Although indices of Black-White dissimilarity may be lower in the South, the relative number of Blacks in urban areas is greater; so the average level of racial isolation within neighborhoods is not much different than in the North. From 1970 to 1990, there was relatively little change in the overall degree of Black isolation, with the average index decreasing from 69 in 1970 to 65 in 1990. In four southern areas—Baltimore, Memphis, Miami, and New Orleans—the Black isolation index was more than 70 in both decades; and in Birmingham, the index of Black isolation rose from 45 to 70 between 1970 and 1990. Only in Norfolk, which was rapidly desegregating, and in Tampa, which had relatively few Blacks, did isolation scores fall below 60. In most cities in the South, as in the North, Blacks were relatively unlikely to share neighborhoods with members of other racial or ethnic groups.

Thus, despite evidence of change in the South, Blacks living within the nation's largest urban Black communities are still highly segregated and spatially isolated from the rest of American society. Of the 30 northern and southern areas examined here, 19 still had Black-White dissimilarity indices in excess of 70 in 1990, and 12 had isolation indices in excess of 70. Either in absolute terms or in comparison to other groups, Blacks remain a very residentially segregated and spatially isolated people.

Recent Trends in Hispanic Segregation

Based on the historical experience of Blacks, recent demographic trends of Hispanics would be expected to have produced increasing levels of segregation during the 1970s and 1980s. In this period, there has been a remarkable resurgence of Hispanic immigration, yielding rapidly growing Hispanic populations in many metropolitan areas. In the Los Angeles metropolitan area, for example, the Hispanic population increased by 1.3 million between 1970 and 1990; Hispanics went from being 28 percent of the population to 38 percent. Because migrant networks channel new arrivals to neighborhoods where immigrants have already settled, such rapid in-migration could be expected to increase the concentration of Hispanics within enclaves and raise overall levels of isolation and segregation (Massey, 1985).

Although spatial assimilation may occur as income rises and the generations succeed one another, these socioeconomic mechanisms occur at a much slower pace than immigration and settlement. During periods of rapid immigration, therefore, segregation levels tend to rise; and the greater and more rapid the immigration, the more pronounced the increase in segregation.

Table 3 presents indicators of Hispanic-White dissimilarity and Hispanic residential isolation for the 30 metropolitan areas containing the largest Hispanic communities in the United States. In a significant subset of these metropolitan areas, Hispanics constitute an absolute majority of the total population, a condition that does not hold for any of the Black communities listed in Table 2. Because large minority populations increase the demographic potential for isolation, and because theorists hypothesize that high minority percentages foment greater discrimination on the part of majority members (Allport, 1958; Blalock, 1967), indices are tabulated separately for areas where Hispanics comprise a majority or near-majority (48 to 49 percent) of the population.

Despite the fact that demographic conditions in these metropolitan areas operate to maximize the potential for segregation, the degree of Hispanic-White residential dissimilarity proved to be quite moderate, and actually decreases over the two decades, going from an average of 55 in 1970 to 47 in 1990. Indices of Hispanic-White segregation were essentially constant in El Paso and Miami, and changed little in San Antonio and Corpus Christi. In Brownsville and McAllen, there were pronounced declines in segregation; but in no case was there an increase in Hispanic segregation from Whites within Hispanic-majority areas.

Indices of isolation, in contrast, were high and rose somewhat from 1970 to 1990. The increases did not stem from an increasing tendency for Whites and Hispanics to live apart, however, but from the large size and rapid growth of the Hispanic population. Isolation indices of 85 and 87 in Brownsville and McAllen mainly reflect the fact that Hispanics represent 82 and 85 percent of the metropolitan populations, respectively. Even if Hispanics were evenly distributed, high levels of Hispanic-White contact are impossible to achieve in areas that are so predominantly Hispanic.

Among Blacks, however, isolation indices in the 80s, as in Chicago and Detroit, generally reflect the intense segregation of Blacks, rather than high Black population percentages; in both these metropolitan areas, Blacks constitute about 22 percent of the population. The contrast in the indices between Hispanics and Blacks is put into perspective by comparing indices for Hispanics in San Antonio with indices for Blacks in northern areas (see Table 1). Although

TABLE 3   Trends in Hispanic Segregation and Isolation in the 30 Metropolitan Areas with the Largest Hispanic Populations, 1970 to 1990

Metropolitan Area	Dissimilarity Indices			Isolation Indices		
	1970[a]	1980[a]	1990[b]	1970[a]	1980[b]	1990[b]
Hispanic majority						
Brownsville-Harlingen, TX	54.0[c]	42.0[d]	39.8	NA	NA	85.2
Corpus Christi, TX	55.9	51.6	47.5	63.5	63.6	67.8
El Paso, TX	49.6	51.2	49.7	71.5	74.1	80.0
McAllen-Pharr, TX	62.0[c]	48.0[d]	37.9	NA	NA	87.4
Miami, FL	50.4	51.9	50.3	46.5	58.3	73.4
San Antonio, TX	59.1	57.2	53.7	67.5	67.5	69.1
Other metropolitan						
Albuquerque, NM	45.7	42.5	41.9	54.4	50.6	53.4
Anaheim-Santa Ana, CA	32.0	41.6	49.9	19.4	31.0	50.1
Bakersfield, CA	5.8	54.5	55.4	34.9	42.1	55.7
Chicago, IL	58.4	63.5	63.2	25.1	38.0	51.3
Dallas-Ft. Worth, TX	42.5	47.8	49.5	18.6	24.0	41.1
Denver-Boulder, CO	47.4	47.4	46.5	27.4	27.5	33.8
Fresno, CA	40.8	45.4	47.8	37.6	44.6	58.7
Houston, TX	45.3	46.4	49.3	26.9	32.8	49.3
Jersey City, NJ	54.8	48.8	42.9	34.5	46.5	56.0
Los Angeles, CA	46.8	57.0	61.0	37.8	50.1	71.5
Nassau-Suffolk, NY	29.1	36.2	42.3	6.0	9.6	22.1
New York, NY	64.9	65.6	65.8	36.1	40.0	66.6
Newark, NJ	60.4	65.6	66.7	16.7	26.3	48.5
Oxnard-Simi Valley, CA	NA	NA	52.3	NA	NA	51.2
Philadelphia, PA	54.0	62.9	62.6	10.6	21.6	42.9
Phoenix, AZ	48.4	49.4	48.1	32.1	32.1	39.8
Riverside- San Bernardino, CA	37.3	36.4	35.8	30.2	31.6	42.7
Sacramento, CA	34.7	36.4	37.0	16.3	16.5	23.9

TABLE 3   (Continued)

Metropolitan Area	Dissimilarity Indices			Isolation Indices		
	1970[a]	*1980*[a]	*1990*[b]	*1970*[a]	*1980*[b]	*1990*[b]
San Diego, CA	33.1	42.1	45.3	19.8	26.9	43.6
San Francisco-Oakland, CA	34.7	40.2	43.9	19.2	19.3	41.1
San Jose, CA	40.2	44.5	47.8	29.6	31.7	47.1
Tampa, FL	56.0	48.4	45.3	25.0	18.2	21.5
Tucson, AZ	52.6	51.9	49.7	46.7	43.1	48.8
Washington, DC	31.8	30.5	40.9	4.3	5.4	22.5
Average	45.3	48.0	49.6	26.5	30.8	45.1

Note: The Massey-Denton computations did not include several metropolitan areas that housed large Hispanic populations in 1990; therefore, additional indices have been taken from Lopez (1981) and Hwand and Murdock (1982). These figures, however, were computed for central cities rather than metropolitan areas and are therefore somewhat higher, thus underestimating increases and overestimating declines in the level of Hispanic-White segregation.

[a] Indices are from Massey and Denton (1987).

[b] Indices from Harrison and Weinberg (1992).

[c] Indices are from Lopez (1981).

[d] Indices are from Hwand and Murdock (1982).

Hispanics constitute 48 percent of San Antonio's population, its Hispanic-White dissimilarity index of 54 is less than that for Black-White indices in any northern area; and San Antonio's Hispanic isolation index of 69 is less than it is for 7 of the 18 black isolation indices.

A better indication of what happens to Hispanics in U.S. cities can be seen by examining segregation measures computed for metropolitan areas where Hispanics do not constitute such a large percentage of the population. On average, indices of Hispanic-White dissimilarity changed little in these areas, moving upward slightly from 45 in 1970 to 50 in 1990. In about one-third of these metropolitan areas—Chicago, Denver, Houston, New York, Phoenix, Riverside, Sacramento, and Tucson—Hispanic segregation remained nearly constant from 1970 to 1990; and in three cases—Albuquerque, Jersey City, and Tampa—indices of Hispanic-White dissimilarity decreased somewhat over the decades. In the remainder of the areas, indices of Hispanic segregation increased. In most cases, the increases were modest; but in several instances, segregation increased substantially over the two decades. In Los Angeles, for example, indices of Hispanic-White segregation increased from 47 to 61; in Anaheim the increase was from 32 to 50. Large increases were also recorded in Nassau-Suffolk,

San Diego, San Francisco, and Washington, D.C. In all these metropolitan areas there were rapid rates of Hispanic population growth and immigration from 1970 to 1990.

Despite these increases, indices of Hispanic-White segregation still remained moderate in 1990. Only 5 of the 24 metropolitan areas displayed indices in excess of 60. In 3 of these—New York, Newark, and Philadelphia—Puerto Ricans predominated; and since 1970, this group has stood apart from other Hispanic populations in displaying uniquely high levels of segregation (Jackson, 1981; Massey, 1981), a pattern largely attributable to the fact that many Puerto Ricans are of African ancestry (Massey and Bitterman, 1985; Massey and Denton, 1989a). The two remaining areas are Los Angeles, which experienced more Hispanic immigration than any other metropolitan area in the country, and Chicago, which contained a large population of Puerto Ricans in addition to a rapidly growing Mexican immigrant community.

Reflecting the increase in the proportion of Hispanics in most metropolitan areas, Hispanic isolation indices rose markedly throughout the nation. In those few areas where rates of Hispanic population increase were relatively slow—Albuquerque, Denver, Phoenix, and Tucson—the level of Hispanic isolation hardly changed;

but as the rate of Hispanic immigration increased, so did the extent of spatial isolation. Given the area's popularity as a destination for Hispanic immigration, Hispanic isolation rose most strongly in Southern California cities, going from 19 to 50 in Anaheim, 38 to 72 in Los Angeles, and 20 to 40 in San Diego.

By the 1990s, isolation indices equaled or exceeded 50 in about half of the metropolitan areas under consideration, but in only two cases—New York and Los Angeles, the two metropolitan areas with the largest Hispanic communities—did the index exceed 60. By way of contrast, only 8 of the 30 Black communities examined earlier had Black isolation indices less than 60. Although contemporary demographic conditions suggest trends toward high segregation and rising isolation among Hispanics, they still do not display the high index ratings characteristic for Blacks in large urban areas.

Recent Trends in Asian Segregation

Although Asian immigration into U.S. urban areas accelerated rapidly after 1970, Asian populations are still quite small compared with either Black or Hispanic populations. Moreover, Asians are more highly concentrated regionally and found in a relatively small number of metropolitan areas. Table 4, therefore, presents indices of Asian segregation and isolation only for the 20 largest Asian communities, rather than the 30 largest.

Again demographic conditions for Asians favor substantial increases in segregation and isolation. In most metropolitan areas, immigration led to the rapid expansion of a rather small 1970 population base. In some areas, the number of post-1970 migrants actually exceeds the size of the original Asian community severalfold. Only 25,000 Asians lived in the Anaheim-Santa Ana metropolitan area in 1970, for example, but by 1990, their number had multiplied ten times, to 249,000. Over the same period, the Asian community of Los Angeles quadrupled, going from 243,000 to 943,000; and Chicago's Asian population grew from 62,000 to 230,000. In such cases where a sudden massive in-migration overwhelms a small, established community, indices of segregation often decrease initially as new arrivals distribute themselves widely, and then increase as these pioneers attract subsequent settlers to the same residential areas.

Such a patter of decreasing and then increasing Asian segregation is the most common pattern of change among the metropolitan areas shown in Table 4. The Asian-White dissimilarity index averaged 44 in 1970, decreased to 36 in 1980, and then increased to 41 in 1990. This basic trend occurred in 12 of the 20 metropolitan areas. In three more areas, an initial decline was followed by no change from 1980 to 1990. Only one area—San Jose—experienced a sustained increase in Asian segregation; but it began from a very low level of segregation in 1970. Four areas displayed uninterrupted declines in segregation across both decades—Boston, Nassau-Suffolk, Newark, and Paterson.

Despite rapid immigration and population growth, Asian segregation indices remained quite moderate in 1990. Increases observed between 1980 and 1990 simply restored the indices to their 1970 levels, yielding little net change over the two decades. Thus, Asian-White dissimilarity indices ranged from the low 30s in Anaheim, Nassau-Suffolk, Newark, Riverside, and Washington to 50 in San Francisco-Oakland. In no metropolitan area did the index of Asian segregation approach the high levels characteristic of Blacks in the nation's largest metropolitan areas.

Rapid Asian immigration into moderately segregated communities did produce rather sharp increases in the extent of Asian isolation, however, consistent with a process of enclave consolidation. The most pronounced increases occurred in areas where Southeast Asian refugees settled in large numbers—Anaheim, where the isolation index rose from 3 in 1970 to 22 in 1990; Fresno, where the increase was from 6 to 33; and San Diego, where the increase was from 6 to 29. Despite these increases, however, Asians still are not very isolated anywhere, including San Francisco-Oakland, where they constitute a higher percentage of the population (21 percent) than in any other metropolitan area. The isolation index of 46 means that Asians in the Bay Area are more likely to share a neighborhood with non-Asians than with each other; and in Los Angeles, which received the highest number of Asian immigrants between 1970 and 1990, the isolation index rose to just under 41. Thus, the largest and most segregated Asian communities in the United States are much less isolated than the most integrated Black communities.

Black Hypersegregation

Despite their apparent clarity, the above data actually understate the extent of Black isolation in U.S. society, because the data only incorporate two dimensions of segregation: evenness, as measured by the dissimilarity

TABLE 4 Trends in Asian Segregation and Isolation in the 20 Metropolitan Areas with the Largest Asian Populations, 1970 to 1990

Metropolitan Area	Dissimilarity Indices			Isolation Indices		
	1970[a]	1980[a]	1990[b]	1970[a]	1980[a]	1990[b]
Anaheim, CA	27.4	24.9	33.3	2.6	7.7	22.4
Boston, MA	49.9	47.4	44.8	8.0	10.5	12.9
Chicago, IL	55.8	43.9	43.2	7.6	8.7	15.9
Dallas, TX	43.9	29.1	40.5	1.7	2.6	9.6
Fresno, CA	35.1	22.9	43.4	5.7	5.3	33.1
Houston, TX	42.7	34.6	45.7	1.5	4.5	15.7
Los Angeles, CA	53.1	43.1	46.3	12.3	15.2	40.5
Minneapolis, MN	45.2	36.9	41.2	3.0	6.2	15.1
Nassau-Suffolk, NY	42.2	34.5	32.4	1.0	2.2	5.9
New York, NY	56.1	48.1	48.4	11.6	14.3	32.8
Newark, NJ	50.2	34.4	29.6	1.5	2.9	7.5
Paterson-Clifton-Passaic, NJ	46.6	40.4	34.4	1.3	3.1	12.1
Philadelphia, PA	49.1	43.7	43.2	2.4	4.0	11.0
Riverside-San Bernardino, CA	31.9	21.5	32.8	2.5	4.1	10.2
Sacramento, CA	47.6	35.5	47.7	11.8	11.6	23.6
San Diego, CA	41.3	40.5	48.1	5.9	11.1	29.1
San Francisco-Oakland, CA	48.6	44.4	50.1	21.0	23.2	46.0
San Jose, CA	25.4	29.5	38.5	5.3	11.6	36.6
Seattle, WA	46.6	33.3	36.5	11.7	12.4	20.0
Washington, DC	36.5	26.8	32.3	2.2	5.7	12.6
Average	43.8	35.8	40.6	6.0	8.3	20.6

[a] Indices are from Massey and Denton (1987).
[b] Indices are from Harrison and Weinberg (1992).

index, and isolation, as measured by the P* index. Massey and Denton (1988, 1989b), however, conceptualize segregation as a multidimensional construct. They contend there are five dimensions of spatial variation; in addition to evenness and isolation, residential segregation should be conceptualized in terms of clustering, concentration, and centralization. This five-dimensional conceptualization of segregation recently has been updated and revalidated with 1990 data (Massey et al., 1996).

Clustering is the extent to which minority areas adjoin one another spatially. It is maximized when Black neighborhoods form one large, contiguous ghetto; and it is minimized when they are scattered, as in a checkerboard pattern. *Centralization* is the degree to which Blacks are distributed in and around the center of an urban area, usually defined as the central-business district. *Concentration* is the relative amount of physical space occupied by Blacks; as segregation increases, Blacks are increasingly confined to smaller, geographically compacted areas.

A high level of segregation on any single dimension is problematic because it isolates a minority group from amenities, opportunities, and resources that affect socioeconomic well-being. As high levels of segregation accumulate across dimensions, however, the deleterious effects of segregation multiply. Indices of evenness and isolation (i.e., dissimilarity and P*), by themselves, cannot capture this multidimensional layering of segregation; therefore, there is a misrepresentation of the nature of Black segregation and an understatement of its severity. Blacks are not only more segregated than other groups on any single dimension of segregation; they are more segregated across all dimensions simultaneously.

Massey and Denton (1993) identified a set of 16 metropolitan areas that were highly segregated—i.e., had an index higher than 60—on at least four of the five dimensions of segregation, a pattern they called "hypersegregation." These metropolitan areas included Atlanta, Baltimore, Buffalo, Chicago, Cleveland, Dallas, Detroit, Gary, Indianapolis, Kansas City, Los Angeles, Milwaukee, New York, Newark, and St. Louis. Within this set of areas, the Black-White dissimilarity index averaged 82, the average isolation index was 71, the mean clustering index was 58, the mean centralization index was 88, and the average concentration index was 83. By way of contrast, neither Hispanics nor Asians were hypersegregated within *any* metropolitan area.

These 16 metropolitan areas are among the most important in the country, incorporating 6 of the 10 largest urban areas in the United States. Blacks in these areas live within large, contiguous settlements of densely inhabited neighborhoods packed tightly around the urban core. Inhabitants typically would be unlikely to come into contact with non-Blacks in the neighborhood where they live. If they were to travel to an adjacent neighborhood, they would still be unlikely to see a White face. If they went to the next neighborhood beyond that, no Whites would be there either. People growing up in such an environment would have little direct experience with the culture, norms, and behaviors of the rest of American society, and have few social contacts with members of other racial groups.

Denton (1994) reexamined the issue of hypersegregation using data from the 1990 Census. According to her analysis, not only has Black hypersegregation continued, in many ways it has grown worse. Of the 16 metropolitan areas defined as hypersegregated in 1980, 14 remained so in 1990. In Atlanta the index of spatial concentration decreased to 59, just missing the criteria for hypersegregation, and in Dallas the isolation index decreased to 58. But both these figures are *just* below the threshold index of 60. All other metropolitan areas that were hypersegregated in 1980 showed an increase on at least one dimension by 1990. In 10 areas, isolation increased; concentration grew more acute in 9 areas; and clustering increased in 8. In Newark and Buffalo, segregation increased in all five dimensions simultaneously; and in Detroit, segregation increased on all dimensions but one.

In short, areas that were hypersegregated in 1980 generally remained so in 1990, and there was little evidence of movement away from this extreme pattern. On the contrary, hypersegregation appears to have spread to several new urban areas during the 1980s. Of the 44 nonhypersegregated metropolitan areas studied by Massey and Denton in 1980, Denton (1994) found that 6 had come to satisfy the criteria by 1990—Birmingham, Cincinnati, Miami, New Orleans, Oakland, and Washington, D.C.—bringing the total number of hypersegregated metropolitan areas to 20. Taken together, these 20 contain roughly 11 million Blacks and constitute 36 percent of the entire U.S. Black population. As already pointed out, the percentage of Hispanics and Asians who are hypersegregated is zero.

Explaining the Persistence of Racial Segregation

A variety of explanations have been posited to account for the unusual depth and persistence of Black segregation in American cities. One hypothesis is that racial segregation reflects class differences between Blacks and Whites—i.e., because Blacks, on average, have lower incomes and fewer socioeconomic resources than Whites, they cannot afford to move into White neighborhoods in significant numbers. According to this hypothesis, Back-White segregation, to some extent, reflects segregation on the basis of income, with poor households, which happen to be predominantly Black, living in different neighborhoods than affluent households, which happen to be disproportionately White.

This explanation has not been sustained empirically, however. When indices of racial segregation are computed within categories of income, occupation, or education, researchers have found that levels of Black-White segregation do not vary by social class (Farley, 1977; Simkus, 1978; Massey, 1979, 1981; Massey and Fischer, 1999). According to Denton and Massey (1988), Black families annually earning at least $50,000 were just as segregated as those earning less than $2,500. Indeed, Black families annually earning more than $50,000 were more segregated than Hispanic or Asian families earning less than $2,500. In other words, the most affluent Blacks appear to be more segregated than the poorest Hispanics or Asians; and in contrast to the case of Blacks, Hispanic and Asian segregation levels fall steadily as income rises, reaching low or moderate levels at incomes of $50,000 or more (Denton and Massey, 1988).

Another explanation for racial segregation is that Blacks prefer to live in predominantly Black neighborhoods, and that segregated housing simply reflects these preferences. This line of reasoning does not square well with survey evidence on Black attitudes, however. Most Blacks continue to express strong support for the ideal of integration. When asked on opinion polls whether they favor "desegregation, strict segregation, or something in-between," Blacks answer "desegregation" in large numbers (Schuman et al., 1985). Blacks are virtually unanimous in agreeing that "Black people have a right to live wherever they can afford to," and 71 percent would vote for a community-wide law to enforce this right (Bobo et al., 1986).

Black respondents are not only committed to integration as an ideal; survey results suggest they also strongly prefer it in practice. When asked about specific neighborhood racial compositions, Blacks consistently select racially mixed areas as most desirable (Farley et al., 1978, 1979, 1994; Clark, 1991). Although the most popular choice is a neighborhood that is half-Black and half-White, as late as 1992, nearly 90 percent of Blacks in Detroit would be willing to live in virtually any racially mixed area (Farley et al., 1994).

Although Blacks express a reluctance about moving into all-White neighborhoods, this apprehension does not indicate a rejection of White neighbors per se, but stems from well-founded fears of hostility and rejection. Among Black respondents to a 1976 Detroit survey who expressed a reluctance to moving into all-White areas, 34 percent thought that White neighbors would be unfriendly and make them feel unwelcome, 37 percent felt they could be made to feel uncomfortable, and 17 percent expressed a fear of outright violence (Farley et al., 1979). Moreover, 80 percent of all Black respondents rejected the view that moving into a White neighborhood constituted a desertion of the Black community. More recently, Jackson (1994) linked the reluctance of Blacks to "pioneer" White areas not only to fears of rejection by White neighbors, but also to an *expectation* of discrimination by real estate agents and lenders.

Thus evidence suggests that racial segregation in urban America is not a voluntary reflection of Black preferences. If it were up to them, Blacks would live in racially mixed neighborhoods. But it is not up to them only, of course; their preferences interact with those of Whites and, thus,

produce the residential configurations actually observed. Even though Blacks may prefer neighborhoods with an even racial balance, integration will not occur if most Whites find this level of racial mixing unacceptable.

On the surface, Whites seem to share Blacks' ideological commitment to open housing. The percentage of Whites on national surveys who agree that "Black people have a right to live wherever they can afford to" approached 90 percent in the late 1970s; and the percentage who disagreed with the view that "White people have a right to keep Blacks out of their [Whites'] neighborhoods," reached 67 percent in 1980. At present, few Whites openly call for the strict segregation of American society (Schuman et al., 1985, 1998; Sniderman and Piazza, 1993; Hochschild, 1995).

However, Whites remain quite uncomfortable with the implications of open housing in practice; only 40 percent, in 1980, said they would be willing to vote for a community-wide law stating that "a homeowner cannot refuse to sell to someone because of their race or skin color" (Schuman and Bobo, 1988). In other words, 60 percent of Whites would vote *against* an open housing law, which, in fact, has been federal law for 25 years.

White support for open housing generally declines as the hypothetical number of Blacks in their neighborhood increases. Whereas 86 percent of Whites in 1978 said they would not move if "a Black person came to live next door," only 46 percent stated they would not move if "Black people came to live in large numbers," and only 28 percent of Whites would be willing to live in a neighborhood that was half-Black and half-White (Schuman et al., 1985). Likewise, the severity of White prejudice toward Blacks increases as the percentage of Blacks in the area increases, a relationship that is *not* observed for Hispanics or Asians (Taylor, 1998).

When questions are posed about specific neighborhood compositions, moreover, it becomes clear that White tolerance for racial mixing is quite limited. According to Farley et al. (1994), 16 percent of Whites responding to a 1992 Detroit survey said they would feel uncomfortable in a neighborhood where only 7 percent of the residents were Black; 13 percent would be unwilling to enter such an area. When the Black percentage reaches 20 percent, one-third of all Whites say they would be unwilling to enter, 30 percent would feel uncomfortable, and 15 percent would seek to leave. A neighborhood about 30 percent Black exceeds the limits of racial tolerance for most Whites; 59 percent would be unwilling to move in, 44 percent would feel uncomfortable, and 29 percent would try to leave. Beyond a 50:50 balance, a neighborhood becomes unacceptable to all except a small minority of Whites; 73 percent said they would not wish to move into such a neighborhood, 53 percent would try to leave, and 65 percent would feel uncomfortable. As was stated, most Blacks feel a 50:50 racial mixture is desirable. This fundamental disparity between the two races has been confirmed by surveys conducted in Milwaukee, Omaha, Cincinnati, Kansas City, and Los Angeles (Clark, 1991).

The discrepancy between Whites' acceptance of open housing in principle and their reluctance to live among Blacks in practice yields a rather specific hypothesis about the nature of trends in Black-White segregation over the past 20 years. Hypothetically, declines in Black-White segregation should be confined primarily to metropolitan areas with relatively small Black populations, because in these places, desegregation can occur without Whites having to share their neighborhoods with too many Black people (Massey and Gross, 1991). If Black people make up 3 percent of the metropolitan population, for example, then complete desegregation yields an average of 3 percent Black within every neighborhood, which is well within most Whites' tolerance limits. If, however, Black people make up 20 percent of the metropolitan population, desegregation would produce neighborhoods that are 20 percent Black, on average, which exceeds the tolerance limits of many Whites, creates instability, and fuels a process of neighborhood turnover. In keeping with this hypothesis, Krivo and Kaufman (1999) show that desegregation between 1980 and 1990 was quite likely where the Black population was small but very unlikely where it was large. As a result, observed declines in segregation during the 1980s were confined largely to metropolitan areas that contained very few Blacks.

Over the last three decades, U.S. metropolitan areas have been transformed by immigration and many have moved well beyond the simple Black-White dichotomy of earlier years, necessitating new approaches to the measurement of racial attitudes. A recent survey in Los Angeles sought to replicate the Detroit survey within an ethnically diverse metropolis. Analysis of these data by Zubrinsky and Bobo (1996) showed that all non-Black groups—Whites, Asians, and Hispanics—attribute a variety of negative traits to Blacks and consider Blacks to be the least desirable neighbors (see, also, Bobo and Zubrinsky, 1996). Blacks experience by far the greatest likelihood of hostility from other groups, and are universally acknowledged to face the most severe housing discrimination. The end result is a clear hierarchy of neighborhood racial preferences in Los Angeles, with Whites at the top, followed by Asians and Hispanics, and Blacks at the bottom. Segregation does not result from Black ethnocentrism so much as from avoidance behavior by other groups, all of whom seek to circumvent potential coresidence with Blacks.

These contrasting racial attitudes create large intergroup disparities in the demand for housing in racially mixed neighborhoods. Given the violence, intimidation, and harrassment that historically have followed their entry into White areas, Blacks express reluctance at being first across the color line. After one or two Black families have moved into a neighborhood, however, Black demand grows rapidly, given the high value placed on integrated housing. This demand escalates as the Black percentage rises toward 50 percent, the most preferred neighborhood configuration; beyond this point, Black demand stabilizes and then falls off as the Black percentage rises toward 100 percent.

The pattern of White, Asian, and Hispanic demand for housing in racially mixed areas follows precisely the opposite trajectory. Demand is strong for homes in all-White areas, but once one or two Black families enter a neighborhood, demand begins to falter as some non-Black families leave and others refuse to move in. The acceleration in residential turnover coincides with the expansion of Black demand, making it likely that outgoing White, Hispanic, or Asian households are replaced by Black families. As the Black percentage rises, overall demand drops ever more steeply, and Black demand rises at an increasing rate. By the time Black demand peaks at the 50 percent mark, practically no other groups are willing to enter and most are trying to leave. Thus, racial segregation appears to be created by a process of racial turnover fueled by the persistence of significant anti-Black prejudice on the part of virtually every other group.

This model of racial change was proposed two decades ago by Schelling (1971), who argued that integration is an unstable outcome because Whites prefer lower minority proportions than Blacks—even though Whites might accept some Black neighbors. Yet by itself, Schelling's explanation is incomplete. Whites can only avoid coresidence with Blacks if mechanisms exist to keep Blacks out of neighborhoods to which they might otherwise be attracted. Whites can only flee a neighborhood where Blacks have entered if there are other all-White neighborhoods to go to, and this escape will only be successful if Blacks are unlikely or unable to follow.

Racial discrimination was institutionalized in the real estate industry during the 1920s and well established in private practice by the 1940s (Massey and Denton, 1993). Evidence shows that discriminatory behavior was widespread among realtors at least until 1968, when the Fair Housing Act was passed (Helper, 1969; Saltman, 1979). After that, outright refusals to rent or sell to Blacks became rare, given that overt discrimination could lead to prosecution under the law.

Black home seekers now face a more subtle process of exclusion. Rather than encountering "White only" signs, they encounter a covert series of barriers. Blacks who inquire about an advertised unit may be told that it has just been sold or rented; they may be shown only the advertised unit and told that no others are available; they may only be shown houses in Black or racially mixed areas and led away from White neighborhoods; they may be quoted a higher rent or selling price than Whites; they may be told that the selling agents are too busy and to come back later; their phone number may be taken but a return call never made; they may be shown units but offered no assistance in arranging financing; or they simply may be treated brusquely and discourteously in hopes that they will leave.

Although individual acts of discrimination are small and subtle, they have a powerful cumulative effect in lowering the probability of Black entry into White neighborhoods. Because the discrimination is latent, however, it is not easily observable, and the only way to confirm whether or not it has occurred is to compare the treatment of both Black and White clients that have similar social and economic characteristics. If White clients receive systematically more favorable treatment, then one can safely conclude that discrimination has taken place (Fix et al., 1993).

Differences in the treatment of White and Black home seekers are measured by means of a housing audit. Teams of White and Black auditors are paired and sent to randomly selected realtors to pose as clients seeking a home or apartment. The auditors are trained to present comparable housing needs and family characteristics,

and to express similar tastes; they are assigned equivalent social and economic traits by the investigator. After each encounter, the auditors fill out a detailed report of their experiences and the results are tabulated and compared to determine the nature and level of discrimination (Yinger, 1986, 1989).

Local fair-housing organizations began to conduct such studies at the end of the 1960s. These efforts revealed that discrimination was continuing despite the Fair Housing Act. A 1969 audit of realtors in St. Louis, for example, documented a pattern and practice of discrimination sufficient to force four realty firms to sign a consent decree with the U.S. Department of Justice wherein they agreed to desist from certain biased practices (Saltman, 1979). Likewise, a 1971 audit study carried out in Palo Alto, California, found that Blacks were treated in a discriminatory fashion by 50 percent of the area's apartment complexes; and a 1972 audit of apartments in suburban Baltimore uncovered discrimination in more than 45 percent of the cases (Saltman, 1979).

Racial discrimination clearly persisted through the 1980s. In one 1983 Chicago study, suburban realtors showed homes to 67 percent of White auditors but only 47 percent of Black auditors (Hintzen, 1983). Another Chicago study done in 1985 revealed that Whites were offered financial information at nearly twice the rate it was offered to Blacks (Schroeder, 1985). One developer working in Chicago's south suburbs refused to deal with Blacks at all; Blacks were always told that no properties were available, even though 80 percent of Whites were shown real estate (Bertram, 1988). In the same study, realtors told 92 percent of Whites that apartments were available but gave this information to only 46 percent of Blacks.

Audit studies of other metropolitan areas reveal similar levels of racial discrimination. According to Yinger's (1986) review of studies conducted in metropolitan Boston and Denver during the early 1980s, Black home seekers had between a 38 and a 59 percent chance of receiving unfavorable treatment, compared to Whites, on any given real estate transaction. Through various lies and deceptions, Blacks were informed of only 65 of every 100 units presented to Whites, and they inspected fewer than 54 of every 100 shown to Whites.

• • •

Realtors were approached by auditors who inquired about the availability of the advertised unit; they also asked about other units that might be on the market. Based on the results, HDS provided evidence that discrimination against Blacks had declined little since 1977. Indeed, it appears the 1977 HUD study may have understated both the incidence and severity of housing discrimination in American cities (Yinger, 1995). According to HDS data, housing was made more available to Whites in 45 percent of the transactions in the rental market and in 34 percent of those in the sales market. Whites received more favorable credit assistance in 46 percent of sales encounters, and were offered more favorable terms in 17 percent of rental transactions. When housing availability and financial assistance were considered together, the likelihood of experiencing racial discrimination was 53 percent in both the rental and sales markets.

• • •

Compared with Blacks, relatively few studies of prejudice and discrimination against Hispanics have been conducted, and there are no national studies that examine attitudes and behaviors concerning Asians. Hakken (1979) found that discrimination against Hispanics in the rental housing market of Dallas was as likely as that against Blacks, and similar results were reported by Feins and colleagues for Boston (Feins et al., 1981). James and Tynan (1986) replicated these results in a study of Denver's sales market, but they found a substantially lower probability of discrimination against Hispanics in the rental market; and despite the relatively high likelihood of discrimination in home sales, in reality, severity of discrimination against Hispanics was not great; the average number of housing units offered to Hispanics was not significantly different than the number offered to non-Hispanic Whites (James and Tynan, 1986).

As with Blacks, however, discrimination against Hispanics appears to have a racial basis. Hakken (1979) found that dark-skinned Chicanos were more likely to experience discriminatory treatment than Blacks, whereas light-skinned Hispanics were less likely to experience such treatment. Consistent with this finding, Massey and Denton (1992) found that Mexicans who identified themselves as mestizos (people of mixed European and Indian origin) were less likely to achieve suburban residence than those who identified themselves as White.

The extent of the racial effect is greater among Caribbean Hispanics, particularly Puerto Ricans, among whom the racial continuum runs from European to African.

Denton and Massey (1989) showed that for Puerto Ricans who identified themselves as Black, housing was as segregated as for U.S. Blacks, whereas those who identified themselves as White experienced low-to-moderate levels of separation. Discrimination was mixed for Caribbean Hispanics who said they were of mixed Black-White origins, but were much closer to the high level of Black segregation. The degree of segregation experienced by racially mixed Caribbean Hispanics was generally greater than that experienced by racially mixed Mexicans, suggesting greater White antipathy toward Africans than Amerindians.

The most complete and systematic data on the treatment of Hispanics in urban real estate markets comes from HUD's 1988 HDS (Yinger, 1995). Results from this study indicate that the overall incidence of housing discrimination was greater for Hispanics than Blacks in the sale market (42 versus 34 percent), but less for Hispanics than Blacks in the rental market (32 versus 45 percent), replicating the earlier results of James and Tynan (1986) in Denver. Also in keeping with the findings of James and Tynan was the fact that the severity of discrimination in the sales market was considerably lower for Hispanics than for Blacks; whereas the marginal probability that an additional housing unit was denied to Blacks was 88 percent, it was only 66 percent for Hispanics. As in earlier research, in the 1988 HDS, race figured prominently in the treatment of Hispanics—dark-skinned Hispanics were much more likely to experience discrimination in the sales market than light-skinned Hispanics (Yinger, 1995). Paradoxically, therefore, recent research on discrimination involving Hispanics reaffirms the conclusion that race remains the dominant organizing principle in U.S. urban housing markets.

Segregation and the Concentration of Poverty

The past two decades have been hard on the socioeconomic well-being of many Americans. The structural transformation of the U.S. economy from goods production to service provision generated a strong demand for workers with high and low levels of schooling, but offered few opportunities for those with modest education and training. In the postindustrial economy that emerged after 1973, labor unions withered, the middle class bifurcated, income inequality grew, and poverty spread; and this new stratification between people was accompanied by a growing spatial separation between them. The stagnation of income proved to be remarkably widespread, and inequality rose not only for minorities—Blacks, Hispanics, and Asians—but also for non-Hispanic Whites (Danziger and Gottschalk, 1995; Levy, 1995; Morris et al., 1994). As a result of their continued racial segregation, however, the spatial concentration of poverty was especially severe for Blacks (Massey and Eggers, 1990; Massey et al., 1991; Krivo et al., 1998). High levels of income inequality paired with high levels of racial or ethnic segregation result in geographically concentrated poverty, because the poverty is localized in a small number of densely settled, racially homogenous, tightly clustered areas, often in an older, urban core abandoned by industry. Had segregation not been in place, the heightened poverty would be distributed widely throughout the metropolitan area (Massey, 1990; Massey and Denton, 1993). By 1990, 83 percent of poor inner-city Blacks lived in neighborhoods that were at least 20 percent poor (Kasarda, 1993).

In a recent paper, Massey and Fischer (2000) broadened this theoretical perspective by arguing that racial segregation interacts with any structural shift that affects the distribution of income, or the spatial configuration of the classes, to concentrate poverty spatially. Specifically, they hypothesize that as racial segregation increases, decreasing incomes, increasing inequality, increasing class segregation, and increasing immigration are more strongly translated into geographic isolation of the poor. Thus, these structural trends produce high and increasing concentrations of poverty for highly segregated groups, but low and falling concentrations of poverty among nonsegregated groups.

Because more than 70 percent of urban Blacks are highly segregated, but 90 percent of all other groups are not, the population of poor experiencing high concentrations of poverty is overwhelmingly Black (Massey and Fischer, 2000). Given the interaction between racial segregation and the changing socioeconomic structure of American society, the issue of race cannot be set aside to focus on the politics of race versus class. Although the implementation of policies that raise average incomes, lower income inequality, and reduce class segregation would lower the spatial isolation of the urban poor, policies to promote the desegregation of urban society would probably have an even greater effect, given segregation's critical role in determining how these factors generate concentrated poverty.

The Consequences of Concentrated Poverty

The argument that the prevalence of concentrated poverty among Blacks decisively undermines the life chances of the Black poor was first made forcefully by Wilson (1987). He argued that class isolation, through a variety of mechanisms, reduced employment, lowered incomes, depressed marriage, and increased unwed childbearing *over and above any effects of individual or family deprivation.* At the time Wilson made this argument, relatively little evidence existed to support it (Jencks and Mayer, 1990), but over the past decade a growing number of studies have accumulated to sustain the basic thrust of Wilson's hypothesis.

In 1988, the Rockefeller and Russell Sage Foundations funded the Social Science Research Council (SSRC) to establish a program of research into the causes and consequences of persistent urban poverty. One SSRC subcommittee—the Working Group on Communities and Neighborhoods, Family Processes, and Individual Development—met regularly over the next eight years to conceptualize and then implement a program of research to determine how concentrated poverty affected social and cognitive development. The ultimate product was a recently published series of studies (Brooks-Gunn et al., 1997) examining the effect of neighborhood conditions on cognitive and social development at three points in the life cycle—early childhood (ages 3–7), late childhood/early adolescence (ages 11–15), and late adolescence (ages 16–19).

The empirical analyses clearly show that socioeconomic inequality is perpetuated by mechanisms operating at the neighborhood level, although the specific pathways are perhaps more complex than Wilson or others imagined. Not only do neighborhood effects vary in their nature and intensity at different stages of the life cycle, they are often conditioned by gender, mediated by family processes, and possibly interactive in how they combine with individual factors to determine social outcomes. Despite these complexities, however, research permits three broad generalizations.

- First, neighborhoods seem to influence individual development most powerfully in early childhood and late adolescence.
- Second, the spatial concentration of affluence appears to be more important in determining cognitive development and academic achievement than the concentration of poverty.
- Third, the concentration of male joblessness affects social behavior more than cognitive development, particularly among Blacks.

These effects persist even after controlling for unobserved heterogeneity. Thus, Wilson's (1987) theory is basically correct—there is something to the hypothesis of neighborhood effects.

One of the most important disadvantages transmitted through prolonged exposure to the ghetto is educational failure. Datcher (1982) estimates that moving a poor Black male from his typical neighborhood (66 percent Black with an average annual income of $8,500) to a typical White neighborhood (86 percent White with a mean income of $11,500) would raise his educational attainment by nearly a year. Corcoran and colleagues (1989) found similar results. Crane (1991) likewise shows that the dropout probability for Black teenage males increases dramatically as the percentage of low-status workers in the neighborhood increases. Residence in a poor neighborhood also decreases the odds of success in the labor market. Datcher (1982) found that growing up in a poor Black area lowered male earnings by at least 27 percent, although Corcoran and colleagues (1989) put the percentage at about 18 percent.

Exposure to conditions typical of the ghetto also dramatically increases the odds of pregnancy and childbirth among teenage girls. According to estimates by Crane (1991), the probability of a teenage birth increases dramatically as the percentage of low-status workers in the neighborhood increases. Similarly, Hogan and Kitagawa (1985) found that living in a very poor neighborhood raised the monthly pregnancy rate among Black adolescents by 20 percent and lowered the age at which they became sexually active. Furstenburg et al. (1987) have shown that attending school in integrated, rather than segregated, classrooms substantially lowers the odds that 15- to 16-year-old Black girls will experience sexual intercourse. Brooks-Gunn et al. (1993) found that the

probability of giving birth before age 29 rose markedly as the percentage of high-income families fell.

In a dynamic **longitudinal analysis** that followed young Black men and women from ages 15 to 30, Massey and Shibuya (1995) found that young men who live in neighborhoods of concentrated male joblessness are more likely to be jobless themselves, controlling for individual and family characteristics, and that Black women in such neighborhoods were significantly less likely to get married.

Massey and Shibuya (1995) also linked concentrated disadvantage to higher probabilities of criminality, a link well-documented by Krivo and Peterson (1996) using aggregate data. The concentration of criminal activity that accompanies the concentration of deprivation accelerates the process of neighborhood transition and, for Blacks, resegregation (Morenoff and Sampson, 1997); it also helps drive up rates of Black-on-Black mortality, which have reached heights unparalled for any other group (Almgren et al., 1998; Guest et al., 1998). The spatial concentration of crime presents special problems for the Black middle class, who must adopt extreme strategies to insulate their children from the temptations and risks of the street (Anderson, 1990; Patillo, 1998).

The quantitative evidence thus suggests that any process that concentrates poverty within racially isolated neighborhoods will simultaneously increase the odds of socioeconomic failure within the segregated group. People who grow up and live in environments of concentrated poverty and social isolation are more likely to become teenage parents, drop out of school, achieve low educations, earn lower adult incomes, and become involved with crime—either as perpetrator or victim.

One study has directly linked the socioeconomic disadvantages suffered by individual minority members to the degree of segregation they experience in society. Using individual, community, and metropolitan data from the 50 largest U.S. metropolitan areas in 1980, Massey et al. (1991) showed that group segregation and poverty rates interacted to concentrate poverty geographically within neighborhoods, and that exposure to neighborhood poverty subsequently increased the probability of male

longitudinal analysis Research conducted over many years so outcomes over time can be observed.

joblessness and single motherhood among group members. In this fashion, they linked the structural condition of segregation to individual behaviors widely associated with the underclass through the intervening factor of neighborhood poverty, holding individual and family characteristics constant. As the structural factor controlling poverty concentration, segregation is directly responsible for the perpetuation of socioeconomic disadvantage among Blacks.

The Road Ahead

This review yields several well-supported conclusions about residential segregation in the United States at the end of the twentieth century.

- First, the extreme segregation of Blacks continues unabated in the nation's largest metropolitan areas, and is far more severe than anything experienced by Hispanics or Asians.
- Second, this unique segregation can in no way be attributed to class.
- Third, although Whites now accept open housing in principle, they have yet to come to terms with its implications in practice. Whites still harbor strong anti-Black sentiments and are unwilling to live with more than a small percentage of Blacks in the neighborhood. As a result, declines in Black-White segregation have been confined almost entirely to metropolitan areas where few Blacks live.
- Fourth, color prejudice apparently extends to dark-skinned Hispanics, and discrimination against both Blacks and Afro-Hispanics is remarkably widespread in U.S. housing markets. Through a variety of deceptions and exclusionary actions, Black access to housing in White neighborhoods is systematically reduced.

- Fifth, White biases and discrimination apparently do not extend to Asians or light-skinned Hispanics, at least to the same degree. In no metropolitan area are Asians or Hispanics hypersegregated; and despite the recent arrival of large numbers of immigrants and rapid rates of population growth, they display levels of segregation and isolation that are far below those of Blacks.
- Sixth, as a result of segregation, poor Blacks are forced to live in conditions of intensely concentrated poverty. Recent shifts in U.S. socioeconomic structure and patterns of class segregation have interacted with Black segregation to produce unusual concentrations of poverty among Blacks. Poor Blacks are far more likely to grow up and live in neighborhoods surrounded by other poor people than poor Whites, Hispanics, or Asians.
- Finally, as a result of their prolonged exposure to high rates of neighborhood poverty, Blacks experience much higher risks of educational failure, joblessness, unwed childbearing, crime, and premature death compared with other groups.

Given the central role that residence plays in determining one's life chances, these results suggest the need to incorporate the effects of racial segregation more fully into theories about the perpetuation of poverty and the origins of the urban underclass. These results also suggest the need to incorporate desegregation efforts more directly into public policies developed to ameliorate urban poverty. All too often, U.S. policy debates have devolved into arguments about the relative importance of race versus class. The issue, however, is not whether race *or* class perpetuates the urban underclass, but how race *and* class *interact* to undermine the social and economic well-being of Black Americans.

Seeing the Big Picture   **How Integrated Is Your Neighborhood?**

The index of dissimilarity is a measure of how residentially segregated one population is from another. A score of 0 would mean groups are randomly distributed throughout a particular area while a score of 100 would mean groups share no social space with one another. What do the index of dissimilarity numbers in Section II of the Appendix tell us about residential segregation in the United States?

22   The Code of the Streets
Elijah Anderson

ELIJAH ANDERSON is William K. Lanman, Jr. Professor of Sociology at Yale University. He is author of *Streetwise: Race, Class and Change in an Urban Community* (1990) and *The Code of the Streets* (1999).

O F ALL THE PROBLEMS BESETTING THE POOR inner-city black community, none is more pressing than that of interpersonal violence and aggression. It wreaks havoc daily with the lives of community residents and increasingly spills over into downtown and residential middle-class areas. Muggings, burglaries, carjackings, and drug-related shootings, all of which may leave their victims or innocent bystanders dead, are now common enough to concern all urban and many suburban residents. The inclination to violence springs from the circumstances of life among the ghetto poor—the lack of jobs that pay a living wage, the stigma of race, the fallout from rampant drug use and drug trafficking, and the resulting alienation and lack of hope for the future.

Simply living in such an environment places young people at special risk of falling victim to aggressive behavior. Although there are often forces in the community which can counteract the negative influences, by far the most powerful being a strong, loving, "decent" (as inner-city residents put it) family committed to middle-class values, the despair is pervasive enough to have spawned an oppositional culture, that of "the streets," whose norms are often consciously opposed to those of mainstream society. These two orientations—decent and street—socially organize the community, and their coexistence has important consequences for residents, particularly children growing up in the inner city. Above all, this environment means that even youngsters whose home lives reflect mainstream values—and the majority of homes in the community do—must be able to handle themselves in a street-oriented environment.

This is because the street culture has evolved what may be called a code of the streets, which amounts to a set of informal rules governing interpersonal public behavior,

Questions to Consider   In "The Code of the Streets" Elijah Anderson chronicles how an individual's environment can create a set of expectations that are at odds with the "dominant" culture. How is "oppositional culture" often detrimental to children and young adults in these communities? How is oppositional culture linked to Anderson's discussion of "street" and "decent" families?

including violence. The rules prescribe both a proper comportment and a proper way to respond if challenged. They regulate the use of violence and so allow those who are inclined to aggression to precipitate violent encounters in an approved way. The rules have been established and are enforced mainly by the street-oriented, but on the streets the distinction between street and decent is often irrelevant; everybody knows that if the rules are violated, there are penalties. Knowledge of the code is thus largely defensive; it is literally necessary for operating in public. Therefore, even though families with a decency orientation are usually opposed to the values of the code, they often reluctantly encourage their children's familiarity with it to enable them to negotiate the inner-city environment.

At the heart of the code is the issue of respect—loosely defined as being treated "right," or granted the deference one deserves. However, in the troublesome public environment of the inner city, as people increasingly feel buffeted by forces beyond their control, what one deserves in the way of respect becomes more and more problematic and uncertain. This in turn further opens the issue of respect to sometimes intense interpersonal negotiation. In the street culture, especially among young people, respect is viewed as almost an external entity that is hard-won but easily lost, and so must constantly be guarded. The rules of the code in fact provide a framework for negotiating respect. The person whose very appearance—including his clothing, demeanor, and way of moving—deters transgressions feels that he possesses, and may be considered by others to possess, a measure of respect. With the right amount of respect, for instance, he can avoid "being bothered" in public. If he is bothered, not only may he be in physical danger but he has been disgraced or "dissed" (disrespected). Many of the forms that dissing can take might seem petty to middle-class people (maintaining eye contact for too long, for example), but to those invested in the street code, these actions become serious indications of the other person's intentions. Consequently, such people become very sensitive to advances and slights, which could well serve as warnings of imminent physical confrontation.

This hard reality can be traced to the profound sense of alienation from mainstream society and its institutions felt by many poor inner-city black people, particularly the young. The code of the streets is actually a cultural adaptation to a profound lack of faith in the police and the judicial system. The police are most often seen as representing the dominant white society and not caring to protect inner-city residents. When called, they may not respond, which is one reason many residents feel they must be prepared to take extraordinary measures to defend themselves and their loved ones against those who are inclined to aggression. Lack of police accountability has in fact been incorporated into the status system: the person who is believed capable of "taking care of himself" is accorded a certain deference, which translates into a sense of physical and psychological control. Thus the street code emerges where the influence of the police ends and personal responsibility for one's safety is felt to begin. Exacerbated by the proliferation of drugs and easy access to guns, this volatile situation results in the ability of the street-oriented minority (or those who effectively "go for bad") to dominate the public spaces.

Decent and Street Families

Although almost everyone in poor inner-city neighborhoods is struggling financially and therefore feels a certain distance from the rest of America, the decent and the street family in a real sense represent two poles of value orientation, two contrasting conceptual categories. The labels "decent" and "street," which the residents themselves use, amount to evaluative judgments that confer status on local residents. The labeling is often the result of a social contest among individuals and families of the neighborhood. Individuals of the two orientations often coexist in the same extended family. Decent residents judge themselves to be so while judging others to be of the street, and street individuals often present themselves as decent, drawing distinctions between themselves and other people. In addition, there is quite a bit of circumstantial behavior—that is, one person may at different times exhibit both decent and street orientations, depending on the circumstances. Although these designations result from so much social jockeying, there do exist concrete features that define each conceptual category.

Generally, so-called decent families tend to accept mainstream values more fully and attempt to instill them in their children. Whether married couples with children or single-parent (usually female) households, they are generally "working poor" and so tend to be better off financially than their street-oriented neighbors. They value hard work and self-reliance and are willing to sacrifice for their children. Because they have a certain amount of faith in mainstream society, they harbor hopes for a better future for their children, if not for themselves. Many of them go to church and take a strong interest in their children's schooling. Rather than dwelling on the real hardships and inequities facing them, many such decent people, particularly the increasing number of grandmothers raising grandchildren, see their difficult situation as a test from God and derive great support from their faith and from the church community.

Extremely aware of the problematic and often dangerous environment in which they reside, decent parents tend to be strict in their child-rearing practices, encouraging children to respect authority and walk a straight moral line. They have an almost obsessive concern about trouble of any kind and remind their children to be on the lookout for people and situations that might lead to it. At the same time, they are themselves polite and considerate of others, and teach their children to be the same way. At home, at work, and in church, they strive hard to maintain a positive mental attitude and a spirit of cooperation.

So-called street parents, in contrast, often show a lack of consideration for other people and have a rather superficial sense of family and community. Though they may love their children, many of them are unable to cope with the physical and emotional demands of parenthood, and find it difficult to reconcile their needs with those of their children. These families, who are more fully invested in the code of the streets than the decent people are, may aggressively socialize their children into it in a normative way. They believe in the code and judge themselves and others according to its values.

In fact the overwhelming majority of families in the inner-city community try to approximate the decent-family model, but there are many others who clearly represent the worst fears of the decent family. Not only are their financial resources extremely limited, but what little they have may easily be misused. The lives of the street-oriented are often marked by disorganization. In the most desperate circumstances people frequently have a limited understanding of priorities and consequences, and so frustrations mount over bills, food, and, at times, drink, cigarettes, and drugs. Some tend toward self-destructive behavior; many street-oriented women are crack-addicted ("on the pipe"), alcoholic, or involved in complicated relationships with men who abuse them. In addition, the seeming intractability of their situation, caused in large part by the lack of well-paying jobs and the persistence of racial discrimination, has engendered deep-seated bitterness and anger in many of the most desperate and poorest blacks, especially young people. The need both to exercise a measure of control and to lash out at somebody is often reflected in the adults' relations with their children. At the least, the frustrations of persistent poverty shorten the fuse in such people—contributing to a lack of patience with anyone, child or adult, who irritates them.

In these circumstances a woman—or a man, although men are less consistently present in children's lives—can be quite aggressive with children, yelling at and striking them for the least little infraction of the rules she has set down. Often little if any serious explanation follows the verbal and physical punishment. This response teaches children a particular lesson. They learn that to solve any kind of interpersonal problem one must quickly resort to hitting or other violent behavior. Actual peace and quiet, and also the appearance of calm, respectful children conveyed to her neighbors and friends, are often what the young mother most desires, but at times she will be very aggressive in trying to get them. Thus she may be quick to beat her children, especially if they defy her law,

not because she hates them but because this is the way she knows to control them. In fact, many street-oriented women love their children dearly. Many mothers in the community subscribe to the notion that there is a "devil in the boy" that must be beaten out of him or that socially "fast girls need to be whupped." Thus much of what borders on child abuse in the view of social authorities is acceptable parental punishment in the view of these mothers.

Many street-oriented women are sporadic mothers whose children learn to fend for themselves when necessary, foraging for food and money any way they can get it. The children are sometimes employed by drug dealers or become addicted themselves. These children of the street, growing up with little supervision, are said to "come up hard." They often learn to fight at an early age, sometimes using short-tempered adults around them as role models. The street-oriented home may be fraught with anger, verbal disputes, physical aggression, and even mayhem. The children observe these goings-on, learning the lesson that might makes right. They quickly learn to hit those who cross them, and the dog-eat-dog mentality prevails. In order to survive, to protect oneself, it is necessary to marshal inner resources and be ready to deal with adversity in a hands-on way. In these circumstances physical prowess takes on great significance.

In some of the most desperate cases, a street-oriented mother may simply leave her young children alone and unattended while she goes out. The most irresponsible women can be found at local bars and crack houses, getting high and socializing with other adults. Sometimes a troubled woman will leave very young children alone for days at a time. Reports of crack addicts abandoning their children have become common in drug-infested inner-city communities. Neighbors or relatives discover the abandoned children, often hungry and distraught over the absence of their mother. After repeated absences, a friend or relative, particularly a grandmother, will often step in to care for the young children, sometimes petitioning the authorities to send her, as guardian of the children, the mother's welfare check, if the mother gets one. By this time, however, the children may well have learned the first lesson of the streets: survival itself, let alone respect, cannot be taken for granted; you have to fight for your place in the world.

Campaigning for Respect

These realities of inner-city life are largely absorbed on the streets. At an early age, often even before they start school, children from street-oriented homes gravitate to the streets, where they "hang"—socialize with their peers. Children from these generally permissive homes have a great deal of latitude and are allowed to "rip and run" up and down the street. They often come home from school, put their books down, and go right back out the door. On school nights eight- and nine-year-olds remain out until nine or ten o'clock (and teenagers typically come in whenever they want to). On the streets they play in groups that often become the source of their primary social bonds. Children from decent homes tend to be more carefully supervised and are thus likely to have curfews and to be taught how to stay out of trouble.

When decent and street kids come together, a kind of social shuffle occurs in which children have a chance to go either way. Tension builds as a child comes to realize that he must choose an orientation. The kind of home he comes from influences but does not determine the way he will ultimately turn out—although it is unlikely that a child from a thoroughly street-oriented family will easily absorb decent values on the streets. Youths who emerge from street-oriented families but develop a decency orientation almost always learn those values in another setting—in school, in a youth group, in church. Often it is the result of their involvement with a caring "old head" (adult role model).

In the street, through their play, children pour their individual life experiences into a common knowledge pool, affirming, confirming, and elaborating on what they have observed in the home and matching their skills against those of others. And they learn to fight. Even small children test one another, pushing and shoving, and are ready to hit other children over circumstances not to their liking. In turn, they are readily hit by other children, and the child who is toughest prevails. Thus the violent resolution of disputes, the hitting and cursing, gains social reinforcement. The child in effect is initiated into a system that is really a way of campaigning for respect.

In addition, younger children witness the disputes of older children, which are often resolved through cursing and abusive talk, if not aggression or outright violence. They see that one child succumbs to the greater physical and mental abilities of the other. They are also alert and attentive witnesses to the verbal and physical fights of

adults, after which they compare notes and share their interpretations of the event. In almost every case the victor is the person who physically won the altercation, and this person often enjoys the esteem and respect of onlookers. These experiences reinforce the lessons the children have learned at home: might makes right, and toughness is a virtue, while humility is not. In effect they learn the social meaning of fighting. When it is left virtually unchallenged, this understanding becomes an ever more important part of the child's working conception of the world. Over time the code of the streets becomes refined.

Those street-oriented adults with whom children come in contact—including mothers, fathers, brothers, sisters, boyfriends, cousins, neighbors, and friends—help them along in forming this understanding by verbalizing the messages they are getting through experience: "Watch your back." "Protect yourself." "Don't punk out." "If somebody messes with you, you got to pay them back." "If someone disses you, you got to straighten them out." Many parents actually impose sanctions if a child is not sufficiently aggressive. For example, if a child loses a fight and comes home upset, the parent might respond, "Don't you come in here crying that somebody beat you up; you better get back out there and whup his ass. I didn't raise no punks! Get back out there and whup his ass. If you don't whup his ass, I'll whup your ass when you come home." Thus the child obtains reinforcement for being tough and showing nerve.

While fighting, some children cry as though they are doing something they are ambivalent about. The fight may be against their wishes, yet they may feel constrained to fight or face the consequences—not just from peers but also from caretakers or parents, who may administer another beating if they back down. Some adults recall receiving such lessons from their own parents and justify repeating them to their children as a way to toughen them up. Looking capable of taking care of oneself as a form of self-defense is a dominant theme among both street-oriented and decent adults who worry about the safety of their children. There is thus at times a convergence in their child-rearing practices, although the rationales behind them may differ.

Self-Image Based on "Juice"

By the time they are teenagers, most youths have either internalized the code of the streets or at least learned the need to comport themselves in accordance with its rules, which chiefly have to do with interpersonal communication. The code revolves around the presentation of self. Its basic requirement is the display of a certain predisposition to violence. Accordingly, one's bearing must send the unmistakable if sometimes subtle message to "the next person" in public that one is capable of violence and mayhem when the situation requires it, that one can take care of oneself. The nature of this communication is largely determined by the demands of the circumstances but can include facial expressions, gait, and verbal expressions—all of which are geared mainly to deterring aggression. Physical appearance, including clothes, jewelry, and grooming, also plays an important part in how a person is viewed; to be respected, it is important to have the right look.

Even so, there are no guarantees against challenges, because there are always people around looking for a fight to increase their share of respect—or "juice," as it is sometimes called on the street. Moreover, if a person is assaulted, it is important, not only in the eyes of his opponent but also in the eyes of his "running buddies," for him to avenge himself. Otherwise he risks being "tried" (challenged) or "moved on" by any number of others. To maintain his honor he must show he is not someone to be "messed with" or "dissed." In general, the person must "keep himself straight" by managing his position of respect among others; this involves in part his self-image, which is shaped by what he thinks others are thinking of him in relation to his peers.

Objects play an important and complicated role in establishing self-image. Jackets, sneakers, gold jewelry, reflect not just a person's taste, which tends to be tightly regulated among adolescents of all social classes, but also a willingness to possess things that may require defending. A boy wearing a fashionable, expensive jacket, for example, is vulnerable to attack by another who covets the jacket and either cannot afford to buy one or wants the added satisfaction of depriving someone else of his. However, if the boy forgoes the desirable jacket and wears one that isn't "hip," he runs the risk of being teased and possibly even assaulted as an unworthy person. To be allowed to hang with certain prestigious crowds, a boy must wear a different set of expensive clothes—sneakers and athletic suit—every day. Not to be able to do so might make him appear socially deficient. The youth comes to covet such items—especially when he sees easy prey wearing them.

In acquiring valued things, therefore, a person shores up his identity—but since it is an identity based on having

things, it is highly precarious. This very precariousness gives a heightened sense of urgency to staying even with peers, with whom the person is actually competing. Young men and women who are able to command respect through their presentation of self—by allowing their possessions and their body language to speak for them—may not have to campaign for regard but may, rather, gain it by the force of their manner. Those who are unable to command respect in this way must actively campaign for it—and are thus particularly alive to slights.

One way of campaigning for status is by taking the possessions of others. In this context, seemingly ordinary objects can become trophies imbued with symbolic value that far exceeds their monetary worth. Possession of the trophy can symbolize the ability to violate somebody—to "get in his face," to take something of value from him, to "dis" him, and thus to enhance one's own worth by stealing someone else's. The trophy does not have to be something material. It can be another person's sense of honor, snatched away with a derogatory remark. It can be the outcome of a fight. It can be the imposition of a certain standard, such as a girl's getting herself recognized as the most beautiful. Material things, however, fit easily into the pattern. Sneakers, a pistol, even somebody else's girlfriend, can become a trophy. When a person can take something from another and then flaunt it, he gains a certain regard by being the owner, or the controller, of that thing. But this display of ownership can then provoke other people to challenge him. This game of who controls what is thus constantly being played out on inner-city streets, and the trophy—extrinsic or intrinsic, tangible or intangible—identifies the current winner.

An important aspect of this often violent give-and-take is its zero-sum quality. That is, the extent to which one person can raise himself up depends on his ability to put another person down. This underscores the alienation that permeates the inner-city ghetto community. There is a generalized sense that very little respect is to be had, and therefore everyone competes to get what affirmation he can of the little that is available. The craving for respect that results gives people thin skins. Shows of deference by others can be highly soothing, contributing to a sense of security, comfort, self-confidence, and self-respect. Transgressions by others which go unanswered diminish these feelings and are believed to encourage further transgressions. Hence one must be ever vigilant against the transgressions of others or even *appearing* as if transgressions will be tolerated. Among young people, whose sense of self-esteem is particularly vulnerable, there is an especially heightened concern with being disrespected. Many inner-city young men in particular crave respect to such a degree that they will risk their lives to attain and maintain it.

The issue of respect is thus closely tied to whether a person has an inclination to be violent, even as a victim. In the wider society people may not feel required to retaliate physically after an attack, even though they are aware that they have been degraded or taken advantage of. They may feel a great need to defend themselves *during* an attack, or to behave in such a way as to deter aggression (middle-class people certainly can and do become victims of street-oriented youths), but they are much more likely than street-oriented people to feel that they can walk away from a possible altercation with their self-esteem intact. Some people may even have the strength of character to flee, without any thought that their self-respect or esteem will be diminished.

In impoverished inner-city black communities, however, particularly among young males and perhaps increasingly among females, such flight would be extremely difficult. To run away would likely leave one's self-esteem in tatters. Hence people often feel constrained not only to stand up and at least attempt to resist during an assault but also to "pay back"—to seek revenge—after a successful assault on their person. This may include going to get a weapon or even getting relatives involved. Their very identity and self-respect, their honor, is often intricately tied up with the way they perform on the streets during and after such encounters. This outlook reflects the circumscribed opportunities of the inner-city poor. Generally people outside the ghetto have other ways of gaining status and regard, and thus do not feel so dependent on such physical displays.

By Trial of Manhood

On the street, among males these concerns about things and identity have come to be expressed in the concept of "manhood." Manhood in the inner city means taking the prerogatives of men with respect to strangers, other men, and women—being distinguished as a man. It implies physicality and a certain ruthlessness. Regard and respect are associated with this concept in large part because of its practical application: if others have little or no regard for a

person's manhood, his very life and those of his loved ones could be in jeopardy. But there is a chicken-and-egg aspect to this situation: one's physical safety is more likely to be jeopardized in public *because* manhood is associated with respect. In other words, an existential link has been created between the idea of manhood and one's self-esteem, so that it has become hard to say which is primary. For many inner-city youths, manhood and respect are flip sides of the same coin; physical and psychological well-being are inseparable, and both require a sense of control, of being in charge.

The operating assumption is that a man, especially a real man, knows what other men know—the code of the streets. And if one is not a real man, one is somehow diminished as a person, and there are certain valued things one simply does not deserve. There is thus believed to be a certain justice to the code, since it is considered that everyone has the opportunity to know it. Implicit in this is that everybody is held responsible for being familiar with the code. If the victim of a mugging, for example, does not know the code and so responds "wrong," the perpetrator may feel justified even in killing him and may feel no remorse. He may think, "Too bad, but it's his fault. He should have known better."

So when a person ventures outside, he must adopt the code—a kind of shield, really—to prevent others from "messing with" him. In these circumstances it is easy for people to think they are being tried or tested by others even when this is not the case. For it is sensed that something extremely valuable is at stake in every interaction, and people are encouraged to rise to the occasion, particularly with strangers. For people who are unfamiliar with the code—generally people who live outside the inner city—the concern with respect in the most ordinary interactions can be frightening and incomprehensible. But for those who are invested in the code, the clear object of their demeanor is to discourage strangers from even thinking about testing their manhood. And the sense of power that attends the ability to deter others can be alluring even to those who know the code without being heavily invested in it—the decent inner-city youths. Thus a boy who has been leading a basically decent life can, in trying circumstances, suddenly resort to deadly force.

Central to the issue of manhood is the widespread belief that one of the most effective ways of gaining respect is to manifest "nerve." Nerve is shown when one takes another person's possessions (the more valuable the better), "messes with" someone's woman, throws the first punch, "gets in someone's face," or pulls a trigger. Its proper display helps on the spot to check others who would violate one's person and also helps to build a reputation that works to prevent future challenges. But since such a show of nerve is a forceful expression of disrespect toward the person on the receiving end, the victim may be greatly offended and seek to retaliate with equal or greater force. A display of nerve, therefore, can easily provoke a life-threatening response, and the background knowledge of that possibility has often been incorporated into the concept of nerve.

True nerve exposes a lack of fear of dying. Many feel that it is acceptable to risk dying over the principle of respect. In fact, among the hard-core street-oriented, the clear risk of violent death may be preferable to being "dissed" by another. The youths who have internalized this attitude and convincingly display it in their public bearing are among the most threatening people of all, for it is commonly assumed that they fear no man. As the people of the community say, "They are the baddest dudes on the street." They often lead an existential life that may acquire meaning only when they are faced with the possibility of imminent death. Not to be afraid to die is by implication to have few compunctions about taking another's life. Not to be afraid to die is the quid pro quo of being able to take somebody else's life—for the right reasons, if the situation demands it. When others believe this is one's position, it gives one a real sense of power on the streets. Such credibility is what many inner-city youths strive to achieve, whether they are decent or street-oriented, both because of its practical defensive value and because of the positive way it makes them feel about themselves. The difference between the decent and the street-oriented youth is often that the decent youth makes a conscious decision to appear tough and manly; in another setting—with teachers, say, or at his part-time job—he can be polite and deferential. The street-oriented youth, on the other hand, has made the concept of manhood a part of his very identity; he has difficulty manipulating it—it often controls him.

Girls and Boys

Increasingly, teenage girls are mimicking the boys and trying to have their own version of "manhood." Their goal is the same—to get respect, to be recognized as capable

of setting or maintaining a certain standard. They try to achieve this end in the ways that have been established by the boys, including posturing, abusive language, and the use of violence to resolve disputes, but the issues for the girls are different. Although conflicts over turf and status exist among the girls, the majority of disputes seem rooted in assessments of beauty (which girl in a group is "the cutest"), competition over boyfriends, and attempts to regulate other people's knowledge of and opinions about a girl's behavior or that of someone close to her, especially her mother.

A major cause of conflicts among girls is "he say, she say." This practice begins in the early school years and continues through high school. It occurs when "people," particularly girls, talk about others, thus putting their "business in the streets." Usually one girl will say something negative about another in the group, most often behind the person's back. The remark will then get back to the person talked about. She may retaliate or her friends may feel required to "take up for" her. In essence this is a form of group gossiping in which individuals are negatively assessed and evaluated. As with much gossip, the things said may or may not be true, but the point is that such imputations can cast aspersions on a person's good name. The accused is required to defend herself against the slander, which can result in arguments and fights, often over little of real substance. Here again is the problem of low self-esteem, which encourages youngsters to be highly sensitive to slights and to be vulnerable to feeling easily "dissed." To avenge the dissing, a fight is usually necessary.

Because boys are believed to control violence, girls tend to defer to them in situations of conflict. Often if a girl is attacked or feels slighted, she will get a brother, uncle, or cousin to do her fighting for her. Increasingly, however, girls are doing their own fighting and are even asking their male relatives to teach them how to fight. Some girls form groups that attack other girls or take things from them. A hard-core segment of inner-city girls inclined toward violence seems to be developing. As one thirteen-year-old girl in a detention center for youths who have committed violent acts told me, "To get people to leave you alone, you gotta fight. Talking don't always get you out of stuff." One major difference between girls and boys: girls rarely use guns. Their fights are therefore not life-or-death struggles. Girls are not often willing to put their lives on the line for "manhood." The ultimate form of respect on the male-dominated inner-city street is thus reserved for men.

"Going for Bad"

In the most fearsome youths such a cavalier attitude toward death grows out of a very limited view of life. Many are uncertain about how long they are going to live and believe they could die violently at any time. They accept this fate; they live on the edge. Their manner conveys the message that nothing intimidates them; whatever turn the encounter takes, they maintain their attack—rather like a pit bull, whose spirit many such boys admire. The demonstration of such tenacity "shows heart" and earns their respect.

This fearlessness has implications for law enforcement. Many street-oriented boys are much more concerned about the threat of "justice" at the hands of a peer than at the hands of the police. Moreover, many feel not only that they have little to lose by going to prison but that they have something to gain. The toughening-up one experiences in prison can actually enhance one's reputation on the streets. Hence the system loses influence over the hard core who are without jobs, with little perceptible stake in the system. If mainstream society has done nothing *for* them, they counter by making sure it can do nothing *to* them.

At the same time, however, a competing view maintains that true nerve consists in backing down, walking away from a fight, and going on with one's business. One fights only in self-defense. This view emerges from the decent philosophy that life is precious, and it is an important part of the socialization process common in decent homes. It discourages violence as the primary means of resolving disputes and encourages youngsters to accept nonviolence and talk as confrontational strategies. But "if the deal goes down," self-defense is greatly encouraged. When there is enough positive support for this orientation, either in the home or among one's peers, then nonviolence has a chance to prevail. But it prevails at the cost of relinquishing a claim to being bad and tough, and therefore sets a young person up as at the very least alienated from street-oriented peers and quite possibly a target of derision or even violence.

Although the nonviolent orientation rarely overcomes the impulse to strike back in an encounter, it does introduce a certain confusion and so can prompt a measure of

soul-searching, or even profound ambivalence. Did the person back down with his respect intact or did he back down only to be judged a "punk"—a person lacking manhood? Should he or she have acted? Should he or she have hit the other person in the mouth? These questions beset many young men and women during public confrontations. What is the "right" thing to do? In the quest for honor, respect, and local status—which few young people are uninterested in—common sense most often prevails, which leads many to opt for the tough approach, enacting their own particular versions of the display of nerve. The presentation of oneself as rough and tough is very often quite acceptable until one is tested. And then that presentation may help the person pass the test, because it will cause fewer questions to be asked about what he did and why. It is hard for a person to explain why he lost the fight or why he backed down. Hence many will strive to appear to "go for bad," while hoping they will never be tested. But when they are tested, the outcome of the situation may quickly be out of their hands, as they become wrapped up in the circumstances of the moment.

An Oppositional Culture

The attitudes of the wider society are deeply implicated in the code of the streets. Most people in inner-city communities are not totally invested in the code, but the significant minority of hard-core street youths who have to maintain the code in order to establish reputations, because they have—or feel they have—few other ways to assert themselves. For these young people the standards of the street code are the only game in town. The extent to which some children—particularly those who through upbringing have become most alienated and those lacking in strong and conventional social support—experience, feel, and internalize racist rejection and contempt from mainstream society may strongly encourage them to express contempt for the more conventional society in turn. In dealing with this contempt and rejection, some youngsters will consciously invest themselves and their considerable mental resources in what amounts to an oppositional culture to preserve themselves and their self-respect. Once they do, any respect they might be able to garner in the wider system pales in comparison with the respect available in the local system; thus they often lose interest in even attempting to negotiate the mainstream system.

At the same time, many less alienated young blacks have assumed a street-oriented demeanor as a way of expressing their blackness while really embracing a much more moderate way of life; they, too, want a nonviolent setting in which to live and raise a family. These decent people are trying hard to be part of the mainstream culture, but the racism, real and perceived, that they encounter helps to legitimate the oppositional culture. And so on occasion they adopt street behavior. In fact, depending on the demands of the situation, many people in the community slip back and forth between decent and street behavior.

A vicious cycle has thus been formed. The hopelessness and alienation many young inner-city black men and women feel, largely as a result of endemic joblessness and persistent racism, fuels the violence they engage in. This violence serves to confirm the negative feelings many whites and some middle-class blacks harbor toward the ghetto poor, further legitimating the oppositional culture and the code of the streets in the eyes of many poor young blacks. Unless this cycle is broken, attitudes on both sides will become increasingly entrenched, and the violence, which claims victims black and white, poor and affluent, will only escalate.

23 Environmental Justice in the 21st Century: Race Still Matters

Robert D. Bullard

ROBERT D. BULLARD is Ware Professor of Sociology and director of the Environmental Justice Resource Center at Clark Atlanta University. He is the author of numerous articles, monographs, and scholarly papers that address environmental justice and public participation concerns. His book, *Dumping in Dixie: Race, Class and Environmental Quality* (1990, 1994, 2000), has become a standard text in the environmental justice field.

Questions to Consider Where is the trash dump, the water treatment plant, or the power plant in your community? In this reading Robert Bullard argues that in all likelihood these environmental dangers are in low-income, black and brown neighborhoods. Why do some communities get "dumped on" while others remain free of any toxic waste sites?

HARDLY A DAY PASSES WITHOUT THE MEDIA discovering some community or neighborhood fighting a landfill, incinerator, chemical plant, or some other polluting industry. This was not always the case. Just three decades ago, the concept of environmental justice had not registered on the radar screens of environmental, civil rights, or social justice groups.[1] Nevertheless, it should not be forgotten that Dr. Martin Luther King, Jr., went to Memphis in 1968 on an environmental and economic justice mission for the striking black garbage workers. The strikers were demanding equal pay and better work conditions. Of course, Dr. King was assassinated before he could complete his mission.

Another landmark garbage dispute took place a decade later in Houston, when African-American homeowners in 1979 began a bitter fight to keep a sanitary landfill out of their suburban middle-income neighborhood.[2] Residents formed the Northeast Community Action Group or NECAG. NECAG and their attorney, Linda McKeever Bullard, filed a class-action lawsuit to block the facility from being built. The 1979 lawsuit, *Bean v. Southwestern Waste Management, Inc.,* was the first of its kind to challenge the siting of a waste facility under civil rights law.

The landmark Houston case occurred three years before the environmental justice movement was catapulted into the national limelight in the rural and mostly African-American Warren County, North Carolina. The environmental justice movement has come a long way since its humble beginning in Warren County, North Carolina, where a PCB landfill ignited protests and over 500 arrests. The Warren County protests provided the impetus for a U.S. General Accounting Office study, *Siting of Hazardous Waste Landfills and Their Correlation with Racial and Economic Status of Surrounding Communities.*[3] That study revealed that three out of four of the off-site, commercial hazardous waste landfills in Region 4 (which comprises eight states in the South) happen to be located in predominantly African-American communities, although African Americans made up only 20 percent of the region's population. More important, the protesters put "environmental racism" on the map. Fifteen years later, the state of North Carolina is required to spend over $25 million to clean up and detoxify the Warren County PCB landfill.

The Warren County protests also led the Commission for Racial Justice to produce *Toxic Wastes and Race,*[4] the first national study to correlate waste facility sites and demographic characteristics. Race was found to be the most potent variable in predicting where these facilities were located—more powerful than poverty, land values, and home ownership. In 1990, *Dumping in Dixie: Race, Class, and Environmental Quality* chronicled the convergence of two social movements—social justice and environmental movements—into the environmental justice movement. This book highlighted African Americans' environmental activism in the South, the same region that gave birth to the modern civil rights movement. What started out as local and often isolated community-based struggles against toxics and facility siting blossomed into a multi-issue, multiethnic, and multiregional movement.

The 1991 First National People of Color Environmental Leadership Summit was probably the most important single event in the movement's history. The Summit broadened the environmental justice movement beyond its early antitoxics focus to include issues of public health, worker safety, land use, transportation, housing, resource allocation, and community empowerment.[5]

The meeting also demonstrated that it is possible to build a multiracial grassroots movement around environmental and economic justice.[6]

Held in Washington, DC, the four-day Summit was attended by over 650 grassroots and national leaders from around the world. Delegates came from all fifty states including Alaska and Hawaii, Puerto Rico, Chile, Mexico, and as far away as the Marshall Islands. People attended the summit to share their action strategies, redefine the environmental movement, and develop common plans for addressing environmental problems affecting people of color in the United States and around the world.

On September 27, 1991, Summit delegates adopted 17 "Principles of Environmental Justice." These principles were developed as a guide for organizing, networking, and relating to government and nongovernmental organizations (NGOs). By June 1992, Spanish and Portuguese translations of the Principles were being used and circulated by NGOs and environmental justice groups at the Earth Summit in Rio de Janeiro.

In response to growing public concern and mounting scientific evidence, President Clinton on February 11, 1994 (the second day of the national health symposium), issued Executive Order 12898, "Federal Actions to Address Environmental Justice in Minority Populations and Low-Income Populations." This Order attempts to address environmental injustice within existing federal laws and regulations.

Executive Order 12898 reinforces the 35-year-old Civil Rights Act of 1964, Title VI, which prohibits discriminatory practices in programs receiving federal funds. The Order also focuses the spotlight back on the National Environmental Policy Act (NEPA), a twenty-five-year-old law that set policy goals for the protection, maintenance, and enhancement of the environment. NEPA's goal is to ensure for all Americans a safe, healthful, productive, and aesthetically and culturally pleasing environment. NEPA requires federal agencies to prepare a detailed statement on the environmental effects of proposed federal actions that significantly affect the quality of human health.

The Executive Order calls for improved methodologies for assessing and mitigating impacts, health effects from multiple and cumulative exposure, collection of data on low-income and minority populations who may be disproportionately at risk, and impacts on subsistence fishers and wildlife consumers. It also encourages participation of the impacted populations in the various phases of assessing impacts—including scoping, data gathering, alternatives, analysis, mitigation, and monitoring.

The Executive Order focuses on "subsistence" fishers and wildlife consumers. Everybody does not buy fish at the supermarket. There are many people who are subsistence fishers, who fish for protein, who basically subsidize their budgets, and their diets, by fishing from rivers, streams, and lakes that happen to be polluted. These subpopulations may be underprotected when basic assumptions are made using the dominant risk paradigm.

Many grassroots activists are convinced that waiting for the government to act has endangered the health and welfare of their communities. Unlike the federal EPA, communities of color did not first discover environmental inequities in 1990. The federal EPA only took action on environmental justice concerns in 1990 after extensive prodding from grassroots environmental justice activists, educators, and academics.[7]

People of color have known about and have been living with inequitable environmental quality for decades— most without the protection of the federal, state, and local governmental agencies. Environmental justice advocates continue to challenge the current environmental protection apparatus and offer their own framework for addressing environmental inequities, disparate impact, and unequal protection.

An Environmental Justice Framework

The question of environmental justice is not anchored in a debate about whether or not decision makers should tinker with risk management. The framework seeks to prevent environmental threats before they occur.[8] The environmental justice framework incorporates other social movements that seek to eliminate harmful practices (discrimination harms the victim) in housing, land use, industrial planning, health care, and sanitation services. The impact of redlining, economic disinvestments, infrastructure decline, deteriorating housing, lead poisoning, industrial pollution, poverty, and unemployment are not unrelated problems if one lives in an urban ghetto or barrio, rural hamlet, or reservation.

The environmental justice framework attempts to uncover the underlying assumptions that may contribute to and produce unequal protection. This framework brings to the surface the ethical and political questions of "who gets what, why, and how much." Some general characteristics of the framework include:

1.   *The environmental justice framework incorporates the principle of the "right" of all individuals to be protected from environmental degradation.* The precedents for this framework are the Civil Rights Act of 1964, Fair Housing Act of 1968 and as amended in 1988, and Voting Rights Act of 1965.

2.   *The environmental justice framework adopts a public health model of prevention (elimination of the threat before harm occurs) as the preferred strategy.* Impacted communities should not have to wait until causation or conclusive "proof" is established before preventive action is taken. For example, the framework offers a solution to the lead problem by shifting the primary focus from *treatment* (after children have been poisoned) to *prevention* (elimination of the threat via abating lead in houses).

Overwhelming scientific evidence exists on the ill effects of lead on the human body. However, very little action has been taken to rid the nation of childhood lead poisoning in urban areas. Former Health and Human Services Secretary Louis Sullivan tagged this among the "number one environmental health threats to children."[9]

The Natural Resources Defense Council, NAACP Legal Defense and Educational Fund, ACLU, and Legal Aid Society of Alameda County joined forces in 1991 and won an out-of-court settlement worth $15–20 million for a blood-lead testing program in California. The *Matthews v. Coye* lawsuit involved the State of California not living up to the federally mandated testing of some 557,000 poor children for lead who receive Medicaid. This historic agreement triggered similar actions in other states that failed to live up to federally mandated screening.[10]

Lead screening is an important element in this problem. However, screening is not the solution. Prevention is the solution. Surely, if termite inspections can be mandated to protect individual home investment, a lead-free home can be mandated to protect public health. Ultimately, the lead abatement debate, public health (who is affected) vs. property rights (who pays for cleanup), is a value conflict that will not be resolved by the scientific community.

3.   *The environmental justice framework shifts the burden of proof to polluter/dischargers who do harm, discriminate, or who do not give equal protection to racial and ethnic minorities, and other "protected" classes.* Under the current system, individuals who challenge polluters must "prove" that they have been harmed, discriminated against, or disproportionately impacted. Few impacted communities have the resources to hire lawyers, expert witnesses, and doctors needed to sustain such a challenge.

The environmental justice framework would require the parties that are applying for operating permits (landfills, incinerators, smelters, refineries, chemical plants, etc.) to "prove" that their operations are not harmful to human health, will not disproportionately impact racial and ethnic minorities and other protected groups, and are nondiscriminatory.

4. *The environmental justice framework would allow disparate impact and statistical weight, as opposed to "intent," to infer discrimination.* Proving intentional or purposeful discrimination in a court of law is next to impossible, as demonstrated in *Bean v. Southwestern Waste*. It took nearly a decade after *Bean v. Southwestern Waste* for environmental discrimination to resurface in the courts.

5. *The environmental justice framework redresses disproportionate impact through "targeted" action and resources.* This strategy would target resources where environmental and health problems are greatest (as determined by some ranking scheme but not limited to risk assessment). Reliance solely on "objective" science disguises the exploitative way the polluting industries have operated in some communities and condones a passive acceptance of the status quo.

Human *values* are involved in determining *which* geographic areas are worth public investments. In the 1992 EPA report, *Securing Our Legacy,* the agency describes geographic initiatives as "protecting what we love."[11]

The strategy emphasizes "pollution prevention, multimedia enforcement, research into causes and cures of environmental stress, stopping habitat loss, education, and constituency building."[12] Geographic initiatives are underway in the Chesapeake Bay, Great Lakes, Gulf of Mexico programs, and the U.S.-Mexican Border program. Environmental justice targeting would channel resources to "hot spots," communities that are overburdened with more than their "fair" share of environmental and health problems.

The dominant environmental protection paradigm reinforces instead of challenges the stratification of people (race, ethnicity, status, power, etc.), place (central cities, suburbs, rural areas, unincorporated areas, Native American reservations, etc.), and work (i.e., office workers are afforded greater protection than farm workers). The dominant paradigm exists to manage, regulate, and distribute risks. As a result, the current system has (1) institutionalized unequal enforcement, (2) traded human health for profit, (3) placed the burden of proof on the "victims" and not the polluting industry, (4) legitimated human exposure to harmful chemicals, pesticides, and hazardous substances, (5) promoted "risky" technologies such as incinerators, (6) exploited the vulnerability of economically and politically disenfranchised communities, (7) subsidized ecological destruction,

(8) created an industry around risk assessment, (9) delayed cleanup actions, and (10) failed to develop pollution prevention as the overarching and dominant strategy.[13]

The mission of the federal EPA was never designed to address environmental policies and practices that result in unfair, unjust, and inequitable outcome. EPA and other government officials are not likely to ask the questions that go to the heart of environmental injustice: What groups are most affected? Why are they affected? Who did it? What can be done to remedy the problem? How can the problem be prevented? Vulnerable communities, populations, and individuals often fall between the regulatory cracks.

Impetus for a Paradigm Shift

The environmental justice movement has changed the way scientists, researchers, policy makers, and educators go about their daily work. This bottom-up movement has redefined environment to include where people live, work, play, go to school, as well as how these things interact with the physical and natural world. The impetus for changing the dominant environmental protection paradigm did not come from within regulatory agencies, the polluting industry, academia, or the "industry" that has been built around risk management. The environmental justice movement is led by a loose alliance of grassroots and national environmental and civil rights leaders who question the foundation of the current environmental protection paradigm.

Despite significant improvements in environmental protection over the past several decades, millions of Americans continue to live, work, play, and go to school in unsafe and unhealthy physical environments.[14] During its 30-year history, the U.S. EPA has not always recognized that many of our government and industry practices (whether intended or unintended) have adverse impact on poor people and people of color. Growing grassroots community resistance emerged in response to practices, policies, and conditions that residents judged to be unjust, unfair, and illegal. Discrimination is a fact of life in America. Racial discrimination is also illegal.

The EPA is mandated to enforce the nation's environmental laws and regulations equally across the board. It is also required to protect all Americans—not just individuals or groups who can afford lawyers, lobbyists, and experts. Environmental protection is a right, not a privilege reserved for a few who can vote with their feet and escape or fend off environmental stressors that address environmental inequities.

Equity may mean different things to different people. Equity is distilled into three broad categories: procedural, geographic, and social equity.

Procedural equity refers to the "fairness" question: the extent that governing rules, regulations, evaluation criteria, and enforcement are applied uniformly across the board and in a nondiscriminatory way. Unequal protection might result from nonscientific and undemocratic decisions, exclusionary practices, public hearings held in remote locations and at inconvenient times, and use of English-only material as the language to communicate and conduct hearings for non-English speaking publics.

Geographic equity refers to location and spatial configuration of communities and their proximity to environmental hazards, noxious facilities, and locally unwanted land uses (LULUs) such as landfills, incinerators, sewer treatment plants, lead smelters, refineries, and other noxious facilities. For example, unequal protection may result from land-use decisions that determine the location of residential amenities and disamenities. Unincorporated, poor, and communities of color often suffer a "triple" vulnerability of noxious facility siting.

Social equity assesses the role of sociological factors (race, ethnicity, class, culture, life styles, political power, etc.) on environmental decision making. Poor people and people of color often work in the most dangerous jobs, live in the most polluted neighborhoods, and their children are exposed to all kinds of environmental toxins on the playgrounds and in their homes.

The nation's environmental laws, regulations, and policies are not applied uniformly—resulting in some individuals, neighborhoods, and communities being exposed to the elevated health risks. A 1992 study by staff writers from the *National Law Journal* uncovered glaring inequities in the way the federal EPA enforces its laws. The authors write:

> There is a racial divide in the way the U.S. Government cleans up toxic waste sites and punishes polluters. White communities see faster action, better results and stiffer penalities than communities where blacks, Hispanics and other minorities live. This unequal protection often occurs whether the community is wealthy or poor.[15]

These findings suggest that unequal protection is placing communities of color at special risk.

The *National Law Journal* study supplements the findings of earlier studies and reinforces what many grassroots leaders have been saying all along: not only are people of color differentially impacted by industrial pollution, they can expect different treatment from the government. Environmental decision-making operates at the juncture of science, economics, politics, special interests, and ethics. This current environmental model places communities of color at special risk.

The Impact of Racial Apartheid

Apartheid-type housing, development, and environmental policies limit mobility, reduce neighborhood options, diminish job opportunities, and decrease choices for millions of Americans.[16] The infrastructure conditions in urban areas are a result of a host of factors including the distribution of wealth, patterns of racial and economic discrimination, redlining, housing and real estate practices, location decisions of industry, differential enforcement of land use and environmental choices, and diminished job communities for African Americans.

Race still plays a significant part in distributing public "benefits" and public "burdens" associated with economic growth. The roots of discrimination are deep and have been difficult to eliminate. Housing discrimination contributes to the physical decay of inner-city neighborhoods and denies a substantial segment of the African-American community a basic form of wealth accumulation and investment through home ownership.[17] The number of African-American homeowners would probably be higher in the absence of discrimination by lending institutions.[18] Only about 59 percent of the nation's middle-class African Americans own their homes, compared with 74 percent of whites.

Eight out of every ten African Americans live in neighborhoods where they are in the majority. Residential segregation decreases for most racial and ethnic groups with additional education, income, and occupational status. However, this scenario does not hold true for African Americans. African Americans, no matter what their educational or occupational achievement or income level, are exposed to higher crime rates, less effective educational systems, higher mortality risks, more dilapidated surroundings, and greater environmental threats because of their race. For example, in the heavily populated South

Coast air basin of the Los Angeles area, it is estimated that over 71 percent of African Americans and 50 percent of whites live in highly polluted areas.[19]

It has been difficult for millions of Americans in segregated neighborhoods to say "not in my backyard" (NIMBY) if they do not have a backyard.[20] Nationally, only about 44 percent of African Americans own their homes compared to over two-thirds of the nation as a whole. Homeowners are the strongest advocates of the NIMBY positions taken against locally unwanted uses or LULUs such as the construction of garbage dumps, landfills, incinerators, sewer treatment plants, recycling centers, prisons, drug treatment units, and public housing projects. Generally, white communities have greater access than people-of-color communities when it comes to influencing land use and environmental decision making.

The ability of an individual to escape a health-threatening physical environment is usually related to affluence. However, racial barriers complicate this process for many Americans.[21] The imbalance between residential amenities and land uses assigned to central cities and suburbs cannot be explained by class factors alone. People of color and whites do not have the same opportunities to "vote with their feet" and escape undesirable physical environments.

Institutional racism continues to influence housing and mobility options available to African Americans of all income levels—and is a major factor that influences quality of neighborhoods they have available to them. The "web of discrimination" in the housing market is a result of action and inaction of local and federal government officials, financial institutions, insurance companies, real estate marketing firms, and zoning boards. More stringent enforcement mechanisms and penalties are needed to combat all forms of discrimination.

Uneven development between central cities and suburbs combined with the systematic avoidance of inner-city areas by many businesses have heightened social and economic inequalities. For the past two decades, manufacturing plants have been fleeing central cities and taking their jobs with them. Many have moved offshore to Third-World countries where labor is cheap and environmental regulations are lax or nonexistent.

Industry flight from central cities had left behind a deteriorating urban infrastructure, poverty, and pollution. What kind of replacement industry can these communities attract? Economically depressed communities do not have a lot of choices available to them. Some workers have

become so desperate that they see even a low-paying hazardous job as better than no job at all. These workers are forced to choose between unemployment and a job that may result in risks to their health, their family's health, and the health of their community. This practice amounts to "economic blackmail." Economic conditions in many people-of-color communities make them especially vulnerable to this practice.

Some polluting industries have been eager to exploit this vulnerability. Some have even used the assistance of elected officials in obtaining special tax breaks and government operating permits. Clearly, economic development and environmental policies flow from forces of production and are often dominated and subsidized by state actors. Numerous examples abound where state actors have targeted cities and regions for infrastructure improvements and amenities such as water irrigation systems, ship channels, road and bridge projects, and mass transit systems. On the other hand, state actors have done a miserable job in protecting central city residents from the ravages of industrial pollution and nonresidential activities valued as having a negative impact on quality of life.[22]

Racial and ethnic inequality is perpetuated and reinforced by local governments in conjunction with urban-based corporations. Race continues to be a potent variable in explaining urban land use, streets and highway configuration, commercial and industrial development, and industrial facility siting. Moreover, the question of "who gets what, where, and why" often pits one community against another.[23]

Zoning and Land Use

Some residential areas and their inhabitants are at a greater risk than the larger society from unregulated growth, ineffective regulation of industrial toxins, and public policy decisions authorizing industrial facilities that favor those with political and economic clout.[24] African Americans and other communities of color are often victims of land-use decision making that mirrors the power arrangements of the dominant society. Historically, exclusionary zoning (and rezoning) has been a subtle form of using government authority and power to foster and perpetuate discriminatory practices.

Zoning is probably the most widely applied mechanism to regulate urban land use in the United States. Zoning laws broadly define land for residential, commercial, or industrial uses, and may impose narrower land-use restrictions (e.g., minimum and maximum lot size, number of dwellings per acre, square feet and height of buildings, etc.). Zoning ordinances, deed restrictions, and other land-use mechanisms have been widely used as a "NIMBY" tool, operating through exclusionary practices. Thus, exclusionary zoning has been used to zone against something rather than for something. With or without zoning, deed restrictions or other devices, various groups are unequally able to protect their environmental interests. More often than not, people-of-color communities get shortchanged in the neighborhood protection game.

In Houston, Texas, a city that does not have zoning, NIMBY was replaced with the policy of PIBBY (place in black's back yard).[25] The city government and private industry targeted landfills, incinerators, and garbage dumps for Houston's black neighborhoods for more than five decades. These practices lowered residents' property values, accelerated physical deterioration, and increased disinvestment in the communities. Moreover, the discriminatory siting of landfills and incinerators stigmatized the neighborhoods as "dumping grounds" for a host of other unwanted facilities, including salvage yards, recycling operations, and automobile "chop shops."[26]

The Commission for Racial Justice's landmark *Toxic Wastes and Race* study found race to be the single most important factor (i.e., more important than income, home ownership rate, and property values) in the location of abandoned toxic waste sites.[27] The study also found that (1) three out of five African Americans live in communities with abandoned toxic waste sites; (2) sixty percent of African Americans (15 million) live in communities with one or more abandoned toxic waste sites; (3) three of the five largest commercial hazardous waste landfills are located in predominately African American or Latino communities and accounts for 40 percent of the nation's total estimated landfill capacity; and (4) African Americans are heavily overrepresented in the population of cities with the largest number of abandoned toxic waste sites, which include Memphis, St. Louis, Houston, Cleveland, Chicago, and Atlanta.

Waste facility siting imbalances that were uncovered by the U.S. General Accounting Office (GAO) in 1983 have not disappeared.[28] The GAO discovered three out of four of the off-site commercial hazardous waste landfills in Region IV (Alabama, Florida, Georgia, Kentucky, Mississippi, North Carolina, South Carolina, and Tennessee) were located in predominately African-American communities. African Americans still made up about one-fifth of the population in EPA Region IV. In 2000, 100 percent of the off-site commercial hazardous wastes landfills in the region is dumped in two mostly African-American communities.

Environmental Racism

Many of the differences in environmental quality between black and white communities result from institutional racism, which influences local land use, enforcement of environmental regulations, industrial facility siting, and where people of color live, work and play. The roots of institutional racism are deep and have been difficult to eliminate. Discrimination is a manifestation of institutional racism and causes life to be very different for whites and blacks. Historically, racism has been and continues to be a major part of the American sociological system, and as a result, people of color find themselves at a disadvantage in contemporary society.

Environmental racism is real. It is just as real as the racism found in the housing industry, educational institutions, employment arena, and judicial system. What is environmental racism and how does one recognize it? *Environmental racism refers to any policy, practice, or directive that differentially affects or disadvantages (whether intended or unintended) individuals, groups, or communities based on race or color.* Environmental racism combines with public policies and industry practices to provide benefits for whites while shifting costs to people of color.[29] Environmental racism is reinforced by government, legal, economic, political, and military institutions.

Environmental decision making and policies often mirror the power arrangements of the dominant society and its institutions. Environmental racism disadvantages people of color while providing advantages or privileges for whites. A form of illegal "exaction" forces people of color to pay costs of environmental benefits for the public at large. The question of who *pays* and who *benefits* from the current environmental and industrial policies is central to this analysis of environmental racism and other systems of domination and exploitation.

Racism influences the likelihood of exposure to environmental and health risks as well as accessibility to health care.[30] Many of the nation's environmental policies distribute the costs in a regressive pattern while providing disproportionate benefits for whites and individuals who fall at the upper end of the education and income scale. Numerous studies, dating back to the seventies, reveal that people of color have borne greater health and environmental risk burdens than the society at large.[31]

Elevated public health risks are found in some populations even when social class is held constant. For example, race has been found to be independent of class in the distribution of air pollution,[32] contaminated fish consumption,[33] location of municipal landfills and incinerators,[34] toxic waste dumps,[35] cleanup of superfund sites,[36] and lead poisoning in children.[37]

Lead poisoning is a classic example of an environmental health problem that disproportionately impacts children of color at every class level. Lead affects between 3 and 4 million children in the United States—most of whom are African-American and Latinos who live in urban areas. Among children 5 years old and younger, the percentage of African-American children who have excessive levels of lead in their blood far exceeds the percentage of whites at all income levels.

In 1988, the federal Agency for Toxic Substances Disease Registry (ATSDR) found that for families earning less than $6,000, 68 percent of African-American children had lead poisoning, compared with 36 percent for white children. In families with income exceeding $15,000, more than 38 percent of African-American children suffer from lead poisoning compared with 12 percent of whites. The average blood-lead level has dropped for all children with the phasing out of leaded gasoline. Today, the average blood-lead level for all children in the U.S. is under 6 ug/dl.[38] However, these efforts have not had the same positive benefits on all populations. There is still work to be done to address the remaining problem. The lead problem is not randomly distributed across the nation. The most vulnerable populations are low-income African-American and Hispanic-American children who live in older urban housing.[39]

Figures reported in the July 1994 *Journal of the American Medical Association* on the Third National Health and Nutrition Examination Survey (NHANES III) revealed that 1.7 million children (8.9 percent of children aged 1 to 5) are lead poisoned, defined as blood-lead levels equal to or above 10 ug/dl.[40] Lead-based paint (chips and dust) is the most common source of lead exposure for children. Children may also be exposed through soil and dust contamination built up from vehicle exhaust, lead concentration in soils in urban areas, lead dust brought into the home on parents' work clothes, lead used in ceramics and pottery, folk medicines, and lead in plumbing.

The Right to Breathe Clean Air

Urban air pollution problems have been with us for some time now. Before the federal government stepped in, issues related to air pollution were handled primarily by states and local government. Because states and local governments did such a poor job, the federal government set out to establish national clean air standards. Congress enacted the Clean Air Act (CAA) in 1970 and mandated the U.S. Environmental Protection Agency (EPA) to carry out this law. Subsequent amendments (1977 and 1990) were made to the CAA that form the current federal program. The CAA was a response to states' unwillingness to protect air quality. Many states used their lax enforcement of environmental laws as lures for business and economic development.[41]

Central cities and suburbs do not operate on a level playing field. They often compete for scarce resources. One need not be a rocket scientist to predict the outcome between affluent suburbs and their less affluent central city competitors.[42] Freeways are the lifeline for suburban commuters, while millions of central-city residents are dependent on public transportation as their primary mode of travel. But recent cuts in mass transit subsidies and fare hikes have reduced access to essential social services and economic activities. Nevertheless, road construction programs are booming—even in areas choked with automobiles and air pollution.[43]

The air quality impacts of transportation are especially significant to people of color who are more likely than whites to live in urban areas with reduced air quality. National Argonne Laboratory researchers discovered that 437 of the 3,109 counties and independent cities failed to meet at least one of the EPA ambient air quality standards.[44] Specifically, 57 percent of whites, 65 percent of African Americans, and 80 percent of Hispanics live in 437 counties with substandard air quality. Nationwide, 33 percent of whites, 50 percent of African Americans, and 60 percent of Hispanics live in the 136 counties in which two or more air pollutants exceed standards. Similar patterns were found for the 29 counties designated as nonattainment areas for three or more pollutants. Again, 12 percent of whites, 20 percent of African Americans, and 31 percent of Hispanics resided in the worse nonattainment areas.

Asthma is an emerging epidemic in the United States. The annual age-adjusted death rate from asthma increased by 40 percent between 1982 and 1991, from 1.34 to 1.88 per 100,000 population,[45] with the highest rates being consistently reported among blacks aged 15–24 years of age during the period 1980–1993.[46] Poverty and minority status are important risk factors for asthma mortality.

Children are at special risk from ozone.[47] Children also represent a considerable share of the asthma burden. It is the most common chronic disease of childhood. Asthma affects almost 5 million children under 18 years. Although the overall annual age-adjusted hospital discharge rate for asthma among children under 15 years old decreased slightly from 184 to 179 per 100,000 between 1982 and 1992, the decrease was slower compared to other childhood diseases,[48] resulting in a 70 percent increase in the proportion of hospital admissions related to asthma during the 1980s.[49] Inner-city children have the highest rates for asthma prevalence, hospitalization, and mortality.[50] In the United States, asthma is the fourth leading cause of disability among children aged less than 18 years.[51]

The public health community has insufficient information to explain the magnitude of some of the air pollution–related health problems. However, they do know that persons suffering from asthma are particularly sensitive to the effects of carbon monoxide, sulfur dioxide's particulate matter, ozone, and nitrogen oxides. Ground-level ozone may exacerbate health problems such as asthma, nasal congestion, throat irritation, respiratory tract inflammation, reduced resistance to infection, changes in cell function, loss of lung elasticity, chest pains, lung scarring, formation of lesions within the lungs, and premature aging of lung tissues.[52]

Nationally, African Americans and Latino Americans have significantly higher prevalence of asthma than the general population. A 1996 report from the federal Centers for Disease Control shows hospitalization and deaths rates from asthma increasing for persons twenty-five years or less.[53] The greatest increases occurred among African Americans. African Americans are two to six times more likely than whites to die from asthma.[54] Similarly, the hospitalization rate for African Americans is three to four times the rate for whites.

A 1994 CDC-sponsored study showed that pediatric emergency department visits at Atlanta Grady Memorial Hospital increased by one-third following peak ozone levels. The study also found that asthma rate among African-American children is 26 percent higher than the asthma rate among whites.[55] Since children with asthma in Atlanta may not have visited the emergency department for their care, the true prevalence of asthma in the community is likely to be higher.

Exploitation of Land, Environment, and People

Environmental decision making and local land-use planning operate at the juncture of science, economics, politics, and special interests that place communities of color at special risk.[56] This is especially true in America's Deep South. The Deep South has always been thought of as a backward land based on its social, economic, political, and environmental policies. By default, the region became a "sacrifice zone," a sump for the rest of the nation's toxic waste.[57] A colonial mentality exists in the South where local government and big business take advantage of people who are politically and economically powerless. Many of these attitudes emerged from the region's marriage to slavery and the plantation system—a brutal system that exploited humans and the land.[58] The Deep South is stuck with this unique legacy—the legacy of slavery, Jim Crow, and white resistance to equal justice for all. This legacy has also affected race relations and the region's ecology. Southerners, black and white, have less education, lower incomes, higher infant mortality, and lower life expectancy than Americans elsewhere. It should be no surprise that the environmental quality that Southerners enjoy is markedly different from that of other regions of the country.

The South is characterized by "look-the-other-way environmental policies and giveaway tax breaks."[59] It is our nation's Third World where "political bosses encourage outsiders to buy the region's human and natural resources at bargain prices."[60] Lax enforcement of environmental regulations has left the region's air, water, and land the most industry-befouled in the United States.

Toxic waste discharge and industrial pollution are correlated with poorer economic conditions. Louisiana typifies this pattern. Nearly three-fourths of Louisiana's population—more than 3 million people—get their drinking water from underground aquifers. Dozens of the aquifers are threatened by contamination from polluting industries.[61] The Lower Mississippi River Industrial Corridor has over 125 companies that manufacture a range of products including fertilizers, gasoline, paints, and plastics. This corridor has been dubbed "Cancer Alley" by environmentalists and local residents.[62] Ascension Parish typifies what many people refer to as a toxic "sacrifice zone." In two parish towns of Geismer and St. Gabriel, 18 petrochemical plants are crammed into a nine-and-a-half-square-mile area. Petrochemical plants discharge millions of pounds of pollutants annually into the water and air.

Louisiana citizens subsidize this corporate welfare with their health and the environment. Tax breaks given to polluting industries have created a few jobs at high cost. Nowhere is the polluter-welfare scenario more prevalent than in Louisiana. The state is a leader in doling out corporate welfare to polluters. A 1998 *Time Magazine* article reported that in the 1990s, Louisiana wiped off the books $3.1 billion in property taxes to polluting companies.[63] The state's top five worse polluters received $111 million dollars over the past decade.

Global Dumping Grounds

There is a direct correlation between exploitation of land and exploitation of people. It should not be a surprise to anyone to discover that Native Americans have to contend with some of the worst pollution in the United States.[64] Native American nations have become prime targets for waste trading.[65] More than three dozen Indian reservations have been targeted for landfills, incinerators, and other waste facilities.[66] The vast majority of these waste proposals were defeated by grassroots groups on the reservations. However, "radioactive colonialism" is alive and well.[67] The legacy of institutional racism has left many sovereign Indian nations without an economic infrastructure to address poverty, unemployment, inadequate education and health care, and a host of other social problems. In 1999, Eastern Navajo reservation residents filed suit against the Nuclear Regulatory Commission to block uranium mining in Church Rock and Crown Point communities.

Hazardous waste generation and international movement of hazardous waste pose some important health, environmental, legal, and ethical dilemmas. It is unlikely that many of the global hazardous waste proposals can be effectuated without first addressing the social, economic, and political context in which hazardous wastes are produced (industrial processes), controlled (regulations, notification and consent documentation), and managed (minimization, treatment, storage, recycling, transboundary shipment, pollution prevention, etc.). The "unwritten" policy of targeting Third-World nations for waste trade received international

media attention in 1991. Lawrence Summers, at the time he was chief economist of the World Bank, shocked the world and touched off an international scandal when his confidential memorandum on waste trade was leaked. Summers writes: "'Dirty' Industries: Just between you and me, shouldn't the World Bank be encouraging MORE migration of the dirty industries to the LDCs?"[68]

Consumption and production patterns, especially in nations with wasteful "throw-away" life styles as the United States, and the interests of transnational corporations create and maintain unequal and unjust waste burdens within and between affluent and poor communities, states, and regions of the world. Shipping hazardous wastes from rich communities to poor communities is not a solution to the growing global waste problem. Not only is it immoral, but it should be illegal. Moreover, making hazardous waste transactions legal does not address the ethical issues imbedded in such transactions.[69] The practice is a manifestation of power arrangements and a larger stratification system where some people and some places are assigned greater value than others.

In the real world, all people, communities, and nations are not created equal. Some populations and interests are more equal than others. Unequal interests and power arrangements have allowed poisons of the rich to be offered as short-term remedies for poverty of the poor. This scenario plays out domestically (as in the United States where low-income and people-of-color communities are disproportionately impacted by waste facilities and "dirty" industries) and internationally (where hazardous wastes from OECD states flow to non-OECD states).

The conditions surrounding the more than 1,900 maquiladoras, assembly plants operated by American, Japanese, and other foreign countries, located along the 2,000-mile U.S.-Mexico border may further exacerbate the waste trade.[70] The industrial plants use cheap Mexican labor to assemble imported components and raw material and then ship finished products back to the United States. Nearly a half million Mexican workers are employed in the maquiladoras.

A 1983 agreement between the United States and Mexico required American companies in Mexico to return waste products to the United States. Plants were required to notify the federal EPA when returning wastes. Results from a 1986 survey of 20 of the plants informed the U.S. EPA that they were returning waste to the United States, even though 86 percent of the plants used toxic chemicals in their manufacturing process. Much of the waste ends up being illegally dumped in sewers, ditches, and the desert. All along the Lower Rio Grande River Valley maquiladoras dump their toxic wastes into the river, from which 95 percent of the region's residents get their drinking water.[71]

The disregard for the environment and public safety has placed border residents' health at risk. In the border cities of Brownsville, Texas, and Matamoras, Mexico, the rate of anecephaly—babies born without brains—is four times the national average. Affected families have filed lawsuits against 88 of the area's 100 maquiladoras for exposing the community to xylene, a cleaning solvent that can cause brain hemorrhages, and lung and kidney damage.

Contaminated well and drinking water looms as a major health threat. Air pollution has contributed to a raging asthma and respiratory epidemic. The Mexican environmental regulatory agency is understaffed and "ill-equipped to adequately enforce its environmental laws."[72] Only time will tell if the North American Free Trade Agreement (NAFTA) will "fix" or exacerbate the public health, economic, and environmental problems along the U.S.-Mexico border.

Setting the Record Straight

The environmental protection apparatus is broken and needs to be fixed. The environmental justice movement has set out clear goals of eliminating unequal enforcement of environmental, civil rights, and public health laws. Environmental justice leaders have made a difference in the lives of people and the physical environment. They have assisted public decision makers in identifying "at-risk" populations, toxic "hot spots," research gaps, and action models to correct existing imbalances and prevent future threats. However, impacted communities are not waiting for the government or industry to get their acts together. Grassroots groups have taken the offensive to ensure that government and industry do the right thing.

Communities have begun to organize their own networks and force their inclusion into the mainstream of public decision making. They have also developed communication channels among environmental justice leaders, grassroots groups, professional associations (i.e., legal, public health, education, etc.), scientific groups, and public policy makers to assist them in identifying "at-risk" populations, toxic "hot spots," and research gaps, and work to correct imbalances.

In response to growing public concern and mounting scientific evidence, President Clinton signed Executive Order 12898. The Executive Order is not a new law. It only reinforces what has been the law of the land for over three decades. Environmental justice advocates are calling for vigorous enforcement of civil rights laws and environmental laws.

The number of environmental justice complaints is expected to escalate against industry, government, and institutions that receive funds. Citizens have a right to challenge discrimination—including environmental discrimination. It is a smokescreen for anyone to link Title VI or other civil rights enforcement to economic disinvestment in low-income and people-of-color communities. There is absolutely no empirical evidence to support the contention that environmental justice hurts **brownfields** redevelopment efforts.

The **EPA** has awarded over 200 Brownfields grants. In 1998, the agency had received some five dozen Title VI complaints. It is worth noting that not a single Title VI complaint involves a Brownfields site. On the other hand, two decades of solid empirical evidence documents the impact of racial redlining by banks, savings and loans, insurance companies, grocery chains, and even pizza delivery companies in thwarting economic vitality in black communities—not enforcement of civil rights laws. Racial redlining was such a real problem that Congress passed the Community Reinvestment Act in 1977.

States have had three decades to implement Title VI of the Civil Rights Act of 1964. Most states have chosen to ignore the law. States need to do a better job assuring nondiscrimination in the application and the implementation of permitting decisions, enforcement, and investment decisions. Environmental justice also means sharing in the benefits. Governments must live up to their mandate of protecting all people and the environment. Anything less is unacceptable. The solution to environmental injustice lies in the realm of equal protection of all individuals, groups, and communities. No community, rich or poor,

---

brownfield An industrial or commercial site that is idle or underused because of real or perceived environmental pollution.
EPA U.S. Environmental Protection Agency. The EPA's Brownfields Program provides direct funding for brownfields assessment, cleanup, revolving loans, and environmental job training.

urban or suburban, black or white, should be allowed to become a "sacrifice zone" or the dumping ground.

Hazardous wastes and "dirty" industries have followed the "path of least resistance." Poor people and poor communities are given a false choice of "no jobs and no development" versus "risky low-paying jobs and pollution." Industries and governments (including the military) have often exploited the economic vulnerability of poor communities, poor states, poor regions, and poor nations for their "risky" operations.

24 Race, Religion, and the Color Line (Or Is That the Color Wall?)
Michael O. Emerson

MICHAEL O. EMERSON is the Allyn and Gladys Cline Professor of Sociology and the Funding Director of the Center on Race, Religion, and Urban Life at Rice University. He has authored many papers and several books on the relationships between race and religion, as well as on neighborhood segregation and immigration issues.

Questions to Consider Michael O. Emerson points out that among the most segregated institutions in the United States are our houses of worship. How much racial separation is there in American religion? Why? Does this racial separation matter, and if so, how? What do we know about multiracial congregations? Why are these racially integrated congregations of interest for understanding race in the United States?

A COUPLE OF YEARS AGO, BISHOP FRED Caldwell, pastor of Shreveport, Louisiana's Greenwood Acres Full Gospel Baptist Church, a large African American congregation, offered a unique proposal. He was offering to *pay* nonblacks to attend his church. So adamant that his church should not be segregated, Bishop Caldwell said that for at least one month he would pay nonblacks five dollars per hour to attend the multiple-hour Sunday morning service, and ten dollars an hour to attend the church's Thursday night service. And he would pay this money out of his own pocket. Bishop Caldwell told the Associated Press, "This idea is born of God. God wants a rainbow in his church." He said the inspiration came to him during a sermon. "The most segregated hour in America is Sunday morning at 11 o'clock. The Lord is tired of it, and I'm certainly tired of it. This is not right."[1]

This story was first reported in the local Shreveport, Louisiana, newspaper, but was soon picked up by papers across the country. The day the story appeared in *USA Today,* ten people sent me online links to the article, often with an e-mail subject heading like "You've got to see this!" The story was soon the talk on radio airwaves and television outlets. Internet chat rooms were talking about it, and people were debating it at the proverbial water cooler.

Pay people to attend worship services? To many, paying people to worship seemed outrageous. Others thought the idea was brilliant, highlighting the racial segregation in houses of worship across the nation. Still others thought the bishop should not focus on the race of those who attended his church, but merely minister to whoever attended. They found his "religious affirmative action" deeply troubling. Discussion spread beyond this simple offer to pay people to attend one church, and turned to whether the racial makeup of congregations matters.

Shortly after this story hit the national news, I was a guest on a two-hour radio call-in show in Baltimore. The show's hosts opened by discussing Bishop Caldwell's offer to pay nonblacks to come to his church, and featured the more general topic of congregational segregation. The issue touched a hot button among the listeners. The hosts kept commenting that their lines were lit up, jammed full. I could hear and feel that the callers were passionate about this topic.

When the first "post-pay-to-attend-offer" Sunday service was held, reporters were eager to see the results. The headlines told the story: "Few take pastor up on offer," said one headline. A year later, a small bit of change had happened. According to a report in one magazine, a year after the offer, about two dozen whites were attending this congregation of thousands, and five whites had become members.[2]

How Segregated Are Religious Congregations?

For a long time, when people studied race relations and inequality, they did not think of religion. But when well over 100 million Americans are attending religious congregations each week, and when 90 percent of Americans say they have a religious faith and believe in a higher being, it seems like a gross oversight not to consider the role of religion. It seems even more of a mistake given that the early giants in the field, such as W. E. B. DuBois, thought it so important that they actually wrote books about it. And like Bishop Caldwell, Martin Luther King, probably the best known advocate for racial equality, called religion the most segregated institution in the nation.

I wanted to piggyback on these giants, so I have spent a number of years researching the relationship between religion and race, and I am delighted to share some of what has been learned with you. One of my first questions was: How segregated are religious congregations? This question did not have an answer other than "very." So my colleagues and I set out to find a more precise answer.

To do so, we decided to study the segregation in two ways. First, we defined homogeneous congregations (80 percent or more of a congregation is of the same race) and mixed race congregations (no one racial group is 80 percent or more of the congregation). We used this cutoff of 80 percent because research done on other

organizations—such as businesses—has found that until another group or groups make up 20 percent or more of an organization, they lack the critical mass to make any significant changes in the organization.

Armed with this definition, we used data collected from a national random sample of congregations. We found that *more than 90 percent* of congregations are racially homogeneous (Figure 1). You have to look hard to find a racially mixed congregation in the United States.

But where you look is important. As Figure 2 shows, the faith tradition matters. Because of the sample size, unfortunately I had to combine all non-Christian congregations—such as Buddhist temples, Muslim mosques, and Jewish synagogues—into one category. When I do that, more than a quarter of all non-Christian congregations are racially mixed. Among Catholic congregations, 15 percent of them are mixed, and among Protestants, just 5 percent are mixed. Why this variation? We found that the larger the religious tradition—the number of people involved in that faith and the number of congregations to chose from—the more segregated it is. To put it most bluntly, the more choices people have of where to worship, the more they choose to be with people who are racially similar to themselves.

We have a more sophisticated way to study the level of congregational segregation. Instead of just studying whether a congregation is or is not racially mixed, we can ask how diverse congregations are by asking: *What is the probability that any two randomly selected people in the congregation will be of different races?* In other words, if you were to walk into a congregation, write the name of each person in attendance on a little slip of paper, put those slips of paper into your hat, mix them up, and then, with your eyes closed, draw out two names, how often would those two people be of different socially defined racial groups? Fifty percent of the time, perhaps, or maybe 30 percent of the time?

Rather than using a hat and slips of paper, we did this process with a statistical formula and a computer. We found that that the average (median) diversity of a congregation in the United States is *just .02*. That means that the probability that any two randomly selected people in a congregation will be of a different races is only 2 percent.

To put that number in context, we did the same calculations for the nation's neighborhoods and schools, both of which are highly segregated, and found that religious

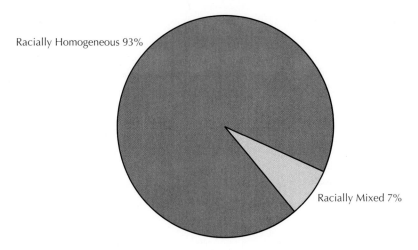

FIGURE 1 **Racial Composition of U.S. Congregations.**
Source: National Congregations Study.

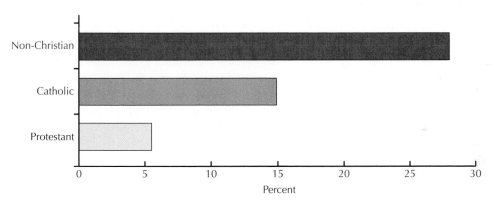

FIGURE 2 **Percentage of Congregations That Are Racially Mixed, by Faith Tradition.**
Source: National Congregations Study.

congregations are *10 times less diverse* than the neighborhoods in which they reside, and *20 times less diverse* than the nation's public schools. When Martin Luther King said that religious congregations are the most segregated institution in the United States, he wasn't kidding. Forget the color line. When it comes to religion in the United States, we have a color wall. Just as China has its great wall, so too does the United States.[3]

So What If Religious Congregations Are Segregated?

Having found out more precisely how segregated religious congregations are, I wondered if it made any difference for race relations and inequality. It does, dramatically so.

Religion has much potential for mitigating racial division and inequality. Most religions teach love, respect, and equality of all peoples. They usually teach of the errors inherent in racial prejudice and discrimination. They often proclaim the need to embrace all people. They speak of the need for fairness and justice. They often teach that selfishness and acting in self-interested ways are counter to the will of the divine.

In the United States, religious faith motivated the fight against slavery. It played an essential role in the Civil Rights movement. It currently is motivating many believers to attempt to reduce the racial divide and injustice. It directs people to value openness and diversity. It guides some to vote in ways that will overcome racial inequality. It motivates others to volunteer in groups working against racial hate and discrimination. For still others, it motivates them to form organizations intent on reducing inequality and strengthening justice. Others are motivated to donate money to such organizations.

Stories of positive actions of religious people and organizations to combat racial division and inequality abound. But in this section, focusing on the structural arrangement of racially segregated religious congregations, I demonstrate the powerful countervailing influences of religion on racialization.

To reflect on this issue properly, let's keep in mind the distinction between macro and micro effects. Part of the irony of religion's role is that in strengthening micro bonds between individuals, religion contributes to within-group sameness, heightens isolation from different groups, and reduces the opportunity to form macro bonds—that is, bonds between groups that serve to integrate a society. The lack of social ties between religious groups across race inhibits movement between them, increasing the importance of group boundaries and social differences. This means that racially segregated congregations lower the probability of intergroup mobility (such as through intermarriage) and heighten the importance of racial boundaries, separate racial identities, and other differences between groups. So though many in the religious community call and work for an end to racial division, the organization of religion into segregated congregations often undercuts their efforts.

The separate groups that are reproduced through religious division result in categorization, for separate groups must be categorized by something—in this case, by race and often by religious and other views. According to

scholars Hamilton and Trolier, categorization has important implications:

> The social categories we develop are more than convenient groupings of individuals that simplify the actual diversities among the people we observe and encounter. They are also categories that can bias the way we process information, organize and store it in memory, and make judgments about members of those social categories.[4]

We all consistently engage in social comparison (Am I smart? Who is good-looking? Who has money?), and research links categorization to at least seven biases:

1. Our brains exaggerate the similarities of ingroup members and their differences from outgroup members.

2. Because people know the outgroup by its perceived differences, outgroup members are identified by these differences, overly homogenizing them.

3. Ingroup favoritism: Even when performing exactly the same actions, ingroup members are evaluated more positively and outgroup members more negatively.

4. We attribute positive behavior of ingroup members to internal traits such as intelligence, and negative behavior to external causes such as a poor home life. We do the exact opposite for outgroup members.

5. Cognitive psychologists find that we have better memories for negative outgroup behaviors than for negative ingroup behaviors.

6. Because our brains tend to overly homogenize outgroups, a negative behavior of an outgroup member is likely to be perceived as characteristic of the entire outgroup. We appear to make the leap from James of Group X shoplifted to people of Group X shoplift.

7. Once people have preconceived stereotypes of an outgroup, they tend to recall only information that confirms their stereotypes, while contradictory evidence is dismissed as an exception. A relative of mine, for example, knew for sure that African Americans were lazy, shiftless, and liars, even though one my relative's closest friends was African American. My relative's explanation? Her friend was not like other African Americans; she was the exception.[5]

Religion contributes to racial division and inequality, then, in that it increases racial categorization, which is a by-product of congregational segregation.

Given human limitations, racially exclusive identities and congregations necessitate another bias. We can call this the ethical paradox of group loyalty. The paradox is that even if made up of loving, unselfish individuals, the group transmutes individual unselfishness into group selfishness.

What does that mean in English? Imagine two groups. Each member of each group is a deeply committed religious person, full of love and concern for others, and has even developed a friendship or two with people of other groups. For historical reasons, one group has more social goods—income, wealth, education, power—than the other group. Despite being made up entirely of unselfish individuals, the two groups will continue to be divided and unequal. How can this be?

Reinhold Niebuhr explored this question way back in 1932 in his book *Moral Man and Immoral Society.*[6] For one thing, he wrote, direct contact with members of other groups is limited, always less than with members of one's own group. People thus know the members of their own group and their needs more deeply, fully, and personally than the members and needs of other groups. Therefore, they attend to the needs of their own group first, precisely because they are moral and loving. How can they turn their backs on the needs of their own group in favor of another group? At the individual level, selfishness is usually considered negative, but at the group level, it is considered moral and just. Indeed, at the group level, it is not selfishness, but morality, service, sacrifice, and loyalty.

We find evidence of this every day. Consider the family. Although we are selfish if we always look out for our individual needs first, it is considered wrong and immoral if we do not consider the needs of our family first, ahead of other families. Your parents would be considered immoral if they did not help pay for their own children's college first. Only if they had extra money (at college prices today, that would be rare!) would they even consider helping other children, but even then, there would be so many other family needs to be met.

So, the approximately 350,000 congregations in the United States, are busy creating group identity and forming

moral persons. Those moral persons, acting morally, are aware of and help their families and the members of their own congregations first, making sure those needs are met before looking to help elsewhere. Because of segregation, this means we help people of our own race—whites helping whites, African Americans helping African Americans, Asians helping Asians, Latinos helping Latinos, and so on.

The problem with this pattern is that the inequality between groups is maintained. Members of groups with the most share it with others of their group. Members of groups with the least are busy trying to meet the needs of others in their group, which because the group has less, are typically bigger needs, trying to be met with less. It is a nasty cycle, even though the people involved are themselves not acting nasty.

We also have another problem, according to Niebuhr. Because the members of a group cannot understand and feel the needs of another group as completely and deeply as those of their own group, reliance on love, compassion, and persuasion to overcome group divisions and inequalities is practically impossible. For this reason, relations between groups are always mainly political rather than ethical or moral (wow, reflect on this statement—it's a doozy). As Niebuhr says, "They will always be determined by the proportion of power which each group possesses at least as much as by any rational and moral appraisal of the comparative needs and claims of each group."[7]

The facts just considered have considerable implications for the perpetuation of racial inequality and stratification. The logic is straightforward: (1) In the United States there is racial inequality in access to valued resources. (2) Access to valued resources—such as jobs, prestige, wealth, and power—is gained in significant part through social ties.[8] (3) For reasons such as social categorization, comparison, and the paradox of ingroup loyalty, people have positive bias for their ingroup and negative bias for outgroups. These three facts suggest that, other factors being equal, any social structure or process that both increases the saliency of group boundaries and reduces interracial ties necessarily reproduces racial inequality. Because the organization of religion in the United States heightens the salience of racial boundaries and reduces interracial ties, it necessarily reproduces racial inequality.[9]

Can We Find a Solution?

So is that it? Must we then conclude that religion really can only entrench and amplify the racial divisions and inequalities that already exist? For the millions of religious people, that would be a pretty disappointing conclusion. But that is not it. If you give it some thought, how could religion change to actually move toward reducing racial division and inequality?

If the whole edifice of evidence against positive effects of religion is built upon the foundation of segregated congregations, what if congregations were not segregated? Could positive changes for racial division and inequality result?

My colleagues and I spent a number of years trying to figure this out. We did so by studying multiracial congregations (those 7 percent of congregations from Figure 1) and, for comparative purposes, racially homogeneous congregations. We conducted telephone interviews, mail surveys, and face-to-face interviews, and we spent lots of time in congregations across the country. I even spent nearly six years in one congregation as it transformed from an all-white congregation to one that no longer had a majority racial group and had people from well over forty nations in attendance.

Social Ties

The first difference we noticed in studying these congregations was the extensive amount of friendships across race that people in these racially mixed congregations had. As an African American woman from Chicago who was a member of a multiracial congregation called Crosstown told us:

> I grew up in a predominantly black church and neighborhood. Crosstown has taught me about other races of people. [The diversity at Crosstown] helped me to develop relationships with people outside my race where I felt they were my friend and we share Christ in our life and that they have the same struggles as I do. . . . I've gotten to know other people on that more personal level.

To test whether this is true more systematically, we conducted a national survey and asked people several questions about the racial composition of their friends and acquaintances. We classified Americans into three groups: those attending racially homogeneous congregations, those attending racially mixed congregations, and those not attending any congregation. One of the questions we asked them was to think of their circle of friends, those people they like to spend time with and keep in regular contact (whether friends from their congregation, neighborhood, work, childhood, etc.). Were all, most, about half, some, or none of their circle of friends the same race as them?

What did we find? Of those attending racially homogeneous congregations, 83 percent said that most or all of their friends were the same race as them. Among those not attending any congregation, 70 percent said most or all of their friends were the same race as them. Here we see a general pattern I often find in my studies. Religion typically serves to intensify general patterns in the larger society. If society is segregated, religion can intensify that segregation through a variety of ways, but most certainly by providing yet another plane of segregation—its congregations.

What is the case, though, for people attending racially mixed congregations? We found a dramatic difference not only from people attending racially homogeneous congregations, but from people not attending congregations. Whereas 83 percent and 70 percent of those two groupings said most or all of their friends were the same race as them, only 36 percent of people attending racially mixed congregation said most or all of their friends were the same race as them. And we found that those 36 percent who did say most of their friends were the same race as them were relatively recent arrivals to their racially mixed congregation.

We found this same pattern for every question we asked about relationships with other people. People not attending congregations are more likely to be interracially married, have best friends who are of a different race, and have more diverse social networks than are those who attend racially homogeneous congregations. But both groups' level of racial diversity in relationships greatly pales compared to that of people in racially mixed congregations.

In terms of creating holes in the color wall, racially mixed congregations seem a promising avenue. But we cannot get ahead of ourselves. For all we know at this point, the folks attending these types of congregations formed their friendships before they started attending their mixed congregation. In fact, perhaps they ended up in such congregations precisely because they had racially diverse friendships to begin with.

So my colleagues and I again set out to find the answer. We went around the country and interviewed about two hundred people attending racially mixed congregations and, for comparison, people attending racially homogeneous congregations. We found two answers. People who attend racially mixed congregations are somewhat more likely to have at some time in their lives attended a racially mixed school or lived in a racially mixed neighborhood. But more than 80 percent of the people in racially mixed congregations said that most of the racial diversity in their friendships came *because of* their involvement in their racially mixed congregation. Indeed, when we did a fancy statistical analysis called logistic regression, we found that by far the most important factor in people's having racially diverse relationships is whether they attend a racially mixed congregation. Representative of this finding, a Salvadorian immigrant living in Los Angeles and attending a racially mixed congregation said that that perhaps 10 percent of the people she new before she started attending her church were of different races, but now, "since I have been at this church the majority of my friends are of different races."

This pattern happens for a couple of reasons. First, of course, people make friends with others in their racially mixed congregation. But the diversity effect of these types of congregations goes even further. After making interracial friends in their congregation, people were often introduced to others in their new friends' networks. For example, Chanel, an African American who attends a racially mixed congregation in the South, met Rosita, a Latina who attends the same congregation, through a women's group at the congregation. They soon became friends. Over time, Rosita would invite Chanel over to her place, for birthday parties or other gatherings, where Chanel would meet and get to know an extended network of other Hispanics. And vice versa. Chanel would invite Rosita to her place for family gatherings, were Rosita met and became friends with an extended network of other African Americans. Their children too became fast friends, and so they often got together so their children could play. And we found that this sort of pattern made people more confident and comfortable getting to know still others of different racial groups. As one man from the Northeast who attends a racially mixed congregation said: "Being in this church has really opened me up to people of all different backgrounds. Now when I meet people of different races at work, I don't just say hello and move on. I am comfortable to get to know them. I've made new friends at work this way."

Attitudes

At a celebration service culminating a weekend of youth events at a Baptist church in the Deep South, families and friends of the youths who had attended were invited for the service. Chase, white, 16 years of age, and due to an accident, in a wheelchair for life, was in attendance that weekend. Not attending any congregation prior to this event, he was invited to this youth weekend by a white classmate who did belong to the church. That Sunday, moved by what he had experienced over the past few days of the youth event, he shared with the congregation that he had found a purpose in this congregation—he had made friends with youth of many different races, and who didn't seem to care at all that he was in a wheelchair. Having talked it over with his parents the day before, he announced, through tears, that he had found a home and that he wanted to become a member of the congregation.

Also in attendance that day were his parents and his brother, Tre. Tre was a longtime devout skinhead. His head shaved nearly clean, he had swastika tattoos all around his upper arms. He had a skinhead symbol tattooed on his chest. And he had a noose tattooed on the full length of this left thigh. He didn't at all like nonwhites: "they're whiners, they steal jobs that belong to us, they're lazy, steal, and they have the government always givin' 'em stuff." He was particularly upset at this church he had come to in support of his brother, Chase. The senior pastor was African American, the associate pastor Hispanic. The entire congregation, in fact, was, in his view, a sickening mix of the different races—black, Hispanic, Asian, and worst of all, whites. What are whites doing here with these people? he thought. He felt ill at the sight. Why hadn't his brother told him who was at this church? And now there was his brother, up front, saying he wanted to become part of this God-forsaken place, even with the support of his parents. Unbelievable! he thought. He was angry, feeling claustrophobic. He just wanted out of this place. But as he described it to me, something happened, something broke inside of him.

> Seein' the people all come up to hug my brother, seein' his happy face, seein' all these different people singin' together, feelin' the power in that, it was somethin'

I ain't never seen or felt before. Not sure how to describe it, just that it felt real, like it was the way things was supposed to be. I felt like some real bad stuff broke inside of me that day. These people weren't all bad people. They were carin' for my brother.

Two weeks later, through tears of his own, Tre joined the church as well, and asked if the African American pastor would come with him later that week to get his white supremacy tattoos removed.

Few stories of change in racial attitudes are as dramatic as this one. But we found a strong pattern of change in the direction of more positive racial attitudes of people that attend these mixed congregations. We found change in all racial groups, but especially among whites. They were the ones who most often had significant changes in their views, and they are the ones who differ the most from their white peers not in mixed race congregations. These changes in attitudes seemed to come about as a result of the newly formed friendships, through preaching and teaching, and through observing those of different races involved in common tasks.

We found these differences across religious traditions. At a multiracial mosque in the Midwest, they had a serious problem. The mosque had people from nations who thought you must *always* remove your shoes when entering the mosque, and people from others nations who thought you must *never* insult Allah by removing your shoes when entering the mosque. Pretty easy to see we've got a problem here. Folks take the shoe issue very seriously, because it is tied to their religion and the proper way to worship. And because the shoe issue was related to nationality, ethnicity, and race, the problem quickly became destructive. People took such offense at the other groups that the mosque leaders decided to put up a screen to divide the shoe removers from the shoe wearers, even though this also divided people by ethnicity and race. But they did not intend to keep it there permanently. After they put it up, the imam began to teach that Allah calls all Muslims to be together, across race, ethnicity, and worship approach. They therefore must find a way to do so in their mosque. Either they would all have to remove their shoes or all wear their shoes, or, the solution he proposed, they would have to accept that whichever people do, they do it out of reverence for Allah, not as a reflection of an inferior ethnicity or culture. Reverence for Allah is what must unite them. Over time, the worshippers came to accept this view, and the screen was eventually

removed, even though some continued to remove their shoes, and some continued to wear their shoes. Friendships across cultures formed, and attitudes about the different groups became more favorable.

Raised Status

This leads to yet another difference we found in these mixed congregations. The congregation I spent years studying made a commitment to go on mission and service trips to each of the nations that members of the congregation were from. When they went on these trips, the appointed leaders were always the people from that country. As the senior pastor of the congregation told me, this worked wonders on the views of his congregants. A Guatemalan cleaning lady who can barely speak English is easy to marginalize in the U.S. context, but when she was the leader on the trip to Guatemala, when she became the person who was fluent in the language, who knew the lay of the land, who had the social connections, who knew what to eat and what to avoid, she came to be seen, this pastor and his congregants told me, in a substantially new light. She was important, she had skills they did not have, and they were dependent upon her. Through evening discussions while on these trips, the congregants came to conclude that social context, not a person's essence, shapes views of their worth and skills. Multiracial congregations, we found, often raise the status of racially different others in the eyes of their members.

As you will recall, segregated congregations contribute to socioeconomic inequality. But we found a different pattern in many mixed race congregations. Because of the social ties between people and changed attitudes, the average education, income, and occupational status of people in these congregations—especially for marginalized groups—were higher than their counterparts not in such congregations. Again, was this the case before or after they came to the congregation? We found that a great deal happened in these congregations that led to increased socioeconomic status after they arrived. Connections were made, child care was provided, and funding was often found that allowed for further schooling. People were hired into jobs that they otherwise might never have known about or had a chance at, because of their connections to others in the congregation well placed in the labor market. It also seems that such congregations help people accrue resources that can gain them access to better heath care, neighborhoods, schools, and other social goods. Mixed race congregations, then, seem to actually reduce the racial divide in inequality.

Bridge Organizations and Sixth Americans

Mixed race congregations are what I call bridge organizations; that is, they gather and facilitate cross-race social ties, creating a "natural" setting where people of different racial groups meet and form relationships, pursuing a common purpose (if you have ever studied contact theory, these types of congregations meet well the conditions necessary for forming friendships and reducing prejudice). So different is the average person in a mixed race congregation compared to the average American outside of these congregations that I call them Sixth Americans. The United States, writes David Hollinger, is really five melting pots;[10] that is, people come from hundreds if not thousands of ethnic backgrounds, but in the United States, they are expected to meld into one of five racial groupings: Indian/Native American, African American/Black, White/Caucasian, Hispanic/Latino/a, or Asian/Asian American.

But people in mixed race congregations, although phenotypically often part of one of these five melting pots, seem to operate outside of their melting pot in most aspects of their social relations. Sixth Americans live in multiple melting pots simultaneously. Minorities among Americans to be sure, Sixth Americans live in a world of primary relationships and associations that are racially diverse. Like other Americans, the Sixth American may work in a racially diverse setting, see racially different others at the grocery store, or perhaps have a friend of a different race. But unlike other Americans, the Sixth American's "world of racial diversity" does not stop here. It is not a racially homogenous world with some diversity sprinkled in; the Sixth American's world is a racially diverse world with some homogeneity sprinkled in. In my book, *People of the Dream,* I argue that these Sixth Americans are a different kind of American. And their congregations, where they gather together to worship, serve, and support one another, despite the failures along the way (which I detail in Chapter 6 of the book), may be harbingers of what is to come.[11]

Conclusion

Religion in the United States is divided by a vast, thick, massive color wall. That color wall has had and has severe implications for racial division and racial stratification. We have ignored the impact of religion on race for too long. Through studying not segregated congregations, but the small percentage of congregations that are racially mixed, I found that despite risks, the overall trends work to reduce racial division and inequality. These findings serve to further amplify the deleterious effects that segregated congregations have on American race relations.

Changing the organization of American religion is not the sole answer to destructive race relations, but it is part of the answer. To that end, several scholars are now pursuing studies of how multiracial congregations form, how to minimize costs and accentuate positives, and how people come to be in these congregations. If you are interested, we invite you to read further by searching out books and other articles on this topic. Humans create their social structures, so change is possible when humans decide their current social structures will no longer do. Will enough decide to make a change, and put enough holes in the color wall to eventually collapse it? Time will tell.

25 Why Are There No Supermarkets in My Neighborhood? The Long Search for Fresh Fruit, Produce, and Healthy Food

Shannon N. Zenk (et al.)

SHANNON N. ZENK is assistant professor in the department of public health, mental health, and administrative nursing at the University of Illinois at Chicago.

Questions to Consider

In a typical middle- to upper-middle-class white suburban neighborhood it is not uncommon to find two, three, or even four supermarkets within a mile or two of one another. Because of their close proximity these stores engage in cutthroat competition. The result is a cheap abundance of fresh fruits, vegetables, and a staggering array of healthy foods. Now think about a poor neighborhood in an inner city. Corner stores, not supermarkets, are the source for grocery shopping. How, according to Professor Zenk and associates, is race and class implicated in having access to large supermarkets? What are the health consequences of having to purchase groceries from corner stores or bodegas rather than a huge supermarket?

FOUR OF THE 10 LEADING CAUSES OF DEATH in the United States are chronic diseases for which diet is a major risk factor.[1] Racial disparities in the burden of these chronic, diet-related diseases are well documented, with African Americans often having the highest morbidity and mortality.[2–5] Because health risks and resources are spatially and socially structured and African Americans disproportionately live in economically disadvantaged neighborhoods, increased attention has been focused on how residential environments shape health and contribute to racial disparities in health.[6–9] An extensive body of literature now associates residence in economically disadvantaged neighborhoods, after control for individual socioeconomic status, with a variety of adverse diet-related health outcomes.[10–12]

Despite numerous research efforts that have examined neighborhood variations in health, relatively little is known about the mechanisms by which neighborhood environments affect health.[13–15] One hypothesis is that economically and socially disadvantaged neighborhoods have inadequate access to healthy foods, thus negatively affecting dietary quality and health. Although the presence of supermarkets may not always be beneficial for neighborhood residents (e.g., if supermarkets displace smaller stores with owners who had positively contributed to and invested in the neighborhood), such large stores can be neighborhood health resources providing generally better availability and selection, higher quality, and lower cost of foods compared with smaller food stores.[16] These food resource factors influence dietary patterns.[17–24] Previous studies have found that fewer supermarkets are located in African American neighborhoods compared with White neighborhoods[25,26] and are located in economically disadvantaged neighborhoods compared with affluent neighborhoods.[16,26–29] Other studies have found no differences in the accessibility of supermarkets according to racial or socioeconomic characteristics of neighborhoods.[30–32] This discrepancy could reflect either differences in the definition of supermarkets or true variability in results across time and place that may be caused by differences in the degree of racial or economic segregation. Lower purchasing power is an often-cited but disputed explanation for the relative scarcity of supermarkets in economically disadvantaged neighborhoods.[33–35]

Analysis of the role of race without regard to poverty and of poverty without regard to race offers an incomplete picture of the potential importance of these factors in shaping the spatial accessibility of supermarkets. Understanding these relationships is critical for informing intervention and policy efforts. Such an understanding is particularly important, given the roles of racial residential segregation and economic restructuring in concentrating poverty in African American neighborhoods of older industrial cities of the Northeast and Upper Midwest.[36–40] Therefore, we sought to determine whether supermarkets are located at farther distances from the center of African American neighborhoods compared with White neighborhoods regardless of neighborhood economic conditions or if racial disparities in supermarket accessibility occur only in higher poverty contexts.

Methods

Setting and Sample

The setting for this study was the Detroit metropolitan area in Michigan. Metropolitan Detroit is characterized by extreme economic inequalities across neighborhoods.[36] Economic inequalities can be traced to the period just after World War II, when highway construction and cheap land outside the city led many industries to relocate to the suburbs.[39,41–43] Between 1950 and 1990, the city of Detroit lost approximately 350, 000 jobs,[41,43,44] largely owing to the relocation of industries to the suburbs, deindustrialization, and other facets of economic restructuring. At the same time, discriminatory federal housing policies and lending practices, racial steering (the act of real estate agents systematically showing African Americans to different neighborhoods than Whites), restrictive covenants, and violence created and reinforced racial residential segregation in metropolitan Detroit. In effect, African Americans were confined to the least desirable, older residential neighborhoods of the city, whereas Whites were able to move to more desirable, newer suburban locations.[35,37,41,44–47] The city of Detroit shifted from 16.2% African American in 1950 to 81.2% African American in 2000,[43,48] a sharp contrast with the 84.8% of metropolitan Detroit residents outside the city limits who identified as non-Hispanic White in 2000.[48] Metropolitan Detroit remains one of the most racially segregated areas in the United States—ranked second overall in residential segregation of African

Americans in 2000.[49] The sample for this study was 869 neighborhoods (we used census tracts as proxies) in the tricounty Detroit metropolitan area. These neighborhoods are located in the city of Detroit and in the tricounty Detroit metropolitan area (Wayne, Oakland, Macomb counties) within a 10-mile buffer of Detroit.

Measures

We used 2000 decennial census data to characterize the neighborhoods. Population density was computed as the total population per square mile (median = 5367.44). Racial composition was defined as the percentage of non-Hispanic African American residents (median = 6.06%). Neighborhood poverty was defined as the percentage of residents below the poverty line (median = 8.21%). . . . Given that 92% of residents in tricounty metropolitan Detroit were either non-Hispanic White (67.3%) or non-Hispanic African American (24.9%), neighborhoods with low proportions of African Americans generally correspond with predominately White neighborhoods.

Supermarkets were defined as supercenters (e.g., Meijer, Super Kmart) and full-line grocery stores (e.g., Farmer Jack, Kroger) associated with a national or regional grocery chain, i.e., a chain with 11 or more retail stores.[50] To identify supermarkets, we obtained a 2001 list of grocery stores from the Michigan Department of Agriculture. We used 2001–2002 paper telephone directories, as well as online telephone directories and company Web sites, in the fall of 2002 to verify the addresses of these supermarkets and to identify additional supermarkets. We con-firmed the address of any supermarket not on the Michigan Department of Agriculture list by telephoning the store. One hundred and sixty supermarkets were identified in Detroit and in the metropolitan area within a 15-mile buffer of Detroit. . . . The additional 5-mile buffer of supermarkets around the sampled neighborhoods helped to ensure that we could calculate supermarket accessibility for neighborhoods at the periphery.

• • •

The nearest supermarket was significantly further away in neighborhoods with a high proportion of African Americans and in the most impoverished neighborhoods compared with neighborhoods with a low proportion of African Americans and the least impoverished neighborhoods, respectively. (These results were adjusted for population density.)

• • •

Among the most impoverished neighborhoods, distance to the nearest supermarket varied considerably by percentage African American, with the nearest supermarket averaging 1.10 to 1.15 miles farther in neighborhoods with medium . . . and high . . . proportions of African Americans, respectively, than in neighborhoods with low proportions of African Americans. . . .

Discussion

Disparities in Supermarket Accessibility

The relationship between neighborhood racial composition and supermarket accessibility varied according to neighborhood poverty level in metropolitan Detroit. The distance to the nearest supermarket was similar among the least impoverished neighborhoods across the 3 tertiles of percentage African American. However, disparities in supermarket accessibility on the basis of race were evident among the most impoverished neighborhoods: the most impoverished neighborhoods in which African Americans resided, on average, were 1.1 miles farther from the nearest supermarket than were the most impoverished White neighborhoods. Most African Americans in tricounty metropolitan Detroit reside in neighborhoods that are in the upper tertile for percentage poor and that have either a high proportion of African Americans (60%) or a medium proportion of African Americans (20%), as defined in this study.

Inadequate accessibility to supermarkets may contribute to less-nutritious diets and hence to greater risk for chronic, diet-related diseases. In a recent qualitative study, Detroit residents reported that lack of access to supermarkets was a barrier to healthy eating.[50] At least 3 previous quantitative studies, all of which examined chain supermarkets, have suggested that closer proximity to supermarkets is associated with better-quality diets.[51–53] The observation that the nearest supermarket averaged 1.1 miles further in the most impoverished neighborhoods in which African Americans resided . . . compared with the most impoverished White neighborhoods . . . is particularly salient, given that 23% and 28% . . . of households in the most impoverished neighborhoods in which African Americans resided did not own a car in 2000.

We began the study with 3 measures of supermarket accessibility: distance to the nearest supermarket, number of supermarkets within a 3-mile radius (considered reachable by car), and potential supermarket accessibility. . . .[54] Because the patterns of these relationships were similar, we present only distance to the nearest supermarket. For all 3 measures, supermarket accessibility was comparable among the least impoverished neighborhoods regardless of neighborhood racial composition, whereas disparities were evident among the most impoverished neighborhoods. The most impoverished neighborhoods in which African Americans resided . . . averaged 2.3 and 2.7 (respectively) fewer supermarkets within a 3-mile radius and had lower potential supermarket accessibility relative to the most impoverished White neighborhoods. . . .

Race appears to be an important factor with respect to supermarket accessibility in the context of more impoverished neighborhoods; 76% of neighborhoods with a high proportion of African Americans were among the most impoverished. The disproportionate representation of African Americans in more impoverished neighborhoods in Detroit can be traced historically. Until the 1940s—a decade in which Detroit's African American population doubled from 149,119 to 300,506 because of the influx of African Americans from the South for manufacturing jobs—African Americans generally resided in central Detroit and east central Detroit.[35,36] Facing overcrowded and substandard housing, African Americans began moving to other parts of the city.[39,55,57] Nevertheless, institutional racism—specifically racial residential segregation—confined African Americans to Detroit neighborhoods that began losing employment opportunities, particularly in the manufacturing industry, in the 1950s.[39,41,44] Between 1948 and 1967, Detroit lost nearly 130,000 manufacturing jobs.[39]

Often confronting strong resistance from Whites, African Americans first moved to nearby neighborhoods in central Detroit.[46,58] Hence, many neighborhoods located in central Detroit[57] transitioned from White to African American in the 1950s and 1960s when African Americans moved in and Whites moved out to newly constructed housing in northeast and northwest Detroit and the suburbs. Businesses closed soon thereafter, particularly after the 1967 racial discord, further compounding the adverse economic impact of the loss of manufacturing jobs.[39,44,59] Hence, the number of abandoned homes and businesses, including grocery stores, grew, and poverty increased substantially.

This pattern of White flight and economic divestment was repeated during several decades across Detroit neighborhoods. Residential patterns of African Americans generally expanded outward in a stepwise progression from central and east central Detroit toward the northern city boundaries and eventually to Southfield, a suburb adjacent to northwest Detroit.[39,44,58] Neighborhoods located in the northernmost portion of Detroit near Eight Mile Road, the infamous African American–White racial dividing line of metropolitan Detroit, and particularly in northwest and northeast Detroit were among the most recent neighborhoods to transition from White to African American. Some neighborhoods, such as those in the far northwest Detroit community of Redford, shifted to African American as late as the 1990s.[44,58,60,61] Similarly, in the suburb of Southfield, the African American population has grown tremendously, from 102 people (0.1% of the population) in 1970 to 42,259 people (54%) in 2000.[58] The number of African Americans in Southfield increased by 48% between 1990 and 2000 alone, despite an increase of only 3% in the city's total population.

This social history of metropolitan Detroit neighborhoods is relevant to our study because, among the least impoverished neighborhoods, all but 1 of the predominately African American neighborhoods with supermarket accessibility equivalent to that of their predominately White counterparts were located in northwest and north central Detroit and in Southfield. An optimistic interpretation of our findings is that supermarkets have newly opened or have remained open in or nearby these middle-income, yet racially transitioning, neighborhoods. This interpretation provides hope that supermarkets will invest or stay invested in African American neighborhoods as long as the residents have sufficient purchasing power to make these outlets profitable. An alternative interpretation of the findings is that among the least impoverished neighborhoods, African American neighborhoods have supermarket accessibility equivalent to that of predominantly White neighborhoods only because the supermarkets located in and nearby are remnants of historically White neighborhoods. Longitudinal data are needed to empirically test these different theories. If these areas remain African American, if they maintain a middle-income population, and if supermarkets remain open in or near these neighborhoods, then economic development may be a key intervention strategy to improve supermarket accessibility in African American neighborhoods. If, conversely, supermarkets close or do not open new sites in these economically stable African American neighborhoods, then factors associated with race are a more likely cause of disparities in supermarket accessibility. Indeed, our finding of disparate supermarket accessibility among the most impoverished neighborhoods by neighborhood racial composition warrants further investigation to identify contributing factors.

• • •

Practice and Policy Implications

The results of the study have several practice and policy implications. Pursuit of these strategies would benefit from a partnership approach between public health professionals and community members to ensure the local relevance of intervention strategies and to enhance community capacity for future intervention efforts.[62] In the first of these implications, the results suggest the critical importance of working to redress fundamental inequalities between African Americans and Whites in order to reduce chronic, diet-related diseases among African Americans.[63] For example, the economic development of African American neighborhoods could be enhanced by policies of creating jobs that pay a fair wage, to improve educational quality and opportunities for adults to increase job skills, to subsidize child care, and to attract new businesses. Second, working to attract supermarkets to economically disadvantaged African American neighborhoods in Detroit is a specific economic development strategy that may directly improve food access. Supermarket development can enhance local economic vitality by (1) providing jobs for residents, (2) increasing the local tax base, (3) making foods available at lower prices, thereby increasing the spending power of residents, and (4) attracting other forms of retail.[34,35,64] Supporting African American ownership of and employment at these supermarkets may be critical to their acceptance and success.[65]

Third, a metropolitanwide planning approach to the food system needs to be pursued.[66] Ideally, the food system would be evaluated holistically to ensure that all communities are served equitably. Fourth, in the short term, inadequate transportation is a significant barrier for residents of economically disadvantaged African American neighborhoods' gaining access to supermarkets.[50] Affordable public transportation needs to be improved by integrating transportation routes with supermarket locations.[67,68]

Fifth, on the basis of our findings of disparate access to supermarkets among the most impoverished neighborhoods by percentage African American residents, efforts to expand the Community Reinvestment Act, a law designed to combat discrimination in commercial real estate lending, may be warranted. Finally, given that racial ideologies are likely to shape the political will to pursue these intervention strategies, public health researchers and practitioners need to work to challenge racial stereotypes in public discourse.[42,43,69]

Helping to contextualize the plight of African Americans historically and spatially and to identify its ramifications for health were the primary intents of this study. We found that the historically influenced concentration of African Americans in higher-poverty neighborhoods in Detroit adversely affects spatial access to supermarkets, a resource of potential great importance in promoting the health of African Americans.

Seeing the Big Picture

Urban Food Deserts: Race, Health, and the Lack of "Real" Food

Compare health outcomes by race in Section III (diabetes, obesity, hypertension) with rates of poverty by race in Section VI of the Appendix. What role do poverty and residential segregation by racial groups play in having access to "healthy foods" found in a supermarket compared to the processed, salty, and fatty foods that dominate corner stores or bodegas?

RACIALIZED OPPORTUNITY IN SOCIAL INSTITUTIONS

Answer the questions that follow.

1. As of 2008, what percentage of the U.S. population do you think was:
   a. Black   _____ %
   b. White   _____ %
   c. Asian   _____ %
   d. American Indian _____ %
   e. Latino   _____ %

2. Who are your three best friends? 1) _____ 2) _____ 3) _____

3. Does the unemployment rate in the United States vary by color or ethnicity? _____

Each of your answers, whether you realize it or not, reflects how you have been shaped by social institutions. Compare your answers on item 1 to the correct percentages as enumerated by the U.S. Bureau of the Census: 12.4 percent black, 67 percent white, 4.4 percent Asian/Pacific Islander, 0.8 percent American Indian, and 14.8 percent Latino.

Did your estimates of the size of these groups differ from the actual numbers? If you said that the black population was around 30 percent or that the Asian population was 10 percent, your answer was similar to the average American response. How do you explain the fact that most people in the United States almost triple-count the black and Asian population? From a sociological perspective, what does the overcounting of the nonwhite population mean?

Item 2 asked you to list your three best friends. How many of the people you listed are from a different race? How many are the same sex as you? If you don't have any best friends who are from a racial background different from your own, why not? Is it that you do not like people from other races? Does this mean you are a racist? Do you only have friends of the same sex? Why?

With regard to item 3, the unemployment rate in the United States does vary by color or ethnicity, with blacks and Latinos twice as likely as whites to be unemployed.

How is the unemployment rate linked to how close people live to areas of high job growth, and how are both of these factors linked to race and ethnicity?

The answers to these questions reflect the ways in which institutions shape how we view the world. Your beliefs, opinions, and attitudes, and the "commonsense" knowledge that guides your moment-to-moment understanding of the world—all may seem to be highly individualistic. Upon closer sociological inspection, however, we see that institutions and other social arrangements influence, mediate, and structure how we think about and come to understand the world in which we live. Think for a moment about your answers to the preceding questions. People of all colors typically overestimate the nonwhite population and underestimate the white population. Perhaps you overestimated the nonwhite population because you live in an all-black or all-Latino neighborhood. When you look out the window or walk down the street, you see that everyone in your neighborhood is like you. That local information is then used to make a judgment about the rest of the United States. But what if you are white and you overestimated the nonwhite population? How do you explain doubling or tripling the black or Asian population? Do you get your information about other racial groups secondhand, from watching television? Might there be a difference between the media's portrayal of race and ethnic relations and what is actually taking place in society? Do you watch professional sports, music videos, or the local television news? Might your estimates reflect something about your television viewing habits? If you do live in a racially segregated neighborhood, might that explain why your best friends are all the same color as you? Do you think you might have close friends from different racial backgrounds if your high school or neighborhood were racially integrated? Why is it that compared to white areas or the suburbs, jobs are often not as plentiful or as well paying in black or Latino neighborhoods?

In Part III, we focus on how race and ethnic identity intersect with the criminal justice system, the labor market, where individuals live and why, and how the media shape our views on race and ethnic relations. The four readings in **Race and Criminal Justice: Oxymoron or an American Tragedy** examine the influence of race and class in the American justice system. Law professor David Cole examines racial disparities in capital punishment sentencing. His research found that courts are more likely to sentence someone to death if the killer is black and the victim white than if the killer is white and the victim black. Who is likely to live or die, controlling for the type of crime committed, varies by race. Kenneth Bolton Jr. and Joe Feagin examine the racism black police officers endure from fellow police as they try to go about their daily responsibilities. Most police officers are not racist, but as their research demonstrates, racism is nonetheless a feature of everyday life that black officers must attend to. Jeffrey Reiman examines a very obvious but unstated fact: People in prison tend to be poor. Put another way, rich people can pay for outstanding legal council. It is not, Reiman argues, that poor people are more prone to criminal behavior; rather, the criminal justice system is rife with racial and economic bias. Finally, Devah Pager's findings about the employment prospects of men with and without criminal records raise troubling questions about the role of race and racism in employment opportunities.

The next section, **How Race Shapes the Workplace,** examines the sociological reasons why economic and occupational outcomes vary by race and ethnicity. The short research summary by Amy Braverman details how a name can signal racial identity and how employers use this information. Roger Waldinger provides historical and contemporary examples of how employment opportunities have changed over time by examining the different occupational niches that ethnic and racial groups occupied in New York City and the conditions that allowed upward mobility for some and economic stagnation for others. Katherine Newman and Catherine Ellis document the work strategies used by fast-food workers in Harlem. The "McJob" experiences of two hundred black and brown respondents in their study challenge a number of "commonsense" assumptions about work at a fast-food restaurant and workers' attitudes about upward mobility. First, Xiaolan Bao and then William Kandel and Emilio Parrado chronicle the ways in which two newly arrived immigrant groups, Chinese laborers in the sweatshops of New York City and Latinos working in poultry plants in the South, are part of an unregulated and exploited workforce that is becoming all too common.

The final section, **Race, Representations, and the Media,** explores how the media shape our views on race and ethnicity. In the first subsection **Drug Dealers, Maids, and Mammies: The Role of Stereotypes in the Media,** Roger Klein and Stacy Naccarato discuss racial bias in local news coverage. Justin Lewis and Sut Jhally use a research project conducted on exposure to *The Cosby Show* as a window into the ways in which racial attitudes and perceptions of mobility are influenced by the television shows people watch. Robert Lichter and Daniel Amundson focus on the invidious ways in which blacks on the nightly news and Latinos in entertainment programming are reduced to a series of degrading stereotypes. These readings ask us to consider how representations of race and ethnicity on the nightly news or on situation comedies shape our worldview. The second subsection, **Crazy Horse Malt Liquor and Athletes: The Tenacity of Stereotypes,** takes two examples of stereotypes that refuse to go away: the image of the savage Indian and the violent black athlete. Debra Merskin deconstructs the meaning of American Indians in popular culture and the consequences of such stereotypical and racist imagery. Finally, Richard Lapchick reports on one unintended consequence of America's romance with professional sports: the cementing of racial stereotypes. Athletes, particularly college athletes, are often subjected to a double standard because their lives are so closely scrutinized by the media. ✳

26 No Equal Justice: The Color of Punishment

David Cole

DAVID COLE was named one of the forty-five outstanding lawyers under the age of forty-five by *The American Lawyer*. He is a professor at Georgetown University Law Center, an attorney with the Center for Constitutional Rights, the chief litigator for *Karen Finley v. National Endowment for the Arts,* and a regular contributor to NPR's *All Things Considered, The Nation* and op-ed pages in major newspapers nationwide. He is the author of *No Equal Justice* (1999).

TONYA DRAKE, A TWENTY-FIVE-YEAR-OLD mother of four on welfare, needed the money. So when a man she hardly knew gave her a $100 bill and told her she could keep the change if she mailed a package for him, she agreed, even though she suspected it might contain drugs. The change amounted to $47.40. The package contained crack cocaine. And for that, Tonya Drake, whose only prior offenses were traffic violations, received a ten-year mandatory minimum prison sentence. When federal judge Richard A. Gadbois, Jr., sentenced her, he said, "This woman doesn't belong in prison for 10 years for what I understand she did. That's just crazy, but there's nothing I can do about it." Had the cocaine in the package been in powder rather than crack form, she would have faced a prison sentence of less than three years, with no mandatory minimum.[1]

Tonya Drake is joined by thousands of prisoners serving lengthy mandatory prison terms for federal crack cocaine violations.[2] What unites them is skin color. About 90 percent of federal crack cocaine defendants are black. Indeed, a 1992 U.S. Sentencing Commission study found

Questions to Consider In *McClesky v. Kemp,* the Supreme Court ruled that even though sentencing disparities were found to be significantly correlated with the race of the defendant, those findings did not necessarily mean there was racist intent in the sentencing. David Cole's research, however, challenges the deeply held belief that the rule of law should be and is applied to all citizens without regard to race, creed, status, or lineage. How do you explain differences in sentencing by race? What would happen if there were a "war on drugs" and the suburbs, rather than the city, were the target? What would white America's response be if millions of young, white, middle-class suburbanites were arrested, sentenced, and put in jail for an extended period of time for recreational marijuana or ecstasy use?

that in seventeen states, not a single white had been prosecuted on federal crack cocaine charges.[3]

Crack cocaine is nothing more than powder cocaine cooked up with baking soda. Wholesalers deal in powder; retailers deal in crack. But under the federal sentencing guidelines, a small-time crack "retailer" caught selling 5 grams of crack receives the same prison sentence as a large-scale powder cocaine dealer convicted of distributing 500 grams of powder cocaine. The U.S. Sentencing Commission has estimated that 65 percent of crack users are white.[4] In 1992, however, 92.6 percent of those convicted for crimes involving crack cocaine were black, while only 4.7 percent were white; at the same time, 45.2 percent of defendants convicted for powder cocaine crimes were white, and only 20.7 percent were black.[5] In Minnesota, where state sentencing guidelines drew a similar distinction between crack and powder cocaine, African Americans made up 96.6 percent of those charged with possession of crack cocaine in 1988, while almost 80 percent of those charged with possession of powder cocaine were white.[6] Sentencing guidelines were ostensibly adopted to eliminate disparity in sentencing, yet the crack/powder distinction has ensured that significant racial inequities remain.

Black defendants have challenged the crack/powder disparity on constitutional grounds, but every federal challenge has failed.[7] The courts, echoing the Supreme Court in *McCleskey,* have held that "mere" statistical disparities do not prove that Congress or the Sentencing Commission adopted the disparities for the purpose of harming African Americans. And it is not wholly irrational to treat crack as more harmful than powder cocaine, because crack is more often associated with violence, is more potent as typically ingested, and is more accessible to low-income people. Accordingly, even though black cocaine offenders in the federal system serve sentences on average five years longer than white cocaine offenders, the courts see no constitutional problem.

In 1995, however, the U.S. Sentencing Commission, which administers the federal sentencing guidelines, concluded that the disparities could not be justified by qualitative differences between the two drugs, particularly as powder cocaine distributors provide the raw material for crack. It proposed to reduce the differential, noting the racial disparities and their corrosive effect on criminal justice generally.[8] Congress and President Clinton responded like politicians; they reframed the issue as whether we should be "tough on crime," and opposed any change. For the first time since the sentencing guidelines were created in 1984, Congress passed a law overriding a Sentencing Commission recommendation to alter the guidelines.[9]

In 1995, the Georgia Supreme Court very briefly took a different approach. Georgia has a "two strikes and you're out" sentencing scheme that imposes life imprisonment for a second drug offense. As of 1995, Georgia's district attorneys, who have unfettered discretion to decide whether to seek this penalty, had invoked it against only 1 percent of white defendants facing a second drug conviction, but against more than 16 percent of eligible black defendants. The result: 98.4 percent of those serving life sentences under the provision were black. On March 17, 1995, the Georgia Supreme Court ruled, by a 4–3 vote, that these figures presented a threshold case of discrimination, and required prosecutors to explain the disparity.[10]

Instead of offering an explanation, however, Georgia Attorney General Michael Bowers took the unusual step of filing a petition for rehearing signed by every one of the state's forty-six district attorneys, all of whom were white. The petition warned that the court's approach was a "substantial step toward invalidating" the death penalty, and would "paralyze the criminal justice system," presumably because racial disparities in other areas might also have to be explained. Thirteen days later, the Georgia Supreme Court took the highly unusual step of reversing itself, and held that the figures established no discrimination and required no justification. The court's new decision relied almost exclusively on the U.S. Supreme Court's decision in *McCleskey.*[11]

The crack/powder differential and the Georgia experience with "two strikes and you're out" life sentences are but two examples of the widespread racial disparities caused by the war on drugs. Between 1986 and 1991, arrests of members of racial and ethnic minorities for all crimes increased by twice as much as nonminority arrests.[12] Yet when that figure is broken down by type of crime, drug offenses were the *only* area in which minority arrests actually increased more than nonminority arrests. The five-year increase in arrests of minorities for drug offenses was *almost ten times* the increase in arrests of white drug offenders.[13]

In 1992, the United States Public Health Service estimated, based on self-report surveys, that 76 percent of illicit drug users were white, 14 percent black, and 8 percent Hispanic—figures which roughly match each group's share of the general population.[14] Yet African Americans make up 35 percent of all drug arrests, 55 percent of all drug convictions, and 74 percent of all sentences for drug offenses.[15] In Baltimore, blacks are five times more likely than whites to be arrested for drug offenses.[16] In Columbus, Ohio, black males are less than 11 percent of the population, but account for 90 percent of drug arrests; they are arrested at a rate eighteen times greater than white males.[17] In Jacksonville, Florida, black males are 12 percent of the population, but 87 percent of drug arrests.[18]

And in Minneapolis, black males are arrested for drugs at a rate twenty times that for white males.[19]

Similar racial disparities are found in incarceration rates for drug offenses. From 1986 to 1991, the number of white drug offenders incarcerated in state prisons increased by 110 percent, but the number of black drug offenders increased by 465 percent.[20] In New York, which has some of the most draconian drug laws in the country—selling two ounces of cocaine receives the same sentence as murder—90 percent of those incarcerated for drugs each year are black or Hispanic.[21] The "war on drugs" is also responsible for much of the growth in incarceration since 1980. Federal prisoners incarcerated for drug offenses increased nearly tenfold from 1980 to 1993, and that increase accounted for nearly three-quarters of the total increase in federal prisoners.[22] The number of state prisoners incarcerated for drug offenses during the same period increased at a similar rate.[23]

The same pattern emerges in the treatment of juveniles. Between 1986 and 1991, arrests of minority juveniles (under age eighteen) for drug offenses increased by 78 percent, while arrests of nonminority juveniles for drugs actually *decreased* by 34 percent.[24] As with adults, black youth are also treated progressively more severely than whites at each successive stage of the juvenile justice process. In 1991, white youth were involved in 50 percent of all drug-related cases, while black youth accounted for 48 percent.[25] Yet blacks were detained for drug violations at nearly twice the rate of whites.[26] Four times as many black juvenile drug cases were transferred to criminal courts for adult prosecution as white cases.[27] And black youth involved in drug-related cases were placed outside the home almost twice as often as white youth. These disparities are only getting worse: from 1987 to 1991, such placement for black juveniles in drug cases increased 28.5 percent, while placement for whites *decreased* 30 percent.[28] The situation in Baltimore is illustrative. In 1980, eighteen white juveniles and eighty-six black juveniles were arrested for selling drugs—already a fairly stark five-to-one disparity. In 1990, the number of white juveniles arrested on drug charges fell to thirteen, while the number of black juveniles arrested grew to 1,304—a disparity of more than one hundred to one.[29]

Thus, the victims of the war on drugs have been disproportionately black. Some argue that this is neither surprising nor problematic, but simply reflects the unfortunate fact that the drug problem itself disproportionately burdens the black community.[30] If more blacks are using and selling drugs, equal enforcement of the drug laws will lead to disproportionate arrests and incarceration of African Americans. Even if that were the case, the fact that the disparities increase at each successive stage of both the criminal and juvenile justice processes suggests that greater drug use by blacks is not the whole story. In addition, as noted earlier, official estimates of drug use by race do not reflect the disparities evident in the criminal justice system, and in fact suggest very little racial disparity in drug use.

The effects of the drug war are difficult to measure. Critics contend that drugs are just as prevalent and cheap today as they were before the crackdown began in the mid-1980s. Proponents point to signs that crack use has declined, and that teen use of drugs generally has also fallen. But it is extremely difficult to say whether these trends are a result of the war on drugs. Scholars find that drug use goes in cycles, but they have never been able to find a correlation between fluctuations in drug use and criminal-law enforcement. One thing is certain, however: the stigmatization and incarceration of such a high proportion of young African-American males for drug crimes will have significant adverse long-term effects on the black community. A criminal record makes it much more difficult to find a legitimate job. We are disabling tens of thousands of young black men at the outset of their careers. The short-term "benefits" of removing offenders from the community may well come back to haunt us in the long term.

Three Strikes

Not so long ago, "three strikes and you're out" was just a baseball slogan. Today, it passes for a correctional philosophy. And here again, African Americans are disproportionately the losers. Between 1993 and 1995, twenty-four states and the federal government adopted some form of **"three strikes and you're out"** legislation, under which repeat offenders face life sentences for a third felony conviction.[31] (Georgia and South Carolina went even further, adopting "two strikes and you're out" laws.) California's three-strikes law, one of the first, was sparked by a repeat offender's

"three strikes and you're out" Laws that require judges to adhere to mandatory minimum sentencing guidelines for a third criminal offense.

abduction and murder of twelve-year-old Polly Klaas in Petaluma in 1993.[32] Under California's version, a second felony conviction doubles the sentence otherwise authorized, and a third felony conviction receives a mandatory twenty-five-year-to-life term, no matter how insubstantial the third conviction, so long as the prior convictions were for "violent" or "serious" crimes. The "three strikes" idea has been wildly popular; 72 percent of California's voters approved it in a popular referendum, and President Clinton himself jumped on the three-strikes bandwagon during the 1994 mid-term election campaign.[33] But the implementation of the laws has led to many problems.

First, the laws lead to draconian results. Jerry Dewayne Williams, for example, received a twenty-five-year sentence for stealing a slice of pizza from four young men at a Los Angeles beach.[34] Another defendant's third strike consisted of stealing five bottles of liquor from a supermarket.[35] In its first two years, California's law led to life sentences for twice as many marijuana users as murderers, rapists, and kidnappers combined.[36] A California Department of Corrections study reported that 85 percent of those sentenced under the law were convicted most recently of a nonviolent crime.[37] Some have argued that focusing on the third strike is an unfair basis for criticism, because most offenders sentenced under the law have long criminal histories.[38] But the law is triggered even where a defendant's prior offenses are in the distant past, the third conviction is for a minor offense, and there is little likelihood that public safety required anything like a life sentence. Robert Wayne Washington, for example, received twenty-five years to life for a minor cocaine possession charge; his prior offenses were two eight-year-old burglaries and an intervening conviction for possession of contraband.[39]

Second, if the purpose of the law is to incapacitate those who would otherwise repeatedly prey on society, it is overinclusive. Most violent criminals have a relatively limited "criminal career," tailing off after ten years or so.[40] An individual's third strike often will not occur until his criminal career is on the wane. Thus, the three-strikes laws will impose life sentences on many offenders who pose little future danger to the community.

Third, such laws increase the costs of administering the criminal justice system. They make police work more dangerous, because a repeat offender facing a life sentence, in the words of Los Angeles Police Department spokesman Anthony Alba, is like "a cornered animal. If he knows he is going to get life in jail, he is definitely going to up the ante in eluding his captors."[41] Once apprehended, many defendants facing a third strike are unwilling to plead guilty, leading to a marked increase in criminal trials. Michael Judge, the chief public defender for Los Angeles County, said, "The law has created the single greatest increase in workload in the thirty years since I've been associated with the criminal justice system."[42] Two years into the California law's existence, an auditor estimated that it had cost Los Angeles County alone an extra $169 million.[43] The increase in criminal trials causes backlogs in the civil justice system, as the courts must increasingly devote themselves to criminal trials; as of 1996, 47 of California's 125 civil courts had to be diverted to hearing criminal cases.[44]

Three-strikes and other mandatory minimum laws have contributed to startling growth in our prison population. From 1980 to 1994, the national prison and jail population increased 195.6 percent.[45] By comparison, the general population increased from 1980 to 1990 by only 9.8 percent.[46] If the prison population continues to grow at the rate of increase from 1995–96, it would top 3.2 million in 2009. California alone has built seventeen new jails in the last fifteen years. Its prison spending has increased over that period from 2 percent to almost 10 percent of its state budget, and it now spends more on corrections than on higher education.[47]

Despite these problems, the three-strikes approach remains extraordinarily popular. Why? One possibility is that, as with many other "get tough" policies, its direct burdens fall disproportionately on minorities. The Georgia case discussed above involving racially disparate application of a two-strikes law is not unique. In California, for example, blacks make up only 7 percent of the general population, yet as of 1996 they accounted for 43 percent of the third-strike defendants sent to state prison. Whites, by contrast, make up 53 percent of the general population in California, but only 24.6 percent of third-strike prisoners. This means that blacks are being imprisoned under California's three-strikes law at a rate 13.3 times that of the rate for whites. And because three-strikes convicts serve such long sentences, their proportion of the prison population will steadily increase; third-strikers comprised 8 percent of the total prison population in 1996, but the California Department of Corrections estimates that by 2024 they will amount to 49 percent.[48] Without a change in direction, the already stark racial disparities in our nation's prisons will only get worse. Yet it is precisely for that reason that there is unlikely to be a change in direction. As long as the effects of this get-tough measure are felt principally in minority communities, there is not likely to be sufficient political pressure for change.

When Is Disparity Discrimination?

As the figures above illustrate, it is beyond dispute that criminal sentencing is marked by stark racial *disparities*. But does this amount to *discrimination*? Everyone agrees that black defendants should not receive harsher penalties simply because they are black, and that criminals who attack white victims should not be punished more severely because the victims were white. But the disparities identified above may be attributable to factors other than race discrimination. Perhaps blacks commit more serious crimes per capita than whites. Social scientists and criminologists have long sought to determine through statistical analysis whether criminal sentencing is impermissibly affected by race, and have reached contradictory conclusions.

In the death penalty setting, as we have seen, most studies conclude that there is discrimination based on the race of the victim, even after controlling for other possible factors. In non–death penalty cases, however, the results are more mixed. In a 1993 study of the racial impact of the federal sentencing guidelines, for example, the U.S. Justice Department's Bureau of Justice Statistics found that although blacks on average received sentences that were almost two years longer than whites, the bulk of this disparity was due to the crack/cocaine sentencing disparity.[49] The study concluded that other racial differences in sentencing for drug trafficking, fraud, and embezzlement could be explained by nonracial factors such as prior prison records, guilty pleas, and severity of offense.[50] But the study also found that even after controlling for such factors, black offenders were 50 to 60 percent more likely to be sentenced for larceny than white offenders, and twice as likely as whites to be sentenced for weapons offenses.[51] Several other studies have concluded that racial disparities in sentencing are largely attributable to race-neutral factors, such as offense severity or prior criminal record.[52] Most criminologists agree that a substantial part—but not all—of sentencing disparity is attributable to blacks committing more

serious crimes than whites.[53] However, all of these findings—both those that find discrimination and those that do not—are plagued by several inescapable problems.

First, in order to determine whether a racial *disparity* is the result of racial *discrimination,* one must compare similar cases. Where defendants similar in all respects but race are treated differently, one may reasonably conclude that discrimination has occurred. The rub lies in defining "similar." As Barbara Meierhoefer has argued,

> There is no disagreement that similar offenders should be sentenced similarly. The problem . . . is that there is no consensus as to what defines "similar offenders." Even outwardly empirical assessments of whether unwarranted disparity has been reduced will be strongly influenced by which offense and offender characteristics are selected to define "similarly situated" offenders.[54]

Thus, for example, critics of the Baldus study used in *McCleskey* have argued that it did not sufficiently identify "similar" cases, and that therefore its conclusion that the remaining disparities were racial in nature was flawed.[55]

Second, even if we could identify and agree on all relevant race-neutral factors that might conceivably explain a disparity, no study can possibly measure all such factors.[56] Some of the most important factors, such as strength of evidence, credibility of witnesses, or the effectiveness of a lawyer's representation, are simply not susceptible to quantification. Quantifiable factors may be missing from available data. No study can absolutely eliminate the possibility that some unaccounted-for race-neutral variable that correlates with race has caused the apparent racial disparity.

Third, statistical studies may also err in the opposite direction, by concealing racial discrimination. A study of sentencing decisions that found that all racial disparities could be explained by offense severity and prior criminal records, for example, might conceal racial discrimination in police or prosecutorial practices. If police officers observe, stop, and arrest blacks at a higher rate than whites because of their race, blacks are more likely to develop criminal records, all other things being equal. Similarly, if prosecutors offer more generous plea bargains to white than black defendants because of their race, black defendants' sentencing reports will reflect higher "offense severity" and more serious criminal records. By focusing only on one stage of the criminal justice system, a statistician may miss discrimination occurring at another stage. At the same time, statistical studies may miss discrimination if, in the aggregate, two forms of discrimination cancel each other out. For example, some biased sentencers might assign a longer sentence for a black-on-black crime because the *defendant* is black; others might impose a shorter sentence because the *victim* is black. If these biases cancel each other out in the aggregate, statistics may conceal actual discrimination.

For these reasons, statistical studies can rarely prove intentional discrimination. But even if none of the sentencing disparities outlined above is attributable to discrimination as the Supreme Court has defined it, they nonetheless raise serious questions about the racial fairness of our criminal justice policy. To see that this is so, one need only imagine the public response if the current racial disparities in criminal justice were reversed. Imagine what kind of pressure legislatures would feel, for example, if one in three young *white* men were in prison or on probation or parole. Imagine what the politics of the death penalty would look like if prosecutors sought the death penalty 70 percent of the time when whites killed blacks, but only 19 percent of the time when blacks killed whites. Or imagine what our juvenile justice policies would be like if white youth charged with drug offenses were four times as likely as black youth to be tried as adults, and twice as likely to be placed outside the home. One thing is certain: the nation would not accept such a situation as "inevitable."

Indeed, turning the tables on some of these statistics is almost beyond comprehension. If the per capita incarceration rate for whites were equal to that for blacks, more than 3.5 million white people would be incarcerated today, instead of 570,000, and we would need more than three times the prison capacity (and prosecution and court capacity) that we currently have. And because white people comprise about 80 percent of the general population, it would be literally impossible for whites to be overrepresented in the prison population to the same degree that black people currently are—four times their representation in the general population.

To see what happens when the criminal law begins to affect large numbers of white middle- and upper-class people, one need only look at the history of marijuana laws. The country's first marijuana users were largely nonwhite, mostly Mexicans.[57] By 1937, every state had criminalized marijuana. In the 1950s, federal penalties for the sale of marijuana ranged from two to five years imprisonment;

a second offense brought a sentence of five to ten years; and a third brought ten to twenty years. State penalties followed suit. In 1956, Congress imposed mandatory minimum sentences for marijuana possession and sale.

In the 1960s, however, marijuana spread to the white middle and upper classes. By 1970, some college campuses reported that at least 70 percent of their student population had tried marijuana. As one author wrote in 1970, "Vast numbers of people have recently adopted the drug as their principal euphoriant; however, by all estimates, the new users are the sons and daughters of the middle class, not the ethnic minorities and ghetto residents formerly associated with marijuana."[58] The harsh penalties imposed when their effect was primarily felt by minorities were no longer acceptable, and marijuana laws were liberalized. As Dr. Stanley Yolles explained in 1970,

> Nobody cared when it was a ghetto problem. Marijuana—well, it was used by jazz musicians or the lower class, so you didn't care if they got 20 years. But when a nice, middle-class girl or boy in college gets busted for the same thing, then the whole community sits up and takes notice. And that's the name of the game today. The problem has begun to come home to roost—in all strata of society, in suburbia, in middle-class homes, in the colleges. Suddenly, the punitive, the vindictive approach was touching all classes of society. And now the most exciting thing that's really happening is the change in attitude by the people. Now we have a willingness to examine the problem, as to whether it's an experimentation, or an illness rather than an "evil."[59]

Police and prosecutors began to leave users alone, and instead targeted dealers and sellers. The courts limited enforcement, using their discretion to invalidate convictions on a variety of grounds. And the legislatures amended the laws, eliminating strict penalties for possession. As one commentator described the development, "In response to the extraordinary explosion in marijuana consumption and the penetration of its use into the mainstream of American life, every state amended its penalties in some fashion between 1969 and 1972, the overall result being a massive downward shift in penalties for consumption-related offenses. Simple possession of less than one ounce was classified as a misdemeanor in all but eight states by the end of 1972."[60] In 1973, Oregon went further and actually decriminalized possession of small amounts of marijuana, and by 1981 ten other states had followed suit.[61]

When the effects of a criminal law reach the sons and daughters of the white majority, our response is not to get tough, but rather to get lenient. Americans have been able to sustain an unremittingly harsh tough-on-crime attitude precisely because the burden of punishment falls disproportionately on minority populations. The white majority could not possibly maintain its current attitude toward crime and punishment were the burden of punishment felt by the same white majority that prescribes it.

Seeing the Big Picture **How Race Tips the Scales of Justice**

Look at Juvenile Drug Offenses in the section on Crime in Section IV of the Appendix. How might Cole explain the huge difference in arrest statistics between blacks and other racial groups?

---

27 Black and Blue: Everyday Racism on the Police Force

Kenneth Bolton Jr. • Joe R. Feagin

KENNETH BOLTON JR. is assistant professor of criminal justice of Southeastern Louisiana University.

JOE R. FEAGIN is professor of sociology at the University of Florida. He is former president of the American Sociological Association. His many Routledge books include: *White Racism* (2nd edition, 2001), *Racist America: Roots, Current Realities, and Future Reparations* (2000), and *The Agony of Education: Black Students at White Colleges and Universities* (1996).

NATIONAL OPINION SURVEYS INDICATE THAT a majority of white Americans believe that serious racial discrimination in most areas is a thing of the past. From this perspective, overt racial hostility and discrimination may once have been problems, but now African Americans have societal access and opportunities at least as good as those of whites. For example, one recent survey asked whites whether they thought that the average black person had health care access, education, wages, and jobs equal to or better than those of the average white person.[1] Some

Questions to Consider Discussions of racism and policing tend to focus on why certain groups are profiled or the social processes that result in incarceration outcomes that are more punitive toward racial minorities compared to whites. What has not been adequately addressed is how black police officers are treated by other, typically white, police officers when they are at the police station or out on patrol. Bolton and Feagin detail the experiences of black police officers who have had to navigate racism in their ranks. How might the racist mistreatment black officers experience shape how they police and their attitudes toward race and racism?

70 percent of whites held to the erroneous belief that black Americans were at least as well off as whites in one or more of these major areas. On a general question, some 71 percent of whites felt that black Americans had societal opportunities *equal to or better than* those of whites, and just one in five felt that black Americans still faced "a lot of discrimination" in society.[2]

Actually, as we have documented in previous chapters and in other books, the evidence against this naive white view is overwhelming, particularly in regard to historically white workplaces and other major economic, political, and social institutions. And it is certainly true of law enforcement agencies. Although our respondents sometimes suggest that certain overt forms of discrimination occur less often in their occupational setting today than in the past, they make clear that even overt racism has by no means ended. In addition, they demonstrate with many experiential accounts that numerous forms of subtle and covert discrimination now operate to block, exclude, and marginalize them in their career and life.

Discriminatory actions by whites are generally buttressed by negative attitudes and ideological constructions. These attitudes use a variety of disguises, ranging from images of black Americans as lazy or incompetent to defensive ideas about the character of discrimination and remedial programs such as affirmative action. Previous research shows that racial discrimination often operates in a context in which many whites deny that it exists at all and, therefore, that black Americans who complain about racism usually do so without justification.[3] The ideological constructions of whites maintain conceptions of white and black people as opposites in perspectives, values, and cultures. Stereotypical notions of these differences are reflected in racist talk, jokes, and cartoons that belittle and humiliate black Americans while reinforcing their subordinate position. In this chapter we continue an examination of the way in which stereotypes and prejudices shape the discrimination that makes the everyday lives of black Americans so painful and difficult.

Here we pay particular attention to the way in which various types of racial hostility and discrimination create a hostile work climate. In workplaces with hostile racial climates, a variety of techniques of control and intimidation, such as racial insults and even physical violence, are employed by whites on a more or less regular basis to thwart or slow the advancement of black employees

beyond their current position. When black law enforcement officers address the racist attitudes and discriminatory behavior of white employees, our respondents indicate they are frequently perceived as threatening. They may face from white colleagues and supervisors a range of responses, not only resentment but also retaliatory actions that seek to contain them and that often result in emotional or physical harm.

Hostile Workplace Climates: Whites Playing the "Race Card"

Conventional white notions notwithstanding, racially hostile workplaces remain common across the United States, not only for black employees but also for many other employees of color.[4] Yet, in spite of the extensive evidence of continuing racism, many white juries and judges often have trouble seeing or remedying this discrimination. For example, in one recent California Court of Appeals ruling, *Etter v. Veriflo Corporation,* white judges concluded that the use of frequent racist epithets against a black male employee (Etter) was not "severe or pervasive" and did not require a legal remedy. The target of the epithets reported that a white supervisor used racially derogatory terms such as "Buckwheat," "Jemima," and "boy" and mocked blacks' pronunciation of words. However, in its decision the court played down the frequency and significance of these terms and ignored Etter's own account and painful experience.[5] Thus, although white judges and juries have become willing at least to listen to black accounts of everyday discrimination, as they did not do in earlier decades, they often find it hard to understand and credit fully the accounts of African Americans about discrimination.

Racist Talk, Jokes, and Cartoons

Half the respondents explicitly discuss encounters in which whites use racist language in conversational settings to refer to them or to other black people. The fact that encounters with these derogatory terms are experienced frequently demonstrates the extent of racist stereotyping and prejudiced thinking of many whites in historically white institutions. Such racist thinking and commentary have often been reported in research studies.[6] Supported and generated within white social groups and grids, this explicitly racist talk and terminology help to promote white solidarity through creating an outside "racial other" that is constantly derided.

Some older respondents note that racist talk was very commonplace when they first joined their law enforcement agency:

> When I first started it was nothing to hear the word "nigger" on the [police] radio. I mean, that was common, because everybody hadn't gotten the word, apparently, that there were some African Americans listening now. Then they went from that to a term that some guy used when he referred to a car with more than two blacks in it as a "load of coal." The first time I heard that, I thought, "Why that son of a bitch; I know what he just said." . . . And a lot of that went on. And then if they realized that I was working, they'd come to me and tell me, well we didn't mean you. And I thought to myself, "What a damned asshole, you meant me."

Although white officers may have altered the terminology according to their needs, the shared negative meaning and intent of this racialized terminology have remained more or less constant. This example illustrates an important point stressed throughout many respondents' discussions of the 1960s and 1970s: although overt forms of racist behavior have become somewhat less visible, the attitudes of many white officers have not dramatically changed. We have previously noted how some white officers have used terms like "TNT" ["typical nigger trouble"] on the police radio. And in the famous trial of the officers who beat Rodney King in Los Angeles, there was some discussion of police radio terminology for black Americans, including the phrase "gorillas in the mist," although a white officer denied that this term had a racial connotation.[7] In the preceding account, the white officers' awareness of the repercussions of their language alters the language to cover their intent, and then they apologize. However, drawing on the totality of his experiences, this respondent understands that they were referring to him.

Another black officer recounts how white officers talked about him as if he did not mind being insulted:

> Well, take for instance my first day. I reported and was told that I'd be riding with another officer who was going to show me around. There was another trooper in the [highway] median and as we, he pulled over into the median to see that trooper to talk, he looked over and saw, you know, that there was another new trooper

there. And he said it as a joke, but it wasn't funny at the time. He used the word "nigger." "Oh, that's just what we need, another fucking 'nigger,'" you know, and laughed, and they laughed and carried on. And I looked, and they could see I wasn't laughing . . . . But I knew they were accustomed to saying that and telling jokes that way, and felt comfortable with it and thought that it was not going to be taken offensively. But, in a period of time, that became taboo, and we really made a lot of progress. . . . Other than that, it's just been, you know, vibes and hearing things from another office when someone doesn't know you're there, and stuff like that.

These reports indicate that numerous white officers are comfortable with racist talk, if nowadays mostly out of the hearing of black officers. They do not seem to care that their joking hurts black officers. Once changes began to be made in departments, racist talk around black officers declined, yet often it continues behind closed doors, as what some researchers call **backstage racism.** With the decline in publicly expressed racist attitudes across the country, many analysts have argued that there is now little racist sentiment in the white community. Yet, studies of what whites do and say just off the public stage, as well as often on the public stage, indicate that this is a greatly mistaken view of racial change. In settings where they feel comfortable, such as with family or white acquaintances, many whites still make blatantly racist comments and perform discriminatory actions that they might not do in public.[8]

Another officer indicates not directly encountering overt racist talk, such as comments using epithets, yet knowing it goes on backstage and behind his back:

> Not directly, indirectly you got those names. What I mean is behind your back basically. . . . You would probably hear them talking about you, or another black officer as you passed by an open door, a cracked door. Or you may have been standing nearby a crowd of white supervisors or white officers, and you would hear that word.

Racist talk just off the public stage takes place as whites vent their anger and frustrations in regard to changing racial relations. It often occurs when whites are gossiping

backstage racism The racism or racist talk individuals engage in when they are privately interacting with same-race friends, family, or co-workers.

and in private conversations, when whites often let their guard down. One officer notes that:

> I've experienced some of the things that I consider to be racism. I was standing there talking with a sergeant. And one of the relief guys who happened to be white— and the sergeant was white—and I was the only black guy there. But you know, how you get accustomed to talking to people and you forget their identity, their culture. . . . It's just a person you're talking to. So he and I were talking and this white guy came up and says, "Sarge, where do I go on my relief duty?" And the sarge, without hesitation, he says, "You got the back fence over there, but the only thing you got to worry about is them little nigger boys trying to climb through the fence." And he looked over at me and he says, "Oh, I'm sorry; I didn't mean to say that." I said, "Well, I know how you are; it's all right." And I did know how he was, you know. I knew his bent; I knew his bent.

Note the comfort level here: these whites understand and employ, usually without thinking, racist constructions to converse about daily occurrences. Often these black officers describe being torn between anger at the insulting nature of the language they are subjected to and some pity for white officers who try to maintain a facade of innocence, only to be revealed as they really are in these everyday moments of routine interaction.

These black officers are quite concerned about the racist jokes and cartoons that are often shared and copied among white officers. Such joking and cartoons serve to denigrate and intimidate black employees and to reinforce the sense of white superiority. Many of the respondents spontaneously discuss how whites in their agency have incorporated jokes into departmental routines. The following account from a very perceptive respondent illustrates how roll calls have served as settings for racist jokes. This ritualistic telling of "the joke" promotes white officer solidarity, reproduces a shared understanding of the subordinate position of people of color, and informs black officers of how many whites still perceive them:

> We had roll calls where everybody would meet at whatever the designated time was for you to start work. . . . There was a long-standing tradition that someone would have the joke for the night. . . . All the ones I've heard, about a month's worth of jokes for the nights that I worked, were all racial jokes. And I didn't like it, and I attempted to find a way to deal

with it. I was talking with an elderly gentleman here, and I mentioned it to him, and he said, "Well, you can't say nothing, because they may shoot you in the back, but, next time, why don't you tell a joke." And I said, "Okay, well I need a joke to tell." And he directed me to another gentleman who was a great storyteller. And there's a guy on the corner, and most people would probably not even consider that the man had any value or what have you. But you know, a real nice man, and he gave me a joke.

He continues with an account of how he fought back against this recurring racist behavior:

> And I wrote it down, and I rehearsed it and practiced it and got before the mirror, and actually I did it, and it took me several weeks. But once I got the joke down, then I had to deal with my nerve to do it. You have to realize that at our roll call at the time, there could have been 200–300 guys in there at any given time at our roll call, and of that, less than 1/2 of 1 percent was black. You understand what I'm saying. So, you know, when you tell your joke, you have to come up front and tell it. Well, I had been pondering it for several days, you know, and this one particular night my hand just shot up, and, of course, the lieutenant who was the watch commander, "Oh we have a rookie with a joke. Let's bring him on up here." And I told the joke the guy had given me about a white female and a black male. And after I told the joke, I laughed and the other black guys almost fell to the floor, but nobody else did. No one said anything. It was just as quiet, like leaving a funeral. And I never heard another joke.

All the jokes told by whites in a particular period were racial jokes, yet another sign of how certain forms of overt racism are still central to society. This example is contextually rich in that it demonstrates many themes about their racialized experiences that are developed by these perspicacious respondents. We see reference to the limited number of black officers in many departments, as well as the importance of sharing knowledge and support among black officers and civilians. We also see clearly the ideological hegemony that whites have in defining black people and in creating a sense of white networking and solidarity through such activities as regular joke telling. Perhaps most interesting here is the way in which a young black officer worked out a thoughtful response to the racism that he faced.

Despite the curtailing of jokes in this particular department, racial joking is still reported by many African Americans inside and outside police institutions. One respondent seeks to illustrate the seriousness with which he regarded a racist cartoon found on the departmental beat sheet by reading from a letter he had written to the chief:

"On [gives recent date] this department used a cartoon depicting a slave ship with the caption, 'The better-equipped slave ships, of course, always carried a spare,' on the beat sheet. This department also used stereotyped comments about 'Rednecks.' I find both comments and cartoon in poor taste and offensive. Many of the minorities in this department also agree with my sentiments in voicing concerns. However, many of the minorities are afraid to verbalize their comments for fear of repercussions. Although we are diverse in our environment, it still seems like we are still promoting racism and negative stereotypes."

Although the whites in the department may have included a "redneck" joke in order to make the slave cartoon less offensive, this officer rightly criticizes both as unnecessarily promoting negative stereotypes of people whom officers interact with more or less daily. It is important to note too that many black officers are both offended and intimidated by such joking and cartoons, and that some fear for their job if they were to let those feelings be known.

Name-Calling and Verbal Threats from White Officers

Clearly, police workplaces are still riddled with instances of overt racism, even though they may be in decline in many departments. Describing black people with epithets and other names is a way that many whites can express ideological conceptions of African Americans. The goals are to denigrate those targeted and to maintain patterns of subordination. One respondent describes his experiences on his first day of work in the 1970s:

You know, it was a real strange experience. The very first day that I reported to the police academy on September 17, the sergeant that was out there in charge walked up to me and said, "You fat-ass nigger, get your ass on that damn scale."

Numerous respondents spontaneously recount experiences in which they have been called derogatory terms by white fellow officers or members of the public. Well into the 1980s, these racist practices were so widespread that in some departments superior officers would counsel new African-American officers on what to expect:

I remember having a conversation with a captain, and he sat me down and he gave me the spiel about, "I want you to know one of the criteria is that you have to have a thick skin. If you can't stand being called a 'nigger' and still do your job, you don't need to be here because you're gonna get called all kinds of names."

Interestingly, this superior officer understood what African-American officers would be subjected to and wanted to make sure that new black officers would accept such behavior without retaliating. Certainly, African Americans do not need to be counseled by white superiors because they encounter name-calling so frequently that they have long ago developed protective mechanisms against it. One respondent illustrates this point:

I've heard that word, must have been well over 10,000 times in my life. But I can't let it affect me. I know who I am; I know what I can do. I know what I have; I know what I've accomplished and no one can take that away from me.

Key here is the frequency of racist names and incidents for African Americans. Racist comments and behavior are far more commonplace than even sensitive whites are likely to know and understand.

The majority of these black women and men indicate that they refuse to accept name-calling within the occupational setting and have, at least a few times, forcefully challenged name callers to cease or face the consequences. One officer discusses her reaction to name-calling at a law enforcement agency party:

I had a white supervisor, and she made a statement. She had a swimming pool and she said, "I just got my pool cleaned, [and now] I let you niggers get in my pool." . . . And at that time, my immediate reactions told me to hit her.

She was restrained in her response in the immediate situation but later filed a complaint with a superior officer, which was dismissed. The only action taken was that the black officer was transferred to another supervisor.

Racialized mistreatment inside and outside the workplace by fellow employees is bad enough for black police officers; when supervisors and other officials participate in, or wink at, such racist actions, their impact is usually more painful and long-lasting. We have noted examples of this participation in discrimination by senior officers and officials throughout this chapter. Racial discrimination supported or ignored by supervisors and senior officers often has very negative effects because the targets of discrimination cannot see a way out. There is no one who can provide help and redress. Most regular white officers tend to orient their discriminatory actions to signals that they receive from more senior white officers. Discriminatory behavior that is winked at or rewarded by these senior officers and officials thus tends to be repeated.[9]

Name-calling was also reported as sometimes being gender oriented. Another female officer comments, "I've had suspects say, 'Bitch, you should be home having babies.'" This form of name-calling seems to be as common in many law enforcement agencies as racist name-calling. Yet these agencies seem to be very slow in protecting women from such harassment and intimidation, and women officers usually lack the political clout in such departments to combat the omnipresent sexist practices.

Police Brutality: Black Officers' Perspectives

Physical violence by police officers is an important form of overt discriminatory behavior that enforces compliance with the status quo and serves as an important reminder to black Americans of the extent to which whites will allow them to participate in a white-controlled society. White police officers have historically controlled black communities, and for that reason there exists in the general framework of black Americans' knowledge of racism some specific knowledge of the centuries-old history of police violence.

The topic of police malpractice remains one of great concern in black communities across the country. Some researchers have described how forceful administration, better police training, and strict police professionalism can reduce unnecessarily violent behavior of police officers and alleviate racial tensions in most cities.[10] In spite of attempts at reform, police malpractice remains a serious problem across the United States. Human Rights Watch, the largest U.S. human rights group, has recently concluded from a study of police behavior in fourteen cities that police "brutality was one of the most serious, enduring and divisive human rights violations in the United States [and] members of the black and Hispanic minorities were the victims in disproportionate numbers."[11]

Our respondents are generally quite aware of the historical patterns of brutality of white officers and of the impact of that violence in shaping black communities' understandings of policing. Indeed, as we have seen, many have witnessed the use of excessive force by white officers or felt threatened by white officers at some point in their life. Still, when discussing their experiences in policing, many respondents were somewhat reticent about discussing the issues of police violence and brutality in interviews. What may have motivated this reluctance could be that most interviews took place in police stations, often with other officers nearby. In addition, it appears that many officers want to reduce tensions at work and lower their stress level. Some, as we have already seen, may fear retaliation by their white counterparts.

Thus, it is very significant that, in some manner, nearly half the respondents addressed varying manifestations of police violence. Some did so in roundabout ways, yet it became clear in the interviews that this is an important issue with which all of them must deal. For example, one officer describes how a past experience with police violence reminds him of the racial nature of police brutality:

> I remember that vividly, where an officer struck a young female with his weapon across the mouth, knocking out several of her teeth. . . . Officers knew he was wrong also and knew that he was prejudiced and was abusive toward African Americans. . . . That would not occur if it had been a white young lady and in a white hospital in a white community.

This incident occurred in a hospital in the daytime and suggests that police brutality has been common and overt. Certainly, incidents such as this serve to keep the victim in a subordinate position and remind other black citizens who witness it, or are aware of it, of what could happen to them.

Another officer suggests that police violence disproportionately affects black prisoners, who are authorities on this subject:

> There has been more brutality on black people going to jail than white folks going to jail. Well, I haven't done a study, but all I can say is what I know here. Just like the guy who was beaten so bad his eye came out of his socket. And there's lot. Some time when I take a different route, some of the prisoners I have in the back of my car say, "What you going to do, take me somewhere and beat me up?" I'll say, "I'm going to take you to jail." . . . So they're expecting you to do something to them because it may have been done before.

This comment implies that white-generated brutality is frequent, although it usually occurs out of the public's view and away from officers not supportive of such violence. Other respondents underscore this point with explanations of how specialized agency divisions that have excluded black officers sometimes have a culture of aggression or violence that becomes accepted, promotes group solidarity, and remains relatively hidden with the agency. For example, one officer discusses the all-white K-9 division: "Now, I've heard stories about a particular dog handler. He would release a dog on anybody and wouldn't care anything about it. I haven't seen it yet. . . . I know it's there."

A respondent from another law enforcement agency discusses how a squad of white officers engaged in severe brutality yet faced little punishment:

> Just a few years ago, we had an incident where this particular little squad of white officers took one black suspect and picked him up from the predominant low socioeconomic area of the city, took him to a baseball park, and did a "ring of fire" on him. A "ring of fire" is where they take this black suspect and put him in the center of a ring of cars and shine their bright lights on him. It's a form of terrorism. . . . A lieutenant filed a long hand-written complaint on it, but nothing ever happened to any of these officers. What the administration did is tore this group apart, took the sergeant that was in charge, and put him in charge of internal affairs. There was nothing we could do because they kind of kept it hush-hush. Nothing was ever done about it. Yep. This is the cruelty I'm telling you about.

Black officers are often reluctant to become involved in such incidents because of fear of retaliation and ostracism.

Administrations that refuse to become involved give implicit support to such behavior, perhaps because of close ties shared with the offending officers or a reluctance to face the wrath of police organizations.

In many respondents' experience, many white officers fear black officers' unity with black communities and seem to feel that black officers can only be "real" police officers to the extent that they do not identify with those communities. More experienced black officers sometimes note that younger black officers are pressured by white officers to prove that they are, in fact, "real" officers by engaging in abusive behavior against black citizens. Thus, one respondent discusses in poignant detail an incident in which his career was negatively affected by white officers' expectations:

> We had a white officer that allegedly beat a black male with a flashlight . . . and the black male received forty-something staples in his head. . . . And I was the supervisor at the time. I came to the scene. . . . And I sent the officers away from the scene, and I stayed there and handled it. I was the only black officer there at that scene. . . . Now I used my head when I sent them away. I knew what I was doing. Now I'm going to show you how blacks can be scrutinized. These are fellow officers. I'm looking out for their safety and the safety of the citizens, okay. Now, you've got a large black crowd accumulating; you've got a black male that's bleeding. You've got two white officers standing over him. Now you've got about 50 blacks coming up. The smartest thing to do is to get those two white officers out of there before more blacks come and say, "There they are; let's get them!" It could create a riot situation, okay? So I got them out of there.
>
> Now, my white officers assumed that I got them out of there so I could solicit complaints. You get what I'm saying? I got them out of there so they wouldn't get killed or have to kill anyone. And I calmed the people down. It worked. We did not have a riot. I told the people, I said, "Well, if you think they are wrong, we'll look into it. And if they are, we will deal with that." But I had to do anything I could do to calm those people down, and I knew these people, and I knew what I needed to do. . . . Now, these officers wrote complaints on me, which they were unfounded, but this is how you're scrutinized. . . . They didn't look at me as an officer; they didn't look at me as trying to calm the situation down; they looked at me as a black just like these people.

Attempting to perform his job to the best of his ability and dissolve a potentially violent situation, this senior officer was perceived by white subordinates as siding with the black community against his police agency. He was ostracized by fellow white officers, chastised by his chief, and forced to the brink of resignation. In his and numerous other officers' experience, whites feel threatened by any suggestion of unity, however inaccurate, between black officers and members of black communities.

The extent of black officer involvement in brutality against black citizens is not known, as no major studies have been undertaken. No respondent described an incident of violence in which he or she participated, although some male respondents did discuss feeling the need to be aggressive at the beginning of their career under pressure from older officers. Numerous respondents indicate that younger black male officers may be more likely to fall under the influence of the policing ideas of white "good old boys" in certain networks that accent excessive violence. However, almost unanimously, the respondents suggest that black officers as a group are less aggressive toward all citizens. The reasons given include a more acute awareness of past police brutality, their own experiences with police brutality, and the fact that many of them live in or near the community that they police, unlike most white officers. One officer explains: "You have a little more respect, I think, for the people you're dealing with. Because if you rode anywhere in the city you'd see the same people out the window. I didn't want to mistreat a guy tonight and see him at the grocery store the next day."

Despite a reluctance to discuss incidents of police violence openly, these black officers are aware of its persistence and its effect of intimidating citizens in black communities. Police violence harms not only particular victims but also the larger black communities, as the victim's experience becomes part of general community knowledge. Although many respondents acknowledge an awareness of excessive violence in their law enforcement agency, only four respondents discussed some actions that they have taken to address violence that they have witnessed or have had knowledge of in their agency. In each instance, they report that they faced retaliation that affected their career. Clearly, the awareness of the possibility of retaliation is intimidating in itself.

Conclusion

> You want to call it progress because there aren't big jokes in the briefing room; the word "nigger" is not used in the briefing room. You'd like to call it progress and to certain people in certain respects, that's exactly what it is. But the hard answer is that those feelings will come out. They're starting to come out in certain policies, in certain decisions that are being made—that is very, very concealed because what you do is you prevent the fact that there is an agenda of making sure this person is kept down [from being revealed].

Much contemporary research has shown that everyday racism, as a manifestation of white authority and power, seeks to suppress the views of those who are dominated and to contain them in traditionally subordinate positions.[12] As we have seen in this [reading], the strategies used by whites at all levels to accomplish such goals range from constructing stereotypes and notions of racial superiority to exhibiting open forms of hostility and recurring discrimination. These black officers provide ample evidence that discrimination by whites maintains the status quo, in part by limiting black participation in historically white institutions. Such white efforts involve ideologically reinforcing the idea of black inferiority and creating institutionalized practices that seek to create constant barriers.

These black officers report that most whites in their job sphere deny that racial discrimination is still a serious problem there, or that they participate in such discrimination. This shifts the blame for continuing racial problems to African Americans, while absolving the collective conscience of white people. The respondents note that when black people point out racist attitudes or acts of discrimination, whites often become defensive or angry. As a result, the complainants frequently face backlash or retaliation. Despite white claims that racial discrimination is dead or dying, these women and men discuss how they daily encounter ways in which whites overemphasize the differences between white and black people, or between black and white communities. Examples include the racist talk that reproduces hoary stereotypes of black inferiority and the racialization of tasks that reinforces notions that black employees cannot competently perform certain job tasks. Finally, our respondents' discussions often illustrate the importance of the techniques recurrently employed by whites to pacify or intimidate black officers. Clearly, hostile racial climates in law enforcement workplaces are still a serious problem in U.S. law enforcement agencies as we move into the twenty-first century.

These law enforcement officers discuss important containment strategies that they have encountered at the hands of whites, thereby providing important insights into how they understand whites. Their reported experiences with everyday discrimination are usually interactive events, and these experiences generally indicate that white and black officers operate from different theories as to the place of whites and blacks in the social world. Our respondents report how being police officers instills in them feelings of pride, purpose, and responsibility, as well as a sense of legitimate authority. However, they report that many encounters with whites revolve around efforts by whites to strip away these feelings and to enforce a subordinate position of black officers to white officers, as well as to white people in general. Therefore, these black officers understand that such containment strategies often foster a sense of white superiority and solidarity that is important to the perpetuation of racial differences and maintenance of different status. The many accounts in the interviews indicate how whites, intentionally or unintentionally, activate their racist notions, employ racist language, and engage in discriminatory behavior in order to conform to the expectations of important others. Constantly, we see the importance of white old-boy networks, for whites generally perform these actions to

be part of a larger group, to show group solidarity. The respondents report in detail how most white officers have access to greater material rewards, as well as to more interpersonal camaraderie and emotional support, because of their membership in the dominant network in their organization.

Our findings provide much evidence for the cumulative and shared general knowledge of discrimination and other aspects of systemic racism that black officers develop over time. They, too, have important networks and support groups that are essential to their survival in a world of daily racism. They learn an array of countering strategies that are essential in their dealing with racism in their workaday lives, strategies that we will examine in detail in the next chapters. Yet, their interviews also indicate that white strategies of containment and restriction are, in part, dependent on this process of sharing among the black officers. In their interviews, these officers note how their experiences with police violence and with racist talk in their department affect them personally. White intimidation is enhanced when black employees communicate information about negative encounters with whites to other black officers, who in turn take defensive precautions because of this information. Those who do not successfully learn these messages or who reject them may find themselves subjected to prolonged periods of harassment. The resulting stress and insecurity produced by white-generated harassment and other forms of discrimination can make an officer's workaday life a living hell.

28 ...and the Poor Get Prison

Jeffrey Reiman

JEFFREY REIMAN is the William Fraser McDowell Professor of Philosophy at American University in Washington, D.C.

Weeding Out the Wealthy

The offender at the end of the road in prison is likely to be a member of the lowest social and economic groups in the country.[1]

This statement in the *Report of the President's Commission on Law Enforcement and Administration of Justice* is as true today as it was over three decades ago when it was written. Our prisons are indeed, as Ronald Goldfarb has called them, the "national poorhouse."[2] To most citizens this comes as no surprise. . . . Dangerous crimes, they think, are committed mainly by poor people. Seeing that prison populations are made up primarily of the poor only makes them surer of this. They think, in other words, that the criminal justice system gives a true reflection of the dangers that threaten them.

In my view, it also comes as no surprise that our prisons and jails predominantly confine the poor. This is not because these are the individuals who most threaten us. It is because the criminal justice system effectively weeds out the well-to-do, so that at *the end of the road in prison,* the vast majority of those we find there come from the lower classes. This weeding-out process starts before the agents of law enforcement go into action. [I argue] that our very definition of crime *excludes* a wide variety of actions at least as dangerous as those included and often worse. Is it any accident that the kinds of dangerous actions excluded are the kinds most likely to be performed by the affluent in America? Even before we mobilize our troops in the war on crime, we have already guaranteed that large numbers of upper-class individuals will never come within their sights.

This process does not stop at the definition of crime. It continues throughout each level of the criminal justice

Questions to Consider   Contrary to the high-profile cases that have recently rocked Wall Street (Enron, Global Crossing, Tyco), few chief executive officers (CEOs) or white-collar administrators serve lengthy (for that matter, any!) jail time for their white-collar crimes. A corporate CEO who has raided his company's pension fund and destroyed the future of thousands of workers typically receives a fine and/or community service for his crime whereas low-level, nonviolent drug dealers are often sentenced to long and hard time in a federal penitentiary. Wealthy lawbreakers, agues Jeffrey Reiman, rarely see the inside of a prison. Why? How is this pattern linked to race?

system. At each step, from arresting to sentencing, the likelihood of being ignored or released or treated lightly by the system is greater the better off one is economically. As the late U.S. Senator Philip Hart wrote:

> Justice has two transmission belts, one for the rich and one for the poor. The low-income transmission belt is easier to ride without falling off and it gets to prison in shorter order.
>
> The transmission belt for the affluent is a little slower and it passes innumerable stations where exits are temptingly convenient.[3]

This means that the criminal justice system functions from start to finish in a way that makes certain that "the offender at the end of the road in prison is likely to be a member of the lowest social and economic groups in the country."

For the same criminal behavior, the poor are more likely to be arrested; if arrested, they are more likely to be charged; if charged, more likely to be convicted; if convicted, more likely to be sentenced to prison; and if sentenced, more likely to be given longer prison terms than members of the middle and upper classes.[4] In other words, the image of the criminal population one sees in our nation's jails and prisons is distorted by the shape of the criminal justice system itself. It is the face of evil reflected in a carnival mirror, but it is no laughing matter.

The face in the criminal justice carnival mirror is also, as we have already noted, very frequently a black face. Although blacks do not make up the majority of the inmates in our jails and prisons, they make up a proportion that far outstrips their proportion in the population.[5] Here, too, the image we see is distorted by the processes of the criminal justice system itself. Edwin Sutherland and Donald Cressey write in their widely used textbook *Criminology* that

> numerous studies have shown that African-Americans are more likely to be arrested, indicted, convicted, and committed to an institution than are whites who commit the same offenses, and many other studies have shown that blacks have a poorer chance than whites to receive probation, a suspended sentence, parole, commutation of a death sentence, or pardon.[6]

William Wilbanks has attacked this conclusion in *The Myth of a Racist Criminal Justice System.*[7] He uses as "perhaps the most important criticism" of the charge that there is discrimination against blacks in arrests the work of Michael Hindelang, which compares the rate at which respondents to the National Crime Survey report being victimized by assailants perceived to be black with the rate at which blacks are arrested for the relevant crimes according to the *UCR,* and finds "that the racial gap in *offending* for robbery, assault, and rape (whether or not an arrest occurred) was almost equal to that found for *arrest* statistics." Wilbanks concludes, "these results indicate that police select black and white arrestees in approximately the same proportion as they are found in the pool of offenders," and thus "argue against police bias in the arrest process."[8] Recent statistics, however, suggest quite the opposite. Consider the following.

In 1998, respondents to the *National Criminal Victimization Survey* reported that approximately 22 percent of

their assailants in violent victimizations (rape, robbery, simple and aggravated assault) were perceived to be black. That same year, the *UCR* indicates that 42 percent of the individuals arrested for these crimes were black. If we drop simple assault on the assumption that it is less often reported to the police than the other violent crimes, the figures change only slightly: 25 percent of violent victimizers are perceived to be black, whereas 44 percent of those arrested for rape, robbery, and aggravated assault are black. These figures indicate that police are arresting blacks almost two times more frequently than the occurrence of their perceived offenses.[9] Because arrest determines the pool from which charged, convicted, and imprisoned individuals are selected, this suggests that deep bias persists throughout the criminal justice system.

I am aware that there are various problems with comparing *UCR* and *NCVS* statistics and various possible explanations for the divergence of black-white arrest rates from the rate at which blacks and whites are perceived offenders. Thus I do not claim that the results just presented prove definitively the presence of racism. Nonetheless, because they come from the statistics that Wilbanks uses as "the most important criticism" of the discrimination thesis, I think they suffice to cast significant doubt on Wilbanks's claim. Thus, I shall treat his thesis as currently unsubstantiated and continue to follow the majority of researchers in holding that the criminal justice system is widely marked by racial discrimination as well as by economic bias.[10] Moreover, I shall shortly present the results of numerous studies that demonstrate this point.

Curiously enough, statistics on differential treatment of races are available in greater abundance than our statistics on differential treatment of economic classes. For instance, although the FBI tabulates arrest rates by race (as well as by sex, age, and geographic area), it omits class or income. Similarly, both the President's Crime Commission report and Sutherland and Cressey's *Criminology* have index entries for race or racial discrimination but none for class or income of offenders. It would seem that both independent and government data gatherers are more willing to own up to America's racism than to its class bias. Nevertheless, it does not pay to look at these as two independent forms of bias. It is my view that, at least as far as criminal justice is concerned, racism is simply one powerful form of economic bias. I use evidence on differential treatment of blacks as evidence of differential treatment of members of the lower classes. There are five reasons for this.

1. First and foremost, black Americans are disproportionately poor. In 1996, while slightly more than one of every ten white Americans received income below the poverty line, nearly three of every ten black Americans did.[11] The picture is even worse when we shift from income to wealth (property such as a home, land, stocks). Blacks in America own one-fifth of the wealth that whites do.[12] Moreover, "the homeownership rate among non-Hispanic whites is more than 50 percent higher than that of blacks." Among homeowners, in 1993, the median equity "was about $50,000 for whites (in 1993 dollars) [and] $29,000 for blacks." Only about 5 percent of black households owned stocks, compared to 25 percent of white households.[13] Unemployment figures give a similarly dismal picture: In 1997, 2.8 percent of white workers were unemployed and 6.5 percent of blacks were. Among those in the crime-prone ages of 16 to 24, 12.7 percent of white youngsters (with no college) and 31.6 percent of black youngsters (with no college)—nearly one of every three—were jobless.[14]

2. The factors most likely to keep one out of trouble with the law and out of prison, such as a suburban living room instead of a tenement alley to gamble in or legal counsel able to devote time to one's case instead of an overburdened public defender, are the kinds of things that money can buy regardless of one's race, creed, or national origin. For example, as we shall see, arrests of blacks for illicit drug possession or dealing have skyrocketed in recent years, rising way out of proportion to drug arrests for whites—though research shows no greater drug use among blacks than among whites. However, drug arrests are most easily made in "disorganized inner-city" areas, where drug sales are more likely to take place out of doors, and dealers are more willing to sell to strangers. Blacks are (proportionately) more likely than whites to live in such inner-city areas and thus more likely than whites to be arrested on drug charges.[15] And one very important reason that blacks are more likely than whites to live in disorganized inner-city areas is that a greater percentage of blacks than whites are poor and unemployed. What might at first look like a straightforward racial disparity turns out to reflect economic status.

3. Blacks who travel the full route of the criminal justice system and end up in jail or prison are close in economic condition to whites who do. In 1978, 53 percent of black jail inmates had pre-arrest incomes below $3,000, compared with 44 percent of whites.[16] In 1983, the median pre-arrest income of black jail inmates was $4,067 and that of white jail inmates was $6,312. About half of blacks in jail were unemployed before arrest, and 44 percent of whites were.[17] In 1991, 30 percent of whites in the prison population and 38 percent of blacks reported no full- or part-time employment during the month before their arrest.[18]

4. Some studies suggest that race works to heighten the effects of economic condition on criminal justice outcomes, so that "being unemployed *and* black substantially increase[s] the chances of incarceration over those associated with being either unemployed or black."[19] This means that racism will produce a kind of selective economic bias, making a certain segment of the unemployed even more likely to end up behind bars.

5. Finally, it is my belief that the economic powers that be in America have sufficient power to end or drastically reduce racist bias in the criminal justice system. To the extent that they allow it to exist, it is not unreasonable to assume that it furthers their economic interests.

For all these reasons, racism will be treated here as either a form of economic bias or a tool that achieves the same end.

In the remainder of this chapter, I show how the criminal justice system functions to *weed out the wealthy* (meaning both middle- and upper-class offenders) at each stage of the process and thus produces a distorted image of the crime problem. Before entering into this discussion, however, three points are worth noting.

First, it is not my view that the poor are all innocent victims persecuted by the evil rich. The poor do commit crimes, and my own assumption is that the vast majority of the poor who are confined in our prisons are guilty of the crimes for which they were sentenced. In addition, there is good evidence that the poor do commit a greater portion of the crimes against person and property listed in the FBI Index than the middle and upper classes do, relative to their numbers in the national population. What I have already tried to prove is that the crimes in the FBI Index are not the only acts that threaten us nor are they the acts that threaten us the most. What I will try to prove in what follows is that the poor are arrested and punished by the criminal justice system much more frequently than their contribution to the crime problem would warrant—thus the criminals who populate our prisons as well as the public's imagination are disproportionately poor.

Second, the following discussion has been divided into three sections that correspond to the major criminal-justice decision points. As always, such classifications are a bit neater than reality, and so they should not be taken as rigid compartments. Many of the distorting processes operate at all criminal-justice decision points. So, for example, while I will primarily discuss the lighthanded treatment of white-collar criminals in the section on charging and sentencing, it is also true that white-collar criminals are less likely to be arrested or convicted than are blue-collar criminals. The section in which a given issue is treated is a reflection of the point in the criminal justice process at which the disparities are the most striking. Suffice it to say, however, that the disparities between the treatment of the poor and the nonpoor are to be found at all points of the process.

Third, it must be borne in mind that the movement from arrest to sentencing is a funneling process, so that discrimination that occurs at any early stage shapes the population that reaches later stages. Thus, for example, some recent studies find little economic bias in sentence length for people convicted of similar crimes.[20] When reading such studies, however, one should remember that the population that reaches the point of sentencing has already been subject to whatever discrimination exists at earlier stages. If, for example, among people with similar offenses and records, poor people are more likely to be charged and more likely to be convicted, then even if the sentencing of convicted criminals is evenhanded, it will reproduce the discrimination that occurred before.

Arrest and Charging

The problem with most official records of who commits crime is that they are really statistics on who gets arrested and convicted. If, as I will show, the police are more likely to arrest some people than others, these official statistics may tell us more about the police than about criminals. In any event, they give us little reliable data about those who commit crimes and do not get caught. Some social scientists, suspicious of the bias built into official records, have tried to devise other methods of determining who has

committed a crime. Most often, these methods involve an interview or questionnaire in which the respondent is assured of anonymity and asked to reveal whether he or she has committed any offenses for which he or she could be arrested and convicted. Techniques to check reliability of these self-reports also have been devised; however, if their reliability is still in doubt, common sense dictates that they would understate rather than overstate the number of individuals who have committed crimes and never come to official notice. In light of this, the conclusions of these studies are rather astounding. It seems that crime is the national pastime. The President's Crime Commission conducted a survey of 10,000 households and discovered that "91 percent of all Americans have violated laws that could have subjected them to a term of imprisonment at one time in their lives."[21]

A number of other studies support the conclusion that serious criminal behavior is widespread among middle- and upper-class individuals, although these individuals are rarely, if ever, arrested. Some of the studies show that there are no significant differences between economic classes in the incidence of criminal behavior.[22] The authors of a recent review of literature on class and delinquency conclude that "Research published since 1978, using both official and self-reported data suggests . . . that there is no pervasive relationship between SES [socioeconomic status] and delinquency."[23] This conclusion is echoed by Jensen and Thompson, who argue that

> The safest conclusion concerning class structure and delinquency is the same one that has been proposed for several decades: class, no matter how defined, contributes little to explaining variation in self-reports of common delinquency.[24]

Others conclude that while lower-class individuals do commit more than their share of crimes, arrest records overstate their share and understate that of the middle and upper classes.[25] Still other studies suggest that some forms of serious crime—forms usually associated with lower-class youth—show up *more frequently* among higher-class persons than among lower.[26] For instance, Empey and Erikson interviewed 180 white males aged 15 to 17 who were drawn from different economic strata. They found that "virtually all respondents reported having committed not one but a variety of different offenses." Although youngsters from the middle classes constituted 55 percent of the group interviewed, they admitted to 67 percent of the instances of breaking and entering, 70 percent of the instances of property destruction, and an astounding 87 percent of all the armed robberies admitted to by the entire sample.[27] Williams and Gold studied a national sample of 847 males and females between the ages of 13 and 16.[28] Of these, 88 percent admitted to at least one delinquent offense.

Even those who conclude "that more lower status youngsters commit delinquent acts more frequently than do higher status youngsters"[29] also recognize that lower-class youth are significantly overrepresented in official records. Gold writes that "about five times more lowest than highest status boys appear in the official records; if records were complete and unselective, we estimate that the ratio would be closer to 1.5:1."[30] The simple fact is that for the same offense, *a poor person is more likely to be arrested and, if arrested charged, than a middle- or upper-class person.*[31]

This means, first of all, that poor people are more likely to come to the attention of the police. Furthermore, even when apprehended, the police are more likely to formally charge a poor person and release a higher-class person *for the same offense.* Gold writes that

> boys who live in poorer parts of town and are apprehended by police for delinquency are four to five times more likely to appear in some official record than boys from wealthier sections who commit the same kinds of offenses. These same data show that, at each stage in the legal process from charging a boy with an offense to some sort of disposition in court, boys from different socioeconomic backgrounds are treated differently, so that those eventually incarcerated in public institutions, that site of most of the research on delinquency, are selectively poorer boys.[32]

From a study of self-reported delinquent behavior, Gold finds that when individuals were apprehended, "if the offender came from a higher status family, police were more likely to handle the matter themselves without referring it to the court."[33]

Many writers have commented on the extent and seriousness of "white-collar crime," so I will keep my remarks to a minimum. Nevertheless, for those of us trying to understand how the image of crime is created, four points should be noted.

1. White-collar crime is costly; it takes far more dollars from our pockets than all the FBI Index crimes combined.

2. White-collar crime is widespread, probably much more so than the crimes of the poor.

3. White-collar criminals are rarely arrested or charged; the system has developed kindlier ways of dealing with the more delicate sensibilities of its higher-class clientele.

4. When white-collar criminals are prosecuted and convicted, their sentences are either suspended or very light when judged by the cost their crimes have imposed on society.

The first three points will be discussed here, and the fourth will be presented in the section on sentencing below.

Everyone agrees that the cost of white-collar crime is enormous. In 1985, *U.S. News & World Report Report* reported that "Experts estimate that white-collar criminals rake in a minimum of $200 billion annually."[34] Marshall Clinard also cites the $200 billion estimate in his recent book, *Corporate Corruption: The Abuse of Corporate Power.*[35] Nonetheless, $200 billion probably understates the actual cost. Some experts place the cost of white-collar crime for firms doing business in the government sector alone at $500 billion a year.[36] Tax evasion alone has been estimated to cost from 5 to 7 percent of the gross national product. For 1997, that would be between $403 and $564 billion.[37]

Let me close with one final example that typifies this particular distortion of justice policy. Embezzlement is the crime of misappropriating money or property entrusted to one's care, custody, or control. Because the poor are rarely entrusted with tempting sums of money or valuable property, this is predominantly a crime of the middle and upper classes. The U.S. Chamber of Commerce estimate of the annual economic cost of embezzlement, adjusted for inflation and population growth, is $12.42 billion—more than four-fifths the total value of all property and money stolen in all FBI Index property crimes in 1997. (Don't be fooled into thinking that this cost is imposed only on the rich or on big companies with lots of resources. They pass on their losses—and their increased insurance costs—to consumers in the form of higher prices. Embezzlers take money out of the very same pockets that muggers do: yours!) Nevertheless, the

FBI reports that in 1997, when there were 1,805,600 arrests for property crimes, there were 17,100 arrests for embezzlement nationwide.[38] Although their cost to society is comparable, the number of arrests for property crimes was *more than 100 times greater* than the number of arrests for embezzlement. Roughly, this means there was one property crime arrest for every $8,000 stolen, and even the language becomes more delicate as we deal with a "better" class of crook.

The clientele of the criminal justice system forms an exclusive club. Entry is largely a privilege of the poor. The crimes they commit are the crimes that qualify one for admission—and they are admitted in greater proportion than their share of those crimes. Curiously enough, the crimes the affluent commit are not the kind that easily qualify one for membership in the club.

And as we have seen, the reluctance to use the full force of the criminal justice system in pursuit of white-collar criminals is matched by a striking reluctance to use the full force of current public and private research organizations to provide up-to-date estimates of its cost. This coincidence is worth pondering by anyone interested in how criminal justice policy gets made and how research and statistics function in the process.

Conviction

Between arrest and imprisonment lies the crucial process that determines guilt or innocence. Studies of individuals accused of similar offenses and with similar prior records show that the poor defendant is more likely to be adjudicated guilty than is the wealthier defendant.[39] In the adjudication process the only thing that *should* count is whether the accused is guilty and whether the prosecution can prove it beyond a reasonable doubt. Unfortunately, at least two other factors that are irrelevant to the question of guilt or innocence significantly affect the outcome: One is the ability of the accused to be free on bail prior to trial, and the second is access to legal counsel able to devote adequate time and energy to the case. Because both bail and high-quality legal counsel cost money, it should come as no surprise that here as elsewhere the poor do poorly.

The advantages of access to adequate legal counsel during the adjudicative process are obvious but still worthy of mention. In 1963, the U.S. Supreme Court handed down the landmark *Gideon v. Wainwright* decision, holding that the states must provide legal counsel to the indigent in all felony cases. As a result, no person accused of a serious crime need face his or her accuser without a lawyer. However, the Supreme Court has not held that the Constitution entitles individuals to lawyers able to devote equal time and resources to their cases. Even though *Gideon* represents significant progress in making good on the constitutional promise of equal treatment before the law, we still are left with two transmission belts of justice: one for the poor and one for the affluent. There is an emerging body of case law on the right to effective assistance of counsel;[40] however, this is yet to have any serious impact on the assembly-line legal aid handed out to the poor.

Needless to say, the distinct legal advantages that money can buy become even more salient when we enter the realm of corporate and other white-collar crime. Indeed, it is often precisely the time and cost involved in bringing to court a large corporation with its army of legal eagles that is offered as an excuse for the less formal and more genteel treatment accorded to corporate crooks. This excuse is, of course, not equitably distributed to all economic classes, any more than quality legal service is. This means that, regardless of actual innocence or guilt, one's chances of beating the rap increase as one's income increases. Regardless of what fraction of crimes are committed by the poor, the criminal justice system is distorted so that an even greater fraction of those convicted will be poor. And with conviction comes sentencing.

Sentencing

The simple fact is that the criminal justice system reserves its harshest penalties for its lower-class clients and puts on kid gloves when confronted with a better class of crook. We will come back to the soft treatment of S&L crooks shortly. For the moment, note that the tendency to treat higher-class criminals more leniently than lower-class criminals has been with us for a long time. In 1972, *The New York Times* did a study on sentencing in state and federal courts. The *Times* stated that "crimes that tend to be committed by the poor get tougher sentences than those committed by the well-to-do," that federal "defendants who

Gideon v. Wainwright The 1963 Supreme Court case that established the right of anyone accused of a crime to have legal counsel even if an individual cannot afford a lawyer.

could not afford private counsel were sentenced nearly twice as severely as defendants with private counsel," and that a "study by the Vera Institute of Justice of the courts in the Bronx indicates a similar pattern in the state courts."[41]

More recently, D'Alessio and Stoltzenberg studied a random sample of 2,760 offenders committed to the custody of Florida Department of Corrections during fiscal year 1985. Although they found no greater sentence severity for poor offenders found guilty of property crimes, they found that poor offenders did receive longer sentences for violent crimes, such as manslaughter, and for moral offenses, such as narcotics possession. Nor, by the way, did sentencing guidelines reduce this disparity.[42] A study of individuals convicted of drunk driving found that increased education (taken as an indicator of higher occupational status) "increase[d] the rate of movement from case filing to probation and decrease[d] the rate of movement to prison." And though, when probation was given, more-educated offenders got longer probation, they also got shorter prison sentences, if sentenced to prison at all.[43]

Chiricos and Bales found that, for individuals guilty of similar offenses and with similar prior records, unemployed defendants were more likely to be incarcerated while awaiting trial, and for longer periods, than employed defendants. They were more than twice as likely as their employed counterparts to be incarcerated upon a finding of guilt. And defendants with public defenders experienced longer periods of jail time than those who could afford private attorneys.[44] McCarthy noted a similar link between unemployment and greater likelihood of incarceration.[45] In his study of 28,315 felony defendants in Tennessee, Virginia, and Kentucky, Champion also found that offenders who could afford private counsel had a greater likelihood of probation, and received shorter sentences when incarceration was imposed.[46] A study of the effects of implementing Minnesota's determinate sentencing program shows that socioeconomic bias is "more subtle, but no less real" than before the new program.[47]

Tillman and Pontell examined the sentences received by individuals convicted of Medicaid provider fraud in California. Because such offenders normally have no prior arrests and are charged with grand theft, their sentences were compared with the sentences of other offenders convicted of grand theft and who also had no prior records. While 37.7 percent of the Medicaid defrauders were sentenced to jail or prison time, 79.2 percent of the others convicted of grand theft were sentenced to jail or prison. This was so even though the median dollar loss due to the Medicaid frauds was $13,000, more than ten times the median loss due to the other grand thefts ($1,149). Tillman and Pontell point out that most of the Medicaid defrauders were health professionals, while most of the others convicted of grand theft had low-level jobs or were unemployed. They conclude that "differences in the sentences imposed on the two samples are indeed the result of the different social statuses of their members."[48]

As usual, data on racial discrimination in sentencing tell the same story of the treatment of those who cannot afford the going price of justice. A study of offender processing in New York State counties found that, for offenders with the same arrest charge and the same prior criminal records, minorities were incarcerated more often than comparably situated whites.[49] A study of sentencing in Miami concludes that when case-related attributes do not clearly point to a given sentence, sentencing disparities are more likely to be based on race.[50] A study of 9,690 males who entered Florida prisons in 1992 and 1993, and who were legally eligible for stricter sentencing under the habitual offender statute, shows that, for similar prior records and seriousness of crime, race had a "significant and substantial" effect: Black defendants were particularly disadvantaged "for drug offenses and for property crimes."[51]

Most striking perhaps is that, in 1993, 51 percent of inmates in state and federal prisons were black and 44 percent of inmates of jails were black, whereas blacks make up only 36.5 percent of those arrested for serious (FBI Index) crimes.[52] Furthermore, when we look only at federal prisons, where there is reason to believe that racial and economic discrimination is less prevalent than in state institutions, we find that in 1986, nonwhite inmates were sentenced, on average, to 33 more months for burglary than white inmates and 22 more months for income tax evasion. In 1989, the average federal sentence for blacks found guilty of violent offenses was 10 months longer than that for whites.[53]

Here must be mentioned the notorious "100-to-1" disparity between sentences for possession of cocaine in powder form (popular in the affluent suburbs) and in crack form (popular in poor inner-city neighborhoods). Federal laws require a mandatory five-year sentence for crimes involving 500 grams of powder cocaine or 5 grams of crack cocaine. This yields a sentence for the first-time offenders (with no aggravating factors, such as possession of a weapon) that is longer than the sentence for kidnapping, and only slightly shorter than the sentence for attempted murder![54] About 90 percent of those convicted of federal crack offenses are black; about 4 percent are white. "As a result, the average prison sentence served by Black federal prisoners is 40 percent longer than the average sentence for Whites."[55] In 1995, the United States Sentencing commission recommended ending the 100-to-1 disparity between powder and crack penalties, and, in an unusual display of bipartisanship, both the Republican Congress and the Democratic President rejected their recommendation.[56]

Sentencing disparities between the races are, of course, not new. An extensive study by the *Boston Globe* of 4,500 cases of armed robbery, aggravated assault, and rape found that "blacks convicted in the superior courts of Massachusetts receive harsher penalties than whites for the same crimes."[57] The authors of a study of almost 1,200 males sentenced to prison for armed robbery in a southwestern state found that "in 1977 whites incarcerated for armed robbery had a greater than average chance of receiving the least severe sentence, while nonwhites had a greater than average chance of receiving a moderately severe sentence."[58] A study of 229 adjudicated cases in a Florida judicial district yielded the finding that "whites have an 18 percent greater chance in the predicated probability of receiving probation than blacks when all other things are equal."[59] A recent study of criminal justice systems in California, Michigan, and Texas by Petersillia confirms the continuation of this trend. "Controlling for the factors most likely to influence sentencing and parole decisions," she writes, "the analysis still found that blacks and Hispanics are less likely to be given probation, more likely to receive *prison* sentences, more likely to receive longer sentences, and more likely to serve a greater portion of their original time."[60] Myers found that "harsher treatment of persons with fewer resources (e.g., female, unemployed, unmarried, black) is . . . pronounced in highly unequal counties."[61]

The federal government has introduced sentencing guidelines and mandatory minimum sentences that might be expected to eliminate discrimination, and many states have followed suit. The effect of this, however, has been not to eliminate discretion but to transfer it from those who sentence to those who decide what to charge—that

is, from judges to prosecutors. Prosecutors can charge in a way that makes it likely that the offender will get less than the mandatory minimum sentence. Says U.S. District Judge J. Lawrence Irving of San Diego, "the system is run by the U.S. attorneys. When they decide how to indict, they fix the sentence."[62] And discrimination persists. To examine the effects of mandatory minimum sentences, Barbara Meierhoefer studied 267,178 offenders sentenced in federal courts from January 1984 to June 1990. She found that whites were consistently more likely than blacks to be sentenced to less than the minimum sentence. The disparity varied from year to year, reaching a high point in 1988, when blacks were 30 percent more likely than whites to receive at least the minimum. Hispanics fared even worse than blacks. Concludes Meierhoefer,

> despite the laws' emphasis on offense behavior, sentences still vary by offender characteristics. . . . Further, both black and Hispanic offenders now receive notably more severe sentences than their white counterparts.
>
> The latter trend suggests that there may be questions to be considered concerning the impact of shifting discretion affecting sentencing from the court to the prosecutor's office.[63]

A growing number of judges are speaking out against the system of sentencing guidelines and mandatory minimum sentences. According to U.S. District Judge Terry Hatter of Los Angeles, "the toughest sentences are now strictly 'applied to basically one group of people: poor minority people." Appellate Judge Gerald W. Heaney of Duluth, Minnesota, conducted his own study "and found that young black men got longer sentences than their white counterparts for similar crimes. Using 1989 data, he compared sentences under the new system with those under the old. The average sentence for black males was 40 months longer, he found, while the average sentence for white males was 19 months longer."[64]

There is considerable evidence that *double discrimination* —by race of the victim and of the offender—affects death penalty sentencing. In Florida, for example, blacks "who kill whites are nearly forty times more likely to be sentenced to death than those who kill blacks." Moreover, among "killers of whites, blacks are five times more likely than whites to be sentenced to death." This pattern of double discrimination was also evidenced, though less pronouncedly, in Texas, Ohio, and Georgia, the other states surveyed. Together, these four states "accounted for approximately 70 percent of the nation's death sentences" between 1972 and 1977.[65]

More recent studies have shown the same pattern. It was on the basis of such research that what may have been the last constitutional challenge to the death penalty was raised and rejected. In the 1987 case of *McCleskey v. Kemp*, evidence of discrimination on the basis of the victim's race was provided by a study by Professor David Baldus, of the University of Iowa, who examined 2,484 Georgia homicide cases that occurred between 1973 (when the current capital murder law was enacted) and 1979 (a year after McCleskey received his death sentence).[66] After controlling for all legitimate nonracial factors—such as severity of crime and the presence of aggravating factors—Baldus found that "murderers of white victims are still being sentenced to death 4.3 times more often than murderers of black victims."[67] The justices of the Supreme Court acknowledged the systemic disparities, but a majority held that the disparities would not invalidate death penalty convictions unless discrimination could be shown in the individual case at hand.

A 1990 report of the General Accounting Office to the Senate and House Committees on the Judiciary reviewed 28 studies on racial disparities in death penalty sentencing and concluded that the race of the victim strongly influenced the likelihood of a death penalty: "[T]hose who murdered whites were found to be more likely to be sentenced to death than those who murdered blacks."[68] Note that all these discriminatory sentences were rendered under statutes that had passed constitutional muster and were therefore presumed free of the biases that led the Supreme Court to invalidate all American death penalty statutes in *Furman v. Georgia* in 1972.

Another study has shown that among blacks and whites on death row, whites are more likely to have their sentences commuted. Also, blacks or whites who have private counsel are more likely to have their execution commuted than condemned persons defended by court-appointed attorneys.[69]

McCleskey v. Kemp A 1987 Supreme Court case that raised the question of racial bias in death penalty cases. The Court found that just because researchers had credibly found statistical patterns of racial bias in death penalty sentencing it did *not* necessarily mean that racial discrimination was the reason for such disparities.

As I have already pointed out, justice is increasingly tempered with mercy as we deal with a better class of crime. The Sherman Antitrust Act is a criminal law. It was passed in recognition of the fact that one virtue of a free enterprise economy is that competition tends to drive consumer prices down, so agreements by competing firms to refrain from price competition is the equivalent of stealing money from the consumer's pocket. Nevertheless, although such conspiracies cost consumers far more than lower-class theft, price fixing was a misdemeanor until 1974.[70] In practice, few conspirators end up in prison, and when they do, the sentence is a mere token, well below the maximum provided in the law.

In the historical *Electrical Equipment* cases in the early 1960s, executives of several major firms met secretly to fix prices on electrical equipment to a degree that is estimated to have cost the buying public well over $1 billion. The executives involved knew they were violating the law. They used plain envelopes for their communications, called their meetings "choir practice," and referred to the list of executives in attendance as the "Christmas card list." This case is rare and famous because it was one in which the criminal sanction was actually imposed. Seven executives received and served jail sentences. In light of the amount of money they had stolen from the American public, however, their sentences were more an indictment of the government than of themselves: *thirty days in jail!*

Speaking about the record of federal antitrust prosecution, Clinard and Yeager write that

> even in the most widespread and flagrant price conspiracy cases, few corporate executives are ever imprisoned; of the total 231 cases with individual defendants from 1955 to 1975, prison sentences were given in only 19 cases. Of a total of 1,027 individual defendants, only 49 were sentenced to prison.[71]

There is some (slight) indication of a toughening in the sentences since antitrust violations were made a felony in 1974 and penalties were increased. "In felony cases prosecuted under the new penalties through March 1978, 15 of 21 sentenced individuals (71 percent) were given terms averaging 192 days each."[72] Nevertheless, when the cost to society is reckoned, even such penalties as these are hardly severe.

After the "anything goes" attitude of the Reagan era, which brought us such highly publicized white-collar skullduggery as the multibillion dollar savings and loan scandal, the 1990s have seen a kind a backlash, with the government under pressure to up the penalties for corporate offenders. Here too, however, progress follows a slow and zigzagging course. Consider, for example, the following series of titles of articles from *The Washington Post:* March 2, 1990. "Criminal Indictments: Training Bigger Guns on Corporations"; April 1, 1990, "Going Soft on Corporate Crime"; April 28, 1990, "Justice Dept. Shifts on Corporate Sentencing" ("Attorney General Dick Thornburgh last month withdrew the Justice Department's longstanding support for tough mandatory sentences for corporate criminals following an intense lobbying campaign by defense contractors, oil companies and other *Fortune* 500 firms."); April 27, 1991, "Corporate Lawbreakers May Face Tougher Penalties."[73] Lest this last one be taken as truly reversing the trend to leniency, note that it reports new sentencing guidelines approved by the U.S. Sentencing Commission, and it points out: "The only penalties set forth by the guidelines are fines and probation because the defendants in such cases are not individuals." Compare this with a statement from Ira Reiner, Los Angeles district attorney, quoted in the first of the articles just listed: "A fine, no matter how substantial, is simply a cost of doing business for a corporation. But a jail term for executives is different. What we are trying to do is to change the corporate culture." Good luck, Ira.

Studies have shown that even though corporate and white-collar lawbreakers are being more frequently brought to justice and more frequently being sanctioned, they still receive more lenient sentences than do those who are sentenced for common property crimes.[74] A study by Hagan and Palloni, which focuses particularly on the differences between pre- and post-Watergate treatments of white-collar offenders, concludes that likelihood of prosecution after Watergate was increased, but that the effect of this was canceled out by the leniency of the sentences meted out:

> the new incarcerated white-collar offenders received relatively light sentences that counterbalanced the increased use of imprisonment. Relative to less-educated common criminals, white-collar offenders were more likely to be imprisoned after Watergate than before, but for shorter periods.[75]

Even after the heightened public awareness of white-collar crime that came in the wake of Watergate and the S&L scandals, it remains the case that crimes of the poor lead to stiffer sentences than the crimes of the well-to-do (see Table 1). Keep in mind while looking at these figures that *each* of the "crimes of the affluent" costs the public more than *all* of the "crimes of the poor" put together.

I do not deny that there has been some toughening of the treatment of white-collar offenders in recent years. Nonetheless, this toughening has been relatively mild, especially when compared with the treatment dealt out to lower-class offenders. Before turning to the "great" scandals of Watergate and the savings and loan industry, here are two "small" cases that illustrate the new developments.

In September 1991, a fire destroyed a chicken-processing plant in Hamlet, North Carolina. When the 100 employees in the plant tried to escape, they found that the company executives had ordered the doors locked "to keep out insects and

TABLE 1   Sentences Served for Different Classes of Crime, 1996–97

	Percent Sentenced to Prison	Average Time Served (in months)
Crimes of the poor		
Robbery	99	60
Burglary	89	28
Auto Theft	63	24
Crime of the affluent		
Fraud	63	16
Tax Law Violation	42	15
Embezzlement	58	9

Source: Sourcebook–1998 (compiled from Tables 5.28 and 6.54, and rounded off).

to keep employees from going outside for coffee breaks, or stealing chickens." Twenty-five workers died in the fire; some were found burned to death at the doors they couldn't open. Another 50 people were injured. The owner of the company and two plant managers were charged with involuntary manslaughter. The outcome: The owner pleaded guilty and was sentenced to 19 years and 6 months in prison. You may or may not think this is severe as a punishment for someone responsible for 25 very painful deaths, but note three revealing facts. First, as part of the plea agreement, the involuntary manslaughter cases against the two plant managers were dismissed, though they surely knew the doors were locked and what the risks were. Second, the owner is eligible for parole after 2½ years. And third, the sentence is "believed to be the harshest judgment ever handed out for a workplace safety violation."[76]

We have seen in this chapter that the criminal justice system is triply biased against the poor. First, there is the economic class bias *among harmful acts* as to which get labeled crimes and which are treated as regulatory matters. Second, there is economic class bias *among crimes* that we have already seen in this chapter. The crimes that poor people are likely to commit carry harsher sentences than the "crimes in the suites" committed by well-to-do people. Third, *among defendants convicted of the same crimes,* the poor receive less probation and more years of confinement than well-off defendants, assuring us once again that the vast majority of those put behind bars are from the lowest social and economic classes in the nation. On either side of the law, the rich get richer . . .

. . . and the Poor Get Prison

At 9:05 A.M. on the morning of Thursday, September 9, 1971, a group of inmates forced their way through a gate at the center of the prison, fatally injured a guard named William Quinn, and took 50 hostages. The Attica uprising had begun. It lasted four days, until 9:43 A.M. on the morning of Monday, September 13, when corrections officers and state troopers stormed the prison and killed 29 inmates and 10 hostages.[77] During those four days the nation saw the faces of its captives on television—the hard black faces of young men who had grown up on the streets of Harlem and other urban ghettos. Theirs were the faces of crime in America. The television viewers who saw them

were not surprised. Here were faces of dangerous men who should be locked up. Nor were people outraged when the state launched its murderous attack on the prison, killing many more inmates and guards than did the prisoners themselves. Maybe they were shocked—but not outraged. Neither were they outraged when two grand juries refused to indict any of the attackers, nor when the mastermind of the attack, New York Governor Nelson Rockefeller, was named vice president of the United States three years after the uprising and massacre.[78]

They were not outraged because the faces they saw on the TV screens fit and confirmed their beliefs about who is a deadly threat to American society—and a deadly threat must be met with deadly force. How did those men get to Attica? How did Americans get their beliefs about who is a dangerous person? These questions are interwoven. People get their notions about who is a criminal at least in part from the occasional television or newspaper picture of who is inside our prisons. The individuals they see there have been put in prison because people believe certain kinds of individuals are dangerous and should be locked up.

I have agued in this chapter that this is not a simple process of selecting the dangerous and the criminal from among the peace-loving and the law-abiding. It is also a process of *weeding out the wealthy* at every stage, so that the final picture—a picture like that that appeared on the TV screen on September 9, 1971—is not a true reflection of the real dangers in our society but a distorted image, the kind reflected in a carnival mirror.

It is not my view that the inmates in Attica were innocent of the crimes that sent them there. I assume they and just about all the individuals in prisons in America are probably guilty of the crime for which they were sentenced and maybe more. My point is that people who are equally or more dangerous, equally or more criminal, are not there; that the criminal justice system works systematically not to punish and confine the dangerous and the criminal, *but to punish and confine the poor who are dangerous and criminal.*

It is successful at all levels. In 1973, there were 204,211 individuals in state and federal prisons, or 96 prisoners for every 100,000 individuals (of all ages) in the general population. By 1979, state and federal inmates numbered 301,470, or 133 per 100,000 Americans. By

1998, there were a total of 1,825,400 persons in state and federal prisons and in the local jails, a staggering 672 for every 100,000 in the population. One in 149 U.S. residents (of all ages and both sexes) was behind bars in 1998. However, of the 1,825,400 inmates in federal and state prisons and in jails, some 1,715,000 are men, virtually all above the age of 18. Because the adult male population in the United States is about 94 million, *this means that roughly one out of every 55 American adult men is behind bars.*[79] This enormous number of prisoners is, of course, predominantly from the bottom of society.

Of the estimated 1.2 million people in state prisons in 1998, one-third were not employed at all (full or part time) prior to their arrests. Just over half were employed at all, thus nearly half were without full-time employment prior to arrest. These statistics are comparable to those in 1986, when 31 percent of state inmates had no pre-arrest employment at all, and 43 percent had no full-time pre-arrest employment.[80] Among jail inmates in 1996, 36 percent were not employed prior to arrest—20 percent were looking for work and 16 percent were not. Approximately half of jail inmates reported pre-arrest incomes below $7,200 a year.[81]

To get an idea of what part of society is in prison, we should compare these figures with comparable figures for the general population. Because more than 90 percent of inmates are male, we can look at employment and income figures for males in the general population in the mid-1990s.

In 1994, 5.4 percent of males, 16 years old and above, in the labor force were unemployed and looking for work. Since it is normally thought that the number of unemployed people who are not looking for work is something less than equal to the number looking, doubling this rate will give us a conservative estimate of the percentage of males above age 16 who are unemployed, looking and not looking. Then, whereas one-third of state prison inmates and 36 percent of jail inmates were unemployed (looking and not looking for work) in the year prior to their arrest, the rate for unincarcerated males above the age of 16, was approximately 11 percent. Prisoners were unemployed at a rate more than three times that of their counterparts in the general population.[82] In 1994, the median income for males, 15 years old and above, with any income at all, was $22,995.[83] This means that half of these males in the

general population with any income at all were earning this amount or less. Compare this to jail inmates, about half of whom earned $7,200 a year or less in the year before they were arrested.

Our prisoners are not a cross section of America. They are considerably poorer and considerably less likely to be employed than the rest of Americans. Moreover, they are also less educated, which is to say less in possession of the means to improve their sorry situations. Of all U.S. prison inmates, 41 percent did not graduate from high school, compared to 20 percent of the U.S. adult population.[84]

The criminal justice system is sometimes thought of as a kind of sieve in which the innocent are progressively sifted out from the guilty, who end up behind bars. I have tried to show that the sieve works another way as well. It sifts the affluent out from the poor, so it is not merely the guilty who end up behind bars, but the *guilty poor.*

. . . The criminal justice system does not simply weed the peace-loving from the dangerous, the law-abiding from the criminal. At every stage, starting with the very definitions of crime and progressing through the stages of investigation, arrest, charging, conviction, and sentencing, the system *weeds out the wealthy.* It refuses to define as "crimes" or as serious crimes the dangerous and predatory acts of the well-to-do—acts that, as we have seen, result in the loss of thousands of lives and billions of dollars. Instead, the system focuses its attention on those crimes likely to be committed by members of the lower classes. Thus, it is no surprise to find that so many of the people behind bars are from the lower classes. The people we see in our jails and prisons are no doubt dangerous to society, but they are not *the danger* to society, not the gravest danger to society. Individuals who pose equal or greater threats to our well-being walk the streets with impunity.

. . . In the present chapter I have argued that the criminal justice system works to make crime appear to be the monopoly of the poor by . . . more actively pursuing and prosecuting the poor rather than the well-off for the acts that are labeled crime. *The . . . effect . . . is to maintain a real threat of crime that the vast majority of Americans believes is a threat from the poor.* The criminal justice system is a carnival mirror that throws back a distorted image of the dangers that lurk in our midst—and conveys the impression that those dangers are the work of the poor.

29 The Mark of a Criminal Record
Devah Pager

DEVAH PAGER is an associate professor of sociology and faculty associate of the Office of Population Research at Princeton University. Her research focuses on institutions affecting racial stratification, including education, labor markets, and the criminal justice system. Pager's current research has involved a series of field experiments studying discrimination against minorities and ex-offenders in the low-wage labor market.

AMONG THOSE RECENTLY RELEASED FROM prison, nearly two-thirds will be charged with new crimes and 40 percent will return to prison within three years. Those who are not reincarcerated have poorer employment and incomes than those without criminal records. But there is strong disagreement over the reasons that ex-offenders do so poorly after release. Does incarceration itself actually lead to lower employment and income? Or do the poor outcomes of ex-offenders merely arise from the environmental and personal histories that sent them to prison in the first place—the broken families, the poor neighborhoods, the lack of education and absence of legitimate opportunities, the individual tendencies toward violence or addiction?[1]

Survey research has consistently shown their incarceration is linked to lower employment and income. Many hypotheses have been proposed for this relationship: the labeling effects of criminal stigma, the disruption of social and family networks, the loss of human capital, institutional trauma, and legal barriers to employment. It is, however, difficult, using survey data, to determine which of these mechanisms is at work and whether, for any given mechanism, the results are due to the effect of imprisonment or to preexisting characteristics of people who are convicted. A further issue, given racial disparities in imprisonment rates, is whether the effect of a criminal record is more severe for African American that it is for white ex-offenders.

> **Questions to Consider**   The rate of recidivism (convicts who return to jail) is extremely high in the United States. Poverty, a lack of formal education, and the disappearance of employment opportunities in the inner city of jobs that pay a living wage create conditions that researchers believe are linked to criminal activity. How difficult is it for someone with a criminal record, a "mark" as this author describes it, to secure employment? Furthermore, how might race play out among those with and without a criminal "mark"? Devah Pager's research findings are shocking.

In the research reported here I sought to answer three primary questions about the mechanisms driving the relationship between imprisonment and employment.[2] First, to what extent do employers use information about criminal histories to make hiring decisions? Second, does race, by itself, remain a major barrier to employment? Its continued significance has been questioned in recent policy debates.[3] Third, does the effect of a criminal record differ for black and white applicants? Given that many Americans hold strong and persistent views associating race and crime, does a criminal record trigger a more negative response for African American than for white applicants?

The Employment Audit

Just as a college degree may serve as a positive credential for those seeking employment, a prison term attaches a "negative credential" to individuals, certifying them in ways that may qualify them for discrimination or social exclusion. Using an experimental audit design, I have been able to isolate that institutional effect, holding constant many background and personal characteristics that otherwise make it very difficult to disentangle cause and effect.[4]

In an employment audit, matched pairs of individuals ("testers") apply for real job openings to see whether employers respond differently to applicants on the basis of selected characteristics. The methodology combines experimental methods with real-life contexts. It is particularly valuable for those with an interest in discrimination, and has primarily been used to study characteristics such as race, gender, and age that are protected under the Civil Rights Act.

Several states, including Wisconsin, have expanded fair employment legislation to protect individuals with criminal records from discrimination by employers, because of their concern about the consequences of the rapid expansion and the skewed racial and ethnic composition of the ex-offender population over the last three decades. Under this legislation, employers are warned that past crimes may be taken into account only if they closely relate to the specific duties required by the job—as, for example, if a convicted embezzler applies for a bookkeeping position, or a sex offender for a job at a day care center. Because of the Wisconsin legislation barring discrimination on the basis of a criminal record, we might expect circumstances to be, if anything, more favorable to the employment of ex-offenders than in states without legal protections.

This audit was conducted between June and December, 2001, in Milwaukee, Wisconsin, which in population, size, racial composition, and employment rate is typical of many major American cities. At the time, the local economy was moderately strong and unemployment rates ranged between 4 and 5.2 percent.[5]

I used two audit teams of 23-year-old male college students, one consisting of two African Americans and the other of two whites. All were bright and articulate, with appealing styles of self-presentation. Characteristics that were not already identical, such as education and work experience, were made to appear identical for the purposes of the audit. Within each team, one auditor was randomly assigned a "criminal record" for the first week; then week by week auditors took turns playing the ex-offender role. The "criminal record" consisted of a nonviolent, felony drug conviction (possession of cocaine with intent to distribute). If the employment application did not request information about previous convictions, ways were found to include that information—for example, by reporting work experience in the correctional facility and citing a parole officer as a reference.

The audit teams applied to separate sets of jobs drawn from the Sunday classified section of the city's major daily newspaper, the *Milwaukee Journal Sentinel,* and from Jobnet, a state-sponsored Web site for employment listings. Since nearly 90 percent of state prisoners have no more than a high school diploma, the job openings chosen were for entry-level positions requiring no previous experience and no education beyond high school (see Figure 1). All openings were within 25 miles of downtown Milwaukee; a majority were in the suburbs or surrounding counties.[6] The survey audited 350 employers, 150 by the white audit team and 200 by the black team.

The audit study focused only on the first stage in the employment process—the stage most likely to be affected by the barrier of a criminal record. Auditors visited the employers, filled out applications, and went as far as they could during that first interview. They did not return for a second visit. Thus our critical variable of interest was the proportion of cases in which employers called the applicant after the first visit. Reference checks were included as an outcome, in the belief that it would be important to have a former employer or parole officer vouch for applicants with criminal records. As it turned out, employers paid virtually no attention to references; only 4 out of 350 actually checked.

Even though employers are not allowed to use criminal background information to make hiring decisions, about three-quarters of employers in this sample explicitly asked if the applicant had ever been convicted of a crime and, if so, for details. A much smaller proportion, just over a quarter, indicated that they would perform a background check (employers are not required to say if they intend to, and this doubtless represents a lower-bound estimate). The use of background checks by employers has been increasingly steadily, however, because of greater ease of access to criminal history information and growing concerns over security.

To what extent are applicants with criminal backgrounds dropped at the beginning of the process? For answers, we turn to the results of the audit.

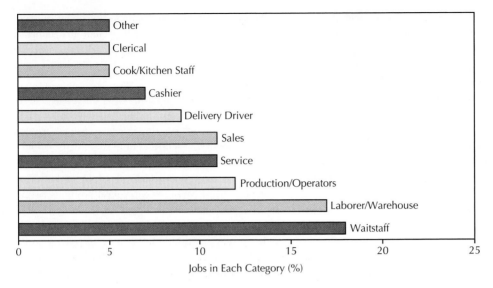

FIGURE 1 The Jobs in the Milwaukee Audit Sample.

The Effects of a Criminal Record and Race on Employment

Given that all testers presented nearly identical credentials, the different responses they encountered can be attributed fully to the effects of race and criminal background.

The results in Figure 2 suggest that a criminal record has severe effects. Among whites, applicants with criminal records were only half as likely to be called back as equally qualified applicants with no criminal record.

The second question involved the significance of race, by itself, in shaping black men's employment prospects,

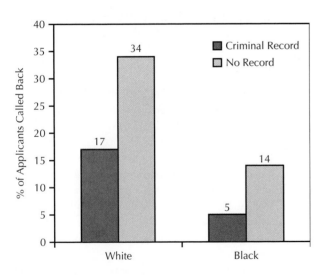

FIGURE 2 The Effect of a Criminal Record in the Milwaukee Audit Sample.

and here too the audit offered an unequivocal answer (Figure 2). The effect of race was very large, equal to or greater than the effect of a criminal record. Only 14 percent of black men without criminal records were called back, a proportion equal to or less than even than the number of whites *with* a criminal background. The magnitude of the race effect found here corresponds very closely to effects found in previous audit studies directly measuring racial discrimination.[7] Since 1994, when the last major audit was reported, very little has changed in the reaction of employers to minority applicants, at least in Milwaukee.

In addition to the strong independent effects of race and criminal record, evidence suggests that the combination of the two may intensify the negative effects: black ex-offenders are one-third as likely to be called as black applicants without a criminal record. It seems that employers, already reluctant to hire blacks, are even more wary of those with proven criminal involvement. None of our white testers was asked about a criminal record before submitting his application, yet on three occasions black testers were questioned. Our testers were bright, articulate young men, yet the cursory review that entry-level applicants receive leaves little room for these qualities to be noticed.

In some cases, testers reported that employers' levels of responsiveness changed dramatically once they had glanced down at the criminal record questions. Employers seemed to use the information as a screening mechanism, without probing further into the context or complexities of the applicant's situation. But in a few circumstances employers expressed a preference for workers who had recently been released from prison because (in one case) "they tend to be more motivated and are more likely to be hard workers" and (in the case of a janitorial job) the job "involved a great deal of dirty work." Despite these cases, the vast majority of employers were reluctant to take a chance on applicants with a criminal record.

The evidence from this audit suggests that the criminal justice system is not a peripheral institution in the lives of young disadvantaged men. It has become a dominant presence, playing a key role in sorting and stratifying labor market opportunities for such men. And employment is only one of the domains affected by incarceration. Further research is needed to understand its effects on housing, family formation, and political participation, among others, before we can more fully understand its collateral consequences for social and economic inequality.

Seeing the Big Picture   **The Link between Race, Education, Employment, and Crime**

In the Appendix look at the unemployment statistics in Section VII, the bachelor's degrees conferred by race in Section I, and the crime statistics in Section IV. How do you think these trends are linked?

30 Kristen v. Aisha; Brad v. Rasheed: What's in a Name and How It Affects Getting a Job

Amy Braverman

AMY BRAVERMAN is a reporter for *University of Chicago Magazine*.

COULD THE NAME AT THE TOP OF A RÉSUMÉ prompt racial discrimination? According to Marianne Bertrand, associate professor in the Graduate School of Business, and MIT economist Sendhil Mullainathan, it can. Answering more than 1,300 help-wanted ads in Boston and Chicago, the researchers sent four résumés—two higher quality, two lower quality, one of each with a black-sounding name—to companies seeking sales, administrative-support, clerical, and customer-service employees. Overall, "white" applicants were called back 50 percent more often than "black" applicants. Brad and Kristen were the top performing white-sounding names, while Jermaine and Ebony got the most callbacks among black-sounding names. Neil, Emily, Rasheed, and Aisha received the fewest callbacks.

> **Questions to Consider** We tend to think of racial discrimination as the denial of rights or opportunities to someone because of his or her race. Is it possible that race discrimination could also include denying someone employment opportunities because that person has a black-sounding name?

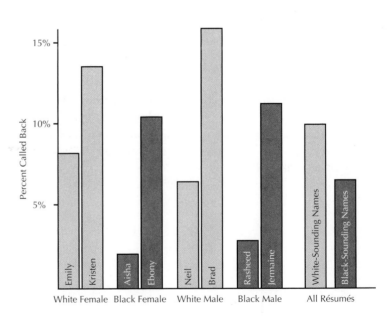

FIGURE 1 Why Brad and Kristen Beat Out Jermaine and Ebony.

31

When the Melting Pot Boils Over: The Irish, Jews, Blacks, and Koreans of New York

Roger Waldinger

ROGER WALDINGER is a professor of race/ethnic/minority relations, urban sociology, and migration and immigration at the University of California, Los Angeles. He is the author of *Still the Promised City? New Immigrants and African-Americans in Post-Industrial New York* (1996) and *Ethnic Los Angeles,* co-edited with Medhi Bozorgmehr (1996).

Questions to Consider   Roger Waldinger makes a number of astute observations about how racial and ethnic groups get sorted into certain occupations. How and in what ways does the historical timing of a group's entry (for example, Irish, Jews, Italians, and Afro-Caribbeans) into the United States affect its economic and social mobility? How does one group come to monopolize one trade or occupation? How are race, ethnicity, upward mobility, and control of local politics linked to upward mobility?

ASSIMILATION IS THE GRAND THEME OF American immigration research. The classic sociological position provided an optimistic counter to the dim assessments of the new immigrants prevalent at the early part of the century. Notwithstanding the marked differences that impressed contemporaries, Robert Park, Ernest Burgess, W. I. Thomas, and others contended that the new immigrant groups would lose their cultural distinctiveness and move up the occupational hierarchy. Milton Gordon's now classic volume distilled the essence of the sociological view: immigrant-ethnic groups start at the bottom and gradually move up; their mobility takes place through individual advancement, not group collective action; in the process of moving up, ethnic groups lose their distinctive social structure; and as ethnics become like members of the core group, they become part of the core group, joining it in neighborhoods, in friendship, and eventually in marriage.

But the image of immigrants moving onward and upward is hard to reconcile with the darker, conflictual side of American ethnic life. Conflict, often of the fiercest kind, runs like a red thread through the history of American ethnic groups. Certainly New Yorkers evince an extraordinary propensity to come to blows over racial and ethnic differences. The latest conflicts pitting blacks against Hasidim and Koreans in Brooklyn or Chinese against Puerto Ricans in Manhattan are but the latest episodes in a longer saga, extending from the anti-Catholic crusades of the 1850s to the school conflicts of the 1890s, to the controversies engendered by the Coughlinites and the German Bund of the 1930s, to the school integration struggles of the 1960s, right up to this day.

The contradiction between ethnic assimilation and ethnic conflict is more apparent than real. Where the classic sociological model goes wrong is not in its depiction of an upward trajectory, but rather in its individualistic assumptions about the process of ethnic change. The story of ethnic progress in America can be better thought of as a collective search for mobility, in which the succession of one migrant wave after another ensures a continuous competitive conflict over resources. Groups move up from the bottom by specializing in and dominating a particular branch of economic life; that specialization goes unchallenged as long as the newest arrivals are content to work in the bottom-level jobs for which they were initially recruited. This [reading] develops the story in the form of brief episodes from the New York experience of four ethnic groups—Irish, Jews, African Americans, and Koreans. Each group is associated with the four successive waves of migration that have swept over New York in the past two hundred years.

The Irish

Nearly one and a half million Irish flocked to the United States between 1846 and 1855 in flight from famine; they converged on the eastern port cities of Boston, Philadelphia, and New York, where, lacking resources, about a quarter stayed. Low levels of education, lack of exposure to industrial or craft work, and lack of capital led the Irish into the lower ranges of manual work, with women taking domestic work and men engaging in insecure, low-paid itinerant employment, especially in construction. Irish progress from the bottom proceeded at a slow pace.

By 1900, however, the Irish had already established themselves in public employment. At the time, the public sector provided relatively few jobs, but this was soon to change. Irish employment in New York City government almost quadrupled between 1900 and 1930, increasing from just under 20,000 to 77,000, while the total number of city workers climbed from 54,000 to 148,000 less than a factor of three.[1]

Irish penetration into the public sector reflected the growing political power of the Democratic machine, which remained Irish dominated. But the machine's hold on local government was met by opposition from WASP reformers. Seeking to break the machine's power by severing the link between political activity and government employment, the reformers installed a civil service system—to little avail. The Irish encountered few effective competitors for city jobs. There was never any serious threat that WASPs would dislodge the Irish. Moreover, the increasingly numerous Poles, Jews, Italians, and others who were just off the boat had little chance of doing well in essay-type exams against the Irish, who were, after all, native English speakers.

The liabilities of the new immigrants lasted hardly a generation; with the Jews' rapid educational and occupational advancement, another competitor entered the scene. But as long as the Irish, through Tammany Hall's grip over city government, could control municipal hiring, interethnic competition posed little threat. Competition was structured in such a way as to minimize the value of Jews' educational advantages. The patronage system functioned unencumbered throughout Tammany's dominance between 1917 and 1933.

The depression severely challenged Irish control over public jobs; LaGuardia's election in 1933 delivered

the coup de grace. Keeping control of City Hall required LaGuardia to undermine the material base of Tammany's power and consolidate his support among groups not firmly under Tammany's tow—the most important of which were the Jews, who had split between LaGuardia and his Tammany opponent in 1933. Both goals could be accomplished in the same way, namely pursuing the administrative changes long championed by the reformers.[2]

The depression and LaGuardia's reforms made city jobs more attractive to highly educated workers, which, under the circumstances, mainly meant Jews. One door at which Jewish competitors knocked was teaching, previously an Irish reserve (as the 1900 statistics show). If Jewish entrance into teaching produced antagonism, far more explosive was the situation in the police force. Twenty-nine thousand men sat for the exam held in April 1939, from whom three hundred were selected to enter the department in 1940. Of these, over one-third were Jews. Not surprisingly, this class of 1940 constituted the first significant proportion of Jews to enter the police.[3]

Jewish-Irish competition produced some other episodes, but conflict between them abated, thanks to the prosperity of the postwar era and the new opportunities it provided. Outmigration to the suburbs and the Sun Belt and mobility into the middle class depleted the ranks of the city's Irish population. By the late 1950s, as Nathan Glazer and Daniel Moynihan noted, so profound was the sense of displacement that the remaining Irish New Yorkers reminded themselves, "There are still some of us left."[4]

Those who are left have kept up the long-established Irish occupational ways. Although the commissioners of the police and fire departments are black and Puerto Rican, respectively, the top brass retains a strongly Irish cast, as does the rank and file. Indeed, the fire department presents a glimpse of New York gone by, with a workforce that is 93 percent white and 80 percent Catholic. Some unions still have a distinctly Irish makeup.[5]

In the 1980s, some of the old niches at last gained new blood, as an influx of new, illegal Irish immigrants fled unemployment in the Republic of Ireland for better times in New York. Whereas black Americans still found the doors of construction unions closed, the new arrivals, dubbed "JFK carpenters," were warmly welcomed by their aging compatriots. Women also retraced the steps of the past, as could be seen from the classified pages of the *Irish Echo,* with its columns of ads for nannies, babysitters, and housekeepers.

The Jews

Although the Jewish presence in New York extends far back, almost to the city's founding, Jews did not become an important, visible element in the city's economic life until the 1880s. Rising anti-Semitism, combined with the pressures of modernization, led to a huge outflow of Jews from Eastern Europe. By 1920, New York, with two million Jews, had become the world's largest Jewish city.

The new arrivals came just when the demand for factory-made clothing began to surge. Many had been tailors in the old country, and although most had worked with needle and thread, they quickly adapted themselves to machine production. As the various components of the clothing industry grew in synergistic fashion, the opportunities for mobility through the ethnic economy multiplied. Through rags, some immigrants found riches; the sweatshop workers who moved to contracting and then to manufacturing, or possibly careers in retailing, filled the newly formed ranks of New York's *alrightniks.*[6]

The Jewish concentration in commerce and clothing manufacture defined their initial place in the ethnic division of labor. Jewish specializations seldom overlapped with the Irish: domestic service and general labor were rarities among the Russians but were common Irish pursuits; by the same token, tailoring and retailing, whether by merchant or peddler, were far more likely to engage Russians than Irish.

As Jews sought to move beyond the ethnic economy, interethnic competition and antagonism grew more intense. The relatively rapid educational progress of younger immigrants and of the second generation prepared them to work outside the ethnic economy, but gentile employers were rarely eager to hire Jews. One study, completed just before the Great Depression, found that the doors of New York's large, corporate organizations—"railroads, banks, insurance companies, lawyers' offices, brokerage houses, the New York Stock Exchange, hotels . . . and the home offices of large corporations of the first rank"—were infrequently opened to Jews.[7] The surge into the schools, and through the schools into the professions, met with resistance from the older, largely Protestant population that dominated these institutions.

In the 1930s, depression and discrimination outside the ethnic economy led many second-generation Jews to seek an alternative in public employment. Although the quest for government jobs, and in particular teaching positions, had started earlier, the straitened circumstances of the 1930s accelerated this search. The quality and quantity of Jews vying for government employment increased, heightening the competitive pressure on the Irish and yielding the antagonism we've already observed.

Jewish-Irish conflict reached its height in the late 1930s; it gradually subsided, replaced by a more explosive, deeply antagonistic relationship with blacks. Although black occupations were more similar to those of the Irish than they were to the Jews', the economic pursuits of Jews put them at odds with blacks on various counts. The Jews dominated small retail activity throughout the city and were particularly prominent in Harlem. The Jewish storeowners in Harlem sold to blacks but preferred not to employ them until protests in the mid-1930s finally forced them to relent. Antagonism toward Jewish shopkeepers in Harlem rose during the 1930s, fueled by the depression and by Jews' broader role as middlemen in the Harlem economy. Frustration boiled over in the riot of 1943, when black Harlemites burned down the stores of Jews in a fury that presaged events to come.[8] Hostility simmered thereafter, reaching the boiling point during the 1960s.

The transformation of the ethnic economy also engendered black-Jewish conflict, rapid Jewish social mobility meant a dwindling Jewish working class; the diminishing supply of Jewish workers had a particularly notable effect on the garment industry, where Jewish factory owners were forced to hire outsiders in growing numbers—first Italians, then blacks. In World War II, desperate for workers, Jewish employers hired blacks in great numbers. By 1950, there were 25,000 African American garment workers, 20,000 more than were working in clothing factories ten years before.[9]

But relations between blacks and Jews proved uneasy. Blacks moved into less-skilled, poorer-paying positions, from which mobility into better-remunerated positions proved difficult. Although the garment unions made explicit efforts to organize black workers and integrate them into union structures, few blacks moved up to elected offices, and none high up in the union hierarchy. To protect jobs from southern competitors, the unions adopted a policy of wage restraint, which inevitably meant a softened stance on union employers at home—much to the dismay of black New York garment workers.[10]

The garment business was the Jewish enclave of the past; Jewish mobility into the middle class had made teaching the Jewish niche of the mid-1960s. As the schools came to serve a growing black population, their role was increasingly contested by black students, parents, and protest organizations. The complaints were various, and not all directly linked to the Jews' prominent role in the school system; but the situation in which so many Jews were teachers and so many schools in black neighborhoods were staffed by Jews inevitably led to conflict. In 1968, a black-dominated school board in Brooklyn dismissed a group of white, largely Jewish teachers and replaced them with a mainly black staff; these actions set off a three-month-long strike by the Jewish-led teachers' union. Although the union eventually won, its victory was pyrrhic, at least concerning black-Jewish relations. Memory of the strike and the resentments it fueled have not significantly changed, even a generation later.[11]

What has altered, however, is the economic position of the Jews. The ethnic economy of the immigrant days remains, but in vestigial form. Although Jews are still active in the garment industry, they mainly concentrate in the designing and merchandising ends. "Goldberg" no longer runs clothing factories; his place has been taken by "Kim" and "Wong," who only employ compatriots, not blacks. The same transformations have changed the face of petty retailing and small landlording—the older flash points of black-Jewish conflict. The Jewish presence in the public sector is also fading fast: working as a city engineer or accountant used to be a Jewish occupation; now these careers engage far many more Patels than Cohens.[12] Only in teaching and in higher education do the Jewish concentrations of the past remain in full force.[13]

A distinctive Jewish role in New York's economy still lives on. It is to be found in the professions, in the persistently high rate of Jewish self-employment, in the prominence of Jews in law, real estate, finance, and the media. But the current Jewish pursuits differ crucially from the older ethnic economy in that they are detached from the dynamics of interethnic composition that characterized earlier periods. In a sense, the material basis that underlay anti-Semitic currents in New York for most of the twentieth century is gone. But its legacy and the many other resources around which groups can compete—status, politics, and territory—ensure continued conflict between Jews and their ethnic neighbors.

The Blacks

In 1890, the black share of the New York population was 1.6 percent—just about what it had been on the eve of the Civil War. But in the 1890s the South started losing blacks due to outmigration, and that loss quickly translated into New York's gain. By 1920, New York housed 150,000 black residents—who, although only 3 percent of the city's population, made New York the country's largest black urban concentration. In the next twenty years, as European immigration faltered and then stopped, and bad conditions in the rural South provided additional reasons to leave, the number of black New Yorkers tripled. Postwar prosperity and a new wave of mechanization down South launched a final, massive flow northward: by 1960, the African American population of New York numbered 1,088,000, of whom approximately 320,000 had moved to the city from other areas (mainly the South) in the previous ten years.[14]

It was not until 1940 that black New Yorkers moved out of the peripheries of the New York economy. At the turn of the century, blacks mainly found work in domestic labor, with 90 percent of black women and 55 percent of black men working in some type of domestic service occupation. Blacks' confinement to domestic service reflected, in part, the unfavorable terms of competition with immigrants, who had evicted them from trades where they had previously been accepted. The continued expansion of New York's economy slowly opened doors in a few manufacturing industries; the shutoff of immigration during World War I and its permanent demise after 1924 further accelerated dispersion into other fields.[15]

But the depression largely put an end to these gains. By 1940, 40 percent of blacks still worked in personal service—a far greater proportion than among the workforce overall.[16] With the advent of World War II doors to other jobs were finally unlocked; manufacturing, in particular, saw very large black employment gains. Yet unlike the case in Chicago or Detroit, the black sojourn in New York's manufacturing sector proved short-lived. Lacking auto factories or steel mills, New York's goods-producing sector was a concentration of low-wage jobs; white workers remained ensconced in the better-paying, more skilled positions. Opportunities for blacks were more easily found in the burgeoning service sector—for example, health care—and in government; hence, blacks quickly dispersed into other fields.

Government, where 35 percent of native-born black New Yorkers worked in 1990,[17] has become the black niche par excellence. The history of black employment in the public sector provides yet another example of the continuing, interethnic competitive conflicts over jobs and economic resources in which New York's ethnic groups have been engaged.

In the early years of the twentieth century, local government, like most other New York employers, closed its doors to blacks: in 1911, the city only employed 511 blacks, almost all of whom were laborers. In the early 1920s, Tammany installed the leader of its black client organization, the United Colored Democracy, as a member of the three-person Civil Service Commission, but black access to public jobs changed marginally. By the late 1920s, the city counted 2,275 black workers on its payroll of whom 900 were in laboring jobs and an additional 700 were in other noncompetitive or per diem positions.[18] The reform regime did more for blacks, pushing black employment above parity by 1940.[19] But these effects occurred as a result of the government's burgeoning payrolls, and they were mainly felt in the black concentrations of hospitals, sanitation, and public works, where more than 80 percent of the city's black job holders worked in 1935.[20] Moreover, blacks remained vulnerable to discriminatory practices, as in the city-owned subway system, where blacks only worked as porters, with the exception of a few stations in Harlem. Most important, the employment system that emerged during the depression put blacks at a structural disadvantage in competition with whites. Lacking the educational skills and credentials needed to qualify for most city jobs, blacks and Puerto Ricans found themselves channeled into noncompetitive positions, of which the single largest concentration was found in the municipal hospital system. From here there were few routes of movement upward, as these bottom-level positions were disconnected from the competitive system, which promoted from within.

Race didn't reach the top of government's agenda until 1965, when John Lindsay arrived in office, the first reformer elected mayor since LaGuardia.[21] Elected with the votes of liberals and minorities, Lindsay lacked his predecessors' commitments to the interests of the largely white, civil service workforce and pledged to increase black and Puerto Rican employment in city agencies. But the new mayor quickly discovered that the civil service structure was not easily amenable to change. Lindsay gradually made progress in reducing the inflated eligibility requirements inherited from the depression, but resistance proved severe when his reforms threatened established white ethnic workers in the better-paid ranks.

Lindsay's main focus, in contrast to earlier reform administrations, was to evade the civil service system and its unionized defenders. The Lindsay administration created new, less-skilled positions for which minority residents could be more easily hired. But this approach never involved large numbers and, more important, left existing eligibility requirements unchallenged, shunting minority recruits into dead-end jobs, where they were marooned.

Lindsay backed off from his confrontations with the civil service system and its defenders in the aftermath of the disastrous 1968 teachers' strike. Where the mayor could both accommodate the unions and pursue his earlier goals of increasing minority employment, he did—mainly by tripling the number of exempt workers and shifting them from agency to agency to avoid the requirement of taking an examination. But in other instances, pressure from civil service interests proved overwhelming. With Abraham Beame's accession to City Hall in 1973, followed in 1977 by Edward Koch, mayoral support for black employment gains vanished for the next sixteen years.

The 1970s and 1980s nevertheless saw dramatic gains in black government employment. Like earlier white ethnic groups that had developed a concentration in public jobs, blacks benefited from simultaneous shifts in the structure of employment and in the relative availability of competing groups.

Changes in the structure of employment came from a variety of sources. The Equal Employment Opportunity (EEO) Act of 1972 prohibited discrimination in local government. By requiring local governments to maintain records on all employees by race and gender and to submit them to the Equal Employment Opportunity Commission, with the clear expectation that governments would show improvement over time, the act also led to institutional changes. As EEO functions were established in each city agency, recruitment and personnel practices changed in ways that benefited previously excluded groups, as recruitment became focused on minority and immigrant communities.

Moreover, the 1972 act provided minority employees with levers to act on more recalcitrant agencies, which they used with greatest effectiveness in the uniformed services. For example, in 1973 the Vulcan Society (the organization of black firefighters) successfully challenged the results of a 1971 exam, leading to an imposition of a 1:3 quota for the duration of that list (1973–79). In 1979, the Guardians and the Hispanic Society challenged the 1979 police officer's exam; court findings of disparate impact led to the imposition of a 33.3 percent minority quota for the duration of the list.

While the advent of affirmative action helped increase access for blacks and other minorities, other changes on the supply side hastened the growth of black employment. Although the city's attraction to its traditional white ethnic labor force had begun to diminish by the 1960s, the fiscal crisis of the mid-1970s decisively exacerbated and extended the city's recruitment difficulties among its traditional workforce. By the time large-scale hiring resumed in the early 1980s, public employment had become a less attractive option than before. Moreover, municipal salaries and benefits took a severe beating during the fiscal crisis; although compensation edged back upward during the 1980s, real gains never recaptured the losses endured during the 1970s. The strength enjoyed by New York's private sector during the 1980s pulled native white workers up the hiring queue and out of the effective labor supply for many city agencies.[22]

In a situation where "the City was hiring a great deal and not turning away anyone who was qualified," as one deputy commissioner told me in an interview, the disparity in the availability of minority and white workers led to rapid recruitment of minority workers. Minorities had constituted only 40 percent of the new workers hired in 1977, making up the majority in only two low-paid occupational categories. By 1987, minorities made up 56 percent of all hires, dominating the ranks of new recruits in five out of eight occupational categories.[23]

Thus, the Koch years of 1977 to 1989 saw the ethnic composition of the municipal workforce completely transformed, notwithstanding the mayor's opposition to affirmative action and the disfavor with which minority leaders greeted his hiring policies. By 1990, whites constituted 48 percent of the 375,000 people working for the city and just slightly more—50 percent—of the 150,000 people working in the agencies that the mayor directly controlled.[24] The declining white presence in municipal employment chiefly benefited blacks. Blacks constituted 25 percent of the city's population and a still smaller proportion of residents who were older than eighteen and thus potentially employable, but made up 36 percent of the city's total workforce and 38 percent of those who worked in the mayoral agencies. Although blacks were still underrepresented in some of the city's most desirable jobs, the earlier pattern of concentration at the bottom was overcome. The municipal hospital system, which employed two-thirds of the city's black employees in the early 1960s, in 1990 employed less than one-fifth, reflecting the dispersion of blacks throughout the municipal sector. And higher-level jobs showed clusters of considerable black overrepresentation as well, with blacks accounting for 40 percent of the administrators and 36 percent of the professionals employed in the direct mayoral agencies.

By 1990, when David Dinkins became New York's first black mayor, the phase of black-for-white succession in municipal employment was nearly complete. Blacks held just over 35 percent of all city jobs; although unevenly represented among the city's many agencies, they were often a dominant presence, accounting for more than 40 percent of employment in six of the ten largest agencies, and more than 50 percent of employment in three of the largest ten.

The comparison with Latinos underlines blacks' advantage in the new ethnic division that has emerged in city government. Whereas the city's Latinos and black populations are equal in number, Latinos hold one-third as many municipal jobs as do blacks. The discrepancies are even greater as one moves up the occupational hierarchy into the ranks of managers and professionals. And blacks have been far more successful than Latinos in gaining new permanent civil service jobs, rather than the provisional appointments on which Latinos have mainly relied. The disparity has not gone unnoticed, as the Commission on Hispanic Concerns pointed out in a 1986 report.[25] Of course, other answers might be invoked to explain Latinos' municipal jobs deficit relative to blacks'. But whatever the precise explanation, Mayor Dinkins's continuing conflicts with the Hispanic community suggest that earlier patterns of interethnic competition over municipal jobs remain alive and well.

The Koreans

In the mid-1960s, just when New York could no longer retain its native population, it reverted back to its role as an immigrant mecca. Immigrants began flocking to New York immediately after the liberalization of U.S. immigration laws in 1965. Their arrival has been the principal driving force of demographic and ethnic change in New York ever since—and will continue to be for the foreseeable future.

In 1965, what no one expected was the burgeoning of Asian immigration. The reforms tilted the new system toward immigrants with kinship ties to permanent residents or citizens. Since there had been so little Asian immigration in the previous fifty years, how could Asian newcomers find settlers with whom to seek reunification? The answer is that kinship connections were helpful, but not essential. The 1965 reforms also created opportunities for immigrants whose skills—as engineers, doctors, nurses, pharmacists—were in short supply. Along with students already living in the United States and enjoying easy access to American employers, these professionals made up the first wave of new Asian immigrants, creating the basis for the kinship migration of less well-educated relatives.

Thus, well-educated, high-skilled immigrants have dominated the Korean influx to the United States and to New York in particular. Although Koreans constitute a small portion of New York's new immigrants—rarely more than 3 percent of the eighty thousand to ninety thousand legal immigrants who come to New York each year—they play an important and very visible role. As middle-aged newcomers with poor English-language skills and often lacking professional licenses, relatively few Koreans have managed to steer a route back into the fields for which they trained. Instead they have turned to small business, setting up new businesses at a rate that few other groups can rival.

Koreans started in fruit and vegetable stores, taking over shops in all areas of the city, regardless of neighborhood composition or customer clientele. From there, Koreans moved on to other retail specialties—dry cleaning, fish stores, novelty shops, and nail salons. By 1980, a third of New York Korean males were already self-employed. The *1991 Korean Business Directory* provides a ready indicator of commercial growth over the 1980s, listing over 120 commercial specialties in which Korean firms are to be found.[26]

The roots of the Korean ethnic economy are found in several sources. The competitive field was open. By the middle to late 1960s, the sons and daughters of Jewish and Italian storekeepers had better things to do than mind a store, and their parents, old, tired, and scared of crime, were ready to sell out to the newcomers from Korea. By the 1980s, the supply of new, native-born white entrepreneurs had virtually dried up. One survey of neighborhood businesses in Queens and Brooklyn found that almost half of the white-owned shops were run by immigrants and that most white businesses were long-established entities, in contrast to the newly founded Korean shops with which they competed.[27]

Another spur to growth came from within the ethnic community. Koreans, like every other immigrant group, have special tastes and needs that are best served by an insider: the growth of the Korean population has created business for Korean accountants, doctors, brokers, hair stylists, and restaurant owners. Although the Korean community is too small to support a huge commercial infrastructure oriented to ethnic needs, the community has utilized its ethnic connections to Korea to develop commercial activities oriented toward non-Korean markets. Active trade relations between South Korea and the United States have provided a springboard for many Korean-owned import-export businesses, of which 119 are listed in the *1991 Korean Business Directory.*

Finally, the social structure of the Korean community itself generates advantages for business success that few other immigrant groups share. Many Koreans emigrate with capital, and those who are cash poor can raise money through rotating credit associations known as *gae.* Because Koreans migrate in complete family units, family members provide a supply of cheap and trusted labor. The prevalence of self-employment means that many Koreans have close ties to other business owners, who in turn are a source of information and support, and the high organizational density of the Korean community—which is characterized by an incredible proliferation of alumni clubs, churches, businessmen's associations—provides additional conduits for the flow of business information and the making of needed contacts. These community resources distinguish the Koreans from their competitors, who are less likely to be embedded in ethnic or family ties that can be drawn upon for help with business information, capital assistance, or staffing problems.

The Koreans have discovered that conflict *need not* be interethnic; there are other sources of threat, and in the 1980s they mobilized Korean merchants on a considerable scale. Like other small business owners, Koreans were unhappy with local government, usually with something that government was doing or was threatening to do. Fruit and vegetable store owners felt that sanitation officials were too conscientious about sidewalk cleanliness, especially since the result of the officials' demands was often a fine that the Korean store owner had to pay. Pressuring the city to relax inspections became a high priority for Korean organizations. In the late 1980s, as the city's fiscal crisis led it to search for new sources of revenue, fiscal planners thought of placing a special tax on dry cleaners. So Korean dry cleaners entered an unusual coalition with the white owners of commercial laundries, and the union that represented the laundryworkers, to roll back the planned tax. Like other small business owners, Korean merchants could also become dissatisfied with government's *failure* to act. The prosperity of the 1980s gave commercial landlords license to raise rents to the maximum, much to the distress of small business owners throughout the city. Koreans joined with their non-Korean counterparts to push for commercial rent control—to no avail.

Although Italians and Jews have largely deserted petty retail trade, they have remained in wholesaling, where the businesses are larger and profits more sizable. Thus Jewish and Italian fruit and vegetable or fish wholesalers have acquired a substantial Korean trade. The encounter has not always been a happy one, as Illsoo Kim recounted in his pathbreaking book: "Especially in their first years of emergence into the fruit and vegetable business, Koreans reported many incidents at the Hunts Point [wholesale] Market. The incidents ranged from unfair pricing and sale of poor-quality produce by the Italian and Jewish wholesalers, to physical threats and beatings administered by competing white retailers."[28] Such conflicts sparked the first mass demonstration by Koreans ever in New York. Although Kim reports that Koreans were subsequently accepted by the wholesaling community, there have been continued incidents and protests, including a recent boycott by Koreans of one of the city's largest fish wholesalers.[29]

In New York, as in almost every other major American city, black neighborhoods have provided new immigrants from Asia and the Middle East with an important economic outlet. To some extent, Koreans and other immigrants have simply replaced older white groups that had long sold to blacks and were now eager to bail out of an increasingly difficult and tense situation. By opening stores in black neighborhoods Koreans were also filling the gap left by the departure of large, nonethnic chain stores, which were steadily eliminating the low-margin, high-cost operations involved in serving a ghetto clientele. Selling to black customers proved fraught with conflict. Small protests erupted in the late 1970s. In 1981 a boycott erupted along 125th Street, Harlem's main commercial thoroughfare, with black leaders calling Korean shop owners "vampires" who came to Harlem to "suck black consumers dry."[30]

Repeated security problems as well as more organized clashes led Korean store owners to establish neighborhood prosperity associations, in addition to those organizations that grouped merchants in a particular retail branch. Thus, alongside groups like the Korean Produce Association or the Korean Apparel Contractors Associations, one finds neighborhood groups like the Korean Merchant Association of the Bronx or the Uptown Korean Merchants Association, which seek "to improve Korean merchants' relations with local residents or communities" while lobbying local police for more effective support.[31]

In 1990 antagonism between black shoppers and Korean merchants erupted in picket lines set up in front of two Korean stores in the Flatbush section of Brooklyn. The clash started with a dispute between a Korean store owner and a black Haitian customer who charged assault; that claim then provoked black activist groups—of fairly dubious repute[32]—to establish a boycott that targeted not only the offending owner, but a neighboring Korean merchant against whom no injury was ever charged.

The boycott lasted for months, choking off business at both stores. Although customers disappeared, the two stores were kept alive by contributions from the organized Korean community, which perceived a broader danger to its economic viability should the boycott succeed. As time went on, government officials were inevitably involved. The boycott became a crisis for Mayor Dinkins, who was widely criticized for not actively seeking an end to the dispute.

The boycott ground to a halt, and a court threw out the legal suit brought by the aggrieved Haitian shopper.

Other, fortunately short-lived boycotts were started in New York even while the Flatbush dispute lingered on. A clash in a nearby Brooklyn area between blacks and a small group of Vietnamese refugees—possibly mistaken for Koreans—showed how quickly tensions generated in one arena could move to another.

Conclusion

The story of New York's Irish, Jews, blacks, and Koreans is richer and more complicated than the occupational histories I've recounted in the preceding pages. But if the [reading's] deliberately one-sided focus provides only a partial account, it reminds us of ethnicity's continuing importance, and not simply because of feelings for one's own kind or animosities toward outsiders. Rather, ethnicity's centrality stems from its role as the mechanism whereby groups of categorically different workers have been sorted into an identifiably distinct set of jobs. In this sense, the ethnic division of labor has been the central division of labor in modern New York. Now, as in the past, distinctive roles in the ethnic division of labor impart a sense of "we-ness" and group interest—ensuring the persistence of ethnic fragmentation and conflict.

Seeing the Big Picture   **Who's Got the "Good" Jobs and Why?**
Look at Section VIII on Occupations in the Appendix. Which racial and ethnic groups monopolize which occupations? How might these trends reflect Waldinger's thesis concerning control of occupations and upward mobility?

 32

"There's No Shame in My Game": Status and Stigma among Harlem's Working Poor
Katherine S. Newman • Catherine Ellis

KATHERINE S. NEWMAN is professor and director of Princeton's Institute for International and Regional Studies. Her 1999 book, *No Shame in My Game: The Working Poor in the Inner City,* won both the Sidney Hillman Book Prize and the Robert F. Kennedy Book Award.

CATHERINE ELLIS is a consulting producer for American RadioWorks®, the documentary unit of American Public Media. She holds a PhD in anthropology from Columbia University.

Questions to Consider   Katherine Newman and Catherine Ellis ask us to imagine what life is like working a "McJob." How do individuals maintain self-respect working at a job that provides little in the way of social status? Is it possible for these workers to find employment that pays a living wage (about $16 an hour in New York City)? What does "No Shame in My Game" mean, and what does this phrase suggest about our attitude toward work?

IN THE EARLY 1990S, THE MCDONALD'S corporation launched a television ad campaign featuring a young black man named Calvin, who was portrayed sitting atop a Brooklyn stoop in his Golden-Arches uniform while his friends passed by to hard-time him about holding down a "McJob." After brushing off their teasing with good humor, Calvin is approached furtively by one young black man who asks, sotto voce, whether Calvin might help him get a job. He allows that he too could use some earnings and that, despite the ragging he has just given Calvin, he thinks the uniform is really pretty cool—or at least that having a job is pretty cool.

Every fast-food worker we interviewed for this study knew the Calvin series by heart: Calvin on the job; Calvin in the street; Calvin helping an elderly woman cross the street on his way to work; Calvin getting promoted to management. They knew what McDonald's was trying to communicate to young people by producing the series in the first place. Fast-food jobs are burdened by a lasting stigma, but one that can be overcome in time. Eventually, so the commercial suggests, the public "dissing" will give way to private admiration as the value of sticking with a job eclipses the stain of a burger flipper's lowly reputation.

One of the moral maxims of American culture is that work defines the person. We carry around in our heads a rough tally that tells us what kinds of jobs are worthy of respect or of disdain, a pyramid organized by the income attached to a particular job, the educational credentials it demands, and the social characteristics of an occupation's incumbents. We use this system of **stratification** (ruthlessly at times) to boost the status of some and humiliate others.[1]

Given our tradition of equating moral value with employment, it stands to reason that the most profound dividing line in our culture is that which separates the working person from the unemployed.[2] Only after this line has been crossed do we begin to make the finer gradations that distinguish a white-collar worker from his blue-collar counterpart, a CEO from a secretary. A whole host of moral virtues—discipline, personal responsibility, pragmatism—are ascribed to those who have found and kept a job, almost any job, while those who have not are dismissed in public discourse as slothful and irresponsible.[3]

We inhabit an unforgiving culture that fails to acknowledge the many reasons some people cross that employment barrier and others are left behind. We may remember, for a time, that unemployment rates are high; that particular industries have downsized millions of workers right out of their jobs; or that racial barriers or negative attitudes toward teenagers make it harder for some people to get jobs than others. Yet in the end American culture wipes out these background truths in favor of a simpler dichotomy: the worthy and the unworthy, the working folk and the lazy deadbeats.

For those on the positive side of the divide, those who work for a living, the rewards are far greater than a paycheck. The employed enter a social world in which their identities as mainstream Americans are shaped, structured, and reinforced. The workplace is the main institutional setting—and virtually the only one after one's school career is over—in which individuals become part of the collective American enterprise that lies at the heart of our culture: the market. We are so divided in other domains—race, geography, family organization, **gender roles,** and the like—that common ground along almost any other lines is difficult to achieve. For our diverse and divided society, participation in the world of work is the most powerful source of social integration.

It is in the workplace that we are most likely to mix with those who come from different backgrounds, are under the greatest pressure to subordinate individual idiosyncrasy to the requirements of an organization, and are called upon to contribute to goals that eclipse the personal. All workers have these experiences in common, even as segregation constrains the real mix of workers, conformity is imposed on some occupations more than others, and the goals to which we must subscribe are often elusive, unreachable, or at odds with personal desire.

The creation of a workplace identity is rarely the task of the self-directed individualist, moving along some preordained path. It is a miracle worked by organizations, firms, supervisors, fellow workers, and by the whole long search that leads from the desire to find a job to the endpoint of landing one. This transformation is particularly fraught for ghetto youth and adults, for they face a difficult job market, high hurdles in convincing employers to take a chance on them, and relatively poor rewards—from a financial point of view—for their successes. But the crafting of an identity is an important developmental

---

stratification How a society ranks its members within a social hierarchy. In the United States, class, power, and social status are the primary sorting mechanisms.

gender roles Beliefs, attitudes, expectations, and behaviors that a society links to one's sex.

process for them, just as it is for their more privileged counterparts.

Powerful forces work to exclude African-Americans, Latinos, and other minorities from full participation in American society. From the schools that provide a substandard education for millions of inner-city kids, to an employment system rife with discrimination, to a housing market that segregates minority families, there is almost no meaning to the notion that Americans all begin from the same starting line.[4] Precisely because this is the case, blasting one's way through the job barrier and starting down that road of acquiring a common identity as mainstream worker is of the greatest importance for black and brown youth in segregated communities. It may be one of the few accessible pipelines into the core of American society and the one with the greatest payoff, symbolic and material.

This paper draws upon a two-year study of fast-food workers and job seekers in central and northern Harlem. Two hundred African-American and Latino workers participated in this study by participating in face-to-face interviews. Sixty of them completed extensive life histories, and a smaller group contributed yearlong personal diaries and permitted the members of our research group to spend extensive periods of time with them, their family members, and their friends. We draw upon all of these data here to explore the nature of values among the working poor in the inner city.

The Social Costs of Accepting Low-Wage Work

While the gainfully employed may be honored over those who stand outside the labor force, all jobs are not created equal. Fast-food jobs, in particular, are notoriously stigmatized and denigrated. "McJob" has become a common epithet meant to designate work without redeeming value. The reasons for this heavy valence are numerous and worthy of deconstruction, for the minority workers who figure in this study have a mountain of stigma to overcome if they are to maintain their self-respect. Indeed, this is one of the main goals of the organizational culture they join when they finally land a job in the restaurant chain we will call "Burger Barn."

Fast-food jobs epitomize the assembly line structure of deskilled service jobs: they are highly routinized, and appear to the untutored observer to be entirely lacking in

discretion—almost military in their scripted nature. The symbolic capital of these routinized jobs can be measured in negative numbers. They represent the opposite of the autonomous entrepreneur who is lionized in popular culture (from *Business Week* to hip-hop).

Burger Barn workers are told that they must, at all cost to their own dignity, defer to the public. Customers can be unreasonably demanding, rude, and demeaning, and workers must count backwards from one hundred in an effort to stifle their outrage. Servicing the customer with a smile is music to management's ears because making money depends on keeping the clientele happy, but it can be an exercise in humiliation for inner-city teenagers. It is hard for them to refrain from reading this public nastiness as another instance of society's low estimation of their worth. But if they want to hold on to these minimum-wage jobs, they soon realize that they have to tolerate comments that would almost certainly provoke a fistfight outside the workplace.

It is well known among ghetto consumers that fast-food crew members have to put up with whatever verbiage comes across the counter. That knowledge occasionally prompts nasty exchanges designed explicitly to anger workers, to push them to retaliate verbally. Testing those limits is an outlet for customers down on their luck, and a favorite pastime of teenagers in particular. This may be the one opportunity they have to put someone else down in public, knowing there is little the worker can do in return.

It is bad enough to be on the receiving end of this kind of abuse from adults, especially white adults, for that has its own reading along race lines. It is, in some respects, even worse to have to contend with it from minority peers, for there is much more personal honor at stake, more pride to be lost, and an audience whose opinion matters more. This no doubt is why harassment is a continuous problem for fast-food workers. It hurts. Their peers, with plenty of anger bottled up for all kinds of reasons extraneous to the restaurant experience, find counterparts working the cash register convenient targets for venting.

Roberta Sampson[5] is a five-year veteran of Burger Barn who has worked her way up to management. A formidable African-American woman, Roberta has always prided herself on her ability to make it on her own. Most of Roberta's customers have been perfectly pleasant people; many have been long-time repeat visitors to her restaurant. But she has also encountered many who radiate disrespect.

> Well, I had alcoholics, derelicts. People that are aggravated with life. I've had people that don't even have jobs curse me out. I've dealt with all kinds.
>
> Sometimes it would get to me. If a person yelled out [in front of] a lobby full of people, "Bitch, that's why you work at Burger Barn," I would say [to myself], "I'm probably making more than you and your mother." It hurts when people don't even know what you're making and they say those things. Especially in Harlem, they do that to you. They call you all types of names and everything.

Natasha Robins is younger than Roberta and less practiced at these confrontations. But she has had to contend with them nevertheless, especially from age-mates who are (or at least claim to be) higher up the status hierarchy than she is. Hard as she tries, Natasha cannot always control her temper and respond the way the firm wants her to:

> It's hard dealing with the public. There are good things, like old people. They sweet. But the younger people around my age are always snotty. Think they better than you because they not working at Burger Barn. They probably work at something better than you.
>
> *How do you deal with rude or unfriendly customers?* They told us that we just suppose to walk to the back and ignore it, but when they in your face like that, you get so upset that you have to say something. . . . I got threatened with a gun one time. 'Cause this customer had threw a piece of straw paper in the back and told me to pick it up like I'm a dog. I said, "No." And he cursed at me. I cursed at him back and he was like, "Yeah, next time you won't have nothing to say when I come back with my gun and shoot your ass." Oh, *excuse* me.

Ianna Bates, who had just turned sixteen the summer she found her first job at Burger Barn, has had many of the same kinds of problems Natasha Robins complains of. The customers who hard-time her are just looking for a place to vent their anger about things that have nothing to do with buying lunch. Ianna recognizes that this kind of thing could happen in any restaurant, but believes it is a special problem in Harlem, for ghetto residents have more to be angry about and fewer accessible targets for one-upmanship. Cashiers in fast-food shops catch the results:

> What I hate about Burger Barn is the customers, well, some of them that I can't stand. . . . I don't want to stereotype Harlem . . . , but since I only worked in Harlem that's all I can speak for. Some people have a chip on their shoulders. . . . Most of the people that come into the restaurant are black. Most of them have a lot of kids. It's in the ghetto. Maybe, you know, they are depressed about their lifestyles or whatever else that is going on in their lives and they just. . . . I don't know. They just are like *urff!*
>
> And no matter what you do you cannot please them. I'm not supposed to say anything to the customer, but that's not like me. I have a mouth and I don't take no short from nobody. I don't care who it is, don't take anybody's crap.

Despite this bravado, Ianna well knows that to use her mouth is to risk her job. She has had to work hard to find ways to cope with this frustration that do not get her into trouble with management:

> I don't say stuff to people most of the time. Mostly I just look at them like they stupid. Because my mother always told me that as long as you don't say nothin' to nobody, you can't never get in trouble. If you look at them stupid, what are they going to do? If you roll your eyes at somebody like that, I mean, that's really nothing [compared to] . . . cursing at them. Most of the time I try to walk away.

As Ianna observes, there is enough free-floating fury in Harlem to keep a steady supply of customer antagonism coming the way of service workers every day of their work lives. The problem is constant enough to warrant official company policies on how Burger Barn's crew members should respond to insults, what managers should do to help, and the evasive tactics that work best to quell an incendiary situation without losing business.[6] Management tries to minimize the likelihood of such incidents by placing girls on the registers rather than boys, in the apparent belief that young men will attract more abuse and find it harder to quash their reactions than their female counterparts.

Burger Barn does what it can to contend with these problems on the shop floor. But the neighborhood is beyond its reach and there too fast-food workers are often met with ridicule from the people they grew up with. They have to learn to defend themselves against the criticism that they have lowered themselves in taking these jobs coming from people they have known all their lives. Stephanie Harmon, who has worked at Burger Barn for over a year, explains that here too she leans on the divide between the worker and the do-nothing:

> People I hang out with, they know me since I was little. We all grew up together. When they see me comin', they laugh and say, "Here come Calvin, here come Calvin sister." I just laugh and keep on going. I say, "You're crazy. But that's OK cause I got a job and you all standing out here on the corner." Or I say, "This is my job, it's legal." Something like that. That Calvin commercial show you that even though his friends tease him and he just brushed them off, then he got a higher position. Then you see how they change toward him.

As Stephanie indicates, the snide remarks of peers and neighbors when a worker first dons a Burger Barn uniform are often replaced with requests for help in getting hired and a show of respect when that worker sticks with the job, shows up with money in her pockets and, best of all, moves into management. Still, the scorn is a burden to endure.

Tiffany Wilson, also a teen worker in a central Harlem Burger Barn, thinks she knows why kids in her community who don't work give her such a hard time. They don't want her to succeed because if no one is making it, then no one needs to feel bad about failing. But if someone claws their way up and looks like they have a chance to escape the syndrome of failure, it must mean everyone could, in theory, do so as well. The teasing, a thinly veiled attempt to enforce conformity, is designed to push would-be success stories back into the fold:

> What you will find in any situation, more so in the black community, is that if you are in the community and you try to excel, you will get ridicule from your own peers. It's like the "crab down" syndrome. . . . If you put a bunch of crabs in a big bucket and one crab tries to get out, what do you think the other crabs would do now? According to my thinking, they should pull him up or push him or help him get out. But the crabs pull him back in the barrel. That's just an analogy for what happens in the community a lot.

Keeping everyone down prevents any particular person from feeling that creeping sense of despair that comes from believing things could be otherwise but aren't.

Swallowing ridicule would be a hardship for almost anyone in this culture, but it is particularly hard on minority youth in the inner city. They have already logged several years' worth of interracial and cross-class friction by the time they climb behind a Burger Barn cash register. More

likely than not, they have also learned from peers that no self-respecting person allows themselves to be "dissed" without striking back. Yet this is precisely what they must do if they are going to survive on the shop floor.

This is one of the main reasons why these jobs carry such a powerful stigma in American popular culture: they fly in the face of a national attraction to autonomy, independence, and the individualist's right to respond in kind when their dignity is threatened. In ghetto communities, this stigma is even more powerful because—ironically—it is in these enclaves that this mainstream value of independence is elaborated and embellished. Film characters from the Superfly variety to the political version (e.g., Malcolm X), rap stars, and local idols base their claims to notoriety on standing above the crowd, going their own way, being beyond the ties that bind ordinary mortals. There are white parallels, to be sure, but this is a powerful genre of icons in the black community, not because it is a disconnected subculture, but because it is an intensified version of a perfectly recognizable American middle- and working-class fixation.

It is therefore noteworthy that thousands upon thousands of minority teens, young adults, and even middle-aged adults line up for jobs that will subject them, at least potentially, to a kind of character assassination. They do so not because they start the job-hunting process with a different set of values, one that can withstand society's contempt for fast-food workers. They take these jobs because in so many inner-city communities, there is nothing better in the offing. In general, they have already tried to get better jobs and have failed, landing instead at the door of Burger Barn as a last resort.

The stigma of these jobs has other sources beyond the constraints of enforced deference. Low pay and poor prospects for mobility matter as well. Fast-food jobs are invariably minimum-wage positions.[7] Salaries rise very little over time, even for first-line management. In ghetto areas, where jobs are scarce and the supply of would-be workers chasing them is relatively large, downward pressure keeps these jobs right down at the bottom of the wage scale.[8]

The public perception (fueled by knowledge of wage conditions) is that there is very little potential for improvement in status or responsibility either. Even though there are Horatio Algers in this industry, there are no myths to prop up a more glorified image. As a result, the epithet "McJob" develops out of the perception that a fast-food worker is not likely to end up in a prestigious position as a general manager or restaurant owner; she is going to spend her whole life flipping burgers.

As it happens, this is only half true. The fast-food industry is actually very good about internal promotion. Shop floor management is nearly always recruited from the ranks of entry-level workers. Carefully planned training programs make it possible for people to move up, to acquire transferable skills, and to at least take a shot at entrepreneurial ownership. Industry leaders, like McDonald's, are proud of the fact that half of their present board of directors started out on the shop floor as crew members. One couldn't say as much for most other Fortune 500 firms.

Nevertheless, the vast majority of workers never even get close to management. The typical entry-level worker cycles through the job in short order, producing an industry average job tenure of less than six months. Since this is just an average, it suggests that a large number of employees are there and gone in a matter of weeks. It is this pattern, a planned operation built around low skills and high turnover, that has given fast-food jobs such a bad name. Although it is quite possible to rise above the fray and make a very respectable living in fast-food management, most crew members remain at the entry level and leave too soon to see much upward movement. Observing this pattern on such a large scale—in practically every town and city in the country—Americans naturally conclude that there is no real future in a job of this kind and anyone with more on the ball wouldn't be caught dead working behind the counter.

The stigma also stems from the low socioeconomic status of the people who hold these jobs. This includes teenagers, immigrants who often speak halting English, those with little education, and (increasingly in affluent communities afflicted with labor shortages) the elderly. To the extent that the prestige of a job refracts the social characteristics of its average incumbents, fast-food jobs are hobbled by the perception that people with better choices would never purposively opt for a McJob. We argue that entry-level jobs of this kind don't merit this scorn: a lot more skill, discretion, and responsibility are locked up in a fast-food job than meets the public eye. But this truth hardly matters where public perception is concerned. There is no faster way to indicate that a person is barely deserving of notice than to point out that they hold a "chump change" job in Kentucky Fried Chicken or Burger King. We "know" this is the case just by looking at the age, skin color, or educational credentials of the people already

on the job: the tautology has a staying power that even the most expensive public relations campaign cannot shake.

It is hard to know the extent to which this stigma discourages young people in places like central Harlem from knocking on the doors of fast-food restaurants in search of employment. It is clear that the other choices aren't much better and that necessity drives thousands, if not millions, of teens and older job seekers to repudiate the stigma associated with fast-food work or learn to live with it.[9] But no one comes into the central Harlem job market without having to contend with the social risks to their identity that come with approaching stigmatized ground.

Tiffany Wilson started working in the underground economy bagging groceries when she was little more than ten years old because her mother was having trouble supporting the family, "checks weren't coming in," and there was "really a need for food" in the family. She graduated to summer youth by the time she was fourteen and landed a job answering phones in a center that dealt with domestic violence cases, referring terrified women to shelters. By the time she was sixteen, Tiffany needed a real job that would last beyond the summertime, so she set about looking—everywhere. As a black teenager, she quickly discovered there wasn't a great deal open to her. Tiffany ended up at Burger Barn in the Bronx, a restaurant two blocks from her house and close enough to her high school to make afterschool hours feasible.

> The first Burger Barn I worked at was because nobody else would take me. It was a last resort. I didn't want to go to Burger Barn. You flip burgers. People would laugh at you. In high school, I didn't wanna be in that kind of environment. But lo and behold, after everything else failed, Martin Paints, other jobs, Burger Barn was welcoming me with open arms. So I started working there.

Tiffany moved to Harlem when she finished high school and found she couldn't commute back to the Bronx. Reluctant to return to the fast-food business, Tiffany tried her luck at moving up, into a service job with more of a white-collar flavor. She looked everywhere for a position in stores where the jobs are free of hamburger grease and hot oil for French fries, stores where clerks don't wear aprons or hair nets. Nothing panned out, despite her best efforts:

> I'm looking at Lerners and Plymouth [clothing stores] and going to all these stores and lo and behold Burger

Barn is there with open arms because I had two years of experience by then.

The new Burger Barn franchise was right in the middle of Harlem, not far from the room she rents over a storefront church. It had the additional appeal of being a black-owned business, something that mattered to Tiffany in terms of the "more cultural reasons why [she] decided to work there." But she confesses to a degree of disappointment that she was not able to break free of entry-level fast-food jobs. With a high-school diploma in hand, Tiffany was hoping for something better.

William Johnson followed a similar pathway to Burger Barn, graduating from summer youth jobs in the middle of high school and looking for something that would help pay for his books and carfare. The Department of Labor gave him a referral to Burger Barn, but he was reluctant at first to pursue it:

> To go there and work for Burger Barn, that was one of those real cloak-and-dagger kind of things. You'll be coming out [and your friends say], "Yo, where you going?" You be, "I'm going, don't worry about where I'm going." And you see your friends coming [to the restaurant] and see you working there and now you be [thinking], "No, the whole [housing] project gonna know I work in Burger Barn." It's not something I personally proclaim or pride and stuff. . . . If you are a crew member, you really aren't shit there. . . . You got nothing there, no benefits, nothing. It was like that [when I was younger] and it's like that now.

William tried every subterfuge he could think of to conceal his job from the kids he knew. He kept his uniform in a bag and put it on in the back of the restaurant so that it would never be visible on the street. He made up fake jobs to explain to his friends where his spending money was coming from. He took circuitous routes to the Barn and hid back by the gigantic freezer when he spotted a friend coming into the store. The last thing William wanted was to be publicly identified as a shift worker at Burger Barn.

In this, William was much like the other teen and young adult workers we encountered. They are very sensitive to stigma, to challenges to their status, and by taking low-wage jobs of this kind they have positioned themselves to receive exactly the kind of insults they most fear. But the fact is that they do take these risks and, in time, latch onto other "narratives" that undergird their legitimacy.

Breaking the Stigma

One of the chief challenges of an organization like Burger Barn is how to take people who have come to them on the defensive and turn them into workers who at least appear on the surface, if not deep in their souls, to enjoy their work. Customers have choices; they can vote with their feet. If ordering french fries at Burger Barn requires them to run a gauntlet of annoyance, rudeness, or diffidence from the person who takes their order, they can easily cross the street to a competitor the next time. It is clearly in the company's interest to find ways to turn the situation around. Ideally, from the industry's viewpoint, it would be best if the whole reputation of these jobs could be reversed. This is what McDonald's had in mind when it launched the Calvin series. But for all the reasons outlined earlier in this chapter, that is not likely to happen, for the conditions that give rise to the stigma in the first place— low wages, high turnover, enforced deference—are not likely to change. Beyond publicizing the opportunities that are within reach, much of which falls on deaf ears, there is little the industry can do to rehabilitate its workers in the eyes of the public and thereby dampen the tension across the counter.

Yet behind the scenes, managers and workers, and peers working together in restaurant crews, do build a moral defense of their work. They call upon timeless American values, values familiar to many, including conservatives, to undergird their respectability. Pointing to the essential virtues of the gainfully employed, Burger Barn workers align themselves with the great mass of men and women who work for a living. "We are like them," they declare, and in so doing separate themselves from the people in their midst who are not employed.

They have plenty of experience with individuals who don't work, often including members of their own families: beggars who come around the restaurants looking for handouts every day; fast-talkers who come into Burger Barn hoping for free food; and age-mates who prefer to deal drugs. In general, these low-wage workers are far less forgiving, and far less tolerant, of these people than are the liberals who champion the cause of the working poor. Since they hold hard, exhausting, poorly paid jobs, they see little reason why anyone ought to get a free ride. What the indigent should do, on this account, is to follow their example: get a job, any job.

Ianna Bates is an articulate case in point. She has had to confront the social degradation that comes from holding a "low job" and has developed a tough hide in response. Her dignity is underwritten by the critique she has absorbed about the "welfare dependent":

> I'm not ashamed because I have a job. Most people don't and I'm proud of myself that I decided to get up and do something at an early age. So as I look at it, I'm not on welfare. I'm doing something.
>
> I'm not knocking welfare, but I know people that are on it that can get up and work. There's nothing wrong with them. And they just choose not to. . . . They don't really need to be on [welfare]. They just want it because they can get away with it. I don't think it's right because that's my tax dollars going for somebody who is lazy, who don't wanna get up. I can see if a woman had three children, her husband left her and she don't have no job cause she was a housewife. OK. But after a while, you know, welfare will send you to school. Be a nurse assistant, a home attendant, something!
>
> Even if you were on welfare, it should be like, you see all these dirty streets we have? Why can't they go out and sweep the streets, clean up the parks. I mean, there is so much stuff that needs to be done in this city. They can do that and give them their money. Not just sit home and not do anything.

Patricia Hull, a mother of five children in her late thirties, couldn't agree more. Patty has worked at Burger Barn for five years now, having pulled herself off of welfare by the sheer determination to be a decent role model for her children. One might imagine that she would be more tolerant of AFDC recipients, since she has been there. She moved up to the Big Apple from Tennessee after her husband walked out on her, hoping to find more job opportunities than the few that were available in the rural south. It took a long time for her to get on her feet and even Patty would agree that without "aid" she would not have made it this far. Still, having finally taken the hard road to a real job, she sees no reason why anyone else should have an easier ride:

> There's so much in this city; it's always hiring. It may not be what you want. It may not be the pay you want. But you will always get a job. If I can work at Burger Barn all week and come home tired and then have to deal with the kids and all of that, and be happy with $125 a week, so can you. Why would I give quarters [to bums on the street]? My quarter is tax-free money for you! No way.

Or, in a variation on the same theme, Larry Peterson reminds us that any job is better than no job. The kids who would dare to hard-time Larry get nothing but a cold shoulder in return because Larry knows in his soul that he has something they don't have: work for which he gets paid.

> I don't care what other people think. You know, I just do not care. I have a job, you know. It's my job. You ain't puttin' *no* food on my table; you ain't puttin' *no* clothes on my back. I will walk tall with my Burger Barn uniform on. Be proud of it, you know.

These views could have come straight from the most conservative Republicans in the country, bent on justifying draconian cuts in the welfare budget. For they trade on a view held by many of the ghetto-based working poor: that work equals dignity and no one deserves a free ride. The difference between them is simply that the working poor know whereof they speak: they have toiled behind the hot grease pits of french-fry vats, they have stood on their feet for eight or nine hours at a stretch, all for the magnificent sum of $4.25 an hour. Virtually all they have to show for their trouble is the self-respect that comes from being on the right side of that gaping cavern that separates the deserving (read working) and the undeserving (read nonworking) poor (Katz 1989).

Other retorts to status insults emerge as well. Flaunting financial independence often provides a way of lashing back at acquaintances who dis young workers for taking Burger Barn jobs. Brian Gray, born in Jamaica but raised in one of Harlem's tougher neighborhoods, knows that his peers don't really think much of his job. "They just make fun," he says. "Ah, you flipping burgers. You gettin' paid $4.25. They'd go snickering down the street." But it wasn't long after Brian started working that he picked up some serious money, serious at least for a teenager in his neighborhood.

> What I did was made Sam [the general manager] save my money for me. Then I got the best of clothes and the best sneakers with my own money. Then I added two chains. Then [my friends] were like, "Where you selling drugs at?" And I'm like, "the same place you said making fun of me, flipping burgers. That's where I'm getting my money from. Now, where are you getting yours from?" They couldn't answer.

Contrary to public perception, most teenagers in Harlem are afraid of the drug trade and won't go near it. They know too many people who are six feet under, in jail, or permanently disabled by the ravages of drugs. If you aren't willing to join the underground economy, where are you going to get the money to dress yourself, go out on the town, and do the other things teens throughout the middle class do on Mom and Dad's sufferance? Most of Harlem's youth cannot rely on their parents' financial support to meet these needs. Indeed, this is one of the primary pressures that pushes young people out into the labor market in the first place, and at an early age. Most workers we interviewed had their first job by the age of fourteen.

What Brian does, then, is to best his mates at their own game by showing them that he has the wherewithal to be a consumer, based on his own earnings. He derives no small amount of pleasure from turning these tables, upending the status system by outdoing his friends on style grounds they value as much as he does.

It might be comforting to suggest that these hard-working low-wage workers were, from the very beginning, different from their nonworking counterparts, equipped somehow to withstand the gauntlet of criticism that comes their way when they start out on the bottom of the labor market. It would be comforting because we would then be able to sort the deserving, admirable poor (who recognize the fundamental value of work and are willing to ignore **stigma**) from the undeserving (who collapse in the face of peer pressure and therefore prefer to go on the dole). This is too simplistic. Burger Barn workers of all ages and colors fully admit that their employment is the butt of jokes and that it has subjected them to ridicule. Some, like Larry Peterson, argue that they don't care what other people think, but even these brave souls admit that it took a long time for them to build up this confidence.

Where, then, does the confidence come from? How do ghetto residents develop the rejoinders that make it possible to recapture their dignity in the face of peer disapproval? To some degree, they can call on widely accepted American values that honor working people, values that float in the culture at large.[10] But this is not enough to construct a positive identity when the reminders of low status—coming from customers, friends, and the

media—are abundant. Something stronger is required: a workplace culture that actively works to overcome the negatives by reinforcing the value of the work ethic. Managers and veteran employees on the shop floor play a critical role in the reinforcement process by counseling new workers distressed by bad-mouthing.

Kimberly Sampson, a twenty-year-old African-American woman, began working at Burger Barn when she was sixteen and discovered firsthand how her "friends" would turn on her for taking a low-wage job. Fortunately, she found a good friend at work who steadied her with a piece of advice:

> Say it's a job. You are making money. Right? Don't care what nobody say. You know? If they don't like it, too bad. They sitting on the corner doing what they are doing. You got to work making money. You know? Don't bother with what anybody has to say about it.

Kim's advisor, a workplace veteran who had long since come to terms with the insults of his peers, called upon a general status hierarchy that places the working above the nonworking as a bulwark against the slights. His point was later echoed by Kim's manager in the course of a similar episode, as she explained:

> Kids come in here . . . they don't have enough money. I'll be like, "You don't have enough money; you can't get [the food you ordered]." One night this little boy came in there and cursed me out. He [said], "That's why you are working at Burger Barn. You can't get a better job. . . ."
>
> I was upset and everything. I started crying. [My manager] was like, "Kim, don't bother with him. I'm saying, *you got a job*. You know. It is a *job*."

Absorbing this defensive culture is particularly important for immigrant workers in Harlem who often find fast-food jobs the first venue where they have sustained interaction with African-Americans who resent the fact that they have jobs at all, much less jobs in their community. Marisa Gonzalez, a native of Ecuador, had a very difficult time when she first began working as a hostess at Burger Barn. A pretty, petite nineteen-year-old, she was selected for the job because she has the kind of sparkle and vivaciousness that any restaurant would want customers to see. But some of her more antagonistic black customers saw her as an archetype: the immigrant who barely speaks a word of English who snaps up a job some native-born English speaker ought to have. Without the support of her

stigma A social mark of disgrace that prevents a person from entering mainstream society. For example, society stigmatizes ex-felons and pedophiles.

bilingual, Latino manager, she would not have been able to pull herself together and get on with the work:

> I wasn't sent to the grill or the fries [where you don't need to communicate with customers]. I was sent to the cash register, even though the managers knew I couldn't speak English. That was only one week after my arrival in the United States! So I wasn't feeling very well at all. Three weeks later I met a manager who was Puerto Rican. He was my salvation. He told me, "Marisa, it's not that bad." He'd speak to me in English, even though he knows Spanish. He'd tell me, "Don't cry. Dry off those tears. You'll be all right, you'll make it." So he encouraged me like no other person in that Burger Barn, especially when the customers would curse at me for not knowing English. He gave me courage and after that it went much better.

Among the things this manager taught Marisa was that she should never listen to people who give her a hard time about holding a job at Burger Barn. Having been a white-collar clerical worker in her native country, it did bother Marisa that she had slipped down the status hierarchy—and it still does. She was grateful, nevertheless, to have a way to earn money and her family was desperate for her contribution. When customers would insult her, insinuating that someone who speaks limited English was of lowly status, she turned to management for help. And she found it in the form of fellow Latino bosses who told her to hold her head up because she was, after all, working, while her critics on the whole were not.

Once these general moral values are in place, many Burger Barn workers take the process one step further: they argue their jobs have hidden virtues that make them more valuable than most people credit. Tiffany Wilson, the young black woman who reluctantly settled for a Burger Barn job when none of the clothing stores she wanted to work for would take her, decided in the end that there was more substance to her job than she credited initially:

> When I got in there, I realized it's not what people think. It's a lot more to it than flipping burgers. It's a real system of business. That's when I really got to see a big corporation at play. I mean, one part of it, the foundation of it: cashiers, the store, how it's run. Production of food, crew workers, service. Things of that nature. That's when I really got into it and understood a lot more.

Americans tend to think of values as embedded in individuals, transmitted through families, and occasionally reinforced by media images or role models. We tend not to focus on the powerful contribution that institutions and organizations make to the creation and sustenance of beliefs. Yet it is clear that the workplace itself is a major force in the creation of a rebuttal culture among these workers. Without this line of defense it would be very hard for Burger Barn employees to retain their dignity. With the support of fellow workers, however, they are able to hold their heads up, not by defining themselves as separate from society, but by calling upon the values they hold in common with the rest of the working world.

This is but one of the reasons why exclusion from the society of the employed is such a devastating source of social isolation. We could hand people money, as various guaranteed income plans of the past thirty years have suggested. But we can't hand out honor. For a majority of Americans, honor comes from participation in this central setting in our culture and from the positive identity it confers.

Franklin Roosevelt understood this during the Great Depression and responded with the creation of thousands of publicly funded jobs designed to put people to work building the national parks, the railway stations, the great highways that criss-cross the country, and the murals that decorate public walls from San Francisco to New York. Social scientists studying the unemployed in the 1930s showed convincingly that people who held **WPA** jobs were far happier and healthier than those who were on the dole, even when their incomes did not differ significantly. WPA workers had their dignity in the midst of poverty; those on the dole were vilified and could not justify their existence or find an effective cultural rationale for the support they received.

This historical example has its powerful parallels in the present. Joining the workforce is a fundamental, transforming experience that moves people across barriers of subculture, race, gender, and class. It never completely eradicates these differences and in some divisive settings it may even reinforce consciousness of them—through glass ceilings, discriminatory promotion policies, and the

---

WPA Works Progress Administration: a New Deal program from the 1930s to provide jobs for the unemployed.

like. But even in places where pernicious distinctions are maintained, there is another, overarching identity competing with forms that stress difference: a common bond within the organization and across the nation of fellow workers. This is what makes getting a job so much more than a means to a financial end. It becomes a crucial developmental hurdle, especially for people who have experienced exclusion before, including minorities, women, the elderly, and teenagers. Any experience that can speak back to the stigma that condemns burger flippers as the dregs, resurrecting them as exemplars of the American work ethic, has extraordinary power.

Those who choose to earn a living in the legitimate job market receive few material rewards for their effort, but they can claim moral legitimacy from the traditional American work ethic. They can't flash large rolls of cash before the eyes of their neighbors, but they can pride themselves on "doing the right thing," avoiding the dangers of the drug trade and the sloth of welfare recipients. While they understand that some people have a legitimate need to receive government assistance, they don't see the payoff of dealing drugs, and this is not an opinion they keep to themselves. Workers with friends or family in the drug trade often implore them to get out, warning them of the dangers, and reasoning that they each make about the same amount of money in a week, while the one involved with drugs has to work longer hours.

Nadine Stevens has worked at Burger Barn since graduating from high school five years ago. By all accounts she lives in one of the most dangerous neighborhoods in Harlem. Her apartment building is the home of an active drug trade and, indeed, the mailboxes were recently removed from the building by police because they were being used for drug transactions. She knows most of the drug dealers who sit on her stoop every day and night, having grown up with them. She and her mother and sister, whose ground-floor apartment faces the street, have seen many young women they know wasted by drugs, and young men killed in their hallway.

Nadine tries to convince the dealers she knows to get out of the trade, and to shoot for getting into management at Burger Barn. She and her sister, Rachael, with whom she works at Burger Barn, recently accosted a young teen they knew on the street whom they suspected of drug running. They told her that if she was desperate for money they'd get her a job at Burger Barn. Sensing the girl's reluctance, Nadine cried, "There's no shame in my game! Come work with me."

The dealers they know argue that the Burger Barn employee is working in a poorly paid, demeaning job and that, furthermore, they couldn't get hired there if they tried. Although their work is dangerous, illegal, and despised by neighbors, they brandish the accoutrements of success glorified in the United States: expensive cars, stylish clothes, and lots of cash. Their honor is measured in dollars, a common American standard that competes for the attention of people otherwise destined to earn little more than the minimum wage.

Anthony Vallo has had to choose on which side of the law to work and, once he secured his Burger Barn job, had to decide what to do about his friends and acquaintances who chose the wrong side. Two of his best friends are in jail. Another friend is dealing drugs and probably isn't far from a jail term himself. What Anthony does is try to maintain a cordial relationship with these guys, but to put as much distance between himself and them as he can without giving offense:

> This friend of mine is selling and stuff like that, but he's my friend. We used to go to school back then. He was like, "Damn, you still doin' that Burger Barn shit? I can get you a real job!" I think he respects me; at least he don't criticize me behind my back. But I try to avoid him, you know.

Drug dealers are not the only problem cases with which Harlem workers must contend. At least until welfare reform began to force women on **AFDC** back into the labor force, many young mothers working low wage jobs were faced with the fork in the road that led either to a job at a place like Burger Barn or public assistance. Since most know a fair number of women who have elected, or had no choice but to opt for, the latter, it takes no small amount of fortitude to go for a minimum-wage job.[11] Indeed, given that AFDC offered greater financial benefits—when health coverage, food stamps, and subsidized housing are part of the package—than these jobs provide, it takes a strong attachment to the work ethic and a willingness to sacrifice elements of one's financial well-being in favor of the dignity that goes with holding a real job.

AFDC Aid to Families with Dependent Children: assistance provided by the federal government to families in economic need.

The Importance of Going to Work

Although having a well-paid, respected career is prized above all else in the United States, our culture confers honor on those who hold down jobs of any kind over those who are outside of the labor force. Independence and self-sufficiency—these are virtues that have no equal in this society. But there are other reasons why we value workers besides the fact that their earnings keep them above water and therefore less in need of help from government, communities, or charities. We also value workers because they share certain common views, experiences, and expectations. The work ethic is more than an attitude toward earning money—it is a disciplined existence, a social life woven around the workplace.

For all the talk of "family values," we know that in the contemporary period, family often takes a backseat to the requirements of a job, even when the job involves flipping burgers. What we are supposed to orient toward primarily is the workplace and its demands. This point could not be made more forcefully than it is in the context of the welfare reform bills of 1996. Public policy in the late 1990s makes clear that poor women are now supposed to be employed even if they have young children. With a majority of women with children, even those under a year of age, in the labor force, we are not prepared to cut much slack to those who have been on welfare. They can and should work like the rest of us, or so the policy mantra goes. This represents no small change in the space of a few decades in our views of what honorable women and mothers should do. But it also reflects the growing dominance of work in our understanding of adult priorities.

We could think of this increasingly work-centered view of life as a reflection of America's waning economic position, a pragmatic response to wage stagnation, downsizing, and international competition: we must work harder. And this it may be. But it is also part of a secular transformation that has been ongoing for decades as we've moved away from home-centered work lives in the agricultural world to employment-centered lives outside the domestic sphere altogether. The more work departs from home, the more it becomes a social system of its own, a primary form of integration that rivals the family as a source of identity, belonging, and friendship. Women like Antonia Piento are not content only to take care of children at home. They want a life that is adult centered, where they have peers they can talk to. Where they might once have found that company in the neighborhood, now they are more likely to find it on the shop floor. Those primary social ties are grounded in workplace relations, hence to be a worker is also to be integrated into a meaningful community of fellow workers, the community that increasingly becomes the source of personal friends, intimate relations and the worldview that comes with them.

Work is therefore much more than a means to a financial end. This is particularly the case when the work holds little intrinsic satisfaction. No one who gets paid for boiling french fries in hot oil thinks they are playing a world-shattering role. They know their jobs are poorly valued; they can see that in their paychecks, in the demeanor of the people whom they serve across the counter, even among some managers. But what they have that their nonworking counterparts lack is both the dignity of being employed and the opportunity to participate in a social life that increasingly defines their adult lives. This community gives their lives structure and purpose, humor and pleasure, support and understanding in hard times, and a backstop that extends beyond the instrumental purposes of a fast-food restaurant. It is the crucible of their values, values that we have argued here are decidedly mainstream.

The working poor sit at the bottom of the occupational structure and feel the weight of disapproval coming down upon their shoulders from better paid, more respectable employees. Yet they stand at the top of another pyramid and can look down the slope toward people they know well who have taken another pathway in the world.

33   Sweatshops in Sunset Park: A Variation of the Late-Twentieth-Century Chinese Garment Shops in New York City

Xiaolan Bao

The late XIAOLAN BAO was a professor of history at California State University Long Branch. She is the author of *Holding Up More Than Half the Sky: Chinese Women Garment Workers in New York City, 1948–1992.*

Questions to Consider   Imagine working twelve hours a day, seven days a week, under physical conditions that are brutal: exposure to lint, physical confinement, sleep deprivation, and chemicals that constantly burn your throat. Your take-home pay at the end of an eighty-four-hour week is about $55. This is not a Jacob Riis description of New York City in 1890 but New York City one hundred years later in the 1990s. Bao's ethnography documents the modern sweatshop and the new immigrants who supply the labor and large profits to the entrepreneurs who are quick to take advantage of young women new to the United States.

ON MARCH 12, 1995, THE *NEW YORK TIMES* carried a report on the Chinese garment shops in the Sunset Park area of Brooklyn, a neighborhood that houses the new Chinese garment production center in New York City. Unlike most of the Chinatown garment shops in Manhattan, many of the Chinese shops in Sunset Park are not unionized. The weak influence of organized labor and law enforcement agencies in the area had virtually turned the industry there into a safety valve for some Chinese employers to extract quick profits while not complying with any labor laws. Incidents of exploitation increased with the expansion of the Chinese garment shops in the area.

The report in the *New York Times,* written by reporter Jane H. Lii, largely confirmed the above observation. The vivid description of life in the shops, based on the reporter's firsthand experience, gripped the hearts of its readers. According to Lii, the shop she worked in for an entire week was "typical of the small, new shops outside Manhattan":

> The steel doors opened into a dim, dusty warehouse. Red and blue rags covered the four windows, shutting out all natural light. Bundles of cut cloth sat piled in haphazard mounds, some stacked taller than a worker. Under fluorescent lights swinging from chains, rows of mid-aged Chinese women hunched over sewing machines, squinting and silent.

Were the working conditions there as horrific as those that splashed across the headlines in city newspapers? Lii's reply indicated that there was "something more complex at work." What, then, was the complexity? Lii reported that the owner of the shop was "actually benevolent, albeit in a harsh way." "She does not pay minimum wage, but she serves her workers tea. She makes them work until midnight, but she drives them home afterward. She uses child laborers, but she fusses over them, combing their ponytails, admiring their painted fingernails, even hugging them." According to Lii, the boss had opened the business only to save her family's honor, for her brother had, among many things, absconded with close to $80,000 owed to his workers in back wages. The shop also was reopened, according to its present owner, in order to provide jobs for those who came from the same region in China and whom she called "our people."

As Lii reported, the situation of the workers in the shop was also complicated. They "sewed virtually non-stop" because they wanted to make money and had no other alternatives without speaking English. They brought their children into the shop to care for them while working. Several children, however, toiled by their mothers' sides to supplement their incomes. It was said that their mothers wanted to instill in them a work ethic by allowing them to do so.

Lii reported that both the employer and her workers considered American labor laws ideal and laudable, but impractical. The workers considered their employer a good boss "precisely because she was willing to violate labor laws and allow their children to work by their sides." The situation was, therefore, "a miserable complicity born of necessity in an insular, immigrant world" or, simply, "a grim conspiracy of the poor," as the reporter concluded. No wonder that the result of working at Sunset Park was pitiful:

> Seven days later, after 84 hours of work, I got my reward, in the form of a promise that in three weeks I would be paid $54.24 or 65 cents an hour (minimum wage is $4.25). I also walked away from the lint-filled factory with aching shoulders, a stiff back, a dry cough and a burning sore throat.

How representative is Lii's seven-day experience in the shops, and how valid is her analysis? In what ways are the conditions in the Sunset Park Chinese shops similar to the union shops in Manhattan's Chinatown, the hub of the Chinese industry in New York City? In what ways are they different? To what extent are the conditions in Sunset Park similar to those of the city's garment shops at the turn of the twentieth century? What are the factors that have led to these similarities and differences? In the era of globalization, what can the conditions in Sunset Park Chinese garment shops tell us about the impact of globalization in the U.S.? This study attempts to answer these questions.

This article is primarily based on the author's historical research of the Chinese garment industry in New York City over the last ten years, her visits to a number of shops in Sunset Park in the late 1990s, and her interviews with several dozen workers in the area.[1] It gives a brief account of the working conditions in the shops and discusses several highly controversial issues in the Sunset Park Chinese community that relate to the garment industry. By presenting a more differentiated picture of the industry, it argues that while labor organizing and law enforcement remain important ways to address labor abuse in the industry, it is imperative for law enforcement agencies, organized labor, and all concerned individuals to understand the complexity embedded in the highly competitive structure of the garment industry, the multidimensional impact of labor legislation and law enforcement, and the need to develop new forms of labor organizing that are informed and responsive to the challenges of the time. Without such an understanding, any effort to curb the sweating phenomenon is likely to be sporadic and without lasting effect on the industry.

Working Environments

The shop where Jane Lii worked and reported is, in large part, typical of the Chinese garment shops in the Sunset Park area. Many of them are housed in former warehouses or converted garages. Because these shops are often hidden behind a steel door and have no sign on the front, one can hardly tell from the outside the nature of the activities inside the shops or, simply, whether there is any activity at all.

Sunset Park offers the Chinese garment industry many advantages. First, the former warehouses and the converted garages there are spacious. Even though they do not provide comfortable working conditions, they offer much more production space than industrial lofts in Manhattan's Chinatown.[2] The 1983 Chinatown Garment Industry Study reports that in 1981, Chinese shops with about 30 sewing machines occupied an average of 6,070 square feet in Soho. These shops were and are still the largest garment shops in the Chinatown area.[3] However, shops in Sunset Park with a similar number of sewing machines can cover as much as 10,000 square feet.[4] The spacious environment of the shops not only allows an effective flow of production, but also provides shop owners with enough space to expand their businesses.

In addition, rents and maintenance fees for buildings in Sunset Park are relatively inexpensive. In the spring of 1998, for example, the owner of a shop, located between Fort Hamilton Parkway and 43rd Street and covering more than 10,000 square feet, told me that she paid only $2,500 a month for a space that accommodates forty workers. For the same money, she could afford only a 4,000-square-foot shop in Manhattan's Chinatown. Maintenance fees are also low. For an additional yearly payment of $100 to

$200, the gas and other equipment and utility lines would be checked by the building owner.[5]

There are, however, many characteristics that Sunset Park shops share with their counterparts in Manhattan's Chinatown. Besides bundles of cut cloth piled up in haphazard mounds in almost any open floor space, there are severe problems with ventilation. Shops that were converted from former warehouses and garages have very few or virtually no windows at all. Conditions are even worse when the employers cover the few windows with rags or newspapers or simply lock the main entrance to conceal operations. In these shops the air is stifling and filled with lint and dust, while workers sew under fluorescent lights in the daytime.[6]

However, unlike Chinatown shops that generally suffer from space limitations, the physical size and working conditions of Sunset Park shops are not all the same. There are shops that have more than thirty workers and cover a space of over 10,000 square feet. There are also shops packed with a dozen sewing machines and piles of cut garments but covering less than 4,000 square feet. These small and big shops are located side by side. However, regardless of the differences, they have something in common. Like their counterparts in Manhattan's Chinatown, there is virtually no space reserved for workers' activities other than sewing. Even in the relatively spacious shops, workers eat their lunch at their sewing machines or at the desks where they work.

Division of Labor

Although the shops in Sunset Park, like those in Manhattan's Chinatown, work on various lines of garments from manufacturers or other contractors, workers mostly produce sportswear and other low-priced women's apparel. The division of labor in the shops varies according to the size of the shop and the line of the garments they produce, but there are in general five kinds of workers on the floor: the sorter, the foreperson, machine operators, pressers, and floor workers.

Garment production starts with the sorter, who separates the cut-up fabrics according to the style of the garments and decides where the work should begin. The cut fabrics are then sent to the machine operators for either sewing or hemming. Machine operators include those workers who sew minor parts of the garments, such as zippers, collars, cuffs and pockets. The garment then passes to the hands of the foreperson, who checks the quality of the sewed or hemmed garments. A quality garment will be sent to buttoners and trimmers who attach buttons, sew buttonholes, and trim extra threads. In its final stage, the garment will be sent to floor workers who hang tags, eliminate irregularities, and put the garments in a transparent plastic bag for shipping.

Like its counterparts elsewhere in the city, the Chinese garment industry in Sunset Park is characterized by its gender hierarchy. The rationale used to justify it is always inconsistent and contradictory. For example, the sorter and pressers, the two highest paid jobs on the shop floor, are almost invariably men. Trimmers, the lowest paid workers, are virtually all women. This arrangement is said to have its basis in women's lack of physical strength to move the bundles of cut-up materials around, and women's intellectual inability to sort the cut-up pieces and to lay out a workable schedule for production. Women are also believed to be too weak to operate the heavy pressing machines and endure the heat generated by them. As a result, they are denied the opportunity to work as a sorter or a presser. What is forgotten in this ungrounded rationale for the gender division of labor on the floor is the duration of strength, which the Chinese call *yin li,* and the extraordinary wisdom to figure out the way to sew the garments with their ever-changing styles. Both of these are necessary qualities of machine operators, who are overwhelmingly women.

It is said that women constitute the majority of machine operators in the shops because the flexible work hours, made possible by the piece-rate system and the larger number of operators in the shops, allow them to fulfill their family responsibilities while working in the shops. This justification ignores the highly competitive environment among the large number of machine operators that is generated by the piece-rate system. Since garment production is seasonal and work tends to be limited in most of the shops, in order to make ends meet, women workers are most likely to utilize every minute available to compete with one another in seizing work and to produce as many garments as they can. This work atmosphere is likely to deprive them of the flexibility that the piece-rate system is supposed to offer.

In addition, as known in the shops, workers' earnings depend not only on the piece rates and the speed at which they work, but also on the kind of work they do. The more mechanical and simple the work is, the faster they can produce, and the more money they can earn. There is no denying that pressers work under extremely stressful conditions, because there are usually only two or three of them in a shop of thirty or more machines and they have to press all the finished garments within a given time. However, their work is simpler than that of machine operators, so they can easily speed up their work after they become used to the structure of the garments and thus increase their incomes. Because there are only a few pressers in a shop, they are protected from the frenetic competition that is a routine part of the lives of machine operators.[7]

Unlike the pressers, machine operators' incomes fluctuate a great deal. Since styles are transient due to the unpredictable nature of fashion, it tends to take much longer for machine operators to get familiar with their work before they can speed up their production. The unpredictable nature of their work also creates more opportunities for their employers to keep wages low by constantly changing their piece rates, which are allegedly based on styles.

Family wages are always invoked to justify not only the higher pay of some traditionally men's work, but also the special payment arrangements in such sections as buttoning and bagging (putting the finished garments into bags). Since piece rates in these two sections are much lower than other sections, employers would subcontract the entire workload to one or two married male workers and allow them to complete the work with the assistance of their families. It used to be said that this arrangement was made to help the men fulfil their traditional gender roles as "rice winners" and to respect Chinese traditional culture. However, this rationale was cast aside in the early 1990s when the male workers left for higher paying jobs and women replaced them in these sections.

As Nancy Green and Susan Glenn have cogently argued, the gender division of labor in the garment industry has never been static.[8] Take the operation of sewing machines for example. Although most sewing machine operators are women, an increasing number of undocumented male workers have taken over these positions in Sunset Park over the last few years. Gender remains at work, however. The recently arrived men could easily take over the traditionally female jobs from women, but the gender identity of their jobs continued to subject them to a position inferior to those in the traditionally men's sections. They are generally believed to be less skilled, physically weak, and hence less manly than the rest of the male workers in the shops.

Fluidity between class and gender lines, generated by the structural flexibility of the garment industry, does not preclude opportunities for upward mobility for female as well as male workers, albeit in different ways and to different degrees. Although most Chinese employers are men and had been workers themselves, an increasing number of women workers have become owners of the garment shops in recent years. This was the case in the shop where reporter Lii worked. Many women employers learned English by attending the free language classes offered by their union or other public institutions. Speaking from fair to good English, they operate their businesses successfully, without the assistance of men. Their past experience as workers and their gender identity may enable them to better understand their women employees. However, this does not guarantee that they will be benevolent bosses, as implied in Lii's report. Recent cases of labor law violations in the Chinese garment shops owned by women have demonstrated that, situated in a highly competitive and marginal position in the city's industry, women employers can be as unscrupulous as their male counterparts.[9]

Wages and Hours

Workers' wages in the Sunset Park garment shops fluctuate greatly, contingent upon the type of work they produce, the level of skill, and the quality and adequacy of work their employer provides. A new hand may earn practically nothing for the first day, while a skilled long-stitch machine operator can earn as much as $600 a week in the high season. In general, as in the case of most Chinatown shops in Manhattan, the sorter, the foreperson, the cleaner(s), and the floor workers are paid by the hour. My interviews show that in 1998 a full-time foreperson or a sorter earned an average of more than six dollars per hour, and the finished garment checkers and cleaners, about three dollars. The rest of the workers in the shops are paid at piece rates. Their incomes vary greatly, ranging from weekly averages of $600 to $700 for a presser; $400 to $500 for a hemmer; $300 to $400 for a single machine operator and buttoner; $250 to $300 for a general machine operator; and $150–$200 for a trimmer. Compared with the union's minimum wages, the above wages of the Sunset Park Chinese garment workers may appear desirable. However, most of these weekly wages are in fact the result of workers' working ten to twelve hours a day. Their work hours are even longer during the busy seasons, with competition mounting in recent years.

Forms of payment are also factors that affect workers' incomes. Like their counterparts in Manhattan's Chinatown, most employers in Sunset Park issue payments in a combination of checks and cash. The portion of the payment received by check is determined by the worker's status or need. For union members, whose number is small in the area, employers tailor the amount of their checks strictly according to the union minimum income requirement for benefit eligibility. However, for nonunion workers, who form the overwhelming majority of the workforce in Sunset Park, the amounts of their checks are either kept below the poverty threshold so that they can maintain eligibility for welfare benefits, or kept in line with the US Immigration and Naturalization Service's basic requirement for financial eligibility for sponsoring the immigration of their family members or relatives into the United States. Working underground, undocumented workers are paid invariably by cash.

Chinese employers argue that workers themselves request various forms of payment. However, my interviews reveal that all workers, regardless of their status, are forced to accept a reduction in their wages, because checks are issued with a deduction of a five to seven percent "handling fee." The same is true for cash payments. Furthermore, piece rates are often not announced before the completion of work and in some shops employers reserve their rights to reduce workers' wages if they consider the wages to be too high.

Researcher Mark Levitan reports that in 1990, 72 percent of the reported incomes of less-skilled blue-collar workers, apparel workers included, were below the poverty threshold for a family of four ($12,674).[10] Underreporting might be a factor in leading to the low-income status of some workers' families. However, what Levitan reported did not appear to be far from reality in the case of Chinese garment workers in New York. My interviews suggest that in the late 1990s the actual average annual income of most Sunset Park Chinese garment workers

was only about $20,000.[11] To sustain their families, many have to work long hours, in violation of U.S. labor laws.

In the shops where the employers still bother to concern themselves with the investigations of law enforcement agencies, workers were required to punch their work cards to show that they were working eight hours a day, even before they start their day's work. My interviews, however, reveal that 90 percent of the workers employed in Sunset Park are working ten to twelve hours a day. During the busy seasons or when orders have to be rushed out, it is not unusual for workers to work unusually long hours, or as Lii indicated, even labor around the clock.

Long hours of work, coupled with the hazardous environment of the shops severely damages workers' health. What happened to Bao Zhi Ni is, indeed, not an isolated case. Her written testimony at a public hearing held by the New York State Assembly Subcommittee on Sweatshops on October 2, 1997, is illustrative of workers' situations:

> My name is Bao Zhi Ni. I am a garment worker. I have worked in the garment factories for close to ten years. For many long hours, I work without proper safety equipment, and under filthy conditions. I work at least ten to twelve hours everyday, but because the bosses depress the wages so low we can only make $20, $30 a day, even though we're working over ten hours . . .
>
> For many long hours I sit at the sewing machine repeating the same motions. I also have to handle heavy bundles of garments every day. Each day at work is an exhausting day. My eyes are tired, and my vision is blurry. My fingers, wrists, shoulders, neck, back, spine, all these parts of my body are inflicted with pain. I started feeling the pain in my lower back five years ago, but I continued to work in the sweatshops. I have no medical benefits.
>
> My shoulders and back hurt constantly. Because I have been forced to work for such long hours, the cartilage between the bones in my back has rubbed away, and I have a pinched nerve. With the pain and the numbness in my left leg, I know that I have muscular and nervous problems. My fingers and wrists hurt. Now, even after just one or two hours of work, my back aches so much that I can barely stand straight. . . . In order to make a living I have no choice but to force myself to work through this pain. Sometimes I can't do it, but I have no choice but to take one or two days off.
>
> Sometimes I have to take one or two weeks off. When I take this time off to heal just a little, my boss

gets angry. The boss will call my house to scold me and say that I'm lazy, tell me that I must go back to work as soon as possible.[12]

My interviews reveal that almost all the garment workers who worked in the industry for more than five years have various health problems. Deng Ying Yi, a long-time labor activist at the Workers Center in Brooklyn run by the Union of Needletrades, Industrial and Textile Employees (UNITE!), is virtually disabled after working in the garment industry for more than ten years, with her nervous system partially damaged. Her case is not unique among workers in Sunset Park. However, most of these nonunionized workers are not covered by any form of health insurance.

To survive in their new homeland, nonunionized workers have to develop their own system to cope with the situation. Many rely heavily on their family ties and community networks. The experience of a Mr. Zhang, who had been a middle-rank official in Guangzhou but who became a finished garment checker in a Sunset Park Chinese garment shop, is indicative of this phenomenon:

> I was already fifty-two when I immigrated to this country. I worked in a garment shop as *cha yi* (Cantonese: a finished garment checker) and my wife *jin sin* (Cantonese: a trimmer). Together, we earned an average of less than $400 a week and we still had to raise a daughter, our youngest daughter who was in her teens and was eligible to come with us when we immigrated to this country. She had to eat, to dress and to go to school. In addition, we had to save money in order to sponsor our two older children to come to the United States. How did we manage to do all this? Well, we relied on our family....
>
> I came with my other five siblings under the sponsorship of a brother. Each of us came with his or her own family. Altogether, it was more than twenty of us who came to New York City on the same day on the same plane. We rented three two-bedroom apartments in this part of Brooklyn because the brother who came earlier told us that rents are much less expensive in this area. Each apartment was shared by two families. My family and my brother's family shared a two-bedroom apartment and we paid a total of $700 for rent and utilities but we ate separately. My family spent a little more than $100 each month on groceries. How did we manage to do this? We bought the cheapest possible food at the market, say, the thirty-nine-cent-a-pound chicken

on sale at Key Foods and the four-head-for-one-dollar broccoli at the street stands in this neighborhood. In addition, my wife and I also picked up empty soda cans and other stuff on our way home from work. If we were lucky, the monthly income from that part of our labor could cover our groceries for an entire week.

> For eight years after we came to this city, we never ate out and never stopped working, eleven to twelve hours a day and seven days a week. Whenever we did not have work to do in our shop my wife and I went to work in another shop.[13]

While family ties are important resources for immigrant workers who came with their families, community networks are the most important assets for undocumented immigrant workers, most of whom did not come with their families. For example, undocumented workers from Wenzhou have contributed money to establish their own "mutual funds." These funds can be used by any member in time of need. This practice has proved to be the most effective way for these workers to survive in time of adversity, since they are denied any social services and benefits in the United States.

As elsewhere in the world, the gendered definitions of roles in the Sunset Park Chinese garment shops, their hierarchical order, and the rationale applied to justify them are shaped by the flexible but highly competitive structure of the garment industry, and have been inherently unstable. This fluidity generates dynamics in the industry, but has also taken a toll on those who labor in the industry. It is by exhausting human resources among the workers and in their community that the nonregulated segment of the garment industry has managed to thrive. Sunset Part is a case in point.

"Co-Ethnic Conspiracy?"

One major aspect of the Chinese garment industry in New York that has generated great interest among some scholars is its co-ethnic nature. Although in recent years more and more garment shops in New York have employers and workers who do not share the same ethnic identity, this is not the case with many of the Chinese garment shops in Manhattan's Chinatown and Brooklyn's Sunset Park. Most Chinese employers continue to hire only workers from major Chinese settlements.

As many studies have pointed out, this co-ethnic nature of the industry has benefited both workers and management.[14] Like their Eastern European counterparts at the turn of the twentieth century, Chinese workers do not have to learn to speak or understand English to work in a garment shop. They can also learn the trade on site and from scratch. In truth, without the industry, many working-class Chinese immigrant families may not have been able to survive.

The co-ethnic nature of the industry is also said to have simplified and humanized management of the shops. Many studies have discussed the particular recruitment pattern of the Chinese shops. Although in recent years a growing number of new immigrant workers have begun to seek employment through advertisements in community newspapers or the help-wanted signs posted in the front of the shops, most employers continue to rely on the recommendations of their workforce for new recruits, and most new immigrant workers obtain their first jobs through their families, friends, and relatives. Some employers also hire job applicants on the spot, without giving them much of a background check. New recruits, especially those who are employed with the recommendations from workers already in the shop, are allowed to use the facilities in the shop to receive on-site training.

Workers can maintain their cultural practices at their workplaces. They celebrate major Chinese festivals in the shops. They also share Chinese food and cooking with one another, listen to the blasting of the closed-circuit Chinese radio broadcasts, and share news about their homeland while working. As Lii noted, although employers in most Chinese shops do not offer their employees overtime payments when they expect workers to work long hours or on weekends, they offer them free rice and water, or even tea in some shops, to eat and drink with their lunch. They also provide lunch or afternoon tea to compensate workers' working on weekends. It is also widely known that most employers in Sunset Park will drive their employees home if their work ends after 11:00 P.M.

Workers who are unfamiliar with the labor laws and their rights in the United States feel obligated to work hard for their employers if their employers are willing to accommodate their needs. The undocumented workers feel particularly grateful to their employers if their employers have offered them any form of protection during immigration or other law enforcement raids. Employers in Sunset Park are known to cover workers up with piles of cut-garments scattered on the floor, or allow them

to use the ladder in the shop to climb to the skylight. These gestures foster gratitude on the workers' part, which they feel obligated to reciprocate.

Many workers find it easy to identify with their employers if they are immigrants and have been workers themselves. Workers who desire upward social mobility look up to their employers as role models, a mirror of their future in the land of opportunity. Workers' empathy with their employers' situation, generated by a mixture of gratitude, fear, and admiration, has often led to their acquiescence to their employers' unscrupulous practices on the shop floor. In some cases this relationship of empathy has become so entrenched that law enforcement agents from outside the Chinese community and Chinese union organizers find it difficult to break. No wonder observers of the industry, like reporter Lii, do not hesitate to call the Sunset Park shop "a miserable complicity born of necessity in an insular, immigrant world." However, this conspiracy theory is too simplistic to explain the complex interdependent relationship between the workers and their employers in the ethnic enclave economy of the United States. It also fails to highlight the imbalance of power embedded in this relationship. Failing to locate the ultimate beneficiaries of this relationship, this theory cannot explain fully the causes of sweated labor in the shops.

Clearly, employers' various forms of accommodation benefit themselves rather than the workers. Let's take the special form of recruitment, for example. Since workers' incomes are based on the work they have accomplished, it will only hurt the new recruits if they are slow to learn their routine of work. However, on-site training allows employers to strengthen their personal ties with the newly hired as well as those who are already in the shop. Paying wages in a mixture of cash and checks or simply by cash also enables the employers to avoid paying taxes, the amounts of which are likely to be much larger than their workers'. A closer investigation of the situation in the industry also reveals that accommodations offered by employers are not unconditional. They are given only to workers who follow the rules they set. Those who refuse to do so are fired, blacklisted, physically assaulted, or subjected to other forms of retaliation.

Most Chinese employers do not force their workers to work long hours. However, production is organized in such a way that workers who do not stay as long as the rest will find themselves in an extremely disadvantageous position. Since there is no limit on work hours in most of the shops and workers who are willing to maximize their work hours can work as long as they wish, those who refuse to do so will end up having only "pork neckbones" (a slang in the Chinatown garment industry, referring to garments difficult to sew), or simply no garments to work on the next morning when they return.

Similar situations occur if a worker is ill and takes sick leave, or refuses to work on Sunday. Employers will hire a replacement worker almost immediately after a laborer fails to show up. Employers will also distribute "chickens in soy sauce" (another slang in the Chinatown garment industry, referring to work easy to sew) or paychecks on Sunday. Under these situations, workers who take a sick day are likely to lose their jobs, and those who do not work on Sunday will miss not only an important opportunity to increase their incomes, but also to get paid in a timely manner. Since workers' wages tend to be withheld by their employers for months in Sunset Park, failing to be present on payday will mean another indefinitely long delay in getting paid. It's no wonder that workers in Sunset Park tend to lament, "We have the option to die but we don't have the option to take a sick day or a rest."

Some employers have also blatantly taken advantage of their workers' acquiescence to maximize their profit. Instances of *zhen jia lao ban* (real and fake bosses) and *yi guo liang zhi* (one country, two systems), stories told by labor activist Deng Ying Yi, are indications of how far employers would go.[15] As Deng recalled, one day workers of a shop came to the UNITE! Workers' Center to seek assistance in collecting their wages. It turned out that their employer had closed the shop after owing them several hundred thousands of dollars in back wages and had vanished without a trace. However, when the State Department of Labor finally undertook this case, the department found it difficult to file charges against the real owner of the shop. The owner, an undocumented immigrant himself, had registered the shop with the name and social security number of an elderly worker and had been signing all the legal documents under this worker's name without informing him. Filing charges against the owner of the shop would mean charges against this worker, who was not the real owner of the shop.[16]

The story of "one country, two systems" is about a peculiar phenomenon in some unionized shops in Sunset Park. According to Deng, although union contracts stipulate that all workers in a union shop are union members and entitled to union benefits, employers of some unionized shops refuse to register their new recruits as union members and keep their wages in the books. Consequently, there are both union and nonunion members in the same shop who are working under very different systems of employment.

My interviews further reveal other forms of discrimination on the floor. For example, some employers offer different piece rates to workers of different immigration status and from different regions in China. Cantonese immigrant workers, who form the majority of the workforce, tend to receive higher piece rates and work relatively regular hours, while non-Cantonese or undocumented workers are denied all these "privileges." Discriminatory treatments have taken a different form in a small number of shops that hire several skilled workers from other ethnic groups. The non-Chinese workers are offered wages and other working conditions that comply with labor laws, while their Chinese fellow workers, who work side by side with them, have to struggle against the grim reality of low pay and long hours of work.[17]

Chinese employers have been so reckless in exploiting workers in their own community that it reinforces the stereotypical image of Chinese workers as the docile "willing slaves" in the Sunset Park area. This image of the workers subjects them to exploitation not only by Chinese employers, but also by shop owners of other ethnic groups. In 1997, the *Sing Tao Daily* reported that seven Chinese workers from a Jewish-owned garment shop came to seek help from the UNITE! Workers' Center. They complained that they had been discriminated against by their Jewish employer who had closed the shop and refused to pay them according to labor laws, as he did to his Hispanic workers.[18]

The most common problem workers face, however, is the failure to receive compensation for their work in a timely manner. Employers benefit tremendously from withholding their workers' wages. Community labor activists estimate that a shop of average size in Sunset Park has thirty-five workers and the lowest wage of garment workers in the area is about $150 per week. If the owner of a shop withholds his/her employees' wages for eight weeks, which is not uncommon in the area, the employer will have more than $40,000 in hand by the end of the eighth week, even if workers in the shop earned the lowest wage in the area. With this $40,000, an employer can open another shop without having to pay interest as they would if borrowing money from a bank.

Regrettably, as union organizers and law enforcement agencies have pointed out, workers tend not to take any legal action against their employers until their employers close down the shops. The reasons are varied. One major reason is the workers' lack of knowledge about their rights and the political operation in their new homeland. With few employment alternatives, many immigrant workers fear that any form of cooperation with law enforcement agencies or organized labor will cost them their jobs. This was particularly the situation before the signing of the Hot Goods Bill by the New York State governor in 1996.[19] Prior to the adoption of this bill, law enforcement agencies had difficulty in helping workers retrieve their back wages if a shop was closed and the employer was hard to locate. As a result, the longer wages were withheld, the more reluctant workers were to report their cases. They feared that their reporting would lead their employers to close the shop for good.

Workers' reluctance to report labor violations on the floor is also compounded by a lack of understanding about the U.S. income tax system. Many are afraid that the amount of money they receive will be reduced by paying taxes if they seek assistance from law enforcement agencies and have to report their back wages to the Internal Revenue Service. Understandably, undocumented workers have additional concerns. Working underground, they fear that a visit from the Department of Labor to their work place will bring in a raid by the Immigration and Naturalization Service.

While workers are often reluctant to take action against their employers, employers are not hesitant to take advantage of workers' fear. According to longtime observers of the community, many employers in the garment industry engage in speculative financial activities with the money they have withheld from their workers, such as gambling or buying high-return but high-risk stocks. Since most of these activities will not lead to their expected outcomes, the employers close down their shops to avoid payments they owe their employees.

There are also employers who simply try to extract larger profits by closing down operations, absconding with the money they have withheld from their employees, and reopening their business under a different name. This was the case where reporter Lii worked. Hence, labor violations are widespread and the turnover rate of many Sunset Park Chinese garment shops is at a record high.[20] This highly unstable situation makes it even more difficult to enforce labor laws in the area, especially in recent years when most of these agencies are understaffed.

Tensions and exploitation in many Chinese garment shops in Sunset Park lay bare the limits of ethnic solidarity in the garment industry. Relegated to the same ethnic economic sector, Chinese employers have to rely on workers in their own community to run their businesses and accommodate workers' needs. However, situated in a marginal position of a highly competitive industry, many employers also do not hesitate to exploit their community ties to maintain their competitive edge in the industry. As in the case with their predecessors in the city's industry, the garment industry offers new Chinese immigrant workers many advantages in working among their own, but it also makes them more vulnerable to exploitation by management on all levels. The degree of labor violation in many Chinese garment shops demonstrates not only the limits of ethnic solidarity but also the devastating impact of the frenetic search for cheap labor on the Chinese community. This impact, as well as the limited nature of ethnic solidarity, will be further explored in the following section.

"The Cantonese vs. the Fujianese"?

One major issue that surfaced constantly during my interviews with workers is their concern about the increasing number of undocumented workers in the industry, most of whom are believed to be from Fuzhou, a major city in the province of Fujian in southeastern China. These newcomers, who speak their own dialect, are often blamed for worsening labor conditions on the shop floor and deteriorating living standards in Sunset Park. They also are charged with undermining workers' solidarity in the industry. Many Cantonese workers believe that there is no way for them to get along well with the Fujianese.

In the course of interviewing workers in Sunset Park, however, I came to know many Cantonese and Fujianese workers who are good friends. I also came to see that although a large number of undocumented workers came from Fuzhou, Fuzhou is not the only place that has sent undocumented Chinese immigrants to the United States.

Undocumented Chinese workers also come from Wenzhou, Guangdong, and almost all the coastal areas of China. There are also some from Malaysia and other Southeast Asian countries. Nevertheless, there is a pronounced tendency in New York's Chinese community to identify all undocumented workers as Fujianese. Stories about how fanatically hardworking they are became a recurring theme in the narratives of almost all the non-Fujianese workers. Fujianese workers were said to be so money-crazy that they would bring their rice cookers to the shops, cook and eat there while working, and even spend the night in the shops if they found any work there.

These undocumented workers are also blamed for having eroded the image of the Chinese in the Sunset Park area. It is said that since they spend so many hours at work, they could even do without a place to stay. It is a general belief in the Sunset Park Chinese community that several dozen immigrants from Fuzhou would share a single one-bedroom apartment, either only spending the night there or using it just for bathing and other purposes while spending their nights in the garment shops. I heard little sympathy for their plight in my interviews with non-Fujianese workers.

Anecdotal as these stories are, recycled repeatedly, they have fostered a profound prejudice against workers from Fuzhou. This prejudice is so prevalent that it often blinds non-Fujianese workers to class conflicts on the shop floor. For example, I came across a group of Cantonese workers who had just been fired by their employer for refusing to work as many hours as he wanted. Rather than blaming their unscrupulous employer, they blamed their unemployment on the workers from Fuzhou whom their employer had hired for lower rates and longer hours of work.

Although all prejudices are unjustified, factors that have contributed to the prejudice against Fujianese workers are worth exploring. My conversation with a Mrs. Deng, a Taishanese worker and a staunch opponent of "those hateful Fujianese," is revealing:[21]

A: As you know, the Chinese garment shops in Sunset Park have a bad name as sweatshops these days. Our lives are miserable. It was all because of those hateful Fujianese. They have taken our jobs. The bosses love them because they don't have family responsibilities and can work twenty-four hours a day in the shop. They are very greedy. What is in their eyes is only money, money, money. Recently we Cantonese have been losing ground in my shop. The Fujianese are taking over. They are everywhere in my shop.

Q: Could you tell me how many workers from Fuzhou are exactly in your shop?

A: Well, I never counted them, but, never mind, let me try. There are a total of about forty machine operators in my shop, one, two, three, yes, three are Cantonese, three are Mandarin speaking from Shanghai and Wuhan, and … [It turned out that only eight out of a total of thirty-five workers in her shop were from Fuzhou and only five out of the nine undocumented workers in her shop came from Fuzhou.]

Q: So the majority in your shop is not Fujianese and the undocumented workers in your shop are not all from Fuzhou.

A: Yes, you are right. My impression was wrong. But still I am nervous about them. Let me tell you something, actually, there are also undocumented workers from Taishan. A village in Taishan is now almost empty, you know, because they had a smuggler in that village, and he had connections with those snakeheads in New York City. The conditions of the undocumented workers from that village are deplorable. I always think that my situation is already miserable enough. [She was collecting welfare benefits at the time of this interview. Her husband just had a surgery and could not work and she had four schoolchildren to raise.] But theirs are even worse. However, I have been told that compared with those from Fuzhou, they seem to be doing fine because many of them have family members or relatives in New York. Those from Fuzhou don't seem to have this advantage and they owe the snakeheads much more money than those from Taishan. Anyway, I should admit that I don't know very much about them because I don't talk to them and they don't talk to me either.

Q: What then made you so angry with them?

A: They work too hard! Whenever there is some work in the shop, especially the easy jobs, they are there. Very often we don't have any work left when we return in the morning. They have finished all the work at night! But we can't do this. We have to go home at night to take care of our families and to have a little rest. We are human beings, you know. But work is money. They have taken away all our money. They are so hateful!

Q: Did your boss ever close the door of the shop at a time like that?

A: No, how could you expect them to do so? Of course not; for the bosses, the sooner they can get the work done the better. So they love those illegal immigrants from Fuzhou. In the past, many garment shop owners had signs on the gates of their shops, saying "Cantonese only," because they were afraid that they would be harassed by the Fujianese gangsters, who are well known for their fearlessness, if they had Fujianese workers in their shops. But now they don't care. They need workers who can work twenty-four hours a day. So the sign on their gates has also changed. It reads "Fujianese only."

The situation has made me really mad. To be honest, who doesn't need money? I too wish that I could work around the clock, if I did not have a family to take care of. I need money too. I don't mind working hard. I was a peasant in China. Rain or shine, I worked outdoors, under conditions much worse than sewing in a garment shop. I wish I could make more money for my family.

But, wait a minute, I sense something wrong with myself in answering your questions. Haven't I somewhat misjudged those undocumented workers from Fuzhou? Yes, I think I have.

Obviously, tension among the workers, ignited by the highly competitive nature of garment organization and accelerated by the manipulation of management, has led to their misjudgment of reality in the shop. Ungrounded as the stories about undocumented workers from Fuzhou are, generated by a mixture of myth and reality, they take a toll on all workers from the same place. This can be seen in the response of a Ms. Wong:

> I think we immigrants from Fuzhou have been treated very unfairly by our own Chinese community. I am not an illegal immigrant. I came with all the papers as a legal immigrant. In addition, unlike the majority of illegal immigrants from the Fuzhou area, I came from the city and with my family. But still, I am looked at as an illegal immigrant because I came from Fuzhou.
>
> I don't speak Cantonese, so I could not find a job in a restaurant or other place. That's how I ended up working in a garment shop.
>
> My husband and I had a hard time looking for a place for our family to stay when we first came. Landlords from other parts of China refused to rent to us, because we are from Fuzhou. People in the community

said we lived like pigs, with several dozen people usually packed in one apartment but registered under only one or two names. So the landlords were scared. Landlords from Fuzhou did not treat us well either. They charged us much higher rents because they knew that we had no choice.

> My husband and I finally got to rent this place because we decided to speak Mandarin and pretended to be from other parts of China when we first met our landlady, who is Cantonese. Yes, now, she knows that we are from Fuzhou but she doesn't care anymore because we have become very good friends, and she says we are the best tenants she has ever had.[22]

Many immigrant workers from Fuzhou whom I interviewed shared her experience. Although almost all immigrant workers from Fuzhou have been affected by the prejudice against them, the undocumented ones among them are the most victimized. A Mr. Dong's response was typical:

> I don't understand why we should be treated like this! We are human beings too! Yes, we work very hard, because we need money to pay back our debts! Yes, many of us share an apartment, because we want to save money. Do we enjoy our lives in this country? Of course not. We are separated from our families and working underground. We are bullied by our bosses, even including those from Fuzhou. They make us work long hours but pay us much less than other workers in the shops. I don't think anyone would like to live a life like ours! But, still, we are not going to give up because we are working for a better life for our families.
>
> My family lives in a village along the Ming River, and I was a fisherman in the village before I came to the United States. I left my home village because the water there was so seriously polluted that there were no edible fish left. I could not make a living for my family by fishing.
>
> Some people ask, "Why don't you go home if life is so hard for you?" But can we? My family has borrowed a lot of money to send me here. My wife and my kids have pinned their hopes on me, yearning for me to bring them to *meiguo* [the beautiful land, which refers to the United States].
>
> In addition, what will folks in my village say if I return home penniless? I remember when I was in the village, I envied those who returned home from the United States. They looked so successful, squandering money like dirt. I wished I could be like them one day. Of course, after I came to the United States, I got to

know that many of them too had been working in a sweatshop, as I do now. If they can make it, I can make it, too. So, I work hard. It is none of anyone's business if I don't eat, don't sleep, and work nonstop.[23]

The strong desire to improve the well-being of their families, reinforced by a degree of vanity for a glamorous return, led the undocumented workers to leave their native land and fall prey to the sweating system in the United States. Although the living conditions of their native land have "pushed" them out of China, it was the underground economy in the United States that has "pulled" them in and lured them to violate U.S. immigration laws.

The experience of the Fujianese garment workers in Sunset Park reminds one of what has happened to each group of newcomers in New York's garment industry. While the constant search for cheap labor brings in different groups of ethnic workers at different points in history, newcomers are always blamed for the cutthroat competition in the industry. This "finger pointing" takes place even within the same ethnic group. As national characteristics were used in the past as a convenient way of explaining the deterioration of working conditions, today regional and dialectal differences, immigration status, and even the location of one's family have become indexes in the Chinese garment industry for differentiating the old from the new, the "human" from the "inhuman," and thereby the excusers from the excused.[24] Labor solidarity in the community is thus undermined by conflicts of interest among workers, as well as elements in the cultural repertoire of the community.

Will Too Much Law Enforcement Kill the Chinese Garment Industry in New York City?

In the late 1990s, a number of Chinese employers in Sunset Park began to react strongly when the New York State Apparel Industry Task Force carried out its mission to enforce labor laws in the city's garment industry. In October 1996, after the task force completed its investigation and charged many Chinese garment shops with labor violations, Chinese employers in Sunset Park launched a massive demonstration to protest the state operation. They called it "adding salt to the wound." Claiming that the law enforcement agency had unjustly labeled all Chinese shops as "sweatshops," Chinese employers held the state

investigation accountable for causing the further decline of Chinese garment industry in the city by providing manufacturers with the justification for withdrawing their work from the Chinese community.

According to the Chinese employers, manufacturers should be blamed for the deteriorating working conditions in the Chinese shops. Since they suppressed piece rates to such an intolerable degree and demanded such quick production and delivery of finished garments, Chinese employers were forced to reduce the piece rates they offered to their workers and expect them to work longer hours in order to remain competitive. In addition, since manufacturers frequently delayed payments for finished work, Chinese employers had to withhold wages to their own workers. Labor law enforcement will kill the Chinese garment industry, they asserted, because only by reducing wages and extending work hours could the industry survive in the highly competitive environment of garment production in New York.[25]

The Chinese employers' accusation against manufacturers is not entirely groundless, given manufacturers' frantic efforts to reduce the costs of labor in recent years. However, as many concerned individuals in the community have rightly pointed out, even though the Chinese garment industry has been hit hard by the outflow of garment production from the city, the sweatshop conditions in the industry are what allow the manufacturers to put a human face on their move from the city.[26]

What has happened since the State Department of Labor established its Apparel Industry Task Force in 1987? Did the efforts of the Task Force lead to the decline of the Chinese garment industry in New York City? Did the industry really decline?

Statistics show that despite the shrinking of the city's share in the U.S. garment industry, the absolute numbers of Chinese shops and their workforce in the past decade or more did not suggest any sign of decline; indeed, they grew. In the early 1980s, there were approximately 500 Chinese shops in the city, largely concentrated in Manhattan's Chinatown and employing an estimated 25,000 Chinese workers. In 1998, there was an estimate of more than 800 Chinese shops, scattered in various parts of the city and employing more than 30,000 Chinese workers.[27]

One specific segment of the Chinese garment industry has declined significantly in recent years, however. It is the number of the unionized shops in Manhattan's

Chinatown. Between 1992 and 1997 the number of garment shops in Manhattan's Chinatown dropped from 608 to 555 and employment declined from 21,015 to 14,887, a loss of more than 6,000 jobs.[28] The decline in the Manhattan's Chinatown garment industry coincided with the rapid growth of the Chinese garment shops in other parts of the city, in particular, Sunset Park in Brooklyn. Although Manhattan's Chinatown remains the center of the Chinese garment industry in New York, with about 500 Chinese shops still clustered in this area, its importance has been significantly reduced by the rapid growth of the Chinese garment industry in other boroughs.

The decline of Manhattan's Chinatown shops has also led to the weakening of union influence on the entire Chinese garment industry in New York City. In the early 1980s, when shops in Chinatown represented an overwhelming majority of the Chinese garment shops in New York City, more than 90 percent of them were unionized. By the end of the 1990s, it is estimated that the UNITE! Local 23-25 represented only half of the Chinese garment shops in the city.[29] The union's influence has declined even in Manhattan's Chinatown, with the percentage of Chinese union shops dropping from more than 90 percent in the early 1980s to fewer than 80 percent by 1997.[30] As a result, membership of the UNITE! Local 23-25—the largest local of the union, with an 85 percent Chinese membership—dropped from 28,083 in 1992 to 22,995 in 1996, a loss of more than 5,000 members.[31]

Despite problems embedded in the unionization of the Chinatown garment industry in earlier years, there are still many significant differences in working conditions between union and nonunion shops. The shrinking percentage of union shops in the Chinese garment industry indicates that more and more Chinese garment workers have been deprived of the benefits and protection to which union members are entitled. It should, therefore, come as no surprise that labor violations are rampant in many nonunion Chinese shops, which have, in turn, undercut working conditions in the union shops.

There is little doubt that manufacturers and retailers should be held accountable for the deteriorating working conditions in the city's garment industry. However, many individuals in the community are also correct in pointing out that it is the sweating system in some Chinese garment shops that has provided them with the most convenient excuse to pull production out of New York City. This is particularly true when politicians of all stripes have recognized a political advantage in promoting the elimination of sweatshops in the U.S., and manufacturers and retailers have also been pressured by consumer groups as well as labor to distance themselves from contract shops labeled as sweatshops.

The Chinese employers' argument that "too much law enforcement will kill the Chinese garment industry in New York City" reminds one of the situations at the turn of the twentieth century. As Nancy Green has noted, during that time when progressive reformers, labor leaders, and state legislators endeavored to improve labor conditions by passing new legislation and enforcing laws, manufacturers also argued that too many constraints would make the landscape of the garment industry disappear altogether from the city.[32] However, the garment industry remains in New York City, and so will the Chinese garment industry, at least for the decade to come.

Some Reflections

Driven by the search for cheap nonunion labor, runaway shops and sweated labor are not unique to the Chinese garment industry, nor are they new in the history of the city's industry. As early as the 1920s the dispersion of garment shops from Manhattan into various parts of the city already became a peculiar aspect in the landscape of New York's garment industry.[33] The Chinese garment industry, as a major part of the city's industry, is no exception in these regards.

The experience of Chinese workers is in many ways similar to that of their predecessors in the city's garment industry, but there are also differences. Particularly in the 1980s and 1990s, these differences were caused by the challenge of the times rather than simply by the cultural characteristics of the Chinese workers. Garment workers in the first half of the twentieth century were able to enjoy improved working conditions, thanks to the strong influence of labor unions and the continuous growth of the city's garment industry. However, Chinese workers in the late twentieth century were increasingly subjected to abusive labor conditions as the city's industry declined rapidly. Their union, plagued by its entrenched bureaucratic culture, could hardly respond to their needs.

As in the case of the city's garment industry in the early twentieth century, law enforcement and labor organizing remain the two most powerful ways to address the problems in the Chinese garment industry. Both law enforcement agents and labor organizers face the challenge of how to understand the complex reality of the garment industry beyond the highly politicized representations of it in political arenas. However, they also have to address different issues in their own realms.

As Mark Levitan has aptly put it, one of the major factors that has undermined significantly the efforts to eliminate sweated labor in the city is that "there are not enough cops on the beat." Despite the growth of sweated labor in the city's garment industry and the politicians' highly emotional pledges to eliminate it, both New York State and federal investigation teams are severely understaffed. According to Levitan, in 1998, there were only twenty-three investigators in the federal office of the Wage and Hour Division that had responsibility for the entire New York City metropolitan area, and only twenty-three out of thirty-four positions in New York City's Apparel Industry Task Force were filled.[34] As a result, in addition to improving their understanding of the dynamics generated by the highly competitive structure of the garment industry, the history and culture of each ethnic group, and the multifaceted impact of their operations, law enforcement agents still have to battle the shortage of hands in carrying out their tasks, a difficult situation that is indeed not of their own making.

Organized labor faces another type of challenge. Never before has UNITE!, the major labor union of the U.S. garment industry, been under so much pressure to reform itself. The parochialism and the culture of business unionism that UNITE! shares with other traditional trade unions have proved to be impotent in this new age of the global economy. Today, with the impressive growth of the community-based labor organizations in New York's Chinatown and other ethnic communities, the question UNITE! faces is no longer whether it is willing to change but whether the change is adequate to maintain its legitimacy as a labor union in the industry.[35] In this era when capital has already globalized its search for inexpensive labor, how can we develop effective organizing strategies that are not only responsive to the needs of U.S. workers but also allow them to join forces with workers in other parts of the world? This is a question very much on the agendas of trade unions as well as concerned individuals in the Chinese community and the city.

34 Hispanics in the American South and the Transformation of the Poultry Industry
William Kandel • Emilio A. Parrado

WILLIAM KANDEL is a sociologist with the Economic Research Service of the U.S. Department of Agriculture, where he conducts research on the geographic dispersion of immigrants and minorities in rural areas and the role of industrial restructuring in demographic change.

EMILIO A. PARRADO is an associate professor of sociology at the University of Pennsylvania.

FINDINGS FROM THE 2000 CENSUS INDICATE two important trends affecting the Hispanic population. The first is the extraordinarily high rate of Hispanic population increase outside of urban areas over the past decade, with growth rates exceeding both metropolitan and nonmetropolitan growth rates for all other racial and ethnic groups (Cromartie 1999; Pérez 2001). In addition, for the first time in U.S. history, half of all nonmetropolitan Hispanics currently live outside the five southwestern states of Arizona, California, Colorado, New Mexico, and Texas (Cromartie and Kandel 2002). The diversity of new rural areas raises questions about forces outside of the Southwest that are attracting migrants, the Hispanic population's assimilation patterns into communities unaccustomed to dealing with immigration, and the connection between structural economic change and Hispanic population growth.

The main objective of this chapter is to link changes in the poultry industry with the growth of the Hispanic population in nonmetropolitan counties in nine southeastern states: Alabama, Arkansas, Georgia, Louisiana, Mississippi, North Carolina, South Carolina, Tennessee, and Virginia. We document the restructuring of the poultry industry and spatially correlate poultry production and areas of Hispanic settlement. Next, given the impact of these population changes on local communities, we examine two case studies to elaborate more directly on the implications of Hispanic growth for the culture, organization, and everyday life of two nonmetropolitan counties in Virginia

Questions to Consider

In 2000, half our nation's foreign-born were from Latin America. This segment represents only about 10 percent of the total U.S. population—less than the 15 percent of the population made up of foreign-born individuals in 1890, but there is an important difference. Early migrations to the United States consisted of mostly white people from Europe. The most recent waves of immigrants are Latino and Asian. Another major difference from past migration patterns is that Latinos from Mexico and Central America are no longer concentrated only in the states that border Mexico. William Kandel and Emilio Parrado examine the ways Latino migration to the southeastern part of the United States has invigorated regions that had been in economic decline, noting that the economic resurgence has resulted largely from the creation of jobs that are dangerous, dirty, unregulated, and exploitive. Do these jobs present new immigrants with a path toward upward mobility or a life of poverty wages?

and North Carolina. Finally, we derive implications for further research to address relations between Hispanics and other minority groups.

New Destinations in Nonmetropolitan America

The degree to which Hispanic residential settlement has expanded outside of traditional migrant-receiving states can be illustrated with 1990 and 2000 Census data. Table 1

TABLE 1   Nonmetropolitan State Populations Ranked by Hispanic
Population Growth

Rank	State	Nonmetro Hispanic Population			Nonmetro Population			Hispanic Share (%)	
		1990	*2000*	*% Change*	*1990*	*2000*	*% Change*	*1990*	*2000*
1	North Carolina	16,714	98,846	491	2,252,775	2,612,257	16	1	4
2	Delaware	1,221	6,915	466	113,229	156,638	38	1	4
3	Alabama	5,198	26,155	403	1,330,857	1,453,233	9	0	2
4	South Carolina	5,830	27,853	378	1,064,088	1,205,050	13	1	2
5	Georgia	26,270	124,296	373	2,126,654	2,519,789	18	1	5
6	Tennessee	7,119	32,737	360	1,579,336	1,842,679	17	0	2
7	Arkansas	9,559	36,504	282	1,310,724	1,434,529	9	1	3
8	Virginia	8,136	28,258	247	1,407,096	1,550,447	10	1	2
9	Mississippi	7,774	24,321	213	1,797,542	1,932,670	8	0	1
10	Minnesota	11,283	34,860	209	1,364,205	1,456,119	7	1	2
11	Iowa	11,807	35,611	202	1,576,857	1,600,191	1	1	2
12	Indiana	12,260	36,921	201	1,581,713	1,690,582	7	1	2
13	Kentucky	8,479	24,465	189	1,905,535	2,068,667	9	0	1
14	Nebraska	16,641	44,564	168	791,050	811,425	3	2	5
15	Wisconsin	11,098	28,893	160	1,560,597	1,723,367	10	1	2
16	Missouri	10,822	27,807	157	1,626,202	1,800,410	11	1	2
17	Pennsylvania	11,004	27,403	149	1,798,645	1,889,525	5	1	1

Sources: U.S. Bureau of the Census 1990, 2000.
Note: Shaded rows are the eight southeastern states highlighted in the study.

presents state-level nonmetropolitan population in absolute and percentage terms for the top seventeen states, sorted by Hispanic population growth rate. Eight of the nine southeastern poultry-producing states appear among the ten states with the fastest-growing nonmetropolitan Hispanic populations; the remaining seven include midwestern states with large beef and pork meatpacking industries.

While Hispanics continue to be overwhelmingly located in metropolitan areas, during the 1990s their nonmetropolitan growth of 70.4 percent exceeded their metropolitan growth rate of 60.4 percent (Cromartie and Kandel 2002). By the decade's end, according to Census 2000 data, Hispanics represented approximately 5.5 percent of the nonmetropolitan population, but had accounted for over 25.0 percent of its growth during the decade. Moreover, Hispanic population growth during the 1990s surpassed total population growth in nonmetropolitan areas in every state except Hawaii.

Widespread media attention on Hispanics in new destinations, however, owes more to their geographic concentration. In 2000, over a third of the 3.2 million rural Hispanics lived in just 109 of all 2,288 nonmetropolitan counties (Cromartie and Kandel 2002).

Since the 1990s, a number of ethnographic studies have documented the immigrants' reception in relatively small communities with few foreign-born residents (Griffith 1995; Guthey 2001; Hernández-León and Zúñiga 2000). The growing nonmetropolitan presence of Hispanics can be attributed to several concurrent trends. First, increased enforcement policies by the Immigration and Naturalization Service to reduce undocumented immigration, ironically, have pushed undocumented migrants away from the traditional migrant-receiving states of California, Arizona, and Texas and into southeastern and midwestern states that previously had few Hispanic migrants (Durand, Massey, and Charvet 2000).

Second, several informants and anecdotal accounts describe labor market saturation in the traditional migrant gateway cities of Los Angeles, Houston, and Chicago and suggest that growing numbers of "pioneer migrants" are seeking employment in new parts of the country. Hispanic settlement in nonmetropolitan areas also was facilitated by an economic recession in the early 1990s in the urban Southwest and other U.S. metropolitan centers. In addition to looking for employment opportunities in nonmetropolitan areas, many Hispanic immigrants may seek to escape problems associated with urban settings, such as poor schools, youth gangs, violence, and expensive and crowded housing.

Third, immigrants are also moving to nontraditional areas because of employers' recruiting efforts to sustain the number of workers needed in industries with less-than-desirable jobs (Johnson-Webb 2002). Consequently, the proportion of Hispanics in industries with low wages and harsh working conditions—meat processing, carpet manufacturing, oil refining, and forestry, to name a few—has increased dramatically since the 1990s (Broadway 1994; Engstrom 2001; Gouveia and Stull 1995; Hernández-León and Zúñiga 2000; Díaz McConnell forthcoming; McDaniel 2002). Because the U.S. Department of Labor does not classify these positions as temporary or highly skilled, firms cannot use special immigration provisions, such as the **H2A** or H2B **visas**, to obtain foreign workers. Information on recruitment practices consists of mostly qualitative journalistic accounts that, nevertheless, describe a host of practices that firms use to recruit workers (Carlin 1999; Katz 1996a, 1996b; Smothers 1996; Taylor and Stein 1999).

An influx of immigrants and newcomers into rural communities often generates conflicting feelings among local residents. Hispanic population growth in many nonmetropolitan places coincides with revived economic activity and reversals of stagnant or declining demographic patterns of previous decades (Broadway 1994; Brown 1993). Nevertheless, immigrant population growth may challenge the ability of rural communities to meet increased demands for social services, particularly schooling for immigrant children, and often increases poverty rates and income inequality (Reed 2001). While immigrants undoubtedly hold the least-desirable and most poorly paid jobs, their presence may exert downward wage pressure on native-born residents working in other low-skilled industries (Massey, Durand, and Malone 2002). Ethnic diversity is viewed by many Americans as a public good that introduces different cultures, languages, and cuisines to native-born residents and reinforces America's cherished self-image as a nation built on the energy and hopes of immigrants

H2A visa A visa granted to a foreign national for temporary or agricultural work in the United States.

(Lapinski et al. 1997). Yet, popular reports suggest a significant level of social conflict in and municipal response from communities that have experienced influxes of immigrants in a relatively short time (Grey 1995; Guthey 2001; Studstill and Nieto-Studstill 2001). We return to these oppositional perspectives that use qualitative descriptions of poultry-producing communities below.

Trends in Poultry Consumption

To see how Hispanic migration to new regions in the southeastern U.S. is related to industrial restructuring, we first consider changes in one of the region's dominant low-skill industries, poultry processing. The poultry industry has been a mainstay in the Southeast for many decades, but since the 1970s, a number of trends have aggregated to influence the demand for labor and, consequently, the settlement patterns of Hispanics. These include (1) increased consumption; (2) increased demand for value-added production; (3) industry consolidation and vertical integration, leading to larger firms; (4) increasing location of production facilities in the Southeast; and (5) the relative attractiveness of meat-processing jobs.

The impetus for changes in the poultry industry began with three consumption trends that strongly influenced the demand for labor. The first was domestic consumption, which grew as the result of two somewhat contradictory trends. In 1977, when beef consumption far exceeded poultry consumption, widely publicized findings from the Framingham Study explicitly outlined health risks associated with red meat in the diet (Dawber 1980). The report's implications were not lost on the American public, which began to eat less beef and more poultry. Per capita poultry consumption doubled between 1977 and 1999, while beef consumption dropped 30 percent over the same period (Figure 1).

Yet, while the Framingham Study represents a milestone event, increasing consumption of fast food in the United States coincided with the growing demand for convenience food. Growth in fast-food franchises such as Kentucky Fried Chicken and marketing through nontraditional outlets such as McDonald's created an enormous demand for a wide variety of chicken products. Within a little over a decade, per capita consumption of poultry surpassed that of beef for the first time since World War II (U.S. Department of Agriculture [USDA] 1960–2000).

The second consumption trend, growth in poultry exports, paralleled domestic demand. Following domestic consumer demand for further-processed products, poultry

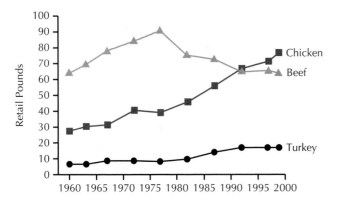

FIGURE 1   Per Capita Consumption of Chicken, Turkey, and Beef, 1960–1999. *Source:* U.S. Department of Agriculture 1960–2000.

firms began supplementing their slaughtering plants with production facilities that cut up chickens and packaged the parts for different segments of the market. Breasts and other white meat met domestic consumption preferences, and dark meat was reserved for the export market. By the mid-1970s, chicken exports had increased significantly, and between 1987 and 2002, they skyrocketed, from 500 million to 6.5 billion pounds (USDA 1960–2000).

The demand for more convenient prepared food generated a precipitous increase in the sale of cut-up poultry and an equally precipitous decline in the sale of whole birds. In 1963, the poultry product mix sold in American supermarkets consisted of 85 percent whole birds and 15 percent cut-up poultry products; by 1997, that proportion was exactly the reverse (Ollinger, MacDonald, and Madison 2000). Consequently, many poultry producers appended "cut-up" operations to their meat-processing plants. The structural shift of value-added production from the retail sector (supermarkets) to the production sector (meat-slaughtering and -processing plants) has had profound consequences for labor demand, and, consequently, for labor supply.

Poultry Industry Concentration and Consolidation

Significant increases in both industry concentration and average poultry plant size have accompanied the trend toward increased consumption. Industrial concentration can often be measured using the "four firm concentration ratio," the proportion of total production controlled by the four largest firms

(Ollinger, MacDonald, and Madison 2000). For the slaughter of chickens, this ratio more than doubled, from 14 percent to 41 percent, between 1963 and 1992; for turkey slaughter, the ratio increased from 23 percent to 45 percent over the same period. Concentration of poultry-processing firms fluctuated, but it also shows an upward trend during the same period. Data after 1992 are not available, but industry reports suggest that this trend continued throughout the 1990s.

Beginning in the late 1940s, firms began to realize greater scale economies by integrating all facets of operation. Under this mode of production, firms contract out to formerly independent chicken farms and provide the chicks, feed, medicines, veterinary services, and other inputs; contracted growers later return grown birds of consistent size and quality to the plant for slaughter (Bugos 1992). Slaughter operations also became more complex as firms responded to increasingly varied consumer and industry demands by adopting cut-up operations and packaging their products in ready-to-sell containers. By controlling all phases of poultry production, such vertically integrated firms could increase their overall profitability while lowering prices; in real terms, the price of poultry dropped by just over 50 percent between 1960 and 1999 (USDA 1960–2000).

Industry consolidation and production have led to larger plants. To measure the extent of industry consolidation, we use proportion of production from firms with four hundred or more employees, a widely used measure developed by the U.S. Bureau of the Census. Beginning in 1967, the proportion of chicken produced by such large plants tripled; by 1992, they accounted for three-quarters of all poultry slaughter and processing (Ollinger, Mac-Donald, and Madison 2000).

Increased consumer demand, growing exports, and industry consolidation trends have combined to expand the demand for labor in the poultry industry. Figure 2 presents employment figures in both the poultry industry and the red meat industry for comparison. The above-noted trends in industry consolidation and plant size also occurred to roughly the same extent in the red meat–processing industry (MacDonald et al. 2000). Yet, as Figure 2 demonstrates, employment in the red meat industry has not grown at all since 1970. In contrast, employment in the poultry industry has grown by 150 percent during the same period, and today it actually exceeds that of the beef industry (U.S. Department of Labor [DOL] 1972–2001).

Geographic Context of Poultry Production

Structural changes in the poultry industry occur in a geographic context. As in most industrial sectors, there is a distinct logic behind the poultry business's economic geography. Poultry can be raised in most areas, and before large firms took over, it was a very competitive industry, because almost anyone could grow chickens almost anywhere. Some locations, however, have certain advantages, and in a competitive market, one seeks advantage by minimizing the most expensive inputs. For poultry, the key inputs are feed and climate. The Southeast, it turns out, has both an ideal climate for raising chickens and access to low-cost grain. Data

from the Census of Agriculture show that the Southeast was producing over half of the nation's chicken slaughter products as early as 1963; in recent years, the proportion has increased to roughly two-thirds (USDA 1960–2000).

The expansion and consolidation of the poultry industry in the Southeast has occurred within the context of a simultaneous economic transformation that, in just a few decades, changed the American South from a relatively depressed region to an economically booming destination (Cobb 1982; Griffith 1995). This economic growth began in the 1960s with the active recruitment of manufacturing industries and promotion of the South as a competitive location for firms seeking a low-wage, non-unionized workforce. With the rediscovery of the Sunbelt as a vacation and retirement destination, the tourism and retirement-community industries expanded significantly.

Tourists and retirees embody two populations which economic development officials everywhere hope to attract, because they use relatively few social services and inject much of their disposable income into the local economy. However, they may unbalance local labor markets, because while they create a large demand for service, construction, and other types of workers, they contribute little, if anything, to the local labor supply.

Hispanics in the Poultry Industry

Attracting workers to the poultry industry is a growing challenge. Nationwide, wages paid in the industry are significantly higher than the minimum wage. However, at

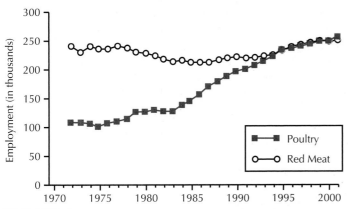

FIGURE 2   Employment in Poultry and Red Meat Products Industry, 1972–2001. *Source:* U.S. Department of Labor, 1972–2001.

$7.39 an hour as of 1997, they had not changed in real terms in more than thirty years and remained among the lowest for manufacturing and food industry employment (Hetrick 1994; U.S. Department of Commerce [DOC] 1967–1997). The wage data we used do not specify region, but wages in southern states were probably below the average. Unionization rates, never high in the South in general, have remained well below 5 percent in meat-processing industries since the early 1980s, according to the Current Population Survey. Poultry processing, like other meat processing, is a relatively hazardous and unattractive occupation, with harsh working conditions that have been continually exposed as bad in media and scholarly accounts (Bjerklie 1995; Sun and Escobar 1999). Moreover, economic growth that began in the early 1980s and continued for almost two decades created employment options that diminished relative incentives for working in the poultry industry.

Under these circumstances, it is not surprising that the poultry industry in the southeastern states has experienced difficulty finding a sufficient supply of local workers willing to accept their wages and working conditions. Consequently, the industry's expansion and concentration within a geographic region whose economic development was already creating an immense demand for low-skilled workers forced the sector to look elsewhere.

As with other low-skill, low-wage industries, the poultry business began actively recruiting immigrants, most coming from Mexico and Central America. Numerous reports have documented the extreme lengths firms have gone to recruit workers for their plants (Barboza 2001). For a region that had low absolute numbers of Hispanics, the size of the poultry-processing workforce has grown significantly.

The results of these recruiting efforts can be seen in Figure 3, which maps the confluence of the location of significant poultry production with Hispanic settlement within the nine southeastern states. Areas denoted by dark gray represent counties in these states which, according to the U.S. Census of Agriculture, ranked, in 1987, 1992, and 1997, within the top 100 chicken-producing counties in the nation. Areas denoted by light gray represent rapid-growth nonmetropolitan Hispanic counties, defined as those in which the Hispanic population grew in absolute and percentage terms by one thousand persons and 150 percent, respectively, between 1990 and 2000. Combining the two patterns yields counties that overlap, shown in solid color. Note that while the rapid Hispanic growth

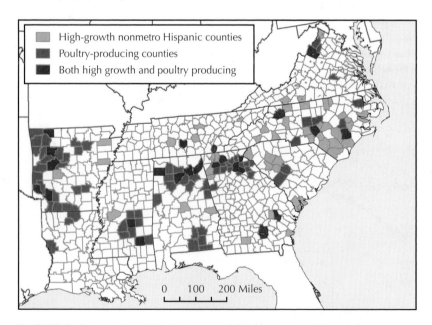

FIGURE 3 **Poultry-Producing and High-Growth Hispanic Counties, Nine Southeastern States, 1990–2000.** *Sources:* U.S. Department of Agriculture, 1987, 1992, 1997; U.S. Bureau of the Census 1990, 2000.

counties are nonmetropolitan, the poultry-growing counties include nonmetropolitan as well as metropolitan counties. Since the Census of Agriculture data refer to where poultry is raised, as opposed to where it is slaughtered and processed, we would expect most of the poultry counties to be in rural, nonmetropolitan areas. Moreover, because of the economics of poultry transportation, we can reasonably assume that most are close to poultry-processing facilities. Thus, contiguous counties in Figure 3 account for a significant number of all counties highlighted.

The proximity of the Hispanic population to poultry-producing regions is unmistakable, and when combined with the qualitative evidence on recruiting practices, it provides a clear picture of the close connection between the poultry industry and Hispanic population growth. Duplin County in North Carolina, for example, has seen its Hispanic population increase by almost seven thousand since the 1990s, owing in no small part to the demand for labor in its Carolina Turkey, Nash Johnson, and Butterball Turkey plants. The Hispanic population in Hall County, Georgia, has grown by twenty-three thousand, not only because of its proximity to Atlanta, but also because of the poultry plants in the town of Gainsville. Marshall County in Alabama employs over three thousand poultry workers, owing to a Tyson Poultry plant in Guntersville, and its Hispanic population has grown by forty-three hundred in the same period.

We have argued that the transformations in this industry correlate with Hispanic population growth in the area. As such, we would expect important changes in the racial and ethnic composition of the labor force working in the poultry industry. However, it is unclear whether Hispanics are replacing or complementing blacks and whites. Figure 4 presents changes in the racial and ethnic composition of the labor force in the meat-processing industry between 1980 and 2000, using Current Population Survey (CPS) data (DOC 1963–1997). Meat processing is a broad category that includes the processing of red meat, pork, turkey, and chicken. However, outside of some pork processing in Mississippi, North Carolina, and Virginia, almost all meat processing in the nine southeastern states consists of poultry processing.

Changes in the racial and ethnic composition of the industry are telling of the potential differential effect of migration on racial groups. Whites have dropped from just under 70 percent to just over 30 percent of the workforce. The proportion of blacks has increased from 30 percent to 50 percent, and the proportion of Hispanics has increased from 1 percent to 17 percent. Figure 2 shows that the actual number of workers in the poultry industry nationwide more than doubled between 1980 and 2001, so the lower percentage of whites does not necessarily indicate that there are fewer whites involved in poultry processing, but it does indicate that there are many more blacks and Hispanics.

Because the CPS tends to undercount Hispanics, these percentages are conservative. To provide some sense of the potential understatement, consider the case of hired farmworkers, another employment group with a high proportion of Hispanics. The National Agricultural Workers Survey,

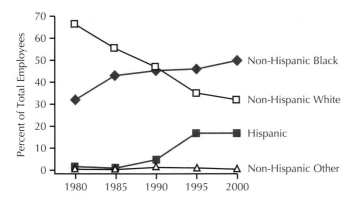

FIGURE 4   Racial and Ethnic Composition of Meat-Processing Industry Employees, Nine Southeastern States, 1980–2000. *Source:* U.S. Department of Commerce, 1963–1997.

considered the most representative survey of farmworkers, places the Hispanic composition of the agricultural farmworker population at more than double the proportion estimated by the CPS.

The National Agricultural Workers Survey evaluates the degree to which immigrant labor complements or substitutes for domestic workers. Hispanics may be replacing non-Hispanic whites, which, assuming the latter are moving into higher-paying jobs, leaves everyone better off. Non-Hispanic blacks may also be leaving the poultry industry in absolute numbers, but their increasing proportion suggests that immigrants may be competing for the same low-skill jobs.

We now turn to case studies of two poultry-producing counties in the Southeast to illustrate how some of the issues noted above—the rapid incorporation of Hispanics into the American South and the consequent impact on receiving communities—manifest in real places. We consider one county in Virginia and one in North Carolina that typify the economic and demographic patterns that we suggest are occurring throughout the southeastern United States.

Accomack County, Virginia, and Duplin County, North Carolina

Accomack County, along the eastern shoreline of Virginia, is the northern part of a slender peninsula at the base of the well-known Delmarva (Delaware-Maryland-Virginia) poultry-producing region. Duplin County, along the southeastern coastal plain of North Carolina, is among the leading turkey-producing counties in the country.

These two nonmetropolitan counties reflect similar population and economic conditions. By 2000 Accomack and Duplin Counties had populations of thirty-eight thousand and forty-nine thousand, respectively, and their 1997 median household incomes of roughly $25,000 and $27,000 were well below the $40,000 and $35,000 averages for Virginia and North Carolina, respectively. Temperate climates in both areas are well suited for raising poultry and growing corn, soybeans, and other feed grains used by the industry. In addition, both counties have long been known for their production of cash crops, including vegetables, fruit, nursery and greenhouse crops, and tobacco. As one drives south from the Maryland border along Virginia's Highway 13 or along I-40 across North Carolina, farmland, food stands, and the occasional tourist

billboard interrupt the rural landscape. Few locations have sizable populations or notable geographies beyond one or two traffic lights; according to one Accomack County resident, "There isn't any town here, there are towns."

Poultry Plants

Virginia ranks eighth or ninth in broiler output, and Accomack County produces about 10 percent of that. Two processing plants, the Tyson plant in Temperanceville and the Perdue plant in the town of Accomac, have been in business for over thirty years and together employed roughly twenty-six hundred persons in 2002. Both Tyson and Perdue are among the top four poultry-producing firms in the nation, and their plants are among the largest in the Delmarva region (Delmarva Poultry Industry [DPI] 2002). Temperanceville is not incorporated; since Accomac is the county seat, it is there that most of the poultry regulation and social-service provision occurs.

North Carolina's annual output of forty-one million turkeys ranks second in the nation, and Duplin County produces one-quarter of that. The poultry industry in the county began in the early 1950s and soon became Duplin County's largest industry. In 1986, Carolina Turkeys built the nation's largest turkey-processing plant in the town of Mount Olive. In 2002, the plant employed close to three thousand workers and had become the world's largest turkey-processing facility, with integrated operations that combined diagnostic labs, research farms, breeder farms, hatcheries, growing farms, and feed mills. Additional poultry plants include Nash Johnson & Sons, Butterball Turkey, and House of Raeford, which together employ an additional twenty-two hundred workers.

Hispanics

Hispanic population growth in Accomack and Duplin Counties during the 1990s illustrates the dramatic inflow of Latinos into southern communities. In 1990, the census counted 450 and 1,015 Hispanics in Accomack and Duplin Counties, respectively. By 2000, the numbers were 1,680 and 7,426, representing increases of 272 and 633 percent, respectively.

These changes altered the racial and ethnic makeup of both counties as they rapidly moved from a biracial white-black population to a multiethnic population with significant Hispanic representation. As of 2000, the population of Accomack had become 62.0 percent white, 31.0 percent black, and 5.5 percent Hispanic, while that of Duplin County had became 55.0 percent white, 29.0 percent black, and 15.0 percent Hispanic. Disaggregating by national origin shows that most Latinos are Mexicans and represent around 65 percent of the Latino population in both counties. Next in line are Guatemalans, 20 percent of Accomack County's Hispanic population, and Hondurans, 15 percent of the same in Duplin County. Differences in the country of origin of the Latino population reflect the highly structured process guiding migration decisions and the role of work, friends, and family networks in determining the destinations of individual migrants (Massey and Espinosa 1997). For example, informants in Accomack County indicate that a sizable portion of the Guatemalan population actually originates from a single *departamento* (province) of the country.

Moreover, while the census captures permanently settled Hispanics, it often undercounts the large number of seasonal agricultural migrant workers who pass through both counties. These annual migratory streams usually begin in Florida or Texas and continue through Georgia and the Carolinas before stopping in the Delmarva Peninsula. Seasonal workers typically work for farm-labor contractors and accompany them from one location to another. While traveling through these counties, in either direction, some migrants find work in the poultry plants and decide to stay. Since poultry work is year-round, those who switch from agricultural work to poultry processing have a greater likelihood of settling permanently.

An example from Duplin County illustrates the close connection between seasonal and permanent migration. One of our interviewees, currently a high-ranking administrator coordinating housing services for one poultry plant, initiated his migration experience when a relative, a former seasonal farmworker, decided to settle in North Carolina. In the late 1970s, growing employment opportunities in the poultry industry provided seasonal workers a channel for upward mobility. After settling in Duplin County, the relative sent word to the interviewee's family about promising employment opportunities in the United States, triggering our interviewee's first U.S. trip in 1980. Most of his brothers and sisters, using his settlement, family networks, and waves of legalizations in the 1980s, followed by the end of the decade. In 2000, his mother immigrated with his youngest sister. Thus, after twenty-two years of experience in the United States, this Mexican family from the State of Veracruz was reconstituted in North Carolina. Only

his father remains in Mexico, despite our interviewee's assurances that life in the United States is not so bad and that the whole family awaits his arrival.

Employment Context

The majority of Hispanic immigrants in Accomack County work in agriculture, not poultry processing, even though the relative size of both industries in the county is roughly the same. In Duplin County, the mix is about equal. Agricultural work typically pays the current minimum wage of $5.15 per hour, although piece-rate pay scales during the harvest season may roughly double this. Poultry plant employment, on the other hand, is year-round work with a starting wage of about $8.00 per hour and includes health and retirement benefits. Any employment progression from agriculture to poultry processing tends to convert residency tenure from temporary to permanent. Some selectivity of legal status occurs; agricultural farmworkers are more likely to be unauthorized than are poultry workers, whose legal documents are more carefully reviewed.

While the processing of poultry is considered year-round work, a significant portion of the workforce cycles through for short periods (Griffith 1995; Horowitz and Miller 1999). Workers may leave because they don't like the work, are using poultry work as stopgap employment between farm-labor jobs, visit family in their home countries, or because they have violated attendance rules. Some also leave to maintain seasonal migration patterns with their undocumented family members. Firms, anticipating that a significant number of hires will leave within months of starting, adjust their wage and benefits structures to reward workers who stay for over six months. According to unofficial estimates and anecdotal reports, turnover rates in poultry plants average from 70 percent annually, with considerable variation by plant. In North Carolina, the high turnover rates permit poultry workers to qualify for programs providing assistance to seasonal workers.

The dynamics of migration and working conditions contribute to the high turnover rate. In addition, crackdowns on undocumented migrants after September 11, 2001, have also affected the stability of poultry employment. There are increasing reports of employees and employers receiving letters from the Social Security Administration notifying them of violations. Employees are notified first, usually because they have used a false or incorrect Social Security number. If the employee does not correct the situation, a letter is sent to the employer, who must notify the employee and terminate employment.

The racial composition of agricultural and poultry workers in Accomack County resembles that found in the nine southeastern states surveyed. Although exact figures do not exist, industry officials estimate the makeup of the poultry-processing workforce nationwide at approximately 50 percent black, 40 percent white, and 10 percent Hispanic. In Duplin County, the Hispanic component in poultry is far greater, approaching 65 percent in one plant.

Within plants, fairly rigid racial and ethnic divisions characterize productive activities, with most whites and some blacks occupying managerial positions and Hispanics confined to manual work in production, packing, mailing, and housekeeping. These divisions have several sources. As one of our informants observed, inability to speak English and low levels of education are central factors in maintaining Hispanics in manual positions. At the same time, what he considered cultural differences also facilitate segregation of activities along racial and ethnic lines.

Labor Market and Demographic Impacts

A central question driving most arguments in favor of or against immigration is the extent to which Hispanic inflows displace or complement local workers. Particularly important is the interaction between Hispanic employment and labor-market outcomes of other minority groups, especially African Americans. While this question well exceeds the scope of this chapter, we contend that labor-market compositional shifts are intertwined with industrial transformations. When such shifts are applied to the poultry industry, we can expect growth in product demand, industrial concentration, and production variability to facilitate demand for Hispanic workers. In this process, Hispanic population inflows do not necessarily imply worker displacement, because all three macrotrends create additional employment.

Some of these expectations are confirmed by our two case studies. Despite very rapid population growth, the unemployment rate declined in Accomack and Duplin Counties, from 9.6 percent to 4.2 percent, and from 8.6 percent to 5.0 percent, respectively, between 1992 and 2000 (DOC 2002). In fact, in 2001, the unemployment rates in both counties were much lower than the nationwide

nonmetropolitan average. In addition, when asked why poultry companies were increasingly hiring Hispanic workers, our informants consistently replied that new jobs were opening up and that nobody else wanted them. This is especially true in Duplin County, with its large, new Carolina Turkeys processing plant. In such a context, the expectation of worker displacement may not be reasonable.

Moreover, informants acknowledged the creation of many skilled positions in, for example, administrative, government, or educational employment for which Hispanics do not qualify. Overall, evidence suggests that while industrial transformations in the poultry industry expanded the demand for low-skilled workers and thus attracted Hispanics, the concomitant and multiplicative effect of economic growth and population increase also facilitated upward occupational mobility and better employment for more educated local residents.

In addition to their racial and ethnic impact on the labor market, Hispanic inflows change the demography of Accomack and Duplin Counties in other ways. Two changes are particularly relevant: gender composition and age distribution.

Gender ratios in these counties vary significantly by racial and ethnic group. According to the 2000 Census, the number of men per 100 women in Accomack County is 94 for whites, 85 for blacks, and 166 for Hispanics. In Duplin County, the gender ratio is 95 for whites, 84 for blacks, and 156 for Hispanics. For the United States as a whole, the gender ratio for Hispanics is 105 men per 100 women. Clearly, the two counties are anomalies within the United States, reflecting the predominantly male component of recent immigration there.

In addition, differences in gender ratios highlight a diverging pattern between Hispanics and blacks. The relative undersupply of women in the Hispanic case contradicts their relative oversupply among African Americans. Studies have found that gender ratios have significant importance in marriage patterns, particularly among blacks, making it more difficult for individuals to find partners in contexts of unbalanced gender markets (Lichter, LeClere, and McLaughlin 1991; Lichter et al. 1992). It is unclear how these patterns will affect the marriage behavior of single Hispanic men and women (Oropesa and Lichter 1994; Parrado and Zenteno In press). If Hispanic men try to find partners in the United States, the relative undersupply of Hispanic women may promote interracial marriage. Alternatively, to the extent that marriage is still constrained across racial and ethnic lines, single men may be forced to return to their local communities to find a partner (Parrado 2002). In this scenario, gender imbalances can also affect patterns of return migration. Given their cultural background, forming a union is still a central personal objective among Hispanics, particularly Mexicans. Conversations with immigrants in these communities suggest that gender imbalances and the difficulties in finding a partner, above and beyond economic success, critically affect settlement decisions.

In addition, gender imbalances have an effect on broader sexual behaviors. Immigrant communities are particularly vulnerable to the proliferation of prostitution and other forms of sexually risky behaviors. Use of prostitutes is particularly prevalent among single and married migrants who leave their families behind, which increases the risk of spreading sexually transmitted diseases, including AIDS. In fact, researchers have hypothesized that migration to the United States is a central contributor to the diffusion of the AIDS epidemic in Mexico, even in rural areas (McQuiston and Parrado 2002; Mishra, Conner, and Magaña 1996). Within the guidelines of the Healthy People objectives established by the U.S. Department of Health and Human Services, Latino organizations in Duplin County have begun to address sexually risky behavior by developing training programs and educational campaigns promoting condom use and AIDS prevention.

The other demographic trait with striking community impacts, age distribution, varies similarly across racial and ethnic groups. Figure 5 plots the percentage of the population in different age groups by race and ethnicity in Duplin County; patterns for Accomack County are very similar. Hispanics represent a much younger population than either blacks or whites. If we look at migration dynamics, the Hispanic percentage peaks very early, at zero to nine years old and again at twenty to twenty-four; it declines at older ages. The two peaks reflect the fact that labor migration is initiated in the early twenties, while children migrate early on or are born following their parents' settlement. The age distribution of blacks and whites is more even, with relatively higher proportions above age forty.

The age distribution of the Hispanic population has affected local communities in these counties in two ways. First, the rapid arrival of school-aged children has increased demand for educational facilities and contributed to school overcrowding. In addition, given the lack of knowledge of English among students and their parents, their arrival has suddenly increased the need for English as a second language (ESL) classes as well as interpreters to facilitate parent-teacher communication. The challenges that immigrants pose for public education systems are particularly relevant; some schools in Duplin County have become 50 percent Hispanic within the space of just a few years. Educators in both counties often find that the new

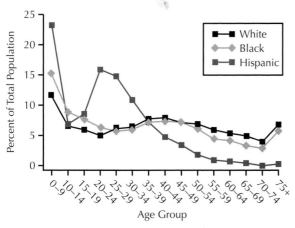

FIGURE 5   Age Distribution, by Race and Ethnicity, Duplin County, North Carolina, 2000.
Source: U.S. Bureau of the Census 2000.

arrivals have little educational background or familiarity with the U.S. educational system. Financing is particularly problematic. In Duplin County, for instance, Carolina Turkeys has recognized the tremendous burden that ESL classes impose on school budgets and now provides financial assistance for their provision.

Second, younger populations increase the prevalence of certain risk behaviors, including crime, alcoholism, and motor vehicle accidents. The higher representation of Hispanics in younger groups makes them particularly vulnerable to such problems, and special programs to address these issues might be required. In addition, age can also affect racial and ethnic relations. Research on neighborhood transitions in cities like Chicago shows that resistance to ethnic change stems not only from the different ethnicity of the arriving population but also from its youth (Flippen 2001). Elderly residents, in particular, may feel threatened by the arrival of younger groups, who they sense can disrupt their way of life or increase their vulnerability to crime. Such feelings can fuel anti-immigrant sentiments among native residents.

Community Impacts and Reaction

Signs of a Hispanic influx into Accomack County in the 1990s generally appeared muted, with only an occasional store sign in Spanish to suggest the presence of Hispanics. From the perspective of social-service delivery, however, indications of a Hispanic presence have cropped up in many small ways. The county court now has a certified court interpreter; previously, anyone with some bilingual ability would be asked to volunteer a translation for defendants. The two health clinics in the area now have Spanish-speaking personnel. The local hospital now uses a commercial phone service to automatically translate conversations. Some county schools have begun canvassing other districts for Spanish-speaking teachers. Employees at the Virginia Employment Commission frequently help Hispanic workers find new or better-paying jobs and often provide emergency food aid, a benefit frequently requested by those just arriving. However, other services, such as securing a driver's license or alcohol counseling, still require people to find their own translator or interpreter. At the community level, Hispanics now enjoy soccer matches all day each Sunday, a local weekly radio program in Spanish, a small Spanish-language newspaper, and church services in Spanish.

In Duplin County, where community impacts are more noticeable, several institutions have emerged that specifically attend to the needs of the Hispanic population and facilitate assimilation and incorporation into U.S. society. Latinos Unidos, for example, provides information about health and legal issues, offers ESL classes, and trains community members to serve local communities. County government has also adapted to the growing Latino community. A leadership program offered through a local college to promote entrepreneurship is now being reformatted into Spanish, an effort that has had a measurable impact on the emergence of Hispanic businesses. Small grocery, video, and music stores cater directly to the Hispanic community and can easily be identified when visiting the counties. In addition, Carolina Turkeys donated two lots to local Hispanic residents on which to construct churches.

Not surprisingly, Hispanic growth is changing the cultural landscape of these communities, from the types of food and consumer goods being sold in stores to the festivities that are celebrated. These changes sometimes occur in conjunction with shifts within the companies that hire Hispanics. For instance, in September 2000, workers from Carolina Turkeys in Duplin County organized an international festival to recognize the growing diversity of the county's Hispanic population. During the successful Semana de la Hispanicidad (Hispanic Heritage Week) in 2001, flags from every Latin American country were posted throughout the company's hallways. Following their lead, black employees decided to celebrate African-American Week in January 2002. In 2002, Carolina Turkeys invited the Mexican consul to give a speech in Duplin County, a widely publicized event that drew over three hundred people, garnered media attention for the Latino population, and created closer links with other groups. Many hope these kinds of initiatives will increase awareness and understanding of the growing diversity of Duplin County's population.

None of the informants we interviewed in Accomack and Duplin Counties suggested that the growth of the Hispanic population had caused concern among community residents, and they offered several reasons for the amenable reception. As part of the Delmarva region, Accomack County has been accustomed for decades to hosting migrants who work in the area's vegetable and grain farms. Moreover, the growth of the Hispanic population here was never as dramatic as it has been in some southeastern towns, such as Siler City, North Carolina, or Dalton, Georgia, where large numbers of Hispanics have recently settled in areas with relatively smaller base populations. In addition, there is increasing recognition of the contribution of the Hispanic population to the local economies. As one informant acknowledged, "We understand that without them, our vegetables wouldn't be picked because we don't have domestic workers that can do the job—or that would want to do the job."

When pressed, however, some of our informants mentioned hearing gripes about job competition between the Hispanic migrant workers and local blacks. Another issue that disturbs local residents in both counties is the trafficking in false driver's licenses, particularly because some of the recipients have little or no driving experience. Hispanic residents, on the other hand, are worried about crime and being targeted for robbery, in particular, because they often carry their money with them or keep their savings in their houses instead of in banks.

Racial and ethnic inequalities in access to housing also create tension. In Accomack County, 82 percent of white households live in owner-occupied housing units, compared with 63 percent of black households, and only 36 percent of Hispanic households. Figures for Duplin County are almost identical. In addition, Hispanics tend to live in overcrowded conditions in both counties, with an average household size of 4.5 persons compared with 2.5 for blacks and whites. Management at Carolina Turkeys in Duplin County and the Tyson and Perdue plants in Accomack County recognize the companies' role in providing adequate rental housing for Hispanic workers and have built homes or purchased house trailers close to their plants.

Conclusions and Policy Implications

In this chapter, we have presented evidence to illustrate how industrial restructuring correlates with changes in labor force composition and, by implication, with patterns of international migration and settlement. If similar trends in industrial development occur in other industries, we can expect them to generate further migration and population change. The visibility of prominent manufacturing firms will require greater attention by policy makers to labor-recruitment practices and the growing number of proposals for changing current immigration policies.

To show how industrial restructuring of the poultry industry plays out at the local level, we presented two case studies of poultry-producing counties in the Southeast, both with similar structural characteristics, but at different phases in their incorporation of Hispanic workers. To the extent that recent local history has been relatively incident free, these vignettes offer some degree of guarded optimism for the incorporation of Hispanic immigrants into the rural South as they create what Haverluk (1998) calls "new communities."

Nevertheless, a central concern of researchers is the degree to which outcomes of industrial development, such as international migration, differentially affect native residents. A sizable literature suggests that the presence of immigrant labor can be significant for wages, benefits, and working conditions (U.S. Department of Labor 1989). Moreover, as the relatively rapid settlement of immigrants in rural communities continues, it may also exacerbate existing patterns of spatial separation and inequality. This may require greater local expenditures on social services and programs that facilitate social integration between new and established residents. Given the geographic proximity of Mexico to the United States, increasing economic integration resulting from the North American Free Trade Agreement, age-specific migration, immigration laws favoring family reunification, and relatively high fertility, Hispanic demographic growth in rural areas will invariably increase. Consequently, many of the issues discussed above will likely continue for the foreseeable future.

Seeing the Big Picture   **How Is Upward Mobility Linked to Education, Occupation, and Immigration?**

In the Appendix, examine the high school dropout rates for Latinos in the Education section (Section I), then look at the occupations where Latinos are clustered, shown in the Occupations section (Section VIII). What does a "good" job require in a postindustrial service economy, and what might this mean for Latino immigrants?

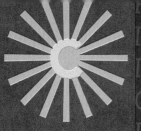

RACE, REPRESENTATIONS, AND THE MEDIA ~
Drug Dealers, Maids, and Mammies: The Role of Stereotypes in the Media

35 Broadcast News Portrayal of Minorities: Accuracy in Reporting

Roger D. Klein • Stacy Naccarato

ROGER D. KLEIN is an associate professor of psychology in education at the University of Pittsburgh.

STACY NACCARATO has an M.Ed. from the University of Pittsburgh.

A STUDY REPORTED LATE LAST YEAR BY THE Project for Excellence in Journalism (Rosenstiel, Gottlieb, & Brady, 2000) suggests that local television news is in trouble. Viewers are abandoning local news in droves, leaving what was once considered "the most popular and trusted source of information in the country" (p. 84). Why are viewers leaving? The report concludes that it is a lack of quality. Carl Gottlieb (personal communication, June 2001), a former television news director and a coauthor of the study, noted that viewers want information, they want value, and they resent the tricks that local news plays to try and hook viewers. The authors believe that local television news is at a crossroad, and they are not particularly optimistic.

But the heart of their report focuses on what successful local news stations do to increase ratings. Surprisingly, the answer is improved quality. One small part of what many successful stations do to improve quality is to reduce crime coverage. They also provide greater context for the crime stories they do cover. They explain crime stories and rather than scaring the audience, they provide balance and relevance. Those findings, we believe, are reasons for optimism. They also connect to the major theme of this article.

> **Questions to Consider**   Think for a moment about your favorite local television news station. How does this news program portray racial minorities in your community? Which groups are likely to be portrayed as victims or criminals? Who is portrayed as being demanding, aggressive, or dangerous? What color are the heroes, authority figures, or experts? Which groups are portrayed negatively, and which are portrayed favorably? How and why does this happen? Roger Klein and Stacy Naccarato explain that biased and sensational news coverage is not what viewers want but reflect the subtle bias in and out of the newsroom.

How are minorities portrayed on local television news? Studies surveying local news in Chicago (Linton & LeBailly, 1998), Los Angeles (Dixon & Linz, 2000), and Philadelphia (Romer, Jamieson, & deCoteau, 1998) have come to similar conclusions. Blacks and Latinos are more likely than Whites to be portrayed as perpetrators. In addition, in two of these studies (Dixon & Linz,

2000; Romer et al., 1998), it has been shown that Whites are overrepresented as homicide victims, compared to crime statistics, whereas Blacks and Latinos are underrepresented as victims. Even local television news stations have acknowledged a problem in the portrayal of minorities. In 1999, San Francisco's KRON-TV produced a two-part series on racism in the news, examining local coverage of minorities and examining race-related issues in their own newsroom (http://www.sfgate.com/cgi-bin/ramhurl.cgi?file=1991/10/21-race_kronv.rm).

In Pittsburgh, we examined 3 weeks of local television newscasts last year and found almost 80% of the references to Blacks, the area's largest minority, to be negative. By contrast, less than two thirds of references to Whites were rated as negative. Put differently, only 22% of stories about Blacks were positive. An almost four-to-one negative-to-positive ratio is troubling.

An equally troubling problem is a lack of context in the crime stories reported on local television news. For example, a rash of murders in Pittsburgh in the spring of 2001 resulted in the total number of homicides through mid-August, exceeding the total in all of 2000. Naturally, there was considerable media attention given to the increase. Local television news presented the bare facts and there was little context. On the other hand, the major local Pittsburgh newspaper, *The Pittsburgh Post-Gazette,* provided context. The focus on context is an important one. Throughout the past two years, about 80% of both the murder victims and the suspects in Pittsburgh have been Black. The broader newspaper coverage, along with editorial coverage (e.g., Craig, 2001), helped readers to understand that the majority of these Black-on-Black homicides appear to have been committed by a small number of people in the African American community. The newspaper also outlined some of the possible causes. Dorfman and Schiraldi (in press) note that White Americans exaggerate the threat of victimization by minorities. They note that Whites believe that they are more likely to be victimized by a member of a minority group, whereas statistics show that they are actually 3 times more likely to be victimized by another White person. The Pittsburgh newspaper does not encourage the readership to view Blacks as dangerous. But television news, with its lack of context, may well contribute to viewers' fears.

Some researchers (e.g., Dixon & Linz, 2000) believe that ethnic misrepresentation on local television news may result in a belief by viewers that the real world is similar to the television world. In data we have collected with different age groups ranging from middle-school students to senior citizens, between 70% and 97% of respondents agree with the statement "Local TV news shows me the way the world really is" (Klein & Cox, 1992, p. 4). One way to interpret these data is by concluding that for many of these Pittsburgh respondents, the television news world has become the real world. Have their attitudes toward African Americans been shaped by the negative-to-positive story ratio described above? Perhaps.

It isn't only adult minorities who are portrayed as criminals on local news. Minority youth are shown as criminals far more often than young Whites (Dorfman & Schiraldi, in press). Actually, it has been shown that the media portray youth of all races as violent, and one study in California (Dorfman, 1993, cited in Dorfman & Schiraldi, in press) demonstrated that less than 2% of stories about youth show their accomplishments. Dorfman (personal communication, June 2001) has suggested that people who have little personal contact with youth tend to view them as violent if they get most of their information about them from print and electronic media.

Are audiences aware of minority misrepresentation? Yes. One study (Linton, 1995) showed that African Americans' main complaint about news coverage was that it contained too much negativity about Blacks and excessive emphasis on crime. A national poll by CNN/ *USA Today*/Gallup (Sharp & Puente, 1994) concluded that almost 40% of Hispanics were upset with news coverage of issues important to them and two thirds of African Americans reported being upset at least once per week by news coverage of Black issues. A national poll of 1,200 children in 1998 conducted by Children Now found that in all of the racial groups surveyed (African American, Asian, Latino, and White), children reported that news media tend to portray African American and Latino people more negatively than White and Asian people, particularly when the news is about young people. A survey of 100 graduate students at the University of Pittsburgh (Klein & Smith, 2000) adds to these findings. Half of the respondents were Black and half were White. Almost 80% of White students and 96% of Blacks agreed that local television news misrepresents minorities, but only 16% of Whites and 30% of Blacks believed that news misrepresents White people. Many of the students also believe that the media intentionally misrepresent minorities. Eighty-six percent of Blacks and 40% of Whites believe misrepresentation is intentional. Although the Black/White opinion difference for this question is statistically significant, the fact that 40% of Whites agreed that news intentionally misrepresents Blacks is itself impressive. Contrast that with only 6% of Whites and 20% of Blacks agreeing that local television news intentionally misrepresents Whites.

Why does local news overrepresent minorities as criminals? First, we should ask why local news overrepresents crime stories in general. The two most common explanations are ratings and convenience: Crime sells and crime stories are easy to do; at least they are easy to do the way most stations do them.

The most common explanations offered for minority misrepresentation are racism and economic gain. Some researchers (e.g., Romer et al., 1998) believe that stations participate in a policy of ethnic blame. They note that Whites own most of the mass media organizations, they influence news content, they want to portray their group favorably, and they blame people of color for their problems. Heider (2000) suggests that some stations and advertisers believe that this ethnic blame approach appeals to a largely White television news audience. The Project for Excellence in Journalism (Rosenstiel et al., 2000) report noted that one third of the local stations surveyed claimed that news content was influenced by advertiser wishes. Finally, Heider has argued that news directors, who are mostly White, suffer from what he calls "incognizant racism"—they are not intentionally racist but rather are simply unaware of their own attitudes.

Given all of these problems, what can be done to try and change local television news? Continuing with Heider's (2000) belief that some newspeople may be unaware of their behavior, we find the work behind the scenes at KRON-TV to be an excellent example of how news personnel can be made aware. The station formed a committee to examine race relations within the news division and worked with San Francisco State University to assess the accuracy and fairness of coverage of the different racial groups living within the viewing area.

Such commitment takes time, cooperation, trust, and management support, and obviously KRON provided that sort of environment. More local news stations should try and follow in their footsteps, but we believe that is much easier to say than do.

Of course, in local television news, ratings and profits are the name of the game. Here, we believe the results of the Project for Excellence in Journalism study are again germane. As mentioned before, they concluded that quality journalism sells. They ranked stations from "A" to "F" based on quality and concluded that "64% of 'A' quality stations were building ratings, a higher percentage than any other grade and nearly double most grades" (Rosenstiel et al., 2000, p. 84). There were some key elements that went into an "A" rating, including greater coverage of the community and longer stories. But master stations (those with consistently high quality rankings and rising ratings over 3 years), as noted before, also aired fewer crime stories. Fewer crime stories may translate into greater profits.

Many local television news stations, however, are set in their ways. For years, news consulting organizations have been promoting emotionalism and sensationalism, and many of the stations have listened. In fact, Carl Gottlieb (personal communication, June 2001) noted that if he were still a news director and was reading his own report recommending quality journalism and less crime coverage, he'd say, "What, are you kidding?" In other words, change will not be easy. But Gottlieb added that out of desperation, out of fear of losing even more viewers, local stations are just beginning to listen.

Notice that it is not suggested that local television news stations eliminate crime stories. But fewer crime stories will almost certainly mean fewer opportunities to misrepresent minorities. Of course, an overall reduction in negative stories does not necessarily mean that the relative imbalance between Black and White crime stories will be reduced.

Again, the Project for Excellence in Journalism found that quality sells and that providing context is also important. By offering context rather than just a very brief 20 seconds of post-homicide or post-robbery video, stations can help to better educate viewers. By focusing more on information and less on sensationalism, there also might be less focus on skin color. Dorfman (1997) has written a handbook on crime coverage for journalists. In the handbook, she encourages reporters covering a homicide to ask a question they often ask when covering a car crash: "Was alcohol involved?" Dorfman says most reporters are not trained to ask the alcohol question at a homicide, but as a public health researcher, Dorfman knows that alcohol is as likely to be involved in a homicide as in a car crash. By improving the nature of crime coverage, reporters can better inform the public about issues that really matter and possibly reduce some of the biases mentioned earlier.

A nationwide study of local news directors (Driscol & Splichal, 1998) supports the belief that news directors are concerned. More than 70% of the 147 news directors responding agreed that their newscasts are scaring members of the community, and 52% agreed that audiences are fed up with this approach. Because local stations are losing viewers and because news directors are sensitive to some of these issues, the time may be ripe for change. But because news is first and foremost a business, it will be more effective to approach stations from a financial angle. Along these lines, recent data from a study by Bushman and Bonnaci (2001) suggest that television viewers are less likely to recall commercial messages when programming has violent content. Although Bushman did not specifically study television news, it is possible that the same principle applies. Advertisers might be interested in these findings.

We also should consider the work of Urban Affairs Professor Donilo Yanich. Yanich (personal communication, June 2001) goes into the community and trains news viewers in critical viewing skills. He suggests that as they watch a news story they use a mental stop—called a critical pause—and that they question a story's purpose and its value. Yanich suggests viewers call local stations when they are concerned or upset by a story. Yanich, who is at the University of Delaware, also has fostered good relationships with local news directors and has been successful in discussing with them the problems created by biased and inadequate crime coverage.

There are also efforts by major news organizations. For example, the Radio and TV News Directors Association (RTNDA) has taken a proactive stand. They have supported efforts to hire people of color in news management roles, promoted the need for diversity in the newsroom, and conducted annual surveys assessing the number of minorities working in news broadcasting. For the current year, the number of minorities in television news hit a record high of 24.6%. Eight percent of news directors were minorities. However, in radio news, minority participation was 10.8%, barely above the decade low set in 2000 (http://www.rtndf.org/news/2001/minsurvey.shtml).

In concluding, we would like to propose that more psychologists become involved in researching television news. Quite a few psychologists study television in general but not the news. We are unclear as to why that is the case. Notice that many of the experts cited herein come from the fields of communications, public health, and urban affairs. We believe that psychologists can make valuable contributions to the research literature and can help to implement change.

36   Television and the Politics of Representation
Justin Lewis • Sut Jhally

JUSTIN LEWIS is professor of communication and deputy head of the School of Journalism, Media and Cultural Studies at Cardiff University. He has written many books and articles on media, politics, and culture, and is currently series editor for the list in *Media and Culture* for Peter Lang Publishers.

SUT JHALLY is author of *The Codes of Advertising: Social Communication in Advertising* and *Enlightened Racism* and co-editor of *Cultural Politics in Contemporary America* and the forthcoming *The Fantasy Factory.* He is founder and executive director of The Media Education Foundation. He is the producer of videotapes *Dreamworlds, Pack of Lies, The Killing Screens, The Date Rape Backlash, Slim Shots, Tough Guise, Killing Us Softly III, Off the Straight and Narrow,* and *Advertising and the End of the World.*

Questions to Consider   Justin Lewis and Sut Jhally use *The Cosby Show* as a way to deconstruct the meaning of race, racial representations, and the role of social class in television. The authors argue that *The Cosby Show,* far from just being a well-written and successful situation comedy, sent a number of messages that were both positive and negative. What were they?

ONE OF THE ABIDING CONCERNS IN contemporary North American culture has been the many attempts to deal with race and racial inequality. Because racism is often understood as a perception dependent on negative or stereotypical images, debates about race often have centered on the issue of representation, with analytical glances increasingly cast toward television, as the main image-maker in our culture.

To make sense of the many competing claims about the way black people are represented on television, we carried out an extensive study based on a content analysis of prime time television together with a series of 52 focus group interviews (made up of 26 white, 23 black, and 3 Latino groups) from a range of class backgrounds. The interviews were designed to probe attitudes about race and the media representation thereof. To facilitate these discussions, each interview began with the viewing of an episode of *The Cosby Show.*

The Cosby Show was chosen because it has, in many ways, changed the way television thinks about the portrayal of African Americans. During the time it took for *The Cosby Show* to go from being innovative to institutional, African Americans became a fairly common sight on network television in the United States. And not just any African Americans: Our content analysis confirmed that we now see a plethora of middle- and upper-middle-class black characters populating our screens. Major black characters—from *ER* to *Sportsnight*—are now much more likely to be well-heeled professionals than blue-collar workers. In this sense, Bill Cosby can be credited with spurring a move toward racial equality on television. Fictional characters on U.S. television always have tended to be middle or upper-middle class—and since the late 1980s, black people have become an equal and everyday part of this upwardly mobile world.

The Cosby Show was, in this sense, more than just another sitcom. It represents a turning point in television culture, to a new era in which black actors have possibilities beyond the indignities of playing a crude and limited array of black stereotypes, an era in which white audiences can accept TV programs with more than just an occasional "token" black character. There is, it seems, much to thank Bill Cosby for. He has, quite literally, changed the face of network television.

At first reading, our study suggested that the upward mobility of black representation precipitated by *The Cosby Show* was an unambiguously positive phenomenon. It appeared, from our focus groups, to promote an attitude of racial tolerance among white viewers, for whom black television characters have become ordinary and routine, and to generate a feeling of pride and relief among black viewers. But *The Cosby Show* and the new generation of black professionals on U.S. television are caught up in a set of cultural assumptions about race and class that complicates the political ramifications of such a trend.

It is true that, in recent decades, the size of the black middle class in the U.S. has grown. This much said, the social success of black TV characters in the wake of *The Cosby Show* does not reflect any overall trend toward black prosperity in the world beyond television. On the contrary, the period in which *The Cosby Show* dominated television ratings—1984 to 1990—witnessed a comparative decline in the fortunes of most African Americans in the United States. The racial inequalities that scarred the United States before the civil rights movement could only be rectified by instituting major structural changes in the nation's social, political, and economic life—an idea informing Great Society interventions in the 1960s and 1970s. Since the election of Ronald Reagan in 1980, both Republican and Democratic administrations generally have withdrawn from any notion of large-scale public intervention in an iniquitous system, committing themselves instead to promoting a global free enterprise economy. This laissez-faire approach has resulted in the stagnation or gradual erosion of advances made by black people during the 1960s. For all the gains made in the fictional world of TV, by almost all demographic measures (such as education, health, levels of incarceration, income, and wealth), the United States remains a racially divided society.

As William Julius Wilson (1987) has documented, maintaining these divisions are a set of socioeconomic conditions that keep most people in their place. The "American Dream" of significant upward mobility is an aspiration that few can or will ever realize. It is an idea sustained by fictions and by anecdotes that focus on the exceptions rather than the rule of class division. If we are to begin any kind of serious analysis of racial inequality in the United States, we must acknowledge the existence of the systematic disadvantages that exclude most people on low incomes in poor neighborhoods—a condition in which black people in the United States have disproportionately been placed—from serious economic advancement.

Left unchecked, it is the laws of free market capitalism—rather than more overt, individual forms of racial discrimination—that reproduce a racially skewed class structure. Most major institutions in the United States have officially declared themselves nonracist and invited black citizens to compete alongside everyone else. This is

important but insufficient. If three white people begin a game of Monopoly, a black player who is invited to join the game halfway through enters at a serious disadvantage. Unless blessed by a disproportionate degree of good luck, the black player will be unable to overcome these economic disadvantages and compete on equal terms. This is, in effect if not in intention, how the United States has treated most of its black citizens: It offers the promise of equal opportunity without providing the means—good housing, good education, good local job opportunities—to fulfill it.

There is a wealth of evidence about the operation of these structural inequalities (see, e.g., Wilson 1987; Hacker 1992). What is remarkable about our culture is that it refuses to acknowledge the existence of class structures, let alone understand how they influence racial inequalities. And yet, at certain moments, we do accept these things as obvious. We expect rich white children to do better than poor black children. We expect it, because we know that they will go to better schools, be brought up in more comfortable surroundings, and be offered more opportunities to succeed. And our expectations would, most often, be proved quite right. The child who succeeds in spite of these odds is a glamorous figure in our culture precisely because he or she has defied these expectations. Unfortunately, our culture teaches us to ignore these social structures and offers us instead a naive obsession with individual endeavor. Instead of a *collective* war on poverty, we have welfare reforms that increase poverty and homelessness in the name of *individual* responsibility.

We would argue that U.S. television—and popular culture generally—is directly culpable for providing an endless slew of apocryphal stories that sustain a cultural refusal to deal with class inequalities and the racial character of those inequalities.

The Upscale World of Television Fiction

Televison in the United States is notable for creating a world that shifts the class boundaries upward. If the path to heaven is more arduous for the rich than the poor, the opposite can be said of entry to the ersatz world of television. Data from the University of Pennsylvania's Cultural Indicators project suggest that, in recent decades, television gives the overwhelming majority of its main parts to characters from middle- and professional class backgrounds, whereas significant working-class roles are few and far between

(Jhally and Lewis 1992). This is in notable contrast to the norms of other English-speaking television programs from countries like Britain and Australia, where working-class characters are much more commonplace. In the United States, the TV world is skewed to such an extent that the definition of what looks normal on television no longer includes the working class. The bias is neither obvious nor clearly stated. On the contrary, television's professionals are generally universalized so that the class barriers that divide working-class viewers from upper-middle TV characters melt away. As some of our working-class viewers said of Cliff Huxtable, he may be a doctor, but he's not as aloof as some of the real doctors they encounter in the non-TV world. This is seen in the words of two respondents:

> I guess he doesn't really seem professional, you know, not the way a doctor would be. The ones I meet are very uppity and they really look down on the lower class. They don't play the status they are in the show. You expect them to be living a much higher class, flashing the money, but they're very down to earth.

Television's characters are thus well-off but accessible. These are pictures of the American Dream, and they are paraded in front of us in sitcoms and drama series night after night. On television, most people, or most people with an ounce of merit, are making it.

But surely, it is only television, isn't it? Most people realize that the real world is different, don't they? Well, yes and no. Our study suggested that the line between the TV world and the world beyond the screen has become, for most people, exceedingly hazy. Many of the respondents in our study would shift from immersion in television's world to critical distance in the same interview, praising *The Cosby Show* at one moment for its realism and criticizing it at another for its lack of realism. Thus, for example, one respondent began with an endorsement of the show's realism: "I think that Cosby is much more true to life; you can put yourself right into the picture. Just about everything they do has happened to you, or you've seen it happen."

Later in the interview, the same respondent criticized the show:

> It's totally a fantasy to me, a fairy tale. . . . I think if you bring the real humdrum of what really life is all about, it would be a total bore. I would much prefer to see a little bit of fairy tale and make-believe.

It seems we watch at one moment with credulity and at another with disbelief. We mix skepticism with an extraordinary faith in television's capacity to tell us the truth. We know that the succession of doctors, lawyers, and other professionals that dominate television's stories is not real, yet we continually think about them as if they were. We have thereby learned to live in the dreams of network executives.

Exceptions to this—perhaps the most notable in recent television history being *Roseanne*—become conspicuous because (at least until the last show in the series when the family wins the lottery) they defy this norm. Simply by being sympathetic and assertively working class, the characters in *Roseanne* stood out from the sea of upscale images that surrounded them. In the United States, there are nearly twice as many janitors as all the lawyers and doctors put together, and yet, on television, the legal or medical professions are run of the mill, whereas to portray a major character as a janitor seems "ostentatiously" class-conscious. The negative response to *thirtysomething* in the 1980s was, in this context, extremely revealing. Here was a show that dealt, fairly intimately, with the lives of a group of middle- and upper-middle-class people. In demographic terms, these characters were the standard fare offered by network television, where most characters of any importance are middle or upper-middle class. Why, then, was this show in particular invariably described, often pejoratively, as a yuppie drama?

The answer tells us a great deal about the way class is represented on television. The show *thirtysomething* was unusual not because it was about young professionals but because it was self-consciously about young professionals. It was difficult to watch an episode without being aware that this was a group of people who were, in class terms, fairly privileged. Here was a show that was conspicuously and unapologetically class-conscious. When most TV characters display a liberal concern for the poor or the homeless, we are invited to applaud their altruism. When characters on *thirtysomething* did so, we were more likely to cringe with embarrassment at the class contradictions thrown up by such philanthropic gestures. Thus, *thirtysomething*'s principal sin was not that it showed us yuppies, but that it made them appear part of an exclusive world that many people will never inhabit. With its coy realism, *thirtysomething* was killjoy television, puncturing the myth of the American Dream.

Although we see echoes of this class consciousness on shows like *Frasier,* they are represented in ways that tend to elide rather than confirm class distinctions. It is not just that Frasier and Niles Crane's high cultural, upper-middle-class affectations are often parodied, but the constant presence of their working-class father reminds us that class background is unimportant.

The prosperous, comfortable world in which most television characters live is generally welcoming, and it is into this world that upscale black characters—from the Huxtables onward—fit like the proverbial glove. It is, we would argue, hard to underestimate the significance of this in the politics of representation. Thus, we can say that to be "normal" on television—the prerequisite for a "positive image"—black characters are necessarily presented as middle or upper-middle class. Indeed, *The Cosby Show* itself used two of television's favorite professions—what, after all, could be more routine than a household headed by a lawyer and a doctor? But unlike *thirtysomething*, it also had to look normal, to portray these wealthy professionals as a regular, "everyday" family. The respondents in our study suggested that the show was particularly skillful and adroit in absorbing this contradiction; indeed, its popularity depends on this combination of accessibility and affluence. Professionals and blue-collar workers can both watch the show and see themselves reflected in it. Social barriers like class or race are absent from this world. They have to be. To acknowledge the presence of such things would make too many viewers uncomfortable. Television has thereby imposed a set of cultural rules on us that give us certain expectations about the way the TV world should be.

The bombardment from this image world makes it difficult for people schooled in the evasive language of North American television to comprehend the world around them seriously. If a serious analysis of class structures is generally absent from our popular vocabulary, then that absence is confirmed by a television environment that makes upward mobility desirable but class barriers irrelevant. As a consequence, when our respondents tried to make sense of class issues thrown up by a discussion of *The Cosby Show,* many were forced to displace the idea of class onto a set of racial categories. This was often the case for our black respondents, who often became enmeshed in the debate about whether the show was "too white" (an idea that, incidentally, the great majority repudiated). Yet, we would argue, the very terms of such a debate involve a misleading syllogism, one that declares that because black people are disproportionately less likely to be upper-middle class, if they become so they have not entered a class category (upper-middle class) but

a racial one (white). One of our black middle-class respondents revealed the confusion involved in this way of thinking when he said, "What's wrong with showing a black family who has those kind of values? I almost said *white* values but *that's not the word I want*" (italics added). The context of a portrayal like *The Cosby Show* is not so much "white culture" (whatever that may be), but "upper-middle-class culture." It is partly by echoing the stilted discourse of U.S. television that many of our respondents found it difficult to make such a distinction.

In creating *The Cosby Show* Bill Cosby can hardly be blamed for playing by the rules of network television. Indeed, what our study makes clear is that it was only by conforming to these cultural limitations that he was able to make a black family so widely acceptable to white TV viewers. This discomfort or distance that most of the white viewers in our study expressed about black television characters was articulated not only in racial terms, but also—albeit indirectly—in class terms. What many white viewers found off-putting about other black sitcoms was not blackness per se but working-class blackness:

> I mean it's not a jive show, like *Good Times*. I think those other shows are more jive, more soul shows, say as far as the way the characters are with making you aware that they are more separate. Where Cosby is more of American down the line thing, which makes everybody feel accepted.
>
> I remember that it (*The Jeffersons*) was a little bit more slapstick, a little bit more stereotypical. They were concerned with racial issues. And it was much more interested in class, and the difference between class, middle class versus working class.
>
> They talk with the slick black accent, and they work on the mannerisms, and I think they make a conscious effort to act that way like they are catering to the black race in that show. Whereas Cosby, you know, definitely doesn't do that. He's upper middle class and he's not black stereotypical. There's a difference in the tone of those shows, completely.

The Price of Admission and Its Political Consequences

Although there may be dimensions to this race/class inflection that go beyond television, the difficulty some white viewers have in inviting black working-class characters into their living rooms is partly a function of television's class premise, in which normalcy is middle and upper-middle class and where working-class characters are, to some extent, outsiders. In terms of the politics of representation, our study raises a difficult question: If black characters must be upscale to be accepted into this image world, is such an acceptance worth the price of admission? To answer this question, we must consider the broader consequences of this representational move.

Among white people, the repeated appearance of black characters in TV's upwardly mobile world gives credence to the idea that racial divisions, whether perpetuated by class barriers or by racism, do not exist. Most white people are extremely receptive to such a message. It allows them to feel good about themselves and about the society of which they are a part. The many black professionals who easily inhabit the TV world suggest to people that, as one of our respondents put it, "There really is room in the United States for minorities to get ahead, without affirmative action."

If affirmative action has become a hot issue in contemporary politics, it is because the tide has turned against it, with states and universities (including our own) buckling under to pressure to abandon the policy. As Gray (1996) suggested in his analysis of the Reagan years, conservatives are able to use their opposition to such policies as a way of mobilizing white votes. Indeed, our study reveals that the opposition to affirmative action among white people is overwhelming. What was particularly notable was that although most white people are prepared to acknowledge that such a policy was once necessary, the prevailing feeling was that this was no longer so.

> I think I've become less enamored of it. I think that when the whole idea was first discussed, it was a very good idea. . . In recent years, I don't think it's necessarily getting anybody anywhere.
>
> I think in a lot of respects it's carried too far and that it results in reverse discrimination because you have quotas to meet for different job positions and that kind of stuff, it's like, a white person no longer has equal opportunity towards a job because you have to fill a quota.
>
> Well, I think it has gone too far, where the white people don't have the opportunities. I think it has come to a point where people should be hired now, not because of their color or their race, but because of what they're able to do. I mean there are people who are much better qualified but can't get hired because they are white, and I don't think that's right. Maybe in the beginning, they needed this. . . but it has gone too far.

There are, of course, circumstances in which a qualified black person will receive a warm reception from employees concerned to promote an "equal opportunities" image. Any cursory glance at social statistics, however, demonstrates that this is because employers are sheepish or embarrassed by current levels of inequality in the workplace. Almost any social index suggests that we live in a society in which black and white people are not equal, whether in terms of education, health, housing, employment, or wealth. So why is affirmative action suddenly no longer necessary? Partly, we would suggest, because our popular culture tells us so.

During our content analysis of the three main networks, we came across only one program that offered a glimpse of these racial divisions. What was significant about this program, however, was that it did not take place in the present, but in the past, during the early days of the civil rights movement. TV was only able to show us racial divisions in the United States by traveling back in time to the "bad old days." Most of the black characters in television's here-and-now seemed blissfully free of such things. Attempts by Hollywood to deal with racial inequality adopt the same strategy. Racism, whether in *Driving Miss Daisy, The Long Walk Home,* or *Amistad,* is confined to the safe distance of history. There are some notable exceptions— such as Spike Lee's work—but the general impression is clear: The social causes of racial inequality are behind us.

Television, despite—and in some ways because of—the liberal intentions of many who write its stories, has pushed our culture backward. White people are not prepared to deal with the problem of racial inequality because they are no longer sure if or why there is a problem. James Patterson and Peter Kim (1992) conducted a survey of contemporary American belief systems:

> In the 1990s, white Americans hold blacks, and blacks alone, to blame for their current position in American society. "We tried to help," whites say over and over, "but blacks wouldn't help themselves." This is the basis for what we've called the new racism. Everything flows from it. It is a change from the hardcore racism that existed in our country's earlier years. It is also a dramatic contrast to the attitude of the 1960s, when many whites, from the President on down, publicly stated that black people were owed compensation for centuries of oppression. (p. 183)

The use of upscale black television characters, our study made increasingly clear, is an intrinsic part of this process.

Television becomes Dr. Feelgood, indulging its white audience so that their response to racial inequality becomes a guilt-free, self-righteous inactivity.

This has saddled us, as Patterson and Kim (1992) suggest, with a new, repressed form of racism. For although television now portrays a world of equal opportunity, most white people know enough about the world to see that black people achieve less, on the whole, than do white people—a discourse emphasized by television news (Entman 1990). They know that black people are disproportionately likely to live in poor neighborhoods, drop out of school, or be involved in crime. Indeed, overall, television's representation of black people is bifurcated—a Jekyll-and-Hyde portrayal in which the bulk of ordinary working-class black Americans have few images of themselves outside of those connected with crime, violence, and drugs.

Media Images: Accentuating the Positive and the Negative

The most striking aspect of the interviews with black Americans in our study was the ubiquity of comments about the role that media images play in how white America looks at them—of how stereotypical images of blacks as criminals affected their own everyday interaction with white society and institutions, as one person put it:

> Nobody can believe that you can actually have the intelligence, the fortitude, the dedication and the determination to go out and earn a decent living to afford you some nice things. The mentality today is that if you're black and you get something, you either got it through drugs or through prostitution.

The role that the media played in the cultivation of this perception was clearly understood. As another of our respondents stated, "We seem to be the only people in the world that TV tries to pick out the negative to portray as characteristic of us. What television is doing to us, I think, is working a hell of a job on us."

For minority groups, then, living in the kind of residential and social apartheid that characterizes much of contemporary America, media images are vital, as they are the primary way that the broader society views them. Black America, after all, is well aware of what white perception of black males in particular can lead to. In the Rodney King case, an all-white suburban jury acquitted four LAPD officers for a brutal beating on the basis that the

person receiving the beating was, in the words of one of the jurors, "controlling the action." When your image of black people is as subhuman criminals, muggers, drug addicts, gang members, and welfare cheats, then even when a black man is lying hogtied on the ground, he is still dangerous, and any action to subdue him becomes justified.

It is not surprising, in this framework, that Bill Cosby's self-conscious attempt to promote a series of very different black images was so well received by the black respondents in our study. But if it is a kind of representational rescue mission, it is one with an almost fairy-tale script. Thus, we can move away from news images of black criminals to fictional images of black lawyers and judges in a matter of network minutes.

In this way, the media images turn real and complex human beings into crude one-dimensional caricatures, which then come to define minority populations for the majority. Perhaps the apotheosis of this bifurcated imagery was the figure of O. J. Simpson. If many white Americans were bemused by the degree to which black Americans felt they had a stake in the innocence of a rich TV celebrity, it was because they did not understand the representational issues at stake. The rush to a judgment of innocence was a mechanism of self-defense against a popular culture that offers a limited and bifurcated view of black life, one that can be symbolized by two characters in the recent history of black representation: Bill Cosby and Willie Horton.

The Cosby Show epitomized and inspired a move in network television toward the routine presentation of black professionals in drama and situation comedy. The flip side to this is the world of the news or so-called reality programming (like *Cops*), in which it is blacks as violent criminals, drug dealers, crackheads, and welfare mothers that dominate the screen. Perhaps the embodiment of this side of the story is Willie Horton, the image used by the Bush presidential campaign in 1988 to scare white America away from voting for Mike Dukakis. (In a now infamous TV campaign ad that is credited with turning the election around, Horton was represented as a crazed murderer, whom the Dukakis prison furlough program, in a moment of foolish liberal dogoodery, allowed out of prison.)

These are the two predominant images of black Americans with which the majority of white people are familiar. The O. J. case was pivotal, as Simpson came to be located precisely at the conjunction between the two. He *was* Bill Cosby (affluent, friendly, smiling, cultured). If he was guilty of brutal double murder, he would *become* Willie Horton. The representational identity of black America as a whole, given the incredible visibility of the case, was the prize at stake.

Writer Anthony Walton (1989) commented on what is at stake in these battles over representation:

> I am recognizing my veil of double consciousness, my American self and my black self. I must battle, like all humans, to see myself. I must also battle, because I am black, to see myself as others see me; increasingly my life, literally, depends upon it. I might meet Bernard Goetz in the subway. . . The armed security guard might mistake me for a burglar in the lobby of my building. And they won't see a mild-mannered English major trying to get home. They will see Willie Horton. (p. 77)

In this context, it is little wonder that black Americans took the Simpson case so personally. His innocence would, in some ways, maintain the representational progress forged by Bill Cosby, whereas his guilt would tilt it back to Willie Horton. He *had* to be innocent because African Americans, like all people, want the world to recognize their humanity and their dignity. In a context in which their identity is at stake, the "evidence" had little relevance. Any story—however implausible—of conspiracy and racism would eradicate the forensics, the DNA tests, and so forth. That is precisely what Johnny Cochran offered the jury and black America, and it was accepted with thanks.

But for white viewers, how can sense be made of this bifurcated world? How can black failure in reality programming be reconciled with television's fictions, so replete with images of black success? How to explain racial inequalities in the context of the racial equality of television's upscale world? Without some acknowledgment that the roots of racial inequality are embedded in our society's class structure, there is only one way to reconcile this paradoxical state of affairs. If black people are disproportionately unsuccessful, then they must be disproportionately less deserving. Although few of our respondents were prepared to be this explicit (although a number came very close), their failure to acknowledge class or racial barriers means that this is the only explanation available. The consequence, in the apparently enlightened welcome white viewers extend to television's black professionals, is a new, sophisticated form of racism. Their success casts a shadow across the majority of black people who, by these standards, have failed. Television, which tells us very little about the structures behind success or failure (Iyengar 1991), leaves white viewers to

assume that the black people who do not match up to their television counterparts have only themselves to blame.

In a rather different way, the effect of *The Cosby Show* on its black audience is also one of flattering to deceive. The dominant reaction of our black viewers to the show was "for this relief, much thanks." After suffering years of negative media stereotyping, most black viewers were delighted by a show that portrayed African Americans as intelligent, sensitive, and successful:

> I admire him. I like his show because it depicts black people in a positive way. It's good to see that black people can be professionals.
> Thank you Dr. Cosby for giving us back ourselves.

The problem with this response is that it embraces the assumption that, on television, a positive image is a prosperous image. This dubious equation means that African Americans are trapped in a position in which any reflection of more typical black experience—which is certainly not upper-middle class—is "stereotypical." As one of our respondents said, even though he was painfully aware that *The Cosby Show* presented a misleading picture of what life was like for most black Americans, "There's part of me that says, in a way, I don't want white America to see us, you know, struggling or whatever." On TV, there is no dignity in struggling unless you win.

This analysis of stereotyping dominates contemporary thought. It is the consequence of a television world that has told us that to be working class is to be marginal. Thus it is that viewers in our study were able to see the Huxtable family on *The Cosby Show* as both "regular" and "everyday" *and* as successful, well-heeled professionals.

For black viewers, this deceit amounts to a form of cultural blackmail. It leaves two choices, either to be complicit partners in an image system that masks the deep racial divisions in the United States or forced to buy into the fiction that, as one respondent put it, "there are black millionaires all over the place," thereby justifying *The Cosby Show* as a legitimate portrayal of average African American life.

The Structural Confines of Network Television

If our story tells us anything, it is that we need to be more attentive to the attitudes cultivated by "normal" everyday television. In the case of representations of race, these attitudes can affect the way we think about "issues" like race and class and, in so doing, even influence the results of elections.

As we have suggested, it does not have to be this way. There is no reason why TV characters cannot be working class and dignified, admirable—or even just plain normal. Bill Cosby's more recent sitcom—*Cosby*—is one attempt to do this, although his enormous popularity as a performer gives him a license that other shows, such as the short-lived *Frank's Place,* do not have. Other television cultures have managed to avoid distorting and suppressing the class structure of their societies; why can't we manage it in the United States?

The American Dream is much more than a gentle fantasy; it is the dominant discourse in the United States for understanding (or misunderstanding) class. It is a cultural doctrine that encompasses vast tracts of American life. No politician would dare question our belief in it, any more than they would publicly question the existence of God. Even though politicians of many different persuasions pay lip service to the dream (it is, in conventional wisdom, "what's great about America"), it is not a politically neutral idea. It favors those on the political right to say that anyone, regardless of circumstance, can make it if they try. In such an egalitarian world, the free market delivers a kind of equity, making public intervention and regulation an unnecessary encumbrance. For government to act to eradicate the enormous social problems in the United States is to defy the logic of the dream. Intervention implies, after all, that the system is not naturally fair, and opportunity is not universal.

The American Dream is, in this context, insidious rather than innocent. It is part of a belief system that allows people in the United States to disregard the inequalities that generate its appalling record on poverty, crime, health, homelessness, and education. It is not surprising that the more fortunate cling to the self-justifying individualism the dream promotes. One of the saddest things about the United States is that sometimes, the less fortunate do too.

The ideological dominance of the American Dream is sustained by its massive presence in popular culture. The television and film industries churn out fable after fable, thereby reducing us to a state of spellbound passivity in which decades of stagnating incomes for many Americans have been accepted with little protest. The success we are encouraged to strive for is always linked to the acquisition of goods, a notion fueled by the ubiquitous language of advertising, in which consumers do not usually see themselves in commercials; rather, they see a vision of a glamorous and affluent world to which they aspire. Underlying the preponderance of middle- and upper-middle-class characters on display is

the relentless message that this is what the world of happiness and contentment looks like. In this context, ordinary settings seem humdrum or even depressing. Not only do we expect television to be more dramatic than everyday life, but, in the United States, we also expect it to be more affluent. We do not want a good story; we want a "classy" setting.

> I liked the background. I like to look at the background on a TV program, I enjoy that. The setting, the clothes, that type of thing. I don't enjoy dismal backgrounds.
> This is nice, it looks good and it's kind of, you accept it; they have a beautiful home and everything is okay.

This is the language of advertising. It is also, now, the discourse of the American Dream. This language is now so much a part of our culture that these attitudes seem perfectly natural. It is only when we look at other television cultures that we can see that they are not.

Few other industrial nations leave their cultural industries to be as dependent on advertising revenue as they are in the United States. In the United States, very little happens in our popular culture without a commercial sponsor. This takes place in a lightly regulated free market economy in which cultural industries are not accountable to a notion of public service but to the bottom line of profitability.

Apart from tiny grants to public broadcasting, the survival of radio and television stations depends almost entirely on their ability to sell consumers (viewers or listeners) to advertisers. Moreover, broadcasters in the United States are required to do little in the way of public service. There are no regulations that encourage quality, diversity, innovation, or educational value in programming. This means that the influence of advertising is twofold. Not only does it create a cultural climate that influences the form and style of programs that fill the spaces between commercials; it also commits television to the production of formulaic programming. Once cultural patterns are established, it is difficult to deviate from them without losing the ratings that bring in the station's revenue.

This is not merely a tyranny of the majority and the logic of the lowest common denominator. A ratings system driven by advertising does not so much favor popularity as the quest for the largest pockets of disposable income. The 1999 season of *Dr. Quinn, Medicine Woman* was cancelled by CBS even though it was regularly the most popular show during its Saturday night time slot. The problem was simply that its viewers were generally not wealthy enough to be of interest to advertisers. The ad-driven chase for well-heeled demographics thereby gives network television an in-built class bias, creating a climate in which portrayals of working-class black characters may make good television but are an unlikely way to attract television's most sought-after demographic group.

Which brings us back to the many representational offshoots of *The Cosby Show.* To be successful and to stay on the air, *The Cosby Show* had to meet certain viewers' expectations. This, as we have seen meant seducing viewers with the vision of comfortable affluence the Huxtables epitomized. Once television has succumbed to the discourse of the American Dream, where a positive image is a prosperous one, it cannot afford the drop in ratings that will accompany a redefinition of viewers' expectations. TV programs that do so are necessarily short-lived. Programs like *Frank's Place, Cop Rock,* or *Twin Peaks* all deviated from a norm, and, although still watched by millions of viewers, they did not attain the mass audience required to keep them on the air. This puts us on a treadmill of cultural stagnation. It is a system in which the bland repetition of fantasies tailored to the interests of wealthier viewers makes sound business sense.

In such a system, *The Cosby Show*'s survival depended on meeting the demands of a formula that pleases as many people as possible and especially its more upscale audience. Our study suggests that it did so with consummate success, pleasing black and white people, blue-collar workers and professionals, all in slightly different ways. The more blue-collar *Cosby* has been less universally embraced, and in this context we should applaud Bill Cosby's attempt to use his popularity to offer audiences a less upscale image.

When our book *Enlightened Racism: The Cosby Show, Audiences, and the Myth of the American Dream* was first published in 1992, we were widely credited with holding *The Cosby Show* responsible for promoting the routine fiction of effortless black success. But this was not the thrust of our argument. *The Cosby Show* and many black professionals portrayed in its wake are genuine attempts to make television's upscale world more racially diverse. The problem is not with individual instances of black success but with a television environment whose structural conditions make a wider array of images less profitable.

37 Distorted Reality: Hispanic Characters in TV Entertainment

S. Robert Lichter • Daniel R. Amundson

S. ROBERT LICHTER is the founder of the Center for Media and Public Affairs, a nonpartisan, nonprofit research and educational organization that conducts scientific studies of news and entertainment media. He is the co-author (with Daniel Amundson) of *Solid Waste Management: Comparing Expert Opinion, Media Coverage, and Public Opinion* (1992).

DANIEL R. AMUNDSON is research director of the Center for Media and Public Affairs. He is co-author (with S. Robert Lichter) of *Solid Waste Management: Comparing Expert Opinion, Media Coverage, and Public Opinion* (1992).

Questions to Consider   Latinos now represent a larger proportion of the total population than do African Americans, but they are mostly invisible on prime-time television. Robert Lichter and Daniel Amundson provide a historical overview of the ways Latinos have been characterized by the media. Have stereotypical depictions of Latinos changed in recent years? Are you able to name five main characters appearing on prime-time television (8 P.M. to 11 P.M. slot) who are Latino? Are these representations favorable? What are the occupations of these Latino characters?

The Past as Prologue

It takes diff'rent strokes to move the world.
— "Diff'rent Strokes" Theme Song

When Kingfish uttered his last "Holy Mackerel, Andy!" in 1953, it marked the end of television's most controversial depiction of blacks. Ironically, the departure of *Amos 'n' Andy* also signaled the end of a brief period of ethnic diversity that would not reappear in prime time for two decades. Several of the earliest family sitcoms were transplanted radio shows set in America's black or white ethnic subcultures. *The Goldbergs* followed the lives of a Jewish immigrant family in New York for twenty years on radio before switching to the new medium in 1949. It featured Gertrude Berg as Molly Goldberg, everyone's favorite Jewish mother. An even more successful series that premiered the same year was *Mama,* which chronicled a Norwegian immigrant family in turn-of-the-century San Francisco. Theme music by Grieg added to the "ethnic" atmosphere, as did accents that made Aunt "Yenny" into a popular character. These white ethnic shows were soon joined by the all-black *Amos 'n' Andy* as well as *Beulah,* which starred the black maid of a white middle-class family.

All these shows relied on stereotypical dialogue and behavior for much of their humor. But social standards were changing, and the new medium created its own demands and perceptions. For example, not only Amos and Andy but even Beulah had been portrayed on radio by white males. When the popular radio show *Life with Luigi* made the switch to TV in 1952, Italian American groups protested its stereotyped portrayal of Italian immigrants. Black groups were equally outraged over *Amos 'n' Andy,* which had been an institution on radio since 1929. As the program evolved, it centered on the schemes of George "Kingfish" Stevens, who combined the soul of Sgt. Bilko with the fate of Ralph Kramden. A small-time con man with big plans that never panned out, he became an immensely popular, lovable loser. His schemes usually pulled in the ingenuous cabbie Andy and the slow-moving janitor Lightnin'.

From Kingfish's fractured syntax ("I'se regusted") to Lightnin's shuffle and falsetto "yazzuh," the series drew on overtly racial stereotypes. The NAACP blasted the portrayal of blacks as "inferior, lazy, dumb, and dishonest," and urged a boycott of Blatz beer, the sponsor. The pressure from civil rights groups probably helped bring the series to a premature end, since it attracted sizeable audiences throughout its two year run.

• • •

While controversy surrounded *Amos 'n' Andy,* little debate attended television's earliest and most high-profile Latino portrayal. From 1950 through 1956, Ziv productions sold 156 episodes of *The Cisco Kid* in syndication to individual stations across the country. Resplendent in his heavily embroidered black costume, Cisco rode across the Southwest righting wrongs and rescuing damsels in distress. He was accompanied by his portly sidekick, Pancho, who served as a comic foil. Pancho was loyal and brave, but his English was every bit as fractured as the Kingfish's. Further, although Cisco and Pancho were positive and even heroic characters, they were often outnumbered by evil and frequently criminal Latino adversaries. In its simplistic presentation that combined positive and negative ethnic stereotypes, *Cisco* set the tone for the *Zorro* series that would follow it on ABC from 1957 through 1959. Thus, these early high-profile representations of Latinos proved a mixed bag, as television's conventions of the day were applied to both network and syndicated fare.

The All-White World

Cisco and *Zorro,* which were aimed at children, outlasted the first generation of ethnic sitcoms for general audiences. By the 1954 season *Mama* was the only survivor of this once-thriving genre. Thus, by the time our study period began, TV's first era of ethnic humor had already come and gone. The urban ethnic sitcoms were replaced by homogeneous suburban settings. There was nothing Irish about the life of Chester Riley, nothing Scandinavian about Jim and Margaret Anderson. The new family shows were all-American, which meant vaguely northern European and carefully noncontroversial. The few remaining ethnics were mostly relegated to minor roles or single episodes.

Just how homogeneous was this electronic neighborhood? From 1955 through 1964, our coders could identify only one character in ten as anything other than northern European on the basis of name, language, or appearance. Such a small slice of the pie got cut up very quickly, and many groups got only crumbs. Just one character in fifty was Hispanic, fewer than one in a hundred was Asian, and only one in two hundred was black.

• • •

Hispanics had virtually no starring roles. For most Hispanic characters, life consisted of lounging in the dusty square of a sleepy Latin town, waiting for the stars to come on stage. Occasionally Hispanics would show up as outlaws in the Old West, but even then mostly as members of someone else's gang. Their comic roles were epitomized by Pepino Garcia, a farmhand for *The Real McCoys*, who functioned mainly as a target of Grandpa Amos McCoy's tirades. Pepino and *The Real McCoys* were replaced in 1963 by Jose Jimenez in the *Bill Dana Show*.

Like their black colleagues, a few stars stood out in a sea of marginal and insignificant roles. A notable exception was Cuban band leader Ricky Ricardo in *I Love Lucy*, played by Desi Arnaz. As the co-star of one of the most popular shows on TV (and coowner of Desilu Productions, along with wife Lucille Ball), Arnaz was a prominent figure in Hollywood. When exasperated by Lucy's schemes and misadventures, Ricky added a comic touch with displays of "Latin" temper and lapses into Spanish. *I Love Lucy* made its mark on television comedy and TV production in general, but it did little for Hispanic characters. The same could be said of another early show with a Hispanic setting, which nonetheless cast Anglos in the major roles. Guy Williams played Don Diego, alias Zorro, the masked champion of the poor and oppressed in old Los Angeles. Their oppressors were evil, greedy Spanish governors and landowners. In one episode Annette Funicello, fresh from the Mickey Mouse Club, showed up as the singing senorita Anita Cabrillo. Despite its "Hispanic" characters, the show was not a generous portrayal of either the people or the culture.

The departure of *Amos 'n' Andy* and *Beulah* all but eliminated black stars. Jack Benny's valet Rochester was one of the few major roles still held by a black in the late 1950s. Black characters didn't even show up in the backgrounds of early shows. Urban settings might feature a black delivery man, porter, or waiter, but black professionals and businessmen were virtually nonexistent. Some westerns like *Rawhide* and *Have Gun, Will Travel* presented a few black cowboys riding the range with their white counterparts. Aside from such occasional and insignificant roles, black characters were simply not a part of the early prime time world.

The Return of Race

In the mid-1960s, the portrayal of ethnic and racial minorities underwent major changes. The proportion of non–northern European roles doubled over the next decade. Before 1965, all racial and ethnic groups to the south or east of England, France, and Germany had scrambled for the one role in ten available to them. Now nonwhite characters alone could count on better than one role in ten. From the first to the second decade in our study [1955–1975], the proportion of English characters was cut in half, while Hispanics became half again as numerous and the proportion of Asians doubled. Blacks were the biggest winners, gaining a dramatic fourteen-fold increase in what had been virtually an all-white landscape.

The invisibility of Hispanics during this period remained more than metaphorical. They were simply not part of television's new ethnic "relevance." Latinos had few continuing prime time roles of any sort during the late 1960s, and certainly no major star parts like Bill Cosby's Alexander Scott. In fact, most Latinos who were cast during this period showed up in episodes of international espionage series that used Central and South American locales. *I Spy* had many episodes set in Mexico, bringing the agents into contact with some positive and many more negative Hispanic characters. In other espionage shows, such as Mission Impossible, the action often centered on a fictitious Central American country, which was inevitably run by a jack-booted junta that could only be stopped by the enlightened Anglo-led team from north of the border.

One of the few exceptions to this pattern was the western *High Chaparral*. Rancher John Cannon had settled in the Arizona territory to found a cattle empire. When his first wife was killed by Apaches, John married Victoria Montoya, the daughter of a wealthy Mexican rancher. The marriage was as much a business move as a romance, since it united the two families. Once tied by marriage, Don Montoya helped John build his herds and produce good breeding stock. Together the two families fought off Apaches and other marauders. Culture clashes between the two families occurred, but usually as a minor part of the plot. Unlike most Mexicans shown in previous westerns, the Montoyas were rich, powerful, sophisticated, and benevolent. In most episodes, Victoria attempted to civilize her more rustic husband and establish a proper home on the range. To be sure, this series still presented semiliterate Hispanic ranchhands, but these portrayals were overshadowed by the Montoyas.

The other exception was the short-lived social relevancy series *Man and the City*. This series presented more contemporary problems of Latinos in an unnamed southwestern city. The show was notable for frequently asserting the dignity and rights of Latinos. For example, in a 1971 segment, a cop is killed in the city's barrio. The police department pulls out all the stops to catch the killers, imposing a curfew and holding suspects incommunicado without legal counsel. All the suspects are Hispanics from the barrio who have little connection to the case. The mayor is forced to intervene and remind the police chief that the city has laws. He demands that all suspects, including minority groups, be given their full rights. The police are reluctant, believing this will impede their investigation. The mayor insists and the police obey his order. They eventually capture a key suspect who helps them catch the killers. There is no indication that racial tensions in the city have ended, merely that one violent episode is over. The groups involved have not learned to like each other; nor are they presented as peacefully coexisting. The point here is that all people have rights and deserve to be treated with dignity and equality. This seems to be the only series that attempted to derive socially relevant plotlines from the barrio.

Not only did the proportion of black characters jump to 7 percent between 1965 and 1975, but the range and quality of roles expanded even more dramatically. In adventure series like *I Spy* and *Mission: Impossible,* blacks moved into their first starring roles in over a decade. Not only were these roles more prominent, they offered a new style of character. Alexander Scott of *I Spy* and Barney Collier of *Mission: Impossible* were competent, educated professionals. These men were highly successful agents whose racial backgrounds were clearly secondary to their bravery and skill. They opened the way for blacks to appear in roles that did not require the actor to be black. There was no more use of poor English, servile shuffling, or popeyed double takes for comic effect. Instead, Collier was presented as an electronics expert and Scott as a multilingual Rhodes Scholar.

The new visibility of blacks quickly moved beyond the secret agent genre. In 1968 the first of television's relevance series managed to convert a negative stereotype into a positive one by casting a young black rebel as a member of *The Mod Squad.* Linc Hayes' militant credentials included an afro haircut, aviator sunglasses, and an arrest during the Watts riots. Not to worry, though. This brooding black rebel was working with the good guys on the L.A.P.D.'s undercover "youth squad," where the dirty dozen met the counterculture every Tuesday at 7:30.

While ABC was coopting the Black Panthers into the establishment, NBC looked to the black middle class for *Julia,* the first black-oriented sitcom in fifteen years. As a dedicated nurse and loving mother in an integrated world, the Julia Baker character looked ahead to *The Cosby Show* rather than backward to *Amos 'n' Andy.* She certainly had more in common with Claire Huxtable than with Kingfish's nagging wife, Sapphire. Unfortunately, she also lacked the vitality and wit of either Sapphire or future mother figures who would be more firmly rooted in black culture, like *Good Times'* Florida Evans.

Julia suffered from the dullness of being a prestige series, just as *The Mod Squad* labored under the hype that attended the relevance series. What they had in common with better-written shows like *I Spy* and *Mission: Impossible* was a tendency to replace the old negative black stereotypes with new positive ones. The authors of *Watching TV* wrote with a touch of hyperbole, "They were no longer bumbling, easygoing, po' folk like Beulah, but rather articulate neo-philosophers just descended from Olympus, though still spouting streetwise jargon."[1] Having discovered that blacks didn't have to be cast as valets and janitors, white writers turned them into James Bonds and Mary Tyler Moores. Thus, as blacks suddenly began to appear on the tube after a decade's absence, they remained invisible in Ralph Ellison's sense. The frantic search for positive characters smothered individuality with good intentions.

Let a Hundred Flowers Bloom

In the early 1970s TV began to broadcast a different message about minorities. The unlikely agent of change was an equal opportunity bigot named Archie Bunker, who excoriated "spics," "jungle bunnies," "chinks," "yids," and every other minority that ever commanded an epithet. When *All in the Family* became the top-rated show within five months of its 1971 premiere, it attracted a barrage of criticism for making the tube safe for ethnic slurs. The producer of public television's *Black Journal* found it "shocking and racist."[2] Laura Hobson, who wrote *Gentlemen's Agreement,* an attack on anti-Semitism, decried its attempt to sanitize bigotry, "to clean it up, deodorize it, make millions of people more comfy about indulging in it."[3] Of course, the point of the show was to poke fun at Archie and all he stood for, as the script and laugh track tried to make clear.

Norman Lear's strategy was to educate audiences by entertaining them instead of preaching at them. So he created a kind of politicized Ralph Kramden, whom audiences could like in spite of his reactionary views, not because of them. He intended that the contrast between Archie's basic decency and his unattractive rantings would prod viewers to reexamine the retrograde ideas they permitted themselves. As Lear put it, the show "holds up a mirror to our prejudices. . . . We laugh now, swallowing just the littlest bit of truth about ourselves, and it sits there for the unconscious to toss about later."[4] As a tool for improving race relations, this approach may have been too subtle for its own good. Several studies suggest that liberals watched the show to confirm their disdain for Archie's views, while conservatives identified with him despite his creator's best intentions.[5] But another legacy of the program was to pioneer a more topical and (by television's standards) realistic portrayal of ethnic relations.

An immediate consequence of *All in the Family* was to introduce the first sitcoms populated by black families since *Amos 'n' Andy*. A year after demonstrating the audience appeal of a white working class milieu not portrayed successfully since *The Honeymooners,* Lear and his partner Bud Yorkin transferred the setting to a black ghetto in *Sanford and Son.* Unlike the integrated middle class world of TV blacks in the late 1960s, *Sanford and Son* revolved around the foibles of a junk dealer in a poor black section of Los Angeles. *Sanford* proved so popular that it soon trailed only *All in the Family* in the Nielsen ratings.

Meanwhile, in an irony Archie would not have appreciated, *All in the Family* spawned not one but two additional black family sitcoms. *The Jeffersons* featured Archie's one-time neighbor George Jefferson as an upwardly mobile businessman whose snobbishness and inverted racism made him almost a black Archie Bunker. *Good Times* was actually a second-generation spinoff. When Archie's liberal nemesis Maude got her own show in 1972, the scriptwriters gave her a quick-witted and tart-tongued black maid named Florida Evans. Two years later the popular Florida got her own show as the matriarch of a family living in a Chicago housing project. This series developed the *Sanford* technique of finding sometimes bitter humor among lower status characters trying to cope with life in the ghetto while looking for a way out of it. Scripts featured ward heelers, loan sharks, abused children, and other facets of life on the edge, in sharp contrast to the comfortable middle class world of *Julia* or the glamorous and exotic locales of *I Spy.*

By this time, other producers, stimulated by Norman Lear's enormous success, were providing sitcoms that drew their characters from minority settings. *What's Happening!!* followed the adventures of three big city high school kids. *Diff'rent Strokes* created an unlikely "accidental family" in which a wealthy white man raised two black kids from Harlem in his Park Avenue apartment, without any serious clash of cultures. This trend almost never extended from the ghetto to the barrio. The one great exception was *Chico and the Man,* a generation-gap sitcom that paired an ebullient young Mexican American with an aging Bunkerish Anglo garage owner. This odd couple clicked with audiences, but the show's success was cut short by the suicide of comedian Freddy Prinze (Chico) in 1977.

Like the black sitcoms, *Chico* used minority culture as a spark to enliven a middle class white world that seemed bland or enervated by comparison. Minority characters of the early 1970s prided themselves not on their similarity to mainstream culture, but on their differences from it. Assimilated characters like Alexander Scott, Barney Collier, and Julia Baker gave way to the racial pride of George Jefferson, Fred of *Sanford and Son,* and Rooster on *Starsky and Hutch.* Where would Fred Sanford or George Jefferson be without their jive talk and street slang? Language was just one way of stressing the differences between racial and ethnic groups.

Minority characters also picked up flaws as they took on more complete roles. Fred Sanford was domineering and could appear foolish. George Jefferson could be as stubborn and narrow-minded as his one-time next-door neighbor. By badgering the interracial couple living upstairs and labelling their daughter a "zebra," he left no doubt about his views. But the thrust of the ethnic sitcom was not to ridicule minority cultures. Instead, racial and ethnic backgrounds were used as an educational tool. The religious, cultural, and other traditions that differentiate minorities from the mainstream were now treated as beneficial rather than problematic. Removed from the confines of the melting pot, these groups offered new approaches to old problems. Television charged them with the task of teaching new ways to the often obstinate world around them. Blacks and Hispanics participated in this era of racial and cultural re-education. It was Chico Rodriguez who taught Ed Brown to relax and be more tolerant on *Chico and the Man.* Benson, the sharp-tongued butler, tried to maintain order amidst the chaos of *Soap,* while steering his employers onto the right track. In one episode he even saved young Billy from the clutches of a religious cult.

The most spectacularly successful effort to combine education with entertainment was a hybrid of the miniseries and "big event" genres. Indeed, *Roots* became the biggest event in television history. This adaptation of Alex Haley's best-selling novel traced the history of four generations of a black family in America, beginning with Kunta Kinte, an African tribesman sold into slavery. It ran for eight consecutive nights in January 1977. When it was over, 130 million Americans had tuned in, including 80 million who viewed the final episode. Seven of the eight episodes ranked among the all-time top ten at that point in television's history. *Roots* created a kind of national town meeting comparable to the televised moon landing or the aftermath of President Kennedy's assassination. It was blamed for several racial disturbances but credited for stimulating a productive national debate on the history of American race relations.

While blacks could look to the high-profile presentation of African American history presented by *Roots*, there was no similar presentation of Hispanic history. If Anglos relied exclusively on Hollywood for information on Latino contributions to American history, their knowledge would extend little further than John Wayne's defense of *The Alamo* against the Mexican "invaders." Illustrations of Latino culture were equally rare. In fact, the only high-profile Hispanic character during this period was Chico Rodriguez. Despite its popularity, *Chico and the Man* was not known as a series that explored Latino culture or Hispanic contributions to American history and culture.

Despite occasional failures, ethnic comedies became the hottest new programming trend of the 1970s. *All in the Family* was the top-rated show for an unprecedented five straight seasons, surpassing previous megahits *I Love Lucy* and *Gunsmoke*. Other top twenty regulars included *Sanford and Son, The Jeffersons,* black comic Flip Wilson's variety show, and *Chico and the Man*. The ethnic wave crested during the 1974–75 season, when a remarkable six of the seven top-rated shows were ethnic sitcoms—*All in the Family, Sanford, Chico, Jeffersons, Rhoda,* and *Good Times.*

If the new decade offered an unaccustomed array of new roles for minorities, it contained some traps as well. Ethnic characters gained more prominent and desirable roles, but also more unflattering ones. Bumblers, buffoons, and bimbos took their place alongside heroes and

sages. For example, Vinnie Barbarino and Juan Epstein were two of the uneducated underachievers on *Welcome Back Kotter*. Barbarino's Italian heritage added ethnic color to his machismo image, while Epstein's ethnic background was contrived for comic effect. He was presented as Buchanan High School's only Puerto Rican Jew. *Good Times* created some negative black characters, such as insensitive building supervisors and abusive politicians. In *What's Happening,* the Thomas family made do without their con man father after he walked out on them. His occasional visits home were usually in search of money for some new scheme. A steady stream of minority characters began to show up as criminals in cop shows like *Kojak, Baretta,* and *Barney Miller.*

Barney Miller also deserves note as one of the most multicultural shows of the time. In the 1975–76 season the squad room contained Polish detective Wojohowicz, Asian American Nick Yemana, African American Harris, and Puerto Rican Chano Amenguale. While Chano was far from perfect he appeared to be a capable officer and no more eccentric than his colleagues on the squad. In the next season Chano was replaced by Detective Baptista, who was a fiery Latina, but not as significant in the squad as Chano. These characters at least served to offset the Hispanic criminals they often arrested.

The late 1970s retained a mix of ethnic heroes and fools in some of the most popular shows of the day. But ethnic characters were beginning to lose their novelty. For instance, *CHiPs* ran from 1977 through 1983 and one of the starring characters was Officer Frank Poncherello. Even though Poncherello was played by the well-known Eric Estrada, Poncherello's Hispanic heritage was all but invisible. It no longer mattered in this series that one of the leads was a Latino. During the 1979 season, three dramatic series were launched with black leads, but none came close to the ratings necessary for renewal. *Paris* starred James Earl Jones as a supercop who ran the station house during the day and taught criminology at night. *The Lazarus Syndrome* featured Louis Gossett as the chief of cardiology in a large hospital. *Harris and Company* focused on the problems of a single parent raising a family. The twist was that this black family was held together not by a matriarch but a middle-aged widower. Thus, Hollywood was at least trying to create some positive role models for black males. But no such efforts extended to Latinos. There were no network series built around a Latino family, Hispanic high school kids, or any of the other patterns found in sitcoms featuring blacks. It would be several years before the short-lived ABC series *Condo* would prominently cast Latinos as middle class characters.

Overall, the 1980s offered little that was new to racial or ethnic minority portrayals in the wake of TV's ethnic revival. These groups continued to be presented more or less as they were in the late 1970s. Despite the continuing presence of racial and ethnic diversity, however, racial themes were no longer in vogue. Integration was assumed as a backdrop, as the prime time world became less polarized. The age of pluralism had arrived, but the thrill was gone. The riots were over, the battles won, and characters got back to their other plot functions. Among these were crime and other wrongdoing. Comedies like *Taxi, White Shadow,* and *WKRP in Cincinnati* continued to present integrated casts, but ethnic characters in dramatic series were often on the dark side of the law.

Ironically, television's multicultural world of the 1980s provided an updated version of the stereotypical Hispanic banditos who populated the westerns thirty years earlier. In the fall of 1980, ABC's controversial sitcom *Soap* introduced a remake of Frito Bandito. Carlos "El Puerco" Valdez was a South American revolutionary playing a love interest of Jessica Tate. They had met when his band kidnapped her for ransom. This plan failed, but after things took a passionate turn, she became a benefactor of his revolution. "El Puerco" led a bumbling, low-budget revolution and he was not above taking time out to romance his new gringo benefactor. "El Puerco" was both Latin lover and bandito with a measure of Jerry Lewis buffoonishness thrown in. Thus, it was down this line that the Frito Bandito's sombrero had been passed—to a fatigue-wearing ne'er-do-well.

There were also more sinister turns in Latino portrayals. Crime shows like *MiamiVice, Hill Street Blues,* and *Hunter* presented Hispanic drug lords as a major nemesis. Trafficking in human misery made these characters rich enough to own cities and sometimes even small countries. They were among the nastiest criminals on TV in the 1980s. There were also petty Hispanic criminals in the slums of *Hill Street Blues* and *Cagney & Lacey.* These small-time hoods, drug addicts, and pimps were less flamboyant than their big-league counterparts, but no less unsavory. Altogether, TV's latest crop of Hispanics included a cruel and vicious group of criminals.

Miami Vice was not only a source of criminal Hispanics—after all the squad was led by the enigmatic Lieutenant Martin Castillo and on the distaff side of the unit was detective Gina Navarro. However inconsistently, the show did attempt to show successful law-abiding Latinos mixed in with the criminal crop. For all of its flaws *Miami Vice* at least attempted to reflect the presence of Latinos in Miami. Contrast this attempt with more contemporary shows like *Baywatch, Acapulco H.E.A.T.,* and others that rarely if ever reference the Hispanic populations in their host cities.

There were occasional attempts to base shows on Hispanic casts, but all proved unsuccessful. In 1983 the Lear-wannabee sitcom *Condo* briefly pitted a bigoted WASP against his Latino next-door neighbors. The following season, the equally short-lived *A.K.A. Pablo* dealt somewhat more seriously with ethnic questions. Focusing on struggling young comic Pablo Rivera and his extended family, the series wrestled with questions about ethnic humor and the preservation of Hispanic culture. Pablo made many jokes about his family and his Mexican American heritage in his nightclub act. This frequently offended his traditionalist parents, who expected him to treat his heritage more respectfully. Despite its brief run, this series was one of the few to deal explicitly with aspects of Latino culture.

A more mixed portrayal appeared in the 1987 series *I Married Dora.* In this fractured fairy tale, Dora Calderon was the housekeeper for widower Peter Farrell and his family. When faced with deportation, Dora and Peter joined in a marriage of convenience. Like many television housekeepers before her, Dora was the voice of wisdom and compassion in the household, but her own illegal status gave her role an ambiguous twist. In 1988, a series called *Trial and Error* was based on Latino characters from the barrio in East Los Angeles. The show revolved around a free-wheeling entrepreneur who ran a souvenir T-shirt company and his upwardly mobile roommate, who was a newly minted lawyer. This series had a lighter touch with less attention to Hispanic culture, but it met with the same quick demise as its predecessors.

Both *A.K.A. Pablo* and *Trial and Error* sprang from the efforts of comedian Paul Rodriguez. It is not uncommon for bankable stars to get their own television series. This is particularly true for stand-up comics, who have taken their nightclub acts into successful series like *Roseanne,*

Home Improvement, Grace Under Fire, and *Seinfeld.* This approach has proven to be a very important avenue onto the screen for blacks. Several exclusively black shows currently on the air are the result of the work of a bankable star. Among those who have followed in the footsteps of Bill Cosby are Keenan Ivory Wayans of *In Living Color,* Martin Lawrence of *Martin,* Mark Curry of *Hangin' with Mr. Cooper,* and Charles Dutton of *Roc.* Unfortunately, this approach has so far been a dead end for Latinos.

Blacks fared better in the 1980s, largely escaping the criminal portrayals of other minorities. When black characters did turn to crime, they were usually small-time criminals driven by desperation. There were even times when their criminal acts were presented as social commentary. For instance, in an episode of *Hill Street Blues,* a black militant occupies a housing project and takes hostages. He threatens to kill them unless the city agrees to keep the project open and fix it up. The man is frustrated and angry that weeks of negotiating led to nothing. The city simply set a new closing date and moved on. Rage and desperation drive him to act and a tense stand-off ensues. In the end, he is mistakenly shot by a police sniper. Everyone is shocked by his desperate act and his tragic death.

Meanwhile, TV turned out numerous positive black role models as diverse as *The Cosby Show's* Heathcliff Huxtable, Mary Jenkins of *227,* Rico Tubbs on *Miami Vice,* and Bobby Hill of *Hill Street Blues.* These shows suggest the diversity of major roles that were at last becoming available to blacks. *227* and *Amen* continued the sharp-tongued tradition of 1970s sitcoms, without the abrasive or objectionable images that had brought criticism. Tubbs and Hill both carried on the tradition of "salt and pepper" law enforcement teams. Hill also represented the educative function of minorities by helping to wean his partner Renko, a southerner, away from residual racist tendencies.

Of course, *Cosby* was the biggest hit of all. This series further developed the low-key humanistic color-blind approach that Bill Cosby has popularized over two decades as *I Spy's* Alexander Scott, high school teacher Chet Kincaid on *The Bill Cosby Show,* and finally in a black version of *Father Knows Best.* The enormous success of this venture led some critics to snipe at Cosby for playing black characters in whiteface to maximize audience appeal. Black psychiatrist Alvin Pouissant, retained by

the show to review scripts for racial authenticity, notes that the criticisms come from white reporters more often than black viewers: "Sometimes it seems they want the show to be 'culturally black'. . . and sometimes it seems they would be happier to see them cussing out white people, a sort of protest sitcom. Some seem to feel that because the family is middle class with no obvious racial problems, that constitutes a denial or dismissal of the black person."[6]

Compared to the plight of TV's Hispanics, debates over whether the Huxtables are divorced from the black experience may seem a luxury, a sign that a one-time out-group has reached a mature phase in its relationship with the Hollywood community. In 1979 organized opposition even persuaded Norman Lear to withdraw a new comedy series at the last minute. *Mister Dugan,* a sitcom about a black congressman, was scheduled to premier on CBS a week after Lear arranged a special screening for the Congressional Black Caucus. The screening was a disaster, with Congressman Mickey Leland calling the lead character "a reversion to the Steppin' Fetchit syndrome."

Lear promptly pulled the show from the schedule. He remarked at the time, "We have a high social conscience, and we want to get the story right. We do not favor the short-term gain over the long-term public interest. Dropping the show was an exercise in that commitment."[7] This was an extraordinary episode in a business often excoriated for caring only about the bottom line. When the medium's most successful producer is willing to withdraw a series on the eve of its broadcast, writing off a $700,000 investment, it shows the power of social commitment in television. The only question is the strength and direction of that commitment.

Moreover, such criticism is belied by the top ten ratings obtained by such diverse families as the Sanfords, Jeffersons, and Evans, not to mention Kunta Kinte and his kin. The success of upper and lower class, matriarchal and patriarchal black family series suggests that television has gone beyond using black characters as a sign of racial diversity. It has begun to show diversity within the black community as well, at last recognizing both the cultural distinctiveness and the universal humanity of this group of Americans. Unfortunately, Hispanics have never played a significant role in television's debate over race relations. When television has explored discrimination, prejudice, or the appropriateness of interracial relationships, it has almost always staged them as a black versus white issue. Whatever racial tensions exist between Latinos and other groups in American society, they have very rarely made it to the small screen.

A Tale of Two Minorities

Black representation continued to increase during the 1990s, as the number of shows with all-black or mostly black casts jumped. Driven largely by the Fox network's quest for new audiences and trademark shows, these new series drew heavily on the struttin' and jivin' characters of the 1970s. Both the 1992 and 1993 seasons featured ten such series, including hits like *Hangin' with Mr. Cooper, Family Matters, Martin,* and *Fresh Prince of Bel Air.* Intense debate has ensued over the quality of these roles and portrayals, which critics disparage as latterday minstrel show stereotypes. However, such complaints have not diminished the popularity of these shows, particularly among black audiences.

Despite continuing controversy, television's portrayal of blacks is in many ways more diverse and substantive than ever before. For instance, on Monday nights viewers could contrast the wealthy Banks family on *Fresh Prince of Bel Air* with the working class Cumberbatches in *704 Hauser Street.* On Tuesday, they could see the struggles of a single mother in *South Central,* followed by the stable two-parent extended family in *Roc.* Then there were the Winslows, a comfortably middle class black family that was a cornerstone of Friday night viewing for years. In addition there were numerous black characters in integrated series such as *L.A. Law, Law & Order, Evening Shade, Love & War, NYPD Blue, In the Heat of the Night,* and *sea Quest DSV.* African Americans were seen as lawyers, judges, police captains, and a host of other roles in these shows.

While shows that were exclusively or mainly about blacks comprised about one eighth of the prime time schedule in 1992–93, only one series in the previous three seasons was based on a Latino family or character. Moreover, that series—the short-lived *Frannie's Turn*—mainly used Hispanic traditions as a comic foil for feminist putdowns. This series revolved around the marriage of a Cuban emigré named Joseph Escobar and his wife, Frannie, an Anglo of unclear ethnic origins. Whatever ethnic and cultural differences may have existed between them were rarely played upon, since most of the plots

dealt with Frannie's quest for equality. However, when aspects of heritage did come up, they frequently reflected poorly on Latinos. For instance, the first episode dealt with Frannie's discovery that Joseph has been sending money to a Cuban liberation movement while telling her to cut the household budget. At one pointin the ensuing argument, she suggests sarcastically, "Who knows, maybe they'll send you the Bay of Pigs decoder ring." In the few episodes that aired, the couple's children seemed oblivious to their heritage, and no effort was made to teach them about their father's culture. Overall, this series made no greater use of ethnicity than *I Love Lucy* did almost forty years earlier.

Otherwise, Latino characters remained largely supporting players or background figures in the prime time schedule. The highest profile in 1992–93 was enjoyed by Daniel Morales, who replaced Victor Sifuentes on *L.A. Law.* Most other recent Latino roles involved lower status jobs or far less airtime in low-rated series. Examples include Chuy Castillo, the cook at the *Golden Palace;* Jennifer Clemente, a very junior attorney in the U.S. Justice Department on *The Round Table;* and detective Rafael Martinez on the *Hat Squad.* There was also Mahalia Sanchez, a bus station cashier in the *John Larroquette Show,* rookie detective James Martinez in *NYPD Blue,* and Paco Ortiz in *Nurses,* none of them starring roles.

The cultural diversity within the Latino community was almost completely absent from prime time. Most Hispanic characters on television came from a "generic" background without reference to national origin or past. Television has rarely pointed out the cultural, historical, or economic differences among different groups within the Latino community. The few shows to make such distinctions, from *Miami Vice* to *Frannie's Turn,* usually did so to place a particular nationality in a negative light. In *Miami Vice,* differing national origins were connected with different types of illegal activities, while in *Frannie's Turn* a Cuban heritage was not a badge of honor. Sadly, the highest-profile Latino characters of the season were Eric and Lyle Menendez, whose murder trial was featured in two made-for-television movies.

An Update

As we have seen, before 1965, prime time was a nearly all-white world populated mainly by generic northern

Europeans, save for the occasional black servant or Mexican bandito. Soon thereafter, the spectrum widened to embrace an array of ethnic and cultural traditions. But various minority groups shared unequally in television's new search for ethnic roots.

Some of these disparities are summarized in Table 1. As the table makes clear, between 1955 and 1986, proportionately fewer Hispanic characters were professionals or executives and more were unskilled laborers. Fewer Hispanics had starring roles, were positively portrayed, or succeeded in attaining their goals. Indeed, according to our 1994 study,[8] the more villainous the character, the sharper the group differences that emerged. Hispanic characters were twice as likely as whites and three times as likely as blacks to commit a crime. Once TV's roster of Hispanic stereotypes solely included the grinning bandito criss-crossed with ammunition belts. More recently, as scriptwriter Ben Stein has observed, "Any time a Cuban or Colombian crosses the tube, he leaves a good thick trail of cocaine behind."[9]

In addition, because of their negative and criminal roles, Latinos stood apart from other characters in the methods they adopted to attain their goals. They were more likely than either whites or blacks to use violence and deceit. If Latinos were distinctive in the means they used to pursue their goals, they also differed in their motivations. Hispanic characters were much more likely to be driven by greed than other characters. More broadly, black characters managed to attain whatever they strove for more often than either whites or Hispanics. In fact, the failure rate among Hispanics was more than double that of blacks. Perusing these figures, it is difficult to resist the conclusion that Hollywood has cracked open the door to black concerns while letting Hispanics serve as window dressing.

Examining character portrayals in 1992, we found that compared to both Anglos and African Americans, television's

TABLE 1 Traits of TV Characters, 1955–1986

	White	Black	Latino
All characters	89%	6%	2%
*Social background**			
Attended college	72	44	**
Lacked high school diploma	25	49	**
Low economic status	22	47	40
Professional or executive	22	17	10
Unskilled laborer	13	16	22
Plot functions			
Starring role	17	15	8
Character succeeded	65	72	54
Character failed	23	16	34
Positive portrayal	40	44	32
Negative portrayal	31	24	41
Committed crime	11	7	22

*Characters were coded only if their backgrounds were clearly indicated by the script.
**Two few characters were coded for meaningful comparisons.
Source: Based on a content analysis of 7,639 prime time characters that appeared in 620 entertainment programs between 1955 and 1986.

Hispanics were low in number, low in social status, and lowdown in personal character, frequently portraying violent criminals. The worst offenders were "reality" shows, whose version of reality often consisted of white cops chasing black and Hispanic robbers. Utilizing the same scientific content analysis approach, we examined the more recent 1994–95 season. We focused on a composite month of prime time entertainment programs broadcast on the four major broadcast networks and in first-run syndication. We found some welcome progress in television's portrayal of Hispanics, combined with some lingering sins of both omission and commission. (These results reflect our analysis of 5,767 characters who appeared on 528 different episodes of 139 prime time series.)

The proportion of Hispanic characters was up but still far below the proportion of Hispanic Americans in the real world. Latinos were "ghettoized" in a handful of series, few of which are still on the air, and few portrayed prosperous, well-educated, authoritative characters. The most striking and hopeful result, however, was a dramatic decline in the portrayal of Hispanics as criminals. Among the major findings:

- *Visibility.* TV's Hispanic presence doubled from 1992 levels. And these characters were more likely to play major roles when they appeared. But the rise was from only 1 to 2 percent of all characters, far below the 10 percent of Americans with Hispanic ancestry in real life. And a majority appeared in only two series, one of which has been canceled.

- *Criminality.* Hispanic characters were less likely to play villains than they were in the 1992 network prime time schedules. The drop in criminal portrayals was down 63 percent (from 16 percent of all Hispanic characters in 1992 and 6 percent in 1994). But even this level of criminality was higher than the 4 percent we found among whites and 2 percent among blacks.

- *New "Realities."* The most striking changes appeared in the cops-and-robbers "reality" shows, such as *COPS* and *America's Most Wanted.* In 1992, a staggering 45 percent of all Hispanics and 50 percent of African Americans who appeared in these shows committed crimes. In 1994–95, the "crime rate" for both minorities plummeted to less than half the previous levels—down from 45 to 16 percent of Latinos and from 50 to 20 percent of blacks portrayed.

Seeing the Big Picture   **How the Media Shape Race Relations**
Section VIII on Occupations in the Appendix shows the racial composition of editors and reporters in the United States. Which groups are over- and underrepresented in these fields? How does a lack of racial minorities in the news production room shape the way racial minorities are presented in the mass media?

38 Winnebagos, Cherokees, Apaches, and Dakotas: The Persistence of Stereotyping of American Indians in American Advertising and Brands

Debra Merskin

DEBRA MERSKIN is an associate professor at the University of Oregon. Her research interests focus on the representation of women and minorities in media, historical studies, and the social influences of the media.

FROM EARLY CHILDHOOD ON, WE HAVE all learned about "Indianness" from textbooks, movies, television programs, cartoons, songs, commercials, fanciful paintings, and product logos.[1] Since the turn of the century, American Indian images, music, and names have been incorporated into many American advertising campaigns and product images. Whereas patent medicines of the past featured "coppery, feather-topped visage of the Indian" (Larson, 1937, p. 338), butter boxes of the present show the doe-eyed, buckskin-clad Indian "princess." These stereotypes are pervasive, but not necessarily consistent—varying over time and place from the "artificially idealistic" (noble savage) to present-day images of "mystical environmentalists or uneducated, alcoholic bingo-players confined to reservations" (Mihesuah, 1996, p. 9). Yet today a trip down the grocery store aisle still reveals ice cream bars, beef jerky, corn meal, baking powder, malt liquor, butter, honey, sour cream, and chewing tobacco packages emblazoned with images of American Indians. Companies that use these images of Indians do so to build an association with an idealized and

Questions to Consider   Driving your Winnebago recreational vehicle (fully loaded 2001 Chieftan model) with Jeep Cherokee in tow, you pull into the Navajo National Park in New Mexico for your much-needed vacation. You sit down, light up a Natural American Spirit Cigarette, open a forty-ounce bottle of Crazy Horse Malt Liquor, and get ready to watch the World Series match between the Atlanta Braves (with their "Tomahawk Chop") and the Cleveland Indians. Each of these products draws on extremely stereotypical imagery of American Indians. Why, according to Debra Merskin, do these stereotypes continue, and what effect do these images have on the way individuals view American Indians?

romanticized notion of the past through the process of branding (Aaker & Biel, 1993). Because these representations are so commonplace (Land O' Lakes maiden, Jeep Cherokee, Washington Redskins logo), we often fail to notice them, yet they reinforce long-held stereotypical beliefs about Native Americans.

Trade characters such as Aunt Jemima (pancake mix), Uncle Rastus (Cream of Wheat), and Uncle Ben (rice) are visual reminders of the subservient occupational positions to which Blacks often have been relegated (Kern-Foxworth, 1994). Similarly, Crazy Horse Malt Liquor, Red Chief Sugar, and Sue Bee Honey remind us of an oppressive past. How pictorial metaphors on product labels create and perpetuate stereotypes of American Indians is the focus of this study. McCracken's (1993) Meaning Transfer Model and Barthes's (1972) semiotic analysis of brand images serve as the framework for the analysis of four national brands. The following sections discuss how stereotypes are constructed and how they are articulated in, and perpetuated through, advertising.

To understand how labels on products and brand names reinforce long-held stereotypical beliefs, we must consider beliefs already in place that facilitated this process. Goings (1994), in his study of African American stereotypes, points out that "Racism was not a byproduct of the Civil War; it had clearly been around since the founding of the nation" (p. 7). Similarly, anti-Indian sentiments did not begin with the subjugation and dislocation efforts of the 1800s. Racial and ethnic images, part of American advertising for more than a century, were created in "less enlightened times" but have become a part of American popular culture and thought (Graham, 1993, p. 35) and persist today. The system of representation thereby becomes a "stable cultural convention that is taught and learned by members of a society" (Kates & Shaw-Garlock, 1999, p. 34).

Part of the explanation for the persistent use of these images can be found in the power and persuasiveness of popular culture representations. Goings's (1994) analysis of Black collectibles and memorabilia from the 1880s to the 1950s is a useful analogy for understanding the construction of Native American stereotypes in popular culture. He suggests that "collectible" items such as salt and pepper shakers, trade cards, and sheet music with images of happy Sambos, plump mammies, or wide-eyed pickaninnies served as nonverbal articulations of racism made manifest in everyday goods. By exaggerating the physical features of African American men and women, and making them laughable and useable in everyday items, these household objects reinforced beliefs about the place of

Blacks in American society. Aunt Jemima, the roly-poly mammy; and Uncle Rastus, the happy slave chef (ironically both remain with us today) helped make Whites feel more comfortable with, and less guilty about, maintenance of distinctions on the basis of race well after Reconstruction. These items were meant for daily use, hence constantly and subtly reinforcing stereotypical beliefs.

Similarly, Berkhofer (1979) suggests that "the essence of the white image of the Indian has been the definition of American Indians in fact and in fancy as a separate and single other. Whether evaluated as noble or ignoble, whether seen as exotic or downgraded, the Indian as image was always alien to white" (p. xv). White images of Native Americans were similarly constructed through children's games, toys, tales, art, and theater of the 1800s. Whereas "Little Black Sambo" tales reinforced the construction of racist beliefs about Blacks, songs such as "Ten Little Indians" or "cowboy and Indian" games similarly framed Indian otherness in the White mind. Goings (1994) makes an important point about the source of the construction of objects that represent this way of thinking:

> It is important to note that Black memorabilia are figures from white American history. White Americans developed the stereotypes; white Americans produced the collectibles; and white American manufacturers and advertisers disseminated both the images and the objects to a white audience. (p. xix)

The maintenance of these kinds of beliefs satisfies the human need for psychological equilibrium and order, finding support and reinforcement in ideology. Defined as "typical properties of the 'social mind' of a group" (van Dijk, 1996, p. 56), ideologies provide a frame of reference for understanding the world. *Racist* ideologies serve several social functions operating to reproduce racism by legitimating social inequalities, thereby justifying racially or ethnically constructed differences. Racist ideology is used to (1) organize specific social attitudes into an evaluative framework for perceiving otherness, (2) provide the basis for "coordinated action and solidarity among whites," and (3) define racial and ethnic identity of the dominant group (van Dijk, 25–27). These beliefs and practices are thereby articulated in the production and distribution of racist discourse.

To every ad they see or hear, people bring a shared set of beliefs that serve as frames of reference for understanding the world around them. Beyond its obvious selling function, advertising images are about making meaning. Ads must "take into account not only the inherent qualities and attributes of the products they are trying to sell, but also the way in which they can make those properties mean something to us" (Williamson, 1978, p. 12).

Barthes (1972) describes these articulations as myth, that is, "a type of speech" or mode of signification that is conveyed by discourse that consists of many possible modes of representation including, but not limited to, writing, photography, publicity, and advertising. Myth is best described by the process of semiology (Barthes, 1972). Semiology "postulates a relation between two terms, a signifier and a signified" (Barthes, 1972, p. 112). The correlation of the terms *signifier, signified,* and *sign* is where associative meaning is made. What we see in an advertisement or product label, at first glance, are basic elements composed of linguistic signs (words) and iconic signs (visuals). Barthes (1972) uses a rose, for example, as a symbol of passion. Roses are not passion per se, but rather the roses (signifier) + concept of passion (signified) = roses (sign). He states that "the signifier is empty, the sign is full, it is a meaning" (Barthes, 1972, p. 113). Another example that involves race is the use of Aunt Jemima for maple syrup. We see the representation of a bandana-clad Black woman who suggests the mammy of the Deep South (signified). When placed on the bottle of syrup (sign), meaning is transferred to the otherwise ambiguous product—care giving, home cooking, and food sharing. The sign is formed at the intersection between a brand name and a meaning system that is articulated in a particular image. Quite simply, a sign, whether "object, word, or picture," has a "particular meaning to a person or group of people. It is neither the thing nor the meaning alone, but the two together" (Williamson, 1978, p. 17).

McCracken (1993, p. 125), who defines a brand as a "bundle or container of meaning," expanded on the Barthesian analysis and developed a framework for understanding the cultural relationship that brands have within society. His anthropological model . . . illustrates the meanings of brands. McCracken shows how brands assume meaning through advertising, combined with consumption behavior, and the nature of common knowledge that consumers bring to this system. The present study expands on this process by adding a reinforcement loop from consumer back to the culture where stereotypes are experienced and recirculated through the system.

A brand can have gendered meaning (maleness/femaleness), social standing (status), nationality (country meaning), and ethnicity/race (multicultural meaning). A brand can also stand for notions of tradition, trustworthiness, purity, family, nature, and so on. McCracken (1993) uses the Marlboro man as an example of these components with which a simple red and white box came to signify freedom, satisfaction, competence, maleness, and a quintessentially American, Western character. The product becomes part of the constellation of meanings that surrounds it and thereby "soaks up" meanings. When the rugged Marlboro man is situated on his horse, on the open plain, almost always alone, the meanings of the constellation become clear—freedom, love of the outdoors, release from the confines of industrialized society—he is a "real man," self-sufficient and individualistic. These meanings become part of a theme made up of prototypical content while simultaneously being "idealizations and not reality itself" (Schmitt & Simonson, 1997, p. 124).

Advertisements are created in such a way as to boost the commodity value of brand names by connecting them to images that resonate with the social and cultural values of a society. These images are loaded with established ideological assumptions that, when attached to a commodity, create the commodity sign. Tools of branding are thereby used to create a particular image in the mind of the consumer. According to van Dijk (1996), this pattern often serves to present an US versus THEM dichotomy, with US being White, "positive, tolerant, modern," and THEM being minorities who are "problematic, deviant and threatening" (pp. 26–27). Hence, attitudes, beliefs, and behavior that are racist serve to support a dominant ideology that focuses on difference and separatism.

These ideas and values are articulated through the construction, maintenance, and perpetuation of stereotypes. Stereotypes are overgeneralized beliefs that

> get hold of the few simple, vivid, memorable, easily grasped, and widely recognized characteristics about a person, reduce everything about the person to those traits, exaggerate and simplify them, and fix them without change or development to eternity. (Hall, 1997, p. 258)

An example is the way the "Indian problem" of the 1800s has been shown in "cowboy and Indian" films. In his analysis of the representation of Indians in film, Strickland (1998, p. 10) asks, "What would we think the American Indian was like if we had only the celluloid Indian from which to reconstruct history?" (Strickland, 1998, p. 10). The cinematic representation includes the Indian as a

> bloodthirsty and lawless savage; the Indian as enemy of progress; the Indian as tragic, but inevitable, victim; the Indian as a lazy, fat, shiftless drunk; the Indian as oil-rich illiterate; the Indian as educated half-breed unable to live in either a white or Indian world; the Indian as nymphomaniac; the Indian as noble hero; the Indian as stoic and unemotional; the Indian as the first conservationist. (Strickland, 1998, p. 10)

Champagne's (1994) analysis of Indians in films and theater suggests that the longevity of James Fenimore Cooper's *Last of the Mohicans,* evidenced by its many film treatments, demonstrates that "Hollywood prefers to isolate its Indians safely within the romantic past, rather than take a close look at Native American issues in the contemporary world" (p. 719).

Natty Bumppo, in James Fenimore Cooper's *Deerslayer,* is a literary example of the male who goes from a state of "uncultured animality" to a state of "civilization and culture" (Green, 1993, p. 327). Larson (1937) describes how this stereotype was translated into a tool for marketing patent medicines:

> No sooner had James Fenimore Cooper romanticized the Indian in the American imagination in his novels than patent-medicine manufacturers, quick to sense and take advantage of this new enthusiasm, used the red man as symbol and token for a great variety of ware. How the heart of the purchaser—filled, like as not, with the heroic exploits of Cooper's Indians— must have warmed as he gazed at the effigy, symbolic of "Nature's Own Remedy." (p. 338)

The female savage becomes an Indian princess who "renounces her own family, marries someone from the dominate culture and assimilates into it" (Green, 1993, p. 327), for example, Pocahontas. From this perspective, Indians are thought of as childlike and innocent, requiring the paternalistic care of Whites; that is, they are tamable. In her study of Indian imagery in *Dr. Quinn, Medicine Woman,* Bird (1996, p. 258) suggests that what viewers see is a White fantasy filled with White concerns around "guilt and retrospective outrage." Green's (1993) analysis of the use of male Indian images in ads posits that Natives continue to be portrayed according to stereotypical images: (1) noble savage (the stoic, innocent, child of nature), (2) civilizable savage (redeemable, teachable), and (3) bloodthirsty savage (fierce, predatory, cultureless, animalistic). Taken together, these studies suggest that

historically constructed images and beliefs about American Indians are at the essence of stereotypical thinking that are easily translated into product images.

To study the articulation of racist ideology in brand images, four currently available national products (Land O' Lakes butter, Sue Bee Honey, Big Chief [Monitor] Sugar, and Crazy Horse Malt Liquor) were analyzed according to Barthes's (1972) semiotic analysis. First, the material object was identified (signifier); second, the associative elements were identified (signified); and, third, these were brought together in what we as consumers recognize as the sign. Company websites, press releases, and product packages were used for visual and textual information. Several attempts to communicate directly with the companies yielded no response. Through this method of analysis we can see how these meanings are transferred to the different products on the basis of both race and gender.

The following section presents a descriptive analysis of Land O' Lakes, Sue Bee Honey, Big Chief (Monitor) Sugar, and Crazy Horse Malt Liquor brand images.

Land O' Lakes

Although not the first national manufacturer to draw on the mystique of Indianness (that honor goes to Red Man Tobacco in 1904), Land O' Lakes is certainly one of the more prominent. In 1921, the Minnesota Cooperative Creameries Association opened for business in Arden Hills, Minnesota. This company served as the central shipping agent for a small group of small, farmer-owned dairy cooperatives (Morgan, 1986, p. 63). In 1924, the group wanted a different name and solicited ideas from farmers. Mrs. E. B. Foss and Mr. George L. Swift came up with the winning name— Land O' Lakes, "a tribute to Minnesota's thousands of sparkling lakes" (p. 63). The corporate website opens with a photograph of a quiet lake amid pine trees and blue sky. The copy under the photograph reads:

> Welcome to Land O' Lakes. A land unlike anywhere else on earth. A special place filled with clear, spring-fed lakes. Rivers and streams that dance to their own rhythms through rich, fertile fields. It's the land we call home. And from it has flowed the bounty and goodness we bring to you, our neighbors and friends.
> (Land O' Lakes, 2000)

In addition, "The now famous Indian maiden was also created during the search for a brand name and trademark. Because the regions of Minnesota and Wisconsin were the legendary lands of Hiawatha and Minnehaha, the idea of an Indian Maiden took form" (Land O' Lakes, 2000). A painting was sent to the company of an Indian maiden facing the viewer, holding a butter carton with a background filled with lakes, pines, flowers, and grazing cows.

At the Land O' Lakes corporate website, the director of communications includes a statement about the maiden image, where he agrees that the logo, the "Indian Maiden," has powerful connotations (Land O' Lakes). Hardly changed since its introduction in the 1920s, he says that Land O' Lakes has built on the "symbolism of the purity of the products" (Burnham, 1992). The company "thought the Indian maiden would be a good image. She represents Hiawatha and the Land of Gitchygoomee and the names of Midwest towns and streets that have their roots in the American Indian population" (Burnham, 1992).

The signifier is thereby the product, be it butter, sour cream, or other Land O' Lakes products. The Indian woman on the package is associated with youth, innocence, nature, and purity. The result is the generic "Indian maiden." Subsequently, the qualities stereotypically associated with this beaded, buckskinned, doe-eyed young woman are transferred to the company's products. Green's "noble savage" image is extended to include the female stereotype.

Sue Bee Honey

The Sioux Honey Association, based in Sioux City, Iowa, is a cooperative of honey producers, yielding 40 million pounds of honey annually (Sioux Honey Association, 2000). Corporate communications describe a change of the product name in 1964 from Sioux Bee to Sue Bee, "to reflect the correct pronunciation of the name" (Sioux Honey Association, 2000). The brand name and image are reinforced on trucks (both real and toys), on the bottles and jars in which the honey is sold, and through collectibles such as coffee mugs and recipe books.

Sue Bee Honey also draws upon the child-of-nature imagery in an attempt to imbue qualities of purity into their products. If we were to view Sue Bee in her full form (as she is shown on many specialty items such as mugs, glasses, and jars) we would see that she is an Indian maiden on top, with braided hair and headband, and a bee below the waist. Changing the spelling of her name from "Sioux Bee" to "Sue

Bee" could be interpreted in a variety of ways—possibly simply as a matter of pronunciation, as the company asserts, or as an effort to draw attention away from the savage imagery stereotypically attributed to members of this tribe and more toward the little girlishness of the image. In this case, the product is honey, traditionally associated with trees and forests and natural places. This association works well with the girl–child Indian stereotype. By placing the girl bee on the package of honey, consumers can associate the innocence, purity, and naturalness attributed to Native American females with the quality of the product.

In the tradition of Pocahontas, both the Land O' Lakes and the Sue Bee maidens symbolize innocence, purity, and virginity—children of nature. The maiden image signifies a female "Indianness." She is childlike, as she happily offers up perhaps honey or butter (or herself) that "is as pure and healthy as she is" (Dotz & Morton, 1996, p. 11). The maiden's image is used to represent attempts to get back to nature, and the association is that this can be accomplished through the healthy, wholesome products of Land O' Lakes. Both images are encoded with socially constructed meanings about female Indian sexuality, purity, and nature.

Monitor Sugar Company

Founded in 1901, the Monitor Sugar Company processes approximately 4% of U.S. beet production into sugar (granulated, powdered, brown, and icing; Monitor Sugar Company, 2000). For 60 years, the company has been producing sugar from beets, relying on the image of an American Indian in full headdress to sell the sugar goods. The products are available on grocery store shelves and in bulk for institution, delivered by trucks with the Big Chief logo emblazoned on the sides.

So, who is this Chief said to represent? Is he a bona fide tribal leader or a composite Indian designed to communicate naturalistic characteristics associated with Indians with the sugar? Green's (1993) savage typology suggests that this individual is a combination of the noble savage (natural) and the bloodthirsty savage (ferocious). He is proud, noble, and natural and yet he is wearing a ceremonial headdress that communicates strength and stoicism.

Crazy Horse Malt Liquor

A 40-ounce beverage that is sold in approximately 40 states (Metz & Thee, 1994), Crazy Horse Malt Liquor is brewed by the Heilman Brewing Company of Brooklyn,

New York. Crazy Horse Malt Liquor employs the image of Tasunke Witko (Crazy Horse) on the label of its malt liquor. On the front of the bottle is an American Indian male wearing a headdress that appears to be an eagle feather bonnet, and there is a symbol representing a medicine wheel—both sacred images in Lakota and other Native cultures (Metz & Thee, 1994).

Image analysis shows that the sign is that of an actual Indian chief. Signified, however, are beliefs about Indians as warriors, westward expansion, how mighty the consumer might be by drinking this brand, and wildness of the American Western frontier.

This brand, perhaps more than any other, has come under public scrutiny because it is the image of a particular person. A revered forefather of the Oglala Sioux tribe of South Dakota, Crazy Horse died in 1877 (Blalock, 1992). The labels feature the prominent image of Chief Crazy Horse, who has long been the subject of stories, literature, and movies. Larger than life, he has played a role in American mythology.

Signifying Green's (1993) bloodthirsty savage image, Crazy Horse Malt Liquor makes use of American myths through image and association. Ironically, Crazy Horse objected to alcohol and warned his nation about the destructive effects of liquor (Specktor, 1995). As a sign, Crazy Horse represents a real symbol of early American life and westward expansionism. He was, according to the vice president of the Oglala Sioux Tribe, a "warrior, a spiritual leader, a traditional leader, a hero who has always been and is still revered by our people" (Hill, 1992; Metz & Thee, 1994, p. 50). This particular image brings together some interesting aspects of branding. Not only is the noble and bloodthirsty savage stereotype brought together in a proud, but ultimately defeated, Indian chief, but also this is an image of a real human being. The association of alcohol with that image, as well as targeting the Indian population, draws on assumptions of alcohol abuse.[2]

Although there are dozens of possible examples of Native images on product labels, ranging from cigarette packages to sports utility vehicles, the examples discussed above illustrate the principles behind semiotics. The four presented here are significant examples of national brands employing stereotypical representations. When people are made aware of these products, they see how these images are consistently found in many products that employ Indian stereotypes either in product names or in their logos.

Many of these signs and symbols have been with us so long we no longer question them. Product images on packages, in advertisements, on television, and in films are nearly the only images non-Indians ever see of Native Americans. The covers of romance novels routinely feature Indian men sweeping beautiful non-Indian women off their feet as their bodices are torn away. These stereotypical representations of American Indians denies that they are human beings, and presents them as existing only in the past and as single, monolithic Indians (Merskin, 1998).

American Indians are certainly not the only racial or ethnic group to be discriminated against, overtly or covertly. Aunt Jemima and Rastus certainly have their origins in dehumanizing, one-dimensional images based on a tragic past. Yet, like Betty Crocker, these images have been updated. Aunt Jemima has lost weight and the bandana, and the Frito Bandito has disappeared (Burnham, 1992). But the Indian image persists in corporate marketing and product labeling.

These are highly visible and perhaps more openly discussed than images that appear on the products we see in grocery store aisles. An Absolut Vodka ad shows an Eskimo pulling a sled of vodka and a GreyOwl Wild Rice package features an Indian with braids, wearing a single feather, surrounded by a circle that represents (according to GreyOwl's distribution manager) the "oneness of nature" (Burnham, 1992). A partial list of others includes Apache helicopter, Jeep Cherokee, Apache rib doormats, Red Man Tobacco, Kleek-O the Eskimo (Cliquot Club ginger ale), Dodge Dakota, Pontiac, the Cleveland Indians, Mutual of Omaha, Calumet Baking Powder, Mohawk Carpet Mills, American Spirit cigarettes, Eskimo pies, Tomahawk mulcher, Winnebago Motor Homes, Indian Motorcycles, Tomahawk missiles, many high school sports teams, and the music behind the Hamm's beer commercials that begins "From the land of sky blue waters." And the list goes on.

Change is coming, but it is slow. For one thing, American Indians do not represent a significant target audience to advertisers. Representing less than 1% of the population, and the most economically destitute of all ethnic minority populations, American Indians are not particularly useful to marketers. Nearly 30% live below the official poverty line, in contrast with 13% of the general U.S. population (Cortese, 1999, p. 117). Without the population numbers or legal resources, it is nearly impossible for the voices of Natives to be heard, unlike other groups who have made some representational inroads. According to Westerman (1989), when minority groups speak, businesses are beginning to listen: "That's why Li'l Black Sambo and the Frito Bandito are dead. They were killed by the very ethnic groups they portrayed" (p. 28).

Not only does stereotyping communicate inaccurate beliefs about Natives to Whites, but also to Indians. Children, all children, are perhaps the most important recipients of this information for it is during childhood that difference is first learned. If, during the transition of adolescence, Native children internalize these representations that suggest that Indians are lazy, alcoholic by nature, and violent, this misinformation can have a life-long impact on perceptions of self and others. As Lippmann (1922/1961) wrote,

> The subtlest and most pervasive of all influences are those which create and maintain the repertory of stereotypes. We are told about the world before we see it. We imagine most things before we experience them. (p. 89)

By playing a game of substitution, by inserting other ethnic groups or races into the same situation, it becomes clear that there is a problem. Stereotypical images do not reside only in the past, because the social control mechanisms that helped to create them remain with us today.

Future research should continue to examine how the advertising and marketing practice of branding contributes to the persistent use of racist images on product labels. This study adds to the sparse literature on media representations of Native Americans in general and adds to Green's (1993) typology by including female counterparts to the male savage stereotypes. Future research could explore more images of Native Americans in ads and on products. Qualitative research with members of different tribes would add depth to this area of study.

Seeing the Big Picture   **The Tomahawk Chop: Racism in Image and Action**

Look though the Appendix and notice the relative quality-of-life measures of American Indians. What is the link between this group's socioeconomic standing and the way they are portrayed in the media?

---

39   Sport in America: The New Racial Stereotypes
Richard E. Lapchick

RICHARD E. LAPCHICK is the DeVos Eminent Scholar Chair and director of the Business Sports Management graduate program in the College of Business Administration at the University of Central Florida.

Questions to Consider   Richard Lapchick asks why athletes are subject to such an intense level of scrutiny by the press. What argument does he make that links race, stereotypes, and celebrity culture to the attitudes most Americans have about student and professional athletes?

Athletes and Crime

The beginning of the twenty-first century brought the hope that many social injustices would be rectified.

However, surveys taken throughout the 1990s indicated that many inaccurate perceptions persisted such as the majority of whites surveyed continuing to believe that most African-Americans are less intelligent, more prone to drug use, more violent, and more inclined towards violence against women than whites are.

Sport culture, as it is currently interpreted, now provides whites with the chance to talk about athletes in a way that reinforces these stereotypes of African-Americans. Because African-Americans dominate the most popular sports, whites tend to "think black" when they think about the major sports.

Each time any athlete gets into trouble, I receive many calls from writers and television producers seeking comments. After a fight involving a basketball or football player, the interrogation invariably includes, "What makes football or basketball players more inclined to get into fights?" I have never been asked this question of a hockey or baseball player, despite the fact that there are as many game fights in those sports.

After a reported incident of domestic violence involving a basketball or football player, the inevitable question is, "What makes football or basketball players more inclined to abuse women?" Equal numbers of hockey and baseball players are accused of domestic violence, yet I have never been asked this question about them.

Each year during the professional drafts in each sport I am asked, "What do you think about colleges and even high school football and basketball players jumping to the pros and missing their chance for an education?" I have never been asked that question about baseball or hockey, tennis or golf players who put higher education on hold to pursue athletic careers.

Shawn Fanning left Northeastern University early to turn pro and earn millions; he was called a genius for founding Napster. The Dean of Northeastern University's School of Engineering told me that one of his biggest problems comes from companies attempting to lure away his top students each year. They leave for the money.

I believe that at least part of the systematic coupling of athletes and crime revolves around racial stereotyping. The media have persistently and consistently suggested that basketball and football players, who happen to be overwhelmingly African-American, are more violent than athletes in other sports and people in society in general. The result is that nearly everyone, including the police, women, fans,

the media, sports administrators, and athletes themselves, believes that certain athletes, especially basketball or football players, are more inclined to be violent in general and violent against women in particular.

Rosalyn Dunlap, an African-American who was a five-time All American sprinter who now works on social issues involving athletes, including gender violence prevention, said, "perpetrators are not limited to any category or occupation. The difference is that athletes who rape or batter will end up on television or in the newspapers. Such images of athletes in trouble create a false and dangerous mindset with heavy racial overtones. Most other perpetrators will be known only to the victims, their families, the police, and the courts."

Once, while speaking to a group of distinguished international fellows at an elite academic institution, I asked members of the audience to write down five words that they would use to describe American athletes. In addition to listing positive adjectives, not one missed including one of the following words: dumb, violent, rapist or drug-user. I regularly meet with NBA and NFL players, as well as with college student-athletes on dozens of campuses. There are a lot of angry athletes who are convinced the public is stereotyping them because of the criminal acts of a few.

Many American men have grown to dislike athletes. A typical man might crave the money and the fame that a pro athlete enjoys, but he recognizes that such athletic success is unattainable for him. After reading all the negative press about athletes, he doesn't want to read that Mike Tyson felt he was treated unfairly by the justice system, knowing full well that Tyson made a reported hundred million dollars in his post-release rehabilitation program. He has little sympathy for the large number of pro athletes signing contracts worth more than ten million dollars a year. He is a micro-thought away from making egregious stereotypes about the "other groups" perceived as stealing his part of the American pie.

Big-time athletes fit the "other groups" category. Whether it is an African-American athlete or coach, or a white coach of African-American athletes, when something goes wrong with a player, a national reaction is likely to be immediate. Tom "Satch" Sanders, who helped the Boston Celtics win eight world championships, is now vice president for player programs for the NBA. His office encourages and guides players to finish their education, prepare for careers after basketball, and adjust to all the attention that NBA stars attract. Sanders presents a view complementary to Dunlap's. He proposes that the public has made a link between the stereotypes for athletes and African-Americans: "Everyone feels that athletes have to take the good with the bad, the glory with the negative publicity. However, no one appreciates the broad-brush application that is applied in so many instances. Of the few thousand that play sports on the highest level, if four or five individuals in each sport—particularly if they are black—have problems with the law, people won't have long to wait before some media people are talking about all those athletes."

APBnews.com released two revealing studies in 2000. The first was a study of NFL players on two teams that made it to the 2000 Super Bowl. The second was a study of the sixteen NBA teams in the 2000 playoffs. In the NFL study, 11 percent of the players had a criminal history. That stood in dramatic contrast to the 35 to 46 percent lifetime arrest rate (taken from extensive studies in California and New York) for adult males under thirty, the same age group as most NFL players. Most NFL players are between 18 and 30 years old although most of those are between the ages of 21 and 30. In the study of NBA players, the arrest rate of those on the sixteen playoff teams was 18 percent, again a fraction of the national figures for their comparable age group of males.

Jeff Benedict's book *Pros and Cons* created a sensation in 1998 by saying that 21 percent of NFL players had arrest records. In an article he coauthored in 1999 for the statistics journal *Chance,* he said that the lifetime arrest rates for the NFL players he documented in *Pros and Cons* was less than half the arrest rate in the general population.

Fans build stereotypes of athletes from media coverage of the athletes and the games. Fans, who are mostly white, observe sport through a media filter that is created by an overwhelming number of white men. There are 1,600 daily newspapers in America employing only nineteen African-American sports columnists. There are only two African-American sports editors who work on newspapers in a city that has professional sports franchises. The fact that the number of sports columnists, as reported in the 2000 conference of the National Association of Black Journalists, has almost doubled from 11 since 1998 is a positive sign. However, there are no African-American sports writers on 90 percent of the 1,600 daily newspapers.

I am not suggesting, nor would I ever suggest, that most or even many of the white news writers are racist. However, they were raised in a culture in which many white people have strong beliefs about what it means to be African-American. The obvious result is that their reporting provides reinforcement of white stereotypes of African-American athletes. According to the National Opinion Research Center Survey, sponsored by the National Science Foundation for the University of Chicago, whites surveyed share the following attitudes:

- Fifty-six percent of whites think African-Americans are more violent.
- Sixty-two percent of whites think African-Americans do not work as hard as whites.
- Seventy-seven percent of whites think most African-Americans live off welfare.
- Fifty-three percent think African-Americans are less intelligent.

Some white writers may have picked up these stereotypes in their own upbringing. When they write about an individual African-American athlete or several African-American athletes who have a problem, it becomes easy to unconsciously leap to the conclusion that fits the stereotype. Sanders said, "Blacks in general have been stereotyped for having drugs in the community as well as for being more prone to violence, However, now more than ever before, young black athletes are more individualistic and they resist the 'broad brush.' They insist on being judged as individuals for everything." But even that resistance can't be misinterpreted by the public and by the writers as off-the-court trash talking.

The athletes of the twenty-first century come from a generation of despairing youth cut adrift from the American dream. When the Center for the Study of Sport in Society started in 1984, one of its primary missions was to help young people balance academics and athletics. Since 1990, its mission has been extended to help young people lead healthy and safe lives.

Today our colleges are recruiting athletes:

- who have witnessed violent death. If an American child under the age of sixteen is killed every two hours with a handgun, then there is a good chance that young athletes will have a fallen family member or friend.
- who are mothers and fathers when they arrive at our schools. There are boys who helped 900,000 teenage girls get pregnant each year. Some student-athletes will leave after four years of college with one or more children who are four or five years old.

- who have seen friends or family members devastated by drugs.

- who have seen battering in their homes. An estimated 3 percent of American men are batterers and an estimated 3 million women are battered each year.

- who were victims of racism in school. Seventy-five percent of all students surveyed by Lou Harris reported seeing or hearing about racially or religiously motivated confrontations with overtones of violence very or somewhat often.

- who grew up as latchkey kids. Either a single parent or two working parents head 57 percent of American families, black and white alike.

Not enough campuses or athletic departments have the right people to help guide these young men and women into their adult lives. College campuses desperately need professionals that can deal with these nightmarish factors.

Academic Issues in College Sport

The amount of media coverage devoted to student-athlete literacy problems seem unique to athletes. The media rarely report that 30 percent of *all* entering freshmen must take remedial English or mathematics. The same holds true for the media's portrayal of student-athlete graduation rates. Although college athletic departments should strive to increase the number of student-athletes who graduate, graduation rates for the student body as a whole have changed. Only 14 percent of entering freshmen graduated in four years. If an athlete does not graduate in four years, some call him dumb; others say the school failed him. Few note that he may be typical of college students.

Don McPherson nearly led Syracuse University to a national championship when he was their quarterback in the 1980s. After seven years in the NFL and CFL, McPherson worked until 1999 directing the Mentors in Violence Prevention (MVP) Program, the nation's largest program using athletes as leaders to address the issue of men's violence against women.

McPherson reflected on the image that associates athletes with a lack of intelligence: "When whites meet an uneducated black athlete who blew opportunities in college or high school, they think he is dumb. They don't question what kind of school he may have had to attend if he was poor, or how time pressures from sport may have affected him. If they don't make it as a pro athlete, they're through without

a miracle. I met lots of 'Trust Fund Babies' at Syracuse. They blew opportunities. No one called them dumb, just rich. We knew they would not need a miracle to get a second chance. I played at Syracuse at a time when being a black quarterback had become more acceptable. But the stereotypes still remained. As a player, people still remember me as a great runner and scrambler. I had not dented their image of the physical vs. intelligent black athlete."

McPherson led the nation in passing efficiency over Troy Aikman and won many awards, including the Maxwell Award, but he was most proud of being the quarterback with the highest passing efficiency rating in the nation. "I should have shattered the image of the athletic and mobile black quarterback and replaced it with the intelligent black quarterback. Unfortunately, stereotypes of football players, mostly black, still prevail. They make me as angry as all the stereotypes of black people in general when I was growing up."

McPherson wore a suit to class and carried the *New York Times* under his arm. But McPherson said that those whites that recognize his style were "surprised and said I was 'a good black man,' as if I were different from other black men. Most students assumed I was poor and that football was going to make me rich. Like many other blacks on campus, I was middle class. My father was a detective and my mother was a nurse."

Irrespective of color or gender, student-athletes graduate at higher rate than non-student-athletes, yet it is difficult to get accurate reporting of this in the press. According to the NCAA's 1999 report:

- Fifty-eight percent of white male Division I student-athletes graduated vs. 57 percent of white male non-athletes. Forty-two percent of African-American male Division I student-athletes graduated vs. 33 percent of African-American male nonathletes.

- Seventy-one percent of white female Division I student-athletes graduated compared to 61 percent of white female nonathletes. Fifty-seven percent of African-American female Division I student-athletes graduated vs. only 43 percent of African-American female nonathletes.

Some disparities do appear when we compare white student-athletes to African-American student-athletes:

- Fifty-three percent of white male Division I basketball student-athletes graduated versus 37 percent of African-American male Division I basketball student athletes.

- Seventy percent of white female Division I basketball student-athletes graduated compared to only 56 percent of African-American female Division I basketball student-athletes.

College sport does not own problems of illiteracy and low graduation rates. They belong to higher education in general and its inheritance of the near bankruptcy of secondary education in some communities.

The publication of graduation rates, long feared by athletic administrators, reveals scandalous rates, but it also shows poor graduation rates specifically for students of color. The predominantly white campuses of most colleges and universities are not welcoming environments for people of color. African-American student-athletes arrive on most campuses and see that only 10 percent of the student body, 3 percent of the faculty, and less than 5 percent of top athletics administrators and coaches look like them. Unless there is a Martin Luther King Center or Boulevard, all of the buildings and streets are named after white people.

In many ways, the publication of graduation rates for student-athletes helped push the issue of diversity to the forefront of campus-wide discussions of issues of race, ethnicity, and gender. Educators finally recognized how they were failing students of color by not creating a conducive, welcoming educational environment.

Drugs and Alcohol Use Among Athletes

A common stereotype depicts athletes as abusing drugs and alcohol. Some athletes do use drugs. CNN Headline news broadcasts stories about famous athletes caught with drugs. Repeated exposure to such reports inflates the size of the problem, but the facts do not reveal widespread abuse among athletes at the professional, college, or even high school level.

According to an extensive 1995 *Los Angeles Times* survey of athletes and the crimes they committed, a total of twenty-two professional and college athletes and three coaches were accused of drug use or a drug-related crime that year. On average, the media reported a story about a new sports figure with a drug problem every two weeks. Center estimates now put the number of sports figures accused of drug-related crimes at fifty per year or one media story per week on average.

Stories about athletes accused of drug use or drug-related crime are and should be disturbing. But those stories are rarely, if ever, put in the context of the

1.9 million Americans who use cocaine each month or the 12.1 million who use heroin throughout their lives. A total of 13 million individuals (6 percent of the American population) use some illicit drug each month, and 17 percent of men in the eighteen-to-twenty-five age group are drug users. Whether it is twenty-two or fifty, athletes who use drugs make up a small fraction of a single percent of the more than 400,000 athletes who play college and professional sports in America.

The NBA's drug policy, which leaves open the possibility of a lifetime ban for any athlete who is caught using drugs, is generally recognized as a model for the sports world. The policy may have stopped a substance abuse problem that predated its inception. According to an APBnews.com report, *Crime in the NBA,* released in June 2000, forty-one players were charged, booked, or arrested in eighty-two instances of crimes more serious than traffic tickets over the course of their time on the rosters of the sixteen NBA playoff teams. The story noted that "it is perhaps a credit to the NBA's antidrug policy that none of the eighty-two incidents noted in the APBnews.com study were related to hard drugs." (Marijuana was cited in six cases.) The forty-one players put the NBA's arrest rate at 18 percent. APB News.com reported that, "By way of comparison, the lifetime arrest rate of the general population as measured in four different studies ranges from 31 to 50 percent."

On the subject of alcohol abuse, the same 1995 *Los Angeles Times* survey of athletes and the crimes they committed, reported that twenty-eight college and professional athletes and four coaches were charged with alcohol-related infractions. None of these thirty-two cases were put in the context of the 13 million Americans who engage in binge drinking at least five times per month. Yet we read about a new athlete with an alcohol problem every eleven days. Such images can fuel an exaggerated sense of crisis in athletics when they are not viewed in full social context.

McPherson remembered being "shocked" when he arrived on Syracuse's campus at how much drinking went on each night among the student body. He felt compelled to call football players he knew on other campuses. "It was the same everywhere. Now when I go to speak on college campuses I always ask. It is worse today. Athletes are part of that culture, but insist that practice and academics crowd their schedules too much to be in bars as often as other students." Student personnel administrators on college campuses acknowledge that abusive drinking is the number one issue on college campuses today.

Athletes and Violence

Media coverage of professional, college, and even high school athletes consistently implies that the violence of sport makes its participants more violent in society.

Are sports any more violent today than they were twenty years ago when no one would have made such an assertion? I don't think so. But the streets and schools across America surely are more violent than they were twenty years ago—there are 2,000 assaults in schools across the nation every hour of every day. The number of American children killed by guns in the 1900s has exceeded the total number of soldiers who died in the Vietnam War. Gun violence obeys no boundaries of race, class, or geography. School shootings occurred in Pearl (Mississippi), Paduka (Kentucky), Jonesboro (Arkansas), and Littleton (Colorado). Violence seems part of the school day.

If one were to put together a lowlights tape of the fights in sports that the public best remembers, I guarantee that most people would list Kermit Washington hitting Rudy Tomjanovich, Latrell Sprewell choking P. J. Carlesimo, and Roberto Alomar spitting at umpire John Hirschbeck. Fear of men of color attacking whites in our society is part of the culture. There is no doubt that the treatment afforded to Washington, Sprewell, and Alomar was measurably different than that given Denver Bronco Bill Romanowski, who is white, after he spit in the face of a black player in 1999.

Most of the stories written about specific athletes who are violent or gender violent are about African-American athletes. Stories about them that appear without appropriate filters of what is going on in society reinforce racial stereotyping.

Athletes and Gender Violence

In the wake of the O. J. Simpson case, any incident involving an athlete assaulting a woman has received extraordinary publicity. The individual cases add up to another stereotype of the new millennium: athletes, especially basketball and football players, are more inclined to be violent towards women than nonathletes are.

Joyce Williams-Mitchell has worked extensively in this field, most recently as the executive director of the Massachusetts Coalition of Battered Women's Service Groups. As an African-American woman, she abhors the image of athletes being more prone to violence against women. "It is a myth. The facts do not bear this out. All the studies of patterns of batterers defined by occupation point to men who control women through their profession. We hear about police, clergy, dentists, and judges. I only hear about athletes as batterers when I read the paper. They are in the public's eye. Men from every profession have the potential to be batterers."

There have been, of course, too many cases of athletes committing assaults on girls and women. As I wrote this section, I received a voice mail message from a reporter: "Have you heard that Corey Dillon is the latest case of an athlete hitting a woman? I guess that depends on when you pick up the message. There may have already been another case!" His message implied that attacks on women by athletes took place hourly.

However, there has never been a thorough, scientific study conclusively showing that athletes are more inclined to violence. Jeffrey Benedict, Todd Crossett, and Mark McDonald wrote the only study that comes close. It was based on sixty-five cases of assault against women that took place on ten Division I campuses over a three year period. Thirteen of the cases involved athletes; seven of the athletes were basketball or football players.

Despite the authors' acknowledgment of both the small number of cases revealed and the fact that the survey did not control for alcohol and tobacco use or the man's attitude toward women (then three main predictors of a male's inclination to gender violence), the press regularly quoted their study without qualification. Media reports never stated that the study came up with only thirteen abusive athletes over three years. They simply said that the study concluded that student-athletes, in particular basketball or football players, committed nearly 20 percent of all campus assaults. Rosalyn Dunlap pointed out that, "This is a racially loaded conclusion. When I was a student-athlete at the University of Missouri, I never thought of keeping myself safe from a 260-pound football player any more than any other man on the street. In fact, male athletes on campus protected me."

The following is a list of data usually missing in the debate about athletes and violence against women.

- In 1994, 1,400 men killed their significant others. In that year, O. J. Simpson was the only athlete accused of murder.

- In 1998, an estimated 3 million women were battered and close to one million were raped. According to various reports in the press in the five years between 1995 and 2000, between seventy and one hundred athletes and coaches were accused of assault against a woman each year.

- The 1999 *Chronicle of Higher Education*'s annual campus crime survey showed that there were a total of 1,053 forcible sex offenses reported in 1997. Fewer than thirty-five student-athletes were arrested in conjunction with these crimes.

Gender violence is a serious problem among American men. The cost of crime to America is pegged at $500 billion per year, according to a National Institute for Justice research report for the Justice Department released in March 1996. Gender assault and child abuse accounted for $165 billion—more than one third of that total.

Rosalyn Dunlap, who worked with The National Consortium for Academics and Sport to create more awareness about the issue, said, "There are no men who should be exempted from being educated about the issue of gender violence although many believe they are. It is a problem for naval commanders, daycare providers, fraternities, guys in a bar, in corporations, in halls of higher education and, yes, on athletic teams. But no more so on athletic teams."

There have been numerous cases in which women brought suits against corporations from harassment and/or assault. The *Boston Globe* gave extensive coverage in the late 1990s to the case against Astra USA, Inc., a chemical company, where women lodged sixteen formal complaints for incidents ranging from sexual harassment to rape. Twenty-nine women brought suit against Mitsubishi for the same reasons. None of the press about Astra suggested that working in a chemical company produced a climate of sexual aggression. At Mitsubishi, no one suggested any relationship between the manufacturing process and gender assault. So why do stories about athletes imply such a linkage to athletics? Does it fit white America's racial imagery?

McPherson believes it does: "Football and basketball mean black. When the public talks about gender violence and athletes, it talks black. No one discusses the problems of golfer John Dailey or Braves manager Bobby Cox. Warren Moon was another story altogether. Problems about athletes hit the papers and people think they detect a pattern because of the seeming frequency. But no one else's problems get in the papers. How do we make legitimate comparisons? With Astra and Mitsubishi, we look at the corporate climate and don't generalize about individuals. But with athletes, especially black athletes, we look at players and look for patterns to add up."

Some observers say athletes are trained to be violent and that we can expect that training to carry over into their homes. If this is true, then what about the training in lethal force we give the police, the Army, the Air Force, the Navy, and the Marines? Will these men also come home and kill? McPherson adds, "There is no logic to connect these cases, but we do fit our stereotypes of African-Americans with such images when we carry through the implication for athletes."

With all the recent publicity about the horrors of gender violence, it would be easy to forget that it was America's big, dirty secret until the O. J. Simpson case made it a notorious subject. Before that trial, few Americans were willing to talk about gender violence. The same unwillingness to confront racism diminishes society's ability to eradicate it. But the situation will never change if it remains unconfronted.

Athletes should take a leadership role on this issue, just as they have on drug abuse and educational opportunity. The MVP Program, organized in 1992 by Northeastern University's Center for the Study of Sport in Society and now headed by Jeff O'Brien, a former football player, has worked on more than sixty-five campuses training male and female athletes to be spokespeople on the issue of gender violence. Each of those schools has become proactive on an issue that has hurt so many women and their families.

Don McPherson insists that "we have to do more to help our youth survive by including our athletes rather than excluding them in helping our youth. The stereotyping of our athletes does not help. We need to be ready with facts to dispute the easy labels."

McPherson and Tom Sanders both argue vigorously that America's athletes not only don't fit the emerging stereotypes about athletes and crime, but the vast majority of professional athletes are extremely positive role models. Sanders said, "when I look at the many NBA players who have their own foundations and who are very involved with giving back to the communities where they play and where they came from, I know they are hurt by the stereotypes." McPherson asserts that "most of the players in the NFL are deeply religious, family-centered men who are constantly giving back to their communities with time and money."

Rosalyn Dunlap wonders when the public and the media will stop being cynical about athletes. "I hear so many people say that if athletes do something in the community that they do it for publicity. Why can't we accept that athletes want to help? Sport and those who play it can help educate us and sensitize us. While we can't ignore the bad news, we should also focus on the overwhelming good news of what athletes do to make this a better world."

I do not believe the stereotypes. However, I do believe the high profile of all professional sports makes it incumbent on those involved to call on sports institutions to demand a higher standard for athletes. Athletes, once challenged, have played a leading role in the battle to educate our children; in the life and death fight against alcohol and drug abuse; and in the attempt to resolve conflicts with reason and not with fists or weapons. Now it is time to challenge them to fight the long overdue battle against gender violence.

The challenge to athletes involved a starting point of confronting the behavior of an individual athlete. Some universities had to make star athletes academically ineligible or expel them from school to convince others that they were serious about education and would not tolerate either poor academic records or athletes violating social norms.

After the tragic death of Len Bias, the nation was forced to recognize that cocaine was not "recreational," but lethal. Schools began random drug testing; the NBA promised to uphold a lifetime ban for players who ignored league drug policies. This ban was necessary to show players as well as their young fans that there could be no tolerance for the use of life-threatening drugs.

The ban will always seem unfair to the player caught with drugs. I am sure Michael Ray Richardson, who was the first NBA player banned for life, still looks in the mirror and asks, "Why me? There were other guys." But the discipline had to start somewhere. What was unfortunate for Richardson was fortunate for the NBA and for society. Action, no matter how symbolic, was critical.

Likewise, when street violence began to invade our rinks, courts, and fields, sport had to take a stand with automatic and serious sanctions that cost players money and cost teams their playing services. No commissioner or director of a players association wanted their entire league and all of its athletes branded as thugs because of those who acted out during the game.

The New England Patriots bit the bullet for all professional sports and decided not to sign draftee Christian Peter, the University of Nebraska's highly acclaimed football player, who carried numerous criminal charges on his record. It was a milestone decision. Patriot owner Robert Kraft felt compelled to take a strong stand immediately after they drafted Peter, despite the fact that he would lose dollars in the draft and could have faced lawsuits from Peter's representatives. The importance of his decision was not only that players would see clear consequences for their actions, but also that children who idolize those players would also see such consequences as relevant to their own choices in life.

Sports figures are in a unique position to effect change. Keith Lee, a six-year NFL veteran who is now the chief operating officer of the National Consortium for Academics and Sport, works to improve race relations among young people. He states, "We need positive role models who can help young people to believe in what they cannot yet see. We need them now more than ever."

Seeing the Big Picture · Television's Interrracial Images: Some Fact, Mostly Fiction

Think for a moment of your three favorite television shows. Now think about watching your two favorite sports teams. Is your social world as integrated as the programming you watch on TV?

Part IV

HOW AMERICA'S COMPLEXION CHANGES

A NATIONALLY DISTRIBUTED, FULL-PAGE magazine advertisement placed by IBM depicts nine of its employees at a business meeting. The employees, presumably managers, are focusing on a white-haired man who is pointing to a chart. The activity depicted is rather mundane—meetings of this type take place thousands of times every business day. What makes this ad exceptional is what it is selling. In large letters across the top of the page, the text of the ad announces "Diversity Works." The employees shown in the hand-drawn advertisement consist, in order, of an older white woman, a black woman, an Asian woman, a white man, an older black man with white hair, two men of ambiguous racial identity, and a white woman in a wheelchair. The racial and ethnic makeup of the cartoon characters in this ad is intended to convey to readers that IBM, as the supporting text tells us, "values individual differences." What is particularly interesting is the lack of white men in this rendering of the inner workings of a large corporation.

IBM may indeed value diversity, but the reality is that the upper ranks of corporate management are still the domain of white men. The bipartisan Glass Ceiling Commission found that white men "hold about 95 of every 100 senior management positions, defined as vice president or above." How corporate America presents its workforce to the public and how diverse the organization actually is, especially as one moves up the occupational ranks, is a contradiction. Perhaps there is a reason this advertisement was a drawing and not an actual photograph of a diverse work environment. What occupations or organizations can you name in which high-status positions reflect the racial, ethnic, and gender composition of the United States? Think about the racial and ethnic composition of members of Congress, or the CEOs of the Fortune 500 companies, or the fifty state governors, or tenured college professors. What is the race and gender of your university or college president? What about the racial or ethnic background

of sports or entertainment celebrities? What patterns emerge, and what do they mean?

We are an incredibly diverse nation. We are reminded of this by advertisements promoting diversity from corporations like IBM, McDonald's, Texaco, Denny's, and Du Pont. We are reminded of this when we are repeatedly told that by the year 2050, about half of U.S. residents will be white and the other half will be black, Asian, and Latino. We are reminded of this when we debate the relative merits of affirmative action, bilingual education, or immigration quotas.

In the public imagination, the idea of ethnic and racial diversity seems to be simultaneously celebrated, feared, and reviled. The United States is promoted as the land of opportunity, but some groups have had more opportunity than others. Why? The United States is defined as a country of immigrants, yet many citizens are fearful that the "new wave" of immigrants will radically change "American" culture. Why? The United States is proclaimed as a color-blind nation, yet inequities based on race and ethnicity are still the norm for a sizable part of the population. If we are a color-blind nation, why is it very likely you will marry someone from the same racial background?

The readings in Part IV examine these contradictions. The four readings in the first section of Part IV, **Race, Ethnicity, and Immigration** focus on the changing complexion of the United States. Stephen Steinberg calls into question the assertion that the United States is a melting pot by pointing out that some groups have never been "melted" into the stew because they were not allowed in the pot.

John Logan documents the rise of black immigrants from Africa and the Caribbean and the unique immigration experiences of these groups. This exceptionally diverse group often gets "lumped" by the media with African Americans or Latinos, but Logan demonstrates that such groupings would be a mistake.

Michael Suleiman examines a community that until very recently received very little attention from the mainstream media. Suleiman describes the ebb and flow of Arab immigrants to the United States and their socioeconomic success relative to other immigrant groups. Mary Waters examines mobility and racial identity construction to explore how race, ethnicity, and opportunity shape the experiences of Afro-Caribbeans in New York City.

The second section, **Race and Romance: Blurring Boundaries,** explores historical and contemporary trends in interracial marriage. Roland Fryer examines both historical trends and current patterns in interracial marriage. His research suggests that falling in love, even across the color line, reflects patterns that privilege one racial minority over another.

Law Professor Randall Kennedy uses popular representations of interracial couples in the media to examine just how much progress we have made in the area of interracial romance. Heather Dalmage explains how and why "racial borders" are patrolled in order to promote racial endogamy.

Kimberly McClain DaCosta examines how the color line is being redrawn within the context of the rise of multiracial families and individuals who define themselves as occupying more than one racial identity.

Finally, in **Living with Less Racism: Strategies for Individual Action,** Meizhu Lui and colleagues propose public policy measures that would start to address racial disparities, and Charles Gallagher suggests ten things we can do to ameliorate racism as we go about our day. ✳

40 The Melting Pot and the Color Line

Stephen Steinberg

STEPHEN STEINBERG is the assistant chair of day studies and a sociologist in the Urban Studies Department at Queens College.

EVERY NATION, UPON EXAMINATION, TURNS out to have been a more or less successful melting pot." So wrote Robert Park, the founder of the famed Chicago School of Sociology, in 1930. It is a testament to Park's prescience that he was able to imagine the melting pot at a time when the United States was ethnically more diverse, and more fragmented, than ever before. During the previous half-century, the nation had absorbed some 24 million immigrants, mostly from Eastern and Southern Europe. These "new immigrants"—Italians, Poles, Russian Jews, Ukrainians, Hungarians and others, far removed geographically and culturally from the people who settled the United States during its first century—were widely believed to be "unassimilable." In Chicago, for example, 70 percent of the population consisted of immigrants and the children of immigrants, and the city was divided into a patchwork of ethnic neighborhoods. In 1921 and 1924, Congress responded with legislation that cut the volume of immigration and instituted national quotas biased against further immigration from Southern and Eastern Europe.

Against this background, Park's dictum provided reassurance that the intermingling of peoples was a universal process and that America's ethnic discord would resolve itself over time. This optimism was shared by Chicago sociologists W. Lloyd Warner and Leo Srole, who conducted field studies of immigrant communities in the 1940s. Warner and Srole argued that appearances were

Questions to Consider

According to the theory of the melting pot, diverse ethnic and racial groups will be thrown together and meld into a new American amalgam that represents the finest cultural aspects of each community. Food is perhaps the easiest way to understand the melting pot perspective. Salsa, not ketchup, is now the number one condiment. There are almost 64,000 pizzerias, almost 7,000 Taco Bells, and 30,000 Asian restaurants in the United States, according to experts in the food industry. But as sociologist Stephen Steinberg argues, not everyone has been allowed into the pot. He suggests "America's melting pot has been inclusive of everybody but blacks." Is his statement about black exclusion from the melting pot justified when we consider African American contributions to popular culture?

deceptive, that the ethnic enclave, though it seemed to nurture isolation and separatism, actually functioned as a decompression chamber, helping immigrants adjust to their new surroundings and preparing the next generation to venture into the mainstream. Whatever its original raison d'etre, the ethnic community actually functioned as an instrument of assimilation.

But if early sociologists were confident about assimilation, a later generation rejected the idea of the melting pot. Ironically, many of these scholars were themselves children of immigrants who have risen to the top of the academic ladder. Their revisionist view of the melting pot can be seen as part of a broader trend among second-generation immigrants: assimilation breeds nostalgia. First-generation immigrants, who are most authentically steeped in ethnic culture, tend to throw it away, often with both hands, as they pursue the opportunities that led them to come to America in the first place. Decades later, their largely assimilated children engage in desperate, but usually futile, efforts to recover the very culture that their parents relinquished. As the children of immigrants entered the ranks of social science, they brought this same nostalgia to their analysis of ethnic trends.

The turning point came with the publication of *Beyond the Melting Pot* in 1970. Scholars Nathan Glazer and Daniel Patrick Moynihan, who had each ascended from immigrant poverty to the ivory tower, concluded from their study of New York City that "the most important thing about the melting pot was that it did not happen." The syntax of this much-quoted passage warrants a moment's reflection. To say that the melting pot "did not happen" is not the same as saying that it was not happening. After all, Park and other theorists of assimilation never claimed that the melting pot was a fait accompli; nor did they project a deadline for the completion of this evolutionary process. Nevertheless, the book's title and argument found a receptive audience. Aside from selling over half a million copies, *Beyond the Melting Pot* marked the beginning of a paradigm shift in the study of ethnicity.

Other books soon appeared that trumpeted the survival of ethnicity over the sinister forces of assimilation. Their titles celebrated *The Decline of the WASP* (1971) and *The Rise of the Unmeltable Ethnics* (1971). A year later, an article in the *New York Times Magazine* proclaimed, "America Is NOT a Melting Pot." Indeed, these writers contended that the United States was undergoing an "ethnic revival" that would resuscitate immigrant cultures. Again, there is a striking historical irony. When ethnic groups were intact and cultural differences pronounced, leading sociologists held that assimilation was inevitable. Several decades later, when these groups had undergone profound transformation, forsaking major elements of their ancestral cultures and assuming comfortable identities as Americans,

the prevailing view was that the melting pot had "never happened."

But such attempts to turn back the clock of assimilation would prove difficult. With the exception of Native Americans, ethnic groups in America are transplanted peoples, far removed in time and space from their original homelands. The necessity of adapting to life in America made assimilation, in Park's words, "progressive and irreversible." By the late 1970s, a number of scholars, myself among them, had begun to argue that the so-called ethnic revival was in fact a symptom of decline, a dying gasp of ethnic consciousness. In fact, all the long-term trends suggested that the melting pot was working as predicted: during the twentieth century, immigrants largely lost their original language and culture, ethnic enclaves dispersed as economic and occupational mobility increased, and the rate of ethnic and religious intermarriage accelerated.

It may be that some observers deny the evident fact of assimilation simply because of the ambiguous terminology that we use to describe it. "Melting pot" conjures up an image of a bubbling cauldron into which immigrants descend—whether they jump or are pushed is another matter—and are quickly dissolved into oblivion. Though rhetorically effective, this imagery obscures the evolutionary nature of assimilation. Correctly understood, it is a process that occurs incrementally across generations. To argue that ethnicity is still an active force in American life—as Glazer and Moynihan did in 1970 and other scholars have repeated ever since—is to beg the crucial question. Just because assimilation isn't complete doesn't mean that it isn't taking place.

How we view assimilation also depends on our conception of culture. Revisionists argue that the melting pot theory is based on a static view, in which the original culture of an immigrant's homeland is simply replaced by American culture. Such critics concede that Italian-Americans, for example, bear little resemblance to Italians in Italy, but they argue that Italian-Americans are nevertheless a distinct community, forged on American soil, complete with its own identity and subculture.

Yet melting pot theorists also realize that immigrant cultures evolve and take new forms as newcomers adapt to life in America. The crucial issue is not whether change occurs, but rather the direction and the end result of that change. The key question is this: will the ethnicity of formerly hyphenated Americans endure, or is it merely a transitional stage in a long-term assimilation? My position has long been that, even if we assume a greater tolerance for diversity than actually exists in American society, the conditions were never promising for a genuine and lasting pluralism.

• • •

Today there is an emerging consensus that the descendants of the great waves of European immigration have reached an advanced stage of assimilation. The most striking evidence is provided by the soaring rates of intermarriage across ethnic lines. According to a 1990 study by sociologist Richard Alba, the percentage of white ethnics aged twenty-five to thirty-four who married outside their own groups was as follows: Germans, 52 percent; Irish, 65 percent; English, 62 percent; Italians, 73 percent; French, 78 percent; Scots, 82 percent; Poles, 84 percent. Even in the case of Jews, for whom intermarriage was historically low, the figure is now thought to approach 50 percent. The conclusion seems inescapable that the melting pot, in the most literal sense, is a reality for groups of European ancestry.

Indeed, sociologists now lump these groups together under the rubric of "Euro-American," thus resolving with a single word the assimilation question that was debated for half a century. It is now conceded that the various nationalities of European descent have become simply "white." As a result, ethnic pluralists and opponents of the melting pot have retreated to a new position: the melting pot does exist, but it is "for whites only." On this view, the common "whiteness" of the Irish, Italians, Poles, Jews and other groups destined them to "melt," even though they were once regarded as distinct races whose cultural and genetic differences rendered them unassimilable. A new genre of "whiteness studies" has documented the process through which these erstwhile pariahs were incorporated into the white majority. The core argument is encapsulated in the titles of several recent books, including *How the Irish Became White, How Jews Became White Folks* and *Whiteness of a Different Color.*

But this argument goes on to hold that the current wave of immigrants, composed mainly of "people of color" from Asia, Latin America and the Caribbean, will not be able to follow in the footsteps of the white ethnics. The fault line dividing ethnic groups in America is no longer nationality or religion, but race. Indeed, a number of scholars have declared that "assimilation theory is dead," since its Eurocentric bias renders it useless for understanding the condition and destiny of people of color.

Aside from racism, the new ethnic pluralists cite several positive factors that, they argue, will spare the new immigrants from the dreaded melting pot. Today's immigrants enter a society that is far more tolerant of ethnic diversity. The ideology of multiculturalism extols ethnic difference and provides institutional mechanisms, such as bilingual education, for the preservation of immigrants' language and culture. As a result, the Asians, Latinos and Caribbeans who make up the new immigration have formed cohesive ethnic communities with flourishing economies and foreign-language media, including cable television, that provide institutional anchorage for language and culture. Furthermore, compared to earlier immigrants, the new immigrants have easy access to their homelands, thanks to telecommunications and cheap airfare. And finally, many new immigrants arrive with education and skills, and often capital as well, and therefore are not forced to compromise their ethnic identities for the sake of economic survival. Indeed, in today's global economy, it is not a handicap but an asset to be multilingual and multicultural.

These are all valid points. The question is whether they add up to the conclusion that assimilation is dead, and that the new immigrants will not "melt" as did their predecessors from Europe. It must be conceded that this is a possible scenario, given what we know about racism as a divisive force in America history. One cannot immediately discount the argument that the melting pot is "for whites only," and that today's immigrants will be prevented from assimilating.

In fact, however, this proposition receives little empirical support from the large body of research on today's immigrants. Indeed, the most compelling evidence leads to the conclusion that, notwithstanding their racial difference, the new immigrants are not only assimilating but are doing so at an even faster rate than did earlier immigrants from Europe.

In retrospect, an early indicator of the eventual assimilation of European immigrants was the rapidity with which they lost their native languages. A pattern emerges with stubborn consistency. Immigrants, of course, retained their native tongues; their children typically were bilingual; and by the third generation, the vast majority were monolingual in English. The virtual eradication of languages in only two generations shows just how fragile culture is, at least once it loses its "survival value" and is severed from the institutions that nourish it. Needless to say, immigrants and their bilingual children were not indifferent to the snuffing out of their native language. But the lesson of history is that sentiment—even passionate loyalty—is not enough to withstand the powerful forces of assimilation.

This process is being reenacted—if anything, at an accelerated pace—among the new immigrants. In a study of Los Angeles based on 1990 census data, David Lopez found that, among Asians, the shift to English monolingualism was nearly universal by the third generation. Consider what this means for family relations. Unless the immigrant grandparents acquire a basic fluency in English, which often is not the case, then grandchildren cannot converse with their grandparents except through the mediation of their bilingual parents.

The picture is somewhat more complex among Latinos, though the overall pattern is still one of rapid language loss. If retention of Spanish were to occur anywhere in the United States, it would be in Los Angeles. Not only do most L.A. Latinos live in predominantly Latino neighborhoods, but the city also has a thriving ethnic press and electronic media. Furthermore, Los Angeles has had an official policy of promoting multiculturalism, including bilingual education and bilingual ballots. Yet Lopez found that 57 percent of third-generation Latinos spoke only English at home. Closer examination of the data revealed that Spanish was retained mainly in households where a foreign-born person—presumably that all-important immigrant grandparent—was present. In the case of Mexican-American youth living in households with no immigrants, only 20 percent spoke Spanish at home.

A study of Cubans in South Florida also found that most young people preferred to speak English at home, even when they were bilingual. Nor was this true only of the middle classes. Among second-generation youth who classified themselves as working class or poor, three-quarters preferred to speak English. Clearly, even though today's society is nominally more conducive to language retention, the new immigrants are moving very rapidly to English monolingualism.

If loss of a native language marks the beginning of the assimilation process, marriage across ethnic lines represents the last (or next to last) stage. Here again, the data do not support either the assumptions or the hopes of the new ethnic pluralists. A study based on the 1990 census found that 40 percent of Asians born in the United States married non-Asians—and these are mostly the children,

not even the grandchildren, of immigrants. The figures ranged from 22 percent among Vietnamese to 31 percent among Japanese, 38 percent among Asian Indians, 46 percent among Chinese, 65 percent among Filipinos and 72 percent among Koreans. These figures are so high that they call into question the very category of race in describing Asian-Americans. Indeed, the level of marriage between Asians of different nationalities is strikingly low, suggesting that they do not see themselves as members of a pan-ethnic Asian "race." Rather, most Asians who intermarry do so with whites, giving rise to speculation that Asians are in the process of "becoming white."

Rates of intermarriage for Latinos are lower than for Asians, but they are high nevertheless. Almost one-third of U.S.-born Hispanics between the ages of twenty-five and thirty-four are married to non-Hispanic whites. Indeed, marriage across racial lines has become so commonplace that some commentators have raised the possibility of a "mestizo America"—a racial mixture that blurs the boundaries among ethnic groups. On this view, it is not a question of minorities being absorbed into the white majority, but rather of a fusing of these diverse peoples into a new amalgam. This is the literal meaning of a "melting pot," and a fulfillment of Robert Park's prescient observation that every nation is a "more or less successful melting pot." Like it or not, and the dissent of the ethnic pluralists is clear, assimilation does appear to be progressive and irreversible, the inexorable by-product of forces put into motion by the very act of immigrating.

•   •   •

Admittedly, this sweeping conclusion, while it captures the main thrust of American ethnic history, does not tell the whole story: in particular, it does not account for the African-American experience. Here we speak of a group that came to America in slave ships, not immigrant steamers. While successive waves of immigrants flowed into the country, first to settle the land and later to provide labor for burgeoning industries, blacks were trapped in the South in a system of feudal agriculture. Even in the North, a rigid color line excluded them from the manufacturing sector. In short, the Industrial Revolution was "for whites only," depriving blacks of the jobs and opportunities that delivered Europe's huddled masses from poverty.

This was the historic wrong that was supposed to be remedied by landmark civil rights legislation in the 1960s.

But by the time most blacks arrived in Northern cities, the manufacturing sector was undergoing a permanent decline, reflecting the impact of labor-saving technology and the export of jobs to low-wage countries. Not only did blacks encounter far less favorable opportunities than did immigrants, not only did they suffer from the economic consequences of past discrimination, and not only did they encounter pervasive racism in the world of work, but they also experienced intense labor competition from yet another huge wave of immigrants, which began in the 1960s and continues to this day.

Though these new immigrants are conspicuous for their "racial" difference, they are not subjected to the all-encompassing system of racial discrimination that was the legacy of slavery. Furthermore, many of these immigrants arrived with education and skills—and sometimes capital as well—that accelerated their mobility and social integration. As noted earlier, Asians and Latinos already display a far greater degree of "residential assimilation" than blacks. And at a time when marriage across racial lines is soaring for Asians and Latinos, it has inched up only slightly for blacks, again indicating that a fundamentally different dynamic is at work. The conclusion is unavoidable: America's melting pot has been inclusive of everybody but blacks.

This is not to deny the obvious fact that there has been enormous progress over the past half-century. Jim Crow is a thing of the past, thanks largely to the black protest movement. The emergence of a large black middle class is another encouraging development, though in my view this does not reflect the deracialization of labor markets so much as the favorable impact of affirmative action policy over several decades. Finally, there has been an unmistakable shift in America's fundamental attitudes toward race. The prominence of blacks among the nation's elites, as well as its pantheon of folk heroes, is stark proof that skin color is no longer a badge of inferiority.

Nevertheless, ours is still a society riven by race. Claims of "progress" invariably depend on comparing the situation today to a retrograde past. The problem here, as James Baldwin observed, is that the crimes of the past are used to gloss over the crimes of the present. When comparisons are made between blacks and whites today, a far less sanguine picture emerges. For example, blacks today earn only three-fifths as much as whites. Furthermore, although the income gap between blacks and whites closed

somewhat in the 1960s, there has been little or no progress since the mid-1970s. So long as nearly a quarter of blacks, and half of black youth, live below the poverty line, these class factors will continue to engender and reinforce racial division.

Even more germane to the question of whether America is a melting pot, black and white Americans are as residentially segregated as ever. Nor is this true only of inner-city blacks. Middle-class blacks also encounter pervasive discrimination in housing, and their arrival into white suburbs usually triggers white flight, resulting in resegregation. It is a mark of the melting pot's failure that African-Americans, whose roots go back to the founding of the nation, are more segregated than even recent immigrants from Asia and Latin America.

In short, despite "progress," ghettoization is still a fact of life. And here we confront a great historical paradox—for these ghettos, the enforced "home" of the nation's racial pariahs, also nourished a vibrant African-American subculture. As sociologist Bob Blauner has observed, while immigrant ghettos "functioned as way stations on the road to acculturation and assimilation," the black ghetto has been permanent, "a continuing crucible for ethnic development and building." And unlike immigrants, who clung to vestiges of cultures ripped from their moorings in distant places, black culture evolved out of the lived experience of black people in America. Instead of isolated fragments selected precisely because they did not interfere with mainstream American culture, black culture is an integral part of the everyday lives of black people. As a result, black culture displays a vitality and dynamism that is generally lacking among the ossifying cultures of the nation's immigrant groups.

Ironically, generations of sociologists have taken precisely the opposite position, on the one hand celebrating the cultures of the nation's immigrant groups and, on the other, holding that blacks were merely "white Americans in black skin," lacking a culture of their own. In the same book where they declared that the melting pot "never happened," Glazer and Moynihan wrote that "it is not possible for Negroes to view themselves as other ethnic groups viewed themselves because—and this is the key to much in the Negro world—the Negro is only an American and nothing else. He has no values and culture to guard and protect." Under a barrage of criticism, Glazer subsequently explained that he meant blacks had no *foreign* culture to guard or protect. However, this only compounds the error, since these foreign cultures—and precisely because they were foreign—were destined to a gradual but inexorable decline. On the other hand, as an indigenous product of the American experience, black culture continues not only to thrive in segregated black communities but also to exert a powerful influence on mainstream American culture.

•   •   •

Throughout this essay, I have emphasized that the melting pot is still at work and that, like past immigrants, today's immigrants from outside the Western Hemisphere will also be fully assimilated at some indeterminate point in the future. The problem, of course, is that we live in the present. It may be our national destiny to become a melting pot, but today the United States is a remarkably polyglot society in which ethnicity flourishes. Despite an overriding trend toward assimilation, ethnic loyalties and attachments remain strong even among segments of older immigrant groups. New immigrants, freshly arrived on American soil, are only at the early stages of the assimilation process. To turn a blind eye to these realities by focusing on long-term trends runs the risk of blotting out the lives and sensibilities of entire communities.

Nor does this warning apply only to ideologues on the political right who, in the name of the melting pot, have waged a relentless crusade against bilingualism, multicultural education and affirmative action. In recent years, a left discourse has emerged that looks "beyond race" and "beyond ethnicity," imagining a post-ethnic future where people are not defined by genes or ancestry. This vision promotes intermarriage across racial and ethnic lines as a way of eliminating, once and for all, the dissonances and conflicts attending racial and ethnic diversity.

For example, historian Gary Nash, a pioneer of multicultural education, has published an essay titled "The Hidden History of Mestizo America," in which he argues that we "need new ways of transcending America's Achilles' heel of race, now that a certain amount of progress has been achieved in living up to our own credo." Like Nash, sociologist Orlando Patterson advocates miscegenation as the ultimate solution to America's intractable race problem. Never mind that African-Americans—not to speak of other ethnic groups—may not wish to miscegenate themselves out of existence. Never mind that it would take generations, if not centuries, to produce the hybrid nation that they envision. Instead of confronting the urgent problems of race in America and addressing the challenges of a multicultural society, these visionaries are throwing in the towel. They use a utopian vision of the melting pot as a façade for moral capitulation.

Let me be clear. There is compelling evidence that the United States will one day become a melting pot, and that this day is approaching faster than ethnic pluralists are willing to acknowledge. From a moral standpoint, however, it is imperative that this melting pot evolve through the operation of historical forces rather than through public policy interventions. It is wrong—to continue the metaphor—to turn up the temperature under the melting pot, or to nudge, cajole or push people into the bubbling cauldron. Any use of state power to undermine ethnicity or to force assimilation is incompatible with democratic principles and violates the rights of ethnic minorities to hold onto their languages and cultures.

The irony of the matter is that, like earlier waves of immigrants, today's newcomers will find their way to the melting pot in due course. So, presumably, will African-Americans, but not until the structures of American apartheid are thoroughly dismantled and the persistent inequalities are resolved. These groups will pursue the personal and social integration that is the promise of the melting pot. But they must do so of their own accord, and not on somebody else's timetable. Here we can take another lesson from history: the carrot, not the stick, has always been the more effective instrument of assimilation.

Seeing the Big Picture   **Who Is Allowed to "Melt" in the Pot? Who Wants To?**
In Section X of the Appendix, do rates of intermarriage support the assertion that the United States is a melting pot? What does the popularity of hip-hop and rap say about the theory of the melting pot?

Who Are the Other African Americans? Contemporary African and Caribbean Immigrants in the United States

John R. Logan

JOHN R. LOGAN is professor of sociology at Brown University. Dr. Logan is co-author, along with Harvey Molotch, of *Urban Fortunes: The Political Economy of Place.* His most recent, edited book, *The New Chinese City: Globalization and Market Reform,* was published by Blackwell in 2001.

A S QUICKLY AS THE HISPANIC AND ASIAN populations in the United States have grown, there has been nearly equal growth among black Americans with recent roots in Africa and the Caribbean. The number of black Americans born in sub-Saharan Africa nearly tripled during the 1990s. The number identifying a Caribbean ancestry increased by over 60 percent. Census 2000 shows that Afro-Caribbeans in the United States number over 1.5 million—more than some more visible national-origin groups, such as Cubans and Koreans. Africans number over six hundred thousand. In some major metropolitan regions, these "new" black groups amount to 20 percent or more of the black population. And, nationally, nearly 25 percent of the growth of the black population between 1990 and 2000 was due to people arriving from Africa and the Caribbean.

This chapter summarizes what is known about these "new" black Americans: their numbers, social backgrounds, and residential locations in metropolitan areas. It makes the following key points:

- It is well known that the socioeconomic profile of non-Hispanic blacks is unfavorable compared to whites, and Asians. There is also striking variation within America's black population. The social and economic profile of Afro-Caribbeans and Africans is far above that of African Americans and even better than that of Hispanics.

- Afro-Caribbeans are heavily concentrated on the East Coast. Six out of ten live in the New York, Miami, and

Questions to Consider   The national narrative on immigration usually focuses on immigrants from Mexico and Central and South America, but there has been a sizable increase in the number of black immigrants from Africa and the Caribbean. There is also a tendency to lump the socioeconomic status and life experiences of new black immigrants from Africa and the Caribbean with African Americans. Professor Logan's research shows that there are some similarities between these populations (e.g., levels of segregation from whites), but these groups are exceptionally diverse. How and in what ways do the experiences of these new groups differ from those of African Americans? Is it the case that the experiences of black African and Caribbean immigrants are similar to those of Latinos? Why and how?

Ft. Lauderdale metropolitan regions. More than half are Haitian in Miami; Haitians are well represented, but outnumbered by Jamaicans, in New York and Ft. Lauderdale.

- America's African population, on the other hand, is much more geographically dispersed. The largest numbers are in Washington, D.C., and New York. In both places, the majority are from West Africa, especially Ghana and Nigeria. East Africa, including Ethiopia and Somalia, is the other main region of origin.

- Like African Americans, Afro-Caribbeans and Africans are highly segregated from whites. But these black ethnic groups overlap only partly with one another in the neighborhoods in which they live. Segregation among black ethnic groups reflects important social differences among them.

- In the metropolitan areas where they live in largest numbers, Africans tend to live in neighborhoods with a higher median income and education level than African Americans and Afro-Caribbeans. In these metro areas, Afro-Caribbeans tend to live in neighborhoods with a higher percentage of homeowners than either African Americans or Africans.

Counting Nonhispanic Blacks in America

The Census Bureau provides different ways of identifying these black populations, depending on the data source that is used.

For data on individuals, the 1990 5 percent Public Use Microdata Sample (1990 PUMS) data files and the Census 2000 1 percent Public Use Microdata Sample (2000 PUMS) make it possible to count the number of African Americans, Afro-Caribbeans, and Africans by combining information on their race, birth, and ancestry. Among non-Hispanic blacks, this study classifies those reporting their ancestry, country of birth, or both in the predominantly black islands of the Caribbean (including such places as Jamaica and Trinidad, but not Guyana) as "Afro-Caribbean." . . .

The Size and Regional Distribution of the Black Population

Census 2000 counted over thirty-five million non-Hispanic blacks, as shown in Table 1. This represents over 12 percent of the U.S. population. The non-Hispanic black population grew by over six million people, a growth rate of almost 21 percent, since the last decennial census. More than nine out of ten of these were African American (based on our classification of persons using 2000 PUMS), but the percentage of other black groups is growing rapidly (from 4 percent in 1990, based on 1990 PUMS data, to 6.1 percent in 2000).

Over 1.5 million blacks can now be classified as Afro-Caribbeans, and over 600,000 can be classified as African. The Afro-Caribbean population grew by more than 618,000 (almost 67 percent), and Africans grew by more than 383,000 (a growth rate of almost 167 percent, approaching a tripling of the African population). These two groups combined, despite being much smaller than

the African-American population, contributed about 17 percent of the six-million-person increase in the non-Hispanic black population during the 1990s. Although not an often recognized part of the American ethnic mosaic, both of these groups are emerging as large and fast-growing populations. Afro-Caribbeans now outnumber and are growing faster than such well-established ethnic minorities as Cubans and Koreans.

Analysis of all 331 metropolitan regions reveals distinct residential patterns for African Americans, Afro-Caribbeans, and Africans. Consider the ten metropolitan regions with the largest representation of the latter two groups. These are listed in Tables 2 and 3. New York, Boston, Washington, D.C., and Atlanta are the metros represented in both tables.

Like African Americans, who are present in large numbers in many metro areas, Africans are dispersed throughout the country. Only a quarter of Africans live in one of the ten largest metropolitan regions, and these metro areas are geographically dispersed. This dispersion, in combination with their smaller numbers, may help explain the "invisibility" of African immigrants in the United States (Arthur 2000). In contrast, Afro-Caribbeans are heavily concentrated in just a few metro areas, all on the East Coast. Six out of ten live in the New York, Miami, and Ft. Lauderdale metro areas; nearly six hundred thousand live in New York alone.

All of the top ten metro regions for Afro-Caribbean populations show growth rates of at least 40 percent since 1990, but four metro areas more than doubled the size of this population. Atlanta saw a fourfold increase in its Afro-Caribbean population, while Orlando nearly tripled its population of this group. With the exceptions of Washington, D.C., and Atlanta, the percentage of the non-Hispanic black population accounted for by Afro-Caribbeans in these top metropolitan regions is quite striking. For instance, over one-quarter of the non-Hispanic black population in the New York and Boston metro areas is Afro-Caribbean.

Jamaicans and Haitians are the two major sources of Afro-Caribbeans in all ten areas shown in Table 2. A majority in Miami (61 percent), West Palm Beach (62 percent), and Boston (57 percent) and a near majority in Newark (49.8 percent) are of Haitian ancestry. Jamaicans are the larger group in Ft. Lauderdale (46 percent), New York (40 percent), Nassau-Suffolk (39 percent), Washington, D.C. (49 percent), and Atlanta (53 percent).

TABLE 1 Composition and Growth of the Non-Hispanic Black Populations of the U.S., 1990–2000

Group	Population		Percentage of Black Population		Percentage of Total Population		Growth
	1990	2000	1990	2000	1990	2000	1990–2000
African American	28,034,275	33,048,095	96.0	93.9	11.3	11.7	17.9
Afro-Caribbean	924,693	1,542,895	3.2	4.4	0.4	0.5	66.9
African	229,488	612,548	0.8	1.7	0.1	0.2	166.9
Non-Hispanic white	188,013,404	194,433,424			75.6	69.1	3.4
Non-Hispanic black	29,188,456	35,203,538			11.7	12.5	20.6
Hispanic	21,836,851	35,241,468			8.8	12.5	61.4
Asian	6,977,447	10,050,579			2.8	3.6	44.0
United States Total	248,709,873	281,421,906			100.0	100.0	13.2

Washington, D.C., and New York have the largest African-born populations (80,281 and 73,851, respectively). The 1990–2000 growth rates exceed 100 percent in all the top metro areas for this population (save Los Angeles–Long Beach at 53.5 percent). Minneapolis–St. Paul saw a 628.4 percent increase in its African population, largely due to refugees from East Africa. In Minneapolis–St. Paul, Africans contribute over 15 percent of the non-Hispanic black population; in Boston, Africans account for nearly 10 percent of non-Hispanic blacks.

In the ten metro areas in Table 3, most Africans were born in West Africa (mainly Nigeria and Ghana) or East Africa (Ethiopia or Somalia). East Africans are the larger source in Minneapolis (61 percent), and they approximately equal West Africans in Los Angeles–Long Beach (37 percent) and Dallas (40 percent). Elsewhere, West Africans predominate: Washington, D.C. (53 percent), New York (69 percent), Atlanta (48 percent), Boston (60 percent), Houston (61 percent), Chicago (58 percent), and Philadelphia (53 percent).

TABLE 2 Metros with Largest Afro-Caribbean Population, 2000

Metro Area	Afro-Caribbean		Percentage of Black Total		Percentage of Metro Total		Growth
	1990	2000	1990	2000	1990	2000	1990–2000
New York, NY	403,198	566,770	20.3	25.7	4.7	6.1	40.6
Miami, FL	105,477	153,255	28.5	34.4	5.4	6.8	45.3
Fort Lauderdale, FL	55,197	150,476	29.6	43.4	4.4	9.3	172.6
Boston, MA–NH	40,825	62,950	20.6	25.6	1.3	1.8	54.2
Nassau–Suffolk, NY	32,210	60,412	17.7	25.5	1.2	2.2	87.6
Newark, NJ	29,818	55,345	7.3	12.1	1.6	2.7	85.6
West Palm Beach–Boca Raton, FL	20,441	49,402	19.8	30.3	2.4	4.4	141.7
Washington, DC–MD–VA–WV	32,440	48,900	3.1	3.7	0.8	1.0	50.7
Orlando, FL	14,872	42,531	10.4	18.4	1.2	2.6	186.0
Atlanta, GA	8,342	35,308	1.1	2.9	0.3	0.9	323.3

TABLE 3   Metros with Largest African-Born Population, 2000

Metro Area	African Born		Percentage of Black Total		Percentage of Metro Total		Growth
	1990	2000	1990	2000	1990	2000	1990–2000
Washington, DC–MD–VA–WV	32,248	80,281	3.0	6.1	0.8	1.6	148.9
New York, NY	31,532	73,851	1.6	3.4	0.4	0.8	134.2
Atlanta, GA	8,919	34,302	1.2	2.9	0.3	0.8	284.6
Minneapolis–St. Paul, MN–WI	3,788	27,592	4.3	15.4	0.1	0.9	628.4
Los Angeles–Long Beach, CA	16,826	25,829	1.8	2.7	0.2	0.3	53.5
Boston, MA–NH	11,989	24,231	6.0	9.8	0.4	0.7	102.1
Houston, TX	9,882	22,638	1.6	3.1	0.3	0.5	129.1
Chicago, IL	8,738	19,438	0.6	1.2	0.1	0.2	122.5
Dallas, TX	7,373	19,134	1.8	3.6	0.3	0.5	159.5
Philadelphia, PA–NJ	5,098	16,344	0.6	1.6	0.1	0.3	220.6

Social and Economic Characteristics of America's Black Populations

We know that the socioeconomic profile of non-Hispanic blacks does not compare favorably to those of whites and Asians. Table 4 offers a comparison based on the 1990 and 2000 PUMS. Less recognized is the diversity within the black population. African Americans have lower educational attainment and median household income and higher unemployment and impoverishment than Afro-Caribbeans and Africans. Afro-Caribbeans and Africans generally compare favorably to America's Hispanic population, while African Americans fare worse. There has been considerable debate about the source of these differences (see, especially, Sowell 1978 and a review of critiques of Sowell's conclusions by James 2002). Thomas Sowell suggests that they are due to cultural gaps, where the thrift and work ethic of immigrants operate in favor of the newer black groups. Mary Waters (1999) reports that Afro-Caribbean immigrants tend to agree with this thesis and that they often seek to distance themselves from an African-American identity; however, she also finds that employers favor Afro-Caribbean workers, in part because they are perceived to be more compliant and more willing to accept inferior wages and working conditions. Winston James (2002) argues that most differences in outcomes are due to immigrant selectivity (see also Takyi 2002a) and that black immigrants, like African Americans and unlike most other immigrant groups, are strongly affected by racial discrimination in the United States.

In sum, Table 4 makes the following points:

- *Nativity:* Over two-thirds of the Afro-Caribbean and nearly 80 percent of the African population is foreign born. The percentage of foreign born in these groups is higher than that of Asians. Not surprisingly, the percentage of foreign born among the group we define as African American is small.

- *Education:* Educational attainment of Africans (14.0 years) is higher than Afro-Caribbeans (12.6 years) or African Americans (12.4 years); indeed, it is higher even than that of whites and Asians.

- *Income:* Median household income of African Americans is lower than that of any other group in the table, lower even than that of Hispanics. Africans and Afro-Caribbeans have much higher median incomes (about $43,000), though these are still well below those of whites and Asians.

- *Unemployment and poverty:* Africans and Afro-Caribbeans also have the lowest rates of unemployment and impoverishment among blacks, comparing favorably to Hispanics. Their position is substantially worse than that of Asians and whites, but Africans' unemployment is not far from that of these two groups.

The social and economic profile of all three black groups generally improved during the 1990s, though the gain in median household income of Afro-Caribbeans was marginal, and the average educational attainment of Africans slipped. Gains for African Americans somewhat

TABLE 4 Social and Economic Characteristics of Non-Hispanic Black Populations in Comparison with Major U.S. Racial and Ethnic Groups, 1990 and 2000

Group	Population	Foreign Born (%)	Years of Education	Median Household Income ($)	Unemployed (%)	Below Poverty (%)
1990						
African American	28,034,275	1.8	11.7	29,251	12.5	32.8
Afro-Caribbean	924,693	72.4	12.1	42,927	9.4	17.8
African	229,488	72.1	14.3	35,041	8.5	24.7
Non-Hispanic white	188,013,404	3.9	12.9	47,481	4.7	11.3
Non-Hispanic black	29,188,456	4.7	11.7	29,850	12.3	32.3
Hispanic	21,836,851	42.7	10.2	35,041	9.9	27.0
Asian	6,977,447	67.5	13.1	54,508	5.0	15.9
2000						
African American	33,048,095	2.2	12.4	33,790	11.2	30.4
Afro-Caribbean	1,542,895	68.3	12.6	43,650	8.7	18.8
African	612,548	78.5	14.0	42,900	7.3	22.1
Non-Hispanic white	194,433,424	4.2	13.5	53,000	4.0	11.2
Non-Hispanic black	35,203,538	6.4	12.5	34,300	11.0	29.7
Hispanic	35,241,468	40.9	10.5	38,500	8.8	26.0
Asian	10,050,579	66.5	13.9	62,000	4.6	13.9

diminished their gap with other non-Hispanic black populations. Very substantial differences in the average socioeconomic standing of these groups remain, though it is unclear how these various characteristics are interrelated. Some studies have shown, for example, that among employed males, there are no differences among black groups in work intensity and motivation to work (Dodoo 1999). There are also additional differences among Africans with different national origins (Takyi 2002b; Kollehlon and Eule 2003).

Residential Patterns within Metropolitan Regions

Another way to evaluate and compare the experiences of these black populations is to look at the degree to which their neighborhoods are segregated from those of other groups and from one another. It was shown above that the socioeconomic conditions of Afro-Caribbeans and Africans are different from those of African Americans; are their residential surroundings also distinct?

This question can be studied through the summary files in which Afro-Caribbeans are identified by ancestry and Africans by country of birth. The 1990 and 2000 population censuses provide the counts necessary to calculate levels of group isolation (the percentage of same-group members in the census tract where the average group member lives); exposure to all non-Hispanic blacks and exposure to whites (defined as the percentage of non-Hispanic blacks and non-Hispanic whites, respectively, in the census tract where the average group member lives); and segregation (the Index of Dissimilarity) from non-Hispanic whites and other black groups (the scores show the percentage of a given group that would have to move to another tract in order for the two groups to be equally distributed). These are indicators of the extent to which a group has developed its own residential enclaves in metropolitan areas. These figures have been calculated by computing levels of isolation, exposure, and dissimilarity in every metropolitan area, then taking a weighted average, giving more weight to areas with more group members.

Table 1 showed that African Americans make up just under 12 percent of the population in the United States, while Afro-Caribbeans and Africans account for 0.5 percent and 0.2 percent, respectively. Thus, if these non-Hispanic black groups were distributed randomly (without regard to in-group preferences or discrimination), their isolation index values would be about 12, 0.5, and 0.2, respectively. Likewise, the exposure scores would match the population percentages of non-Hispanic blacks and whites in Table 1. Dissimilarity is a measure of evenness and thus captures how equally members of a given group are distributed across tracts compared to another group. A dissimilarity score of less than 30 is generally thought to indicate low segregation, scores between 30 and 55 indicate moderate segregation, and scores above 55 indicate high segregation.

Table 5 shows that exposure to whites is low and declining for each black group. Africans have the highest exposure to whites (in 2000, just under half of the people in the neighborhood where an average African person lived was white); Afro-Caribbeans now have the lowest exposure to whites (29.9 percent) among black groups. Conversely, dissimilarity scores indicate high, though

slightly declining, segregation of all non-Hispanic black groups from whites. All dissimilarity scores from non-Hispanic whites are in excess of 60 percent.

The percentage of African Americans in the neighborhood where an average African American person lives declined from 54.3 percent in 1990 to 49.4 percent in 2000. Because of their smaller size, other black groups have much lower isolation scores, though these were on an upward trajectory in the 1990s. While they live in neighborhoods where their own group tends to be a small minority, Afro-Caribbeans' neighborhoods are, on average, close to 50 percent black. Africans, on the other hand, live in neighborhoods where blacks are outnumbered by whites (though they did increase their exposure to blacks from 23.3 percent to 28.3 percent).

Segregation of black groups from one another, as measured by the Index of Dissimilarity, is declining, but it is strikingly high. (Note that these average values are not symmetrical because the average segregation of group *x* from group *y* is weighted by the number of group *x* residents; segregation of group *y* from group *x* is weighted by the number of group *y* residents.) Caution should be exercised in interpreting these figures, however. Because

TABLE 5   Segregation of Black Populations, National Metro Averages

		African Americans	Afro-Caribbeans	African Born
Exposure to whites	1990	33.4%	33.5%	56.7%
	2000	33.3	29.9	46.3
Segregation from whites	1990	68.6	74.1	69.6
	2000	65.0	71.8	67.8
Isolation (exposure to own group)	1990	54.3	12.5	1.8
	2000	49.4	15.3	3.3
Exposure to blacks	1990	56.1	47.3	23.3
	2000	51.8	47.3	28.3
Segregation from African Americans	1990	—	46.6	68.9
	2000	—	42.5	59.2
Segregation from Afro-Caribbeans	1990	62.3	—	66.7
	2000	56.3	—	60.3
Segregation from Africans	1990	75.8	66.1	—
	2000	66.7	60.0	—

Africans and Afro-Caribbeans are found in very small numbers in many metropolitan areas, the national averages include many values for metro areas where the score is unreliable. It will be more revealing to assess dissimilarity scores among black groups in places like New York, Washington, D.C., and Atlanta, where all three are found in larger numbers. These data are shown in Tables 6 and 7.

Table 6 describes residential patterns for Afro-Caribbeans in the ten largest metropolitan areas for this population. Segregation from whites is very high in all of them, increasing in some areas, while declining in others. Exposure to whites, however, varies greatly—from living in neighborhoods that are less than a quarter white and majority black (New York, Miami, and Newark) to living in neighborhoods where whites make up as much as 40 percent of the population (Boston, West Palm Beach, and Orlando). Segregation from African Americans is only in the moderate range (35–45), indicating that Afro-Caribbeans' neighborhoods overlap substantially with those of African Americans. Segregation from Africans is substantially higher, though it remains within the moderate range. New York is the one case where both Afro-Caribbeans and Africans are present in large numbers, and segregation between these two groups is in the high range.

Table 7 shows segregation measures in the ten largest metropolitan areas for the African born. Exposure of Africans to whites declined significantly in all ten regions; it was extremely low in New York (17.0 percent) and near or above 50 percent only in Minneapolis–St. Paul, Boston, Dallas, and Philadelphia. Segregation from whites is in the high range in all cases, though falling in some of them. At the same time, Africans' exposure to blacks is growing, though it is much lower for Africans than for Afro-Caribbeans.

The table generally confirms the national pattern in which Africans are surprisingly segregated from African Americans and Afro-Caribbeans, though these values generally declined during the last decade. Washington, D.C., and Atlanta offer the possibility that where their populations are larger, Africans' neighborhoods may overlap more with those of other blacks. However, the case of New York shows that such a tendency is not inevitable.

Blacks' Neighborhood Characteristics

Non-Hispanic black groups are residentially segregated from whites and from each other. Do they also live in neighborhoods of different quality? (For research on this same question in the 1970–1980 period, see Adelman et al. 2001.) This final section of this chapter analyzes selected neighborhood characteristics for the average group member: the neighborhood's median household income (in constant dollars for 1990 and 2000), the percentage of group

TABLE 6 Segregation of the Ten Metro Regions with Largest Afro-Caribbean Population in Census 2000

Metro Area	Exposure to whites		Segregation from whites		Exposure to blacks		Segregation from African Americans		Segregation from Africans	
	1990	2000	1990	2000	1990	2000	1990	2000	1990	2000
New York, NY	15.4%	11.8%	81.8%	82.7%	62.2%	64.0%	40.2%	39.2%	62.6%	57.7%
Miami, FL	23.9	15.0	66.6	68.1	49.6	54.1	50.6	47.3	66.1	59.0
Fort Lauderdale, FL	52.8	36.6	56.1	57.2	36.3	43.6	44.4	34.6	69.8	67.5
Boston, MA–NH	42.7	40.7	76.4	73.2	42.8	39.3	41.3	34.9	63.4	54.5
Nassau–Suffolk, NY	45.5	36.7	76.8	75.2	38.0	38.7	40.8	36.4	68.7	48.8
Newark, NJ	26.2	22.9	79.8	78.0	60.8	60.0	40.5	37.8	59.7	47.7
West Palm Beach–Boca Raton, FL	46.1	47.3	69.7	60.2	41.5	34.6	42.7	44.0	83.0	74.4
Washington, D.C.–MD–VA–WV	40.8	34.6	67.0	64.6	43.0	43.3	55.2	48.4	44.9	42.5
Orlando, FL	62.8	42.4	52.9	58.1	26.0	32.6	49.1	40.2	67.3	65.4
Atlanta, GA	48.8	36.2	69.0	61.8	46.6	52.3	53.6	39.8	56.8	48.2

TABLE 7   Segregation of the Ten Metro Regions with Largest African-Born Population in Census 2000

Metro Area	Exposure to whites		Segregation from whites		Exposure to blacks		Segregation from African Americans		Segregation from Afro-Caribbeans	
	1990	2000	1990	2000	1990	2000	1990	2000	1990	2000
Washington, D.C.–MD–VA–WV	47.7%	37.5%	62.7%	63.1%	34.6%	36.7%	62.9%	58.2%	44.9%	42.5%
New York, NY	29.9	17.0	71.6	78.0	38.4	47.0	62.1	48.5	62.6	57.7
Atlanta, GA	53.1	39.4	67.2	63.6	39.7	43.2	57.4	54.0	56.8	48.2
Minneapolis–St. Paul, MN–WI	78.0	59.2	73.0	68.4	11.2	21.9	66.1	50.0	79.3	73.5
Los Angeles–Long Beach, CA	44.7	34.4	59.4	59.9	17.1	19.9	68.3	60.6	65.8	61.1
Boston, MA–NH	55.5	47.5	68.2	63.7	22.4	26.6	64.7	48.9	63.4	54.5
Houston, TX	46.8	33.0	68.2	67.9	23.7	27.3	71.3	64.7	61.6	54.8
Chicago, IL	51.7	45.1	78.0	72.7	29.1	31.0	80.5	71.2	73.2	66.3
Dallas, TX	66.4	49.0	64.8	60.0	15.5	19.6	74.3	64.2	72.9	66.4
Philadelphia, PA–NJ	56.8	49.2	78.1	70.2	34.5	38.7	72.2	61.9	68.0	58.8

members who own their homes, and the percentage of residents (over age twenty-five) with a college education. These are characteristics of the neighborhoods in which an average group member lives, rather than of the groups themselves (these were shown previously in Table 4).

Table 8 shows that non-Hispanic blacks, regardless of ethnicity, live in worse neighborhoods, on average, than do non-Hispanic whites, with one exception—Africans exceed whites in the educational attainment of their neighbors.

More relevant here are the differences among black populations:

- *Income:* The average African American lives in a census tract with a median income of $35,679, while the

average Afro-Caribbean lives in a census tract with a median income of $41,328. Africans live in more advantaged neighborhoods with a median income of $45,567 (though this is still more than $7,000 below the neighborhood median income of an average non-Hispanic white).

- *Homeownership:* The average African American lives in a tract where 53.1 percent of the residents own their homes. This is higher than the other black groups, and to some extent it reflects the advantage of having lived for more generations in the United States. The average Afro-Caribbean lives in a tract where 49.8 percent of the residents own homes. Although

TABLE 8   Neighborhood Characteristics of the Average Group Member, National Metro Averages

Group	Median Household Income ($)		Percentage Homeowners		Percentage College Educated	
	1990	2000	1990	2000	1990	2000
African American	31,548	35,679	49.8	53.1	14.0	17.5
Afro-Caribbean	39,970	41,328	44.1	49.8	17.5	20.3
African born	44,715	45,567	44.7	47.2	28.8	29.3
Non-Hispanic white	47,683	52,637	67.6	70.7	23.8	29.0

lower than the national average for African Americans, this deficit is largely due to their concentration in the New York metro area, where this group is mainly found in inner-city neighborhoods. Regional comparisons of this neighborhood characteristic show that Afro-Caribbeans fare much better than African Americans in New York and somewhat better in Washington, D.C., and Atlanta. The average African lives in a tract where 47.2 percent of neighbors are homeowners.

- *Education:* The average African lives in a neighborhood where 29.3 percent of residents have a college education, compared to 29 percent for an average non-Hispanic white. This reflects the very high educational attainment of the Africans who have been able to immigrate to the United States. By contrast, the average African American lives in a neighborhood where 17.5 percent of residents have a college education, while 20 percent of an average Afro-Caribbean person's neighbors have a college education.

Table 9 provides a closer look at the metro areas where Afro-Caribbeans are most numerous. Homeownership in their neighborhoods, as noted above, is especially low in New York (and Newark and Boston as well, where they also are concentrated in the inner city). Their neighborhoods are relatively less affluent and less educated in New York. In other metro areas in the table, homeownership in their neighborhoods is actually well above the national average for African Americans. Afro-Caribbeans live in relatively affluent neighborhoods in Nassau–Suffolk (which is all suburban), Washington, D.C., and Atlanta and in neighborhoods with a relatively high education level in Washington, D.C., Atlanta, and Boston.

Similar information is given in Table 10 for the top ten metro areas of Africans. Their neighborhoods have especially high levels of education in Washington, D.C., but in several other metro areas, the percentage of neighbors with a college degree is higher than the national average for whites' neighborhoods: Atlanta, Los Angeles–Long Beach, Houston, Chicago, and Dallas. Exceptionally low are the education levels in New York and Philadelphia. Africans also live in especially affluent neighborhoods in Washington, D.C., with a median income of over $57,000—again, well above the national average for whites' neighborhoods. These income levels are lowest in New York and Minneapolis. Finally, Philadelphia stands out for high homeownership in Africans' neighborhoods (over 60 percent), while in New York, homeownership is exceptionally low (less than 25 percent).

TABLE 9 **Neighborhood Characteristics of the Average Afro-Caribbean Resident**

Metro Area	Median Household Income ($)		Percentage Homeowners		Percentage College Educated	
	1990	*2000*	*1990*	*2000*	*1990*	*2000*
New York, NY	39,410	38,758	31.0	35.1	15.5	18.2
Miami, FL	33,665	33,873	53.8	58.1	13.9	15.0
Fort Lauderdale, FL	35,403	39,621	59.2	64.3	13.3	17.0
Boston, MA–NH	40,825	42,463	36.9	42.3	22.5	26.1
Nassau–Suffolk, NY	63,190	64,241	73.7	75.9	21.4	23.5
Newark, NJ	44,036	45,216	39.6	41.9	17.9	20.5
West Palm Beach–Boca Raton, FL	33,061	38,114	54.9	62.2	12.5	17.5
Washington, DC–MD–VA–WV	53,864	57,218	51.9	57.6	31.5	35.7
Orlando, FL	38,210	39,252	59.6	60.0	17.2	18.1
Atlanta, GA	46,267	50,911	57.9	61.9	27.1	29.9

TABLE 10 Neighborhood Characteristics of the Average
African-Born Resident

Metro Area	Median Household Income ($)		Percentage Homeowners		Percentage College Educated	
	1990	2000	1990	2000	1990	2000
Washington, DC–MD–VA–WV	55,784	57,143	47.0	50.4	37.5	39.5
New York, NY	40,145	35,243	24.3	24.2	22.7	20.3
Atlanta, GA	43,049	48,614	45.1	49.8	30.0	30.5
Minneapolis–St. Paul, MN–WI	36,321	37,679	46.4	44.0	31.2	27.9
Los Angeles–Long Beach, CA	49,075	47,009	41.9	42.9	26.9	29.8
Boston, MA–NH	43,138	42,925	37.9	40.2	27.3	28.2
Houston, TX	41,298	46,531	39.2	48.8	30.9	30.9
Chicago, IL	40,700	45,509	41.0	47.4	30.7	34.3
Dallas, TX	45,671	49,347	38.2	43.6	35.0	33.1
Philadelphia, PA–NJ	43,811	41,647	60.2	60.7	25.4	23.1

Conclusion: The Increasing Diversity of America's Black Populations

All of these analyses point in a similar direction. Black Americans of all ethnic backgrounds are highly segregated from whites and disadvantaged in comparison to them. Yet, beneath this communality born of the color line are substantial differences between the majority of blacks with historical origins in the United States and new, growing minorities from the Caribbean and Africa. Nearly 17 percent of recent growth in the black population is due to increases in these new groups. Particularly in metro areas where they constitute 20 percent or more of the black population, an increasingly urgent social and political question is whether common problems associated with race will outweigh differences linked to national origins (Logan and Mollenkopf 2003). Scholars generally agree that the differences are substantial and that black immigrants have limited prospects of assimilation either into mainstream American society or into the African-American minority (Kasinitz 1992; Ho 1991). In some places with a long history of black ethnic diversity, such as New York City, the differences have appeared to be divisive in political races

(Rogers 2004). But some studies have shown that majority-black institutions are capable of successfully incorporating newcomers (Foerster 2004).

The newcomers have numerous advantages compared to African Americans. Their own education levels and incomes tend to be higher. Not only do they typically live in somewhat different neighborhoods, but in most metro areas, these neighborhoods have a higher socioeconomic standing.

Comparable diversity has been documented among Hispanics (particularly contrasting South Americans and Cubans with Mexicans, Central Americans, and Dominicans) and Asians (among whom Indians and Filipinos present a very different profile than Chinese or Koreans). The American public is used to thinking in terms of the broader racial and ethnic categories—Hispanic, Asian, black. Certainly in the history of black-white relations in this country, the distinctions between blacks of different social class or national origin have paled in comparison to their common treatment. We may nevertheless be moving into an era when those distinctions become more salient and when we must think not only in terms of majority and minority groups but in terms of a nation of many minorities.

42

The Arab Immigrant Experience
Michael W. Suleiman

MICHAEL W. SULEIMAN is University Distinguished Professor in the Department of Political Science at Kansas State University. He has written and co-edited numerous works in the field of Arab American studies, including *U.S. Policy on Palestine from Wilson to Clinton* and *Arab Americans: Continuity and Change.*

Questions to Consider   Since 9/11 the media seem to have discovered the Arab American population in the United States, but this group has had significant presence in this country for almost 150 years. In this article Suleiman maps Arab migration to the United States and the "Americanization" process this group, like almost all immigrant groups to this country, has experienced. He suggests that an ambiguous racial status and racism were used to deny citizenship to Arab immigrants. How and why did this happen?

Introduction

In 1977, William E. Leuchtenburg, the prominent American historian, remarked, "From the perspective of the American historian, the most striking aspect of the relationship between Arab and American cultures is that, to Americans, the Arabs are a people who have lived outside of history."[1] Professor Leuchtenburg could have just as accurately made the same observation about Arabs in America.

Ignorance about Arab Americans among North Americans at large means that, before looking at more detailed accounts of the Arab-American experience, we may benefit from a quick overview of Arab immigration to North America and what the Arab-American communities here have been like.

There have been two major waves of Arab immigration to North America. The first lasted from the 1870s to World War II and the second from World War II to the present. Members of the two waves of immigrants had somewhat different characteristics and faced different challenges in the social and political arena. Any examination of the immigrant communities must take into account these differences. As we shall see, the two communities began to come together in the 1960s, especially after the 1967 Arab-Israeli war,[2] and this rapprochement must also be taken into account.

The term "Arab Americans" refers to the immigrants to North America from the Arabic-speaking countries of the Middle East and their descendants. The Arabic-speaking countries today include Algeria, Bahrain, Egypt, Iraq, Jordan, Kuwait, Lebanon, Libya, Mauritania, Morocco,

Oman, pre-1948 Palestine and the Palestinians, Qatar, Saudi Arabia, Sudan, Syria, Tunisia, United Arab Emirates, and Yemen. Somalia and Djibouti are also members of The League of Arab States and have some Arabic-speaking populations. Most Arab immigrants of the first wave came from the Greater Syria region, especially present-day Lebanon, and were overwhelmingly Christian; later immigrants came from all parts of the Arab world, but especially from Palestine, Lebanon, Syria, Egypt, Iraq, and Yemen, and had large numbers of Muslims among them. Although most Muslim Arab immigrants have been Sunni (reflecting the population in the region), there is a substantial Shi'a minority. Druze started immigrating in small numbers late in the nineteenth century.

Immigrants from the Arabic-speaking countries have been referred to and have referred to themselves by different names at different times, including Arabs or Arabians, but until World War II the designation Syrian or Syrian-Lebanese was used most often. The changeability of the name may indicate the absence of a definite and enduring identity, an issue that is discussed later. For the purposes of this chapter, the various names are used interchangeably, but the community primarily is referred to as Arab or Arab American.[3]

It is impossible to determine the exact number of Arab immigrants to North America, because U.S. and Canadian immigration officials have at different times used different classification schemes. Until 1899 in the United States, for instance, immigration statistics lumped the Arabs with Greeks, Armenians, and Turks. For this and other reasons, only estimates can be provided.

According to U.S. immigration figures, which generally are considered to be low, about 130,000 Arabs had immigrated to the United States by the late 1930s.[4] Estimates of the size of the Arab-American community by scholars and community leaders vary widely. A conservative estimate is that there were approximately 350,000 persons of Arab background in the United States on the eve of World War II.[5] In the 1990s, the size of the Arab community in the United States has been estimated at less than one million to the most frequently cited figure of two and one-half to three million.[6]

Numerous reasons have been given for the first wave of Arab immigration to America, which began in large numbers in the 1880s, but the reasons usually fall into two categories: push and pull factors, with the push factors accorded greater weight.

Most scholars argue that the most important reasons for emigration were economic necessity and personal advancement.[7] According to this view, although the economy in geographic or Greater Syria (a term encompassing the present-day countries and peoples of Syria, Lebanon, the Palestinians, Israel, Jordan, and possibly Iraq) registered some clear gains in the late nineteenth and early twentieth centuries, this progress was uneven in its impact and did not manifest itself in a sustained manner until "after emigration to the New World began to gather momentum."[8] The economy of Mount Lebanon suffered two major crippling blows in the mid-1800s. The first was the opening of the Suez Canal, which sidetracked world traffic from Syria to Egypt and made the trip to the Far East so easy and fast that Japanese silk became a major competitor for the Lebanese silk industry. The second blow came in the 1890s, when Lebanese vineyards were invaded by phylloxera and practically ruined.[9]

Also contributing to the economic stress in the Syrian hinterland was a rapid increase in population without a commensurate increase in agricultural or industrial productivity. Many families found that the subsistence economy could support only one child, who eventually inherited the farm or household. Other male children had to fend for themselves, and emigration to a New World of great wealth became an irresistible option.[10]

Many Lebanese Christians, who constituted most of the early Arab arrivals in North America, emphasize religious persecution and the lack of political and civil freedom as the main causes of their emigration from lands ruled by an oppressive Ottoman regime.[11] Under Ottoman rule, Christians in the Syrian province were not accorded equal status with their Muslim neighbors. They were subjected to many restrictions on their behavior and often suffered persecution. These oppressive conditions worsened and discriminatory actions occurred more often as the Ottoman rulers became weaker and their empire earned the title of the "Sick Man of Europe." As the power of the sultan declined, the local rulers began to assert greater authority and power, which they at times used to suppress and oppress further their subjects, particularly Christians. In part, this persecution took place in response to the increased power and prestige of "Christian" Europe and the encroachment of its rulers on Ottoman sovereignty. This effect, combined with the Christian population's desire for greater equality, threatened the Muslim public's sense of security. Like the "poor white trash" of the American South at the time of the Civil War and the Civil Rights Movement, the Muslim population in the Syrian province was poor and oppressed—but it still enjoyed a social status that was superior to that of the non-Muslims, particularly the Christians. The threat of losing that "high" status made many Muslims susceptible to suggestions from local Ottoman rulers that their Christian neighbors were the cause of rather than companions in their troubles. The worsened social and economic conditions in Syria in the mid-1800s and the beginning of the disintegration of feudalism, especially among the Druze, produced social turmoil that erupted in sectarian riots in which thousands of Christians perished.[12] Many Christian Lebanese, especially Maronites, cite the 1860 disturbances and massacres as the main factor contributing to the exodus from their homeland.

In addition to the economic, political, and social causes of the early Arab immigration to North America, some incidental factors should be cited. Among these are improved transportation and communication facilities worldwide, development of steam navigation that made the sea voyage safer and shorter, and aggressiveness of agents of the steamship companies in recruiting new immigrant passengers. Although American missionaries often actively discouraged Syrians or Arabs from migrating to the United States, their very presence as model Americans, their educational activities, and their reports about American life ignited a desire, especially among the graduates of American schools and colleges in Syria, to emigrate to America.

After the feasibility and profitability of immigration to the United States and to "America" in general were well established, chain migration became the norm, with immigrants making it possible for the ambitious and the disgruntled in the old homeland to seek newer horizons. Those wanting to escape military service in the **Ottoman** army and those craving freedom from oppression and the liberty to speak and publish without censorship or reprisal left their homeland quickly and stealthily and sought what they thought would be a temporary refuge in America.

The Early Arab Community in America

Before World War II, most Arabs in America were Christians who came from the Mount Lebanon region of geographic Syria. Especially until the turn of the century, these travelers were mainly poor, uneducated, and illiterate in any language. They were not trained for a particular profession. As unskilled workers, after they learned the rudiments of the English language, they could work in factories and mines. However, such jobs were taxing and monotonous and, most importantly, did not offer opportunities for the fast accumulation of wealth, which was the primary objective of these early Arab arrivals. Farming presented them with the added hardships of isolation, loneliness, and severe weather conditions. Peddling therefore was an attractive alternative. It did not require much training, capital, or knowledge of English. With a few words of English learned on the run, a suitcase (*Kashshi*)

Ottoman Empire An empire covering parts of Europe, Asia, and Africa that dominated that region from the thirteenth century until World War I.

full of notions (e.g., needles, thread, lace) provided by a better-established fellow Lebanese or other Arab supplier, probably a relative who helped bring them to the New World, many new arrivals often were on the road hawking their wares only a day or so after they landed in America. Success in peddling required thrift, hard work, very long hours, the stamina to endure harsh travel conditions (mostly walking the countryside on unpaved roads), and not infrequently, the taunting and insults from children or disgruntled customers. These conditions were made tolerable for most early Arab arrivals by their vision of a brighter economic future and the concomitant prestige they and their families would eventually acquire in the old country. When they could afford to do so, they switched to the "luxury" of a horse and buggy and later to a dry-goods store.[13]

Before World War I, Arabs in North America thought of themselves as sojourners, as people who were in, but not part of, American society. Their politics reflected and emulated the politics of their original homeland in substance and style, because they were only *temporarily* away from home. In New York, *Kawkab America* (*Kawkab Amirka*), the first Arabic-language newspaper established in North America, declared in its very first issue its unequivocal support for the Ottoman sultan, whose exemplary virtues it detailed at length.[14] All other newspapers had to define in one way or another their attitude toward and their relationship with the Ottoman authorities. Although *Kawkab America* was pro-Ottoman, at least initially, *Al-Ayam* (*al-Ayyam*) was the most vehement opponent of the Ottoman authorities, a role it later shared with *Al-Musheer* (*al-Mushir*).[15] It excoriated the cruelty and corruption of Ottoman rulers, especially in the Mount Lebanon region. It also called for rebellion against the Turkish tyrants and urged its readers to exercise their freedom in America to call for freedom back home. Other newspapers, including *Al-Hoda* (*al-Huda*) and *Meraat-ul-ul-Gharb* (*Mir'at al-gharb*), fell between these two extremes of total support or clear rejection of Ottoman authority.

The orientation of early Arab Americans toward their homeland meant that their political activities were also focused on issues that were important in their country or village of origin. There was communal solidarity, but the community was a collective of several communities. The sectarian and regional disputes that separated the Arabs back home were also salient in this "temporary" residence. The newspapers they established were in the main socializing agencies conveying the messages of their sectarian leadership. Because the Orthodox already had their *Kawkab America, Al-Hoda* was set up to represent and speak for the Maronites. Later, *Al-Bayan (al-Bayan)* proclaimed itself the newspaper of the Druze.[16] Within each community there were rivalries and competing newspapers, each claiming to be the best defender or representative of its sect.

World War I was a watershed event for Arabs in North America, cutting them off from their people back home. This separation from the homeland became almost complete with the introduction of very restrictive quota systems in the United States and Canada after World War I, which practically cut off emigration from Arab regions. These developments intensified the community's sense of isolation and separation, simultaneously enhancing its sense of solidarity. One consequence was a strengthening of the assimilationist trend—a trend already reinforced by the American-born children of these Arab immigrants.

The substance and style of the Arab community's politics changed after the war, with a clear realization that they had become part of American society. Intersectarian conflicts became less intense and fewer in number. Calls for unity were heeded more often. For instance, Syrian-Lebanese clubs formed regional federations that joined together to form a national federation.[17] A process of socialization into American politics resulted in greater participation in voting and party membership and in public and political service at local or state levels. "Syrian" Republican and Democratic Clubs were formed in the United States, and the arena for political competition changed as the Arab community became part of the American body politic. There also emerged a clear change in matters of style—generally for the better. By the 1930s and 1940s, conflicts became fewer and somewhat less personal, and the language of discourse became much less offensive.

Whereas first-generation Arabs in America managed as best they could in an alien environment, their children were thoroughly immersed in American society and culture—and their first or only language was English. Consequently, English-language newspapers and journals were established to cater to young Americans of Arab heritage.[18] Eastern churches began to translate some of the liturgy and conduct part of the services in English to prevent the loss of members,[19] although many members left the church nonetheless. Some intellectuals, including some of the most celebrated Arab-American writers and poets, took advantage of the blessings of freedom and democracy in North America to attack the tyranny and corruption of the clergy, especially in the old homeland but also in America. Some also expressed atheistic or agnostic views, and others left their old churches and joined new ones.[20]

As Arabs assimilated in American society, they also worked harder for a better image of themselves and their people in the old homeland. More effort was spent on campaigns to inform Americans about the rich Arab heritage. In the political arena, especially in the United States, there were many, serious efforts to get the government to support foreign policy positions favored by the Arab community, especially in regard to Palestine. During World War I and its aftermath, the main political preoccupation of the Arabic-speaking groups in North America was to achieve the liberation of their homelands from Ottoman rule and to provide economic assistance to their starving relatives, especially in the Mount Lebanon region. To accomplish these objectives, their leaders set up relief committees, raised funds, and sent money and supplies whenever it was possible to do so. They also urged Arab young men in the United States to join the American armed forces to help their new country and to liberate their old homeland.[21] Leaders organized campaigns to have their people buy American Liberty bonds to help with the war effort.[22]

After the war, the Arabs in America were divided over the destiny of the regions liberated from Ottoman rule. In general, there was a strong sentiment among the Maronites to support French control over Syria and Lebanon under the League of Nations' Mandate.[23] Others argued for complete independence, viewing France as a new occupying power.[24] On the question of Palestine, there was general agreement in support of the Palestinian-Arab population and for eventual, if not immediate, independence. There was widespread opposition to Zionism as a movement bent on establishing a Jewish state there.[25] Arabs in America showed their support for the Palestinians through lectures, publications, fund raising, and political lobbying, especially with U.S. government officials.[26]

Until World War I, Arabs in North America may be considered sojourners exhibiting many traits of a middleman minority—a community whose members primarily engage in one particular specialized activity such as migrant farm work or peddling. Substantial numbers of Arabs in America engaged in commerce, most often beginning as peddlers commissioned by their own countrymen. Their objective was to make the greatest amount of money in the shortest possible time to help their families in the old country and eventually to retire in comfort in their village or neighborhood. In the meantime, they spent as little as possible of their income in America, often living in crowded tenements and, while on the road, in barns or shacks to avoid expensive hotel costs. They did not live rounded lives, allowing themselves no luxuries and finding contentment and solace in family life. Because they could pull up stakes anytime, they sought liquidity in their economic enterprises. Long-term investments were avoided. For that reason, in addition to other advantages, they preferred peddling, dry goods stores, restaurants, the professions, and a cottage industry in lace and needlework. In all of these activities, their primary contacts were with other Arab Americans, especially relatives or people from the same town, religious sect, or geographic region.[27] They developed few lasting relationships with "Americans." *Al-Nizala,* the term the Arab-American community used to refer to itself, is a name that clearly describes its status and purpose. It means a temporary settlement, and it was used in contrast to "the Americans" to indicate the alien or stranger status of Arabs in America. At first, Arabs in America formed their own residential colonies, especially in New York and Boston. Even when they did not, they encouraged within-group marriage, frequently praising its virtues and especially pointing out the disadvantages of marrying "American" girls. In other words, they resisted assimilation, even after their intellectuals began to urge acculturation to life in America.[28]

Arabs in America, sharing an attitude common to other middleman or sojourner communities, were charged with being "clannish, alien, and unassimilable."[29] Such attitudes were fairly common among influential American journalists and public officials, who also viewed Arabs as inferior to whites. In the economic field, Arabs were sometimes seen as parasites, because they allegedly did not engage in any productive industry, merely being engaged in trade. They were sometimes attacked as a drain on the American economy, because they sent part of their income back home.[30]

The Process of Americanization

Arab immigrants soon found out that the land of opportunity was also strewn with hardship and an "unwelcome" mat. In response to insults and charges of inferiority, they did occasionally defend themselves.[31] However, to add injury to insult, the U.S. and Canadian authorities began to claim that Arabs had no right to naturalization and citizenship because they allegedly were Asian and did not belong to the white race.[32] This problem of racial identification and citizenship traumatized the Arabic-speaking community. In their attempt to resolve this crisis, the "Syrians" searched for their roots and found them in their *Arab* background, which ensured them Caucasian racial status and therefore eligibility for U.S. citizenship—or so they argued.[33] Beginning in 1909, Arabic-speaking individuals from geographic Syria began to be challenged in their citizenship petitions. It was not until 1914, however, that George Dow was denied a petition to become a U.S. citizen because, as a "Syrian of Asiatic birth," he was not a free white person within the meaning of the 1790 U.S. statute.[34] In 1915, the Dow decision was reversed based on the argument that the pertinent binding legislation was not that of 1790 but the laws of 1873 and 1875, and in accordance with these, Syrians "were so closely related to Europeans that they could be considered 'white persons.'"[35] Despite this precise and authoritative language, "Syrians" in the United States continued to be challenged and to feel insecure about their naturalization status until the period of 1923 to 1924.[36]

Even during World War II, the status of Arabs remained unclear. In 1942, a Muslim Arab from Yemen was denied U.S. citizenship because "Arabs as a class are not white and therefore not eligible for citizenship," especially because of their dark skin and the fact that they are "part of the Mohammedan world," separated from Christian Europe by a wide gulf.[37] On the other hand, in 1944, an "Arabian" Muslim was granted citizenship status under the 1940 Nationality Act, because "as every schoolboy knows, the Arabs have at various times inhabited parts of Europe, lived along the Mediterranean, been contiguous to European nations and been assimilated culturally and otherwise by them."[38]

Apart from the legal battles to ensure they were allowed to reside in their new homelands, especially in the United States, Arabic-speaking persons had to figure out what identity best fit their indeterminate status. They knew who they were and had a very strong sense of personal identity centered first and foremost in the family. There were, however, other lesser but still important identities related to clan, village, or sect. Because these identities were strong, a "national" identity could remain amorphous or at least indeterminate, shifting from one orientation to another with relative ease and without much psychological dislocation. In practical terms, the Arabic-speaking people in North America functioned as a collective of communities whose bonds of solidarity beyond the family were mainly related to sect or country, such as Maronite, Orthodox, Muslim, Druze, and Palestinian affiliations. Before World War II, the primary or most acceptable designation for the group was "Syrian." However, when Lebanon emerged as a country in the 1920s, some Maronites, especially N. Mokarzel, the editor and publisher of *Al-Hoda,* spearheaded a campaign to get the community to change its name to Lebanese, because Lebanon was where most of its members originally came from.[39] The campaign was not a big success, although many of the clubs did change their name to Syrian-Lebanese.[40]

Another and more important identity crisis occurred when these peripatetic sojourners realized that they had to decide whether to become "settlers" or return to the old homeland. It had become increasingly difficult for them to function as temporary aliens. After World War I, it became clear to large numbers of Arabs in North America that it was not possible to go "home" again and that the United States and Canada were their homes.[41] This change from sojourner to permanent settler necessitated and was accompanied by other changes in the way Arabs in America thought and in the way they behaved. The substantial investments they had made in homes, property, and real estate in the old country lost their original purpose, and much more attention was paid to material improvements and investments in their new countries. In the United States, one manifestation was the migration by substantial numbers of the New York Arab community from the rundown and extremely crowded tenements of Manhattan to the nicer environment of South Ferry in Brooklyn and beyond.[42]

Arabs in America saw that they had to become full-fledged Americans. Assimilation became strongly and widely advocated, and citizenship training and naturalization were greatly encouraged. Although outmarriage was still not favored, some now claimed that success in such situations was possible if the American partner (usually female) was a "good" person who behaved in a conservative or traditional manner.[43] Along the same lines, Arab women were told to retain the modesty code of the old homeland.[44]

Although Arab women in America constituted a major asset to their kinfolk, they also presented the community with many difficulties, primarily related to issues of honor and modesty. This problem was most acute among the Druze, some of whom asked to restrict or totally ban the immigration of Druze women to America. Among Christians, women peddlers were a big concern. The complaints and areas targeted for reform included the act of peddling itself, the personal appearance and dress of the woman peddler, the distance she covered and whether she had to stay away from home overnight, and her demeanor or behavior. These problems were viewed as especially serious because large numbers had decided to stay in America and wanted to become "acceptable" to the host society. The preference was for Arab women to help their kinfolk by crocheting or sewing at home or by minding their family's store. Work in factories was also acceptable, although not favored, especially among the rising middle-class Arab Americans.[45]

The decision to settle in America meant setting a higher priority on children's education for boys and girls. This was viewed as more important than any contribution the children might make to the family's economic welfare. The result was a marked improvement in women's education and an increase in the number of male and female graduates from universities and professional institutions.

Another consequence of the decision to stay in America was that parents and children had to learn to be good Americans, and they flocked to citizenship classes. Parents attended English-language classes and studied the American governmental system in preparation for their new role as American citizens. Americanization was seen as a process of shedding old loyalties, the traditional culture, and the Arabic language. The children therefore grew up barely aware of their Arabic heritage.

Although the assimilationist approach began to gain favor and was encouraged by the leadership, it was not presented in ideological terms. Often, it took the form of a suggestion that Arabs should no longer feel like strangers in their new country and that they should make a positive contribution to American society.[46] Nevertheless, in the heyday of the melting pot approach to assimilation, the Arabs in America strove to remove any differences, except perhaps food and music, that separated them from the general American population. They also neglected or chose not to teach their children Arabic or to instill into them much pride of heritage.[47] The result was that, by World War II, Arabs in North America were, for all practical purposes, an indistinguishable group from the host society. It took a second wave of immigration and other developments to rekindle interest in their Arab heritage and to revive them as an ethnic community.

Post–World War II Immigration

The second wave of Arab immigration brought to North America a much more diverse population, one that differed greatly from the early pioneering group. Whereas the first-wave immigrants came almost exclusively from the area of Greater Syria and were overwhelmingly Lebanese, the new immigrants came from all parts of the Arab world, including North Africa. Unlike early arrivals, who were predominantly Christian, the new immigrants were Christians and Muslims.

The two groups' reasons for immigration were also somewhat different. In addition to economic need and the attraction of a major industrial society, new immigrants often were driven out of their homes as a result of regional conflicts (e.g., Palestine-Israel, Arab-Israeli, Iraq-Iran, Iraq-Kuwait) or civil wars (e.g., Lebanon, Yemen) or as a consequence of major social and political changes in the homeland that made life difficult, especially for the wealthy or the middle class in Egypt, Iraq, Syria, and other countries. The search for a democratic haven, where it is possible to live in freedom without political or economic harassment and suppression by the government was a strong motivation, even more so than during the earlier period, that affected much larger numbers of individuals. To these political and economic motivations can be added a psychological one. The great improvements in transportation and communication facilitated the process of immigration, and by making the world seem smaller, they made it much easier for people to accept the notion of migration to other parts of the world, especially to the United States and Canada.

Whereas the early Arab immigrants were mainly uneducated and relatively poor, the new arrivals included large numbers of relatively well-off, highly educated professionals: lawyers, professors, teachers, engineers, and doctors. Many of the new immigrants began as students at American universities who decided to stay, often as a result of lack of employment opportunities back home or because of the unstable political conditions in the homeland—conditions that often threatened imprisonment or death for returnees.[48] Besides these comparatively affluent immigrants, especially in the 1990s, relatively large numbers of semieducated Arabs, primarily engaged in commerce, came to North America as political refugees or as temporary residents to escape the wars and violence of the Middle East region.

An important difference between members of the two immigration waves is the way each group thought of itself in terms of American society and politics. First-wave immigrants were viewed and thought of themselves as mere sojourners staying in the United States on a temporary basis with the primary or sole purpose of making a fortune they could enjoy back home. This orientation remained dominant at least until World War I and probably well into the 1920s. Such a stance meant that they avoided participation in American society beyond taking care of basic needs such as commerce. They were "Syrians" or "Arabians" and sought to establish their own churches, clubs, or newspapers. They sought (and preached to their people) not to "meddle" in the affairs of the host society. They were anxious not to offend their hosts, not to break the law, and not to behave in a manner offensive to Americans, but they also tried not to imitate American social customs (i.e., Americanize), not to mix socially with Americans, and not to intermarry. Although most did not participate in politics much beyond voting, they nevertheless expressed pride in the occasional Arab who was able to make it as a city alderman, political party functionary, or a candidate for local political office.

The change from these conditions came slowly and as a result of changes in the world around them, especially World War I, the Ottomans' oppressive treatment of their subjects in the Syria-Lebanon region, and the success of Zionism in securing Western, especially British and

American, support for its objective of establishing a Jewish homeland in Palestine.

Immigrants who arrived after World War II came with a well-defined view of democracy and the role of citizens in it—ideas they had learned in their homeland but that had originally been imported from Europe and America. Their higher level of education and social status gave them greater confidence about participating in American politics almost as soon as they arrived in their new country. Even when they thought about returning to their Arab homeland, they were anxious to live full and productive lives in the United States or Canada for themselves and their children. The Arab-American community today constitutes a combination of the diversities of the early and more recent immigrants. In addition to the sectarian and mainly social clubs that the early immigrants formed, new political organizations were gradually established. In the United States, Syrian Democratic and Syrian Republican clubs were formed in the 1920s and 1930s. These were, as the Arab Democratic and Arab Republican clubs are today, adjuncts to the main two major parties designed to encourage political participation and to integrate Arabs into the American body politic. What was new and significant was the establishment of bona fide Arab-American pressure groups and voluntary associations whose main function has been to protect themselves against harassment from private groups or public agencies and to influence policy in the United States and Canada concerning different parts of the Arab World or Middle East.

As World War I had marked a watershed for the early Arab immigrants, the 1967 Arab-Israeli war did for the entire community. The older and newer Arab-American communities were shocked and traumatized by the 1967 war. In particular, they were dismayed and extremely disappointed to see how greatly one-sided and pro-Israeli the American communications media were in reporting on the Middle East.[49] The war itself also produced soul-searching on the part of many Arab Americans, old and new, and often reinforced or strengthened their Arab identity. This group included many members already active in various Palestinian, Syrian, and Lebanese clubs, which were mainly social in nature.

By 1967, members of the third generation of the early Arab immigrants had started to awaken to their own identity and to see that identity as Arab, not "Syrian." Elements of this third generation combined with politically

sophisticated immigrants to work for their ethnic community and the causes of their people in the old homelands. The result was establishment of the Association of Arab-American University Graduates (AAUG) in late 1967, which was the first post–World War II national, credible, nonsectarian organization seeking to represent diverse elements of the Arab-American community and to advance an Arab rather than regional or country orientation.

To the AAUG, however, American hostility to "Arabs" and the concept of Arabism was so extreme and so widespread among policy makers and the general public that influencing the political process or public policy, especially in the United States, seemed futile. The Republican and Democratic parties were almost completely and solidly one-sided in their support of Israel and in their hostility to Arab causes, even though the United States had huge economic and military assets in the region and was on the friendliest terms with most leaders and countries of the Arab world. The AAUG sought support from or identified with other individuals and groups. Among these were a few politicians such as Senator William Fulbright and others who were courageous enough to voice criticism of U.S. policy in the Middle East, other minority or disenfranchised groups in American society, and some intellectuals who began to criticize the administration and its policies.

The AAUG's first priority was the need to provide accurate information about the Arab world and Arabs in North America and to distribute this literature to the public at large, wherever access was possible. It sought to educate the Arab countries and people about the true nature of the problems facing the region and to educate Arab intellectuals and political leaders about U.S. and Canadian policies and the American political process. While the AAUG sought mainly to inform and educate, it also performed other tasks, because no other organizations existed to perform them. Among the tasks to which the AAUG devoted some time and effort were political lobbying, attacks against defamation of and discrimination against Arabs and Arab Americans, and activism among Arab Americans to get them to participate in politics.

These ancillary tasks were later championed and performed by newer organizations. The National Association of Arab Americans (NAAA) was formed in 1972 in the United States to act as a political lobby to defend and advance Arab-American interests and causes. In 1980, in response to the continuing slanders and attacks against Arabs and Arab Americans, the American-Arab Anti-Discrimination Committee (ADC) was established and quickly drew widespread support from the varied elements of the Arab community. In 1985, the Arab American Institute (AAI) was formed, primarily to encourage Arab Americans to become active in the American political arena.[50]

Building a New Future

To get a feel for how the Arab community has fared in America, it is useful to review some of the challenges and concerns that Arabs have faced in their new homeland and how they have coped with building a new future. Among the most important issues with which Arabs in America have had to wrestle is the definition of who they are, their sense of identity as a people, especially as they encountered and continue to encounter bias and discrimination in their new homeland.

Although Arabs in the United States and Canada constitute an ethnic group, they were not an ethnic minority in their old homeland. Their new identity has been shaped by many factors but especially by continuing interactions between conditions in the old and new homelands and by the interplay between their perceptions of themselves and how others see them. The early immigrants spoke Arabic and came from a predominantly Arabic culture and heritage, but they did not think of themselves as "Arabs." The main bond of solidarity among them at that time was based on familial, sectarian, and village- or region-oriented factors. The plethora of names by which they were known in the New World reflects their lack of "national" identity and ignorance or confusion on the part of the host society. Another factor in this process was the American, especially U.S., obsession with the idea of race and the various attempts early in this century to classify every immigrant group, no matter how small, by its racial composition.[51] The early Arabic-speaking groups were called Asians, "other Asians," Turks from Asia, Caucasian, white, black, or "colored."

Although immigration officials and the general press looked down on Arabic-speaking peoples, they nevertheless viewed them as part of the "white race," at least for the first thirty years or so of their presence in North America. These authorities then decided those immigrants were not white. With their very identity questioned and maligned, the reaction of the early Arab Americans was to try to refute what they saw as demeaning and untrue charges. They argued that they were very much part of the white race.[52] Stung by accusations of inferiority in terms of scientific and technological accomplishments, Syrian-Arab Americans developed a two-cultures thesis long before C. P. Snow discussed it.[53] Their argument, which became popular in the community, especially among Arab literati, was that, although America was the most advanced country in the world in science, technology, and industrialization, the East was spiritually superior.[54] Coming from the Holy Land, they offered themselves as guides and instructors to Americans in their search for and desire to experience the life and times of Jesus—where he was born, preached, was crucified, and rose from the dead.[55] Arab Americans spoke and wrote about the "spiritual" East in terms that suggested perpetuity: it was always so and would always be so. By accident or not, these writers in essence condemned the East to an absence of material progress and desire to produce such for all time.

The emphasis on Eastern spirituality, although useful in making Arabs feel good about themselves compared with "materialist" Americans, still left Arabs in America with little cultural heritage to offer their American-born children. The result often was to ignore their Arab heritage and, especially beginning in the 1920s, to emphasize almost full assimilation in American society. As the children grew up immersed in American society and culture while simultaneously exposed to a smattering of Arabic words at home and some Arabic food and music, they often found themselves experiencing an identity crisis of some kind, mainly resulting in rootlessness, ambiguity, and a fractionalized personality.[56] These were the reactions of some of the Arab-American literati of the post–World War II period. The very culture of their own country denied them the privilege of being openly proud of their heritage. They sometimes dealt with this awkward situation by complaining about American prejudice and discrimination against Arabs and by simultaneously denigrating their own people and heritage—if only to ingratiate themselves with their readers, their fellow Americans.[57]

The 1967 war changed the situation radically. Israel, in the short period of seven days, defeated the Arab armies. The Arab people generally felt let down and humiliated. Arabs in America, both newcomers and third-generation descendants of the early pioneers, deeply resented the extreme partisanship America and Americans (especially the U.S. government and people) showed toward Israel and the occasional hostility toward Arabs. The consequence was for Arab Americans to shake off their malaise and to organize. Their first goal was to fight against the negative stereotyping of Arabs. Their second was to help modify American policy toward the Middle East and make it more balanced. In the process, sectors of the well-established older community de-assimilated. They began openly to call themselves Arab and to join political groupings set up to defend Arab and Arab-American causes.[58] Arab Americans also began to organize conferences and publish journals and books in defense of their cause. They wrote fiction, poetry, and memoirs declaring pride in and solidarity with Arabs and the Arab community in America.

Open Arab-American pride in their heritage and activism on behalf of their cause does not, however, mean that prejudice against them ceased. On the contrary, many in the community feel that prejudice and discrimination have increased. Different reasons have been advanced to explain the prejudice and discrimination that Arabs encounter in North America, and different individuals and groups have emphasized what they believe to be the main cause or the one most pertinent to their situation.

The most popular explanation for the negative stereotypes Americans hold about Arabs is that they are ignorant of the truth because they have not read or have read inaccurate and false reports about Arabs and have not come into contact with Arabs. According to this view, the stereotypes are mainly the result of propaganda by and on behalf of Zionist and pro-Israeli supporters. The primary objective of this propaganda has been to deprive Arabs, especially Palestinians, from presenting their case to the American public and the American political leadership.[59]

In this view, the attempt to deny Arabs and Arab Americans a public voice also extends to the political arena. In this way, it becomes a "politics of exclusion" in an attempt to prevent debate on any issues that reflect poorly on Zionists or Israel. It also smears and defames Arab candidates for political office to defeat them and exclude them from effective participation in political decision making. This "political racism" is presumed to be ideological in nature and not necessarily directed against Arabs or Arab Americans as a people or as an ethnic community.[60]

Another view sees hostility and violence against Arabs and Arab Americans as anti-Arab racism. This hostility is seen as part of the native racist attitudes and is believed to be present in all sectors of American society, not just among fringe groups. Somewhat related to this view is "jingoistic racism," which is directed at whatever foreign enemy is perceived to be out there.[61] Because of the many recent conflicts in the Middle East in which the United States directly or indirectly became involved and where incidents of hijacking and hostage taking occurred, many Americans reacted negatively against a vaguely perceived enemy next door, often not distinguishing between Arabs and Muslims or between Arabs and any foreigner who "looks" Arab.[62]

Still another view of negative Arab stereotypes, at least in the United States, argues that these ideas are "rooted in a core of hostile archetypes that our culture applies to those with whom it clashes."[63] According to this argument, most of the elements that constitute the Arab image in America are not unique to Arabs but also have been applied to other ethnic groups, especially blacks and Jews in the form of racism and anti-Semitism. These negative stereotypes have been transferred to a new group, the Arabs or Arab Americans.

Part of the negative stereotyping and hostility many Americans harbor toward Arabs is based on the latter's alleged mistreatment of their women. It is rather ironic, therefore, that Arab-American women find themselves the subject of prejudice, discrimination, and hostility at the hands of American men and women. This is often the result of hostility based on race, color, or religion.[64]

Arab-American women have had more problems than their male counterparts in defining an acceptable or comfortable identity. The problem is multifaceted and affects different sectors differently. Women who have come from the most traditional countries of the Arab world have experienced a greater restriction of their freedom in the United States. This is primarily the result of an inability on the part of traditional husbands, fathers, and brothers to deal with the nearly complete freedom accorded to women in American society. Just as important is the inability of the women to participate fully in the United States because they do not know the language, lack the necessary education, and are unfamiliar with American customs. They are not psychologically ready to countenance, let alone internalize, certain mores pertaining to the public display of affection and male-female interaction. Because many cannot drive and probably do not have a car, they find themselves much more isolated than they were back home, where they often had a vibrant and full life, albeit within the confines of the family and female friends.[65]

Among middle-class, first-generation Arab-American women, there is perhaps not much adjustment necessary. They usually follow the somewhat liberal mores they brought with them from the old homeland. On the other hand, Arab girls reaching their adolescence in the United States are likely to experience more problems as a result of the potential clash between traditional child-rearing practices and the freer atmosphere found in North America.[66]

Among better-educated, young Arab-American women, the issue of identity is both more subtle and more openly discussed. Like their male Arab-American counterparts, these women suffer from and are offended by the hostility against Arabs and Arab Americans. They also find American views of how women are allegedly treated in the Arab world to be inaccurate and grotesque. Nevertheless, they would like to expand the rights of Arab women and to improve the quality of their lives. They resent and reject any attempt on the part of Arab-American men to define what their role should be in maintaining Arab culture and mores in North America. In particular, they want to reject the notion that family honor resides in women and that the way a woman behaves, especially concerning her modesty and sexuality, can bring honor or dishonor to the family. They do not wish to be the conveyors or transmitters of tradition and culture—at least not as these are defined by men or as they prevail in the old homeland.[67]

Women and men in the Arab-American community of the 1990s find that the "white" racial classification that the early Syrian-Arab community worked so hard to attain is flawed. In practical daily interactions, Arabs in America are often treated as "honorary whites" or "white but not quite."[68] In reaction to this situation, at least four different orientations have been advocated. For the majority, especially among the older and well-established Christian community, there is some disgruntlement but general passivity about the discrimination and the prejudice that accompany their "white but not quite" status, and they work to remove these negative attitudes. Others, especially the Arab American Institute, have argued

for a special designation of Arabs in the United States as a minority (e.g., the Hispanics) or as a specific census category encompassing all peoples of the Middle East.[69] Still others, especially some young, educated Arab-American women, have expressed a preference for the designation "people of color."[70] This would place them as part of a larger category that includes most of the federally recognized minorities in the United States. There are also those who resent being boxed into one category. Their sense of identity is multifaceted; they are men or women; Arab, American, Muslim or Christian; white or dark skinned; and so on. They think of themselves in different ways at different times or in different contexts, and they argue for getting rid of such categories or for the use of more descriptive categories that recognize different aspects of their background, culture, or physical appearance.[71]

The search for an adequate or comfortable identity for Arabs in America has been guided and perhaps complicated by the need to feel pride in their heritage and simultaneously avoid prejudice and discrimination in their new homeland. For most, the search is neither successful nor final. They continue to experience marginality in American society and politics, and they try to overcome this in various ways. Some resort to ethnic denial; they deemphasize their Arab or Islamic background by claiming a connection with what they believe is a more acceptable appearance in America. Instead of proclaiming their Arabism, for instance, they claim that they are Lebanese or Egyptian. Some may even deny their heritage altogether, claiming to be Greek or Italian. Some new arrivals instead choose ethnic isolation. They are unwilling to change themselves and do not believe they can change the host society.

Among those who want full integration or assimilation into American society, especially middle-class Arab Americans, many emphasize the strong cultural link between Arabs and Americans. They refuse to give up and continue to work hard to show where the dominant American view is wrong. For most, accommodation is the easiest and most comfortable stance. These men and women consciously or subconsciously act in ways that reduce their difference from the American dominant group. They attempt "to pass."[72] Others, especially those who seek material success, especially those who are in public professions (e.g., television, radio, movies), often give in and convert to the prevailing view. Not infrequently, the very individuals who are looked down on by the Arab-American community are selected to speak for and represent the Arabs in America.[73]

The Arab-American Community in the 1990s

After more than a century of immigration, it is clear that the basic reasons Arabs came are no different from those that drove or attracted other groups to come here. They came because of the promise of a quick fortune and a sense of adventure; the threat of war or economic disaster; education, training, technology; and the thrill of living in a free democratic system. Whatever their reasons, true integration and full assimilation have eluded them. In part, this is the result of the many developments leading to the debunking of the notion of a melting pot and the greater tolerance of a multicultural society. The more important reason, however, has been the hostility the host society has shown toward Arab immigrants.[74]

Nevertheless, Arabs in America have done very well. Since the 1960s, there has always been at least one representative of Arab background in the U.S. Congress (e.g., James Abourezk, Mary Rose Oakar, Mark Joe [Nick] Rahall II). Others have served as state governors (e.g., Victor Atiyeh, OR) or on the White House staff (e.g., John H. Sununu). Similarly, individuals of Arab descent have been elected to the Canadian parliament (e.g., Mac Harb, Mark Assad) and to provincial legislatures. Many of these individuals have faced difficulties in attaining their positions because they were of Arab background. Some have found it useful to de-emphasize or deny that background to get or maintain their positions. Most also have not been strong or vocal supporters of Arab or Arab nationalist causes.

Nonetheless, ethnic pride is more openly displayed by an increasing number of political candidates at local, state, and national levels.[75]

Arab Americans have done well and fared better economically than the general population average in many areas. The 1980 and 1990 U.S. census data show that Arab Americans reach a higher educational level than the American population as a whole. According to the 1990 census, 15.2 percent of Arab Americans have "graduate degrees or higher"—more than twice the national average of 7.2 percent. Household income among Arab Americans also tends to be higher than the average. Arab Americans have also done well in professional, management, and sales professions.[76]

Although many Arabs in America have reached the highest level of their profession in almost all professions,[77] the American media primarily highlight the negative achievements of Arabs and Muslims. Quite often, the media announce the Arab or Islamic origin or affiliation of anyone accused of a terrorist act—even before they know whether the perpetrator is Arab or Muslim. In the case of positive role models such as Michael DeBakey or Ralph Nader, the media often never mention their Arab background. One reason is that "some [too many] have found it necessary to hide their origins because of racism."[78] Lists of prominent Arab Americans occasionally are published in the press to inform the public about the community's accomplishments, but the fact that such lists are compiled indicates that Arab Americans feel the sting of negative stereotyping and try to correct the bad publicity. Despite the fact that Arabs have lived in America for more than a century and despite their major successes, they are still struggling to be accepted in American society. Full integration and assimilation will not be achieved until that happens.[79]

43 Ethnic and Racial Identities of Second-Generation Black Immigrants in New York City
Mary C. Waters

MARY C. WATERS is a professor of sociology at Harvard University. She is the author of *Ethnic Options: Choosing Identities in America* and the co-author of *From Many Strands: Ethnic and Racial Groups in Contemporary America.*

> **Questions to Consider**   Based on her research of West Indians and Haitian Americans in New York City, Mary Waters found that first-generation black immigrants "tended to distance themselves from American blacks." Why? What does this "distancing" strategy say about the way American blacks are perceived by new immigrant groups? How is racism *within* a racial group possible?

THE GROWTH OF NONWHITE VOLUNTARY immigrants to the United States since 1965 challenges the dichotomy that once explained different patterns of American inclusion and assimilation—the ethnic pattern of assimilation of European immigrants and the racial pattern of exclusion of America's nonwhite peoples. The new wave of immigrants includes people who are still defined racially in the United States but who migrate voluntarily and often under an immigrant preference system that selects for people with jobs and education that put them well above their coethnics in the economy. Do the processes of immigration and assimilation for nonwhite immigrants resemble the processes for earlier white immigrants? Or do these immigrants and their children face very different choices and constraints because they are defined racially by other Americans?

This [reading] examines a small piece of this puzzle—the question of the development of an ethnic identity among the second generation of black immigrants from the Caribbean. While there has been a substantial amount of interest in the identities and affiliations of these immigrants, very little research has been conducted on the identities of their children. The children of black immigrants in the United States face a choice about whether to identify as black American or whether to maintain an ethnic identity reflecting their parents' national origins. First-generation black immigrants to the United States have tended to distance themselves from American blacks, stressing their national origins and ethnic identities as Jamaican or Haitian or Trinidadian, but they also face overwhelming pressures

in the United States to identify only as blacks (Foner 1987; Kasinitz 1992; Stafford 1987; Sutton and Makiesky 1975; Woldemikael 1989). In fact, they have been described as "invisible immigrants," because rather than being contrasted with other immigrants (for example, contrasting how Jamaicans are doing relative to Chinese), they are compared with black Americans. The children of black immigrants, because they lack their parents' distinctive accents, can choose to be even more invisible as ethnics than their parents. Second-generation West Indians in the United States most often will be seen by others as merely "American"—and must actively work to assert their ethnic identities.

The types of racial and ethnic identities adopted by a sample of second-generation West Indians[1] and Haitian Americans in New York City are explored here, along with subjective understandings these youngsters have of being American, being black American, and being their ethnic identity. After a short discussion of current theoretical approaches to understanding assimilation among the second generation, three types of identities adopted by the second generation are described and the different experiences of race relations associated with these identities are traced. Finally this [reading] suggests some implications for future patterns of identity development. . . .

Interviews with first-generation immigrants and their American coworkers reveal a great deal of tension between foreign-born and American-born blacks in both the working-class and the middle-class work sites. Long-standing tensions between newly arrived West Indians and American blacks have left a legacy of mutual stereotyping. (See Kasinitz 1992.) The immigrants see themselves as hardworking, ambitious, militant about their racial identities but not oversensitive or obsessed with race, and committed to education and family. They see black Americans as lazy, disorganized, obsessed with racial slights and barriers, with a disorganized and laissez-faire attitude toward family life and child raising. American blacks describe the immigrants as arrogant, selfish, exploited in the workplace, oblivious to racial tensions and politics in the United States, and unfriendly and unwilling to have relations with black Americans. The first generation believes that their status as foreign-born blacks is higher than American blacks, and they tend to accentuate their identities as immigrants. Their accent is usually a clear and unambiguous signal to other Americans that they are foreign born.

The dilemma facing the second generation is that they grow up exposed to the negative opinions voiced by their parents about American blacks and to the belief that whites respond more favorably to foreign-born blacks. But they also realize that because they lack their parents' accents and other identifying characteristics, other people, including their peers, are likely to identify them as American blacks. How does the second generation handle this dilemma? Do they follow their parents' lead and identify with their ethnic identities such as Jamaican or Haitian or West Indian? Or do they try to become "American" and reject their parents' ethnic immigrant identities? . . .

Theoretical Approaches to Assimilation

Theories derived from the experiences of European immigrants and their children in the early twentieth century predicted that the more time spent in the United States, the more likely second-generation youths were to adopt an "American identity" and to reduce ties to the ethnic identities and culture of their parents. This "straight-line" assimilation model assumes that with each succeeding generation, the groups become more similar to mainstream Americans and more economically successful. For instance, Warner and Srole's (1945) study of ethnic groups in Yankee City (Newburyport, Massachusetts) in the early 1930s describes the generational march from initial residential and occupational segregation and poverty to residential, occupational, and identificational integration and Americanization.

However, the situation faced by immigrant blacks in the 1990s differs in many of the background assumptions of the straight-line model. The immigrants do not enter a society that assumes an undifferentiated monolithic American culture but rather a consciously pluralistic society in which a variety of subcultures and racial and ethnic identities coexist. In fact, if these immigrants assimilate, they become not just Americans but black Americans. The immigrants generally believe that it is higher social status to be an immigrant black than to be an American black. Second, the economic opportunity structure is very different now from what it was at the beginning of the twentieth century. The unskilled jobs in manufacturing that enhanced job mobility for immigrants' children at the turn of the century have been lost as economic restructuring in the United States has shifted to a service economy (Gans 1992). The immigrants also are quite varied in the skills they bring with them. Some arrive with advanced educations and professional qualifications to take relatively well-paying jobs, which put them ahead of native American blacks (for example, Jamaican nurses). Others are less skilled and face difficulties finding work in the United States. Finally, the degree of residential segregation faced by blacks in the United States, whether foreign born or American born, has always been, and continues to be, of a much higher order than the segregation faced by foreign-born white immigrants (Lieberson 1980; Massey 1990). Thus, even with occupational mobility, it is not clear that blacks would be able to move into higher-status neighborhoods in the orderly progression that Warner and Srole (1945) describe in their Yankee City study of European ethnic succession. A further complication for the black second generation is that part of being a black American involves dealing with American racism. Because immigrants and black Americans report a large difference in the perception and expectation of racism in American society, part of becoming American for the second generation involves developing a knowledge and perception of racism and its subtle nuances. . . .

Patterns in the Second Generation

The interviews suggest that while the individuals in this study vary a great deal in their identities, perceptions, and opinions, they can be sorted into three general types: identifying as Americans, identifying as ethnic Americans with some distancing from black Americans, or identifying as an immigrant in a way that does not reckon with American racial and ethnic categories.

A black American identity characterized the responses of approximately 42 percent of the eighty-three second-generation respondents interviewed. These youngsters identified with other black Americans. They did not see their "ethnic" identities as important to their self-image. When their parents or friends criticized American blacks or described what they perceived as fundamental differences between Caribbean-origin people and American blacks, these youngsters disagreed. They tended to downplay a national-origin identity and described themselves as American.

Another 30 percent of the respondents adopted a very strong ethnic identity that involved a considerable amount of distancing from American blacks. It was important for these respondents to stress their ethnic identities and for other people to recognize that they were not American blacks. These respondents tended to agree with parental judgments that there were strong differences between Americans and West Indians. This often involved a stance that West Indians were superior to American blacks in their behaviors and attitudes.

A final 28 percent of respondents had an immigrant attitude toward their identities, as opposed to American-identified youth or ethnic-identified youth. Most, but not all, of these respondents were more recent immigrants themselves. A crucial factor for these youngsters is that their accents and styles of clothing and behavior clearly signaled to others that they were foreign born. In a sense, their identity as an immigrant people precluded having to make a "choice" about what kind of American they were. These respondents had a strong identity, such as Jamaican or Trinidadian, but did not evidence much distancing from American blacks. Rather their identities were strongly linked to their experiences on the islands, and they did not worry much about how they were seen by other Americans, white or black.

A number of factors influence the type of identity the youngsters develop. They include the class background of the parents, the social networks in which the parents are involved, the type of school the child attends, and the family structure. All of these factors affect the ability of parents and other family members to shield children from neighborhood peer groups that espouse antischool values.

The type of identity and outlook on American race and ethnic relations that the youngsters developed was strongly related to their social class and its trajectory. The ethnic-identified youngsters were most likely to come from a middle-class background. Of the eighty-three second-generation teens and young adults interviewed, 57 percent of the middle-class teens identified ethnically, whereas only 17 percent of the working-class and poor teens identified ethnically.[2] The poorest students were the most likely to be immigrant or American identified. Only one out of the twelve teens whose parents were on public assistance identified ethnically. The American identified, perhaps not surprisingly, were also more likely to be born in the United States—67 percent of the American identified were born in the United States, as opposed to only 13 percent of the immigrant identified and 42 percent of the ethnically identified.

Parents with more education and income were able to provide better schools for their offspring. Among the respondents, some of the middle class had moved from the inner-city neighborhoods they had originally settled in to middle-class neighborhoods in the borough of Queens or to suburban areas where the schools were of higher academic quality and more likely to be racially integrated. Other middle-class parents sent their children to Catholic parochial schools or to citywide magnet schools such as Brooklyn Tech or Stuyvesant. Thus, the children were far more likely to attend schools with other immigrant children and with other middle-class whites and blacks, although some of the Catholic high schools were all black in enrollment.

The children of middle-class parents who did attend the local high schools were likely to be recent immigrants who had an immigrant identity. Because of their superior education in the West Indies, these students were the best in the local high schools, attended honors classes, and were bound for college. The children of middle-class parents who identified as American and were pessimistic about their own future opportunities and adopted antischool ideologies were likely to have arrived early in their lives and to have attended New York City public schools in inner-city areas from an early age.

The social networks of parents also influenced the type of identity the children developed. Regardless of social class, parents who were involved in ethnic voluntary organizations or heavily involved in their churches seemed to instill a strong sense of ethnic identity in their children. Parents whose social networks transcended neighborhood boundaries seemed to have more ability to provide guidance and social contacts for their children.

The two neighborhood schools where we interviewed the teenagers were among the five most dangerous schools in New York City—they were inadequate facilities with crumbling physical buildings, high dropout rates, and serious problems with violence. Both schools were all minority, with over 90 percent of the student body composed of black students, both American and foreign born. The students who attended these schools and were not in the separate honors track (which was overwhelmingly filled with newly arrived immigrants) faced very limited future options, even if they managed to graduate.

Finally, the family structure and the experience of migration itself have a profound effect on the degree of control parents have over teenage children. Many families are composed of single working mothers and children. These mothers have not been able to supervise their children as much as they would like, and many do not have any extended family or close friends available to help with discipline and control. Even families with two spouses present often have been apart for long periods because one spouse preceded the family in migration. Often children have been left in the islands or sent ahead with relatives to New York, with the parents often struggling to reassert authority after the family reunites. The generational conflict that ensues tends to create greater pressure for students to want to be "American" to differentiate themselves from parents.

Ethnic Response

All of the teenage respondents reported comments by their parents about American blacks that were very similar to those recorded in our interviews with the first generation. The differences were in how the teens interpreted what their parents were saying. In general, the ethnic-identified teens agreed with their parents and reported seeing a strong difference between themselves and black Americans, stressing that being black is not synonymous with being black American. They accept their parents' and the wider society's negative portrayals of poor blacks and wanted to avoid any chance that they will be identified with them. They described the culture and values of lower-class black Americans as lacking discipline, a work ethic, good child-rearing practices, and respect for education. They contrast these failures with the values of their parents' ethnic groups, which include an emphasis on education, strict discipline for children, a strong work ethic, and social mobility. They try to impress that they are Jamaican or Haitian and most definitely not black American. This allows them less dissonance with their parents' negative views of American blacks. They do not reject their parents' culture and identities but rather reject the American social system that would identify them as black American and strongly reject the African American peer group culture to which they would be assigned by whites and others if they did not consciously transmit their ethnic identities.

Although society may define the second generation on the basis of skin color, the second-generation ethnic teens believed that being black American involves more than merely having black skin. One young woman criticized American blacks in this way:

> Some of them [black Americans] think that their heritage includes not being able to speak correctly or walk correctly, or act loud and obnoxious to make a point. I don't think they have to do that. Just when I see black Americans, it depends on how I see you on the street. Walking down the street with that walk that moves a little bit too much. I would say, I'd think you dropped out of high school.

These teens also differentiated themselves from black Americans in terms of their sensitivity to racism, real or imagined. Some of the ethnic-identified second generation echo the feelings we heard from the first generation that American blacks are too quick to use race as an explanation or excuse for not doing well:

> There was a time back in the, '40s and, '50s and, '60s or whenever when people was actually trying to keep down black people and stuff like that. But, you know, some black people now, it's like they not actually trying to make it better, you know? Some are just like, people are like, oh, this place is trying to keep me down, and they sulk and they cry about it, and they're not really doing that much to help themselves.

. . . It's just like hyping the problem if they keep [saying] everything is racial, everything is racial.

The second-generation teens who are doing well try to understand how it is that they are so successful when black Americans are not—and often they chalk it up to family values. They say that their immigrant families have close-knit family values that stress education. Aware of, and sometimes sharing, the negative images of black Americans that the whites they encounter believe, the second generation also perceives that whites treat them better when they realize they are not "just" black Americans. When asked if they benefited ever from their ethnicity, they responded "yes": "It seems white Americans don't tend to put you in the same category as black Americans." Another respondent said:

> The West Indians tend to go that extra step because they, whites, don't usually consider them really black Americans, which would be working class. They don't consider them, I guess, as black. They see them as a person.

The dilemma for the second generation is that while they have a strong sense of their own identities as very different from black Americans, this was not clear to other people. Often both whites and blacks saw them as just black Americans and did not notice that they were ethnically different. When people did comment on their ethnic difference it was often because of the way they talked and the way they walked. These two characteristics were cited as reasons that whites and other blacks gave for thinking those of the second generation were not "really black." Whites tend to let these children know that they think of them as exceptions to the rule, with the rule being that most blacks are not good people. However, these young people also know that unless they tell people of their ethnicity, most whites have no idea they are not black Americans.

Many of these teens coped with this dilemma by devising ways to telegraph their identities as second-generation West Indians or Haitians. One girl carried a Guyanese map as part of her key chain so that when people looked at her keys they would ask her about it and she could tell them that her parents were from Guyana. One young woman described having her mother teach her an accent so that she could use it when she applied for a job or a place to live. Others just try to work it into conversation when they meet someone. This means that their self-identification is almost always at odds with the identifications others make of them in impersonal encounters in American society and that, as a result, they must consciously try to accentuate their ethnic identity:

Q: When a form or survey asks for your race what do you put down?

A: Oh boy, that is a tough one. It's funny because, you know, when we fill applications I never know what to check off, you know. I'm serious. 'Cause they have Afro-American, but they never have like Caribbean. They do have white, Chinese. To tell the truth, I would like to be called Caribbean, West Indian. Black West Indian.

The teens who were around many black Americans felt pressure from their peers to be part of the group and identify as black American. These teens would consciously talk about passing for American at some points and passing for Haitian or Jamaican at others by changing the way they talked or acted:

> When I'm at school and I sit with my black friends and, sometimes I'm ashamed to say this, but my accent changes. I learn all the words. I switch. Well, when I'm with my friends, my black friends, I say I'm black, black American. When I'm with my Haitian-American friends, I say I'm Haitian. Well, my being black, I guess that puts me when I'm with black Americans, it makes people think that I'm lower class. . . . Then, if I'm talking like this [regular voice] with my friends at school, they call me white.

American-Identified Second Generation

The American-identified second-generation teenagers differed in how little they stressed their immigrant or ethnic identities to the interviewers. They follow a path that is more similar to the model posed in the straight-line theory. They stress that they are American because they were born here, and they are disdainful of their parents' lack of understanding of the American social system. Instead of rejecting black American culture, it becomes their peer culture, and they embrace many aspects of it. This brings them in conflict with their parents' generation, most especially with their parents' understandings of American blacks. They most definitely assimilate to black America; they speak black English with their peers, they listen to rap music, and they accept the peer culture of their black American friends. They are aware of the fact that they are considered black American by others and that they can be accused of "acting white" if they don't speak black English and behave in particular ways. Most included their ethnic identities as background, but none of them adopted the stance that they were not, in a major sense, black American. When asked about ethnic background and how other people think of it, one respondent replied:

Q: What is your ethnic background?

A: I put down American because I was born up here. I feel that is what I should put down. . . .

Q: What do other people think you are?

A: Black American because if I don't say. . . . Like if they hear my parents talk or something they always think they are from Jamaica. . . . But they just think I am black American because I was born up here.

Many of these teens discuss how they do not control how others see them:

A: Some people just think I am American because I have no accent. So I talk like American people. I don't talk Brooklynese. They think I am from down south or something. . . . A lot of people say you don't look Haitian. I think I look Haitian enough. I don't know, maybe they are expecting us to look fresh off the boat. I was born here and I grew up here, so I guess I look American and I have an American accent.

Q: If people think you are black American do you ever do anything about it?

A: No, I don't. If they ask me if I am American, I say yes. If they ask me where my parents are from, I tell them Haiti.

In fact, they imply that being a black American is more stylish and "with it" than being from the islands:

A: I consider myself a black American. When I think of a black American I don't think of them as coming from the West Indies.

Q: Any characteristics that come to mind?

A: I would not think of someone in a suit. I would think of a regular teenager. I would think of a regular person. I think of someone that is in style.

Q: What about someone from the islands?

A: Jamaicans. They dress with neon colors. Most of the girls wear gold and stuff like that.

Some of the young people told us that they saw little if any difference between the ethnic blacks and the American blacks. Many stressed the Caribbeanization of black New York and described how all the Americans were interested in being Caribbean now:

A: It use to be Jamaicans and American blacks did not get along because everyone was afraid of Jamaicans. But now I guess we are closer now. You tell an American that you are Jamaican and it is no big deal. Americans are acting more like Jamaicans. Jamaicans are acting like Americans.

Q: What do you mean by acting like each other?

A: Sure there are a lot of Americans out there speaking patois. And then all the Jamaicans are coming over here and they are like "Yo, what's up" and they are like that. Pretty soon you can't really tell who is Jamaican and who is American.

However, the parents of the American-identified teens have expressed to their children the same negative impressions of American blacks that the ethnic-identified teens reported. These teenagers report many negative appraisals of American blacks by their parents:

> They always say Haiti is better in this way or in that way. They say the kids here have no respect. The kids here are brought up without any supervision. My father is always talking about they [American blacks] be hanging out on the corner. And he says you won't find Haitians doing that. My mom always says you will marry a Haitian. Why are you talking to those American boys?

This young Haitian American teen tries to disagree with her mother and to temper her mother's interpretations of American blacks:

Q: Are there any characteristics or traits that come to mind about Haitian Americans?

A: Not really. I don't really—cause most people are Haitian American if they are born here. . . . Like me, I don't know if I act like a Haitian or do I have Haitian characteristics, but I'm mostly—like everything I do or like is American. My parents, they do not like American blacks, but they feel that they are lazy. They don't want to work and stuff like that from what they see. And I feel that, um,

I feel that way too, but sometimes it won't be that person's fault, so I try to stick up for them. And my mother is like, yeah, you're just too American.

In marked contrast to the ethnic-identified teens, though, the American-identified teens disagreed with their parents' statements about American blacks, reluctantly agreed with some of it but provided qualifications, or perhaps, most disturbingly, accepted the appraisals as true of American blacks in general and themselves as American blacks. This young Trinidadian American swallows her parents' stereotypes and applies them directly to herself:

Q: How close do you feel in your ideas about things to West Indians?

A: Not very close. My feelings are more like blacks than theirs. I am lazy. I am really lazy and my parents are always making comments and things about how I am lazy. They are always like, in Trinidad you could not be this lazy. In Trinidad you would have to keep on working.

The fact that the teens are identifying as American and that their parents have such negative opinions of Americans causes some conflict. The teens either adopt a negative opinion of themselves or disagree with their parents' assessments of American blacks. But it is not just their parents who criticize black Americans. These youngsters are very aware of the generalized negative view of blacks in the wider culture. In answer to the question, "Do whites have an image of blacks?" all of them responded that whites have a negative view of blacks, seeing them as criminal, lazy, violent, and uncaring about family. Many of the teenagers prefaced their remarks by saying that they did not know any whites but that they knew this is what whites thought through the mass media and through the behaviors of whites they encountered in buses, trains, and stores. This mostly involved incidents such as whites protecting their handbags when the teenagers arrived or store clerks following them and expecting them to shoplift. This knowledge that the society in which they live devalues them because of their skin color and their identity affected these teens deeply.

Immigrant-Identified Teens

The more recently arrived young people who still identify as immigrant differed from both the ethnic- and the American-identified youth. They did not feel as much pressure to "choose" between identifying with or distancing from black Americans as did either the American or the ethnic teens. Strong in their national-origin identities, they were neutral toward American distinctions between ethnics and black Americans. They tended to stress their nationality or their birthplace as defining their identity. They also pointed to their experiences growing up and attending school in a different country. This young man had dreadlocks and a strong Jamaican accent. He stresses his African roots and lets his Jamaican origin speak for itself:

Q: What is your ethnicity? For example, when forms or surveys ask what your ethnic group or ancestry is what do you put?

A: African.

Q: Do you ever put Jamaican or anything?

A: No, not really. Only where Jamaican comes up is if someone asks where you're from. I'll say I am from Jamaica.

Q: What do people usually think you are?

A: They say I am Jamaican.

Q: They know that immediately?

A: Yeah.

Q: How do they know?

A: I change my voice. I don't have to tell them. I think it's also because of my locks sometimes and the way I carry myself, the way I dress.

While an ethnic-identified Jamaican American is aware that she might be seen by others as American and thus actively chooses to present herself as Jamaican, an immigrant-identified Jamaican could not conceive of herself as having a choice, nor could she conceive of being perceived by others as American. While an ethnic-identified teen might describe herself as Jamaican American, for the immigrant teen Jamaican would be all the label needed. Most teens in this category were recent immigrants. The few U.S.-born teens classified as immigrant identified had strong family roots on the islands, were frequent visitors to the islands, and had plans to return to live there as adults. A crucial factor that allows these youngsters to maintain this identity is that their accents and styles of clothing and behavior clearly signaled to others that they were foreign born.

Q: How important is it to you that your friends think of you in terms of your ethnicity?

A: Oh, very important. You know, I try hard not to lose my roots, you know, when I come to the United States. A lot of people who come here try to lose their accent, you know. Even in the workplace, you know, because they fear what other people might think of them. Even in the workplace. Me, I never try to change, you know, the way I am. I always try to, you know, stay with them, the way of my culture.

Q: So it's something you want people to recognize?

A: Yeah, definitely, definitely, absolutely.

Q: Why?

A: Why? I'm proud of who I am, you know. I'm proud of where I'm from and I'm not going to change because somebody might not like the way I walk, talk or dress, you know.

The importance of birthplace was stressed repeatedly by the immigrant identified as they stressed their difference from American-born coethnics:

Q: What would you put on a form or survey that asked about your ethnicity?

A: I'll say I'm Jamaican. You gotta say where you come from.

Q: And do you think of yourself more as a Jamaican or more as an American?

A: I think of more of a Jamaican' cause it's, I wasn't born here. I was born in Jamaica and was there for fourteen years.

Q: And what about kids who are born in America, but their parents were born in Jamaica?

A: Well, you see that is the problem. You see, kids whose parents are Jamaican, they think that, well, they are Jamaican. They need to recheck that they're Americans 'cause they was born in the country and they wasn't born outside the country. So I think they should, you know, know more about American than Jamaican.

Some who adopt this strong identity with the immigrant country were born in the United States, but the combination of strong family roots on the island, frequent visits, and plans to go live there when they are older allows them to think of themselves as not really American at all. This is especially easy to do in the public high schools where there are large numbers of freshly arrived youngsters from the islands.

Q: What do you think your race is?

A: Well, I'm black. I consider myself black. I don't consider myself black American, Afro-American and stuff like that because it's hard to determine, you know, for a person as an individual to determine himself to be Afro-American. . . . I'll be more a Guyanese person because certain things and traditions that I am accustomed to back home, it's still within the roots of me. And those things have not changed for a long period of time, even though you have to adapt to the system over here in order to get ahead and cope with what is going on around you.

While the ethnics tended to describe people as treating them better when they described their ethnic origins, and the Americans tended to stress the antiblack experiences they have had and the lack of difference between the foreign born and the American, the immigrant teens spoke about anti-immigrant feelings and discrimination and responded with pride in their national origins.

Contrasting Identities

In some sense one can see each of these identities as an embrace of one identity and an opposition to another. The American-identified youth are assimilating, in fact, to the American black subculture in the neighborhood. They are adapting to American black cultural forms, and they do so in distinction to their parents' ethnic identities and the wider mainstream white identities. These students adopt some of the "oppositional" poses that American black teenagers show toward academic achievement, the idea of America, the idea of opportunity, and the wider society (Fordham 1988; Ogbu 1990; Portes and Zhou 1993). They also are opposed to their parents' outlooks and ideas, stressing that what worked as a life strategy and a child-raising technique in the islands does not work in the United States. These teens tend to adopt a peer culture of racial solidarity and opposition to school authorities. What is clear from the interviews is that this stance is in part a socialized response to a peer culture, but the vast majority of it comes about as a reaction to their life experiences. Most specifically, the teens respond to their experiences with racial discrimination and their perceptions of blocked social mobility. The lives of these youngsters basically lead them to reject their parents' immigrant dream of individual social mobility and to accept their peers' analysis of the United States as a place with blocked social mobility where they will not move far.

The American-identified teens do not seem aware of the scholarly literature and the perceptions among ethnic- and immigrant-identified youngsters that the foreign born are of higher social status than the American born. In the peer culture of the neighborhood and the school, these teenagers describe a situation in which being American offers higher social status than being ethnic. For instance, several youngsters described "passing" as black American in order not to be ridiculed or picked on in school:

> I used to be scared to tell people that I was Haitian. Like when I was in eighth grade there were lots of Haitians in the ESL classes, and people used to beat them up. They used to pick on them. I said to myself I am going to quiet down, say I am American.

When asked about the images others held of being from the islands, most of the teens described neutral attributes, such as styles of dress. However, many who identified as Americans also described negative associations with the immigrants' identities. The Jamaicans said most people thought of drug dealers when they thought of Jamaicans. A few of the teens also intimated that people from the islands were backward in not knowing how to live in a big city, both in appreciating the wonders of the city and being street smart to avoid crime and hassles with other people. In terms of the former attribute, the teens described people from the islands who were not accustomed to shopping in big malls or having access to a wide variety of consumer goods.

Not one of the American-identified teens voiced the opinion of the overwhelming majority of the ethnic teens that whites were more likely to like the foreign born. In part, this reflected the differences the groups had in their contact with whites. Most of the inner-city ethnic-identified teens had almost no contact with whites, except for teachers. They also are in schools where the vast majority of the students are foreign born or second generation. The larger number of middle-class teens who were ethnic-identified were more likely to have white classmates in citywide magnet high schools, in parochial schools, or in suburban schools or workplaces.

The inner-city American-identified teens also voiced more positive appraisals of black Americans than did the immigrant- or the ethnic-identified teens. Their descriptions reflect the reality of living in neighborhoods where there is crime and violence. A majority of the American-identified teens said that a good trait of black Americans is that they work hard and they struggle. These are the very same children whose parents describe black Americans

primarily as lazy and unwilling to take advantage of the opportunities available to them. The children seem to be perceiving a reality that the parents cannot or will not.

Many of these teens live in neighborhoods that are all black and also attend schools that are all black. So, aside from teachers, these young people have almost no contact with white Americans. This does not stop them from absorbing the fact that whites have negative stereotypic views of blacks. But unlike the middle-class blacks who come in contact with whites who tell them that they are "good blacks," these youths live in the urban areas associated with crime, they dress like the typical black urban youth, and they talk with Brooklyn accents and black American slang. When they do encounter whites in public places, the whites do not ask about their parents' backgrounds.

Q: Have you ever experienced any discrimination or hostility in New York?

A: From being Trinidadian no. But because of being black, you know, everybody stereotypes. And they say "blacks, they tend to steal, and stuff like that." So, like, if I am walking down the street and a white lady go by and they smile and I smile. They put their bag on the other side.

The parents of these teens grew up in situations where blacks were the majority. The parents do not want their children to be "racial" in the United States. They define "being racial" as being overly concerned with race and with using race as an excuse or explanation for lack of success at school or on the job. The first generation tends to believe that, while racism exists in the United States, it can be overcome or circumvented through hard work, perseverance, and the right values and attitudes. The second generation experiences racism and discrimination constantly and develops perceptions of the overwhelming influence of race on their lives. These teens experience being hassled by police and store owners, not being given jobs, even being attacked on the streets if they venture into white neighborhoods. The boys adopt black American culture in their schools, wearing flattops, baggy pants, and certain types of jewelry. This contributes to the projection of the "cool pose," which in turn causes whites to be afraid of them. This makes them angry and resentful. The media also tell these youngsters that blacks are disvalued by American society. While parents tell their children to strive for upward mobility and to work harder in the face of discrimination, the American-identified teens think the rewards for doing so will be very slim.

This causes a wide gulf between the parents and their children. These parents are absolutely terrified of their children becoming Americans. For the children, to be American is to have freedom from the strict parental controls of the immigrant parents. This is an old story in the immigrant saga, one visible in novels and movies about conflicts between Jewish and Italian immigrants and their children. But the added dimension here is that these parents are afraid of the downward social mobility that becoming an American black represents to them. And this idea is reinforced constantly to these parents by whites who tell them that they are better than American blacks.

One question about how things had changed since the civil rights movement shows the different perceptions of the teens about race in American society. The ethnically identified gave answers I suspect most white Americans would give. They said that things are much better for blacks now. They state that blacks now can ride at the front of the bus and go to school with whites. The irony, of course, is that I was sitting in an all black school when they told this story. The vast majority of the American-identified teens state that things are not better since the civil rights movement; the change is that discrimination now is "on the down low," covered up, more crafty. Some pointed out that we were in an all-black school. The result of these different world views is that the parents' view of an opportunity structure that is open to hard work is systematically undermined by their children's peer culture and, more important, by the actual experience of these teens.

On the other hand, the ethnic-identified teens, whose parents are more likely to be middle class and doing well or who attend parochial or magnet schools, see clearer opportunities and rewards ahead, despite the existence of racism and discrimination. Their parents' message that hard work and perseverance can circumvent racial barriers does not fall on unreceptive ears. The ethnic-identified youngsters embrace an identity derived directly from their parents' immigrant identity. Such an identity is in opposition to their peers' identities and in solidarity with their parents' identities. These youngsters stress that they are Jamaican Americans and that, while they may be proud

of their racial identity as black, they see strong differences between themselves and black Americans. They specifically see their ethnic identities as keys to upward social mobility, stressing, for instance, that their parents' values of hard work and strict discipline help them to succeed in the United States when black Americans fail. This ethnic identity is very much an American-based identity—it is in the context of American social life that these youngsters base their assumptions of what it means to be Jamaican or Trinidadian. In fact, the pan-ethnic identities of Caribbean or West Indian often are the most salient label for these youngsters, as they see little differences among the groups and it is more important to differentiate themselves as second-generation Americans. The distancing that these teens show from black Americans often leads them to accept many negative stereotypes of black Americans. These youngsters tend to have ethnic friends from a West Indian background, white American friends, and very few, if any, black American friends.

The immigrant-identified teens are different from either of the other two, because of how they think about who they are not as well as how they think about who they are. These teens have a strong identity as Jamaican or Trinidadian, but this identity tends to be related to their interactions with other Jamaicans or Trinidadians rather than their interactions with black or white Americans. These youngsters identify with their homelands or their parents' homelands, but not in opposition to black Americans or in opposition to white Americans. They tend to be immersed in the immigrant community, to have friends who are all the same ethnicity or from other islands. They tend to be more recent arrivals. Unlike the ethnically identified, however, they do not distance themselves from American blacks, and they have neutral or positive attitudes and relations with them. At the same time, they see themselves as different from, but not opposed to, black Americans.

These identities are fluid and change over time and in different social contexts. We found cases of people who describe identifying very strongly as black American when they were younger and who became more immigrant identified when they reached high school and found a large immigrant community. Most new arrivals to the United States start out as immigrant identified, and the longer they stay in the United States, the more they begin to think of themselves in terms of American categories. The kind of social milieu the child faces, especially the school environment, has a strong influence on the outcome. A school with many black Americans creates pressure to identify racially; likewise a neighborhood and school with many immigrants makes it possible to avoid thinking much about American categories. In the face of much pressure not to follow the rules and not to succeed academically, youngsters who are doing well in school and do value education increasingly come to stress their ethnic backgrounds as an explanation for their ambition and success.

The American racial classification system that pushes toward an either/or—"black or white"—designation of people makes the immigrant option harder to hold onto. When others constantly identify the individual as black and refuse to make distinctions based on black ethnicity, pressure builds for the individual to adapt his or her identity to that outside identification—either to say "Yes, I am black," and to accept categorization with black Americans or to resent the characterization and strongly make an ethnic identification as Trinidadian American. The American myopia about ethnic differences within the black community makes the middle-ground immigrant identity unstable. Because every young person is aware of the negative images held by whites and the wider society of black Americans, the acceptance of an American black identity also means the acceptance of the oppositional character of that identity. Oppositional identities, as Ogbu (1990) clearly argues, are self- and group-affirming identities for stigmatized groups—defining as good and worthy those traits and characteristics that are the opposite of those valued by the majority group. This tends to draw the aspirations of the teens downward.

Implications of the Patterns

Some of the distancing shown by the ethnic-identified teens vis-à-vis underclass black identity is the same as that exhibited by middle-class black Americans. Elijah Anderson (1990) has noted that middle-class blacks in a gentrifying neighborhood in Philadelphia use various verbal and nonverbal strategies to convey to others that they are not from the ghetto and that they disapprove of the ghetto-specific behaviors of the blacks who live

there. Being an ethnic black in interactions with whites seems to be a shorthand way of conveying distance from the ghetto blacks. Thus, the second generation reserves their ethnic status for use as an identity device to stress their distance from poor blacks and to stress their cultural values, which are consistent with American middle-class values. This same use of an ethnic identity is present among first-generation immigrants of all social classes, even those in racially segregated poor neighborhoods in New York.

The second generation in the segregated neighborhoods, with little chance for social mobility, seems to be unaware that status as a black ethnic conveys higher social status among whites, in part because they have not had much contact with whites. The mass media convey to them the negative image of American blacks held by whites but do not convey to them the image among intellectuals, middle-class whites, and conservative scholars, such as Thomas Sowell, that they have cultural capital by virtue of their immigrant status. They do get the message that blacks are stereotyped by whites in negative ways, that the all-black neighborhoods they live in are violent and dangerous, and that the neighborhoods of whites are relatively safe. They also encounter a peer culture that values black American cultural forms. The immigrant culture of struggle, hard work, and educational success that their parents try to enforce is experienced in negative ways by these youngsters. They see their parents denying them privileges that their American peers enjoy and, unlike the middle-class youth, they do not automatically associate hard work, lack of dating and partying, and stress on scholastic achievement with social mobility. In the peer culture of the school, immigrant- and ethnic-identified teens tend to be the best students. In the neighborhood inner-city schools, newly arrived immigrants who have attended better schools in the islands tend to outperform the students who have spent their lives in substandard New York City public schools. This tends to reinforce the association between ethnicity and school success—and the more American-identified teens adopt an adversarial stance toward school.

Warner and Srole (1945), in their study of Yankee City in the 1930s, report that it is the socially mobile white ethnics whose ties to the ethnic group and the ethnic identity decline. In their work, those individuals stuck in the lower classes turned to their ethnic identities and groups as a sort of consolation prize:

> Our class system functions for a large proportion of ethnics to destroy the ethnic subsystems and to increase assimilation. The mobile ethnic is much more likely to be assimilated than the nonmobile one. The latter retains many of the social characteristics of his homeland. . . . Some of the unsuccessfully mobile turn hostile to the host culture, develop increasing feelings of loyalty to their ethnic traditions, become active in maintaining their ethnic subsystems, and prevent others from becoming assimilated. But, generally speaking, our class order disunites ethnic groups and accelerates their assimilation. (p. 284)

It could be that the process will be exactly the opposite for black immigrants and black ethnics. In this case, the more socially mobile cling to ethnic identity as a hedge against their racial identity. The less mobile blacks see little advantage to stressing an ethnic identity in the social worlds in which they travel, which are shared mostly with black Americans. Stressing an ethnic identity in that context risks being described as "acting white," being seen as rejecting the race and accepting the white stereotypes, which they know through their everyday lives are not true.

The changes in race relations in the United States since the 1960s are very complicated and most surely involve a mixing of class and race. Some white Americans are trying to see the difference between ghetto inner-city blacks, whom they fear and do not like, and middle-class blacks, whom they do not fear and with whom they would like to have contact, if only to prove to themselves that they are not racist or, in a more formal sense, to meet their affirmative goals.

Middle-class blacks realize this and try to convey their class status in subtle and not so subtle ways (Feagin 1991). The immigrants also utilize the fact that New Yorkers tend to use foreign-born status as a proxy for the class information they are seeking. The white New Yorkers we interviewed do notice differences among blacks, and they use ethnic differences as clues for class differences. If the association found here between social class and ethnic identity is widespread, this perception could become a self-fulfilling prophesy. It could be that the children of poor parents will not keep an ethnic identity and the children whose parents achieve social mobility will keep the ethnic identity. This will reinforce the image in the minds of whites that the "island people" are "good blacks," thus giving the edge in employment decisions and the like to ethnic blacks over American blacks.

On the other hand, it remains to be seen how long the ethnic-identified second generation will continue to identify with their ethnic backgrounds. This also is related to the fact that whites tend to make racial judgments about identity when it comes to blacks. The second generation does not have an accent or other clues that immediately telegraph their ethnic status to others. They are aware that, unless they are active in conveying their identities, they are seen as black Americans, and that often in encounters with whites, the status of their black race is all that matters. It could be that by the time they have children, they will have decided that the quest not to be seen as a black American will be a futile one.

Seeing the Big Picture   **Is a Nonethnic Racial Identity Possible?**

The four readings in this section recall a saying appropriate to this material: "You can change your ethnicity, but you can't change your race." Is this expression true or false? Why?

44

Guess Who's Been Coming to Dinner? Trends in Interracial Marriage over the 20th Century

Roland G. Fryer Jr.

ROLAND G. FRYER JR. is assistant professor of economics, Harvard University, and Faculty Research Fellow, National Bureau of Economic Research, both in Cambridge, Massachusetts. His e-mail address is rfryer@fas.harvard.edu.

WHILE BLACK–WHITE PARITY HAS NOT YET been achieved in the United States, many gauges relating to economic and political empowerment have shown extraordinary convergence. Over the past 40 years, for instance, the black–white ratio of median earnings for male full-time workers increased from .50 to .73 (Welch, 2003) and the racial disparity in life expectancy decreased from 6.8 to 5.3 years (author's calculations using data from the National Center of Health Statistics). For the first time, recent cohorts of black and white children with similar backgrounds enter school on equal footing (Fryer and Levitt, 2004).

But in the most intimate spheres of life—religion, residential location, marriage, and cohabitation—far less convergence has occurred. Martin Luther King Jr. famously noted in a number of his speeches that "the 11 o'clock hour on Sunday is the most segregated hour in American life" (for example, see King, 1956). Today, an estimated 90 percent of Americans worship primarily with members of their own race or ethnicity (Stodgill and Bower, 2002). Residential segregation, though lower today than in 1970, remains remarkably high. In a typical American city, 64 percent of blacks would have to change neighborhoods to ensure an even distribution of blacks across the city (Cutler, Glaeser, and Vigdor, 1999). Even friendship networks within seemingly integrated public schools are remarkably

> ### Questions to Consider
>
> In *Loving v. Virginia* (1967) the U.S. Supreme Court ruled that antimiscegenation laws were unconstitutional. Simply put, the Court argued that the federal government had no right to intervene in or prohibit matters of intimacy between consenting adults. One would expect that almost fifty years later people would have married in considerable numbers across the color line. It is true that the number of interracial marriages has increased considerably, but the number is still relatively small (about 7 percent of all marriages). What is most interesting from a sociological perspective is that marriages across the color line are not random. Some racial groups are more likely to marry across the color line than others. Which groups tend to engage in exogamy or marry "out" of their race more than the others, and why? What's the basis for your answer?

segregated; the typical student has .7 friends of a different race (Echenique and Fryer, forthcoming).

Historically, there was a distinction between economic and political equality on one side and social equality on the other (Woodward, 1955). Courts often stated that blacks would be made equal under the law but remain subordinate in informal, intimate spheres of life. In *Plessy v. Ferguson* (163 U.S. 537 [1896]), the U.S. Supreme Court argued that integration in schools, parks, railroads, and courts could not be mandated because they were private, social concerns. The last civil rights to be granted pertained to the laws governing to social interactions, like whom to marry and where to live.

In this paper, I focus on one aspect of social intimacy—marriages across black, white, and Asian racial lines. The paper begins with a brief history of the regulation of race and romance in America. Then, using census data from 1880 to 2000, an analysis of interracial marriage uncovers a rich set of cross-section and time-series patterns.

Marrying across racial lines is a rare event, even today. Interracial marriages account for approximately 1 percent of white marriages, 5 percent of black marriages, and 14 percent of Asian marriages. Among married whites, 0.4 percent choose to marry blacks and 0.6 percent choose to marry Asians. Among married blacks, 4.6 percent intermarry with whites and 0.5 percent with Asians. Asians intermarry almost exclusively with whites—white spouses comprise 13.2 percent of all Asian marriages and blacks roughly 1 percent.

The data are most consistent with a Becker-style marriage market model [Becker, 1973] in which objective criteria of a potential spouse, his/her race, and the social price of intermarriage are central. The evidence in favor of the classic Becker model is far from overwhelming and hinges on several plausible (but untestable) assumptions. Yet it is the only hypothesis I test that does not contradict the data in important ways, after testing a range of theories, including a social exchange theory of marriage that dominates the sociology literature and a marriage theory based on random search and social interactions.

Ultimately, social intimacy is a way of measuring whether or not a majority group views a minority group on equal footing. In most information-based theories of discrimination, stereotyping, stigma, and inequality, social intimacy leads to less discrimination and improved outcomes for racial minority groups (for example, Fryer and Jackson, 2003; Rosch, 1978; see also Loury, 2002, for a conceptual discussion of racial stigma). Relatedly, Patterson (1982) argues that "social death," the treating of individuals as less than full persons, is the real historical tragedy of racial relations in the United States.

The primary movation for this paper was to explore the division between political and social inequality in the unlovely history of *black–white* relations in America and how

interracial intimacy may be a more appropriate barometer for the closing of the divide than labor market statistics, but some of the more interesting patterns in the data concern *Asian* intermarriage. As a group, Asians did not face the intensity or longevity of social ostracism endured by blacks, but for many years the U.S. placed strict quotas on immigrants from Asia. This legacy may explain why the time-series patterns look so similar to those for blacks. The civil rights movement was liberating for all racial groups.

A Brief History of Romance, Regulation, and Race

When slavery replaced indentured servitude as the primary source of labor in the upper regions of the South during the last decades of the seventeenth century, whites began to work in close contact with blacks. In some cases, coworkers became intimate and blurred the color line (Moran, 2003). Antimiscegenation laws (laws that forbade marrying across racial lines) became a way to draw a distinction between black and white, slave and free. The Chesapeake colonies, now Maryland and Virginia, were the first to enact statutes that punished whites for racial mixing. In Virginia, the law instructed that a white spouse be banished from the colony within three months of an interracial wedding. This penalty was increased to six months in jail in 1705. In Maryland, if a white woman married a black man she became a slave to her husband's master. Interracial marriage laws also ensured that blacks could not have access to inheritance. Over time, bans on interracial marriage and corresponding social taboos were also directed at Asian groups like Chinese, Japanese, and Filipinos—especially in Western states. However, miscegenation has always been legal for Native Americans and Hispanics.

Table 1 provides dates for the permanent repeal of antimiscegenation laws, by state. The first column shows the twelve states that never had laws against black–white marital unions. The second column shows states that repealed such laws before 1900. The third column shows states that repealed such laws after 1900, but before the 1967 U.S. Supreme Court decision in *Loving v. Virginia* (388 U.S. 1), which held such laws to be unconstitutional. The final column shows the states that repealed their laws only after the Supreme Court ruling.

Looking back, one obvious question is why more states didn't drop their bans on interracial marriage after the passage of the 14th Amendment to the U.S. Constitution

TABLE 1   **Permanent Repeals of Antimiscegenation Laws, by State**

Never had such laws	Repealed before 1900	Repealed after 1900, before **Loving**	Repealed after **Loving**
Alaska	Illinois (1874)	Arizona (1962)	Alabama
Connecticut	Iowa (1851)	California (1948)	Arkansas
Hawaii	Maine (1883)	Colorado (1957)	Delaware
Kansas[a]	Massachusetts (1843)	Idaho (1959)	Florida
Minnesota	Michigan (1883)	Indiana (1965)	Georgia
New Hampshire	Ohio (1887)	Maryland (1967)	Kentucky
New Mexico[a]	Pennsylvania (1780)	Montana (1953)	Louisiana
New Jersey	Rhode Island (1881)	Nebraska (1963)	Mississippi
New York[b]		Nevada (1959)	Missouri
Vermont		North Dakota (1955)	North Carolina
Washington[a]		Oregon (1951)	Oklahoma
Wisconsin		South Dakota (1957)	South Carolina
		Utah (1963)	Texas
		Wyoming (1965)	Tennessee
			Virginia
			West Virginia

[a]Had laws, but repealed them before statehood.

[b]Had a law against interracial sex when it was a Dutch colony (New Amsterdam).

in 1868, which attempted to make sure that slaves would receive the rights of citizens by requiring "equal protection of the laws." Indeed, six states in the North, Midwest, and West repealed antimiscegenation laws at about this time, and a few Southern states temporarily dropped bans on interracial marriage. But the Southern states soon reversed course.

For instance, in an Alabama 1872 state Supreme Court decision, *Burns v. State* (48 Alabama 195), the court dropped bans on interracial marriage by appealing to the Civil Rights Act of 1866 and the 14th Amendment to argue that marriage was a contract and blacks now had the right to enter contracts with whites. But immediately following the removal of the Northern troops from the South, officials began to delineate sharply between political equality and social equality. Political equality was the formal access to governmental processes, whereas social equality involved informal relations between neighbors, friends, and family. In 1877, the Alabama Supreme Court reversed its decision in *Green v. State* (58 Alabama 190), concluding that the Civil Rights Act of 1866 was not meant to overturn antimiscegenation laws. The court rejected the idea that marriage was simply a contract between individuals. Instead, the court insisted that "homes are nurseries of the states" and that public officials were entitled to regulate marriage to promote the general good. The court argued that equal-protection laws were not violated so long as both parties were equally punished, and the court also declared that it was "under no obligation to promote social equality."

Even the famous 1954 school desegregation decision in *Brown v. Board of Education of Topeka Kansas* (347 U.S. 483), which was a fundamental breakthrough on the road to civil rights, did not bring an end to bans on interracial marriage. Six months after the *Brown* decision, the Supreme Court, without dissent, refused to hear an appeal by Linnie Jackson who was convicted under an Alabama statute barring interracial marriage. Alabama argued that *Brown* did not apply to antimiscegenation because the ruling only involved public services and facilities. One justice described the court's view on desegregation and antimiscegenation at this time by saying (as quoted in Moran, 2003), "One bombshell at a time, please!"

It was at the intersection of sexual freedom and civil rights that antimiscegenation laws would finally be eliminated. In the 1965 case of *Griswold v. Connecticut* (381 U.S. 479), the Supreme Court struck down a Connecticut statute that limited the use of contraception by married couples. The decision declared that marriage was an institution "intimate to the degree of being sacred." Two years later, the case of *Loving v. Virginia* held that all bans on interracial marriages were unconstitutional—forcing 16 states to allow interracial marriage.

Trends in Interracial Marriage over the Twentieth Century

To study the patterns of interracial marriage over time, I use data from the Integrated Public Use Microdata Series based on U.S. Census Data for 1880–2000. Interracial pairings are made using the "spouse location" variable which allows one to search through a census household to identify a given person's spouse, and then to identify demographic data about the spouse. An interracial marriage is defined as a marriage between two individuals who report a different race when the census is taken. Three racial groups are analyzed: Asians, blacks, and whites. All other racial groups and individuals without valid responses to race are dropped from the sample. Other racial categories were omitted because their definitions have not remained constant over time and very often the sample of intermarriages involving these groups is too small. Unless otherwise specified, the denominator used to calculate the rates of intermarriage for a racial group is the number of married persons within that group.

Racial Intermarriage Relative to All Marriage

Figure 1 shows trends in interracial marriage for whites, blacks, and Asians over time. Panel A documents the trends in interracial marriage among whites. In 1880, interracial marriages among whites and blacks or Asians were extremely rare (less than 0.1 percent of all white marriages). Whites were more likely to intermarry with blacks than Asians, though this trend eventually reversed. For the first 100 years of the time series, the share of white male–black female marriages remained under 0.1 percent, trended up from 1980 through 2000, and peaked in the latter years at 0.2 percent. White female–black male unions increased from 0.10 percent in 1970 to 0.45 percent in 2000.

White intermarriages with Asians follow a very different pattern. White male–Asian female matches were quite rare from 1880 to 1960. In 1960, this level was rising dramatically. These marriages continued to increase nearly

ten-fold over the next 40 years, and today are the most common interracial marriage. White female marriages with Asian men followed a similar, though less pronounced, trajectory.

Black males and females have similar trends of miscegenation across the twentieth century, though the level of interracial mixing is quite different, as shown in Panel B of Figure 1. Rates of interracial marriage between blacks and other racial groups remained flat from 1880 to 1970. Between 1970 and 2000, black men exhibit an almost six-fold increase in intermarriage with whites. Currently, almost 6 percent of black male marriages are with whites. Black females exhibit similar trends, although the timing of the increase is later and the raw prevalence of interracial marriages is less for black females. Roughly 2.9 percent of black female marriages are to white men. Black men and women are equally unlikely to marry Asians.

In 1880, approximately 1 percent of Asian men intermarried with whites. Rather than increase monotonically over time, the share of Asian men intermarrying with whites rises until 1940 and then decreases. Asian females exhibit the opposite pattern, showing dramatic increases in intermarriage with whites until 1980 and then a slow decrease. Until 1960, Asian men were more likely than Asian women to intermarry with whites. By the 2000 census, however, this trend had reversed. Asian women are almost twice as likely to marry a white person as Asian men.

In our sample, Asians comprise 1.4 percent, blacks 11.3 percent, and whites the remainder. It is quite remarkable, in a purely statistical sense, that white males and Asian females are the most prevalent interracial marriage. However, the fact that black–Asian intermarriage occurs so rarely could theoretically be due to their relatively small shares of the population, and need not imply negative preferences for one another—later we explore this possibility—but unadjusted means of interracial marriages need to be interpreted with care.

Figure 1 calculates intermarriage rates relative to all married people. However, the propensity of racial groups to marry has fluctuated substantially over time. If rates of intermarriage are divided by all people, not just by individuals who are married, some different patterns emerge.

Overall marriage rates have declined in recent decades. For instance, between 1962 and 2004 the marriage rate for black women has declined steadily from

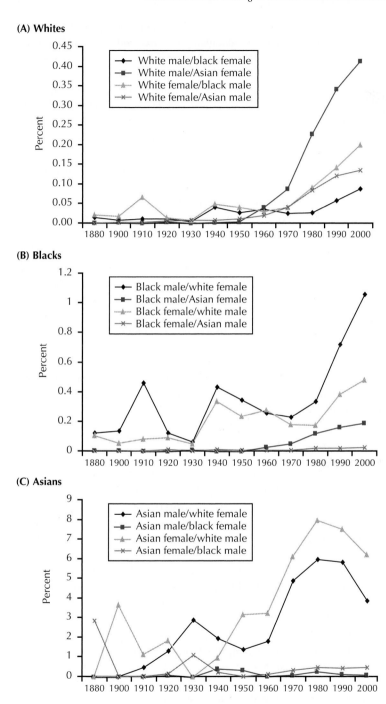

(A) Whites

(B) Blacks

(C) Asians

FIGURE 1 Percent of Whites (A), Blacks (B), and Asians (C) Marrying Out of Race, Excluding Foreign-Born, Counting All Persons *(as a percent of all marriages).*

62 to 36 percent (based on author's calculations using the Current Population Survey). Marriage rates among whiles have decreased from 84 to 64 percent.

If rates of intermarriage are divided by all people, then white men and white women show essentially similar trends as in Panel A of Figure 1: a low level of intermarriage until 1960—typically less than 0.05 percent—followed by a sharp increase in all categories of miscegenation. By 2000, 0.4 percent of white men had married an Asian female and 0.1 percent had married a black female, while 0.2 percent of white women had married a black male and 0.15 percent had married an Asian male. Asians and blacks also exhibit remarkably similar time-series patterns to that displayed in Figures IB and IC, though the magnitudes are substantially smaller because the denominator contains all persons rather than only married persons.

Intermarriage by Education Level

There seems to be some conventional wisdom that interracial marriages are concentrated among those with lower levels of education. But while this claim used to be true several decades ago, the pattern has reversed itself. Interracial marriages are now more concentrated among the those with higher levels of education.

For this analysis, I divide education level into four categories: high school dropout (less than 12 years of education), high school degree, some college (enrolled in college but not graduated), and college degree or more. Individuals without valid educational attainment responses were dropped from the sample. The analysis is also limited to the period between 1940 and 2000, because detailed data on educational attainment are only available in the census after 1940. (Before 1940, the census only asks whether or not a person is literate, not their educational attainment.)

From 1940 to 1960, whites with less than a high school level of education were the most likely to intermarry, at a rate of about 0.1 percent of all marriages, while intermarriage among higher-educated groups was essentially zero. In the 1960s and 1970s, whites with higher education levels begin to show a marked increase in miscegenation rates while intermarriage rates among the least-educated tailed off just a bit. In 2000, white men with some college education or more than a college education had

intermarriage rates above 0.4 percent, and white women in these education categories had intermarriage rates above 0.25 percent.

The pattern for Asians is similar to that of whites. From 1940 to 1960, about 8–12 percent of the marriages of Asian men with less than a high school education were outside the race. For Asian men with higher levels of education, the rate of intermarriage was typically 1–2 percent in these years. But the rate of intermarriage for low-educated Asian men has since plummeted to 1 percent in 1990 and almost zero by 2000, while the rate of intermarriage for Asian men with college education or more had risen above 4 percent by 1980. Asian women show a similar pattern, although the timing is a little different. Asian women of all education levels were very unlikely to intermarry in 1940, with all education levels having intermarriage rates under 2 percent. But from 1950 to 1980, Asian women with a high school education or less were more likely to intermarry than those with more education, at rates of 8–10 percent. But by 2000, intermarriage rates for Asian women with less than a high school education had dropped again, to 2 percent, while intermarriage rates for Asian women with a college education or more had risen to 8 percent.

Blacks follow this same general pattern, with a twist. Between 1940 and 1960, the least educated blacks were the most likely to intermarry, with intermarriage rates typically between 0.6 and 1.0 percent of all marriages. But during the 1960s and 1970s, the prevalence of intermarriage rates among this education group changed little, while those with more education increased intermarriage rates. By 2000, blacks with some college education were the most likely to intermarry, with an intermarriage rate of 2.5 percent for black men and 1.1 percent for black women (who are generally less likely to intermarry than black men). However, blacks are also much less likely than whites or Asians to possess a college or higher-level degree. Adjusting for the relative numbers of individuals in each educational category, more-educated blacks experience a sharper increase in their intermarriage rates than their less-educated counterparts. With this adjustment, the patterns of racial intermarriage by level of education are strikingly similar across all racial groups.

Military Service and Intermarriage

Soldiers are forced to interact and trust individuals of various ethnic and racial groups; the price for not doing so can be large. Romano (2003) provides a detailed historical description of interracial mixing in America since World War I, emphasizing the role of the military and of war in shaping preferences towards interracial marriage. To date, there has been no statistical analysis of members of the military versus civilians in the proclivity to intermarry. The data collected for this paper show that while military service seems to have had little effect on rates of intermarriage from 1940 to 1960, black and white veterans have had higher rates of intermarriage than nonveterans since then.

From 1940 to 1960, white veterans and nonveterans had very similar rates of racial intermarriage at 0.1–0.2 percent. As rates of intermarriage rise, the rate of intermarriage for white veterans rose faster than for nonveterans. By 2000, the intermarriage rate of white veterans was 1.3 percent versus a rate of 0.9 percent for nonveterans. Similarly, black veterans and nonveterans have very similar rates of intermarriage from 1940 to 1960, at about 1 percent. But as rates of racial intermarriage rise for both groups, the increase is faster for black veterans. By 2000, black veterans had an intermarriage rate of 6.9 percent, compared to 4.3 percent for black nonveterans.

In this area, Asians do not follow a similar pattern to blacks or whites. From 1940 to 1970, the intermarriage rate for Asian veterans was similar to that of nonveterans in the range of 10–15 percent. However, when rates of intermarriage increased for both groups in the 1970s, the rate for Asian nonveterans increased more quickly. By 2000, the racial intermarriage rate was 35 percent for nonveteran Asians versus only 24 percent of veteran Asians.

With the current data, it is impossible to distinguish between selection (individuals who enter the military are those who would be more inclined to intermarry) and treatment (the military experience cultivates a demand for interracial intimacy). The latter possibility is bolstered by the fact that the time-series variation fits with historical data on the integration of military units (MacGregor, 1985). The Armed Forces were fully segregated through World War II. President Harry Truman ordered an end to racial segregation in the late 1940s, and racially integrated units started during the Korean War. The trend has continued since. The military is currently believed to be as racially integrated as any U.S. institution, although blacks may still lag in officer representation, especially at the highest ranks (MacGregor, 1985).

Fitting Theories of the Family to Facts about Interracial Marriage

A number of facts emerged from the analyses in the preceding sections. White male–Asian female marriages are the most common interracial marriage, comprising 20 percent of all Asian female marriages and 35 percent for domestic-born Asian women. White female–black male is the second most common pairing, constituting 6 percent of black male marriages. Asian–black marriages are virtually nonexistent. Adjusting for the relative supply of each racial group in the population provides a different portrait of interracial marriage—particularly for intermarriage with Asians whose small numbers can make the raw calculations deceiving. Intermarriage rates differ substantially by education, geographic considerations, and veteran status. The most striking patterns are those concerning the reversal in the role of education in intermarriage. In the middle of the twentieth century, the least educated were more likely to be in an interracial marriage, but by the end of the century, the most educated were the most likely to intermarry.

In this section, we investigate the extent to which three theories of interracial marriage can account for this rich set of facts. The first theory is the most well known in sociology: social exchange theory (Merton, 1941). The remaining two are economic models: a search model and a Becker-style marriage-market model (Becker, 1973).

Social Exchange Theories

The leading theory in sociology for explaining intermarriage between racial groups is social exchange theory. This approach was originally laid out in Merton (1941); Blau (1964) and Kalmijn (1993) offer some interesting extensions of the basic model. The ideas are similar to some models of hedonic pricing in economics (Rosen, 1974).

Let individuals be represented by a vector of characteristics: attractiveness, sense of humor, height, weight, race, gender, family wealth, criminal record, and so on. Suppose the value of a person in a marriage market depends on that person's objective value, given a person's vector of characteristics, and the societal cost of marrying an individual with such characteristics. Further, assume that all else equal, marrying across racial lines is a cost.

The predictions of the social exchange theory are clear. For whites, given they are believed to be on top of the social hierarchy, interracial marriage will always come at a social cost, though interracial marriage with whites is a benefit to other groups. In equilibrium, then, whites must be compensated for their higher social status by intermarrying with racial minorities who possess more redeeming qualities. In minority–white marriages, the minorities will have superior objective characteristics—like being more attractive or intelligent—than their white mates. Thus, the social exchange model refers to a trade between objective characteristics and social status.

Social exchange theory is successful at capturing some elements of the data. For example, if one assumes that the societal cost of intermarriage fell sharply during the 1960s, then one can explain the increase in miscegenation after that time. If one further assumes that the societal cost of marrying Asians differs (in specific ways) from intermarrying with blacks, the relative magnitudes of Asian and black intermarriage with whites can be obtained. Further, a more general model of social exchange in which societal costs of interracial marriage decrease as objective value increases picks up further subtleties in the data.

However, this theory fails to explain the characteristics of who marries whom in interracial unions, which is really the key prediction. If anything, the average education of blacks who chose to intermarry is less than the average education of those who intramarry (despite the fact that higher-educated blacks are the most likely to intermarry—they are outnumbered by blacks with less education). This is a direct contradiction of the theory.

---

45 Captain Kirk Kisses Lieutenant Uhura: Interracial Intimacies—The View from Hollywood
Randall L. Kennedy

RANDALL L. KENNEDY is a professor of law at Harvard Law School. His areas of research and interest include the intersection of racial conflict and legal institutions in American life. He is author of *Interracial Intimacies: Sex, Marriage, Identity and Adoption* (2003) and *Race, Crime, and the Law (1997)*.

IN 1960 THERE WERE ABOUT 51,000 BLACK-WHITE married couples in the United States; in 1970, 65,000; in 1980, 121,000; in 1991, 213,000; and in 1998, 330,000. In other words, between 1960 and 2000, black-white mixed marriages increased more than six-fold. But not only are mixed marriages becoming more numerous; they are also becoming more common among people who are younger and more fertile. Previously, participants in such marriages tended to be older than other brides and grooms. Frequently they were veterans of divorce, embarking on second or third marriages. In recent years, though, interracial couples have been marrying at younger ages than their pioneering predecessors,

Questions to Consider   How many television shows and movies can you name in which the love interests are interracial couples? Now list the number of those interracial couples that were a black man and a white woman. Is it still true, as law Professor Randall Kennedy suggests, that the only way Hollywood would pair a black man, even a superstar like Denzel Washington, with a white woman, would be for him to be "paralyzed from the waist down" as in the movie *The Bone Collector* (1999)?

and have shown a greater inclination to raise children and pursue all of the other "normal" activities that married life offers.

Given the low historical baselines against which trends today are measured, it is easy to exaggerate the scope of black-white marital integration. It should therefore be stressed that mixed marriages remain remarkably rare, comprising a mere .6 percent of the total marriages in 1998, for instance, when 330,000 couples out of 55,305,000 overall had one black and one white partner. Moreover, blacks' racial isolation on the marriage market appears to eclipse that of other people of color. The percentages of Native Americans and Asian Americans marrying whites are much larger than the percentage of blacks doing the same.[1] Professor Nathan Glazer is correct, then, in stating that "blacks stand out uniquely among the array of ethnic and racial groups in the degree to which marriage remains within the group." Among the complex reasons for this social isolation are aggregate subjective evaluations of marriageability, beauty, personality, comfort, compatibility, and prestige that favor certain groups over others. At the dawn of the twenty-first century, a wide array of social pressures continue to make white-black marital crossings more difficult, more costly, and thus less frequent than other types of interethnic or interracial crossings.

Still, even taking into account the peculiar persistence of the black-white racial divide, the trajectory of this form of **miscegenation** is clear: through turbulent times and in the face of considerable opposition, the number of black-white marriages has been increasing consistently (albeit slowly) for at least forty years. Reinforcing this growth is the fact that interracial marriage has become compatible with lofty ambitions across a variety of fields—not only entertainment but government service, scholarship, the philanthropic sector, business, and the professions. The Thomas-Lamp marriage is indicative of this trend. So, too, are the unions of William Cohen (former senator from Maine and secretary of defense in the Clinton administration) and his black wife; Peter Norton (inventor of widely used computer software) and his black wife;[2] and Franklin Raines (former director of the Office of Management and Budget and chief executive officer of Fannie Mae) and his white wife. Furthermore, despite the substantial influence of the black-power

miscegenation The "mixing" of different racial groups—that is, marrying, cohabiting, having sexual relations and children with a partner from outside of one's racially or ethnically defined group.

backlash, some African Americans whose positions make them directly dependent upon black public opinion have managed to marry whites without losing their footing. A good example is Julian Bond, the chairman of the board of directors of the NAACP, whose wife is white.

There are other signs, too, that black-white interracial romance has become more broadly accepted and even, in certain contexts, quite fashionable. One such indicator is advertising. Advertisers seek to persuade people to buy goods and services by increasing awareness of them and associating them with imagined pleasures. In the past, advertisers targeting general audiences with the lure of romance have typically—indeed, overwhelmingly—used couples of the same race. But these days, at least occasionally, interracial couples are being deployed as enticements to shop at Nordstrom's, Club Monaco, or Wal-Mart, or to purchase furniture from IKEA, jeans from Guess, sweaters from Tommy Hilfiger, cologne from Calvin Klein, shampoo from Procter & Gamble, or watches from Gucci.

Television programming also signals important changes in sexual attitudes. Prior to the 1960s, portrayals or even insinuations of black-white interracial romance were virtually nonexistent on TV. The November 22, 1968, episode of the popular science-fiction series *Star Trek* marked a breakthrough in showing a kiss shared by the legendary (white) Captain James T. Kirk and (black) Lieutenant Uhura. Remarkably, however, the characters were not portrayed as actively *wanting* to kiss each other; instead they were *forced* to do so by a villain who captured Kirk's vessel, the starship *Enterprise,* and usurped the will of its crew. Not until 1975 did network television portray a married black-white couple, Tom and Helen Willis, who occupied a prominent place on the popular sitcom *The Jeffersons.* The show, a spinoff of Norman Lear's *All in the Family,* was about an eponymous black family whose patriarch, the hardworking but obnoxious George Jefferson, was obsessed with upward mobility, or what the theme song referred to as "movin' on up." The Willises lived in the same expensive apartment building as the Jeffersons. Although George constantly taunted the couple, calling them zebras, the families ultimately merged when the Jeffersons' son married the Willises' daughter.[3] Since the 1970s, depictions of interracial intimacies have remained rare on commercial television, though they do surface occasionally. In 1989 the short-lived *Robert Guillaume Show* presented viewers with a romance between a divorced black marriage counselor and his white secretary. The following year, the upstart Fox television network reluctantly aired *True Colors,* a situation comedy centered on the marriage of a black dentist (with two teenage sons) and a white schoolteacher (with a live-in mother and a teenage daughter). According to the show's creator, executives at the three older networks (ABC, CBS, and NBC) expressly stated that they were afraid the interracial marriage would alienate potential advertisers and dissuade at least some local affiliates from broadcasting the program. Notwithstanding cold feet at the top, writers have in the last decade or so succeeded in convincing television executives to air more entertainment fare featuring, or at least noting the existence of, interracial intimacy. Indeed, several of the most popular and influential shows of the 1990s portrayed transracial romances. Sometimes the racial aspect of the relationship was highlighted, as in *L.A. Law*'s dramatization of a black lawyer feeling that he must choose between his white lover and his job as an elected representative of a mainly black constituency. Sometimes it was ignored, as on *Ally McBeal,* where race matters seldom if ever arose in conversations between the white woman attorney and the black male physician with whom she was infatuated. On occasion, on-screen interracial relationships failed. The producers of *ER,* for example, terminated a romance between a black male doctor and a white colleague, not in deference to viewer opposition but because the black actor involved objected. He complained that whereas his character had always been obnoxious in his dealings with black women, he was now being shown as sympathetic in his treatment of the white woman. On other programs, interracial romance was permitted to blossom. In 1994, for example, on *In the Heat of the Night,* the white sheriff of a town in the Deep South married a black woman on-screen,[4] and in 1997, a network production of *Cinderella* paired a black actress in the title role with a Filipino Prince Charming, to great popular acclaim.[5]

In some venues, nonfictional portrayals of interracial intimacy have been sensationally negative, as on confessional talk shows that, for a while at least, uniformly depicted transracial relationships as troubled, weird,

or pathological.[6] In other contexts, however, television programs have acknowledged the gamut of personalities and emotions to be found among those who happen to be involved in interracial intimacies. In the fall of 1999, the Public Broadcasting System (PBS) aired *An American Love Story,* a ten-hour documentary film by Jennifer Fox that chronicled the lives of an interracial family: Bill Sims, a black man; Karen Wilson, a white woman; and their two daughters, Cecily and Chaney. Wilson and Sims first met in 1967, at a resort where he was playing piano in a rhythm-and-blues band and she was vacationing with her parents. He was the son of a cleaning woman and a steelworker who was also a Baptist minister; her father was a machinist, and her mother was a grocery clerk. When their courtship began, Bill was eighteen and Karen seventeen. Neither set of parents objected to the relationship, and both urged the couple to marry after Wilson got pregnant (though they in fact did not do so until the child was six years old).

Whites in Wilson's hometown of Prospect, Ohio, strongly condemned her romance with Sims. Her supposed friends ostracized the couple, and the local sheriff jailed Sims on several occasions for no other reason than to harass him. In 1972 they moved with their baby daughter to Columbus, but even in this larger, less isolated locale, they encountered overt hostility. They suspected bigots of killing their dog and setting their car afire in a successful campaign to frighten them away. They moved again, this time to Flushing, New York, where they hoped to find a more openminded community.

Over the years, the Wilson-Sims family subsisted largely on Karen's reliable earnings as a manager, supplemented by Bill's spotty wages as, among other things, a carpenter, mail carrier, and musician. At the price of some tedium, *An American Love Story* shows its subjects engaged in all the quotidian tasks of daily life—cooking, cleaning, resting, seeking comfort, venting frustration—that have little or nothing to do with racial differences. It also shows them facing various nonracial crises, including Karen's hysterectomy and Bill's alcoholism. Almost inevitably, though, racial difficulties surface to menace the couple and their children. Among the most poignant segments of the series are wrenching scenes from Cecily's years as an undergraduate at Colgate College, where tyrannical black classmates tell her, essentially, that if she wants to be their friend, she must refuse to join a predominantly white sorority and, more generally, defer to their black-separatist sensibilities. She declines their terms, and they retaliate; she is hurt. Throughout, the television audience is privy to the conflict.[7]

The creators of *An American Love Story* wanted to document an interracial marriage that spanned the final decades of the twentieth century. Its subjects, for their part, wanted to change perceptions through education; this ambition constituted the principal explanation offered by the Sims-Wilson clan for permitting their family life to be examined in such a public manner. Education was also the primary aim cited by the program's director, Jennifer Fox, a white woman who credited her own love affair with a black man with opening her eyes to important areas of American life to which she had previously been blind.[8]

On the big screen, too, recent years have seen an increase in both the number and the quality of depictions of interracial intimacy. There was a time, not so long ago, when the scarcity of such portrayals made keeping track of them easy; now, because of their increasing numbers and variety, that task is much more difficult. True, the fear of an adverse audience response can still cause cautious film producers to suppress interracial romance, not only through their choice of projects but even in their handling of plot points. In John Grisham's novel *The Pelican Brief* (1992), for instance, the protagonists become lovers, but in the screen version (1993), there is no romance; the relationship remains resolutely platonic. The reason for this alteration is obvious: the male lead is played by a black actor (Denzel Washington), and the female lead by a white actress (Julia Roberts). There are, moreover, scores of other examples of black actors apparently being singled out for Hollywood's cold shoulder treatment lest they mirror real-life interracial erotic excitement. Prominent among these desexualized roles are Will Smith's character in *Men in Black* (1997) and Wesley Snipes's in *Murder at 1600* (1997). This approach led one wag to remark, in reference to *The Bone Collector* (1999), that the only way Denzel Washington would ever be shown "getting the girl" was if he played a man paralyzed from the waist down. That being said, a number of major motion pictures released in the past decade have followed actors

and actresses of all complexions in their pursuit of sexual pleasures across color lines, and have done so with a boldness that probably would not have been tolerated in the environment that generated *Guess Who's Coming to Dinner?* Examples include the explicit erotic grapplings of Lawrence Fishburne and Ellen Barkin in *Bad Company* (1995), Wesley Snipes and Natassia Kinski in *One Night Stand* (1997), Reese Witherspoon and Bookeem Woodbine in *Freeway* (1996), Warren Beatty and Halle Berry in *Bulworth* (1998), Tom Cruise and Thandie Newton in *Mission: Impossible 2* (2000), Julia Stiles and Sean Patrick Thomas in *Save the Last Dance* (2000), and Halle Berry and Billy Bob Thornton in *Monster's Ball* (2001).[9] In increasing numbers of films, moreover, interracial intimacy has been emerging as simply one part of a larger story in which racial difference is of little or no significance. This is an important development because presuming the normalcy of interracial intimacy—treating it as "no big deal"—may be more subversive of traditional norms than stressing the racial heterodoxy of such relationships. Although examples of this presumption can be found in several films (e.g., *Pulp Fiction* [1994], *Cruel Intentions* [1999], and *Mystery Men* [1999]), the most significant was the blockbuster *The Bodyguard* (1992), which starred Kevin Costner and Whitney Houston.

• • •

Perhaps the most potent influence in creating new possibilities for interracial intimacy is that wielded by individuals engaged in (or born of) transracial dating, marriage, and parenting. This population, numbering in the hundreds of thousands, exhibits tremendous variety. One generalization that can properly be made about it, however, is that it is becoming increasingly vocal. There was a time, not so long ago, when the vast majority within this group sought invisibility; now, by contrast, many of its members seek recognition and are establishing or joining advocacy organizations devoted to publicizing their views and institutionalizing their presence. Announcing the formation of the Association of Multi-Ethnic Americans (AMEA) in November 1988, Carlos Fernandez declared:

> We who embody the melting pot . . . stand up, not merely as neutrals in interethnic conflicts, but as intolerant

participants against racism from whatever quarter it may come. . . . We are the faces of the future. Against the travails of regressive interethnic division and strife, we can be a solid core of unity bonding the peoples of all cultures together in the common course of human progress.

People involved in interracial intimacies used to voice quiet requests for simple protection against intimidation and violence. Now their demands are becoming more ambitious. One of these has to do with racial labeling. Many interracial couples object to standardized forms that compel them to designate their children either merely "black" or merely "white." Similarly, many who identify themselves as "mixed"—or "mulatto" or "half-and-half" or "multiracial"—bridle at classificatory regimes that impose singular racial identifications, as if everyone must be *only* white *or* black *or* Latino *or* Asian (etc., etc.). Prior to the census of 2000, the United States Census Bureau counted individuals according to that assumption. But after a good deal of prodding by AMEA and similar groups, the bureau decided to broaden the menu boxes available for indicating racial affiliation. Rather than being limited to only one box, respondents are now authorized to check whatever boxes they deem applicable, though the census bureau continues to decline to offer a separate "multiracial" box.[10] One complaint leveled against the traditional "check one box" regime is that it fosters confusion and inaccuracy—describing as "black," for example, people who are also partly white or partly Native American or partly Asian. Susan Graham, the (white) founder of Project RACE (Reclassify All Children Equally) notes that her "child has been white on the U.S. Census, black at school, and multiracial at home, all at the same time." Beyond the issue of statistical inaccuracy, the system has more personal ramifications, in that it compels mixed individuals to select for recognition only one aspect of their composite background, and thereby subordinate all the other aspects.

The census bureau's multiple-box-checking initiative addresses some but by no means all of the objections raised by critics.[11] Some contend that even the option of checking several boxes indicates, in effect, that multiracial individuals are only parts of other communities, rather than constituent members of a distinct multiracial community of their own. Some observers protest, moreover, the continuation of *any* racial scheme of classification, however it may be supplemented or repackaged. Whatever one may think of the ideas propounded by these various dissidents, it is clear that they are flexing their political muscles as never before and affecting hearts and minds in fundamental ways. They are not content to accept inherited conventions but insist instead on adding their own preferences to America's cultural mix. Professor Maria P. P. Root has demanded a Bill of Rights for racially mixed people, which would include the rights to identify one's race differently in different situations, to change one's racial identity over a lifetime (and more than once), to have loyalties to and identifications with more than one racial group, and to be able freely to choose whom to befriend and love. The winner of the 1995 Miss USA beauty pageant objected to being pegged as "black." "If people are going to know me," Chelsi Smith explained, "it's important for them to know that I'm black and white and that it hasn't been a disadvantage." Tiger Woods likewise does not enjoy being referred to as the first "black" or "African American" golf superstar, believing that those labels obscure other aspects of his ancestry that are just as important to him. He has therefore coined the term "'Cablinasian'—[for] Caucasian, Black, Indian, Asian"—to describe himself.[12] The coinage has proved controversial.[13] Many people, mainly blacks, have accused him of wanting to flee an African American identity that whites will impose upon him regardless of his preferences. ("When the black truck comes around," one observer quipped, "they're gonna haul his ass on it.") Such reactions notwithstanding, the real point here is that Root, Smith, Woods, and tens of thousands more like them have felt sufficiently self-assured to speak up, and have received substantial support in doing so. Their conduct mirrors and strengthens a new force in America: the will of people engaged in or born of multiracial relationships, who have begun to insist upon public recognition of the full complexity of their lives.

Across the country, scores of interracial support groups have sprung up, among them MOSAIC (Multiethnics of Southern Arizona in Celebration); A Place for Us (North Little Rock, Arkansas); I-Pride (Interracial

Intercultural Pride, Berkeley, California); MASC (Multiracial Americans of Southern California, Los Angeles, California); F.C. (Families of Color) Communiqué (Fort Collins, Colorado); Interracial Family Alliance (Augusta, Georgia); Society for Interracial Families (Troy, Michigan); 4c (Cross Cultural Couples & Children, Plainsboro, New Jersey); the Interracial Club of Buffalo; the Interracial Family Circle of Washington, D.C.; and HONEY (Honor Our New Ethnic Youth, Eugene, Oregon). On college campuses, students can join organizations such as FUSION (Wellesley), Kaleidoscope (University of Virginia), Students of Mixed Heritage and Culture (SMHAC, Amherst), Half 'n' Half (Bryn Mawr), and Mixed Plate (Grinnell). These groups offer forums in which people can meet others in their situation, disseminate relevant information, debate, and organize. Although most of these organizations lack deep roots, many display a vigor and resourcefulness that suggest they will survive into the foreseeable future. They stem from and represent a community in the making. It is a community united by a common demand that the larger society respect and be attentive to people who either by descent or by choice fall outside the conventional racial groupings—people who are partners in interracial couples, parents of children whose race is different from their own, and children whose race differs from their parents'. The members of this community want whites to cease viewing them as products or agents of an alarming mongrelization. They want blacks to stop regarding them as inauthentic and unstable in-betweeners. They want security amid the established communities from which they have migrated. They want to emerge from what the writer Lise Funderberg has aptly called the "racial netherworld." They want to enjoy interaction with others without regret or fear, defensiveness or embarrassment. They want respect.

Seeing the Big Picture

Love May Be Blind, but It's Not Color-Blind

Look at Section X in the Appendix. All things being equal, one would think that if people choose to marry across the color line these unions would be randomly distributed—that is, we would observe similar marriage rates across racial categories. But we don't. What do these data suggest about intergroup relations?

Discovering Racial Borders

46   *Heather M. Dalmage*

HEATHER M. DALMAGE is an associate professor of sociology at the School of Policy Studies at Roosevelt University, Chicago. She is the author of *Tripping on the Color Line: Black–White Multiracial Families in a Racially Divided World* (2000) and a national expert on interracial relationships. She is editor of *The Multiracial Movement: The Politics of Color* (2003).

Questions to Consider   Heather M. Dalmage explains how racial borders are "policed" to discourage individuals from falling in love across the color line. How and in what ways (if any) were racial borders enforced in your own life so that dating across the color line was not very likely to happen? How would your family react if your new romantic partner was from a racial category different from your own? Given that such unions are often stigmatized, what strategies do interracial couples employ, according to Dalmage, to dismiss such views and normalize their own relationship?

Border Patrolling

The belief that people ought to stick with their own is the driving force behind efforts to force individuals to follow prescribed racial rules. Border patrollers often think (without much critical analysis) that they can easily differentiate between insiders and outsiders. Once the patroller has determined a person's appropriate category, he or she will attempt to coerce that person into following the category's racial scripts. In *Race, Nation, Class: Ambiguous Identities*, Etienne Balibar and Immanuel Wallerstein observe that "people shoot each other every day over the question of labels. And yet, the very people who do so tend to deny that the issue is complex or puzzling or indeed anything but self-evident."[1] Border patrollers tend to take race and racial categories for granted. Whether grounding themselves in essentialist thinking or hoping to strengthen socially constructed racial categories, they believe they have the right and the need to patrol. Some people, especially whites, do not recognize the centrality and problems of the color line, as evinced in color-blind claims that "there is only one race: the human race" or "race doesn't really matter any more." Such thinking dismisses the terror and power of race in society. These individuals may patrol without being aware of doing so. In contrast, blacks generally see patrolling the border as both problematic and necessary.

While border patrolling from either side may be scary, hurtful, or annoying, we must recognize that blacks and whites are situated differently. The color line was imposed by whites, who now have institutional means for maintaining their power; in contrast, blacks must consciously and actively struggle for liberation. Repeatedly, people in multiracial families have told me, "The one thing that David Duke and Louis Farrakhan agree on is that we should not exist." What is not analyzed are the different historical legacies that bring both men to the same conclusion. The only form of borderism in which blacks engage is border patrolling, although they can act on prejudicial feelings and discriminate. After centuries of systemic control, only whites can be racist. As Joe Feagin and Hernán Vera explain, "black racism would require not only a widely accepted racist ideology directed at whites, but also the power to systematically exclude whites from opportunities and rewards in major economic, cultural, and political institutions."[2] White and black border patrollers may both dislike interracial couples and multiracial families, but their dislike comes from different historical and social perspectives. Moreover, border patrolling tends to take place intraracially: whites patrol whites, and blacks patrol black and multiracial people.

White Border Patrolling

Despite the institutional mechanisms in place to safeguard whiteness, many whites feel both the right and the obligation to act out against interracial couples. If a white person wants to maintain a sense of racial superiority, then he or she must attempt to locate motives and explain the actions of the white partner in the interracial couple. A white person who crosses the color line threatens the assumption that racial superiority is essential to whites. The interracially involved white person is thus often recategorized as inherently flawed—as "polluted."[3] In this way, racist and **essentialist** thinking remains unchallenged.

Frequently white families disown a relative who marries a person of color, but several people have told me that their families accepted them again once their children were born. The need to disown demonstrates the desire to maintain the facade of a pure white family.[4] By the time children are born, however, extended family members have had time to shift their racial thinking. Some grant acceptance by making an exception to the "rule," others by claiming to be color blind. Neither form of racial thinking, however, challenges the color line or white supremacy. In fact, both can be painful for the multiracial family members, who may face unending racist compliments such as "I'll always think of you as white."

The myth of purity is maintained by controlling white women's wombs. Thus, white women are patrolled more harshly than white men are. The regulations women face have not always been overtly displayed but have developed within the culture's conception of the *family ethic,* an ideal extant since the arrival of the early settlers that has influenced perceptions of proper work and home roles for white, middle-class family members.[5] The proper family should have a male breadwinner and patriarch and a female who makes her husband and obedient children her life's central work. According to Mimi Abramowitz, the family ethic "has made [women] the guardians of family and community morality, expected them to remain pious and chaste and to tame male sexuality, and defined them as weak and in need of male protection and control."[6] Ultimately, the family ethic has kept white women under

essentialism The false idea that individuals or groups have an immutable fundamental nature that exists outside of society. An essentialist statement would be that all women are nuturing.

the control of white men. In *Whiteness Visible: The Meaning of Whiteness in American Literature and Culture,* Valerie Babb notes that images depicting white women as helpless and in need of white men's protection grew against a backdrop of a developing patriarchy. White women faced particularly harsh regulations because the "loss of sexual purity through intercourse with other races endangers visible race difference, a key driving force behind an ideology of whiteness that gives political, economic, and social advantage to those with 'appropriate' race lineage."[7] The myth of white racial purity required white women to give birth to the offspring of white men—and only white men. Unfortunately, many white women have played active roles in maintaining this myth of purity. For instance, in 1897 one wrote: "If it takes lynching to protect women's dearest possession from drunken, ravening beasts, then I say lynch a thousand a week if it becomes necessary."[8] Today many white women who give birth to children of color give them up for adoption, fearing that as mothers of children of color they will become pariahs in their families and society at large.[9] Such complicity has worked to strengthen the color line and white-supremacist abuses.

It has been argued that white women should be protected because they are the gatekeepers of racial purity.[10] Any white woman who would trade in her white privilege and connections to white male power must be dismissed as unnaturally bad and bizarre. Julie, a white mother recently divorced from her black husband, has contended with white border patrolling and its underlying images. One incident (although not the only one) occurred while she was on a date with a white physician:

> He asked to see a picture of my daughter. I handed it to him. He was very clever; he asked, "Is her dad from the U.S.?"
>
> I think he was praying her dad was Spanish, and he could deal with that, anything but black. I could tell it bothered him, so I said, "Listen, I can see by the look on your face that there is obviously a problem here, so why don't we just talk about it right now."
>
> He said, "You want to know the truth? Well, I have a real problem with the fact that you slept with a black man." Then he went on with the whole, "You're such a pretty and intelligent woman; why would you marry a black man?"

Her date was drawing on the interlocking imagery of race and sex and what it means to be a good white woman. In his attempt to explain away Julie's behavior, he searched for motives, implying that only unattractive, unintelligent white women sleep with and marry black men. Further, the fact that she slept with a black man removed her eligibility as a white woman. She is assumed to be fundamentally and essentially changed. Perhaps he feared that his white purity would be contaminated with blackness through this bad white woman. Perhaps he felt threatened because he could not immediately detect her racial flaw. He may have begun to discover the mutability of race, which could undermine his own sense of racial superiority. While all people of color face some form of racist imagery in a white racist society, Julie notes the centrality and power given to racist images directed specifically against black people and interracially involved whites and blacks: "I think he was praying her dad was Spanish, and he could deal with that, anything but black."

Black men are seen "as a constant threat" to patriarchal whiteness.[11] Abby Ferber writes: "A photograph of a white woman with an Asian American man, for example, does not have the same symbolic power. The image of interracial sexuality between a white woman and a black man is pregnant with meaning in the American imagery. Powerful enough to serve as a symbol of all interracial sexuality."[12] White women who enter into interracial relationships with black men are often treated as aberrant, misguided white trash who are in this relationship solely for sex or rebellion. Barbara gained forty pounds because she "got tired of being mistaken for a prostitute." She explains, "It's assumed that the only reason you're involved in the relationship is because you're sexually depraved. . . that you've got to be the dregs of society to get involved or you want to hurt somebody." Women may be explained away as money or status seekers.[13] Often when we are out, people will ask Philip what he does for work. After learning he's an attorney, they don't bother to ask me what I do. This could be a gender issue; in a **patriarchal** world men are seen as the subjects, women the objects. But I often wonder how much it has do with assumptions about uncovering the motive behind our relationship—that I have traded my white status for his occupational and class status.[14]

The strength of racist images is manifested in the comments directed at women who are assumed to be good,

patriarchal Refers to a society organized so that men dominate women.

upstanding white women. June, a businesswoman who is raising two biracial sons in suburban New Jersey, commented, "I think America still hates [white] women who sleep with black men. And when they see you with these children, they want to believe you adopted them, which is usually the first question people will ask: 'Did you adopt them?' I always just say, 'No, I slept with a black man.'"

June's comments highlight a few issues. First, she does not specify who constitutes "America." Whites may hate these women because they threaten the color line that maintains white privilege and power. At the same time, blacks may hate them because they threaten the unity of African Americans. Second, several white women talked to me about the frequency of the adoption question—one more attempt to explain their behavior. If women who appear to be good turn out to be polluted, white border patrollers become nervous. Their inability to tell "us" from "them" calls into question their own racial identity. The more the border patroller clings to an identity of racial superiority, the more he or she looks for ways to explain away these aberrant white women. Third, like June, many interracially married white women resist allowing whites to recategorize them in an attempt to regain or maintain a sense of superiority. "No, I used the good-old fashioned method" is a common retort to such questioners.

Not all white women resist border patrollers. Many succumb to the hostility and end their relationships with black men. Several white women told me they had temporarily ended their interracial relationship, each citing border patrolling as the reason. For instance, Barbara, the woman who gained forty pounds to avoid being seen as a prostitute, said:

> When I met my husband, he was the sweetest, kindest—he was a wonderful human being, everything I was looking for except for the color and at one point I was really apprehensive about it. The race thing really bothered me 'cause I didn't like being stared at and I didn't like people hating me. I didn't like how black women viewed me, and to white men I was a possession. It's like, "you crossed the line." You know the feeling, like you have to be the lowest of the low to be with an African American. "Who are you trying to hurt?" It was just really sick. So I went away for a while.

Although she did eventually marry this "wonderful human being," she needed time away to think about race on a more sophisticated level—time to question her internalization of racist images and the color line.

The stereotype of black male sexuality converges with the myth of the chaste and virtuous good white woman, making white female–black male relationships the ones most patrolled by whites.[15] White men contend with a different type of border patrolling in a society that privileges both whiteness and maleness. Historically, white men who interracially marry were reported to come from lower economic classes and were at times designated as crazy.[16] Today the more common image that white interracially married men face is of being in the relationship solely for sex. These men may be seen as committing an individual transgression but are not held responsible for protecting whiteness. In her study of white supremacist publications, Abby Ferber found that "while relationships between white women and black men are condemned, and described as repulsive, relationships between white men and black women were common and remain beyond condemnation."[17] The lack of imagery about white male–black female relations reflects a history of silence among whites concerning their complicity in the rape of black women. Moreover, in a society in which whiteness (and maleness) represents power, privilege, and unearned advantage, many white men view their privilege in the world as normal. They risk "outing" these taken-for-granted privileges when they talk about race.[18]

The white men with whom I spoke were split about the importance of—even the existence of—border patrolling. Unlike black men, black women, and white women, they did not consistently talk about the effects of racialized images. When I asked, "As an interracially married white man, how do you think others view you?" responses were split: half the men spoke of border patrollers; the other half denied the importance of race in their lives and society. The first few times I heard white men deny or disregard the importance of racism and border patrolling, I was surprised. It took me some time and several more interviews to make sense of this.

Joe, the first interracially married white man I interviewed, lived in a predominantly white, upper-class community about an hour from New York City. With his infant daughter on his lap and a tape recorder on the table, he began to unfold the details of his life. I asked how he thinks others view him. He responded, "I can't worry about what other people think. For a long time my wife worried, but once she got over that, we had a big wedding. . . . It took a lot to convince her that's how we should think about it, and I think she's more comfortable with that." He said that they do not have problems as an interracial couple, that everything is smooth. We were chatting after the interview when his wife walked into the room. She began to cite several problems they had faced because of their interracial relationship. When she referred to each incident, he nodded in agreement.

Several months later I interviewed Raymond, a white interracially married man living on Chicago's north side. Drinking coffee in a local café, he discussed the meaning of race in his life. When I asked him about how others view him, he replied staunchly, "I don't know, and I don't care. I never thought about it. I don't think about it. What do they think when they see my wife and me together? Pardon my language, but I don't give a shit what they think; I just don't give a shit. I go for months, and that never occupies my mind."

These men may be proving masculinity through a show of strength, rugged individualism, and disinterest and thus verbally disregard border patrolling and racial images. Each, however, repeatedly claimed that race does not matter. Instead, they believed the focus "should be on ethnic backgrounds" or on the fact that "we are all Americans." Men who did not want to recognize racial images tended not to recognize the privilege associated with whiteness, drawing instead on notions of meritocracy. Whether or not they recognized differences, they did not recognize power. Nevertheless, they used their power as white males to create a racial discussion with which they felt comfortable. For instance, Joe's comfort came from not having to hear any racially derogatory comments: "If somebody would make a derogatory comment, I would just say, 'My wife is black.' Usually I wouldn't even have to say, 'I don't want to hear comments like that'—they would just stop." Whiteness is about privilege and power. It is a privilege to be able to set the parameters of racial discussions and expect that others will comply. Moreover, the power of these professional white men overrides the power that white border patrollers may have to influence them.

In addition to proving masculinity, these men may be attempting to downplay the prevalent stereotype that interracial couples are together for sexual reasons only. For instance, Raymond repeatedly stated that his relationship was not about "jungle fever," a phrase that filmmaker Spike Lee popularized to suggest that interracial couples are attracted only because of sexual curiosity. At the end of our interview I asked Raymond if there was anything else he wanted to say. He answered, "Let people know that this is not about jungle fever. Race does not matter. I love my wife." His repeated references to jungle fever reflected his awareness of border patrolling despite his claim of color-blindness. Rather than critically thinking about race and the origins of such stereotypes, he defensively dismisses the significance of race.

Some white men did recognize and address the importance of racial images, border patrollers, and the relationship between race and power. The common thread for these men was that they had friendships and networks with black males before meeting their spouse. Through these male friends they began to recognize the privileges that remain invisible to so many other white men. The importance of friendships with black males cannot be understated. White men sit in a position of power because of both their race and sex. When sex differences are removed as a factor in their relationships, they can understand more clearly the ways in which race mediates power relations. This is not as obvious to white men who are introduced to blackness (and thus whiteness) through intimate relations with a woman.

Clancy, a fifty-year-old white man who grew up outside Chicago, had black roommates and friends in college. By the time he met his wife he understood from his buddies the effects of racism in society. He spoke in detail about the border patrolling he faced from the white teachers at the Chicago elementary school where he taught after getting married: "My wife and I walked into a meeting with the white teachers and the people from the neighborhood, and it sent those people into conniptions. I won't forget that. It was my first year teaching there, and from then on it was like, 'God have mercy on my soul,' I was a dead person in that school and that stayed with me for seventeen years—the whole time I was there." In this case, Clancy's teaching position was continually threatened by white border patrollers.

Peter, a white minister living on Chicago's South Side, had graduated from a black seminary in the southern United States. As the only white in many situations, he was immersed in black culture. The privileges and power bestowed on whites in a system of whiteness and the richness of black culture became visible to him. Like Clancy, he recognized and addressed the border patrolling he encountered from whites. In the following case, Peter had just been named the pastor of a white church in a white working-class neighborhood in Cleveland: "I had gotten moved to a white church. That turned out to be two years from hell. The church did not want me to be appointed there. They actually had a special meeting after they got wind of who was coming; 95 percent of the church did not want me there because I was interracially married. The first church meeting I was at, the chair asked for further motions. One person said, 'I make a motion that the reverend resign from this church.'" Peter laughed about the absurdity of the situation and then continued: "The first sermon, attendance was over one hundred; everyone came out to see the show. From then on, attendance never got above sixty, so basically about forty people boycotted the whole time I was there. I had people who still attended but resigned all their offices." In addition, church members began a letter-writing campaign to the bishop accusing Peter of various wrongdoings—for example, claiming he had taken all the Bibles out of the church. Peter and his family eventually moved to a black church in Chicago. The Ohio church members who had resigned their offices returned to them after he left.

Privileges granted to people with white skin have been institutionalized and made largely invisible to the beneficiaries. With overwhelming power in society, why do individual whites insist on border patrolling? As economic insecurity heightens and demographics show that whites are losing numerical majority status, the desire to scapegoat people of color, especially the poor, also heightens. As whites lose their economic footing, they claim white skin as a liability. Far from recognizing whiteness as privilege, they become conscious of whiteness only when defining themselves as innocent victims of "unjust" laws, including affirmative action.[19] In their insecurity they cling to images that promote feelings of superiority. This, of course, requires a racial hierarchy and a firm essentialist color line. Border patrolling helps to maintain the myth of purity and thus a color line created to ensure that whites maintain privileges and power.

Black Border Patrolling

Some blacks in interracial relationships discover, for the first time, a lack of acceptance from black communities. Others experienced border patrolling before their marriage, perhaps because of hobbies and interests, class, politics, educational goals, skin tone, vernacular, or friendship networks. Patrolling takes on new proportions, however, when they go the "other way" and marry a white person. While all relationships with individuals not seen as black are looked down on, relationships with whites represent the gravest transgression. Interracially married black women and men often believe they are viewed as having lost their identity and culture—that they risk being seen as "no longer really black." Before their interracial marriage, most called black communities their home, the place from which they gained a sense of humanity, where they gained cultural and personal affirmation. During their interracial relationship many discovered black border patrolling. Cathy Cohen suggests that "those failing to meet indigenous standards of blackness find their life chances threatened not only by dominant institutions or groups, but also by their lack of access to indigenous resources and support."[20] Interracially involved blacks needed to carefully weigh their decision to cross the color line.

George, a black man, lives with his wife, Dorothy, a white woman, and their two young children in Montclair, New Jersey, a racially mixed suburb of New York City. I drove along the town's big, clean, tree-lined streets one Sunday morning to meet with George in his home. During our interview he explained that he had dated a white girl in high school and was aware of how blacks and whites respond to such a relationship. Nonetheless, a recent event at his Manhattan workplace troubled him. Bill, a black male coworker, told him:

"I couldn't marry a white woman. How about you?"

I said, "I am married to a white woman."

"You joking me, George! Big strong handsome brother like you!"

I said, "Yo, man, I don't know what all that handsome stuff you comin' with."

He said, "All jokes aside, George, you telling me you went the other way?"

I said, "There's nothing wrong with that."

And he's like "Oh, George, I don't believe it."

He was just solemn after that and looked down, so I said, "Bill, does that mean we're not going to be friends anymore?"

He goes, "No, man, you still my man."

He gave me the ole handshake; I said, "Bill, no, man, you frontin' now."

He said, "I'm just surprised, you know. You never told me about your wife."

The implication here is that a "strong brother" would not sell out his community like this; only weak men would do that. Before this confrontation George had been an integral part of many conversations at work about race, racism, and black culture. After it he found "they'll be talking about something totally in the black culture. I come into the room and be listening; and when I would put my opinion in, the conversation would end—just like that. The room goes empty. . . . because I'm married to a white woman, blacks figure my culture is gone; it's shot." He is accused of having lost connectedness to African Americans, being weak, and marrying a white woman to escape his blackness.

Blacks in interracial relationships defend themselves against accusations of weakness, neurosis, and betrayal. In *Black Skin, White Masks,* Frantz Fanon writes about black men in interracial relationships: "I marry white culture, white beauty, white whiteness. When my restless hands caress those white breasts, they grasp white civilization and dignity and make them mine."[21] In his psychoanalytic interpretation of the effects of **colonization** and racism, Fanon suggests that many black men who intermarry suffer from neurosis created in a world in which black men are not valued and thus do not value themselves. They think that a relationship with a white woman will validate them—that is, whiten them. Of black women, Fanon writes, "It is because the Negress feels inferior that she aspires to win admittance into the white world."[22] Without acknowledging the pain caused by border patrolling and the desire many interracially married blacks have to maintain strong ties with other blacks, Fanon labels black men and black women in interracial relationships as pathological and neurotic.

colonization When one country controls another in order to seize resources, such as land, gold, timber, or ivory, or to enslave its population.

More recently, Paul Rosenblatt and his colleagues conducted a study of forty-two multiracial couples in the Minneapolis–St. Paul area. They conclude that many African Americans feel that "it is inappropriate to choose as a partner somebody from the group that has been oppressing African Americans."[23] Many black border patrollers have an overriding concern about loyalty to the race. If an individual is not being loyal, then he or she is explained away as weak, acting in ways that are complicit with the oppression of other black Americans. In "Essentialism and the Complexities of Racial Identity," Michael Eric Dyson suggests, "Loyalty to race has been historically construed as primary and unquestioning allegiance to the racial quest for freedom and the refusal to betray that quest to personal benefit or the diverting pursuit of lesser goals. Those who detour from the prescribed path are labeled 'sellouts,' 'weak,' 'traitors,' or 'Uncle Toms.'"[24] Thus, black men and women face differing social realities and forms of patrolling.

An overwhelming percentage of black-white couples involve a black male and a white female at a time when there are "more single women in the black community than single men."[25] Many black men are hindered by a racist educational system and job market that make them less desirable for marriage. Many others are scooped into the prison industrial complex. High-profile athletes and entertainers who marry white women confirm for many that black men who are educated and earn a good living sell out, attempting to buy white status through their interracial relationship.[26] Beyond issues of money and status, many black women see black male–white female interracial relationships "as a rejection of black women's beauty, [and] as a failure to acknowledge and reward the support that black women give black men."[27] In *Rooted against the Wind,* Gloria Wade-Gayles writes about the pain and feeling of rejection that black women experience when they see black men with white women:

> We see them, and we feel abandoned. We feel abandoned because we have been abandoned in so many ways, by so many people, and for so many centuries. We are the group of women furthest removed from the concept of beauty and femininity which invades almost every spot of the planet, and as a result, we are taught not to like ourselves, or, as my student said, not to believe that we can ever do enough or be enough to be loved or desired.[28]

Black women and men may both feel a sense of rejection when they see an interracial couple, but for each that sense of rejection comes from a different place. In a society in which women's worth is judged largely by beauty—more specifically, **Eurocentric** standards of beauty—black women are presumed to be the farthest removed from such a standard. Men's worth is judged largely by their educational and occupational status, two primary areas in which black men are undermined in a racist system. Black men with few educational and job opportunities lack status in the marriage market. Thus, when black men see a black woman with a white man, they may be reminded of the numerous ways in which the **white-supremacist** system has denied them opportunities. The privilege and power granted to whites, particularly to white males, is paraded in front of them; and they see the black women in these relationships as complicit with the oppressor.

I met Parsia, a successful businesswoman and a black interracially married mother living in Connecticut, through a family friend. Having grown up in a close-knit African American community, she was uncertain if she wanted to marry interracially and risk losing the support of that community. Now happily married and the mother of a beautiful little girl, she is still very aware of border patrolling. For this reason she prefers not to bring her husband to some areas in Harlem and to black-centered events:

> African Americans do view blacks in interracial relationships as turncoats. There is a pervasive belief in the African American community that it is much more difficult to maintain your identity in an interracial relationship. I believe that once blacks see me as part of an interracial couple, it changes their perception of me right away. They disrespect me as another black person, and then they just disregard my belonging to the community, and suddenly I become the outsider—an outsider because I am with him.

Eurocentric The view that European culture is superior to all other cultures in the world; implies that European culture should be the yardstick by which all other cultures are measured.

white supremacist A person who believes in the supremacy of the white race.

Her fears are not unfounded. One day she and her husband were walking in Philadelphia when a young black man accosted them:

> If I had been alone and this young brother was hassling me in any way, I would have stopped, turned around, and said, "Look, why are you bothering me? What's the deal here?" But I didn't feel at all that I could have this conversation with this young man. He was so hostile, and the source of his hostility was totally his perception of black-white relationships, and there was nothing I could say to change that perception.

This young border patroller may be responding to a belief that Parsia is a race traitor. She is no longer an insider worthy of respect but an outsider who signifies neurosis in the form of self-hate and community betrayal—perhaps the highest form of betrayal. The prospect of rejection by other African Americans is enough for many blacks to deny, hide, or avoid interracial relationships. Border patrolling from other blacks, racism from whites, and the prospect of struggling alone in a racist society seem too high a price; so many who enter interracial relationships end them in short time.

Today there are no longer legal sanctions against interracial marriage, but de facto sanctions remain. At times, family and friends exert pressure to end the interracial relationship; at other times, pressure may come from the border patrolling of strangers. Even if the relationship is clandestine, thoughts of how friends, family members, co-workers, employers, and the general public might respond can deter people from moving forward in a relationship. In each of the following cases the couples did get back together eventually, but all the black women took some time away from the relationship to make this choice.

Lisa met her white husband when she was a college student at a historically black college in the South.

> [I was] the only female in the jazz orchestra, [so] there were all these [black] guys saying, "Why are you with this white guy?" And one band member would make racial comments about "Don't marry whitey, don't trust whitey, don't do this for whitey." This guy in the band tried to talk me out of marrying Peter. I had some apprehension, so I broke up with him and told him I did not want to develop a relationship.

Parsia explains why she temporarily ended her relationship before finally deciding to marry her white husband, Joe:

> When I met Joe, I was really resistant to dating across racial lines. No way would I do that. It took me a very long time to get over that and deal with those feelings, biases, and expectations. I expected friends would feel very uncomfortable socializing with us. I still do believe that there is a certain language that blacks have when we are apart from other races, when we are alone socially. That's a very important part of my life, and I expected that I might lose that, and that was a very fearful thing for me. The more I felt him getting closer, the more I started seeing the possibility of longevity in the relationship, the more afraid I got. I was terrified that I would be in an interracial relationship for the rest of my life, so I pulled back in a big way and we broke up. There was definitely a shame and a guilt I had to get over because I felt that by dating interracially I was betraying black men.

Her fear reflects her reliance on other African Americans for mutual support in a white-supremacist system. Moreover, her observation that "there is a certain language that blacks have when we are apart from other races" indicates a shared cultural identity that creates and demands the enforcement of borders.

In some cases parents and family reinforce reservations about crossing over. Quisha, like Parsia, broke up with her white boyfriend, Raymond, because she needed time to think about what life would be like in an interracial relationship. "I was really excited about him and told my mom, and she just had a heart attack because he was white. I totally did not expect this from her. She would call everyday and was just hammering it into me to just forget this—and so I really badly and abruptly broke it off with Raymond. He was a real gentleman; he kept calling to find out what happened, and I totally blew him off." She explained her underlying fears as she discussed how she handles people staring at her: "I can feel my grandmother and my mother and my aunts disapproving in those stares, so that's intimidating." Lisa, Parsia, and Quisha all married the men they had left, but they needed time to think about risks, their own understandings of race and community, and what it means to be a black woman in the United States.

They are three of the many black women in interracial relationships who challenge the idea that white men are responsible for the low number of black female–white male interracial marriages. Theorists attempting to explain motives behind interracial marriages have often pointed to the low number of these marriages as evidence that white men are choosing not to marry black women.[29] These theorists suggest that white men are least likely to intermarry with black women because they would gain nothing in these marriages: no money, no status. My research, however, demonstrates the power of black women. The stories they share directly challenge long-held motive myths that imply that black women would marry white men if only white men would choose them. On the contrary, in each of the relationships just discussed, the black woman instigated a breakup. Perhaps their understanding of what it means to be strong, dedicated, and connected to black communities is responsible for the lower numbers of black female–white male marriages.

Border patrolling plays a central role in life decisions and the reproduction of the color line. As decisions are made to enter and remain in an interracial relationship, the color line is challenged and racial identities shift. Many blacks spoke of the growth they experienced because of their interracial relationship and border patrolling. Parsia explains, "I used to be real concerned about how I would be perceived and that as an interracially married female I would be taken less seriously in terms of my dedication to African American causes. I'm not nearly as concerned anymore. I would hold my record up to most of those in single-race relationships, and I would say, 'Okay, let's go toe to toe, and you tell me who's making the biggest difference,' and so I don't worry about it anymore." Identities, once grounded in the presumed acceptance of other black Americans, have become more reflective. Acceptance can no longer be assumed. Definitions of what it means to be black are reworked. Likewise, because of border patrolling, many whites in interracial relationships began to acknowledge that race matters. Whiteness becomes visible in their claims to racial identity.

Conclusion

Unlike transracially adopted and multiracial people who are raised across the color line, people in interracial relationships discover borderism when they decide to cross the line. This unique form of discrimination, grounded in a racist and segregated society, is always at work even when multiracial family members are not present. Yet by examining the experiences of multiracial family members, we can see the myriad ways in which the color line is both reproduced and resisted. Because interracially married people are often raised in single-race worlds, they have internalized borderism. Thus, part of the decision to become involved interracially includes the need to overcome internalized borderist thoughts. Most of them begin questioning color-blind and essentialist perspectives and learn to understand race as more fluid and complex. Skin color and physical features become just one set of criteria used to think about community and belonging. Many of the people I interviewed referred to this growth process (although not all interracially married people accept the invitation to rethink race).

In a society that often rejects people who cross the color line, individuals involved in such relationships have much to consider before making a permanent commitment. Given the significance of race in our society, a basic choice that all couples contend with is whether or not to stay together in the face of borderism. A few individuals claimed that there was no decision; they fell in love, and that was it. For most others, however, a life across the color line and facing borderism did not look all that inviting and in fact was enough to cause some to terminate their relationships.[30] While the number of people involved in interracial relationships is not known, we do know that in 1995 the census bureau estimated that there were only 246,000 black-white interracial marriages in the United States.[31] This is quite a small percentage considering that in the same year there were more than 50 million total marriages.[32] Borderism and its various components are strong and painful enough to keep black-white interracial marriages the least common marriage pattern for both blacks and whites.

47 Redrawing the Color-Line? The Problems and Possibilities of Multiracial Families and Group Making

Kimberly McClain DaCosta

KIMBERLY MCCLAIN DACOSTA is associate professor of African and African American studies and of social studies at Harvard University. DaCosta is interested in the intersection of cultural ideas about race and the family and is currently completing a book on efforts to create a multiracial collective identity in the United States, based on interviews and fieldwork with members of organizations for interracial families and people of mixed descent.

It is my belief that the next generation's principal task will be the hard and painful one of destroying color-caste in the United States.
—W. LLOYD WARNER[1]

A FTER TIGER WOODS WON THE 1997 MASTERS Tournament, he quickly became the poster boy of multiracialism—the well-adjusted, hugely successful, mixed race child with two devoted, loving, and *married* parents. Woods's rising public profile mirrored and symbolized the increasingly public profile of mixed descent persons. By the 1990s, multiracial families and multiracial identity were given more attention in the media, portrayed in such a positive way that one could be excused if one forgot the powerful stigma previously heaped upon intermarried couples and their families. Woods's success and embrace by the American public lent credibility to assertions that multiraciality was "old news"—that this had been going on for centuries (by which people usually meant interracial sex, not family), and that Americans were no longer shocked by this anymore.

Yet the emergence of multiracial families represents a significant historical shift, particularly when we consider the efforts made to prevent and conceal family ties across racial boundaries. The emergence of a multiracial identity as the expression of such family ties is a major shift as well. Given that race as a mark of identity (rather than an

Questions to Consider   In 2000 the U.S. Census Bureau allowed individuals to check more than one racial category in the decennial census. Although there is a long history of "multiracials" in the United States, the effect of institutionalizing the mixed race or multiracial category has carved out a distinct social identity that challenges the way we typically think about racial categories. Within the context and acceptance of a multiracial movement one can now claim, as Professor DaCosta points out, a "Japanese and Mexican" or a "black and Irish" identity. How might these "new" identities redraw the color line? How might you respond when someone explains to you they are "black, white, and little bit Latina" or "Italian, Asian, and Puerto Rican"?

uncomplicated descriptor of a biological reality) only developed in the twentieth century, and that the major period of growth in marriages across racial categories did not begin until the 1960s, this shift has taken place in a relatively short period of time. In the last decade, the idea of "multiracial community" has developed a social and cultural presence in the United States. Since the struggle over the census in the 1990s, references to "multiracials" regularly appear in the popular press, in academic literature, and in the marketplace, and the creation of multiracial organizations has continued unabated. Due to the efforts of people in those organizations, in conjunction with increasing rates of intermarriage, the multiracial family is no longer a contradiction in terms. Rather than "melting" into traditional racial groups, people of mixed race are elaborating a distinct sense of groupness as "multiracial." At the same time, they are asserting specific mixed ethnoracial identifications such as "Japanese and Mexican" or "black and Irish."

How then should we evaluate the impact and significance of multiracial group making? How is the color line being redrawn? The definition of race—a basic concept for describing social differences and inequalities in the United States—is in the process of changing. But in what ways and with what impact?

It is impossible to evaluate the impact of multiracial politics without attention to historical and social contexts. Without such contexts, it is tempting to conclude, as many have, that the collective efforts of multiracials are inherently progressive, inherently regressive, or even irrelevant. Appearing on the Oprah Winfrey show, for example, a black/white woman explains to the audience that as a multiracial person she can be a bridge to promote understanding between racial groups. In hearings over changes to racial classification, opponents to the possibility of the state enumerating mixed descent persons invoke the specter of **apartheid** South Africa, suggesting that new categories will create an escape hatch from blackness. At around the same time, some scholars claim that Asian outmarriage reflects Asian self-hatred and is an attempt to leave behind a stigmatized group. Still others state that the issue is "old news," not important enough to waste time commenting on it.

The social and historical contexts will allow us to make sense of what multiracials are doing today and that make such blanket assessments of multiracial politics less defensible. For the multiracial movement is about race and family—cultural categories, not static institutions—the meanings of which depend on context. This being the case, there can be no definitive answer to the question "are multiracial politics progressive or regressive?" Such evaluations will differ according to individual identities and political intentions. More useful than evaluations of the logic of racial categories or intermarriage in the abstract, then, are historically grounded and ethnographically parsed accounts that show us what is different between now and the past and that ask what these categories mean to the people who feel invested in organizing around them.

apartheid The state-sanctioned and legally enforced policy of racial segregation instituted by South Africa.

Family Matters

According to Drake and Cayton (1993 [1945]), "Social segregation is maintained, in the final analysis, by **endogamy**—the rule that Negroes must marry Negroes, and whites must marry whites—and by its corollary that when an intermarriage does "accidentally" occur, the child must automatically be classed as a Negro no matter how white his skin color."[2]

In order to understand multiracial group making—its rise, shape, contents, and possible impact—one must not only denaturalize race but denaturalize the family, for the construction of the American family and race are joint historical and cultural processes that are mutually determinative. Racial classifications and antimiscegenation policies facilitated the creation of sharp divisions between social groups, defined them as racially different, and in so doing shaped the cultural common sense in which racial difference and the division of families along racial lines appears to be natural. Despite the possibility of legal marriage across racial boundaries, the normative family is still monoracial, and racial affiliation exacts a kind of loyalty that disqualifies intimate connections across racial categories. The realization that they are misfits in this context motivates multiracial actors to challenge the prevailing race/family nexus.

This struggle is apparent in the stories told by my respondents. While the interracial unions in my respondents' families were legally sanctioned, some struggled with the discretionary acts of disowning by their monoracial parents that mimicked the economic impacts that antimiscegenation laws once had. For most intermarried couples and families, however, what is at stake lies in the terrain of relatedness, emotional connection, the sense of cultural loss and gain, and the recognized reflection of the self in one's child—all structured by the racial dimension of the normative family.

The legalization of intermarriage, along with popular representations of multiracial families as heterosexual and nuclear leads to interpretations of multiracial families as an interesting "flavor" of the normative family. While it is clear that the heterosexual nuclear family is accorded material and social privilege in U.S. society, and that most of the contemporary discussion of multiracial

endogamy The custom of marrying only within one's racial, ethnic, or social group.

families concerns heterosexual couplings, it misses the point to see multiracial families as an interesting variation on the theme of the heterosexual nuclear family. Rather, multiracial families—and multiracial politics broadly conceived—should be understood as part of an historical transformation in kinship, ideology, and social relations that have come about as the result of conflict, contradiction, and struggle.

Yet just how far we have come is a matter of debate. Although antimiscegenation laws are unconstitutional, intermarriage remains rare, especially so between blacks and whites. Moreover, a nontrivial percentage of people (of all racial groups) still disapprove of intermarriage. While the social climate for intermarried couples and families has certainly improved in the last several decades, Drake and Cayton's observations of Chicago in the 1930s describe all too well the state of intermarriage today, especially for blacks. They found that while blacks had made gains in governmental and economic areas, only "very moderate" gains had been made in "spatial and family relations." They concluded that while intermarriage is legally permitted, "it is generally discouraged." "[I]nformal social controls among both Negroes and whites," they wrote, "keep the number of such marriages small despite the fact there are no legal prohibitions against them" (1993 [1945], 127).

Of course, the same degree of separation is not found between Asians and whites and Latinos and whites. Intermarriage rates with whites for Asians, Latinos, and Native Americans are comparable to those of Southern and Eastern European immigrants in the early twentieth century who, through intermarriage with American-born whites, expanded the definition of who is white. With each generation in the United States and as income and education levels rise, Latinos and Asians are more likely to marry whites. This has prompted Roger Sanjek (1994) to argue that we may be seeing a "race-to-ethnicity" conversion for Hispanics and Asians, but not for African Americans.

Despite very low intermarriage rates for blacks, which testify to a firmer racialized boundary separating blacks from other groups, assertions by multiracials—even those of African descent—that they are not "just black" confounds that once defining feature of the color line to which DuBois ([1903] 1996) referred a century ago. Multiracial activists' demand for a recognition of mixedness challenges the categorical nature of the American racial classification system which, until 1997, recognized membership in only one category. As such, it is in direct opposition to the logic of the one-drop rule—the key mechanism that maintained that color line. Moreover, their efforts disrupt what the one-drop rule firmly established, namely the racial basis of kinship in which relatedness across racial boundaries is not socially recognized.

In everyday life, not just in official categories, the definition of blackness (and consequentially of white, Asian, Indian, and Latino identities) is shifting as well. So while in the 1930s Drake and Cayton (1993 [1945]) observed that the "children of mixed matings" are "always defined as Negroes," an understanding that prevailed through the 1980s, this is no longer as certain as it once was. Mariah Carey, for example, is not understood (or marketed) as a black singer, despite being of African descent, just as respondents with an ambiguous physical appearance and who lack cultural credentials are not necessarily accepted by blacks as (authentically) black, nor are they necessarily seen as sharply different by nonblacks despite knowledge of their African ancestry.

Racial Options?: Choice and the Limits of Choice

Twenty-six years ago, in the conclusion of her study on the Lumbee Indians of Robeson County, North Carolina, Karen Blu stated that "there is no 'right' to choose one's 'racial' ancestry, as race is currently conceived, but if race and ethnicity become progressively intertwined in a new way, it is possible that being Black will, in years to come, be more a matter of individual choice and less a matter of assignment by others" (1980, 210). Students of race and ethnicity in the United States often note that a key difference between the ways Americans experience ethnic and racial identities is the degree of choice one has to identify (or not) in ethnic or racial terms. This distinction is based on the historical experience of European immigrants. As the voluntary and involuntary factors that held together European immigrant ethnic communities (for example, residential segregation, discrimination, prejudice, religious affiliation) have declined, so too has the salience of ethnicity in the lives of their descendants (Alba 1990; Gans 1979; Lieberson 1985; Waters 1990). For these white ethnics, ethnicity is chosen rather than ascribed and expressions of ethnic identity are largely symbolic in content.

In her often-cited book *Ethnic Options: Choosing Identities in America,* Mary Waters (1990) found that not only did her white respondents choose which ethnicity to be, but also whether to be ethnic *at all*. Moreover, ethnic identity held few negative consequences for her respondents. It did not limit whom they could marry, determine where they could live, their employment prospects, or who their friends were. In contrast, the literature is replete with examples showing the continued prevalence and salience of ethnoracial ascription for nonwhites. The third and fourth generation Japanese and Chinese Americans Mia Tuan studied report that "others consistently expect them to identify ethnically (e.g., as Chinese or Japanese) or racially as Asian and be knowledgeable about Chinese or Japanese 'things' and express dissatisfaction when they are not" (Tuan 1998, 156). Attributions of racial difference are consequential for African Americans whether or not they choose to assert a racial identity, even for middle-class blacks who conform to white middle-class norms of behavior (Bell 1992; Cose 1992; Fordham 1997).[3] Racial options—the ability to choose whether to identify or be identified in racial terms—have been elusive.

Events of the last decade, however, suggest that we need to revisit the question of whether or not "racial options" are in the making. The institutionalized option to choose multiple racial affiliations in official race counts represents a racial option "on paper." The flexibility exhibited by respondents in how they describe, display, and perform their ethnoracial identities makes clear that indeed racial identification and categorization are somewhat malleable. But how much can this be said to approximate the kind of symbolic ethnicity found among white ethnics?

In all the ways ethnic identity did not matter for Waters's respondents, racial identity *did* matter for mine. Regardless of how much they chose to identify themselves as mixed, they faced resistance from institutions, peers, and even family members. When they wished not to have to identify themselves in racial terms, others *did* classify them in racial terms, and not necessarily in the ways they wished to be classified. Moreover, *how* they looked mattered very much in what types of identity expressions were likely to be authenticated by others. The dark-skinned person who identifies as white—or even mixed—must still work very hard to get others to treat him as such. In other words, not all heritages can equally be chosen or discarded at will. That their efforts have been met with suspicion and resistance is telling of lingering opposition to treating what are considered racial distinctions as just another form of ethnicity.

A key aspect of the optional character of white ethnicity is its costlessness. Unlike the ethnic identifications of white ethnics, for my respondents "being" mixed race or marrying someone of a different race had significant costs. Some intermarried respondents were "disowned" by their parents. For others, racial difference within the family was sometimes a source of tension that distorted emotional connections between family members. Moreover, for mixed descent respondents, asserting a mixed racial identification threatened their belonging within ethnic communities.

Yet while racial identification for multiracials is not entirely voluntary or costless, there is a way in which multiracial identification looks like the symbolic ethnicity of whites. Waters (1990) explains the apparent paradox that while ethnicity is a matter of choice, relatively costless and inconsequential in her respondents' lives, her respondents "cling tenaciously to their ethnic identities." They do so, she argues, because symbolic ethnicity actually reconciles two contradictory impulses in the American character—the desire for both individuality *and* conformity. "Having an ethnic identity is something that makes you both special and simultaneously part of a community. It is something that comes to you involuntarily through heredity, and at the same time it is a personal choice. And it allows you to express your individuality in a way that does not make you stand out as in any way different from all kinds of other people" (Waters, 1990, 150).

Similarly, the idea that racial identity can be freely chosen appeals to the high value Americans place on individualism. The novelty of a mixed racial identity makes one stand out against dominant modes of identification. At the same time, the elaboration of a sense of multiracial group identity makes one feel as if one belongs to a community where one is, if only in one's perceived marginality, just like everyone else. The irony here is that while the discourse of choice in racial identification suggests we as individuals are determining for ourselves who we want to be, in fact we are "choosing" within a given set of epistemological, social, and political conditions that make only certain choices possible.

Scholars have sometimes described the trajectory of white ethnicity from a consequential group affiliation to a largely symbolic one as a transition from "being" to "feeling" ethnic (Bakalian 1993). "People desperately wish to 'feel' ethnic," Steinberg argues, "precisely because they have all but lost the prerequisites of 'being' ethnic." (1989, 63). In this respect, the multiracial example is perhaps best understood as a move in the opposite direction. Elaborations of multiracial collective identification represent an attempt to move *from* "feeling" *to* "being" multiracial. For some of my respondents, that feeling of being mixed race was largely a feeling of not fitting into any ethnoracial community. For others it was based on a feeling of being a part of both. The construction of multiracial organizations, the push for official designation of mixed race status—these are moves to make multiracials appear more real in a culture that elevates ethnicity and race as primary markers of personhood—to not only feel multiracial, but also to "be" multiracial in civic and social life.

The dividing line between what constitutes racial versus ethnic difference in the United States has always fallen fairly close to the line marking whom one would consider marrying and what ancestry one would publicly claim. Yet according to this barometer, some racialized distinctions—particularly American Indian status—have also been treated as "ethnic" ones—interesting "decorations" to the family tree that have little consequence in everyday life. Of course, the symbolic aspect of American Indian identity has only been inconsequential for persons of mixed background, whose native ancestry is generations removed, and who do not live on reservations. While to date visible non-European ancestry has been consequential, particularly for persons of African descent, one can certainly imagine a time in the not too distant future where being Asian, Mexican, and even black will increasingly be treated and *experienced* (much like American Indian ancestry is currently treated by whites who claim it)—symbolically. As this generation of mixed descent persons have children of their own, who may cross even more racialized boundaries, they are likely to encourage their children to "embrace" all of their ancestry. As such, the proliferation of racial identifiers that individuals use is likely to expand. The consequences of such racial identifications and the nature of the connections to those racialized communities, however, will largely depend on where they live, whom they live with, and what they look like.

The Future of Multiracial Group Making

I have discussed in detail how the multiracial example draws our attention to the hegemonic, yet hidden assumptions about the American family—namely that families are monoracial—and how racial homogeneity has been fundamental to how families are constructed. But what does the multiracial example teach us about ethnoracial group making? In the process of elaborating what they share with each other, and seeking public recognition for themselves, multiracials make the mixed position a socially recognizable one. As the idea that multiracials exist is further institutionalized, it is appropriate to evaluate in what sense this "group" will come to be like traditional ethnoracial groups.

Like panethnic formations among Latinos, Asian Americans, and American Indians in the United States, the construction of multiracial community is profoundly shaped by state policies. These panethnic formations arose out of a context in which the state "lumped" together groups who consider themselves to be distinct on some basis deemed salient (such as shared language or presumed racial similarity). In response, these distinct cultural and linguistic groups began to assert a common identification (Espiritu 1992; Nagel 1995; Omi and Winant 1994). Collective identification, generally speaking, followed categorization.

The assertion of a collective identification among "multiracials" emerges out of a different relationship to the state. Unlike Latinos, Asians, and American Indians, "multiracials" have not been lumped together for the purposes of racial classification or the administration of social policies. Neither were they counted separately in racial statistics nor was social policy developed to deal with them as a class of people. Multiracials began to coalesce in response to social and cultural pressures that defined them as misfits and that stigmatized interracial families. They *sought* a state classification as a remedy to those grievances.

Now that the state classifies mixed race people as such, one of the key factors motivating multiracial mobilization in the 1990s is no longer available. Additionally, the prejudice and stigma associated with interracial marriage and families have declined significantly. Even in the absence of those initial motivating factors, however, it seems likely that collective mobilization around multiracial identification will continue for the foreseeable future.

First, mixed race organizations have become increasingly institutionalized. The Mavin Foundation has professionalized what began as grassroots, minimally organized community building efforts. Matt Kelley, its founder and president, has assembled a paid staff that operates a Web site, runs community outreach activities, and acts as a kind of clearinghouse for information on mixed race people and issues of race and social justice. The foundation publishes a quarterly magazine (*Mavin: The Mixed Race Experience*), the production values of which rival those of most national monthlies—a far cry from the photocopied newsletters irregularly produced by local community organizations in the 1990s. Moreover, through its Campus Awareness and Compliance Initiative, sponsored jointly with HIF, AMEA, and the Level Playing Field Institute, it aims to ensure that the MOOM [mark one or more] option is fully institutionalized in federal agencies.[4]

Groups like Mavin, as well as campus organizations and academic classes, focused on mixed race people are manifestations of ongoing attempts to create and sustain mixed race community. Once established, people have vested interests in maintaining them, as they provide jobs, income, and a public platform for members. These venues for expressing and exploring multiracial identity are likely to thrive, as the "two or more races" population is expected to grow significantly in the next decade. Recent population estimates show the "two or more races" population was the third fastest growing group between 2003 and 2004 (behind Hispanics and Asians) (Files 2005). While demographic statistics cannot predict whether multiracial collective identification will be meaningful to this population, the ongoing institutionalization of mixed race identity will encourage such an identification. For example, schools are required to ask students if they are "of two or more races," and given the opportunity to identify themselves this way, many people will. With statistics on this population, school administration will likely craft programs for such students, further encouraging such an identification. Indeed this is already happening. In 1988 when students at Harvard formed a discussion group for mixed race students, they knew of no other such group. By 2005, the ninth annual Pan-Collegiate Mixed Race Conference took place while one of the largest professional associations of student affairs personnel inaugurated a standing committee on multiracial student affairs, alongside its committees for Asian, African American, Latino, and Native American students.[5]

While the educational arena will likely encourage multiracial identification, so too will the market. The juggernaut of consumer capitalism has taken up multiracialism. As long as mixed race retains its air of hipness and authenticity, marketers will continue to exploit it. As long as the population that identifies itself as mixed race continues to grow, business will court "it," developing products to meet its putative needs and helping to make multiracials in the process. Five years after Census 2000, multiracial community is increasingly translocal, Web based, and media driven. The advent of high-speed global communications technology in the 1990s has allowed those previously isolated by geography to "come together" virtually. These virtual communities are cheap to start up and to run and so will likely continue. Not incidentally, the low cost and wide reach of Web communications has greatly facilitated the creation of companies selling mixed race consumer products. Increasingly, mixed race organizations, Web communities, and entrepreneurs engage in a symbiotic relationship, with each Web site giving links to each other, and in so doing reinforcing their raison d'etre.

While mixed racial identifications have become further institutionalized through state codification, it is not clear to what extent "multiracials" will make demands on the state on behalf of multiracials as a group. To date, self-appointed spokespersons for multiracials limit themselves to ensuring that federal agencies collect multirace data and to calls to investigate the extent to which multiracials have unique health care needs.[6] At this time, the multiple race population is not a protected class for the purposes of antidiscrimination efforts, which may be the next battle multiracial activists wage. The political commitments of younger organized multiracials, however, appear to be left leaning. Participants in Mavin, the leaders of Mixed Media Watch, and my respondents largely consider themselves to be politically progressive and antiracist. They are skeptical of the claims that race does not matter by conservatives who point to their multiple racial identifications as proof of its irrelevance. There is a strong impulse among these respondents to avoid essentializing a set of differences that distinguish multiracials from others. Yet through the debate over official classification and the organizations in which they explore what they share as a group, racial mixedness is constituted as an adequate principle upon which to act.

There is an inescapable irony of group making that in seeking to undermine the foundations of American racial thinking, they reaffirm racial thinking as well. While activists and parents describe their use of multiple terms for indicating their racial identity as "revolutionary" or simply "accurate," it is also true that the logic of mixed race stems from the same underlying logic that preceded it—that individuals have race, and when they combine sexually we get "racial mixture." Both ideas assume there is race, it is carried in the body, and its mixed through sexual reproduction.

While those who fought official enumeration of mixed race status challenged the prevailing way that race was categorized, they stopped short of challenging the principle of racial classification itself. While seeming to challenge the racial state, multiracial activists *affirmed* the right of the state to label individuals in racial terms by arguing that it has a *duty* to label them in ways that fully recognize the possibility of boundary crossing. This can only entrench the underlying notion that individuals are made of "racial stuff" (albeit of more than one type) and that their racial composition ought to be recognized by that ultimate symbolic agency—the state. Their activism recognizes, indeed *welcomes* the right of the state to record a race for each of its members (even if individuals "self-identify"). This is a striking acceptance of the racial state, in and through which the category of race was created and through which it is reproduced.

Yet this irony is not limited to this movement. "The reproduction of ethnicity and the reinforcement of its pragmatic salience," writes Comaroff, "is as much a function of efforts directed at its erosion as it is of activities that assert its positive value" (Comaroff 1987, 315). If race is where you locate your difficulties, race is where you look for solutions. "Race" seems like an efficacious basis upon which to act.

The construction of multiracial community, like pan-ethnic constructions and movements for ethnic renewal, is a flexible, sometimes strategic and sometimes contradictory phenomenon. It creates new racial subjects while conforming to the preexisting U.S. racial order, as it provides a crucial consciousness-raising tool with which to make demands on the state. It undermines rigid modes of racial thinking in the United States while multiplying the available ways of naming racial difference. While mixed race people may identify *with* each other, they eschew the notions of racial sameness that racial identity usually entails. While a collective mixed race identity is

potentially subversive, it may be readily absorbed into the existing racial order, in which multiraciality comes to be seen as simply another racial category, robbed of its critical content.[7] The meaning of multiracial will be affected by the political alignments, demographics, and economic pressures of all other groups.

Critics of the group-making project among multiracials claim that "the multiracial community" is a fabrication. After all, mixed race people come in a variety of "mixes." As such, as a group they share no ancestry in common. Nor do they necessarily share language, religion, or culture. They are not, in other words, a "real" ethnic group. Yet the fabricated aspect of multiracial group making that its critics find so troubling is precisely what makes studying this phenomenon so valuable. The notion of "fabrication" has a double meaning, signifying both an act of creation (which captures the constructed nature of groups) and a *deception,* in which the ways we tend to perceive groups in everyday life (as durable, real, substantial entities) masks the reality that groups do not exist as such, but rather are the products of a complex work of *group making.* All ethnoracial groups are constructed. In the project of making multiracials, however, the ways in which such construction proceeds are just more obvious.

The Family's Role in Racial Change

Multiracial activists have used the state as a means through which to gain symbolic recognition not only of their racial identity, but of their families as well. The multiracial family, some believe, serves as proof that America's racial problems can be overcome. I dub this the "family thesis," inspired by Benjamin DeMott's critique of contemporary racial politics. In his book, *The Trouble with Friendship,* DeMott (1998 [1995]) critiques what he calls "the friendship thesis" that underlies many putative solutions offered in culture and politics for healing racial division. According to DeMott, embedded within the "friendship thesis" is the "certainty that one-on-one, black-white relations can be relied on to resolve race problems." In a similar vein, the "family thesis" suggests that if we all just intermarried and had children together our problems would be resolved.

Historical and cross-cultural analyses show the problems with such an idea. First, rather than bringing about social equality, intermarriage tends to follow other indicators of social equality (such as educational achievement) between groups. But more to the point, it is questionable that personal relations can resolve what is wrought institutionally with the help of the state, no matter how intimate and caring those personal relations are. The hierarchies of relatedness that my respondents hold, which structure their sense of trust, affinity, and beliefs about others (despite growing up in interracial families), suggest that more than intimate and empathetic relations between individuals is needed to bring about social change. Empathy is limited in its capacities to bring about social change, since people can cultivate empathy for specific individuals while keeping intact their basic (negative) beliefs about the categories of people from which those individuals come. This is why assertions that people in intermarriages and multiracial individuals are less prejudiced natural bridges across the racial divide are problematic. It is easy to make exceptions for one's kin, marking them as the exception to the negative rule for others of a particular group, thus leaving the line of demarcation intact.

The complexities of interracial intimacy revealed through the stories of my respondents are cautionary tales with implications for how we interpret intermarriage statistics as barometers of racial change. In his influential study of white ethnicity Richard Alba writes, "By far the most impressive evidence of the diminishing power of ethnicity among whites is the rising tide of interethnic marriage. Marriage is a sensitive barometer of social integration because it involves great social intimacy" and links together members of families in regular contact (1990, 11–12). In contemporary interpretations of intermarriage patterns, families are assumed to engage in regular contact and to be intimate—to care for one another in a variety of ways (physically, financially, and emotionally). In the process, children are assimilated into one ethnic group (usually the dominant one) or act as bridges between those of their parents. This formulation imagines intermarriage as the sine qua non of assimilation: a cultural merger that produces children who embody that merging.

While interracial families are imagined as sites where racial differences meet and melt (away), racialized differences among family members create variable experiences for the members of such families. The family, as feminist scholars have argued for decades, is not a monolithic unit, and members within families have divergent and competing interests. For my respondents, race often formed

the ground of those competing interests. In other words, while intermarriage may be common for some groups, it does not follow that it is either preferred or without controversy for either the partners in a marriage or their children, to say nothing of the ethnoracial communities with which they are engaged.

While invaluable for helping us understand changes in identification and marriage patterns, such statistics are very crude instruments for understanding meaning and tell us very little about practice—how and why people think of themselves in such terms and how they behave on the basis of them. When we rely on demographics to tell our stories we are merely recording and elaborating the preconstructed categories of the state and of social movements and are unable to say anything about whether and in what ways such categories are meaningful.

My point here is both methodological and epistemological. We need qualitative ethnographic work to understand meaning and process and we also need to question on what basis the assortment of people who marked boxes on the census can be considered a social group. Analyzing the statistics on racial identification tells us about patterns, but before we begin to make inferences about what those patterns say about group boundaries, the existence of groups, or the "groupness" of groups, we need to know something about meaning and practice.

Family's Radical Potential

All this is not to say that interracial kinship lacks a radical *potential*. Though I am cautious about interpreting multiracial identification and rising rates of intermarriage as signs of fading ethnoracial boundaries, I do believe that these developments, along with a growing public discussion of interracial intimacy, reflect and signal significant changes in the nature of racial division in the United States. The attempt to obtain some form of multiracial classification grew out of a desire to make visible those bonds that are easily elided—a recognition of not only a varied racial heritage, but of *relationships*. The MOOM option institutionalizes and records in statistical form a trace of those relationships.

For many of my respondents, parenting mixed race kids provided a powerful means through which they were able to extend their sense of obligation, empathy, and likeness beyond the circle of their ethnic group of origin. The notion that one can change one's people, to embrace the "other," is a potentially powerful tool to begin healing social divisions because it says that such social boundaries are artificial, and despite the very real consequences of those boundaries, through love and work they can be overcome.

The experience of living within interracial families allowed many of my respondents to overcome the racial categories that have almost always served to mark others outside one's moral domain, emphasizing the difference, and even the inhumanity, of the Other. It strikes me that the multiracial movement has its most radical potential in this vein. Presentations of multiracial family *as* families lessen the presumed distance across racial categories. Kinship symbolically bridges the imagined distance between racial groups. I am reminded of Patricia Williams's observation of a white woman suckling a black child. She writes:

> Is there not something unseemly in our society about the spectacle of a white woman mothering a black child? A white woman giving totally to a black child; a black child totally and demandingly dependent for everything, sustenance itself, from a white woman. The image of a white woman suckling a black child . . . Such a picture says, there is no difference; it places the hope of continuous generation of immortality of the white self in a little black face.

Given the pitfalls of family imagery mentioned earlier, images of the family are only truly transformative if they extend the cultural obligation to care for and about others *outside* the limits of both genealogical relatives *and* racial groups. One respondent tried to put into words how he saw this potential:

> The way that a multiracial person sees the world—we come in so many different shades that I realize I can't look at someone and tell what they are any more. They could be black and white. They could be the same mixture that I am and look totally different or look very similar. So walking down the street, I can't look at someone and immediately conclude that I'm not related to them in some way, maybe not immediately but somewhere back in history we probably had some common ancestors, you know. Who knows? I really don't know. I can't say as a fact. So in a sense you start walking down the street and you look at everyone and see everyone as being related to you. Now, if you do that how can you discriminate against someone if you acknowledge that they're related to you? You can't discriminate against your brother or sister. What line,

what rules—what lines of demarcation are you going to use to say this is us, this is them, these are the haves, these are the have-nots. You start to break them down. So the people can then start seeing or recognizing that—we are talking about the whole idea of one common humanity, you know, and I think that's a part of multiracial identity. The more you learn about multiracial people you just see multiracial people. This is what they look like. They're not so different as I thought. You know, so-and-so might not be so different. So that's why I really like to promote a multiracial outlook.

Seeing oneself in the other, as Jessica Benjamin (1988) argued, opposes the breakdown of mutual recognition that allows members of one category to see themselves as apart and above (or below) that leads to domination. It is this sense—that they are visible yet not seen—that motivates the action of the people who have been most involved in the multiracial movement. An acknowledgment of their social existence is something they understand to be crucial to eroding the color line. The issue is as much emotional as it is structural.

Understanding the emergence of multiracial families as a politicization of kinship helps clarify, if not the political implications of multiracial politics, then how multiracials understand the meaning of the actions in which they are engaged. The meaning of multiracial movement for its participants cannot be grasped merely at the cognitive level, where analysts of multiracial politics insist on grounding their critiques (for example, chastizing notions of racial accuracy or the use of fractional language as a reification of race). The notion of racial coherence put forth by respondents and evident in the idea that multiracial identification is expressive of a "whole self," should be understood not as a ground of politics, but as its effect—a response to the social conditions that create, sustain, and reproduce racial division.

The opposition between race and mixed race reaffirms boundaries between categories (white/black/Asian and so forth) even as the vocabulary of kinship brings together categories of bodies previously isolated outside of the sphere of family. So while multiracialism may reinscribe racial thinking by leaving intact the idea of race, it also calls attention to the peculiar history of the United States that denies social and sexual mixing across boundaries and helps us understand the role of such denial in supporting white domination.

The notion that one can choose one's racial identification disrupts the notion of genealogical descent as well. Such a notion says that people can choose *not* to identify with one of their ancestors' categories, or may choose to identify with a group to which none of their ancestors belonged, as did Mandy Rodriguez. Moreover, while some people might claim a multiracial identity, their children might not necessarily retain such an understanding of themselves.

While perhaps not revolutionary, the emergence of multiracial families as such represents a significant transformation in the logic (or illogic) underpinning dominant American racial discourse. The increasing prevalence and acceptance of intermarriage is a redefinition of permissible objects of sexual passion, as well as a redefinition of kinship. Multiracial families (and multiracial politics more broadly) do not necessarily challenge the biologistic and genealogical logic of race or family. Instead, they undercut the twin pillars of racial formation—hypodescent and antimiscegenation—creating the space by which the racialized family and familized notions of race are undermined.

While the multiracial family has long been a cultural contradiction in terms, that is no longer the case. The formation of collective organizations for multiracial families and their assertions that they are indeed families challenges a fundamental feature of American racial domination, yet its implications are not entirely clear. Intermarriage patterns and the political and cultural response to them and to mixed racial identity have always been linked to the broader system of racial domination that demarcates white from black (and less rigidly, white from other ethnoracial groups), and the fates of those of African descent (whether one is putatively "mixed" or not) have always been linked. While the possibility exists that the greater visibility of multiracial families will lead to more acceptability of all kinds of relations across racial boundaries—beginning with intimate and familial ones and corresponding with spatial and social ones—this does not mean, of course, that the problem that defined America in the twentieth century—the color line—has not followed us into the twenty-first.

Seeing the Big Picture   Interracial Marriage and the Blurring of the Color Line

Look at Figure 35 "Interracial Married Couples" in the Appendix. Why is it that so few individuals marry across the color line? What would it take for these numbers to radically change?

48   Policy Steps toward Closing the Gap

Meizhu Lui, Bárbara J. Robles, Betsy Leondar-Wright, Rose M. Brewer, and Rebecca Adamson

Meizhu Lui is the executive director of United for a Fair Economy (UFE).

Bárbara J. Robles taught Latino public policy at the LBJ School of Public Affairs at the University of Texas at Austin from 1998 to 2005. She has a PhD in economics from the University of Maryland at College Park.

Betsy Leondar-Wright is UFE's communications director. A longtime economic justice organizer and researcher, she is the author of *Class Matters: Cross-Class Alliance Building for Middle-Class Activists* (New Society Publishers, 2005).

Rose M. Brewer, PhD, is associate professor and Morse Alumni Distinguished Teaching Professor of African American & African Studies at the University of Minnesota and a contributing editor to *Souls,* an interdisciplinary journal of the Institute for Contemporary Black History at Columbia.

Rebecca Adamson, a Cherokee, is founder and president of First Nations Development Institute (1980) and founder of First Peoples Worldwide (1997).

Questions to Consider   The authors provide a number of proposals for achieving socioeconomic equality between the races. How and in what ways does everyone benefit from living in a society where there is greater social equality? As you read each suggestion, ask yourself if you believe that these calls for greater social justice are politically possible. Would most Americans sign on to these plans to create a more just society? If it seems as though their proposal might be too difficult to implement, what would you do to convince the public that achieving racial equality would benefit all of society?

THIS LIST IS BY NO MEANS COMPREHENSIVE, but perhaps it can spark more energy to tackle the issue of wealth building for communities of color, and for all those currently without economic security.

First Steps: Human Assets

Education has been an important tool in creating white advantage. It was a crime to teach African slaves to read and write; Latinos have been disadvantaged by English-only classrooms; Native Americans were forced into assimilationist school settings, and Asians had to sue to go to school with whites.

In today's economy, more than ever, you need an education to get ahead. Even for a menial job, a high school diploma is often required. Current mechanisms for public school funding—largely local property taxes—enable wealthier families in white suburbs who pay more property taxes to have more dollars invested in their public schools. Disparity in funding produces disparities in educational outcomes, and perpetuates a class and race divide. The infusion of federal dollars to invest more in communities that are poor could help close the gap.

As unionized jobs in manufacturing have shrunk, higher education has become an even more important ticket to a job at a decent wage with benefits. Professor Hubie Jones, former dean of the Boston University School of Social Work and a longtime community activist, grew up with his single mom in Harlem, New York. Without the possibility and promise of free higher education at the City College, he says, he would not have had the motivation to work hard in school in order to get that ticket up and out. Gangs and drugs would have been the only option.

Free public universities came about in 1862, the same year as the Homestead Act, when the Morrill Act established land-grant colleges in every state. Their purpose was to provide knowledge and skills to the newly landed masses.[1] Public institutions of higher education were the ticket out of poverty for many people of color who could not afford tuition at private colleges. Today, affordable higher education is moving out of reach for many of our children.

The federal government spends $55 billion on student aid, but the mix has been changing. Seventy-seven percent of that aid is in loans, not grants, a reversal of past policies. With tax cuts mostly for the wealthy, and the resulting budget shortfalls, states have been spending less on their public colleges, and tuitions have been growing at a faster rate than family income. The new welfare policies set in 1996 have led to a decline in enrollment of low-income women in college. Before the Temporary Assistance for Needy Families (TANF) program, forty-two states allowed women to count college attendance as employment in order to qualify for benefits: after TANF, only twenty-six states still allowed this option.[2] We can change the mix back again, and raise new taxes to invest in public colleges. A well-educated populace is the cornerstone of democracy, and the cornerstone is crumbling.

For those who don't speak English as their first language, English classes are the first stepping-stones to success. It is not possible to get a decent job without English skills. Some immigrants are not literate in their native language and need extended classes. Some come with degrees from other countries, and can learn English quickly. For all of them, long waiting lists for free or affordable classes prevent them from obtaining this skill so essential for entry of limited English speakers into the U.S. workforce. On the other hand, so that non–English speakers do not get cheated out of their assets, or miss out on the benefits of programs for which they qualify, English-only policies must be rejected.

One big health problem can wipe out a lifetime of savings. The cost of care for a premature baby in a neonatal intensive care unit can be $500,000. In 1999, one quarter of the families that filed for bankruptcy cited health problems and the related costs as the reason.[3]

A 2000 study found that people of color are more likely to be uninsured than non-Hispanic whites, and are less likely to have job-based health insurance.[4] Thirty percent of Latinos, 25 percent of African Americans, 20 percent of Asian Americans and Pacific Islanders, and 17 percent of Native Americans are uninsured.[5] (The relatively low percentage rate of uninsured Native Americans is mostly due to their access to Indian Health Services as opposed to private or Medicaid coverage.[6]) Medicaid, which cares for the poor in inner cities and rural areas, is increasingly underfunded, as states face budget crises.

Universal coverage is possible. In 1983, Hawaii received permission from the federal government to require all employers to provide insurance to employees. In 1993, they were able to pool all their public dollars to create one big statewide insurance system. Not only were they able to provide health, dental, and mental health coverage for all, but the system was also able to save public dollars through a competitive bidding system.[7]

Hitting a Stride: Income Assets

One of the main reasons that nonwhite people were shut out of asset building was because they were restricted to no wage or low-wage jobs. From African slaves in the South to Latino day laborers on the street corners of Los Angeles, people of color have been denied fair compensation for their labor power. They have been limited to jobs that whites did not and do not want, were excluded from unions, paid taxes to work, and have always been the last hired and the first fired.

Jobs are needed that provide the cash income to cover day-to-day needs, *with something left over to build savings,* the basis for financial wealth. Today, income disparity lays the groundwork for future wealth disparities. Thomas Shapiro, in *The Hidden Cost of Being African American: How Wealth Perpetuates Inequality,* analyzed the impact of income on wealth. Once basic living expenses are met, each additional dollar of annual income generates $3.26 in net worth over a person's lifetime. Wealth disparity grows because of differences in income. For example, the difference in net worth between someone making $30,000 a year and someone making $60,000 a year is nearly $100,000.[8] Income includes not just wages and salaries based on working, but cash supports for those who are unemployed, retired, or parents of small children.

In Bárbara Robles's class at the LBJ school at the University of Texas in Austin, students simply did not believe her when she told them that the minimum wage means a family must live on $10,000 a year. Over 27 million workers make less than $8 dollars an hour; of these workers, 16.8 million are adults twenty-five and over; more than 16 million are women; 22 million are white; 4.2 million are black; and more than 17.5 million work full-time.[9] The present federal minimum wage of $5.15 an hour translates into an annual income of $10,712. The Economic Policy Institute has done several studies that reveal that an increase in the minimum wage would primarily benefit full- and part-time workers of low-income families,[10] which are disproportionately headed by single women of color. It would require raising the minimum wage to at least $8.10 an hour as of 2004 for a family of four to move above the official poverty line.[11] Around the country, people are organizing for more than the minimum wage: they are demanding a living wage. Since the cost of living varies across the country, communities are calculating costs particular to their cities. For example, in San Francisco voters approved a city living wage of $8.50 an hour in 2003; this will put over $100 million per year into the pockets of roughly fifty-four thousand workers.

And what about a maximum wage? In most countries, the ratio of CEO pay to worker pay has been around 40 to one. In the United States in 2004, the ratio of CEO pay to the average workers pay was 431 to 1.[12] Rep. Martin Sabo of Minnesota wants to curb that excess. His Proposed Income Equity Act would prevent corporations from claiming tax deductions on any executive pay that totals over 25 times what a company's lowest paid workers are earning.

The poorest group in the United States is women of color and their children. As Miami resident Thelma Brown puts it, "[C]ertified nursing assistants in Miami start at $5.75 an hour with no benefits. Day care costs ninety to one hundred dollars every two weeks per kid; then you have

to pay rent, electricity, food, and everything else. A single mom can't live on one job at that rate."[13] They require government help to survive. For many years, it was mainly white women who received welfare payments. Attieno Davis, a longtime African American activist, remembers how empowering it was for black women in the 1960s to realize that they were *entitled* to these benefits, too. Latinos also were underenrolled, since no outreach was conducted in Spanish, nor were there Spanish-speaking workers in welfare offices. However, President Reagan's caricature of "welfare queens," stereotyped as a woman of color, created backlash. In 1996, the program changed to Temporary Assistance to Needy Families. To quality for the meager payments, women cannot have assets of more than $1,000 in some states.

One positive tax provision for the poor is the Earned Income Tax Credit (EITC). It was born out of the welfare debates in the late 1960s and early 1970s. At the time, President Nixon was proposing a guaranteed income to all families with children, regardless of whether the parent(s) worked. It is amazing today to remember that Nixon was proposing such a progressive policy. But Democratic senator Russell Long of Louisiana felt that the Nixon proposal would discourage people from working. His alternate proposal provided tax relief to low-income workers, rather than guaranteed income for all. The EITC was passed in 1975. Its annual budget rose from $2 billion to $12 billion between 1980 and 1992. According to the 2001 Census, forty-three million people were living in low-income working families with children, and two out of every three poor families with children had at least one parent working. The EITC has lifted more families with children out of poverty than any other government program.[14]

Low-wage workers use the money they receive from the EITC for investments in education and savings, as well as to help them pay daily living expenses.[15] In order to encourage savings. Ray Boshara from the New America Foundation suggests that a portion of EITC refunds could be channeled directly into a basic savings account.[16] The Center on Budget and Policy Priorities found that EITC funds are often spent locally, serving as an economic development tool for low-income neighborhoods.[17]

Decent pay and accumulation of assets is hard to come by if you are not allowed citizenship. As we have seen, immigrant status has been a major barrier to economic equality for people of color. Jeannette Huezo, a political refugee from El Salvador, has lived and worked in Boston for fifteen years. However, she had to leave four of her children behind when she fled, and they are not allowed to reunite; she has been sending money home to support them. Salvadorans in the United States send remittances back home that now amount to half of the Salvadoran economy. Being forced into low-paid jobs because of their tenuous legal status, coupled with the need to send money home, makes it difficult to build assets in either country. The National Coalition for Dignity and Amnesty developed a proposal for a federal Freedom Act. It would legalize undocumented immigrants currently living in the United States and create a status of "temporary residency" for future migrants, who would be eligible for permanent residency after three years.

People of color should be hired into jobs for which they are qualified and to rise to the level of their capabilities. Affirmative action, won through the Civil Rights Movement, did bring many more people of color into middle-income jobs where they could begin to save, buy homes, and build wealth. However, the gap is still not closed. Over their working lifetime, African Americans with a college degree can expect to earn $500,000 less than equally qualified white people.[18] Asians do fine getting in on the ground floor and moving up, but then encounter glass ceilings: an Asian with a college degree had median annual earnings in 1993 of $36,844; comparably qualified whites made $41,094.[19] The need for affirmative action and government enforcement of non-discrimination laws is far from over.

Going the Distance: Financial Assets

Over the course of history, the federal government has used public resources to create wealth-building starter kits as well as continuing subsidies for whites, and has removed assets from people of color and denied them the benefits given to whites. In recent years, the white middle class has taken a hit: overall, it's shrinking, and general economic inequality has reached the levels of the Gilded Age at the turn of the last century. As a result, more and more academics, advocates, foundations, and public officials are recognizing that income alone is not enough to lift a family out of poverty. While this attention is not mainly because of wide recognition of the racial wealth gap, there is an opportunity to bring race into the conversation.

It's not that there aren't federal asset policies currently in place. The government spends approximately $355 billion a year in direct outlays and tax expenditures (allowing tax breaks for certain kinds of income). However, they are not named as asset policies, and they disproportionately benefit those who already have assets.[20] As we have seen, the net worth of people of color is far below that of whites.

While there are many ways to group asset-building opportunities, the Asset Policy Initiative of California has designed a framework that is simple and user-friendly. They see that strategies in four areas are needed. *Asset accumulation* is about policy strategies that encourage families to save; *asset leveraging* policies help low-wealth families use their limited savings to get loans for larger assets such as home and business ownership. Unfortunately, if there are not *asset preservation* assistance programs, often low-wealth people lose everything they have to predatory lenders. And finally, "*asset creation*" goes beyond individual strategies; communities can gain control over development in their own neighborhoods and rural communities.

Asset Accumulation

New thinking on how to help low-income people save money has been inspired by Michael Sherradan's groundbreaking book *Assets and the Poor: A New American Welfare Policy.* Sherradan and others recognize that income-support programs do not foster asset accumulation.[21]

Individual Development Accounts (IDAs) are nontaxable matching funds savings accounts that can be used—and used *only*—toward purchasing a home, retirement, education, starting a business, or other asset-accumulating endeavors. The outside matching source comes either from the public or private sector. Generally, the program has been targeted to the working poor, those who have a low but stable income in which some money can be set aside. Foundations and local banks have both provided funding to augment savings on the part of the poor. There are about 250 neighborhoods participating in IDA programs across the country, many in communities of color. The National Council of La Raza and the First Nations Development Institute have developed projects for Latinos and Native peoples.

Pilot IDA programs funded privately have encouraged policy change. According to the Corporation for Enterprise

Development (CFED), since 1993, twenty-nine states and the District of Columbia have passed laws in support of IDAs. Thirty-two states have included IDA initiatives in their welfare reform programs and seven states have instituted state-funded IDA programs. In 1998, a federal pilot program of savings incentives for the poor was enacted, with $125 million over five years set aside for matching individual savings. While on the one hand this legislation helps to make the IDA idea more visible, it is not on a scale to be truly transformative.[22]

Another promising idea involves investing in our future: our nation's children. It is every parent's dream to leave their child a nest egg. And wouldn't it be great if everyone could be born with a trust fund! An impossible dream? Just such a program was instituted in England, sponsored by Prime Minister Tony Blair's Labor Party. In 2003, the British Parliament established what has become known as "baby bonds," a small child trust fund for each newborn in the country. Modest amounts of public funds will be deposited and invested for each newborn infant, and made available for withdrawal at the age of eighteen. If a child is given an initial deposit of $1,000, and then the parent makes a yearly contribution of $500, matched by another $500 from an outside source, this would translate into $40,000 available to eighteen-year-olds to use toward education, starting a business, or putting a down payment on a home.[23]

In 2005, a bill to create a similar program was introduced in Congress by an unusual alliance of conservative Republicans and progressive Democrats. The America Saving for Personal Investment, Retirement, and Education Act (the ASPIRE Act of 2005) proposed that a $500 KIDS Account be established for every newborn child. Children in households earning below the national median income would be eligible for a supplemental government contribution of up to $500. Additional benefits would include tax-free earnings, matched savings for lower income families, and financial education. Here is a program that provides a double incentive for lower income people to save: no taxes on the savings account, and matched government contributions for the poor.

Whether such new asset subsidiary programs should be universal or targeted to people of color is a strategic question. In any case, additional resources for outreach, translation, and other mechanisms to ensure inclusion must be part of the program.

Asset Leveraging

When you have some savings, you can either keep them, or use them to leverage more assets through making bigger investments.

Rotating savings and credit associations (ROSCA) have been an important strategy utilized by immigrant households in order to start a small business, purchase a home, or pay for a child's education. This strategy has origins in many different ethnic groups from East Asia, Latin America, the Caribbean, the Near East, and Africa. The Vietnamese ROSCA is called a *hui,* the Ethiopian is *ekub,* Jamaican is *partners,* Dominican, *san,* Korean, *keh,* and Cambodian *tong-tine.*[24]

A ROSCA is formed among family members, friends, and kin groups. They require participants (usually five or more people) to pay in a monthly sum agreed upon by the group. A participant can make a request to borrow the month's pool of money, or there may be an agreed-upon sequence for withdrawal—tax- and interest-free, since these transactions take place outside of the mainstream economic structure. This continues until all members have had access to the funds. The system is based on trust and social pressure. Thus, if members do not return the money at some point, their reputation in the community is tainted, something they are usually not willing to risk.

A *Philadelphia Inquirer* reporter sat in on a ROSCA meeting. "A Vietnamese *hui* group listened as one member asked to break the payout schedule and let her have that month's collection. . . . [T]he group sat in judgment on her needs, then let her take the tax-free, no-interest pot of $14,000." But because ROSCAs are part of an unregulated, unprotected financing system, they have no recourse in case of theft. While sometimes immigrants do not trust banks, banks also do not make it easy to deposit ROSCA dollars. They treat deposits as belonging to an individual or household, and have no category to accommodate this unique form of savings. They report any deposit of more than $10,000 to the Internal Revenue Service. Without a financial institution to hold the money, one member has to keep the mounting dollars under his or her bed. A policy that recognized ROSCAs as a micro lending system, and allowed the money to be banked and borrowed tax-free, would build on existing community customs and help rather than hinder these activities.

Another way to use your small savings to leverage larger loans without worrying about a financial institution charging excessive fees and interest is to join a community credit union. The credit union movement was essentially a response to mainstream financial institutions' neglect of marginalized groups. Community Development Credit Unions (CDCU) provide basic financial services such as check cashing and small loans at fair rates to their members within a restricted area or community.[25] They are member based and member governed; some are based in churches or community organizations. One of the problems plaguing poor communities is that the meager resources present in poor communities tend to flow out of them.[26] In response to this problem, CDCUs keep local money in the community, as well as draw in outside money.[27] The resources accrued from CDCUs are then channeled back into the community and are used to respond to its various needs.

Usually, the first asset leveraged from savings is a home to live in. Expanding opportunities for home ownership are critical in closing the racial wealth divide. Home equity is one of the first building blocks for wealth, and is the most significant source of assets for people of color. For blacks, 62 percent of their net worth is held in homes; for Latinos, 51 percent. For white families, housing accounts for only 32 percent of their net worth. Given the history of federal subsidies for home ownership for whites, targeted funding for people and communities of color is now needed.

The Community Reinvestment Act of 1977 (CRA) came out of community struggles demanding access to banks and mortgage companies. Evidence was compiled showing that financial institutions engaged in discriminatory lending practices based on race, age, and location, instead of on an applicant's creditworthiness. These discriminatory practices had contributed to the decline of low-income and minority neighborhoods. The CRA required banks to lend in low-income communities, and federal banking regulators were mandated to maintain a close watch on financial institutions to ensure that they were meeting the needs of local communities. Communities of color were successful in getting the federal government to use its powers to stop private industry from providing affirmative action in lending to whites.

Through the CRA, significant strides were made during the 1990s as major banking institutions increase

lending toward affordable housing and economic development to assist low-income people.[28] Over $20 billion has been invested in low-income neighborhoods and communities of color thanks to the CRA.[29]

Asset Preservation

Home ownership has been a double-edged sword for many home owners of color. It is a struggle first to gain access to fair loan terms, and another to try and keep the home. If we were to dig beneath the home ownership figures, which provide only a snapshot in time, we would find a lot more turnovers of home ownership among people of color than among whites. Lending predators target the weak—those unfamiliar with the rules of the game.

ACORN's Mary Gaspar described her ordeal: "Here's how my nightmare started: I got a check in the mail from Household Finance with an offer to refinance our home.... Household was misleading and dishonest. I received my first bill and it was $13,000 more than I thought it was going to be! I have seen how Household preys on people who are economically desperate as well as middle-class people like us." ACORN (Association of Community Organizations for Reform Now) responded by putting public pressure on Household Finance by holding demonstrations at their annual shareholder meetings. They were joined in their efforts by members of United for a Fair Economy's Responsible Wealth project. Proxy votes given to ACORN members by Responsible Wealth members who owned shares allowed Mary to tell her story—*inside* the halls of wealth, usually barred to the people of color whose hard-earned homes were being stolen from them. Having shareholders and ACORN members speaking with one voice brought Household to the table to discuss changing its behavior.[30]

Mortgage foreclosure has been another impediment to maintaining home ownership. A report done by the Family Housing Fund in Minneapolis found that the major reason home owners default on mortgage payments is job loss or a significant reduction in income; other causes include health emergencies and separation or divorce. While home ownership rates have increased, so have instances of foreclosure.

Foreclosure prevention is an important tool in stabilizing home owners at risk of losing their homes and neighborhoods by preventing houses from becoming vacant and boarded up. Between 1991 and 1997, the Mortgage

Foreclosure Program (MFP) carried out by the Family Housing Fund assisted close to seventeen hundred home owners and helped to reinstate the mortgages of over half of them within the St. Paul and Minneapolis area.[31] Foreclosure prevention counseling provides a more affordable way for home owners to stabilize their home ownership, compared to going through a mortgage insurer. It costs an average of $2,800 to help a home owner reinstate a mortgage, while with a mortgage insurer it could cost $10,000 to $28,000, depending on the insurer and the location of the home.[32] Ana Moreno, a housing consultant who conducted the study, contends that "[p]rograms that promote home ownership for households with very low incomes need to be linked to the full continuum of homeownership support services—pre-purchase education and counseling, financial assistance, post-purchase support, and delinquency and foreclosure prevention."[33]

Even with a home, you can spend your final years in poverty, if you have no retirement account from which to draw. Social security was invented to protect U.S. workers from this risk: it is the country's most successful insurance program. While 10 percent of those over age sixty-five live in poverty today, without social security that rate would be almost 50 percent.[34] Occupations held mostly by African Americans and Latinos were excluded initially, but all employment sectors were included beginning in 1950. Social security was also expanded to include not only retirement benefits, but also benefits to disabled workers and the families of workers who have died.

Because people of color have less income from stock holdings or capital gains than whites, social security is especially important to them: it is the sole source of income for 40 percent of elderly African Americans. The shorter life span of African American men means that both survivor and disability benefits go disproportionately to African Americans. While African Americans make up 12 percent of the U.S. population, 23 percent of children receiving social security survivor benefits are African American, as are about 17 percent of disability beneficiaries.[35]

Private pension plans are also an important asset. They provide retirement income, often as an employment benefit. The loss of unionized manufacturing jobs in the 1990s led to the loss of this asset for many. Laid off from auto and steel jobs which opened up to them during World War II, African Americans in particular have had to shift to jobs in the low-wage service sector, which do not provide employer-sponsored pension plans. In 2001, the mean value of the retirement account of a black family was $12,247, compared to $10,206 for a Latino family and $65,411 for a white family.[36]

For those who are fortunate to have jobs with pensions, there has been a change from defined benefit plans, in which workers receive a defined percentage of their wages, based on age and years of service, to defined contribution plans, in which employers and/or employees contribute a defined amount of money into a plan, but they do not guarantee that the money will still be there when you retire. The risk has been shifted to the worker. The AFL-CIO news related the story of Wanda Chalk, an African American employee at Enron. She had worked at Enron for fifteen years and had stock options worth $150,000, which were to generate income for her retirement. But due to Enron's fraudulent dealings, when Enron crashed, so did she. She lost her job, her stock value dropped to zero, and her retirement security went up in smoke.

Privatizing social security could produce the same effect. Preservation of assets, not risky schemes that could fail when you need the money most, needs to remain the cornerstone of retirement plans. As a society, we should not revert to a pre-Depression system, where our elders are at risk of dying in poverty.

Asset Creation

Even if a few individuals of color hold greater assets, that will not be enough to close the racial wealth divide. Just because in 2004 Bill Cosby was worth $540 million in assets, and just because the Unanues, owners of Goya Foods, were worth $700 million, it doesn't help those members of their racial groups who are stuck at the bottom. Assets need to be utilized to expand wealth for the community as a whole.

For example, Native land was given away to railroad owners and, in 1887, tribal land was broken into individual plots. Over the years, more and more Native owners lost their plots, resulting in a checkerboard pattern of landownership in what should have been tribally owned territory. In 2002, the Northwest Area Foundation, funded by heirs of James J. Hill, head of the Great Northern Railroad, who grew rich from the displacement of Ojibwes in Minnesota, made voluntary reparations. They gave $20 million in seed money for a buyback. Now millions of acres are back under tribal control.

In the 1970s, the inner city of Battle Creek, Michigan, became an economically depressed area, due to the closing of a military base nearby; by 1990, there were fifty recognized crack houses within a mile of downtown. Battle Creek Neighborhoods Incorporated, a community development financial institution, stepped in. Their approach has been to focus on lending to people who are willing to buy particular community blocks rather than to buyers of housing units scattered throughout the city. Their loans come with a requirement to improve the property and to participate in improving the quality of life on the block. For example, they sponsor "best of neighborhood" contests—Best Front Porch, Best Back Yard, Best Group Effort—that encourage home maintenance and improvement. Brenda Sue Woods wasn't going to participate in the Porch contest at first, but then decided to try. When

she took first place, "I was just screaming like I won something on The Price Is Right." The emphasis on neighborhoods will enable housing values to rise in the area.

The Hawai'i Alliance for Community-Based Economic Development, a statewide nonprofit organization, provides loans not to individuals, but to groups. For example, a group of young people put in a proposal with the goal of "reconnection with their elders." One of the ways they used the loan was for a community van to transport those elders to needed services.

In a variety of locations, nonprofit organizations and government entities are experimenting with wealth-creation frameworks that are "inclusive, community-driven, and action oriented, protecting community, cultural, and environmental concerns while shielding individual private rights."[37] These efforts are road signs to the future.

---

49 Ten Things You Can Do to Improve Race Relations

Charles A. Gallagher

CHARLES A. GALLAGHER is professor and chair of the Department of Sociology, Social Work and Criminal Justice at La Salle University in Philadelphia. His research focuses on racial and social inequality, immigration, urban sociology, and the ways in which the media, the state, and popular culture construct, shape, and disseminate ideas of race. He has published articles on the sociological functions of color-blind political narratives, how racial categories expand and contract within the context of interracial marriages, race theory, racial innumeracy, and how one's ethnic history shapes perceptions of privilege.

> **Questions to Consider**   Photocopy and pass along my "Ten Things You Can Do to Improve Race Relations" to family, friends, teachers, spiritual leaders, brothers, and sisters. Please contact me with any additions you might have for my list. I can be reached at gallagher@lasalle.edu.

THE STUDY OF RACE AND ETHNIC RELATIONS in the United States can be a rather depressing and disempowering undertaking. Ongoing institutional racism in education, employment, housing, lending, and law enforcement; continued wealth and income disparities between racial groups; and the persistence of racial prejudice and discrimination in most spheres of social life may leave one with the impression that nothing can be

done to improve race relations. The modern civil rights movement was three hundred years in the making, and while movement toward racial equality has been substantial, racism and racial inequality still infect our nation and poison civic life. Such prejudice and inequality persist in part because changing the institutional barriers that allocate occupational and educational opportunity is a slow and difficult task. Upward mobility for different racial and ethnic groups is typically measured in generations rather than decades or years. One is tempted to throw one's hands in the air and yell, "There is nothing I can do!!!" But there is. You have the power to influence your family, friends, and peers by discussing the topics raised in this class. At the individual, interpersonal, and community level you can engage in activities to promote equal opportunity while building bridges between people from different racial backgrounds. Understanding the root causes of ethnic and racial inequality in the United States and examining in this class the facts, theories, evidence, and examples that pertain to such inequality will allow you to explain to others why racism and racial and ethnic inequality remain so stubbornly part of our culture. You now have the sociological tools to calmly, intelligently, and rationally engage in conversations with other adults about racism in America and what individuals, institutions, and the government *could* and *should* do to fashion a society where equal opportunity exists for all groups. Following are ten simple things you can do as you go about your day to raise your own and other people's consciousness about race relations and racial justice in America.

1. Talk to Your Family

Respectfully engage your friends and family in what you learned in this class. If you have family members that are racist or use stereotypes, ask them politely and nonjudgmentally why they harbor such animosity towards a whole group of people. Did they have a bad experience with someone from that group? Ask them if they have ever been the target of animosity or hatred because of their race, ethnic background, religion, or nationality. How did such an encounter make them feel? Were their parents or grandparents ever subject to such prejudice or discrimination? Why? Ask them if they think their prejudice or racism violates the American creed of equal treatment and opportunity for all regardless of group membership. If they believe in the American creed, how do they reconcile their racism or prejudice? Ask them if they believe in the golden rule that states "do unto others as you would have them do unto you."

2. Avoid Sterotypical Language

Be mindful that certain words or phrases typically mean the person is about to use stereotypes to describe a group. When you hear someone say "All black people do this … ,"

or "Latinos always like to … ," or "I never met a white person who could … ," a red flag should go up that stereotypes are in use. Politely ask if they are referring to an individual encounter with someone from another group or if they mean to speak for thirty-eight million blacks, forty million Latinos, ten million Asians, two hundred million whites, or 2.5 million American Indians in this country. Ask the person if they really believe *all people* in that group actually share the same behaviors and attitudes. Is it possible that certain behaviors or beliefs only appear in one racial or ethnic group and not another?

3. Racism Isn't Funny

Don't tolerate racist jokes. If you hear a joke being told that disparages someone because of his or her group membership, stop the person from telling the joke. If they insist on finishing, ask them why they don't like black people or white people or Asians or Catholics or whomever they are ridiculing in their attempt at humor. You have many retorts to such simplistic and retrograde behavior. You might say "Hey, I don't think putting down other people is funny," or "I have gay friends, I don't want to hear you trashing them," or "My brother-in-law is black (or white or Asian or Catholic or Jewish, etc.) and I think he's great." Be willing to "take the stand" about what is appropriate public discourse. If you do not speak up and let the person know that such remarks are socially inappropriate, you are condoning their beliefs and behavior. Inaction is a form of action.

4. Be Introspective

Think back to reading 17, in which Robert Merton discussed the unprejudiced nondiscriminator. This person was not prejudiced, nor did she discriminate against anyone in any way. How can we live our lives so social or peer pressure do not push us toward racist, prejudiced, or bigoted beliefs or actions? If you find yourself being a prejudiced nondiscriminator (fair-weather illiberal) or an unprejudiced discriminator (fair-weather liberal), ask yourself how you got there. Be introspective and honest about why you acted or behaved a certain way toward someone from a different ethnic or racial group. What scared you about the situation that made you deviate from your core beliefs or values? Did you overreact? Were you defensive? If you could relive that experience, what would you do differently? Is it possible you were socialized or taught to react the way you did? What role did peer pressure play in your actions? The most important thing you can do is to think critically about the root causes of your anxieties, attitudes, and actions. Be introspective and be willing to change how you think about groups different from your own.

5. Be a Good Citizen—Vote

Vote in every election. Take the time to find out candidates' positions on policies that have implications for race relations. Do not support a politician whose campaign rhetoric is racially divisive or attempts to win votes by manipulating racial (or class) fears. Knowing what the issues are (and are not) requires reading a newspaper every day.

6. TV, Rap, Rock: Appeals to the Lowest Common Denominator

When you watch television, realize that you are under constant bombardment by the most simplistic and stereotypical images of ethnic and racial groups. Ask yourself which racial and ethnic groups are on prime time and how those groups are represented. Are whites, blacks, Asians, Latinos, or American Indians in a wide range of roles, or are some groups more likely to be maids, gangbangers, exotics, or lawyers? Why? What you watch on television is not just entertainment. The mass media provide the images, symbols, and narratives that shape the way we understand society. The media cement existing stereotypes and construct expectations about where groups should be placed in America's racial hierarchy. The television industry uses stereotypes to make racial inequality look like the "normal" order of society. How are you are being manipulated by the programs you watch?

7. Learn Your Family's History

Take time to talk to the elderly people in your life. Ask your parents, aunts and uncles, neighbors, and spiritual leaders in your community about how race relations have changed since they were children. Ask your parents, grandparents, and other relatives about the *Brown* decision, the Civil Rights movement, Martin Luther King, Jr.'s assassination, the American Indian Movement (AIM),

La Raza, and the L.A. riots. How do they explain these events? What were they doing as these monumental events unfolded? Your elders are resources. Talk to them about the past and the present.

8. Teach through Example

Be a positive role model to all the younger people in your life. If you are of college age or older, you probably have a number of children and young adults who look up to you for moral guidance. If they hear you use foul language, then in all likelihood they will too. If you speak and act in a racist manner, they will learn your racism. Explain to those who view you as a role model what it means to live in a multiracial, multiethnic society. Explain to them what the American creed and the "golden rule" mean.

9. Step Out of Your Comfort Zone

Involve yourself in activities that place you in an environment where you will be exposed to people from different racial and ethnic backgrounds. Think about attending museums, music events, ethnic festivals, restaurants, supermarkets, shops, or any other public place where you will share space with people different from yourself.

10. Know Thyself

Did you grow up in a community that was racially homogenous? Was your house of worship pretty much composed of people who looked like you? Are your best friends all of the same race? Was your elementary school segregated? How about your high school? What did it look like in terms of racial composition? Do you think being raised in a segregated environment shapes racial attitudes? How? How do you think being the only racial minority in most social settings might shape a person's views of race relations? Have your ideas about race changed since you were fifteen years old? How and why? Reflect on these questions and write your answers as an essay. Circulate what you write to your friends and family. Set up a meeting to have a discussion on what you wrote and what their views on race relations in the United States are.

"If You're Not Part of the Solution, You're Part of the Problem."

RACE BY THE NUMBERS ~
America's Racial Report Card

Introduction

How are the race categories used in Census 2000 defined?

"White" refers to people having origins in any of the original peoples in Europe, the Middle East, or North Africa. It includes people who indicated their race or races as "White" or wrote in entries such as Irish, German, Italian, Lebanese, Near Easterner, Arab, or Polish.

"Black or African American" refers to people having origins in any of the black racial groups of Africa. It includes people who indicated their race or races as "Black, African Am., or Negro" or wrote in entries such as African American, Afro American, Nigerian, or Haitian.

"American Indian and Alaska Native" refers to people having origins in any of the original peoples of North and South America (including Central America), and who maintain tribal affiliation or community attachment. It includes people who indicated their race or races by marking this category or writing in their principal or enrolled tribe, such as Rosebud Sioux, Chippewa, or Navajo.

"Asian" refers to people having origins in any of the original peoples of the Far East, Southeast Asia, or the Indian subcontinent. It includes people who indicated their race or races as "Asian Indian," "Chinese," "Filipino," "Korean," "Japanese," "Vietnamese," or "Other Asian," or wrote in entries such as Burmese, Hmong, Pakistani, or Thai.

"Native Hawaiian and Other Pacific Islander" refers to people having origins in any of the original peoples of Hawaii, Guam, Samoa, or other Pacific Islands. It includes people who indicated their race or races as "Native Hawaiian," "Guamanian or Chamorro," "Samoan," or "Other Pacific Islander," or wrote in entries such as Tahitian, Mariana Islander, or Chuukese.

"Some other race" was included in Census 2000 for respondents who were unable to identify with the five Office of Management and Budget race categories. Respondents who provided write-in entries such as Moroccan, South African, Belizean, or a Hispanic origin (for example, Mexican, Puerto Rican, or Cuban) are included in the Some other race category. (U.S. Census 2000)

Compare total U.S. population to trends shown in Appendix figures.

Compare the size of the total population at the bottom of the page to the trends observed in figures in the Appendix. Is the group overrepresented? For example, Figure 26 shows us that 89% of all lawyers are white although whites make up 74% of the total U.S. population. Whites are overrepresented in the field of law. Or is it the case that a group is underrepresented? Figure 27 shows us that 5% of all physicians are Latinos but Latinos make up 15% of the total U.S. population. Latinos are underrepresented as physicians.

The U.S. population is 74% white (including Latinos who define themselves as white). The total U.S. population comprises: non-Hispanic white, 67%; black, 12.4%; Latino, 14.8%; Asian, 4.4%; and American Indian, 0.8%.

FIGURE 1 Changes to Race and Ethnicity Categories on the U.S. Census, 1790–2000.

Year	Categories included	Categories eliminated
1790	Free White male/female, Non-taxed Indian, Slaves (3/5 of a person)	
1870	White, Black, mulatto, quadroon, octoroon, Indian	Non-taxed Indian, slaves, free White
1890	White, Black, mulatto, quadroon, octoroon, Indian, Japanese, Chinese	
1900	Black, White, Japanese, Chinese, Indian	Mulatto, quadroon, octoroon
1910	Black, White, Japanese, Chinese, Indian, mulatto	
1930	White, Black, Japanese, Chinese, Indian, Hindu, Korean, Mexican	Mulatto
1940	White, Black, Japanese, Chinese, Indian, Hindu, Korean	Mexican
1950	White, Black, Japanese, Chinese, American Indian	Hindu, Korean
1960	White, Black, Japanese, Chinese, American Indian, Hawaiian, part-Hawaiian, Aleut, Eskimo	
1980	White, Black or African American, American Indian and Alaska Native, Asian, Native Hawaiian and Other Pacific Islander	
2000	"check all that apply" system implemented	

Source: Dispatches from the Color-Line: The Press and Multiracial America. Suny Press 2007 Catherine R. Squires.

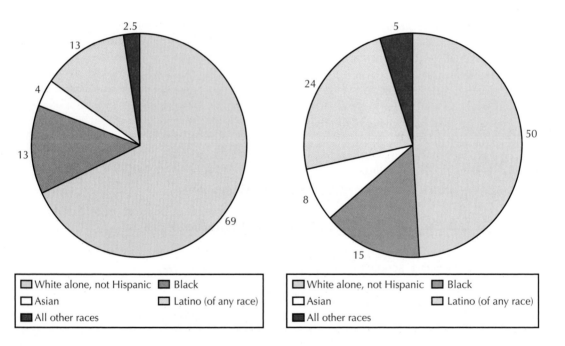

FIGURE 2 Population of the U.S. 2000 and Projected 2050. *Source:* Data from U.S. Census Bureau, 2004, "U.S. Interim Projections by Age, Sex, Race, and Hispanic Origin," http://www.census .gov/ipc/www/usinterimproj/.

The U.S. population is 74% white (including Latinos who define themselves as white). The total U.S. population comprises: non-Hispanic white, 67%; black, 12.4%; Latino, 14.8%; Asian, 4.4%; and American Indian, 0.8%.

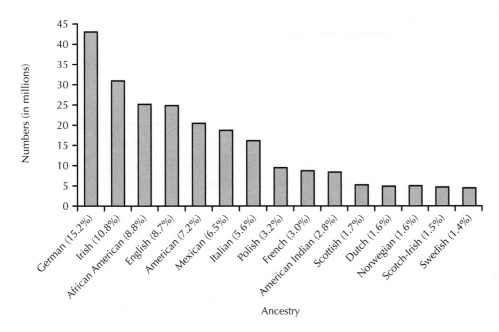

FIGURE 3 **Fifteen Largest Ancestries.** *Source:* Data from U.S. Census Bureau, Census 2000 special tabulation. *Note:* Percent of total population in parenthesis. Data based on sample.

Section I: Education

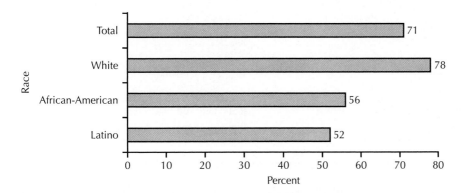

FIGURE 4 **High School Graduation Rates for 2002.** *Source:* Data from Manhattan Institute, Education Working Paper No. 8, February 2005.

The U.S. population is 74% white (including Latinos who define themselves as white). The total U.S. population comprises: non-Hispanic white, 67%; black, 12.4%; Latino, 14.8%; Asian, 4.4%; and American Indian, 0.8%.

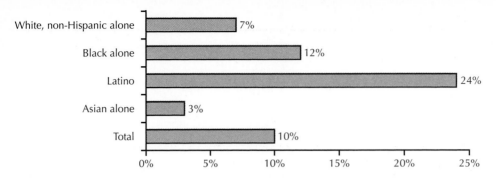

FIGURE 5 **High School Dropout Rates for 2004.** *Source:* Data from Child Trends' calculations of U.S. Census Bureau, *School Enrollment—Social and Economic Characteristics of Students: October 2004: Detailed Tables:* Table 1.

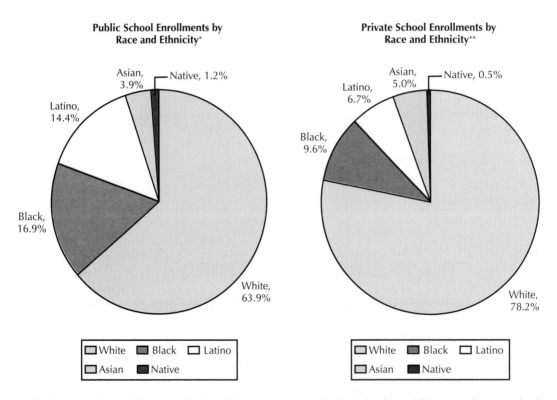

*90% of all school age children attend public school.   **10% of all school age children attend private school.

FIGURE 6 **Racial Composition of Public and Private Schools.** *Source:* Data from Common Core of Data, 1997–98 and Private School Survey, 1997–98.

The U.S. population is 74% white (including Latinos who define themselves as white). The total U.S. population comprises: non-Hispanic white, 67%; black, 12.4%; Latino, 14.8%; Asian, 4.4%; and American Indian, 0.8%.

FIGURE 7 Degrees Conferred.

Racial/Ethnic Group	BA	MA	Law	MD	PhD
White	70.0	60.3	83.0	68.6	81.0
Black	8.7	7.8	4.4	6.7	7.0
Latino	6.3	4.4	6.6	6.4	5.0
Asian	6.2	4.8	7.4	15.6	6.0
Native American	0.7	0.5	0.5	1.4	<1

Source: Data from U.S. Department of Education, National Center for Education Statistics, Integrated Postsecondary Education Data System (IPEDS), Fall 2003, National Postsecondary Student Aid Study (NPSAS; 2000), and NSF/NIH/USED/USDA/NASA, Survey of Earned Doctorates by U.S. Citizens, 2003.

Section II: Housing

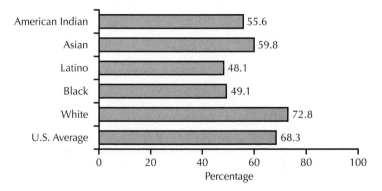

FIGURE 8 **Homeownership Rates for 2003.** *Source:* Data from U.S. Bureau of the Census: Home Ownership Rates by Race and Ethnicity of Householder, Annual Statistics 2003.

FIGURE 9 Index of Dissimilarity for the USA.

	Black	Latino	Asian	Native American
Dissimilarity Index 2000 (weighted averages)	64	51	41	33

Source: Data from U.S. Bureau of the Census, 2000 Summary File 1.
Note: A zero on this index would mean that racial groups are evenly integrated throughout a city. A score of one hundred means complete racial segregation among groups.

The U.S. population is 74% white (including Latinos who define themselves as white). The total U.S. population comprises: non-Hispanic white, 67%; black, 12.4%; Latino, 14.8%; Asian, 4.4%; and American Indian, 0.8%.

Figure 10   Segregation from Whites in the Largest 10 Metropolitan Areas.

Metropolitan Area	Population (millions)	Black	Latino	Asian
Los Angeles—Long Beach	9.5	67.5	63.2	48.3
New York	9.3	81.8	66.7	50.5
Chicago	8.3	80.8	62.1	44.4
Philadelphia	5.1	72.3	60.2	43.8
Washington, DC	4.9	63.1	48.4	39.0
Detroit	4.4	84.7	45.7	45.9
Houston	4.2	67.5	55.7	49.4
Atlanta	4.1	65.6	52.5	45.2
Dallas	3.5	59.4	54.1	45.0
Boston	3.4	65.7	58.8	44.9

Source: Data from John R. Logan, Brian Stults, and Reynolds Farley. 2004. "Segregation of Minorities in the Metropolis: Two Decades of Change" Demography 41: 1–22. For more information, see http://browns4.dyndns.org/cen2000_s4.

Note: A zero on this index would mean that racial groups are evenly integrated throughout a city. A score of one hundred means complete racial segregation among groups.

Section III: Health

FIGURE 11   Health Disparities by Race.

	White	Black	Latino	Asian	AI/NA
Heart disease (%)	26.9	40.1	27.7	5.4	n/a
Premature deaths (%)	14.7	31.5	23.5	n/a	36.0
High blood pressure (%)	31.1	43.2	18.6	16.3	20.7
Overweight and obesity rate (%)	55.3	65.8	57.6	35.9	61.6
Birthrate (births/1000)	11.7	16.1	22.6	16.5	13.8
Infant mortality (death/1000)	5.7	13.5	5.4	4.7	9.7
Rate of teen births (births/1000)	28.5	68.3	83.4	18.3	53.8
Cases of HIV (rates 100K)	12.3	18.4	39.7	8.6	16.9
Distribution of new AIDS cases (%)	31.1	48.2	18.5	1.3	0.5
Tuberculosis (rates 100K)	1.5	12.6	10.4	27.8	6.8
Cigarette smoking (%)	23.3	21.7	18.5	13.7	38.4

Source: Data from U.S. Bureau of the Census, updated July 2005.

The U.S. population is 74% white (including Latinos who define themselves as white). The total U.S. population comprises: non-Hispanic white, 67%; black, 12.4%; Latino, 14.8%; Asian, 4.4%; and American Indian, 0.8%.

FIGURE 12   Percentage of Americans Uninsured by Race.

	Uninsured Non-Elderly	Uninsured Children
White	13%	6%
Black	21%	9%
Latino	34%	20%
Other	19%	15%
USA	16%	10%

Source: Data from National Health Interview Survey, 2003.

Section IV: Crime

FIGURE 13   Percentage of Crime in the U.S. by Race and Ethnicity.

	White	Black	Asian	Native American
Murder & non-negligent manslaughter	42.5	55.4	1.4	0.7
Forcible rape	58.7	38.7	1.5	1.1
Robbery	42.8	55.4	1.2	0.6
Aggravated assault	61.7	36.0	1.3	1.0
Burglary	67.2	30.8	1.1	0.9
Larceny-theft	67.9	29.2	1.6	1.4
Motor vehicle theft	57.4	39.8	1.8	0.9
Arson	74.7	23.6	0.8	0.9
Violent crime	57.5	40.3	1.3	0.9
Property crime	66.9	30.4	1.5	1.2

Source: Data from U.S. Bureau of Justice Statistics, 2002.

The U.S. population is 74% white (including Latinos who define themselves as white). The total U.S. population comprises: non-Hispanic white, 67%; black, 12.4%; Latino, 14.8%; Asian, 4.4%; and American Indian, 0.8%.

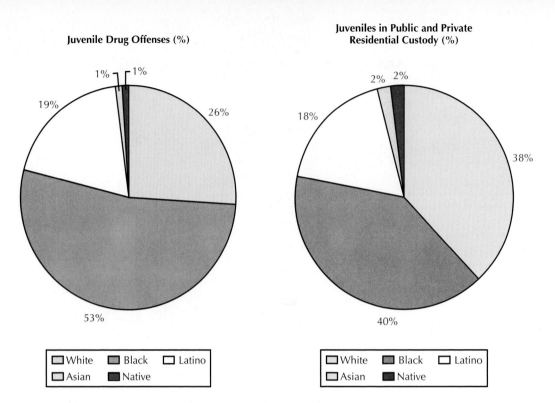

Juvenile Drug Offenses (%)

Juveniles in Public and Private Residential Custody (%)

| White | Black | Latino |
| Asian | Native | |

| White | Black | Latino |
| Asian | Native | |

FIGURE 14 **Juvenile Crime Statistics.** *Source:* Data from U.S. Bureau of Justice Statistics, 2002.

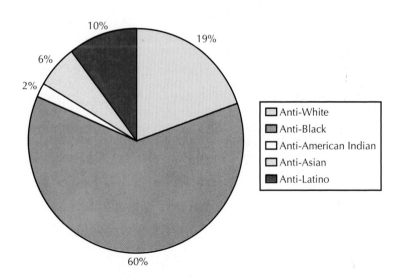

- Anti-White
- Anti-Black
- Anti-American Indian
- Anti-Asian
- Anti-Latino

FIGURE 15 **Hate Crimes by Race.** *Source:* FBI's Uniform Crime Report, 2003.

The U.S. population is 74% white (including Latinos who define themselves as white). The total U.S. population comprises: non-Hispanic white, 67%; black, 12.4%; Latino, 14.8%; Asian, 4.4%; and American Indian, 0.8%.

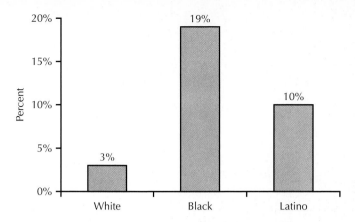

FIGURE 16 **Lifetime Chances of Going to Prison.**
Source: Data from U.S. Bureau of Justice Statistics, 2001.

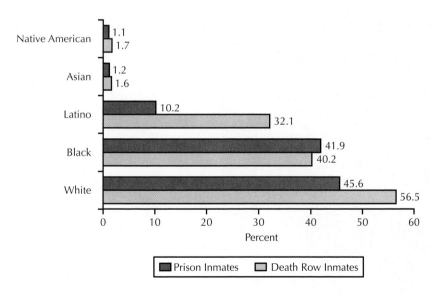

FIGURE 17 **Prison and Death Row Inmates.** *Source:* Data from U.S. Department of Justice and Death Row USA Spring 2004.

The U.S. population is 74% white (including Latinos who define themselves as white). The total U.S. population comprises: non-Hispanic white, 67%; black, 12.4%; Latino, 14.8%; Asian, 4.4%; and American Indian, 0.8%.

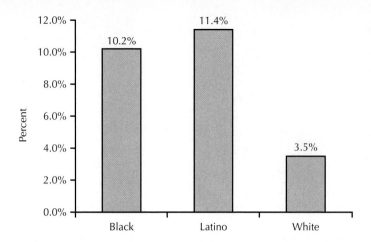

FIGURE 18 **Likelihood of Being Searched during a Traffic Stop.** *Source:* Data from U.S. Bureau of Justice Statistics, 2002.

Section V: Computers

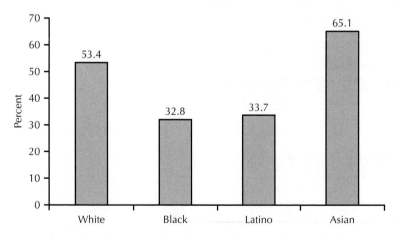

FIGURE 19 **Families Who Own Computers (Income $15–30K, 2000).** *Source:* Data from U.S. Bureau of the Census.

The U.S. population is 74% white (including Latinos who define themselves as white). The total U.S. population comprises: non-Hispanic white, 67%; black, 12.4%; Latino, 14.8%; Asian, 4.4%; and American Indian, 0.8%.

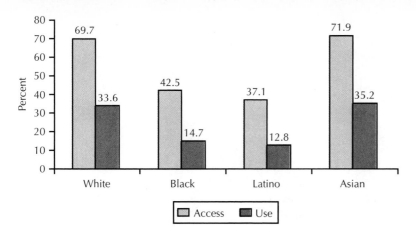

FIGURE 20   Computer Access and Use by Children 3–17 Years Old.
Source: Data from U.S. Bureau of the Census.

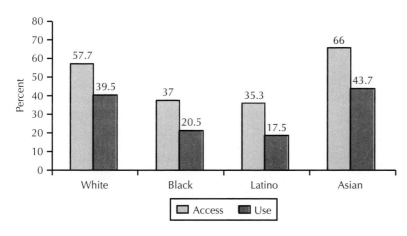

FIGURE 21   Computer Access and Use by Persons 18 and Older.
Source: Data from U.S. Bureau of the Census.

Section VI: Income, Weath, and Poverty

FIGURE 22   Median Household Income, 2007.

White	Black	Latino	Asian
$54,920	$33,916	$38,679	$66,103

Source: http://www.census.gov/Press-Release/www/releases/archives/income_wealth/012528.html.

The U.S. population is 74% white (including Latinos who define themselves as white). The total U.S. population comprises: non-Hispanic white, 67%; black, 12.4%; Latino, 14.8%; Asian, 4.4%; and American Indian, 0.8%.

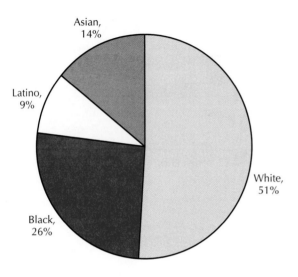

The Poor: Households with Incomes
between $2500 and $4999

Asian,
14%

Latino,
9%

White,
51%

Black,
26%

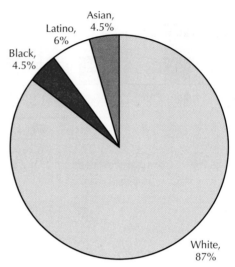

The Rich: Households with Incomes
over $250,000

Asian,
4.5%

Latino,
6%

Black,
4.5%

White,
87%

FIGURE 23   Who Is Rich, Who Is Poor.

FIGURE 24   Poverty in the United States.

	White	Black	Latino	Asian
% of population living in poverty (2002)	17.6	29.9	13.4	24.5
Related kids under 18 in families living in poverty (2001)	8.9	30.0	27.4	11.1
Working Poor (%) (1998)	6.9	13.6	19.2	n/a
Poverty (%) (2003)	8.2	24.3	22.5	11.8

Source: Data from U.S. Bureau of the Census, 2001–2003.

The U.S. population is 74% white (including Latinos who define themselves as white). The total U.S. population comprises: non-Hispanic white, 67%; black, 12.4%; Latino, 14.8%; Asian, 4.4%; and American Indian, 0.8%.

Section VII: Employment

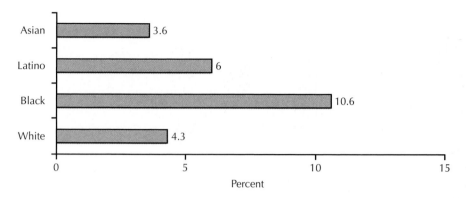

FIGURE 25 **Unemployment Statistics.** *Source:* U.S. Bureau of Labor Statistics, 2004–2005.

Section VIII: Occupations

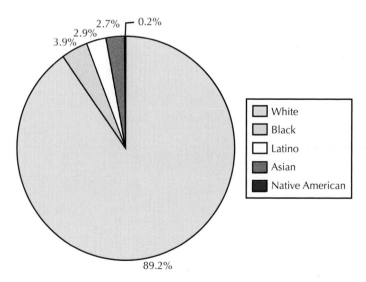

FIGURE 26 **Lawyers by Race and Ethnicity.** *Source:* Data from U.S. Census Bureau 1 Percent Public Use Microdata Sample Surveys, 201. *Note:* Numbers are the percent of the population.

The U.S. population is 74% white (including Latinos who define themselves as white). The total U.S. population comprises: non-Hispanic white, 67%; black, 12.4%; Latino, 14.8%; Asian, 4.4%; and American Indian, 0.8%.

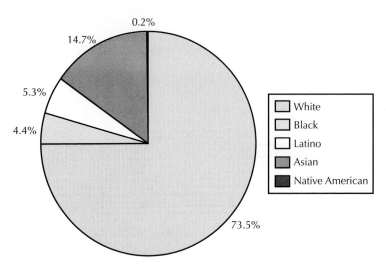

FIGURE 27 **Physicians and Surgeons by Race and Ethnicity.** *Source:* Data from U.S. Census Bureau 1 Percent Public Use Microdata Sample Surveys, 201. *Note:* Numbers are the percent of the population.

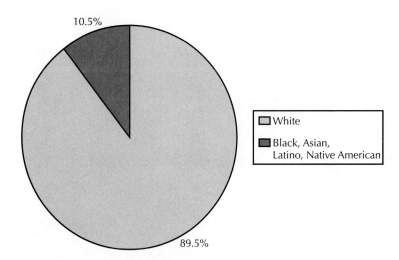

FIGURE 28 **Washington D.C. National Press Corps Reporters and Editor by Race and Ethnicity.** *Source:* Data from Unity, 2004. *Note:* Numbers are the percent of the population.

The U.S. population is 74% white (including Latinos who define themselves as white). The total U.S. population comprises: non-Hispanic white, 67%; black, 12.4%; Latino, 14.8%; Asian, 4.4%; and American Indian, 0.8%.

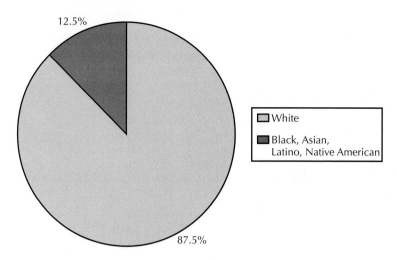

12.5%

87.5%

- ☐ White
- ■ Black, Asian, Latino, Native American

FIGURE 29 **Newsrooms Nationwide by Race and Ethnicity.**
Source: Data from Unity, 2004. *Note:* Numbers are the percent of the population.

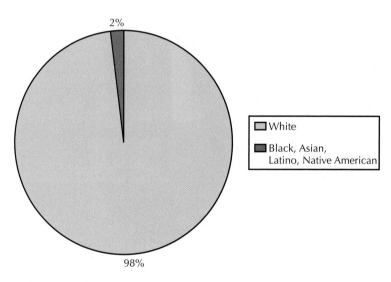

2%

98%

- ☐ White
- ■ Black, Asian, Latino, Native American

FIGURE 30 **CEOs of Fortune 500 Companies by Race and Ethnicity.** *Source:* Data from Christian Science Monitor, October 31, 2005. *Note:* Numbers are the percent of the population.

The U.S. population is 74% white (including Latinos who define themselves as white). The total U.S. population comprises: non-Hispanic white, 67%; black, 12.4%; Latino, 14.8%; Asian, 4.4%; and American Indian, 0.8%.

FIGURE 31   Other Occupations by Race and Ethnicity.

	White	Black	Latino	Asian	Native American
Registered Nurses	80.4	8.9	3.4	5.5	0.4
Engineers	80.9	4.2	3.9	9.2	0.3
Police Supervisors	81.4	9.5	6.1	0.5	0.9
Police/Detectives	76.6	11.4	8.5	1.4	0.7
College Instructors	79.7	5.6	4.5	8.1	0.4
Judges/Hearing Examiners/JPs/some Arbitrators	82.1	12.0	3.4	1.4	0.9
Clergy	81.8	8.4	3.9	4.1	0.7
Information Technology	73.8	7.6	5.1	11.4	0.3
School Teachers	81.8	9.0	5.7	1.8	0.5

Source: Data from U.S. Census Bureau 1 Percent Public Use Microdata Sample Surveys, 201.

Section IX: Government

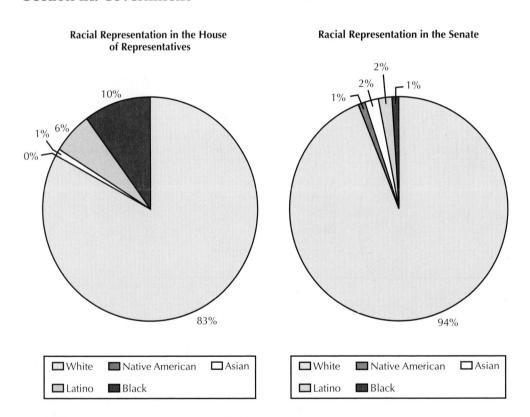

FIGURE 32   **Racial Representation in 109th Congress.** *Source:* Data from U.S. House of Representatives, House Press Gallery; U.S. Senate, Daily Press Gallery, Minority Senators.

The U.S. population is 74% white (including Latinos who define themselves as white). The total U.S. population comprises: non-Hispanic white, 67%; black, 12.4%; Latino, 14.8%; Asian, 4.4%; and American Indian, 0.8%.

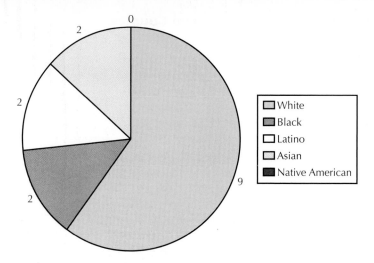

FIGURE 33   Racial Representation in the Presidential
Cabinet 2005. *Source:* House Press Gallery: *The President's Cabinet;*
The White House.

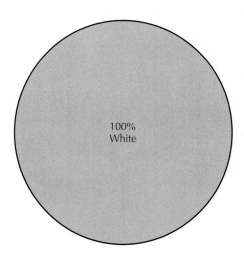

FIGURE 34   Race of Presidents in
the United States, as of October 2008.

The U.S. population is 74% white (including Latinos who define themselves as white). The total U.S. population comprises: non-Hispanic white, 67%; black, 12.4%; Latino, 14.8%; Asian, 4.4%; and American Indian, 0.8%.

Section X: New Boundaries: Immigration and Interracial Couples

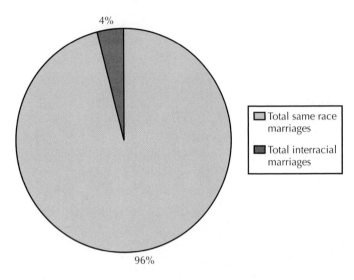

4%

96%

Legend:
- Total same race marriages
- Total interracial marriages

FIGURE 35 Interracial Married Couples 2003.

Source: Data from U.S. Census Bureau, *Statistical Abstract of the United States: 2004–2005.*

FIGURE 36 Ten Largest Cities and Their Multiracial Populations 2000.

Place	Total population		Two or more races population		
	Rank	*Number*	*Rank*	*Number*	*Percent*
New York, NY	1	8,008,278	1	393,959	4.9
Los Angeles, CA	2	3,694,820	2	191,288	5.2
Chicago, IL	3	2,896,016	3	84,437	2.9
Houston, TX	4	1,953,631	4	61,478	3.1
Philadelphia, PA	5	1,517,550	10	33,574	2.2
Phoenix, AZ	6	1,321,045	8	43,276	3.3
San Diego, CA	7	1,223,400	5	59,081	4.8
Dallas, TX	8	1,188,580	12	32,351	2.7
San Antonio, TX	9	1,144,646	9	41,871	3.7
Detroit, MI	10	951,270	18	22,041	2.3
Honolulu, HI	46	371,657	6	55,474	14.9
San Jose, CA	11	894,943	7	45,062	5.0

Source: Data from U.S. Census Bureau, Census 2000 Restricting Data (Public Law 94–171) Summary File, Table PL1.

The U.S. population is 74% white (including Latinos who define themselves as white). The total U.S. population comprises: non-Hispanic white, 67%; black, 12.4%; Latino, 14.8%; Asian, 4.4%; and American Indian, 0.8%.

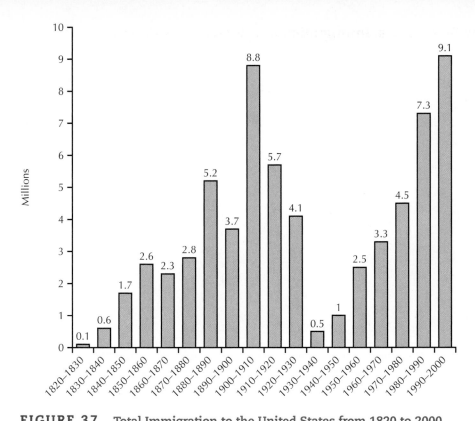

FIGURE 37 **Total Immigration to the United States from 1820 to 2000, by Decade.** *Source:* Data from U.S. Immigration and Naturalization Service.

The U.S. population is 74% white (including Latinos who define themselves as white). The total U.S. population comprises: non-Hispanic white, 67%; black, 12.4%; Latino, 14.8%; Asian, 4.4%; and American Indian, 0.8%.

FIGURE 38 Settlement Patterns of Immigrants.

		Immigrants		Share of Population	
		2000	*1990*	*2000*	*1990*
1	Los Angeles–Long Beach	3,449,444	2,892,456	36.2%	32.7%
2	New York, NY	3,139,647	2,285,024	33.7%	26.8%
3	Chicago, IL	1,425,978	885,081	17.2%	11.9%
4	Miami, FL	1,147,765	874,569	50.9%	45.1%
5	Houston, TX	854,669	440,321	20.5%	13.3%
6	Orange County, CA	849,899	575,108	29.9%	23.9%
7	Washington, DC	832,016	489,641	16.9%	11.6%
8	Riverside–San Bernardino, CA	612,359	360,643	18.8%	13.9%
9	San Diego, CA	606,254	428,810	21.5%	17.2%
10	Dallas, TX	591,169	234,522	16.8%	8.8%
11	Oakland, CA	573,144	337,435	24.0%	16.2%
12	San Jose, CA	573,130	347,201	34.1%	23.2%
13	San Francisco, CA	554,819	441,290	32.0%	27.5%

Source: Data from John R. Logan. 2006. "Settlement Patterns of Immigrants in Metropolitan America" in Mary Waters and Reed Ueda (eds.), *The New Americans: A Handbook to Immigration Since 1965.* Harvard University Press, forthcoming.

The U.S. population is 74% white (including Latinos who define themselves as white). The total U.S. population comprises: non-Hispanic white, 67%; black, 12.4%; Latino, 14.8%; Asian, 4.4%; and American Indian, 0.8%.

Notes and References

READING 2

References

Aptheker, Herbert, ed. 1974. *A Documentary History of the Negro People in the United States.* Secaucus, NJ: Citadel.

Boskin, Joseph. 1966. *Into Slavery: Radical Decisions in the Virginia Colony.* Philadelphia: Lippincott.

Catterall, Helen. 1937. *Judicial Cases Concerning American Slavery and the Negro.* 5 vols. Washington, DC: Negro University Press.

Davidson, Basil. 1961. *The African Slave Trade.* Boston: Little, Brown.

Donnan, Elizabeth, ed. 1965. *Documents Illustrative of the History of the Slave Trade to America.* 4 vols. New York: Octagon.

Elkins, Stanley. 1976. *Slavery: A Problem in American Institutional and Intellectual Life.* Chicago: University of Chicago Press.

Federal Writers Project. 1969. *The Negro in Virginia.* New York: Arno.

Franklin, John Hope. 1974. *From Slavery to Freedom: A History of American Negroes.* New York: Knopf.

Jordan, Winthrop. 1968. *White over Black: American Attitudes toward the Negro, 1550–1812.* Chapel Hill: University of North Carolina Press.

Morgan, Edmund S. 1975. *American Slavery, American Freedom: The Ordeal of Colonial Virginia.* New York: Norton.

Mullin, Gerald. 1974. *Flight and Rebellion: Slave Resistance in Eighteenth-Century Virginia.* New York: Oxford University Press.

Mullin, Michael, ed. 1975. *American Negro Slavery: A Documentary History.* New York: Harper & Row.

Phillips, Ulrich B. 1966. *American Negro Slavery: A Survey of the Supply, Employment and Control of Negro Labor as Determined by the Plantation Regime.* Baton Rouge: Louisiana State University Press.

Redding, J. Saunders. 1973. *They Came in Chains.* Philadelphia: Lippincott.

Stampp, Kenneth M. 1956. *The Peculiar Institution.* New York: Knopf.

Tannenbaum, Frank. 1963. *Slave and Citizen: The Negro in the Americas.* New York: Random House.

READING 3

Notes

1. *San Francisco Chronicle,* 14 September 1982, 19 May 1983. Ironically, the 1970 Louisiana law was enacted to supersede an old Jim Crow statute which relied on the idea of "common report" in determining an infant's race. Following Phipps's unsuccessful attempt to change her classification and have the law declared unconstitutional, a legislative effort arose which culminated in the repeal of the law. See *San Francisco Chronicle,* 23 June 1983.

2. The Mormon church, for example, has been heavily criticized for its doctrine of black inferiority.

3. Thomas F. Gossett notes:

   Race theory . . . had up until fairly modern times no firm hold on European thought. On the other hand, race theory and race prejudice were by no means unknown at the time when the English colonists came to North America. Undoubtedly, the age of exploration led many to speculate on race differences at a period when neither Europeans nor Englishmen were prepared to make allowances for vast cultural diversities. Even though race theories had not then secured wide acceptance or even sophisticated formulation, the first contacts of the Spanish with the Indians in the Americas can now be recognized as the beginning of a struggle between conceptions of the nature of primitive peoples which has not yet been wholly settled. (Thomas F. Gossett, *Race: The History of an Idea in America* [New York: Schocken Books, 1965], p. 16.)

   Winthrop Jordan provides a detailed account of early European colonialists' attitudes about color and race in *White over Black: American Attitudes Toward the Negro, 1550–1812* (New York: Norton, 1977 [1968]), pp. 3–43.

4. Pro-slavery physician Samuel George Morton (1799–1851) compiled a collection of 800 crania from all parts of the world which formed the sample for his studies of race. Assuming that the larger size of the cranium translated into greater intelligence, Morton established a relationship between race and skull capacity. Gossett reports that:

   In 1849, one of his studies included the following results: The English skulls in his collection proved to be the largest, with an average cranial capacity of 96 cubic inches. The Americans and Germans were rather poor seconds, both with cranial capacities of 90 cubic inches. At the bottom of the list were the Negroes with 83 cubic inches, the Chinese with 82, and the Indians with 79. (Ibid., p. 74.)

On Morton's methods, see Stephen J. Gould, "The Finagle Factor," *Human Nature* (July 1978).

5. Definitions of race founded upon a common pool of genes have not held up when confronted by scientific research which suggests that the differences *within* a given human population are greater than those between populations. See L. L. Cavalli-Sforza, "The Genetics of Human Populations," *Scientific American,* September 1974, pp. 81–89.

6. Arthur Jensen, "How Much Can We Boost IQ and Scholastic Achievement?" *Harvard Educational Review* 39 (1969):1–123.

7. Ernst Moritz Manasse, "Max Weber on Race," *Social Research* 14 (1947):191–221.

8. Quoted in Edward D. C. Campbell, Jr., *The Celluloid South: Hollywood and the Southern Myth* (Knoxville: University of Tennessee Press, 1981), pp. 168–70.

9. Marvin Harris, *Patterns of Race in the Americas* (New York: Norton, 1964), p. 56.

10. Ibid., p. 57.

11. After James Meredith had been admitted as the first black student at the University of Mississippi, Harry S. Murphy announced that he, and not Meredith, was the first black student to attend "Ole Miss." Murphy described himself as black but was able to pass for white and spent nine months at the institution without attracting any notice (Ibid., p. 56).

12. A. Sivanandan, "From Resistance to Rebellion: Asian and Afro-Caribbean Struggles in Britain," *Race and Class* 23(2–3) (Autumn–Winter 1981).

13. Consider the contradictions in racial status which abound in the country with the most rigidly defined racial categories—South Africa. There a race classification agency is employed to adjudicate claims for upgrading of official racial identity. This is particularly necessary for the "coloured" category. The apartheid system considers Chinese as "Asians" while the Japanese are accorded the status of "honorary whites." This logic nearly detaches race from any grounding in skin color and other physical attributes and nakedly exposes race as a juridical category subject to economic, social and political influences. (We are indebted to Steve Talbot for clarification of some of these points.)

14. Gordon W. Allport, *The Nature of Prejudice* (Garden City, NY: Doubleday, 1958), pp. 184–200.

15. We wish to use this phrase loosely, without committing ourselves to a particular position on such social psychological approaches as symbolic interactionism, which are outside the scope of this study. An interesting study on this subject is S. M. Lyman and W. A. Douglass, "Ethnicity: Strategies of Individual and Collective Impression Management," *Social Research* 40(2) (1973).

16. Michael Billig, "Patterns of Racism: Interviews with National Front Members," *Race and Class* 20(2) (Autumn 1978):161–79.

17. "Miss San Antonio USA Lisa Fernandez and other Hispanics auditioning for a role in a television soap-opera did not fit the Hollywood image of real Mexicans and had to darken their faces before filming." Model Aurora Garza said that their faces were bronzed with powder because they looked too white. "'I'm a real Mexican [Garza said] and very dark anyway. I'm even darker right now because I have a tan. But they kept wanting me to make my face darker and darker" (*San Francisco Chronicle,* 21 September 1984). A similar dilemma faces Asian American actors who feel that Asian character lead roles inevitably go to white actors who make themselves up to be Asian. Scores of Charlie Chan films, for example, have been made with white leads (the last one was the 1981 *Charlie Chan and the Curse of the Dragon Queen*). Roland Winters, who played in six Chan features, was asked by playwright Frank Chin to explain the logic of casting a white man in the role of Charlie Chan: "'The only thing I can think of is, if you want to cast a homosexual in a show, and get a homosexual, it'll be awful. It won't be funny . . . and may be there's something there . . .'" (Frank Chin, "Confessions of the Chinatown Cowboy," *Bulletin of Concerned Asian Scholars* 4(3) (Fall 1972)).

18. Melanie Martindale-Sikes, "Nationalizing 'Nigger' Imagery Through 'Birth of a Nation,'" paper prepared for the 73rd Annual Meeting of the American Sociological Association, 4–8 September 1978, San Francisco.

19. Jordan, *White over Black,* p. 95; emphasis added.

20. Historical focus has been placed either on particular racially defined groups or on immigration and the "incorporation" of ethnic groups. In the former case the characteristic ethnicity theory pitfalls and apologetics such as functionalism and cultural pluralism may be avoided, but only by sacrificing much of the focus on race. In the latter case, race is considered a manifestation of ethnicity.

21. The degree of antipathy for these groups should not be minimized. A northern commentator observed in the 1850s: "An Irish Catholic seldom attempts to rise to a higher condition than that in which he is placed, while the Negro often makes the attempt with success." Quoted in Gossett, op. cit., p. 288.

22. This analysis, as will perhaps be obvious, is essentially DuBoisian. Its main source will be found in the monumental (and still

largely unappreciated) *Black Reconstruction in the United States, 1860–1880* (New York: Atheneum, 1977 [1935]).

23. Alexander Saxton argues that:

    North Americans of European background have experienced three great racial confrontations: with the Indian, with the African, and with the Oriental. Central to each transaction has been a totally one-sided preponderance of power, exerted for the exploitation of nonwhites by the dominant white society. In each case (but especially in the two that began with systems of enforced labor), white workingmen have played a crucial, yet ambivalent, role. They have been both exploited and exploiters. On the one hand, thrown into competition with nonwhites as enslaved or "cheap" labor they suffered economically; on the other hand, being white, they benefited by that very exploitation which was compelling the nonwhites to work for low wages or for nothing. Ideologically they were drawn in opposite directions. *Racial identification cut at right angles to class consciousness.* (Alexander Saxton, *The Indispensable Enemy: Labor and the Anti-Chinese Movement in California* [Berkeley and Los Angeles: University of California Press, 1971], p. 1; emphasis added.)

24. Selig Perlman, *The History of Trade Unionism in the United States* (New York: Augustus Kelley, 1950), p. 52; emphasis added.

25. Whether southern blacks were "peasants" or rural workers is unimportant in this context. Some time during the 1960s blacks attained a higher degree of urbanization than whites. Before World War II most blacks had been rural dwellers and nearly 80 percent lived in the South.

26. See George Gilder, *Wealth and Poverty* (New York: Basic Books, 1981); Charles Murray, *Losing Ground* (New York: Basic Books, 1984).

27. A brilliant study of the racialization process in Britain, focused on the rise of "mugging" as a popular fear in the 1970s, is Stuart Hall et al., *Policing the Crisis* (London: Macmillan, 1978).

28. The case of Vincent Chin, a Chinese American man beaten to death in 1982 by a laid-off Detroit auto worker and his stepson who mistook him for Japanese and blamed him for the loss of their jobs, has been widely publicized in Asian American communities. On immigration conflicts and pressures, see Michael Omi, "New Wave Dread: Immigration and Intra–Third World Conflict," *Socialist Review* 60 (November–December 1981).

READING 4

Notes

1. Charles Hirschman, "America's Melting Pot Reconsidered," *Annual Review of Sociology* 9 (1983): 397–423.

2. Robert E. Park, *Race and Culture* (Glencoe, IL: Free Press, 1950), p. 150 (italics added).

3. Robert E. Park and Ernest W. Burgess, *Introduction to the Science of Society* (Chicago: University of Chicago Press, 1924), p. 735.

4. Janice R. Hullum, "Robert E. Park's Theory of Race Relations" (M.A. thesis, University of Texas, 1973), pp. 81–88; Park and Burgess, *Introduction to the Science of Society,* p. 760.

5. Milton M. Gordon, *Assimilation in American Life* (New York: Oxford University Press, 1964), pp. 72–73.

6. Ibid., p. 71.

7. Silvia Pedraza, *Political and Economic Migrants in America: Cubans and Mexicans* (Austin: University of Texas Press, 1985), pp. 5–7; Richard Alba, *Ethnic Identity: The Transformation of White America* (New Haven, CT: Yale University Press, 1990), p. 311; J. Allen Williams and Suzanne T. Ortega, "Dimensions of Assimilation," *Social Science Quarterly* 71 (1990):697–709.

8. Milton M. Gordon, *Human Nature, Class, and Ethnicity* (New York: Oxford University Press, 1978), pp. 67–89.

9. Gordon, *Assimilation in American Life,* pp. 78–108.

10. See Will Herberg, *Protestant—Catholic—Jew,* rev. ed. (Garden City, NY: Doubleday, Anchor Books, 1960).

11. Milton M. Gordon, "Models of Pluralism: The New American Dilemma," *Annals of the American Academy of Political and Social Science* 454 (1981):178–88.

12. Alba, *Ethnic Identity,* p. 3.

13. Stanley Lieberson and Mary Waters, "Ethnic Mixtures in the United States," *Sociology and Social Research* 70 (1985): 43–53; Cookie White Stephan and Walter Stephan, "After Intermarriage," *Journal of Marriage and the Family* 51 (May 1989):507–19.

14. Nathan Glazer and Daniel P. Moynihan, *Beyond the Melting Pot* (Cambridge, MA: M.I.T. Press and Harvard University Press, 1963).

15. Andrew M. Greeley, *Ethnicity in the United States* (New York: Wiley, 1974), p. 293.

16. Ibid., pp. 295–301.

17. Ibid., p. 309.

18. William L. Yancey, D. P. Ericksen, and R. N. Juliani, "Emergent Ethnicity: A Review and Reformulation," *American Sociological Review* 41 (June 1976):391–93. See also Greeley, *Ethnicity in the United States,* pp. 290–317.

19. Talcott Parsons, "Full Citizenship for the Negro American? A Sociological Problem," in *The Negro American,* edited by Talcott Parsons and Kenneth B. Clark (Boston: Houghton Mifflin, 1965–66), p. 740.

20. James Geschwender, *Racial Stratification in America* (Dubuque, IA: Brown, 1978), p. 58.

21. Gordon, *Human Nature, Class, and Ethnicity,* pp. 73–78. See also Clifford Geertz, "The Integrative Revolution," in *Old Societies and New States,* edited by Clifford Geertz (New York: Free Press, 1963), p. 109.

22. Edna Bonacich, "Class Approaches to Ethnicity and Race," *Insurgent Sociologist* 10 (Fall 1980):11.

23. Frederik Barth, "Introduction," in *Ethnic Groups and Boundaries: The Social Organization of Culture Difference* (Oslo: Universitetsforlaget, 1969), pp. 10–17.

24. Susan Olzak, "A Competition Model of Collective Action in American Cities," in *Competitive Ethnic Relations,* edited by Susan Olzak and Joane Nagel (Orlando, FL: Academic Press, 1986), pp. 17–46.

25. Ronald Bailey and Guillermo Flores, "Internal Colonialism and Racial Minorities in the U.S.: An Overview," in *Structures of Dependency,* edited by Frank Bonilla and Robert Girling (Stanford, CA: privately published by a Stanford faculty–student seminar, 1973), pp. 151–53.

26. G. Balandier, "The Colonial Situation: A Theoretical Approach," in *Social Change,* ed. Immanuel Wallerstein (New York: Wiley, 1966), p. 35.

27. Pablo Gonzalez-Cassanova, "Internal Colonialism and National Development," in *Latin American Radicalism,* edited by Irving L. Horowitz et al. (New York: Random House, 1969), p. 130; Bailey and Flores, "Internal Colonialism," p. 156.

28. Bailey and Flores, "Internal Colonialism," p. 156.

29. Bob Blauner, *Racial Oppression in America,* (New York: Harper & Row, 1972), p. 55. Our analysis of internal colonialism draws throughout on Blauner's provocative discussion.

30. Stokely Carmichael and Charles Hamilton, *Black Power* (New York: Random House, Vintage Books, 1967), pp. 2–7.

31. Guillermo B. Flores, "Race and Culture in the Internal Colony: Keeping the Chicano in His Place," in *Structures of Dependency,* edited by Bonilla and Girling, p. 192.

32. Michael Hechter, *Internal Colonialism* (Berkeley: University of California Press, 1975), pp. 9–12; Michael Hechter, "Group Formation and the Cultural Division of Labor," *American Journal of Sociology* 84 (1978):293–318; Michael Hechter, Debra Friedman, and Malka Applebaum, "A Theory of Ethnic Collective Action," *International Migration Review* 16 (1982):412–34. See also Geschwender, *Racial Stratification in America,* p. 87.

33. Joe Feagin and Bonnie Mitchell, "America's Non-European Cultures: The Myth of the Melting Pot," in *The Inclusive University: Multicultural Perspectives in Higher Education,* edited by Benjamin Bowser, Gale Auletta, and Terry Jones (forthcoming).

34. Carol B. Stack, "Sex Roles and Survival Strategies in an Urban Black Community," in *Women, Culture and Society,* edited by Michelle Zimbalist Rosaldo and Louise Lamphere (Stanford, CA: Stanford University Press, 1974), p. 128; Ronald Angel and Marta Tienda, "Determinants of Extended Household Structure: Cultural Pattern or Economic Need?" *American Journal of Sociology* 87 (1981–82):1360–83.

35. Joan W. Moore, "American Minorities and 'New Nation' Perspectives," *Pacific Sociological Review* 19 (October 1976): 448–55; Michael Omi and Howard Winant, *Racial Formation in the United States* (New York: Routledge & Kegan Paul, 1986), pp. 47–49.

36. Bonacich, "Class Approaches to Ethnicity and Race," p. 14.

37. Mario Barrera, *Race and Class in the Southwest,* (Notre Dame, IN: University of Notre Dame Press, 1979), pp. 201–203; Bonacich, "Class Approaches to Ethnicity and Race," p. 14.

38. Bonacich, "Class Approaches to Ethnicity and Race," pp. 14–15.

39. Edna Bonacich and John Modell, *The Economic Basis of Ethnic Solidarity* (Berkeley: University of California Press, 1980), pp. 1–37. For a critique, see Eugene Wong, "Asian American Middleman Minority Theory: The Framework of an American Myth," *Journal of Ethnic Studies* 13 (Spring 1985):51–87.

40. Quoted in Michael Albert et al., *Liberating Theory* (Boston: South End Press, 1986), p. 35.

41. Philomena Essed, *Understanding Everyday Racism* (Newbury Park, CA: Sage, 1991), pp. 30–32.

42. Ibid., p. 32.

43. Patricia Hill Collins, *Black Feminist Thought: Knowledge, Consciousness, and the Politics of Empowerment* (Boston: Unwin Hyman, 1990), pp. 40–48.

44. Denise A. Segura, "Chicanas and Triple Oppression in the Labor Force," in *Chicana Voices: Intersections of Class, Race and Gender,* edited by Teresa Cordova et al. (Austin, TX: Center for Mexican American Studies, 1986), p. 48.

45. Omi and Winant, *Racial Formation in the United States,* pp. 75–76.

46. Howard Winant, "Racial Formation Theory and Contemporary U.S. Politics," in *Exploitation and Exclusion,* edited by Abebe Zegeye, Leonard Harris, and Julia Maxted (London: Hans Zell, 1991), pp. 130–40.

47. James C. Scott, *Domination and the Arts of Resistance* (New Haven, CT: Yale University Press, 1990); John Gaventa, *Power and Powerlessness* (Urbana: University of Illinois Press, 1980).

48. Scott, *Domination and the Arts of Resistance,* p. 116.

49. Sterling Stuckey, *Slave Culture* (New York: Oxford University Press, 1987), pp. 27, 42–46.

READING 5

Notes

1. All racialized social systems operate along white supremacist lines. See Charles W. Mills, *Blackness Visible* (Ithaca, NY: Cornell University Press, 1998).

2. I make a distinction between race and ethnicity. Ethnicity has a primarily sociocultural foundation, and ethnic groups have exhibited tremendous malleability in terms of who belongs. In contrast, racial ascriptions (initially) are imposed externally to justify the collective exploitation of a people and are maintained to preserve status differences. The distinction I make was part of a debate that appeared recently in the *American Sociological Review*. For specialists interested in this matter, see Bonilla-Silva, "The Essential Social Fact of Race," *American Sociological Review* 64, no. 6 (1999): 899–906.

3. Herbert Blumer was one of the first analysts to make this argument about systemic rewards received by the races ascribed the primary position in a racial order. See Herbert Blumer, "Reflections on Theory of Race Relations," pp. 3–21 in *Race Relations in World Perspective*, edited by A. W. Lind (Honolulu, HI: University of Hawaii Press, 1955). Du Bois's argument about the psychological wages of whiteness has been used recently by Manning Marable, *How Capitalism Underdeveloped Black America;* and by David Roediger, *The Wages of Whiteness.*

4. This point has been made by Michel Omi and Howard Winant, *Racial Formation in the United States;* Winant, *Racial Conditions.*

5. I am referring to cases such as Haiti. Nonetheless, recent research has suggested that even in such places, the abolition of slavery did not end the racialized character of the social formation. See Michel-Rolph Troillot, *Haiti, State Agency Nation: Origins and Legacy of Duvalierism* (New York: Monthly Review Press, 1990).

6. For a similar argument, see Floya Anthias and Nira Yuval-Davis, *Racialized Boundaries: Race, Nation, Gender, Colour, and the Anti-Racist Struggle* (London, England: Tavistock, 1992).

7. For an early statement on this matter, see Hubert M. Blalock, Jr., *Toward a Theory of Minority-Majority Group Relations* (New York: John Wiley and Sons, 1967). For a more recent statement, see Susan Olzack, *The Dynamics of Ethnic Competition and Conflict* (Stanford, CA: Stanford University Press, 1992).

8. Nineteenth-century nation-building processes throughout Latin America included the myth of racial democracy and color- or race-blindness. This facilitated the struggles for independence and the maintenance of white supremacy in societies wherein white elites were demographically insignificant.

For discussions pertinent to this argument see the excellent collection edited by Michael Hanchard, *Racial Politics in Contemporary Brazil* (Durham and London: Duke University Press, 1999).

9. See my "The Essential Social Fact of Race," *American Sociological Review* 64, no. 6 (December 1999): 899–906.

10. On this point, see Warren Whatley and Gavin Wright, *Race, Human Capital, and Labor Markets in American History,* Working Paper #7 (Ann Arbor, MI: Center for Afroamerican and Africa Studies, University of Michigan, 1994). For an incisive discussion, see Samuel L. Meyers, Jr., "Measuring and Detecting Discrimination in the Post–Civil Rights Era," pp. 172–197 in *Race and Ethnicity in Research Methods,* edited by John H. Stanfield II and Rutledge M. Dennis (London: Sage Publications, 1993).

11. Michael Reich, "The Economics of Racism," in *Racial Conflict, Discrimination, and Power: Historical and Contemporary Studies,* edited by William Barclay, Krishna Kumar, and Ruth P. Simms (New York: AMS Press, 1976), p. 224.

12. Omi and Winant, *Racial Formation in the United States,* 64.

13. On the invention of the white race, see Theodore W. Allen, *The Invention of the White Race,* Vol. I (London: Verso, 1994). On the invention of the "Indian" race, see Robert E. Berkhoffer, *The White Man's Indian* (New York: Vintage, 1978). On the invention of the black and white races, see Winthrop Jordan, *White over Black.*

14. A classic book on the ideological binary construction of the races in the United States is Thomas Gossett, *Race: The History of an Idea in America* (Dallas, TX: Southern Methodist University Press, 1963). For an analysis of an earlier period in the Americas, see Tzevetan Todorov, *The Conquest of America: The Question of the Other* (New York: Harper Colophon, 1984).

15. On this matter, I stated in my recent debate in the pages of the *American Sociological Review* with Mara Loveman that "'race,' like 'class' or 'gender,' is *always contingent* but is also *socially real.* Race operates 'as a shuttle between socially constructed meanings and practices, between subjective and lived, material reality' (Hanchard 1994:4)." (901). Michael G. Hanchard, *Orpheus and Power* (Princeton, NJ: Princeton University Press, 1994).

16. This last point is an extension of Nicos Poulantzas' view on class. Races—as classes—are not an "empirical thing"; they denote racialized social relations or racial practices at all levels. Poulantzas, *Political Power and Social Classes* (London: Verso, 1982), p. 67.

17. For a full discussion, see my "The Essential Social Fact of Race." For a similar argument, see Teresa Amott and Julie Matthaei, *Race, Gender, and Work: A Multicultural Economic History of Women in the United States* (Boston, MA: South End Press, 1996).

18. Frederick Barth, "Introduction," pp. 9–38 in *Ethnic Groups and Boundaries: The Social Organization of Culture Difference,* edited by F. Barth (Bergen, Norway: Universitetsforlaget, 1969).

19. For the case of the Jews, see Robert Miles, *Racism After "Race Relations"* (London: Routledge, 1993). For the case of the Irish, see Allen, *The Invention of the White Race.*

20. For a recent excellent discussion on ethnicity with many examples from the United States, see Stephen Cornell and Douglas Hartmann, *Ethnicity and Race: Making Identities in a Changing World* (London: Pine Forge Press, 1998).

21. Roediger, *The Wages of Whiteness.* See also Noel Ignatiev, *How the Irish Became White* (New York: Routledge, 1995).

22. For identity issues among Caribbean immigrants, see the excellent edited collection by Constance R. Sutton and E. M. Chaney, *Caribbean Life in New York City: Sociocultural Dimensions* (New York: Center for Migration Studies of New York, 1987).

23. Barth, "Introduction," 17.

24. A few notable discussions on this matter are Ira Berlin, *Slaves Without Masters: The Free Negro in Antebellum South* (New York: Pantheon, 1975); John Hope Franklin, *From Slavery to Freedom: A History of the Negro Americans* (New York: Alfred Knopf, 1974); August Meir and Elliot Rudwick, *From Plantation to Ghetto* (New York: Hill and Wang, 1970).

25. The motivation for racializing human relations may have originated in the interests of powerful actors, but after social systems are racialized, all members of the dominant race participate in defending and reproducing the racial structure. This is the crucial reason why Marxist analysts (e.g., Cox, Reich) have not succeeded in successfully analyzing racism. They have not been able to accept the fact that after the phenomenon originated with the expansion of European capitalism into the New World, it acquired a life of its own. The subjects who were racialized as belonging to the superior race, whether or not they were members of the dominant class, became zealous defenders of the racial order.

26. Hillel Ticktin, *The Politics of Race: Discrimination in South Africa* (London: Pluto, 1991), p. 26.

27. The classic book on this is Paula Giddings, *When and Where I Enter: The Impact of Black Women on Race and Sex in America* (New York: Bantam, 1984). See also Nancy Caraway, *Segregated Sisterhood: Racism and the Politics of American Feminism* (Knoxville, TN: University of Tennessee Press, 1991).

28. This argument is not new. Analysts of the racial history of the United States have always pointed out that most of the significant historical changes in this country's race relations were accompanied by some degree of overt violence. See Harold Cruse, *Rebellion or Revolution* (New York: William Morrow, 1968); Franklin, *From Slavery to Freedom;* and James W. Button, *Blacks and Social Change: Impact of the Civil Rights Movement in Southern Communities* (Princeton, NJ: Princeton University Press, 1989).

29. This point is important in literature on revolutions and democracy. On the role of violence in the establishment of bourgeois democracies, see Barrington Moore, Jr., *Social Origins of Dictatorship and Democracy* (Boston, MA: Beacon Press, 1966). On the pivotal role of violence in social movements, see Frances Fox Piven and Richard A. Cloward, *Poor People's Movements: Why They Succeed, How They Fail* (New York: Vintage, 1979).

30. The notion of relative autonomy comes from the work of Poulantzas (*Power and Social Classes*) and implies that the ideological and political levels in a society are partially autonomous in relation to the economic level; that is, they are not merely expressions of the economic level.

31. Paul Gilroy, *"There Ain't No Black in the Union Jack": The Cultural Politics of Race and Nation* (Chicago, IL: University of Chicago Press, 1991), p. 17.

32. See Ellis Cose, *The Rage of a Privileged Class: Why Are Black Middle Class Angry? Why Should America Care?* (New York: HarperCollins, 1993); Lawrence Otis-Graham, *Member of the Club: Reflections on Life in a Racially Polarized World* (New York: HarperCollins, 1995).

33. In addition to the work by Joe R. Feagin and Hernán Vera already cited, see Lawrence Bobo, J. Kluegel, and R. Smith, "Laissez Faire Racism: The Crystallization of a Kinder, Gentler, Antiblack Ideology," and, particularly, Mary R. Jackman, *Velvet Glove: Paternalism and Conflict in Gender, Class and Race Relations* (Berkeley, CA: University of California Press, 1994).

34. Curiously, historian Eugene Genovese made a similar argument in his book *Red and Black.* Although he still regarded racism as an ideology, he stated that once it "arises it alters profoundly the material reality and in fact becomes a partially autonomous feature of that reality." *Red and Black: Marxian Explorations in Southern and Afroamerican History* (New York: Pantheon, 1971), p. 340.

35. Stuart Hall, "Race Articulation and Societies Structured in Dominance," in *Sociological Theories: Race and Colonialism,* edited by UNESCO (Paris: UNESCO, 1980), p. 336.

36. Actions by the Ku Klux Klan have an unmistakably racial tone, but many other actions (choosing to live in a suburban neighborhood, sending one's children to a private school, and opposing government intervention in hiring policies) also have racial undertones.

READING 6

Reference

Council of Economic Advisers. 1998. *Changing America: Indicators of Social and Economic Well-Being by Race and Hispanic Origin.* Washington, D.C.: U.S. Government Printing Office.

READING 7

Notes

1. Navarro, V. (1990). Race or class versus race and class: Mortality differentials in the United States. *Lancet, 336,* 1238–1240.

2. Braithwaite, R. L., & Taylor, S. E. (1992). *Health issues in the black community.* San Francisco: Jossey-Bass.

3. Furino, A. (Ed.). (1992). *Health policy and the Hispanic.* Boulder, CO: Westview Press.

4. Livingston, I. L. (1994). *Handbook of black American health: The mosaic of conditions, issues, policies, and prospects.* Westport, CT: Greenwood Press.

5. Zane, N.W.S., Takeuchi, D.T., &Young, K. N. S. (Eds.). (1994). *Confronting critical health issues of Asian and Pacific Islander Americans.* Thousand Oaks, CA: Sage.

6. National Center for Health Statistics. (1994). *Health, United States, 1993.* Hyattsville, MD: U.S. Department of Health and Human Services.

7. Sorlie, P. D., Backlund, E., Johnson, N. J., & Rogot, E. (1993). Mortality by Hispanic status in the United States. *JAMA, 270,* 2464–2468.

8. Vega, W. A., & Amaro, H. (1994). Latino outlook: Good health, uncertain prognosis. *Annu Rev Public Health, 15,* 39–67.

9. Fingerhut, L. A., & Makuc, D. M. (1992). Mortality among minority populations in the United States. *Am J Public Health, 82,* 1168–1170.

10. Lin-Fu, J. S. (1993). Asian and Pacific Islander Americans: An overview of demographic characteristics and health care issues. *Asian Am Pacific Islander J Health, 1,* 20–36.

11. Chen, M. S. (1993). A 1993 status report on the health status of Asian American and Pacific Islanders: Comparisons with *Healthy People 2000* objectives. *Asian Am Pacific Islander J Health, 1,* 37–55.

12. Crews, D. E. (1994). Obesity and diabetes. In N.W.S. Zane, D. T. Takeuchi, & K.N.J. Young (Eds.), *Confronting critical health issues of Asian and Pacific Islander Americans* (pp. 174–208). Thousand Oaks, CA: Sage.

13. Smith, E. M. (1993). Race or racism? Addiction in the United States. *Ann Epidemiol, 3,* 165–170.

14. Smith, J. P., & Welch, F. R. (1989). Black economic progress after Myrdal. *J Econ Lit, 27,* 519–564.

15. Hernandez, D. J. (1993). *America's children: Resources from family, government and the economy.* New York: Russell Sage Foundation.

16. National Center for Health Statistics. (1994). *Excess deaths and other mortality measures for the black population: 1979–81 and 1991.* Hyattsville, MD: U.S. Public Health Service.

17. Kochanek, K. D., Maurer, J. D., & Rosenberg, H. M. (1994). Why did black life expectancy decline from 1984 through 1989 in the United States? *Am J Public Health, 84,* 938–944.

18. Cooper, R. S. (1993). Health and the social status of blacks in the United States. *Ann Epidemiol, 3,* 137–144.

19. Freeman, H. P. (1993). Poverty, race, racism, and survival. *Ann Epidemiol, 3,* 145–149.

20. Rowley, D. L., Hogue, C. J. R., Blackmore, A. C., Ferre, C. D., Hatfield-Timajchy, K., et al. (1993). Preterm delivery among African-American women: A research strategy. *Am J Prev Med, 9*(Suppl.), 1–6.

21. Castro, K. G. (1993). Distribution of acquired immunodeficiency syndrome and other sexually transmitted diseases in racial and ethnic populations, United States: Influences of life-style and socioeconomic status. *Ann Epidemiol, 3,* 181–184.

22. Mullings, L. (1989). Inequality and African-American health status: Policies and prospects. In W. A. VanHome & T. V. Tonnesen (Eds.), *Twentieth century dilemmas—Twenty-first century prognoses* (pp. 154–182). Madison: University of Wisconsin, Institute on Race and Ethnicity.

23. Cooper, R. S., Steinhauer, M., Schatzkin, A., & Miller, W. (1981). Improved mortality among U.S. blacks, 1968–78: The role of antiracist struggle. *Int J Health Serv, 11,* 511–522.

24. Jackson, J. S., Brown, T. N., Williams, D. R., Torres, M., Sellers, S. L., & Brown, K. (1995). Perceptions and experiences of racism and the physical and mental health status of African Americans: A thirteen year national panel study. *Ethn Dis, 5*(1).

25. Williams, D. R. (1995). Poverty, racism and migration: The health of the African American population. In S. Pedraza & R. G. Rumbaut (Eds.), *Immigration, race, and ethnicity in America. Historical and contemporary perspectives.* Belmont, CA: Wadsworth.

26. Wilson, W. J. (1987). *The truly disadvantaged.* Chicago: University of Chicago Press.

27. Haan, M., Kaplan, G., & Camacho, T. (1987). Poverty and health: Prospective evidence from the Alameda County Study. *Am J Epidemiol, 15,* 989–998.

28. Harburg, E., Erfurt, J., Chape, C., Havenstein, L., Scholl, W., & Schork, M. A. (1973). Sociological stressor areas and black-white blood pressure: Detroit. *J Chronic Dis, 26,* 595–611.

29. McCord, C., & Freeman, H. P. (1990). Excess mortality in Harlem. *N Engl J Med, 322,* 173–177.

30. Massey, D. S., & Gross, A. B. (1993). *Black migration, segregation, and the spatial concentration of poverty.* Irving B. Harris Graduate School of Public Policy Studies Working Paper, Ser. 93-3, University of Chicago.

31. Gabarino, J., Dubrow, N., Kostelney, K., & Pardo, C. (1992). *Children in danger: Coping with the consequences of community violence.* San Francisco: Jossey-Bass.

32. Williams, D. R. (1991). Social structure and the health behavior of blacks. In K. W. Schaie, J. S. House, & D. Blazer (Eds.), *Aging, health behaviors and health outcomes* (pp. 59–64). Hillsdale, NJ: Erlbaum.

33. Herd, D. (1985). Migration, cultural transformation and the rise of black liver cirrhosis mortality. *Br J Addict, 80,* 397–410.

34. Davis, R. M. (1987). Current trends in cigarette advertising and marketing. *N Engl J Med, 316,* 725–732.

35. Singer, M. (1986). Toward a political economy of alcoholism. *Soc Sci Med, 23,* 113–130.

36. Levin, M. (1988). The tobacco industry's strange bedfellows. *Bus Soc Rev, 65,* 11–17.

37. Wilson, T. W., & Grim, C. E. (1991). Biohistory of slavery and blood pressure differences in blacks today. *Hypertension, 17*(Suppl. I), 122–128.

38. Jackson, F. L. C. (1991). An evolutionary perspective on salt, hypertension, and human genetic variability. *Hypertension, 17*(1, Suppl. 1), 129–132.

39. Curtin, P. D. (1992). The slavery hypothesis for hypertension among African Americans: The historical evidence. *Am J Public Health, 82,* 1681–1686.

40. Williams, D. R. (1992). Black-white differences in blood pressure: The role of social factors. *Ethn Dis, 2,* 126–141.

41. Baquet, C. R., Horm, J. W., Gibbs, T., & Greenwald, P. (1991). Socioeconomic factors and cancer incidence among blacks and whites. *J Natl Cancer Inst, 83,* 551–557.

42. Rogers, R. G. (1992). Living and dying in the U.S.A.: Sociodemographic determinants of death among blacks and whites. *Demography, 29,* 287–303.

43. Greenberg, M., & Schneider, D. (1994). Violence in American cities: Young black males is the answer, but what was the question? *Soc Sci Med, 39,* 179–187.

44. Lillie-Blanton, M., Anthony, J. C., & Schuster, C. R. (1993). Probing the meaning of racial or ethnic group comparisons in crack cocaine smoking. *JAMA, 269,* 993–997.

45. Krieger, N., & Fee, E. (1994). Social class: The missing link in U.S. health data. *J Health Serv, 24,* 25–44.

46. Otten, M. C., Teutsch, S. M., Williamson, D. F., & Marks, J. S. (1990). The effect of known risk factors on the excess mortality of black adults in the United States. *JAMA, 263,* 845–850.

47. Schoendorf, K. C., Hogue, C. J. R., Kleinman, J. C., & Rowley, D. (1992). Mortality among infants of black as compared with white college-educated parents. *N Engl J Med, 326,* 1522–1526.

48. Krieger, N., Rowley, D. L., Herman, A. A., Avery, B., & Phillips, M. T. (1993). Racism, sexism, and social class: Implications for studies of health, disease, and well-being. *Am J Prev Med, 9*(Suppl.), 82–122.

49. Kessler, R. C., & Neighbors, H. W. (1986). A new perspective on the relationships among race, social class, and psychological distress. *J Health Soc Behav, 27,* 107–115.

50. Williams, D. R., Takeuchi, D., & Adair, R. (1992). Socioeconomic status and psychiatric disorder among blacks and whites. *Soc Forces, 71,* 179–194.

51. Eller, T. J. (1994). *Household wealth and asset ownership, 1991* (U.S. Bureau of the Census, Current Population Reports, P70–34). Washington, DC: U.S. Government Printing Office.

52. Miller, J. E., & Korenman, S. (1994). Poverty and children's nutritional status in the United States. *Am J Epidemiol, 140,* 233–243.

53. Hogue, C. J. R., Buehler, J. W., Strauss, L. T., & Smith, J. C. (1987). Overview of the National Infant Mortality Surveillance (NIMS) project: Design, methods, results. *Pub Health Rep, 102,* 126–138.

54. Williams, D. R., Lavizzo-Mourey, R., & Warren, R. C. (1994). The concept of race and health status in America. *Pub Health Rep, 109,* 26–41.

55. King, G., & Williams, D. R. (1995). Race and health: A multi-dimensional approach to African American health. In S. Levine, D. C. Walsh, B. C. Amick, & A. R. Tarlov (Eds.), *Society and health: Foundation for a nation.* New York: Oxford University Press.

56. Williams, D. R. (Ed.). (1995). Special issue on racism and health. *Ethn Dis, 5.*

57. Maxwell, N. L. (1994). The effect on black-white wage differences in the quantity and quality of education. *Indust Labor Relations Rev, 47,* 249–264.

58. U.S. Bureau of the Census. (1991). *Money income of households, families, and persons in the United States* (Current Population Reports, Ser. P-60, No. 174). Washington, DC: U.S. Government Printing Office.

59. Dressler, W. W. (1993). Health in the African American community: Accounting for health inequalities. *Med Anthropol Q, 7,* 325–345.

60. Collins, S. M. (1983). The making of the black middle class. *Soc Problems, 10,* 369–382.

61. Wilhelm, S. M. (1987). Economic demise of blacks in America: A prelude to genocide? *J Black Studies, 17,* 201–254.

62. Cooper, R. (1984). A note on the biological concept of race and its application in epidemiologic research. *Am Heart J, 108,* 715–723.

63. Robinson, J. (1984). Racial inequality and the probability of occupation-related injury or illness. *Milbank Q, 62,* 567–590.

64. Polednak, A. P. (1993). Poverty, residential segregation, and black/white mortality rates in urban areas. *J Health Care Poor Underserved, 4,* 363–373.

65. LaVeist, T. A. (1989). Linking residential segregation and infant mortality in U.S. cities. *Social Soc Res, 73,* 90–94.

66. Polednak, A. P. (1991). Black-white differences in infant mortality in 38 standard metropolitan statistical areas. *Am J Public Health, 81,* 1480–1482.

67. Council on Ethical and Judicial Affairs, American Medical Association. (1990). Black-white disparities in health care. *JAMA, 263,* 2344–2346.

68. Klag, M. H., Whelton, P. K., Coresh, J., Grim, C. E., & Kuller, L. H. (1991). The Association of skin color with blood pressure in U.S. blacks with low socioeconomic status. *JAMA, 265,* 599–602.

69. Keith, V. M., & Herring, C. (1991). Skin tone and stratification in the black community. *Am J Sociol, 97,* 760–778.

READING 8

Notes

1. Most particularly and influential, Steele's book *The Content of Our Character: A New Vision of Race in Race,* published in 1990; and Thernstrom's 1997 book, *America in Black and White: One Nation, Indivisible.*

2. Mary Patillo-McCoy's book, *Black Picket Fences,* traces the development of the black middle class.

3. Data from this section, as well as a fuller discussion of the details, can be found in *The Hidden Cost of Being African American.*

4. William Julius Wilson makes this case, especially for jobs, in his 1987 book *The Truly Disadvantaged.* Christopher Jencks and Meredith Phillips present the black-white education gap argument in *The Black-White Test Score Gap,* 1998.

5. The full multiple regression results can be found in *The Hidden Cost of Being African American.*

6. *The Wealth of Hispanic Households: 1996 to 2002.* Kochhar, Rakesh. The Pew Hispanic Center. October, 2004.

READING 9

References

Adams, R. 1969. "The Unorthodox Race Doctrine of Hawaii." Pp. 81–90 in *Comparative Perspectives on Race Relations,* edited by M. Tumin. Boston: Little, Brown.

Ballhatchet, K. 1980. *Race, Sex, and Class Under the Raj.* London: Camelot.

Bennett, L., Jr. 1962. *Before the Mayflower: A History of the Negro in America, 1619–1962.* Chicago: Johnson.

Berry, B. 1963. *Almost White.* New York: Macmillan.

———. 1965. *Race and Ethnic Relations,* 3rd ed. New York: Houghton Mifflin.

Bilbo, T. G. 1947. *Take Your Choice: Separation or Mongrelization.* Poplarville, MS: Dream House Publishing.

Blalock, H. M., Jr. 1967. *Toward a Theory of Minority-Group Relations.* New York: Capricorn Books.

Blaustein, A. P., and C. C. Ferguson, Jr. 1957. *Desegregation and the Law.* New Brunswick, NJ: Rutgers University Press.

Burma, J. G. 1946. "The Measurement of Passing." *American Journal of Sociology* 52: 18–22.

Cannon, P. 1956. *A Gentle Knight: My Husband. Walter White.* New York: Rinehart.

Catterall, H. T., ed. 1926–1937. *Judicial Cases Concerning American Slavery and the Negro.* Vols. 1–5. Washington, DC: Carnegic Institute.

Daniel, G. R. 1992. "Beyond Black and White: The New Multiracial Consciousness." Pp. 333–341 in *Racially Mixed People in America,* edited by M. P. P. Root. Newbury Park, CA: Sage.

———. 2000. *More Than Black: Multiracial Identity and the New Racial Order.* Philadelphia: Temple University Press.

Davis, F. J. 1991. *Who Is Black? One Nation's Definition.* University Park: Pennsylvania State University Press.

———. 1995. "The Hawaiian Alternative to the One-Drop Rule." Pp. 115–131 in *American Mixed Race: The Culture of Microdiversity,* edited by Naomi Zack. Lanham, MD: Rowman and Littlefield.

Day, D. 1979. *The Adoption of Black Children: Counteracting Institutional Discrimination.* Lexington, MA: Lexington Books.

Domínguez, V. R. 1986. *White by Definition: Social Classification in Creole Louisiana.* New Brunswick, NJ: Rutgers University Press.

Durkheim, E. 1960. *The Division of Labor in Society.* Translated by G. Simpson. New York: Free Press.

Eckard, E. W. 1947. "How Many Negroes Pass?" *American Journal of Sociology* 52: 498–503.

Fernandez, C. A. 1995. "Testimony of the Association of Multiethnic Americans Before the Subcommittee on Census, Statistics, and Postal Personnel of the U.S. House of Representatives." Pp. 191–210 in *American Mixed Race: The Culture of Microdiversity,* edited by Naomi Zack. Lanham, MD: Rowman and Littlefield.

Foster, E. 1998. "Jefferson Fathered Slave's Last Child." *Nature,* November 5, pp. 27–28.

Gist, N. P., and R. Dean. 1973. *Marginality and Identity.* Leiden: Brill.

Graham, S. R. 1995. "Grassroots Advocacy." Pp. 185–189 in *American Mixed Race: The Culture of Microdiversity,* edited by N. Zack. Lanham, MD: Rowman and Littlefield.

Grosz, G. 1989. "From Sea to Shining Sea: A Current Listing of Interracial Organizations and Support Groups Across the Nation." *Interrace* 1: 24–28.

Gwaltney, J. L. 1980. *Drylongso: A Self-Portrait of Black America.* New York: Vintage.

Haizlip, S. T. 1994. *The Sweeter the Juice: A Family Portrait in Black and White.* New York: Simon and Schuster.

Haley, A. 1976. *Roots: The Saga of an American Family.* Garden City, NY: Doubleday.

Haley, A., and D. Stevens. 1993. *Queen.* New York: Avon.

Harris, M. 1964. *Patterns of Race in the Americas.* New York: Walker.

Hoetink, H. 1967. *Caribbean Race Relations: A Study of Two Variants.* London: Oxford University Press.

Howard, A. 1980. "Hawaiians." Pp. 449–452 in *Harvard Encyclopedia of American Ethnic Groups,* edited by S. Themnstrorn. Cambridge, MA: Harvard University Press.

Jorge, A. 1979. "The Black Puerto Rican Woman in Contemporary American Society." Pp. 134–141 in *The Puerto Rican Woman,* edited by Edna Acosta-Belén. New York: Praeger.

Ladner, J. A. 1977. *Mixed Families: Adopting Across Racial Boundaries.* Garden City, NY: Anchor/Doubleday.

Lew, J. 2000. "Guidance on Aggregation and Allocation of Data on Race for Use in Civil Rights Monitoring and Enforcement." OMB Bulletin No. 00-02. Washington, DC: Office of Management and Budget.

Myrdal, G., R. Sterner, and A. M. Rose. 1944. *An American Dilemma.* New York: Harper and Row.

Nakashima, C. L. 1992. "An Invisible Monster: The Creation and Denial of Mixed-Race People in America." Pp. 162–178 in *Racially Mixed People in America,* edited by M. P. P. Root. Newbury Park, CA: Sage.

Nicholls, D. 1981. "No Hawks or Pedlars: Levantines in the Caribbean." *Ethnic and Racial Studies* 4: 415–431.

Ottley, R. 1943. *New World A-Coming.* Cleveland: World Publishing.

Page, C. 1996. *Showing My Color.* New York: Harper and Collins.

Reed, T. E. 1969. "Caucasian Genes in American Negroes." *Science* 165: 762–768.

Rose, A. M. 1956. *The Negro in America.* Boston: Beacon Press.

Russell, K., M. Wilson, and R. Hall. 1992. *The Color Complex: The Politics of Skin Color Among African Americans.* Orlando, FL: Harcourt Brace.

Solaun, M., and S. Kronus. 1973. *Discrimination Without Violence.* New York: John Wiley.

Stoddard, E. R. 1973. *Mexican Americans.* New York: Random House.

Trillin, Calvin. 1986. "American Chronicles: Black or White." *New Yorker,* April 14, pp. 62–78.

Valverde, K-L. C. 1992. "From Dust to Gold: The Vietnamese Amerasian Experience." Pp. 144–161 in *Racially Mixed People in America,* edited by M. P. P. Root. Newbury Park, CA: Sage.

Van Den Berghe, P. L. 1971. "Racial Segregation in South Africa: Degrees and Kinds." Pp. 37–49 in *South Africa: Sociological Perspectives,* edited by H. Adam. New York: Oxford University Press.

Vander Zanden, J. W. 1972. *American Minority Relations,* 3rd ed. New York: Ronald.

Wagley, C., ed. 1963. *Race and Class in Rural Brazil,* 2nd ed. Paris: UNESCO.

Watson, G. 1970. *Passing for White: A Study of Racial Assimilation in a South African School.* London: Tavistock.

White, W. 1948. *A Man Called White: The Autobiography of Walter White.* New York: Viking.

Williams, G. H. 1995. *Life on the Color Line: The True Story of a White Boy Who Discovered He Was Black.* New York: Dutton.

Williams, T. K. 1996. "Race as Process: Reassessing the 'What Are You?' Encounters of Biracial Individuals." Pp. 191–210 in *The Multiracial Experience,* edited by M. P. P. Root. Newbury Park, CA: Sage.

Williamson, J. 1980. *New People: Miscegenation and Mulattoes in the United States.* New York: Free Press.

READING 10

Notes

1. U.S. Congress, *American Indian Policy Review Commission: Final Report,* vol. 1 (Washington, D.C.: Government Printing Office, 1977), 3.

2. See, e.g., Haunani-Kay Trask, *From a Native Daughter: Colonialism and Sovereignty in Hawai'i* (Monroe, Maine: Common Courage, 1993) and Roger MacPherson Furrer, ed., *He Alo á He Alo (Face to Face): Hawaiian Voices on Sovereignty* (Honolulu, Hawaii: American Friends Service Committee–Hawai'i, 1993).

3. 3528 U.S. 495 (2000).

4. Http://www.doi.gov/nativehawaiians/.

5. See S. James Anaya, "The Native Hawaiian People and International Human Rights Law: Toward a Remedy for Past and Continuing Wrongs," *Georgia Law Review* 28 (1994), 309–64.

6. Vine Deloria Jr., "The American Indian Image in North America," *Encyclopedia of Indians of the Americas,* vol. 1 (St. Clair Shores, Mich.: Scholarly Press, 1974), 43.

7. Paula D. McClain and Joseph Stewart Jr., *"Can We All Get Along?" Racial and Ethnic Minorities in American Politics* (Boulder, Colo.: Westview, 1998), 6, citing John Higham, *Strangers in the Land: Patterns of American Nativism, 1860–1925* (Westport, Conn.: Greenwood, 1963).

8. 180 U.S. 261 (1901).

9. Felix S. Cohen, *Handbook of Federal Indian Law,* reprint ed. (Albuquerque: University of New Mexico Press, 1972), 268.

10. Jack Utter, *American Indians: Answers to Today's Questions* (Lake Ann, Mich.: National Woodlands, 1993), 30–31.

11. William Quinn Jr., "Federal Acnowledgment of American Indian Tribes? The Historical Development of a Legal Concept," *American Journal of Legal History* 34 (October 1990): 331–63.

12. 56 *Federal Register* 47, 325 (1991).

13. 25 Code of Federal Regulations 83.7 (a)–(g) (1991).

14. 25 *U.S.C.* chapter 1, section 1, 961.

15. 25 *U.S.C.* chapter 1, 962.

16. William W. Quinn Jr., "Federal Acknowledgment of American Indian Tribes: Authority, Judicial Interposition, and 25 C.F.R. Sec. 83," *American Indian Law Review* 17 (Fall 1992): 48.

17. Quinn, "Federal Acknowledgment of American Indian Tribes," 52.

18. Felix Cohen, "The Erosion of Indian Rights, 1950–1953: A Case Study in Bureaucracy," *Yale Law Journal* 62 (February 1953): 352.

19. Letter from Carol A. Bacon, acting director of the Office of Tribal Services, Bureau of Indian Affairs, 3 December 1991. The author has copy of the letter.

20. 108 Stat., 709.

21. See U.S. Congress, House, "A Bill to Provide for Administrative Procedures to Extend Federal Recognition to Certain Indian Groups, and for Other Purposes," 105th Cong., 2d sess., 1998, H. Rept. 1154. As of this writing—May 1999—none of these bills has become law.

22. Ellen Barry, "Agency Willing to Relinquish Power to Recognize Tribes," *Boston Globe,* 26 May 2000, B1.

23. 118 U.S. 948 (1998).

24. See, e.g., Trask, *From a Native Daughter,* and Anaya, "The Native Hawaiian People," 309.

25. Allogan Slagle, "Unfinished Justice: Completing the Resoration and Acknowledgment of California Indian Tribes," *American Indian Journal* 13, no. 4 (Fall 1989): 325–45.

26. William W. Quinn Jr., "The Southeast Syndrome: Notes on Indian Descendant Recruitment Organizations and Their Perceptions of Native American Culture," *American Indian Quarterly* 14, no. 2 (Spring 1990): 147–54.

27. Jackie J. Kim, "The Indian Federal Recognition Procedures Act of 1995: A Congressional Solution to an Administrative Morass," *The Administrative Law Journal of the American University* 9, no. 3 (Fall 1995): 899–932.

28. See http://www.doi.gov/bia/bar/indexq.htm for statistical details of the acknowledgment project's efforts.

29. Donald Fixico, *Termination and Relocation: Federal Indian Policy, 1945–1960* (Albuquerque: University of New Mexico Press, 1986).

30. 67 Stat., B132.

31. 110 Stat., 130.

32. N.C. Public Laws, 1953, chapter 874, p. 747.

33. 70 Stat., 254.

34. David E. Wilkins, "Breaking into the Intergovernmental Matrix: The Lumbee Tribe's Efforts to Secure Federal Acknowledgment," *Publius: The Journal of Federalism* 23 (Fall 1993): 123–42.

35. McClain and Stewart, "Can We All Get Along?" 6.

36. Bart Vogel, "Who Is an Indian in Federal Indian Law?" in *Studies in American Indian Law,* ed. Ralph Johnson (Pullman: Washington State University, 1970), 53.

37. C. Matthew Snipp, *American Indians: The First of This Land* (New York: Russell Sage Foundation, 1989), 34.

38. Snipp, *First of This Land,* 33.

39. Cohen, *Handbook,* 2.

40. Snipp, *First of This Land,* 33.

41. 29 Stat., 321.

42. Abdul G. Kahn, *Report on the Indian Definition Study* (Washington, D.C.: Department of Education, 1980).

43. Kahn, *Indian Definition Study,* 56.

44. Joane Nagel, *American Indian Ethnic Renewal: Red Power and the Resurgence of Identity and Culture* (New York: Oxford University Press, 1996), 243.

45. Brian Stackes, "Planned Bureau of Indian Affairs Regulations Stir Concerns Among Tribal Leaders," *Indian Country Today,* 18 August 2000, 1.

46. Russell Thornton, "Tribal Membership Requirements and the Demography of 'Old' and 'New' Native Americans," in *Changing Numbers, Changing Needs: American Indian Demography and Public Health,* ed. Gary D. Sandefur, Ronald R. Rindfuss, and Barney Cohen (Washington, D.C.: National Academy Press, 1996), 110–11.

47. See, e.g., Francis Paul Prucha, *American Indian Treaties: The History of a Political Anomaly* (Berkeley, Calif.: University of California Press, 1994) and Robert A. Williams Jr. *Linking Arms Together: American Indian Treaty Visions of Law and Peace, 1600–1800* (New York: Oxford University Press, 1997).

48. 16 Stat., 566.

49. 7 Stat., 391.

50. 7 Stat., 391.

51. Cesare Marino, "Reservations," in *Native America in the Twentieth Century: An Encyclopedia,* ed. Mary B. Davis (New York: Garland Publishing, Inc., 1996), 544–56.

52. Vine Deloria Jr. and Clifford M. Lytle, *American Indians, American Justice* (Austin: University of Texas Press, 1983), 58.

53. Deloria and Lytle, *American Indians,* 58.

54. John H. Moore, "The Enduring Reservations of Oklahoma," in *State & Reservation: New Perspectives on Federal Indian Policy,*

ed. George Pierre Castile and Robert L. Bee (Tucson: University of Arizona Press, 1992), 92–109.

55. See Robert F. Heizer, *The Destruction of California Indians* (Lincoln: University of Nebraska Press, 1993) for a first-rate account of what these nations experienced from 1847 to 1865.

56. Title 18, *U.S. Code,* section 1151.

57. Council of Economic Advisers, *Changing America: Indicators of Social and Economic Well-Being by Race and Hispanic Origin* (Washington, D.C.: Government Printing Office, 1998), 4.

58. www.census.gov/prod/2001 pubs.

59. Russell Thornton, *American Indian Holocaust and Survival: A Population History Since 1492* (Norman: University of Oklahoma Press, 1987).

60. www.census.gov/prod/2001pubs.

61. Russell Thornton, "What the Census Doesn't Count," *New York Times,* 23 March 2001, A21.

62. C. Matthew Snipp, "The Size and Distribution of the American Indian Population: Fertility, Mortality, Migration, and Residence," in *Changing Numbers, Changing Needs: American Indian Demography and Public Health,* ed. Gary D. Sandefur, Ronald R. Rindfuss, and Barney Cohen (Washington, D.C.: National Academy Press, 1996), 42–43.

63. Snipp, "The Size and Distribution," 39.

64. Snipp, *The First of This Land,* 171.

65. Snipp, *The First of This Land,* 165.

66. Lawrence H. Fuchs, *The American Kaleidoscope* (Hanover, N.H.: Wesleyan University Press, 1990), 329.

READING 11

Notes

1. For an extended discussion of the critical transnational approach to immigration, see Espiritu (2003). Certainly, I am not the first scholar to apply a critical transnational framework to the study of Asian Americans. Oscar Campomanes (1997), Sucheta Mazumdar (1990), Shirley Hune (1989), and others have written persuasively on the importance of conducting Asian American studies through an "international" frame.

2. For a detailed account of the disputes over the classification of Asian Americans in the 1980 and 1990 censuses, please see Espiritu (1992, ch. 5).

3. According to the 2000 census, 10.2 million reported that they were *only* Asian. An additional 1.7 million people reported that they were Asian and at least one other race (Barnes and Bennett 2002, 3).

4. In 1990 the Japanese American share of the Asian American population was 12 percent, and the five largest Asian American groups were Chinese (23 percent), Filipino (19 percent), Asian

Indian (11 percent), Korean (11 percent), and Vietnamese (8 percent).

5. According to the 2000 U.S. census, approximately 850,000 people reported that they were Asian and white, and 360,000 reported that they were two or more Asian groups (Barnes and Bennett 2002, table 4). The debate over the classification of multiracials in the 2000 census often posed the interests of multiracial Asian Americans—the right to claim their full heritage—in opposition to the civil rights needs of pan-Asian America—the possible loss of political clout that is tied to numbers (see Espiritu 2001, 31). Refusing this "splitting," Asian American multiracial organizations rejected the "stand-alone multiracial" category and endorsed the "check more than one" format because the latter would allow them to identify as multiracial *and* "still be counted with their Asian American brethren and sisters" (King 2000, 202). This stance suggests that multiracial Asian and pan-Asian identities need not be mutually exclusive.

References

Barnes, Jessica, and Claudette E. Bennett. 2002. *The Asian Population 2000.* Washington: U.S. Department of Commerce.

Blauner, Robert. 1972. *Racial Oppression in America.* New York: Harper & Row.

Campomanes, Oscar. 1997. "New Formations of Asian American Studies and the Questions of U.S. Imperialism." *Positions* 5(2): 523–50.

Daniels, Roger. 1988. *Asian America: Chinese and Japanese in the United States Since 1850.* Seattle: University of Washington Press.

Davis, Angela. 1997. "Interview with Lisa Lowe—Angela Davis: Reflections on Race, Class, and Gender in the USA." In *The Politics of Culture in the Shadow of Capital,* edited by Lisa Lowe and David Lloyd. Durham, N.C.: Duke University Press.

Espiritu, Yen Le. 1992. *Asian American Panethnicity: Bridging Institutions and Identities.* Philadelphia: Temple University Press.

———. 2001. "Possibilities of a Multiracial Asian America." In *The Sum of Our Parts: Mixed Heritage Asian Americans,* edited by Teresa Williams-Leon and Cynthia L. Nakashima. Philadelphia: Temple University Press.

———. 2003. *Home Bound: Filipino American Lives Across Cultures, Communities, and Countries.* Berkeley: University of California Press.

Espiritu, Yen Le, Dorothy Fujita Rony, Nazli Kibria, and George Lipsitz. 2000. "The Role of Race and Its Articulations for Asian Pacific Americans." *Journal of Asian American Studies* 3(2): 127–37.

Hayano, David. 1981. "Ethnic Identification and Disidentification: Japanese-American Views of Chinese Americans." *Ethnic Groups* 3(2): 157–71.

Hossfeld, Karen. 1994. "Hiring Immigrant Women: Silicon Valley's 'Simple Formula.'" In *Women of Color in U.S. Society,* edited by Maxine Baca Zinn and Bonnie Thornton Dill. Philadelphia: Temple University Press.

Hune, Shirley. 1989. "Expanding the International Dimension of Asian American Studies." *Amerasia Journal* 15(2): xix–xxiv.

Ichioka, Yuji. 1988. *The Issei: The World of the First Generation Japanese Americans, 1885–1924.* New York: Free Press.

Iwasaki, Naomi. 1999. "Pan-Asian What?" *Asian American Revolutionay Movement Ezine,* http://www.aamovement.net/narratives/panasian.html (accessed December 4, 2003).

Kang, Laura Hyun Yi. 1997. "Si(gh)ting Asian/American Women as Transnational Labor." *Positions* 5(2): 403–37.

King, Rebecca Chiyoko. 2000. "Racialization, Recognition, and Rights: Lumping and Splitting Multiracial Asian Americans in the 2000 Census." *Journal of Asian American Studies* 3(2): 191–217.

Kurashige, Scott. 2000. "Panethnicity and Community Organizing: Asian Americans United's Campaign Against Anti-Asian Violence." *Journal of Asian American Studies* 3(2): 163–90.

Lim, Linda Y. C. 1983. "Capitalism, Imperialism, and Patriarchy: The Dilemma of Third-World Women Workers in Multinational Factories." In *Women, Men, and the International Division of Labor,* edited by June Nash and Maria Patricia Fernandez-Kelly. Albany: State University of New York Press.

Ling, Susie Hsiuhan. 1984. "The Mountain Movers: Asian American Women's Movement in Los Angeles." M.A. thesis, University of California at Los Angeles.

Liu, William. 1976. "Asian American Research: Views of a Sociologist." *Asian Studies Occasional Report* 2: whole issue.

Lott, Juanita. 1976. "The Asian American Concept: In Quest of Identity." *Bridge* (November): 30–34.

Lowe, Lisa. 1991. "Heterogeneity, Hybridity, Multiplicity: Marking Asian American Differences." *Diaspora* 1(1, Spring): 25–44.

———. 1996. *Immigrant Acts: On Asian American Cultural Politics.* Durham, N.C.: Duke University Press.

Mazumdar, Sucheta. 1990. "Asian American Studies and Asian Studies: Rethinking Roots." In *Asian Americans: Comparative and Global Perspectives,* edited by Shirley Hune et al. Pullman: Washington State University Press.

Misir, Deborah N. 1996. "The Murder of Navroze Mody: Race, Violence, and the Search for Order." *Amerasia Journal* 22(2): 55–76.

Nguyen, Viet Thanh. 2002. *Race and Resistance: Literature and Politics in Asian America.* New York: Oxford University Press.

Omatsu, Glenn. 1994. "'The Four Prisons' and the Movements of Liberation: Asian American Activism from the 1960s to the 1990s." In *The State of Asian America: Activism and Resistance in the 1990s,* edited by Karin Aguilar-San Juan. Boston: South End.

Omi, Michael. 1993. "Out of the Melting Pot and into the Fire: Race Relations Policy." In *The State of Asian Pacific Americans: Policy Issues to the Year 2000.* Los Angeles: LEAP Asian Pacific American Public Policy Institute and UCLA Asian American Studies Center.

Omi, Michael, and Howard Winant. 1986. *Racial Formation in the United States: From the 1960s to the 1980s.* New York: Routledge & Kegan Paul.

Ong, Aihwa. 1996. "Citizenship as Subject Making: New Immigrants Negotiate Racial and Ethnic Boundaries." *Current Anthropology* 25(5): 737–62.

Ong, Paul. 1989. "California's Asian Population: Past Trends and Projections for the Year 2000." Los Angeles: Graduate School of Architecture and Urban Planning.

———. 2000. "The Asian Pacific American Challenge to Race Relations." In *The State of Asian Pacific Americans: Transforming Race Relations,* edited by Paul Ong. Los Angeles: LEAP Asian Pacific American Public Policy Institute and UCLA Asian American Studies Center.

Ong, Paul, and Suzanne J. Hee. 1993. "The Growth of the Asian Pacific American Population." In *The State of Asian Pacific Americans: Policy Issues to the Year 2000.* Los Angeles: LEAP Asian Pacific American Public Policy Institute and UCLA Asian American Studies Center.

———. 1994. "Economic Diversity." In *The State of Asian Pacific Americans: Economic Diversity, Issues, and Policies,* edited by Paul Ong. Los Angeles: LEAP Asian Pacific American Public Policy Institute and UCLA Asian American Studies Center.

Sacks, Karen, and Nancy Scheper-Hughes. 1987. "Introduction." *Women's Studies* 13(3): 175–82.

Saito, Leland. 1998. *Race and Politics: Asian Americans, Latinos, and Whites in a Los Angeles Suburb.* Urbana and Chicago: University of Illinois Press.

Sassen, Saskia. 1992. "Why Migration." *Report on the Americas* 26(1, July): whole issue.

Shah, Bindi. 2002. "Making the 'American' Subject: Culture, Gender, Ethnicity, and the Politics of Citizenship in the Lives of Second-Generation Laotian Girls." Ph.D. diss., University of California at Davis.

Shankar, Rajiv. 1998. "Foreword: South Asian Identity in Asian America." In *A Part, Yet Apart: South Asians in Asian America,* edited by Lavina Dhingra Shankar and Rajini Srikanth. Philadelphia: Temple University Press.

Shinagawa, Larry Hajime, and Gin Yong Pang. 1996. "Asian American Panethnicity and Intermarriage." *Amerasia Journal* 22(2): 127–52.

Smith, James P., and Barry Edmonston, eds. 1997. *The New Americans: Economic, Demographic, and Fiscal Effects of Immigration.* Washington, D.C.: National Academy Press.

Strobel, Leny Mendoza. 1996. " 'Born-Again Filipino': Filipino American Identity and Asian American Panethnicity." *Amerasia Journal* 22(2): 31–54.

Takaki, Ronald. 1989. *Strangers from a Different Shore: A History of Asian Americans.* Boston: Little, Brown.

U.S. Department of Commerce. U.S. Census Bureau. 2002. "Coming to America: A Profile of the Nation's Foreign Born (2000 Update)." *Census Briefs: Current Population Survey, February 2002.* Washington: U.S. Census Bureau.

U.S. Immigration and Naturalization Service (USINS). 1997. *Statistical Yearbook of the Immigration and Naturalization Service, 1995.* Washington: U.S. Government Printing Office.

Wong, Paul. 1972. "The Emergence of the Asian-American Movement." *Bridge* 2(1): 33–39.

Zhou, Min. 1999. "Coming of Age: The Current Situation of Asian American Children." *Amerasia Journal* 25(1): 1–27.

Zhou, Min, and James V. Gatewood. 2000. "Introduction: Revisiting Contemporary Asian America." In *Contemporary Asian America: A Multidisciplinary Reader,* edited by Min Zhou and James V. Gatewood. New York: New York University Press.

READING 12

References

Bean, Frank D., and Gillian Stevens. *America's Newcomers and the Dynamics of Diversity.* New York: Russell Sage Foundation, 2003. This book explores the significance of immigration for America, including its implications for loosening racial and ethnic boundaries.

Davis, F. James. *Who Is Black? One Nation's Definition.* University Park, PA: Pennsylvania State University Press, 1991. Davis details the history of the "one-drop rule" in the United States.

Gerstle, Gary. "Liberty, Coercion, and the Making of Americans." In *The Handbook of International Migration,* edited by Charles Hirschman, Philip Kasinitz, and Josh DeWind. New York: Russell Sage Foundation, 1991. A history of racial categories and how they have changed.

Loewen, James. *The Mississippi Chinese: Between Black and White.* Cambridge, MA: Harvard University Press, 1971. Loewen shows how Chinese immigrants changed their racial classification from almost black to almost white.

Nobles, Melissa. *Shades of Citizenship: Race and the Census in Modern Politics.* Stanford, CA: Stanford University Press, 2000. A history or racial categories in the Census in the United States.

Perlmann, Joel, and Mary C. Waters, eds. *The New Race Question: How the Census Counts Multiracial Individuals.* New York: Russell Sage Foundation, 2002. This anthology examines the history of racial enumeration, the likely effects of the Census change in the race question, and possible policy implications for the future.

Qian, Zhenchao. "Breaking the Racial Barriers: Variations in Interracial Marriage Between 1980 and 1990." *Demography* 34, 2 (1997), 263–276. This study illustrates the growing trends in interracial marriage.

Waters, Mary C. "Multiple Ethnicities and Identity in the United States." In *We Are a People: Narrative and Multiplicity in Constructing Identity,* edited by Paul Spikard and W. Jeffrey Burroughs. Philadelphia: Temple University Press, 2000. Water examines the different ways interracial couples identify their children.

READING 13

Notes

1. FUBU (For Us By Us) is a black-owned manufacturer of urban, hip-hop style clothing.

2. For an excellent overview of how the media construct a view of race relations that is overly optimistic, see Benjamin DeMott, *The Trouble with Friendship: Why Americans Can't Think Straight About Race* (New York: The Atlantic Monthly Press, 1995).

3. The Gallup Organization, "Black/White Relations in the U.S." (June 10, 1997):1–5; David Shipler, *A Country of Strangers: Blacks and Whites in America* (New York: Vintage Books, 1998).

4. For an insightful discussion of how neoconservative writers like Dinesh D'Souza distort history and contemporary race relations, see David Theo Goldberg, "The New Segregation," *Race and Society* 1, no. 1 (1998).

5. Dinesh D'Souza, *The End of Racism: Principles for a Multiracial Society* (New York: Free Press, 1995); Ellis Cose, *Color-Blind: Seeing Beyond Race in a Race-Obsessed World* (New York: Harper Collins, 1997).

6. David Moore, "Americans Most Important Sources of Information: Local News," *The Gallup Poll Monthly,* 2–5 September 1995; David Moore and Lydia Saad, "No Immediate Signs That Simpson Trial Intensified Racial Animosity," *The Gallup Poll Monthly,* 2–5 October 1995; Kaiser Foundation, *The Four Americas: Government and Social Policy Through the Eyes of America's Multi-Racial and Multi-Ethnic Society* (Menlo Park, CA: Kaiser Family Foundation, 1995).

7. A. C. Nielsen, *Information Please Almanac* (Boston: Houghton Mifflin, 1997).

8. John Lewis and Sut Jhally, "Affirming Inaction: Television and the New Politics of Race," in *Marxism in the Postmodern Age: Confronting the New World Order,* edited by A. Callari, S. Cullenberg, and C. Biewener (New York: Guilford Press, 1995).

9. For an outstanding discussion of how color blindness is used politically by neoconservatives, see Amy Ansell, *New Right, New Racism: Race and Reaction in the United States* (New York: New York University Press, 1997); Howard Winant, *Racial Conditions: Politics, Theory, Comparisons* (Minneapolis: University

of Minneapolis Press, 1994); Stephen Steinberg, *Turning Back: The Retreat from Racial Justice in American Thought and Policy* (New York: Beacon Press, 1995); Eduardo Bonilla-Silva, *White Supremacy and Racism in the Post–Civil Rights Era* (Boulder: Lynne Rienner Publishers); and Michael Omi, "Racism," in *The Making and Unmaking of Whiteness,* edited by Birget Brander Rasmussen, Eric Klineberg, Irene J. Nexica, and Matt Wray (Durham: Duke University Press, 2001).

10. Ruth Frankenberg, "The Mirage of an Unmarked White-ness," in *The Making and Unmaking of Whiteness,* edited by Birget Brander Rasmussen, Eric Klineberg, Irene J. Nexica, and Matt Wray (Durham: Duke University Press, 2001).

11. David Theo Goldberg, *Racial Subjects: Writing on Race in America* (Thousand Oaks, CA: Routledge, 1997), 55; see also Charles Jaret, *Contemporary Racial and Ethnic Relations* (New York: Harper Collins, 1995), 265–270.

12. Leslie G. Carr, *Color-Blind Racism* (Thousand Oaks, CA: Sage Publications, 1997), 108; see also David Carroll Cochran, *The Color of Freedom: Race and Contemporary American Liberalism* (New York: State University of New York Press, 1999).

13. Mary Waters, *Ethnic Options: Choosing Identities in America* (Berkeley: University of California Press, 1990); Charles A. Gallagher, "Playing the Ethnic Card: Using Ethnic Identity to Negate Contemporary Racism," in *Deconstructing Whiteness, Deconstructing White Supremacy,* edited by Ashley Doane and Eduardo Bonilla-Silva (Lynne Rienner Publishers, forthcoming 2002).

14. Ashley W. Doane Jr., "Dominant Group Identity in the United States: The Role of 'Hidden' Ethnicity in Intergroup Relations," *The Sociological Quarterly* 38, no. 3 (1997): 378.

15. Joe Feagin and Melvin Sikes, *Living With Racism: The Black Middle Class Experience* (Boston: Beacon Press, 1994).

16. The Gallup Organization, "Black/White Relations in the U.S.," 10 June 1997, 1–5.

17. Kaiser Foundation, *The Four Americas: Government and Social Policy Through the Eyes of America's Multi-Racial and Multi-Ethnic Society* (Menlo Park, CA: Kaiser Family Foundation, 1995).

18. Howard Schuman et al. (1997), 193.

19. U.S. Bureau of the Census, *Housing Vacancies and Home Ownership Annual Statistics* (Washington D.C.: U.S. Government Printing Office, 1999).

20. U.S. Bureau of the Census, *Asset Ownership of Households* (Washington D.C.: U.S. Government Printing Office, 1993); see also *Black Wealth/White Wealth: A New Perspective on Racial Inequality* (New York: Routledge, 1995).

21. John J. Macionis, *Sociology,* 7th ed. (Saddle River, NJ: Prentice Hall, 1999).

22. Diana B. Henriques, *New York Times,* 4 July, 2001, p. A1.

23. U.S. Department of Health and Human Services, *National Center for Chronic Disease Prevention and Health Promotion,* 1998; Centers for Disease Control and Prevention, National Center for Health Statistics, *Monthly Vital Statistics Report* 46 (2001).

24. Feagin, 2000.

25. Karen Gullo, *The Atlanta Journal and Constitution,* 12 March 2001, p. A7.

26. Jim Abrams, *The Atlanta Journal and Constitution,* 2 December 2000, p. A9.

27. Laura Parker and Peter Eisler, *USA Today,* 6–8 April 2001, p. A1.

28. Frankenberg (2001), p. 76.

29. Lawrence Bobo and James R. Kluegel, "Status, Ideology, and Dimensions of Whites' Racial Beliefs and Attitudes: Progress and Stagnation," in *Racial Attitudes in the 1990s: Continuity and Change,* edited by Steven A. Tuch and Jack K. Martin (Westport, CT: Praeger, 1997), p. 95.

30. Carr, p. x.

31. David Roediger, *The Wages of Whiteness: Race and the Making of the American Working Class* (New York: Verso Press, 1991), p. 137.

32. Cited in David Roediger, "The White Question," *Race Traitor* (Winter 1993): 104.

READING 15

Notes

I am grateful for comments on earlier drafts of this paper from Margaret Chin, Jennifer Lee, an anonymous reviewer—and from my fellow authors in this volume.

1. These categories are constructions, but they also contain populations experiencing all the pleasures and pains of being located in a hierarchy. And although I am often discussing constructions, I will forgo the practice of putting all racial, national, and related names and labels between quotes, except for unusual racial stereotypes.

2. The two races may not be called that openly, but ambiguous pejoratives have long been part of the American vocabulary, for example *underclass* now, and *pauper* a century earlier (Gans 1995). Since races are social constructions, their names will depend in large part on who does the naming—and whose names become dominant in the public vocabulary.

3. Puerto Ricans are still often described as immigrants, even though they have been American citizens for a long time and their move from the island to the mainland is a form of interstate mobility. Racial, class, and linguistic considerations have undoubtedly influenced this labeling.

The same dominant-race thinking led Irving Kristol and other neoconservatives to argue in the 1960s that blacks were similar enough to the white European immigrants to be able to adopt and act on immigrant values. They also assumed that blacks would then assimilate like immigrants, ignoring such facts as that blacks had originally come as slaves, not immigrants; had been here several centuries; and had not yet been allowed by whites to assimilate. Thirty years later, many whites ignore the same facts to propose the newest immigrants as role models for blacks.

4.   Much less is said about black Hispanics, including Puerto Ricans, who suffer virtually all of the discriminatory and other injustices imposed on African-Americans.

5.   Some highly placed whites are already worrying, for example in a *Time* cover story by William Henry III (1990), but then similar whites worried a century earlier what the then arriving Catholic and Jewish newcomers would do to *their* country. The current worries are as meaningless as the old ones, since they are based on extrapolations of current patterns of immigration, not to mention current constructions of (nonwhite) race and (Hispanic) ethnicity.

6.   Hacker (1996) notes, for example, that the term "white trash" is no longer in common use. Indeed, for reasons worth studying, the more popular term of the moment is "trailer trash," which nonetheless seems to be applied solely to poor whites.

7.   In this respect, the United States differs from many other countries in the Western hemisphere, where blacks who have managed to become affluent are treated, within limits, as whites.

8.   Not only might they perceive it more angrily than I am here doing, but they might be angrier about it than about the present hierarchy, simply because it is new but no great improvement. One result could be their constructions of new racial identities for themselves that depart drastically from the ones future nonblacks consider reasonable.

9.   Being far fewer than Asians in number, South Asians are nationally not very visible now. Moreover, for religious and other reasons, South Asian immigrants have so far often been able to discourage their children from intermarrying.

10.   My observations on multiracial constructions and people have benefited from many conversations with Valli Rajah.

11.   Between 1970 and 1994, the number of people in interracial marriages grew from 676,000 to more than three million (Fletcher 1997). In 1990, biracial children made up 4 percent of all children, increasing from half a million in 1970 to about two million that year. The largest number were Asian-white children, followed by Native American–white and African American–white ones (Harrison and Bennett 1995).

12.   Some observers currently estimate that 70 percent of all Japanese and Japanese-Americans are intermarried, mostly with whites. Since they came to the United States as families long before 1965, this estimate may supply a clue about what will happen to second-, third-, and later-generation descendants of other Asian-American populations.

13.   Presumably class position will affect how other descendants of old Southern mulatto and creole populations (Dominguez 1986) will be classified.

14.   In the political debates over the racial categories to be used in the Year 2000 Census, vocal multiracials preferred to be counted as and with various people of color. African-Americans and other officially recognized racial groups also indicated their opposition to a multiracial category, being reluctant to reduce the power of their numbers or the federal benefits that now go to racial minorities (e.g., Holmes 1996).

15.   Kohne (1996) reports that light-skinned biracial Columbia University students who identify as whites also apply for scholarships as blacks. But then, four decades earlier, I met Italian-Americans in Boston's West End who took Irish names in order to obtain jobs in Irish-dominated city hall.

16.   The practice of quantifying racial bloods has a long history in Europe and the United States, thanks to both eugenics and slavery. Perhaps it will disappear when enough people have to start counting three or more races. However, people also still use blood fractions when they marry across religions, so that the notion of racial, ethnic, or religious "blood" is by no means obsolete.

17.   They are also different, for "one and the same person may be considered white in the Dominican Republic or Puerto Rico . . . 'colored' in Jamaica, Martinique, or Curacao . . . [and] a 'Negro' in Georgia" (Hoetink 1967, xii).

18.   This account is based mainly on the data summarized in Fiola 1990 and Skidmore 1992, the classic analysis of the Brazilian racial system in Skidmore 1993, Adamo's 1983 case study of race and class in Rio de Janeiro, and the sociopolitical analyses by Marx (1995, 1996). I am indebted to Anthony Marx for guiding me into the literature on Brazil, although there is still precious little social research, especially with current data, in English.

19.   No one has so far paid much attention to who is constructed as exotic and why, except the multiracial people, mostly women, to whom it is applied. Some of them benefit because they are sought by industries that hire workers with exotic facial features; but women without these occupational interests resent such labeling because it turns them into sexual objects.

Industries that employ workers with exotic features, facial and otherwise, such as the fashion and entertainment industries, play an interesting, and probably unduly influential, role in the country's public racial construction.

20.   Even now, at the close of the twentieth century, whites who argue that America is a "Christian" nation are pursuing a politics of identity as much as of religious dominance.

21.   I am indebted to my Columbia University colleague, biologist Robert Pollack, for my understanding of this phenomenon.

22. Originally, people drew on nineteenth-century and earlier comparisons of apes and humans, with those determined to be closer to apes in facial appearance being thought inferior. Brain size was also used, at least until scientific research debunked its relevance, and the researchers also discovered that it did not correlate with status. The final blow was the discovery that the much maligned Neanderthalers had larger brains than *Homo sapiens.*

23. Ears have served mainly as anchors for adornment, although protruding ones have sometimes been brought surgically closer to the head.

24. Now that some young women show their navels or wear bathing suits with uncovered buttocks, these could become eligible for racial typing.

25. Constructionists in the social sciences and the humanities have so far mainly emphasized that races, like other human notions, are socially constructed, but social scientists have paid little attention to the actual construction process and its participants. What we know about that process comes mostly from scholars who analyze racial images over time, in literature or the popular culture, and have collected process information as part of their work.

26. Forced Chinese labor was also recruited for the cotton plantations, but the Chinese workers turned out to be inefficient cotton pickers and thus managed to avoid becoming slaves.

27. I am indebted to Roderick Harrison and especially Manuel de la Puente of the U.S. Bureau of the Census for materials that clarified this set of responses.

28. Social scientists on the staff of the Census Bureau and the Bureau of Labor Statistics spend part of their time analyzing the large number of private races that people supply in answer to open-ended questions to produce the small number of public ones reported by the federal government.

29. For some similar practices by Jews in post-Holocaust Germany, see Rapaport 1997, 166–67.

30. For example, one of Waters's respondents explained that she traced her bad moods to "the Irish in me," while "all of the good things" were Italian (Waters 1990, 25). Embryo clinics are asked by some of their customers to supply sperm and egg donors of similar ethnic origin, in one case to obtain an "Irish background, or at least light hair and light eyes" (Kolata 1997, 34). As a result, ethnicity may be so racialized that it is not very voluntary, although voluntary ethnicity may also be used to achieve voluntarily chosen racial features.

31. Needless to say, traumatic and long-lasting economic decline is a more likely cause for a public recognition of class in America.

References

Adamo, Samuel C. 1983. "The Broken Promise: Race, Health and Justice in Rio de Janeiro, 1890–1940." Ph.D. diss., University of New Mexico.

Alba, Richard D. 1990. *Ethnic Identity.* New Haven: Yale University Press.

Dominguez, Virginia R. 1986. *White by Definition.* New Brunswick: Rutgers University Press.

Feagin, Joe R., and Michael P. Sykes. 1994. *Living with Racism.* Boston: Beacon.

Fields, Barbara J. 1990. "Slavery, Race and Ideology in the United States of America." *New Left Review* 15:95–108.

Fiola, Jan. 1990. "Race Relations in Brazil: A Reassessment of the 'Racial Democracy' Thesis." Occasional Papers Series no. 34. University of Massachusetts Latin American Studies Program, Amherst.

Fletcher, Michael A. 1997. "More Than a Black-White Issue." *Washington Post National Weekly Edition,* May 26, 34.

Frey, William H. 1996. "Immigration, Domestic Migration and Demographic Balkanization in America." *Population and Development Review* 22:741–63.

Gans, Herbert J. 1992. "Second Generation Decline: Scenarios for the Economic and Ethnic Futures of the post-1965 American Immigrants." *Ethnic and Racial Studies* 15:173–92.

————. 1995. *The War against the Poor.* New York: Basic.

Gerber, Eleanor, and Manuel de la Puente. 1996. "The Development of and Cognitive Testing of Race and Ethnic Origin Questions for the Year 2000 Census." In Bureau of the Census, *1996 Annual Research Conference.* Washington: Government Printing Office.

Gitlin, Todd. 1995. *The Twilight of Common Dreams.* New York: Metropolitan.

Gordon, Milton M. 1964. *Assimilation in American Life.* New York: Oxford University Press.

Hacker, Andrew. 1996. Foreword to *The Coming Race War?* by Richard Delgado. New York: New York University Press.

Harrison, Roderick J., and Claudette Bennett. 1995. "Racial and Ethnic Diversity." In *State of the Union: America in the 1990s,* vol. 2, *Social Trends,* edited by Reynolds Farley. New York: Russell Sage Foundation.

Henry, William, III. 1990. "Beyond the Melting Pot." *Time,* April 9, 29–32.

Hoetink, Harry. 1967. *The Two Variants in Caribbean Race Relations.* London: Oxford University Press.

Holmes, Steven. 1996. "Census Tests New Category to Identify Racial Groups." *New York Times,* December 4, A25.

Ignatiev, Noel. 1995. *How the Irish Became White.* New York: Routledge.

Kalmijn, Matthijs. 1991. "Status Homogamy in the United States." *American Journal of Sociology* 93:496–523.

Kohne, Natasha G. 1996. "The Experience of Mixed-Race Women: Challenging Racial Boundaries." Unpublished senior thesis, department of sociology, Columbia University, New York.

Kolata, Gina. 1997. "Clinics Selling Embryos Made for 'Adoption.'" *New York Times,* November 23, 1, 34.

Loewen, James W. 1988. *The Mississippi Chinese.* 2d ed. Prospect Heights, Ill.: Waveland.

Marris, Peter. 1996. *The Politics of Uncertainty.* New York: Routledge.

Marx, Anthony W. 1995. "Contested Citizenship: The Dynamics of Racial Identity and Social Movements." *International Review of History* 40, supplement 3: 159–83.

———. 1996. "Race-Making and the Nation-State." *World Politics,* January, 180–208.

Mintz, Sidney W. 1989. *Caribbean Transformations.* New York: Columbia University Press.

Morganthau, Tom. 1995. "What Color Is Black?" *Newsweek,* February 12, 63–67.

Newman, Katherine. 1993. *Declining Fortunes.* New York: Basic.

Rapaport, Lynn. 1997. *Jews in Germany after the Holocaust.* Cambridge: Cambridge University Press.

Rodriguez, Clara E. 1989. *Puerto Ricans: Born in the U.S.A.* Boston: Unwin Hyman.

Roediger, David R. 1991. *Wages of Whiteness.* London: Verso.

Rumbaut, Ruben G. 1997. "Ties That Bind: Immigration and Immigrant Families in the United States." In *Immigration and the Family,* edited by Alan Booth, Ann C. Crouter, and Nancy Landale. Mahwah, N.J.: Erlbaum.

Sanjek, Roger. 1994. "Intermarriage and the Future of the Races in the United States." In *Race,* edited by Steven Gregory and Roger Sanjek. New Brunswick: Rutgers University Press.

Skidmore, Thomas L. 1992. "Fact and Myth: Discovering a Racial Problem in Brazil." Working paper 173. Helen Kellogg Institute for International Studies, University of Notre Dame.

———. 1993. *Black into White.* Durham: Duke University Press.

Stonequist, Everett V. 1937. *The Marginal Man.* New York: Scribner's.

Waters, Mary. 1990. *Ethnic Options: Choosing Identities in America.* Berkeley: University of California Press.

READING 18

Notes

1. See Kevin R. Johnson, "The Antiterrorism Act, the Immigration Reform Act, and Ideological Regulation in the Immigration Laws: Important Lessons for Citizens and Noncitizens," *St Mary's Law Journal* 28 (1997): 841–69. See generally James Morton Smith, *Freedom's Fetters: The Alien and Sedition Laws and American Civil Liberties* (Ithaca, NY: Cornell University Press, 1956); see also James X. Dempsey and David Cole, *Terrorism and the Constitution: Sacrificing Civil Liberties in the Name of National Security* (Los Angeles: First Amendment Foundation, 1999).

2. Richard Delgado and Jean Stefancic, "Images of the Outsider in American Law and Culture: Can Free Expression Remedy Systemic Social Ills?" *Cornell Law Review* 77, no. 6 (1992): 1258; Cynthia Kwei Yung Lee, "Race and Self-Defense: Toward a Normative Conception of Reasonableness," *Minnesota Law Review* 81 (1996): 402–52; Margaret M. Russell, "Race and the Dominant Gaze: Narratives of Law and Inequality in Popular Film," *Legal Studies Forum* 15 (1991): 243; see also Jody Armour, "Stereotypes and Prejudice: Helping Legal Decisionmakers Break the Prejudice Habit," *California Law Review* 83, no. 3 (May 1995): 733.

3. Natsu Taylor Saito, "Symbolism Under Siege: Japanese American Redress and the 'Racing' of Arab Americans as 'Terrorists," *Asian Law Journal* 8, no. 1 (May 2001): 11–26.

4. See Susan M. Akram, "Scheherezade Meets Kafka: Two Dozen Sordid Tales of Ideological Exclusion," *Georgetown Immigration Law Journal* 14 (1999): 54.

5. Edward W. Said, "A Devil Theory of Islam," *The Nation,* August 12, 1996, 28; see also Ahmed Yousef and Caroline F. Keeble, *The Agent: The Truth Behind the Anti-Muslim Campaign in America* (UASR Publishing Group, 1999).

6. See Nabeel Abraham, "Anti-Arab Racism and Violence in the United States," in *The Development of Arab-American Identity,* ed. Ernest McCarus (Ann Arbor, MI: University of Michigan Press, 1994); Jack G. Shaheen, *Reel Bad Arabs: How Hollywood Vilifies a People* (New York: Olive Branch Press, 2001); see also the archived reports of the American-Arab Anti-Discrimination Committee on anti-Arab hate crimes, http://www.adc.org.

7. See Nabeel Abraham, "The Gulf Crisis and Anti-Arab Racism in America," in *Collateral Damage: The New World Order at Home and Abroad,* ed. Cynthia Peters (Boston: South End Press, 1991), 255–78; see also Michael J. Whidden, "Unequal Justice: Arabs in America and United States Antiterrorism Legislation," *Fordham Law Review* 69, no. 6 (May 2001): 2825, and Suad Joseph, "Against the Grain of the Nation—The Arab," in *Arabs in America: Building a New Future,* ed. Michael W. Suleiman (Philadelphia: Temple University Press, 1999).

8. Alfred M. Lilienthal, "The Changing Role of B'nai B'rith's Anti-Defamation League," *Washington Report on Middle East Affairs,* June 1993, 18; Anti-Defamation League of B'nai B'rith, *Pro-Arab Propaganda in America: Vehicles and Voices: A Handbook* (New York: Anti-Defamation League of B'nai B'rith, 1983). The Middle East Studies Association (MESA) has passed two resolutions criticizing the ADL for defaming students, teachers,

and researchers as "pro-Arab propagandists." See Betsy Barlow, "Middle East Studies Association Condemns ADL Philadelphia Office," *Washington Report,* January–February 1997, 72; Phebe Marr, "MESA Condemns Blacklisting," *Washington Report,* December 17, 1984, 8.

9. See Ian F. Haney López, "Institutional Racism: Judicial Conduct and a New Theory of Racial Discrimination," *Yale Law Journal* 109, no. 8 (June 2000); see also Akram, "Scheherezade Meets Kafka," which traces the contemporary targeting of Arabs and Muslims in immigration enforcement (see n. 4).

10. For analysis of the balancing of necessary security measures and democratic values in response to terrorism, see Symposium, "Law and the War on Terrorism," *Harvard Journal of Law and Public Policy* 25 (Spring 2002); "Responding to Terrorism: Crime, Punishment, and War," *Harvard Law Review* 115 (2002): 1217–38; Peter Margulies, "Uncertain Arrivals: Immigration, Terror, and Democracy after September 11," *Utah Law Review* (2002): 481.

11. Ian F. Haney López, "The Social Construction of Race: Some Observations on Illusion, Fabrication, and Choice," *Harvard Civil Rights–Civil Liberties Law Review* 29, no. 1 (Winter 1994).

12. Michael Omi and Howard Winant, *Racial Formation in the United States: From the 1960s to the 1980s* (New York: Routledge and Kegan Paul, 1986).

13. Ibid., 68–69.

14. See Saito, "Symbolism Under Siege" (see n. 3).

15. *St Francis Coll. v. Al-Khazraji,* 481 US 604, 610n4 (1987).

16. See Abraham, "Anti-Arab Racism and Violence" (see n. 6).

17. López, "Institutional Racism" (see n. 9); M. Cherif Bassiouni, introduction to *The Civil Rights of Arab-Americans,* ed. M. Cherif Bassiouni (Washington, DC: Association of Arab-American University Graduates, 1974). For analysis of the negative impacts of Operation Boulder (code name for Nixon's 1972 policy) on the civil rights of Arab Americans, see Abdeen M. Jabara, "Operation Arab: The Nixon Administration's Measures in the United States After Munich," in Bassiouni, *Civil Rights of Arab-Americans,* 1–14.

18. Bruce Hoffman, *Terrorism in the United States and the Potential Threat to Nuclear Facilities* (Santa Monica, CA: Rand Corporation, 1986), 11, 15.

19. Ibid., 16.

20. Ibid., 12–15.

21. "Domestic Terrorism in the 1980s," *FBI Law Enforcement Bulletin,* October 1987, 13.

22. Chris Lutz, ed., *They Don't All Wear Sheets: A Chronology of Racist and Far Right Violence, 1980–1986* (Atlanta, GA: Center for Democratic Renewal, 1987); Anti-Defamation League of B'nai B'rith, *Extremism on the Right: A Handbook* (New York: Anti-Defamation League of B'nai B'rith, 1988).

23. Abraham, "Anti-Arab Racism and Violence," 157 (see n. 6).

24. Lilienthal, 18 (see n. 8).

25. Anti-Defamation League, *Pro-Arab Propaganda* (see n. 8).

26. Lilienthal, 18 (see n. 8).

27. Amy Kaufman Goott and Steven J. Rosen, *The Campaign to Discredit Israel* (Washington, DC: American Israel Public Affairs Committee, 1983); Jonathan S. Kessler and Jeff Schwaber, *The AIPAC College Guide: Exposing the Anti-Israel Campaign on Campus* (Washington, DC: American Israel Public Affairs Committee, 1984).

28. Paul Findley, *They Dare to Speak Out: People and Institutions Confront Israel's Lobby* (Westport, CT: Lawrence Hill, 1985); Naseer Aruri, "The Middle East on the U.S. Campus," *The Link* 18, no. 2 (May–June 1985); Edward Tivnan, *The Lobby: Jewish Political Power and American Foreign Policy* (New York: Simon and Schuster, 1987); Rachelle Marshall, "PACmen," *The Nation,* June 6, 1987; Rachelle Marshall, "The Decline of B'nai B'rith: From Protector to Persecutor," *Washington Report on Middle East Affairs,* April 1989, 19.

29. Delinda C. Hanley, "ADL and AJC Demand Muslim Panelists Be Excluded," *Washington Report on Middle East Affairs,* January–February 2002, 83.

30. Ibid.

31. Ibid.

32. Rick Paddock, "A Spy for the Anti-Defamation League: Did a Liberal Civil Rights Group Get Caught with Its Binoculars Up?" *Cal. J.,* June 1, 1993, 2.

33. Abdeen Jabara, "The Anti-Defamation League: Civil Rights and Wrongs," *Covert Action,* no. 45 (Summer 1993): 28–29; see also San Francisco District Attorney's Office, "Organizational Victims of ADL Espionage" (1993), reprinted in *ADC Times,* May–June 1993, 21 (on file with Susan M. Akram).

34. Jabara, "The Anti-Defamation League," 30–31 (see n. 33).

35. Ibid., 31.

36. Ibid.; Jim McGee, "Jewish Group's Tactics Investigated," *Washington Post,* October 19, 1993.

37. Dennis Opatrny and Scott Winokur, "Israeli Man Held by Israel Linked to Spy Case," *San Francisco Examiner,* February 12, 1993; Jabara, "The Anti-Defamation League," 29 (see n. 33).

38. Bob Egelko, "Jewish Defense Group Settles S. F. Spying Suit," *San Francisco Chronicle,* February 23, 2002; Dennis King and Chip Berlet, "ADLgate," *Tikkun* 8 (July–August 1993): 31; Dennis Opatrny and Scott Winokur, "Police Said to Help Spy on Political Groups," *San Francisco Examiner,* March 9, 1993.

39. Final Settlement, *American-Arab Anti-Discrimination Committee v. Anti-Defamation League,* Civil Action No. 93-6358 RAP (C.D. Cal. 1999).

40. See McGee, n. 36.

41. Jabara, "The Anti-Defamation League," 37 (see n. 33).

42. Michael Gillespie, "Los Angeles Court Hands Down Final Judgment in Anti-Defamation League Illegal Surveillance Case," *Washington Report on Middle East Affairs,* December 1999, 43.

43. An ADL advertisement in the *New York Times,* May 11, 1997, entitled "We Hate Keeping Files on Hate," claims: "For 83 years, ADL has considered it our duty to collect and process information on racists, anti-Semites and extremists by monitoring and analyzing publications of all kinds and to share our findings to help focus American public opinion on the dangers of bigotry and hatred" (copy on file with Susan M. Akram).

44. Abraham, "Anti-Arab Racism and Violence," 187 (see n. 6).

45. Ibid.

46. Shaheen, *Reel Bad Arabs,* 9 (see n. 6).

47. Ibid., 11.

48. Ibid., 15.

49. Ibid., 31–33.

50. Abraham, "Anti-Arab Racism and Violence," 188–92 (see n. 6).

51. Michael Guido, "Let's Talk About City Parks and the Arab Problem," cited in Abraham, "Anti-Arab Racism and Violence," 191 (see n. 6).

52. Governor Milliken quoted in Abraham, "Anti-Arab Racism and Violence," 196 (see n. 6).

53. *New York Times,* "Mondale Camp Returns Funds to U.S. Arabs," August 25, 1984.

54. Stephen Franklin, "Arab-Americans Fall Victim to Mideast: Kuwaiti Ship Flagging Sparks Fears," *Chicago Tribune,* July 12, 1987.

55. Editorial, "The Untouchables," *The Nation,* March 21, 1987.

56. Dean E. Murphy, "Mrs. Clinton Says She Will Return Money Raised by a Muslim Group," *New York Times,* October 26, 2000.

57. Neil MacFarquhar, "Saudi Sheik Regrets Giuliani Turning Down His Donation," *New York Times,* October 13, 2001.

58. Laurie Goodstein and Tamar Lewin, "Victims of Mistaken Identity, Sikhs Pay a Price for Turbans," *New York Times,* September 19, 2001; Tamar Lewin and Gustav Niebuhr, "Attacks and Harassment Continue on Middle Eastern People and Mosques," *New York Times,* September 18, 2001.

59. Lynne Duke, "Islam Is Growing in U.S. Despite an Uneasy Image," *Washington Post,* October 24, 1993.

60. Michael W. Suleiman, "The Arab Immigrant Experience," introduction to *Arabs in America,* 18 (see n. 7).

61. Editorial, "Don't Judge Islam by Verdicts," *Orlando Sentinel,* March 8, 1994.

62. Bernard Weinraub, "39 American Hostages Free After 17 Days," *New York Times,* July 1, 1985.

63. House Committee on the Judiciary, Subcommittee on Criminal Justice, *Ethnically motivated violence against Arab-Americans: Hearing before the Subcommittee on Criminal Justice of the Committee on the Judiciary,* 99th Cong., 1986, 57, 64.

64. *New York Times,* "Bomb Kills Leader of U.S. Arab Group," October 12, 1985.

65. Abraham, "Anti-Arab Racism and Violence," 171 (see n. 6).

66. Ibid., 172.

67. American-Arab Anti-Discrimination Committee, *1991 Report on Anti-Arab Hate Crimes: Political and Hate Violence Against Arab Americans* (Washington, DC: American-Arab Anti-Discrimination Committee Research Institute, 1992), 6.

68. Abraham, "Anti-Arab Racism and Violence," 204 (see n. 6).

69. Jim McGee, "Ex-FBI Officials Criticize Tactics on Terrorism," *Washington Post,* November 28, 2001.

70. Bassiouni, *Civil Rights of Arab-Americans* (see n. 17).

71. Elaine Hagopian, "Minority Rights in a Nation-State: The Nixon Administration's Campaign against Arab-Americans," *Journal of Palestine Studies 5,* nos. 1 and 2 (Autumn–Winter, 1975–76): 97–114.

72. Ibid., 102.

73. Noam Chomsky, *Pirates & Emperors: International Terrorism in the Real World* (Montreal: Black Rose Books, 1987), 117–30.

74. Ibid., 123.

75. Ibid., 118.

76. Emily Sachar, "FBI Grills NY Arab-Americans," *Newsday,* January 29, 1991.

77. Lisa Belkin, "For Many Arab-Americans, FBI Scrutiny Renews Fears," *New York Times,* January 12, 1991.

78. On March 1, 2003, the INS was reorganized into the US Immigration and Customs Enforcement (ICE) and the US Citizenship and and Immigration Services (CIS) agencies. For ease of reference this article will continue to refer to "INS" or "immigration services," because all events referred to occurred prior to the agency reorganization.

79. David Cole, "Guilt by Association: It's Alive and Well at INS," *The Nation,* February 15, 1993, 198–99.

80. *United States v. Palestine Liberation Organization,* 695 F. Supp. 1456 (S.D.N.Y. 1988), rejecting the US government's efforts to close the PLO office used in connection with its role as Permanent Observer to the United Nations; see also *Palestine Information Office v. Shultz,* 853 F.2nd 932 (D.C. Cir. 1988), and *Mendelsohn v. Meese,* 695 F. Supp. 1474 (S.D.N.Y. 1988), challenging the constitutionality of law requiring closure of the Palestine Information Office in Washington, DC.

81. House Committee on the Judiciary, Subcommittee on Administrative Law and Governmental Relations, *Legislation to Implement the Recommendations of the Commission on Wartime Relocation and Internment of Civilians: Hearing on HR 442 Before the Subcommittee on Administrative Law and Governmental Relations,* 100th Cong., 1987, 67 (submission of Investigations Division of the Immigration and Naturalization Service, emphasis added).

82. Memorandum from Investigations Division, Immigration and Naturalization Service, Alien Border Control (ABC) Group IV–Contingency Plans 16 (November 18, 1986), with attachments including INS, "Alien Terrorists and Undesirables: A Contingency Plan" (1986) (on file with Susan Akram).

83. John A. Scanlan, "American-Arab—Getting the Balance Wrong—Again!" *Administrative Law Review* 52, no. 1 (Winter 2000): 363–68.

84. Sharon LaFraniere and George Lardner, "U.S. Set to Photograph, Fingerprint all New Iraqi and Kuwaiti Visitors," *Washington Post,* January 11, 1991.

85. Immigration and Nationality Act (INA) Sec. 212(a) (27)–(29), 8 U.S.C. Sec. 1182(a) (27)–(29) (1952) (repealed 1990).

86. 22 U.S.C. Sec. 2691 (1988) (denying waiver to noncitizens connected with the Palestine Liberation Organization as well as representatives of organizations advocating totalitarian government).

87. The "PLO exception" is codified as INA Sec. 212(a), 8 U.S.C. Sec. 1182(a).

88. For the Supreme Court decision in the lengthy litigation, see *Reno v. American-Arab Anti-Discrimination Committee,* 525 US 471 (1999), citing other published federal court decisions in the case. For an example of the commentators on the implications of the case, see Hiroshi Motomura, "Judicial Review in Immigration Cases after AADC: Lessons from Civil Procedure," *Georgetown Immigration Law Journal* 14 (2000).

89. Dempsey and Cole, *Terrorism and the Constitution,* 33–34, discussing LA Eight case (see n. 1).

90. Senate Select Committee on Intelligence, *Nomination of William H. Webster: Hearings before the Select Committee on Intelligence of the United States Senate,* 100th Cong., 1st sess., 1987, 95 (emphasis added).

91. *American-Arab Anti-Discrimination Committee v. Reno,* 119 F. 3rd 1367, 1370 (9th Cir. 1997).

92. *American-Arab Anti-Discrimination Committee v. Meese,* 714 F. Supp. 1060 (C.D. Cal. 1989).

93. INA Sec. 212(a) (3) (B) (iii), 8 U.S.C. Sec. 1182(a) (3) (B) (iii) (emphasis added). After September 11, Congress further expanded the definition of "terrorist activity."

94. Gerald L. Neuman, "Terrorism, Selective Deportation and the First Amendment after *Reno v. AADC," Georgetown Immigration Law Journal* 14 (2000): 322–27.

95. *Reno v. American-Arab Anti-Discrimination Committee,* 525 US 471–72 (1999). In reaching that conclusion, the Court relied on INA Sec. 242(g), 8 U.S.C. Sec. 1252(g): "Except as provided in this section and notwithstanding any other provision of law, no court shall have jurisdiction to hear any cause or claim by or on behalf of any alien arising from the decision or action by the Attorney General to commence proceedings, adjudicate cases, or execute removal orders against any alien under this Act."

96. Stephen H. Legomsky, *Immigration and Refugee Law and Policy,* 3rd ed. (New York: Foundation Press, 2002), 86.

97. See Akram, "Scheherezade Meets Kafka," 52n4 (see n. 4).

98. *Rafeedie v. INS,* 688 F. Supp. 729 (D.D.C. 1988), *aff'd in part, rev'd in part, remanded,* 880 F.2nd 506 (D.C. Cir. 1989).

99. *Rafeedie v. INS,* 688 F. Supp., 734–35.

100. *Rafeedie v. INS,* 880 F.2nd, 516.

101. Antiterrorism and Effective Death Penalty Act of 1996, Public Law 104–132, *U.S. Statutes at Large* 110 (1996): 1213; see Whidden, "Unequal Justice," 2841–83, for summary of the genesis of AEDPA and analysis of its impact on Arabs and Muslims (see n. 7).

102. Illegal Immigration Reform and Immigrant Responsibility Act of 1996, Public Law 104-208, *U.S. Statutes at Large* 110 (1996): 3009.

103. Akram, "Scheherezade Meets Kafka," 52, 52n4, listing post-1996 secret evidence cases (see n. 4).

104. See *National Security Considerations Involved in Asylum Applications: Hearings Before the Senate Judiciary Committee on Technology, Terrorism, and Government Information,* 105th Cong., 1998, FDCH Political Transcripts, 5–14 (testimony of INS General Counsel Paul Virtue).

105. AEDPA at Sec. 303 (f) (2) (B) and at Sec. 504 (e) (3) (C).

106. For a general summary of the Iraqi Seven cases by the lead counsel, see Niels W. Frenzen, "National Security and Procedural Fairness: Secret Evidence and the Immigration Laws," *Interpreter Releases* 76 (1999): 1681n31.

107. *National Security Considerations Involved in Asylum Applications: Hearings Before the Senate Judiciary Committee on Technology, Terrorism, and Government Information,* 105th Cong., 1998, FDCH Political Transcripts, 23–27 (statement of R. James Woolsey).

108. ACLU of Florida, "Palestinian Professor Challenges His Detention by INS as Illegal," May 14, 2002, http://www.aclufl.org/alnajjarhabeasrelease051402.html.

109. *In re Anwar Haddam,* 2000 BIA LEXIS 20, 1 (BIA December 1, 2000).

110. *Al-Najjar v. Reno,* 97 F. Supp. 2nd 1329, 1333–34 (S.D. Fla. 2000).

111. *Al-Najjar v. Ashcroft,* 257 F.3rd 1330, 1336–68 (2001) (stating that the attorney general had the authority to detain al-Najjar indefinitely).

112. *Al-Najjar v. Ashcroft,* 257 F.3rd 1262, 1274 (11th Cir. 2001).

113. For discussion of the facts and legal decisions in the Haddam case, see *In re Haddam,* No. A22-751-813 (BIA September 10, 1998), *aff'd; In re Anwar Haddam,* 2000 BIA LEXIS 20, 1 (BIA December 1, 2000); Akram, "Scheherezade Meets Kafka," 79–81, analyzing the INS proceedings against Haddam (see n. 4).

114. *Matter of Nasser Ahmed,* No. A90-674-238 (Immigration Court, June 24, 1999) (decision following remand); see also Dempsey and Cole, *Terrorism and the Constitution,* 128–31, discussing case (see n. 1).

115. *United States v. Rahman,* 189 F.3rd 88, 103 (2nd Cir. 1999).

116. Philip G. Schrag, *A Well-Founded Fear: The Congressional Battle to Save Political Asylum in America* (New York: Routledge, 2000), 42–44, 134, 137, 148, 162, 164, 217.

117. "How Did He Get Here?" *60 Minutes,* CBS, March 14, 1993.

118. Thomas Alexander Aleinikoff, David A. Martin, and Hiroshi Motomura, *Immigration and Citizenship: Process and Policy,* 4th ed. (St. Paul, MN: West Group, 1998), 863–71, 1028–29 (discussing summary exclusion provisions of 1996 immigration reforms).

READING 19

Notes

1. Raphael Tardon, "Richard Wright Tells Us: The White Problem in the United States," *Action,* 24 Oct. 1946. Reprinted in Kenneth Kinnamon and Michel Fabre, *Conversations with Richard Wright* (Jackson, Miss., 1993), 99. Malcolm X and others used this same formulation in the 1960s, but I believe that it originated with Wright, or at least that is the earliest citation I have found so far.

2. This is also Toni Morrison's point in *Playing in the Dark: Whiteness in the Literary Imagination* (Cambridge, Mass., 1992).

3. Richard Dyer, "White," *Screen* 29 (fall 1988): 44.

4. I thank Michael Schudson for pointing out to me that since the passage of civil rights legislation in the 1960s whiteness dares not speak its name, cannot speak in its own behalf, but rather advances through a color-blind language radically at odds with the distinctly racialized distribution of resources and life chances in American society.

5. Walter Benjamin, "Madame Ariane: Second Courtyard on the Left," from *One-Way Street* (London, 1969), 98–99.

6. Richard Slotkin, *Gunfighter Nation: The Myth of the Frontier in Twentieth Century America* (New York, 1992); Eric Lott, *Love and Theft* (New York, 1993); David Roediger, *Wages of Whiteness* (New York, 1992); Michael Rogin, "Blackface White Noise: The Jewish Jazz Singer Finds His Voice," *Critical Inquiry* 18 (spring 1992).

7. Robin Kelley, *Hammer and Hoe* (Chapel Hill, N.C., 1990); Lizabeth Cohen, *Making a New Deal* (Cambridge, 1991); George Sanchez, *Becoming Mexican American* (New York, 1993); Edmund Morgan, *American Slavery, American Freedom* (New York, 1975); John Hope Franklin, *The Color Line: Legacy for the Twenty-first Century* (Columbia, Mo., 1993).

8. Alexander Saxton, *The Rise and Fall of the White Republic* (New York, 1992); Roediger, *Wages;* Michael Rogin, *Ronald Reagan, the Movie: And Other Episodes in Political Demonology* (Berkeley, 1987); Michael Rogin, "Blackface"; Michael Rogin, "'Democracy and Burnt Cork': The End of Blackface, the Beginning of Civil Rights," presented at the University of California Humanities Research Institute Film Genres Study Group, November 1992.

9. See Kenneth Jackson, *Crabgrass Frontier: The Suburbanization of the United States* (New York, 1985); and Douglas S. Massey and Nancy A. Denton, *American Apartheid: Segregation and the Making of the Underclass* (Cambridge, Mass., 1993).

10. I thank Phil Ethington for pointing out to me that these aspects of New Deal policies emerged out of political negotiations between the segregationist Dixiecrats and liberals from the North and West. My perspective is that white supremacy was not a gnawing aberration within the New Deal coalition but rather an essential point of unity between southern whites and northern white ethnics.

11. Records of the Federal Home Loan Bank Board of the Home Owners Loan Corporation. City Survey File, Los Angeles, 1939, Neighborhood D-53, National Archives, Washington, D.C., box 74, records group 195.

12. Massey and Denton, *American Apartheid,* 54.

13. John R. Logan and Harvey Molotch, *Urban Fortunes: The Political Economy of Place* (Berkeley, 1987), 182.

14. Ibid., 114.

15. Ibid., 130.

16. See Gary Gerstle, "Working-Class Racism: Broaden the Focus," *International Labor and Working Class History* 44 (fall 1993): 36.

17. Logan and Molotch, *Urban Fortunes,* 168–69.

18. Troy Duster, "Crime, Youth Unemployment, and the Black Urban Underclass," *Crime and Delinquency* 33 (Apr. 1987): 308.

19. Ibid., 309.

20. Massey and Denton, *American Apartheid,* 55.

21. Logan and Molotch, *Urban Forunes,* 113.

22. Robert D. Bullard, "Environmental Justice for All," in *Unequal Protection: Environmental Justice and Communities of Color,* ed. Robert Bullard (San Francisco, 1994), 9–10.

23. Massey and Denton, *American Apartheid,* 61.

24. Gertrude Ezorsky, *Racism and Justice: The Case for Affirmative Action* (Ithaca, N.Y., 1991), 25.

25. Logan and Molotch, *Urban Fortunes,* 116.

26. Jim Campen, "Lending Insights: Hard Proof That Banks Discriminate," *Dollars and Sense* 191 (Jan.–Feb. 1991): 17.

27. Mitchell Zuckoff, "Study Shows Racial Bias in Lending," *The Boston Globe,* 9 October 1992, 1, 77, 78.

28. Paul Ong and J. Eugene Grigsby III, "Race and Life-Cycle Effects on Home Ownership in Los Angeles, 1970 to 1980," *Urban Affairs Quarterly* 23 (June 1988): 605.

29. Massey and Denton, *American Apartheid,* 108.

30. Gary Orfield and Carol Ashkinaze, *The Closing Door: Conservative Policy and Black Opportunity* (Chicago, 1991), 58, 78.

31. Logan and Molotch, *Urban Fortunes.*

32. Campen, "Lending Insights," 18.

33. Gregory Squires, "'Runaway Plants,' Capital Mobility, and Black Economic Rights," in *Community and Capital in Conflict: Plant Closings and Job Loss,* ed. John C. Raines, Lenora E. Berson, and David McI. Gracie (Philadelphia, 1982), 70.

34. Gertrude Ezorsky, *Racism and Justice: The Case for Affirmative Action* (Ithaca, N.Y., 1991), 15.

35. Orfield and Ashkinaze, *The Closing Door,* 225–26.

36. McClatchy News Service, "State Taxes Gouge the Poor, Study Says," *Long Beach Press-Telegram,* 23 April 1991, A1.

37. "Proposition 13," *UC Focus* (June–July 1993): 2.

38. William Chafe, *The Unfinished Journey* (New York, 1986), 442; Noel J. Kent, "A Stacked Deck: Racial Minorities and the New American Political Economy," *Explorations in Ethnic Studies* 14 (Jan. 1991): 11.

39. Kent, "Stacked Deck," 13.

40. Melvin Oliver and James Johnson, "Economic Restructuring and Black Male Joblessness in United States Metropolitan Areas," *Urban Geography* 12 (Nov.–Dec. 1991); Gerald David Jaynes and Robin M. Williams, Jr., eds., *A Common Destiny: Blacks and American Society* (Washington, D.C., 1989); Reynolds Farley and Walter R. Allen, *The Color Line and the Quality of Life in America* (New York, 1987); Melvin Oliver and Tom Shapiro, "Wealth of a Nation: A Reassessment of Asset Inequality in America Shows at Least 1/3 of Households Are Asset Poor," *Journal of Economics and Sociology* 49 (Apr. 1990); Jonathan Kozol, *Savage Inequalities: Children in America's Schools* (New York, 1991); Cornell West, *Race Matters* (Boston, 1993).

41. Orfield and Ashkinaze, *Closing Door,* 46.

42. Ibid., 206.

43. Bart Landry, "The Enduring Dilemma of Race in America," in Alan H. Wolfe, *America at Century's End* (Berkeley, 1991), 206; Franklin, *Color Line,* 36–37.

44. Kathleen Hall Jamieson, *Dirty Politics: Deception, Distraction, and Democracy* (New York, 1992), 100.

45. Mary Edsall and Thomas Byrne Edsall, *Chain Reaction* (New York, 1991).

46. Nathan Glazer makes this argument in *Affirmative Discrimination* (New York, 1975).

47. I borrow the term "overdetermination" here from Louis Althusser, who uses it to show how dominant ideologies become credible to people in part because various institutions and agencies independently replicate them and reinforce their social power.

48. Rogena Schuyler, "Youth: We Didn't Sell Them into Slavery," *Los Angeles Times,* 21 June 1993, B4.

49. Ibid.

50. Jim Newton, "Skinhead Leader Pleads Guilty to Violence, Plot," *Los Angeles Times,* 20 Oct. 1993, A1, A15.

51. Antonin Scalia, quoted in Cheryl I. Harris, "Whiteness as Property," *Harvard Law Review,* 106 (June 1993): 1767.

52. Ibid.

53. The rise of a black middle class and the setbacks suffered by white workers during deindustrialization may seem to subvert the analysis presented here. Yet the black middle class remains fragile, far less able than other middle-class groups to translate advances in income into advances in wealth and power. Similarly, the success of neoconservatism since the 1970s has rested on securing support from white workers for economic policies that do them objective harm by mobilizing counter-subversive electoral coalitions against busing and affirmative action, while carrying out attacks on public institutions and resources by representing "public" space and black space. See Oliver and Shapiro, "Wealth of a Nation." See also Logan and Harvey, *Urban Fortunes.*

54. Johnny Otis, *Upside Your Head! Rhythm and Blues on Central Avenue* (Hanover, N.H., 1993).

55. Mobilizations against plant shutdowns, for environmental protection, against cutbacks in education spending, and for reproductive rights all contain the potential for pan-ethnic antiracist organizing, but, too often, neglect of race as a central modality for how issues of employment, pollution, education, or reproductive rights are experienced isolates these social movements from their broadest possible base.

56. Walter Benjamin, "Madame Ariane: Second Courtyard on the Left," from *One-Way Street* (London, 1969), 98, 99.

READING 20

References

Blumer, Herbert. 1958. "Racial Prejudice as a Sense of Group Position." *Pacific Sociological Review* 1: 3–7.

Bobo, Lawrence D. 1988. "Attitudes Toward the Black Political Movements: Trends, Meaning, and Effects on Racial Policy Attitudes." *Social Psychology Quarterly* 51(4): 287–302.

———. 1999. "Prejudice as Group Position: Microfoundations of a Sociological Approach to Racism and Race Relations." *Journal of Social Issues* 55(3): 445–72.

———. 2000. "Reclaiming a DuBoisian Perspective on Racial Attitudes." *Annals of the American Academy of Political and Social Science* 568: 186–202.

Bobo, Lawrence D., and Devon Johnson. 2004. "A Taste for Punishment: Black and White Americans' Views on the

Death Penalty and the War on Drugs." *Du Bois Review* 1: 151–80.

Bobo, Lawrence, and James R. Kluegel. 1997. "Status, Ideology, and Dimensions of Whites' Racial Beliefs and Attitudes: Progress and Stagnation." In *Racial Attitudes in the 1990s: Continuity and Change,* edited by Steven A. Tuch and Jack K. Martin. New York: Praeger.

Bobo, Lawrence, James R. Kluegel, and Ryan A. Smith. 1997. "Laissez-Faire Racism: The Crystallization of a Kinder, Gentler Antiblack Ideology." In *Racial Attitudes in the 1990s: Continuity and Change,* edited by Steven Tuch and Jack K. Martin. New York: Praeger.

Bobo, Lawrence D., and Ryan A. Smith. 1998. "From Jim Crow Racism to Laissez-Faire Racism: The Transformation of Racial Attitudes." In *Beyond Pluralism: The Conception of Groups and Group Identities in America,* edited by Wendy F. Katkin, Ned Landsman, and Andrea Tyree. Urbana, Ill.: University of Illinois Press.

Bobo, Lawrence D., and Mia Tuan. Forthcoming. *Prejudice in Politics: Group Position, Public Opinion, and the Wisconsin Treaty Rights Controversy.* Cambridge, Mass.: Harvard University Press.

Bobo, Lawrence, and Camille L. Zubrinsky. 1996. "Attitudes on Residential Integration: Perceived Status Differences, Mere In-group Preference or Racial Prejudice?" *Social Forces* 74(3): 883–909.

Bonilla-Silva, Edward. 2001. *White Supremacy and Racism in the Post–Civil Rights Era.* Boulder, Colo.: Lynne Rienner.

Charles, Camille Z. 2000. "Neighborhood Racial-Composition Preferences: Evidence from a Multiethnic Metropolis." *Social Problems* 47(3): 379–407.

———. 2003. "The Dynamics of Racial Residential Segregation." *Annual Review of Sociology* 29: 67–107.

Citrin, Jack, Donald Green, and David O. Sears. 1990. "White Reactions to Black Candidates: When Does Race Matter?" *Public Opinion Quarterly* 54: 74–96.

Cohen, Cathy J. 1999. *The Boundaries of Blackness: AIDS and the Breakdown of Black Politics.* Chicago: University of Chicago Press.

Collins, Randall. 2001. "Ethnic Change in Macrohistorical Perspective." In *Problem of the Century: Racial Stratification in the United States,* edited by Elijah Anderson and Douglas S. Massey. New York: Russell Sage Foundation.

Dawson, Michael C. 1994. *Behind the Mule: Race and Class in African American Politics.* Princeton, N.J.: Princeton University Press.

———. 2000. "Slowly Coming to Grips with the Effects of the American Racial Order on American Policy Preferences." In *Racialized Politics: The Debate on Racism in America,* edited by David O. Sears, James Sidanius, and Lawrence D. Bobo. Chicago: University of Chicago Press.

———. 2001. *Black Visions.* Chicago: University of Chicago Press.

Dawson, Michael C., and Ravana Popoff. 2004. "Reparations: Justice and Greed in Black and White." *Du Bois Review* 1: 47—92.

Farley, Reynolds, Charlotte Steeh, Maria Krysan, Tara Jackson, and Keith Reeves. 1994. "Stereotypes and Segregation: Neighborhoods in the Detroit Area." *American Journal of Sociology* 100(3): 750–80.

Feagin, Joe R. 2001. *Racist America: Roots, Current Realities, and Future Reparations.* New York: Routledge.

Fields, Barbara J. 1982. "Ideology and Race in American History." In *Region, Race, and Reconstruction: Essays in Honor of C. Vann Woodward,* edited by J. Morgan Kousser and James M. McPherson. New York: Oxford University Press.

Gans, Herbert J. 1999. "The Possibility of a New Racial Hierarchy in the Twenty-first-Century United States." In *The Cultural Territories of Race: Black and White Boundaries,* edited by Michele Lamont. New York: Russell Sage Foundation.

Holt, Thomas, 2000. *The Problem of Race in the Twenty-first Century.* Cambridge, Mass.: Harvard University Press.

Jackman, Mary R. 1994. *The Velvet Glove: Paternalism and Conflict in Gender, Class, and Race Relations.* Berkeley: University of California Press.

Kim, Claire Jean. 2000. *Bitter Fruit: The Politics of Black-Korean Conflict in New York City.* New Haven, Conn.: Yale University Press.

Kinder, Donald R., and Lynn M. Sanders. 1996. *Divided by Color: Racial Politics and Democratic Ideals.* Chicago: University of Chicago Press.

Klinkner, Philip, and Rogers Smith. 1999. *The Unsteady March: The Rise and Decline of Racial Equality in America.* Chicago: University of Chicago Press.

Kluegel, James R., and Lawrence D. Bobo. 2001. "Perceived Group Discrimination and Policy Attitudes: The Sources and Consequences of the Race and Gender Gaps." In *Urban Inequality: Evidence from Four Cities,* edited by Alice O'Connor, Chris Tilly, and Lawrence D. Bobo. New York: Russell Sage Foundation.

Kluegel, James R., and Eliot R. Smith. 1986. *Beliefs About Inequality: Americans' Views About What Is and What Ought to Be.* New York: Aldine de Gruyter.

Krysan, Maria. 2000. "Prejudice, Politics, and Public Opinion: Understanding the Sources of Racial Policy Attitudes." *Annual Review of Sociology* 26: 135–68.

Lamont, Michele. 2000. *The Dignity of Working Men: Morality and the Boundaries of Race, Class, and Immigration.* Cambridge, Mass.: Harvard University Press.

Lee, Taeku. 2002. *Mobilizing Public Opinion: Black Insurgency and Racial Attitudes in the Civil Rights Era.* Chicago: University of Chicago Press.

Liptak, Adam. 2003. "Texas Governor Pardons 35 Arrested in Tainted Sting." *New York Times,* August 23.

McConahay, John B. 1986. "Modern Racism, Ambivalence, and the Modern Racism Scale." In *Prejudice, Discrimination, and Racism,* edited by John F. Dovidio and Samuel Gaertner. Orlando, Fla.: Academic Press.

McWhorter, John. 2000. *Losing the Race: Self-sabotage in Black America.* New York: HarperCollins.

Rashbaum, William K. 2003. "Woman Dies After Officers Mistakenly Raid Her Home." *New York Times,* May 17.

Sears, David O. 1988. "Symbolic Racism." In *Eliminating Racism: Profiles in Controversy,* edited by Phyllis A. Katz and Dalmas A. Taylor. New York: Plenum.

Sears, David O., and Jack Citrin. 1985. *Tax Revolt: Proposition 13 and Something for Nothing in California.* Cambridge, Mass.: Harvard University Press.

Sears, David O., Collette van Laar, and Rick Kosterman. 1997. "Is It Really Racism? The Origins of White Americans' Opposition to Race-Targeted Policies." *Public Opinion Quarterly* 61: 16–53.

Sengupta, Somini. 2001. "September 11 Attack Narrows the Racial Divide." *New York Times,* October 10.

Smith, Eliot R. 1993. "Social Identity and Social Emotions: Toward New Conceptualizations of Prejudice." In *Affect, Cognition, and Stereotyping: Interactive Processes in Group Perception,* edited by Diane M. Mackie and David L. Hamilton. New York: Academic Press.

Sniderman, Paul M., and Thomas Piazza. 1993. *The Scar of Race.* Cambridge: Harvard University Press.

Steele, Claude. 1998. "A Threat in the Air: How Stereotypes Shape Intellectual Identity and Performance." In *Confronting Racism: The Problem and the Response,* edited by J. L. Eberhardt and Susan T. Fiske. Thousand Oaks, Calif.: Sage Publications.

Thernstrom, Stephan, and Abigail Thernstrom. 1997. *America in Black and White: One Nation, Indivisible.* New York: Simon & Schuster.

Thompson, J. Phillip. 1998. "Universalism and Deconcentration: Why Race Still Matters in Poverty and Economic Development." *Politics and Society* 26: 181–219.

Torres, Kimberly C., and Camille Z. Charles. 2004. "Metastereotypes and the Black-White Divide: A Qualitative View of Race on an Elite College Campus." *Du Bois Review* 1: 115–50.

Waters, Mary C. 1999. *Black Identities: West Indian Immigrant Dreams and American Realities.* Cambridge, Mass.: Harvard University Press.

Yinger, John. 1998. "Housing Discrimination Is Still Worth Worrying About." *Housing Policy Debate* 9: 893–927.

Zuberi, Tukufu. 2001. *Thicker Than Blood: How Racial Statistics Lie.* Minneapolis: University of Minnesota Press.

Zubrinsky, Camille L., and Lawrence Bobo. 1996. "Prismatic Metropolis: Race and Residential Segregation in the City of Angels." *Social Science Research* 24: 335–74.

READING 21

References

Allport, G. 1958. *The Nature of Prejudice.* Garden City, N.Y.: Doubleday Anchor.

Almgren, G., A. Guest, G. Imerwahr, and M. Spittel. 1998. Joblessness, family disruption, and violent death in Chicago: 1970–1990. *Social Forces* 76: 1465–1494.

Anderson, E. 1990. *Streetwise: Race, Class, and Change in an Urban Community.* Chicago: University of Chicago Press.

Bertram, S. 1988. *An Audit of the Real Estate Sales and Rental Markets of Selected Southern Suburbs.* Homewood, Ill.: South Suburban Housing Center.

Blalock, H.M., Jr. 1967. *Toward a Theory of Minority-Group Relations.* New York: Wiley.

Bobo, L., H. Schuman, and C. Steeh. 1986. Changing racial attitudes toward residential integration. Pp. 152–169 in *Housing Desegregation and Federal Policy,* ed. Chapel Hill: University of North Carolina Press.

Bobo, L., and C. Zubrinsky. 1996. Attitudes on residential integration: Perceived status differences, mere in-group preference, or racial prejudice? *Social Forces* 74:883–909.

Brooks-Gunn, J., G. Duncan, and J. Aber, eds. 1997. *Neighborhood Poverty: Context and Consequences for Children.* New York: Russell Sage.

Brooks-Gunn, J., G. Duncan, P. Klebanov, and N. Sealand. 1993. Do neighborhoods influence child and adolescent development? *American Journal of Sociology* 99:353–395.

Clark, W. 1991. Residential preferences and neighborhood racial segregation: A test of the Schelling segregation model. *Demography* 28:1–19.

Corcoran, M., R. Gordon, D. Laren, and G. Solon. 1989. Effects of family and community background on men's economic status. Working Paper 2896, National Bureau of Economic Research, Cambridge, Mass.

Crane, J. 1991. The epidemic theory of ghettos and neighborhood effects on dropping out and teenage childbearing. *American Journal of Sociology* 96:1226–1259.

Danziger, S., and P. Gottschalk. 1995. *America Unequal.* Cambridge: Harvard University Press and the Russell Sage Foundation.

Datcher, L. 1982. Effects of community and family background on achievement. *The Review of Economics and Statistics* 64:32–41.

Demerath, N., and H. Gilmore. 1954. The ecology of southern cities. Pp. 120–125 in *The Urban South,* R. Vance and

N. Demerath, eds. Chapel Hill: University of North Carolina Press.

Denton, N. 1994. Are African Americans still hypersegregated? Pp. 49–81 in *Residential Apartheid: The American Legacy,* R. Bullard, J. Grigsby III, and C. Lee, eds. Los Angeles: CAAS Publications, University of California.

Denton, N., and D. Massey. 1988. Residential segregation of Blacks, Hispanics, and Asians by socioeconomic status and generation. *Social Science Quarterly* 69:797–817. 1989. Racial identity among Caribbean Hispanics: The effect of double minority status on residential segregation. *American Sociological Review* 54:790–808. 1991. Patterns of neighborhood transition in a multiethnic world. *Demography* 28:41–64.

Duncan, O., and B. Duncan. 1957. *The Negro Population of Chicago: A Study of Residential Succession.* Chicago: University of Chicago Press.

Farley, R. 1977. Residential segregation in urbanized areas of the United States in 1970: An analysis of social class and racial differences. *Demography* 14:497–518.

Farley, R., S. Bianchi, and D. Colasanto. 1979. Barriers to the racial integration of neighborhoods: The Detroit case. *Annals of the American Academy of Political and Social Science* 441:97–113.

Farley, R., H. Schuman, S. Bianchi, D. Colasanto, and S. Hatchett. 1978. "Chocolate city, vanilla suburbs": Will the trend toward racially separate communities continue? *Social Science Research* 7:319–344.

Farley, R., C. Steeh, M. Krysan, T. Jackson, and K. Reeves. 1994. Stereotypes and segregation: Neighborhoods in the Detroit area. *American Journal of Sociology* 100:750–780.

Feins, J., R. Bratt, and R. Hollister. 1981. *Final Report of a Study of Racial Discrimination in the Boston Housing Market.* Cambridge: Abt Associates.

Fix, M., G. Galster, and R. Struyk. 1993. An overview of auditing for discrimination. Pp. 1–68 in *Clear and Convincing Evidence: Measurement of Discrimination in America,* M. Fix and R. Struyk, eds. Washington, D.C.: The Urban Institute Press.

Frey, W., and R. Farley. 1994. Changes in the segregation of Whites from Blacks during the 1980s; Small steps toward a more integrated society. *American Sociological Review* 59:23–45. 1996. Latino, Asian, and Black segregation in U.S. metropolitan areas: Are multiethnic metros different? *Demography* 33:35–50.

Furstenburg, F. Jr., S. Morgan, K. Moore, and J. Peterson. 1987. Race differences in the timing of adolescent intercourse. *American Sociological Review* 52:511–518.

Guest, A., G. Almgren, and J. Hussey. 1998. The ecology of race and socioeconomic distress: Infant and working age mortality in Chicago. *Demography* 35:23–34.

Hakken, J. 1979. *Discrimination Against Chicanos in the Dallas Rental Housing Market: An Experimental Extension of the Housing Market Practices Survey.* Washington, D.C.: Office of Policy Development and Research, U.S. Department of Housing and Urban Development.

Harrison, R., and D. Weinberg. 1992. Racial and ethnic residential segregation in 1990. Paper presented at the annual meeting of the Population Association of America, Denver, April 13.

Helper, R. 1969. *Racial Policies and Practices of Real Estate Brokers.* Minneapolis: University of Minnesota Press.

Hintzen, H. 1983. *Report of an Audit of Real Estate Sales Practices of 15 Northwest Chicago Real Estate Sales Offices.* Chicago: Leadership Council for Metropolitan Open Communities.

Hochschild, J. 1995. *Facing up to the American Dream: Race, Class, and the Soul of the Nation.* Princeton: Princeton University Press.

Hogan, D., and E. Kitagawa. 1985. The impact of social status, family structure, and neighborhood on the fertility of Black adolescents. *American Journal of Sociology* 90:825–855.

Hwang, S., and S. Murdock. 1982. Residential segregation in Texas in 1980. *Social Science Quarterly* 63:737–748.

Jackson, P. 1981. Paradoxes of Puerto Rican segregation in New York. Pp. 109–126 in *Ethnic Segregation in Cities,* C. Peach, V. Robinson, and S. Smith, eds. London: Croom Helm.

Jackson, T. 1994. The other side of the residential segregation equation: Why Detroit area Blacks are reluctant to pioneer integration. Paper presented at the Russell Sage Foundation Multi-City conference.

James, F., and E. Tynan. 1986. Segregation and discrimination against Hispanic Americans. Pp. 83–98 in *Housing Discrimination and Federal Policy,* J. Goering, ed. Chapel Hill: University of North Carolina Press.

Jencks, C., and S. Mayer. 1990. The social consequences of growing up in a poor neighborhood. Pp. 111–186 in *Inner City Poverty in the United States,* L. Lynn, Jr., and M. McGeary, eds. Washington, D.C.: National Academy of Sciences.

Kantrowitz, N. 1973. *Ethnic and Racial Segregation in the New York Metropolis.* New York: Praeger.

Kasarda, J. 1993. Inner city concentrated poverty and neighborhood distress: 1970–1990. *Housing Policy Debate* 4(3):253–302.

Krivo, L., and R. Kaufman. 1999. How low can it go? Declining Black-White segregation in a multi-ethnic context. *Demography* 36:93–110.

Krivo, L., and R. Peterson. 1996. Extremely disadvantaged neighborhoods and urban crime. *Social Forces* 75:619–648.

Krivo, L., R. Peterson, H. Rizzo, and J. Reynolds. 1998. Race segregation, and the concentration of disadvantage: 1980–1990. *Social Problems* 45:61–80.

Levy, F. 1995. Incomes and income inequality. Pp. 1–58 in *State of the Union: America in the 1990s,* Farley, ed. New York: Russell Sage.

Lieberson, S. 1980. *A Piece of the Pie: Blacks and White Immigrants Since 1880.* Berkeley: University of California Press.

Lopez, M. 1981. Patterns of interethnic residential segregation in the urban Southwest, 1960 and 1970. *Social Science Quarterly* 62:50–63.

Massey, D. 1979. Effects of socioeconomic factors on the residential segregation of Blacks and Spanish Americans in United States urbanized areas. *American Sociological Review* 44:1015–1022. 1981. Hispanic residential segregation: A comparison of Mexicans, Cubans, and Puerto Ricans. *Sociology and Social Research* 65:311–322. 1985. Ethnic residential segregation: A theoretical synthesis and empirical review. *Sociology and Social Research* 69:315–350. 1990. American apartheid: Segregation and the making of the underclass. *American Journal of Sociology* 96:329–358.

Massey, D., and B. Bitterman. 1985. Explaining the paradox of Puerto Rican segregation. *Social Forces* 64:306–331.

Massey, D., G. Condran, and N. Denton. 1987. The effect of residential segregation on Black social and economic well-being. *Social Forces* 66:29–57.

Massey, D., and N. Denton. 1987. Trends in the residential segregation of Blacks, Hispanics, and Asians. *American Sociological Review* 52:802–825. 1988. The dimensions of residential segregation. *Social Forces* 67:281–315. 1989a. Residential segregation of Mexicans, Puerto Ricans, and Cubans in U.S. metropolitan areas. *Sociology and Social Research* 73:73–83. 1989b. Hypersegregation in U.S. metropolitan areas: Black and Hispanic segregation along five dimensions. *Demography* 26:373–393. 1992. Racial identity and the spatial assimilation of Mexicans in the the United States. *Social Science Research* 21:235–260. 1993. *American Apartheid: Segregation and the Making of the Underclass.* Cambridge: Harvard University Press.

Massey, D., and M. Eggers. 1990. The ecology of inequality: Minorities and the concentration of poverty, 1970–1980. *American Journal of Sociology* 95:1153–1189.

Massey, D., and M. Fischer. 1999. Does rising income bring integration? New results for Blacks, Hispanics, and Asians in 1990. *Social Science Research* 28:316–326. 2000. How segregation concentrates poverty. *Ethnic and Racial Studies* 23:670–691.

Massey, D., and E. Fong. 1990. Segregation and neighborhood quality: Blacks, Hispanics, and Asians in the San Francisco metropolitan area. *Social Forces* 69:15–32.

Massey, D., and A. Gross. 1991. Explaining trends in residential segregation 1970–1980. *Urban Affairs Quarterly* 27:13–35.

Massey, D., A. Gross, and M. Eggers. 1991. Segregation, the concentration of poverty, and the life chances of individuals. *Social Science Research* 20:397–420.

Massey, D., and Z. Hajnal. 1995. The changing geographic structure of Black-White segregation in the United States. *Social Science Quarterly* 76:527–542.

Massey, D., K. Shibuya. 1995. Unraveling the tangle of pathology: The effect of spatially concentrated joblessness on the well-being of African Americans. *Social Science Research* 24: 252–366.

Massey, D., M. White, and V. Phua. 1996. The dimensions of segregation revisited. *Sociological Methods and Research.* 25:172–206.

Morenoff, J., and R. Sampson. 1997. Violent crime and the spatial dynamics of neighborhood transition: Chicago, 1970–1990. *Social Forces* 76:31–64.

Morris, M., A. Bernhardt, and M. Hancock. 1994. Economic inequality: New methods for new trends. *American Sociological Review* 59:205–219.

Moskos, C., and J. Butler. 1996. *All That We Can Be: Black Leadership and Racial Integration the Army Way.* New York: Basic Books.

Patillo, M. 1998. Sweet mothers and gangbangers: Managing crime in a Black middle-class neighborhood. *Social Forces* 76:747–774.

Saltman, J. 1979. Housing discrimination: Policy research, methods, and results. *Annals of the American Academy of Political and Social Science.* 441:186–196.

Schelling, T. 1971. Dynamic models of segregation. *Journal of Mathematical Sociology* 1:143–186.

Schneider, M., and J. Logan. 1982. Suburban racial segregation and Black access to local public resources. *Social Science Quarterly* 63: 762–770.

Schroeder, A. 1985. *Report on an Audit of Real Estate Sales Practices of Eight Northwest Suburban Offices.* Chicago: Leadership Council for Metropolitan Open Communities.

Schuman, H., and L. Bobo. 1988. Survey-based experiments on White racial attitudes toward residential integration. *American Journal of Sociology* 2:273–299.

Schuman, H., C. Steeh, and L. Bobo. 1985. *Racial Attitudes in America: Trends and Interpretations.* Cambridge: Harvard University Press.

Schuman, H., C. Steeh, L. Bobo, and M. Krysan. 1998. *Racial Attitudes in America: Trends and Interpretations.* Cambridge: Harvard University Press.

Simkus, A. 1978. Residential segregation by occupation and race in ten urbanized areas, 1950–1970. *American Sociological Review* 43:81–93.

Sniderman, P., and T. Piazza. 1993. *The Scar of Race.* Cambridge: Harvard University Press.

Taylor, M. 1998. The effect of racial composition on racial attitudes of Whites. *American Sociological Review* 63:512–535.

Turner, E. and J. Allen. 1991. *An Atlas of Population Patterns in Metropolitan, Los Angeles and Orange Counties.* Occasional Publication

in Geography No. 8. Northridge, Calif.: Center for Geographical Studies, California State University at Northridge.

U.S. Bureau of the Census. 1979. The Social and Economic
Status of the Black Population in the United States: An
Historical View, 1790–1978. Current Population Reports,
Special Studies Series P–23, No. 80. Washington, D.C.:
U.S. Government Printing Office.

Wilson, W. 1987. *Truly Disadvantaged: The Inner City, the Underclass, and Public Policy.* Chicago: University of Chicago Press.

Yinger, J. 1986. Measuring racial discrimination with fair housing audits: Caught in the act. *American Economic Review*
76:991–993. 1985. The racial dimension of urban housing
markets in the 1980s. Pp. 43–67 in *Divided Neighborhoods:
Changing Patterns of Racial Segregation,* G.A. Tobin, ed. Newbury Park, Calif.: Sage Publications. 1989. Measuring discrimination in housing availability. Final Research Report
No. 2 to the U.S. Department of Housing and Urban
Development. Washington, D.C.: The Urban Institute.
1995. *Closed Doors, Opportunities Lost: The Continuing Costs of
Housing Discrimination.* New York: Russell Sage.

Zubrinsky, C., and L. Bobo. 1996. Prismatic metropolis: Race
and residential segregation in the City of Angels. *Social Science Research* 25: 335–374.

READING 23

Notes

1. Robert D. Bullard, 1994, *Dumping in Dixie: Race, Class and
   Environmental Quality.* Boulder, CO: Westview Press.

2. Robert D. Bullard, "Solid Waste Sites and the Black Houston Community," *Sociological Inquiry* 53 (Spring 1983):
   273–288.

3. U.S. General Accounting Office (1983), *Siting of Hazardous
   Waste Landfills and Their Correlation with Racial and Economic
   Status of Surrounding Communities,* Washington, DC: Govern-
   ment Printing Office.

4. Commission for Racial Justice (1987), *Toxic Wastes and Race
   in the United States,* New York: United Church of Christ.

5. Charles Lee, 1992, *Proceedings: The First National People of
   Color Environmental Leadership Summit,* New York: United
   Church of Christ Commission for Racial Justice.

6. Dana Alston, "Transforming a Movement: People of Color
   Unite at Summit against Environmental Racism," *Sojourner*
   21 (1992), pp. 30–31.

7. William K. Reilly, "Environmental Equity: EPA's Position,"
   EPA Journal 18 (March/April 1992): 18–19.

8. R. D. Bullard and B. H. Wright, "The Politics of Pollution:
   Implications for the Black Community," *Phylon* 47 (March
   1986): 71–78.

9. Robert D. Bullard, "Race and Environmental Justice in the
   United States," *Yale Journal of International Law* 18 (Winter
   1993): 319–335; Robert D. Bullard, "The Threat of Environmental Racism," *Natural Resources & Environment* 7 (Winter 1993): 23–26, 55–56.

10. Louis Sullivan, "Remarks at the First Annual Conference on
    Childhood Lead Poisoning," in Alliance to End Childhood
    Lead Poisoning: Final Report, Washington DC: Alliance to
    End Childhood Lead Poisoning, October, 1991, p. A-2.

11. Bill Lann Lee, "Environmental Litigation on Behalf of Poor,
    Minority Children, *Matthews v. Coye*: A Case Study," paper pre-
    sented at the Annual Meeting of the American Association for
    the Advancement of Science, Chicago (February 9, 1992).

12. Ibid., p. 32.

13. Ibid.

14. Robert D. Bullard, "The Environmental Justice Framework:
    A Strategy for Addressing Unequal Protection," paper pre-
    sented at Resources for the Future Conference on Risk
    Management, Annapolis, MD (November 1992).

15. Paul Mohai and Bunyan Bryant, "Race, Poverty, and the
    Environment," *EPA Journal* 18 (March/April 1993): 1–8;
    R. D. Bullard, "In Our Backyards," *EPA Journal* 18 (March/
    April 1992): 11–12; D. R. Wernette and L. A. Nieves,
    "Breathing Polluted Air," *EPA Jounal* 18 (March/April 1992):
    16–17; Patrick C. West, "Health Concerns for Fish-Eating
    Tribes?" *EPA Journal* 18 (March/April 1992): 15–16.

16. Marianne Lavelle and Marcia Coyle, "Unequal Protection,"
    National Law Journal (September 21, 1992): S1–S2.

17. Robert D. Bullard, ed., *Confronting Environmental Racism:
    Voices from the Grassroots,* Boston: South End Press, 1993,
    chapter 1; Robert D. Bullard, "Waste and Racism: A Stacked
    Deck?" *Forum for Applied Research and Public Policy* 8 (Spring
    1993): 29–35; Robert D. Bullard (ed.), *In Search of the New
    South—The Black Urban Experience in the 1970s and 1980s*
    (Tuscaloosa, AL: University of Alabama Press, 1991).

18. Florence Wagman Roisman, "The Lessons of American Apart-
    heid: The Necessity and Means of Promoting Residential Racial
    Integration," *Iowa Law Review* 81 (December 1995): 479–525.

19. Joe R. Feagin, "A House Is Not a Home: White Racism and
    U.S. Housing Practices," in R. D. Bullard, J. E. Grigsby, and
    Charles Lee, eds., *Residential Apartheid: The American Legacy,*
    Los Angeles: UCLA Center for Afro-American Studies Pub-
    lication, 1994, pp. 17–48.

20. Eric Mann, *L.A.'s Lethal Air: New Strategies for Policy, Organiz-
    ing, and Action,* Los Angeles: Labor/Community Strategy
    Center, 1991, p. 31.

21. Jim Motavalli, "Toxic Targets: Polluters That Dump on
    Communities of Color Are Finally Being Brought to Justice,"
    E Magazine, 4 (July/August 1997): 29–41.

22. Joe Bandy, "Reterritorializing Borders: Transnational Environmental Justice on the U.S./Mexico Border," *Race, Gender, and Class* 5 (1997): 80–103.

23. Bunyan Bryant and Paul Mohai, *Race and the Incidence of Environmental Hazards* (Boulder, CO: Westview Press, 1992); Bunyan Bryant, ed., *Environmental Justice,* pp. 8–34.

24. R. Pinderhughes, "Who Decides What Constitutes a Pollution Problem?" *Race, Gender, and Class* 5 (1997): 130–152.

25. Diane Takvorian, "Toxics and Neighborhoods Don't Mix," *Land Use Forum: A Journal of Law, Policy and Practice* 2 (Winter 1993): 28–31; R. D. Bullard, "Examining the Evidence of Environmental Racism," *Land Use Forum: A Journal of Law, Policy, and Practice* 2(Winter 1993): 6–11.

26. For an in-depth examination of the Houston case study, see R. D. Bullard, 1987, *Invisible Houston: The Black Experience in Boom and Bust.* College Station, TX: Texas A&M University Press, pp. 60–75.

27. Ruth Rosen, "Who Gets Polluted: The Movement for Environmental Justice," *Dissent* (Spring 1994): 223–230; R. D. Bullard, "Environmental Justice: It's More than Waste Facility Siting," *Social Science Quarterly* 77 (September 1996): 493–499.

28. Commission for Racial Justice, *Toxic Wastes and Race in the United States,* pp. xiii–xiv.

29. U.S. General Accounting Office, *Siting of Hazardous Waste Landfills and Their Correlation with Racial and Economic Status of Surrounding Communities,* Washington, DC: U.S. General Accounting Office, 1983, p. 1.

30. Robert D. Bullard, ed., *Confusing Environmental Racism: Voices from the Grassroots,* Boston: South End, 1993; Robert D. Bullard, "The Threat of Environmental Racism," *Natural Resources & Environment* 7 (Winter 1993): 23–26; Bunyan Bryant and Paul Mohai, eds., *Race and the Incidence of Environmental Hazards,* Boulder, CO: Westview Press, 1992; Regina Austin and Michael Schill, "Black, Brown, Poor and Poisoned: Minority Grassroots Environmentalism and the Quest for Eco-Justice," *The Kansas Journal of Law and Public Policy* 1 (1991): 69–82; Kelly C. Colquette and Elizabeth A. Henry Robertson, "Environmental Racism: The Causes, Consequences, and Commendations," *Tulane Environmental Law Journal* 5 (1991): 153–207; Rachel D. Godsil, "Remedying Environmental Racism," *Michigan Law Review* 90 (1991): 394–427.

31. Bullard and Feagin, "Racism and the City," pp. 55–76; Robert D. Bullard, "Dismantling Environmental Racism in the USA," *Local Environment* 4 (1999): 5–19.

32. W. J. Kruvant, "People, Energy, and Pollution," in D. K. Newman and Dawn Day, eds., *The American Energy Consumer,* Cambridge, Mass.: Ballinger, 1975, pp. 125–167; Robert D. Bullard, "Solid Waste Sites and the Black Houston Community," *Sociological Inquiry* 53 (Spring 1983): 273–288; United Church of Christ Commission for Racial Justice, *Toxic Wastes and Race in the United States,* New York: Commission for Racial Justice, 1987; Dick Russell, "Environmental Racism," *The Amicus Journal* 11 (Spring 1989): 22–32; Eric Mann, *L.A.'s Lethal Air: New Strategies for Policy, Organizing, and Action,* Los Angeles: Labor/Community Strategy Center, 1991; D. R. Wernette and L. A. Nieves, "Breathing Polluted Air: Minorities are Disproportionately Exposed," *EPA Journal* 18 (March/April 1992): 16–17; Bryant and Mohai, *Race and the Incidence of Environmental Hazards;* Benjamin Goldman and Laura J. Fitton, *Toxic Wastes and Race Revisited,* Washington, DC: Center for Policy Alternatives, NAACP, and United Church of Christ, 1994.

33. Myrick A. Freedman, "The Distribution of Environmental Quality," in Allen V. Kneese and Blair T. Bower (eds.), *Environmental Quality Analysis,* Baltimore: Johns Hopkins University Press for Resources for the Future, 1971; Michael Gelobter, "The Distribution of Air Pollution by Income and Race," paper presented at the Second Symposium on Social Science in Resource Management, Urbana, Illinois (June 1988); Gianessi et al., "The Distributional Effects of Uniform Air Pollution Policy in the U.S.," *Quarterly Journal of Economics* (May 1979): 281–301.

34. Patrick C. West, J. Mark Fly, and Robert Marans, "Minority Anglers and Toxic Fish Consumption: Evidence from a State-Wide Survey in Michigan," in Bryant and Mohai, *Race and the Incidence of Environmental Hazards,* pp. 100–113.

35. Robert D. Bullard, "Solid Waste Sites and the Black Houston Community," *Sociological Inquiry* 53 (Spring 1983): 273–288; Robert D. Bullard, *Invisible Houston: The Black Experience in Boom and Bust,* College Station, TX: Texas A&M University Press, 1987, chapter 6; Robert D. Bullard, "Environmental Racism and Land Use," *Land Use Forum: A Journal of Law, Policy & Practice* 2 (Spring 1993): 6–11.

36. United Church of Christ Commission for Racial Justice, *Toxic Wastes and Race;* Paul Mohai and Bunyan Bryant, "Environmental Racism: Reviewing the Evidence," in Bryant and Mohai, *Race and the Incidence of Environmental Hazards;* Paul Stretesky and Michael J. Hogan, "Environmental Justice: An Analysis of Superfund Sites in Florida," *Social Problems* 45 (May 1998): 268–287.

37. Marianne Lavelle and Marcia Coyle, "Unequal Protection: The Racial Divide in Environmental Law," *National Law Journal,* September 21, 1992.

38. Agency for Toxic Substances Disease Registry, *The Nature and Extent of Lead Poisoning in Children in the United States: A Report to Congress,* Atlanta: U.S. Department of Health and Human Resources, 1988, pp. 1–12.

39. J. Schwartz and R. Levine, "Lead: An Example of the Job Ahead," *EPA Journal* 18 (March/April 1992): 32–44.

40. Centers for Disease Control and Prevention, "Update: Blood Lead Levels—United States, 1991–1994," *Mortality and Morbidity Weekly Report* 46, no. 7 (February 21, 1997): 141–146.

41. James L. Pinkle, D. J. Brody, E. W. Gunter, R. A. Kramer, D. C. Paschal, K. M. Glegal, and T. D. Matte, "The Decline in Blood Lead Levels in the United States: The National Health and Nutrition Examination Survey (NHANES),"*Journal of the American Medical Association* 272 (1994): 284–291.

42. Arnold W. Reitze, Jr., "A Century of Air Pollution Control Law: What Worked; What Failed; What Might Work," *Environmental Law* 21 (1991): 1549.

43. For an in-depth discussion of transportation investments and social equity issues, see R. D. Bullard and G. S. Johnson, eds., *Just Transportation: Dismantling Race and Class Barriers to Mobility.* Gabriola Island, BC: New Society Publishers, 1997.

44. Sid Davis, "Race and the Politics of Transportation in Atlanta," in R. D. Bullard and G. S. Johnson, *Just Transportation,* pp. 84–96; Environmental Justice Resource Center, *Sprawl Atlanta: Social Equity Dimensions of Uneven Growth and Development,* a report prepared for the Turner Foundation, Atlanta: Clark Atlanta University (January 1999).

45. D. R. Wernette and L. A. Nieves, "Breathing Polluted Air: Minorities Are Disproportionately Exposed," *EPA Journal* 18 (March 1992): 16–17.

46. CDC, "Asthma—United States, 1982–1992." *MMWR* 43 (1995): 952–955.

47. CDC, "Asthma Morality and Hospitalization among Children and Young Adults—United States, 1980–1993." *MMWR* 45 (1996): 350–353.

48. Anna E. Pribitkin, "The Need for Revision of Ozone Standards: Why Has the EPA Failed to Respond?" *Temple Environmental Law & Technology Journal* 13 (1994): 104.

49. CDC/NCHS, *Health United States* 1994, DHHS Pub. No. (PHS) 95-1232, Tables 83, 84, 86, 87.

50. CDC, "Asthma—United States, 1982–1992." *MMWR* 43 (1995): 952–955.

51. CDC, "Disabilities among Children Aged Less Than or Equal to 17 years—United States, 1991–1992." *MMWR* 44 (1995): 609–613.

52. U.S. EPA, "Review of National Ambient Air Quality Standards for Ozone, Assessment of Scientific and Technical Information," OAQPS Staff Paper, Research Triangle Park, NC: EPA, 1996; Haluk Ozkaynk, John D. Spengler, Marie O'Neil, Jianping Xue, Hui Zhou, Kathy Gilbert, and Sonja Ramstrom, "Ambient Ozone Exposure and Emergency Hospital Admissions and Emergency Room Visits for Respiratory Problems in Thirteen U.S. Cities," in American Lung Association, *Breathless: Air Pollution and Hospital Admissions/Emergency Room Visits in 13 Cities,* Washington, DC: American Lung Association, 1996; American Lung Association, *Out of Breath: Populations-at-Risk to Alternative Ozone Levels,* Washington, DC: American Lung Association, 1995.

53. Centers for Disease Control and Prevention, National Center for Environmental Health, Division of Environmental Hazards and Health Effects, Air Pollution and Respiratory Branch, "Asthma Mortality and Hospitalization Among Children and Young Adults—United States, 1980–1993," *Morbidity and Mortality Weekly Report,* 45 (1996).

54. Centers for Disease Control, "Asthma: United States, 1980–1990,"*MMWR* 39 (1992): 733–735.

55. Mary C. White, Ruth Etzel, Wallace D. Wilcox, and Christine Lloyd, "Exacerbations of Childhood Asthma and Ozone Pollution in Atlanta," *Environmental Research* 65 (1994): 56.

56. R. D. Bullard, "The Legacy of Apartheid and Environmental Racism," *St. John's Journal of Legal Commentary* 9 (Spring 1994): 445–474.

57. Donald Schueler, "Southern Exposure," *Sierra* 77 (November/December 1992): 45.

58. Robert D. Bullard, "Ecological Inequities and the New South: Black Communities Under Siege." *Journal of Ethnic Studies* 17 (Winter 1990): 101–115; Donald L. Bartlett and James B. Steele, "Paying a Price for Polluters," *Time* (November 23, 1998), pp. 72–80.

59. Schueler, "Southern Exposure," p. 46.

60. Ibid., pp. 46–47.

61. James O'Byrne and Mark Schleifstein, "Drinking Water in Danger," *The Times Picayune,* February 19, 1991, p. A5.

62. Conger Beasley, "Of Poverty and Pollution: Keeping Watch in Cancer Alley," pp. 39–45.

63. Bartlett and Steele, "Paying a Price for Polluters," p. 77.

64. Conger Beasley, "Of Pollutions and Poverty: Deadly Threat on Native Lands," *Buzzworm,* 2 (5) (1990): 39–45; Robert Tomsho, "Dumping Grounds: Indian Tribes Contend with Some of the Worst of America's Pollution," *The Wall Street Journal* (November 29, 1990); Jane Kay, "Indian Lands Targeted for Waste Disposal Sites," *San Francisco Examiner* (April 10, 1991); Valerie Taliman, "Stuck Holding the Nation's Nuclear Waste," *Race, Poverty & Environment Newsletter* (Fall 1992): 6–9.

65. Bradley Angel, *The Toxic Threat to Indian Lands: A Greenpeace Report.* San Francisco: Greenpeace, 1992; Al Geddicks, *The New Resource Wars: Native and Environmental Struggles Against Multinational Corporations,* Boston: South End Press, 1993.

66. Jane Kay, "Indian Lands Targeted for Waste Disposal Sites," *San Francisco Examiner* (April 10, 1991).

67. Ward Churchill and Winona la Duke, "Native America: The Political Economy of Radioactive Colonialism," *Insurgent Sociologist* 13 (1) (1983): 61–63.

68. Greenpeace, "The Logic Behind Hazardous Waste Export," *Greenpeace Waste Trade Update* (First Quarter 1992): 1–2.

69. Dana Alston and Nicole Brown, "Global Threats to People of Color," pp. 179–194 in R. D. Bullard, ed., *Confronting Environmental Racism: Voices from the Grassroots,* Boston: Southend Press, 1993.

70. Roberto Sanchez, "Health and Environmental Risks of the Maquiladora in Mexicali," *Natural Resources Journal* 30(1) (1990): 163–186.

71. Beatriz Johnston Hernandez, "Dirty Growth," *The New Environmentalist* (August 1993).

72. T. Barry and B. Simms, *The Challenge of Cross Border Environmentalism: The U.S. Mexico Case,* Albuquerque, NM: The Inter-Hemispheric Education Resource Center, 1994.

READING 24

Notes

1. Boston, John. 2003. "At Long Last, Going to Church Finally Pays." Online [cited 7 August 2003]. Available from http://www.the-signal.com/News/ViewStory.asp?storyID-2906.

2. Olson, Ted. 2004. "Fred Caldwell: Paying the Price for Unity." *Today's Christian,* July/August.

3. Excerpted from Emerson, Michael O. 2006. *People of the Dream: Multiracial Congregations in the United States.* Princeton, NJ: Princeton University Press, Chapter 2.

4. Hamilton, David L., and Tina K. Trolier. 1986. "Stereotype and Stereotyping: An Overview of the Cognitive Approach." In *Prejudice, Discrimination, and Racism,* eds. John F. Davidio and Samuel L. Gaertner, 127–63, Orlando, FL: Academic Press, p. 188.

5. These seven biases are the result of several research works. See Hewstone, Miles, Jos Jaspers, and Mansur Lalljee. 1992. "Social Representations, Social Attribution and Social Identity: The Intergroup Images of 'Public' and 'Comprehensive.'" *European Journal of Social Psychology* 12:241–69; Hogg, Michael A., and Dominic Abrams. 1988. *Social Identifications: A Social Psychology of Intergroup Relations and Group Processes.* London: Routledge; Howard, John W., and Myron Rothbart. 1980. "Social Categorization and Memory for In-group and Out-group Behavior." *Journal of Personality and Social Psychology* 38:301–10; Linville, Patricia W., Peter Salovey, and Gregory W. Fischer. 1986. "Stereotyping and Perceived Distributions of Social Characteristics: An Application to Ingroup-Outgroup Perception." In *Prejudice, Discrimination, and Racism,* eds. John F. Dovidio and Samuel L. Gaertner, 165–208, Orlando, FL: Academic Press; Tajfel, Henri. 1978. "Social Categorization, Social Identity and Social Comparison." In *Differentiation Between Social Groups: Studies in the Social Psychology of Intergroup Relations,* ed. Henri Tajfel, 61–76, London: Academic Press; Taylor, S. E. 1981. "A Categorization Approach to Stereotyping." In *Cognitive Processes in Stereotyping and Intergroup Behavior,* ed. D. L. Hamilton, 83–114, Hillsdale, NJ: Erlbaum; Wilder, D. A. 1981. "Perceiving Persons as a Group: Categorization and Ingroup Relations." In *Cognitive Processes in Stereotyping and Intergroup Behavior,* ed. D. L. Hamilton, 213–57, Hillsdale, NJ: Erlbaum.

6. Niebuhr, Reinhold. 1932. *Moral Man and Immoral Society: A Study in Ethics and Politics.* New York & London: C. Scribner's.

7. Niebuhr 1932:xxii–xxiii.

8. Hechter, Michael. 1987. *Principles of Social Solidarity.* Berkeley: University of California Press, p. 41.

9. This section was excerpted from Emerson, Michael O., and Christian Smith. 2000. *Divided by Faith: Evangelical Religion and the Problem of Race in America.* New York: Oxford University, Chapter 8.

10. Hollinger, David. 1995. *Postethnic America: Beyond Multiculturalism.* New York: Basic Books.

11. Much but not all of this section is excerpted from Emerson, Michael O. 2006. *People of the Dream,* Chapters 4 and 7.

READING 25

Notes

1. National Center for Health Statistics, Centers for Disease Control and Prevention. Deaths—leading causes. Available at: http://www.cdc.gov/nchs/fastats/lcod.htm. Accessed February 13, 2004.

2. Fried VM, Prager K, MacKay AP, Xia H. Chartbook on trends in the health of Americans. In: *Health, United States, 2003.* Hyattsville, Md: National Center for Health Statistics, 2003.

3. Jemal A, Thomas A, Murray T, Thun M. Cancer statistics, 2002. *CA Cancer J Clin.* 2002;52:23–47.

4. Ries Lag, Eisner MP, Kosary CL, et al., eds. SEER cancer statistics review, 1973–1999. Bethesda, Md: National Cancer Institute; 2002. Available at: http://seer.cancer.gov/csr/1973–1999. Accessed February 13, 2004.

5. *Healthy People 2010: Understanding and Improving Health.* Washington, DC: US Dept of Health and Human Services, 2001. Also available at: http://web.health.gov/healthypeople/document. Accessed January 1, 2005.

6. Fitzpatrick K, LaGory M. *Unhealthy Places: The Ecology of Risk in the Urban Landscape.* New York, NY: Routledge; 2000.

7. Lillie-Blanton M, LaVeist T. Race/ethnicity, the social environment, and health. *Soc Sci Med.* 1996;43:83–91.

8. Macintyre S, Maciver S, Sooman A. Area, class, and health: should we be focusing on places or people? *J Soc Policy.* 1993;22:213–234.

9. Yen J, Syme SL. The social environment and health: a discussion of the epidemiologic literature. *Annu Rev Public Health.* 1999;20:287–308.

10. Ellen I, Mijanovich GT, Dillman K. Neighborhood effects on health: exploring the links and assessing the evidence. *J Urban Aff.* 2001;23:391–408.

11. Pickett KE, Pearl M. Multilevel analyses of neighborhood socioeconomic context and health outcomes: a critical review. *J Epidemiol Community Health.* 2000;55:111–122.

12. Robert SA. Socioeconomic position and health: the independent contribution of community socioeconomic context. *Annu Rev Sociol* 1999;25:489–516.

13. Diez Roux AV. Investigating neighborhood and area effects on health. *Am J Public Health.* 2001;91:1783–1789.

14. Hillemeier MM, Lynch J, Harper S, Casper M. Measuring contextual characteristics for community health. *Health Serv Res.* 2004;38:1645–1717.

15. Macintyre S, Ellaway A, Cummins S. Place effects on health: how can we conceptualize, operationalize, and measure them? *Soc Sci Med.* 2002;55:125–139.

16. Mantovani RE, Daft L, Macaluso TF, Welsh J, Hoffman K. *Authorized Food Retailers' Characteristics and Access Study*. Alexandria, Va: US Dept of Agriculture, 1997.

17. Cheadle A, Psaty BM, Curry S, et al. Community-level comparisons between the grocery store environment and individual dietary practices. *Prev Med* 1991;20:250–261.

18. Cohen NL, Stoddard AM, Sarouhkhanians S, Sorensen G. Barriers toward fruit and vegetable consumption in a multiethnic worksite population. *J Nutr Educ.* 1998;30:381–386.

19. Drewnowski A, Specter SE. Poverty and obesity: the role of energy density and energy costs. *Am J Clin Nutr* 2004;79:6–16.

20. French SA, Story M, Jeffery RW. Environmental influences on eating and physical activity. *Annu Rev Public Health.* 2001;22:309–335.

21. Furst T, Connors M, Bisogni CA, Sobal J, Falk LW. Food choice: a conceptual model of the process. *Appetite.* 1996;26:247–266.

22. Glanz K, Basil M, Mailbach E, Goldberg J, Snyder D. Why Americans eat what they do: taste, nutrition, cost, convenience, and weight control concerns as influences on food consumption. *J Am Diet Assoc.* 1998;98:1118–1126.

23. Huang K. Role of national income and prices. In: Frazao E, ed. *America's Eating Habits: Changes and Consequences.* US Dept of Agriculture, 1999;161–171. Agriculture Information Bulletin No. 750.

24. Reicks M, Randall J, Haynes B. Factors affecting vegetable consumption in low-income households. *J Am Diet Assoc.* 1994;94:1309–1311.

25. Race and place matter for major Chicago area grocers. Chicago, Ill: Metro Chicago Information Center: Available at http://www.mcic.org. Accessed January 3, 2005.

26. Morland K, Wing S, Diez Roux A, Poole C. Neighborhood characteristics associated with the location of food stores and food service places. *Am J Prev Med.* 2002;22:23–29.

27. Alwitt LF, Donley TD. Retail stores in poor urban neighborhoods. *J Consum Aff.* 1997;31:139–164.

28. Chung C, Myers SL. Do the poor pay more for food? An analysis of grocery store availability and food price disparities. *J Consum Aff.* 1999; 33:276–296.

29. Cotterill RW, Franklin AW. *The Urban Grocery Store Gap.* Storrs, Conn: Food Marketing Policy Center, University of Connecticut, 1995.

30. Cummins S, Macintyre S. A systematic study of an urban foodscape: the price and availability of food in Greater Glasgow. *Urban Stud.* 2002;39:2115–2130.

31. Cummins S, Macintyre S. "Food deserts"—Evidence and assumption in health policy making. *BMJ.* 2002; 325:436–438.

32. Jones SJ. *The Measurement of Food Security at the Community Level: Geographic Information Systems and Participating Ethnographic Methods* [dissertation]. Chapel Hill, NC. University of North Carolina at Chapel Hill, 2002.

33. Donohue RM. *Abandonment and Revitalization of Central City Retailing: The Case of Grocery Stores* [dissertation]. Ann Arbor, Mich: University of Michigan, 1997.

34. The business case for pursuing retail opportunities in the inner city. Boston, Mass: The Boston Consulting Group and The Initiative for a Competitive Inner City, 1988. Available at: http://www.icic.org. Accessed January 3, 2005.

35. The changing models of inner city grocery retailing. Boston, Mass: The Initiative for a Competitive Inner City, 2002. Available at: http://www.icic.org. Accessed January 3, 2005.

36. Jargowsky PA. *Poverty and Place: Ghettos, Barrios, and the American City.* New York, NY: Russell Sage Foundation, 1997.

37. Massey DS, Denton NA. *American Apartheid: Segregation and the Making of the Underclass.* Cambridge, Mass: Harvard University Press, 1993.

38. Massey, DS, Fischer MJ. How segregation concentrates poverty. *Ethn Racial Stud.* 2000;23:670–691.

39. Sugrue TJ. *The Origins of the Urban Crisis: Race and Inequality in Postwar Detroit.* Princeton, NJ: Princeton University Press, 1996.

40. Wilson WJ. *The Truly Disadvantaged: The Inner City, the Underclass, and Public Policy.* Chicago, Ill: University of Chicago Press, 1987.

41. Farley R, Danziger S, Holzer HJ. *Detroit Divided.* New York, NY: Russell Sage Foundation, 2000.

42. Geronimus AT. To mitigate, resist, or undo: addressing structural influences on the health of urban populations. *Am J Public Health.* 2000;90:867–872.

43. Schulz A, Williams DR, Israel B, Lempert LB. Racial and spatial relations as fundamental determinants of health in Detroit. *Milbank Q.* 2002;80:677–707.

44. Darden JT, Hill RC, Thomas J, Thomas R. *Detroit: Race and Uneven Development.* Philadelphia, Pa: Temple University Press, 1987.

45. Collins CA, Williams DR. Segregation and mortality: the deadly effects of racism. *Social Forum.* 1999;14:495–523.

46. Thomas JM. *Redevelopment and Race: Planning a Finer City in Postwar Detroit.* Baltimore, Md: The Johns Hopkins University Press, 1997.

47. Williams DR, Collins CA. Racial residential segregation: a fundamental cause of racial disparities in health. *Public Health Rep.* 2001;116:404–416.

48. *Michigan Metropolitan Information Center 2000 Census Demographic Characteristics.* Detroit, Mich: The Center for Urban Studies, Wayne State University. Available at: http://www.cus.wayne.edu/census/censuspubs.aspx. Accessed January 3, 2005.

49. Iceland J, Weinberg DH, Steinmetz E. *Racial and Ethnic Residential Segregation in the United States: 1980–2000.* Washington, DC: US Government Printing Office, 2002. US Census Bureau, Series CENSR-3.

50. Kieffer E, Willis S, Odoms-Young A, et al. Reducing disparities in diabetes among African American and Latino residents of Detroit: the essential role of community planning focus groups. *Ethn Dis.* 2004;14:S1-27–S1-37.

51. Laraia BA, Siega-Riz AM, Kaufman JS, Jones SJ. Proximity to supermarkets is positively associated with diet quality index for pregnancy. *Prev Med.* 2004;39:869–875.

52. Morland K, Wing S, Diex Roux A. The contextual effect of the local food environment on residents' diets: the atherosclerosis risk in communities study. *Am J Public Health.* 2002;92:1761–1767.

53. Wrigley N, Warm D, Margetts B, Whelan A. Assessing the impact of improved retail access on diet in a "food desert": a preliminary report. *Urban Stud.* 2002;39:2061–2082.

54. Zenk SN. *Neighborhood Racial Composition, Neighborhood Poverty, and Food Access in Metropolitan Detroit: Geographic Information Systems and Spatial Analysis* [dissertation]. Ann Arbor, Mich: University of Michigan, 2004.

55. Hartigan J. *Racial Situations: Class Predicaments of Whiteness in Detroit.* Princeton, NJ: Princeton University Press, 1999.

56. Zunz O. *The Changing Face of Inequality: Urbanization, Industrial Development, and Immigrants in Detroit, 1880–1920.* Chicago, Ill: University of Chicago Press, 1982.

57. McWhirter C. Life of one street mirrors city's fall: racial fears trigger white flight in '50s. *The Detroit News.* June 17, 2001.

Available at: http://www.detnews.com/specialreports/2001/elmhurst. Accessed January 5, 2005.

58. Metzger K, Booza J. *African Americans in the United States, Michigan, and Metropolitan Detroit.* Detroit, Mich: Center for Urban Studies, Wayne State University, 2002. Center for Urban Studies Working Paper Series, No. 8.

59. McWhirter C. 1967 Riot sent street into wrenching spiral: once stable block withers as property owners desert. *The Detroit News.* June 18, 2001. Available at: http://www.detnews.com/specialreports/2001/elmhurst. Accessed January 5, 2005.

60. *1990 Census Subcommunity Profiles for the City of Detroit.* Detroit, Mich: Southeast Michigan Census Council, 1993.

61. *2000 Census Subcommunity Profiles for the City of Detroit.* Detroit, Mich: United Way Community Services, 2001.

62. Israel BA, Schulz AJ, Parker EA, Becker AB. Review of community-based research: assessing partnership approaches to improve public health. *Annu Rev Public Health.* 1998;19:173–201.

63. James SA. Primordial prevention of cardiovascular disease among African Americans: a social epidemiological perspective. *Prev Med.* 1999;29:S84–S89.

64. Pothukuchi K. Attracting supermarkets to inner city neighborhoods: economic development out of the box. *Econ Dev Q.* In press.

65. *The African American Grocery Shopper 2000.* Washington DC: Food Marketing Institute; 2000.

66. Pothukuchi K, Kaufman JL. Placing the food system on the urban agenda: the role of municipal institutions in food system planning. *Agric Human Values.* 1999;16:213–224.

67. Ashman L, Vega J, Dohan M, Fisher A, Hipper R, Romain B. *Seeds of Change: Strategies for Food Security for the Inner City.* Los Angeles, Calif: University of California Los Angeles; 1993.

68. Gottlieb R, Fisher A, Dohan M, O'Connor L, Parks V. *Homeward Bound: Food-Related Transportation Strategies for Low Income and Transit Dependent Communities.* Los Angeles, Calif: University of California Transportation Center, 1996. Available at: http://www.foodsecurity.org/homewardbound.pdf. Accessed February 13, 2004.

69. Cohen HW, Northridge ME. Getting political: racism and urban health. *Am J Public Health* 2000;90:841–842.

READING 26

Notes

1. Jim Newton, "Judges Voice Anger over Mandatory U.S. Sentences," *L.A. Times,* 21 August 1993, A1.

2. As of 1995, there were 14,000 people in prison for federal crack convictions, 80 percent of whom were black. Ronald

Smothers, "Wave of Prison Uprisings Provokes Debate on Crack," *N.Y. Times,* 24 October 1995, A18.

3. H. R. Rep. No. 104-272 at 20 (1995), reprinted in 1995 U.S.C.C.A.N. 335,353 (citing U.S. Sentencing Commission study).

4. *United States v. Armstrong,* 517 U.S. 456 (1996) (Stevens, J., dissenting) (citing United States Sentencing Commission, Special Report to Congress: *Cocaine and Federal Sentencing Policy,* 39, 161, 1995).

5. *United States v. Clary,* 846 F. Supp. 768, 787 (E. D. Mo. 1994); see also *United States v. Walls,* 841 F. Supp. 24, 28 (D.D.C. 1994).

6. *State v. Russell,* 477 N.W. 2d 886, 887 n.1 (Minn. 1991). In the Eastern District of Missouri, 98.2 percent of defendants convicted of crack cocaine charges from 1988 to 1992 were black. *United States v. Clary,* 846 F. Supp. at 786.

7. See, e.g., *United States v. Richardson,* 130 F. 3d 765 (7th Cir. 1997); *United States v. Andrade,* 94 F. 3d 9 (1st Cir. 1996); *United States v. Teague,* 93 F. 3d 81 (2d Cir. 1996), *cert. denied,* 117 S. Ct. 708 (1997); *United States v. Lloyd,* 10 F. 3d 1197 (6th Cir. 1993), *cert. denied,* 513 U.S. 883 (1994); *United States v. Jackson,* 67 F. 3d 1359 (8th Cir. 1995), *cert. denied,* 517 U.S. 1192 (1996).

8. United States Sentencing Comm., Special Report to the Congress, *supra* note 4.

9. In 1997, the Sentencing Commission recommended reducing rather than eliminating the disparity, and the Clinton Administration supported the proposal. As of this writing, Congress has not acted on the recommendation.

10. *Stephens v. State,* 1995 WL 116292 (Ga. S. Ct. Mar. 17, 1995).

11. *Stephens v. State,* 456 S.E. 2d 560 (Ga. 1995).

12. American Bar Association, *The State of Criminal Justice,* 9 (February 1993) (23 percent minority increase, 10 percent nonminority).

13. Id.

14. Jerome G. Miller, *Search and Destroy: African American Males in the Criminal Justice System,* 81 (New York: Cambridge Univ. Press, 1996).

15. Marc Mauer & Tracy Juling, The Sentencing Project, *Young Black Americans and the Criminal Justice System: Five Years Later,* 12 (1995).

16. David J. Rothman, "The Crime of Punishment," *New York Rev. of Books,* 17 February 1994, 34, 37.

17. Jerome G. Miller, *Search and Destroy, supra* note 14.

18. Id.

19. Id.

20. Marc Mauer, *Intended and Unintended Consequences: State Racial Disparities in Imprisonment,* 10 (Sentencing Project, Jan. 1997).

21. Human Rights Watch, *Cruel and Unusual: Disproportionate Sentences for New York Drug Offenders,* 2 (March 1997).

22. Dep't of Justice, Bureau of Justice Statistics Bulletin, *Prisoners in 1994,* 10, Table 13 (1995).

23. Id. at 11, Table 14 (state prisoners incarcerated on drug offenses increased from 19,000 in 1980 to 186,000 in 1993).

24. American Bar Association, *State of Criminal Justice, supra* note 12.

25. Office of Juvenile Justice and Delinquency Programs, *Juvenile Court Statistics 1991,* 25, Table 35, 71, Table 114 (May 1994). In this source, Hispanic youth were included in the "white" racial category.

26. 13,800 black juveniles were detained for drug violations, as compared to 7,400 white juveniles. Id. at 74, Table 118, 28, Table 39.

27. Id. at 29, Table 40.

28. Id. at 25, Table 37.

29. National Center on Institutions and Alternatives, *Hobbling a Generation: Young African American Males in the Criminal Justice System of America's Cities: Baltimore, Maryland* (September 1992).

30. See, e.g., Randall Kennedy, "The State, Criminal Law, and Racial Discrimination: A Comment," 107 Harv. L. Rev. 1255 (1994). For a detailed response, see David Cole, "The Paradox of Race and Crime: A Comment on Randall Kennedy's 'Politics of Distinction," 83 Geo. L.J. 2547 (1995); see also Randall Kennedy, "A Response to Professor Cole's 'Paradox of Race and Crime,'" 83 *Geo. L.J.* 2573 (1995).

31. National Institute of Justice, Department of Justice, *Three Strikes and You're Out: A Review of State Legislation,* 1 (September 1997); Tom Rhodes, "Third Strike and Pizza Thief Is Out for 25 Years," *The Times,* 4 April 1996 (available on NEXIS).

32. Maura Dolan & Tony Perry, "Justices Deal Blow to '3 Strikes,'" *L.A. Times,* 31 June 1996, A1.

33. Id.; see also The President's Radio Address, Weekly Comp. Pres. Doc. 1493 (July 16, 1994) (supporting "three strikes and you're out" provision in federal crime bill).

34. Rhodes, *supra* note 31.

35. Daniel B. Wood, "Softer Three-Strikes Law Brings Wave of Appeals," *Christian Science Monitor,* 24 June 1996, 3.

36. Christopher Davis, Richard Estes, and Vincent Schiraldi, "Three Strikes": The New Apartheid (Report of the Center on Juvenile and Criminal Justice, San Francisco, March 1996).

37. Fox Butterfield, "Tough Law on Sentences Is Criticized," *N.Y. Times,* 8 March 1996, A14.

38. See, e.g., Andy Furillo, "Most Offenders Have Long Criminal Histories," *Sacramento Bee,* 31 March 1996, A1.

39. Id.

40. William Spelman, *Criminal Incapacitation,* 15 (New York: Plenum Press, 1994) ("the typical criminal career lasts only 5 to 10 years"); 1 *Criminal Careers and Career Criminals,* 94

(Alfred Blumstein et al., eds.) (Washington, D.C.: National Academy Press, 1986) (same).

41. Daniel B. Wood, "LA Police Lash Out Against Three Strikes," *Christian Science Monitor,* 29 March 1996, 3.

42. Fox Butterfield, *supra* note 37.

43. Id.

44. Ian Katz, "Bull Market in Prisons and Knee-Jerk Politics," *The Guardian,* 25 May 1996 (available on NEXIS).

45. Bureau of Justice Statistics, *Sourcebook of Criminal Justice Statistics—1995,* Table 6.11 (1996).

46. Ann Golenpaul, ed., *Information Please Almanac,* 829 (Boston: Houghton Mifflin, 1997).

47. Ian Katz, *supra* note 44.

48. Christopher Davis, et al., *supra* note 36.

49. Douglas C. McDonald & Kenneth E. Carlson, *Sentencing in the Federal Courts: Does Race Matter? The Transition to Sentencing Guidelines, 1986–90: Summary,* 1–2 (Washington, D.C.: Bureau of Justice Statistics, 1993).

50. Id. at 13–17.

51. Id. at 16–17.

52. See, e.g. Stephen Klein, Joan Petersilia, and Susan Turner, "Race and Imprisonment Decisions in California," 247 *Science* 812–16 (Feb. 16, 1990) (studying California sentences and concluding that race did not improve the accuracy of predicting what type of punishment offenders would receive); Alfred Blumstein, "On the Racial Disproportionality of United States Prison Populations," 73 J. of Crim. L. & Crim. 1259 (1983) (finding little evidence of racial bias in incarceration for serious crimes); but see Jerome Miller, *Search and Destroy, supra* note 14 (reviewing studies finding evidence of racial discrimination); Crutchfield, et. al, "Analytical and Aggregation Biases in Analysis of Imprisonment: Reconciling Discrepancies in Studies of Racial Disparity," 31 J. of Res. In Crime & Delinquency 178 (1994) (critiquing prior studies for aggregating information in a way that might conceal discrimination; finding evidence of discrimination).

53. Michael H. Tonry, *Malign Neglect: Race, Crime, and Punishment in America,* 29 (New York: Oxford Univ. Press, 1995).

54. Barbara S. Meierhoefer, "Individualized and Systemic Justice in the Federal Sentencing Process," 29 Am. Crim. L. Rev. 889, 891 (1992).

55. William Wilbanks, *The Myth of a Racist Criminal Justice System* (Monterey, CA: Brooks/Cole, 1986).

56. Stephen P. Klein, *Racial Disparities in Sentencing Decisions,* 5 (Santa Monica, CA: Rand, 1991).

57. Unless otherwise indicated, the information in the next two paragraphs is drawn from Bonnie Whitebread, "Marijuana Prohibition," 56 U.Va. L. Rev. 983 (1970).

58. Whitebread, 56 Va. L. Rev. at 1096.

59. Gertrude Samuels, "Pot, Hard Drugs, and the Law," *N.Y. Times Magazine,* 15 February 1970, 14.

60. Richard J. Bonnie, "The Meaning of 'Decriminalization': A Review of the Law," Contemporary Drug Problems 277, 278 (Fall 1981).

61. Id. at 279; see also Bureau of Justice Statistics, U.S. Dept of Justice, *Drugs, Crime and the Justice System,* 84–85 (1992) (reporting that when large numbers of white middle-class youth were arrested for marijuana possession in the late 1960s and early 1970s, public complaints led Congress and eleven states to decriminalize or reduce substantially the penalties for that crime).

READING 27

Notes

1. Richard Morin, "Misperceptions Cloud Whites' View of Blacks," *Washington Post,* July 11, 2001, p. A01.

2. "Washington Post/Kaiser/Harvard Racial Attitudes Survey," *Washington Post,* July 11, 2001, p. A01.

3. See Joe R. Feagin, Hernan Vera, and Pinar Batur, *White Racism: The Basics,* 2nd ed. (New York: Routledge, 2001), especially chapters 7 and 8.

4. See Joe R. Feagin and Melvin P. Sikes, *Living with Racism: The Black Middle Class Experience* (Boston: Beacon Press, 1994); Yanick St. Jean and Joe R. Feagin, *Double Burden: Black Women and Everyday Racism* (New York: M. E. Sharpe, 1998); and Joe R. Feagin, *Racist America: Roots, Current Realities, and Future Reparations* (New York: Routledge, 2000).

5. *Etter v. Veriflo Corporation,* 67 Cal. App. 4th 457, 79 Cal. Rptr. 2d 33 (1st Dist. Cr. App. 1998). We summarize here the discussion in Joe R. Feagin and Karyn D. McKinney, *The Many Costs of Racism* (Lanham, MD: Rowman & Littlefield, 2003), chapter 1; see also Steven Keeva, "A Bumpy Road to Equality: Panelists Say Courts Are Backpedaling on Minority Issues," *ABA Journal* (1996): 32.

6. See Feagin, *Racist America,* chapters 3–4.

7. See Feagin, Vera, and Batur, *White Racism,* chapter 5.

8. Kristen Myers and Passion Williamson, "Race Talk: The Perpetuation of Racism through Private Discourse," *Race & Society* 4 (2001): 3–26.

9. For the general point in the sociological literature, see Ruth A. Wallace and Alison Worl, *Contemporary Sociological Theory,* 4th ed. (Englewood Cliffs, NJ: Prentice Hall, 1995), pp. 290–92.

10. David L. Carter and Thomas Barker, "Administrative Guidance and Control of Police Officer Behavior: Policies, Procedures, and Rules," in *Police Deviance,* ed. Thomas Barker and David L. Carter (Cincinnati: Anderson, 1991), pp. 13–28.

11. Jonathan Wright, "Rights Group Says Police Brutality Rife in U.S." (Reuters, 1998), 1.

12. See Feagin, Vera, and Batur, *White Racism;* and Feagin and Sikes, *Living with Racism.*

READING 28

Notes

1. *The Challenge of Crime in a Free Society: A Report by the President's Commission on Law Enforcement and Administration of Justice* (Washington, DC: Government Printing Office, 1967).

2. Ronald Goldfarb, "Prisons: The National Poorhouse," *New Republic,* November 1, 1969, pp. 15–17.

3. Philip Hart, "Swindling and Knavery, Inc.," *Playboy,* August 1972, p. 158.

4. Compare the statement, written more than half a century ago, by Professor Edwin H. Sutherland, one of the major luminaries of twentieth-century criminology:

   First, the administrative processes are more favorable to persons in economic comfort than to those in poverty, so that if two persons on different economic levels are equally guilty of the same offense, the one on the lower level is more likely to be arrested, convicted, and committed to an institution. Second, the laws are written, administered, and implemented primarily with reference to the types of crimes committed by people of lower economic levels [E. H. Sutherland, Principles of Criminology (Philadelphia: Lippincott, 1939), p. 179].

5. For example, in 1991, when blacks made up 12 percent of the national population, they accounted for 46 percent of the U.S. state prison population. BJS, *Survey of State Prison Inmates,* 1991, p. 3.

6. Edwin H. Sutherland and Donald R. Cressey, *Criminology,* 9th ed. (Philadelphia: Lippincott, 1974), p. 133. The following studies are cited in support of this point (p. 133, note 4): Edwin M. Lemert and Judy Roseberg, "The Administration of Justice to Minority Groups in Los Angeles County," University of California Publications in Culture and Society 2, no. 1 (1948), pp. 1–28; Thorsten Sellin, "Race Prejudice in the Administration of Justice," *American Journal of Sociology* 41 (September 1935), pp. 212–217; Sidney Alexrad, "Negro and White Male Institutionalized Delinquents," *American Journal of Sociology* 57 (May 1952), pp. 569–74; Marvin E. Wolfgang, Arlene Kelly and Hans C. Nolde, "Comparisons of the Executed and the Commuted among Admissions to Death Row," *Journal of Criminal Law, Criminology, and Police Science* 53 (September 1962), pp. 301–11; Nathan Goldman, *The Differential Selection of Juvenile Offenders for Court Appearance* (New York: National Council on Crime and Delinquency, 1963); Irving Piliavin and Scott Briar, "Police Encounters with Juveniles," *American Journal of Sociology* 70 (September 1964), pp. 206–14; Robert M. Terry, "The Screening of Juvenile Offenders," *Journal of Criminal Law, Criminology, and Police Science* 58 (June 1967), pp. 173–81. See also

Ramsey Clark, *Crime in America* (New York: Simon & Schuster, 1970), p. 51: "Negoes are arrested more frequently and on less evidence than whites and are more often victims of mass or sweep arrests"; and Donald Taft, *Criminology,* 3rd ed. (New York: Macmillan, 1956), p. 134:

Negroes are more likely to be suspected of crime than are whites. They are also more likely to be arrested. If the perpetrator of a crime is known to be a Negro the police may arrest all Negroes who were near the scene—a procedure they would rarely dare to follow with whites. After arrest Negroes are less likely to secure bail, and so are more liable to be counted in jail statistics. They are more liable than whites to be indicted and less likely to have their case nol prossed or otherwise dismissed. If tried, Negroes are more likely to be convicted. If convicted they are less likely to be given probation. For this reason they are more likely to be included in the count of prisoners. Negroes are also more likely than whites to be kept in prison for the full terms of their commitments and correspondingly less likely to be paroled.

7. William Wilbanks, *The Myth of a Racist Criminal Justice System* (Monterey, Calif.: Brooks/Cole, 1987).

8. Ibid., pp. 64–65.

9. *Sourcebook—1998,* p. 186, Table 3.26; p. 342, Table 4.10, *UCR—1998;* pp. 228.

10. For an overview of this double distortion, see Thomas J. Dolan, "The Case for Double Jeopardy: Black and Poor," *International Journal of Criminology and Penology* 1 (1973), pp. 129–50.

11. *StatAbst—1998,* p. 480, Table 762. See also Karen Pennar, "The Rich Are Richer—And America May Be the Poorer," *Business Week,* November 18, 1991, pp. 85–88.

12. Francine Blau and John Graham, "Black-White Differences in Wealth and Asset Composition," *Quarterly Journal of Economics* (May 1990), p. 323; David Swinton, "The Economic Status of African Americans during the Reagan-Bush Era: Withered Opportunities, Limited Outcomes, and Uncertain Outlook," in *The State of Black America* (New York: National Urban League, 1993), p. 138.

13. *Economic Report of the President,* February 1998, pp. 130–31.

14. *StatAbst—1998,* p. 407, Table 651.

15. Michael Tonry, "Racial Politics, Racial Disparities, and the War on Crime," *Crime & Delinquency* 40, no. 4 (October 1994), pp. 483, 485–86.

16. *Sourcebook—1981,* p. 463.

17. *StatAbst—1988,* p. 175, Table 304.

18. BJS, *Profile of Inmates in the United States and England and Wales, 1991* (October 1994, NCJ145863), p. 13.

19. Theodore Chiricos and William Bales, "Unemployment and Punishment: An Empirical Assessment," *Criminology* 29, no. 4 (1991), p. 718.

20. "An offender's socioeconomic status . . . did not impact sentence length for any of the property offenses." Stewart J. D'Alession and Lisa Stolzenberg, "Socioeconomic Status and the Sentencing of the Traditional Offender," *Journal of Criminal Justice* 21 (1993), p. 73. The same study did find that lower-socioeconomic-status offenders received harsher sentences for violent and moral-order crimes. Another study that finds no greater likelihood of incarceration based on socioeconomic status is Michael Benson and Esteban Walker, "Sentencing the White-Collar Offender," *American Sociological Review 53* (April 1988), pp. 294–302. And yet another found higher-status offenders to be more likely to be incarcerated: David Weisburd, Elin Waring, and Stanton Wheeler, "Class, Status, and the Punishment of White Collar Criminals," *Law and Social Inquiry 15* (1990), pp. 223–41. These last two studies are limited to offenders convicted of white-collar crimes, and so they deal with a sample that has already been subject to whatever discrimination exists in the arrest, charging, and conviction of white-collar offenders.

21. Isidore Silver, "Introduction to the Avon edition of *The Challenge of Crime in a Free Society*" (New York: Avon, 1968), p. 31.

22. This is the conclusion of Austin L. Porterfield, *Youth in Trouble* (Fort Worth, Tex.: Leo Potishman Foundation, 1946); Fred J. Murphy, M. Shirley, and H. L. Witmer, "The Incidence of Hidden Delinquency," *American Journal of Orthopsychiatry 16* (October 1946), pp. 686–96; James F. Short, Jr., "A Report on the Incidence of Criminal Behavior, Arrests, and Convictions in Selected Groups," *Proceedings of the Pacific Sociology Society, 1954,* pp. 110–18, published as vol. 22, no. 2 of *Research Studies of the State College of Washington* (Pullman: State College of Washington, 1954); F. Ivan Nye, James F. Short, Jr., and Virgil J. Olson, "Socioeconomic Status and Delinquent Behavior," *American Journal of Sociology 63* (January 1958), pp. 381–89; Maynard L. Erikson and Lamar T. Empey, "Class Position, Peers and Delinquency," *Sociology and Social Research 49* (April 1965), pp. 268–82; William J. Chambliss and Richard H. Nagasawa, "On the Validity of Official Statistics; A Comparative Study of White, Black, and Japanese High-School Boys," *Journal of Research in Crime and Delinquency* 6(January 1969), pp. 71–77; Eugene Dolescal, "Hidden Crime," *Crime and Delinquency Literature 2, no. 5* (October 1970), pp. 546–72; Nanci Koser Wilson, *Risk Ratios in Juvenile Delinquency* (Ann Arbor, Mich.: University Microfilms, 1972); and Maynard L. Erikson, "Group Violations, Socioeconomic Status, and Official Delinquency," *Social Forces 52, no. 1* (September 1973), pp. 41–52.

23. Charles R. Tittle and Robert F. Meier, "Specifying the SES/Delinquency Relationship," *Criminology 28, no. 2* (1990), p. 292.

24. Gary F. Jensen and Kevin Thompson, "What's Class Got to Do With It? A Further Examination of Power-Control Theory," *American Journal of Sociology 95,* no. 4 (January 1990), p. 1021.

25. This is the conclusion of Martin Gold, "Undetected Delinquent Behavior," *Journal of Research in Crime and Delinquency* 3, no. 1 (1966), pp. 27–46; and of Sutherland and Cressey, *Criminology,* pp. 137, 220.

26. Cf. Larry Karacki and Jackson Toby, "The Uncommitted Adolescent: Candidate for Gang Socialization," *Sociological Inquiry 32* (1962), pp. 203–15; William R. Arnold, "Continuities in Research—Scaling Delinquent Behavior," *Social Problems* 13, no. 1 (1965), pp. 59–66; Harwin L. Voss, "Socio-economic Status and Reported Delinquent Behavior," *Social Problems,* 13, no. 3 (1966), pp. 314–24; LaMar Empey and Maynard L. Erikson, "Hidden Delinquency and Social Status," *Social Forces* 44, no. 4 (1966), pp. 546–54; Fred J. Shanley, "Middle-Class Delinquency As a Social Problem," *Sociology and Social Research* 51 (1967), pp. 185–98; Jay R. Williams and Martin Gold, "From Delinquent Behavior to Official Delinquency," *Social Problems* 20, no. 2 (1972), pp. 209–29.

27. Empey and Erikson, "Hidden Delinquency and Social Status," pp. 549, 551. Nye, Short, and Olson also found destruction of property to be committed most frequently by upper-class boys and girls, "Socioeconomic Status and Delinquent Behavior," p. 385.

28. Williams and Gold, "From Delinquent Behavior to Official Delinquency."

29. Gold, "Undetected Delinquent Behavior," p. 37.

30. Ibid., p. 44.

31. Comparing socioeconomic status categories, "scant evidence is found that would support the contention that group delinquency is more characteristic of the lower-status levels than other socioeconomic status levels. In fact, only arrests seem to be more characteristic of the low-status category than the other categories." Erikson, "Group Violations, Socioeconomic Status and Official Delinquency," p. 15.

32. Gold, "Undetected Delinquent Behavior," p. 28 (emphasis added).

33. Ibid., p. 38.

34. "Stealing $200 Billion the Respectable Way," *U.S. News & World Report,* May 20, 1985, p. 83.

35. Marshall B. Clinard, *Corporate Corruption: The Abuse of Corporate Power* (New York: Praeger, 1990), p. 15.

36. August Bequai, "High-Tech Security and the Failings of President Clinton's Commission on Critical Infrastructure Protection," *Computer and Security* 17 (1998), pp. 19–21.

37. Michael Levi, *Regulating Fraud: White-Collar Crime and the Criminal Process* (London: Tavistock, 1987), p. 33; *StatAbst—1998,* p. 456, Table 721.

38. *UCR–1998,* p. 210, Table 29.

39. See, for example, Theodore G. Chiricos, Philip D. Jackson, and Gordon P. Waldo, "Inequality in the Imposition of a Criminal Label," *Social Problems* 19, no. 4 (Spring 1972), pp. 553–72.

40. A good summary of these developments can be found in Joel Jay Finer, "Ineffective Assistance of Counsel," *Cornell Law Review* 58, no. 6 (July 1973), pp. 1077–1120.

41. Lesely Oelsner, "Wide Disparities Mark Sentences Here," *The New York Times,* September 27, 1972, p. 1.

42. Stewart J. D'Alession and Lisa Stolzenberg, "Socioeconomic Status and the Sentencing of the Traditional Offender," *Journal of Criminal Justice* 21 (1993), pp. 71–74.

43. Barbara C. Nienstedt, Marjorie Zatz, and Thomas Epperlein, "Court Processing and Sentencing of Drinking Drivers," *Journal of Quantitative Criminology* 4, no. 1 (1988), pp. 39–59.

44. Theodore Chiricos and William Bales, "Unemployment and Punishment: An Empirical Assessment," *Criminology* 29, no. 4 (1991), pp. 701–24.

45. Belinda R. McCarthy, "A Micro-Level Analysis of Social Control: Intrastate Use of Jail and Prison Confinement," *Justice Quarterly* 7, no. 2 (June 1990), pp. 334–35.

46. Dean J. Champion, "Private Counsels and Public Defenders: A Look at Weak Cases, Prior Records, and Leniency in Plea Bargaining," p. 143.

47. T. Miethe and C. Moore, "Socioeconomic Disparities under Determinate Sentencing Systems: A Comparison of Pre-guideline and Postguideline Practices in Minnesota," *Criminology* 23, no. 2 (1985), p. 358.

48. Robert Tillman and Henry Pontell, "Is Justice 'Collar-Blind'?: Punishing Medical Provider Fraud," *Criminology* 30, no. 4 (1992), pp. 547–73, quote from p. 560.

49. James F. Nelson, "Hidden Disparities in Case Processing: New York State, 1985–1986," *Journal of Criminal Justice* 20 (1992), pp. 181–200.

50. J. D. Unnever and L. A. Hembroff, "The Prediction of Racial/Ethnic Sentencing Disparities," *Journal of Research in Crime and Delinquency* 25 (1988), p. 53.

51. C. Crawford, T. Chiricos, and G. Kleck, "Race, Racial Threat, and Sentencing of Habitual Offenders," *Criminology* 36, no. 3 (1998), pp. 481–511.

52. BJS, *Prisoners in 1994,* August 1995 (NCJ-151654), p. 9; BJS, *Prison and Jail Inmates, 1995,* p. 10; *Sourcebook—1994,* Table 4.11, p. 388.

53. *Sourcebook—1987,* pp. 376, 491, 518; *Sourcebook–1992,* p. 492, Table 5.21.

54. *Criminal Justice Newsletter,* March 1, 1995, p. 3; *Criminal Justice Newsletter,* April 17, 1995, p. 5.

55. McDonald, Douglas, and Carlson, *Sentencing in the Federal Courts: Does Race Matter?* (Washington, D.C.: BJS, 1993), cited in Michael Tonry, "Racial Politics, Racial Disparities, and the War on Crime," *Crime & Delinquency* 40, no. 4 (October 1994), p. 487.

56. Ronald Smothers, "Wave of Prison Uprisings Provokes Debate on Crack," *The New York Times,* October 24, 1995, p. A12.

57. "Blacks Receive Stiffer Sentences," *Boston Globe,* April 4, 1979, pp. 1, 50f.

58. Randall Thomson and Matthew Zingraff, "Detecting Sentencing Disparity: Some Problems and Evidence," *American Journal of Sociology* 86, no. 4 (1981), pp. 869–80, especially p. 875.

59. J. Unnever, C. Frazier, and J. Henretta, "Race Differences in Criminal Sentencing," *Sociological Quarterly* 21 (Spring 1980), pp. 197–205, especially p. 204.

60. J. Petersillia, "Racial Disparities in the Criminal Justice System: A Summary," *Crime & Delinquency* 31, no. 1 (1985), p. 28. See also G. Bridges and R. Crutchfield, "Law, Social Standing and Racial Disparities in Imprisonment," *Social Forces* 66, no. 3 (1988), pp. 699–724.

61. M. Myers, "Economic Inequality and Discrimination in Sentencing," *Social Forces* 65, no. 3 (1987), p. 761.

62. Mary Pat Flaherty and Joan Biskupic, "Rules Often Impose Toughest Penalties on Poor, Minorities," *The Washington Post,* October 9, 1996, p. A26.

63. Barbara S. Meierhoefer, *The General Effect of Mandatory Minimum Prison Terms: A Longitudinal Study of Federal Sentences Imposed* (Washington, D.C.: Federal Judicial Center, 1992), especially pp. 1, 20, 25. Between October 1989 and 1990, 46 percent of whites received federal sentences below the mandatory minimum, but 32 percent of blacks did. *Sourcebook—1991,* p. 542, Table 5.43.

64. Mary Pat Flaherty and Joan Biskupic, "Rules Often Impose Toughest Penalties on Poor, Minorities."

65. William J. Bowers and Glenn L. Pierce, "Racial Discrimination and Criminal Homicide under Post-Furman Capital Statutes," in H. A. Bedau, ed., *The Death Penalty in America* (New York: Oxford University Press, 1982), pp. 206–24.

66. *McCleskey v. Kemp,* 107 S. Ct. 1756 (1987). The research central to this case was that of David Baldus, reported in D. Baldus, C. Pulaski, and G. Woodworth, "Comparative Review of Death Sentences: An Empirical Study of the Georgia Experience," *Journal of Criminal Law and Criminology* 74 (1983), pp. 661–725. Other studies that support the notion of discrimination in capital sentencing based on race of victim are R. Paternoster, "Race of Victim and Location of Crime: The Decision to Seek the Death Penalty in South Carolina," *Journal of Criminal Law and Criminology* 74, no. 3 (1983), pp. 754–88; R. Paternoster, "Prosecutorial Discretion in Requesting the Death Penalty: A Case of Victim Based Racial Discrimination," *Law and Society Review* 18 (1984), pp. 437–78; S. Gross

and R. Mauro, "Patterns of Death: An Analysis of Racial Disparities in Capital Sentencing and Homicide Victimization," *Stanford Law Review* 37 (1984), pp. 27–120; Radelet and Pierce, "Race and Prosecutorial Discretion in Homicide Cases," *Law and Society Review* 19 (1985), pp. 587, 615–19.

67. Anthony G. Amsterdam, "Race and the Death Penalty," in S. Gold, ed., *Moral Controversies* (Belmont, Calif.: Wadsworth, 1993), pp. 268–69.

68. U.S. General Accounting Office, Report to the Senate and House Committees on the Judiciary, *Death Penalty Sentencing: Research Indicates Pattern of Racial Disparities* (February 1990), especially p. 5.

69. Marvin E. Wolfgang, Arlene Kelly, and Hans C. Nolde, "Comparison of the Executed and the Commuted among Admissions to Death Row," in *Crime and Justice in Society,* ed. Quinney pp. 508, 513.

70. "Antitrust: Kauper's Last Stand," *Newsweek,* June 21, 1976, p. 70. On December 21, 1974, the Antitrust Procedures and Penalty Act was passed, striking out the language of the Sherman Antitrust Act, which made price fixing a misdemeanor punishable by a maximum sentence of one year in prison. According to the new law, price fixing is a felony punishable by up to three years in prison. Because prison sentences were a rarity under the old law and usually involved only 30 days in jail when actually imposed, there is little reason to believe the new law will strike fear in the hearts of corporate crooks.

71. Marshall Clinard and Peter Yeager, *Corporate Crime* (New York: Free Press, 1980), pp. 291–92.

72. Ibid., p. 153.

73. *The Washington Post,* March 2, 1990, pp. A1, A20; April 1, 1990, p. C3; April 28, 1990, pp. A1, A14; April 27, 1991, p. A6.

74. K. Johnson, "Federal Court Processing of Corporate, White Collar, and Common Crime Economic Offenders over the Past Three Decades," *Mid-American Review of Sociology* 11, no. 1 (1986), pp. 25–44.

75. J. Hagan and P. Palloni, "'Club Fed' and the Sentencing of White-Collar Offenders Before and After Watergate," *Criminology* 24, no. 4 (1986), pp. 616–17. See also J. Hagan and P. Parker, "White-Collar Crime and Punishment: The Class Structure and Legal Sanctioning of Securities Violations," *American Sociological Review* 50 (1985), pp. 302–16.

76. John P. Wright, Francis T. Cullen, and Michael B. Blankenship, "The Social Construction of Corporate Violence: Media Coverage of the Imperial Food Products Fire," *Crime & Delinquency* 41, no. 1 (January 1995), pp. 23–24; Laurie Grossman, "Owner Sentenced to Nearly 20 Years over Plant Fire," *The Wall Street Journal,* September 15, 1992, p. A10.

77. Tom Wicker, *A Time to Die* (New York: Quadrangle, 1975), pp. 311, 314.

78. Ibid., p. 310.

79. *Sourcebook—1987,* p. 486, BJS, *Correctional Populations in the United States, 1985,* p. 10, Table 2.6; *StatAbst—1988,* p. 13, Table 13; BJS, *Prisoners in 1998* (NCJ175687); BJS, *Prison and Jail Inmates at Midyear 1998* (NCJ173414); U.S. Bureau of the Census, Current Population Reports, Series PPL-57, U.S. Population Estimates by Age, Sex, Race, and Hispanic Origin: 1990–1996.

80. BJS, *Survey of State Prison Inmates,* 1991, p. 3.

81. BJS, *Criminal Offender Statistics,* at http://www.ojp.usdoj.gov/bjs/crimoff.htm (last revised December 5, 1999); and BJS, *Profile of Jail Inmates 1996* (April 1998, NCJ164620).

82. *Economic Report of the President,* February 1998, p. 331, Table B-43.

83. *Economic Report of the President,* February 1998, p. 320, Table B-33.

84. BJS, *Criminal Offender Statistics,* "Comparing Federal and State Prison Inmates."

References

Anderson, David. *Crime and the Politics of Hysteria: How the Willie Horton Story Changed American Justice.* New York: Times Books, 1995.

Clinard, Marshall. *Corporate Corruption: The Abuse of Power.* New York: Praeger, 1990.

Day, Kathleen. *S & L Hell: The People and the Politics Behind the $1 Trillion Savings and Loan Scandal.* New York: Norton, 1993.

Lusane, Clarence. *Pipe Dream Blues: Racism and the War on Drugs.* Boston: South End Press, 1991.

Lynch, Michael, and E. Britt Patterson. *Race and Criminal Justice.* New York: Harrow & Heston, 1991.

Miller, Jerome. *Search and Destroy: African-American Males in the Criminal Justice System.* New York: Cambridge University Press, 1996.

Pearce, Frank, and Lauren Snider. *Corporate Crime.* Toronto: University of Toronto Press, 1995.

Pizzo, Stephen, et al. *Inside Job: The Looting of America's Savings and Loans.* New York: McGraw-Hill, 1989.

Simon, David, and Stanley Eitzen. *Elite Deviance,* 6th ed. Boston: Allyn & Bacon, 1999.

Timmer, Doug, and Stanley Eitzen. *Crimes in the Streets and Crimes in the Suites.* Boston: Allyn & Bacon, 1989.

READING 29

Notes

1. For discussions of the effect of incarceration, see, e.g., J. Grogger, "The Effect of Arrests on the Employment and Earnings of Young Men," *Quarterly Journal of Economics* 110 (1995): 51–72; B. Western, "The Impact of Incarceration on Wage Mobility and Inequality," *American Sociological Review* 67, no. 4 (2002): 526–46.

2. This research is reported in D. Pager, "The Mark of a Criminal Record," *American Journal of Sociology* 108, no. 5 (2003): 937–75. IRP thanks the University of Chicago Press for permission to summarize the article.

3. See, for example, D. Neal and W. Johnson, "The Role of Premarket Factors in Black-White Wage Differences," *Journal of Political Economy* 104, no. 5 (1996): 869–95; S. Steele, *The Content of Our Character: A New Vision of Race in America* (New York: Harper Perennial, 1991).

4. The method of audit studies was pioneered in the 1970s with a series of housing audits conducted by the Department of Housing and Urban Development, and was modified and applied to employment by researchers at the Urban Institute in the early 1990s. M. Turner, M. Fix, and R. Struyk, *Opportunities Denied, Opportunities Diminished: Racial Discrimination in Hiring* (Washington, DC: Urban Institute Press, 1991).

5. Bureau of Labor Statistics, Local Area Unemployment Statistics. Last accessed March 2003. http://www.bls.gov/lau/home.htm.

6. Over 90 percent of recent, entry-level job openings in Milwaukee were located in the outlying counties and suburbs, and only 4 percent in the central city. J. Pawasarat and L. Quinn, "Survey of Job Openings in the Milwaukee Metropolitan Area: Week of May 15, 2000," Employment and Training Institute Report, University of Wisconsin–Milwaukee, 2000.

7. M. Bendick, Jr., C. Jackson, and V. Reinoso, "Measuring Employment Discrimination through Controlled Experiments," *Review of Black Political Economy* 23 (1994): 25–48.

READING 31

Notes

1. Stephen Erie, *Rainbow's End* (Berkeley: University of California Press, 1988), 88–89.

2. Thomas Kessner, *Fiorella H. LaGuardia* (New York: McGraw-Hill, 1989); Charles Garrett, *The LaGuardia Years* (New Brunswick, NJ: Rutgers University Press, 1961).

3. A survey of the surviving members of the class indicates that 38 percent were Catholic and 36 percent Jewish, with Russia and Ireland the leading countries of origin of the respondents' grandparents (Richard Herrnstein et al., "New York City Police Department Class of 1940: A Preliminary Report" [unpublished manuscript, Department of Psychology, Harvard University, n. d.])

4. Nathan Glazer and Daniel P. Moynihan, *Beyond the Melting Pot* (Cambridge, MA: MIT Press, 1969).

5. Data on the ethnic composition of the fire department are from *Equal Employment Opportunity Statistics: Agency Full Report* (New York: New York City Department of Personnel, 1990); data on the religious composition are from Center for Social Policy and Practice in the Workplace, *Gender Integration in the Fire Department of the City of New York* (New York: Columbia University School of Social Work, 1988), p. 41.

6. Roger Waldinger, *Through the Eye of the Needle* (New York: New York University Press, 1986).

7. Heywood Broun and George Britt, *Christians Only* (New York: Vantage Press, 1931), 244.

8. Dominic Capeci, *The Harlem Riot of 1943* (Philadelphia: Temple University Press, 1977), 172.

9. Waldinger, *Through the Eye of the Needle,* 109–10. Employment data calculated from the census apply to employed persons twenty-five to sixty-four years old only. "Blacks" refers to native-born African Americans only. Data calculated from the Public Use Microdata Samples (U.S. Bureau of the Census, *Census of Population, 1940,* Public Use Microdata Samples [Computer file] [Washington, DC: U.S. Dept. of Commerce, Bureau of the Census, producer, 1983; Ann Arbor, MI: Inter-university Consortium for Political and Social Research, distributor, 1984]; U.S. Bureau of the Census, Census of Population, 1950, Public Use Microdata Samples [computer file] [Washington, DC: U.S. Dept. of Commerce, Bureau of the Census, and Madison: University of Wisconsin, Center for Demography and Ecology, producers, 1984; Ann Arbor, MI: Inter-university Consortium for Political and Social Research, distributor, 1984]).

10. Hasia Diner, *In the Almost Promised Land* (Westport, CT: Greenwood Press, 1977), presents a favorable account of the response among the Jewish trade union elite to the black influx into the garment industry; see chap. 6. Herbert Hill has offered a far more critical account in numerous writings, most important, "The Racial Practices of Organized Labor: The Contemporary Record," in *Organized Labor and the Negro,* edited by Julius Jacobson (New York: Doubleday, 1968), 286–337. For a judicious balancing of the issues, see Nancy Green, "'Juifs et noirs aux etats-unis: La rupture d'une 'alliance naturelle,'" *Annales, E.S.C., 2*(March–April 1987): 445–64.

11. Diane Ravitch, *The Great School Wars* (New York: Basic Books, 1974).

12. Roger Waldinger, "The Making of an Immigrant Niche," *International Migration Review* 28(1)(1994).

13. "The Debate Goes On," *Alumnus: The City College of New York* 87(1)(Winter 1992):8–11.

14. Emmanuel Tobier, "Population," in *Setting Municipal Priorities,* edited by Charles Brecher and Raymond Horton (New York: New York University Press, 1981), 24.

15. Data are from U.S. Bureau of the Census, *Occupations at the 1900 Census* (Washington, DC: GPO, 1904). See also Herman Bloch, *The Circle of Discrimination* (New York: New York University Press, 1969).

16. Data are from the U.S. Bureau of the Census, *Census of Population, 1940.*

17. Calculated from the U.S. Bureau of the Census, *Census of Population and Housing, 1990,* Public Use Microdata Sample (a Sample): 5-Percent Sample (computer file) (Washington, DC: U.S. Dept. of Commerce, producer, 1993; Ann Arbor, MI: Inter-university Consortium for Political and Social Research, distributor, 1993).

18. Colored Citizens' Non-Partisan Committee for the Re-election of Mayor Walker, *New York City and the Colored Citizen* (n.d. [1930?]), LaGuardia Papers, Box 3530, New York Municipal Archives.

19. Calculated from U.S. Bureau of the Census, *Census of Population, 1940,* Public Use Microdata Samples. Also see Edwin Levinson, *Black Politics in New York City* (New York: Twayne, 1974).

20. Ira Katznelson, *Black Men, White Cities* (New York: Oxford University Press, 1973), 82.

21. For a more detailed discussion of the Lindsay period, see Roger Waldinger, "The Ethnic Politics of Municipal Jobs," working paper no. 248, UCLA Institute of Industrial Relations, Los Angeles, 1993.

22. Raymond Horton, "Human Resources," in *Setting Municipal Priorities,* edited by Charles Brecher and Raymond Horton (New York: New York University Press, 1986). See also Roger Waldinger, "Changing Ladders and Musical Chairs," *Politics and Society* 15(4) (1986–87):369–402, and "Making of an Immigrant Niche."

23. City of New York, Citywide Equal Employment Opportunity Committee, *Equal Employment Opportunity in New York City Government, 1977–1987* (New York: Citywide Equal Employment Opportunity Committee, 1988), 6.

24. Data are from unpublished EEOC reports from the New York City Department of Personnel, New York Board of Education, New York City Transit Authority, and New York City Health and Hospitals Corporation.

25. City of New York, Mayor's Commission on Hispanic Concerns, *Report* (New York: Mayor's Commission on Hispanic Concerns, 1986), 109.

26. *1991 Korean Business Directory* (Long Island City, NY: Korean News, 1991).

27. Roger Waldinger, "Structural Opportunity or Ethnic Advantage: Immigrant Business Development in New York," *International Migration Review* 23(1)(1989):61.

28. Illsoo Kim, *The New Urban Immigrants* (Princeton, NJ: Princeton University Press, 1981), 51.

29. Pyong Gap Min, "Cultural and Economic Boundaries of Korean Ethnicity: A Comparative Analysis," *Ethnic and Racial Studies* 14(2) (1991):235.

30. Lucie Cheng and Yen Espiritu, "Korean Businesses in Black and Hispanic Neighborhoods," *Sociological Perspectives* 32(4) (1989):521.

31. Illsoo Kim, "The Koreans: Small Business in an Urban Frontier," in *New Immigrants in New York,* edited by Nancy Foner (New York: Columbia University Press, 1987), 238.

32. Tamar Jacoby, "Sonny Carson and the Politics of Protest," *NY: The City Journal* 1(4)(1991): 29–40.

READING 32

Notes

1. The research for this chapter was made possible by generous grants from the Russell Sage, Ford, Rockefeller, Spencer, and William T. Grant Foundations. A revised version of this chapter appears in Newman 1999.

2. There are further shades of gray below the line of the employed that distinguish those who are searching for work and those who have accepted their fate as nonworkers, with the latter suffering the greatest stigma of all.

3. For more on the moral structure associated with work and achievement of the American dream, see Hochschild 1995.

4. See Wilson 1996, Massey and Denton 1993, Hacker 1992, and Urban Institute 1991.

5. All names and identifying information have been changed to protect confidentiality.

6. Hochschild 1983 documents similar attempts in the airline industry. One airline holds a mandatory seminar for flight attendants to teach them "anger-desensitization" when dealing with rude and demeaning customers.

7. In areas experiencing exceptionally tight labor markets—including much of the Midwest in the late 1990s—wages for these jobs are climbing above the minimum-wage line.

8. This is one of the many reasons why increasing the minimum wage is so important. Ghettos have such impoverished job bases to begin with that they are almost always characterized by slack labor markets. Only when the labor supply outside ghetto walls has tightened down to almost impossible levels do we begin to see this tide lift inner-city boats. Eventually employers do turn to the workers who are low on their preference queues (as we learned in the 1980s during the Massachusetts miracle), but these conditions are, sadly, rare and generally short-lived.

9. Indeed, over a five-month period in 1993 there were fourteen job applicants for every job opening at two different Burger Barns in Harlem (Newman and Lennon 1995).

10. The fact that Harlem residents rejected for these jobs hold these values is some evidence for the preexisting nature of this mind-set—although these rejects had already piled up

work experience that may have contributed to the sharpening of this alternative critique.

11. It should be noted that women on welfare and women in low-wage jobs are not necessarily two distinct groups. Many women find it necessary to go back and forth between holding a low-wage job and relying solely on welfare, and many supplement one form of income with the other (not to mention other income from friends, family, and unreported work), since neither source alone provides enough money to support a family (see Edin 1994).

References

Anderson, Elijah. 1990. *Streetwise.* Chicago: University of Chicago Press.

Edin, Kathryn. 1994. "The Myths of Dependency and Self-Sufficiency: Women, Welfare, and Low-Wage Work." Unpublished paper. Department of Sociology and Center for Urban Policy Research, Rutgers University.

Hacker, Andrew. 1992. *Two Nations.* New York: Ballantine.

Hochschild, Arlie. 1983. *The Managed Heart.* Berkeley: University of California Press.

Hochschild, Jennifer L. 1995. *Facing Up to the American Dream.* Princeton: Princeton University Press.

Katz, Michael. 1989. *The Undeserving Poor.* New York: Pantheon.

Massey, Douglas S., and Nancy A. Denton. 1993. *American Apartheid.* Cambridge: Harvard University Press.

Newman, Katherine S. 1999. *No Shame in My Game: The Working Poor in the Inner City.* New York: Knopf/Russell Sage Foundation.

Newman, Katherine S., and Chauncy Lennon. 1995. "The Job Ghetto." *American Prospect,* summer, 66–67.

Urban Institute. 1991. *Opportunities Denied, Opportunities Diminished.* Report 91–9. Washington: Urban Institute Press.

Waller, Maureen. 1996. "Redefining Fatherhood: Paternal Involvement, Masculinity, and Responsibility in the 'Other America.'" Ph.D. diss., Princeton University.

Wilson, William Julius. 1996. *When Work Disappears.* New York: Knopf.

READING 33

Notes

1. Unless otherwise noted, the following discussion is primarily based on these sources and the information provided by Liang Huan Ru, the former veteran union organizer in Brooklyn.

2. I use "Manhattan's Chinatown" because new Chinatowns have recently emerged in other boroughs of New York City, such as Queens and Brooklyn.

3. Abeles, Schwartz, Haechel & Silverblatt, Inc., *The Chinatown Garment Industry Study* (hereafter *Study*) (New York: International Ladies' Garment Workers' Union Local 23–25 and the New York Skirt and Sportswear Association, 1983), 55. For the sizes of the shops in Manhattan's Chinatown, see *Study,* 49–59.

4. See for example, the weekly special issue of the *Sing Tao Daily* (hereafter *STD*), March 8, 1998, 7.

5. My visit to the shop and interview with the shop owner.

6. One woman worker told me in an interview that it was so hot inside her shop in summer that sometimes she simply could not help crying while trying to rush out her work.

7. Experienced pressers began to lose this advantage in more and more Chinese garment shops in recent years, largely due to the increased competition from undocumented male workers. Unable to compete with the low wages accepted by the latter, they too had to face economic insecurity in the industry. I am indebted to a reminder from Liang Huan Ru, an organizer of UNITE! Local 23–25, and May Ying Chen, vice president of UNITE!, for this piece of information. What, however, must be kept in mind is that while competition has mounted among pressers in recent years, women machine operators also faced competition from undocumented workers.

8. See Susan Glenn, *Daughters of the Shtetl: Life and Labor in the Immigrant Generation* (Ithaca, New York: Cornell University Press, 1990), 90–131, and Nancy Green, *Ready-to-Wear and Ready-to-Work: A Century of Industry and Immigrants in Paris and New York* (Durham: Duke University Press, 1997), 161–87.

9. The most recent case was the one at 446 Broadway in November 1997, in which a young woman employer closed her shop after withholding a large sum of money in back wages from her employees. The case was covered by most major newspapers inside and outside the Chinese community. See, for example, *New York Times,* December 14, 1997.

10. See "Opportunity at Work: The New York City Garment Industry" (New York: Community Service Society of New York, 1998), 39.

11. This observation has been supported by recent coverage in Chinese community newspapers. For example, as covered in *World Journal* (hereafter *WJ*) in 1996, the monthly income of an elderly couple who worked in a Chinese garment shop was $1,800 and $2,200, respectively. Given the depressed piece rates in the last two years and the seasonal nature of the industry, this observation, based on interviews with workers in Sunset Park, does not seem to be far away from reality.

12. Directly quoted from "Behind Closed Doors: A Look into the Underground Sweatshop Industry," a report by the New York State Assembly Sub-Committee on Sweatshops (New York, November 1997), 59–61.

13. Interview by the author on April 13, 1998.

14. See, for example, Bernard Wong, "The Role of Ethnicity in Enclave Enterprises: A Study of the Chinese Garment Factories in New York City," *Human Organization* 46 (2), 1987: 120–9.

15. "One country, two systems" is the Chinese state policy in Hong Kong after the former British colony was returned to China in 1997.

16. Cases like this are not unheard of in the Chinese garment industry in Manhattan's Chinatown as well as other boroughs of the city. See, for example. The Chinese Staff and Workers Association, *Zhi Gong Zhi Sheng* (January 1994).

17. I was told that this small number of workers from other ethnic groups were likely to have worked for the former owner of the shop and the Chinese employer employed them as part of the deal when he/she purchased the business. I was also told that some Chinese employers deliberately kept these workers to protect their businesses from harassment by Chinese gangsters, who tended not to attack shops with non-Chinese workers for fear that their illicit activities would be known beyond the Chinese community.

18. *STD,* December 19, 1997.

19. The "Hot Goods Bill" was signed into law on July 2, 1996. This bill has established "additional methods of obtaining restitution for unpaid apparel industry workers from contractors, manufacturers, and retailers." For a further discussion of this bill, see "Behinds Closed Doors," 4.

20. The *Study* has reported that at the end of 1981, 28 percent of all Chinese shops in Chinatown had been in business for less than one year and close to half of them had been in operation for less than two years (p. 68). However, in the late 1990s, as many workers have pointed out, the Chinese garment shops in Sunset Park are often opened and closed down within months.

21. Taishan is a county in Guangdong Province. Immigrants from this county are also generally called "Cantonese."

22. Interview by the author on July 2, 1998.

23. Interview by the author on June 21, 1998.

24. Immigration status and whether one is living with their family have become important indexes because much of the Chinese community has chosen to believe that legal immigration and family life are the norms throughout the history of the community, however invalid this belief is.

25. For a summary of their arguments, see *STD,* April 22, 1998.

26. For different voices in the community, see, for example, the weekly special issues of *STD,* May 17, 1998 and June 28, 1998.

27. The estimate of 800 Chinese shops is based on an adding of the approximate 500 shops in Manhattan and the more than 300 shops in Brooklyn and other boroughs. More than 30,000 workers were estimated by the community press in the end of 1997. See *STD,* December 22, 1997.

28. These statistics are provided by the Research Department of the New York State Department of Labor.

29. In 1997, when the union signed a new contract with Chinese employers, the three Chinese contractors' associations represented only 406 shops in the city. This was later reported in most Chinese community newspapers. See, for example, *STD,* February 23, 1998.

30. This percentage of Chinatown union shops in 1997 is based on a comparison of the number of garment shops in the Chinatown area provided by the state labor department, which is not classified according to ethnicity, and the estimate of Chinatown union organizers and the Chinese newspapers. See, for example, *STD,* December 22, 1997 and April 29, 1998 and *WJ,* February 28, 1998.

31. These statistics are provided by the UNITE! Research Department. The estimated percentage of the local's Chinese membership in this study is consistent with the numbers provided by the local.

32. Green, *Ready-To-Wear,* 50.

33. See Nancy Green, "Sweatshop Migrations: The Garment Industry between Home and Shop," in *The Landscape of Modernity: Essays on New York City, 1900–1940,* eds. David Ward and Olivier Zunz (New York: Russell Sage Foundation, 1992), 213–32.

34. Mark Levitan, *Opportunity at Work: The New York City Garment Industry* (New York: Community Service Society of New York, 1998), 59.

35. One of the most active community-based labor organizations in New York's Chinatown in the last two decades is the Chinese Staff and Workers' Association.

READING 34

References

Barboza, David. 2001. "Meatpackers' Profits Hinge on Pool of Immigrant Labor." *New York Times* (Dec. 21).

Bjerklie, Steve. 1995. "On the Horns of a Dilemma: The U.S. Meat and Poultry Industry." In *Any Way You Cut It: Meat Processing and Small-Town America,* ed. D. D. Stull, M. J. Broadway, and D. Griffith, 41–60. Lawrence: University Press of Kansas.

Broadway, Michael J. 1994. "Hogtowns and Rural Development." *Rural Development Perspectives* 9: 40–46.

Brown, Dennis. 1993. "Changes in the Red Meat and Poultry Industries: Their Effect on Nonmetropolitan Employment." *Agricultural Economic Report* 665. Washington, DC: Economic Research Service, U.S. Department of Agriculture.

Bugos, G. E. 1992. "Intellectual Property Protection in the American Chicken-Breeding Industry." *Business History Review* 66: 127–168.

Carlin, Michael. 1999. "Even Tougher on Farm Labor?" *Raleigh News and Observer* (July 28).

Cobb, James C. 1982. *The Selling of the South: The Southern Crusade for Industrial Development, 1936–1990.* Baton Rouge: Louisiana State University Press.

Cromartie, John. 1999. "Race and Ethnicity in Rural Areas." *Rural Conditions and Trends* 9 (2): 9–19.

———, and William Kandel. 2002. "Did Residential Segregation in Rural America Increase with Recent Hispanic Population Growth?" Poster presented to the Meetings of the Population Association of America, Atlanta, GA, May 8–11.

Dawber, Thomas. 1980. *The Framingham Study.* Cambridge, MA: Harvard University Press.

Delmarva Poultry Industry, Inc. (DPI) 2002. http://www. dpichicken.org/

Díaz McConnell, Eileen E. Forthcoming. "Latinos in the Rural Midwest: Historical Context and Contemporary Challenges." In *Apple Pie and Enchiladas: Latino Newcomers and the Changing Dynamics of the Rural Midwest,* ed. J. Chapa, A. Millard, and R. Saenz. Austin: University of Texas Press.

Durand, Jorge; Douglas S. Massey; and Fernando Charvet. 2000. "The Changing Geography of Mexican Immigration to the United States: 1910–1996." *Social Science Quarterly* 81: 1–16.

Engstrom, James. 2001. "Industry and Immigration in Dalton, Georgia." In *Latino Workers in the Contemporary South,* ed. A. Murphy, C. Blanchard, and J. A. Hill, 44–56. Athens: University of Georgia Press.

Flippen, Chenoa. 2001. "Neighborhood Transition and Social Organization: The White to Hispanic Case." *Social Problems* 48 (3): 299–321.

Gouveia, Lourdes, and Donald D. Stull. 1995. "Dances with Cows: Beefpacking's Impact on Garden City, Kansas, and Lexington, Nebraska." In *Any Way You Cut It: Meat Processing and Small-Town America,* ed. D. D. Stull, M. J. Broadway, and D. Griffith, 85–108. Lawrence: University Press of Kansas.

Grey, Mark A. 1995. "Pork, Poultry, and Newcomers in Storm Lake, Iowa." In *Any Way You Cut It: Meat Processing and Small-Town America,* ed. D. D. Stull, M. J. Broadway, and D. Griffith, 109–128. Lawrence: University Press of Kansas.

Griffith, David. 1995. "Hay Trabajo: Poultry Processing, Rural Industrialization, and the Latinization of Low-Wage Labor." In *Any Way You Cut It: Meat Processing and Small-Town America,* ed. D. D. Stull, M. J. Broadway, and D. Griffith, 129–152. Lawrence: University Press of Kansas.

Guthey, Greig. 2001. "Mexican Places in Southern Spaces: Globalization, Work and Daily Life in and around the North Georgia Poultry Industry." In *Latino Workers in the Contemporary South,* ed. A. Murphy, C. Blanchard, and J. A. Hill, 57–67. Athens: University of Georgia Press.

Haverluk, Terrence W. 1998. "Hispanic Community Types and Assimilation in Mex-America." *Professional Geographer* 50 (4): 465–480.

Hernández-León, Rubén, and Víctor Zúñiga. 2000. "'Making Carpet by the Mile': The Emergence of a Mexican Immigrant Community in an Industrial Region of the U.S. Historic South." *Social Science Quarterly* 81: 49–66.

Hetrick, Ron L. 1994. "Why Did Employment Expand in Poultry Processing Plants?" *Monthly Labor Review* (June): 31–34.

Horowitz, Roger, and Mark J. Miller. 1999. "Immigrants in the Delmarva Poultry Processing Industry: The Changing Face of Georgetown, Delaware and Environs." Occasional Paper No. 37, Julián Samora Research Institute, Michigan State University.

Johnson-Webb, Karen D. 2002. "Employer Recruitment and Hispanic Labor Migration: North Carolina Urban Areas at the End of the Millennium." *Professional Geographer* 54 (3): 406–421.

Katz, Jesse. 1996a. "The Chicken Trail: How Migrant Latino Workers Put Food on America's Table." *Los Angeles Times* (Nov. 10).

———. 1996b. "Poultry Industry Imports Labor to Do Its Dirty Work." *Los Angeles Times* (Dec. 8).

Lapinski, John S., et al. 1997. "Trends: Immigrants and Immigration." *Public Opinion Quarterly* 61: 356–383.

Lichter, Daniel T.; F. B. LeClere; and D. K. McLaughlin. 1991. "Local Marriage Market and the Marital Behavior of Black and White Women." *American Journal of Sociology* 96: 843–867.

Lichter, Daniel T., et al. 1992. "Race and the Retreat from Marriage: A Shortage of Marriageable Men?" *American Sociological Review* 57 (6): 781–799.

MacDonald, James, et al. 2000. "Consolidation in U.S. Meatpacking." *Agricultural Economic Report* 322–785. Washington, DC: Economic Research Service, U.S. Department of Agriculture.

Massey, Douglas S.; Jorge Durand; and Nolan Malone. 2002. *Beyond Smoke and Mirrors: Mexican Immigration in an Era of Economic Integration.* New York: Russell Sage.

Massey, Douglas S., and Kristin E. Espinosa. 1997. "What's Driving Mexico-U.S. Migration? A Theoretical, Empirical, and Policy Analysis." *American Journal of Sociology* 102 (4): 939–999.

McDaniel, Josh M. 2002. "Immigrants and Forest Industries in Alabama: Social Networks and Pioneer Settlements." Paper presented at the Immigration and America's Changing Ethnic Landscapes Conference, Athens, GA, Apr. 12–14.

McQuiston, Chris, and Emilio A. Parrado. 2002. "Migration and HIV Risks among Mexicans: Evidence from Participatory Action Research." Unpublished manuscript.

Mishra, Shiraz I.; Ross F. Conner; and J. Raúl Magaña, eds. 1996. *AIDS Crossing Borders.* Boulder, CO: Westview Press.

Ollinger, Michael; James MacDonald; and Milton Madison. 2000. *Structural Change in U.S. Chicken and Turkey Slaughter.* Agricultural Economic Report 787. Washington, DC: Economic Research Service, U.S. Department of Agriculture.

Oropesa, R. S., and D. Lichter. 1994. "Marriage Markets and the Paradox of Mexican American Nuptiality." *Journal of Marriage and the Family* 56: 889–908.

Parrado, Emilio A. 2002. "International Migration and Men's Marriage in Mexico." Unpublished Manuscript.

———, and René Zenteno. In press. "Gender Differences in Union Formation in Mexico: Evidence from Marital Search Models." *Journal of Marriage and Family.*

Pérez, Laura. 2001. "The Changing Geography of Latinos: Evidence from Census 2000." Paper presented to the American Sociological Association Meetings, Anaheim, CA.

Reed, Deborah. 2001. "Immigration and Males' Earnings Inequality in the Regions of the United States." *Demography* 38: 363–373.

Smothers, Ronald. 1996. "Unions Head South to Woo Poultry Workers." *New York Times* (Jan. 30).

Studstill, John D., and Laura Nieto-Studstill. 2001. "Hospitality and Hostility: Latin Immigrants in Southern Georgia." In *Latino Workers in the Contemporary South,* ed. A. Murphy, C. Blanchard, and J. A. Hill, 68–81. Athens: University of Georgia Press.

Sun, Lena H., and Gabriel Escobar. 1999. "On Chicken's Front Line." *Washington Post* (Nov. 28–Dec. 1).

Taylor, Marisa, and Steve Stein. 1999. "Network Helps Recruit Immigrants for U.S. Job Market." *Fort Worth Star-Telegram* (July 4).

U.S. Bureau of the Census. 1990. *Census of Population.* Summary Tape File 3. Washington, DC.

———. 2000. *Census of Population.* Summary Tape File 1. Washington, DC.

U.S. Department of Agriculture. Economic Research Service (USDA.ERS). *Poultry Yearbook,* 1960–2000, various issues. Washington, DC.

U.S. Department of Commerce (DOC). 1963–1997. *Current Population Survey.* Earnings Supplement, various years. Washington, DC.

———. 1967–1997. *Census of Manufactures.* Industry Series, various years. Washington, DC.

———. 2002. *Local Area Unemployment Statistics.* Washington, DC. http://www.bls.gov/lau

U.S. Department of Labor (DOL). 1972–2001. *Occupational Employment Statistics.* Washington, DC.

———. Bureau of International Labor Affairs. 1989. *The Effects of Immigration on the U.S. Economy and Labor Market.* Washington, DC.

READING 35

References

Bushman, B., & Bonnaci, A. (2001). *Sex and violence impair memory for commercials.* Unpublished manuscript, Iowa State University.

Children Now. (1998, May 6). *A different world: Children's perceptions of race and class in media.* Oakland, CA: Author.

Craig, J. G. (2001, August 12). Murder most murky. *Pittsburgh Post-Gazette,* p. E-3.

Dixon, T. L., & Linz, D. (2000). Race and the misrepresentation of victimization on local television news. *Communication Research, 27,* 547–573.

Dorfman, L. (1997). *Reporting on violence: A handbook for journalists.* Berkeley, CA: Berkeley Media Studies Group.

Dorfman, L., & Schiraldi, V. (in press). Off balance: Youth, race and crime in the news. *Crime and Delinquency.*

Driscol, P., & Splichal, S. L. (1998). *Legal concerns in TV newsrooms: A national survey of local television news directors.* Paper presented at the annual convention of the Association for Educators in Journalism and Mass Communication, Baltimore.

Heider, D. (2000). *White news: Why local news programs don't cover people of color.* Mahwah, NJ: Lawrence Erlbaum Associates.

Klein, R. D., & Cox, R. C. (1992). *Audience reactions to local TV news: An extension.* Paper presented at the annual meeting of the American Psychological Association, Washington, DC.

Klein, R. D., & Smith, B. (2000). *Reactions of Black and White students to local TV news.* Unpublished manuscript, University of Pittsburgh.

Linton, C. (1995). *Multicultural news in Chicago: Does it make the grade? Ethnic leaders rate the* Chicago Tribune *and* Sun-Times. Evanston, IL: Gannett Urban Journalism Center, Northwestern University.

Linton, C. C., & LeBailly, R. K. (1998). *African-American and Latino views of local Chicago TV news* (Working Paper WP-98-15). Chicago: Institute of Policy Research, Northwestern University.

Romer, D., Jamieson, K. H., & deCoteau, N. J. (1998). The treatment of persons of color in local television news. *Communication Research, 25,* 286–305.

Rosenstiel, T., Gottlieb, C., & Brady, L. E. (2000). Time of peril for TV news. *Columbia Journalism Review, 39,* 84–92.

Sharp, D., & Puente, M. (1994, July 26). Minorities consider the media unfair. *USA Today,* p. 1A.

READING 36

References

Entman, R. 1990. "Modern Racism and the Images of Blacks in Local Television News." *Critical Studies in Mass Communication* 7 (4, December): 332–345.

Gray, H. 1996. *Watching Race: Television and the Struggle for Blackness.* Minneapolis: University of Minnesota Press.

Hacker, A. 1992. *Two Nations: Black and White, Separate, Hostile, Unequal.* New York: Scribner.

Iyengar, S. 1991. *Is Anyone Responsible?* Chicago: University of Chicago Press.

Jhally, S. and J. Lewis. 1992. *Enlightened Racism: The Cosby Show, Audiences, and the Myth of the American Dream.* Boulder, CO: Westview.

Patterson, J. and P. Kim. 1992. *The Day America Told the Truth.* New York: Dutton.

Walton, A. 1989. "Willie Horton and Me." *The New York Times Magazine,* August 20, section 6, p. 77.

Wilson, W. J. 1987. *The Truly Disadvantaged.* Chicago: University of Chicago Press.

READING 37

Notes

1. Harry Castleman and Walter Podrazik, *Watching TV: Four Decades of American Television* (New York: McGraw-Hill, 1982), 208.

2. Ibid., 226.

3. Laura Z. Hobson, quoted in Christopher Lasch, "Archie Bunker and the Liberal Mind," *Channels,* October/November 1981, 34.

4. Quoted in Castleman and Podrazik, *Watching TV,* 227.

5. See Richard Adler, ed., *All in the Family: A Critical Appraisal* (New York: Praeger, 1979).

6. Quoted in William Raspberry, "Cosby Show: Black or White?" *Washington Post,* 5 November 1984.

7. Quoted in *Time,* 19 March 1979, 85.

8. S. Robert Lichter and Daniel R. Amundson, *Distorted Reality: Hispanic Characters in TV Entertainment* (Washington, DC: Center for Media and Public Affairs, 1994).

9. Quoted in *Time,* 19 March 1979, 85.

READING 38

Notes

1. Many people have preferences about terms used to describe America's indigenous peoples. "American Indian" is commonly used, as is "Native American, Native, and Indian." These terms are used interchangeably in recognition of individual preferences, without disregarding the weight each word carries.

2. Lawsuits are currently underway to limit Heilman Breweries' use of the name Crazy Horse Liquor (Specktor, 1995). Several states have outlawed the sale of the beverage (Specktor, 1995). Also under review are important legal issues such as a tribe's sovereign power to exercise civil jurisdiction and the Witko family's right to protect the image of their ancestor.

References

Aaker, D., & A. L. Biel. (1993). *Advertising's role in building strong brands.* Mahwah, NJ: Lawrence Erlbaum.

Barthes, R. (1972). *Mythologies.* New York: The Noonday Press.

Berkhofer, R., Jr. (1979). *The white man's Indian: Images of the American Indian from Columbus to the present.* New York: Vintage Books.

Bird, S. E. (1996). Not my fantasy: The persistence of Indian imagery in *Dr. Quinn, Medicine Woman.* In S. E. Bird (Ed.), *Dressing in feathers: The construction of the Indian in American popular culture* (pp. 245–262). Boulder, CO: Westview Press.

Blalock, C. (1992). Crazy Horse controversy riles Congress: Controversies over Crazy Horse Malt Liquor and Black Death vodka. *Beverage Industry, 83*(9), 1–3.

Burnham, P. (1992, 27 May). Indians can't shake label as guides to good buys. *The Washington Times,* p.E1.

Champagne, D. (1994). *Native America: Portrait of the peoples.* Detroit: Visible Ink.

Cortese, A. J. (1999). *Provocateur: Images of women and minorities in advertising.* New York: Rowman & Littlefield Publishers, Inc.

Dotz, W., & Morton, J. (1996). *What a character! 20th century American advertising icons.* San Francisco: Chronicle Books.

Goings, K. W. (1994). *Mammy and Uncle Mose: Black collectibles and American stereotyping.* Bloomington, IN: Indiana University Press.

Graham, R. (1993, 6 January). Symbol or stereotype: One consumer's tradition is another's racial slur. *The Boston Globe,* p. 35.

Green, M. K. (1993). Images of American Indians in advertising: Some moral issues. *Journal of Business Ethics, 12,* 323–330.

Hall, S. (1997). *Representation: Cultural representations and signifying practices.* London: Sage.

Hill, R. (1992). The non-vanishing American Indian: Are the modern images any closer to the truth? *Quail* (May), 35–37.

Kates, S. M., & Shaw-Garlock, G. (1999). The ever-entangling web: A study of ideologies and discourses in advertising to women. *Journal of Advertising 28*(2), 33–49.

Kern-Foxworth, M. (1994). *Aunt Jemima, Uncle Ben, and Rastus: Blacks in advertising yesterday, today, and tomorrow.* Westport, CT: Praeger.

Land O' Lakes. (2000). [On-line]. Available: http://www.landolakes.com

Larson, C. (1937). Patent-medicine advertising and the early American press. *Journalism Quarterly, 14*(4), 333–339.

Lippmann, W. (1922/1961). *Public opinion.* New York: Macmillan & Company.

McCracken, G. (1993). The value of the brand: An anthropological perspective. In D. Aaker & A. L. Biel (Eds.), *Brand equity is advertising: Advertising's role in building strong brands.* Mahwah, NJ: Lawrence Erlbaum.

Merskin, D. (1998). Sending up signals: A survey of American Indian media use and representation in the mass media. *The Howard Journal of Communications, 9,* 333–345.

Metz, S., & Thee, M. (1994). Brewers intoxicated with racist imagery. *Business and Society Review, 89,* 50–51.

Mihesuah, D. A. (1996). *American Indians: Stereotypes and realities.* Atlanta, GA: Clarity Press.

Monitor Sugar Company. (2000) [On-line]. Available: http://members.aol.com/asga/mon.htm.

Morgan, H. (1986). *Symbols of America.* New York: Penguin Books.

Schmitt, B., & Simonson, A. (1997). *Marketing aesthetics: The strategic management of brands, identity, and image.* New York: The Free Press.

Sioux Honey Association. (2000). [On-line]. Available: http://www.suebeehoney.com.

Specktor, M. (1995, January 6). Crazy Horse exploited to peddle liquor. *National Catholic Reporter, 31*(10), 3.

Strickland, R. (1998). The celluloid Indian. *Oregon Quarterly* (Summer), 9–10.

van Dijk, T. A. (1996). *Discourse, racism, and ideology.* La Laguna: RCEI Ediciones.

Westerman, M. (1989, March). Death of the Frito bandito: Marketing to ethnic groups. *American Demographics, 11,* 28–32.

Williamson, J. (1978). *Decoding advertisements: Ideology and meaning in advertising.* New York: Marion Boyars.

READING 41

References

Adelman, Robert M., Hui-shien Tsao, Stewart E. Tolnay, Kyle D. Crowder. 2001. "Neighborhood Disadvantage among Racial and Ethnic Groups: Residential Location in 1970 and 1980." *Sociological Quarterly* 42: 603–32.

Arthur, John A. 2000. *Invisible Sojourners: African Immigrant Diaspora in the United States.* New York: Praeger.

Dodoo, F. Nii-Amoo. 1999. "Black and Immigrant Labor Force Participation in America." *Race and Society* 2: 69–82.

Foerster, Amy. 2004. "Race, Identity, and Belonging: 'Blackness' and the Struggle for Solidarity in a Multiethnic Labor Union." *Social Problems* 51: 386–409.

Ho, Christine. 1991. *Salt-Water Trinnies: Afro-Trinidadian Immigrant Networks and Non-assimilation in Los Angeles.* New York: AMS Press.

James, Winston. 2002. "Explaining Afro-Caribbean Social Mobility in the United States: Beyond the Sowell Thesis." *Comparative Studies in Society and History* 44: 218–62.

Kasinitz, Philip. 1992. *Caribbean New York.* Ithaca, NY: Cornell University Press.

Kollehlon, Konia T., and Edward E. Eule. 2003. "The Socioeconomic Attainment Patterns of Africans in the United States." *International Migration Review* 37: 1163–90.

Logan, John R., and John Mollenkopf. 2003. *People and Politics in America's Big Cities.* New York: Drum Major Institute for Public Policy.

Rogers, Reuel R. 2004. "Race-Based Coalitions among Minority Groups: Afro-Caribbean Immigrants and African-Americans in New York City." *Urban Affairs Review* 39: 283–317.

Sowell, Thomas. 1978. "Three Black Histories." In *Essays and Data on American Ethnic Groups,* ed. Thomas Sowell. Washington, DC: Urban Institute.

Takyi, Baffour K. 2002a. "Africans in the Diaspora: Black-White Earnings Differences among America's Africans." *Ethnic and Racial Studies* 25: 913–41.

———. 2002b. "The Making of the Second Diaspora: On the Recent African Immigrant Community in the United States of America." *Western Journal of Black Studies* 26: 32–43.

Waters, Mary. 1999. *Black Identities: West Indian Immigrant Dreams and American Realities.* Cambridge, MA: Harvard University Press.

READING 42

Notes

1. See William E. Leuchtenburg, "The American Perception of the Arab World." In George N. Atiyeh, ed., *Arab and American Cultures* (Washington, DC: American Enterprise Institute for Public Policy Research, 1977), p. 15.

2. Although it is possible to speak of several waves of Arab immigration to North America (e.g., 1880s to World War I, World War I to World War II, 1945 to 1967, 1968 to the present), there have been two main waves: from the 1880s to World War II and from World War II to the present. The major differences in the character and composition of the immigrant populations can be detected primarily between these two groups.

3. Unless otherwise indicated, references to the Arab community include the Arabs in Canada and those in the United States. Because of the much smaller numbers of Arabs in Canada, leadership on major issues usually has come from the Arab community in the United States.

4. See appendixes 1 and 2 in Gregory Orfalea, *Before the Flames: Quest for the History of Arab Americans* (Austin, TX: University of Texas Press, 1988), pp. 314–15. There were about 11,000 Arabs in Canada in 1931. For more on the subject of Arab immigration to Canada, see Baha Abu-Laban, *An Olive Branch on the Family Tree: The Arabs in Canada* (Toronto: McClelland and Stewart, 1980).

5. This is the official U.S. government figure cited in Philip Hitti's "The Emigrants," published in the 1963 edition of the *Encyclopedia of Islam* and reproduced in *Al-Hoda, 1898–1968* (New York: Al-Hoda Press, 1968), p. 133. A much larger estimate of 800,000 (Lebanese) was given by Ashad G. Hawie, *The Rainbow Ends* (New York: Theo. Gaus' Sons, 1942), pp. 149, 151.

6. This figure does not include the Arab community in Canada, which has fewer than 400,000 persons today. For estimates of Arab immigration to Canada, see Baha Abu-Laban, *An*

Olive Branch on the Family Tree: The Arabs in Canada (Toronto: McClelland and Stewart, 1980) and Ibrahim Hayani's chapter in Michael Suleiman, ed., *Arabs in America: Building a New Future* (Philadelphia: Temple University Press, 1999). Philip M. Kayal gave the low estimate in 1974 for Arabs in the United States but provided a revised estimate much closer to the generally accepted figure in 1987. See his "Estimating Arab-American Population," *Migration Today* 2, no. 5 (1974): 3, 9, and "Report: Counting the 'Arabs' Among Us," *Arab Studies Quarterly* 9, no. 1 (1987): 98–104.

7. See Philip K. Hitti, *The Syrians in America* (New York: George H. Doran, 1924), p. 48; Alixa Naff, *Becoming American: The Early Arab Immigrant Experience* (Carbondale, IL: Southern Illinois University Press, 1985), p. 83; Samir Khalaf, "The Background and Causes of Lebanese/Syrian Immigration to the United States before World War I." In Eric J. Hooglund, ed., *Crossing the Waters: Arabic-Speaking Immigrants to the United States before 1940* (Washington, DC: Smithsonian Institution Press, 1987), pp. 17–35; and Charles Issawi, "The Historical Background of Lebanese Emigration: 1800–1914." In Albert Hourani and Nadim Shehadi, eds., *The Lebanese in the World: A Century of Emigration* (London: I.B. Tauris, 1992), pp. 13–31. See also Baha Abu-Laban, "The Lebanese in Montreal." In Albert Hourani and Nadim Shehadi, eds., *The Lebanese in the World: A Century of Emigration* (London: I.B. Tauris, 1992), pp. 227–42.

8. Charles Issawi, "The Historical Background of Lebanese Emigration: 1800–1914." In Albert Hourani and Nadim Shehadi, eds., *The Lebanese in the World: A Century of Emigration* (London: I.B. Tauris, 1992), p. 22.

9. Philip K. Hitti, *The Syrians in America* (New York: George H. Doran, 1924), pp. 49–50. See also Akram Fouad Khater, "'House' to 'Goddess of the House': Gender, Class, and Silk in 19th-Century Mount Lebanon," *International Journal of Middle East Studies* 28, no. 3 (1996): 325–48.

10. For an informed and intelligent discussion on this and related issues, see Louise Seymour Houghton's series of articles entitled "Syrians in the United States," *The Survey* 26 (1 July, 5 August, 2 September, 7 October, 1911), pp. 480–95, 647–65, 786–803, 957–68.

11. For an early account of Arab immigration to the United States and to North America in general, which cites religious persecution as the reason for migration, see Basil M. Kherbawi, "History of the Syrian Emigration," which is part seven of Kherbawi's *tarikh al-Wilayat al-Muttahida* (*History of the United States*) (New York: al Dalil Press, 1913), pp. 726–96, published in Arabic.

12. See Leila Tarazi Fawaz, *An Occasion for War: Civil Conflict in Lebanon and Damascus in 1860* (Berkeley, CA: University of California Press, 1995). See also, Mikha'il Mishaqa, *Murder, Mayhem, Pillage and Pluder: The History of Lebanon in the 18th and 19th Centuries.* Translated by Wheeler M. Thackston, Jr. (Albany, NY: State University of New York Press, 1988).

13. See Louise Seymour Houghton's series of articles entitled "Syrians in the United States," *The Survey,* 26 (1911), pp. 480–95; and Alixa Naff, *Becoming American: The Early Arab Immigrant Experience* (Carbondale, IL: Southern Illinois University Press, 1985), pp. 128–200. For Canadian statistics, see Baha Abu-Laban, *An Olive Branch on the Family Tree: The Arabs in Canada* (Toronto: McClelland and Stewart, 1980).

14. *Kawkab America* (15 April 1892): 1, English section. The English titles of Arabic newspapers cited here are provided as originally used. The titles in parentheses are the transliterations used by the Library of Congress.

15. Even though *Kawkab America* was published for about seventeen years, only copies of the first four years are available; the others have been lost.

16. See Motaz Abdullah Alhourani, "The Arab-American Press and the Arab World: News Coverage in Al-Bayan and Al-Dalil" (master's thesis, Kansas State University, Manhattan, KS, 1993).

17. For a history of the organizational and political activities of Arabic-speaking groups in the United States during this period, see James Ansara, "The Immigration and Settlement of the Syrians" (master's thesis, Harvard University, Cambridge, MA, 1931).

18. Among these, the most important journal was *The Syrian World,* published and edited by Salloum Mokarzel. A useful publication is the *Annotated Index to the Syrian World, 1926–1932* by John G. Moses and Eugene Paul Nassar (Saint Paul, MN: Immigration History Research Center, University of Minnesota, 1994).

19. See Philip M. and Joseph M. Kayal, *The Syrian-Lebanese in America: A Study in Religion and Assimilation* (Boston, MA: Twayne Publishers, 1975).

20. A good account of the most prominent of these writers is provided by Nadira Jamil Sarraj, *Shu'ara' al-Rabitah al-Qalamiyah* (Poets of the Pen League) (Cairo, Egypt: Dar al-Ma'arif, 1964), published in Arabic.

21. See, for instance, Ameen Rihani, "To Syrians in the [American] Armed Forces," *As-Sayeh (al-Sa'ih)* (16 September 1918): 2, published in Arabic.

22. Advertisements and editorials in support of American Liberty bonds were found in most Arabic publications of that period, including *Al-Hoda* and *Meraat-ul-Gharb.*

23. See, in particular, *Syria Before the Peace Conference* (New York: Syrian-Lebanese League of North America, 1919).

24. This was the view often voiced after French entrenchment in Syria and Lebanon in the late 1920s and the 1930s.

25. For a summary of these views, see "Editors and Arabian Newspapers Give Opinions on Zionism," *The Jewish Criterion* (5 July 1918): 16–17.

26. Among the more active participants in public lectures and writings on this issue were Ameen Rihani and F. I. Shatara. The

Arab National League was established in 1936, and members spoke out on Palestine and other issues. For coverage of these and other activities related to the Palestine issue, see *Palestine & Transjordan* for that period. See also "A Communique from the Arab National League," *As-Sayeh* (6 August 1936): 9.

27. On the occupations of emigrant Arabs, especially in North America and specifically about those engaged in commerce, see Salloum Mokarzel, *Tarikh al-tijara al-Suriyya fi al-mahajir al-Amrikiyya* (*The History of Trade of Syrian Immigrants in the Americas*) (New York: Syrian-American Press, 1920), published in Arabic. On peddling activity, see Alixa Naff, *Becoming American: The Early Arab Immigrant Experience* (Carbondale, IL: Southern Illinois University Press, 1985), pp. 128–200.

28. The Arabic press of the period was replete with such advice.

29. Edna Bonacich, "A Theory of Middleman Minorities," *American Sociological Review* 38 (1973): 591.

30. Prejudice against Arabs in America was widespread, and there was also some discrimination, especially in the southern United States. See, for instance, Nancy Faires Conklin and Nora Faires, "'Colored' and Catholic: The Lebanese in Birmingham, Alabama." In Eric J. Hooglund, ed., *Crossing the Waters: Arabic-Speaking Immigrants to the United States before 1940* (Washington, DC: Smithsonian Institution Press, 1987), pp. 69–84.

31. See, for instance, H. A. El-Kourie, "Dr. El-Kourie Defends Syrian Immigrants," *Birmingham Ledger* (20 September 1907) and "El-Kourie Takes Burnett to Task," *Age-Herald* (Birmingham, AL) (20 October 1907): 6.

32. In 1908, Canada issued the Order-in-Council, P.C. 926, which severely restricted Asiatic immigration. Negative attitudes about "Syrians," mistaking them for "Turks," also were a factor in reducing the level of Arab immigration to Canada. See Baha Abu-Laban, "The Lebanese in Montreal." In Albert Hourani and Nadim Shehadi, eds., *The Lebanese in the World: A Century of Emigration* (London: I.B. Tauris, 1992), p. 229.

33. See Kalil A. Bishara, *The Origins of the Modern Syrian* (New York: Al-Hoda Publishing House, 1914), published in English and Arabic.

34. See *Ex Parte Dow,* 211 F. 486 (E.D. South Carolina 1914) and *In Re Dow,* 213 F. 355 (E.D. South Carolina 1914).

35. *Dow v. United States et al,* 26 F. 145 (4th Cir. 1915).

36. See Joseph W. Ferris, "Syrian Naturalization Question in the United States: Certain Legal Aspects of Our Naturalization Laws," Part II, *The Syrian World* 2, no. 9 (1928): 18–24.

37. *In Re Ahmed Hassan,* 48 F. Supp. 843 (E.D. Michigan 1942).

38. *Ex Parte Mohriez,* 54 F. Supp. 941 (D. Massachusetts 1944).

39. See the Arabic edition of *Al-Hoda, 1898–1968* (New York: Al-Hoda Press, 1968).

40. *The Syrian Voice* changed its name to *The Syrian and Lebanonite Voice* in the late 1930s.

41. See M[ichael A.] Shadid, "Syria for the Syrians," *Syrian World* 1, no. 8 (1927): 21–24, and see "'Syria for the Syrians' Again: An Explanation and a Retraction," *Syrian World* 3, no. 4 (1928): 24–28.

42. For an excellent early study of New York Arabs, see Lucius Hopkins Miller, "A Study of the Syrian Communities of Greater New York," *Federation* 3 (1903): 11–58.

43. This was the message often presented in *Al-Akhlaq (al-Akhlaq)* (*Character*) in the 1920s.

44. See the various articles in the Arabic press by Afifa Karam and Victoria Tannous.

45. This issue occupied the Arab community for a long time and was almost a weekly subject in the main newspapers until peddling activity dwindled in the late 1920s. See, for instance, Afifa Karam's (untitled) article about women peddlers and the *Kashshi* in *Al-Hoda* (14 July, 1903): 2.

46. See, for instance, Habib I. Katibah, "What Is Americanism?" *The Syrian World* 1, no. 3 (1926): 16–20; W. A. Mansur, "The Future of Syrian Americans," *The Syrian World* 2, no. 3 (1927): 11–17, and see "Modern Syrians' Contributions to Civilization," *The Syrian World* 4, no. 5 (1930): 7–14.

47. The question about whether to teach Arabic to their children was a controversial issue in the 1920s and hotly debated in two main journals, *The Syrian World* and *Al-Akhlaq.*

48. See Michael W. Suleiman, "A Community Profile of Arab-Americans: Major Challenges and Concerns," *Arab Perspectives* (September 1983): pp. 6–13.

49. See Ibrahim Abu-Lughod, ed., *The Arab-Israeli Confrontation of June, 1967: An Arab Perspective* (Evanston, IL: Northwestern University Press, 1970).

50. Michael W. Suleiman, "Arab-Americans and the Political Process." In Ernest McCarus, ed., *The Development of Arab-American Identity* (Ann Arbor, MI: University of Michigan Press, 1994), pp. 37–60.

51. See "Dictionary of Races or Peoples." In *United States Reports of the Immigration Commission* (Washington, DC: Government Printing Office, 1911).

52. The details of these appeals are discussed in Michael W. Suleiman, "Early Arab-Americans: The Search for Identity." In Eric J. Hooglund, ed., *Crossing the Waters: Arabic-Speaking Immigrants to the United States before 1940* (Washington, DC: Smithsonian Institution Press, 1987), pp. 37–54.

53. C. P. Snow, *The Two Cultures and the Scientific Revolution* (Cambridge, England: Cambridge University Press, 1961).

54. This became a popular theme among many Arab-American writers. See, for instance, Abraham Mitry Rihbany, *A Far Journey* (Boston, MA: Houghton-Mifflin, 1914).

55. Abraham Mitrie Rihbany, *The Syrian Christ* (Boston, MA: Houghton-Mifflin, 1916).

56. See Evelyn Shakir, "Pretending to Be Arab: Role-Playing in Vance Bourjaily's 'The Fractional Man,'" *MELUS* 9, no. 1 (1982): 7–21. See also Vance Bourjaily, *Confessions of a Spent Youth* (New York: Bantam Books, 1961).

57. See, for instance, William Peter Blatty, *Which Way to Mecca, Jack?* (New York: Bernard Geis Associates, 1960).

58. See Ali Shteiwi Zaghel, "Changing Patterns of Identification among Arab Americans: The Palestine Ramallites and the Christian Syrian-Lebanese" (Ph.D. diss., Northwestern University, 1977).

59. Much has been written in this vein. For a lengthy bibliography, see Michael W. Suleiman, *The Arabs in the Mind of America* (Brattleboro, VT: Amana Books, 1988). For a Canadian-Arab activist's view, see Sheikh Muhammad Said Massoud, *I Fought as I Believed* (Montreal: Sheikh Muhammad Said Massoud, 1976).

60. Helen Hatab Samhan, "Politics and Exclusion: The Arab American Experience," *Journal of Palestine Studies* 16, no. 2 (1987): 11–28.

61. Nabeel Abraham, "Anti-Arab Racism and Violence in the United States." In Ernest McCarus, ed., *The Development of Arab-American Identity* (Ann Arbor, MI: University of Michigan Press, 1994), pp. 155–214.

62. For documentation, see, for instance, *1990 ADC Annual Report on Political and Hate Violence* (Washington, DC: American-Arab Anti-Discrimination Committee, 1991). For Canadian statistics, see Zuhair Kashmeri, *The Gulf Within: Canadian Arabs, Racism and the Gulf War* (Toronto: James Lorimer & Co., 1991).

63. Ronald Stockton, "Ethnic Archetypes and the Arab Image." In Ernest McCarus, ed., *The Development of Arab-American Identity* (Ann Arbor, MI: University of Michigan Press, 1994), p. 120.

64. See the various essays and poems in Joanna Kadi, ed., *Food for Our Grandmothers: Writings by Arab-American and Arab-Canadian Feminists* (Boston, MA: South End Press, 1994).

65. See Louise Cainkar, "Palestinian Women in the United States: Coping with Tradition, Change, and Alienation" (Ph.D. diss., Northwestern University, 1988).

66. See Charlene Joyce Eisenlohr, "The Dilemma of Adolescent Arab Girls in an American High School" (Ph.D. diss., University of Michigan, 1988).

67. For an excellent study on Arab-American women, see Evelyn Shakir, *Bint Arab: Arab and Arab American Women in the United States* (Westport, CT: Praeger, 1997).

68. Joseph Massad, "Palestinians and the Limits of Racialized Discourse," *Social Text* 11, no. 1 (1993): 108.

69. The attempt has failed, at least so far. See the 16 September 1997 letter to Katherine K. Wellman of the Office of Management and Budget sent on Arab American Institute (AAI) stationery and signed by Helen Hatab Samhan (AAI), Samia El Badry (Census 2000 Advisory Committee), and Hala Maksoud, American-Arab Anti-Discrimination Committee.

70. Lisa Suhair Majaj, "Two Worlds: Arab-American Writing," *Forkroads* 1, no. 3 (1996): 64–80. See also different entries in Joanna Kadi, ed., *Food for Our Grandmothers: Writings by Arab-American and Arab-Canadian Feminists* (Boston, MA: South End Press, 1994).

71. See, for instance, Pauline Kaldas, "Exotic." In Joanna Kadi, ed., *Food for Our Grandmothers: Writings by Arab-American and Arab-Canadian Feminists* (Boston, MA: South End Press, 1994), pp. 168–69.

72. See Nabeel Abraham, "Arab-American Marginality: Mythos and Praxis." In Baha Abu-Laban and Michael W. Suleiman, eds., *Arab Americans: Continuity and Change* (Belmont, MA: AAUG Press, 1989), pp. 17–43.

73. See Michael W. Suleiman, "American Views of Arabs and the Impact of These Views on Arab Americans," *Al-Mustaqbal Al-Arabi* 16 (1993): 93–107, published in Arabic.

74. Milton Gordon states that the absence of a hostile attitude on the part of the host society is a key factor in the integration and assimilation of immigrants. See his *Assimilation in American Life: The Role of Race, Religion, and National Origins* (New York: Oxford University Press, 1964).

75. These attitudes were evident in a 1998 survey of Arabs active in U.S. politics, an analysis of which I plan to publish.

76. For analyses of some of the 1980 and 1990 U.S. census data, see John Zogby, *Arab America Today: A Demographic Profile of Arab Americans* (Washington, DC: Arab American Institute, 1990), and Samia El-Badry, "The Arab-American Market," *American Demographics* (January 1994): 22–27, 30. See also "CPH-L-149 Selected Characteristics for Persons of Arab Ancestry: 1990," U.S. Bureau of the Census, 1990 Census of Population and Housing, C-P-3-2, Ancestry of the Population in the United States: 1990.

77. Examples include Michael DeBakey in medicine (heart surgery); Elias Corey in chemistry (1990 Nobel Prize winner); Casey Kasem, Danny Thomas, and Paula Abdul in entertainment; Helen Thomas in journalism; Doug Flutie in sports (1984 Heisman Trophy winner); and Ralph Nader in consumer advocacy.

78. Casey Kasem, "We're Proud of Our Heritage," *Parade* (*Kansas City Star*) (16 January 1994): 1.

79. See Lisa Suhair Majaj, "Boundaries: Arab/American." In Joanna Kadi, ed., *Food for Our Grandmothers: Writings by Arab-American and Arab-Canadian Feminists* (Boston, MA: South End Press, 1994), pp. 65–84.

READING 43

Notes

1. The families of the teens were from twelve different countries including Jamaica (31 percent); Trinidad (21 percent); Guyana (16 percent); Barbados (10 percent); Haiti (10 percent); Grenada (5 percent); and a few each from the smaller

islands of Montserrat, Saint Thomas, Anguilla, Saint Lucia, Dominica, and Nevis.

2. Middle class was defined as having at least one parent with a college degree or a professional or business position. Working class was defined as a parent with a low-skill job; poor were students whose parents were not currently employed.

References

Anderson, E. 1990. *Streetwise: Race, Class, and Change in an Urban Community.* Chicago: University of Chicago Press.

Feagin, J. R. 1991. "The Continuing Significance of Race—Antiblack Discrimination in Public Places." *American Sociological Review* 56(1): 101–116.

Foner, N. 1987. "The Jamaicans: Race and Ethnicity Among Migrants in New York City." In *New Immigrants in New York,* edited by N. Foner. New York: Columbia University Press.

Fordham, S. 1988. "Racelessness as a Factor in Black Students' School Success: Pragmatic Strategy or Pyrrhic Victory?" *Harvard Education Review* 58(1) (February).

Gans, H. J. 1992. "Second-Generation Decline: Scenarios for the Economic and Ethnic Futures of Post-1965 American Immigrants." *Ethnic and Racial Studies* 15 (April):173–192.

Kasinitz, P. 1992. *Caribbean New York: Black Immigrants and the Politics of Race.* Ithaca, NY: Cornell University Press.

Lieberson, A. 1980. *A Piece of the Pie: Blacks and White Immigrants Since 1980.* Berkeley: University of California Press.

Massey, D. 1990. "American Apartheid: Segregation and the Making of the Underclass." *American Journal of Sociology* 96(2) (September): 329–357.

Ogbu, J. U. 1990. "Minority Status and Literacy in Comparative Perspective." *Daedalus* 119(2) (Spring):141–168.

Portes, A., and M. Zhou. 1993. "The New Second Generation: Segmented Assimilation and Its Variants." *Annals of the American Academy of Political and Social Sciences* 530 (November): 74–96.

Stafford, S. B. 1987. "Language and Identity: Haitians in New York City." In *Caribbean Life in New York City: Sociocultural Dimensions,* edited by C. R. Sutton and E. M. Chaney. New York: Center for Migration Studies.

Sutton, C. R., and S. P. Makiesky. 1975. "Migration and West Indian Racial and Ethnic Consciousness." In *Migration and Development: Implications for Ethnic Identity and Political Conflict,* edited by H. I. Safa and B. M. Du Toit. Paris: Mouton.

Warner, W. L., and L. Srole. 1945. *The Social Systems of American Ethnic Groups.* New Haven, CT: Yale University Press.

Woldemikael, T. M. 1989. *Becoming Black American: Haitian and American Institutions in Evanston, Illinois.* New York: AMS Press.

READING 44

Notes

1. Throught history, interracial intimacy has been taboo, and there may be considerable underreporting of interracial marriage. This bias likely changes over time and may influence the time-series variation as well as the cross-sectional estimates. The estimates are likely lower bounds on the amount of interracial marriage that actually occurs. Yet, because interracial marriage is concrete and verifiable, this concern is less in the marriage data than question regarding cohabitation, dating, or sexual preferences.

References

Becker, Gary. 1973. "A Theory of Marriage: Part I." *Journal of Political Economy,* 81(4): 813–46.

Blau, Peter M. 1964. *Exchange and Power in Social Life.* New York: Wiley.

Cutler, David, Edward Glaeser, and Jacob Vigdor. 1999. "The Rise and Decline of the American Ghetto." *Journal of Political Economy,* 107(3): 455–506.

Echenique, Federico, and Roland Fryer. Forthcoming. "A Measure of Segregation Based on Social Interactions." *Quarterly Journal of Economics.*

Fryer, Roland, and Mathew Jackson. 2003. "Categorical Cognition: A Psychological Model of Categories and Identification in Decision Making." National Bureau of Economic Research Working Paper 9579.

Fryer, Roland, and Steven Levitt. 2004. "Understanding the Black–White Test Score Gap in the First Two Years of School." *Review of Economics and Statistics,* 86(2): 447–64.

Kalmijn, Matthijs. 1993. "Trends in Black/White Intermarriage." *Social Forces,* 72(1): 119–46.

King, Martin Luther, Jr. 1956. "Paul's Letter to American Christians." Sermon delivered at Dexter Avenue Baptist Church, Montgomery, Alabama, on November 4, 1956. In *Knock at Midnight: Inspiration from the Great Sermons of Reverend Martin Luther King, Jr.,* ed. Clayborne Carson and Peter Holloran. New York: Warner Books, 1998.

Loury, Glenn. 2002. *The Anatomy of Racial Inequality.* Cambridge, MA: Harvard University Press.

MacGregor, Morris. 1985. *Integration of the Armed Forces 1940–1965.* Defense Studies Series. Washington, DC: Center of Military History, United States Army.

Merton, Robert K. 1941. "Intermarriage and the Social Structure: Fact and Theory." *Psychiatry,* August, 4(8): 361–74.

Moran, Rachel. 2003. *The Regulation of Race and Romance.* Chicago: University of Chicago Press.

Patterson, Orlando. 1982. *Slavery and Social Death: A Comparative Study.* Cambridge, MA: Harvard University Press.

Romano, Renee. 2003. *Race Mixing: Black–White Marriage in Post-war America.* Cambridge: Harvard University Press.

Rosch, Eleanor. 1978. "Principles of Categorization." In *Cognition and Categorization,* ed. E. Rosch and B.B. Lloyd, 27–48. Hillsdale, NJ: Erlbaum.

Rosen, Sherwin. 1974. "Hedonic Prices and Implicit Markets: Product Differentiation in Pure Competition." *Journal of Political Economy,* 82(1), 34–55.

Stodgill, Ron, and Amanda Bower. 2002. "Welcome to America's Most Diverse City." *Time,* in partnership with CNN, August 25. http://www.time.com/time/nation/printout/0,8816,340694,00.html.

Welch, Finis. 2003. "Catching Up: Wages of Black Men." *American Economic Review,* 93(2): 320–25.

Woodward, C. Vann. 1955. *The Strange Career of Jim Crow.* New York: Oxford University Press.

READING 45

Notes

1. "Over 93 percent of whites and of blacks marry within their own groups, in contrast to about 70 percent of Asians and of Hispanics and less than one-third of American Indians." Roderick J. Harrison and Claudette E. Bennett, "Racial and Ethnic Diversity," in Reynolds Farley, ed., *State of the Union: America in the 1990s—Vol. Two: Social Trends* (1995), 165.

   When people of Latino and Asian ancestry marry exogamously, "their spouses are very likely to be white; interracial marriages in the United States [have seldom] involved the mixing of two minority groups" (Ibid.).

2. Reflecting on his marriage, Peter Norton once mused, "Other than sex itself, why do you want to spend your life in the company of a woman as opposed to a best male friend? Part of the answer has to do with the wonderful, bizarre, inexplicable differences between male psychology and female psychology. Well, in the same vein, why would you want to spend your life with a person from the same ethnic background? You miss the frisson" (quoted in David Owen, "The Straddler," *The New Yorker,* January 30, 1995).

3. Roxie Roker, the black actress who played Helen Willis, was herself married to a white man. The popular musician Lenny Kravitz is their son. See Lynn Norment, "Am I Black, White, or in Between?," *Ebony,* August 1995; "Roxie Roker, 66, Who Broke Barrier in Her Marriage on TV's *Jeffersons*," *New York Times,* December 6, 1995.

4. Denise Nicholas, who played the character whom the sheriff married, actively shaped the public image of her role, particularly with respect to the interracial relationship. Nicholas felt that the characters "should either break [the relationship] off or get married because oftentimes, historically, interracial relationships were back-alley affairs, hidden and

lied about, particularly in the South. It became really important to me that the [characters] do something dignified; I didn't want my character to be cheap" ("Denise Nicholas and Carroll O'Connor Wed on TV Drama 'In the Heat of the Night,'" *Jet,* May 9, 1994). It should be recalled that the basis for the television series was the film of the same name (1967), which featured a thoroughly bigoted white sheriff (played by Rod Steiger, in an Academy Award–winning performance).

5. ABC's hugely successful musical production starred Brandy as Cinderella and Paolo Montalban as the prince. Taking the role of Prince Charming's mother, the queen, was a black actress, Whoopi Goldberg, while the king was played by a white actor, Victor Garber. See Veronica Chambers, "The Myth of Cinderella," *Newsweek,* November 3, 1997; "Cinderella TV Music Special Produces Spectacular Rating for ABC," *Jet,* November 24, 1997.

6. Such depictions were no accident. When television producers sought guests for these programs, they advertised for people who had had *bad* experiences in or on account of interracial relationships. It was this bias that gave rise to episodes such as "Woman Disowned by Her Family for Dating a Black Man" on *Jenny Jones* and "Blacks and Blondes: White Girls Dating Black Guys for Sex, Style, and Status" on *Geraldo.*

7. Several months after *An American Love Story* aired, Cecily Wilson married a white union organizer whom she had met on a blind date. See "Weddings: Cecily Wilson, Gregory Speller," *New York Times,* May 7, 2000.

8. Fox has stated that she was surprised by some of her relatives' negative reactions to her interracial relationship, and surprised, too, by the regularity of the racial mistreatment her black lover suffered. In retrospect, she observes, "it was almost like I was deluded or something; I thought I was living in a different world than I was living in" (quoted in Paula Span, "Modern Family Life in Black and White: PBS Documentary Chronicles an Interracial Marriage," *Washington Post,* September 9, 1999).

9. Two excellent coming-of-age films that evoke the hazards and rewards of teenage interracial dating in the 1950s are Robert De Niro's *A Bronx Tale* (1993) and Barry Levinson's *Liberty Heights* (2000).

10. Although they failed to persuade the United States Census Bureau to offer the "multiracial" box for the 2000 census, multiracialist reformers have succeeded in convincing a number of state governments—including those of Georgia, Illinois, Florida, Indiana, Michigan, and Ohio—to require that such a box be provided on state forms that collect racial data. They have also managed to convince several important private institutions, among them Harvard University, to add a "multiracial" category alongside the other, more familiar and

established, choices. See Tanya Kateri Hernandez, "'Multiracial' Discourse: Racial Classifications in an Era of Color-Blind Jurisprudence," *Maryland Law Review* 57 (1998): 97, 98 n. 4.

11. When the racial-classification issue was decided for the 2000 census, the person in charge of the supervisory agency was Franklin Raines, a black man married to a white woman. Franklin and Wendy Raines had two children who themselves faced this classification dilemma. See Julia Malone, "Facing the Racial Question: More Categories in the Census," *The Atlanta Journal and Constitution,* October 15, 1997.

12. Woods made his views known on Oprah Winfrey's television show soon after he won the prestigious Masters golf tournament. See Greg Couch, "Woods: I'm More Than Black," *Chicago Sun-Times,* April 22, 1997, p. 1.

13. In a satirical essay entitled "The Mulatto Millennium," Danzy Senna facetiously defined "Cablinasian" thus:

A rare exotic breed found mostly in California. This is the mother of all mixtures. . . . A show mulatto, with great performance skills, the Cablinasian will be whoever the crowd wants him to be, and can switch at the drop of a dime. Does not, however, answer to the name Black. . . . Note: If you spot a Cablinasian, please contact the Benetton Promotions Bureau. [In Claudine Chiawei O'Hearn, ed., *Half and Half: Writers on Growing Up Biracial and Bicultural* (1998), 26.]

For a powerful defense of Woods's position, see Gary Kamiya, "Cablinasian like Me," Salon.com, April 1997. For a critique, see Leonard Pitts, "Is There Room in This Sweet Land of Liberty for Such a Thing as 'Cablinasian'? Face It, Tiger: If They Say You're Black, Then You're Black," *Baltimore Sun,* April 29, 1997.

READING 46

Notes

1. Etienne Balibar and Immanuel Wallerstein, *Race, Nation, Class: Ambiguous Identities* (New York: Verso, 1991), 71.

2. Joe Feagin and Hernán Vera, *White Racism* (New York: Routledge, 1995), ix–x.

3. Abby L. Ferber, *White Man Falling: Race, Gender and White Supremacy* (New York: Roman and Littlefield, 1998), 100.

4. Naomi Zack, *Race and Mixed Race* (Philadelphia: Temple University Press, 1994).

5. Mimi Abramowitz, *Regulating the Lives of Women: Social Welfare Policy from Colonial Times to the Present* (Boston: South End Press, 1996).

6. Ibid., 3.

7. Valerie Babb, *Whiteness Visible: The Meaning of Whiteness in American Literature and Culture* (New York: New York University Press, 1998), 76.

8. Grace Elizabeth Hale, *Making Whiteness: The Culture of Segregation in the South, 1890–1940* (New York: Vintage Books, 1998), 109.

9. See, for instance, Gail Folaron and McCartt Hess, "Placement Considerations for Children of Mixed African American and Caucasian Parentage," *Child Welfare League of America* 72, 3 (1993): 113–135.

10. See for instance, Ferber, *White Man Falling.*

11. Ibid.

12. Ibid., 104.

13. Robert Merton, "Intermarriage and the Social Structure: Fact and Theory," *Psychiatry* 4 (1941): 361–374; see also Matthijs Kalmijn, "Trends in Black/White Intermarriage," *Social Forces* 72, 1 (1996): 119–146.

14. Merton, "Intermarriage"; Kingsley Davis, "Intermarriage in Caste Societies," *American Anthropologist* (September 1941): 388–395.

15. Ferber, *White Man Falling.*

16. Zack, *Race and Mixed Race;* Joel Williamson, *New People: Miscegenation and Mulattoes in the United States* (New York: New York University Press, 1984).

17. Ferber, *White Man Falling,* 103.

18. Kate Davy, "Outing Whiteness." *Theatre* 47, 2 (1995): 189–205.

19. Charles Gallagher, "White Reconstruction in the University," *Socialist Review* 24, 1 and 2 (1995): 165–188.

20. Cathy J. Cohen, "Contested Membership: Black Gay Identities and the Politics of AIDS," in *Queer Theory/Sociology,* ed. Steven Seidman (Cambridge, Mass.: Blackwell, 1996), 365.

21. Frantz Fanon, *Black Skins, White Masks* (New York: Grove), 83.

22. Ibid., 60.

23. Paul C. Rosenblatt, Terri A. Karis, and Richard D. Powell, *Multiracial Couples: Black and White Voices* (Thousand Oaks, Calif.: Sage, 1995), 155.

24. Michael Eric Dyson, "Essentialism and the Complexities of Racial Identity," in *Multiculturalism: A Critical Reader,* ed. David Theo Goldberg (Cambridge, Mass.: Blackwell, 1994), 222.

25. Rosenblatt et al., *Multiracial Couples,* 150.

26. Ibid., 151.

27. Ibid.

28. Gloria Wade-Gayles, *Rooted against the Wind* (Boston: Beacon, 1996), 110.

29. David Heer, "Negro-White Marriages in the United States," *Journal of Marriage and the Family* 28 (1966): 262–273; Kalmijn, "Trends"; Merton, "Intermarriage"; Davis, "Intermarriage in Caste Societies."

30. Although many people break up permanently, I interviewed individuals who eventually made the decision to commit to an interracial marriage.

31. Claudette Bennett, "Interracial Children: Implications for a Multiracial Category" (paper presented at the annual meeting

of the American Sociological Association, Washington, D.C., 1995).

32. Rosenblatt et al., *Multiracial Couples,* 5.

READING 47
Notes

1. "A Methodological Note" in Drake and Cayton (1993) [1945].
2. *Black Metropolis,* p. 127.
3. The strength and consequences of the tendency to racialize those of African descent in the United States is underscored by the persistent attempts of immigrants of African descent from the Caribbean and African continent to *emphasize* their cultural and linguistic differences from African Americans so as to escape the consequences of such racialization (Waters 1999).
4. OMB Directive 15 guidelines mandated federal agency compliance by 2003. As of 2006, the Education Department had not yet implemented the MOOM option. In August 2006, however, Education Department officials released a proposal for a plan to allow students to mark multiple racial categories that, if adopted, would comply with the federal guidelines.
5. The American College Personnel Association has an estimated 8,000 members.
6. Mavin Foundation has been quite involved in expanding the tracking and donation of bone marrow by mixed race people. They assert that mixed race people in need of bone marrow have difficulty finding matches because they are of mixed race.
7. Winant (1994) contrasts hegemony with domination. Rather than being silenced or repressed, hegemony incorporates opposition and difference (with modification) into the social order, as it robs opposition of its critical content.

References

Alba, R. (1990). *Ethnic Identity: The Transformation of White America.* New Haven, CT, Yale University Press.

Bakalian, A. (1993). *Armenian-Americans: From Being to Feeling Armenian.* New Brunswick, NJ, Transaction Publishers.

Bell, D. (1992). *Faces at the Bottom of the Well.* New York, Basic Books.

Blu, K. (1980). *The Lumbee Problem: The Making of an American Indian People.* Cambridge, UK, Cambridge University Press.

Comaroff, J. L. (1987). "Of Totemism and Ethnicity: Consciousness, Practice and the Signs of Inequality." *Ethnos* 52: 301–323.

Cose, E. (1992). *Rage of a Privileged Class: Why Do Prosperous Blacks Still Have the Blues?* New York, Harper Perennial.

DeMott, B. (1998 [1995]). *The Trouble with Friendship: Why Americans Can't Think Straight about Race.* New Haven, Yale University Press.

Drake, S. C. and H. Cayton. (1993 [1945]). *Black Metropolis: A Study of Negro Life in a Northern City.* Chicago, University of Chicago Press.

DuBois, W. E. B. ([1903] 1996). *The Souls of Black Folk. The Oxford W. E. B. DuBois Reader.* E. J. Sundquist. New York and Oxford, MI, Oxford University Press.

Espiritu, Y. L. (1992). *Asian American Panethnicity: Bridging Institutions and Identities.* Philadelphia, Temple University Press.

Files, J. (June 10, 2005). Report Describes Immigrants as Younger and More Diverse. *The New York Times:* 12.

Fordham, S. (1997). *Blacked Out.* Chicago, University of Chicago Press.

Gans, H. J. (1979). "Symbolic Ethnicity: The Future of Ethnic Groups and Cultures in America." *Ethnic and Racial Studies* 2: 1–20.

Lieberson, S. (1985). Unhyphenated Whites in the United States. *Ethnicity and Race in the U.S.A.: Toward the Twenty-first Century.* R. D. Alba. New York, Routledge: 159–180.

Nagel, J. (1995). "American Indian Ethnic Renewal: Politics and the Resurgence of Identity." *American Sociological Review* 60(6): 947–965.

Omi, M. and H. Winant. (1994). *Racial Formation in the United States: From the 1960s to the 1990s.* New York, Routledge.

Sanjek, R. (1994). Intermarriage and the Future of Races in the United States. *Race.* S. Gregory and R. Sanjek. New Brunswick, NJ, Rutgers University Press: 103–130.

Steinberg, S. (1989). *The Ethnic Myth: Race, Ethnicity, and Class in America.* Boston, Beacon Press.

Tuan, M. (1998). *Forever Foreigners or Honorary Whites? The Asian Ethnic Experience Today.* New Brunswick, NJ, Rutgers University Press.

Waters, M. (1990). *Ethnic Options: Choosing Ethnic Identities in America.* Berkeley, University of California Press.

Waters, M. C. (1999). *Black Identities: West Indian Immigrant Dreams and American Realities.* Cambridge, MA, Harvard University Press.

Winant, H. (1994). Racial Formation and Hegemony: Global and Local Developments. *Racism, Modernity and Identity on the Western Front.* A. Rattansi and S. Westwood. Cambridge, UK, Polity Press. 266–289.

READING 48

References

Agres, Bob. "Community Building in Hawai'i," in *The Nonprofit Quarterly,* Summer 2005.

Anderson, Sarah, John Cavanagh, Scott Klinger, and Liz Stanton, *Executive Excess 2005.* Boston and Washington, DC: Institute for Policy Studies and United for a Fair Economy, 2005. http://www.faireconomy.org/press/2005/EE2005.pdf (accessed September 8, 2005).

Boshara, Ray, Reid Cramer, and Leslie Parrish. *Policy Options to Encourage Savings and Asset Building by Low-Income Americans,* New America Foundation, Discussion Draft. January 28, 2004. www.newamericafoundation.org

Brown, Michael K. "Race in the American Welfare State: The Ambiguities of 'Universalistic' Social Policy Since the New Deal." *Without Justice for All: The New Liberalism and Our Retreat from Racial Equality.* Adolph L. Reed, editor. Boulder, CO: Westview Press, 1999.

Collins, Chuck, and Felice Yeskel. *Economic Apartheid in America: An Economic Primer on Economic Inequality and Insecurity.* New York: The New Press, 2000.

Ginsberg, Thomas, and Paola Ochoa (contributor). "Immigrants Pool Money, Find Success." *Philadelphia Inquirer,* Nov. 17, 2003.

Henry J. Kaiser Family Foundation. "New Report Provides Critical Information About Health Insurance Coverage and Access for Racial and Ethnic Minority Groups." Washington, DC, Aug. 1, 2000. http://www.kff.org/uninsured/upload/13342_1.pdf (accessed December 16, 2004).

Isbister, John. *Thin Cats: The Community Development Credit Union Movement in the United States.* Davis, CA: Center for Cooperatives, University of California, 1994.

Moreno, Ana. *Mortgage Foreclosure Prevention: Program and Trends.* Minneapolis: Family Housing Fund, December 1998.

Muhammad, Dedrick, Attieno Davis, Meizhu Lui, and Betsy Leondar-Wright. *The State of the Dream 2004: Enduring Disparities in Black and White.* Boston: United for a Fair Economy, 2004.

Orr, Doug. "Social Security Isn't Broken." *Dollars & Sense,* 256 (2004).

Phillips, Katherin Ross. *Who Knows About the Earned Income Tax Credit?* Washington, D.C.: Urban Institute, Jan. 1, 2001. http://www.urban.org/UploadedPDF/anf_b27.pdf, p. 1.

Policy Link. "Community Reinvestment Act: Why use the tool?" http://www.policylink.org/EquitableDevelopment/content/tools/56/20-all? (Accessed December 4, 2003).

Price, Derek, Lumina Foundation for Education, *Inequality in Higher Education: The Historic and Continuing Significance of Race,* panel on Colorlines Conference, Harvard Law School Civil Rights Project, Aug. 30, 2003.

Root Cause. *Community Impact Report.* Miami, FL: November 11, 2003. http://users.resist.ca/~mangus/CIR_eng.pdf (accessed 1/8/05).

Shapiro, Thomas. *The Hidden Cost of Being African American: How Wealth Perpetuates Inequality.* New York: Oxford University Press, 2004.

Shapiro, Thomas. PowerPoint presentation at Center for American Progress panel on wealth inequality, September 23, 2004.

Sherradan, Michael. *Assets and the Poor: A New American Welfare Policy.* Armonk, NY: M. E. Sharpe, 1991.

Sklar, Holly, Laryssa Mykyta, and Susan Wefald. *Raise the Floor Wages: Wages and Policies That Work for All of Us.* New York: Ms. Foundation for Women, 2001.

Spriggs, William E. "African Americans and Social Security: Why the Privatization Advocates Are Wrong," *Dollars & Sense,* 256 (2004): 18.

United for a Fair Economy, *Annual Report.* 2002.

U.S. Department of Health and Human Services, Substance Abuse and Mental Health Services Administration, *National Household Survey on Drug Abuse.* Rockville, MD: 1998. http://oas.samhsa.gov/nhsda/NHSDAsumrpt.pdf (accessed December 19, 2004).

Woo, Deborah. *Glass Ceilings and Asian Americans: The New Face of Workplace Barriers,* Walnut Creek, CA: AltaMira Press, 2000.

Notes

1. Brown, 9.
2. Price, 2003.
3. Sklar et al., 2001, 122.
4. Henry J. Kaiser Family Foundation, 1.
5. Ibid., 2.
6. Ibid., 4.
7. U.S. Department of Health and Human Services.
8. Shapiro, *Hidden Cost,* 2004, 52.
9. Sklar et al., 2001, 90.
10. Collins and Yeskel, 2000, 182.
11. Ibid.
12. Anderson et al., 2005, 1.
13. Root Cause, 2003.
14. Sklar et al., 2001, 118.
15. Phillips, 2001.
16. Boshara et al., 2004, 1.
17. Sklar et al., 2001, 118.
18. Muhammad et al., 2004, 7.
19. Woo, 2000, 104.
20. Shapiro, PowerPoint, 2004.
21. Sherradan, 1991, 3–7.
22. Brown, 17.
23. Shapiro, *Hidden Cost,* 2004, 185.
24. Ginsberg and Ochoa, 2003, B1.
25. Isbister, 1994, 2.
26. Ibid., 5.
27. Ibid.
28. Policy Link, 2003.
29. Ibid.
30. United for a Fair Economy, 2002.
31. Moreno, 1998, 6–7.
32. Ibid., 1.
33. Ibid., 17.
34. Orr, 2004, 14.
35. Spriggs, 2004, 18.
36. Muhammad et al., 2004, 17.
37. Agres, 2005, 37.

Credits

READING 1

"How Our Skins Got Their Color" by Marvin Harris, from *Our Kind: Who We Are, Where We Came From and Where We Are Going,* pp. 112–114. Copyright © 1989 by Marvin Harris. Reprinted by permission of HarperCollins Publishers, Inc.

READING 2

"Drawing the Color Line" by Howard Zinn, from *A People's History of the United States,* pp. 23–38, by Howard Zinn. Copyright © 1980 by Howard Zinn. Reprinted by permission of HarperCollins Publishers, Inc.

READING 3

"Racial Formations" by Michael Omi and Howard Winant, from *Racial Formation in the United States,* Second Edition, Michael Omi and Howard Winant, eds. Copyright © 1994 by Routledge, Inc. Reproduced by permission of Routledge, Inc., part of the Taylor & Francis Group.

READING 4

"Theoretical Perspectives in Race and Ethnic Relations" by Joe R. Feagin and Clairece Booher Feagin, from *Racial and Ethnic Relations,* Sixth Edition, by Joe R. Feagin and Clairece Booher Feagin. Copyright © 1990 Pearson Education. Reprinted by permission of Pearson Education, Inc., Upper Saddle River, NJ.

READING 5

"Racialized Social System Approach to Racism" by Eduardo Bonilla-Silva, from *White Supremacy and Racism in the Post-Civil Rights Era* by Eduardo Bonilla-Silva. Copyright © 2001 by Lynne Rienner Publishers. Reprinted with permission.

READING 6

"An Overview of Trends in Social and Economic Well-Being, by Race" by Rebecca M. Blank, from *America Becoming: Racial Trends and Their Consequences,* Vol. 1, National Academies Press, 2001, pp. 21–39. Reprinted with permission.

READING 7

"The Color of Health in the United States" by David R. Williams and Chiquita Collins. Copyright © 2002. Reprinted by permission of The Annual Review.

READING 8

"Transformative Assets, the Racial Wealth Gap, and the American Dream" by Thomas Shapiro. Reprinted by permission of the National Urban League.

READING 9

"Defining Race: Comparative Perspectives" by F. James Davis, from *Mixed Messages: Multiracial Identities in the "Color-Blind" Era,* edited by David Brunsma.

READING 10

"A Tour of Indian Peoples and Indian Land" by David E. Wilkins, from *American Indian Politics and the American Political System,* pp. 11–40. Copyright © 2002. Reprinted by permission of Rowman & Littlefield Publishers, Inc.

READING 11

"Asian American Panethnicity: Contemporary National and Transnational Possibilities" by Yen Le Espiritu. From *Not Just Black and White: Historical and Contemporary Perspectives on Immigration, Race, and Ethnicity in the United States.* © 2004 Russell Sage Foundation, 112 East 64th Street, New York, NY 10021. Reprinted by permission.

READING 12

"Beyond Black and White: Remaking Race in America" by Jennifer Lee and Frank Bean. © 2003 by American Sociological Association. All rights reserved. Reprinted from *Contexts* by permission of American Sociological Association via RightsLink.

READING 13

"Color-Blind Privilege: The Social and Political Functions of Erasing the Color Line in Post-Race America" by Charles A. Gallagher, from the *RGC Journal Special Edition on Privilege,* Abby L. Ferber and Dena R. Samuels, co-editors, Vol. 10, No. 4, 2003.

READING 14

"The Ideology of Colorblindness" by Lani Guinier and Gerald Torres, reprinted by permission of the publisher from *The Miner's Canary: Enlisting Race, Resisting Power, Transforming Democracy,* pp. 38–39, 42–48, Cambridge, Mass.: Harvard University Press. Copyright © 2002 by Lani Guinier and Gerald Torres.

READING 15

"The Possibility of a New Racial Hierarchy in the Twenty-First Century United States" by Herbert J. Gans, from *The Cultural Territories of Race,* edited by Michele Lamont. Copyright © 1999 University of Chicago and the Russell Sage Foundation. Reprinted by permission of the University of Chicago Press.

READING 16

"Race Prejudice as a Sense of Group Position" by Herbert Blumer, from *The Pacific Sociological Review,* Vol. 1, No. 1, Spring 1958, pp. 3–7. Reprinted by permission of Dean S. Dorn for the Pacific Sociological Association.

READING 17

"Discrimination and the American Creed," essay by Robert K. Merton, from *Discrimination and National Welfare,* edited by Robert M. MacIver. Copyright 1949 by the Institute for Religion and Social Studies. Reprinted by permission of HarperCollins Publishers, Inc.

READING 18

"Race and Civil Rights Pre–September 11, 2001: The Targeting of Arabs and Muslims," by Susan M. Akram and Kevin R. Johnson, originally published as part of a longer article, "Race, Civil Rights, and Immigration Law after September 11, 2001: The Targeting of Arabs and Muslims" in the *NYU Annual Survey of American Law* 58, No. 3 (2002): 295–356 [58 N.Y.U. Ann. Surv. Am. L. 295 (2002)].

READING 19

"The Possessive Investment in Whiteness: Racialized Social Democracy" by George Lipsitz, from *American Quarterly* 47:3 (1995), pp. 369–387. Copyright © The American Studies Association. Reprinted with permission of The Johns Hopkins University Press.

READING 20

"Laissez-Faire Racism, Racial Inequality, and the Role of the Social Sciences" by Lawrence D. Bobo, in *The Changing Terrain of Race and Ethnicity.* © 2004 Russell Sage Foundation, 112 East 64th Street, New York, NY 10021. Reprinted with permission.

READING 21

"Residential Segregation and Neighborhood Conditions in U.S. Metropolitan Areas" by Douglas S. Massey, from *America Becoming: Racial Trends and Their Consequences,* Vol. 1, pp. 391–434, National Academies Press. Copyright © 2001. Reprinted with permission.

READING 22

"The Code of the Streets" by Elijah Anderson, from *The Code of the Streets.* Originally in *The Atlantic Monthly,* 273, No. 5, May 1994. Copyright © 1994 by Elijah Anderson. Reprinted with the permission of Elijah Anderson.

READING 23

"Environmental Justice in the 21st Century: Race Still Matters" by Robert D. Bullard, from *Phylon,* 2001, Vol. 49, No. 3–4, pp. 151–171. Copyright © 2001 Phylon. Reprinted by permission.

READING 24

"Race, Religion, and the Color Line (Or Is That the Color Wall?)" by Michael O. Emerson. Reprinted by permission of the author.

READING 25

"Why Are There No Supermarkets in My Neighborhood? The Long Search for Fresh Fruit, Produce, and Healthy Food" by Shannon N. Zenk (et al.). From "Neighborhood Composition, Neighborhood Poverty, and the Spatial Accessibility of Supermarkets in Metropolitan Detroit" by Shannon Zenk (et al.) *American Journal of Public Health,* April 2005, Vol. 95, No. 4, pp. 660–667. Copyright © American Public Health Association. Reprinted with permission of The American Public Health Association.

READING 26

"No Equal Justice: The Color of Punishment" by David Cole, from *No Equal Justice: Race and Class in the American Criminal Justice System.* Copyright © 1998 by David Cole. Reprinted by permission of The New Press, (800) 233–4830.

READING 27

"Black and Blue: Everyday Racism on the Police Force" by Kenneth Bolton Jr. and Joe R. Feagin. From *Black in Blue* edited by Kenneth Bolton Jr. and Joe R. Feagin, pp. 43–92.

READING 42

"The Arab Immigrant Experience" by Michael W. Suleiman, as it appears in *Arabs in America: Building a New Future,* edited by Michael Suleiman. Reprinted by permission of Temple University Press. Copyright © 1999 by Temple University. All rights reserved.

READING 43

"Ethnic and Racial Identities of Second-Generation Black Immigrants in New York City" by Mary C. Waters, from *The New Second Generation,* edited by Alejandro Portes. Copyright © 1996 Russell Sage Foundation, 112 East 64th Street, New York, NY 10065. Reprinted with permission.

READING 44

"Guess Who's Been Coming to Dinner? Trends in Interracial Marriage over the 20th Century" by Roland G. Fryer Jr., from *Journal of Economic Perspectives,* Vol. 21, Number 2, Spring 2007, pp. 71–90.

READING 45

"Captain Kirk Kisses Lieutenant Uhura: Interracial Intimacies— The View from Hollywood" by Randall Kennedy, from *Interracial Intimacies* by Randall Kennedy, © by Randall Kennedy. Used by permission of Random House, Inc. and Fish and Richardson.

READING 46

"Discovering Racial Borders" by Heather M. Dalmage, from *Tripping on the Color Line: Black-White Multiracial Families in a Racially Divided World* by Heather Dalmage. Copyright © 2000 by Heather Dalmage. Reprinted by permission of Rutgers University Press.

READING 47

"Redrawing the Color Line? The Problems and Possibilities of Multiracial Families and Group Making" by Kimberly McClain DaCosta, from *Making Multiracials: State, Family, and Market in the Redrawing of the Color Line* by Kimberly McLain DaCosta. Copyright © 2007 by the Board of Trustees of the Leland Stanford Jr University. All rights reserved. Used with the permission of Stanford University Press, www.sup.org.

READING 48

"Policy Steps toward Closing the Gap" by Meizhu Lui, Barbara J. Robles, Betsy Leondar-Wright, Rose M. Brewer, and Rebecca Adamson, from *The Color of Wealth.*

READING 49

"Ten Things You Can Do to Improve Race Relations" by Charles A. Gallagher. Copyright © 2004 by Charles A. Gallagher. Reprinted by permission of the author.